ENGENDERING PSYCHOLOGY

WOMEN AND GENDER REVISITED

SECOND EDITION

FLORENCE L. DENMARK

Pace University

VITA CARULLI RABINOWITZ

Hunter College of the City University of New York

JERI A. SECHZER

Pace University

PEARSON

Boston ■ *New York* ■ *San Francisco*
Mexico City ■ *Montreal* ■ *Toronto* ■ *London* ■ *Madrid* ■ *Munich* ■ *Paris*
Hong Kong ■ *Singapore* ■ *Tokyo* ■ *Cape Town* ■ *Sydney*

Series Editor: Kelly May
Series Editorial Assistant: Adam Whitehurst
Marketing Manager: Karen Natale
Editorial-Production Service: Omegatype Typography, Inc.
Composition Buyer: Linda Cox
Manufacturing Buyer: JoAnne Sweeney
Cover Administrator: Kristina Mose-Libon
Electronic Composition: Omegatype Typography, Inc.

For related titles and support materials, visit our online catalog at www.ablongman.com.

Between the time Website information is gathered and then published, it is not unusual for some sites to have closed. Also, the transcription of URLs can result in typographical errors. The publisher would appreciate notification where these errors occur so that they may be corrected in subsequent editions.

Library of Congress Cataloging-in-Publication Data

Denmark, Florence.
    Engendering psychology : women and gender revisited / Florence Denmark, Vita
Rabinowitz, Jeri Sechzer.
      p.   cm.
    ISBN 0-205-40456-1 (alk. paper)
    1. Women—Psychology.   2. Sex role—Psychological aspects.   3. Sex discrimination
against women.   4. Feminist theory.   I. Rabinowitz, Vita Carulli.   II. Sechzer, Jeri A.
III. Title.

HQ1150.D45 2004
155.6'33—dc22

                                                                              2004044693

Printed in the United States of America

10   9   8   7   6   5   4   3   2   1   09   08   07   06   05   04

To our feminist colleagues and students in the psychology of women

and

To our husbands,
Robert Wesner,
Jack Rabinowitz,
Philip Sechzer,
who provided unwavering support

and

To our children,
who always root for us

CONTENTS

PREFACE

We three are longtime friends and collaborators in research on women and gender. In our many far-ranging discussions about women, reflecting our different backgrounds, areas of expertise, and points of view, we came to believe that we could make a significant contribution to the psychology of women and gender. That conviction resulted in the first edition of our textbook, in which we set out to write the kind of text that we thought was missing and sorely needed. We entitled it *Engendering Psychology* after an article one of us (FLD) published in 1994 in the *American Psychologist* about the need for psychology in general and the psychology of women in particular to take a *gendered perspective* on issues. Such a perspective is not simply a focus on women or "women's issues," but rather an analytic approach to understanding theories, research, policies, and practices from the perspectives of women and men. To take a gendered perspective is to recognize that gender is a major basis for social differentiation throughout the world, and that gender affects people's experiences and viewpoints about virtually everything. Such a perspective helps us ask and answer questions about, for example, whether there are gender-related patterns in how people form relationships or succeed at school and work.

In the first edition of our text, we covered critical topics that were omitted or shortchanged in other texts, such as international and cross-cultural studies, disability and sexuality, and issues relating to aging. We featured a chapter on race and ethnicity and one on the origins of stereotypes in myths and religions, both of which were unprecedented at the time. Beyond covering topics that were not treated in depth elsewhere, we incorporated perspectives and scholarship that were often generally lacking in psychological texts, such as historical perspectives on current issues, scientific comparisons between women and men wherever relevant, and the inclusion of pertinent interdisciplinary material. We produced a book that was recognized as different, nuanced, and exciting by reviewers, and was highly regarded by students and instructors alike.

Since the first edition of *Engendering Psychology* appeared in 2000, a considerable amount of significant new research and scholarship on women and gender has been produced. Without eliminating all the unique and valuable material and insights from the first edition, we have, in the second edition, identified and incorporated new trends in the field. We carefully selected what research to include from among a large number of excellent studies from all over the world. Thus, we have included new research on sexual orientation, gender in the classroom, gender and achievement in school and work, women's friendships and relations with their families, sexuality and health as people age, sexual dysfunction, depression, violence and exploitation of women, and suicidality.

Because of the centrality of reproductive issues and parenting to women and men, and the sheer amount of new research on those topics, we have written a separate chapter, Chapter 10, called Parenting and Reproductive Issues. Chapter 13, Issues in Mental Health, has been substantially revised and expanded to include new perspectives on depression, eating disorders, and treatments as well as new sections on personality disorders, suicide, and parasuicidality. We have added hundreds of new references to the second edition.

We have also maintained and strengthened the gendered perspective that usefully informed our first edition. As with the first edition, the second edition presents issues in their complexity and richness, without sacrificing excitement or clarity. To an extent that is not always found in psychology of women texts, our treatment of issues is based solidly on scientific evidence and presented in a balanced manner. More important than any particular additions to this revised text are the depth and breadth of our coverage of topics. For example, throughout the text we integrate new developments from biological and biomedical research into our social, cultural, and feminist orientation. Wherever appropriate, we address the challenge that evolutionary psychology has posed for feminist scholarship. And, more than do other texts on the psychology of women, we consider women in their evolving social, cultural, and ethnic contexts. We take a comparative approach that looks at women across cultures and ethnicities. We consider girls and women across the life span, and examine sex differences and similarities. Although our primary focus is on the psychology of women, our text takes gender seriously and contains a great deal of information on men and boys as well as women and girls. Thus, our book is suitable for courses in the psychology of women and in gender courses more generally.

We have written this book primarily for undergraduate classes in the psychology of women. However, it can also be used for courses on gender or women's studies. As a text it can stand alone or be used in conjunction with a book of readings or other material that an instructor would assign. In addition, sections of this volume can be used as a supplement to courses that include units on gender roles, gender issues in developmental psychology, human sexuality, and so on. With its wealth of references, this volume encompasses recent as well as classic studies and thus can serve as a valuable resource for advanced students and faculty conducting research on women. Although this text provides an unusually thorough discussion of a wide range of topics germane to the psychology of women and gender, it is by no means exhaustive. The subject of each chapter alone yields enough information to fill an entire volume. Readers interested in pursuing topics in greater depth can make use of citations and further readings to locate additional information.

The organization of this book combines a developmental and topical approach. All chapters are self-contained and can be readily rearranged according to a given instructor's preference. The text consists of 14 chapters and an epilogue. The first chapter sets the tone for the book beginning with an exploration of the meanings of sex and gender, discusses gender stereotypes and discrimination in society and in science, and provides guidelines for the conduct of gender-fair research. The origins of gender stereotypes are revealed in Chapter 2 in a unique and extensive review of mythology and religion that reaches back to its roots in earliest civilizations. In Chapter 3, we feature a special contribution on Culture, Ethnicity, Race, and Class by Professor June Chisholm, who is an expert in this area. However, our interest in psychological aspects of culture, race, ethnicity, and class is not confined to any one chapter and so is reflected throughout the text. Chapter 4, Biology of Sex and Gender, incorporates basic as well as current findings relevant to sex and gender. Other chapters examine the psychological development of girls and women. Topics here incorporate how females grow up (Chapter 5), aspects of their abilities and achievement (Chapter 6), and their work lives and careers (Chapter 7). Included also are separate chapters on human sexuality (Chapter 8), intimate relationships (Chapter 9), parenting and reproductive issues (Chapter 10), and growing older (Chapter 11).

The remaining chapters are devoted to more topics of vital importance to the lives of girls and women—violence and exploitation (Chapter 12), and mental and physical health (Chapters 13 and 14). These chapters examine issues from a historical perspective as well as from psychosocial and cultural perspectives and bring in new scholarship and fresh views on topics such as elder abuse, female infanticide, gay bashing, changing patterns of eating disorders, and the intersection of ethnicity and race with physical and mental health. The epilogue raises questions about the future realities and potentialities of women's and girls' experiences and forecasts trends in the study of women and gender.

Special features include a detailed outline at the beginning of each chapter, with a glossary of relevant terms, a series of questions, and suggestions for additional readings at the end of each chapter designed to stimulate critical thinking and discussion. For the second edition, a completely new Instructor's Manual has been developed by Professor Maram Hallak of the Borough of Manhattan Community College of the City University of New York.

We have many varied goals for this edition. We hope that readers of *Engendering Psychology: Women and Gender Revisited* will internalize a valuing of women and their own lives and experiences. Beyond that, readers should come to understand the concept of gender as a social construct in contrast to the concept of sex, which denotes biological classification into female and male, as well as to recognize the importance of equality of power and the subsequent need for activism and change.

More specifically, readers should grow in some of the following ways:

1. *Deeper understanding of women.* Individual women may find validation and a sense of empowerment in being a woman and in being part of a larger group of women with common concerns and experiences. Men may be better able to connect with the experiences of their female family members, friends, and other significant women in their lives.

2. *The knowledge that "woman" is a diverse and multifaceted category.* Women must be looked at with regard to all aspects of their lives other than only their sex and gender.

3. *Critical thinking skills.* Through learning about the psychology of women, readers will be able to perceive human behavior more accurately and more equitably and to evaluate psychological research critically.

4. *An appreciation that women have been and continue to be an oppressed group globally.* By understanding the plight of women, we gain insight about other oppressed groups and how gender intersects with other systems of discrimination.

5. *Future concerns.* Readers can renew and increase their interest in and commitment to working toward social, legal, political, and health changes that advance women and other nondominant groups.

If this book guides and enlightens without being overwhelming and encourages a cooperative dialogue among students and instructors and women and men, then it will have accomplished the authors' intent. We want to encourage the development of an informed, critical, and committed student, one who, inspired by a gendered perspective, is prepared to confront issues and effect change in the twenty-first century.

ACKNOWLEDGMENTS

We wish to acknowledge the invaluable contributions made by the following individuals. First we are grateful to June Chisholm of Pace University, who not only contributed Chapter 3 on culture, ethnicity, race, and class, but also greatly expanded our outlook on diversity throughout this book. We thank Maram Hallak of Borough of Manhattan Community College for the fine Instructor's Manual and Test Bank that accompanies this book.

We have special thanks for Kelly May, Psychology Editor at Allyn and Bacon, for encouraging us and staying on top of this project. We also appreciate the competence and hard work on our behalf by many others at Allyn and Bacon, with special thanks to Pamela Lasky, Marketing Manager.

We are indebted to our many colleagues and students, many from Pace University, Hunter College, and the Graduate Center of the City University of New York, who have superbly educated us about many of the topics covered in this text and offered special support during this process. These include Darlene DeFour of Hunter College; Roseanne Flores of Hunter College; Jim Gordon of Hunter College; Anne Griffin of Cooper Union; Rebecca Huselid of Hunter College; Margery Kalb, a graduate of Pace University; Jessica Kindred of the Graduate Center of CUNY; Herbert Krauss of Pace University; Lori Klausner of Hunter College; Victoria O'Donnell of the State University of New York at Albany; Catherine Ryan of the National League of Nursing; Deborah Tolman of San Francisco State College; and Virginia Valian of Hunter College and the Graduate Center of CUNY. We also appreciate the helpful comments of this edition's reviewers: Lisa Harrison, California State University, and Marion Mason, Bloomsburg University. The authors wish to cite their students at Pace University, Hunter College, and CUNY, and Maram Hallak's students at Borough of Manhattan Community College, CUNY.

We were especially fortunate to have students at Pace University who provided us with valuable research assistance. Rachele Flora and Lani Sherman were especially helpful in tracking down references and doing library research. Rachel Caplan, Michelle Marquez, and Steve Salbod from Pace were also helpful to us.

We owe a special debt of gratitude to Rachel Gorman of Hunter College, who contributed on every level to this text, and whose ideas, work habits, and warm and ready sense of humor cannot be overstated. We are especially grateful for her invaluable contribution to Chapter 13, "Issues in Mental Health."

Last but not least, we thank our respective husbands, Robert Wesner, Jack Rabinowitz, and Philip Sechzer, for their commitment to the importance of our work and their pride in our accomplishments.

Florence L. Denmark
Vita C. Rabinowitz
Jeri A. Sechzer

ABOUT THE AUTHORS

FLORENCE L. DENMARK

Florence L. Denmark is an internationally recognized scholar and researcher. She received her Ph.D. from the University of Pennsylvania in social psychology. Denmark's current position is the Robert Scott Pace Distinguished Research Professor at Pace University in New York, where she served as chair of the psychology department for 13 years. Denmark has published extensively on the psychology of women and gender and has long been an energetic force in advancing psychology internationally, particularly as it concerns the psychology of women and human rights.

Florence Denmark served as the eighty-eighth president of the American Psychological Association and has been an active member of many of its boards and committees, including the Council of Representatives and Board of Directors. She is a fellow of 12 APA divisions and served as president of APA Divisions 1, 35, and 52. In addition, Florence Denmark was president of the International Council of Psychologists, the Eastern Psychological Association, the New York State Psychological Association, and Psi Chi. She was also a vice president of the New York Academy of Sciences. She has four honorary doctorates and is the recipient of many awards, including APA's Distinguished Contributions to Education and Training, Public Interest, and the Advancement of International Psychology. Florence Denmark is currently an APA/NGO representative to the United Nations and continues to teach graduate courses at Pace University. Recently, she was elected Chair of the United Nations NGO Committee on Aging. She received the 2004 Gold Medal Award for Life Achievement in Psychology in the Public Interest from the American Psychological Foundation.

VITA CARULLI RABINOWITZ

Vita C. Rabinowitz is Professor and Chair of the Department of Psychology at Hunter College of the City University of New York (CUNY) and is a member of the social-personality doctoral program at the Graduate Center of CUNY. With Virginia Valian, she co-directs Hunter's Gender Equity Project (GEP), which seeks to help women faculty in the natural and social sciences flourish at Hunter. The GEP is partially funded by a National Science Foundation ADVANCE Institutional Transformation Award.

Rabinowitz received her doctorate in social psychology from Northwestern University, where she developed her lifelong love of research methodology from Donald T. Campbell and Thomas D. Cook. Her current research and writings are in the area of sex and gender bias in behavioral and biomedical research, feminist perspectives on research methods, and the advancement of women and gender equity in academia.

JERI ALTNEU SECHZER

Jeri A. Sechzer is Visiting Professor of Psychology at Pace University. She received her Ph.D. in behavioral neuroscience from the University of Pennsylvania. Sechzer's main research and publications primarily concern sex and gender issues in behavioral and biomedical science, behavioral neuroscience, bioethics, and values in science. She has recently begun to address issues of religion, psychology, and gender.

Sechzer is a fellow of the American Psychological Association (Division 35, Psychology of Women, Division 6, Behavioral Neuroscience and Comparative Psychology, and Division 52, International Psychology), the American Association for the Advancement of Science (AAAS), the New York Academy of Medicine, and the New York Academy of Sciences. She has been the recipient of many honors and awards. Some of these include the Leadership Award of the Exxon Education Foundation, the Outstanding Women in Science Award of the Association for Women in Science (AWIS, New York Chapter), and the Wilhelm Wundt Award of the New York State Psychological Association for her scientific contributions to psychology.

JUNE F. CHISHOLM

June F. Chisholm is Professor of Psychology at Pace University and Adjunct Professor at New York University Medical Center. She is a clinical psychologist who worked for many years as a Senior Psychologist in the outpatient psychiatric department at Harlem Hospital Center, providing psychological services to an ethnically diverse, primarily poor, urban population. She has a small, part-time private practice in Manhattan. Her clinical and research interests include issues in the psychological treatment of Women of Color, psychological assessment of children and adults, parenting, community psychology, violence, and prejudice in the theory and practice of psychology.

CHAPTER 1

EXPLORING SEX AND GENDER

Ignorance about women pervades academic disciplines in higher education, where the requirements for the degree seldom include thoughtful inquiry into the status of women, as part of the total human condition.
—Carolyn Sherif

Psychology has nothing to say about what women are really like, what they need and what they want, essentially, because psychology does not know.
—Naomi Weisstein

It may be a pleasure to be "we," and it may be strategically imperative to struggle as "we," but who, they ask, are "we"?
—Ann Snitow

We exist at moments, at the margins and among ourselves. Whether or not we have transformed the discipline of psychology, and whether or not we would like to, remain empirical and political questions. . . . At the level of theory, methods, politics, and activism, it is safe to say that feminist psychology has interrupted the discipline.
—Michelle Fine

It feels glorious to "reclaim an identity they taught [us] to despise."
—Michelle Cliff

[A]s historians and sociologists have begun to identify the ways in which the development of scientific knowledge has been shaped by its particular social and political context, our understanding of science as a social process has grown.
—Evelyn Fox Keller

They say that women talk too much. If you have worked in Congress you know that the filibuster was invented by men.
—Clare Boothe Luce

If you are going to generalize about women, you'll find yourself up to here in exceptions.
—Dolores Hitchens

Remember, Ginger Rogers did everything Fred Astaire did, but she did it backwards and in high heels.
—Faith Whittlesey

It has been more than 35 years since Sherif and Weisstein penned the preceding sentiments that reverberated throughout psychology. More recently, the field of the psychology of women has begun to correct its **androcentric (male-centered) bias** and the literature on the psychology of women continues to expand. One of the authors of this textbook, Florence Denmark, commented in 1980 that women in psychology had gone from "rocking the cradle to rocking the boat." In fact, there are now several journals (*Feminism and Psychology, Sex Roles,* and *The Psychology of Women Quarterly*) exclusively concerned with women and gender. The psychology of women is also interdisciplinary because it is informed by research conducted across a wide number of disciplines, such as biology, sociology, anthropology, history, media studies, economics, education, and linguistics.

As Fine suggests in the preceding quote, however, "interrupting" the discipline of psychology means that psychology has been made to pause and reconsider its theoretical assumptions and where they have led us. This reconsideration is a first step in transforming the discipline and the social structures that have impeded the progress of women in society. Today women and the issues that they care about receive greater attention from scientists, researchers, and laypersons. Few would dispute that women have made great strides in North America over the last quarter century. Yet clearly not all women have thrived. Subtle, and sometimes not-so-subtle, forces continue to support belief systems, traditions, and practices that are sources of inequity between females and males.

In this chapter, we will discuss the distinctions between sex and gender. The chapter also explores and critically examines traditional approaches to psychological research and the biases therein. Psychological research, like any research enterprise, is subject to the perils of researchers' own stereotypes and attitudes, which affect the way women and female psychologists are perceived. Sexism in both society and science is explored and gender-fair solutions for sexism in research will be considered. Feminist research, due to its critique of scientific procedures and findings, is particularly suited to uncovering biases that are related to race, ethnicity, disability, and sexual orientation as well as gender. Feminists in psychology have begun to focus on the societal forces that afford privilege for some at the expense of others. Therefore, feminist psychologists are positioned at the forefront of social change as they uncover bias in society and science and advance the study and understanding of girls and women.

To make psychology a stronger science and profession that better serve the public interest, certain changes are necessary. Specifically, sensitivity to issues concerning women, gender, and diversity must be emphasized. Psychology should include a gender perspective in its domains of science, practice, education,

and public interest. Psychology must make visible women's viewpoints and experiences. **Engendering psychology** refers to cultivating a psychology in which gender considerations are mainstreamed or integrated throughout the discipline (Denmark, 1994). In addition to distinguishing between sex and gender, this chapter will discuss the obstacles faced and the advances made in research as sensitivity to gender issues becomes more and more salient in psychology.

DISTINCTION BETWEEN SEX AND GENDER

The girl pictured in Figure 1.1 is mystified by the distinction between sex and gender. Let us investigate the meanings of these terms to clear up her confusion.

The Limits of Biology

The terms **sex** and **gender** are often misunderstood and misused. All animals, including humans, are differentiated by sex, but only humans are differentiated by gender. Sex, very simply, refers to the biological differences in the genetic composition and reproductive structures and functions of men and women. Two biological sexes exist in mammals and in many non-mammalian species, although recent controversies question the actual number of biological sexes that exist (see Chapter 4).

Biological differences between females and males exist on many levels: chromosomal, genetic, hormonal, and neurological. There is widespread misinformation and lack of understanding of these processes and interrelationships. For example, people's unfounded beliefs concerning hormones make the distinction of sex even more confusing. Many individuals believe that estrogen and progesterone are uniquely female hormones, while androgens are hormones that belong exclusively to males. However, all these hormones are found in both men and women, but in varying concentrations.

Why Gender?

Biological differences between men and women become social distinctions in most societies. Though

FIGURE 1.1   The Sex–Gender Distinction

gender is based on sex, it is actually comprised of traits, interests, and behaviors that societies place on or ascribe to each sex. In psychology as in all sciences, research findings are put into a theoretical framework to give meaning and coherence to facts and to generate future research. Two major theories with sharply contrasting perspectives currently vying for influence in the social sciences, including psychology, are sociobiology and social construction theory.

Evolutionary psychology (or **sociobiology**) was first formulated by E. O. Wilson, who argued

that psychological traits are selected in a population because they are adaptive and help maintain that population. In other words, psychological traits are subject to the same evolutionary processes as are physical traits, and natural selection helps shape aspects of social behavior and social thinking (Denmark, Rabinowitz, & Sechzer, 2000). Proponents of this view hold, for example, that women were bred to be mothers and men to be providers because the biological, sexually differentiated roles maximize the survival of the human species (Wilson, 1975). According to Wilson (1975), in early history, men were predominantly responsible for hunting in the wild, which required cognitive and motor skills such as mental rotation and good hand–eye coordination in order to be successful. Women, who were primarily in charge of raising and protecting children and gathering nearby fruits and vegetables, would have less need of such skills and thus did not develop them. Such differences are said to have impacted on the abilities and traits carried by men and women today (Denmark, Rabinowitz, & Sechzer, 2000). In Wilson's own words:

> It pays males to be aggressive, hasty, fickle, and undiscriminating. In theory it is more profitable for females to be coy, to hold back until they can identify the male with the best genes . . . human beings obey this biological principle faithfully. (1978, p. 156)

Evolutionary psychologists also propose that different preferences for males and females in regards to mate selection are biologically defined rather than culturally determined. For example, men place more emphasis on the physical attractiveness of their mates than do women, who are more interested in men's ability to be providers (Buss, 1994). This has to do with the fact that men are often faced with the problem of identifying women who are fertile and healthy enough to bear offspring, which is thought to be associated with attractiveness, whereas women are concerned with finding a mate who is willing to provide for her and her child, a task that would be difficult for her to undertake alone.

Although evolutionary theory has gained some popularity, it is more important to note that the theory attempts to explain conditions only after the fact. The theory provides a possible explanation for events that occurred in the past, but is not amenable to testing. In addition, the theory overlooks data that do not support the evolutionary framework and fails to consider the fact that women also engage in tasks that required skills traditionally considered to be within the male domain, such as spatial abilities (Smuts, 1995).

The second theory, **social constructionism,** is often traced to French philosopher Michel Foucault (1978). In contrast to evolutionary theorists, social constructionists believe that human behavior is shaped by historical, cultural, and other environmental conditions rather than from a biological perspective. This view further suggests that human behavior does not have essential elements that have universal meanings across times, places, and circumstances. Thus, the meaning of behavior will also change across time and place. Behavior can be best understood by examining its historical, cultural, and social milieu. Throughout this text we will see the impact of social construction on gender. For instance, as we will see in Chapter 8, the meaning of a sexual act depends on the particular context in which it occurs. Thus, men who have sex with other men while they are in prison rarely consider themselves, or are considered by others, gay.

In an age of technological advancement in much of the Western industrial economies, the different life experiences of males and females are not due mainly to hormones or reproductive capacities, but primarily to the *social context* that determines gender, that is, what is considered "feminine" and what is "masculine." By social context, we mean the total social sphere in which people find themselves: their personal history, immediate situation, society, and culture. The social context influences and determines the beliefs and behaviors that many people mistakenly believe are directly linked to being female or male. Gender is also more than just a category. Gender is a set of experiences and activities that comprises being female and male; and to a greater or lesser extent, all females and males are involved in the ongoing, day-to-day activities that make up "doing" gender (West & Zimmerman, 1987), or living up to society's prescriptions for gender based on their sex.

Gender is a social construction that refers to how differences between girls and boys and women and men are created and explained by society. It refutes notions that most differences between women and men are due to biology and are normal and immutable. The concept of gender underscores the fact that while we may observe many different behaviors and attitudes between women and men, there is not necessarily a biological basis for those differences. For example, gender is quickly constructed, even for the newborn. A visit to a greeting card shop will demonstrate that foremost on the mind of those who congratulate new parents is the sex of the newborn. Girls' cards are dominated by themes of daintiness and physical attractiveness. Boys' cards are dominated by themes of strength and sports. The difference between the types of cards for female and male infants reveals how early gender is constructed, and how the ideals for each sex are based on images that maximize the differences between females and males. For example, within 24 hours of birth, mothers and fathers were more likely to describe female infants as softer, finer featured, and smaller than male infants even though male and female infants overall were not significantly different from each other in terms of birth weight, birth length, or overall appearance and facial features (Rubin, Provenzano, & Luria, 1974). Nothing much has changed since 1974.

Although classified ads no longer specify the sex of the applicants employers are seeking, consider the following listing for a fictitious position. As you read the description, think about your own match with this position.

> *We are looking to hire the ideal member of the female sex. Applicants should be compassionate, patient, and kind. A nurturing woman is preferred.*

In actuality, the traits listed here refer to aspects of the female *gender* and not the female *sex*. Many women, perhaps yourself included, possess these attributes; however, many women do not conform to this stereotypical characterization. In fact, some *men* are more suited to this description than some women!

Now consider the following position:

> *We are looking to hire the ideal member of the female gender. Essential requirements: must have breasts and have given birth for this position as a baby's wet nurse.*

The second ad demonstrates the incorrect usage of the term female *gender.* Possession of breasts, having given birth, and the capacity to nurse a baby are traits limited only to biological females and the correct term is female *sex.*

This leads us to a very important question. If some critical behaviors or traits are not due to biologically based differences, what is the purpose of creating such differences? Psychologists sometimes disagree about this, and we address this issue later. But first, we need to consider some of the psychological processes that are involved in how beliefs about gender and gender-related activities are adopted and maintained by individuals.

Beliefs about Gender

Many theoreticians assert that children are *socialized* to act in accordance with their cultural dictates, presumably through the societal rewards and punishments that accompany adoption of society's values and norms. This influence of culture throughout the life span leads to the reinforcement and perpetuation of gender stereotyping. This view is known as the **cultural approach** to explaining the origin of gender stereotypes from a sociocultural perspective (Deaux & Kite, 1993).

A second framework, the **structural approach,** emphasizes the common positions that certain groups occupy within the social structure. Rather than stressing early socialization experiences, adherents of this approach focus on the ongoing structural and social role requirements that channel our experience, from the family to the societal level. For example, occupational roles were found to be a strong determinant of the traits ascribed to women and men, outweighing gender information (Deaux & Kite, 1993).

Beliefs about gender might also be explained from a cognitive perspective. **Stereotyping** is one example of a more general categorization process that is necessary in order for people to deal with the complexities of human existence. To cope with a potentially unmanageable amount of information, people learn to streamline information processing by grouping people into manageable categories based on some similarity among members.

For most people, the words *male* and *female* conjure up very different images. Beyond anatomical and physical characteristics, these words bring to mind generalized notions of two very different types of behaviors, personality traits, and other attributes. These stereotypes depict men as stronger, more rational, objective, aggressive, and outgoing, and women as weaker, more emotional and submissive, but warm and caring. Specific characteristics considered socially desirable for males differ from those considered socially desirable for females: Males should be aggressive, assertive, independent, unemotional, dominant, not easily influenced, better in math and science, unexcitable, decisive. Females should be tactful, gentle, aware of others' feelings, dependent, insecure, indecisive, emotional, but not aggressive.

These and other beliefs or stereotypes of female and male are evident in the United States. They can also be found in most, if not all, major societies in both western and eastern cultures. At a time when women have expanding opportunities for advancement and empowerment, portrayals of women that exemplify these stereotypes continue to oppress them and limit their many prospects for change.

Many real-life examples of stereotyping can be found in discrimination cases that have been brought before the courts. Imagine that you had worked for a number of years at a Fortune 500 firm in the United States. You had established a strong track record by being praised for your work by clients, winning new clients for the firm, working extremely hard and to high standards. Each year, a few individuals make partner. Based on your stellar performance, which exceeds the performance of many other women as well as men, you expect to be made a partner of the firm even though there are only a few partners, about 1 percent, who are women. Instead of receiving a partnership, however, you are told that you have interpersonal problems, that you are too "macho," and that you need a "course at charm school." A colleague even advises you to wear makeup if you want to be seriously considered for partner (*Hopkins v. Price Waterhouse*, 1985, p. 117). What would you do? Ann Hopkins lived through these experiences and decided to take the accounting firm of Price Waterhouse to court (see Box 1.1).

According to cognitive social psychologists, at root in the Hopkins case is the notion of **stereotypes.**

Box 1.1

Psychology, Stereotyping, and the Law: The Case of *Hopkins v. Price Waterhouse*

Susan Fiske and her colleagues, Donald Bersoff, Eugene Borgida, Kay Deaux, and Madeline Heilman, took psychological findings about the character and operation of stereotyping into sex discrimination litigation. The case, well-known in legal circles, involved the employment of Ann Hopkins at Price Waterhouse (a leading accounting firm). Hopkins was, by virtually all accounts, a competent, committed, hardworking, and effective professional. Although successful in her job, Hopkins was denied partnership, and she promptly filed a complaint in federal court. Social psychologist Susan Fiske testified on her behalf, primarily citing research findings on stereotyping, conditions that encourage it, indicators that reveal it, consequences of it, and remedies to prevent it. The judge ruled in Hopkins's favor, and Price Waterhouse, not surprisingly, appealed. After Hopkins's appellate victory, the case eventually was reviewed by the U.S. Supreme Court. Although research on sex stereotyping had been introduced in other legal proceedings (e.g., Goodman & Croyle, 1989), review by the Supreme Court made this case unique. It was the first such case to examine psychological research on sex stereotyping. The American Psychological Association entered with an amicus curiae (friend of the court) brief, expanding psychology's involvement. The result, possibly attributable in part to psychology's role, was victory for Hopkins.

Source: From "Resolving Legal Questions with Psychological Data," by E.F. Loftus, 1991, *American Psychologist, 46*, pp. 1046–1047.

In general, stereotypes are generalized and oversimplified beliefs about groups of people (Harré & Lamb, 1986). Whereas prejudice refers to an attitude toward a group, which is usually negative such as hostility or dislike, stereotypes are widely shared and socially validated beliefs or cognitions about whole groups of people that are then applied to individual members of that group (Lott, 1995). Stereotypes, the outcome of normal human cognitive processes called categorization, are highly efficient and organize much of what we perceive in the social world (Fiske & Taylor, 1991). For example, we quickly perceive a person's sex, race, occupation, or ethnicity, and we then form impressions based on this limited information. These impressions are not necessarily accurate ("Tim's sister is a president of a major university. I'll bet she doesn't have children"). The content of stereotypes will vary based on how they are cognitively organized, for example, around age, status, or gender, and who holds the stereotypes. For instance, many young people believe that the elderly tend to be lonely, but in actuality, one study showed that adolescents were just as likely to report feeling lonely when alone as the aged (Larson, Csikszentmihalyi, & Graef, 1982).

We next look more closely at **gender stereotypes,** that is, how females and males are represented. How are gender stereotypes expressed? How do gender stereotypes develop? What is the relationship of sexism to stereotypes? What are the implications of both racism and sexism for women of color?

Gender Stereotypes

Gender is often classified into feminine and masculine qualities or behaviors and is prone to stereotyping as a result. Classic research conducted in the 1970s and 1980s (e.g., Broverman, Vogel, Broverman, Clarkson, & Rosenkrantz, 1972; Deaux & Emswiller, 1974; Spence, Helmreich, & Stapp, 1974) found that women were evaluated as more communal and expressive than men and that men were believed to be more competent, agentic, and instrumental than women. Moreover, these differences extended beyond evaluations to beliefs about

occupations and appropriate roles. People who are not labeled feminine or masculine are termed *androgynous* individuals, because they have a mixture of the traits traditionally assigned to one sex or the other (e.g., Bem, 1974).

Do we know what factors are crucial to the formation of stereotypes, especially gender stereotypes? Recent research has explored some of the factors that may be involved in their formation. Eagly (1987) suggests that the typical social roles performed by men and women in society call for the characteristics that people have come to associate with each sex. Men have come to occupy positions that require attributes such as agency, independence, instrumentality, and task orientation, whereas women have tended to occupy positions that require communality, emotional expressiveness, and nurturance. According to Eagly, men and women develop the personality characteristics needed to fill certain roles. Thus, she feels that men and women are born with the same personality potential, but the different social roles they play dispose the individual to select and develop some personality characteristics at the expense of others. In another social role analysis, Hoffman and Hurst (1990) found that objective sex differences in personality are not necessary for the formation of gender stereotypes; the mere fact of the division of labor based on sex is sufficient. In this more cognitive explanation, gender stereotypes arise to justify or rationalize gender roles.

In her review of the literature, Valian (1998) takes a cognitive approach by emphasizing that the most salient and distinctive social role occupied by women is motherhood, and the most obvious characteristic of motherhood is physical nurturance. Throughout human history, women have borne, nursed, and cared for infants. This has constrained women's mobility, and thus it made sense for them to remain at home and assume child-care and homemaking responsibilities. This act of physical nurturance is extrapolated to the personality realm, so that women are seen—regardless of whether they really are—as more psychologically nurturing as well. According to Valian, the perception of this single salient difference creates and amplifies other gender stereotypes.

Cross-cultural research has suggested that some aspects of gender stereotypes are remarkably similar across cultures. For example, in one major study of "typical characteristics" of women and men, Williams and Best (1990) asked college students in 25 countries to rate the extent to which each of 300 adjectives was associated with males and females. In at least 19 of the countries, males were associated with the following adjectives: *adventurous, aggressive, autocratic, daring, dominant, enterprising, forceful, independent, masculine, stern,* and *strong.* Women were associated with the following adjectives: *affectionate, feminine, sensitive, sentimental, submissive,* and *superstitious.* In some countries (such as Japan and Nigeria), male-associated terms were rated more favorably than female-associated terms, and in other countries (such as Italy and Brazil), female-associated terms were perceived as more positive. Interestingly, the only major societal variable that differed between the countries with the positive and negative stereotypes for women and men was religion. Countries with religious traditions in which females were visible in religious ceremonies and were portrayed as virtuous and powerful (e.g., as deities and saints) had much more positive views of women than did countries whose religious traditions did not feature women prominently. (See Chapter 2 for a discussion of mythology and religion.)

Unfortunately, perceived similarities among females (or males) may be inaccurate and perpetuate the formation of faulty gender stereotypes (Deaux & Kite, 1993). Interest in exploring racial and ethnic stereotypes, as well as gender stereotypes, arose in psychology at least in part due to the rise of feminism (Deaux, 1995).

Gender schemas are structures that allow a person to organize information related to gender by linking gender labels to objects, traits, and behaviors. Children learn to categorize information based on gender at a young age and demonstrate this knowledge in their preferences for play, toys, and playmates (Martin & Little, 1990). The degree to which children display gender stereotyping is thought to represent the strength of their gender schemas (Templeton, 1999). A study conducted by Templeton (1999) found

that a group of 6-year-old children demonstrated gender-schematic processing and interpreted ambiguous situations in terms of gender regardless of their level of gender stereotyping (Templeton, 1999).

Many children are stigmatized by the outside world as well as by their families for exhibiting atypical gender behavior. Several gay men report having experienced painful childhoods because they were "gentle and sensitive" boys, and their parents were unable to accept their atypical interests and possible homosexuality. In recent years, professionals have worked to educate people about the fact that although extreme gender nonconformity in childhood is associated with a homosexual or bisexual identity in adulthood, neither of these is a disorder. Despite progress that has been made in understanding this, many children exhibiting atypical gender behavior are still tormented and teased (Crawford, 2003). This reinforces the idea that stereotypes based on gender are still in existence and can be expressed in a wide variety of domains.

In considering how stereotypes are organized, we first need to consider the basis for their organization. Because an individual's sex is typically highly visible and salient to observers (race, ethnicity, and age are other examples), sex is a foundation for cognitive categorization. The result is a number of gender stereotypes that are based on whether a person is perceived to be male or female. Furthermore, when researching the stereotypes that people hold, many gender stereotypes may actually be a mixture of sex, race, and/or class (see Box 1.2). Not only are the characteristics ascribed to men and women different, but these same characteristics also have different amounts of desirability.

The extent to which gender stereotypes reflect actual gender comparisons between men and women is debatable. Whatever "truth" does exist within the roles ascribed to men and women may originate in biology or environment, or be a function of the interaction of the two. However, it is dangerous to take a gender stereotype and apply it to every individual, no matter how truthful it might seem to be at a group level (Deaux & Kite, 1993). Yet gender-associated processes are often so deeply ingrained and subtle

Box 1.2 _____

Stereotypes of Women
by Race and Class

BLACK WOMEN	WHITE WOMEN
Hostile	Warm
Dirty	Vain
Emotional	Dependent
Superstitious	Intelligent

MIDDLE-CLASS WOMEN	LOWER-CLASS WOMEN
Intelligent	Talkative
Ambitious	Irresponsible
Competent	Dirty
Happy	Dependent

Source: Adapted from "Race × Class Stereotypes of Women," by H. Landrine, 1985, *Sex Roles, 13,* pp. 65–75.

that most of us do not even realize how strongly they affect our behavior, thoughts, feelings, language, interactions with others, and the structures of social institutions. Some psychologists have proposed that it may be more beneficial to explore the ways in which gender differences are produced rather than to debate about the extent and truth of their existence. For example, psychologists could study girls with exceptionally high math abilities to determine what has influenced their abilities, whether it is biological or social, and focus more on ways to create more equal opportunities for girls (Halpern, 1986; Hyde & Linn, 1986).

Returning to the example of Ann Hopkins, the testimony of a cognitive psychologist at the trial pointed out that a number of conditions encouraged the use of gender stereotypes for *outgroups,* or individuals who are not perceived as members of one's own group. These conditions included the following: Hopkins's near-solo status in the firm; her job, which was traditionally held by men; her personal attributes that made her fit for her job as a manager but that were not typical for women and that could "create dissatisfaction among their subordinates." Further-

more, female stereotypes are elicited when judgments are made of ambiguous traits, such as an individual's "warmth," "collegiality," or "interpersonal skills." It was Hopkins's gender, not her track record, that was narrowly evaluated and became the primary category by which she was judged. Future research needs to consider the institutionalization of discrimination by examining the environment or "playing field" in which women are evaluated.

In sports, for example, athletes, coaches, and referees expect that the playing field will be level; that is, players from all teams must subscribe to the same rules in order for fairness and equality to prevail. In social life, however, playing fields are not necessarily level and exert considerable influence in facilitating or negating the stereotyping process. One playing field that concerns us is that of science, including psychology. As we will see, science is not isolated and immune from antifemale prejudices, stereotypes, and discrimination.

SEX DISCRIMINATION IN SOCIETY AND SCIENCE: BLATANT, SUBTLE, AND COVERT

Sex Discrimination in Society

Sex discrimination, the harmful and unequal treatment of individuals due to their sex, is a function of both internal processes, such as cognitive categorization that underlies much stereotyping, and the power that men have to invoke antifemale prejudices through everyday practices that deny women the very privileges that men enjoy. Before reading on, answer the questions in Box 1.3.

According to Benokraitis and Feagin (1995), **sexism** produces greater disadvantages for women than for men because it is women who are targeted more frequently. Although men may experience discrimination due to other social variables (religion, age, race, or sexual preference), their gender neutralizes these other sources of discrimination. Being female, on the other hand, predicts discrimination more than other variables. In many domains, including achievement, simply being male advantages men and simply being female disadvantages women. In addi-

Box 1.3_____

A Self-Study

Using the scale below, indicate how often the event has happened to you over the course of your life.

1   2   3   4   5   6

the event   *the event*
never   *happened*
happened   *almost*
                        all the time

Answer 1: If the event has NEVER happened to you.
Answer 2: If the event happened ONCE IN A WHILE.
Answer 3: If the event happened SOMETIMES.
Answer 4: If the event happened A LOT.
Answer 5: If the event happened MOST OF THE TIME.
Answer 6: If the event happened ALMOST ALL THE TIME.

1. How many times have people made inappropriate or unwanted sexual advances to you because you are a woman?
2. How many times have you been treated unfairly by your coworkers, fellow students, or colleagues because you are a woman?
3. How many times have you wanted to tell someone off for being sexist?
4. How many times have you been denied a promotion or a raise because you are a woman?
5. How many times have you been picked on, hit, pushed, shoved, or threatened with harm because you are a woman?
6. How many times have you been forced to listen to sexist jokes or degrading sexual jokes?
7. How many times have you gotten into an argument or fight about something sexist that was done or said to you or to somebody else?
8. How many times have people failed to show you the respect that you deserve because you are a woman?
9. How many times have you been treated unfairly by teachers or professors because you are a woman?
10. How many times have you been treated unfairly by your boyfriend, husband, or other important man because you are a woman?

Source: Adapted from "The Schedule of Sexist Events: A Measure of Lifetime and Recent Sexist Discrimination in Women's Lives," by E. A. Klonoff and H. Landrine, 1995, *Psychology of Women Quarterly, 19,* pp. 439–472.

_____

tion, being female is braided with additional social variables, such as age, race or ethnicity, and social class, to produce greater disadvantage (Benokraitis & Feagin, 1995).

Blatant Sexism.   After answering the questions in Box 1.3, you may notice that the behaviors you experienced varied along a number of dimensions. According to Benokraitis and Feagin, sexism varies as a function of its visibility, intentionality, and ease of documentation. **Blatant sexism** occurs when women are treated in a transparently harmful and unequal way. Physical violence, sexist jokes, degrading language, sexual harassment, unequal treatment under the law or in employment fall into this category. The effects of blatant sexism, such as inequality in employment, are well documented (see Chapter 7).

Subtle Sexism.   **Subtle sexism** is less apparent than blatant sexism because it is less visible to others as well as to ourselves. Benokraitis and Feagin make the point that we have internalized negative cultural messages regarding the inferiority of women, despite all of our outward attempts to say that we believe in the equality of women. For example, when three or four male faculty members congregate in a parking lot to chat, other faculty merely think they are sharing information or passing the time of day together and wave as passing by the group. When three or four female faculty members form a group, however, other faculty members may feel they can joke to the threesome or foursome that they are forming a "cabal." When men form a group, onlookers do not experience any message except a wave or inattention. For a cluster of women, however, the message is different. When they form a group, it is inferred to be for the sinister purpose of plotting, intrigue, or conspiracy. According to Benokraitis and Feagin, subtle sexism is not necessarily manipulative, intentional, or malicious; however, it can be. Furthermore, it can be documented, though it is difficult to do so because many people do not perceive it as a threat.

Covert Sexism.   Distinctive from blatant and subtle forms of sexism, **covert sexism** is intentional, hidden, and frequently hostile. This form of sexism refers to behavior that is deliberate in attempting to thwart women and assure their failure. Applications for jobs or promotions are "lost" but then found after the job is filled or the promotion occurs. Covert sexism can be very difficult to prove or document, and strategies, such as sabotage of a woman on the job, are easy to deny (Benokraitis & Feagin, 1995).

Sex Discrimination in Science

According to most traditional definitions, **science** is a knowledge-based activity that depends on facts accumulated through systematic and objective questioning, hypothesis testing, methodological study, analysis, and presentation. In most college classrooms, science is presented as a dispassionate activity (Rabinowitz & Sechzer, 1993). As conventionally presented, a scientist is not sentimental, irrational, emotional, or imprecise (Fausto-Sterling, 1992b; Rabinowitz & Sechzer, 1993). Historians of science,

however, have pointed to a number of errors and shortcomings in science (e.g., Jacklin, 1981). Vita Rabinowitz and Susan Weseen (1997) have noted that "As in other scientific fields, the history of psychology is replete with examples of failures to replicate results, peculiar omissions and preoccupations, and misinterpretations of findings" (p. 626). Commonly, different scholars interpret the "same findings" quite differently at different times. To take just one example, American social psychologists (with the important exception of Solomon Asch) have tended to interpret Asch's famous research on the effects of group pressure as supporting the notion that people are conforming, and this interpretation has gained force over time. European psychologists (and Asch himself) saw the same work as suggesting that people are remarkably independent of group pressure (Asch, 1951; Friend, Rafferty, & Bramel, 1990). Gender comparisons in science are particularly fraught with difficulty and subject to misinterpretation.

Men's prominence in the history of the field of psychology parallels sex role stereotypes pervading our society. Psychology might have more accurately been called the psychology of men (see Box 1.4). Most research in the first half of the twentieth century was carried out by men, with a predominance of male participants. In the rare event that a study did include some female participants, male–female differences were not explored. In fact, close to 95 percent of all early research never looked at male–female comparisons (Denmark, 1976; Sechzer, Griffin, & Pfafflin, 1994).

The few studies carried out in the early years of the twentieth century that did look at male–female differences (and were carried out by male investigators) overwhelmingly concluded that females were inferior partly based on an idea called the *variability hypothesis.* This hypothesis, which was prominent in the early 1900s, posited that males were more variable than females on many dimensions and that this greater variability of males indicated their higher status and greater potential. However, Leta Hollingworth, a female psychologist conducting research during this time, and her colleagues found no female–male differences in variability (Denmark & Fernandez, 1993).

BOX 1.4

A Psychologist Remembers

In 1991, the annual conference of the American Psychological Association was held in San Francisco. A friend of the authors of this text attended the meetings and has told this story widely:

I was standing at a publisher's book stall and was admiring their new textbook on the psychology of women. It was very enjoyable to consider the scope and depth of recent scholarship on women, as many of the topics were long neglected. I made a few comments to the publisher's representative. Within a few moments, I noticed that another psychology professor joined me and the bookseller in the book stall. A couple of minutes later, I heard the professor ask: "Where are your psychology of men textbooks?"

I have to say, in all honesty, that without missing a beat, I wheeled around, quickly scanning his badge for his name and university affiliation, and advised him, in as nonchalant a voice as I could gather: "Why don't you examine any introductory psychology textbook published before 1978. Most of the human subjects, and even the rats, were white and male."

The psychologist looked taken aback at first and then his facial expression changed and he looked down. After about 10 seconds, he nodded his head up and down slowly and looked back up and said, "I need to think about this, don't I." I nodded back. He smiled and walked away.

I went back to paging through the new textbook. At that moment, I knew that psychology, and some psychologists, were being challenged during a wholesale change in the production of psychological knowledge. It was a great moment.

Source: Leonore Loeb Adler, personal communication, August 1991.

In 1914, Hollingworth found that when birth weight and length of neonates were examined, the female sex (if any) was favored in terms of variability (Montague & Hollingworth, 1914). Hollingworth also concluded that women's physical and mental performance did not fluctuate according to the phases of the menstrual cycle, as had been previously surmised (Hollingworth, 1914). Lowie and Hollingworth (1916) reported that the objective evidence of cross-cultural, biological, and psychological studies did not support the notion of innate female inferiority. Thus, not only did Hollingworth and her colleagues refute the variability hypothesis based on scientific research; but they also elucidated the gender bias underlying the hypothesis. Yet, during this period the history of the field of psychology tended to neglect women's roles and contributions to the field—a serious omission, as the reader will see (Russo & Denmark, 1987).

Viola Klein (1950) aptly summarized our cognitive heuristics or shortcuts in describing male versus female behavior. She pointed out our cultural tendency to note a wide variation in male abilities and dispositions while summarizing women in homogenous terms. Klein keenly noted a fact regarding stereotyping in research that was carried out well into the 1960s: Male researchers tended to note the wide individual difference of men ("us") but tended to view women as a distinct psychological type ("them") (Denmark & Fernandez, 1993). "Whether she is strong-willed or meek, single-minded or hesitant, gentle or quarrelsome—she is supposed to possess a particular version of whatever trait she manifests and her stubbornness or submissiveness, her capriciousness or lack of humor will be found 'typically feminine' " (Klein, 1950, p. 4).

In the late nineteenth and early twentieth centuries, myths about women's inferiority pervaded society. The popularity of Social Darwinism, or "survival of the fittest," reinforced the belief that men were superior to women as a result of natural selection based on sex. Early female psychologists had their hands full, attempting to disprove notions such as the debilitating effect of the menstrual cycle on women and women's emotional fragility (see Box 1.5). As psychoanalytic theory became more popular, female psychologists were forced to contend with concepts such as penis envy and inferior superego development in women. As these beliefs grew more widespread, the disadvantaged position of women in psychology became more salient (Denmark & Fernandez, 1993).

As social psychology and human learning blossomed as fields in psychology, so too did the idea that social factors in behavior were important in understanding gender differences (Denmark & Fernandez, 1993).

Research that focuses on male–female differences due to biology or early socialization contributes, in some instances, to the notion that women are deficient. This notion "is seen in the explanations for women's lack of achievement motivation, their excessive fear of success, their lack of self-confidence, or their desire for children" (Kahn & Yoder, 1989, p. 424). Such research contributes to the status quo because it reflects

---

BOX 1.5_____

G. Stanley Hall

G. Stanley Hall is considered to be one of the founders of modern psychology. Most accounts of Hall focus on his early concerns with functionalism, that is, the study of mental functions and adaptive processes. Many functionalists were influenced by Darwin's evolutionary theory, which Hall used to support his theory of sex differences. Leslie Diehl (1988) maintains that, excepting scholarship by feminists (Rosenberg, 1982; Shields, 1975), most historians have ignored Hall's interest in women's nature and sex differences. Hall, in fact, was a leader of the movement against coeducation in the early part of the twentieth century. Although males and females were represented in most grade schools and high schools by the turn of the century, the fledgling presence of women in colleges and universities renewed the controversy. His views on evolution influenced his theory of human development (G. S. Hall, 1904, in Diehl, 1988).

Adolescence was a period of biological differentiation that necessitated different roles for men and women in life as well as in education. It was especially during the period of adolescence that Hall thought women should be separated from men due to the danger of damage to the female reproductive system. Coeducation could potentially feminize men in Hall's view. Furthermore, coeducation was both an attack on the role of women as mothers and therefore on the future of humanity. Furthermore, in Hall's view, "the truest measures of the effects of education on the development of the reproductive organs were the reduced number of marriages among female college graduates and the smaller number of children produced" (Diehl, 1988, p. 300). Hall's views were hardly unanimously accepted by the public or psychologists, but he singled out feminists for special attack, charging them with wanting to deny the monthly pain of menstruation of young girls (1908, p. 10240) and with trying to "escape the monthly function" (1904, p. 609) in their research and theorizing.

Hall's writings on the topic have enjoyed near obscurity but his role in the lives of women undergraduates was potentially more potent. Hall was a chief administrator at Clark University from 1888 through 1920. In 1889, he prevailed with the board of trustees at Clark to deny women admission to the university and later, under public and state pressure, took a stance that would void women's chance to be fully admitted to undergraduate and master's programs. Yet he did enroll women in graduate programs. According to Diehl, the paradox of the psychological theoretician and administrator was due to the fact that to Hall, women students were unusual and not typical of women in general. Alternatively, perhaps the women at Clark University appealed to Hall's own proclivities as a theoretician. For example, just as Hollingworth enrolled at Columbia where there were instructors who shared her perspective on sex differences, Hall himself could have attracted female students who ascribed to his own views on sex differences (Rosenberg, 1982).

the belief that differences between men and women, attributed to either biology or early socialization, are permanent and intractable (Kahn & Yoder, 1989; Prilleltensky 1989). Furthermore, such research can sound as though it is blaming the victim as the context in which these differences emerge is left unexamined and unchallenged (Kahn & Yoder, 1989; Ryan, 1971).

Attention to social and contextual variables yields correctives to many long-standing truisms in sex difference research. For example, for many years scientists concluded that boys were naturally better at math than girls (Benbow & Stanley, 1980). However, many factors other than biology could account for this finding. In a study of mathematically gifted girls and boys (Fox, 1987), girls were significantly less confident in their abilities than were their male counterparts. In fact, girls take fewer math courses in high school than boys do (Peterson & Crockett, 1987). Moreover, the perceived usefulness of mathematics plays a role in the discrepancy between males and females. As females tended to perceive less utility for mathematics in the future, so too did their test scores diminish (Hilton, 1987).

Motivation could also help explain the differences. Denmark and Francois (1987) have noted that, because studies have shown that enjoying math may be considered unfeminine, performing well "on the SAT mathematics test may not be very important to girls. They might not consider themselves 'high achievers' even if they did receive high scores" (p. 65). As noted much earlier by Fennema and Sherman (1977), math *ability* has also been confounded with math *training,* as well as with parents' attitudes, teachers' attitudes, and informal math experiences.

A meta-analysis of gender differences (Hyde, Fennema, & Lamon, 1990) comprising the testing of 3 million persons found no gender differences in math ability with the one exception of the area of problem solving. Here males scored noticeably higher beginning in high school, with the differences increasing during college. Males hold the belief that "math is for men" much more strongly than girls and women do. This suggests that it is not necessarily true that women are deterred from math courses and math-related activities because of their own beliefs,

but it may be that boys and men behave toward girls and women with a subtle pressure not to achieve in math and science (Hyde et al., 1990). For further information on gender differences in mathematical aptitude, see Chapter 6.

FEMINIST PERSPECTIVES AND IDEOLOGY

The feminist movement has raised the consciousness of both women and men revealing how our everyday lives and social norms reinforce male dominance. Although there have been individual women who have acted to change male dominance or patriarchy in their own particular spheres, feminist movements arose to develop and implement broad-based social actions to challenge a whole range of social and cultural traditions regarding sex and gender (Stockard & Johnson, 1992). The beginnings of **feminism** date back to 1903 with the founding of the Women's Social and Political Union (WSPU) in Britain by Emmeline Pankhurst and her daughters, which initiated the **"first wave of feminism"** (Humm, 1992). In the United States, the first formally organized convention for women's rights was held in 1848 in Seneca Falls, New York. The conference, attended by three hundred people and organized by Elizabeth Cady Stanton and Lucretia Mott, produced a document endorsing women's rights, the Declaration of Sentiments, which paralleled the Declaration of Independence.

Feminism: Not a "Brand Label"

The term *feminism* was not used until the twentieth century and refers to the belief that women and men are equal and should be equally valued as well as have equal rights (Offen, 1988). Feminism has a broad-based perspective and encompasses several different ideologies, each with a unique frame of reference. Yet, many of these theories and viewpoints intersect and are not strictly exclusive. All, however, criticize the ways in which women have been "oppressed, repressed, and suppressed" and "celebrate the ways in which so many women have 'beaten the system,' taken charge of their own destinies, and encouraged each other" (Tong, 1989, pp. 1–2).

There is not one type of feminist, just as there is not one type of sexist. Feminism is a broad movement that enables researchers to adopt different perspectives of feminism as they conduct research and generate theory. The term *feminist* does not accurately portray the various views that inform the scholarship that is considered feminist. The term *feminist,* however, is many times used by nonfeminists as a caricature of individuals who are characterized by negative traits as discussed later.

One viewpoint, **socialist feminism,** does not focus on individuals, but on social relations and how social institutions preserve and promote male dominance. Socialist feminism emphasizes the need to change our economic system as a precondition to gender equality. Economic and sexist oppression are seen as fundamental aspects of society that reinforce each other. For example, most social feminists believe that a few wealthy white people exploit the working class and all men exploit women.

Socialist feminists often study the relationship of inequalities stemming from social class, race, and ethnicity as well as from gender. Socialist feminism stresses unity and integration, both in the sense of integrating all aspects of women's lives and in the sense of producing a unified feminist theory (Tong, 1989). These groups call for a fundamental restructuring of social institutions and social relationships.

Radical feminism, a second feminist perspective, focuses on the control of women by men. Whereas socialist feminists emphasize both economic and sexist oppression, the position of radical feminists is that men's oppression of women is primary and serves as a model for all other oppression (e.g., economic and racial). The goal of radical feminism is the abolition of class and gender inequality and the creation of a new culture and society based on a more balanced integration of female and male power. Radical feminists also believe that in order to end the oppression of women, it is necessary to establish women-centered systems and beliefs. Therefore, change is needed on all levels.

The theory of radical feminism is still evolving and therefore is not as well developed as those of the other feminist groups. One reason is that unlike the other feminist groups, radical feminists reject feminisms rooted in theories developed by men. The theory of radical feminism must be developed by women and must be based on women's experiences. Because of oppression, women have had few chances to come together to understand their experiences and to develop theories (Rosser, 1992). Research in this domain often looks at sexuality and violence against women in order to understand the origin of males' greater power in our society.

A third feminist perspective, **cultural feminism,** seeks to emphasize the characteristics and qualities of women that have been devalued and ignored in our society—qualities such as female tendencies toward being nurturing, caring, and concerned for the needs of others. Cultural feminism supports the idea that our society should acknowledge and honor unpaid work contributed by women in our culture.

A fourth feminist perspective, **liberal feminism,** focuses on equality. This perspective defines a feminist as one who believes that females are entitled to total social and legal equality with males, and who supports revisions in values, mores, and laws in order to achieve this equality. This feminist perspective also believes that males and females are more alike than different, and that if given similar, equal opportunities and situations, men and women will behave similarly.

Liberal feminism is sometimes referred to as "equal opportunity feminism" (Stockard & Johnson, 1992). Liberal feminists do not seek special privileges but demand that everyone receive consideration without discrimination on the basis of gender. For almost three decades, liberal feminists have championed for changes in our language, changes in how the media represent women, and even changes in religious practices. According to Stockard & Johnson (1992), "These attempts have met with such success that some authors have suggested that we are in a postfeminist era" (p. 18).

The label *feminist* is considered somewhat stigmatizing by some, and many people therefore tend to avoid classifying themselves as such. Yet the same people will express views consistent with those of liberal feminism. For example, in a recent teaching experience, one of the authors asked the class how many of them would call themselves feminists and she got a minimal positive response. However, when she asked them how many believed in justice and equality for all races, classes, and sexes, they responded unanimously in the affirmative.

THE FEMINIST CRITIQUE IN PSYCHOLOGY

Feminists are not antiscience. Indeed many prominent feminist researchers within psychology have dedicated their careers to demonstrating how rigorous scientific research can dispel myths and stereotypes harmful to women. Feminist researchers, like feminists in other domains, vary in the problems that they tackle and the specific research methods that they use to approach problems.

Research and theorizing on gender comparisons continue and are popular among some feminists. Some feminist psychologists focus almost exclusively on differences between women and men in their writing and research (e.g., Belenky, Clinchy, Goldberger, & Tarole, 1986; Gilligan, 1982). According to these authors, gender differences are important and show, for example, that women are more caring, more interpersonally effective in leadership skills, and have other special characteristics. These characteristics are consistent with many gender stereotypes of women as distinct from men and men's stereotypical cluster of traits.

Other feminist research psychologists have tended to find fewer gender differences than have researchers such as Gilligan and others who depend on case histories and alternative research approaches (Eagly, 1995a). While noting that some large gender differences have been found in psychology, such as women smiling much more than men (Hall, 1984), these feminist psychologists have argued that most differences are zero to moderate in size (Hyde & Plant, 1995). Furthermore, they say that by focusing on differences, the similarities, which are more numerous and equally important, become obscured. As we shall see throughout this book, women and men are more alike than they are different.

The above example of a gender difference, women smiling more than men, is explained by Hyde

and Plant as due to the social dominance of men in interpersonal situations (Hyde & Plant, 1995). These researchers argue that research that focuses on gender differences does not help promote the causes of women and the social change that is needed. Furthermore, problems in gender comparison research revolve around difficulties in defining and measuring differences, and in removing values in the interpretation of results. Continuing to focus on differences between males and females may serve to keep women in inferior social positions. Researchers with this perspective (e.g., Hyde & Plant) advocate integrating feminist research into each area of psychology, which would obviate any need for a separate study of the psychology of women. Focusing instead on similarities, which are more common, may help women more easily gain legal and social parity with men. Conversely, others have argued that a focus on similarity has obscured important gender differences and that a focus on such differences could "enhance women's ability to understand the antecedents of inequality and to improve their status in society" (Eagly, 1995b, p. 155).

We now know that although sex differences have been studied in psychology since its inception, it is often not clear precisely what is being studied. Terms such as *sex, gender, male, female, masculine,* and *feminine* have been used too loosely or inclusively to describe everything from the biological sex of participants to the social or situational factors considered appropriate to males and females. Whenever females and males are compared and differences assessed, so many uncontrollable variables are correlated with biological sex that we can never know which variable played a causal role in a gender difference. For instance, female and male groups in any one study may be different in height, body fat composition, educational background, social skills, athletic experience, eating habits, and a host of other variables too numerous to measure. Feminist researchers have pointed to the dangerous and unscientific tendency to interpret gender differences as originating in innate biological differences—sex differences—without evidence supporting those claims (Rabinowitz & Sechzer, 1993).

It is by now well known that many long-established "sex differences," on reexamination, are bound by historical, social, cultural, and contextual factors and do not endure over time, populations, or situational context. For example, as we will see in Chapter 6, the difference in mathematical ability between males and females is shrinking over time in the United States. Many gender differences have been reinterpreted as power or status differences. Moreover, the conventional focus on sex differences in the psychological literature obscures the many ways in which males and females are similar.

Biases in Research

Over 30 years ago, coinciding with the women's movement in the 1970s, a few feminist psychologists began raising questions about how we did research in psychology and related fields, including **bias in research methods.** They noted, for example, that the research questions posed reflected men's interests and concerns more than women's and that gender-role stereotypes affected all aspects of the research. They pointed out that male research participants were much more commonly used than female participants and that findings based on males were indiscriminately generalized to females. Increasingly, feminists noticed that the bias in the choice of research participants, with its attendant biases in many other aspects of the research, was rampant in animal research as well as human research, and in health and biomedical research as well as behavioral and social research (Sechzer, Denmark, & Rabinowitz, & 1993; Sechzer, Zmitrovich, & Denmark, 1985). In some cases, findings based solely on male animals have been generalized to human females (Sechzer, Griffin, & Pfafflin, 1994)! Over the past four decades, clear progress has been made in psychology toward the conduct of gender-fair research. There is recent evidence that related fields such as biomedicine are following suit, due largely to a federal mandate established in the mid-1990s to include women (and ethnic minorities) in research that is relevant to both males and females. But progress in the conduct of nonsexist research in biomedicine, health, and some areas of research prac-

tice in psychology has been slow and, in certain quarters, grudging. Let us briefly review how feminist psychologists, along with psychologists of color, gay male and lesbian psychologists, and other scholars who represent disenfranchised groups in psychology and society, are changing the practice of psychological research.

Traditional, Nonsexist, and Feminist Approaches to Research

Among many, but by no means all researchers, there is increased understanding and acceptance of the fact that science is not, and cannot be, value-free. Our values arise from our experience of our gender, race, cultural and ethnic background, social class, and other influences, and they enrich at the same time that they constrain our work. Values affect all phases of a research project from the choice of what to study to the conclusions drawn from the results. Pervasive beliefs about the objectivity of science prevent us from seeing the nature and limits of scientific knowledge, and have worked to preserve the status quo in society (Rabinowitz & Sechzer, 1993).

Rabinowitz and Sechzer (1993) and Denmark, Russo, Frieze, and Sechzer (1988) have reviewed many of the issues that arise in the nuts and bolts of conducting more gender-fair research, such as the formulation of research questions, the conduct of the literature review, the choice of research participants and research designs, the operationalization of variables, and the analyzing and interpretation of results. These issues are discussed next.

Question Formulation.   Traditional psychology has begun its analysis from men's experience, particularly white middle-class men's experiences. Questions have been asked about the conditions under which females are cognitively impaired, but not about when males are so impaired, just as they have been asked about male sexual arousal far more often than about female sexual arousal. In psychological research in general, the concentration has been on topics such as aggression, conflict, dominance, work achievement, and cognitive processes and has downplayed topics such as affiliation, cooperation, family issues, and emotional processes. As an essential corrective to male bias in psychology, the experiences, concerns, and perspectives of girls and women need to be better integrated into mainstream psychology.

Reviewing the Psychological Literature.   Most researchers get their ideas from reading other people's work. Many bodies of literature are rife with sexist assumptions and research practices, and are unreliable guides for feminist research. While analyzing scholarly literature, we need to identify likely sources of bias and consider how different research participants, treatments, designs, and measures might affect the results of the study.

Sample Selection.   Descriptions of participants in the research report typically include their sex. This is largely due to scientific convention, but also reflects assumptions that sex is a variable that affects results. There is a serious problem with conceptualizing sex (along with other participant characteristics) as an independent variable. It is a descriptive that is inherently confounded. It has obvious biological (genetic, hormonal, physiological), psychological (developmental, experiential), and sociocultural (socialization, economic, educational, political) components. Sex of research participants is not manipulable. Males and females are not randomly assigned to their gender, and gender comparisons are thus fraught with problems in interpretation, as we have already noted.

Research Design.   There are few topics in psychology for which it is safe to assume that gender is completely irrelevant. Feminist psychologists remind the scientific community that gender matters, and that we need to reflect this in our research. For instance, they caution that gender is a complex independent variable; if it is used as an independent variable, it needs to be taken apart (unpacked) and analyzed so that we can better understand which of the many facets of gender may be important in a given area. Beyond our participants, we need to take into account the sex of experimenters, confederates, and other people involved in our research.

It is by now a truism in research methodology that the choice of research design depends on the research question. Causal questions call for experimental designs when they are ethical and feasible to implement. But despite their unique advantages in permitting causal inferences, experiments frequently do not illuminate the processes underlying the relationships among variables, and, as we have noted, they are poor vehicles for understanding variables that are attributes such as gender, race, culture, and class. Given what many feminist researchers have found to be the inherent sexism of traditional scientific psychology, more and more feminists are exploring the use of alternative research methods, particularly qualitative methods, in their work. Qualitative research methods are particularly helpful in capturing the rich array of personal, situational, and structural factors that shape, and are shaped by, women and girls (Riger, 1992).

Operationalizations.   Females and males throughout the life span differ in the ideas, objects, and events to which they are exposed, the behaviors that they are able to practice, and the outcomes that they receive in the real world. For these reasons, we expect them to enter any experimental situation with different orientations, attitudes, perceptions, expectations, and skills. It has been pointed out by feminist theorists that the methods used in research experiments are not neutral, and the chosen method can shape and constrain findings (Crawford & Kimmel, 1999). Females and males respond to the same stimuli quite differently, and we need to determine the meaning to participants of experimental stimuli, tasks, and tests before assuming that all respondents share the researchers' perceptions and assumptions. Current writings in the field of psychology indicate that feminist research is moving toward models that acknowledge and take into account the fact that feminism is not monolithic in its politics or philosophy (Akman et al., 2001).

Data Analysis and Interpretation.   We have already discussed some of the most serious problems in testing for and interpreting gender differences. We need to be sure not to exaggerate or minimize such differences.

Oversimplified conclusions regarding gender differences can provide seemingly scientific justifications for stereotyping and discriminatory practices.

Guidelines for avoiding sexism in psychological research were developed for conducting gender-fair research (Denmark et al., 1988). As both experienced research psychologists and psychology students conduct research, they need to confront and reduce the potential for sexism at all stages of the research process. Box 1.6 provides a series of bias-related research problems and gender-fair research solutions.

Mapping Solutions for Gender-Fair Research

It is important when reporting gender differences to avoid value judgments about the direction of the differences, because these kinds of judgments have been used against women in the past. Thus, male rationality has been contrasted with female emotionality, male dominance with female submission, male independence with female dependence, and so on. The unspoken assumption underlying such evaluations is that if a response is more associated with females than males, there must be something wrong with it.

These critiques and correctives of traditional scientific practice, born in the 1970s, have woven their way into mainstream psychology. Increasingly, the insights and perceptions of 1990s feminist theory are changing our conceptions of the socially and culturally structured differences among people, and promising to change the practice of psychology still further (Sechzer, Griffin, & Pfafflin, 1994; Stewart, 1998). According to a leading feminist theorist and methodologist Abigail Stewart, contemporary feminist theories have even more to offer psychology. Stewart wrote specifically of improving and enriching research in personality, but her analysis has broader implications for all of psychology. She points to six areas wherein feminist theories can help us get behind invalid and limiting assumptions that render research less exciting and revealing than it might be, and she holds forth the promise of enriching psychological research generally.

Specifically, the practices that Stewart (1998) calls for are these:

1. Look for what has been left out of traditional research in an area, because features of women's experience have been left out of the discipline. For instance, the assumption that everyone has an equal chance of succeeding or failing to get what they want is not likely to be valid.

2. Analyze your own position as it affects your understanding and the research process. Our positions as educated middle-class professionals bias how we view all aspects of the research, even how we see the routine process of obtaining informed consent. Our participants' understanding of events, stimuli, and tests needs to become central to our analyses.

3. Use gender as an analytic tool, a category of analysis, as a socially constructed concept that has different and layered meanings in different cultural and historical contexts.

4. Consistent with the notion of gender as an analytic tool, gender is not (only) about difference but it is also about dominance or power relations. As Stewart notes, power is a critical aspect of gender requiring analysis in our research.

5. Explore other aspects of social position. Given the power dimension of gender, and moved by the evidence of the importance of power relations within groups of women who differ by race, culture, and class, for example, Stewart argues that we must consider how all aspects of structural power in a culture shape and define gender and the research topic under investigation.

6. Give up the search for a unified self: Individual personalities derive from multiple and conflicting forces. One is not, for example, entirely dominant or subordinate, but dominant and subordinate along particular dimensions and in particular contexts.

We conclude, along with Stewart, that contemporary theoretical and epistemological advances in feminist analyses can be mined for insights into how to improve theory and research in psychology, especially if they devote far greater attention to cultural diversity.

Feminist psychologist Hope Landrine challenges psychology in a multicultural world to develop

Box 1.6

Sexism-Related Research Problems and Gender-Fair Research Solutions

Science produces knowledge, but it is also a *human and social process*. Therefore, the production of knowledge can be affected by human values and assumptions, which can impact at one or more stages of the research process. The result, which many reviews of the literature support, is that science can produce highly biased knowledge, especially when conducting human research related to gender, race, ethnicity, disability, sexual preference, or socioeconomic status.

The following guidelines, although focused on gender, are based on principles that can be applied to other forms of bias as well.

QUESTION FORMULATION

Problem: Gender stereotypes that are associated with the topic being studied can bias question formulation and research outcomes.

Example: Some studies have defined leadership only in terms of dominance, aggression, and other styles that emphasize characteristics congruent with a male stereotype.

Correction: Recognize the existence of a range of leadership styles, including those that emphasize egalitarian relationships, negotiation, conflict resolution, and consideration of others. The limits of any definition that is used should be specified.

RESEARCH METHODS

Problem: The selection of research participants is based on stereotypic assumptions and does not allow for generalizations to other groups.

Example: On the basis of stereotypes about who should be responsible for contraception, only females are looked at in studies of contraception.

Correction: Both sexes should be studied before conclusions are drawn about the factors that determine use of contraception.

Problem: The sex and race of research participants, experimenters' confederates, and persons in direct contact with the participants are not specified. Potential interactions of sex and race or other variables may create unexplained variance.

Example: More helping behavior by males rather than females is found in studies that use a young female confederate who needs help. Such results may be a function of the sex of the confederate or an interaction of participant and confederate rather than a difference due to the gender of the research participants.

Correction: Control for or vary sex and race of persons involved in the research. Try to include experimenters and participants who are members of racial minorities. At a minimum, specify the sex and race of everyone involved in the research.

DATA ANALYSIS AND INTERPRETATION

Problem: Serendipitous gender differences are reported, but no report is made when differences are not found. Care must be taken to avoid giving a skewed image of the actual data.

Example: "In analyzing data, we found that males and females differed significantly on . . . "

Correction: Any nonhypothesized sex or gender differences should be reported and the need for replication indicated to assure that the difference is not artifactual. When gender differences are not found and where such an observation is relevant, this too should be reported so that future research could confirm or disconfirm the lack of any nonhypothesized gender differences.

Problem: Misleading implications of findings of gender differences are not addressed. Statistical significance is not clearly distinguished from the substantive significance.

Example: "The spatial ability scores of women in our sample are significantly lower than those of the men, at the .01 level." The reader is left to assume that perhaps women should not become architects or engineers.

Correction: "The spatial ability scores of the women are significantly lower than those of the men, at the .01 level. Successful architects score above 32 on our spatial ability test . . . ; engineers score above 31. . . . Twelve percent

(continued)

BOX 1.6   Continued

of the women and 16% of the men in our sample score above 31; 11% of the women and 15% of the men score above 32."

CONCLUSIONS

Problem: Results based on one sex are generalized to both.

Example: Threshold measurements in shock sensitivity for rats have been standardized for males, but are often generalized to both sexes.

Correction: There should be empirically determined norms for male and female study

participants that reflect differences in weight, body fat, and so on.

Problem: Evaluative labeling is used for results.

Example: Male aggressiveness is used as the standard of acceptability. Females are described as unaggressive or submissive.

Correction: Use neutral, objective descriptions, such as "the mean score for the aggression measure was higher for males than females."

Source: From "Guidelines for Avoiding Sexism in Psychological Research: A Report of the Ad Hoc Committee on Nonsexist Research," by F. L. Denmark, N. F. Russo, I. H. Frieze, and J. A. Sechzer, 1988, *American Psychologist, 43,* pp. 582–584. Copyright 1988 by American Psychological Association. Reprinted by permission of the publisher.

---

explicit theoretical frameworks through which sociocultural variables and differences will become salient. Specifically, Landrine calls for models for understanding cultural variables, a theory of the relationship between culture and behavior that neither romanticizes cultures nor renders difference deviant. She writes (Landrine, 1985):

> Culture is not just an additional variable that demarcates the local limits of otherwise universal gender-related principles and gender differences, nor is it simply an additional, moderating variable whose inclusion will allow researchers to account for a larger percentage of the variance in human behavior. Rather, culture is us, it is each of us, and thus only it can be known, revealed, and discovered in social science. Researchers need to understand that European American culture is the structure and content of feminist psychology and is the only thing that is discovered and revealed in feminist data, constructs, therapies, and theories on gender. (pp. 65–75)

Landrine concludes that culture will be regarded with dignity, and the sociology of knowledge in feminist scholarship advanced, only when all cultures are treated with equal respect.

FORMAL RECOGNITION OF THE PSYCHOLOGY OF WOMEN

The field of the psychology of women emerged in an effort to help rectify the problems discussed previously. Feminism became an important issue during the 1960s, as the women's liberation movement increased its activity. During this time, women's centers, women's studies programs, and college courses about women and their contribution to psychology were developed. One of us offered the first doctoral course ever in the psychology of women.

The psychology of women itself basically encompasses all psychological issues pertaining to women and their experience. This includes male gender-role behavior mediated by interactions with females. Official acceptance of the field within psychology came in 1973 when the American Psychological Association (APA) established **Division 35,** the Division of the Psychology of Women (Denmark & Fernandez, 1993).

The impact of the growth of the psychology of women, both in the United States and internationally, is shown by the following events. APA's nonsexist research guidelines (discussed earlier in this chapter), promoted through the efforts of Division 35 activities, have opened the way for the adoption of non-sexist guidelines in many disciplines besides psychology, including sociology and anthropology. The adoption of a form of these guidelines has occurred in many other countries as well. The preparation of nonracist, nonageist, and nonheterosexist guidelines was the direct result of the landmark APA guidelines. As Division 35 grew, it functioned to provide a forum for the development of an in-depth focus on understanding both the psychological and the social realities of women. Courses in the psychology of women are now taught in many countries, including Israel, Ireland, the Netherlands, Costa Rica, and Argentina as well as the United States.

The psychology of women affects all of psychology by highlighting methodological biases and emphasizing the need to use representative samples to yield generalizable data. In addition, the psychology of women or gender has blossomed into an interdisciplinary field—women's studies. The cross-fertilization of women's studies and psychology has resulted in an increased awareness of class, culture, and racial issues. The psychology of women continues to give rise to feminist pedagogy, which fosters the development of feminist identity, shared leadership during the learning process, and integration of emotional and factual learning, resulting in greater overall congruence and enhanced self-esteem.

Ethnic Minority Women

Just as there is no universal male experience, no female experience is universal. Women, like men, vary greatly in their ethnicities, cultures, classes, ages, and life experiences. Psychologists are increasingly acknowledging and studying diverse groups of women. Unfortunately, the vast majority of classical research focuses on White, middle-class women, and perspectives of women of color and poor women are virtually absent from psychology (Reid, 1993).

Pamela Trotman Reid has urged psychologists to analyze women in multiple contexts, to expand our focus to include multiple races and classes in our studies, and to consider gender alongside other major status characteristics. She has challenged psychology, particularly the psychology of women, to deal honestly and fully with female ethnicity and class (Reid, 1993).

Racial, ethnic, and class stereotypes interact with gender to promote subordination. Women may be in triple jeopardy, suffering oppression on the basis of gender, race or ethnicity, and class. As a result of being discriminated against and excluded because of both race and class, a woman may readily come to accept society's attribution of inferiority because of her gender. These factors have interesting ramifications for research with minority women, whose experience is unique (Hunter College Women's Studies Collective, 1995).

Today, some researchers are likely to be meticulous in providing demographic information about the populations they have studied. However, this effort is not sufficient. Although the race and social class of participants are included as descriptors, they are typically not evaluated as factors that affect the experience and shape the responsiveness of participants. For example, in research on college students, we see little or no recognition of the privilege associated with being White, middle class, and well educated. Questions about the impact of race remain reserved for people of color, and queries on social class are saved for working-class and poor people (Reid, 1993).

Ethnic minority women in the field of psychology have unfortunately been few and far between, and the history of ethnic minority female psychologists is minimal. Until 1940, only four Black universities offered psychology as a major, and few Blacks attended predominantly White universities. Sadly, the involvement of Asian, American Indian, and Hispanic women in psychology is even less monitored.

EMERGENCE OF THE PSYCHOLOGY OF MEN AS A DISTINCT FIELD

Basically, the study of psychology has been the psychology of men. More recently, men have come together in an attempt to better understand themselves within the context of social institutions that nurture and give rise to sexist values, and the context of their proscribed and strictly masculine gender role. The American Psychological Association recently established Division 51, the Society for the Psychological Study of Men and Masculinity.

Men, like women, have been affected by emotional and psychological boundaries. Herbert Goldberg was a prominent figure of this movement in the 1970s. His book, *The New Male,* stresses a man's need to become more sensitive to the emotional and physical aspects of the self (1980). In fact, some researchers have found that adherence to certain aspects of the male gender role can be detrimental to men's mental health and self-image.

In response to this, small groups of men were formed all over the nation in an effort to educate and raise consciousness regarding this issue. The first Men and Masculinity conference was held in 1974 (Lamm, 1977) and has continued to meet regularly to this day. The primary function of these conferences is to provide an arena for the concern that males in the United States (and elsewhere) are prevented from actualizing their full potential as human beings, and for discussion about the harm that assigning female and male gender roles can cause.

Many spin-offs have resulted from these male consciousness-raising experiences, and political repercussions were felt in the form of efforts to change laws that discriminate against men in their roles as fathers and as husbands, that is, divorce legislation, child custody, and visitation. Currently, **the men's movement** has diversified to include various groups across the country (Gross, Smith, & Wallston, 1983), such as antisexist groups and groups that are all male and believe that males have suffered because of the actions of feminist women. This particular aspect of the 1990s men's movement is epitomized by individuals such as Robert Bly, who rails against men's "softness" and emphasizes their need to reestablish their "truly" masculine identity.

Today, an ongoing debate regarding the impact of the feminist movement on boys and men still exists in the United States, the United Kingdom, and Australia. These debates are referred to as "about the boys." In the realm of education, several writers, therapists, and educationists directly attack the women's movement for the damage that it has done to boys. The position is taken by those with this belief that girls' success is achieved at the expense of boys. Boys are referred to as the "new disadvantaged" (Foster, Kimmel, & Skelton, 2001). Despite these arguments, the women's movement has only sought to place women on an equal plane with men. Its goal is not to place men and boys in a disadvantaged position, but to provide both genders with equal treatment and equal opportunity.

PSYCHOLOGICAL RESEARCH AND SOCIAL CHANGE

Historically, psychology is a field that has focused on changing people. Techniques for changing behavior, increasing knowledge about oneself, and decreasing unhealthy or unproductive thoughts and actions are used in numerous educational and treatment environments. Yet research has shown that the strength of these techniques alone is often not enough to effect individual change. Problems that are ingrained in society's structural fabric require more than individual modifications in behaviors and attitudes to solve them. Social institutions and environments that allow women to be victimized and treated unequally must be changed.

According to Kahn and Yoder (1989), the psychology of women can serve to foster rather than inhibit social change. For psychology to facilitate this process, psychologists and their students need to understand how behavior is shaped by external forces and also to imagine a society in which the roles, health, and issues pertinent to women are addressed so that solutions enhance women's well-being. Psychological research that concentrates on changing establishments such as the workplace, academic settings, business institutions, and the family looks at real people within complex social environments. The subsequent chapters of this text assemble the research and findings that will help shape, we hope, a psychology of social change in the future.

Currently, the psychology of women involves critiques of conventional constructs, research methods, and practices, as well as developing new forms of scholarship and practice that include feminist insights and values (Marecek, Kimmel, Crawford, & Hare-Mustin, 2003). Research and practice should take into account the various contexts in which men and women behave and recognize gender as a characteristic of a population (Reid, 2002). Although feminist efforts have helped women to become acknowledged in the field of psychology, there is still a need for sustained attention to more inclusive research and practice (Chin & Russo, 1997).

SUMMARY

The terms *sex* and *gender* are distinct. Sex refers to biological and genetic differences. Gender refers to the different clusters of traits, interests, and behaviors that societies ascribe to each sex. Although some traits and abilities are statistically different between the sexes, due to either socialization or biology, many "differences" in behavior are nonexistent, small, or moderate. Evolutionary psychology is important because it takes into consideration the biological differences historically believed to exist between the sexes; however, it is not testable and does not take into account the fact that women currently engage in many of the activities that were previously considered to be solely performed by men. The social constructionist perspective in psychology examines how differences are created and then used to justify nonneutral differences between men and women, which ultimately prove to be disadvantageous to women.

Theoreticians and researchers have developed different explanations for beliefs about gender. Some psychologists believe that gender is an outcome of socialization (cultural approach). Others believe gender is an outcome of the varying positions that women and men occupy in society (structural approach). Yet other psychologists have focused on the stereotypes, that is, cognitive rules of thumb that are widely held, oversimplified beliefs. Individuals use stereotypes when they cope with information. These gender stereotypes, or beliefs about what is appropriately feminine or masculine behavior, are influenced by sex, race, and class. The stereotypes associated with gender affect an individual's access to resources and power but so too does the environment or social context in which women care for others and engage in paid employment.

Sex discrimination underlies both everyday life and the practice of science. Sexism constantly reproduces the power inequities of women on a daily basis and varies along a number of dimensions. There are different types of sexism: blatant, subtle, and covert. Historically, myths about women's inferiority pervaded psychological science as well as society as witnessed in the difficulties women had in achieving parity with men in higher education. Paradoxically, some researchers insist on sex differences between men and women but note the superiority of women to men along a number of psychological dimensions. Psychologists themselves are divided regarding the implications of sex difference research. Feminists in psychology, just as "women" themselves, are not a homogenous group. The term *feminist* when used by itself does not accurately portray the various views which inform scholarship that is considered feminist. Some of the types of feminists identified were social feminists, radical feminists, and liberal feminists.

In science, values influence the questions asked, the methods pursued, and the interpretation of data. A variety of problems and biases occur in research. Some of these are exclusion of women as research participants, publication bias, gender differences in self-report, and an overreliance on college-age participants. Further problems in research concern the difficulty in discerning confounds. Are observed differences due to gender or are they due to status and power? Feminists have critiqued traditional research strategies and provided a number of solutions for gender-fair research. Such solutions hinge on accepting that science can never be completely value-neutral. In this context, social change brought about by psychological research promises to challenge the status quo. The psychology of women and gender has received recognition by the American Psychological Association. The importance of ethnicity, race, and class to the conduct of research will only enhance the production of knowledge that aims to maximize women's well-being.

Now that we have initiated the process of bringing women into focus, the next chapter will review the origins of the stereotypes and images of women that remain with us today.

KEY TERMS

Androcentric bias (p. 2)
Bias in research methods (p. 18)
Blatant sexism (p. 11)
Covert sexism (p. 12)
Cultural approach (p. 6)
Cultural feminism (p. 16)
Division 35 (p. 22)
Engendering psychology (p. 3)
Evolutionary psychology (p. 4)
Feminism (p. 15)

First wave feminism (p. 15)
Gender (p. 3)
Gender schemas (p. 9)
Gender stereotypes (p. 8)
Liberal feminism (p. 16)
Men's movement (p. 24)
Radical feminism (p. 16)
Science (p. 12)
Sex (p. 3)
Sex discrimination (p. 10)

Sexism (p. 10)
Social constructionism (p. 5)
Socialist feminism (p. 16)
Sociobiology (p. 4)
Stereotypes (p. 7)
Stereotyping (p. 6)
Structural approach (p. 6)
Subtle sexism (p. 11)

DISCUSSION QUESTIONS

1. What is the difference between sex and gender?

2. What are the processes that underlie the development of beliefs regarding gender?

3. What are the problems with research that focuses on gender differences?

4. Develop a list of the ways that sexism interacts with ageism or classism or racism. For example, what are the traits that women might be ascribed with if they are young, Hispanic, and poor versus the traits of women who are old, Black, and middle class? Describe why this may occur.

5. What is feminism? How has feminism positively impacted on research in psychology?

6. What are the positive and negative aspects of evolutionary psychology?

FURTHER READINGS

Benokraitis, N. V., & Feagin, J. R. (1995). *Modern sexism: Blatant, subtle, and covert discrimination* (2nd ed.). Englewood Cliffs, NJ: Prentice Hall.

Biaggio, M. & Hersen, M. (2000). *Issues in the psychology of women.* New York: Kluwer Academic/Plenum Publishers.

Bohan, J. S. (1992). *Seldom seen, rarely heard: Women's place in psychology.* Boulder, CO: Westview Press.

Chrisler, J. C., Golden, C., & Rozee, P. D. (Eds.). (2004). *Lectures on the Psychology of Women* (3rd ed.). New York: McGraw-Hill.

Denmark, F. L., & Paludi, M. A. (Eds.). (1993). *The psychology of women: A handbook of issues and theories.* Westport, CT: Greenwood Press.

Faludi, S. (1991). *Backlash: The undeclared war against American women.* New York: Crown.

Fine, M., Weis, L., Powell, C., & Wong, L. M. (1997). *Off white: Readings on race, power, and society.* New York: Routledge Press.

Tavris, C. (1992). *The mismeasure of woman: Why women are not the better sex, the inferior sex, or the opposite sex.* New York: Touchstone.

Chapter 2

THE IMPLICATIONS OF MYTHOLOGY AND RELIGION FOR WOMEN AND GENDER

From 3000 B.C.E. to C.E. 1100, man's view of himself as superior in all ways to women soon became enshrined in the law and custom of the world's earliest civilizations, those of the Near East. [A] Woman became a chattel first of her father, then of her husband, then of her son.
—Reay Tannahill

There are many scapegoats for our sins, but the most popular one is providence.
—Mark Twain

Those who say religion has nothing to do with politics do not know what religion is.
—Mohandas K. Gandhi

You may go over the world and you will find that every form of religion which has breathed upon this earth has degraded women. There is not one which has not made her subject to man.
—Elizabeth Cady Stanton

Psychology enlightens our understanding of all behavior and experience, including religious beliefs and practice. In fact, the psychology of religion is one of the oldest areas in all of psychology. Some of psychology's earliest leading figures, including William James and G. Stanley Hall, wrote extensively on this topic. In the 1970s the American Psychological Association established Division 36, the Division of the Psychological Study of Religious Issues, which recognizes the significance of religion both in the lives of people and in the discipline of psychology. The division is open to anyone with an interest in the opportunities and tensions that exist between psychology and religion (Nielson, 2000).

People's experiences and opinions of religious constructs and institutions are inextricably tied to gender. Research shows that there are female–male differences in all aspects of religious experience from extrinsic practices such as attendance at religious services to intrinsic beliefs and values such as spirituality. Despite the fact that women around the world are far more involved in religious activities than men, women are still far less likely than men to be formal religious leaders.

And, as we shall see, since earliest history, myths and religions have embodied images of women as inferior—socially, culturally, and biologically—which have since become entrenched in other cultural representations. In more recent times, we see these depictions in the economy, with underpaid and undervalued female employees at virtually all career levels (Blier, 1984). As social movements arise to threaten the social order vis à vis the status of women,

"it has been a recurrent phenomenon that corresponding 'scientific' theories emerge that implicitly defend the *status quo*"(Blier, 1984, p. vii).

How did these gender stereotypes and images come about? When and why did they arise and how were they maintained? What is the place of women in our society and how did that place develop? What are some of the ways in which women in various times and places have attempted to affect change?

This chapter addresses these questions. To answer them we need a historical context, "for every human event is the product of the interplay of the forces of the past and the responses of the forces of the present" (Swidler, 1976, p. 4). A historical context is especially relevant in pursuing and understanding societal attitudes and the status of women. Thus it is essential to explore how attitudes toward women developed in past societies and why and how they are prevalent in today's society. We will also see whether attempts to change attitudes about the status of women in the past were successful. Finally, we will discuss how these images of women enshrined in mythology and religion are affecting women's lives in contemporary society.

MYTHOLOGY AND RELIGION

Women as a Source of Evil

There exist many stories in early myths and religions about the creation of man and woman and about the evil, destructiveness, and mysteries of women. Many are familiar with the story of Pandora in classical Greek mythology. Pandora was the first mortal woman in Greek mythology; out of curiosity, she opened the cover of a forbidden jar containing Hope together with all the evils of mortals. Hope alone remained in the jar, but the evils within flew out and were scattered throughout the world and "for mortals devised sorrowful troubles." Pandora is seen as the origin of all the world's evils (Morford & Lenardon, 1995).

In the history of India, both female and male deities were worshiped. Traces of these beliefs and practices are found in the mythology that apparently predated the beginning of religion in India, as well as in the rural cultural traditions as far back as the third millennium B.C.E. The ancient goddess who was considered to have high power came to be named **Shakti.** She was held to be able to create as well as destroy, and the term *to have shakti* meant to have the energy of creation and destruction. In primitive times, this power was thought of as *femininity.* So the goddess, or "mother" as she was called, who can bring forth life is also the purveyor of death. The critical association that India has made throughout 4,000 years of worship and religious development is that this "primordial femininity" needs the control of a "primordial masculinity" (Carmody, 1989, p. 42) that is considered consistent, cerebral, and without fervor. It was thought that if this ancient goddess was not controlled she would create turmoil and upheaval through the excess use of her energy. According to Carmody, the social constraints on women still found in Hindu society have found sanction in this primitive concept of the nature of the female.

Perhaps the most famous story portraying the evil of women is found in the story of Genesis in the Old Testament of the Hebrews. Adam and Eve, the first man and woman, were placed in the Garden of Eden by the Lord. They were forbidden by the Lord to eat fruit from the tree of knowledge. Eve could not resist temptation. She ate the fruit of the tree and gave the fruit to Adam. And, as the serpent told them, they each "knew both good and evil" (Genesis III:5). For succumbing to temptation, Adam and Eve were punished by the Lord by being forced to leave the Garden of Eden. For Eve's punishment for what she had done, she was told by the Lord, "I

will greatly multiply thy sorrow and thy conception; in sorrow shalt thou bring forth children; and thy desire shall be to thy husband, and he shall rule over thee" (Genesis III:16). Eve then, as the first woman, is seen as the source of original sin and as responsible for the fall of humanity. She is also seen as subordinate to her husband and subject to his rule. And, although "Genesis symbolically depicts the change of status for *both* woman and man, sadly it has been the woman's loss rather than the man's that has been emphasized" (Carroll, 1983, p. 16). In most Western religions Eve is considered the source of original sin, on which many theological principles are based.

Historian Leonard Swidler has written in great detail about the story of Eve in Genesis, and it is worthwhile to consider his work. He tells that there are two traditions about Eve. The first, before her Fall (before she is beguiled by the serpent and eats fruit from the forbidden tree) depicts her as the equal of man. But then, after the Fall, she is depicted as subject to man. These two traditions are to be found in the older scriptural tradition in the Yahwist story of creation (Swidler, 1976). Some aspects of these two views of women do emerge early in the formation of traditional religions, but the prelapse view fades with time, with a focus on the postlapse events that reversed the ideal universe attained in the Garden of Eden. Swidler summarizes this in a quote by Tavard:

> There were two traditions [that came to develop] about woman. The one corresponded to the order of society, in which woman, though protected by many laws, was inferior to man. The other echoed the legends of the origins as recorded in the Yahwist text: originally woman was the higher and better part of mankind. (Swidler, 1976, pp. 27–28)

The prelapse tradition or state of woman seems not only to have faded but also to have been lost. In the focus on the postlapse tradition, women are clearly depicted as different from and secondary to males—incomplete, an aberration, and in other derogatory terms. This is found in special concern about women's reproductive functioning. For example, menstruating women in Judaism are depicted as unclean, particularly in Orthodox Judaism. (In other religions and cultures, menstrual blood is also considered a pollution.) In the New Testament, there is the image of woman as Madonna (Virgin Mary), and in tradition there is the image of woman as whore (Mary Magdalene). This sends double messages about female sexuality (these dichotomies will be discussed further in Chapter 8).

There are parallels to these legends throughout the myths and religions across various cultures, which have been interwoven into the religions of the East and West. Even when goddesses and women were accorded power in these sagas, these powers were still associated with some form of evil, destructiveness, or mystery.

Primitive Cultures. Both men and women in non-literate societies have handed down culture and myths that were unique to their "sex-specific roles and needs" (Carmody, 1989, p. 36). Many of the attitudes and practices of these cultures, as well as those from obsolete religions, have left their mark on the major world religions. Primitive cultures were polytheistic, believing in special gods and goddesses with none as the supreme being. Males were gods of wisdom, water, thunder, and war; females were goddesses of the moon, fertility, summer, birth, and fruits of the earth. The myths and the gods and goddesses that participated in them became "woven tightly into the fabric of early religion" (Tannahill, 1982, p. 53). The time period we speak of for primitive societies throughout the world ranged from the various parts of the **Stone Age** through the **Bronze Age.** The **Paleolithic Age** (Old Stone Age) ranged from more than 25,000 B.C.E. to 10,000 B.C.E.; the **Mesolithic Age** from 10,000 to about 7000 B.C.E., and the **Neolithic Age** from 7000 to about 3500 B.C.E. The Bronze Age ranged from about 3500 B.C.E. to 1000 B.C.E. (The designations **B.C.E.** [before the common era] and **C.E.** [common era], used originally in some circles to avoid the Christian references in the designations B.C. [Before Christ] and A.D. [*Anno domini,* in the year of the Lord], have gained wider use and are most likely to be used even more broadly in the future. We use B.C.E. and C.E. in this book.) Table 2.1 describes these primitive ages.

The various pantheons (gods and goddesses) in these primitive cultures featured females in prominent

TABLE 2.1 Ages for Primitive Societies: 25,000 B.C.E. to 1000 B.C.E.

1. The Paleolithic Age ranged from more than 25,000 B.C.E. to 10,000 B.C.E.

2. The Mesolithic Age ranged from 10,000 B.C.E. to about 7000 B.C.E.

3. The Neolithic Age ranged from 7000 B.C.E. to about 3500 B.C.E.

4. The Bronze Age ranged from 3500 B.C.E. to about 1000 B.C.E.

roles. In Stone Age cultures, goddesses abounded, and there were many matriarchal cultures in which women alone were thought to be responsible for offspring. Here, a child's legitimacy depended on knowing who the mother was. In this era, people believed in **parthenogenesis** because the process of sexual reproduction was not yet discovered. In contrast, in patriarchal cultures, which developed later, the paternity of the child had to be proved, because inheritance, bloodline, and legitimacy were established through the father. In many primitive tribes in Europe, Asia, and North America, matrilinear social organization granted women important rights over their children and principal roles in tribal decisions and rules (Carmody, 1989).

In these nonliterate societies, women played an important part as gatherers of food and probably provided more food on a continual basis than did the men, who were hunters. Women and their goddesses were tied to fertility of the earth and human fertility. The female divinities were associated not only with fertility and life but also with death. According to Gimbutas (1982), among Old European statues only 2 to 3 percent of the total number are of males; the rest are of females.

Despite these powerful images in which women were portrayed as fertility goddesses and earth mothers, they were, at the same time, perceived as threatening and a source of fear. In Sumerian literature (the Sumerian kingdom existed from about 2800 to 2360 B.C.E.), the fertility goddess, Inanna, was quite powerful. This goes back to early Neolithic times when women were believed to be the sole child makers, as well as cultivators of the soil. In somewhat later Babylonian times (2067 to 2025 B.C.E.), the fertility goddess and earth mother Ishtar (a variation of Inanna), was not always thought of as kind and gentle. There was something uncontrollable about her, and when roused she became warlike and destructive, revealing that sex has its deadly as well as a life-giving side. Other goddesses, such as Anath of ancient Canaan, were seen as shrewish and bloodthirsty (Noss, 1949; Ringgren & Strom, 1967; Tannahill, 1982).

In Egypt, also during the second millennium (2000 B.C.E. to 1000 B.C.E.), gods first appeared as animals, but then gradually assumed human forms, though often with some animal parts. The ankh, originally the Egyptian symbol of the generative principles of both women and men, has come to represent the female. It is shown in Figure 2.1. Goddesses also became known and worshiped, although they too were less powerful than and subordinate to the male gods. One exception was Isis. As the goddess of fertility, Isis was also versed in magic. Isis is usually represented with a cow's horns and a lunar or solar disk. By about 1500 B.C.E., she had become one of the most renowned of goddesses. She was so popular that Isis cults of worship extended and survived as far as Spain, North Africa, and Germany for centuries and was known as late as the second century B.C.E. Although worshiped as a fertility goddess, Isis, with her magic powers over life and death, was adored yet feared (Anderson & Zinsser, 1988; Ringgren & Strom, 1967). Thus, although women in mythology have been worshiped for their power to give life, they have also been feared and resented for their power to take it away (Lederer, 1968; Tannahill, 1982). Isis is represented in Figure 2.2.

Women and the Moon. Many goddesses were known as moon goddesses: Ishtar of Babylonia and Isis of Egypt, as discussed previously; Aphrodite and Artemis of Greece; Astarte, worshiped by the Canaanites, early Hebrews, and Phoenicians; and Cybele and Hecate, worshiped by the Greeks. In these times, the moon was still closely associated with women and fertility, and the moon goddesses were worshiped for their power to create life and growth. The words *menses* and *menstruation* also relate to the moon. Menstruation means "moon change" (*mens* refers to

ANKH

The ankh is the oldest amuletic device of Egypt. The heiroglyphic sign of the ankh means "life," "living," and "everlasting life." It refers not only to the earthly world but also, and perhaps more importantly, to the afterlife, the second life, that of the spirit.

The symbol of the ankh combines the generative principles of man and woman in a single design. The loop represents the feminine reproductive organs while the remainder that of the male.

Another interpretation is that of a dam thrown across the Nile, which forms a lake of life-giving waters. The upright is the Nile, the cross bar the dam and the loop the lake.

FIGURE 2.1   The Ankh

Source: From Clive Barrett's *The Egyptian Gods and Goddesses,* Diamond Books, London, reproduced by permission of the author.

FIGURE 2.2   Isis

Source: From Clive Barrett's *The Egyptian Gods and God-desses,* Diamond Books, London, reproduced by permission of the author.

both the moon and the month) (Lederer, 1968, p. 35). This association of the moon and women can be traced back to nonliterate cultures that believed that the light of the moon was crucial for growth. Rather than the sun, the moon was thought to germinate seeds and stimulate plant growth. People in these cultures also believed that without the power of the moon women could not bear children nor animals their young. Thus the moon became the symbol of fertility for tribes that had not yet discovered the sex-

ual basis of reproduction. It was believed that the moon was able to impregnate women. This belief was so potent that women would sleep on their abdomens in order to prevent the light of the moon from falling there and would also rub spittle on their abdomens to prevent pregnancy (Harding, 1971).

These nonliterate people believed that women "must be of the same nature of the moon, because of their monthly cycle which is of the same duration as the moon" (Harding, 1971, p. 21). Later, as these early societies became agricultural and tribes settled down, it was necessary to have a system of planting and searching for edible roots and fruits to feed the people. Women then had the responsibility for all planting and harvesting; because of their moon nature, it was thought that they and only they had the power to make things grow.

In later mythology, these beliefs came to focus on the concept of moon goddesses who had the power of fertility and were the givers of life, but also had the negative side of the destructiveness of nature and death. This duality of the moon goddess means that, although she produces light and thus understanding and intelligence, under certain conditions her light "may also produce darkness, her intelligence may result in confusion . . . and may pass over into madness" (Harding, 1971, p. 24). Although in many religions the bright and dark aspects of the moon were represented by one goddess, in some religions they are represented by two. The early Greeks recognized Selene as the goddess of both phases of the moon, but sometime later each phase of the moon came to be represented separately by different goddesses; Aphrodite came to represent the light moon while Hecate represented the dark side. The waxing phase of the moon represented the power of growth; the waning phase of the moon represented the power of destruction and death. During the moon's dark phase, storms and floods, destruction by pests, as well as ghosts were feared but expected. These two phases of the moon, good and evil, have also been compared with women's nature. The waxing and waning of the moon has been associated with women's instability. The moon also came to be considered a source of inner emotional storms and conflict and in this way could influence the onset of lunacy, that is, intermittent insanity, supposed to change in intensity with the phases of the moon (Harding, 1971). Current notions of women's instability can be traced all the way back to these "mythical" lunar associations. As late as 1971, many superstitions related to the moon were still found in isolated areas of Europe, Great Britain, and the southern part of the United States (Harding, 1971).

Another important concept among primitive tribes was of *mana*. *Mana* is a Melanesian term for the widespread belief in an occult force or some supernatural power that is different from persons or spirits. Mana is either good or bad, and refers to one's experience of a powerful and silent force in things or other persons. This force is believed to be able to go from objects in nature to humans, between persons, and back to nature. Mana is thought to permeate everything, but especially the alien and unusual (Hays, 1964; Noss & Noss, 1984). Although both men and women are subject to the experience of mana in others, women, with their powers of the moon, menstruation, and fertility, seem alien or unusual and mysterious. Thus it was believed that women were filled with mana, which could be positive but, more important, negative. This concept of mana is another way of perceiving women as ambivalent; their negative or bad mana can lead to sickness, mutilation, terror, and even death in men. This belief would in time result in attempts to protect men from the bad mana of women and would later be entwined into developing religious and social forms to protect men from the "dangerous sex" (Hays, 1964, pp. 34–38).

Magic and fear were also associated with women because of their monthly period and menstrual blood. Blood was seen as a positive, intrinsic power, a vitalizing and revitalizing agent, and was used in many magical rituals and in dealing with the gods and spirits. There was no understanding of the cause and meaning of menstrual blood and so it was considered magical. Box 2.1 describes the taboo of blood and menstruation.

The specialness of menstruation may have caused envy among men, who were "denied" this power, and no cultural rite, no matter how intensely practiced, could endow males with the power to menstruate and to bear children. Whether menstruation was recog-

---

BOX 2.1

The Second Taboo: Blood and Menstruation

While the first taboo among primitive tribes was incest, the second taboo was blood. In the prehistoric period, blood was considered as life. Early writings concluded that blood was not only crucial for life but that it was "the essence of life itself" (Tannahill, p. 43). Blood held a mystical meaning especially with regard to menstruation with significance regarding the position of men and women. It is most likely that the taboo regarding menstruation came about through ignorance not through deliberate sexism.

The real meaning of menstruation was unknown not only to primitive tribes and the Hebrews whose treatment of women during menstruation is discussed later, but it was not until recent times that scientists elucidated the biological function of menstruation. To prehistoric society menstrual blood was magical. To these people it was magical because losing blood did not cause pain, illness, or even death. There was little understanding, but mystical wonder that this blood flowed for several days and then stopped. It was only seen in women, young women, and brought about a certain element of fear. With this, menstrual blood was associated with power of women who menstruated and this concept of awesome power persisted even as late as the seventeenth century and perhaps still does in some parts of the world (Harding, 1971; Tannahill, 1982).

Source: From "The Second Taboo" in *Sex in History* (p. 43), by R. Tannahill, 1982, New York: Stein and Day. Copyright 1980, 1982 by Reay Tannahill.

nized as a puberty rite among primitive tribes is un-certain, but among some of these early tribes there were attempts by men to imitate the menarche. According to Tannahill (1982) the practice of *subincision* evolved as a puberty rite in primitive tribes and was continued in some tribes into the twentieth century in central Australia and New Guinea. This puberty rite was actually a type of mutilation by which the "underside of the penis was split from the point nearest the scrotum, sometimes for a little as an inch, sometimes for almost its whole length" (Tannahill, 1982, p. 44). The blood that ensued was referred to as "men's menstruation" (Tannahill, 1982, p. 44). This association of magic power with menstrual blood and hence with women was to be used by magicians and sorcerers even as late as the seventeenth century.

However, as formal religions began to develop and incorporate myths, women were granted less and less power. Menstruation came to be considered taboo, and restrictions including isolation were placed on women during their menstrual period. Even in some primitive societies today, women are physically isolated in huts during their menstrual period (Small, 1999). Tannahill (1982) suggests that perhaps in the beginning the women may not have protested these restrictions if their menstrual periods pained and distressed them. The recurring theme was that women were unclean, unstable, and primitive. We shall discuss these taboos again in the various religions in which they were adopted and still exist in one form or another. But regardless of how these restrictions or taboos developed, they did not favor women, but oppressed them. As formal religions coevolved with patriarchy, men were considered important—the representative of the species—and women were considered variants of men. This perception has its roots in the biblical story of Creation, described earlier. In other creation myths, such as that of Pandora, who was created by Zeus, man is always created first, the more important of the species and the more "normative." Woman is created second, a variant or different version of man. These beliefs or attitudes have been maintained with "the division of responsibility, opportunity, and privilege that still prevails between male and female humans, and the

patterns of psychological interdependence that are implicit in this division" (Dinnerstein, 1976, p. 4).

China Before Confucius

Perception of Female and Male.   In China, perhaps as early as 1000 B.C.E., unknown philosophers (several centuries before Confucius) distinguished between energy modes that acted together in every natural object, the *yin* and the *yang*. The yang is described as masculine: active, warm, dry, bright, procreative, positive. According to Noss (1949), "it [the yang] is seen in the sun, in anything that is brilliant, the south side of a hill, the north side of a river, fire" (p. 295). The yin is described as a mode of energy in a lower and slower key. Yin is "fertile and breeding, dark and cold, wet, mysterious, secret; the female or negative principle in nature. It is seen in the shadows, quiescent things, the north side of a hill, the shadowed south bank of a river" (Noss, pp. 295–296). Men and women are the product of the interrelationship of these two energy sources in varying degrees. They show differing proportions of each, men being celestial or predominantly *yang* and of great worth; women are earthly, predominantly *yin* and of little account.

Here too, early in the East, we can find the dominance and superiority of males over females. If we explore further and trace the development of many of the world's major religions, we will see that they progressed in lockstep with the development of patriarchy, "a form of social organization in which descent and succession are traced through the male line" (Young, 1987, p. 21).

RELIGIONS ORIGINATING IN INDIA

The world's great religions were born in what we call the Middle East and South Asia (formerly, India was considered part of the Far East) (Noss & Noss, 1984, p. i). Buddhism, Hinduism, and Jainism, the chief religions of India, have remained largely in India and Asia, while Judaism and Christianity have spread to Europe and the Americas. Islam, although largely represented in the Middle East, has also spread to the Western world in increasing numbers.

The religions of India represent the transition of a people from **polytheism** to **pantheism;** that is, from the belief in and worship of many gods to the precept that God is not a personality, but that God, the universe, and the human soul are all one and the same; there is no distinction anywhere (Zaehner, 1958).

The major religions of India are interrelated and based on the classical Indian creed, the **Vedic** literature. Early Hinduism built further on this literature, whereas Jainism and Buddhism began as a rejection of these doctrines. All these religions offer a path to salvation as a way to meet their people's need to adjust to life and the world. The motive of Hindu, Jainist, and Buddhist thought has been to "*escape* from the degrading . . . experiences and misleading appearances of the physical world into mental and spiritual realms that have an unshakable reality and guarantee eternal satisfaction" (Noss, 1949, p. 97). Hinduism is based on the belief that man's error is in his "*thinking:* his miseries due to fallacies in his conception of things" (Noss, 1949, p. 97); Jainism, however, primarily emphasizes "*behavior,* how one acts; one must behave so as to avoid contamination by matter, defiling as pitch and destructive of all spirituality of being" (Noss, 1949, p. 98). Early Buddhism identifies the chief errors of man in the area of "*feeling;* it is our desires that must be reined in and prevented from flooding us with misery" (Noss, 1949, p. 98). Although all three religions are in basic agreement with each other on the necessity of seeking salvation, each has a different approach to the path of salvation. We shall see that these basic doctrines, especially that of early Hinduism, had a serious impact on women and continue to do so. To understand the development of restrictions on the people of India, especially on women, it is necessary to pursue the history of the development of these religions.

Brahmanism and Early Hinduism: The Transition from Polytheism to Pantheism

The Aryan Immigration. Sometime around 1500 B.C.E. (the second millennium), organized tribes of people, known as Aryans, traveled in hordes into northwest India and began their centuries-long conquest of this enormous country. The Aryans were tall and light-skinned Indo-Europeans who proceeded to conquer the Dasas (Dasyus), darker-skinned tribes of India. The Dasas were a people of mixed origin and diverse ethnic composition. History shows them to have had well-developed systems of art and architecture, which combined to produce the Bronze Age. They had a religion of which many ideas and beliefs would help to germinate *Hindu* doctrines of reincarnation and the law of Karma. The Dasas primarily worshiped mother-goddesses, the bull, and a special fertility god (Noss & Noss, 1984; Ringgren & Strom, 1967). Several centuries would pass before the Indo-Europeans completely conquered this vast land. In doing so the Indo-Europeans "were eventually to remake, and be remade by India" (Noss & Noss, 1984, p. 73). Figure 2.3 shows the invasion of the Indo-Europeans (Indo-Aryans) and their spread throughout India.

After defeating and subjugating the Dasas, the Aryans settled into tribes and gradually became a pastoral and agricultural people. The family life of the existing non-Aryan (Dasa) tribes was matriarchal with matrilineal descent and inheritance. Goddesses figured very importantly in their religious ceremonies. There was a sense of mutuality between non-Aryan men and woman in which each one's role was recognized, appreciated, and supported (Carroll, 1983). The Aryans changed all this and enforced *their* patriarchal system on the Dasas, which restricted the power and roles of women. Yet even in this early period, women certainly fared better than they would later on as India continued to develop. In contrast to the matrilineal system, each Aryan tribe had a chieftain called a *rajah* who made the rules of the tribe and also protected its members. The father (*pitar*) was the head of the family, the master of the household, and the owner of its property. He was also the family priest. The wife and mother (*matar*) during this early period was relatively free and much less isolated than her female descendants would be. Although she had authority in her home over her children and Black servants, the mother was still subject to restriction by her husband, but not rigidly so. This would not be typical of Brahmanism or later Hinduism.

Like the Dasas, the Aryans worshiped various deities, male, female, and animal but began to de-

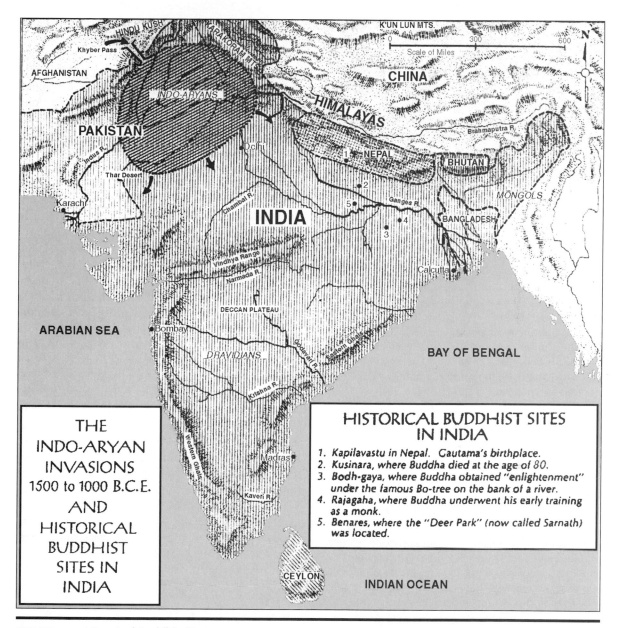

FIGURE 2.3   Historical Buddhist Sites

Source: From *Man's Religions* (pp. 99–128), by J. B. Noss, 1949, New York: Macmillan. Copyright
© 1949. Adapted by permission of Pearson Education, Inc., Upper Saddle River, NJ.

velop religious texts now known as classic Vedic literature in which the gods, goddesses, and their powers were glorified. By the end of the seventh century B.C.E., the Aryans had a well-established social stratification system that eventually became the *caste* or *varna system* (Carroll, 1983; Noss, 1949; Noss & Noss, 1984). This social system was based on color (*varna*) and appears to have developed from the

Aryan's firm rules of **endogamy** and **exogamy,** which forbade marriage outside one's racial group and also with near kin. The austere enforcement "undoubtedly was influenced more by their [Aryans] being outnumbered by a subject, black-skinned, allegedly inferior people" (Carroll, 1983, p. 23). Although the first division of society was based on "unadulterated race or color discrimination . . . *varna (caste)* became a method of separation and discrimination by virtue of *jati,* or birth, and then by color" (Carroll, 1983, p. 23). There is still some controversy about the meaning of *caste* (Carroll, 1983; Noss, 1949; Noss & Noss, 1984). The four original castes were the *Brahmans, Kshatriyas, Vaisyas,* and *Sudras.* They are described in Table 2.2.

As the caste system became more rigid, its impact on women soon proved to be severe. "Not only did Hindu thought and scriptures relegate females to a lowly status, but they were assigned the low caste standing of Sudras, irrespective of the caste into which they were actually born. They were doubly damned as women and as Sudras and were therefore banned by decree . . . from contact with the scriptures, deities and Brahmins" (Carroll, 1983 p. 15). This is an excellent example that demonstrates how, in places with racial and ethnic discrimination, we also find discrimination and oppression of women.

The Brahmans, who evolved as the highest and most powerful caste, wrote voluminous texts showing a growing sense of the principle of unity in the universe. This became a pantheistic doctrine in which **Brahma** (sometimes referred to as Brahman) was declared the creator of the universe and the *ultimate reality.* The Brahma was all that was objective and all that was subjective. Thus, according to the Brahmans, the man and the universe are all one, the Brahma. While the concept of Brahma as the one god or the ultimate reality developed, two doctrines were adopted that would succeed in permanently altering the outlook of India well into the present time. These were the doctrine of *transmigration of souls* (**reincarnation** or Samsara) and the *law of* **Karma.** Transmigration of souls or Samsara states that

> the soul of man who dies does not, except in the case of one who turns into indistinguishable oneness with Brahma, pass into a permanent state of being in heaven or hell or elsewhere; the soul, rather, is reborn into another existence which will terminate in due time and necessitate yet another birth. The nature of the next birth will be determined by The Law of Karma, the notion that one's status in the present life is the result of one's thoughts and deeds in the past life. Karma had an ethical consequence fixing one's lot in future existences. (Noss, 1949, pp. 122–123)

These two doctrines had strong social consequences. The lower castes were looked at as having sinned in their previous existence, whereas the upper castes,

TABLE 2.2   The Caste System

The different castes originally were

1. The **Brahmans,** the priests who would become the highest caste with the color white as its distinction.
2. The **Kshatriyas,** the warrior and official caste with red for its color.
3. The **Vaisyas,** which consisted of peasants and craftsmen with yellow as its color of distinction.
4. The **Sudras,** the servant and slave caste.

There was also the untouchable caste (the pariahs or outcasts) who were not permitted to have anything to do with the other castes.

The Brahmans or priests eventually became the highest caste, with the Kshatriyas next. Brahmans were rapidly increasing in number and made religion and the search for knowledge their life work. The Brahmans were raised to great prestige because of the superstitious regard of the people for sacrificial prayer. However, it took a long time for the caste stratification to change India proper. The people of pre-Aryan and early Aryan India were not too affected by the caste system, and even as late as the fourth century B.C.E. there was a fairly flexible structure between the two upper castes (Carroll, 1983; Noss, 1949; Noss & Noss, 1984; Ringgren & Strom, 1967).

Source: From *A History of the World's Religions* (9th ed.) by Noss & Noss, © 1994.

especially the Brahmans, were considered, according to the doctrine, to have led exemplary previous lives. These doctrines acted to reinforce the social discrimination of the caste system. This negative aspect of life, the constant reincarnation or rebirths and the fear of one's next existence, brought about a great pessimism in the Indian people. Hindus called the process of rebirth *the Wheel* and studied and worked on how to escape it and become one with Brahma, thus achieving eternal salvation (Moksha, or freedom from Karma and reincarnation). We shall see in the section on later Hinduism that the adoption of these two doctrines had even greater impact on women.

Toward the close of this early period, the Brahmans were growing in number and power and gradually became the elite of the caste system. The priests or Brahmans now occupied the central power in India. They performed sacrifices as part of the path to achieving freedom from rebirth and reincarnation; the deities, however, held less significance. It was the sacrifice that would achieve the desired result.

The caste system was still not in its final form, but hard and fast rules were being drawn. On the one hand, a member of the Brahman caste had every right to enjoy his exalted position because of the good deeds he had performed in his previous lives, which entitled him to his high position. Along with this standing, he had every right to expect that after death he would indeed achieve salvation with Brahma. On the other hand, especially for lower castes and for outcasts, escape from the Wheel of Karma appeared to be a hopeless situation, and people who understood these concepts became extremely pessimistic. They faced the seemingly eternal continuation of the cruel round of rebirth and the hopelessness of escaping the law of Karma. Gradually, a great depression spread throughout the entire country. The people of the second caste, the Kshatriyas, were now becoming discontented with their position, but to question the law of Karma would be seen as the worst of heresies. However, two heresies did arise that, while they rejected Brahmanism, still sought a way to salvation and release from reincarnation and the law of Karma.

Jainism and Buddhism

During the sixth century B.C.E., there was a religious awakening in India that was the result of the spreading pessimism described previously. This awakening was apparent first in the great rejection of Brahmanism and the rise of two new religions, Jainism and Buddhism, which the Brahmans considered heresies. There was an urgency about this movement or rebellion. People saw these new religions as an answer and as a means of escaping from their growing misery and the doctrine of birth, rebirth, and Karma. The usual philosophical speculation or priestly sacrifices did not help. It was the caste system under which the individual suffered most. These two religions and the later development within Hinduism emerged as the three major Eastern religions, each of which involved concepts of reincarnation and salvation. In each, we find many examples of the domination of the male over the female (Noss, 1949).

Jainism. In its rejection of early Hinduism or Brahmanism, Jainism was essentially atheistic and extremely ascetic. According to Webster's dictionary, *ascetic* is the practice or way of life characterized by contemplation and rigorous self-denial for religious purposes. Critical minds objected to the idealism of Brahmanism that resolved the substantial world of the everyday into a single unknowable entity—Brahma. Yet they believed in the doctrine of reincarnation (Samsara) and Karma. Although they believed in the reality of the physical world, they also believed that it was possible to achieve Moksha and transcend one's physical state to become one with the universe, but not with any supreme being.

The founder of Jainism was Mahavira (Great Man or Hero). He was born in India, lived from 599 to 527 B.C.E., and was said to have come from the second highest caste, Kshatriya. His father was said to have been a wealthy rajah and Mahavira and his family lived in great luxury. Mahavira married and had a daughter, but he was never contented with his princely life. It is believed that at 30 years of age he gave up his wealth, family, and belongings to practice asceticism and complete withdrawal from all worldly things. He eventually joined a group of monks and took their pledge to neglect his body and forsake all care of it and to suffer all calamities arising from divine powers or man or animals.

Mahavira was to wander naked for years searching for a way of release from the cycle of birth, death, and rebirth. He became convinced that "(1) saving one's soul from evil (purging contamination from the soul) is impossible without practicing the severest asceticism, and (2) that maintaining the purity and integrity of one's own soul involved practicing *ahisma* or noninjury to any and all living beings" (Noss, 1974, p. 108). In his wanderings, he refused raw food of any kind and accepted in his begging bowl only that food that had been left over by the person or persons for whom it was originally prepared.

After 13 years of wandering, Mahavira finally came to a town called Grimbibhikagama not far from a sal tree. There, in a deep meditation, he is said to have had the experience of a complete and full **Nirvana.** He had finally achieved a complete victory over his body as well as the needs and desires that keep one attached to the physical world. After this, Mahavira began his journey all over India, teaching people his way or path to salvation and making converts. At the age of 72 he cut all worldly ties and sought the practice of self-starvation (*sallakhana*). On his death it was said with certainty that he was finally liberated from rebirth and reincarnation.

Mahavira's path to salvation necessitated taking of the Five Worldly Vows that he developed for his system of asceticism. These vows include

> *(1) Not to kill, (2) Not to speak untruth, (3) Not to steal, (4) Renunciation of all sexual pleasure. I shall not give way to sensuality, nor cause others to do so, nor consent to it in others, (5) Renunciation of all attachments, whether to little or much, small or great, living or lifeless things; neither shall I myself form such attachments, nor cause others to do so, nor consent to their doing it. (Noss, 1949, pp. 99–100)*

Mahavira had specific comments about women regarding the fourth vow: "The greatest temptation in the world [is] women. . . . Men forsooth say, 'These are the vessels of happiness.' But this leads them to pain, to delusion, to death, to hell, to birth as hell-beings or brute beasts" (Noss, 1949, p. 113).

For some time after the death of Mahavira, women were excluded from pursuing the higher forms of perfection and release and were not permitted to enter the temples. For the Jain text says,

> *Infatuation, aversion, fear, disgust and various kinds of deceit are ineradicable from the minds of women; for women, therefore, there is no Nirvana. Nor is their body a proper covering: therefore they have to wear a covering. In the womb, between the breasts, in their naval and loins, a subtle emanation of life is continually taking place. How can they be fit for self-control? A woman may be pure in faith and even occupied with a study of the sutras or the practice of a terrific asceticism: in her case there will still be no falling away of karmic matter. (Campbell, 1962, p. 237)*

The Jains subsequently became divided into two groups, the more liberal Shvetambras and the conservative Digimbaras. The first group admitted women to their monastic orders and assumed that they had a chance to enter Nirvana (to achieve salvation) without being reborn as a man; the Digimbaras, however, persisted in their conservative ways and adhered to the original "vows," accepting their founder's verdict about women, that they are the cause of "all sinful acts" (Noss, 1974, p. 116). Women in this group were excluded from higher forms of perfection and release and were not admitted to their temples. The Digimbaras felt that women could not achieve salvation until they were reborn as men. That was the only hope that women had.

The Five Great Vows could apply only to Jainist aesthetics. For the layperson these vows were relaxed, especially the fourth vow regarding renunciation of sexual pleasures. This vow now stated that one should always be faithful to husband or wife and be pure in thought and word. Jainist ideology did have some effect on Indian thought, and some of the doctrines were to be subsequently adopted in later Hinduism. Jainism today numbers about 2 million adherents, mainly in the Bombay area of India. This religion never spread beyond India, as did Buddhism.

Buddhism.   Although Buddhism came about nearly a generation after Jainism, it still shares some of the same motives and principles, most notably a world-denying movement of escape as a means of achieving salvation, but still in a different way. Although it was based on worldly renunciation, Buddhism was moderate in comparison with Jainism. Siddhartha Gautama, the founder of Buddhism, lived about 2,500 years ago (536–476 B.C.E.) in India, and the religion he founded spread beyond India to Nepal and then came to embrace most of Asia. It is now quite popular in the United States. See Figure 2.3 for historical Buddhist sites.

Similar to the life of Mahavira, Gautama was born to a wealthy family in northern India. According to the many legends about his life, Gautama is said to have been protected from all hardships. His father was a chieftain of the Sakya clan, a warrior group, and was determined that his son should not have to learn about or experience the hardships of life or know about old age, disease, suffering, and death. While still young, Gautama married his cousin and soon after their son was born. Yet with all the riches he and his family were accustomed to, he became dissatisfied and unhappy. Legend has it that a god appeared to him in the form of a very feeble and fragile old man, and for the first time Gautama began to learn about suffering and old age. When a second apparition appeared, that of a diseased man, Gautama learned for the first time about physical illness and misery. Finally, Gautama saw yet another specter. It was the body of a dead man on a funeral pyre. Thus he came to learn about the awful fact of death. These sights continued to distress him and he was unable to find peace. Sometime later Gautama was confronted with a fourth specter, an ascetic monk in a yellow robe. This monk had apparently gained true peace within his soul, and it is said that Gautauma learned how "freedom from the miseries of old age, disease and death could be won" (Noss & Noss, 1984, p. 108). For some time after these apparitions, Gautama had thoughts about leaving his family and going out into the world in a homeless state as a religious mendicant. He did this shortly after his son was born.

He too wandered for six years throughout India, testing Brahman and Jainist philosophy with different teachers in different places to see whether he could realize the "realm of nothingness" through various practices. He also tested the extreme asceticism of Jainist philosophy. But he was disappointed with both. Gautama pursued all kinds of meditation with no effect. He did not give up, and over time his thinking became much more meaningful as a result of all his religious experiences. Gautama did not follow the extreme ascetic practice of the Jains nor did he return to his former state of pleasure and lust. Instead, he sought a middle path toward renunciation and salvation. Gautama finally came to a place called Bodhigaya and, similar to Mahavira's sal tree, he is said to have sat under a fig tree, which afterward came to be called the Knowledge or Bodhi-tree. There he entered a deep meditation, which totally freed him from all desire for worldly things, and he was able to attain enlightenment or Nirvana, the experience he had sought for so long, "a state of fulfillment and release from the bondage of worldly existence (Samsara)" (Carmody, 1989, p. 237). Gautama realized that when one reached enlightenment, one was free of desire and the suffering it caused, and that he had been able to escape into a higher form of consciousness. The Buddhist scriptures say that Gautama passed into a state of awareness and knew neither satisfaction or dissatisfaction.

From then on Gautama became the Buddha, the enlightened one. After this enlightened state had passed, he knew that he had to teach this way of salvation to all who would listen. The Buddhist order was then established. At that time in India, the caste system was not fully in place, and members of any caste were welcome to join the new order. Many Kshatriyas and those of lower castes as well as some Brahmans joined his order, now known as the Sangha.

Basic rules were written and customs adopted: the wearing of a yellow robe, the requirement for a shaven head, carrying a begging bowl, and daily meditation. Members of the order also had to follow the ten precepts of Buddha listed in Table 2.3.

TABLE 2.3 The Ten Precepts of Buddha

All Buddhists undertook to obey the precepts. They included

1. Refrain from destroying life (*ahisma*).
2. Do not take what is not given.
3. Abstain from unchastity.
4. Do not lie or deceive.
5. Abstain from intoxicants.
6. Eat moderately and not after noon.
7. Do not look on at dancing, singing, or dramatic spectacles.
8. Do not affect the use of garlands, scents, or unguents, or ornaments.
9. Do not use high or broad beds.
10. Do not accept gold or silver.

As you can see, the first 4 vows of Buddha are the same as that in the Jainist order. The remaining 6 vows of Buddha detail aspects of the Jains' 5th vow but in a moderate way to show the middle path between the two. As described earlier, the 5th vow of the Jains was to renounce all attachments. Buddhist philosophy, like the Jains' philosophy, was essentially atheistic or agnostic.

Source: From *A History of the World's Religions* (9th ed.) by Noss & Noss, © 1994.

One became a Buddhist by "taking refuge in the 'three jewels' that Buddhists treasure—the Buddha himself, the *Dharma* (teaching), and the Sangha (the Buddhist order)" (Carmody, 1989, p. 68).

In its beginning, Buddhism was more egalitarian than other Indian religions and than it would later become. Buddha gave the same teachings to female as well as male disciples, and they were all taught that the same spiritual path to salvation was open to all, regardless of gender. Sometime around the beginning of the common era and after the death of Buddha, a theological controversy emerged among Buddhists, some of whom engaged in efforts to prove that women were inferior to men and therefore incapable of the highest order of attainment. Orders of monks and nuns were established with the creation of rules for both. But there were special rules that applied only to the nuns. Among these rules, known as The Eight Chief Rules, supposedly formulated by Buddha himself, "were the most notable and the most stifling" (Barnes, 1987, p. 118). These rules included a requirement that each nun treat every monk as her senior and superior. Nuns were forbidden ever to revile or admonish any monk. All formal ceremonies had to be carried out under the guidance or in the presence of monks, as was the settlement of penances for any erring nuns.

Early concepts of Buddhism charged its followers to love all humans with a mother's love. Interestingly, this charge involved only sons but says nothing about daughters: "As a mother, even at the risk of her own life, protects her son, her only son, so let him [the follower] cultivate love without measure toward all beings." Although Buddhism eventually adopted the general bias toward women and clearly went along with the Indian tendency to subject women to men's control, Buddhism did give women another option not available in Brahmanism or Jainism. There were many female Buddhist teachers who lectured on the responsibilities of wives and husbands and household management. Moreover, laywomen also could become Buddhists by following a less rigorous path and still gain merit. It was the laywomen who financially supported most of the Buddhist orders regardless of caste or gender. These groups of women were also a major force in the survival and spread of Buddhism.

However, Buddhism eventually lost ground to Hinduism in India. It is still very prominent in many Asian countries and has spread to the United States and other Western countries. The total number of Buddhists in the world is about 350 million. Most of the schools of Buddhism that exist today have become fully egalitarian, offering greater opportunities within the teachings to women. Many of the problems that women in Buddhist countries (China, Japan, and Tibet) face today have more to do with entrenched social values than with Buddhist theories and practices. Figure 2.4 illustrates the spread of Buddhism through the Middle East.

Later Hinduism

As Brahmanism (early Hinduism) failed to hold its people through its priestly sacrifices and its philoso-

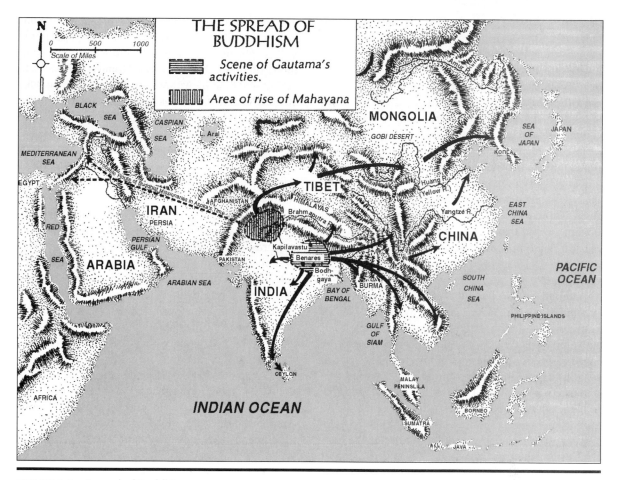

FIGURE 2.4   Spread of Buddhism

Source: From *Man's Religions* (pp. 99–128), by J. B. Noss, 1949, New York: Macmillan. Copyright © 1949.

phy, a compelling need developed to escape from increasing pessimism. This motivated people to attempt to find a practical means to achieve relief from their growing misery. The Kshatriyas formed the major group that did not like either the social or religious implications of Brahmanism. Its idealistic model struck many as absurd. As we discussed earlier, Jainism and then Buddhism expressed their revolt and offered a different path to salvation, rejecting the sacrificial system of Brahmanism as useless and misleading. These new religions also refused to give

Brahmans "first place or prescriptive rights in discovering the way from misery to freedom" (Noss & Noss, 1984, pp. 177–178).

In the turmoil that ensued during the rise of Jainism and Buddhism, Brahmanism began, of necessity, to change. Instead of using tactics against Jainism and Buddhism or outlawing these religions, Brahmans declared that many of the principles of these two "heretical" religions were valid and proceeded to adopt them. One was the principle of noninjury to living beings, or *Ahimsa,* which resulted in the renunciation by many of eating meat and the gradual development of vege-tarianism. This doctrine, together with the concept of reincarnation, brought about the veneration of the cow, a widespread feature of the Hindu religion. All parts of the cow, including its excreta, were hallowed and the killing of one was punishable by death. In many areas of India today, particularly in the villages, the cow is still a sacred animal. Another adaptation came from Buddhism: The Brahmanists included in their principles the moral desirability of quenching desire and in this way prepared for the final entrance to Nirvana. Hinduism was now on its way to being redefined. Three ways to achieve release from misery and pessimism and three paths to salvation were worked out and clearly specified. The first of these, and of relevance to the status of women, was the *Way of Works* or the *Karma Marga*.

Indian society had by now become patriarchal, particularly in marriage. Marriage by mutual consent between bride and bridegroom was discouraged and **polygamy** was actively encouraged, especially for the upper castes, for the purpose of transmitting esteemed male traits and improving bloodlines. Of great importance was the Way of Works, which governed how to carry out rites, ceremonies, and duties that would add to one's merit toward achieving salvation. The *Code of Manu,* which was a list of rules of life, was well established by 200 B.C.E. There was a list of "man's debts" that he owed in order to achieve good works. There was of course a separate Way of Works for women. Women's duty was to meekly serve their men: "In childhood, a female must be subject to her father, in youth to her husband, and when her lord is dead to her sons; a woman must never be independent" (Noss & Noss, 1984, p. 188). There were also restrictions regarding meals; wives had to eat separately from their husbands and were also to be the last in the family to be fed. "The most excellent of all good works that she can do is to seek to please him by manifesting perfect obedience to him." Included in the Way of Works is the custom of **suttee,** one of the oldest customs for women. The Code of Manu states, "She must on the death of her husband allow herself to be burnt alive on the same funeral pyre; then everybody will praise her virtue" (Noss & Noss, 1984,

p. 181). This custom, once widely practiced in India, is now forbidden by law. It is, however, apparently still practiced in the religious circles of some religions of India (Ward, 1999). Isolated instances of self-immolation by widows are still taking place, despite strict precautions taken by the police.

From the thirteenth to the eighteenth century in India, female infanticide was practiced. In the extreme, Brahmanic religion sanctioned this, along with the practice of suttee and a ban on widow remarriage. All these practices were part of the devaluation of women (Robinson, 1985).

Female infanticide is discussed in Chapters 3, 4, 12, and 14 as an ongoing practice in several Asian countries. With particular concern about this practice in India, Robinson (1985) wrote that female infanticide has been outlawed and was virtually eradicated in that country. However, female infanticide is still carried out and may even be increasing in parts of India. Some families apparently feel that it is too costly to raise daughters given the costs of dowries and weddings. Indian sons are better able than daughters to hold prestigious jobs and bring money into the family. In other circumstances, women have so little emotional and financial support from partners, family, or other sources that, in desperation, they neglect their infants until they die (Ward, 1999). Scrimshaw (1984) has depicted infanticide as follows:

> *Perhaps the greatest tragedy in today's world is that modern contraceptives and even induced abortion have not sufficiently replaced infanticide as a means of fertility control. Further, infanticide has been superceded in many societies by abandonment, neglect, and differential care rather than methods of fertility control less costly in terms of lives and resources.* (p. 462)

Throughout the centuries Hinduism became more flexible and liberal. Six different systems or approaches to reach salvation gradually developed. One of these included the Yoga system, a practice of the mental discipline of meditation and concentration as the way to release and salvation. Childhood marriage was outlawed along with infanticide and suttee. Modern legislation in India now permits divorce and legislates that women have the same political rights as men. Western religion and science have had an impact on Hinduism in its approach to education, social welfare, and women. A wider variety of opinion and disagreement about religion is now tolerated. Intellectual freedom has unfolded so that adherents of Hinduism could deny aspects of the teachings as long as they did not break completely with the code of social regulations (e.g., dietary restriction, marriage laws, and cow veneration). In the twentieth century, accepting the advances of science and technology, secular groups formed. These groups raise more radical issues including the rejection of all religion. They condemned the pessimistic tone of Hinduism and its world-denying perspective.

The concept of the exclusiveness of castes is finally crumbling under the weight of globalization and modernization. For example, in today's world, castes must travel together on modern transportation and work in the same environment. In 1948, when India became independent from Great Britain, India abolished "untouchability" and forbade its practice, but it has taken a long time for this integration to take place. Additional changes took place. Mahatma Gandhi, who was a champion of women's rights, set changes in motion so that women would be considered capable of attaining salvation. The Constitution of 1947 banned discrimination of women in all social, political, and economical matters.

In the late 1970s, birth control promoted by the government of Prime Minister Indira Gandhi was opposed. However, in 1980, during her second administration, family planning began to be practiced. The reasons for this were twofold: The population in India in 1981 was in excess of projections, and birth control was crucial to the effort to improve the health and welfare of Indian women.

Because women in India were considered to be among the most neglected, many Hindu reformers began to focus on the needs of women and to champion education for them. Their efforts improved the status of women, and education became available to all females. Tradition, however, hampered the efforts of reformers and still continues to subvert their successors' endeavors (Carroll, 1983).

Although these changes have been positive for women, the force of tradition still impedes progress. Even in current times, tradition keeps wives subservient to their husbands. In the late 1970s, there were reports of suicide among women, most of whom had been highly educated and who had been married only a short time. At first, it was thought that they had been murdered by their husbands who had tired of them and sought a dowry that a new wife would bring. Analysts later speculated that many were overwhelmed by the changes brought about by marriage and found that they could not cope with the move to a new household and restrictions of marriage and, in some cases, motherhood. After their education, they had envisioned broader and more liberal horizons and, failing that, they had become extremely depressed (Carmody, 1989).

In rural areas the pressures on women were comparable. The patterns of life were traditional, essentially untouched by the events occurring after India gained its independence in 1947. These patterns have continued, even with the positive changes. Hindu festivals include god and goddess worship. According to Carmody (1989), "the majority of Hindus, men as well as women, have sought to improve their Karma, make a living, prosper with healthy children all by worshipping gods and goddesses" (pp. 59–60). In small villages and outlying areas, contemporary reforms have had little impact. These people still today rely on ancient traditions and worship of gods and goddesses, along with their understanding of the concepts of reincarnation and rebirth.

Education appears to be one of the most important changes necessary for the improvement of conditions for women. "[R]eligion has historically been and continues to be one of the main inhibitors of the education of females" (Caroll, 1983, p. 55). Religion could be a positive influence if certain aspects of Hinduism were modified or eliminated. Carroll (1983) has speculated on whether such reform could be accomplished and the conditions under which reform could progress. She feels that without a centralized authority or a charismatic leader in India, the potential for the advancement of women is poor. On the other hand, there are now only 90 women for every 100 men in India. The female–male ratio in India actually decreased from 972 to 1,000 in 1901 to 900 to 1,000 in 2000 (Saravate, 2000).

There are more than 795 million Hindus in the world; 700 million of these religious adherents live in India, representing 80 percent of the country's population.

Summary of Religions Arising in India

In this review of the religions of India we have looked at the ways in which women were perceived and treated from ancient times. These gender stereotypes, formulated thousands of years ago, have continued to be maintained in one form or another to the present. We have also considered the changes in the status of women, both positive and negative, throughout these thousands of years. In the early development of Hinduism (Brahmanism), we saw negative changes for women that, as Hinduism developed further, became even worse, starting with the change from a matrilineal society to a patriarchal society. In early Jainism, there were few if any improvements for women, except for the one branch of Jainists who accepted women as capable of reaching enlightenment and salvation. Buddhism showed the most improvement for women overall as the religion matured. Although experiencing many changes for women in the religious, social, and economic areas, later Hinduism is still burdened by a tradition that offers a poor outlook for change. Today, although modified regarding their attitudes toward women, these religions are still plagued with the images developed in their formative periods. Many practices still abound, from infanticide, suicide of educated women, and the continued importance of dowries. Domestic violence is also coming to light and many if not most of the victims are women of India's elite (Pandey, 2003).

We will continue to explore these considerations as we move on to the other major religions from their inception to more modern times.

MONOTHEISTIC RELIGIONS

The prevailing ideas of the religions of India differ profoundly from those that developed in the Middle East. Noss (1974) has provided a concise description of these differences. **Monotheism,** the belief in one God who reveals himself to his people, had replaced polytheism and pantheism. In monotheistic religions, God is the creator and sustainer of the universe and is anthropomorphized as a person with a proclaimed interest in good moral behavior. Monotheistic religion is a way of comprehending and mastering life rather than negating it as in the religions of pantheism. Asceticism or self-denial is not considered crucial whereas nature is a created reality—"a stage on which the drama of divine–human relationship is enacted" (Noss, 1974, p. 334). This relationship is brought about by God, not man.

Monotheism is a revealed religion belonging to Judaism, Christianity, and Islam; in contrast, the religions of India are those in which people, by discipline and reflection, obtain their own enlightenment and achieve salvation. In monotheistic religions, people turn to a single source of revelation from a great God, whereas in the Indian religions people seek many sources of help to achieve salvation. Thus, monotheistic religions, with few exceptions, give great importance to the human community and consider the relationship between God and humans as a "person-to-person encounter in which the moral element is prominent" (Noss, 1974, p. 355).

Judaism was the first monotheistic religion to develop in the Middle East and marked this transition from pantheism and polytheism. Centuries later Judaism gave rise to Christianity, and although the two religions may have influenced each other historically, each has its own internal dynamism and distinct characteristics. Islam was the last monotheistic religion to develop and did so in the midst of Judaism and Christianity. It was surely influenced by some of their beliefs and practices. Although monotheism is almost exclusively associated with these three religions, it may also be seen now in some specific Hindu groups and perhaps even elsewhere (Parrinder, 1983). The development toward a monotheistic theology began almost four millennia ago, and even though monotheism was a latecomer on the stage of history, it nevertheless has had profound effects on the development of Western civilization.

Although we are cognizant of the contributions of monotheistic religions, we are also concerned with the attitudes and beliefs about females and males that these religions encompassed. We will see that the attitudes and beliefs about women and men that we find today were profoundly shaped by these religions from their inception thousands of years ago that carried over to Western culture. The late Juanita Williams (1987) wrote about the perception of women as a necessary evil throughout history. Some of her thoughts are summarized in Box 2.2.

The basic source of traditional attitudes toward women and men in Judaism and Christianity derives from the story of Genesis in the Old Testament. As we showed earlier, virtually all major religions have a strong emphasis on the two sexes acting in ways consistent with a patriarchal society. This is especially evident in Judaism and Christianity. The Adam and Eve story shows that because of Eve's gullibility and treachery she brings about the downfall of Adam and of succeeding generations. Consequently, she is condemned to suffer childbirth, work hard, and to be a faithful and submissive wife. The Adam and Eve story can be perceived as a rationale for patriarchy.

Judaism: From Polytheism to Monotheism

With a history going back 4,000 years, Judaism is the oldest of the revealed religions. The belief in one God is the basis of the Jewish religion, and it is believed that this God is the creator and ruler of the universe and is eternal, transcendent, and the only god to be worshiped. God communicates to his people through the prophets, and Moses is considered to be the most illustrious of all the prophets throughout the history of Judaism. In a covenant made 4,000 years ago, God promised Abraham a land for all his generations. On Mount Sinai, God revealed the Ten Commandments and the Torah to Moses (Flower, 1997). The Torah contains the five Books of Moses (Genesis, Exodus, Leviticus, Numbers, and Deuteronomy). The Torah is the "ultimate, unchanging word of Divine Law" (p. 6). To most Jews, God is all-knowing and all-seeing and he and he alone can reward or punish. It is believed that one day God will send the Messiah who will be a descendent of David. Then the age of the redemption will begin and the dead will be resurrected.

The oldest of the revealed religions, Judaism has survived for over 4,000 years in spite of conquests, exile, anti-Semitism, and slaughter. In the 1930s anti-Semitism, which had been prevalent throughout Europe, increased dramatically with the rise of Hitler. It culminated in the Nazi Holocaust in which over 6 million Jews were put to death in gas chambers during World War II. When these horrendous facts become known after the war, it shocked and devastated the international community. It was decided that a separate state was needed for the protection and

---

BOX 2.2

Women as Property

During most of the history of Western civilization, women have always been regarded basically as property and with no rights of their own. A creed of early Puritan belief was the requirement that women be kept in a subordinate position. John Milton, a Puritan poet, insisted strongly on the inferiority of women and the need for men to guard their authority over women to deter them from foolish action. He expressed a theme of woman as an intrusive nuisance in a man's world in his *Paradise Lost*, when he has Adam mournfully ask, after the transgression, why God created "this novelty on earth, this fair defect," instead of filling the world with men, or finding some other way to generate mankind (Rogers, 1966).

This mythic perception of woman as a necessary evil has successfully survived the evolution of ideas and intellectual changes. The basic ideas of woman's inferiority and unfitness to be man's equal continue to be thematically important in determinants of attitudes toward her.

safety of those Jews who had survived. On May 14, 1948, the United Nations voted to establish the state of Israel. The creation of a separate state in Palestine for Jews was seen by the Jewish people as fulfillment of the promise made by God to Abraham and Moses millennia earlier. Jews still believe that they were "chosen by God to be an example of light and love to all mankind" (Flower, 1997, p. 6) through the teachings as revealed to Moses.

Denomination of Judaism.   In the mid-1800s, egalitarian movements in Europe and advances in science brought changes in Judaism. Many no longer wanted to accept that the Torah was revealed as was believed in Orthodox Judaism. Changes in ritual and dietary law were also desired. Under the guidance of Rabbi Isaac Wise (1819–1900), the Reform movement began. It is the most liberal branch of Judaism and is still evolving. Basically, Reform Judaism emphasizes the ethics of Judaism rather than the rituals and dietary laws. Women and men sit together in the synagogue rather than separated as in Orthodox Judaism. In the Orthodox religion, when a boy reaches age 13, he enters adulthood with rite of Bar Mitzvah. In Reform Judaism, both boys and girls partake in this rite—but with girls the rite is called Bat Mitzvah. Commentaries on and interpretations of the law became part of Reform practice. These were radical and very progressive changes and not everyone was happy with them. Instead, a middle ground soon developed in Europe—Conservative Judaism.

Two concepts or ideologies dominate Conservative Judaism. The first stresses the centrality of religion in Jewish life; the second is a strong sense of tradition, history, and the continuity of Jewish life. Professor Solomon Schechter, a leader in the Conservative movement, spoke of the "organic unity" of Jewry (Noss, 1974, p. 415). Tradition is stressed, both in ritual and dietary law, but there are commentaries on and interpretations of the laws. As in Reform Judaism, both women and men sit together and both girls and boys partake in the rite of adulthood at age 13. The Conservative movement has not been very successful in Europe or in Israel but is in the United States where it contains the largest membership of all

the branches of Judaism. The Conservative movement also gave rise to the Reconstructionist branch of Judaism, somewhat to the left of Conservatism. Rabbi Mordecai Kaplan, a former Conservative rabbi, was the founder of Reconstructionism. This branch of Judaism allows a wide spectrum of clergy, from traditional practice to left-wing ideology. Reconstructionism also believes that religion evolves with social change. These are just some basic differences among these branches of Judaism. There are many other differences, especially with regard to the interpretation of the Bible and ritual and dietary law.

Holidays.   All branches of Judaism observe five major holidays. These include Rosh Hashanah, which occurs in September or October and ushers in the Jewish New Year, and eight days later, Yom Kippur, the Day of Atonement. Yom Kippur is a 24-hour period of fasting and is spent mainly in the synagogue atoning for sins committed against God and praying for forgiveness for the year. It is the most sacred day of the year. Hanukkah, the Festival of Lights, begins in December, often very close to Christmas. This is a commemoration of the victory of Judas Maccabaeus in the second century C.E. and the rededication of the temple in Jerusalem. Passover (*Pesach*), observed in March or April, celebrates the liberation of the Jews from bondage in Egypt by the intervention of God through the Prophet Moses. Passover occurs very close to Easter. Seven weeks after Passover, Jews celebrate Pentecost (Shabuoth). This commemorates the giving of the law to Moses on Mount Sinai.

Population of Jews.   The world Jewish population has begun to slow. The estimated strength of world Jewry in 2002 was approximately 13,295,000 compared with previous estimates of at least 14 million in 1998. Almost 6.2 million live in North America, about 5 million in Israel, 1.5 million in Europe, 400,000 in Central and South America, 103,000 in Australia and New Zealand, 88,000 in Africa, and about 47,000 in Asia. These are estimated figures because of the difficulty of reaching so many unaffiliated Jews. The total may be more than actually reported here (Jewish Virtual Library of the American–Israeli Cooperative Enterprise, 2004).

The Religion of the Early Hebrews.   Judaism, like Hinduism, started an ethnic religion. As in the other religions, stereotypes of women in Judaism developed along with the early development of the Hebrew religion and continued with the Judaic order that followed. These stereotypes are still evident today. To appreciate how these stereotypes took shape, we need to look back at the history and foundation of Judaism through the common era.

The story of the founding of Judaism is the story of Abraham and his wife, Sarah. It is recorded in detail in the books of Genesis and Exodus from the Hebrew Bible or Old Testament. Although the Bible provides the most complete history of the development of the religion of the Jews, the story of Abraham and several other writings have been considered oral traditions, passed down through generations. There was no reliable record of written Hebrew before the tenth century B.C.E., which, as we will see, was after the Hebrews escaped from Egypt under the leadership of Moses and settled in the land of Canaan (Cahill, 1998; Parrinder, 1983). The Hebrews were members of an ancient northern Semitic tribe and were the ancestors of the Jews and descendents of the patriarchs of the Hebrew Bible or Old Testament (*Encyclopedia Britannica,* 1999).

It is speculated that Abraham was born about 1900 B.C.E. near a place called Ur in Babylonia, along the border of Mesopotamia. Abraham married Sarah and sometime later the family settled in Harran, close to the Arabian desert. It was here that a voice came to Abraham and said:

> *Get thee out of thy country, and from thy kindred,*
> *from thy father's house, unto the land that I will show*
>   *thee.*
> *And I will make of thee a great nation, and I will bless*
>   *thee,*
> *and make thy name great; and be thou a blessing.*
> *(Genesis 12:1,2)*

Abraham gave his allegiance to this God who had spoken to him and proceeded to take his family to Canaan (Palestine), where he built an altar to wor-

ship his God, whom he called El Shaddai. Soon, a famine came to Canaan and Abraham and Sarah went to Egypt, where they prospered greatly. God revealed himself again to Abraham and made a covenant with him. He would be Abraham's God and God to all his generations. He promised to give Abraham and his descendants the land of Canaan (Genesis 17:1–9). But Abraham was unhappy because he and Sarah did not have any children. God promised that she would soon have a child and said that Abraham's child and all the children of his descendants should be circumcised at eight days "and my covenant shall be in your flesh for an everlasting covenant" (Genesis 17:10–14). By this covenant between God and man, the children of Abraham would not be able to forget God and God would never forget them. Sarah conceived and bore a son whom she named Isaac and who was circumcised at eight days old as God had instructed.

As recorded in Genesis, God tested Abraham, telling him to take his son Isaac and "offer him up" on a mountain for sacrifice to his God. Abraham obeyed and was prepared to slay his son, but at the critical moment, God's messenger stopped him, saying that now God knew Abraham was in awe of him and God provided a ram for the sacrifice instead of Isaac (Genesis 22:1–18). Noss (1974) has suggested that the story of Isaac lays the foundation for the substitution of animals for sacrifice instead of humans. This was the first crucial episode in the formation of Judaism.

Abraham and his descendants prospered in Canaan but once again it is told that a famine came and decimated the land. So, Abraham and Sarah's descendants left Canaan and made their way to Egypt. For generations they flourished in Egypt until about 1580 B.C.E., when the Egyptians began to expel many groups. The descendants of Abraham were not expelled and continued to live peacefully. Sometime during the thirteenth century B.C.E., a "mad pharaoh, Ramses II, came to power" (Noss & Noss, 1984, p. 359). He decided to build great works—cities and temples—and, because he needed large numbers of unpaid laborers, made slaves of the Hebrews.

The story of the Exodus and of Moses, the greatest prophet in the Hebrew Bible, is so well known that it will be described only briefly here. For many years the Hebrews were in bondage in Egypt. God was revealed to Moses and instructed him what to do to escape the Egyptians. This came about when the Hebrews fled across the Red Sea, which God parted for them. They escaped, and when they were safely across the sea, God closed the sea, destroying the Egyptians who had tried to follow the Hebrews. This is the event known as Passover, which Jews all over the world celebrate in the spring (Cahill, 1998; Noss & Noss, 1984).

The leadership of Moses makes its greatest contribution to Judaism after the crossing of the Red Sea. During the wandering of the Hebrews in the desert, Moses acted as an intermediary between his people and God. He went up on Mount Sinai where God was again revealed to him. God wanted to make another covenant with the Hebrew people. The terms of the covenant were inscribed on two tablets; the first was the Ten Commandments and the second was the **Torah** (Exodus 20:1–22). The Hebrews, carrying the sacred tablets in the Ark of the Covenant (Noss, 1974, p. 365), wandered in the desert for 40 years until they reached the border of Canaan and prepared to invade it. Moses was not to enter Canaan and died before the invasion. His young general, Joshua, replaced him. The invasion was a long process and took years of fighting but finally the Hebrews succeeded. The Hebrews captured and entered Canaan (Palestine) and captured Jerusalem. This was the promised land to which God had led them.

It is estimated that the Hebrews entered Canaan or Palestine about 1200 B.C.E. From the time they entered Canaan they were known as Israelites. This name would not change until late in the fifth century B.C.E. when they would become known as Jews (*Encyclopedia Britannica*, 1999).

The kingdom of Judah was established in the southern part of Canaan, and Solomon was made their king. He erected a temple for the worship of God about 930 B.C.E. According to custom, the temple was the only site where Jewish prayer and sacrifice could be carried out and was under the supervision of the priestly order. A pilgrimage to the temple was mandatory. However, in 597 B.C.E. Neb-

uchadnezzer, the king of Babylon, sacked Jerusalem and reduced the entire area to rubble. The temple in Jerusalem was destroyed. Nebuchadnezzer took captives and carried away the king, all the nobles, and many other renowned groups to Babylon (Kings 24:14–16). Others who were able fled to Egypt and surrounding countries in the Mediterranean. The rest of the Israelites continued to stay on in Judah. The change in the status of the Israelites who survived the fall of Jerusalem was so profound that the name *Hebrew* was dropped and history has spoken of them as Judeans or Jews, of which the latter has continued to the present time (Noss, 1974). In Babylonia, the Jews were permitted comparative freedom to live their old way of life. Although no longer able to worship and offer sacrifice to God at the temple in Jerusalem, the only place they knew, the Jews maintained their faith. They established places to meet, teach, pray, and hold religious discussions. Meetings were held on the Sabbath and the discussions became the origin of the sermon and were standard. These practices foreshadowed what would become the synagogue and the official writing down of the oral tradition of the Torah, which would include the place of women.

About 50 years later (539 B.C.E.), Babylon was captured by Cyrus the Great, the founder of the Persian Empire. He allowed the Jews to return to Jerusalem and Judah. The temple was rebuilt and priests again became dominant. Distinct from the temple, synagogues began to develop in Jerusalem and throughout Judah. There were also many different groups: the Edomites, Sodomites, and Samaritans, as well as other religious Jewish sects who held specific thoughts about women. The hopes of the Jews to rebuild the kingdom of Judah were not to be realized even a century later.

By the fifth century B.C.E., the Jews had become dependent on their own religious authorities even though they were under Persian rule. The supreme authority was the high priest in the temple in Jerusalem. The scribes began to write down the oral tradition of the Torah (the Hebrew Bible) and other sacred writings that would become Hebrew law. Those who had special talents for preaching in the synagogues would later be known as rabbis or teachers and would become part of the group known as the Pharisees.

This was the beginning of the period of formative Judaism that began around 450 B.C.E. in Palestine. It was during this time that Judaism began to take root and of which we have written records (Noss & Noss, 1984). Attitudes toward women began to be clearly defined and included in the religious scriptures. There were many social and cultural forces during the several hundred years that the scriptures were being written down that would help shape the perspectives of women and the restrictions on them that would evolve.

The writing of the scriptures and the final shape of the Hebrew Bible would take until the first century C.E. to be completed. It was put into its present canon and fixed about 90 C.E.—that is, no longer subject to change. Some years later, the leading rabbis of the first and second centuries C.E. codified the interpretations and commentary on the oral law and compiled them in the form of the Mishna, which was the first part of the **Talmud.** The second part of the Talmud, the Gemara, included the commentaries and discussions on the Mishna and completed the Talmud. The Talmud functioned as a guide for the operative conduct of Jewish life and also contained an important section describing the place of women in Jewish life. Carmody (1989) has commented that "[T]he Hebrew bible is our best source about the *religious experience* of women before the Common Era" (p. 135) and that the Talmud is the most "important document about the *official status* of women in Judaism of the Common Era" (p. 135).

Swidler (1976) describes the sociocultural forces in which formative Judaism developed. For most of this time, Jewish women lived in a patriarchal society. It was assumed that men were in charge of all affairs, from leadership to teaching to legislation. Women were considered lesser than men and they were to follow them. This was essentially the general pattern, although there were famous biblical exceptions in which women were heroines and leaders. This inferior status of women was the general model in the ancient world of the Middle East (Palestine, Egypt, Babylonia, etc.), also known as the Fertile Crescent.

Most of these civilizations were male dominated. Men were in charge of the government, ran businesses, administered the law and education, and often controlled theology and religious practices. Women were second-class citizens without any power or prestige. *The Social World of Ancient Israel* (Matthews & Benjamin, 1995) provides additional information on women in the Israelite patriarchy.

However, by the fifth and fourth centuries B.C.E. in many parts of classical Greek society, Hellenism (Box 2.3) flourished. Here, as well as in Egypt and Rome, Hellenistic society was essentially individualistic and the status of women was considerable. Women had greater freedom, they took part in sports, and they owned and ran businesses. In some of these societies, women in rural areas had greater freedom than those in the cities. In the Hellenistic period the status of women in marriage was also elevated. Marriage continued to be monogamous for both partners, and there was an equal right for either partner to seek divorce for infidelity. Inheritance laws favored women. In the Hellenistic world, there was also an increase in sensitivity toward children and animals. This was in contrast to earlier Greek society and other societies in which women were frequently classed as inferior *along* with children and slaves. In Greece, these changes were especially noted in and around Sparta, where society was more individualistic, but not as much for society in Athens and Macedonia, where societal structures tended to be more patriarchal.

In contrast, the status of Jewish women during this same period seems to have reached a nadir in Western history (Bullough, 1974). Swidler has suggested that because the Hellenistic culture was so attractive and pervasive, many Jews saw it as a threat to Jewish identity. In protecting the Jewish character, they proceeded to insulate the Jewish community from these influences. They expanded restrictions on one-half of their community, the female half, in order to remove them from the pervading influence of Hellenism. This action prevented the higher status of Hellenistic women from reaching and influencing women in the Jewish community. This helped to ensure the procreation and survival of Judaism as a part of carrying out the Covenant with God.

Box 2.3

Hellenism

Hellenism relates to the cultural model generated by Alexander the Great of Greece. Hellenism came to dominate the Near East and eastern Europe in the late centuries B.C.E. through the early centuries of the C.E. and spread through the Middle East, affecting the Hebrews during the period of formative Judaism. Hellenism combined unprecedented religious and racial tolerance. Many Hebrews, particularly women, welcomed Hellenism but the plain people were slow to respond to its precepts. The Hebrew scribes and rabbis for obvious reasons strongly opposed this new culture (Carmody, 1989, p. 236; Noss & Noss, 1994, p. 395).

Source: From *A History of the World's Religions* (9th ed.) by Noss & Noss, © 1994.

Attitudes of Major Jewish Groups. As noted, this period was the time of the writing of the Hebrew scriptures, and by 90 C.E. this canon or doctrine was fixed and no longer subject to change. These writings also "fixed" the images and perceptions of women and the laws and restrictions to be placed on them. Three major groups of men came to have important influence on the religious customs and rituals of the Jews in Palestine: the *Pharisees,* the *Essenes,* and the *Sadducees.*

The Pharisees. The Pharisees were devoted to the written Torah or Bible and were concerned with moral obedience. They perceived "woman as 'in all things inferior to man' as 'evil' as 'overcome by the spirit of fornication' " (Swidler, 1976, p. 56). According to Swidler, this could hardly be without wide social effects.

The Essenes. They lived in different parts of the country. Their beliefs were similar to those of the Pharisees. These extremely pious men had no women and renounced all sexual desire. They thought of women as a distraction. Their writings express misogynism (hatred of women).

The Sadducees. They were the ruling hierarchy and separated themselves from the general public. They believed in the written law. They were liberal in their time and favored the Greek style of life. Like the Essenes, they did not survive.

The Rabbis. They evolved from the Pharisees after 70 C.E. They believed that one had to live by the scriptures. Rabbinic Judaism developed in an already highly structured patriarchal system. Although they did write positive evaluations of women, overall they gave women a disadvantaged status. Women were subordinate to man in every facet of life, whether religious, social, or legal; they were of inferior mind and function. Within their subordinate position, women were depicted favorably by the rabbis. Some examples of positive images of women include "He who has no wife dwells without good, without help, without joy, without blessing, without atonement" (Genesis Rabbah, 18:2). Rabbis praised women for being supportive, resourceful, and self-sacrificing. They wrote of the sadness and darkness that descends at the death of one's wife. Nonetheless, the rabbis produced a concept of Judaism in this well-established patriarchal society that presented a world with men at the center. The laws that the rabbis wrote were perceived as "divinely ordained" (Baskin, 1984) and only considered a woman in relationship to a man; her duty was to be completely under his control and to contribute to his comfort. If women realize their obligations, they are revered and honored and their praises loudly sung. If they do not fulfill their responsibilities, their husbands can divorce them, punish them, and treat them harshly, for which there is no protection. On the other hand, a woman could not divorce her husband or seek refuge from him. In the case of adultery by either the wife or the husband, the punishment was death by stoning. But for the man there was little castigation if he had sex with an unmarried woman. (Niditch [1991], however, has speculated about how strictly these laws were implemented for both men and women.) There were exceptions to these denigrating perceptions of women. In the history of the development of Judaism, many women were heroines; Esther, who saved her people, and Ruth, who accepted the God of her mother-in-law, are examples. The only woman described in the book of Jewish laws (the Talmud) as learned in Jewish law is Beruriah, the wife of a rabbi. But then she is later transformed into an adulteress who commits suicide (Baskin, 1984).

The Synagogue.   Women were not permitted to take an active role in the development of rabbinic Judaism nor were they permitted to have the religious education that men could have. Study of the Torah and other scriptures was closed to women by several but not all groups. They could not assume an equal part in religious practices. They were separated from men in the synagogue, but it is not clear just when this practice started. It apparently did not exist in earlier temple worship. Archeological studies of the first-century synagogues do not show separation of men and women. However, it was believed that separation would prevent distraction of the men from their prayers by avoiding sexual arousal by the women. Women had to enter their section of the synagogue by certain gates, but were forbidden entrance if they were menstruating or were within seven days of their cycle. Women were placed in a court either behind the men or in a gallery above the men. The separation was seen as just one part of the distinctions between men and women and became a principle for temple worship (now only for Orthodox practice) (Swidler, 1976).

Menstruation.   The responsibility of the husband was to produce children, but it also became a responsibility of the wife. The writers of biblical law had contemptuous feelings about the way women's reproductive systems functioned. Menstrual blood was now seen as totally incompatible with any ritual worship or sacrifices made to God. A woman was declared unclean from the beginning of her menstrual period until seven days had passed. After her child was born, she was considered unclean for 40 days after the birth of a

boy, but for 80 days after the birth of a girl (Carmody, 1989). As discussed earlier, menstrual blood and other bodily secretions were deemed a pollution in other cultures as well (Douglas, 1969; Swidler, 1976), and, as we have seen and will continue to see, this was not unique to Judaism. Additional laws state that whatever a menstruating woman touches or sits on is impure. If a man has intercourse with a menstruating woman, he shall be unclean for seven days, and every bed on which he lies shall be unclean (Leviticus, 15:23–34). A more severe punishment for this practice is possible, in which the man and woman are cut off from their people (Leviticus, 20:18).

The life of women during the time of formative Judaism was negative. Women remained uneducated and were considered property of their husbands. They were castigated for their reproductive function and considered unclean. Polygamy was permissible for men, but **polyandry** was not permitted for women. On the other hand, while women were separated from men and from their religious practice, men did appreciate women's many skills and contributions. These were mainly involved in household activities, procreation (especially if a boy was born), child rearing, and other domestic talents. Husbands were not always harsh and abusive, but often loving and caring. However, in their early morning prayers, men thanked God for not creating them as women. Across the centuries, these concepts of Jewish women were undoubtedly internalized so that women not only accepted their inferior status and treatment, but also considered themselves to be inferior and to deserve such treatment.

In his review of the condition of women in the period of formative Judaism, Swidler concludes that the markedly inferior status of women and the potent misogynism during this phase were not mitigated by the sincere affection that men showed their wives and children (Swidler, 1976). The religious and patriarchal structures that were written into the Bible and other scriptures surely had an overwhelming influence on the history of Jewish life and Judaism, which continues to the present time.

In more recent times, feminist ideas have begun to enter Jewish discourse and there have been increasing efforts at reform. Conservative, Reform, and

Reconstructionist Judaism, although still embroiled in controversies concerning the status of women, have undergone many changes. Feminists are involved in all branches of Judaism, working to make transformations that are acceptable to today's women. Women and men, too, have expended considerable effort in Orthodox Judaism to modify the laws that have kept women on the fringes of religious practice and under the restrictions on marriage and divorce. While women have been ordained as rabbis and cantors in Reconstructionist, Reform, and Conservative Judaism, they have not been able to do so in Orthodox Judaism. A major problem for Orthodox women is in the area of divorce. Divorce is so strictly controlled by the men that for so many women, it has been literally impossible to obtain a divorce. There is also an apparent increase in domestic violence among Orthodox groups, although we do not know the precise percentage that violence occurs among Orthodox Jews (Forman & Maier, 1997; Silver, 1998; DeVoe & Borges, 2004). Even with the positive changes that have taken place, many Jewish women feel that until actual changes are made in the laws of rabbinic Judaism, women will still be dealing with a patriarchical structure in which women are not equal to men in their capacity for religious participation.

Christianity

Christianity is the most widespread of the great religions and has the largest numbers of adherents. It is a monotheistic religion with a wide range of beliefs based on the work of Jesus of Nazareth, who lived for about 30 years in Palestine and was crucified by the Romans sometime between 29 and 33 C.E. Jesus was a Jew as were his chief followers, the Apostles, who accepted him as the "Christ," the anointed or chosen one (*Encyclopedia Britannica*, 1999; Noss, 1974). Jesus Christ is generally considered "God and Man" (Flower, 1997, p. 19). Most Christians believe that Jesus is divine, the Son of God, but was made a man and came down to Earth to carry out God's will and that he died on the cross for their sins. They believe that Jesus was resurrected from the dead after three

days and for the next 40 days, based on testimony of contemporary witnesses, was seen by his disciples on many occasions and then ascended to heaven. For many if not most Christians, the meaning of Christ's death is salvation. Salvation depends on "the grace, the divine favor of God, shown in the atonement for man's sins by the death of Jesus Christ on the cross" (Flower, 1997, p. 25). Jesus, although he is divine, walks among his followers on Earth. He "is present in them and they in Him, in their belief and trust" (p. 25). In this way, "Christians do not worship a dead hero, but the living Christ" (Parrinder, 1983, p. 420).

Christians believe Jesus to be the Messiah or Christ as was prophesied in the Hebrew Bible and "in unique relation to God whose son He was declared to be" (Flower, 1997, p. 19). Christ is from the Greek—*Khristos*—which is a translation from the Hebrew word *mashiah* (anointed one). This is the name Jesus was called when the budding faith was being communicated to the people outside of Palestine. Christians consider Jesus to be the "human face of God" (p. 19). He is the way to reach God. "I am the way, and the truth and the life. No one comes to the father but by me" (John 14:6). Christians are able to draw close to God by following Jesus' life and teachings.

Although monotheistic, the belief in one God often incorporates the doctrine of the Trinity—the Father, the Son, and the Holy Spirit. The Nicene Creed explains this in that "the one God is revealed in three persons: the Father, the Son and Holy Spirit. They are three persons in the same substance and as such are united—but yet separate" (Flower, p. 24). This concept of the Trinity is not accepted by all branches of Christianity.

Also important is the Bible. The Bible for Christians is comprised of the Old Testament (the Hebrew Bible) and the New Testament. The New Testament is considered by Christians to be the fulfillment of the Old Testament, because the figure of Jesus and his life and teachings as told in the Gospels, fulfill the prophesies of the coming Messiah as written in the Old Testament.

Through Jesus' **Apostles,** the Christian faith spread through the Greek and Roman world. By the year 315 C.E., the Emperor Constantine granted religious tolerance for Christians and equality with other religions (it would not be made the official religion until the end of the 4th century). This became the basis of civilization for the Middle Ages in Europe. As Christianity continued to spread, major separations developed as a result of differences in doctrine and practice. These separations include the Roman Catholic Church, which acknowledges the bishop of Rome, the pope; the Eastern or Orthodox Church; and the Protestant denominations, which began during the sixteenth century C.E. Reformation. However, all branches of Christianity recognize the authenticity of the Bible.

There are sacraments carried out in all branches of Christianity. A sacrament is a ritual defined as "an outward and visible sign of an inward spiritual grace. It is through the sacraments that God, through the Holy Spirit, is present in mankind" (Flower, 1997, pp. 26–27). The Roman Catholic and Eastern churches recognize seven sacraments: baptism, confirmation, marriage, ordination, reconciliation, anointing of the sick, and the Eucharist (communion). Some Protestant churches observe only the two main sacraments— baptism and communion.

Holidays.   Christians also observe several major holidays. Lent, a 40-day preparation leading up to Easter, commemorates the 40 days that Jesus spent in the wilderness before beginning his ministry as well as the 40 years that the Jews spent wandering in the desert. Good Friday, falling sometime during March or April, is the day of the Crucifixion of Jesus Christ and is a day of sadness followed by the joy of resurrection on Easter Sunday, which is a major festival. Forty days after Easter is Ascension Day, which commemorates the ascension of Jesus into heaven. Ten days after the ascension of Jesus is Pentecost, the day on which the Holy Spirit descended on all of Jesus' Apostles and was received by about 3,000 believers. The Pentecost (fiftieth day) is also a Hebrew holiday coming fifty days after the second day of Passover. Pentecost is also known as the Hebrew festival Shabuoth (the festival of fruits). The festival Christmas, held on December 25, celebrates the nativity of Jesus. It is often a time for gifts, family gatherings, singing carols, and feasting.

Population.   There are now about 2.1 billion Christians worldwide—33 percent of the world's population, a number that has stabilized over many decades. Approximately 1 billion are Roman Catholic, 360 million are Protestant, and 220 million are Eastern Orthodox. About 80 million are Anglican Christians and 175 million are from other churches outside the main category of Christianity but are in some way related to Protestantism. In East Asia, Christians are not highly visible and total approximately 75 million. There are factions of Christians in other areas of the world (World Evangelization Research Center, 2003; *Encyclopedia Britannica*, 1999).

Jesus and the Development of Christianity

The story of Christianity is the story of Jesus of Nazareth, but it is also the story of a religion that developed from the faith "that in its founder God was made manifest in the flesh and dwelt among them" (Noss, 1974, p. 417). After the Resurrection, when the disciples came to believe that Jesus was God on Earth, the key elements of the Christian doctrine were in place. Jesus did not write down his teachings and relied on his disciples to carry out his work and preach what he taught. The major sources of his teachings come from the Gospels and the **Epistles** in the New Testament, composed after Jesus' death.

Jesus was born about 4 B.C.E. (Smith, 1994). Prior to his birth, as told in the Gospels, the angel Gabriel was sent by God to the virgin girl Mary in Nazareth. He told her that she would conceive and give birth to a son called Jesus. Mary replied that she was a virgin and asked how this could be (Luke 1:34). The angel replied that the "Holy Spirit will come on you, and the power of the Most High will overshadow you. Therefore the child to be born will be called holy, the son of God" (Luke 1:26–38). Mary became pregnant. Some months later Mary and her husband Joseph began their travel to Bethlehem. We are familiar with the story of how Joseph and Mary could not find proper lodgings and so Jesus was born in a manger. The Gospel of Luke tells that when the shepherds heard an angel say, "To you is born this day in the City of David a Savior, who is Christ the Lord," in

David's city, the shepherds traveled to Bethlehem and found Mary with her infant (Luke 2:8–20). When Jesus was eight days old, he was circumcised, according to the Jewish law, and Mary and Joseph went to the temple in Jerusalem to offer a sacrifice in honor of Jesus' birth.

The world in which Jesus grew up and started his ministry was a complex one. The Jews had been under foreign influence and were oppressed under Roman rule. The concept of monotheism as well as the problem of keeping the people from straying from their religion and from being influenced by other groups created a great deal of tension. Proposed resolutions ranged from outward rebellion, to accommodation, to remaining within society and revitalizing Judaism by adhering strictly to the law, to withdrawing into their community to continue with their celibate lives, praying, fasting, and keeping the Sabbath while awaiting the Messiah as prophesied in the Hebrew Bible. Jesus wanted change. Instead of holiness and strictly adhering to the ritual law, Jesus stressed God's compassion and questioned whether the social system that the code of holiness structured was truly a compassionate one. That difference would be important in the splitting off from Judaism and the development of Christianity.

There is little known or written about Jesus' early life. It has been assumed (but is undocumented) that his earthly parents, Mary and Joseph, were common people who led quiet religious lives, making the yearly trip to pray in the temple in Jerusalem on Passover as was the custom. It was also thought that Jesus worked as carpenter with his father and other family members.

When Jesus was about 30 years old, he had a profound experience. This came about when he was baptized by John. John came out of the desert where he had lived the life of an ascetic. He appeared quite suddenly on the shore of the Jordan River with an important message: "Repent! for the Kingdom of Heaven is at hand" (Matthew 3:2). John was certain the end of the present age was at hand and that the Messiah would judge the people. Only those who repented could face the day of wrath that would take place. He said that the Messiah was already begin-

ning his task. John went on to preach throughout Palestine. He took those convinced of the need to repent down to the Jordan River, immersed them into the water to signify their repentance and the washing away of their sins against the Lord. He became known as John the Baptist. John preached social and individual righteousness. He attracted much attention but denied being the Messiah; instead he professed to prepare the way for the people to accept the Messiah. Jesus came to him asking to be baptized. John immersed Jesus in the water of the Jordan River. As Jesus came out of the water, "He saw the heavens opened, the spirit descending on him like a dove; and a voice came from heaven, Thou art my beloved son in whom I am well pleased" (Mark 1:10–11).

Immediately after his baptism, Jesus went into the Judean wilderness for 40 days and nights. He did not eat; he was tempted by the Devil but refused to yield. It is this 40-day period that Christians observe as Lent. Soon after Jesus returned from the wilderness, John the Baptist was arrested for his preaching. Jesus then crossed the Jordan and began to make his way to Galilee. He accepted the first of his disciples—Simon Peter and his brother Andrew, and James and his brother John. Jesus' message was urgent, proclaiming the good news from God that "the time is fulfilled and the Kingdom of God is at hand; repent, and believe this good news" (Mark 1:15). This was the beginning of his ministry.

Jesus started his ministry by speaking in the synagogue, and as the crowds grew larger, he preached to the people in marketplaces and open fields. The Gospels tell of the miracles that Jesus performed—at the wedding feast at Cana, where he changed water into wine; his healing of a child in Capernum; the multiplication of loaves of bread and fishes; raising Lazarus from the dead; and calming the terrible storm on the Sea of Galilee. Palestine and its territories and areas in the time of Christ is shown in Figure 2.5.

Jesus' message was clear. "The appointed time has been fulfilled, and the kingdom of God has drawn near. Be repentant you people, and have faith in the good news"(Mark 1:15). Jesus attracted enormous crowds. His preaching was lucid and understandable to the ordinary Jew. He told the people that the new

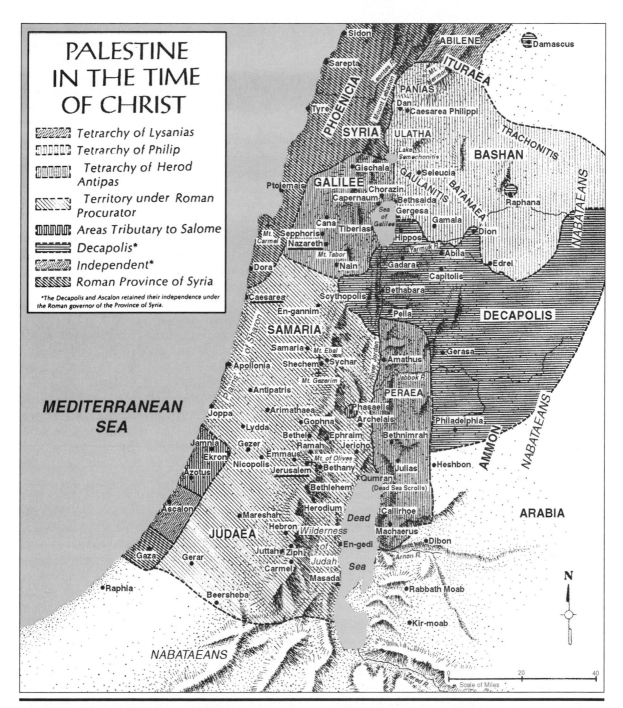

FIGURE 2.5   Palestine in the Time of Christ

Source: From *Man's Religions* (pp. 99–128), by J. B. Noss, 1949, New York: Macmillan. Copyright © 1949. Adapted by permission of Pearson Education, Inc., Upper Saddle River, NJ.

age was dawning and that when it came, the reign of God would be supreme. He taught that God's will was ultimate and that everyone should have faith in his powers. He impressed on the people that faith and obedience to God's will were vital and would lead to the love and understanding of God and enable the people to walk in the ways of God. He assured them that by accepting the will of God, all of them might enter into the kingdom—but only if they repented and returned to the true loyalty of God (Flower, 1997; Noss, 1974).

Jesus' teaching can be summed up by his Sermon on the Mount, preached to an enormous crowd. In his sermon, Jesus spoke of overturning the status quo that was adhered to by the Pharisees and Sadducees. It can be found in its entirety in Matthew (Matthew 5:3–12). Jesus also gave a simple prayer, "The Lord's Prayer" (Matthew 6:9–13). This prayer, said with reverence and humility, became a fundamental prayer for Christians and is recited throughout the world.

Although Jesus' teaching attracted large numbers of Jews wherever he went in Palestine, it soon became evident that not enough people were heeding his message. Until this time Jesus had been preaching to his fellow Jews, but later he carried his ministry to non-Jews. Jesus claimed that purity of the heart was absolutely more important than the ritual cleansing required by Judaic law. Jesus declared that people could break the law in thought as well as in deed. His popularity aroused the concerns and anger of some religious groups, especially the Pharisees, who held to the legality of Judaism and Judaic law, as well as that of the Sadducees, who were the priestly rulers and whose power depended on the goodwill of the Romans. Concern arose about whether Jesus was indeed the promised King of the Jews or the Messiah. His increasing popularity seemed to suggest that people would accept him as such. Jesus did not directly call himself the Messiah, focusing instead on teaching the ways of God and the way to reach God. However, when called the Messiah by his disciples, Jesus affirmed this as a revelation from God. Several days before his crucifixion, Jesus rode into Jerusalem to celebrate the forthcoming Passover. Although he rode

on a donkey, it was perceived that he did so in the style of a ruler. The people expected Jesus to declare that he was the king and rise up against Rome. But Jesus had denied this, saying that the Kingdom of God was not literal. Many of his followers were disillusioned, including Judas, one of his own disciples. Jesus had come to be considered dangerous in the eyes of the leaders who, with the disillusioned Judas, arranged for his arrest. The Passover supper Jesus shared with his Apostles before his arrest is known as The Last Supper. Jesus was charged with blasphemy—that he claimed to be the Messiah and the Son of God. The Roman rulers sanctioned the arrest of Jesus and passed the death sentence with insurrection as the reason. His death was by crucifixion on a Friday. John, Jesus' most beloved Apostle, as well as Jesus' mother, Mary, Salome, Mary Magdalene, and Mary, the mother of the Apostle James, stayed there until Jesus died. Crucifixion was not a Jewish but a Roman method of capital punishment. Many Jews as well as others were said to have been crucified as rebels on meager evidence (Flower, 1997; Parrinder, 1993; Smith, 1994).

Jesus foretold that he would be put to death and at the Passover meal tried to prepare the Apostles for his departure. Jesus told them that through his death the disciples would understand the need for his sacrifice and would understand the significance of his death for the salvation of all humanity.

Jesus' body was taken off the cross and buried. Two days later, on Sunday, the tomb was found empty by Mary Magdalene; Mary, the mother of James; and other women. This was the day of the resurrection of Jesus, to be known as Easter Sunday. Jesus then began to reappear to his Apostles in corporeal form. Now the Apostles began to understand who Jesus was. He told the meaning of his life and death—he came to "minister and give His life, a ransom in exchange for many" (Mark 10:45). "His death was to free the people from sin and reconcile them with God, with whom they would then live in harmony. He was the ultimate, perfect sacrifice" (Flower, 1997, pp. 21–22). Thus, after Jesus, no additional sacrifice would be necessary. His work would be carried out by his Apostles, who would proclaim him the Messiah.

Forty days after the Resurrection, Jesus ascended to heaven. Ten days later, at the Jewish festival of the Pentecost, the Apostles gathered in a room in Jerusalem. Suddenly, they heard a noise like a stiff breeze that proceeded to fill the entire room. Tongues of fire appeared and descended on each of the Apostles who then began to speak in different languages. This was the Holy Spirit of which Jesus had spoken (Acts 1:9–11; 2:1–4). Thus, the Holy Spirit of God was deemed to have "endowed His followers with its power" (Flower, 1997, p. 22). Now Jesus' Apostles were enabled to continue with his ministry, invested with the Holy Spirit, and act as Jesus' representatives on Earth. The Resurrection, Ascension, and return of Jesus became the focus of Christianity. To Christians, it seemed that in his willingness to suffer death for the redemption of humanity, Jesus gave to them the clearest understanding of the quality of "the redemptive love for God himself" (Noss, 1974, p. 437).

Through the continuing efforts of Jesus' Apostles, especially **Paul** (St. Paul), the new faith spread through Persia, Asia, and Africa, reaching across the sea to Rome. At that time, Christianity began to adapt to the different beliefs and cultures of these countries.

Jesus and Women in Pre-Christian Palestine

Quite early in Jesus' ministry, women formed an important part of the crowds that followed him. The Gospels tell of his egalitarian attitude toward women. Jesus had sensitive and sympathetic relations with many women such as Martha and Mary, the sisters of Lazarus, whom Jesus brought back from the dead. As related earlier, women stayed by him during and after his crucifixion, and after the Resurrection, his first appearance was to the women who found his tomb empty. Carmody (1989) has written about Jesus' stance toward women. She describes how the Gospels tell of Jesus' teachings about divorce. In rejecting divorce, Jesus spoke of the unity of man and woman as being "one flesh," which bound both to the marriage (Mark 10:17–31). The prevailing law at the time gave men exclusive control over the right to divorce. The denial of divorce would be a positive benefit to women, protecting them from abandonment and

poverty, and keeping them from being set adrift in a male-centered society. Jesus rejected the custom that it was one's duty to marry and procreate. He felt that if a man or woman wanted to have a life of religious service, then an unmarried state was permissible. In this way, Jesus made it possible for men as well as women to lead a monastic life. Jesus also spoke against a double standard for morality and marital fidelity. Yet, he did not absolutely reject the patriarchal culture that was part of Judaism and that of other cultures. He felt that men should be the ones to set moral examples in the community. As evidence of this, 12 men, but no women, became his Apostles, although he did accept women as his students, something the rabbis of the time would never permit (Carmody, 1989).

The Gospels also relate that Jesus prevailed against Jewish customs, especially the prohibition against activity on the Sabbath, for which he was severely criticized. He healed many, including women, on this holy day of rest. He dealt compassionately with all kinds of women among them prostitutes and women who were "unclean" (menstruating) according to the law and who were to be shunned (Thurston, 1998). In his positive attitude toward women, Jesus not only took from Judaism what would be important for his own teachings, but also transcended the laws of Judaism as well. His new movement, not yet called Christianity, seemed to accept and welcome women. Carmody (1989) quotes Ben Witherington who, in explaining why Christianity differed from Judaism, said, "Thus, the community of Jesus, both before and after Easter, granted women *together* with men (not segregated from men . . .) an equal right to participate fully in the family of faith. This was a right that women did not have in contemporary Judaism or in many pagan cults" (Witherington, 1984, p. 127).

As we turn to the development of Christianity and the role of women in this new religion, we will explore whether these attitudes toward women were maintained.

Catholicism

Christianity began after the death of Jesus. In the development and spread of Christianity, the concept of the church as a teaching authority became prominent. It began with the postulate that "God came to earth in the person of Jesus Christ to teach people how to live in this world so as to inherit eternal life" (Smith, 1994, p. 22). As Christianity spread throughout Rome, it was initially subject to official persecution, but by 380 C.E., it became the official religion of the Roman Empire. It essentially continued until 1054 C.E. when it divided into the Eastern Orthodox Church and the Roman Catholic Church. Then, in the sixteenth century, another great division occurred with the Protestant Reformation.

Roman Catholics see their church as beginning with Jesus and Peter and continuing through an unbroken succession of 20 centuries of popes to the present time. They see the Protestants as beginning in 1517 and the Eastern Orthodox Church as beginning with the earlier splits from the Catholic Church.

Protestants see their churches in the direct historical line of succession from the early churches of the first and second centuries. Protestants disagree on various issues, but all denominations try to make their congregations more or less like the congregations of the first century of Christianity. Throughout the 20 centuries of Christianity, particularly in Roman Catholicism, there has been conflict between two motifs in the theological understanding of male–female relations: equivalence and subordination. This conflict between the two views, one that affirmed the equivalence of man and woman as human persons and the other that defined woman as subordinate to men socially and even ontologically, can be traced through the whole of Christian history (Carroll, 1983).

The traditional biblical references for both of these basic positions have come from Paul's letters. Paul, an Apostle of Jesus, has been considered the "second founder of Christianity" (Noss, 1974, p. 441). He was very important in the spread of Christianity throughout the Roman Empire. Before 65 C.E., Paul wrote to the Galatians the *equivalence* position: "There is no such thing as Jew and Greek, slave and free, male and female; for you are all one person in Christ Jesus" (Paul's Letter to the Galatians 3:28).

There is evidence that early Christianity regarded redemption by Jesus as overturning systems of social discrimination, bringing all persons to a new status before God. But beginning with the post-Pauline period, the social order, according to the concept of subordination, demanded that men as husbands have authority over women, both as wives and children. Wives must act as obedient followers and carry out the commands of the husband, as must children and servants. This theology of subordination has been maintained by insinuating that women are, in fact, morally, ontogenically, logically, and intellectually inferior to the man and therefore less capable of an independent life. A woman's inferior status can lead to sin when she acts independently. The *subordinate* position implies that:

> As in all the churches of the saints, the women should keep silence in the churches. For they are not permitted to speak, but should be subordinates, as even the law says. If there is anything they desire to know, let them ask their husbands at home. For it is shameful for a woman to speak in church. (Paul's First Letter to the Corinthians, 14:34–35)

Paul's letter of equivalence suggests that early **Pauline** Christianity accepted the radical egalitarianism of Jesus and his movement. But according to Carmody (1989), the church did not accept Paul's vision and intent to define the Christian community on an egalitarian basis. The patriarchalism of the Judaic culture and the contemporary Hellenistic culture (which was different then from that in early Judaism) began to penetrate the church's vision for family life and the community. Whether this was the reason for Paul's subordinate position has not been clarified. The theme of subordination has never been the sole view of women in Christianity, although for much of its history it has been the dominant and official one. The concept of equivalence has been present, but only recently has it come to be the dominant view and then only by liberal churches. Equivalence takes the creation story of Genesis, in which both male and female are created in the image of God, as *normative.*

After the split from the Eastern Orthodox Church, the Roman Catholic Church continued to evolve. If it were true that Jesus Christ came to Earth to teach people how to obtain eternal life, it was crucial for his teachings to continue. The Gospels may not be sufficient because they contained ambiguities. If the Bible is studied individually, it may be given different interpretations. From these problems arose the concept of a "supreme court to adjudicate between truth and error" (Smith, 1994, p. 223). The formation of such a teaching authority resulted in the doctrine of "papal infallibility." The earthly head of the Catholic Church is the pope, successor to St. Peter in the Bishopric of Rome. The doctrine of papal infallibility asserts that "when the Pope speaks officially on matters of faith and morals, God protects him from error" (Smith, 1994, p. 223).

A second concept that developed in Catholicism was the Church as the Sacramental Agent—to know what sacraments should be done and to be able to carry them out. As indicated earlier, the Roman Catholic Church observes seven sacraments, paralleling the important moments and needs during one's lifetime. Two need to be repeated often: reconciliation (confession) and the Church's central sacrament, the Mass, also known as the Holy Eucharist or communion.

These two concepts of the Church as a *teaching authority* and a *sacramental agent* are two of the most important central perspectives in Roman Catholicism. There are other important aspects of the Catholic Church but they are beyond the scope of this section.

The Virgin Mary. Catholic tradition has it that Mary, the only mortal born without original sin, although a virgin, conceived and gave birth to Jesus Christ, the Son of God. She is the principal saint, also known as the Blessed Virgin Mary, Our Lady, and the Mother of God (from the Greek *theotokos*). Her name in Hebrew is Miriam.

The events of Mary's life and the birth of Jesus as told in the New Testament have already been reviewed. Although few other details of her life are mentioned or implied, tradition has it that she was the daughter of St. Anne and St. Joachim and that she was presented and dedicated at the temple in Jerusalem as a virgin at a young age. According to a doctrine issued in the fifth century C.E., Mary was "assumed" directly into heaven. However, it was not until 1950 that Pope Pius XII's bulla *Munifcentissimus Deus* made Mary's assumption into heaven an article of faith. In 1854, the Roman Catholic Church proclaimed the dogma of the Immaculate Conception—declared in the bulla *Ineffabilis Deus* of Pope Pius IX, according to which Mary was conceived without original sin. The Roman Catholic Church also teaches that Mary was freed from actual sin by a special grace of God (*Encyclopedia Britannica,* 1999).

While Catholics but not all Protestant denominations have accepted the pope's 1950 bulla, Mary's virginity has served as an important symbol of Christianity's ascetic ideal, almost since the church was organized. From the earliest times in the Catholic Church, it was believed that Mary's intercession was especially effective on behalf of humanity, and since the Middle Ages, the most prevalent expressions of Marian devotion have been the recitations of the rosary. According to the Church, Mary is the mediatrix of all graces. The study of doctrine about Mary is called Mariology and the veneration and devotion to Mary is called Mariolatry (*Columbia Encyclopedia,* 1993).

Devotion to Mary has increased in many parts of the world and in some cases has been carried to an idolatrous extreme. Mary is the most famous and venerated of mother figures, and she has grown to be an immense personality throughout the world. It is claimed that 2 billion Hail Marys are said daily. Why is this happening? Why did 5 million people, many non-Christian, visit Lourdes this year to drink the healing waters and 10 million travel to Mexico City to pray to Mary, Our Lady of Guadalupe? Why the need to talk with her?

Apparitions of Mary have been reported for centuries but have always been infrequent events. Each apparition was said to have been accompanied by miraculous healings, messages from heaven, and other signs of supernatural intervention. Sightings were reported in New York City in 1970, and in 1981, sightings began in Medjugorje in Bosnia. There Mary is said to have appeared to six young peasants and has continued to deliver messages to them. No fewer than 11 million believers have flocked to the site.

Theologians and clergy are uneasy about these sightings, which seem to have multiplied out of proportion. The church as yet has not made a definitive statement about the sightings but is asking serious questions concerning the sudden rise in appearances of Mary.

One explanation for the increase in the frequency of appearances of Mary is that the emotional need for her is so irresistible to a profoundly troubled world that people, even those without an obvious link to Mary, are being drawn to her. It is known that in the Muslim world, Mary is revered as a pure and holy saint, but it is remarkable to many that large numbers of Muslims are making pilgrimages to Christian shrines (*Life Magazine,* 1996).

It also seems that more feminists are rediscovering the feminine symbol that Mary presents. As the Bible's most famous and revered woman, Mary may now have become a symbolic player in the fight for the ordination of women. These women point out that Pope John Paul II loves Mary and visits Mary shrines—yet he stands by the long-term rationale for a males-only priesthood. This dichotomy is also seen in the fact that Mary adorns the banners of the liberals seeking a more prominent role for women in all the churches, but, at the same time, Mary glorifies the banners of the many conservatives who want to preserve the ministries as all-male. Despite intransigence, the fight is having an effect. The church is beginning to redefine women's roles and, according to many clergy, the all-male celibate priesthood may be endangered, a sign that culture may be stronger than theology. With the elevation of Mary today, whether as a symbol for feminists or as solace for a sorely troubled world, her cultural importance now seems to far transcend more dogmatic or institutional boundaries than could ever have been anticipated.

Current Issues.   While Catholic women are seeking ways to be given a more responsible role in the church, major events concerning Catholic priests and sexual abuse have been made public. In the early twenty-first century, there have been many revelations about priests and sexual abuse of young boys. These shocking events had apparently been taking place for decades. Some priests began to serve jail sentences with the unfortunate murder of one of them

(Alternet; American Catholic, 2003; Bader, 2002; Just for Catholics, 2003).

This scandal shook all aspects of the church community—priests, laypeople, and bishops. Although the hierarchical system of the church finally worked to address the problems of pedophilia and cover-ups, many of the lay members of the church demanded explanations, accountability, and a resolution to affect change. Some have felt that celibacy may well be a factor and that the future of the church will surely involve a debate over this centuries-old practice. In the Protestant churches clergy are allowed to marry (American Catholic, 2003). In addition, there has been a history of married Protestant clergy entering the Catholic Church who have been permitted to continue their marital state. These events may inadvertently help women in their efforts to play an important role in the church.

Eastern Orthodoxy

The Eastern Orthodox Church has far more similarities to than differences from the Catholic Church. Both observe the same sacraments but while they believe in a teaching authority, two differences are evident. The Catholic Church regards as doctrine the Immaculate Conception, the Assumption of Virgin Mary, and others. The Eastern Orthodox Church considers these as "additions" that Orthodox Christians may or may not choose to endorse (Smith, 1994).

In the Roman Catholic Church, dogmas are, in the final analysis, pronounced by the pope. In contrast, Eastern Orthodoxy believes that God's truth is revealed through the "conscience of the Church" or Christian consensus. Thus the Eastern Church does not have a pope but the titular head of the church is the patriarch of Constantinople. Church dogmas reflect the consciences of the Orthodox Christians (Noss, 1974; Smith, 1994).

While Eastern Orthodoxy may seem more egalitarian, it, too, like Catholicism, maintains that an all-male clergy was part of God's plan for the church. So it, too, is imbued with the patriarchal system that has only recently shown signs of changing (Carmody, 1989).

Protestantism. On October 31, 1517, Martin Luther began this theological and ecclesiastical opposition to Catholicism by nailing his Ninety-Five Theses to the church door in Wittenberg, Germany. The causes that led to the break from Roman Catholicism are complex and still being debated. However, the basic cause was the development of a new concept of philosophy of Christianity. Luther's interest was to restore to all Christians the liberty of the Gospel. And, because men and women were both created in the image of God, they shared the fundamental abilities and the rights to this liberty.

Although Luther disagreed with Roman Catholic positions on some major issues, his arguments and references were generally conservative doctrinal positions very much in the mainstream of ancient and medieval Christian theology. Luther rejected the concept of papal authority and considered it idolatrous because it prevented the type of critical deliberation that would avoid limitations and errors. Many Protestants believe that God speaks to his people through the Bible and insist that every word and letter in it was dictated by God. Thus, the Bible contains no historical, scientific, or other errors.

Another concept in Protestantism is the importance of private religious experience in which what is experienced must be the work of the Holy Spirit. For Protestants, the Bible presents the clearest picture of God's goodness and the way the people can relate to it. In this way "The Bible is, for Protestants, ultimate" (Smith, 1994, p. 229).

There is some recognition that with each individual's encounter with God's Word in the Bible as a centering force in her or his religion, there can be uncertainty and risks. If one misreads the Bible, different truths may emerge. The formation of different groups within Protestantism may be evidence of these different interpretations of the Bible. In addition, other differences among the Protestant denominations are in their church government. Nevertheless, Protestants, regardless of their denomination, prefer these problems to the security of doctrines or institutions that they consider to be fallible.

Although the mainstream Protestant reform groups abolished celibacy among priests (and Christian monasteries), they did not immediately substitute a new inclusion of women in the Protestant married clergy. Therefore, Reformation on the whole did not have a liberating effect on women.

In beginning this section on Protestantism, we noted that one reason for the break from Catholicism was that Luther wanted to restore to all Christians the liberty of the Gospel. And, because men and women were created in the image of God, they shared the basic capacities and rights related to this liberty (Carmody, 1989, p. 174). On the other hand, the reformers kept with the patriarchal tradition that advocated silence and submission of women based on the order of creation (man was created first in the image of God and woman created second) and based on the punishment for the sin of Eve. However, in time, cultural changes with regard to women were made.

One of the most critical distinctions among the major divisions of the Protestant Reformation was church government. It was these differences that ultimately most influenced the places of women in Protestant churches.

There are four basic divisions of Protestantism, all dating from the sixteenth-century Reformation: the Lutherans, the Reformed, the Anglicans, and the Anabaptists.

The Lutherans. Luther initiated the Reformation in Germany. The important ecclesiastical appointments were made from the top down—from the princes of each German state (e.g., Saxony, Prussia). There was no democracy. When the Lutheran Church came to the United States, it was not until 1918 that somewhat democratic reforms were made (Evans, 1976).

The other half of the Lutherans were the Scandinavians. These nations all had powerful and somewhat democratic parliaments as well as kings. Sweden, Denmark, and Norway all adopted Lutheranism as their state religion and were later joined by Finland. All these churches were generally ruled by their somewhat democratic parliaments. Scandinavian Lutheranism followed Scandinavians to the United Sates. They spoke well for women. But it was not until 1938 that the Norwegian parliament began to ordain women. By 1958, European Lutheran churches and many of those in the United States began to ordain women as clergy.

The Reformed Tradition.   Sometimes called the Calvinist tradition, the Reformed tradition has historically fought over Calvin's doctrines of predestination. This tradition began in the Swiss city-state Canton of Zurich by Zwingli in 1518. Zwingli advocated free will in opposition to Calvin's position. Zwingli's position has been accepted by almost all Reformed churches today.

The original Reformed churches were historically somewhat democratic because the church government was modeled after their elected city-state governments. Middle-class males, but not poor males, could vote. With few exceptions, women could not. Reformed churches spread to cities in Switzerland, Germany, and Holland; to some French cities, a few Hungarian towns, the Church of Scotland (the Presbyterians); to the Scotch-Irish in Northern Ireland; and to many English cities (the Congregationalists or "Puritans"). When the churches emigrated to North America, many split off (e.g., the Church of Scotland became the "Christian Church" or "disciples of Christ").

The Reformed churches all had democratic governments that encouraged education for all their members, including women. Their clergy was highly educated (in the United States). Members of the Reformed churches founded Harvard, Yale, Princeton, and many other colleges.

The Anglican Tradition.   This tradition split with the church of Rome. It began in 1532 when King Henry VIII of England decided to divorce in order to marry Anne Boleyn. The king broke with the pope, seized control of all churches in England, as well as church land and property for himself and his allies. He eliminated all who opposed his "religious" reforms, replacing them with his friends and associates.

In the beginning the Anglican Church differed little from the Catholic Church except that church authorities were appointed directly by the king and, of course, divorce was permissible. The Bible was translated and published in English. By 1551, mar-

ried clergy were permitted. The Anglican Church remained completely hierarchical in government; Anabaptist (Brownists) and Reformed (Puritans, Congregationalists, Presbyterians) churches were now organized illegally in urban and working-class areas (Langer, 1948).

There were many conflicts between the English kings and parliament that existed well into the next century. Since 1660, the governing power of the Anglican Church in England has remained partly democratic. The Protestant Episcopal Church in the United States was organized as an American denomination separate from the English state church after the Revolutionary War (Ahlstrom, 1972).

The Anabaptist Churches.   These were originally working-class and peasant churches of the Reformation and were opposed by Lutheran state authorities, Roman Catholic state authorities, Reformed church authorities, and Anglican English state authorities. The movement was started in Switzerland by Felix Mantz about 1525. Women were part of this local congregation and may have already started to vote in its decision-making process. The congregation was expelled in 1526 for opposing infant baptism (Williams, 1962). The Anabaptist movement rapidly spread across northern and central Europe, organizing house churches of the poor, often led by ex–Roman Catholic clergy. They were opposed by local authorities almost everywhere. Women played a major role in town events and even in a military battle in Munster, Germany.

Regarding the role of women in the Anabaptist movement, Williams (1962), in summarizing the sixteenth-century Anabaptist movement, stated that "Nowhere else in the Reformation Era were women so nearly the peers and companions in the faith and martyrdom in missionary enterprise. . . .The Anabaptist insistence on the conventional principle of freedom of conscience for all adult believers and thereby the extension of the priesthood of the Christophorous laity to women constituted a major breach in the patriarchalism and a momentous step in the Western emancipation of women" (pp. 506–507).

Thus far, our discussion has provided some concept of the principles of Protestantism and the major divisions within it in which women have played some part, depending on their particular group membership. We can also see that in the Reformation, the patriarchal system was still functioning. Rather than discussing in more detail the role and progress of women in each of the groups within these divisions, we will describe events in the **Puritan** groups and in the **Quakers**. In the Puritan groups, women suffered severely and many were killed; whereas beginning in the seventeenth century in England and then in the United States, the Quakers became very important in pioneering leadership in the emancipation of women.

Puritanism.   Puritanism did not develop in England until the late sixteenth century and was brought to America soon after. English Puritans elaborated on the relations between female and male in marriage. The Puritan husband was to be the benevolent ruler; the wife, although a subordinate partner, was to be a docile helpmate to her husband in all things. This view of family harmony had another side, a constant suspicion that women (and servants) were secretly rebellious against authority. This was frequently thought to be more prevalent among women than men, because women were the "weaker vessel." This was thought to be the fact because "the Devil [could] more easily prevail in her and . . . continues to resort to women as the easier victim of temptation" (Perkins, 1596). Perkins specified that one of the reasons women easily succumb to the devil is that they are by nature insubordinate and wish to repudiate their divinely appointed inferiority to men. This makes women an easy target for the devil.

Whether this was one of the concepts that led to the association of women with witchcraft is uncertain. However, there were witchcraft trials and burning of witches long before Puritanism developed in England. In 1431, the French heroine Jeanne d'Arc was burned at the stake as a witch by the English. After that, the French were decidedly unenthusiastic about witchcraft trials. However, thousands of "witches," mostly peasant women with local enemies, were convicted and burned during that century in Germany, Scotland, and Spain. Accusations of witchcraft existed among Catholics and Protestants and

were found on both sides of the Atlantic. Almost all the victims were women, although some men were also convicted as witches.

The Puritans who came to America brought the same ideology along with them. Puritanism flourished in Massachusetts, which was a bastion of Puritan orthodoxy. The elaboration on relations between husband and wife continued with the idea of women's subordination. The suspicions of witchcraft were augmented by a now-famous Puritan tract on witches—Cotton Mather's 1689 *Memorable Providences, Relating to Witchcrafts and Possession.* This book was probably one of the causes of the 1692 Salem witch trials. Cotton Mather was one of the clergy in Salem (Ahlstrom, 1972).

In the summer of 1692, hysteria concerning witches, provoked in part by the Puritan clergymen, gripped Salem village. The governor of Massachusetts created a special court to try suspected witches, and by that autumn, twenty people were hanged. Most were local women, but two Puritan clergymen had also been victims of witchcraft associations and were convicted. All died protesting their innocence. The verdict was often based on "eyewitness" testimony, including neighbors who were certain that they saw the victims do impossible things such as floating through the air and changing themselves into nonhuman animals. Although twelve local clergymen actively opposed the trials, warning about the dangers of such testimony, three clergymen actively supported the trials. Interestingly, Cotton Mather's father, Increase Mather, wrote about these cases, attacking the Salem witchcraft court decisions. Finally, Massachusetts Governor Phipps was convinced by Increase Mather's manuscript that innocent people had been falsely convicted and hanged. He disbanded the court and ended the trials in late 1692 (Ahlstrom, 1972).

Although many people in Massachusetts probably believed witches did exist, this was in part provoked by the sermons and writing of the clergy. The Massachusetts clergy became more interested in fair trials than witch-hunts. The people in Massachusetts gradually became disgusted with these trials after the Salem events, and they were never again repeated in

America. One of the trial judges, Samuel Sewell, later made a very sad public confession in church that he had been wrong at the witchcraft trials (Ahlstrom, 1972; Smith, Handy, & Loetscher, 1960).

Quakerism.   Quakerism continued these Puritan attitudes but was more charismatic and egalitarian. This was especially because of a woman, Margaret Fell, and George Fox's beliefs about Eve. They believed in women's subordination to men because of Eve's part in the Fall; they also proclaimed that this condition of subordination *ended* when a woman accepted Jesus Christ as Savior, because her original equal position to men before the Fall was then automatically restored by God. Therefore, Christian women should now actively proclaim God's word in public, just as women such as the Samaritan woman at the well, Mary Magdalene, and Lydia did in the New Testament. The parallelisms of Adam's fall and Christ's new salvation and reconciliation for humans has been a traditional theme in Christian theologies (Ahlstrom, 1972).

George Fox (1624–1691) searched for the Holy Spirit during the English Civil War and actively began to travel and preach a mystical or spiritual version of Christianity about 1648. The traditional date for the founding of the Society of Friends or Quakers is 1652, when Fox held a crucial organizational meeting at Swarthmore Hall in England, the home of some of his most loyal associates, as well as patrons Thomas Fell (1595–1658) and his wife, Margaret Fell (1614–1702).

The Quakers treated all members, men and women, as "saved in Christ" and therefore equal in church roles and responsibilities. They abandoned separate clergy, believing that all their adult members, both men and women, were "priests" or clergy. Fox, Margaret Fell, and other Quakers, both men and women, became aggressive missionaries, which landed their members in jail (and sometimes hanged) in both England and America. Fox himself visited America where some Quakers had already settled.

Another Quaker, William Penn, obtained a charter from the English king to create a place of settlement and refuge for Quakers in America in the new colony of Pennsylvania in 1681. The Quakers in America had formerly helped Roger Williams and Anne Hutchinson create the colony of Rhode Island (1636) and were the first English settlers of New Jersey (1674) (Ahlstrom, 1972; Smith, Handy, & Loetscher, 1960).

Some important examples of Quaker women taking active roles were Mary Fischer, Ann Austin, Mary Clark, and Mary Dyer, who attempted to preach Quaker Christianity in the closed Puritan state of Massachusetts between 1651 and 1655. Mary Fisher and Ann Austin were jailed naked for five weeks and inspected for bodily tokens of witchcraft, and their library of over 100 books was confiscated. Mary Clark was severely whipped, held in prison for ten weeks, and then expelled to Rhode Island. Mary Dyer was hanged (Ahlstrom, 1972; Irwin, 1979).

Religion differed in different areas of the colonies. While Massachusetts was the stronghold of Puritanism, Rhode Island became home for dissidents, with the middle colonies having many Quakers, especially Pennsylvania. The southern colonies were mainly loyal to the Church of England, although Maryland was settled by Roman Catholics. Nevertheless, the major influence was that of the Puritans made up of British believers who themselves had emigrated to America to find "religious liberty."

Eventually, the concept of patriarchal order began to be overcome, but only in the Christian movements in the nineteenth century as a result of the Enlightenment. This allowed modern Christians to identify with redemption and reform in the direction of egalitarian rights and opportunities, a way to justify the equivalence of all persons and to provide access to opportunities for self-expression. This shift was basic for all modern theologies of liberation, including the feminism that arose in the nineteenth- and twentieth-century drives for women's suffrage in the United States. This feminist movement was the biggest single change in public concepts of women in the last two centuries. These concepts are highly evident today in women's continuing struggle for equality with men.

Thus, the early "narrow thought in Christianity, as much as in any other religion, restricted the acceptance of women as full human beings" (Carroll, 1983) and is still with us today. The classic in Western literature that has most systematically argued for the general biological inferiority of women has been Plato's *Republic*. Included in this theme is the mythical belief that women have weaker brains and weaker educational needs than men, which was previously supported by "scientific" data. These resultant attitudes are still encountered daily by girls and young women embarking on education in science, mathematics, law, medicine, and other allegedly masculine fields.

In religious hierarchy, power and prestige have been reserved exclusively for males. Until very recently in most denominations, only men could be priests, ministers, or rabbis. Although the first female Protestant cleric was ordained in 1853, it was not until 1972 that the first female Reform rabbi was ordained, and in 1976 the first female Episcopal priest was ordained. At first, their positions were highly controversial, but as time passed, though still subject of some dispute, their numbers have increased. At present, the Catholic Church does not have female clergy, although Roman Catholic women can now participate in the Mass as lectors and in the distribution of the Eucharist. Nuns have become more independent and involved in the community, and there is a strong movement toward equality in the church.

Islam

There are millions of Muslim women in the many Muslim countries throughout the world. Complex elements comprise the picture of the Islamic woman; that is, the basic Islamic rites and aspects of its interpretation in each of the Muslim countries, as well as the politics of each of these countries, make it difficult to write about the place of women in Islamic society, especially at this critical moment in history.

A *Muslim* is "one who submits" or "one who commits *himself* to Islam." The word *Islam* means "submission" or "surrender." "One who thoughtfully

declares, 'I am a Muslim' has done more than affirm *his* membership in a community. . . . [He is saying] 'I am one who commits himself to God' " (Adams, 1965, p. 496). In the beginning, Islam was a challenge to other religions, primarily Judaism and Christianity. The force and clarity of Islamic thought have great appeal for those who have accepted it. It has been estimated that at least 1 billion people now consider themselves adherents to Islam, and the number is increasing. Since its inception, Islam has held to its one basic scripture, which has been preserved in its initial textural purity. The Qur'an (or Koran), the Bible of the Muslims, was revealed to Muhammed, the Muslim prophet, about 531 C.E. (Noss & Noss, 1984; Ringgren & Strom, 1967).

Pre-Islamic Arabia. At the time of Muhammad's birth, the Arabian peninsula was populated by seminomadic tribes. They were neither politically nor spiritually united; their main loyalty was to the tribe. It was an inhospitable land, and tribes were forced to move from one area to another along this peninsula, seeking a more favorable climate in which they could find food and water. The Arabian people had a polytheistic religion and worshiped many gods and goddesses, animals, demons, wells, and stones, similar to the tribes Abraham had lived among.

Muhammad was born about 570 C.E. in Mecca, a small town in western Arabia. It is said that Muhammad's father, a Quraysh Cherish of the Hashemite clan, died before Muhammad was born. His mother died when Muhammad was 6 years old, and he was brought up first by his paternal grandfather and then by his uncle. Growing up in impoverished circumstances surely shaped Muhammad's feelings about poor people. He was angered by the social inequities and the mistreatment of women and children, and he condemned female infanticide (Carroll, 1983; Ringgren & Strom, 1967).

Muhammad entered the service of Khadija, the widow of a wealthy merchant. Khadija was attracted to Muhammad and admired his ability to assist her in the management of her trading business. Muhammad married Khadija when he was 25 and she was 40. It was said that she had considerable influence on his thoughts, especially about the social problems in Arabia. She also had sufficient wealth so that he was free to pursue his meditations. Khadija and Muhammad had six children, but only his daughter Fatima survived him and lived to see her father's Islam grow and prosper. Khadija died in 621 C.E. Until then, she was Muhammad's only wife. After Khadija's death, Muhammad took four wives, which was then permitted by the Koran (Carmody, 1989; Carroll, 1983; Ringgren & Strom, 1967).

When he was 40 years old, Muhammad began to receive revelations from the God, Allah. Khadija supported his belief that Allah had chosen him to be a prophet. Khadija became known as the First Mother of the Faithful and was his first convert. Her uncle Waraqah also believed in Muhammad's visions and decided that he was the successor of Moses and was destined to be the prophet of his Arab people for his God, Allah. At first Muhammad spoke about his revelations only to his family circle, but soon Allah commanded him to preach to his tribe, where he obtained his first disciples.

But many members of Muhammad's own tribe were hostile to his ideas. His main supporters were liberated slaves and poor people. Muhammad began to preach a consistent monotheism.

> *Say Allah is One*
> *The Eternal God*
> *He begot none,*
> *Nor was he begotten*
> *None is equal to him*
> *Koran 81.I–14 [cp. Rev.6.12–14]. Pelican trs.,*
> *p. 17, II.3–11.*

Eventually, more and more tribes followed Muhammad, converting to Islam. When about 60 of his converts moved to Yathrib, he went there himself in 622 C.E. This town would eventually be named after him, The Prophet's City, *madinal an-nabi* or Medina. This event marked the beginning of the Muhammadan era. After his followers abandoned their old tribal groups in Mecca, strong enmity developed between the new religionists and the Meccans. This triggered a holy war in the cause of the God, Allah.

Muhammad and his new Islamites became strong enough to attack Mecca, and in 630 C.E. it was conquered. Muhammad began the ritual of the pilgrimage to the holy city of Mecca, which became a precedent for all rituals and which still survives. Muhammad died in Medina on June 8, 632 C.E., at about the age of 59. He was buried in Mecca. By then he and the new Islam held sway over nearly the entire Arabian peninsula.

Muhammad's revelations are preserved as originally written in the Qur'an (meaning reading or recitation), or Koran. The Qur'an was not completed until after Muhammad's death, partly through writings and by relying on oral tradition. In volume it is comparable to the New Testament. To faithful Muslims, the Qur'an is the very word of Allah brought down and revealed to Muhammad, just as the Ten Commandments had been revealed to Moses on Mount Sinai (Ringgren & Strom, 1967). Let us look at what is in the Qur'an and what it means for the status of women both during the formative period of Islam and in current times.

The Qur'an. In the doctrine of the Qur'an, the "absolute oneness of God" is its principal tenet. "There is no God but Allah, and Muhammad is his prophet." This is the Islamic creed. Allah is omnipotent and omniscient (all-powerful and all-knowing). Polytheism and the Christian belief in the Trinity are denied. All is dependent on the will of Allah. There will be judgment and retribution; the good will enter Paradise and the wicked are damned to Hell. The patriarchs of the Jews as well as Jesus are all considered prophets and the recipients of revelations by Allah, but the absolute and perfect revelation came through Muhammad, who is the last in the long succession of prophets.

The basic plan of worship in the Qur'an involves the Five Pillars of Islam, which are the demands made of all adherents of Islam. These are described in Table 2.4.

Male circumcision is not mandated by law in the Qur'an but is generally observed in all Muslim countries. Pork is regarded as unclean and the eating of it is prohibited, as is the drinking of alcohol (Ringgren & Strom, 1967).

TABLE 2.4   The Five Pillars of Islam

The five basic demands are

1. **The Creed:** There is no God but Allah.
2. **The Ritual Prayer:** It is now said five times a day at fixed hours.
3. **Almsgiving:** A kind of tithe for the poor and sick and for other purposes.
4. **Fasting:** Total abstinence from food and drink and sexual intercourse from sunrise to sunset during the month of Ramadan.
5. **Pilgrimage to Mecca:** This is obligatory for any believer once during *his* lifetime if *he* can possibly undertake it.

Source: From *World Religions* (pp. 503–504) edited by Geoffrey Parrinder. Copyright © 1983 by the Hamlyn Publishing Group Ltd. Reprinted by permission of Facts on File, Inc.

Impact of Islam on Women.   Many pre-Islamic traditions were carried over to Islam, but others were not. There were both patriarchal and matriarchal systems at the time of Muhammad, but Islam abolished all matriarchy. Women were no longer controlled by their families but by their husbands and their husbands' relatives. But despite the patriarchal system of most pre-Islamic marriages, the woman retained blood kinship with her tribe and could seek protection with her own tribe if maltreated by her husband. Polyandry gave way to polygamy (Ringgren & Strom, 1967).

Muhammad was familiar with the doctrines of Christianity and Judaism. He disapproved of the celibacy of Christianity. He did not equate women with evil and uncleanliness. Muhammad was sympathetic to women and concerned with their treatment, especially of widows. He did not consider women's menstruation as unclean or menstrual blood as pollutions, although he did order women not to pray during this time and precluded their presence at the **Mosque.** The question of whether women should attend the Mosque engaged the attention of Muslim doctors. Many, if not most, preferred that women not pray in the Mosque, but they were constrained by tradition, which said that women could not be prevented from attendance but may not be perfumed.

The Qur'an is clear about full religious responsibility for women. Women are directed to participate in the stated obligations equally with men. In practice, however, this was not carried out. It is said that Muhammad allowed women to pray in the Mosque with him, while other stories say that this was possible only with the permission and presence of the husband. Muhammad replaced the practice of polyandry with polygamy but restricted the practice to only four wives. There was a proviso that all wives were to be treated equally. He did this out of concern for the large numbers of women whose husbands were killed in battle and who needed to be taken care of. Divorce was not to be undertaken rashly by husbands. Although under Islam divorce benefited men, stipulations allowed divorced women to keep their dowries, and they were to be sent away with kindness and no loss of reputation. Previously, women were punished if they had committed adultery by being beaten or even stoned to death. This punishment was not in the Qur'an but originated from the Torah of the Jews. Muhammad modified this law and urged leaders to let the accused go on the premise that it is better to make an error in forgiveness than in punishment (Noss, 1974).

However, a few years after Muhammad's death, conditions for women worsened under the rule of Umar, who succeeded him. Umar attempted to limit women to praying at home. After much opposition even from his wife and son, he virtually succeeded in this by appointing separate imams (teachers) for men and women. He also prevented Muhammad's wives from making pilgrimages but later changed his decision. Umar supported the trend toward excluding women from taking part in religious life and in all communal aspects of that life. This practice of *exclusion* was one of two significant factors in early Islam that contributed to the rapid decline of the status of women. The other factor was the seclusion of women. J. I. Smith (1985) describes *seclusion* as a custom beginning specifically with the prophet's relegation of his wives to a separate place apart from normal social interaction with men. Women stayed at home and were not permitted to speak directly with men. Any conversation had to be carried out with a curtain between them. This led to the direct withdrawal of women from normal society, which came to be essentially a male society. Seclusion in this new religion resulted in a diminished role for women. Smith argues that the practice of seclusion would not have come about if the men of the time had not encouraged it. The institution of *hijah*, or seclusion behind a curtain, was said to be a divine revelation by Allah. The freedoms that women had enjoyed became virtually nonexistent.

The custom of *veiling* also diminished the role of women in this early period of Islam. Women had to keep their faces covered if they went out. Many women also covered one of their eyes. This practice, which emphasized both the obedience of women and their chastity, pervaded all Muslim lands.

It seems apparent that at no time during or immediately after the time of the prophet did women hold strong positions of leadership in the religious sphere. Only a few women in the very early days of Islam served as collectors and transmitters of traditions or in public affairs. The practices of exclusion and seclusion kept women from making any progress. There appears to be no convincing evidence that the establishment of Islam, and the social revolution that ensued, expanded opportunities for women that were previously not available to them. The establishment of Islam as a religiocultural system reduced the chances for women to participate in public life. J. I. Smith (1985) argues that codification of the laws in the Qur'an taken as divine revelation and the imposition of seclusion alleged to be based on divine revelation were crucial factors that increased the exclusion of women. The rapid implementation of exclusion and seclusion that followed Muhammad's death should be seen as the predominant attitude of men about the unsuitability of women to take part in public life and leadership. Women were willing to submit to these restrictions and accept that they were a part of divine revelation. Smith suggests strongly that considerable investigation needs to be done to obtain a clearer picture of the status of women at the time of the prophet.

Current Status of Women in Islam. As Islam spread it gained converts from Arab countries and from non-Arab countries such as Iran, Malaysia, Pakistan, and Indonesia (where in the 1970s only about 15 percent of the population was Muslim and now is the largest Muslim country in the world).

As indicated earlier, a woman's role as a Muslim depends on the varying laws and cultures in different countries as well as the economy of these countries and the social conditions. Agricultural societies have begun to urbanize with an increase in industry and technological development, which has had both positive and negative effects on women. State systems were able to lower infant and maternal mortality and increase life expectancy, but at the same time increased population growth also increased the burdens of childbearing particularly among poor women. And, even though there are educational efforts to address illiteracy, women have not benefited very much. However, when women from upper classes are educated, they have many more alternatives from which to choose. In many poor Islamic countries the practice of exclusion has not turned out to be practical, because Muslim men cannot afford to keep their wives secluded; they are needed to work and help support their families.

When the United States–led alliance toppled the Taliban in Afghanistan in November 2001, a direct effect was that women and girls had greater freedom to play a role in public life. They were able to take advantage of educational programs, health care, and could seek employment. In Kabul, the capital, women and girls were protected under the International Security Assistance Force (ISAF). Yet even in Kabul many Afghan women faced threats from civilians or armed men. Outside of Kabul, where the ISAF was not present, there was much lawlessness and Afghan women faced serious threats to their physical safety. The practice of wearing a **"burqa"** is no longer the law and the woman and/or her husband could make the decision of whether to wear one. Yet many women have great fear about going out without a veil or burqa (Human Rights Watch News, 2003).

In other Islamic countries there has been heightened discussion about the status of women. This has come about because of the continued growth and development of society. As a result of increased communication and travel, Muslims can take advantage of new information that is constantly being made available. Others have felt that their institutions and religious practices are inadequate. So, on the one hand, Muslims have unfulfilled expectations because of restrictions of freedom, and on the other hand, many feel they are losing touch with their Islamic identity (An-Naim, 2002). Women in several Islamic countries are demanding more rights and are beginning to fight Muslim law.

There are now only two countries in which women must be covered—Saudi Arabia and Iran. In Iran, dress restrictions had eased but controls have since tightened (Anatomy of a Cover-up, 2003). In Saudi Arabia, although women are completely covered, they can work with men. Many of these women are professionals who are highly educated. In other countries there are positive and negative events in progress. Sharia laws were implemented in the state of Zamfara in Nigeria, with one consequence being that women and men may no longer travel together in public. Women in Kuwait cannot vote. In early 2003 a bill to give women this right was defeated by a small minority but women are continuing to fight. A progressive law to protect the human rights of women was introduced. The federal Sharia court challenged it and directed the president to amend the law so that it would conform with Islamic injunctions (R. M. Pal, 2002).

In Turkey, issues are very different. Turkey is a secular country, and Sharia law is banned yet women are fighting for the right to wear a head scarf. Colleges can bar women from attending classes if they wear a head scarf or refuse to remove it; women cannot have their pictures taken for a driver's license while wearing a head scarf. In this secular country the modest head scarf has become the focus of a divisive struggle. One problem in how to resolve this issue concerns Turkey's efforts to join the European Union (Moore, 2000).

As the struggle for women's rights takes place in several Islamic countries, other countries have tightened restrictions for women. Thus, there is no definitive way to characterize the status of Islamic women. The war in Iraq, the continuing turmoil in the Middle East amid terrorist activities and military action, and the increasing influence of the Islamic fundamentalists in conflict with the Western way of life, has made the status of Islamic women highly uncertain and a state that remains to be determined (Sechzer, 2003).

SUMMARY

In this chapter we reviewed the major Eastern and Western cultures to determine sources of gender stereotypes still manifest. We traveled back in history to the beginnings of these stereotypes in mythology and religion. The early development of specific religions was recounted and validated how attitudes toward women and their treatment evolved along with the evolution of the religions. It did not matter the religion one followed or the society one lived in; all had negative attitudes about women and placed restrictions on them. We discussed the impact of these attitudes and restrictions on women and how they functioned. We found that even way back in history, women and some men did make attempts to change some of the worst conditions for women. But, at least until recently, few changes succeeded. When changes were made they were often reversed with shifts in political power, and in some societies, restrictions were intensified for ideological, political, or economic reasons.

Because these stereotypes are so enshrined in each of our cultures and religious practices, we are not totally aware of the breadth and depth of our compliance and continued acceptance of them in our ongoing daily life. Until recently, many of us have not even questioned their validity. The emergence of feminist theology will have a profound effect on some basic tenets of traditional religions, which may bring about changes in religious laws that had been considered immutable.

There are now many critiques and questions that dispute the traditional patriarchal concepts, texts, and practices. The continuing development and spread of women's rights movements throughout most of the world appear to be forcing some initial changes in the way religions treat women and the way women experience their religion. These changes may be the only hope for many religions to continue to grow and function in the twenty-first century.

Even small changes will have a substantial impact on society in general but especially for women.

Societal change has often come about through manipulation and transformation of the religious institutions and beliefs that have always served to maintain the status quo. We have seen that in the many periods throughout civilization, the fortunes of women changed along with religious transformations as well as through political changes and developments in science and technology. These transformations will profoundly affect both Western and Eastern cultures and those in the developing world in ways that we cannot possibly anticipate.

KEY TERMS

Apostle (p. 54)
B.C.E. (p. 30)
Brahma (p. 38)
Bronze Age (p. 31)
Burqa (p. 70)
C.E. (p. 31)
Endogamy (p. 38)
Epistle (p. 55)
Exogamy (p. 38)
Karma (p. 38)
Mesolithic Age (p. 31)

Monotheism (p. 46)
Mosque (p. 69)
Neolithic Age (p. 31)
Nirvana (p. 40)
Paleolithic Age (p. 31)
Pantheism (p. 36)
Parthenogenesis (p. 31)
Paul (p. 59)
Pauline (p. 60)
Polyandry (p. 53)
Polygamy (p. 44)

Polytheism (p. 36)
Puritan (p. 65)
Quaker (p. 65)
Reincarnation (p. 38)
Shakti (p. 30)
Stone Age (p. 31)
Suttee (p. 44)
Talmud (p. 51)
Torah (p. 50)
Vedic (p. 36)

DISCUSSION QUESTIONS

1. Are you a participating member of your religious group? If yes, are there restrictions affecting women?

2. Are the attitudes toward girls and women in your religious or cultural group restrictive or liberal? Do they still reflect the stereotypes described in this chapter?

3. What changes have been made concerning women's roles in your religious group or in your particular house of worship? Were you involved in achieving these changes?

4. What changes do you feel are still needed in your or other religious or cultural groups to make it possible for women to participate equally with men?

5. Do you approve of women becoming priests, ministers, rabbis, or other religious leaders? What major changes would these women bring about in the major religions?

6. How would you describe the daily home life and workday of ordained women religious leaders?

7. Should lesbians be permitted to study and become active religious leaders?

FURTHER READINGS

Carroll, T. F. (1983). *Women, religion and development in the Third World.* New York: Praeger.

Goldenberg, N. R. (1985). *Changing of the gods: Feminism and the end of traditional religions.* Boston: Beacon Press.

Haddad, Y. Y., & Findley, E. B. (Eds.). (1984). *Women, religion and social change.* Albany: State University of New York Press.

Morford, M. P. O., and Lenardon, R. J. (1995). *Classical mythology* (5th ed.). White Plains, NY: Longman Publishers.

Sharma, A. (Ed.). (1987). *Women in World religions.* Albany: State University of New York Press.

CHAPTER 3

CULTURE, ETHNICITY, RACE, AND CLASS

JUNE F. CHISHOLM, PH.D. *

If I didn't define myself for myself, I would be crunched into other people's fantasies for me and eaten alive.
—Audre Lorde

If Rosa Parks had taken a poll before she sat down in the bus in Montgomery, she'd still be standing.
—Mary Frances Berry

I've been in America since I was eight months old, and I have lived here with my parents, two siblings, and two grandparents. My parents are both from India, and they want me to practice the same culture as they did. However, the culture around me is the American culture. So the question is, Do I practice the culture of the society that surrounds me or should I exercise the Indian values as my parents taught me?
—Sneha Upadhyay, age 17
   Asian Indian

Sometimes I feel discriminated against, but it does not make me angry. It merely astonishes me. How can they deny themselves the pleasure of my company? It's beyond me.
—Zora Neale

*Dr. June F. Chisolm has specially written this chapter for this text. She is currently on the faculty at Pace University.

*Being Nigerian, I have never really understood the whole idea of racism
and discrimination. One could argue that this is because Nigeria is one
of the few countries that have blacks in the majority (one out of every five
Africans is Nigerian), but I actually believe that there is a very different
cultural mentality there than here in the United States. . . . In this country
where all people are declared equal by law there is still an underlying
rejection and fear of people of color. For us not to consider ourselves
inferior we have to connect to our own culture. My parents believe that
this will give us the pride and strength needed to face adversity and
overcome any obstacles. . . .*
—Nneka Nnaoke Ufere, age 14
   Nigerian

*Some of us come from the poorest locales in the nation; some of
us from very privileged backgrounds. Some of us are biracial or
multiracial; some of us are disabled; some of us are lesbians or
bisexuals. We come from all different ethnic, cultural, and spiritual
traditions. We are immigrants, some of us. We are mothers, some of us.
We are beauties, inner and outer. We are heroines. We are winners,
every one of us. We are poets. We are the present. And, make no
mistake, we are the future.*
—Iris Jacob, age 18
   Biracial

*With the changing demographics occurring in the United States,
psychology must make substantive revisions in its curriculum, training,
research and practice. Without these revisions, psychology will risk
professional, ethical and economic problems because psychology will
no longer be a viable professional resource to the majority of the U.S.
population.*
—Christine C. Iijima Hall

*The mainstream assumptions of normative behavior will be infused by
that behavior of people of color. Instead of solely valuing independence,
interdependence will be also aspired as a desirable trait. Instead of
viewing separation as a mature developmental response, other cultural*

values will be offered as alternatives. For instance, the Japanese concept of amae *positively emphasizes the feeling of filial dependence and parental indulgence. Along these lines, learned cognitive patterns that are culturally biased (e.g., locus of control and self-efficacy) will be reexamined. For instance, instead of solely valuing internal locus of control and self-reliance as modes of action, the role played by destiny, fate, and karma will provide alternative acceptable options.*

—Lillian Comas-Diaz

In the beginning of the twenty-first century, as was true in the 1980s and 1990s, I am recognized as being a woman of color and, by those choosing political correctness, an African American woman. *Women of Color* came to replace the older term, *minority women,* which connotes powerlessness and inferiority, because of the efforts of the National Institute for Women of Color formed in 1981 by Sharon Parker and Veronica Collazo; this feminist organization serves as an umbrella group linking many organizations dealing with issues or mutual concerns of women from a variety of ethnic backgrounds (Frost-Knappman, 1994).

Today, more than ever before, in New York City I am often greeted with the question "Where are you from?" Years ago, this question, when asked by another person of color, meant "From what southern state are your people from?" That is, it was understood that I was a citizen of the USA, a Black woman living in the North, but that my roots were southern. The question now means "What country are you from?" and reflects the changing demographics of immigrant groups in the United States of America, especially in urban cities. The question also reflects one of the several effects of **globalization.** Globalization and continued industrialization have catapulted issues associated with gender from localities entrenched in class, ethnic, national, and regional concerns affecting some women to an international arena broadening the salience and impact to women worldwide, albeit in varying degrees. This idea will be explored later in this chapter.

In the 1970s, I was recognized by those choosing political correctness as an Afro-American woman and, in solidarity with oppressed women in developing countries, a Third World woman. Ten years before that, I was recognized, with some temerity by the "establishment," as a Black. In my childhood, I was either a Negro (or Negress for those who also recognized my sex) or Colored. Back then, to be called Colored by some individuals was positive and affirming because, for them, the term connoted a connection and solidarity with people of color around the world. For others, using the term was negative because it referred exclusively to American Blacks and all that is inherent in our "inferior" status in America.

Today, "Black" continues to have similar connotations. For some, it is an umbrella term recognizing the solidarity with people of the Black Diaspora, that is, people dispersed throughout the world whose ancestors are of African descent (Landrine, 1995). For others, it is a racial designation in which race is either viewed as a biological, or genetic, fact or a social construction with scientific, sociopolitical, moral, and economic ramifications.

I consider myself fortunate to have been raised within a cohesive, nurturing network of family, friends, and neighbors who enabled me to live through decades of designations and redesignations with an intact sense of self as a confident, intelligent, and capable person who chose to pursue a career in the field of psychology. Some might question the degree of my intactness, considering this career choice and the role the field has had and continues to have in perpetuating stereotypic views about "people like me." Nonetheless, for more than two decades I have been a practicing clinical psychologist and an educator who has worked with women, men, and children from a variety of cultural, ethnic, and socioeconomic backgrounds. The following discussion on culture, ethnicity, race,

class, and gender is based in part on a critical review of the literature and my work experience.

As evident in the quotations at the beginning of this chapter and my opening personal statement, any meaningful discussion on this topic, especially as it relates to women of color, requires the use of labels and terms that, for clarity, must be defined. This chapter discusses **gender** with respect to culture, race, ethnicity, and class by focusing on women in the revised major U.S. ethnic–racial groupings: White (Euro American), Black/African American, American Indian/Alaska Native, Native Hawaiian/ Other Pacific Islander, Asian, Some Other Race, and two ethnicity categories—Hispanic/Latino and Not Hispanic/Not Latino.

It is to be noted, that the term **African American** is an **ethnocultural group;** a grouping of people rather than a racial category, even though its use in discussions on race ignores this distinction. The term **Hispanic** refers to all people of Spanish origin and includes a variety of nationalities, ethnicities, and races. **Chicanos** and **Chicanas** are men and women of Mexican origin. **Latinos** and **Latinas** are men and women from Latin America. Some politically conscious women prefer the term *Latina* to *Hispanic.* For American women of color of Asian descent the preferred term is **Asian American,** even though the term is overinclusive, referring to people whose ancestors are from China, Japan, Korea, India, Southeast Asia, and South Asia (Bradshaw, 1994; Reeves & Bennett, 2002). Likewise the term **American Indian** refers to anyone whose ancestors are from one of the 587 American Indian tribes.

The sections on demography and mental and physical health use the U.S. Census Bureau racial categories: White, Black, Asian/Pacific Islander, American Indian/Alaska Native, and Hispanic (although this is not a racial group). The terms *White* and *Black* as used by the Census Bureau are problematic. A Hispanic can be any race. The term **White** subsumes many ethnocultural groups (e.g., Anglo Americans, Irish Americans, Italian Americans, Polish Americans). The term **Black** is used for African Americans, people from the Caribbean (e.g., West Indians), Black Hispanics, and recent immigrants from Africa.

The following passage from a text entitled *Culture, Ethnicity and Mental Illness* (Griffith & Baker, 1993) illustrates the confusion surrounding ethnic–racial categorization, the consequences of which are problematic for the theory and practice of psychology:

> The African American population of the United States is a heterogeneous group of individuals who may speak other languages in addition to English. They have different ethnic heritages and skin color. In the early part of this century, they were called Negroes or people of color. As a result of the civil rights activity of the 1960s and the "Black is beautiful" movement, many of these people preferred simply to be called blacks, although some preferred the designation African American. Because the former terminology refers explicitly to skin color and excludes any reference to cultural heritage, some have found it inadequate, preferring to be called African Americans (Pinderhughes, 1989). However, "black," "Afro-American," and "African American" continue to be used interchangeably to denote nonwhites born in the United States who are descendants of African slaves, as well as [emphasis mine] recent immigrants from the West Indies, Brazil, and a host of other countries, including those in Africa. (p. 148)

African American, when so broadly applied, tends to be too inclusive and runs the risk of missing significant differences related to cultural heritage, national origin, and experience of oppression among people of color of African descent. Moreover, it is unlikely that people of color who are not descendants of African slaves from the United States would refer to themselves as African American, despite any physical resemblance to African Americans. For example, a person of African descent (i.e., parents are African immigrants) who was born in the United States but whose ancestors were not slaves in America would not readily identify with being called an African American, because the term refers to African ancestors who were slaves during the slavery period in American history.

The diversity in the United States of America in the twenty-first century has made it increasingly more difficult for many who reside in this country to be identified in ways consistent with their view of themselves. Indeed, the psychological literature now reflects what has been common knowledge among those identified as being "ethnic"; individuals often identify as being multi-ethnic, that is, they acknowledge having multiple ethnic identities, the salience determining which one(s) is/are operating at any given time determined by the social context (Hornsey & Hogg, 2000; Sedikides & Brewer, 2001). Another difficulty, in part, is based on the labeling of "subordinate" racial–ethnic groups into categories by governmental agencies and policy makers that reflect the psychosociopolitical landscape of group relations in contemporary American society.

Panethnicity, a term that refers to the development of coalitions among ethnic–racial subgroups, has emerged in some segments of American society enabling these subgroups a collective voice to be heard as they confront oppressive and discriminatory laws/policies (e.g., coalition of American Indian tribal groups, coalition among Latinos and Asian Americans) (Espiritu, 1992; Schaefer, 2001).

HISTORICAL OVERVIEW OF THE EXPERIENCES OF PEOPLE OF COLOR IN AMERICA

Ogbu (1994) points out the importance of appreciating the historical power relations between minority and majority groups. Even with an appreciation of diversity, one must still acknowledge the effects of varying sociopolitical relations that each minority group has with the dominant group within a temporal/social context. That is, the origin and nature of these sociopolitical relations are not merely functions of minority culture or in fact how it is perceived by the majority culture. It varies with each minority–majority group pair, reflecting much more than the characteristics of the minority group but also the zeitgeist about the status of the "other" within a minority–majority classification (e.g., subjugation as in slavery, colonization, immigration) at the time of the initial contact.

African Americans: Immigrants Not by Choice

From 1619 to 1863 the institution of slavery was the plight of the ancestors of African Americans; the socioeconomic forces and racism generated during that period have been perpetuated through the years by the direct, organized, and secret methods of groups such as the Ku Klux Klan, economic and legal methods such as Jim Crow laws in the South, and more covert forms of institutionalized racism and discrimination such as redlining in African American communities (subtle but definite strategies for maintaining segregated residential communities, discrimination in hiring, etc.).

Traditionally, African American women have had more or less equal status with African American men within the family (Davenport & Yurich, 1991). African American women of necessity have always worked outside the home and have been strong and independent within the family. African American women have traditionally been socialized to be caretakers (Comas-Diaz & Greene, 1994). The traditional feminine role for U.S. women to be homemakers, that is, wife and mother who remains home with the children, often was not an option for African American women, resulting in a strengthening of feelings of competency and skills of independence born out of the African tradition and survival of slavery (Smith, Burlew, Mosley, & Whitney, 1978).

American Indians: Indigenous Americans

American Indians were defeated in wars, subjugated through treaties, and forced to relocate and live on reservations as a conquered people. Their historical status approximates that of traditional or classical colonialism. A woman's identity in traditional Indian life is firmly rooted in her spirituality, extended family, and tribe (Green, 1980; Jaimes, 1982; LaFromboise, Berman, & Sohi, 1994; Welch, 1987). Although both Indian men and women suffer the consequences of societal dislocation and the denial of basic human rights, women's lives have been particularly affected by the pressing effects of acculturation into the dominant society. Although tribes differed in terms of the specific roles and behavior expected of women, most Indian women experienced greater flexibility and power than did women in European societies. The traditional roles and status of American Indian women

were undermined by European colonizers who perceived American Indian women's conduct as subversive to their intended style of sociopolitical and religious order (LaFromboise, Heyle, & Ozer, 1990). Missionary activity led to the Christian conversion of many American Indians. American Indian children were forcibly separated from their families and placed in boarding schools to become "civilized," that is, reject their culture while embracing the culture of the colonizers (Tafoya, 1989; Udall, 1977). Women's roles and power within tribes today vary among Indian communities and according to clan and family structure (LaFromboise, Heyle, & Ozer, 1990).

Hispanic Americans: Immigrants Not by Choice and Voluntary Immigrants

People of Latin American descent are a heterogeneous group that includes new immigrants and descendants of some of the original Spanish speakers, people with different national origins, and those who do as well as those who do not identify closely with their ethnic heritage (Ginorio, Gutierrez, Cauce, & Acosta, 1995).

Chicanos (Mexican Americans), who make up 60 percent of the Latino population (Portes & Truelove, 1987), trace their historical origins to Mexico, which was defeated as a nation in its attempts to maintain and expand its possessions in what is now the United States. Treaties were signed between the two nations. Yet, Mexicans who remained or migrated to the United States were usually not covered by political agreements between the two sovereign nations (Lindsey, 1980). Historically, Chicanas have been ascribed an inferior status to men. Both the economic system and the church sanctioned continued dominance and sexual abuse by men (Nieto-Gomez, 1976). "Church tradition has directed the women to identify with the emotional suffering of the pure, passive, bystander, the Virgin Mary" (Nieto-Gomez, 1976, p. 228). From this identification with the Virgin Mary as the ultimate role model, the concept of marianisma (the ideal of womanliness in Latino cultures) grew along with the expectation that the woman would passively endure injustices committed against her. The concept of marianisma has been linked with child-rearing attitudes and behaviors in Latino families. Empirical studies report that Latino families are more protective of their children than are White or African American families and that Latino families are more child centered, placing greater emphasis on the mother–child relationship than on the spousal relationship (Durret, O'Bryant, & Pennebaker, 1975; Ginorio et al., 1995).

A similar situation is found in Puerto Rican society, which accounts for 15 percent of the Latino population, and Puerto Rican women tend to experience similar conflicts as Chicanas (Rivers, 1995). Puerto Rico was acquired by the United States at the end of the Spanish American War. The high rate of unemployment on the island has contributed to the migration of Puerto Ricans to the United States during the past 45 years (Ginorio et al., 1995).

The socioeconomic profile of Cuban Americans, who constitute 5 percent of the Latino population, is different from the other groups; the demographic picture of Cuban Americans mirrors the national averages with respect to education and economic status (Portes & Truelove, 1987). Those Cuban immigrants who came to the United States between 1959 and 1965, forming the "first wave," settling in Miami, Florida, were successful because (1) they received federal economic benefits due to their status as political refugees; (2) they were educated, professional people; and (3) they formed an ethnic enclave economy that has supported more recent immigrants (Nelson & Tienda, 1985).

The most rapidly expanding Latino subgroup, which comprises 20 percent of the Latino population, is a heterogeneous grouping that includes Central American refugees (e.g., from El Salvador), white-collar and professional workers from South America (e.g., Argentina, Uruguay), and migrants from the Caribbean (Ginorio et al., 1995).

The "Great Society" of the 1960s and 1970s in the United States paved the way for aid to immigrants. In 1965 the Immigration and Nationality Act Amendments stressed family unification and encouraged more non-Europeans to immigrate to the States. In the 1980s the debate over high immigration levels led to compromise legislation including the separate status and processing of refugees. In 1994, the Census reported that 22.3 million Americans were foreign born.

Asian Americans

In the 1800s America was viewed as a society that welcomed immigrants. It was during this time that a million Irish immigrants fled to the United States as a result of the potato famine. France made a gift of the Statue of Liberty to the United States, which was dedicated by President Cleveland in 1886. The Supreme Court ruled in 1898 that a man born in California to Chinese parents is a U.S. citizen (*United States v. Wong Kim Ark*).

The first wave of voluntary immigration of Chinese occurred among those seeking fortunes in gold around 1848. Subsequent importation of Chinese laborers to the United States was recommended by the U.S. government for the establishment of a transcontinental railroad and to cultivate lands in California. The subsequent immigration laws and naturalization laws functioned to protect the economic interest of the prevailing Eurocentric interests. These various forms of oppression have ramifications for Asian women immigrants because they faced the problems of sexism within their own cultures and also the racism and sexism of the dominant White culture (Rohrbaugh, 1979). Traditional Asian families have a long history of oppression and exploitation of women. Women are subordinate to men and subject to male authority and control (Song, 1993). Over 90 percent of the initial Asian immigrants were men (Kim & Otani, 1983), because of legal restrictions and a cultural tendency for women to remain at home.

In the early 1900s there was growing concern about immigration (the 1910 Census indicated that the population in America was 92 million of which 13.5 million were "foreign born"). The concern resulted in policy changes in which quotas favoring northern Europeans were implemented. The combination of exclusion and antimiscegenation laws (laws prohibiting interracial marriage) acted to suppress the presence of Asian women in the United States to such a degree that the imbalance in the gender ratio was still high as recently as 1970 (Kim & Otani, 1983). Legal restrictions on the immigration of Asian women, laws that revoked citizenship for any U.S. woman who married an "alien ineligible for citizenship" (e.g., the 1922 Cable Act), and the artificial community of single Asian men created by these laws influenced to a great degree both the status and the role of Asian women when they finally did arrive. After the Japanese attacked Pearl Harbor launching America into World War II, Japanese Americans were detained in internment camps and their property confiscated.

In the 1950s non–Western Hemisphere immigrants were limited; the Immigration and Nationality Act gave preference to highly skilled workers. The number of Asian Americans and Pacific Islanders doubled between 1981 and 1994, from 4.2 million to 8.8 million. Between 1980 and 1991, 46.2 percent of all immigrants admitted to the United States came from Asia. During the 1980s immigrants from China, Korea, and the Philippines came to America and added to the large populations already here from those countries. These immigrants, many highly educated, came basically for family reunification and through employment provisions of the immigration laws. Another group of immigrants and refugees, fleeing from war and unstable economic and political conditions, came from countries of East and Southeast Asia (e.g., Vietnam, Laos, Cambodia, Burma, and China).

Differences between older and younger generations of Asian women are found in (1) employment status (older women are employed in service jobs or factory jobs, especially the garment industry, whereas younger women's employment resembles the distribution for European American women (Glenn, 1986); (2) education (second- and third-generation Asian women are better educated); and (3) the values and lifestyles of the younger generation are less traditional than those of their parents and grandparents and are often a source of conflict (Almquist, 1989).

Asian Americans have been called the "model minority" due to *apparent* upward mobility and socioeconomic success in comparison to other American minority groups. But within the Asian community, many, including Asian American women, have not enjoyed such success (Chow, 1985; Wong, 1983).

The last decade of the twentieth century saw controversy in the efforts to streamline citizenship processing for eligible individuals while attempting to reduce the number of immigrants. California voters passed Proposition 187, which denied school and health benefits to noncitizens including children; the courts later blocked its implementation. In 1996 the House of Representatives voted 259–169 to declare English the official language of the federal government. The test for U.S. citizenship required by the Immigration and Naturalization Service (INS) has become the subject for political debate: Its administration varies in each of the 33 INS districts; some argue that it is too easy, some argue too difficult, and some advocate that the test should be administered only in English.

The daily lives and activities within the communities of many African, American Indian, Asian, Latin American women and women of color from other backgrounds may not be directly affected by American racism and sexism. However, they are linked by racial oppression in both an historical and contemporary sense. That is, each group has been uniquely influenced by its history prior to its arrival to the United States as well as experiences in this country. Consequently, a positive sense of these women's psychological well-being, if it develops at all, unlike their White counterparts, evolves from a complex, internal conundrum of positive personal and collective heritage, plus racism, sexism, immigration, acculturation, assimilation, discrimination, and stereotyping.

THEORETICAL AND EMPIRICAL RESEARCH ON PEOPLE OF COLOR: THE SHIFT FROM A "MINORITY" TO "MULTICULTURAL" PARADIGM

Empirical research in which race is a part of the research design is a well-established tradition that has produced a body of knowledge about "minorities" that is widely known and accepted in many scientific circles, albeit with ambivalence, because of the social ramifications of the group investigated. Few studies were designed to highlight racial variations as a major thrust of the research. The practice of grouping individuals into categories such as Black and White that stem from a sociopolitical system structured to protect the **hegemony** (i.e., the domination and power of certain groups) has produced an extensive body of findings based on flawed methodology and lacking rigor, but nonetheless reflecting the bias of the particular researcher, as well as conforming, in a general way, to the socially constructed "truths" about the "races" studied (Abreu, 2001; American Psychological Association, 2003; Betancourt & Lopez, 1993; Graham, 1992; Helms & Talleyrand, 1997).

Graham (1992) argues that while the percentage of studies on African Americans in mainstream psychology has always been low (3.6 percent), there is a growing trend of exclusion of such studies so that in the 1990s the field is in danger of becoming "raceless." Scarr (1988) boldly states:

> There should be no qualms about the forthright study of racial and gender differences; science is in desperate need of good studies that highlight race and gender variables, unabashedly, to inform us of what we need to do to help underrepresented people to succeed in this society. Unlike the ostrich, we cannot afford to hide our heads for fear of socially uncomfortable discoveries. (p. 56)

To better understand the points raised in the preceding section, let us look at a hypothetical research project in which a researcher is interested in the relationship between problem-solving ability and the capacity for logical reasoning. The researcher designs an experiment with a methodology that appears to be objective (i.e., an apparatus is used that contains buttons, panels, and slots). To open the device to obtain a prize, subjects will have to independently combine two different procedures—first pressing the correct button to release a marble and then inserting the marble into the appropriate slot to open a panel. The researcher, interested in developmental issues and cross-cultural differences, conducts this experiment with different populations (e.g., White American children and adults and Liberian children and adults). He finds that White American children under the age of 10 were unable to solve the problem, whereas the American adult group was very successful. However, neither the Liberian adult nor Liberian child group was able to solve the problem. One might be tempted to conclude that Liberian adults do not problem solve as well as American adults. Such a conclusion would be false and misleading, but nevertheless would be consistent with previous scientific findings suggesting that Blacks are less intelligent than Whites. However, a finding that shows a difference in performance on some measure between two groups does not automatically mean that the difference reflects *deviancy* or a *deficiency* among the sample that scored lower. In fact, our hypothetical study was actually a real study conducted by Cole and his colleagues (Cole, Gay, Glick, & Sharp, 1971). In a follow-up study, the methodology was changed; that is, the apparatus used to assess problem-solving abilities among a Liberian population was constructed from materials familiar and common in Liberian culture and, not surprisingly, the findings were reversed: The Liberian sample performed better than the American sample!

The traditional theoretical models that have been used at various points in the history of American psychology to understand and explain the nature and experiences of "minority" groups are instructive in highlighting the complex, complementary relationship between psychological thought and prevailing societal views. For example, the **inferiority model** comprises a vast array of theories that explicitly or implicitly link African Americans' status in society to inherent genetic defects (Jensen, 1985; Shockley, 1971). That is, as a group, African Americans are believed to be genetically inferior to Caucasians, and this inferiority accounts for their marginal status. While this model has been rejected by most social scientists, the controversial book *The Bell Curve* (Herrnstein & Murray, 1994) raised the issues once again in the 1990s. In the 1900s, Irish Americans were one of the immigrant groups similarly understood from this model as being genetically flawed. Based on the results of "mental tests" administered on their arrival at Ellis Island, they were deemed "feebleminded."

The **cultural deprivation model** frames the condition of the minority group, most notably African Americans and Latinos, within the context of **racism,** prejudice, and discrimination. This model explains ethnic identity, self-esteem, school failure, chronic unemployment, family disturbances, and higher rates of more serious psychiatric disorders in terms of oppressive environmental circumstances. Critics of this model point out that it tends to overlook the strengths, competencies, and skills of the group thereby unwittingly perpetuating stereotypic views (Jones, 1991; Landrine, 1995; Moynihan, 1965).

Stereotypic views about other ethnic–racial groups have also been perpetuated through inadequate theoretical formulations and biased research. For example, while the image of the **model minority** may fit some Asian Americans, such as some Japanese, some Chinese, and some Koreans, other Asian groups experience high unemployment (Wong, 1983; Wong & Hayashi, 1989). Moreover, few of these studies examined gender differences (Chow, 1985) and many misstate the status of Asian American women, who, in general, have not attained the same advantages associated with their male counterparts.

Vazquez-Nuttall, Romero-Garcia, and De Leon (1987) reviewed studies that measured the perceptions of masculinity and femininity of Hispanic American women in North America and questioned the traditional concept that Hispanic culture is one of male dominance and female submissiveness, conceding that the dynamics of the relationships were often more complex than the stereotypes. Indeed, the stereotype of dominant male and submissive female roles in the Mexican American family is not supported by research that includes an analysis of class, urban–rural, regional, and generational differences (Hurtado, Hayes-Bastista, Burciaga, Valdez, & Hernandez, 1992). This complexity is especially true for women who have come into contact with European American culture by pursuing education and careers.

The research of Hayes-Bastista cited in a report by Winkler (1990) on the impact of poverty found evidence of "cultural vitality." For example, poor Latinos were twice as likely to live in traditional family structures compared to either poor Blacks or Whites;

Latinos had the highest rates of working males, higher life expectancy, with a 50 percent lower rate of violent deaths compared to Blacks and 20 percent lower compared to Whites. Additionally, immigrant Latinos exhibited healthier behavior than Latinos born in this country. While there is little doubt that poverty is clearly stressful, is damaging to a sense of well-being, and results in numerous and complex disadvantages, Hayes-Bastista's research provides evidence of more complex dynamics at play that involve strengths as well as weaknesses.

The research cited that was conducted by people of color within psychology supports Greenfield's (1994) ideas about the importance of an **insider's perspective** in the framing of research and interpretation of data. An *insider* social scientist is someone who is from the culture or group being researched. In contrast, an outsider social scientist with an **outsider's perspective** is someone who is not from the culture or group that he or she researches. Greenfield (1994) argues that psychology as a whole, in its attempts to be objective, has overlooked this important phenomenon as a variable influencing the scientific method and the subsequent interpretation of the database generated, while functioning, albeit unconsciously, as "unacknowledged" insiders of Euro-American culture. The outsider's perspective tends to involve the imposition of assumptions about the psychological phenomenon in question, with serious ramifications. It would be a mistake to conclude from Greenfield's analysis that the problem of scientific bias in research on ethnicity, race, gender, and class can be resolved by promoting more research conducted by insiders. Without doubt, more research conducted by insiders is desirable. However, the point to be made here is that a balance between the research generated by insiders and outsiders is necessary. Achieving a balance may reduce if not eliminate the deleterious impact of poorly framed research questions, inadequate methodology, and misleading interpretation of findings on ethnic–racial minorities that misinforms the scientific community as well as the community at large.

It is noteworthy that women scholars studying gender raise similar concerns about the psychological understanding of women's experiences that, until recently, was based on theories and research developed by men in a male-dominated profession (Denmark & Paludi, 1993; Miller, 1976; Unger, 1981). Denmark, Russo, Frieze, and Sechzer (1988) stress the importance of developing guidelines for conducting nonracist, nonsexist research.

Additionally, the use of supplemental texts to complement traditional texts points out the limitations and misconceptions that persist within the traditional mainstream approaches. However, these texts do little to reform the enterprise that produces them. Information about women presented in the psychological literature on gender has been expanded and improved by the inclusion of chapters focusing on culture, ethnicity, race, and class as relevant to all aspects of psychological functioning.

The **multicultural perspective** in psychology focuses on how group differences with respect to culture, ethnicity, and race should be addressed and included into theoretical discourse and research that recognizes the integrity of the group and views diversity as a resource rather than a social problem. According to the American Psychological Association (2003):

> The integration of the psychological constructs of racial and ethnic identity into psychological theory, research, and therapy has only just begun. Psychologists are starting to investigate the differential impact of historical, economic, and sociopolitical forces on individuals' behavior and perceptions. Psychology will continue to develop a deeper knowledge and awareness of race and ethnicity in psychological constructs and to actively respond by integrating the psychological aspects of race and ethnicity into the various areas of application in psychology. (p. 395)

The goals of the multicultural perspective are persuasive; its positive impact on the field will hinge on the extent to which concepts and categories of race and ethnicity reflect dynamic intergroup relations subject to change rather than reified, immutable explanatory frames. For example, in medicine some physicians fail to diagnose certain diseases in individuals because the individuals they are examining are members of groups not known to carry those diseases; thus, the physician's "understanding" of race–ethnicity prevents him or her from "seeing" the symptoms of a disease (Graves, 2001).

Campbell (1967) warned psychologists about the danger of perpetuating ethnic stereotyping by the practice of using race as a variable in comparison studies. Azibo (1988) criticizes the scientific basis of a comparative racial paradigm that reinforces the view that a Eurocentric perspective sets the norms by which the African American experience, as well as the experiences of other ethnic groups in the United States, is evaluated and consequently found to be deviant. This approach omits an analysis of within-group variation.

FEMINIST PERSPECTIVES

Scholarship within the feminist literature presents an alternative view, but until recently it has also been the victim of the narrow scope that tends to misinform and misconstrue the nature of woman by using a framework that is too inclusive and all encompassing. Women scholars critiqued the dominant U.S. institutions and ideologies for being patriarchal and accused mainstream psychology for being "womanless" (Crawford & Marecek, 1989). However, their analyses failed to consider distinctions in class or racial and ethnic inequalities. Espin (1994) acknowledges the narrow-sightedness of some feminists in psychology and agrees with several feminists of color (Anzaldua, 1990; Combahee River Collective, 1979; hooks, 1984; Lorde, 1984) that "White middle class women do not 'own' feminism, nor is feminism irrelevant to the experiences of Women of Color" (p. 265).

The current epistemology and methodology of psychological thought and practice attempt to revise our understanding of the human condition by examining the psychological significance of cultural, ethnic, racial, and economic influences on individual and group differences. Alternative perspectives for psychological understanding of the human condition are emerging. This understanding reflects contemporary national and international, sociopolitical, and economic realities shaping psychological inquiry and scientific knowledge about human behavior. It appears that the psychological community has become aware of sufficient anomalies in the theoretical models and the tradition of scientific practice and, as Kuhn (1970) has argued in his thesis about the structure of scientific revolutions, has embarked on investigations that will lead the profession to a new set of commitments as well as a new basis for the practice of the field.

In 1970 Toni Cade Bambara asked, "How relevant are the truths, the experiences, the finding of white women to black women? Are women after all simply women?" Cole (1986) eloquently expresses the dilemma:

> . . . to address our commonalities without dealing with our differences is to misunderstand and distort that which separates as well as that which binds us as women. Patriarchal oppression is not limited to women of one race, ethnic group, women in one class, women of one age group or sexual preference, women who live in one part of the country, women of any one religion, or women with certain physical abilities or disabilities. While oppression of women knows no such limitations, we cannot, therefore, conclude that the oppression of all women is identical. . . . That which women have in common must always be viewed in relation to the particularities of a group, for even when we narrow our focus to one particular group of women it is possible for differences within that group to challenge the primacy of what is shared in common. For example, what have we said and what have we failed to say when we speak of "Asian American women"? (pp. 2, 3)

In 1851, at a women's rights convention in Ohio, Sojourner Truth (1797–1883) one of the early feminists of color, articulated these differences when she spoke out against male delegates who warned women that they were going beyond their true natures when they wished to participate in the world of men.

> That man over there says that women need to be helped into carriages and lifted over ditches, and to have the best place everywhere. Nobody ever helps me into carriages or over mud puddles, or gives me any best place! And ain't I a woman? Look at me! I could work as much and eat as much as a man—when I could get it—and bear the lash as well! And ain't I a

woman? I have borne thirteen children, and seen most all sold off to slavery and when I cried out with my mother's grief, none but Jesus heard me! And ain't I a woman?" (Schneir, 1972, p. 177)

Yamada (1983), an Asian American feminist, asserts that Women of Color experience a double bind in their efforts to be heard by many White majority women who, she observes, act as though they need to be educated about the plight of Women of Color instead of educating themselves. Simultaneously they convey the unspoken request that Women of Color talk about what is acceptable and not criticize the values of their dominant White counterparts. She adds, "Asian female interests—which may include focus on family rather than self, fatalism, obedience, inhibition, passivity, self-restraint and adaptiveness—are all positions that are often rejected and criticized as negative role types by White middle-class feminist formulations on sexist oppression" (p. 93).

CULTURE

Discussions on culture and, to a lesser extent, ethnicity, in psychology texts are becoming more prevalent even though the subject is still deemed by social scientists to be contained within the domain of anthropology. The increasing cultural diversity of the United States challenges the field of psychology (science and practice) into an awareness of the need to develop cultural sensitivity and competencies with respect to theory, practice, and psychological research. Moreover, psychologists need a better understanding of cultural, ethnic, racial, and socioeconomic realities as they impact on gender. Psychologists need to develop an explicit theoretical model through which sociocultural variables and differences are meaningfully explored. Research citing ethnic differences and speculations about the cultures of others without some theoretical foundation ultimately obscures the relevance of culture while perpetuating the very conditions the focus on diversity supposedly challenges (hooks, 1992).

Bullivant (1984), an anthropologist, defines **culture** as a group's program for survival in and adaptation to its environment. The cultural program consists of knowledge, concepts, and values shared by group members through systems of communication. Culture also consists of the shared beliefs, symbols, and interpretations within a human group. Other social scientists view culture as consisting of the symbolic, ideational, and intangible aspects of human societies. For instance, the way you make sense of things depends on your way of making meaning in the world, that is, your worldview. Each individual makes unique meanings, but these meanings also have universal human qualities influenced by cultural factors; culture, therefore, is composed of all those things that people have learned and is reflected in actions, beliefs, values, fears, and the traditions evident throughout their history (APA, 2003).

Landrine (1995) suggests that the ways in which psychologists, as social scientists, have traditionally construed meaning from behavior, with behavior defined as "superficial–mechanical movements irrespective of context," results in comparative studies about women of different ethnic groups who vary in the frequency or prevalence of a specific behavior. The danger in this kind of analysis lies in the mistaken assumption that the "specific behavior," operationally defined, has identical or similar meanings across ethnic, cultural, and gender boundaries. This researcher proposes a **"contextualistic behaviorism"** perspective that emphasizes that "behaviors" have no a priori categorical meanings but must be understood and defined through a careful analysis of the context in which the behavior occurs. What this suggests is that seemingly identical "behavior" across cultural, ethnic, and gender groups may in fact be categorized in different ways because the "behavior-in-context" changes the meaning depending on the referent group. The example cited of the research findings about the higher incidence of unprotected anal intercourse as a risk factor for HIV infection among young Latinas and the approach to effectively deal with this risk factor with this group of women illustrates the application of this perspective to research and intervention (see Landrine, 1995, pp. 9–11). It was found that "anal sex" meant something quite different for this young Latina group of women than it did for gay men. Specifically, by engaging in anal

sex, these young women could meet the sexual demands of their boyfriends while complying with the larger cultural norm to remain virgins until marriage. According to this culture, virginity means that the young women have not engaged in vaginal intercourse, thus keeping the hymen intact. Once the researchers understood the meaning of the behavior-in-context, that is, the significance of anal sex for these young women, the campaign to eliminate this high-risk behavior among this population was different from the one launched to educate gay men about the dangers of this high-risk behavior.

An **ecological model,** derived from field theory, often used within community psychology, is another possible theoretical perspective for the meaningful study of culture, ethnicity, race, and gender. Kurt Lewin (1935) formulated that human behavior is a function of the interaction of the person and environment: $B = f(P,E)$ "a person's behavior in any situation is jointly determined by the characteristics of that situation, *as he perceives them* [emphasis mine], and by the particular behavioral dispositions of which he is possessed at that time" (Carson, 1969). Roger Barker (1968) and his colleagues at the Midwestern Psychological Field Station of the University of Kansas identified "environments" or what he termed, **"behavior settings."** A behavior setting is a basic environmental unit that entails the naturally occurring spatial and temporal features that surround behavior and the appropriate behavioral match. As an example, Barker uses the analogy of how one comes to understand the behavior of a first baseman in a baseball game. To observe only the player's behavior would not enable one to comprehend the game that gives meaning to the player's actions. Learning about the aspirations and attitudes of the individual players would also give little understanding of the game. In contrast, by attending more to the game around the player, the ecological environment of the player is made visible (Barker, 1968).

The point to be made here is that theoretical models do exist within psychology that may be more germane to conceptualizing the multiplicative variables of culture, ethnicity, race, and gender as they impact on "behavior." Spelman (1988) suggests that one way to better understand gender and what it means to be a woman or man is to focus not only on what all women and all men seem to have in common but also on the meaning of what all women and all men do not have in common because of cultural, ethnic, racial, and class differences. Examining both the commonalities and differences is to ask about the extent to which **gender identity** coexists with these other aspects of identity.

Gender Socialized Behavior

According to Miller (1976), the *dominants,* that is, those in power, label their *subordinates* as substandard, defective, and inferior. The preferred roles in the culture are reserved for the dominants, and they define the acceptable roles for the *subordinates* such as providing services that *dominants* do not want to perform. This is evident when looking at the different status of men and women. Figure 3.1 humorously depicts the polarization of the sexes into two mutually exclusive groups.

One of the earliest and most pervasive tasks of childhood is learning to be a "psychological" male

"Which one of us is the opposite sex?"

FIGURE 3.1   The Polarization of the Sexes
© Leung/Rothco. Reprinted with permission.

or female, a task that is generally accomplished by the age of three (Bussey & Bandura, 1984; Libby & Aries, 1989). Boys are raised to be independent, self-reliant, aggressive, and achievement oriented to a greater extent than are girls. Low (1989) found that sexual restraint and industriousness were instilled in girls in about forty cultures, while boys received such training in fewer than five cultures. Chodorow (1979) proposed that the female identity is based on attachment to the mother, whereas the male's is based on detachment. The individual's relationship to the mother in childhood is then posited to give rise to a specific style of thinking and behavior in adulthood. For the female, this style is person centered or relational—that is, the social context influences thinking and problem solving—while for the male, it is object centered or nonrelational. Feminist theorists argue that the relational behavior identified by many to be female, is more properly understood as a method of oppression designed by men, for women (Hogg & Frank, 1992). It is suggested to be a mechanism of social control for the purpose of excluding one gender from attaining equal access to the social power resources of the other (Hare-Mustin & Maracek, 1988).

Constructs of race, gender, and class help to explain the position of oppressed women nationally and internationally. Gender, ethnicity, and socioeconomic class are core components of an individual's identity. In studies of 14 countries, Williams and Best (1990) examined how individuals believe themselves to be (the actual self), how they would like to be (the ideal self), and how males and females should be (the ideology of gender). They found small cultural variations in the actual or ideal self, but large cultural variations in the ideology of gender. Specifically, in countries with high socioeconomic development and a high proportion of Protestant Christians, there were highly educated women, and large percentages of women were employed outside the home. In those countries the gender ideology was egalitarian. In other cultures, especially those with large proportions of Muslims, such as India, Pakistan, and Nigeria, the gender ideology emphasized the desirability of differences between men and women.

Of special interest is Japan, because it is a modern country with a gender ideology that is still relatively traditional. But as Iwao (1993) observes, the gender ideology is very different among those born during the 1930–1946, the 1946–1955, and the 1955–1970 periods.

Gender-Role Inequality and Abuse

The general pattern around the world is that men have more status and power than women, but this difference is not the same across cultures (Rosaldo & Lamphere, 1974). Cultures differ in the degree of gender inequality. Inequality in this context is meant to convey more than "unequal treatment." It includes the heuristic view that the functions ascribed to women, and hence women themselves, are subordinate in status to men (i.e., **sexism**). In some cultures this subordinate status involves a pejorative devaluation of women and women's work, which creates a diminished quality of life for them or, in extreme cases, threatens their very lives. The underlying ideology of this unequal treatment has been called **hostile sexism** in the psychological literature (Glick & Fiske, 2001). Hostile sexism resembles other forms of prejudice typically directed toward groups who are seen as threats to the in-group's status and power. In contrast, **benevolent sexism,** despite its oxymoronic quality, is a subjectively favorable, chivalrous ideology that offers protection and affection to women who embrace conventional roles, roles that perpetuate their inequality in a patriarchal society. In some ways its effects are more pernicious than hostile sexism because men and women, but especially women, embrace this ideology; thus, women tend to be more tolerant of sexist behavior and its consequences on their "inferior" status because they perceive the motivation for the behavior as being protective (Glick & Fiske, 2001).

Even in cultures in which an ideal of gender equality is stated explicitly, as in Mao's China, the practice is inconsistent with the ideal. In band societies there is often male–female reciprocity and complementarity rather than hierarchy (Triandis, 1994). In stratified societies, socioeconomic and gender inequalities are often correlated. In Africa, for example, in the non-Muslim areas, the status of women was fairly equal to the status of men until the colonial powers took over (Etienne & Leacock, 1980). Under colonization economic exploitation occurred and gender inequality increased.

One index of gender inequality is the percentage of illiterates who are women. In general, it is desirable to have an equal number of men and women who are literate, as is the case in Scandinavia and Switzerland. In many of the developing countries, however, far more women than men are illiterate. Even in the United States, women did not match the education levels of men until the late 1970s (Triandis, 1994). A second index of gender inequality is the gender–earnings ratio, which indicates how much women earn as a percentage of what men earn. In general, women earn less than men. Figure 3.2 shows the gender disparity of earnings between men and women by ethnicity.

Indices of gender abuse include the prevalence of wife abuse, **genital mutilation** of girls and young women, acid throwing, infanticide, and elder abuse (the majority of whom are women). Although husbands can no longer legally beat their wives in the United States, and wives in the United States can legally sue their husbands for damages, the practice remains a reality for far too many women and their families. In India, the phenomenon of bride burning has increased in the past 20 years.

An Islamic court in Nigeria recently overturned an earlier decision that had condemned a divorced mother, Amina Lawal, who had given birth to a child conceived outside of marriage, to be stoned to death. Her case received worldwide attention, drawing sharp criticism from the Nigerian president and the international community. Some hailed the court's decision as a triumph for Islamic justice, while others, who are seen as being conservative, adamantly denounced the ruling, claiming that there was no justice (New York Times, 2003).

It is beyond the scope of this discussion to review and/or critique Islamic law. What is important to note in this discussion about gender-role inequality and abuse is that the man who was presumably sexually involved with Ms. Lawal and the father of her child was not charged because he had three witnesses testify that he had not been involved with Ms. Lawal and that

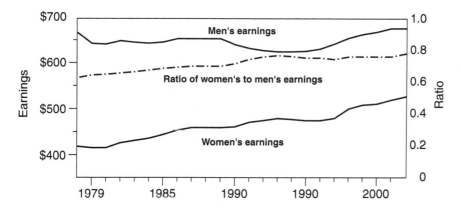

Chart 1. Median usual weekly earnings of full-time wage and salary workers in constant (2002) dollars by sex, 1979–2002 annual averages.

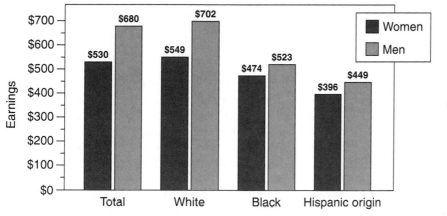

Chart 2. Median usual weekly earnings of full-time wage and salary workers by sex, race, and Hispanic origin, 2002 annual averages.

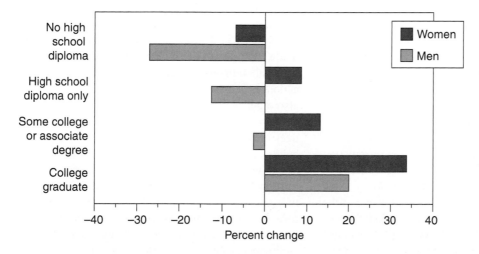

Chart 3. Percent change in median usual weekly earnings from 1979 to 2002 by educational attainment and sex.

Note: Data relate to earnings of full-time wage and salary workers 25 years and older. Changes are calculated from constant-dollar annual averages.

FIGURE 3.2   Gender Disparity of Earnings

Source: U.S. Department of Labor Bureau of Labor Statistics. Highlights of Women's Earnings in 2002. Report 972 (pp. 1–37), September 2003.

(continued)

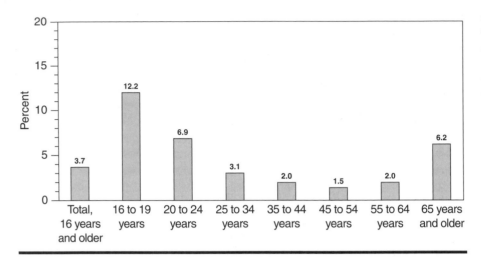

Chart 4. Percent of women with earnings at or below the Federal minimum wage by age, 2002 annual averages.

Note: Data relate to female wage and salary workers paid hourly rates.

FIGURE 3.2   Continued

"evidence" was sufficient according to the law. Men in the United States, prior to the developments in the field of DNA testing, used similar defenses when accused of sexual relations with women and subsequent impregnation.

Clitordiction and *infibulation* (technical terms for what is more commonly called female genital mutilation) of girls are practiced in many parts of Africa and the Middle East (see Figure 3.3). According to the World Health Organization, more than 80 million females have been subjected to genital mutilation in Africa, which ranges from the removal of the foreskin of the clitoris to removal of the clitoris and labia with unsterilized equipment and without anesthesia, and the two sides of the vulva sewn together. The practice reflects tribal customs and societal values and is considered a significant aspect of a woman's identity. Some men, believing that women's sexual organs are unclean and that clitordiction/infibulation "purifies" women, will not marry women who have not undergone the procedure (Heise, 1994).

What is so inconceivable to those outside of the cultures in which these practices are condoned is that they are performed by women and are viewed as a rite of passage. The plight of 19-year-old Fauziya Kasinga, who sought asylum in the United States after fleeing Togo when she was 16 to escape having a tribal member "scrape my woman parts off," has drawn international attention and condemnation of this type of gender abuse. The outcry from Westerners has focused on the medical health hazards for these girls and young women rather than attack the belief systems that condone the practice. Apropos of this, legislators in several states including New York, responding to reports that the practice of genital mutilation is occurring in the United States by immigrants from those countries in which the practice is tradition, are modeling bills based on a federal bill introduced by U.S. Representative Pat Schroeder that made genital mutilation illegal in the United States.

Although one can feel appalled by the beliefs and actions of some women that affect not only them but also other women in their culture, it undoubtedly is much more difficult to examine the beliefs and practices in one's own culture that, to others outside that culture, are equally appalling and perceived to be abusive to women. An example from American history is illustrative. It is noteworthy that in the nineteenth century, doctors in England and the United States performed clitoridectomies on women as a viable treatment for masturbation, nymphomania, and psychological problems (Abusharaf, 1998).

In the United States, the recent medical practice of discharging a mother and her newborn child within

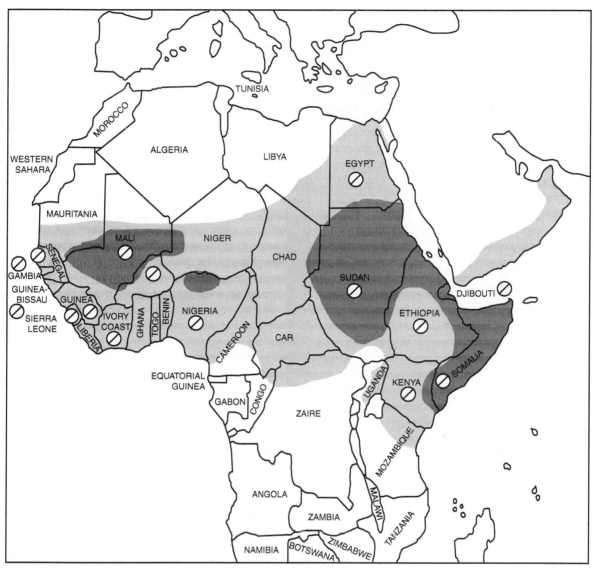

● Excision (cutting of the clitoris and all or part of the labia minora)

● Infibulation (cutting of the clitoris, labia minora, and part of the labia majora and stitching together of most of the vaginal opening)

⊘ Over half of all women and girls mutilated

FIGURE 3.3   Countries in Which Genital Mutilation of Women and Girls Is Widely Practiced, Early 1980s

Source: From *World Watch,* 2(2), (WDC, March–April 1989). Copyright 1989 by the Worldwatch Institute. Reprinted by permission.

48 hours of delivery and, most recently, discharging women having had mastectomies within 48 hours of surgery, has prompted legislation to stop these practices that seem, at best, insensitive to the emotional and physical vulnerability of women at these times and, at its worst, dangerous to their health and the health of the newborn. The policy for early discharge apparently stems from guidelines established by third-party payers (insurance companies) based on greed, albeit couched in terms of cost-effective treatment.

In some parts of the world, most notably China, South Korea, India, and Nepal, studies have shown that girls often receive inferior medical care and education and less food than their brothers (Landes, Foster, & Cessna, 1995). In India and China many women use sonograms and amniocentesis to learn whether they are carrying a girl; if they are, the fetus is frequently aborted (Heise, 1994).

Within the past decade, researchers have identified different types of elder abuse including physical abuse, psychological abuse, material abuse, financial abuse, violation of rights, active neglect, passive neglect, and psychological neglect. In 1984, a California study conducted by the California State Department of Social Services found that the typical abuse victim was female (73 percent) and about 78 years of age; almost two-thirds of the abused were White (65 percent), Unknown (17.8 percent), followed by Hispanics (8.8 percent), Black (7.5 percent) and Other (2.2 percent) (Landes et al., 1995).

AMERICAN CULTURE

In the United States, the distinction among groups based on cultural heritage is a hierarchical stratification scheme consisting of a *dominant* culture and a variety of *subcultures*. The **dominant culture** (1) owns and controls the means of production and commerce; (2) has the power to grant and take away livelihoods; (3) owns and controls the channels of communication in the society; (4) decides what, how, and who gets addressed in the media; (5) promotes those aspects of culture in the media that are considered valuable; and (6) excludes, denigrates, or makes invisible those aspects of culture that it considers inferior or of less

value. The people identified as being members of the dominant culture are afforded privileges denied those deemed nonmembers because of real or perceived differences that impact the quality of life for both the dominant and subordinate groups. Assumptions of white male supremacy and **white privilege** predominate in American value systems, worldview, and social institutions (Bullivant, 1984; McIntosh, 1988; McLemore, 1991; Triandis, 1994). Wise (2002) states,

> *That which keeps people of color off-balance in a racist society is that which keeps whites in control: a truism that must be discussed if whites are to understand our responsibility to work for change. Each thing with which "they" have to contend as they navigate the waters of American life is one less thing whites have to sweat: and that makes everything easier, from finding jobs, to getting loans, to attending college. (p. 107)*

A *subculture* is one of those cultures that does not exert the same power and influence in the society at large. These cultures are often portrayed by the dominant culture as being of less value (e.g., portrayed as marginal, primitive, unsophisticated, exotic, mysterious, etc.). Ironically, aspects of these cultures are frequently "borrowed" by the dominant culture and "valued" when they can be put to profitable commercial use. Examples include American Indian jewelry, music stemming from the African American experience (the blues, gospel, jazz), and ethnic cuisines.

Glazer and Moynihan (1970) propose that the "melting pot" metaphor describing the cultural composition of the United States in reality does not provide an accurate description. To strengthen their point, they discuss how Jews, Italians, and the Irish of New York City chose to retain their old-world heritages. Similarly, other groups have not relinquished cultural characteristics in order to become totally "Americanized."

Within ethnic groups, there are different perspectives on the role of ancestral cultural history. At one extreme are some scholars on the African American experience and some African Americans who question the significance of African roots to contemporary life. This view, that the experience of slavery and subsequent discrimination are mainly responsible for a distinctive African American culture, is challenged by others who point to the fact that Africans who survived slavery and adapted to the customs and traditions of European Americans had a culture that must have affected the nature of their adaptation (Sudarkasa, 1988). At another extreme are Japanese Americans who place so much importance on ancestral history that they label every generation since emigration from Japan with a distinctive name. First-generation Japanese Americans born and raised in Japan are called **Issei;** second-generation Japanese Americans who were born in the United States and experienced American backlash during World War II resulting in the internment of many Japanese Americans are called **Nisei;** third-generation Japanese Americans are called **Sansei** (Greenfield, 1994; Kumekawa, 1993).

The need to recognize the differences as well as the common experiences women share involving race and gender can be seen when one considers the different stereotypes about women and women of color that for the latter are based not only on their gender but also on their racial designation. Gender stereotypes affect how women and men think of themselves and how they evaluate their own behavior as well as the behavior of others. For Women of Color stress is often the result of significant role strain as we try to accommodate to different cultural expectations and values simultaneously.

African American women have been stereotyped as "Aunt Jemima," "Mammy," "Sapphire," "whore," and "super woman"(Greene, 1992; Young, 1989), as "matriarchs," and as the prototypical "welfare recipient" (e.g., a lazy single woman who continues to have children out of wedlock for a larger welfare check). The American Indian woman has been stereotyped as the "squaw," a term that became synonymous with "drudge" and/or "prostitute" (Witt, 1976). The contemporary image of the American Indian woman from Hollywood is an American Indian Princess, Pocahontas. Hispanic American women have been variously stereotyped as a passive, submissive, male-dominated, all-suffering woman or as a loud, histrionic, hot-tempered "Carmen Miranda" type (Rivers, 1995). The predominant stereotypic image for the

Asian American woman is one of reserve, passivity, and sexual attractiveness. They defer to males, elders, and authority figures (Chan, 1987; Fujitomi and Wong, 1976). These different stereotypes of women share a common theme, but their differences reflect conscious and unconscious operations in the collective psyche of Americans about race and ethnicity.

In the following sections on ethnicity and race, gender is secondary to the discussion in an attempt to better elucidate how ethnicity and race become primary, inextricable aspects of identity for people of color, regardless of gender. While gender differences in identity exist in relation to ethnicity and race, the sociopolitical reality of racism in American society and its pervasive impact on all sectors of society, including the scientific community, calls for separate consideration of race from gender, at least initially. To do otherwise seems more likely to obscure rather than illuminate the spectrum of socially transmitted values that are internalized in varying ways by Women of Color.

ETHNICITY

In anthropological terms, an ethnic group is generally understood to designate a population that is largely self-perpetuating; shares fundamental cultural values, realized in overt unity in cultural forms; makes up a field of communication and interaction; and has a membership that identifies itself, and is identified by others, as constituting a category distinguishable from other categories of the same order (Narroll, 1964). Barth (1969) stresses that ethnic groups are categories of ascription and identification by the actors themselves, and thus have the characteristic of organizing interaction between people. When someone is identified as being a member of an ethnic group, that individual supposedly shares with that group many complex characteristics such as language, customs, traditions, physical characteristics, religion, and ancestral origin. **Ethnicity** is a key aspect of one's identity. Erikson (1950) began to develop a framework for understanding how the individual is linked to the ethnic group and society. He viewed identity as a process located in the core of the individual, and yet also in the core of his or her communal culture. Ethnic identity may remain hidden and outside of awareness. Its effects on feelings, thoughts, perceptions, expectations, and actions of people toward others are not readily understood; nonetheless, it is maintained by a boundary (Barth, 1969). The following self-descriptions offered by these two individuals during a workshop on cultural sensitivity are illustrations:

> I'm Syrian and Italian—pure on each side. To belong to both of these ethnic groups where I grew up meant being inferior. I have mixed feelings about my ethnic background because Italians are associated not only with food but with the underground and I have had to be connected with that emotionally. In the Syrian aspect of my life, they have not had a good historical reputation and are considered sort of sleazy—so you might say I come from a kind of underground sleaze. (Pinderhughes, 1989, p. 41)
>
> I now realize my father taught us to hate being Black. We couldn't go out of the house until we straightened our hair—he was ashamed of being Black, and I used to envy kids whose fathers taught them to feel proud. I have to work hard to overcome this—even now. (Pinderhughes, 1989, p. 41)

For some individuals and groups (e.g., some English-speaking Whites and some ethnic minorities), ethnicity as a defining characteristic of personality and group identity at the conscious and unconscious levels may no longer retain its salience. **Symbolic ethnicity,** involved with the more visible aspects of ethnic heritage (e.g., acknowledging ceremonial holidays, eating ethnic food, wearing ethnic clothing on ceremonial occasions) does not bind the individual to adhere to the shared customs and traditions of the past. In other words the term suggests that ethnicity has shifted from the center of identity to the periphery, that other identities may have more of an impact on what one does, how one thinks, and with whom one chooses to affiliate (Gans, 1979; Schaefer, 2001).

For example, I met with a young Korean man for a psychological consultation. He had been in the United States for four years and is the father of two young children who were born in the United States. He was experiencing emotional conflict about the best ways to raise his children who have never been to Korea and are not acquainted with traditional Korean customs. He is raising his children the "American way" because they are "Americans" and he wants them to be successful here. In contrast to traditional Korean child-rearing practices, his child-rearing methods apparently involve much less discipline, and less of an emphasis on honor, self-sacrifice, and respect for self and others.

African Americans and many individuals from the Asian and Hispanic populations are often reluctant to give up ethnic customs and traditions learned early in life in favor of Eurocentric middle-class American values and lifestyles that may be contrary to their beliefs. African Americans have fought to overcome cultural dominance and discrimination and, through efforts such as the civil rights movement, have sought to understand and maintain our cultural heritage.

The designation of *African American woman* presents three aspects of identity, ethnicity, race, and gender, as a totality, an entity. However, I don't think of myself as an *African American* and a *woman;* I am *myself,* which includes but is not limited to both conscious and unconscious conceptions of what an *African American woman* is all about. Yet, I am well aware that in this society, my experiences will reflect a blend of racial, ethnic, and gender influences that, depending on the referent group of the moment, will determine which of these facets of my identity takes precedence over the others. That is, while I share much in common with women of different ethnic and racial backgrounds, I also will have experiences that are more in common with men who share my ethnic and racial heritage.

The cultural indicators of the ethnic boundary may change as well as the cultural characteristics of the members and the organizational form of the ethnic group. However, what becomes crucial in understanding the impact of ethnicity on psychological functioning are those mechanisms that permit the continued existence of the ethnic group. Barth (1969) makes the cogent point that ethnic groups persist as significant units despite constant interaction with persons of different cultural/ethnic backgrounds because of shared criteria and signals for identification and shared codes and values that structure the very nature of such interactions. It is interesting to note that colleagues who have run workshops on racial–ethnic awareness and identity have shared with me their observations that many White attendees do not think of themselves in terms of "having" an ethnicity or "being" ethnic. "Ethnicity" is something they associate more with "minorities." Any discussion on ethnicity in American culture must address the racial climate of American society, because this racial climate fosters the political stratification of dominant versus subordinate groups based on presumed ethnic–racial groupings.

According to Goffman (1959), all interethnic relations are maintained by a set of rules that govern interethnic social encounters. Based on Erikson's views on the centrality of ethnicity to one's identity and Goffman's discussion on the systemic rules that shape and maintain interethnic encounters, ethnicity needs to be distinguished from race in psychological research and discourse. Within the psychological literature there are those who are proposing that the constructs of ethnicity and race be merged into a broader construct (Phinney, 1996). Based on the preceding discussion, combining ethnicity and race for research purposes would seemingly obscure rather than clarify the meaning and usage of both in psychology. I concur wholeheartedly with those who state that race is not ethnicity (Helms & Talleyrand, 1997). Instead, what needs to occur among those studying ethnicity and gender is a shift away from a psychology of groups to a psychology of group processes analyzed on various levels (e.g., intrapsychic, interpersonal, institutional and structural, and sociocultural) (Unger, 1995). According to the Multicultural Guidelines of the American Psychological Association (APA, 2003), ethnicity refers to the acceptance of the group mores and practices of one's culture of origin and the associated sense of belonging. Moreover, it is understood that one can have multiple ethnic identities operating differentially at various times. In short, the differences within ethnic groups will undoubtedly prove to be larger than the differences between ethnic groups, a finding contemporary research on gender differences has shown to

be the case (Abe-Kim, Okazaki, & Goto, 2001; Comas-Diaz, 2001).

RACE IN AMERICA

Race matters in America. To the non-White person in America, race is the most important defining factor in all aspects of life (West, 1994). Race takes on a cultural significance as a result of the social processes that sustain majority–minority status (Pinderhughes, 1989). The subordinate status assigned to persons with given physical traits and the projections made on them are used to justify exclusion from or inclusion within the society. The responses of both those who are dominant, and therefore exclude, and the victims who are subordinate, and therefore are excluded, become part of their cultural adaptation. The meaning assigned to class status as well as racial categorization is determined by the dynamics of stratification and stereotyping. Hopps (1982) suggests that true understanding of minority status requires understanding of the various levels of oppression endured by the group. While discrimination and exclusion have existed in this country for a number of groups classified as minorities, oppression has been the most severe, deeply rooted, persistent, and intractable for people of color (Hopps, 1982). Surveys on the attitudes of the majority (Whites) concerning minorities (Blacks, Hispanics for instance) show that attitudes do change often within one generation, especially during periods of social upheaval. Also, research suggests that more progress toward equality was made during the 1950s and 1960s than in the last 20 years of the twentieth century; this trend is termed **symbolic racism,** as it reflects subtler forms of prejudice in which race is not directly expressed but nonetheless is the subtext for opposition to policy changes/issues related to race relations (Sindanius, Bobo, & Pratto, 1996).

Apropos of contemporary forms of covert institutionalized racism, Patricia Williams, a law professor (and a woman of color), recounted her experience with the "new rhetoric of racism" encountered when she was in the market to buy a new home out of state. The transaction with the bank (conducted by telephone) to obtain a mortgage had gone smoothly (e.g., she met all of the criteria) up until the bank received her "corrected" contract by mail (the loan officer at the bank had, in error, checked off "White" in the box on the fair housing form and Ms. Williams had crossed it out). The attitude of the bank changed dramatically (e.g., requests for more money, more points, a higher interest rate); "race" was never mentioned as a reason for the stalled process. The bank cited increased "economic risk"; translated this means it was concerned about "white flight" and decreased property values in the area that heretofore had been protected by redlining. She threatened to sue and was able to procure the loan on the original terms (Williams, 1997).

Theories and research on the complexities in the relationship between self and racial–ethnic identity have shown when people are secure in their identities, they can act with greater openness to others of different cultural backgrounds. However, when people internalize negative images of their ethnic backgrounds, learning values from the larger society conflicting with those of their family, they can develop a sense of inferiority and self-hate that manifests in different ways (Cobbs, 1972; Klein, 1980).

Subordinates can and have coped with the power imbalance between them and the dominants through **horizontal hostility** (Pharr, 1988); that is, members of a subordinate group expressing hostility in a horizontal direction toward one's own kind. Consequently, there may be infighting among members of a subordinate group. According to Pharr (1988), "we may see people destroying their own neighborhoods, displaying violence and crime toward their own kind, while respecting the power of those that make up the norm" (p. 61). Self-hatred is often the result of the internalization of the dominant group's beliefs that those who are subordinates are substandard, defective, and inferior.

The form self-hatred takes varies from subordinate group to subordinate group. For example, among African Americans, both men and women, the preference for light skin and devaluation of dark skin indicates negative views about the self. One of my patients takes great pride in the fact that she comes from the town in a southern state known for its single,

light-skinned African American women. These women are sought out by African American men who are interested in either maintaining or improving their social status and seek to marry a light-skinned African American woman. Another patient, who is Puerto Rican, recalled with great sadness a conference on Latina women she attended. According to her, the Latina women present seemed to divide and splinter off into antagonistic groups in which inclusion or exclusion was seemingly determined by fluency in Spanish and degree of accentedness in English.

An important factor contributing to the **assimilation** or **acculturation** of the minority group is whether the group is a **voluntary minority** or an **involuntary minority.** Ogbu (1994) states that voluntary or immigrant minorities are people (and their descendants) who have voluntarily come to the United States because they believe that the move will ultimately lead to more economic opportunities and greater political freedom. These expectations continue to influence the way the immigrants perceive and respond to obstacles confronting them in American society (e.g., discrimination). Voluntary minorities do relatively well in education and employment, especially after mastering the language. What is important is that they apparently do not interpret their presence and/or reception in the United States in terms of having been forced on them by Euro-Americans. On the other hand, involuntary minorities are people and their descendants who were originally forced against their will by Euro-Americans through slavery, conquest, and colonization to marginally participate in American society. They tend to define themselves and their cultures in opposition to the cultural values of the majority. Examples of both types include people of color from the Caribbean (e.g., Jamaican Americans) and African Americans, respectively. Although both experience oppressive racism and sexism, West Indian Americans tend to be more successful than their African American counterparts (Brice, 1982).

Featherston (1994) makes the point that Women of Color "live theater of the absurd" daily in their efforts to negate negative assumptions imposed from without and to create internal frames of reference that facilitate authentic self-awareness and expression. She quotes Toni Morrison who, on a segment of Bill Moyers' television series, *World of Ideas,* which I happened to see and remember as having a lasting impression, made the following statement about Black–White race relations in America:

> *To make an American, you had to have all these peo-ple from all these different classes, different countries, different languages feel close to one another. So what does an Italian peasant have to say to a German burgher, and what does an Irish peasant have to say to a Latvian? You know, really, they tended to balkanize. But what they could all do is not be Black. So, it is not coincidental that the second thing every immigrant learns when he gets off the boat is the word "nigger." In that way, he's establishing oneness, solidarity, and union with the country. That is the marker. That's the one. Well, these were people who were frightened. I mean, I would be. You go to a strange country, maybe you have some friends there. You need a job. You've cut your bridges. You've said something is terrible back home. You go, and you emigrate, you go some-place else. And if it's under duress, you are facing chaos. And when you are facing chaos, you have to name it, or violate it, or control it in some way. So you want to belong to this large idea, you want to belong. And one learns very quickly what to belong to. And you belong to this non-Black population which is everywhere. But it serves. It serves. It has always served economically a lot of forces in this country. (Feathesrton, 1994, preface)*

A cursory review of the history of race in Amer-ica supports Morrison's assertions; from 1840 to the early and midtwentieth century, the categories "white" and "Caucasian" gradually overlapped and fused such that European immigrants previously perceived as dis-tinct and separate groups (e.g., Alpine, Anglo-Saxon, Celt, Iberic, Teutons, Hebrew, Mediterranean, Nordic, etc.) found common ground in their "whiteness" in re-sponse to the migration of African Americans to the north and west of the country (Blackwell, Kwoh, & Pastor, 2002; Jacobson, 1998; Rothenberg, 2001; Swain, 2002). Jacobson (1998) states,

> *It is not just that various white immigrant groups' eco-nomic successes came at the expense of nonwhites, but*

> *that they owe their now stabilized and broadly recog-nized whiteness itself in part to these nonwhite(s). (p. 9)*

One of the psychological consequences of racial categorization into "White" and "non-White" groups is the impact on identity for both groups. White racial identity received scant attention in the literature until Helms's (1984, 1990, 1995) model proposed that Whites go through similar stages of racial identity as non-Whites: contact, disintegration, reintegration, pseudoindependence, immersion/emersion, and au-tonomy. Recently, another model has been proposed that challenges the assumptions of the earlier models. Rowe, Behrens, and Leach (1995) propose that the racial development of Whites is fundamentally dif-ferent from that of non-Whites because the former are not forced to deal with the ill effects of oppression; for these researchers, white racial development in-volves the development of a white racial conscious-ness (WRCD), that is, attitudes and beliefs of Whites toward non-Whites that perpetuate perceived differ-ences and consequent differential status of both groups in society.

Numerous models on Black racial identity have been developed and modified over the years to apply to other ethnic minorities (e.g., Latinos, biracial per-sons) as well as other subordinate groups (women, gays) vis-à-vis the dominant culture (Downing & Roush, 1985; Kerwin & Ponterotto, 1995; Reynolds & Pope, 1991; Ruiz, 1990). Atkinson, Morton, and Sue (1998) developed a generic cultural identity model that can be applied to all minority groups. It consists of five stages: conformity, dissonance, resis-tance, introspection, and integrative awareness.

Racial categorization is arguably questionable, confusing, and tends to have adverse effects on those identified as being members of the ethnic group (Be-tancourt & Lopez, 1993; Spickard, 1992). The Cen-sus Bureau has divided the American population into four major races: White, Black, Asian/Pacific Is-lander, and American Indian/Eskimo/Aleut. In the 1970s the Census added Hispanic origin, a group that had previously been labeled "Spanish speaking" or "Spanish surnamed." People who felt they did not fit into these categories could choose "Other."

In 1994, the Census Bureau began hearings to consider adding new categories to the present census choices. They found that Arab Americans, for example, are unhappy with their official designation of "White, non-European." Many Native Hawaiians want to be redesignated as American Indians rather than Pacific Islander, reflecting historical accuracy. Some Hispanics want the Census Bureau to classify them in terms of race not ethnic origin and to replace the term *Hispanic* with *Latino.* For those with this view, the term *Hispanic* recalls the colonization of Latin America by Spain and Portugal and has become as offensive as the term *Negro* became for African Americans.

Survey results show that people would prefer to be identified as Puerto Rican, Colombian, Cuban, and so on. About one in three Black Americans would like the Census Bureau to adopt the term *African American.* People from the Caribbean, however, tend to prefer being labeled by their country of origin such as Jamaican or Haitian American. Africans who are not American also find the term inaccurate. It is imperative that the rich diversity in individual differences that exists within each of these groups not be overlooked.

Scientists in the fields of biology and genetics have been challenging the conventional racial categories of Black, White, and Asian, based mostly on phenotype, that is, observable differences in skin color, hair texture, and the shape of one's eyes and nose, as meaningful ways of organizing information about the variability among people (Begley, 1995). When other variables such as genes or traits are used as criteria for race categorization, surprising combinations occur. Jared, a biologist, for example, groups Asians, Native Americans, and Swedes together based on the common characteristic of their shovel-shaped incisors (Begley, 1995). Norwegians, Arabians, north Indians, and the Fulani of northern Nigeria can be considered a racial group because they alone share in common the lactase enzyme that digests milk sugar; other Africans, Japanese, and American Indians are lactase deprived and hence could be considered another racial group.

As mentioned earlier, there is an extensive literature in psychology on race and the use of race as a variable in comparison studies. Many psychological researchers, along with biologists, acknowledge that race is more a social construction than a genetic or biological reality (APA, 2003). Some advocate combining ethnicity and race into a single construct (Phinney, 1996), while others advocate revising the construct race to distinguish it from constructs such as ethnicity and minority (Landrine, 1995; Helms & Talleyrand, 1997).

CLASS

In psychology, **class** is discussed in terms of socioeconomic status of the individual or group that signifies, among other things, one's degree of success in achieving a quality of life, standard of living, and lifestyle idealized in the American Dream. Presumably, the higher the socioeconomic level, the better the quality of life and the more successful are those who attain it. Conversely, the lower the socioeconomic status, the less successful the individual is in attaining a desirable standard of living, which, according to democratic ideals, is possible for all. Class, defined by income, education, and power and analyzed solely in terms of its relationship with various psychological constructs, such as intelligence, locus of control, achievement motivation, mental health, and the like, obscures the vulnerabilities of designated minorities who are barred from participating as equal players in the capitalistic marketplace of the United States and who suffer from **classism.** When gender, race, and ethnicity are included in discussions on class, the politics of deeply institutionalized policies and practices of discrimination and the resilience of racial–ethnic and gender hierarchies become apparent.

For example, Sidel's (1993) assessment of poverty in the United States indicates that poverty affects women and ethnic minority families more than others. Single mothers are more likely to be poor than any other demographic group, affecting not only their psychological well-being and physical health, but also exposing their children to stress associated with poverty. The *feminization of poverty,* a phrase originally coined by sociologist Diana Pearce (Sidel,

1993), refers to social and economic factors resulting in the increased percentage of poor women and children. These include the rapid growth of female-headed families, a labor market that continues to discriminate against female workers, and unpaid domestic responsibilities traditionally reserved for women (e.g., child care).

The manner in which women experience the adverse effects of exclusion based on race, gender, and class can and does differ among and within minority groups. Racial differences between Puerto Rican American and Asian American women can also be observed and foster different responses from the majority group. Distinctions in linguistic and cultural patterns may also, in part, account for differences in responses. For example, degree of accentedness, especially for Spanish-speaking people, tends to correlate negatively with the listener's perception and impression of the speaker's ability and competence (Ryan & Carranza, 1975; Ryan, Carranza, & Moffie, 1977; Steinhart, 1992). Research findings on Asian Americans have led to erroneous notions about their successful adaptation and contributed to the image of Asian Americans as the *model minority*. While the image may be true for some Asian Americans such as the Japanese, Chinese, and Koreans, other Asian groups experience high unemployment (Wong, 1983; Wong & Hayashi, 1989). Moreover, few of these studies examined gender differences (Chow, 1985) and so misstate the status of Asian American women who, in general, have not attained the same advantages associated with their male counterparts. In sum, every woman, regardless of her race–ethnicity and socioeconomic status, is vulnerable to the ill effects of oppression and discrimination.

The ill effects of oppression and discrimination are evident among women and men who report experiencing a sense of marginality and/or invisibility as a function of their race, ethnicity, and/or gender (Chisholm, 1996; Comas-Diaz & Greene, 1994). By marginality, I mean to suggest that many individuals experience a profound schism between their public and private presentations of self, which reflects an awareness of how the dominant "other" perceives (misperceives by "not seeing," stereotyping, etc.)

them in those settings away from family, friends, and neighborhood (e.g., work, school, business) in which there is interaction between designated majority and minority individuals. The "not seeing" results in a sense of invisibility despite the fact that the individual may be highly visible, that is, invisible in terms of influence while being visible in terms of tokenism. The individual experiencing marginality exists uncomfortably in the worlds of both the dominant other and the minority group and is perceived and treated differently by both. In the world of work, for example, the marginal person is defined by his or her race and gender as well as competence. In personal life, he or she often feels set apart from family and friends who experience whatever his or her "successes" may be, as determined by the dominant group, as a moving away from the minority group, sometimes literally as in leaving the old neighborhood, or emotionally.

QUALITY OF LIFE AMONG WOMEN OF COLOR

Each group of ethnic minority women has been uniquely influenced by its history prior to its arrival in the United States as well as its experiences in this country. Former Secretary of Health and Human Services Margaret M. Heckler acknowledged that large differences between the health status of Whites and ethnic minorities exist; individuals from minority groups are not as healthy and die at a younger age than those of the White majority. Various explanations have been given including high-risk behavior, inadequate or absence of health insurance, poverty, poor access to health care, racism, and discrimination (Squyres, Jacobs, & Quiram, 1996; Utsey & Payne, 2000; Utsey, Ponterotta, Reynolds, & Cancelli, 2000; Utsey, Chae, Brown, & Kelly, 2002).

Mental Heath

Mirowsky and Ross (1980) discuss two competing hypotheses in studies of the relation between ethnic status and psychological distress. The first, the *minority status perspective,* asserts that the extent to which an ethnic group is both a minority group and disadvantaged, the chronic social stressors associated with the disadvantaged position will produce greater distress, that is, ethnic differences in psychological distress are due primarily to social class effects. The other hypothesis, the ethnic culture perspective, states that the psychological well-being of ethnic minorities varies with different cultural patterns in terms of beliefs, values, and lifestyles, that is, there are ethnic effects that are both positive and negative on mental health over and above social class effects (Murguia, Zea, Reisen, & Peterson, 2000).

The woman of color who accepts the American standard for femininity, womanhood, and female attractiveness is vulnerable to lowered self-esteem and even self-hatred because of her inability to readily change facial features, hair texture, and skin color, despite the fantastic claims of the lucrative cosmetic industry, which caters to women, ethnic minority women in particular, striving to achieve the impossible (Kaw, 1993; Rivers, 1995; Root, 1995).

Misdiagnoses of mental disorders among people of color have been reported in the literature. African American and Puerto Rican patients are less likely than White patients to be diagnosed as having a psychotic affective disorder and more likely to be diagnosed as having schizophrenia (Garb, 1997; Thomas & Sillen, 1979). Patients from the lower socioeconomic classes are more often assessed to be more seriously disturbed than patients from the higher social economic classes. Moreover, women patients are more often seen to be more disturbed than their male counterparts presenting with identical problems (Atkinson & Hackett, 1998). Among immigrants, misdiagnoses of mental disorders by service providers unfamiliar with culture-bound syndromes has been reported (Oquendo, Horwath, & Martinez, 1992). For example, among Latinas, *ataque de nervios* is a condition characterized by a sense of being out of control in which uncontrollable shouting, attacks of crying, trembling, heat in the chest rising into the head, verbal or physical aggression, dissociative experiences, fainting, and suicidal gestures may occur. This condition may be misconstrued by the Western practitioner as somatization, hysteria, and/or an affective disorder.

Women of color have been found to experience high levels of depression and anxiety (Kessler, 2000a;

Kuo, 1984; LaFromboise et al., 1990; Myers et al., 2002; Pyant & Yanico, 1991). An American Psychological Association report indicated that among American Indians, the typical client seeking help from an Indian Health Service–supported outpatient reservation-based mental health service unit, is depressed, anxious, and/or experiencing situational crises such as domestic violence, disruption, or victimization and has been or is currently using drugs or alcohol (Jacobs, Dauphinais, Gross, & Guzman, 1991). Additionally, tragedies occur frequently in Indian communities involving motor vehicle accidents, homicide, and suicide (Indian Health Service, 1989). Consequently it is widely speculated that primary mental health issues for American Indian women are trauma and a cycle of unresolved grief and mourning (LaFromboise, Bennett, James, & Running Wolf, 1995; Root, 1992).

Many studies have found a significant relationship between mental disorders and degree of acculturation of people of color (Escobar, 1993; Smart & Smart, 1995). For example, higher rates of acute depression are sometimes reported for immigrant versus nonimmigrant Latinas (Vega, Warheit, & Meinhardt, 1984), while other studies have shown that the U.S.-born Latinas report more depression than do immigrant Latinas (Ginorio et al., 1995). It is speculated that for the highly acculturated Latina, conflicts between cultural expectations and achievement in the majority culture in the face of discrimination generate high levels of stress (Amaro & Russo, 1987).

While women of color tend to have more positive attitudes toward mental health services and use them more frequently than their male counterparts (Gary, 1987), accurate diagnosis and effective treatment are often impeded by stereotypical attitudes, gender-role bias (Chisholm, 1996; Comas-Diaz & Jacobsen, 1991; Jackson & Greene, 2000; Sue, 1988; Thomas & Sillen, 1979), and linguistic bias directed toward non-English-speaking and/or bilingual clients (Malgady, Rogler, & Constantino, 1987).

Turner and Turner (1992) found in a survey among psychologists listed in the National Register of Health Service Providers in Psychology that race–ethnicity of the therapist, not gender or age, was a significant factor in therapy outcome for a large percentage of ethnic minority clients. Ethnic minority therapists were more likely to report having ethnic minority clients as well as White clients than were the White therapists in the sample. The Turners surmised:

> White therapists, based on socialization and experience, have certain attitudes—including negative attitudes and stereotypes about various categories of people. A minority client enters the mental health system and needs to be evaluated and treated, but he/she also has attitudes about people who are likely to be the service providers. When therapist and client meet, the therapist's negative attitudes and stereotypes lead

> him/her to both expect certain behavior from the client and that he/she behave in certain ways. The African American client *or* ethnic minority client *[emphasis mine]* reacts to these expectations and behaviors, and behaves in such a way as to fulfill the expectations. The therapist notes that the client has behaved in a way consistent with his/her racial attitudes and stereotype and continues to behave in ways consistent with those attitudes and stereotypes. Since *no* authentic *[emphasis mine]* encounter takes place, one of the two gives up and leaves the relationship. (p. 8)

See Box 3.1 for a discussion of cross-ethnic counseling.

Box 3.1

Cross-Ethnic Counseling

The following clinical vignette illustrates a worst-case scenario involving an upper-middle-class White male psychiatrist and a poor, young urban African American woman patient who had been referred by the psychiatrist to see me for a psychological assessment to evaluate for mental retardation and a personality disorder.

L., a 17-year-old, African American single female was being seen once a week in psychotherapy sessions with a White male psychiatrist. A nurse's entry in her chart had suggested the possibility of suicidal behavior because the patient had indicated during the intake screening that she had taken an overdose of vitamin C. The therapist dismissed the possibility of a suicide attempt because "everyone knows that vitamin C won't kill you. She's probably slow." I interviewed her and obtained the following information. She was prone to violent outbursts in which she would physically fight against two or more people, males or females, when she felt provoked. She had no psychiatric history or record of misconduct or violence. L. and her boyfriend of ten months were talking about getting married within the next two years. The emergence of the violent outbursts began several months after the sudden death of her beloved mother and the consequent mistreatment by an older sister with whom she was forced to live. Her sister allegedly told L. that since their mother was dead, she was now the mother, and L. had to obey her and live by her rules or else. Her bereavement was complicated by her intentional refusal to feel grief, sadness, and anger over her loss. Moreover, the lack of emotional support

by her family and the dire financial circumstances of staving off homelessness by living with a sister whom she despised contributed to her emotional state. L. had a mercurial quality of becoming hostile and belligerent, while at other times displaying a soft-spoken, sensitive, and compassionate concern for others. She understood her fighting in terms of being easily irritated and as a way of ensuring her safety and of protecting her boyfriend, who, since her mother's death, was the only other person in the world she cared about. What was most significant about her violent behavior was the extent to which she provoked these attacks and her sense of gratification in dealing with them. In relating each incident she became "alive," eager to talk about her moves and countermoves, and the harm inflicted on the others. She rarely fought with only one other person; being outnumbered was key to experiencing the "high." She seemed to have little awareness of her provocative behavior or its self-destructiveness. For instance, she described two physical altercations, one in which she deliberately fought back with a gang of girls who attacked her because she had "dissed" (disrespected) one of them, and the other involving her fighting single-handedly with a group of boys who had "dissed" her boyfriend in her presence. The significance of the history and current behavior of this young woman, which at the very least would raise the question of depression and suicidal risk, was apparently misconstrued, overlooked, or, worse, not elicited in the clinical interviews with the treating physician.

In an attempt to educate psychologists on how to provide effective psychological services to individuals who are culturally, ethnically, and/or racially different from themselves, graduate training programs are offering courses designed to teach cultural competencies and sensitivities to different customs and worldviews (APA, 2003).

Physical Health

Gender and race affect longevity. The average life expectancy for women in 2001 was 79.8 years. The life expectancy for a White woman was the highest at 80.2 years. For Black women it was 75.5 years, slightly higher than that of White men (75.0 years) but much higher than that of Black men (68.6 years). For Hispanic women, it was 77.1 years and for American Indian women it was 76.2 years. Data for Asian and Pacific Islander Americans were not available. Women will continue to have longer life expectancies, according to the U.S. Census Bureau projections (Leigh, 1994; Squyres et al., 1996), but will be sicker (Sechzer et al., 1996; National Center for Health Statistics, 2003).

Cardiovascular Disease, Cancer, and Stroke. Heart disease is the leading cause of death for women, followed by cancer and stroke, with the exception of unintentional injuries as the third cause of death among American Indian women. The death rates among women vary depending on race and age. Overall, Black women have higher death rates than White women for most of the major causes of death other than suicide. Black women are more than one and a half times as likely to suffer heart disease, nearly twice as likely to have a stroke, and over two and a half times as likely to die from diabetes (Chideya, 1995; Landes, Foster, & Cessna, 1994; Squyres et al., 1996; Villarosa, 1994; White, 1994) (see Table 3.1).

Four and a half times as many Black women are murdered than are White women and nine times as many die of AIDS (see Table 3.2 and 3.3). Black and White women under age 50 have essentially equal incidence rates of breast cancer. However, after that age, White women have consistently higher rates than their Black counterparts, but survival rates are not similar.

According to the 1983–1989 SEER (Surveillance, Epidemiology, and End Results) Program of the National Cancer Institute, the five-year survival rate was 81 percent for White women and 64 percent for Black women, a difference the Institute called "significant" (Landes et al., 1994) (see Figure 3.4). Asian and Pacific Islander women have higher death rates and lower five-year survival rates than White women for most types of cancer (American Heart Association, 2004).

Obesity. Obesity is one of the health-related lifestyle conditions that is a major problem for Black and Hispanic women, who have been found to have a higher rate of obesity than White women (American Heart Assoc., 2004; Landes et al., 1994; Squyres et al., 1996). Nearly 60 percent of all American Indian women on reservations in 1987 and 63 percent of urban American women were found to be obese. Similar findings exist for Pacific Islanders, Native Hawaiian women, and Samoan women (Leigh, 1994). During adolescence and adulthood, body mass index (BMI) and the prevalence of obesity begin to increase with age among Black women and are linked to diets of poverty that are high in fat and low in fruits and vegetables. Of particular concern is the location of the excess fat. Fat that deposits more in the central part of the body has been linked to increased cardiovascular risk factors including hypertension, diabetes mellitus, and plasma lipid abnormalities. The attitudes toward body weight and weight control among Women of Color are seemingly more tolerant to the extent that being overweight or obese is not necessarily equated with being unattractive.

Cigarette Smoking. The hazards of cigarette smoking affect not only the smoker but also everyone with whom she comes in contact (e.g., children, spouse through secondhand smoke, fetus if the smoker is pregnant). Cigarette smoking has declined among Black and White women since the 1980s but has not changed among Hispanic women (Haynes, Harvey, Montes, Nickens, & Cohen, 1990; Leigh, 1994; Squyres et al., 1996). Surveys show that Asian American women have the lowest rate of smoking; the prevalence rates vary among American Indians (American Heart Association, 2004).

TABLE 3.1   Life expectancy at birth, at 65 years of age, and at 75 years of age, according to race and sex: United States, selected years 1900–2001

[Data are based on death certificates]

SPECIFIED AGE AND YEAR	ALL RACES			WHITE			BLACK OR AFRICAN AMERICAN[1]		
	Both Sexes	Male	Female	Both Sexes	Male	Female	Both Sexes	Male	Female
At birth				*Remaining life expectancy in years*					
1900[2,3]	47.3	46.3	48.3	47.6	46.6	48.7	33.0	32.5	33.5
1950[3].............	68.2	65.6	71.1	69.1	66.5	72.2	60.8	59.1	62.9
1960[3].............	69.7	66.6	73.1	70.6	67.4	74.1	63.6	61.1	66.3
1970	70.8	67.1	74.7	71.7	68.0	75.6	64.1	60.0	68.3
1980	73.7	70.0	77.4	74.4	70.7	78.1	68.1	63.8	72.5
1985	74.7	71.1	78.2	75.3	71.8	78.7	69.3	65.0	73.4
1990	75.4	71.8	78.8	76.1	72.7	79.4	69.1	64.5	73.6
1991	75.5	72.0	78.9	76.3	72.9	79.6	69.3	64.6	73.8
1992	75.8	72.3	79.1	76.5	73.2	79.8	69.6	65.0	73.9
1993	75.5	72.2	78.8	76.3	73.1	79.5	69.2	64.6	73.7
1994	75.7	72.4	79.0	76.5	73.3	79.6	69.5	64.9	73.9
1995	75.8	72.5	78.9	76.5	73.4	79.6	69.6	65.2	73.9
1996	76.1	73.1	79.1	76.8	73.9	79.7	70.2	66.1	74.2
1997	76.5	73.6	79.4	77.1	74.3	79.9	71.1	67.2	74.7
1998	76.7	73.8	79.5	77.3	74.5	80.0	71.3	67.6	74.8
1999	76.7	73.9	79.4	77.3	74.6	79.9	71.4	67.8	74.7
2000[4].............	77.0	74.3	79.7	77.6	74.9	80.1	71.9	68.3	75.2
2001[5].............	77.2	74.4	79.8	77.7	75.0	80.2	72.2	68.6	75.5
At 65 years									
1950[3].............	13.9	12.8	15.0	—	12.8	15.1	13.9	12.9	14.9
1960[3].............	14.3	12.8	15.8	14.4	12.9	15.9	13.9	12.7	15.1
1970	15.2	13.1	17.0	15.2	13.1	17.1	14.2	12.5	15.7
1980	16.4	14.1	18.3	16.5	14.2	18.4	15.1	13.0	16.8
1985	16.7	14.5	18.5	16.8	14.5	18.7	15.2	13.0	16.9
1990	17.2	15.1	18.9	17.3	15.2	19.1	15.4	13.2	17.2
1991	17.4	15.3	19.1	17.5	15.4	19.2	15.5	13.4	17.2
1992	17.5	15.4	19.2	17.6	15.5	19.3	15.7	13.5	17.4
1993	17.3	15.3	18.9	17.4	15.4	19.0	15.5	13.4	17.1
1994	17.4	15.5	19.0	17.5	15.6	19.1	15.7	13.6	17.2
1995	17.4	15.6	18.9	17.6	15.7	19.1	15.6	13.6	17.1
1996	17.5	15.7	19.0	17.6	15.8	19.1	15.8	13.9	17.2
1997	17.7	15.9	19.2	17.8	16.0	19.3	16.1	14.2	17.6
1998	17.8	16.0	19.2	17.8	16.1	19.3	16.1	14.3	17.4
1999	17.7	16.1	19.1	17.8	16.1	19.2	16.0	14.3	17.3
2000[4].............	18.0	16.2	19.3	18.0	16.3	19.4	16.2	14.2	17.7
2001[5].............	18.1	16.4	19.4	18.2	16.5	19.5	16.4	14.4	17.9

(continued)

TABLE 3.1   Continued

SPECIFIED AGE AND YEAR	ALL RACES			WHITE			BLACK OR AFRICAN AMERICAN[1]		
	Both Sexes	Male	Female	Both Sexes	Male	Female	Both Sexes	Male	Female
At 75 years									
1980	10.4	8.8	11.5	10.4	8.8	11.5	9.7	8.3	10.7
1985	10.6	9.0	11.7	10.6	9.0	11.7	10.1	8.7	11.1
1990	10.9	9.4	12.0	11.0	9.4	12.0	10.2	8.6	11.2
1991	11.1	9.5	12.1	11.1	9.5	12.1	10.2	8.7	11.2
1992	11.2	9.6	12.2	11.2	9.6	12.2	10.4	8.9	11.4
1993	10.9	9.5	11.9	11.0	9.5	12.0	10.2	8.7	11.1
1994	11.0	9.6	12.0	11.1	9.6	12.0	10.3	8.9	11.2
1995	11.0	9.7	11.9	11.1	9.7	12.0	10.2	8.8	11.1
1996	11.1	9.8	12.0	11.1	9.8	12.0	10.3	9.0	11.2
1997	11.2	9.9	12.1	11.2	9.9	12.1	10.7	9.3	11.5
1998	11.3	10.0	12.2	11.3	10.0	12.2	10.5	9.2	11.3
1999	11.2	10.0	12.1	11.2	10.0	12.1	10.4	9.2	11.1
2000[4].	11.4	10.1	12.3	11.4	10.1	12.3	10.7	9.2	11.6
2001[5].	11.5	10.2	12.4	11.5	10.2	12.3	10.8	9.3	11.7

[1]Data shown for 1900–60 are for the nonwhite population.

[2]Death registration area only. The death registration area increased from 10 States and the District of Columbia in 1900 to the coterminous United States in 1933. See Appendix II, Registration area.

[3]Includes deaths of persons who were not residents of the 50 States and the District of Columbia.

[4]Life expectancies (LEs) for 2000 were revised and may differ from those shown previously. LEs for 2000 were computed using population counts from Census 2000 and replace LEs for 2000 using 1990-based postcensal estimates.

[5]Life expectancies for 2001 were computed using 2000-based postcensal estimates.

Notes: Populations used for computing life expectancy and other life table values for 1991—1999 are postcensal estimates of U.S. resident population, based on the 1990 census. See Appendix I, Population Census and Population Estimates. Beginning in 1997 life table methodology was revised to construct complete life tables by single years of age that extend to age 100. (Anderson RN. Method for Constructing Complete Annual U.S. Life Tables. National Center for Health Statistics. Vital Health Stat 2(129). 1999.) Previously abridged life tables were constructed for 5-year age groups ending with the age group 85 years and over. Life table values for 2000 and 2001 were computed using a slight modification of the new life table method due to a change in the age detail of populations received from the U.S. Census Bureau. Data for additional years are available. See Appendix III.

Sources: Centers for Disease Control and Prevention, National Center for Health Statistics, National Vital Statistics System; Grove RD, Hetzel AM. Vital statistics rates in the United States, 1940–1960. Washington: U.S. Government Printing Office, 1968; life expectancy trend data available at www.cdc.gov/nchs/about/major/dvs/mortdata.htm; Arias E, Anderson RN, Kung HC, Murphy SL, Kochanek KD. Deaths: Final data for 2001. National vital statistics reports. Vol 52 no 3. Hyattsville, Maryland: National Center for Health Statistics. 2003.

TABLE 3.2 Leading causes of death and numbers of deaths, according to sex, race, and Hispanic origin: United States, 1980 and 2001

[Data are based on death certificates]

SEX, RACE, HISPANIC ORIGIN, AND RANK ORDER	1980		2001[1]	
	Cause of death	*Deaths*	*Cause of death*	*Deaths*
All persons				
. . .	All causes	1,989,841	All causes	2,416,425
1	Diseases of heart	761,085	Diseases of heart	700,142
2	Malignant neoplasms	416,509	Malignant neoplasms	553,768
3	Cerebrovascular diseases	170,225	Cerebrovascular diseases	163,538
4	Unintentional injuries	105,718	Chronic lower respiratory diseases	123,013
5	Chronic obstructive pulmonary diseases	56,050	Unintentional injuries	101,537
6	Pneumonia and influenza	54,619	Diabetes mellitus	71,372
7	Diabetes mellitus	34,851	Influenza and pneumonia	62,034
8	Chronic liver disease and cirrhosis	30,583	Alzheimer's disease	53,852
9	Atherosclerosis	29,449	Nephritis, nephrotic syndrome, and nephrosis	39,480
10	Suicide	26,869	Septicemia	32,238
Male				
. . .	All causes	1,075,078	All causes	1,183,421
1	Diseases of heart	405,661	Diseases of heart	339,095
2	Malignant neoplasms	225,948	Malignant neoplasms	287,075
3	Unintentional injuries	74,180	Unintentional injuries	66,060
4	Cerebrovascular diseases	69,973	Cerebrovascular diseases	63,177
5	Chronic obstructive pulmonary diseases	38,625	Chronic lower respiratory diseases	59,697
6	Pneumonia and influenza	27,574	Diabetes mellitus	32,841
7	Suicide	20,505	Influenza and pneumonia	27,342
8	Chronic liver disease and cirrhosis	19,768	Suicide	24,672
9	Homicide	18,779	Nephritis, nephrotic syndrome, and nephrosis	18,852
10	Diabetes mellitus	14,325	Chronic liver disease and cirrhosis	17,393
Female				
. . .	All causes	914,763	All causes	1,233,004
1	Diseases of heart	355,424	Diseases of heart	361,047
2	Malignant neoplasms	190,561	Malignant neoplasms	266,693
3	Cerebrovascular diseases	100,252	Cerebrovascular diseases	100,361
4	Unintentional injuries	31,538	Chronic lower respiratory diseases	63,316
5	Pneumonia and influenza	27,045	Diabetes mellitus	38,531
6	Diabetes mellitus	20,526	Alzheimer's disease	38,090
7	Atherosclerosis	17,848	Unintentional injuries	35,477
8	Chronic obstructive pulmonary diseases	17,425	Influenza and pneumonia	34,692
9	Chronic liver disease and cirrhosis	10,815	Nephritis, nephrotic syndrome, and nephrosis	20,628
10	Certain conditions originating in the perinatal period	9,815	Septicemia	17,931
White				
. . .	All causes	1,738,607	All causes	2,079,691
1	Diseases of heart	683,347	Diseases of heart	610,638
2	Malignant neoplasms	368,162	Malignant neoplasms	479,651

(continued)

TABLE 3.2   Continued

SEX, RACE, HISPANIC ORIGIN, AND RANK ORDER	1980		2001[1]	
	Cause of death	Deaths	Cause of death	Deaths
White (continued)				
3	Cerebrovascular diseases	148,734	Cerebrovascular diseases	140,465
4	Unintentional injuries	90,122	Chronic lower respiratory diseases	113,819
5	Chronic obstructive pulmonary diseases	52,375	Unintentional injuries	85,964
6	Pneumonia and influenza	48,369	Diabetes mellitus	57,180
7	Diabetes mellitus	28,868	Influenza and pneumonia	54,774
8	Atherosclerosis	27,069	Alzheimer's disease	50,348
9	Chronic liver disease and cirrhosis	25,240	Nephritis, nephrotic syndrome, and nephrosis	31,345
10	Suicide	24,829	Suicide	27,710
Black or African American				
. . .	All causes	233,135	All causes	287,709
1	Diseases of heart	72,956	Diseases of heart	77,674
2	Malignant neoplasms	45,037	Malignant neoplasms	62,170
3	Cerebrovascular diseases	20,135	Cerebrovascular diseases	19,002
4	Unintentional injuries	13,480	Unintentional injuries	12,462
5	Homicide	10,172	Diabetes mellitus	12,305
6	Certain conditions originating in the perinatal period	6,961	Homicide	8,226
7	Pneumonia and influenza	5,648	Human immunodeficiency virus (HIV) disease	7,844
8	Diabetes mellitus	5,544	Chronic lower respiratory diseases	7,589
9	Chronic liver disease and cirrhosis	4,790	Nephritis, nephrotic syndrome, and nephrosis	7,274
10	Nephritis, nephrotic syndrome, and nephrosis	3,416	Septicemia	5,880
American Indian or Alaska Native				
. . .	All causes	6,923	All causes	11,977
1	Diseases of heart	1,494	Diseases of heart	2,402
2	Unintentional injuries	1,290	Malignant neoplasms	2,155
3	Malignant neoplasms	770	Unintentional injuries	1,361
4	Chronic liver disease and cirrhosis	410	Diabetes mellitus	644
5	Cerebrovascular diseases	322	Cerebrovascular diseases	574
6	Pneumonia and influenza	257	Chronic liver disease and cirrhosis	533
7	Homicide	217	Chronic lower respiratory diseases	427
8	Diabetes mellitus	210	Suicide	321
9	Certain conditions originating in the perinatal period	199	Influenza and pneumonia	318
10	Suicide	181	Nephritis, nephrotic syndrome, and nephrosis	236
Asian or Pacific Islander				
. . .	All causes	11,071	All causes	37,048
1	Diseases of heart	3,265	Malignant neoplasms	9,792
2	Malignant neoplasms	2,522	Diseases of heart	9,428
3	Cerebrovascular diseases	1,028	Cerebrovascular diseases	3,497
4	Unintentional injuries	810	Unintentional injuries	1,750
5	Pneumonia and influenza	342	Diabetes mellitus	1,243
6	Suicide	249	Chronic lower respiratory diseases	1,178
7	Certain conditions originating in the perinatal period	246	Influenza and pneumonia	1,171
8	Diabetes mellitus	227	Suicide	634

SEX, RACE, HISPANIC ORIGIN, AND RANK ORDER	1980		2001[1]	
	Cause of death	*Deaths*	*Cause of death*	*Deaths*
9	Homicide	211	Nephritis, nephrotic syndrome, and nephrosis	625
10	Chronic obstructive pulmonary diseases	207	Homicide	543
Hispanic or Latino				
. . .	—	—	All causes	113,413
1	—	—	Diseases of heart	27,090
2	—	—	Malignant neoplasms	22,371
3	—	—	Unintentional injuries	9,523
4	—	—	Cerebrovascular diseases	6,416
5	—	—	Diabetes mellitus	5,663
6	—	—	Homicide	3,331
7	—	—	Chronic liver disease and cirrhosis	3,301
8	—	—	Chronic lower respiratory diseases	2,832
9	—	—	Influenza and pneumonia	2,722
10	—	—	Certain conditions originating in the perinatal period	2,227
White male				
. . .	All causes	933,878	All causes	1,011,218
1	Diseases of heart	364,679	Diseases of heart	295,556
2	Malignant neoplasms	198,188	Malignant neoplasms	248,146
3	Unintentional injuries	62,963	Unintentional injuries	55,493
4	Cerebrovascular diseases	60,095	Chronic lower respiratory diseases	54,561
5	Chronic obstructive pulmonary diseases	35,977	Cerebrovascular diseases	53,428
6	Pneumonia and influenza	23,810	Diabetes mellitus	26,917
7	Suicide	18,901	Influenza and pneumonia	23,744
8	Chronic liver disease and cirrhosis	16,407	Suicide	22,328
9	Diabetes mellitus	12,125	Nephritis, nephrotic syndrome, and nephrosis	15,241
10	Atherosclerosis	10,543	Chronic liver disease and cirrhosis	15,048
Black or African American male				
. . .	All causes	130,138	All causes	145,908
1	Diseases of heart	37,877	Diseases of heart	37,016
2	Malignant neoplasms	25,861	Malignant neoplasms	32,679
3	Unintentional injuries	9,701	Unintentional injuries	8,537
4	Cerebrovascular diseases	9,194	Cerebrovascular diseases	7,907
5	Homicide	8,274	Homicide	6,780
6	Certain conditions originating in the perinatal period	3,869	Human immunodeficiency virus (HIV) disease	5,328
7	Pneumonia and influenza	3,386	Diabetes mellitus	5,049
8	Chronic liver disease and cirrhosis	3,020	Chronic lower respiratory diseases	4,187
9	Chronic obstructive pulmonary diseases	2,429	Nephritis, nephrotic syndrome, and nephrosis	3,186
10	Diabetes mellitus	2,010	Influenza and pneumonia	2,813
American Indian or Alaska Native male				
. . .	All causes	4,193	All causes	6,466
1	Unintentional injuries	946	Diseases of the heart	1,358
2	Diseases of heart	917	Malignant neoplasms	1,103
3	Malignant neoplasms	408	Unintentional injuries	908

(continued)

TABLE 3.2   Continued

SEX, RACE, HISPANIC ORIGIN, AND RANK ORDER	1980		2001[1]	
	Cause of death	*Deaths*	*Cause of death*	*Deaths*
American Indian or Alaska Native male (continued)				
4	Chronic liver disease and cirrhosis	239	Chronic liver disease and cirrhosis	309
5	Cerebrovascular diseases	163	Diabetes mellitus	276
6	Homicide	162	Suicide	259
7	Pneumonia and influenza	148	Cerebrovascular diseases	217
8	Suicide	147	Chronic lower respiratory diseases	200
9	Certain conditions originating in the perinatal period	107	Influenza and pneumonia	160
10	Diabetes mellitus	86	Homicide	146
Asian or Pacific Islander male				
. . .	All causes	6,809	All causes	19,829
1	Diseases of heart	2,174	Diseases of heart	5,165
2	Malignant neoplasms	1,485	Malignant neoplasms	5,147
3	Unintentional injuries	556	Cerebrovascular diseases	1,625
4	Cerebrovascular diseases	521	Unintentional injuries	1,122
5	Pneumonia and influenza	227	Chronic lower respiratory diseases	749
6	Suicide	159	Influenza and pneumonia	625
7	Chronic obstructive pulmonary diseases	158	Diabetes mellitus	599
8	Homicide	151	Suicide	458
9	Certain conditions originating in the perinatal period	128	Homicide	375
10	Diabetes mellitus	103	Nephritis, nephrotic syndrome, and nephrosis	320
Hispanic or Latino male				
. . .	—	—	All causes	1,068,473
1	—	—	Diseases of heart	14,195
2	—	—	Malignant neoplasms	11,825
3	—	—	Unintentional injuries	7,157
4	—	—	Cerebrovascular diseases	1,982
5	—	—	Homicide	2,756
6	—	—	Diabetes mellitus	2,590
7	—	—	Chronic liver disease and cirrhosis	2,410
8	—	—	Suicide	1,576
9	—	—	Chronic lower respiratory diseases	1,482
10	—	—	Human immunodeficiency virus (HIV) disease	1,437
White female				
. . .	All causes	804,729	All causes	1,068,473
1	Diseases of heart	318,668	Diseases of heart	315,082
2	Malignant neoplasms	169,974	Malignant neoplasms	231,505
3	Cerebrovascular diseases	88,639	Cerebrovascular diseases	87,037
4	Unintentional injuries	27,159	Chronic lower respiratory diseases	59,258
5	Pneumonia and influenza	24,559	Alzheimer's disease	35,634
6	Diabetes mellitus	16,743	Influenza and pneumonia	31,030
7	Atherosclerosis	16,526	Unintentional injuries	30,471
8	Chronic obstructive pulmonary diseases	16,398	Diabetes mellitus	30,263

	1980		2001[1]	
SEX, RACE, HISPANIC ORIGIN, AND RANK ORDER	*Cause of death*	*Deaths*	*Cause of death*	*Deaths*
9	Chronic liver disease and cirrhosis	8,833	Nephritis, nephrotic syndrome, and nephrosis	16,104
10	Certain conditions originating in the perinatal period	6,512	Septicemia	14,435
Black or African American female				
. . .	All causes	102,997	All causes	141,801
1	Diseases of heart	35,079	Diseases of heart	40,658
2	Malignant neoplasms	19,176	Malignant neoplasms	29,491
3	Cerebrovascular diseases	10,941	Cerebrovascular diseases	11,095
4	Unintentional injuries	3,779	Diabetes mellitus	7,256
5	Diabetes mellitus	3,534	Nephritis, nephrotic syndrome, and nephrosis	4,088
6	Certain conditions originating in the perinatal period	3,092	Unintentional injuries	3,925
7	Pneumonia and influenza	2,262	Chronic lower respiratory diseases	3,402
8	Homicide	1,898	Septicemia	3,245
9	Chronic liver disease and cirrhosis	1,770	Influenza and pneumonia	2,958
10	Nephritis, nephrotic syndrome, and nephrosis	1,722	Human immunodeficiency virus (HIV) disease	2,516
American Indian or Alaska Native female				
. . .	All causes	2,730	All causes	5,511
1	Diseases of heart	577	Malignant neoplasms	1,052
2	Malignant neoplasms	362	Diseases of heart	1,044
3	Unintentional injuries	344	Unintentional injuries	453
4	Chronic liver disease and cirrhosis	171	Diabetes mellitus	368
5	Cerebrovascular diseases	159	Cerebrovascular diseases	357
6	Diabetes mellitus	124	Chronic lower respiratory diseases	227
7	Pneumonia and influenza	109	Chronic liver disease and cirrhosis	224
8	Certain conditions originating in the perinatal period	92	Influenza and pneumonia	158
9	Nephritis, nephrotic syndrome, and nephrosis	56	Nephritis, nephrotic syndrome, and nephrosis	131
10	Homicide	55	Septicemia	72
Asian or Pacific Islander female				
. . .	All causes	4,262	All causes	17,219
1	Diseases of heart	1,091	Malignant neoplasms	4,645
2	Malignant neoplasms	1,037	Diseases of heart	4,263
3	Cerebrovascular diseases	507	Cerebrovascular diseases	1,872
4	Unintentional injuries	254	Diabetes mellitus	644
5	Diabetes mellitus	124	Unintentional injuries	628
6	Certain conditions originating in the perinatal period	118	Influenza and pneumonia	546
7	Pneumonia and influenza	115	Chronic lower respiratory diseases	429
8	Congenital anomalies	104	Nephritis, nephrotic syndrome, and nephrosis	305
9	Suicide	90	Essential (primary) hypertension and hypertensive renal disease	234
10	Homicide	60	Alzheimer's disease	188
Hispanic or Latino female				
. . .	—	—	All causes	50,096
1	—	—	Diseases of heart	12,895
2	—	—	Malignant neoplasms	10,546

(continued)

TABLE 3.2   Continued

SEX, RACE, HISPANIC ORIGIN, AND RANK ORDER	1980		2001[1]	
	Cause of death	*Deaths*	*Cause of death*	*Deaths*
Hispanic or Latino female (continued)				
3	—	—	Cerebrovascular diseases	3,434
4	—	—	Diabetes mellitus	3,073
5	—	—	Unintentional injuries	2,366
6	—	—	Influenza and pneumonia	1,413
7	—	—	Chronic lower respiratory diseases	1,350
8	—	—	Nephritis, nephrotic syndrome, and nephrosis	965
9	—	—	Certain conditions originating in the perinatal period	959
10	—	—	Chronic liver disease and cirrhosis	891

. . . Category not applicable.

— Data not available.

[1]Figures for homicide and suicide include September 11, 2001 related deaths for which death certificates were filed as of October 24, 2002.

Notes: For cause of death code numbers based on the *International Classification of Diseases, 9th Revision* (ICD–9) in 1980 and ICD–10 in 2001.

Sources: Centers for Disease Control and Prevention, National Center for Health Statistics, National Vital Statistics System; *Vital statistics of the United States, vol II, mortality, part A,* 1980. Washington: Public Health Service. 1985; Anderson RN, Smith BL. Deaths: Leading causes for 2001. National vital statistics reports. vol 52 no 9. Hyattsville, Maryland: National Center for Health Statistics. 2003.

According to a nationwide survey conducted by the Centers for Disease Control and Prevention, the smoking habits of youth suggested a disturbing trend in the 1990s. Among Black youth, smoking rates had increased 80 percent since 1991 from 12.6 percent to 22.7 percent; 39.7 percent of white teenagers reported cigarette use, an increase from 30.9 percent in 1991. More than one-third of Hispanic students smoked cigarettes, up from about 25 percent in 1991 (Stolberg, 1998).

Education

Regardless of education, on average, men still earn more than women at every level of education. The greatest disparity exists for women with professional degrees (60 percent of what men earn) and for those who did not finish high school (65 percent) (Chideya, 1995; Landes et al., 1994; Ortiz, 1994; U.S. Dept. of Labor, 2002) (see Table 3.4).

The proportion of all women attending institutions of higher education rose from 47 percent in 1976 to 55 percent in 1993. By 1993, Asian and Hispanic women made the greatest gains in enrollment over those years (304 percent and 215 percent increase, respectively) (Foster, Squyers, & Jacobs, 1996; Squyres et al., 1996). As of 1994, about 63.2 percent of female high school graduates enrolled in college compared to 60.6 percent of all high school graduates. In 1992–1993, women obtained a larger percentage (59 percent) of associate degrees (two-year college) than men; women earned 54 percent of the

TABLE 3.3 AIDS Cases by Sex, Age at Diagnosis, and Race/Ethnicity, Reported through December 2001, United States

MALE AGE AT DIAGNOSIS (YEARS)	WHITE, NOT HISPANIC		BLACK, NOT HISPANIC		HISPANIC		ASIAN/PACIFIC ISLANDER		AMERICAN INDIAN/ALASKA NATIVE		TOTAL[1]	
	No.	(%)	No.	(%)	No.	(%)	No.	(%)	No.	(%)	No.	(%)
Under 5	535	(0)	2,165	(1)	783	(1)	17	(0)	12	(1)	3,515	(1)
5–12	346	(0)	498	(0)	284	(0)	10	(0)	6	(0)	1,146	(0)
13–19	916	(0)	1,020	(0)	570	(0)	26	(0)	23	(1)	2,555	(0)
20–24	7,938	(3)	7,590	(3)	4,520	(4)	181	(3)	84	(4)	20,337	(3)
25–29	38,967	(12)	26,595	(12)	17,138	(14)	675	(13)	351	(17)	83,794	(12)
30–34	71,345	(23)	46,088	(20)	28,377	(23)	1,161	(22)	536	(26)	147,600	(22)
35–39	71,995	(23)	51,302	(22)	27,047	(22)	1,169	(22)	473	(23)	152,124	(23)
40–44	52,653	(17)	41,395	(18)	19,215	(16)	927	(17)	303	(15)	114,585	(17)
45–49	32,116	(10)	24,839	(11)	10,937	(9)	558	(10)	134	(7)	68,635	(10)
50–54	17,498	(6)	12,959	(6)	5,861	(5)	301	(6)	63	(3)	36,718	(5)
55–59	9,337	(3)	6,987	(3)	3,242	(3)	177	(3)	37	(2)	19,801	(3)
60–64	5,139	(2)	3,819	(2)	1,769	(1)	76	(1)	18	(1)	10,829	(2)
65 or older	4,249	(1)	3,242	(1)	1,455	(1)	76	(1)	17	(1)	9,048	(1)
Male subtotal	313,034	(100)	228,499	(100)	121,198	(100)	5,354	(100)	2,057	(100)	670,687	(100)
FEMALE AGE AT DIAGNOSIS (YEARS)												
Under 5	502	(2)	2,153	(3)	770	(3)	17	(2)	13	(3)	3,460	(2)
5–12	196	(1)	521	(1)	223	(1)	10	(1)	0	(0)	953	(1)
13–19	295	(1)	1,250	(1)	316	(1)	8	(1)	4	(1)	1,873	(1)
20–24	1,774	(6)	4,844	(6)	1,625	(6)	46	(6)	36	(8)	8,328	(6)
25–29	4,831	(16)	11,876	(15)	4,364	(14)	116	(14)	69	(14)	21,266	(15)
30–34	6,818	(22)	18,055	(22)	6,418	(21)	146	(18)	105	(22)	31,564	(22)
35–39	6,244	(20)	18,351	(21)	5,878	(22)	142	(18)	95	(20)	30,733	(21)
40–44	4,199	(14)	13,221	(14)	3,950	(16)	121	(15)	61	(13)	21,560	(15)
45–49	2,307	(7)	6,922	(8)	2,249	(8)	74	(9)	48	(10)	11,607	(8)
50–54	1,309	(4)	3,447	(4)	1,245	(4)	37	(5)	22	(5)	6,062	(4)
55–59	816	(3)	1,865	(3)	750	(2)	29	(4)	18	(4)	3,479	(2)
60–64	519	(2)	1,103	(1)	411	(1)	29	(4)	5	(1)	2,069	(1)
65 or older	1,044	(3)	1,073	(1)	355	(1)	28	(3)	4	(1)	2,507	(2)
Female subtotal	30,854	(100)	84,681	(100)	28,554	(100)	803	(100)	480	(100)	145,461	(100)
Total[2]	343,889		313,180		149,752		6,157		2,537		816,149	

[1]Includes 545 males and 89 females whose race/ethnicity is unknown.
[2]Includes 1 person whose sex is unknown.

111

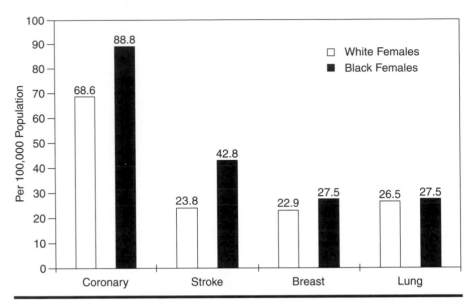

FIGURE 3.4   Age-Adjusted Death Rates for Heart Attack, Stroke, Breast and Lung Cancer for White and Black Females (United States: 1990 Final Mortality)

Source: National Center for Health Statistics and the American Heart Association. From "Mental Health Issues in African-American Women," by J. F. Chisholm, 1996, *Women and Mental Health: Annals of the New York Academy of Sciences, 789,* p. 165. Copyright 1996 by the New York Academy of Sciences. Reprinted with permission.

bachelor's degrees (four-year college); however, they earned fewer degrees at the graduate level (Foster et al., 1996; Squyres et al., 1996). Educational attainment was typically lower among Hispanics of both sexes than among Blacks or Whites. Ginorio et al. (1995) conclude that Latinas (Hispanic women) receive less familial and institutional support for educational achievement than do Latinos (Hispanic men) and are more likely to be encumbered by societal gender-role responsibilities. Those Latinas who do achieve academic success are accordingly less likely to be married and less **gender stereotyped** than their counterparts who do not attend college or attain college degrees. The proportion of women to have had 12 or more years of schooling increased most dramatically between 1970 and 1991 among Black women. Women of Asian descent, regardless of whether they were born in this country, are more

likely than other women between the ages of 25 and 54 to have had four or more years of college.

In 2002, women generally were more likely than men to have some college, but men were more likely to have earned an associate's degree and bachelor's degree (Spraggins, 2003). However, the trend appears to be that women are beginning to earn more advanced degrees than are men. The statistics on the educational attainment of ethnic minority women present a variable picture. More Black women than Black men earned a bachelor's degree in 2002. Asians and Pacific Islanders as a group were more likely than non-Hispanic Whites to have earned at least a college degree; however they were also more likely than Whites to have less than a ninth grade education. Educational attainment also varies among Hispanics; for instance, Cubans, Puerto Ricans, and South Americans are more likely to have at least a high school education than are

TABLE 3.4 Median Usual Weekly Earnings of Full-Time Wage and Salary Workers in Constant (2002) Dollars by Sex, Race, and Hispanic Origin, 1979–2002 Annual Averages

YEAR AND SEX	TOTAL, 16 YEARS AND OVER	WHITE	BLACK	HISPANIC ORIGIN
Both Sexes				
1979	$553	$568	$456	$444
1980	541	555	439	432
1981	536	549	444	422
1982	539	552	437	428
1983	536	548	447	428
1984	537	554	443	427
1985	548	567	442	430
1986[1]	562	580	456	434
1987	566	581	455	431
1988	563	576	459	424
1989	559	573	447	418
1990[1]	549	565	439	405
1991	548	569	448	402
1992	553	575	448	404
1993	562	582	452	405
1994[1]	561	580	446	389
1995	561	580	448	385
1996	560	577	442	387
1997[1]	562	580	447	393
1998[1]	576	600	469	408
1999[1]	592	618	480	415
2000[1]	600	615	488	412
2001	605	620	494	421
2002	609	624	498	423
Women				
1979	418	422	388	361
1980	415	419	383	356
1981	414	417	389	359
1982	426	431	387	363
1983	432	436	397	368
1984	437	442	397	368
1985	443	449	402	366
1986[1]	455	461	413	378
1987	459	465	417	380
1988	460	465	421	380
1989	459	467	422	377
1990[1]	462	471	411	371
1991	472	480	415	376

(continued)

TABLE 3.4 Continued

YEAR AND SEX	TOTAL, 16 YEARS AND OVER	WHITE	BLACK	HISPANIC ORIGIN
Women (continued)				
1992	477	486	421	379
1993	482	491	426	383
1994[1]	479	490	416	366
1995	476	486	416	358
1996	477	489	414	361
1997[1]	482	496	419	355
1998[1]	503	515	440	371
1999[1]	511	521	441	375
2000[1]	513	521	448	379
2001	520	530	459	392
2002	530	549	474	396
Men				
1979	669	684	522	503
1980	646	661	505	484
1981	642	661	507	475
1982	650	669	496	479
1983	648	663	503	470
1984	645	660	499	473
1985	649	666	486	471
1986[1]	656	678	499	468
1987	656	681	494	463
1988	656	679	507	449
1989	655	675	487	441
1990[1]	642	658	481	424
1991	635	651	482	416
1992	629	646	478	426
1993	626	642	480	424
1994[1]	627	657	481	412
1995	631	664	482	410
1996	636	662	470	406
1997[1]	646	665	483	415
1998[1]	659	677	515	429
1999[1]	667	689	527	438
2000[1]	671	694	525	429
2001	680	701	526	443
2002	680	702	523	449
Women's Earnings As Percent of Men's[2]				
1979	62.5	61.7	74.3	71.7
1980	64.3	63.5	75.8	73.6
1981	64.5	63.1	76.7	75.6

YEAR AND SEX	TOTAL, 16 YEARS AND OVER	WHITE	BLACK	HISPANIC ORIGIN
1982	65.5	64.4	78.0	75.7
1983	66.6	65.7	78.9	78.3
1984	67.6	67.0	79.6	77.8
1985	68.2	67.4	82.8	77.7
1986[1]	69.3	67.9	82.7	80.7
1987	69.9	68.2	84.4	82.1
1988	70.1	68.5	83.0	84.6
1989	70.1	69.2	86.5	85.6
1990[1]	71.9	71.5	85.5	87.6
1991	74.3	73.7	86.1	90.5
1992	75.8	75.2	88.1	89.1
1993	77.1	76.5	88.8	90.4
1994[1]	76.4	74.5	86.5	88.8
1995	75.4	73.2	86.3	87.3
1996	75.0	73.8	88.1	89.0
1997[1]	74.5	74.6	86.8	85.6
1998[1]	76.3	76.1	85.4	86.5
1999[1]	76.5	75.7	83.7	85.7
2000[1]	76.4	75.1	85.2	88.4
2001	76.4	75.6	87.2	88.5
2002	78.1	78.2	90.7	88.2

[1]The comparability of historical labor force data has been affected at various times by methodological and conceptual changes in the Current Population Survey (CPS). For an explanation, see the Explanatory Notes and Estimates of Error section of the February 2003 and subsequent issues of *Employment and Earnings,* a monthly BLS periodical.

[2]These figures are computed using unrounded medians and may differ slightly from percents computed using the rounded medians displayed in this table.

Note: Persons of Hispanic origin may be of any race; thus they are included in both the white and black population groups. The Consumer Price Index research series using current methods (CPI-U-RS) is used to convert current dollars to constant dollars.

Source: U.S. Department of Labor Bureau of Labor Statistics. Highlight of Women's Earnings in 2002. Report 972. September 2003, pp. 1–37.

Mexicans (McKinnon, 2003; Reeves & Bennett, 2003; Ramirez & de la Cruz, 2003).

The fields of study in which the most notable gains for women occurred were business and management. Between 1971 and 1990, the proportion of business and management degrees awarded to women rose from 9 percent to 46 percent at the bachelor's level and from 4 percent to 34 percent at the master's level. After declining in the 1970s and 1980s, degrees earned in psychology, social sciences, and education rose in the 1990s. Important inroads were also made

by women in the life, physical, and computer sciences (Foster et al., 1996; Squyres et al., 1996).

Employment

In the twenty-first century two processes—"globalization" and the "feminization of migration," involving the migration of Women of Color from the Third World to Western, industrialized countries such as the United States to work—have broadened and transferred the realm of women's work squarely on the labor of these new immigrants (Castles & Miller, 1998; Ehrenreich & Hochschild, 2002; Momsen, 1999). Ehrenreich and Hochschild (2002) write,

While the European or American woman commutes to work an average twenty-eight minutes a day, many nannies from the Philippines, Sri Lanka, and India cross the globe to get to their jobs. . . . Third World migrant women achieve their success only by assuming the cast-off domestic roles of middle and high income women in the First World—roles that have been previously rejected, of course, by men. And their "commute" entails a cost we have yet to fully comprehend. (p. 3)

In the early 1990s, 59 million women aged 16 years and older were employed or looking for work, or 58 percent of the total female labor force; 74 percent of all women in the workforce were in their childbearing years (18 to 44 years). The greatest labor force participation was among women between 35 to 44 years of age (77 percent). Over 55 percent of all working women are employed in the following traditionally female occupations: administrative support including clerical, service, health treatment occupations (e.g., nurses, dietitians, physician's assistants), and non-college-level teachers. Many American Indian women work primarily in federal and local government jobs. Others are employed as artists, poets, university instructors, heavy equipment operators, truck drivers, and small farmers.

While Latinas have the lowest labor force participation, the participation is not equal among the major Hispanic groups in the United States; there are major differences for both men and women in labor force participation, with Chicanos having the highest participation rate among males and Cuban women having the highest participation rate among females. For both genders, Puerto Ricans have the lowest participation rate (Ginorio et al., 1995).

As with Black American women, Asian American women, compared with other groups of women, tend to be employed outside the home because they need a second income as Asian men earn less than do White men (Chan, 1991). According to Chu (1988), Filipina women are employed at a higher rate than men because of their high educational levels, whereas Vietnamese women are employed at the lowest rates

in part because of lack of skills relevant to the type of employment. Reporting on census data for Los Angeles County from 1980, Chu (1988) reports that Korean and Vietnamese women were overrepresented in the lower-paying jobs and underrepresented in managerial and professional jobs. The percent of Filipina and Asian Indian women working in managerial and professional jobs was higher. She also noted that more than half of Japanese women were in white-collar occupations as were Chinese women.

Recent surveys indicate that 57 percent of all married women over 16 years of age are employed. The percentage of working wives' earnings to family income varied by race: 38 percent for Black working wives, 32 percent for Hispanic wives, and 31 percent for White working wives (Foster et al., 1996). The main reason for the varying percentages was that more Black wives were year-round, full-time workers (64 percent) compared to 53 percent of White wives and 51 percent of Hispanic wives. Additionally White husbands earned more than Black or Hispanic husbands, although earnings for wives varied little. Consequently, Black wives' salaries were 83 percent of their husbands', Hispanic wives earned 74 percent as much as their husbands, and White women earned 68 percent as much as their husbands.

More women and ethnic minority men and women are working in companies at a professional level than ever before; however, their progress has often been confined to the lower levels of management, a barrier dubbed the "glass ceiling." The Department of Labor has defined this phenomenon as "artificial barriers based on attitudinal or organizational bias that prevent qualified individuals from advancing upward in their organization into management level positions." This results in the exclusion of White women and ethnic minority men and women from the centers of power where important decisions are made. In general, minorities have plateaued at lower levels of the workforce than women (Cyrus, 1993). Stress among professional Women of Color in the corporate world can overwhelm (Campbell, 1993). This stress is more than the typical stress relating to managing homes and families while dealing with office politics and meeting deadlines. The highly competitive atmosphere with its oppressive overtones not only separates ethnic minority women from their White colleagues but also tends to place them in opposition to their ethnic minority male professional counterparts. Says Audrey Chapman, a therapist and human relations trainer in Washington, DC, specializing in stress management seminars for women professionals, "The women exhibit a lot of psychosomatic pain in their backs and necks. They have severe menstrual cramps. The pain isn't so much physical as it is mental. Stress leads to the real killers . . . hypertension, diabetes, and strokes" (Campbell, p. 107).

Family Type

Silverstein and Auerbach (2002) express the following view on contemporary families in America:

> *Trying to conform to a single version of family life is not just doomed to failure, but unnecessary. Intimate relationships and good-enough parenting are always difficult to achieve. However, if people attempt to conform to idealized myths, they are making the difficult challenge of raising healthy children even more difficult. Rather than trying to find the "one right way," parents need to be flexible and creative in seeking strategies that work for their particular family. (p. 15)*

Parenting is one of the important functions of family life, regardless of family type. Box 3.2 provides major aspects of parenting.

In 1998, the percent of White married-couple families was 80.8 percent, down from 89 percent in 1970. The percent of Black married-couple families dropped to 46.6 percent from 68 percent 28 years ago. Among Hispanic families, 69 percent were married-couple families and women headed 23.2 percent of family households. However, there were significant differences among Hispanic subgroups. For example, among Cuban Americans 80.7 percent were married-couple families, and among Mexican Americans 72 percent were married-couple families. The proportion of married-couple families among Asian and Pacific Islanders was higher than that for any other group (i.e., 81.7 percent in 1998, down from 82 percent in 1990).

An increase in single-parent homes is a trend that can be seen among all ethnic–racial groups. Families headed by women among Puerto Ricans were 37.7 percent. The proportion of families headed by women has increased among Blacks and Whites, from 28 percent in 1970 to 46.7 percent in 1998, and from 9 percent to 14 percent, respectively (Rein, 2001). Forty-five percent of American Indian households are headed by women (LaFromboise et al., 1995), 42 percent of those women are under the age of 20 when they have their first child, and many never marry (Snipp & Aytac, 1990). Chu (1988) noted that the divorce rate for Asian Americans was much lower than for other women; thus proportionally fewer Asian women are single heads of households than other groups of women. However, differences exist among Asian groups; the divorce rate was higher among Japanese Americans compared with Vietnamese Americans; the divorce rate for Korean women was relatively high also (Root, 1995).

In 1998, 9.3 percent (19.4 million) of all adults who had ever been married were divorced. Among women, 12.2 percent of Black women, 10.2 percent of White women, and 8.4 percent of Hispanic women were divorced (U.S. Census Bureau, 1998).

SUMMARY

This chapter reviewed and discussed a few of the traditional psychological theories and empirical research on people of color (the minorities). The concept of gender and the salience of including, in fruitful ways, an analysis of culture, ethnicity, race, and class into discussions on gender and socialized behavior were explored. A brief historical overview of the experiences of women from four ethnic minority groups (African Americans, American Indians, Hispanic Americans, and Asian Americans), as well as a summary of quality-of-life issues facing them, was presented.

The scope of psychological inquiry into culture, race, ethnicity, and gender to date has seemingly been limited to identifying and appreciating the diversity among ethnic groups in general and among ethnic

Box 3.2

Highlight on Parenting

Effective parenting enables parents to encourage and facilitate the development of healthy, well-adjusted children who are prepared to deal with the vicissitudes of life. By definition, effective parenting presupposes that the quality of the parent–child relationship and parenting skills are sound. In 1990 the U.S. Department of Health and Human Services sponsored a conference that reviewed research on successful families. The following characteristics were found among strong, healthy families: communication, encouragement of individuals, expressing appreciation, commitment to family, religious/spiritual orientation, social connectedness, ability to adapt, clear roles, and time together (Foster et al., 1996). Each of these characteristics may have different definitions and requirements by ethnic group.

A child having matured in a family that facilitated these characteristics has achieved a harmonious balance between one's private, inner reality of the self and experience, and one's public presentation of self in the outer (social) reality. Conversely, ineffective parenting as evidenced in the research on violent youth, for example, indicates disturbances in the parent–child relationship that interfere with a child's development, predisposing the child to later difficulties. Given the ethnic and multicultural diversity as well as social class differences within contemporary American society, no one model or ideal child-rearing method exists (Fantini & Cardenas, 1980). There must be a recognition of the community values, the dignity inherent in local cultural customs, and the need for tolerance in relating to cultural diversity. While it is beyond the scope of this chapter to examine the differences in child rearing among and between people of color of different socioeconomic status and ethnocultural backgrounds, it is worthwhile to acknowledge that differences in child rearing relative to our pluralistic society may impact on the issues raised in this discussion.

Recent thinking about family systems and our understanding of unconscious motivations helps to expand our knowledge about the transmission of family patterns across generations. Not only explicit family rules but also powerful implicit rules allow the expression of certain feelings and inhibit others. The concept of *quality time* may also serve to illustrate the ideas cited. In one sense the term seems euphemistic in that it serves to assuage the guilt and, in some instances, contradict the common sense of some parents who, realizing that while they are away from their children, parenting responsibilities must be delegated to others, or in many cases to the children themselves (e.g., latchkey children). Alternatively quality time alludes to a psychological space in which ideas, attitudes, fantasies, expectations, intentionality, parent–child schemes, and skills about parenting determine the characteristics of the actual parenting. Achieving quality time on a regular, consistent basis has become close to impossible for all types of families, especially dual-career families, working-class families in which both parents have one or more jobs, and single-parent families. For some the issue is child supervision while parents are working, a much more fundamental concern than quality time with children. This is poignantly illustrated in the tragic circumstances in New York City of the recent deaths of a 9-year-old girl and her 17-month-old brother. A fire broke out in their home when they were left home alone without supervision while their mother (a single parent with two jobs), who had decided to go on to work when the baby-sitter failed to arrive, was working her shift at McDonald's (Khan & Mohajer, 2003).

I am reminded of a conversation I had with a colleague whose children are now grown. She said that one advantage of being in academia was the flexible schedule. All through her children's childhood and adolescence she prided herself in "being" there for them. She was disturbed by a recent conversation with her adult daughter whose recollection of her mother during those years was quite different; the daughter felt that her mother had always been preoccupied with work and not "all there." Fabe and Wikler (1978) describe four factors that affect how a working mother will adapt to parenting: (1) the demands of her work, (2) her attitudes about her job, (3) her use of child care, and (4) her personal reaction to motherhood. Even with the involvement of the father in child care, the stress and strain of being responsive to the child's needs and fulfilling other, often conflicting, responsibilities may impact on child rearing vis-à-vis the emotional availability of the parent and the quality of the parent–child interactions; this is especially true for people of color who face discrimination based on cultural or ethnic–racial prejudice.

women in particular as it pertains to gender. What is also needed and to date has not been done is an analysis into the ethnic boundary that defines the group, that is, the social boundaries structuring social life. As discussed earlier in the chapter, social boundaries involve a complex organization of behavior and social relations such that the nature of interactions among people are in a sense determined by unconscious cuing of being fellow members of an ethnic group or not. It thus entails the assumption that the two are fundamentally "playing the same game," and there is the potential for diversification and expansion of their social relationship to cover eventually all different sectors and domains of activity. On the other hand, a dichotomization of others as strangers, or outsiders, implies a recognition of limitations on shared understandings and interactions. The status of a given group within society helps determine whether the ethnic meaning for a given group or individual becomes positive, ambivalent, or negative, which bears greatly on how the group and the individual behave.

For Women of Color in the United States, race, gender, and class are so intertwined that manifestations of their presence constantly permeate our lives. The fictions ascribed to us form a socially constructed reality or pseudo-reality of stereotypic images idealized and devalued by society at large, and internalized by us in varying degrees. These images capture the shadow rather than the essence of our lives, thereby limiting opportunities, and possible experiences, hence curtailing our potential and prohibiting what could be. Similar sentiments are expressed by other women who, while not directly subjected to oppressive forces because of race, nonetheless feel and are oppressed by other forms of discrimination prevalent in our society. Engendering psychology and including in meaningful ways the influences of culture, race, ethnicity, and class will provide psychologists with the tools necessary to shatter the fictive images that destroy us and pave the way for self-definitions that affirm and appreciate our differences as well as our commonalities.

KEY TERMS

Acculturation (p. 96)
African American (p. 77)
American Indian (p. 77)
Asian American (p. 77)
Assimilation (p. 96)
Behavior setting (p. 86)
Benevolent sexism (p. 88)
Black (p. 77)
Chicanos and Chicanas (p. 77)
Class (p. 98)
Classism (p. 98)
Contextualistic behaviorism (p. 86)
Cultural deprivation model (p. 83)
Culture (p. 85)
Dominant Culture (p. 92)
Ecological model (p. 86)

Ethnicity (p. 93)
Ethnocultural group (p. 77)
Gender (p. 77)
Gender identity (p. 87)
Gender stereotype (p. 113)
Genital mutilation (p. 88)
Globalization (p. 76)
Hegemony (p. 82)
Hispanics (p. 77)
Horizontal hostility (p. 96)
Hostile sexism (p. 88)
Inferiority model (p. 82)
Insider's perspective (p. 83)
Involuntary minority (p. 96)
Issei (p. 93)
Latinos and Latinas (p. 77)

Model Minority (p. 83)
Multicultural perspective (p. 83)
Nisei (p. 93)
Outsider's perspective (p. 83)
Panethnicity (p. 78)
Racism (p. 83)
Sansei (p. 93)
Sexism (p. 88)
Symbolic ethnicity (p. 74)
Symbolic racism (p. 95)
Voluntary minority (p. 96)
White (p. 77)
White privilege (p. 92)

DISCUSSION QUESTIONS

1. Are the commonalities among women of different cultures, ethnicities, races, and social classes greater than their differences, such that the "truths" about one group of women are relevant and true for different groups of women? If yes, why? If no, why not?

2. In what ways do culture, ethnicity, race, gender, and class influence your sense of identity?

3. Discuss how a Woman of Color from a "voluntary minority" might respond differently than a woman from an "involuntary" minority to discrimination or prejudice experienced in the workplace.

4. Discuss the assertion that traditional feminist thought about gender causes Women of Color to experience a double bind.

5. In what ways have traditional theories and research methodology within mainstream psychology perpetuated gender and ethnic stereotypes? What steps should psychologists take to reduce and eventually eliminate these types of bias in research?

6. Are Asian American women the model minority? If, yes, why? If no, why not?

7. Define marginality. In what ways do oppression and discrimination contribute to men and women experiencing a sense of marginality?

8. Should race and ethnicity be merged into a single construct within psychology? If yes, why? If no, why not?

9. In her essay on White privilege, Peggy McIntosh (1988) listed some of the privileges she has as a White woman. Create a listing of the privileges people enjoy by virtue of their gender, sexual orientation, social class, age, or physical condition. Discuss how systems of privilege operate in United States society.

FURTHER READINGS

Anzaldua, G. (Ed.). (1990). *Making face, making soul—Haciendo caras: Creative and critical perspectives by feminists of color.* San Francisco: Aunt Lute Foundation.

Azibo, D. A. (1988). Understanding the proper and improper usage of the comparative research framework. *Journal of Black Psychology,* 15, 81–91.

Cole, J. (Ed.). (1986). *All American women: Lives that divide, ties that bind.* New York: Macmillan.

Jacob, I. (2002). *My sisters' voices: Teenage girls of color speak out.* New York: Holt.

Landrine, H. (Ed.). (1995). *Bringing cultural diversity to feminist psychology: Theory, research, and practice.* Washington, DC: American Psychological Association.

Ogbu, J. (1994). From cultural differences to differences in cultural frame of reference. In P. Greenfield & R. Cocking (Eds.), *Cross-cultural roots of minority child development* (pp. 365–391). Hillsdale, NJ: Erlbaum.

Pinderhughes, E. (1989). *Understanding race, ethnicity, and power: The key to efficacy in clinical practice.* New York: Free Press.

Song, Y., & Kim, E. (Eds.). (1993). *American mosaic: Selected readings on America's multicultural heritage.* Upper Saddle River, NJ: Prentice Hall.

CHAPTER 4

BIOLOGY OF SEX AND GENDER

Anatomy is Destiny.
—Sigmund Freud

Although the girl is not yet a woman, her record to date offers convincing evidence that the gender identity gate is open at birth . . . and that it stays open at least for something over a year after birth.
—John Money

For questions of inheritance, legitimacy, paternity, succession to title, and eligibility to certain professions, modern Anglo-Saxon legal conditions required that newborns be registered as male or female.
—Anne Fausto-Sterling

As Darwin demonstrated . . . we males have been born the fittest for three billion years. From that constantly on-the-make little tree mouse (the lemur . . .) to Mailer the magnificent, the DNA of the male Y chromosome has programmed us to lead our sisters.
—Edgar Berman, *The Compleat Chauvinist*

IS ANATOMY DESTINY?

Can We Change Sex and Orient Gender?

Can we change sex and orient gender or was Freud correct when he said that "anatomy is destiny" (Freud, 1924)? In the 1970s these questions came to focus on the now classic story of "John and Joan." This well-known case, which took place in 1963, involved a set of normal male twins. At 7 months of age one of the twins, John, developed phimosis, an abnormal condition whereby the foreskin around the penis tightens and prevents urination. It is a serious condition requiring circumcision, (removal of the foreskin of the penis) to relieve the problem. During the surgical circumcision, which was carried out using a cautery, John's penis was accidentally burned and ablated (amputated). After much discussion and consultation, John was taken to the Johns Hopkins University in Baltimore where the family consulted with Dr. John Money, a renowned sex researcher, to determine how to handle this case of **ablatio penis.** On Dr. Money's advice it was decided that it would be best to rear John as a girl. The family was instructed on how to treat the child in a gender-appropriate way. John's name was changed to "Joan." Within the following year, an orchidectomy (removal of the testes) was performed. Sometime later, further surgery was carried out and a vagina was constructed for Joan.

The development of Joan was monitored with yearly visits to the Johns Hopkins Hospital. A psychiatric team, which included female therapists, was located in the family's area, and they arranged a program to foster female identification and role modeling for Joan. The treatment was reported to be progressing successfully with the acceptance of the child as Joan. Money (1975) reported on Joan's progress:

> Although the girl is not yet a woman, her record to date offers convincing evidence that the gender identity gate is open at birth for a normal child no less than for one born with unfinished sex organs or one who was prenatally over or underexposed to androgen [male hormone], and that it stays open at least for something over a year after birth. (p. 98)

Money continued to write on the success of this case of sex reassignment, believing that the outcome reinforced a social-learning theory of sexual identity.

In 1975, when Joan was about 12 years old, she had, according to reports, developed as a normal female, confirming Money's projection that being raised as a female would override the masculinizing effect of male genes and early male hormone output. He strongly believed that sexual identity and sexual behavior was simply a matter of upbringing (Money, 1975; Money & Tucker, 1975). As Joan approached pubertal age she began to receive female hormones, developing breast tissue. The perception was that she continued to function as a normal female.

Long-term follow-up studies by others revealed that several psychiatrists had examined Joan when she was 13. The psychiatrists' findings and conclusions seemed to conflict strongly with those reported by Money. They found that Joan was having significant psychological problems concerning her ambivalence with a female role. It became apparent that she was never really content with being a girl, suspecting that she was really a male ever since she was in second grade. Joan had developed a masculine gait, which was ridiculed by her classmates. She also showed interest in what were then commonly considered as male occupations. By the time Joan was 14 years old, she started to rebel at her female persona. She sought other medical treatment. Joan stopped taking estrogens, had a mastectomy, and started taking male hormones. Joan then reverted to the male status he had always wanted and began to use his original name, John. Over a period of time John had a phalloplasty, a surgical procedure to form a penis. When John was 25 years old he married a woman who already had a family. Scientists report that John now is happily married, is strictly heterosexual, although he still suffers from the psychic trauma of his early life and is still bitter about his treatment (Diamond & Sigmundson, 1997; Holden, 1997; Pinel, 2003).

This case has been followed since the 1960s. It received widespread recognition, which in turn influenced many scientific and social disciplines. Numerous texts, including those in psychology, sociology, and women's studies were rewritten to assert that "conventional patterns of masculine and feminine behavior can be altered. It also casts doubt on the theory that major sex differences, psychological as well as anatomical, are immutably set by the genes at conception" ("Biological Imperatives," 1973). At that time, the newly stated and rapidly accepted view was seen as validation of a theory that gender identity will depend on the child's upbringing and environment and one that, as of this writing, still influences physicians and theorists and can still be found in the literature. This belief is based on assumptions that (1) individuals are psychosexually neutral at birth and (2) healthy psychosexual development is dependent on the appearance of the genitals. These assumptions appear to have been influenced strongly by Money and his colleagues (Diamond & Sigmundson, 1997). Because of Money's prominence in the scientific community at the time, such assumptions became entrenched in the academic and medical communities. And, although Joan's reversion to a male occurred at 14 years of age, and the longitudinal data have been made available, many textbooks do not reflect these later findings.

Pinel (1993, 2003), in his careful and complete review of Joan's case of sex reassignment, regarded it as "scientifically regrettable that so much of a theoretical and philosophical superstructure has been built on the supposed results of a single, uncontrolled and unconfirmed case" (p. 293). Pinel believes that the practice of surgical sex reassignment at (or around) birth should be stopped. These essentially irreversible procedures should be decided at puberty and the emergence of the subject's sexual identity with an appropriate and acceptable treatment carried out.

In contrast to Money's nurture over nature views, Diamond, a reproductive biologist, has proposed an interactive model of gender identity (Diamond, 1982) that he calls the *biased interaction model*. In this model, sexuality and gender are influenced by environmental forces, but the environmental influence is profoundly affected by the individual's biological makeup (genes and hormones). Gender identity and sexuality are the outcome of the interaction of the two (biology and environment). The fact that the majority of individuals have a gender identity that fits with their biological sex is consistent with Diamond's theory.

Also inconsistent with a strict environmental view of gender identity are studies of a group of children in the Dominican Republic by Imperato-McGinley and her associates (Imperato-McGinley & Peterson, 1976;

Imperato-McGinley, Peterson, Gaultieret, & Sturla, 1979), which are described in Box 4.1.

It is not clear how much we can learn about the normal development of gender identity from studies of children with anomalous biological conditions. Clearly, more research with various populations is needed. At the present time, however, gender identity is best viewed as the product of an interaction between biology and the environment.

Nature versus Nurture: Development of Gender Identity

For decades, the relative influence of nature (biology and anatomy) versus nurture (social and cultural learning and the environment) on human development and gender identity has been debated. Freud's psychoanalytic theory postulates a model for gender identity for the male and for the female that has been one of the most influential theories in the history of psychology and psychiatry. Freud's concepts, which stress anatomy, give little attention to the role of society and learning in shaping behavior, particularly in the development of gender identity. Freud's theory of psychosexual development was based on his belief in the superiority of the male and the phallus. He formulated three stages of early sexual development that we all pass through and that occur in distinctive ontogenetic stages. Freud's theory of psychosexual development is presented in detail in Chapter 5.

Questions and criticisms of Freud's theory have been raised in part because it overemphasizes biological determinants of sexual development, setting the stage for the nature versus nurture controversy. The John and Joan case was used to support nurture over nature as evidence for the malleability of sexual identity and, thus, that anatomy is *not* destiny ("Anatomy *Is* Destiny," 1997). Many textbooks and instructors have continued to cite the case of John and Joan to support this theory, even though John's reversion to his male self demonstrates that so many important aspects of sexual differentiation are indeed biologically determined (Diamond & Sigmundson, 1997; Holden, 1997; Reiner, 1997). The consequences of this are major because, as we will see later on in this chapter, many babies are born with ambiguous genitalia and

Box 4.1_____

Nature versus Nurture

In addition to support from human and animal studies for Diamond's theory, additional evidence has come from the work of Julianne Imperato-McGinley and her associates. For several years they studied a group of male pseudohermaphrodites in the Dominican Republic. These children had normal male sex chromosomes (XY) and male gonads, but they had an inherited enzyme deficit due to a genetic defect that resulted in improperly formed external genitalia at birth. They presented an incompletely formed scrotum that looked like labia and a very small penis that looked like a clitoris with a partially formed vagina. The uneducated parents and probably the physicians who delivered these babies were unaware of any problems. The parents proceeded to raise the children as females.

When the "girls" reached puberty, normal male testosterone production began, causing their penis to fully develop. Puberty was also associated with the onset of other masculine behaviors. The girls indeed became boys. It was most surprising, that despite their rearing as girls, the psychological orientation of the majority of these children also changed and their gender identity became male with all the typical male behaviors and attitudes. Therefore, despite all the environmental forces in their rearing, there was little effect once their biological systems changed.

From the results of these studies, it was apparent that biology was the ultimate influence on their sexuality and on their final gender identity. This is in accordance with the outcome that Diamond's theory predicted. Imperato-McGinley and her colleagues believe that their findings provide evidence that when the sex of rearing, even for a prolonged period, is contrary to the child's biological sex, in the end, the biological sex will prevail if at puberty normal hormone production takes place (Imperato-McGinley & Peterson, 1976; Imperato-McGinley et al., 1979).

This type of pseudohermaphroditism will be discussed in further detail in the section Testicular Feminization Syndrome.

---

internal sexual organs. And, while the policy has been to surgically alter these infants, current reassessment of this practice is occurring. New data increasingly show that sexual anatomy and its appearance may be less critical in determining gender identity than is the prenatal hormonally differentiated brain. As we will see, the psychosexual neutrality or plasticity "gate" that Money (1975) postulated to stay open for at least a year after birth may in fact have a much narrower window early in embryonic life when intrauterine hormone exposure virilizes or feminizes the brain and determines **sexual dimorphism.**

SEX DETERMINATION, DIFFERENTIATION, AND REPRODUCTION

Reproduction and therefore the survival of the species are the evolutionary goal of all organisms. Species that do not have effective reproductive mechanisms will not survive very long.

How and by what process do males become males and females become females? And what are the consequences if the process goes awry? There are many factors that affect the process of becoming female or male. As shown in Figure 4.1, the stage is set with chromosomes and genes.

Chromosomes and Genes

Simple organisms such as amoeba and paramecia reproduce by splitting in two to create a pair that is genetically identical to the parent or original organism before division. More complex organisms, including humans, reproduce by combining genetic material of both parents to create an offspring. Each parent donates a reproductive cell known as a gamete or germ cell; the male contributes a **sperm** cell and the female an **ovum** or egg cell. These two cells combine or fuse to create a single cell, which will develop into the offspring. One of the benefits of this reproductive process is that, when genetic material from different cells is combined, genetic diversity is increased and the transmission or inheritance of undesirable traits to the ensuing offspring are lessened or avoided.

FIGURE 4.1 Chromosomes and Genes
Copyright Miriam Strulle

Sexual determination and differentiation is an intricate process that is *only initiated* at the time of conception. Conception is just the first part of the process to determine the sex and sexual development of the offspring. Every cell in our bodies, other than the sperm and egg (ova), contains two sets of **chromosomes** in its nucleus arranged in pairs (called *diploid*)—23 from the mother and 23 from the father making a total of 46 chromosomes (the sperm and ova have only one set of 23 chromosomes). Twenty-two pairs of the chromosomes appear identical and are known as autosomes (independent), which determine the organism's physical development independently of its sex.

The twenty-third pair is the sex chromosomes, which will initiate the process toward development of a male or female. The female is represented by the X chromosome and the male by the Y chromosome. The cells of females all contain two chromosomes of one type, XX; the cells of males have one of each, X and Y. The presence of the Y chromosome differentiates the male from the female. The female always contributes an X chromosome. The male can contribute either an X or a Y. If the male contributes an X chromosome, the offspring is is on its way to be female with a pair of XX chromosomes; if a Y chromosome is contributed, the offspring is on its way to be male with an XY chromosome. The functional unit of the chromosome is the gene, and every chromosome consists of several thousands of genes (Carroll & Wolpe, 1996; Hunter, 1995; Masters, Johnson, & Kolodny, 1995; Schatten & Schatten, 1983). The genetic information that controls the development of an organism is contained in the DNA that make up these chromosomes, as seen in Figure 4.2.

The production of the gametes, the male and female reproductive cell or sperm and ova (*gamete* is from the Greek *gamos* meaning "marriage"), differs from that of the somatic cells of the body, each with its 23 pairs of chromosomes. The gametes are produced by the division of special cells in the **ovaries** and **testes** and result in cells that have only one-half the normal number of chromosomes, called haploid cells in contrast to diploid cells with 23 pairs. If the gametes too had 23 pairs of chromosomes they would, on merging, produce an organism with 46 pairs or 92 chromosomes. In the male, the division of special cells into sperm cells results in one-half of the sperm cells having an X chromosome and the other half a Y chromosome. In the female, division will result in each half of the ova having an X chromosome. Therefore, instead of 23 *pairs* of chromosomes, sperm and ova contain only 23 *single* chromosomes, one member of each pair. An ovum is the largest cell in the human body, approximately the size of the head of a pin. Its yolk contains nutrients to sustain its growth for a few days. On the other hand, sperm are one of the smallest cells in the body and swim by lashing their long tails back and forth to propel them forward (flagellation). The testes produce billions of cells across the life cycle of the male (Carroll & Wolpe, 1996; Rathus, Nevid, & Fichner-Rathus, 1997).

Fertilization, Conception, and Sex Determination

Fertilization, the union of the sperm and egg, requires the production of ova (eggs) and sperm. Schatten and Schatten (1983) have stated that at birth about 400,000 unripe ova are present in the female ovary. On the other hand, the testes continue to produce billions of cells from puberty on. The process of fertilization, conception, and sexual determination is a complex one. Masters et al. (1995) and Schatten and

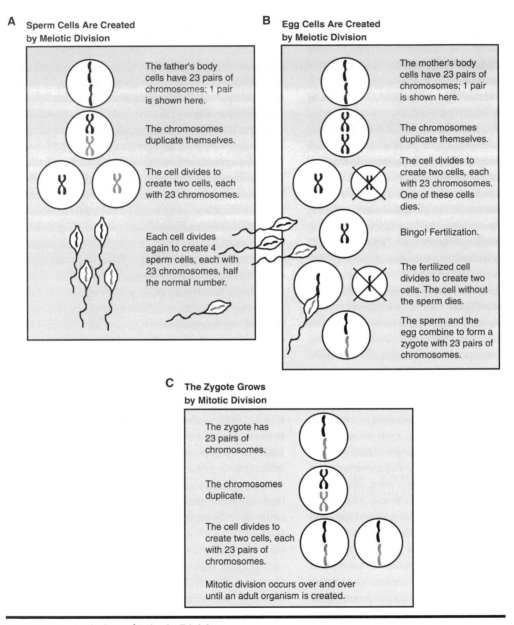

A Sperm Cells Are Created by Meiotic Division

The father's body cells have 23 pairs of chromosomes; 1 pair is shown here.

The chromosomes duplicate themselves.

The cell divides to create two cells, each with 23 chromosomes.

Each cell divides again to create 4 sperm cells, each with 23 chromosomes, half the normal number.

B Egg Cells Are Created by Meiotic Division

The mother's body cells have 23 pairs of chromosomes; 1 pair is shown here.

The chromosomes duplicate themselves.

The cell divides to create two cells, each with 23 chromosomes. One of these cells dies.

Bingo! Fertilization.

The fertilized cell divides to create two cells. The cell without the sperm dies.

The sperm and the egg combine to form a zygote with 23 pairs of chromosomes.

C The Zygote Grows by Mitotic Division

The zygote has 23 pairs of chromosomes.

The chromosomes duplicate.

The cell divides to create two cells, each with 23 pairs of chromosomes.

Mitotic division occurs over and over until an adult organism is created.

FIGURE 4.2 Meiotic and Mitotic Division

Source: From *Biopsychology* (4th ed.) (p. 36), by John P. J. Pinel, 2000, Boston: Allyn and Bacon. Copyright © 2000 by Pearson Education. Reprinted by permission of the publisher.

Schatten (1983) have provided excellent reviews and detailed descriptions of this entire process. Each ova contains a different assortment of chromosomes, thus having a tremendous potential for genetic diversity in the offspring, especially when combined with genetic material of the male. After puberty, on about the fourteenth day of the menstrual cycle, one ovary will produce a ripened ovum each month, which is gently drawn from the surface of the ovary into the Fallopian tube by the movement of cilia (tiny hairlike structures). If fertilization occurs, it is usually in the upper part of the Fallopian tube, not in the uterus. If the egg is not fertilized, it disintegrates in about 48 hours.

After ejaculation into the **vagina,** healthy sperm swim rapidly into the female's reproductive system. Although as many as 200 million or more sperm are in the vagina, only about a few thousand ever reach the Fallopian tubes and only about 200 actually get near the egg. Most sperm spill out of the vagina or clump together and are immobilized, and never reach the female's cervix. Others are damaged or enter the empty Fallopian tube. This appears to be nature's way to assure that only the healthiest sperm get a chance to fertilize the egg. The Y sperm have been shown to move faster than the X sperm, thus increasing their chances of reaching an ovum and increasing the chance of conceiving a male.

Sperm can stay in the reproductive tract for several hours in a process called **capacitation** that enables the sperm to penetrate the egg. During capacitation, sperm secrete a chemical (acrosin) that dissolves the **zona pellucida,** the jellylike coating around the egg. The egg can enhance this process by embracing the sperm with tiny outgrowths called microvilli on its surface. The egg pulls the sperm inside via these microvilli and moves its nucleus to meet that of the sperm. To prevent penetration by other sperm (polyspermy), an electrical block, temporary but rapid, occurs within thousandths of a second once the sperm attaches itself to the ova's surface. The second block comes about when microscopic vesicles from the ova's membrane begin to secrete proteins that form a hard protective coat that pushes all the other sperm away. After the sperm actually enters the egg, it penetrates through the ova's cytoplasm until it meets the nucleus. The sperm's movements are controlled by the beating of its tail. The nucleus of the ova has been shown to quickly migrate toward the sperm. The two nuclei meet and their nuclei fuse, combining the DNA from the mother and the father. The intricate process of fertilization may take at least 24 hours. It begins with the first contact that the sperm makes with the surface of the egg, but fertilization is not considered to have taken place until the genetic material from the egg and the sperm combine (Masters et al., 1995; Schatten & Schatten, 1983).

Upon fertilization, a single cell is produced—the **zygote.** The zygote contains 23 chromosomes contributed by the sperm and 23 from the egg. These 46 chromosomes with their genetic material will initiate the programming for the inherited characteristics such as eye color, hair color, skin color, and blood type. Two of these chromosomes, the sex chromosomes, will determine the sex of the developing embryo. Because eggs have only X chromosomes, it is the genetic nature of the sperm penetrating and activating the egg that is the primary determining factor of the sex of the resulting zygote, as shown in Figure 4.2 (Hunter, 1995; Masters et al., 1995; Schatten & Schatten, 1983).

About 30 to 36 hours after fertilization takes place in the Fallopian tube, the single-celled zygote starts to divide, first into two cells, then the two cells into four cells, and so on. Division continues, forming smaller and smaller cells that increase in number. This small mass is called a *morula*. It begins to travel down the Fallopian tube toward the **uterus,** propelled by cilia (hairlike structures) of the Fallopian tube, and will reach it in about five to seven days. Once it enters the uterus, the morula implants itself in the lining of the uterus. There it will continue to develop and receive nourishment from the placenta, which is a mass of tissues formed on the wall of the uterus through which the fetus will receive nutrients and oxygen and through which it will eliminate its waste products. Once the zygote is implanted in the uterus, **conception** is complete. This product of conception is known as the *conceptus*. For the first eight weeks of pregnancy or gestation, the conceptus is called an **embryo.** From the ninth week until birth it is called a **fetus** (Carroll & Wolpe, 1996; Masters et al., 1995). Schatten and Schatten (1983) have written that "Fertilization is the riskiest of all biological processes. No other basic, necessary physiological mechanism is so chancy, so fragile, and so clearly a matter of life or death. If successful, the union of sperm and egg bridges the generations and ensures survival of the species" (p. 34). Striking changes take place during pregnancy in both the embryo or fetus and the mother to be. The nine months of gestation are divided into three-month periods called **trimesters.** The process from fertilization to implantation in the uterus is shown in Figure 4.3.

Sexual Differentiation and Gestation

When conception is complete, the genetic sex of the embryo is determined. Genetic determination is not enough, however. There is a significant amount of differentiation necessary to complete what we now recognize as the adult male or female. When the genetic material from each parent is combined, sexual differentiation leads to specific physical differences between males and females. This process is essentially controlled by genetic and hormonal mechanisms. Although genetic coding has predestined the embryo to become a male or female, prior to the differentiation process the fetus is sexually neutral. Dur-

ing the first weeks of development, the male and female embryos are anatomically identical and undifferentiated. By the fifth and sixth weeks of pregnancy, two primitive gonads begin to form. They are bipotential; that is, they can develop into ovaries or testes. Two paired primitive duct systems also develop that will form in both female and male embryos—the Müllerian ducts and the Wolffian ducts, respectively. At this point, differentiation appears to depend on the male. For the testes to develop, another step in genetic control must take place. The Y chromosome carries a sex-determining gene, the H-Y gene, which produces an antigen (the H-Y antigen) that stimulates the transformation of the undifferentiated gonads into testes. If the H-Y antigen is not present, the primitive gonads will always develop into ovaries. Thus, unless the H-Y antigen is present, a female will develop.

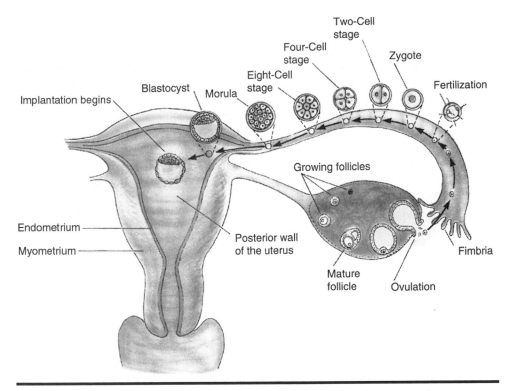

FIGURE 4.3 The Ovarian Cycle, Conception, and the Early Days of the Germinal Stage

Source: From *Human Sexuality in a World of Diversity* (p. 307), by S. A. Rathus, J. S. Nevid, and L. Fichner-Ratus, 1997, Boston: Allyn and Bacon. Copyright © 1997 by Allyn and Bacon. Reprinted by permission.

Other proteins along the Y chromosome have also been hypothesized to initiate the testes-forming process but these mechanisms are still poorly understood (Hunter, 1995; Ohno, 1979; Rathus, Nevid, & Fichner-Rathus, 1998).

Once the testes begin to develop, other aspects of differentiation occur at three different levels: the internal sex structures, the external genitals, and the brain. These are predominantly controlled by hormones. And even if the sex chromosome pattern is that of the male, XY with 46 chromosomes, without a sufficient amount of the male hormone testosterone at the critical time, anatomic development will be female. Such abnormalities will be discussed further on in this chapter.

Internal Sexual Structures. By the seventh to eighth week in most males, the testes begin to develop. The newly forming testes begin to secrete two different chemicals. One chemical, a Müllerian duct–inhibiting substance, causes substantial shrinking of the ducts, which almost disappear instead of developing into female internal organs. The male hormone **testosterone,** an **androgen,** is the second substance to be secreted and is the principal hormone produced by the testes. Testosterone stimulates the development of the Wolffian ducts into internal male organs—the epididymis, vas deferens, seminal vesicles, and ejaculatory ducts. In certain tissues, testosterone is then converted to or acts like a prohormone for the formation of dihydrotestosterone, which results in the development of the penis, scrotum, and prostate.* Testosterone and dihydrotestosterone are androgens, hormones that stimulate masculinization (Carroll & Wolpe, 1996).

In contrast, differentiation of internal female structures does not appear to depend on hormones, but only on the lack of testosterone. Ovaries develop about the twelfth week of gestation, but even if this is delayed, the Müllerian duct system will continue its development into a uterus, Fallopian tubes, and part of the vagina. Without sufficient amounts of testosterone, the Wolffian system in the now designated female will shrink with only tiny remnants remaining.

*Testosterone and other androgens are secreted in varying amounts by the ovaries and the adrenal cortex, as well as by the testes, and serve different functions at different stages of life (Gilman, Rall, Nies, & Taylor, 1990).

By the fourteenth week of gestation, there is a clear difference in the internal structure of the male and female embryo. The course and development of internal sexual structures is seen in Figure 4.4.

External Genitals and Hormones. As we have noted, the external genitals for both male and female develop from the same tissue. Male and female organs that develop from the same tissue are known as *homologous* organs.

In the seventh week of gestation, the external genitals of both male and female still look the same. The undifferentiated tissue from which genitalia will develop exists as a mound of skin or a tubercle beneath the umbilical cord. In females, the external genitals develop under the influence of female hormones now beginning to be produced by the placenta and by the mother. The clitoris, vulva, and remaining sections of the vagina can be seen by the eighth week. In the male, stimulation by androgens beginning at the eighth week causes the folds of tissue that would otherwise develop into vaginal lips in the female to grow together to form the cylindrical shaft of the penis. The tissue that would develop into the clitoris in the female now develops into the glans of the penis in the male. Other surrounding tissue differentiates into the outer vaginal lips in the female or the scrotum in the male that will eventually contain the testes.

Ovaries and testes develop first in the abdomen during fetal life and remain there through early development. The ovaries begin to descend into the pelvis and testes into the scrotum when the child is about 5 years of age. The development of external genitalia is seen in Figure 4.5.

Hormones play a crucial role in the development of males and females. Endocrine glands such as the gonads begin to secrete hormones directly into the bloodstream, which are then carried to the target organs. For example, the ovaries produce **estrogen** and **progesterone,** the two major female hormones. Estrogen is critical for the development of female sexual characteristics throughout fetal development and in later life, while progesterone acts to regulate the menstrual cycle and, when the female reaches puberty, prepares the uterus for implantation of the embryo and pregnancy. The testes produce androgens (e.g.,

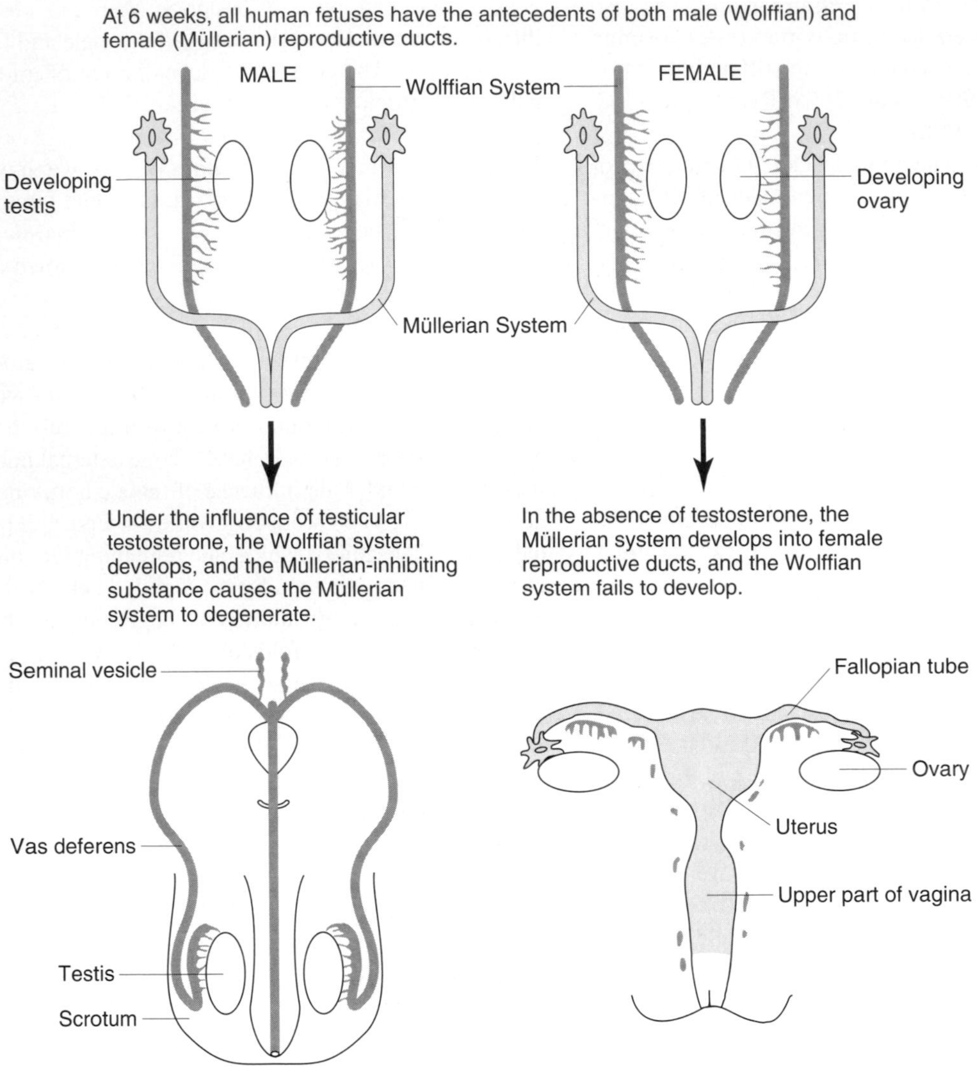

At 6 weeks, all human fetuses have the antecedents of both male (Wolffian) and female (Müllerian) reproductive ducts.

MALE — Wolffian System — FEMALE

Developing testis

Developing ovary

Müllerian System

Under the influence of testicular testosterone, the Wolffian system develops, and the Müllerian-inhibiting substance causes the Müllerian system to degenerate.

In the absence of testosterone, the Müllerian system develops into female reproductive ducts, and the Wolffian system fails to develop.

Seminal vesicle

Vas deferens

Testis

Scrotum

Fallopian tube

Ovary

Uterus

Upper part of vagina

FIGURE 4.4   Development of Internal Reproductive Systems

Source: From *Biopsychology* (4th ed.) (p. 51), by John P. J. Pinel, 2000, Boston: Allyn and Bacon. Copyright © 2000 by Pearson Education. Reprinted by permission of the publisher.

testosterone), also critical for the male. A male fetus will develop female characteristics if androgens are not secreted at the correct time or if the fetus, due to some defect, is insensitive to androgens. These anomalies will be described later in this chapter.

Brain Differentiation and Dimorphism.   Differentiation of the male and female brain begins during

prenatal life starting at about 12 weeks and develops into a sexually dimorphic organ. Hormones in the blood of the fetus have a critical and timely influence. Much of our evidence comes from experiments on animals in which fetal brain development can be monitored and the influence of hormones can be measured directly. One of the most important *structural* differences between male and female brains is in the

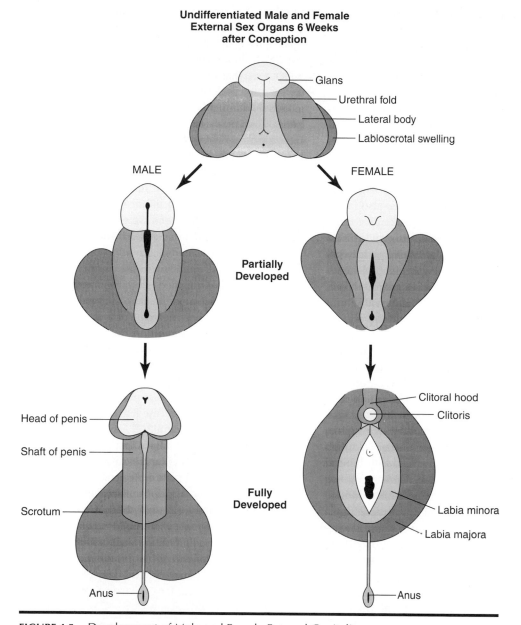

FIGURE 4.5   Development of Male and Female External Genitalia

Source: Biopsychology (4th ed.) (p. 52), by John P. J. Pinel, 2000, Boston: Allyn and Bacon. Copyright © 2000 by Pearson Education. Reprinted by permission of the publisher.

number and location of certain types of nerve connections (synapses) in the hypothalamus. In prenatal sexual differentiation, in the presence of androgen stimulation, the brain develops in a male pattern. In the absence of androgen stimulation, the brain develops in a female direction. This hormonal programming starts to take place during prenatal life and determines the type of patterning and function of the hypothalamus and the pituitary gland. Thus, females will have a cyclic sex hormone production and menstrual cycles, while males will have a generally constant level of hormone production. Therefore, female fertility becomes cyclic, whereas male fertility is continuous. This is probably one of the most *important* sex differences in female–male brain function. Prenatal hormone effects on the developing brain may also influence later behaviors, such as sexual behavior, assertiveness, and aggression (Goldman, 1978; McEwen, 1981; Rubin, Reinisch, & Haskett, 1981).

The brains of men on average are larger than the brains of women, but men on average are also larger than women. There are two hemispheres of the brain connected by a large band of fibers, the *corpus callosum*. Although they can interact with each other, they do not usually have the same functions. Many functions are *lateralized*—that is, they are located primarily in one hemisphere. The left hemisphere is primarily involved in language and participates in analyzing information and performing serial functions such as verbal ability—speaking, understanding speech, ability to read and write. The right hemisphere appears specialized for perceptive function, drawing, reading, essentially synthesizing simple information to construct complex objects. In the 1970s Sperry, his associates, and other neuroscientists showed evidence that the right hemisphere of women's brains share language capabilities with the left hemisphere, while in men, language resides mainly in the left hemisphere. Therefore, a stroke in the left hemisphere of a women will result in fewer deficits in language ability than would occur in men with a similar brain injury (Carlson, 2002; Levy, 1990). In Chapter 6, the complex issue of lateralization in ability and achievement is discussed in detail.

In the introduction to this chapter we reviewed the classic case of John and Joan and the final outcome of this case of sex reassignment. The significance of prenatal hormone exposure to the developing brain was one aspect that was not considered at the time that the decision was made to feminize John. Now we know more about the implications of brain development as it is influenced by the intrauterine hormonal milieu. Sexual dimorphism in the brain was first reported by Raisman and Field (1971). More in-

formation has emerged since that time, as indicated in this section, and will be discussed further in other sections of the chapter. However, from our review of sexual determination and differentiation, it should be understood that the structure that may be critical for psychosexual development and adaptation is not anatomy—but the brain.

Gestation and Fetal Development.   The length of gestation in humans ranges from 36 to 38 weeks and is divided into 3-month (12-week) periods or trimesters.

By the end of the first trimester, the fetus begins to resemble a very small infant. It is about 10 centimeters (4 inches) long and weighs about 19 grams (2/3 ounce). From the end of the twelfth week, fetal development consists of the enlargement and differentiation of the already existing structures.

By the end of the fourteenth week (now the second trimester), movements or "quickening" of the fetus are felt, and by the eighteenth week, the fetal heartbeat can be heard. During the twentieth week, the fetus begins to open its eyes, and in the twenty-fourth week, it becomes light sensitive and can hear sounds. Movements become more vigorous and the fetus displays sleep and wake periods.

By the third trimester, the fetus develops fat pads and its skin becomes wrinkled and is covered with fine downlike hair, which will disappear before birth. In the seventh month, the fetus turns in the uterus and presents a head-down position in preparation for delivery. If it does not turn, then delivery will be a *breech* presentation (feet first) that will require special skills by the obstetrician during delivery to rotate the infant to a head-down position. By the time of delivery, the average full-term normal infant weighs 3,300 grams (7.5 pounds) and is an average of 50 centimeters (20 inches) long (Carroll & Wolpe, 1996; Masters et al., 1995).

Sexual Selection

The possibility of influencing the sex of a fetus has intrigued women and men throughout time. The historical literature abounds with techniques recommended to control the sex of offspring. The ancient Greeks, among them Pythagoras (580–500 B.C.E.), thought that the noble parts of the fetus derived from male semen, while the base or coarse parts of the fetus derived from female semen. The Greek physician Hippocrates and philosopher Democritus of Abdera, both of whom lived between 460 and 370 B.C.E., also had specific assumptions about how sex was determined. Hippocrates believed that the male fetus formed on the right side of the womb and the female on the left. Democritus believed that each testis played an important role in sexual determination; females originated from the left testis and males from the right (Cadden, 1993; Hunter, 1995). According to Mittwoch (1977), this distinction between right and left influenced and indeed led to the general concept of *rightness* being associated with maleness and *leftness* being associated with females, and with the usual sexist attributes. This led to recommendations for special positions during intercourse.

The Hippocratic corpus (a collection of writings by physicians during Hippocrates' time that also claims to include some of those by Hippocrates himself) held the belief that both parents contribute seed arising from all parts of their bodies to form the fetus, a process known as *pangenesis.* This theory was used to explain the resemblance of the offspring to their parents and other members of the family. Another view of the ancient Greeks, which has also been attributed to Hippocrates, is the belief in two seeds, one contributed by each parent. The philosopher Aristotle (384–322 B.C.E.) also held specific beliefs about reproduction. First, in contrast to the Hippocratic corpus, Aristotle believed that only one seed was necessary for reproduction and that was from the male. Aristotle designated different values based on the poles of temperatures; warm is better than cool; dry is better than wet. With reference to sex, the male, who is warm, became the superior sex. For Aristotle, the female is cooler, which immediately earned her a lower place in the natural order, and her lack of warmth was responsible for the difference in her reproductive role. Because males are warmer, they have sufficient heat to process their nutrients into semen; females, according to Aristotle, lack sufficient heat and can produce only menstrual blood, which, however, has characteristics that help to form the fetus. Aristotle also held other sexist attitudes. His warm and cold poles of temperature, which defined males as superior and females as inferior, also translate to ability and activity on the part of the male and the opposite, inability and passivity, for the female. Aristotle believed that females were a type of deformed males. Females are representative of either "the weakness of the father's seed or the intractability of the mother's material or some external condition which has, by default, produced a daughter" (Cadden, 1993, p. 24). Aristotle also thought that if the parents had intercourse in a wind coming from the north, a male fetus would form and, in a south wind, a female would result.

Throughout the span of history, many of these concepts persisted. During the late Middle Ages, varieties of these same doctrines, especially those of Aristotle, continued to be espoused in modified forms. Similar beliefs and other legends appeared throughout the Oriental world of Persia, Mesopotamia, and India. Down through the centuries, from ancient Greece until the nineteenth century, there was little progress in the scientific understanding of the reproductive process and sexual determination and so these beliefs were paramount. Hunter (1995) details the very gradual development of knowledge about reproduction by physicians, scientists, and philosophers across these centuries. One interesting concept is the *preformist* or *ovist* theory of reproduction in which the offspring is considered to be already preformed in the egg. The view held by eminent anatomists during the sixteenth and seventeenth century (e.g., William Harvey [1578–1657] and Reguier de Graaf [1641–1673]) was that all living things derive from eggs. Although the microscope was first built in 1595 by Hans and Zacharias Jansen, it was very rudimentary. This preformist view held until improved models of the microscope became available. In the mid 1600s Anton van Leeuwenhoek began to build more powerful microscopes. By 1678, using one of his microscopes, he reported the discovery of semen—the first factual description of spermatozoa (http://www.ucmp.berkley.edu/leeuwenhoek.html; Hunter, 1995, p. 3). In the ensuing centuries there continued to be increasing research into the anatomical and physiological bases of the reproductive process. We now have a much more precise understanding of this process, with meticulous details on reproduction.

Nevertheless, many myths about how to determine the sex of the fetus have continued into our current time. Some examples of such myths are seen in Box 4.2.

However, there are known scientific and medical reasons for sexual selection. Some inherited diseases may affect one sex more than the other (e.g., hemophilia affects more males than females). With the development of amniocentesis, performed around the sixteenth week of gestation, and other techniques, the sex of the fetus can easily be determined, although such information is not routinely provided. While this procedure is necessary for determining the risk of chromosomal abnormalities in pregnant women over age 30, it also has the advantage of discovering sex-linked abnormalities. The question of abortion in such cases, as well as the aborting of a fetus of the unpreferred sex, has raised moral, ethical, and social issues in many countries. In some countries such as China, a one-child policy is in effect in an effort to control overpopulation. The incidence of infanticide, primarily of females, is thought to be used to allow for the subsequent birth of a male child. Carroll and Wolpe (1996) report that as of 1992 some 60 million babies, all female, fail to be accounted for in China, India, Pakistan, Bangladesh, Nepal, Egypt, and western Asia. It is believed that female infanticide as well as neglect to the point of death for female babies, who are given less food and medical treatment, are the reasons for the inability to account for these female babies.

An American volunteer working at an orphanage in Guangzhou, China, was devastated when she observed the bodies of abandoned girls carted away in wheelbarrows to be disposed of by the garbage collectors. Reports are that the government and State Family Planning Commission in China are trying to correct the situation (Herbert, 1997). China maintains a one-child policy with tight restrictions on the number of births. Sex-selective abortion is thought to have decreased the incidence of female infanticide, but there is still a large number of missing girls in China. A recent article published in the United Kingdom cites that over 116 males were recorded for every 100 females born in China. The ratio is thought to be primarily due to sex-selective abortion and that female infanticide has become infrequent (Gittings, 2002). Nevertheless, the group Gendercide Watch is unable to derive reliable statistics on the number of girls who die every year from infanticide. Data are complicated by unreliability and ambiguity. Yet, they estimate such casualties in the hundreds of thousands with sex-selective abortions likely to account for an even higher incidence of "missing girls" (http://gendercide.org/case_infanticide.html).

In 2000, the New York Times reported that many "illegal" children are born in secret and never registered and that it has become even more difficult to monitor pregnancies (Rosenthal, 2000). Johansson and Nygren as early as 1991 have claimed that this practice of unreported births of girls may well ac-

---

Box **4.2**

Current Myths of Sexual Determination

The fascination with and interest in sexual determination and selection have continued. In many countries, including Western countries, some myths also persist. For example, many men still believe that it is the woman who determines the sex of the fetus, not withstanding the available knowledge that only the male has the Y chromosome. It is not uncommon that women who give birth to females are blamed for their baby's sex, and in some societies men divorce their wives and marry other women in the hope of siring a male heir (Masters et al., 1995). There is some evidence that creating an acidic or alkaline environment in the vagina will affect the type of sperm (X or Y) to reach the ova in the Fallopian tube. Having intercourse on specific days prior to ovulation is also considered to favor the fertilization of a female or male. Other formulas and diet regimes for sexual determination regularly appear in the literature and will doubtless keep doing so.

count for a large proportion of these "missing girls." However, recent data are not available.

Although government regulations in China prohibit many of these practices, they need to be strictly enforced. Family planning programs and counseling will play an important part in reducing selective abortion as well as female infanticide.

In 1998, a group of physicians at a fertility center in Virginia reported that they are now able to "stack the odds" that a couple can have a baby of the sex that they prefer. This group has developed a DNA detector technique for sorting the X- from the Y-bearing sperm based on the amount of DNA present (the Y-bearing sperm have less DNA than the X-bearing sperm). The physicians at the center report a high success rate in sex selection. The couples that they have helped range from those who have a sexual preference in order to avoid transmitting sex-linked genetic diseases to those who already have a child of one sex and would like one of the other sex. This technique has raised questions about the ethics of such selection procedures and the safety in the long term of such techniques (Kolata, 1998).

WHAT HAPPENS IF SOMETHING GOES AWRY?

Incidents of abnormal sexual development have been noted since ancient times, but without any understanding of their origin. These disorders not only occur in humans but also have their counterparts in diverse animal species (Hunter, 1995). Early observations focused on the abnormal appearance of the external genitalia and later included the gonads. As science and technology advanced, we have gained a better comprehension of the basis of many of these sexual abnormalities. Prenatal development and differentiation are the consequences of carefully coordinated developmental processes. Each stage of prenatal development carries the risk of irregularities that can result in abnormal or atypical sexual differentiation. Three major causes of abnormal differentiation have been determined: (1) sex chromosome disorders, (2) genetic or hormonal conditions, and (3) exposure of the fetus to prescribed drugs or drugs that the mother ingested herself. We will review here some of the major disorders that can occur.

Sex Chromosome Disorders

As described earlier, there are normally 46 chromosomes (23 pairs), which include one pair of sex chromosomes, XX or XY. An infant can be born with one or more extra sex chromosomes or with only one sex chromosome. This abnormality takes place after fertilization and during the meiosis (cell division) stage when the fertilized ovum begins to divide. These disorders have a variety of effects on physical appearance, may lead to different physical and psychological clinical syndromes, and can affect sexual behavior.

Klinefelter's Syndrome. This syndrome affects 1 in 500 males and occurs when a genetic male has an extra X chromosome. This happens when an ovum with an extra X chromosome is fertilized by a Y sperm resulting in an XXY embryo, giving the offspring a total of 47 instead of 46 chromosomes. The Y chromosome then triggers the development of male genitalia, but because of the extra X chromosome the genitalia are prevented from developing normally. Because testosterone production is reduced, men with Klinefelter's syndrome may have a small penis and small testes. Surface virilization, including pubic and axillary hair, are usually normal. These men are usually tall with a feminized body shape and most often develop gynecomastia (enlarged breasts). They appear to have a low sex drive, may be impotent, and seem to be passive, with low levels of ambition, thought to be due to their low testosterone levels. Klinefelter's syndrome is found in about 1 in 700 live births, but is not usually detected until puberty or early adulthood. Testosterone therapy, especially during adolescence, will improve the condition and facilitate development of secondary sexual characteristics (Hunter, 1995; Masters et al., 1995).

Turner's Syndrome. This disorder is the most common chromosome disorder in females. Although the incidence is 1 in 100 at conception, it drops significantly to 1 in 1,000 females at birth. It has been estimated that about 98 percent of embryos or fetuses with an X0 (zero) chromosomal constitution will not survive (Short, 1982). Turner's syndrome comes about when an ovum without any X chromosome is fertilized by an X sperm. This gives the offspring only 45 chromosomes and is designated as X0. However, if an ovum without an X chromosome is fertilized by a Y chromosome, the ovum will die.

Although external genitalia appear normal in Turner's syndrome, the ovaries never develop properly and are called *streak gonads* (Hunter, 1995). The typical female with Turner's syndrome is short, perhaps due to abnormal bone growth, with skin folds over the neck that appear to be webbed. Birth marks on the skin are also common. Though external genitalia appear normal, menstruation is absent because the ovaries are nonfunctional, and therefore these females are sterile. Occasionally, however, menstruation and even pregnancy have been reported. There may also be abnormalities of the cardiovascular and lymphatic systems. Breast development and menstruation may be induced with hormone therapy but the problems of height and infertility have not been successfully treated. These girls show less involvement in social activities and have more academic problems than non–Turner's syndrome girls (Rathus, Nevid, & Fishner-Rathus, 1998).

XYY Syndrome and XXX Syndrome. Chromosomal disorders in which there is an extra X or Y chromosome are rare. They occur at the time of fertilization, when a normal ovum with one X chromosome is fertilized by a sperm that has two Y chromosomes (XYY) or two X chromosomes (XXX). An XXX condition can also come about when an ovum with two X chromosomes is fertilized by a normal sperm with an X chromosome. Although these individuals may grow up as normal males and females, they may have some genital abnormalities and decreased fertility or infertility. Some of these individuals may show signs of slight mental retardation. There is at present no known treatment for these syndromes.

Genetic or Hormonal Conditions

Pseudohermaphroditism. A **pseudohermaphrodite** is one who is born with gonads (internal sex organs) that match her or his sex chromosomes, but whose genitals (external sex organs) appear to be that of the other sex. There are two categories of this condition.

Adrenogenital Syndrome (AGS). This type of *female* pseudohermaphrodite has ovaries, Fallopian tubes, a uterus, and a 46 XX chromosome constitution, and has normal fertility potential and yet the genitals are masculinized. Masculinization of the genitals can range from mild enlargement of the clitoris to the formation of a penis-like structure or even the development of a true penis. Labia may be fused, resembling a scrotum. The genitals appear to be so strongly male that the actual sex of the infant can be wrongly identified.

The most frequent cause of AGS, an inherited disorder, involves an enzyme block of the adrenal glands, resulting in the production of excessive amounts of androgens. When this happens, the female fetus is exposed to abnormal amounts of androgens at a crucial period of prenatal development. The genitals are masculinized to varying degrees depending on the amount of male hormone secreted. If an early diagnosis is not made, the adrenal glands will continue their abnormal production of androgens, and masculinization will persist throughout the girl's development. If a diagnosis of AGS is made at birth or shortly thereafter, treatment can begin in early childhood so that normal androgen output can be attained. Plastic surgery can later modify the appearance of the genitals. Because the internal organs remain normal, fertility may also be normal and pregnancy may even be possible. Today, if a baby is born with questionable male genitals, a chromosome analysis can easily be carried out, thus assuring early treatment of this disorder.

Yet even with early treatment, the behavior of AGS girls may be somewhat different from that of normal girls. AGS girls may show a higher rate of "tomboyism." They may prefer boys to girls as playmates and show little interest in activities associated with girls: playing with dolls, playing house, and imitating the mother's activities. Although there is no problem with their gender identity, AGS females show delayed dating and may have considerable difficulty in establishing close relationships. The question of the incidence of bisexual or lesbian tendencies has been raised regarding AGS females (Carroll & Wolpe, 1996; Hoyenga & Hoyenga, 1993; Hunter, 1995; Masters et al., 1995).

Testicular Feminization Syndrome. This is a type of *male* pseudohermaphrodite and is an inherited condition in which testosterone and other androgens have no effect on the fetus. These androgen-insensitive male pseudohermaphrodites have a 46 XY chromosome pattern and have testes, but are born with female genitals. Even though testosterone secretion at the crucial time in neonatal development is normal, because the fetus is insensitive to it, differentiation occurs as it does in females, with the formation of a clitoris, labia, and vagina. However, in this type of disorder, the fetal testes do produce the Müllerian-inhibiting substance (to which the fetus is sensitive). The Müllerian ducts will shrink and prevent the growth of a uterus and Fallopian tubes, but a vagina ending in a blind pouch can develop.

At birth, the testicular feminized infant resembles a normal female unless the testes have descended into the labia and can be identified on examination of the groin. These children are usually reared as girls with normal development until around puberty. The lack of menstruation brings about medical investigation and a diagnosis is made. There can even be some breast development in these adolescents because the testosterone produced metabolizes into estrogen to which the body is sensitive. These "girls" have a very feminine appearance; that is, they have physical characteristics highly prized by society. When testicular feminization is extreme, some feel it is best that these children be raised as girls.

A second type of male pseudohermaphroditism is known as the *5-alpha-reductase syndrome* or the *Dominican Republic syndrome,* an endocrine defect referred to earlier in this chapter. In this disorder, an inherited enzyme defect in genetically 46 XY males results in improper formation of male genitalia, even though prenatal testosterone concentration is normal. This is an inherited condition due to a recessive gene. There is a lack of the enzyme that facilitates the conversion of testosterone to dihydrotestosterone, the androgen needed for closure of the scrotum and growth of the penis. Since 1976, Imperato-McGinley and her colleagues have been involved in studies of these children in the villages of the Dominican Republic. When these babies are born, they appear anatomically to be females, with normal internal sex structures but

a small, clitoris-like penis and incompletely formed scrotum resembling the labia. They are reared as girls. The parents are unaware that anything is wrong with these children. However, when these "girls" reach puberty, there is an acceleration of testosterone; they develop male genitalia with all the secondary male sex characteristics and are then considered true males. Despite being reared as females, in many if not most of the cases their gender identity changes to male. The transition from female to male has been problematic. Whether they are accepted as true males is still questionable. Thus the forces of socialization have little effect when their hormones come into play at puberty. Imperato-McGinley and her coworkers believe that these studies show that even when a person is reared in a manner counter to his or her biological sex, biological sex will prevail if normal hormones are produced at puberty (Imperato-McGinley et al., 1979). As noted earlier, Imperato-McGinley's findings also fail to support Money's earlier theories of nurture and lend support to Diamond's biased interaction model concepts, both of which were discussed in the beginning of this chapter (Pinel, 1993).

True Hermaphroditism or Intersexuality. This disorder is defined as the "possession, at birth, of both male and female characteristics in the gonads and/or in the internal or external genitalia" (Jacobs, 1969, p. 214). The word *hermaphrodite* comes from the Greek god Hermes and Aphrodite, the goddess of sexual love and beauty. According to the Greek legend, Hermaphroditus, the son of Hermes and Aphrodite, became half female and half male when his body fused with that of a nymph with whom he fell in love.

The condition appears to be exceptionally rare. Such individuals are born with both testicular and ovarian tissue, with a variable distribution of each type of tissue. Combinations of these tissues vary; there may be one testis and one ovary or a mixture of both ovarian and testicular tissue (ovotestis). When the gonads are well defined as an ovary or testis, the ovary tends to be found on the left side and the testis on the right. In extreme cases, both testes and ovaries are fully formed.

In the majority of cases, the chromosome constitution of true hermaphrodites is 46 XX compared with 46 XY chromosomes. Because there is testicular tissue, true hermaphrodites usually show signs of masculinization in their external genitalia. Yet, development of breast tissue can appear at puberty. A uterus is frequently present with a Fallopian tube on one side and a vas deferens and epididymis on the other. Both male and female duct systems may also be present on opposite sides of the body. The extent of the development of these structures depends on the amount of ovarian and testicular tissue and the extent of hormone action during fetal life. Although the chromosome constitution of these individuals may be female (46XX) or male (46XY), their sex is considered ambiguous and so too is their gender identity (Hunter, 1995).

Although the condition appears to be quite uncommon, it is difficult to estimate the percentage of intersexuals. Fausto-Sterling (1993) quotes Money as suggesting that intersexuals may constitute as much as 4 percent of the population. In her article, "The Five Sexes," Fausto-Sterling includes both the true hermaphrodites and the pseudohermaphrodites. Her "five sexes" include male; female; true hermaphrodites, whom she calls *herms;* the pseudohermaphrodites described previously: *merms,* males who have testes and some type of female genitalia but no ovaries; and *ferms,* females who have ovaries with some type of male genitalia but no testes. Fausto-Sterling traces the history of hermaphroditism and shows concern about surgical sex assignment or correction when these conditions are diagnosed. She feels that these individuals are compelled by society to choose an established gender role and stay with it. The selection of gender began in Europe during the Middle Ages and has continued until recently. "For questions of inheritance, legitimacy, paternity, succession to title, and eligibility for certain professions, modern Anglo-Saxon legal conditions require that newborns be registered as male or female" (Fausto-Sterling, 1993, p. 22). Fausto-Sterling raises questions about why this is necessary and points to an apparent cultural need to keep a clear and consistent division between the two sexes. She feels that intersexuals should be permitted to develop as such. For her, a new ethic of medical treatment would come about whereby the oppositions—"patient and physician, parent and child, male and female, heterosexual and homosexual—would be dissolved" (Fausto-Sterling, 1993, p. 24).

While Fausto-Sterling's ideal world seems far away, a number of intersexuals who have had corrective surgery have found each other primarily through the Internet. They have joined together to protest surgical correction. They want to establish a pattern whereby intersexuals will be free to grow and develop with their combination of male and female characteristics and make their own way. It is a group that we shall certainly hear more from in the near future. The social, ethical, and psychological implications are being brought before the public.

Prenatal Drug Exposure

Drugs taken at any time during pregnancy that can cross the placental barrier can cause damage to the embryo or fetus, which may have many serious consequences including malformations called *teratogenic.*

When pregnant women are given hormones as part of medical treatment, the hormones enter the circulation and cross the placental barrier. The embryo or fetus exposed to these hormones often suffers detrimental effects. For example, if a pregnant woman is given male hormones or drugs mimicking male hormones, the AGS syndrome can result, depending on the amount of drug and the time of pregnancy during which the drugs are administered. Synthetic female hormones can result in malformation of the penis (Masters et al., 1995; Wilson, 1990). The behavior of these children may also be affected. Boys who were exposed to female hormones have been found to be lower in assertiveness and, compared with other males, have less athletic ability. They were perceived as less likely to indulge in physical activity than normal boys. Girls exposed to female hormones during gestation demonstrated heightened femininity (Ehrhardt, Grisanti, & Meyer-Bahlburg, 1977; Masters et al., 1995). Antibiotics that cross the placental barrier may also have adverse effects on the embryo and fetus. More research is needed on new drugs available that may also affect the developing embryo and fetus.

Alcohol. When a pregnant woman consumes alcohol, it circulates throughout her body and also through the fetus. Excessive and repeated amounts of alcohol throughout pregnancy may result in the neonate developing withdrawal symptoms. Alcoholism can also result in vitamin depletion, biochemical imbalance, small-for-dates babies, premature births, or even prenatal death. Physical malformations can occur as part of the **fetal alcohol syndrome,** which include pre- and postnatal growth defects; small brain; joint, limb, or heart malformations; and, most critically, mental retardation (Carroll & Wolpe, 1996; Hyde, 1996).

Other Addictive Drugs.   Heroin, morphine, cocaine, amphetamines, and marijuana may also lead to consequences similar to those of the fetal alcohol syndrome. Many pregnant women are not single drug abusers but polydrug abusers, which places their babies at a very high risk for teratogenic and other defects. The question of whether cocaine abuse will affect the developing fetus has received positive and negative answers. Recent data suggest that cocaine, too, has adverse effects on the developing fetus. The effect of drugs taken by the father before conception is not as well documented as for the pregnant woman taking drugs, but recent work has suggested that damage to the sperm and their genetic material may occur, with serious effects on the embryo (Lester, Latasse, & Seifer, 1998).

BIOLOGICAL CHANGES
ACROSS THE LIFE SPAN

From the time of birth (the neonatal period) until the child begins to reach puberty, circulating levels of gonadal hormones are very low, reproductive organs are undeveloped, and males and females differ little in general appearance. Although the sexual organs are immature, the adrenal glands of infant girls begin to produce small amounts of estrogen and the undeveloped testes of males produce small amounts of testosterone.

Puberty

By the time the child reaches 6 or 7 years of age, she or he is well aware of the anatomical differences between boys and girls and most probably between the mother and father. Children soon become aware of intimacy and privacy and usually develop a sense of modesty about exposing their bodies. Subsequently,

children are likely to engage in sexual exploration to learn more about these differences.

Puberty represents a period of transition between childhood and adulthood during which an adolescent growth spurt takes place, secondary sex characteristics develop, and fertility is achieved. Puberty is also the time when there is an increase in hormones, often a sudden increase. As puberty approaches, the ovaries begin to function and the testes increase functioning. The adrenal cortex also starts to enlarge and increases its output of steroids, which include the sex hormones. As hormone levels increase, the concentrations in the two sexes begin to differ (Hoyenga & Hoyenga, 1993; Pinel, 1993, 2003). Puberty begins in girls between 8 and 13 years and between 9.5 and 13.5 years in boys (McAnulty & Burnette, 2004).

In pubertal females, estrogen levels rise and feminization takes place. Estrogen levels increase to about eight times their level in childhood, along with an increase in progesterone, which help the breasts to develop and the uterus to reach its adult size. The hips and thighs begin to accumulate fat to produce the typical female shape. The ovaries also produce some androgen (testosterone), which results in the growth of pubic and underarm hair and in some cases acne. The first indication that puberty has started is the growth spurt and the beginning of breast development, which will continue for several years. Breast growth can begin as early as 8 years of age or as late as 13 years of age. The appearance of pubic hair becomes noticeable shortly after the breasts begin to grow. During this same time, the uterus begins to enlarge and the vagina lengthens. The first menstruation, the *menarche,* occurs as the breasts become fully developed and after the peak growth spurt. Although the menarche is the most obvious indication of sexual maturation, it actually occurs several years after puberty begins. Yet, it presents a dramatic change in the female in contrast to the male, for which there is no single and dramatic sign to indicate when his sperm are viable or that he is now fertile. A girl's awareness of her bodily changes is often accompanied by strong emotional and psychological reactions, especially as she recognizes the fact that she will have a menstrual period on a monthly basis and that she is now fertile. Earlier in the twentieth century, the age at menarche was almost 16 years, but this has gradually decreased. Nutrition, heredity, socioeconomic conditions, family size, and psychological factors all may influence the age at which the first menstruation occurs It can vary from as early as 8 years to as old as 16 or later, again with differences in ethnic and minority groups (Basow, 1986; Beal, 1994; Hoyenga & Hoyenga, 1993; Marshall & Tanner, 1969; Masters et al., 1995; Pinel, 1993).

In pubertal males, androgen hormone levels rise to almost 18 times what they were during childhood; however, the adolescent growth spurt and masculinization begin some two years later than feminization for girls. The first change seen in the male is the growth of the testes, then of the penis and the accessory male sex organs: the prostate, seminal vesicles, and epididymis. The increase in androgen levels results in the development of muscle tissue and body hair. Boys' estrogen levels also increase and in some cases lead to breast enlargement. Although usually transient, it is an embarrassing condition for a young boy, and he may be subjected to much ridicule. This is commonly followed by a growth spurt, with the development of pubic and facial hair as well as underarm hair. Boys' sweat glands become active and their voices deepen. One certain indication of puberty is the sexual interest that boys begin to show. As puberty proceeds, boys begin to have frequent erections, thoughts about sex, "wet dreams," and their first ejaculations. This is the phase when boys may show a renewed interest in masturbating. Boys have different emotional and psychological responses to their first ejaculation and the realization that they are now fertile. Boys generally begin to show genital development at an average of 11.6 years and reach adult size at about 14.9 years (Beal, 1994; Carroll & Wolpe, 1996; Doyle, 1989; Masters et al., 1995; Pinel, 1993).

The developmental changes that take place during puberty are seen in Figure 4.6. The mature reproductive systems of the female and male are shown in Figures 4.7 and 4.8.

Menstruation and the Menstrual Cycle

The **menstrual cycle** averages about 28 days, but can range from 15 to 45 days. The cycle is usually set with the girl's first menstruation. The human female at birth

has about 400,000 primary follicles in her ovaries. The female reproductive system is shown in Figure 4.7 and can be compared with the male reproductive system in Figure 4.8. As described earlier, each follicle contains an egg or ovum. With each menstrual cycle, an ovum is released into the Fallopian tube from the ovary and begins its trip down the Fallopian tube for possible fertilization and implantation in the uterus.

The menstrual cycle is divided into four phases. The **follicular phase** is the initial phase, beginning after the last menstrual period has ended. It lasts from about 6 to 13 or 14 days. During this phase, estrogen released from the ovaries stimulates the regrowth of the *endometrium,* the inner layer of the uterus, which has diminished after the last menstrual period. At the same time, the follicles in the ovary begin to ripen with the next ovum to be released.

In the **ovulation phase,** the second phase, the follicle matures and swells. This phase ends when the follicle ruptures, releasing the ovum. During the third phase, the **luteal phase,** a group of cells, the *corpus luteum,* forms in the space that previously held the now-ruptured follicle. For the next 10 to 12 days, the corpus luteum, a small pouchlike gland, secretes additional estrogen and progesterone via stimulation by the hypothalamus. These hormones act to increase the growth of the endometrium in the uterus and to improve the blood supply so that, if the ovum is fertilized, the uterus will be prepared to implant and nourish a fertilized egg. If within this time the ovum is not fertilized, the continued high levels of progesterone and estrogen are a signal to the hypothalamus to decrease production of hormones. When this occurs, the corpus luteum begins to degenerate, and about 2 days before the end of the normal menstrual cycle, estrogen and progesterone levels decrease rapidly and the luteal phase ends.

The fourth and final phase of the cycle is the **menstrual phase.** During this phase, the endometrial cells lining the uterus shrink and slough off. The uterus contracts in order to expel the dead tissue along with blood, which passes from the uterine cavity through the cervix into the vagina. It is these contractions that cause menstrual cramps, which for some women become extremely painful. Other possible effects of the menstrual cycle, such as PMS (premen-

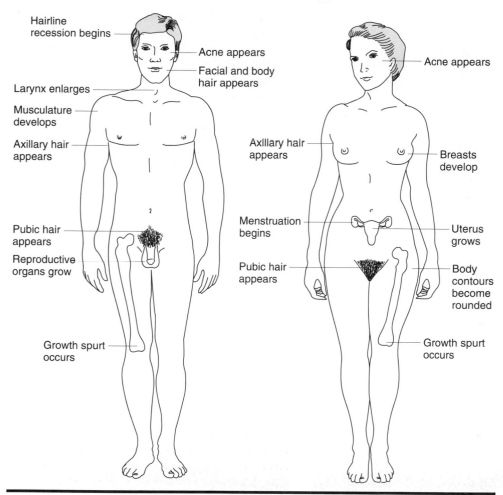

FIGURE 4.6 Changes Occurring in Males and Females during Puberty
Source: Biopsychology (4th ed.), by John P. J. Pinel, 2000, Boston: Allyn and Bacon. Copyright © 2000 by Pearson Education. Reprinted by permission of the publisher.

strual syndrome), are discussed in Chapter 13. The menstrual flow is known as *menses,* which lasts from about 3 to 7 days. The first day is known as Day 1 of the cycle, which begins after the menstrual cycle ends. The follicular phase begins again and the cycle is repeated (Carroll & Wolpe, 1996; Hoyenga & Hoyenga, 1993; Hyde, 1996). The phases of the menstrual cycle and hormonal changes are shown in Figure 4.9.

Thus far in this chapter, we have described the process of ovulation, fertilization, conception, and gestation. The next area we explore is the process of menopause, which marks the termination of the reproductive life of the female.

Menopause

Just as the age of menarche has decreased, the age of menopause has increased, making the reproductive range of women much longer than it had been. In the last century, menopause started in a woman's middle forties, but now the age has increased into the late forties or early fifties (Carroll & Wolpe, 1996).

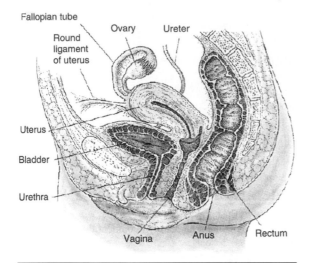

FIGURE 4.7   The Female Reproductive System
This cross-section locates many of the internal sex organs that compose the female reproductive system. Note that the uterus is normally tipped forward.
Source: From *Human Sexuality in a World of Diversity* (3e, p. 65), by S. A. Rathus, J. S. Nevid, and L. Fichner-Rathus, 1997, Boston: Allyn and Bacon. Copyright © 1997 by Pearson Education. Reprinted by permission of the publisher.

The term **menopause** refers to the period in which menstruation gradually ends, most commonly between 46 and 50 years of age (Rathus, Nevid, & Fichner-Rathus, 1998). For the woman, this interval symbolizes a gradual passage from being able to reproduce to becoming infertile. During menopause, estrogen production gradually declines, resulting in the cessation of menstruation. As the ovaries age, they cannot respond to stimulation from the anterior pituitary gland to produce estrogen and progesterone. Often, one of the first signs of menopause is irregular menstrual cycles. Excessive bleeding during a cycle may also occur. A woman may have amenorrhea (lack of a cycle) for several months, followed by one or more cycles, but then the menstrual flow gradually ends. Menstruation usually does not stop suddenly, but gradually wanes. Menopause is considered to have occurred when a year has passed without a menstrual cycle.

As estrogen levels decrease, often fluctuating in the early stages of menopause, the primary sex organs are affected. The clitoris and labia become smaller. Due to the lack of estrogen, the vaginal wall is al-
tered, and the vagina often becomes dry and can cause painful intercourse. The ovaries and uterus also begin to undergo changes. Decreased estrogen production also affects the secondary sex characteristics: a decrease in hair on the head and in the pubic area, loss of tone in the breasts, and sometimes the appearance of hair on the upper lip and chin. Wrinkling of the skin may also begin. One of the most important changes is the loss of bone density, resulting in **osteoporosis.** The aging woman with increasingly brittle bones is at a heightened risk for fracture of the hip and vertebrae. A full discussion of osteoporosis is given in Chapter 14.

The age at which menopause occurs and the symptoms experienced throughout this transition period vary greatly from woman to woman. Even though the ovaries stop producing progesterone and all but a small amount of estrogen, the adrenal glands continue to produce various amounts of these hormones. In many women, the vacillation of hormone levels causes *hot flashes.* Hot flashes are the most common symptom, affecting about 75 percent of women. The typical hot flash is defined by women as a transient sensation of flushing, sweating, and heat. These sensations are often accompanied by palpitations of the heart and anxiety and can be followed by chills. The terms *hot flash, flush,* and *night sweat* are all used to describe the same symptoms. Symptoms may occur weekly or every few hours. They may last a few seconds to several minutes. Because hot flashes tend to occur more often during the night, women complain of being awakened suddenly and suffer from insomnia. Hot flashes may also be accompanied by headaches. Some women experience mood and other emotional changes that become distressing. Chapter 11 describes some of these changes with a particular focus on psychological and social effects of menopause (Bates, 1981; Carroll & Wolpe, 1996; Kronenberg, 1990; Rathus, Nevid, & Fichner-Rathus, 1998).

Treatment of Symptoms.   The treatment of menopausal symptoms and concern about preventing heart disease and osteoporosis are ongoing issues. While the incidence of cardiovascular disease (CVD) in premenopausal women is significantly less than that of men, CVD increases markedly after menopause.

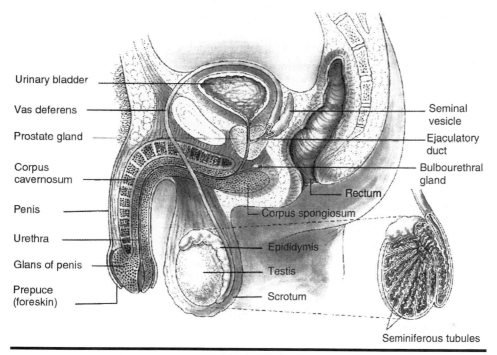

Urinary bladder

Vas deferens

Prostate gland

Corpus cavernosum

Penis

Urethra

Glans of penis

Prepuce (foreskin)

Seminal vesicle

Ejaculatory duct

Bulbourethral gland

Rectum

Corpus spongiosum

Epididymis

Testis

Scrotum

Seminiferous tubules

FIGURE 4.8   The Male Reproductive System
The external male sex organs including the penis and the scrotum.
Source: From *Human Sexuality in a World of Diversity* (3e, p. 103), by S. A. Rathus, J. S. Nevid, and L. Fichner–Rathus, 1997, Boston: Allyn and Bacon. Copyright © 1997 by Pearson Education. Reprinted by permission of the publisher.

This change has been attributed to the loss of estrogen, which protects women against cardiovascular disorders. The use of hormone replacement therapy (HRT) for these purposes has conflicted with the reported increased risk of cancer of the uterus and breast, and not only is HRT no protection for heart disease but also a suggestion exists that there is an increased risk of heart disease. The National Institutes of Health terminated estrogen and progesterone (used to prevent or minimize the development of uterine cancer) trials, but the estrogen alone study still continues. However, HRT has been shown to slow down the loss of bone density especially when combined with other factors such as nutrition and exercise (Galsworthy, 1994; Henderson, Stampfer et al., 1991; National Institutes of Health, 2003).

Thus, the question of taking estrogen must be considered and a risk–benefit ratio established. It seems to be all right for short-term use to relieve acute menopausal symptoms. Different women have different risk–benefit ratios depending on genetic and lifestyle factors. The decision to take HRT is a personal one that should be made with a physician. There is continuing work by many pharmaceutical companies to develop new drugs and treatments to replace estrogen and reduce the risk of uterine and breast cancer. The drug Evista is one such replacement. It is reported to prevent bone loss and also work as estrogen does to decrease cholesterol. This drug apparently carries no risk for cancer of the uterus and breast, and it may be able to be used by women either at risk for breast cancer or who have had breast cancer. The drugs Fosomax, Actonel, and others are now used extensively by postmenopausal women and women with osteoporosis to reduce bone loss and increase bone density. Other drugs, such as salmon calcitonin (Miacalcin) administered nasally, can also reduce bone loss. Any of these drugs must

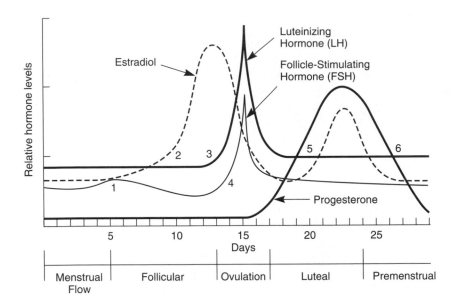

Phases of the human menstrual cycle

1. In response to an increase in FSH, small spheres of cells called ovarian follicles begin to grow around individual egg cells (ova).

2. The follicles begin to release estrogens such as estradiol.

3. The estrogens stimulate the hypothalamus to increase the release of LH and FSH from the anterior pituitary.

4. In response to the LH surge, one of the follicles ruptures and releases its ovum.

5. The ruptured follicle under the influence of LH develops into a corpus luteum (yellow body) and begins to release progesterone, which prepares the lining of the uterus for the implantation of a fertilized ovum.

6. Meanwhile, the ovum is moved into the Fallopian tube by the rowing action of ciliated cells. If the ovum is not fertilized, progesterone and estradiol levels fall, and the walls of the uterus are sloughed off as menstrual flow and the cycle begins once again.

FIGURE 4.9 Hormones during the Menstrual Cycle

Source: Biopsychology (2nd ed.) (p. 63), by John P. J. Pinel, 1993, Boston: Allyn and Bacon. Copyright © 1993 by Pearson Education. Reprinted by permission of the publisher.

be taken under a physician's supervision and in the smallest effective dose for each patient.

Male Climacteric

In men, the pattern of aging and reproductive change is very different from that of women. There is no def-inite end to male fertility, no recognizable sign of its termination, as with the cessation of menstrual flow during menopause. Sperm production decreases after 40 years, but men can still be fertile into their eight-ies. And, although testosterone levels decrease after age 55, there is no rapid and major drop in hormone levels as there is in women.

Only about 5 percent of men experience a condition called the *male climacteric,* sometimes erroneously referred to as *male menopause.* The male climacteric has been defined as a syndrome experienced by men over age 60, marked by some or all of the following symptoms: "weakness, tiredness, poor appetite, decreased sexual desire, reduction or loss of potency, irritability and impaired ability to concentrate" (Masters, Johnson, & Kolodny, 1994, p. 265). These symptoms occur because of decreased testosterone levels but can be improved or even reversed with testosterone treatment. On experiencing any of these symptoms, men may think that they are suffering from a serious disease, but on seeking a physician's help they can be treated successfully.

However, other problems are more common than the climacteric in aging men. One is the enlargement of the prostate gland, believed to be a consequence of decreasing hormone levels. Approximately 10 percent of men develop this problem at about 40 years of age, but the incidence increases to almost 50 percent by age 80. The enlarged prostate causes urinary problems ranging from difficulty in initiating urination to nocturnal frequency. Surgery can alleviate these symptoms by removal of the part of the enlarged gland that is pressing against the urethra. To date nonsurgical treatment has not been very successful. Prostate cancer is also a disease that tends to develop in men over age 50. Approximately 70 percent of men with prostate cancer are over age 65 and 80 percent of men who are 80 years or older have prostate cancer (McAnulty & Burnette, 2004). The incidence is higher in African American males, who are twice as likely to die from it than are White males. On the other hand, Hispanic American, American Indian, and Asian American men have a lower incidence of prostate cancer. Various treatments from surgery to female hormone treatment to radiation and implantation of radium seeds have been successful but carry risks. For example, surgery may result in permanent erectile dysfunction and often temporary incontinence. Radiation causes less of these effects. Some men forego any treatment and still live full and happy lives (McAnulty & Burnette, 2004).

Sexuality and Ageism

In Western cultures, sex has been considered an activity primarily for the young and healthy and not for the older or elderly couple. These myths do not hold up. The need for intimacy and pleasure generally found in sexual activity does not disappear when a woman reaches menopause or when a man's hormonal levels decrease. The biological changes described here do not automatically terminate sexual function, and aging alone does not diminish sexual interest in either males or females. However, in both men and women, aging, with its associated biological changes, does affect the nature of sexual function. The process of aging in both women and men is fraught with psychological consequences that vary across cultures. *Ageism,* prejudice against people because they are old, is a well-known phenomenon in the United States and other industrialized countries. In some other societies, aging is accompanied with high-level recognition and deference. In most Western cultures, ageism is a much more negative experience for women than for men. The psychological consequences of aging and the strategies for coping with these changes are described in Chapter 11.

SUMMARY

This chapter began with a history of the nurture versus nature theory from the 1970s that involved the sex reassignment of a baby and the consequences of this drastic procedure. Then we described the simplest elements of the reproductive process—the ovum and the sperm. We took you through the concepts of fertilization and conception, the development of the fetus, and the birth of the offspring. The risks and consequences at each stage of the reproductive process should serve to alert young as well as older people to the importance of prenatal education to assure the development of normal and healthy babies.

We have also described biological changes across the life span from the onset of puberty through the onset of the menstrual cycle to the end of the reproductive life of the female. We also included changes in men around their climacteric and concluded the chapter with problems of sexuality and ageism in both females and males.

In presenting the details of these processes, it should be evident that a vast amount of scientific and technological advances has become available and, as a result, has given us increased knowledge about the biology of sex and gender. Finally, an understanding of these ontological (developmental) processes early in this volume should assist the reader in relating to the chapters that follow.

KEY TERMS

Ablatio penis (p. 122)
Androgens (p. 129)
Capacitation (p. 127)
Chromosomes (p. 123)
Conception (p. 127)
Embryo (p. 127)
Estrogen (p. 129)
Fetal alcohol syndrome (p. 139)
Fetus (p. 127)
Follicular phase (p. 140)

Hormone (p. 129)
Luteal phase (p. 140)
Menopause (p. 142)
Menstrual cycle (p. 140)
Menstrual phase (p. 140)
Ovulation phase (p. 140)
Osteoporosis (p. 142)
Ovaries (p. 125)
Ovum (p. 124)
Progesterone (p. 129)

Pseudohermaphrodite (p. 136)
Sexual dimorphism (p. 124)
Sperm (p. 124)
Testes (p. 123)
Testosterone (p. 129)
Trimester (p. 127)
Uterus (p. 127)
Vagina (p. 127)
Zona pellucida (p. 127)
Zygote (p. 127)

DISCUSSION QUESTIONS

1. How do you feel about John Money's decision to reassign the sex of the 7-month-old baby, especially in light of the failure of his *nurture* not *nature* theory?

2. How do you think you would respond if "John" were your child and this terrible accident occurred?

3. How important is it for pregnant women to get prenatal education regarding prenatal drug exposure to make certain that their fetuses will not be exposed and risk abnormalities?

4. Do you think that intersexuals should be allowed to grow up without being subjected to a sex assignment without their consent? What possible psychological problems would they need to cope with under either circumstance?

5. As a female, what were your thoughts and feelings when your menstrual cycle began? When did you realize that you were then capable of becoming pregnant?

FURTHER READINGS

Boswell, J. (1980) *Christianity, social tolerance, and homosexuality: Gay people in western Europe from the beginning of the Christian era to the fourteenth century.* Chicago: University of Chicago Press.

Cadden, J. (1993) *The meanings of sex differences in the Middle Ages.* Cambridge, UK: Cambridge University Press.

Fausto-Sterling, A. (1992). *Myths of gender: Biological theories about women and men.* (2nd ed.). New York: Basic Books.

Tavris, C. (1992). *The mismeasure of women.* New York: Simon & Schuster.

CHAPTER 5

GROWING UP

What are little girls made of, made of?
What are little girls made of?
Sugar and spice and everything nice;
And that's what little girls are made of, made of.
—Mother Goose

Boys were listened to and shown how to do things, which would seem to
convey the message that what they have to say is important and that they
are mastering new skills. Girls, on the other hand, were treated gently,
and at the same time, with a lack of full attention and an imposing of
opinions and values. The gentle treatment would seem to convey the
message that they are fragile and docile.
—Phyllis Bronstein

In the older times it was seldom said to little girls, as it always has been
said to boys, that they ought to have some definite plan, while they were
children, what to be and do when they were grown up. There was usually
but one path open before them, to become good wives and housekeepers.
And the ambition of most girls was to follow their mothers' footsteps in
this direction: a natural and laudable ambition. But girls, as well as boys,
must often have been conscious of their own peculiar capabilities,—must
have desired to cultivate and make use of their individual powers.
—Lucy Larcom

The only trouble here is they won't let us study enough. They are so
afraid we shall break down and you know the reputation of the College is
at stake, for the question is, can girls get a college degree without
ruining their health?
—Ellen Henrietta Swallow Richards

. . . all children have creative power.
—Brenda Ueland

Creative minds have always been known to survive any kind of bad training.
—Anna Freud

How would I have turned out, I wonder sometimes, had I grown up in a house that stifled enterprise by imposing harsh and senseless discipline? Or in an atmosphere of overindulgence, in a household where there were no rules, no boundaries drawn? My mother certainly understood the importance of discipline, but she always explained why some things were not allowed. Above all, she tried to be fair and to be consistent.
—Jane Goodall

This chapter considers various issues pertaining to the development of gender roles in childhood and adolescence. Girls' development may usefully be viewed separately from boys' development because girls face distinct challenges during the course of their childhoods (see Box 5.1).

Gender-role and personality development are described in this chapter in the context of several psychological paradigms, including psychoanalytic, social learning, and cognitive-developmental theories. Distinctions between a feminine and masculine sense of morality are highlighted, and theories proposed by Freud, Kohlberg, and Gilligan are contrasted. Freudian theory links children's moral capacity to their development of a superego at the resolution of the Oedipal conflict. Kohlberg elucidates a developmental series of moral reasoning stages that is hierarchical in nature and based on research with only male

BOX 5.1

The Wonder (and Worry) Years

There may be no such thing as *child* development anymore. Instead, researchers are now studying each gender's development separately and discovering that boys and girls face very different sorts of challenges. Here is a rough guide to the major phases in their development.

	GIRLS	BOYS
0–3 years	Girls are born with a higher proportion of nerve cells to process information. More brain regions are involved in language production and recognition.	At birth, boys have brains that are 5 percent larger than girls' (size doesn't affect intelligence) *and* proportionately larger bodies—disparities that increase with age.
4–6 years	Girls are well suited to school. They are calm, get along with others, pick up on social cues, and reading and writing come easily to them.	The start of school is a tough time as boys must curb aggressive impulses. They lag behind girls in reading skills, and hyperactivity may be a problem.
7–10 years	Very good years for girls. On average, they outperform boys at school, excelling in verbal skills while holding their own in math.	While good at gross motor skills, boys trail girls in finer control. Many of the best students, but also nearly all of the poorest ones, are boys.
11–13 years	The start of puberty and girls' most vulnerable time. Many experience depression; as many as 15 percent may try to kill themselves.	A mixed bag. Dropout rates begin to climb, but good students start pulling ahead of girls in math skills and catching up some in verbal ones.
14–16 years	Eating disorders are a major concern. Although anorexia can manifest itself as early as 8, it typically afflicts girls starting at 11 or 12; bulimia at 15.	Entering adolescence, boys hit another rough patch. Indulging in drugs, alcohol, and aggressive behavior are common forms of rebellion.

Source: From "Boys Will Be Boys," by B. Kantrowitz and B. Kalb, 1998, May 11, *Newsweek,* pp. 54–60.

children. Gilligan, on the other hand, describes two different styles of moral reasoning adopted by girls and boys that emerge in the context of their differential upbringing. We also consider evolutionary psychology's concept of gender-role development. In addition, the chapter illustrates prevailing images of femininity and masculinity in Western society. These gender representation stereotypes play an influential role in shaping young children's attitudes and emerging gender identity formation. Next, the chapter examines additional forces influencing gender role development, beginning with parenting and prenatal experiences, and continuing with socialization aspects such as language, play, media, school, and peers. The increase in biological and social distinctions between the sexes that emerge during puberty and adolescence is discussed. Finally, the chapter will examine how demographic variables, specifically race and class, influence gender comparisons.

EXPECTATIONS AND GENDER ROLES

When American couples elect to find out the sex of their child during the mother's pregnancy, gender-role expectations and assignments may be set in motion even at this prenatal stage. Maccoby and Jacklin

(1974) reported that U.S. men prefer to have male children. Similarly, Jaccoma and Denmark (1974) noted that couples in the United States often hope that the firstborn child will be male, based on the assumption that if a female child is born afterward, she will have an older brother to look out for her (Denmark, Nielson, & Scholl, 1993; Jaccoma & Denmark, 1974). In contrast, a Canadian study (McDougall, 1999) indicated that all parents preferred at least one child of each sex; neither girls nor boys were preferred as first-born by either women or their husbands/partners. However, those women who did have a sex preference for firstborns preferred sons. In the United States, men tend to prefer sons to daughters as their firstborn child. They also prefer sons as the majority in three-child families and desire a son if only one child is born (Hamilton & Mayfield, 1999).

The preference for sons may be declining in North America, yet it is still strong in other parts of the world, especially in developing countries. Women and men both have a preference for sons according to surveys in Botswana, Tunisia, and Morocco (Campbell & Campbell, 1997; Obermeyer, 1996). Preference for boys is more extreme in Asian countries such as Taiwan and Korea. Reasons given include economic reasons, continuation of the family name, support of parents in old age, and companions for fathers (Sohoni, 1994). In Bangladesh, parents prefer sons to daughters (Nosaka, 2000). In India and China, the desire for sons is so intense that female fetuses are aborted or, even worse, female infants are killed, regardless of the fact that such acts are forbidden (Neft & Levine, 1997). In addition, in China, prenatal scans are utilized to thwart the birth of unwanted daughters and thus ensure the birth of sons. If indeed the scan determines that the fetus is female, the fetus is aborted. Consequently, in the past decade, China has had the largest gap between male and female births in the world, with a ratio of 144 to 100 (Eckholm, 2002). Regrettably, the sex of children can influence how parents perceive and interact with them. For instance, a Swedish study demonstrated that parents tended to play less with children who did not correspond with their preference (Stattin & Klackenberg-Larsson, 1991).

Often, as the time for delivery nears, preparations are made for the new infant, such as the selection of the nursery room color and décor and the purchase of gender-appropriate toys and clothing. Blue is the traditionally appropriate color for newborn boys' clothing, bedding, and room, and pink is the traditional color for girls. A survey of birth congratulatory cards by students of Maram Hallak, a Pace University adjunct professor, indicated that for newborn girls and newborn boys, "girl" cards are mostly pastel and pinkish colors, with pictures such as stuffed animals and flowers. On the other hand, "boy" cards contain darker colors and images of trucks, cars, airplanes, and other vehicles (M. Hallak, personal communication, July 16, 2003). Furthermore, verbal messages of expressiveness such as sweetness and sharing are more prominent on girl than boy cards (Bridges, 1993). Gender stereotyping continues beyond infancy into childhood. Initially, children may receive soft, cuddly toys to play with that may vary according to their sex. For example, it is considered unusual for the growing female child to be given "male" toys such as footballs and trucks. In a study analyzing the maintenance of gender stereotypes in Halloween costumes, both female and male costumes contained a high proportion of hero costumes. Nonetheless, female costumes, for the most part, depicted beauty queens, princesses, and other archetypes of traditional femininity. Masculine costumes stressed the warrior theme of masculinity and were more likely to include villains, especially agents or symbols of death (Nelson, 2000). In children's artwork, stereotypes exist that "only girls use pink," "only boys draw wars," and "girls draw people and boys draw guns" (White, 1998).

Before the woman becomes pregnant, various strategies may be employed to influence the sex of the embryo. As we learned in Chapter 4, the mother's sex chromosome is consistently an X or "female" chromosome and the father's sex chromosome may be either a female X or a male Y chromosome. An XX chromosome pairing during fertilization and conception will initiate the process toward the development of a female embryo; an XY chromosome pairing will initiate the process toward male development.

In addition to the early beliefs and practices described in Chapter 4 to influence the sex of the offspring, current beliefs and practices may be based on more reliable scientific data. Women who conceive during times when their vaginal environments are strongly acidic are more likely to have girls, suggesting that a strongly acidic environment may weaken or be highly detrimental to the male Y chromosome (Rathus, 1988). Hyde and DeLamater (1999) also report that women who conceive during times when their vaginal environment is expected to be strongly acidic are more likely to produce girls. Timing of fertilization may also be a factor in determining the embryo's sex. Although the Y chromosome is faster, it does not endure as long as the X chromosome. Therefore, if fertilization takes place slightly before ovulation when the ovum (egg) is not completely mature, it is more likely that the embryo will be female. In this circumstance, the sperm must remain in the female's reproductive tract until the egg is fully mature, which increases the probability that the more enduring X chromosome will outlast the Y chromosome. However, if fertilization occurs right after ovulation when the ovum is fully mature, the greater speed of the Y chromosome may enable it to reach and fertilize the ovum before the X chromosome, making it more probable that the embryo will be a male (Nevid, Fichner-Rathus, & Rathus, 1995). Furthermore, age differences between wives and husbands may influence the sex of the firstborn child. Couples with large gaps in age, with husbands being older than their wives, tend to have firstborn sons. Alternatively, in couples with a small age difference, with wives being older than husbands, it is more likely for a daughter to be the firstborn child (Manning, 1998).

PSYCHOLOGICAL THEORIES ON GROWING UP

Three major psychological theories attempt to explain gender-role development: the *psychoanalytic* perspective, the *social learning* theory, and the *cognitive-developmental* approach.

Freud's *psychoanalytic theory* posits that children ultimately learn to adopt the female or male role through identification with the same-sex parent, passing through several fixed stages of psychosexual development. Female and male infants begin life in the oral stage of development. The mouth is the original erogenous zone, and babies derive nourishment and pleasure entirely from their oral experiences of sucking and feeding. Initially the mother serves as the love object for both girls and boys, and there is little psychological differentiation between the sexes. During the anal phase of development, emphasis is shifted away from the infant's feeding experiences involving the mouth, and toilet training assumes a prominent position. Throughout the oral and anal stages of development, girls and boys remain psychologically similar. The onset of the phallic stage during the preschool years ushers in the development of disparate gender roles. At this time, girls and boys discover that they are anatomically different, a revelation that is pivotal in the developing relationship with both parents. Boys discover that they have a penis and take great pride in this organ. Oedipal struggles ensue in which boys harbor sensual feelings for their mothers and resent their fathers as rivals in the competition for the mother's affection. To resolve the guilt inspired by these emotions and to mitigate the intense fear that their fathers will punish them with castration, boys abandon their mothers and identify with their fathers. The process of identification with the father involves internalizing the father's ideals, values, and behaviors and acquiring a masculine gender identity.

The experience of girls during the phallic stage is drastically different. When they discover they don't have a penis, girls grow angry with their mothers because they perceive themselves to have been castrated, and they develop penis envy. An Electra complex ensues in which girls develop sensual feelings toward their fathers and resent their mothers. Eventually acknowledging that identification with the father is hopeless, they accept their mother as a role model, but often with lingering ambivalence. Thus, children of both sexes develop images of gender that are largely based on the personalities of their parents.

This theory of development, while creative and innovative, is unscientific in nature and denigrates women. By emphasizing the presence or absence of a penis as the pivotal element of gender differentiation, Freud's model of psychosexual development inherently asserts the superiority of the male sex. From a Freudian perspective, latency is a phase of relative calm, when the drives recede into the background and the passions of infantile sexuality are repressed to permit space for concentrated attention to mastery of school and social situations outside of the family. Children during this period tend to defensively shun opposite-sex peers, partly as a means to avoid the (re)emergence of latent sexuality.

Prompted by physiological changes of puberty, the genital stage heralds the powerful reactivation of sexuality. Unlike earlier phases, however, adolescent sexuality entails the search for a nonincestuous love object. Of course, in a psychoanalytic view, derivatives of earliest relationships with parents will always impact mature object choice. For example, the new object may represent aspects of the original parent figure or may encompass opposite characteristics, representing a rebellion against the parent. From a traditional Freudian point of view, the goal of the genital stage is mature sexuality, defined as sexual intercourse, with the aim of reproduction. Contemporary psychoanalytic theory has expanded the acceptable sexual activities associated with mature sexuality. Freud's theory cannot be tested or verified as it applies to adolescents and adults (see Chapter 11).

Unlike the psychoanalytic approach, *social learning theory* emphasizes the power of the surrounding social environment in influencing children's development of gender images. Although this approach shares Freud's view that children internalize gender images through imitation of their parents, social learning theory proposes that others' reactions serve as the main motivation for internalizing these images. The principle of reinforcement states that reward after the performance of a specific behavior will increase the possibility that this behavior will be performed more frequently in the future. Behaviors followed by punishments will be subsequently abandoned. Relating to gender development, children are consequently rewarded for performing actions that are stereotypically associated with their sex. Hence, they are more likely to adopt gender-typed behaviors into their repertoire. Gender-inappropriate behaviors, which often elicit punishment and criticism from parents, are relinquished.

The concepts of imitation and observational learning are key to the paradigm of social learning theory. Children have a tendency to copy the behaviors they view others performing. They actively observe what other people are doing and may store up this information to guide them in the future. Therefore, according to this theory, children acquire gender roles by imitating and observing the behaviors of their same-sex parent. However, children may have their own conceptions about appropriate behavior for girls and boys; neither psychoanalytic nor social learning theory accounts for this possibility.

The *cognitive-developmental perspective* emphasizes the role of the child in her or his own socialization. Based on the model of cognitive development advanced by Piaget and Inhelder, children's shifting cognitive organization underlies their development of gender roles. Children learn their own *gender identity* at an early age and choose to form their own images of behaviors and traits appropriate to their sex. The concept of gender identity forms around 2 years of age. At this same time, girls and boys recognize their sex and begin to identify with their same-sex parent. However, gender remains a fluid construct in their minds, and they do not recognize the permanency of being female or male until *gender constancy* is achieved. Gender identity becomes a crucial aspect of personal identity once girls and boys realize that their sex is a fixed characteristic. Role models are a springboard for this process; eventually, children use gender as a classification principle and create schemas, or mental categories, organized in terms of gender. They impose structure on their world and actively choose to behave according to these gender-typed rules.

Like social learning theory, the cognitive-developmental view proposes that gender-role learning is a function of a general process in which children use cues from their social environment to form notions of gender-appropriate behavior. Thus, children seek out patterns and roles that dictate the functioning of females and males and follow these rules as a way to adapt to social demands (Kohlberg, 1966). The primary weakness of cognitive-developmental theory is that it is incomplete; it does not account for the entire process of gender-role socialization. Kohlberg's theory, for example, states that children desire to follow social rules in order to master the social environment, yet the theory fails to explain why these social rules are built around gender (Kohlberg, 1966).

In support of cognitive-developmental theory, a 1994 report states that knowledge about gender begins as early as the first year of infancy (Poulin-Dubois, Serbin, Kenyon, & Derbyshire). (See Bem's [1981] gender schema theory discussed later in this chapter.) At one year of age, infants can match voices with faces according to gender, at least for female stimuli. Because this knowledge about gender is based on the perceptual characteristics of each gender group, its development is likely to precede the development of knowledge about female- or male-typed activities and traits associated with each sex (Poulin-Dubois et al., 1994). Toddlers, especially boys, are more likely to comply with the demands of the same-sex parent. This may be because of perceived similarities with this parent (Power, McGrath, Hughes, & Manire, 1994). All theories are incomplete but each adds something to the explanation of gender-role development.

MORAL DEVELOPMENT

Moral development is another area in which misconceptions about gender exist. Despite the attention to gender differences in moral development, contemporary psychologists tend to be wary of overgeneralizations that foster misconception. Developmental theories positing gender differences may inadvertently promote unduly monolithic dichotomies. The moral development of females and males is always fluid and multidimensional, distinctions are far from pristine; contemporary theorists from most orientations thus lean toward a conceptualization of moral development that emphasizes greater androgyny and synthesis (Benjamin, 1988; Bernstein, 1993; Chodorow, 1989). Several noted researchers on child development have differentiated between the moral development of females and males. Four such scholars are Freud, Piaget, Kohlberg, and Gilligan.

Freud

According to Freudian theory (as noted earlier in this chapter), children resolve their Oedipal conflicts through identification with the same-sex parent, which results in the acquisition of the superego. The superego fills a self-judgmental function in the child and serves to promote the child's morality. Freud believed that the superego was less developed in girls, because

their identification with the same-sex parent was more ambivalent than that of boys. As a result, girls were assumed to have more vague conceptions of morality than boys did.

Freud concluded that females would not solve moral problems through a rational, impersonal set of rules based on society's values. Rather, they would base their reasoning on their feelings about the people involved and the particular situation. As we mentioned earlier, Freud's theories have been criticized for their unscientific nature and lack of empirical evidence, as well as their obvious gender bias. Gender differences in superego development have been much deliberated and debated, and may give rise to differing prevalence or manifestations of moral development among females and males. For the girl, Freud (1925) proposed that penis envy galvanizes a daughter to turn away from her mother and toward her father. But because the threat of punishment and castration is physically nonspecific and more nebulous, Freud reasoned that the ensuing weaker power of repressive forces resulted in a less well-developed superego in girls.

Contemporary Freudians have expanded and modified Freud's views. For example, Bernstein (1993) has noted that clinical evidence attests to the strength of the female superego. Bernstein has also pointed to the paradox that, throughout history, women have been the keepers of morality while men's role has been a duality of making the rules and being tacitly permitted to break them. Adultery may be seen as one instance of this pervasive double standard. Bernstein has attributed this outcome to two aspects of Freud's work. First, Freud chose a quality that tended to be ascribed to men, that is, firmness, as desirable for moral development. The allegedly firmer, more inflexible structure of the male superego was seen as a purely positive quality. However, as Bernstein has described, the flexibility characteristic of the female superego may be equally positive. Any attribute will have both positive and negative aspects. Second, Bernstein has asserted that Freud's insistence on the Oedipus complex as the core source of moral development is extremely problematic. Bernstein and others (see also Sagan, 1989) point to the pivotal, complex contributions of pre-Oedipal development to the superego structure of both females and males.

In general, contemporary psychoanalytic theory is inclined to understand the Oedipal phase and its reverberations in generally more metaphorical and relational terms, and to view female–male development and morality as perhaps at times specifically different but not better or worse (Greenberg & Mitchell, 1983; Kalb, 2002). Greenberg and Mitchell (1983) have pointed out that, despite its rootedness in drive theory, the Oedipal constellation is intrinsically relational in its embeddedness in the interpersonal (as well as intrapsychic) interaction among three participants. Each person's conscious and unconscious plays on the others, in a continually interpenetrating cycle of influence. Contemporary analysts of most orientations tend to place more weight than did Freud on the child's response to a real other, permitting greater reciprocal influence between the intrapsychic and the real, relational environment, including the gender contribution of each member of the relational milieu (Benjamin, 1998; Chodorow, 1978; Pine, 1990; Slochower, 1996).

Piaget

Piaget developed a theory of moral development derived largely from his theory of cognitive development. This theory involves two distinct stages of moral development. Piaget (1932) used males as his point of departure or as a normative model of moral development, and mostly assumed that his theory

would generalize to girls. The first stage, **morality of constraint** (or heteronomous morality), characterizes children's moral judgments until they are approximately 9 or 10 years of age. In this stage, children base their moral judgments on what is deemed appropriate by the adults surrounding them. These children tend to base moral judgments on objective consequences. They believe that rules are immutable and believe in imminent justice or natural retribution for wrongdoing (Piaget, 1932).

The second stage in Piaget's theory is **morality of cooperation** (or autonomous morality). Children in this stage base their moral judgments on intentions rather than consequences, moving from an objective to a subjective orientation. They regard rules as social conventions modifiable by majority wish and realize the foolishness of believing in imminent justice. Piaget believed that interactions with one's peers were crucial for moving from the first stage to the second (Piaget, 1932).

Kohlberg

Drawing on Piaget's theoretical framework, Kohlberg theorized that there were three distinct levels of moral development, each one characterized by two stages, as shown in Table 5.1. To develop his theory, Kohlberg gave children moral dilemmas in which several different choices were apparent. He classified the morality of the course of action selected by

TABLE 5.1   Kohlberg's Stages of Moral Development

STAGE	BASIS OF MORAL REASONING
Preconventional Level	
Stage 1: Punishment and Obedience Orientation	Consequences of actions
Stage 2: Naïve Hedonistic Orientation	Obtaining rewards and personal interests
Conventional Level	
Stage 3: Good Boy–Good Girl Orientation	Gaining others' approval
Stage 4: Social-Order-Maintaining Orientation	Conforming to society's rules
Postconventional Level	
Stage 5: Social Contract/Legalistic Orientation	Balancing the value of community rights and individual rights
Stage 6: Universal Ethical Principle Orientation	Respect for universal human rights

the children based on the reasons given for their decisions.

In the first level of moral development, **preconventional reasoning,** children base moral decisions on the consequences of their actions. Rewards and punishments signal whether a behavior is good or bad. Stage 1 is called the punishment and obedience orientation because it emphasizes children's unswerving acceptance of the rule of authority. Children adopt the moral prescriptions of authority as their own and do not perceive the possibility of other perspectives. In Stage 2, the naïve hedonistic orientation, children have developed the capacity to recognize the existence of alternative points of view and base moral decisions on maximizing their own rewards and self-interest (Kohlberg, 1976).

At the second level of moral development, **conventional reasoning,** individuals abide by internal moral standards that are based entirely on those of parents and/or society. Stage 3 has been termed the good boy–good girl orientation. In this stage, individuals are apt to uphold social norms and seek approval from others whom they know personally. In Stage 4, the social-order-maintaining orientation, individuals incorporate the perspective of unknown people when making moral decisions. They believe that the laws and rules of society are wholly applicable to all members of society (Kohlberg, 1976).

Some individuals achieve the highest level of moral development, **postconventional reasoning,** in adolescence or early adulthood. However, most individuals do not reach this point. At this level, morality is completely internalized and based on abstract principles and values. Individuals in Stage 5, the social contract/legalistic orientation, believe that the rule system of society represents only one possible system of social order. They perceive inconsistencies between the rights and values of individuals and the rules of law that govern them. Hence, moral reasoning considers community rights versus individual rights. Kohlberg's highest stage of moral development, Stage 6, is termed the universal ethical principle orientation. In this stage, individuals have developed a moral standard based on universal human rights that sometimes transcend the laws of society. They utilize ethical standards to guide them in making moral decisions (Kohlberg, 1976).

Limitations of Kohlberg's theory were that his studies were conducted largely with boys as participants and the stimulus materials were male oriented. Not surprisingly, he found that only males achieved the highest level of moral development. Because Kohlberg's results found gender differences favoring men, psychologists found Kohlberg's methods and results flawed. Kohlberg's student, Carol Gilligan, conducted studies that resulted in a more gender-fair, if problematic, theory of moral development.

Gilligan

Although Kohlberg developed his theory by presenting children of various ages with hypothetical dilemmas, Gilligan felt that this experiment limited the criteria for judgment of children's morality level to their use of abstract, detached justice. Using Kohlberg's scales, women typically scored at Stage 3 of development (Gilligan, 1982), at which morality is experienced as shared, conventional, socially/interpersonally agreed upon, and corresponds to pleasing others and being helpful. In Stage 4, rules supersede relationships. In Stages 5 and 6, universal ideals of justice are paramount. Thus, higher levels of morality are equated with deductive reasoning—objective, nonemotional though independent, individual, noninterpersonal mental processes—and the differentiation between morality and law (Kohlberg, 1981). Traditionally, female modes of morality are thus relegated to a position of inferiority by Kohlberg's standards. Gilligan termed Kohlberg's version of morality the *justice perspective* because it focused on contractual obligations and principles of reciprocity. She proposed that other moral concerns and values exist, such as care, compassion, and concern for others (Gilligan, 1982). Gilligan has given voice to the paradox that traditionally cultivated female traits, such as nurturance and relatedness, are not valued as exemplary morality in Western culture. She has posited that assertion and autonomy, typically thought of as male strengths, perpetuate a biased value system and a version of morality that emphasizes rules, objective reason, and independence over emotion, connectedness, and interdependence. This "care perspective" highlights the significance of sustaining interpersonal relationships. Moral decisions are made on the basis of maintaining personal relationships and fostering sensitivity to the needs of others. Gilligan linked the two different conceptions of morality to the distinct patterns of psychological development experienced by females and males. In noting that women are most often the primary caregivers to children, Gilligan, following Chodorow (1978) and others, supplants Freud's, Piaget's, and Kohlberg's belief of women's inferior morality with her view that females' pre-Oedipal experience of relationship and identification with their mother's nurturer role results in their greater capacity for empathy and relatedness. Because Gilligan believed female development centers on attachment to the mother, she posited that women would utilize the care perspective when making moral decisions. Conversely, men's more objective, detached morality grows out of their experience of disidentification and separation from their mothers. Thus, male development emphasizes independence and separation from the mother. Hence, the justice perspective is more aligned with their developmental experience.

In place of presenting children with hypothetical dilemmas, Gilligan and her colleagues asked them (both females and males) to describe an actual moral dilemma that they had confronted at some point. The research found that females, more than males, tended to discuss issues of trust, friendship, and concern for others (Gilligan, 1982).

In sum, Gilligan and her colleagues found that females' moral dilemmas tended to emphasize care, whereas males' moral dilemmas tended to emphasize fairness and justice (Gilligan & Attanucci, 1988). However, subsequent studies suggest that these differences more often reflect the kinds of problems actually experienced by females and males rather than differences in their own personal value systems.

Cosse (1992) infers from Gilligan's work that the female developmental pathway is based on interpersonal, empathetic relatedness. Female morality in adolescence and beyond is guided by an empathetic understanding of person, context, and situation. Males, on the other hand, follow a pathway that leads to their personal autonomy. They follow an internalized set of rules that is applicable in all situations. In early adulthood, females and males are confronted with the task of integrating these pathways for a complete morality.

Gilligan's perspective on morality is an important critique of Kohlberg's theory because it exposes the bias against women implicit in this theory. Gilligan believes that these two paths to morality are different, but equal, and that there is nothing inherently better or worse in either approach to making moral judgments. Her theory of morality gives a positive view of characteristics that have been continually disparaged by placing value on interpersonal attachment and relationships. All of these attributes—caring, relationships, and concern for others' feelings—were previously devalued because they were thought to interfere with the male attributes of logic and reason.

However, we must exercise some caution in accepting Gilligan's perspective. This theory suggests that women and men display very different types of moral thinking, with women emphasizing the care perspective and men the justice perspective. However, Jaffee and Hyde (2000) found that both women and men were prone to using a combination of the justice and care perspectives in moral decision-making processes. In addition, Gilligan's claim that Kohlberg's theory does not adequately speak to women may have been premature, as more recent studies of his theory indicate that women and men score at about the same moral level.

Recently, a similar gender predisposition in moral judgment has been established cross-culturally. In a study of the moral reasoning of Mexican and Anglo American college students, between the ages of 18 and 25 years old, it was found that in terms of care, females scored higher than males and Mexican Americans scored higher than Anglo Americans. (Gump, 2000). Interestingly, no differences were found in the justice perspective. Furthermore, another study on moral reasoning in African Americans demonstrated that, with regard to dating, the majority of both females and males offered more responses from the justice standpoint (Weisz, 2003). However, empirical support for Gilligan's conceptualization of moral development is inconsistent. Additional research is needed to determine whether females and males reason differently about moral dilemmas.

Gilligan has recently written a book (2002) on pleasure. Girls cloak themselves in self-sacrificing femininity and boys hide behind disconnection, according to Gilligan. Both are essentially dishonest and preclude authentic joy and pleasure.

IMAGES OF FEMININITY AND MASCULINITY

As young children develop socially and cognitively, their images of gender take on a more complex form. Very early on, girls' identification with a nurturer who is typically of the same sex promotes the development of a high degree of nurturance, relatedness, and more permeable boundaries. In contrast, boys traditionally have been seen to need to disidentify with their female caretakers, resulting in a pull toward autonomy, power, and greater separation–individuation.

It is possible that young children's gender identification will prove to be dysfunctional, as in the case of **gender identity disorder** (GID). Children who are diagnosed with GID typically display an array of marked cross-gender role behaviors and often express the wish to belong to the other sex. These children may feel an aversion to or actively avoid gender-role behaviors associated with their own sex. Children with GID show both affective and cognitive gender confusion (Zucker et al., 1993). It has been reported that children with GID have an inherited predisposition for affective disorder. This predisposition may be manifested in early childhood with a tendency to display states of anxiety. For example, young boys with GID tend to display shy and inhibited behavior and have an aversion to rough and aggressive play (Coates, 1995).

GID tends to decrease with age. Apparently, children become less inclined to evaluate their own sex negatively or ambivalently as they mature. This may merely reflect a growing adherence to conventional gender stereotypes. It could also be a manifestation of achievement of concrete operational thought, enabling the children to appreciate the invariant nature of gender (Zucker et al., 1993).

Children's personal gender-role orientation may increase or decrease in flexibility in middle childhood and adolescence, depending on several factors. Girls tend to be more flexible than boys in their preferences for engaging in gender-typical or gender-atypical behavior as well as in their standards for the behavior of others. It often seems more acceptable (to both parents and peers) for girls to play baseball or dress like "tomboys" than it is for boys to play with dolls or paint their nails. Young boys are more likely to present themselves as sex typed when in front of their peers as opposed to when alone (Banerjee, 2000). Children tend to view their social environment in more rigid terms than adolescents do. In both girls and boys, flexibility of gender roles for both themselves and others increases from middle childhood to adolescence, perhaps because of the change in perceived flexibility of the child's social environment. One study conducted on a kibbutz in Israel showed that adolescent females expressed more liberal attitudes regarding gender roles than did adolescent boys (Kulik, 1998). A study carried out in Egypt, a society with extremely differentiated roles for women and men, reported that neither girls nor boys conveyed egalitarian attitudes regarding gender roles. However, girls were significantly more likely to articulate less traditional opinions than boys (Mensch, 2003). In general, the degree of gender-role flexibility exhibited by children and adolescents represents complex developmental and socialization processes (Katz & Ksansnak, 1994).

Children's images of gender play an important role in such areas as popularity in elementary school (Adler, Kless, & Adler, 1992; Powlishta, Serbin, Doyle, & White, 1994), conceptions of personal power (Dyson, 1994), self-esteem (Orr & Ben-Eliahu, 1993), and motivation and personal goals for adolescents (Gibbons et al., 1993). All of these areas are salient in terms of personality formation and healthy adjustment. In elementary school, children's peer cultures may be stratified by sex (Adler et al., 1992). In-group/out-group bias may play a role in the development of gender prejudice, because elementary school children tend to attribute positive traits to members of their own sex and negative traits to the other sex (Powlishta et al., 1994). The tendency to associate exclusively with classmates of one's own sex is a pervasive one. Children are especially attuned to this when there is a danger of being teased about one's secret romantic intentions in having a friend of the other sex (Adler et al., 1992; Dyson, 1994; Powlishta et al., 1994). In general, children's relationships with their peers have a strong influence on how children view the roles of females and males in society as well as how their self-concepts are developed (Witt, 2000).

This polarization of peer groups into female and male cliques may contribute to the generation and reinforcement of gender-role ideals for "feminine" and "masculine" behavior. An elementary school child's popularity may in fact be determined by her or his adherence to the students' gender-role ideals. However, this is more the case with boys than with girls, and conceptions of gender-typical behavior have actually become more flexible over the years. Whereas boys were once characterized as purely active and girls as passive, boys' and girls' behavior now incorporates elements of both genders (Adler et al., 1992). In an American study it was found that girls and boys were more similar than different. In spite of this, boys were still more liable than girls to engage in more controlling acts and domineering interactions in same-sex pairs, whereas girls were more likely than boys to use a combination of collaborative and informing acts (Leaper, 1999). Nevertheless, in some countries, such as India, traditional gender roles are still affirmed in the formal education setting. In primary schools, girls are given nurturing or domestic tasks with limited authority such as sweeping, cleaning, caring for others, and playing teacher. Alternatively, boys engage in more energetic, aggressive and physical activities, which require more strength and ability (Bhattacharjee, 1999). During latency, one reason children adhere to same-sex peer groups is because sexuality is repressed, and opposite-sex peers threaten the suppression that is needed to permit focus on cognitive/school growth and social development outside the family (with nonincestuous objects).

In a study of adolescents and college students, more males than females defined conventional masculine attributes as masculine, whereas more females than males viewed these traits as equally connected with masculinity and femininity. Conventional feminine and neutral attributes were judged similarly by both. Male self-esteem was significantly related to the men's conventional masculinity, whereas female self-esteem did not depend on any gender-related attributes. Both female and male self-esteem benefited from having a self-image that was not stereotypically feminine or masculine (Orr & Ben-Eliahu, 1993).

Findings from this study also suggest that gender differences in self-esteem do not emerge until young adulthood, when males tend to perceive themselves as more worthy than females. It appears, then, that masculinity is the stronger predictor of self-esteem, perhaps because society tends to reward masculine traits to a greater extent than feminine traits (Orr & Ben-Eliahu, 1993). In schools, girls' perceptions of competence and importance are undermined. Teachers encourage boys to be more assertive while girls are valued more for their appearance than for their accomplishments (Orenstein, 1994). Irvine (1986) points out that girls are less likely to speak up in class than boys, and this is reinforced by teachers calling on boys more often than girls. Oftentimes, girls respond to this gender bias by losing confidence in themselves and forming thoughts, feelings, and opinions of low self-esteem.

Adolescents' images of women's roles differ cross culturally. In the Philippines, Guatemala, and the United States, teenagers who were shown images of women working in an office and images of women preparing food described the women in terms of contentment or dissatisfaction. Filipino adolescents also described these women in terms of their apparent organization or disorganization. Guatemalan respondents described both women in terms of hope, hard work, betterment, and family. In the United States, on the other hand, the women were described in terms of their level of contentment and "niceness" (Gibbons et al., 1993).

It is difficult to identify a specific cultural variable resulting in these particular responses, especially in light of the commonality of many of the responses. In all three samples, the women cooking were described as mothers who were cooking for others. These women were perceived in terms of their relationships with other people. The women engaged in office work were also described similarly in all three samples; traits such as hardworking and wanting something more out of life were attributed to them by respondents from all three countries. However, teenagers from the United States and the Philippines described these women as yearning or dreaming.

Guatemalans connected this yearning to achieving goals or betterment of the self or the family. The adolescents' interpretations of the drawings may reflect not only their views of women and their roles but also images of their own futures (Gibbons et al., 1993).

In sum, images of gender and its requirements for appropriate behavior begin developing at a very young age and are continually reinforced by the child's surroundings.

CHILDREN'S ATTITUDES TOWARD FEMALES AND MALES

In addition to environmental factors, the gendered images and stereotypes employed by children are a function of their development, especially cognitive development (Biernat, 1991; Bigler & Liben, 1992; Liben & Signorella, 1993). Bem's **gender schema theory** suggests that children create knowledge structures that organize gender-related information in memory and are used to evaluate new information according to gender. Gender schemas might include knowledge about the physical appearances of females and males; their typical interests, activities, and personality traits; and expectations about how females and males will react to different situations (Bem, 1981).

Children's gender schemas may be more or less flexible, and this flexibility or rigidity will affect their attitudes toward both females and males. Younger children are more inclined to classify information into very strict gender categories. Stimuli labeled as female or male will have several different traits ascribed to it by these children based on this distinction alone (Biernat, 1991). In a study on children's evaluations of gender roles in a home context, children were provided with imagined scenarios in which their stereotypical knowledge was assessed. Most of the children displayed gender stereotypes, such as choosing a girl to help a mother with cooking and a boy to help a father with building (Schuette, 2000).

As children grow older, gender remains a cue for stereotyping a stimulus, but other cues are acknowledged as well. In addition, older children are cognitively capable of understanding that many characteristics are shared by both sexes and are not in the unique domain of one or the other. Paradoxically,

however, a bipolar view of femininity and masculinity seems to develop with age. Although older children are more open to the idea of a woman expressing masculine traits and a man expressing feminine ones, certain feminine and masculine features (e.g., physical characteristics) are deemed mutually exclusive by these children—more so than by their younger counterparts (Biernat, 1991).

Toy preference is an effective means of gauging children's attitudes toward gender. Bussey and Bandura (1992) found that children chose to play with so-called same-gender toys from as young as 30 months. Boys were more strongly opposed to cross-gender toys than girls were, sometimes attempting to have the stereotypic feminine objects removed rather than merely ignoring them. More recently, significant preferences for gender-stereotyped toys were found by the age of 18 months (Serbin, 2001). By 3 years of age, gender-typical toy choices are well established (Eisenberg, Martin, & Fables, 1996). These differences persist throughout childhood (Rodgers, Fagot, & Winebarger, 1998). Apparently, children adopt traditional patterns of gender-linked conduct from an early age. Society tends to perpetuate gender preferences for toys. For example, in toy stores, there is a clear gender-type separation for school-aged children in that there are specified boy and girl aisles. The girl aisles contain mostly dolls, household toys, makeup-kits, and jewelry, whereas the boy aisles are filled with sports toys, action figures, cars, and trucks (M. Hallak, personal communication, July 16, 2003). Despite these typical gender preferences, girls are more likely to play with nontraditionally feminine toys (e.g., transportation toys and sports equipment) than boys are to play with nontraditionally masculine toys (e.g., dolls) (Etaugh & Liss, 1992).

Frey and Ruble (1992) found a similar tendency among boys and girls; boys were more likely to restrict themselves to gender-typed toys—at times, even when the cross-gender toy was more attractive. Frey and Ruble suggest that society's attribution of greater power and competence to males may make girls more motivated than boys to adopt cross-gender behavior. It is also possible that girls' definition of gender-appropriate behavior expands to include gender-neutral as well as stereotypically feminine behavior, whereas boys define gender-appropriate behavior exclusively in terms of stereotypically masculine behavior (Frey & Ruble, 1992).

Although younger children do tend to be more rigid with regard to gender-role consistency, the degree of this rigidity varies with the individual. Children with more flexible norms about gender-role violation may choose a course of action based on factors other than gender, such as attractiveness (Lobel & Menashri, 1993). A preschooler's standards for gender-appropriate or inappropriate behavior are affected by the child's environment, specifically the parents' values as mediated by their surrounding culture. In a Canadian study, a gender-sorting task involving parents and children revealed a shift in the perceived function of some traditionally stereotyped toys. When parents played with girls, there was a greater flexibility in the categories of toys with which they played. Nevertheless, when parents played with boys, the majority of time was spent playing with masculine toys (Wood, 2002).

Fagot, Leinbach, and O'Boyle (1992) found that toddlers and preschoolers who demonstrated a more pronounced tendency to label nonhuman items (animals and objects) in gender-stereotyped ways generally had mothers who initiated gender-typical play more often, responded more positively to their children's gender-typed play, and initiated less other-gender play with them. In general, these mothers expressed more traditional attitudes concerning appropriate behavior for women and traditional roles within the family and rated their own personality as containing fewer other-gender traits. This factor may be partially responsible for determining a child's attitude toward gender and toward members of either sex who engage in cross-gender behavior.

Conversely, increased father participation in child rearing during the preschool and elementary school years was found to contribute to more nontraditional views regarding employment as well as less conservative expectations for child rearing. Adolescents tended to express conventional or less conventional attitudes toward the gender roles of their parents in keeping with the atmosphere in which they were raised (Williams, Radin, & Allegro, 1992). Unfortunately, it has been shown that paternal involvement in child rearing is conditional—ethnicity,

gender-role identity, and perceived skill at child care tasks all apparently influence the father's level of contribution. Specifically, African American ethnicity, androgynous gender role identity, and higher perceived mental ability predicted increased involvement (Sanderson, 2000).

Cross-Cultural Gender Attitudes in Children

In a more global sense, developing gender attitudes in children is a function of the culture in which they are raised. A study conducted in Canada focusing on South Asian immigrants found that South Asian communities and family structure remained male dominated, regardless of acculturation. Gender roles were preserved through segregation of males and females, control of social activities of girls, and arranged marriages. Furthermore, adolescent girls professed high social penalties connected to protest and dissent (Talbani, 2000). Alternatively, in Jamaica, female-headed households are prevalent, with women serving as both the primary economic provider and the child caretaker in the home. Possibly as a result of this, a tendency for a cultural preference for girls in Jamaica has been noted by researchers (Sargent & Harris, 1992).

Jamaican children of both sexes begin performing household chores at a young age, but boys are supervised much less closely than girls are. Parents express higher expectations for their daughters both academically and economically. In fact, parents' differing attitudes favoring female over male children may be reflected in sex differences in terms of health and growth (improved health and growth for female children), patterns of child abandonment (boys being more frequently abandoned than girls), and decisions of foster and adoptive parents (to adopt female rather than male children). Statistics in all of these areas parallel the Jamaican cultural preference for girls (Sargent & Harris, 1992).

Portuguese children were found to begin acquiring knowledge of gender stereotypes at age 5, and to continue developing this knowledge beyond age 11. Across all age levels, knowledge of gender stereotypes varied inversely with socioeconomic status, suggesting that Portuguese middle- and upper-class families place a greater emphasis on traditional gender roles. Like Brazilian, Venezuelan, and Chilean children, Portugese children, especially girls, tended to know more about the female stereotype than the male stereotype. In these countries, the female stereotype is reported to be more favorable than the male stereotype (Neto, Williams, & Widner, 1991). Therefore, knowledge of the preferred stereotype might come more readily.

In Botswana, on the other hand, women are not regarded as highly. Children of both sexes hold the attitude that women are more suited to domestic careers (e.g., housecleaner), or careers in aesthetics (e.g., hairdresser) and caregiving (e.g., nurse). Men, on the other hand, were rated as the best candidates for positions of leadership (e.g., mayor), in technology (e.g., engineer), and in academia (e.g., professor). Apparently, Botswanan children perceive "women's work" as less prestigious than "men's work." Unfortunately, the female children also viewed themselves as better suited for women's work (Mbawa, 1992).

Finally, in the United States, boys have been traditionally socialized to become future breadwinners for their families, whereas female socialization has involved preparation for domestic roles as wife and mother. Whereas personality and attractive appearance are seen as essential characteristics for females, males are usually encouraged to be achievement oriented, competitive, and aggressive. Although such priorities eventually have ramifications for career choices (a phenomenon strikingly similar to that of Botswana), change is happening toward more gender-fair attitudes (Denmark, Nielson, & Scholl, 1993). Correspondingly, in South Africa, a child-focused, child-guided grassroots movement called GEM (Girls Education Movement) was initiated in March 2003 by the parliament of the Republic of South Africa (http://gem.giv.za). This group has established specific goals and objectives in order to improve the quality of education for both girls and boys, prevent gender biases and the abuse of women, as well as create equal opportunities for women.

Nevertheless, there is evidence in other countries of a continuing gender bias. An Australian study found that the breadwinner role is still associated with the paternal figure (Whelan & Lally, 2002). As a rule,

parents openly encourage gender-stereotyped behavior in their children; for example, household chores may be assigned according to the child's sex (e.g., boys' taking out the garbage and girls' doing dishes). Such gender stereotyping impacts children's assessments of gender roles. In an American study focusing on gender roles in a home context, children were asked to assign helpers for parents in stereotypical activities. The majority of children opted for the stereotypically appropriate child to help the parent (e.g., the girl to help the mother with cooking and the boy to help the father with building) (Schuette, 2000). The assignment of gender-stereotyped chores may play a role in determining a child's household behavior in adulthood. In addition, children are influenced by their parents' roles in household tasks. However, the majority of U.S. parents make some nontraditional chore assignments (Lackey, 1989). Another study in the Unites States showed that the parental division of household labor when boys are very young has a positive effect on their involvement in household chores as adults (Cunningham, 2001).

Overall, attitudes toward gender-appropriate behavior tend to be differentiated among children worldwide, whether their bias is occasionally in favor of women or, more commonly the case, of men. These attitudes begin developing at a very early age and continue to affect individuals into adulthood, thus creating a culture in which one sex or the other has the upper hand. Such stereotypes are perpetuated most potently at the individual level within the child's own family.

PARENTING

In recent years it has become clear that parents do not bear as much responsibility for socialization into gender roles as was once thought. Other factors, such as the child's own need to feel like a girl or a boy and peer influence, may play a far more significant role in gender stereotyping. The media, schools, and even language all play a role in shaping the formation of children's gender schemata, as will be discussed in the next section of this chapter. Yet researchers maintain that parents do play a significant role in childhood gender socialization. Adults will often attribute dispositions to their children based on a number of factors, including logical inferences from the children's actual behavior, the parents' emotions, and preexisting beliefs influenced by class, culture, and personal values. In turn, these parental perspectives interact with the child's own perspective (Dix, 1993).

Many individual, cultural, and gender differences may stem from the way that adults understand the dispositions and competencies of their children. Subsequently, by expressing their views of the dispositions they attribute to their children, parents directly influence children's views of who they are and how they should act. Children feel motivated to conform to these acquired self-attributions and to the expectations implied by these dispositional labels (Dix, 1993).

The Baby X experiment (Seavey, Katz, & Zalk, 1975) pointed to a marked difference in graduate students' interaction with a female infant according to whether they were informed that the infant was a girl or a boy. Both female and male adults chose a gender-stereotyped toy (a Raggedy Ann doll) to interact with the 3-month-old infant when the child was described as female. Males had significantly less contact with the infant than did females in the no-gender-information condition. Even though the infant was female, 57 percent of the male students and 70 percent of the female students thought the baby was male in the no-name condition. The subjects readily found cues to support their gender guess. Thus, those who said the baby was a girl referred to the infant's softness and fragility.

When replicated with both a female and a male infant and using undergraduate students as research participants, stereotyped behavior regarding toy choice was even more pronounced (Sidorowicz & Lunney, 1980). In this study, toy choice was greatly influenced by gender label. When the female or male infant was reported to be a boy, the vast majority of participants chose a football to interact with the baby. In contrast, regardless of the infant's sex, a doll was the overwhelming choice when the infant was labeled with a female name. Attributions about the infant were similar to those in the earlier study in the gender-neutral condition. Clearly, adults' perception of infants' gender influences their interactions with the infant.

In general, parents tend to foster boys' autonomy and girls' dependence. Whereas boys are socialized to take a more active, mastery-oriented stance toward their environment, girls are discouraged from taking new risks and from mastering new situations on their own. For example, parents have been found to encourage and reward boys' involvement in physically active games requiring large motor coordination while steering girls toward calmer, safer activities (Rosen & Peterson, 1990). Parents play with girls and boys differently, tending to talk more with their daughters and engage in more active games with their sons. Parents also encourage gender-appropriate activities by providing children with gender-typed toys and clothing (Will, Self, & Datan, 1976). When interacting with their children, parents display a stronger tendency to assist girls with their endeavors, even when this help is not necessary. In addition, whereas boys are subtly encouraged to roam away from parental supervision, girls are discouraged from such independence-producing behavior. This is true even at the level that chores are assigned: boys are usually responsible for taking out the garbage and raking leaves; girls attend to indoor duties (Denmark, Nielson, & Scholl, 1993). Thus, parents support high levels of dependency in girls (Denmark, Nielsen, & Scholl, 1993; Rosen & Peterson, 1990).

Children often model their behavior after that of their parents. For example, household responsibilities relegated to one sex or the other in a particular family tend to be viewed as women's work or men's work by the children raised in that particular family. These perceptions are often distorted; for example, a child might assume that men are better drivers simply because the family's lifestyle has the father doing more of the driving.

Studies comparing the developmental outcomes of children reared in heterosexual homes and in homes with one or more lesbian parents suggest that, in large part, children in both homes progress similarly in major developmental categories (e.g., Patterson, 1992, 1994; Steckel, 1987). Interestingly, children in homes with one or more lesbian mothers appear to be less aggressive and more positive than children reared with heterosexual mothers (Steckel, 1987). Charlotte Patterson, who has done extensive work in this area, conducted a study in 1994 that compared grade school children living with either heterosexual or lesbian mothers on a number of dimensions. Results from this research indicate that children living with lesbian mothers expressed their feelings, both positive and negative, more often than did children in homes with heterosexual mothers. One interpretation may be that children who are in homes with lesbians as primary caregivers may be encouraged to recognize their affective states and to verbalize feelings and related experiences (Patterson, 1994).

Marital quality differentially affects parents' interactions with their daughters and sons. Fathers who are less satisfied with their marriage tend to behave and feel more globally negative toward their daughters, regardless of their daughters' behavior. Less satisfied married mothers are more likely to respond negatively to negative verbalizations from their sons. These mothers also negate their daughters when the daughters behave in an assertive manner inconsistent with a traditional feminine gender role (Kerig, Cowan, & Cowan, 1993).

Explanations proposed for these phenomena provide insight into the effect that parents might have on their children's gender-role socialization. It is possible that distressed mothers look to their daughters for emotional support, because nurturing is traditionally a feminine function. This family dynamic would have negative consequences for the daughter's relationship with her father. On the other hand, fathers may be more likely to transfer disappointment in a marriage on to a female child. This is probable because a father's role as husband tends to influence his role as father. A third suggestion is that because fathers usually withdraw emotionally from their wives in the face of marital distress, they may also withdraw from their daughters. Girls may develop an assertive and assiduous style to gain the attention of their emotionally distant fathers, which could have the unfortunate effect of fostering their fathers' further negativity toward them (Kerig et al., 1993).

Sons of parents who are lower in marital satisfaction not only may be passive observers of the reciprocity of negative affect taking place between their parents but also may become involved in, and socialized into, such interactions with their maritally dis-

tressed mothers. It is possible that this phenomenon provides a mechanism through which intergenerational transfer of marital dysfunction might take place. As for maritally dissatisfied mothers negating their daughters' assertive behavior, this tendency may reflect an attempt by these mothers to socialize their daughters into an interactional style that they themselves experience in the marital relationship (Kerig et al., 1993).

It is apparent that the emotional quality of the relationships between marital partners and their children affects parents' interaction styles with their daughters and sons. These differing interaction styles foster discrete notions in the child of the social roles of females and males. When the mothers' and fathers' feelings about their marital partners affects the quality of the parent–child relationship, the significance of gender in the development of the family system begins to emerge (Kerig et al., 1993).

Single Parenting

Many children are raised in single-parent households, either due to death of a parent, divorce, or other circumstances. The parent responsible for the primary care of these children is usually hardworking and devoted to the children's welfare. However, single-parent homes have their own set of ramifications for children's gender-role attitudes. As the absent parent is usually the father, and fathers tend to encourage gender-appropriate behavior more strongly than mothers do, one would expect that children raised in single-parent homes would display more androgynous behaviors.

Consistent with the above prediction, preschool-aged boys in female-headed households are typically less aggressive and less likely to engage in rough-and-tumble, stereotypically masculine play. This may result from single mothers' tendency to be more protective of their children than mothers with a partner in the home, and the lack of a father to balance out the mother's caution by encouraging the son's independence and risk taking. Lack of a male role model may be another reason for this tendency (Leaper, Smith, Sprague, & Schwartz, 1991).

However, some boys in this situation may develop an exaggerated masculine style to compensate for feelings of uncertainty about their gender identity. These boys tend to have difficulty establishing close relationships, depend excessively on the male peer group, rebel against the authority of adult males, and avoid anything perceived to be feminine (Biller, 1981). Indeed, Stevenson and Black's (1988) meta-analytic review found support for this tendency in the literature: Older boys in homes from which the male caretaker was absent tended to demonstrate more aggressive and other stereotypically masculine behavior. This may be a reason that some impoverished, single, African American mothers described their male children as significantly more difficult than female children (Jackson, 1993). This may be a function of boys' tending to be more active than girls and thus more difficult to socialize, especially when their mothers work full time. The characteristics enumerated here tend to preclude mothers' involvement with their own children. This may perpetuate a cycle in which many of these children, having suffered the emotional absence of a father and a mother, are unresponsive to their own children as adults. All impoverished families are potential candidates for this syndrome.

Girls, on the other hand, seem less directly influenced by father absence, possibly because the father is a less salient role model for them. However, in adolescence, girls from female-headed households may have some difficulty interacting comfortably with males. Although girls from homes with a widowed mother seem anxious and inept around males, girls from divorced homes act more sexually assertive. A possible explanation is that girls from widowed homes are less exposed to men. Girls from divorced homes, on the other hand, may be more exposed to men because their mothers are more likely to date. They may see their mothers interacting with these men in a flirtatious way and follow their example, generalizing this way of behaving as one in which to socialize with all males.

While mother absence results in the reversal of traditional gender roles in the home, having a father as the primary caregiver has less effect on children's gender-role behavior. A possible explanation for this is the greater likelihood for children living with their fathers to come into contact with a female *parent fig-*ure (either the child's own mother, a female relative, a nanny, or a baby-sitter) than for children living with their mothers to be exposed to a male parent figure and role model. Children living with their fathers tend to have a more balanced experience in terms of female and male adult figures.

In Williams, Radin, and Allegro's study (1992) of adolescents raised primarily by their fathers, increased father participation in child rearing contributed to more nontraditional gender views of parenting. However, assessments of a role-reversed parenting arrangement differed for girls and boys. Sons tended to see more advantages than disadvantages, stating that their relationship with their fathers was enhanced. Daughters, on the other hand, regretted missing the contact with their mothers that they felt they needed.

Parents of each sex have distinct qualities and values to offer to their children. The next section will explore some of the differences between women and men as parents and how this affects children.

Effects of Parents on Children

Several early studies showed that fathers tended to stereotype their children according to sex to a greater degree than mothers did (Maccoby & Jacklin, 1974). This was true as early as infancy, when the child did not yet display salient gender-typed traits. Fathers tended to view their newborn sons as "firmer, larger featured, better coordinated, more alert, stronger, and hardier," while describing newborn daughters as "softer, finer featured, more awkward, more inattentive, weaker, and more delicate" (Rubin, Provenzano, & Luria, 1974). This trend continued as their offspring developed into childhood.

Lewis (1972) analyzed the behavior of mothers and infants and found additional evidence that parents do change their behavior measurably as a function of the sex of the child. For six months or so, infant boys have more physical contact with their mothers than do infant girls, but by the time boys are 6 months old, this relationship reverses and girls receive more physical as well as nontactile contact.

Fathers may spend less time with their infants than mothers do, but father–infant interaction is more playful than mother–infant interaction (Clarke-Stewart, 1978; Parke, 1978). Fathers' play with infants tends to be more vigorous and physical than mothers' play. Mothers' play is often more intellectually oriented, possibly involving verbalization (e.g., nursery rhymes) and conventional games (e.g., peek-a-boo). Mothers are also more likely than fathers to use toys to stimulate their infants (Clarke-Stewart, 1978; Lamb, 1979; Parke, 1978).

Parents have been found to attend to, stimulate, and interact with infants of their own sex more than with infants of the other sex (Parke, 1978). This is especially true of fathers, who tend to make more trips to visit their male newborns in the hospital, engage their infant sons in more play, and display more physical affection to them (Belsky, 1979; Field, 1978; Lamb, 1979; Weinraub & Frankel, 1977). Mothers also display a tendency to imitate, talk to, and play with their infant daughters more than with their sons. The special interest parents show their same-sex offspring may enhance the parents' attractiveness to their children, making it more likely that the children will seek their same-sex parents out as companions and role models.

The extra stimulation that boys receive from their fathers may have important consequences for male development. Boys may reciprocate their fathers' interest and affection, which may be the reason that boys typically prefer interacting with their fathers rather than their mothers by their second birthday (Belsky, 1979; Lamb, 1979). Fathers also provide a special sort of stimulation for their sons, which teaches them competencies that they are unlikely to learn from others. Indeed, research has shown that infant boys who were fatherless showed less interest in manipulating novel objects than did boys from intact families (Parke, 1978). Moreover, in a study on the influence of father involvement and the functioning of children, the presence of a father was linked with better cognitive development and greater perceived competence by children (Dubowitz, 2001). Although girls benefit from interaction with their fathers, father absence is typically associated with more negative consequences in male than in female children. This may be partially explained by the lack of a father figure, but another reason might be the difficulty encountered by mothers attempting to discipline their sons singlehandedly.

Fathers' tendency to reinforce gender differences in their sons and daughters is especially pronounced in the area of physical activity. Fathers involve boys in more active and physical play than girls (Rosen & Peterson, 1990). Fathers are also more likely to reward girls for positive, compliant behavior and to reward boys for assertiveness (Kerig et al., 1993).

A strong relationship exists between boys' masculinity and their fathers' personalities, namely, that boys who are masculine have fathers who are both affectionate and powerful (Hetherington, 1967; Mussen & Rutherford, 1963; Payne & Mussen, 1956). But the converse does not hold true; there is very little evidence of a parallel relationship between mothers' personalities and their daughters' femininity. In fact, paternal personality characteristics actually tend to influence girls' gender typing more than maternal traits.

Both parents express different views of their daughters and of their sons, and treat them accordingly. Girls are viewed as more truthful, and parents relate to them with more physical closeness and warmth. Boys, on the other hand, are disciplined more harshly. Girls are attended to when they ask for help, whereas boys' attempts at assertiveness are reinforced by their parents (Fagot, Hagan, Leinbach, & Kronsberg, 1985; McDonald & Parke, 1986; Ross & Taylor, 1989).

In general, fathers see child care as the mother's primary responsibility and view their role as "helping out" and being the primary provider. They often use gender-specific excuses for spending less time with their children than their wives do, such as the fact that work keeps them away or that they are impatient with young children (LaRossa & LaRossa, 1981; McHale & Huston, 1985; McKee, 1982). Interestingly, fathers from the lower socioeconomic bracket tend to spend more time with their children than other fathers do (Cohen, 1998).

Despite the tendency for a father to spend less time with children, in the United States the father may play many roles in his family—that of provider, decision maker, nurturer, husband, and father (McAdoo, 1986). Contrary to popular belief, men can and often do fulfill their children's needs for emotional support and understanding. In fact, children in single-parent homes headed by fathers rate their fathers as more nurturing than children in two-parent homes rate either parent. Fathers feel they best express their love to their children by how well they take care of them, whereas children express their love by how well they cooperate and show deference to their fathers (Hanson, 1986).

It is clear that the father plays a highly salient role in a child's psychosexual development and sex typing, more so than the mother does. Johnson (1963, 1977) argues that while mothers treat their sons and daughters more alike than do fathers, fathers develop distinctly discrepant styles of interaction with their female and male children that lead the children to develop feminine and masculine traits. According to Johnson, fathers teach daughters to be feminine by interacting with them in a warmly indulgent, protective, and mildly flirtatious way. With sons, on the other hand, fathers act demanding and critical, insisting that the boys display traditionally masculine behaviors and shun feminine ones. The father socializes both girls and boys toward independence, but in different ways—boys toward instrumental competence within the male peer group and girls toward eventual establishment of an expressive role within a new family context.

Why do men perpetuate gender roles more ardently than do women? Some claim that it is because men are concerned with maintaining the power and status advantages they currently enjoy. Another explanation is that men are simply transmitting to others the stronger pressure that they themselves have experienced for conforming to the culturally prescribed male gender role.

However, besides parenting styles, other factors have an impact on gender differentiation. The next section will discuss the various socializing events that affect gender.

SOCIALIZING FORCES

Language

Most of an individual's relations with the social world are mediated by language, and the learning of language is one of the first and most important tasks facing a developing child. Children's development of gender identity and gender role may be inextricably bound up with the acquisition of language (Constantinople, 1979). The labels that children learn (e.g., boy, girl, man, woman, daddy, mommy) help them to form the categories around which they build a fundamental understanding of gender and to guide their thinking about this concept. For this reason, linguistic sexism can have a pervasive influence on children's developing gender identity.

Language is not neutral; it differentiates women from men. **Linguistic sexism** refers to the perpetuation and reinforcement of sexist ideology through the content of a language (Nilsen et al., 1977). In addition to separating women and men, the English language actually favors men, affording them greater power over women. Linguistic sexism in the English language takes one of three distinct forms: ignoring women, defining women, or deprecating women.

The English language tends to *ignore women* by extending male terms to refer to humans as a whole. For example, when talking about the human species, people still frequently refer to it as *man* or *mankind.* Yet girls and women make up close to 52 percent of the human race, making them the majority.

The use of *he* as a generic pronoun referring to both boys and girls and men and women usually results in the listener or reader imagining a male as the subject of the sentence (Cole, Hill, & Dayley, 1983). In fact, most of the antecedents to the pronoun *he* in textbooks refer only to men, not to men and women (Bertilson, Springer, & Fierke, 1982). It is only natural that children's exposure to this form of linguistic sexism would affect their image of their own sex as well as that of the other sex. In fact, according to Hyde (1984), most elementary school children have learned to think of males when they hear *he* in a gender-neutral context and do not know that *he* can refer to both males and females. Because they are exposed to a constant stream of information using the masculine gender as normative, they learn to think of the typical person as male. This is an important step toward the cultural assumption that the male is normative and the female atypical or deviant.

Society also tends, through language, to *define women* in terms of their relationship to men. For example, a woman is often referred to as so-and-so's wife, widow, or daughter. In addition, the frequency with which women give up their surnames for their husbands' names on marrying stems from the ancient patriarchal tradition of viewing a woman as her husband's possession. Changing one's name implies that the person is changing or losing some aspect of his or her identity. Finally, language *deprecates or devalues women* and has done so throughout history. Misogyny is pervasive in classical literature. In addition, when we note the number of words indicative of sexual promiscuity, we find well over 200 such words to describe a sexually active woman but just over 20 words to describe lustful men (Stanley, 1977). Even with parallel terms, the female counterpart of a male term often has a more negative connotation (e.g., bachelor–spinster, master–mistress, etc.).

Play and Competition

A strong preference for one's own sex is exhibited when children are observed in play. This preference begins in the toddler period, continues through the preschool years, and increases during middle childhood (Fagot, 1991; Serbin, Moller, Powlishta, & Gulko, 1991). Girls' preference for members of their own sex as playmates appears as early as the age of 2, whereas this preference in boys is not as clear until about three years of age (Hayden-Thomson, Rubin, & Hymel, 1987). This preference for others of the same sex has been observed in many other cultures and seems to follow roughly the same time course, emerging in the toddler period and increasing through middle childhood (Shepard, 1991). In general, sex dominates children's decisions to play with or avoid another child, often overruling other characteristics such as race and ethnicity.

One reason children prefer their own sex is that they simply get along better, with similar styles of interaction and similar interests. The key factor in compatibility seems to be the partner's social responsiveness, with girls being more responsive and cooperative, whereas boys are often more assertive and domineering. Boys also appear to enjoy rough-and-tumble play more than girls do and are therefore more likely to initiate it with each other (Rosen & Peterson, 1990).

Another reason for children's seeking out members of their own sex as playmates is their need to establish a gender identity. Once children become aware that they are members of one gender group, they are motivated to stick with that group. Shared gender membership is even more important to children than are mutual interests, and as a result, children increasingly spend time exclusively with those of the same sex. Within their respective play groups, girls and boys socialize one another into traditional gender-role behavior by punishing those who deviate from gender role appropriate activities with critical remarks, abandoning play with the friend who persists in doing something that appears gender-inappropriate, or trying to get the friend to do something else. Children are more careful to play with gender-appropriate toys when another child is present than when they are alone, even if the peer is not actually interacting with them (Serbin, Connor, Buchardt, & Citron, 1979). Apparently, children are eager for their peers to view them engaged in only gender-appropriate behavior.

Research has found many gender differences in children's play. In addition to engaging in more rough-and-tumble play, boys are more physically aggressive than girls and are more likely to display anti-social behavior. In particular, boys are often targets of aggressive content in marketing and are more desensitized to aggressive content than girls are (Klinger, 2001). Boys also seem to be more impulsive than girls. There is strong evidence that boys engage in more exploratory and curiosity-seeking behavior. Boys play outside more than girls do and tend to play competitive and challenging games more often. Boys also play in larger groups than do girls (Rosen & Peterson, 1990).

The games and physical activities of boys also serve as preparation for what they will do when they grow up. In competitive sports they experience victory and defeat. Effort and experience become salient; they learn to try harder, to reach a bit higher each time, and gradually and steadily improve the development of achievement skills and competitive behavior skills. They also learn that failures are commonplace and do not necessarily indicate that an individual is inadequate. For girls, on the other hand, both competition and winning are fairly unfamiliar experiences (Denmark, 1975). Box 5.2 describes the different types of toys commonly given to girls and boys.

BOX 5.2

Toys for Girls and Boys

Girls are more likely to get passive toys, such as dish sets, clothes, and coloring books. They may get toy ovens, irons, and sewing machines. The more elaborate models of these toy household appliances actually work, and so girls can start ironing and baking at an early age. Many of these toys are realistic representations of the things that girls may do later in life. Girls may also get dollhouses in which they can move furniture and play house. Their dolls can be handled like real babies: fed, diapered, and even bathed. These toys prepare girls for futures as mothers and homemakers.

Boys are more likely to get toys that encourage creativity and manipulation: chemistry sets, erector sets, toy trains, and tool chests. Boys are also more likely to get mobile toys, action toys, and sports equipment. The toys that boys get are often connected with action and exciting occupations, such as being a cowboy, a policeman, or an astronaut. For the most part, however, these toys do not represent occupations likely to be entered by most young men. Seldom does a boy get a toy briefcase and a bunch of papers to shuffle in an imitation of an adult's likely role.

Source: From *Masculine and Feminine: Gender Roles over the Life Cycle* (2nd ed.), by M. Richmond-Abbott, 1992, New York: McGraw-Hill.

In middle childhood, avoidance of the other sex increases and becomes quite salient. For example, boys may tend to run from girls, claiming that they have "cooties." Contact that does take place between the two groups is often tinged with romantic or sexual overtones (Adler et al., 1992). Such contact appears to be a prelude to the shift that takes place in the teenage years, when interest in members of the other sex becomes acceptable among one's peer group and may lead to dating.

The Media

Television, which exerts a significant influence on children's attitudes toward gender, overwhelmingly stereotypes feminine and masculine roles. Prime-time shows tend to portray women as young, unemployed, family bound, and/or sexual objects. Even those shown in responsible roles are commonly searching desperately for a man. Although females on prime-time television are more likely to have jobs than in the past, oftentimes a female character's occupational status is unspecified. Females represented in comedies have lower-paying, less prestigious jobs and are half as likely as males to be bosses (Glascock, 2001). Prime-time males, on the other hand, are depicted as tough, cool American men who are engaged in violent, mobile occupations and have numerous female admirers (Signorelli, 1989). Soap operas and comedy shows also tend to portray female characters as inferior to male characters. The majority of animated spokes-characters used in television advertisements are male, reinforcing the idea that males are more significant than females (Peirce, 1999). Not only are television commercial characters given more prominence if they are male, but White male characters are emphasized over Black male characters. These commercial images perpetuate prejudice against both women and African Americans (Coltraine, 2000).

Cartoons aimed at young children provide some of the most sexist depictions of females and males in the media. Male characters and male themes predominate in most cartoons. As a result, boys will rarely watch female-centered cartoons, and girls, in contrast, will be exposed mainly to male-centered cartoons.

A popular children's animated television show in the early 1990s depicted superheroes called the "Teenage Mutant Ninja Turtles." Elementary school children enacting original episodes of these shows typically excluded girls from their stories. Although a girl was able to obtain a part after some negotiation, she was required to fit the specifications of the superhero script, which typically emphasized her desirability and did not place her on equal footing with the male characters. Another cartoon show about the "X-Men" gave females a greater role in superhero play. Yet boys enacting episodes of this show continued to exclude girls from their play because of their romantic associations in the show; elementary school boys did not wish to be victims of teasing for this type of association with girls in the class (Dyson, 1994). Like other forms of media, video games have a significant effect on children's gender identity. Popular video games such as those made for Nintendo and Sony Playstation foster traditional gender roles. For example, women are portrayed as sex objects and violent/aggressive males are socially acceptable (Dietz, 1998).

Children's Literature

In an analysis of five sets of primary readers cross culturally, all of the countries' texts studied were found to subscribe to the traditional gender-role stereotypes. Almost all of the texts (with the exception of the Swedish readers) were found to portray fewer female characters than male characters. At least during the 1970s, some Russian, Rumanian, and Swedish texts depicted women in less traditional roles, but only the Swedish texts showed men or boys in nurturant or nontraditional roles (Denmark & Waters, 1977).

However, children's literature has improved greatly since that time, when studies showed that males dominated the stories, titles, and illustrations in popular children's books (Purcell & Stewart, 1990; Sadker, Sadker, & Klein, 1991). In spite of these changes, some gender stereotyping remains; there are still more male supporting characters, female characters are more likely to need help than are male characters, and males are more likely to be the ones to assist them (McDonald, 1989). Classic children's literature, however, prolifically read to children by their parents and studied in school, is highly gender stereotyped. While females constitute over 51 percent of the population, they are represented in less than that amount in children's literature (Gooden, 2001).

A colleague who has been teaching a course on the psychology of women at the University of Manitoba in Winnipeg, Canada, conducted an informal study of college students' favorite fairy tales from childhood. She found that her students, primarily young women, overwhelmingly chose Cinderella as their favorite fairy tale of childhood. Distant second- and third-place choices were Snow White and Sleeping Beauty (M. Johnson, personal communication, May 15, 1998). It is striking that their most revered character from early childhood, Cinderella, is portrayed as a passive female who is powerless and must sit at home in anticipation of her prince's arrival. Similarly, happy endings in fairy tales depict gender stereotyping in that heroines do little more than "sit, wish, and wait for marriage" (Turkel, 2002). The fairy tales that pervade young children's lives broadcast highly stereotypic views of women and men. Independent, courageous, and active heroines, such as Dorothy in the Wizard of Oz, were atypical for their time (Turkel, 2002).

Advertising

Children today, as never before in history, are bombarded with adult advertising of increasing sophistication and power. Advertisements in magazines, on billboards, and on television contain many subtle messages encouraging gender stereotyping. Much of the advertising for women is directed at convincing them to purchase products that will make them more attractive. The message in these advertisements is that women who are natural are not good enough and can improve by using the product in question. Many of these advertisements also suggest that older women are unnoticed and unworthy, and it is incumbent on women to stave off the aging process; if they do age, it is their own fault for not trying hard enough to stop the clock (Kilbourne, 1987).

Advertisements also tend to portray women as childish, cutesy, dumb, or uninformed. Studies show that females are overrepresented in television commercials featuring domestic products and underrepresented in those that do not (Bartsch, 2000). Furthermore, these ads for cleaning products depict housewives who are unable to clean successfully or overjoyed when they actually can. These childlike and trivializing portrayals of women make it difficult to take them seriously and may even convey the message that women are dumb and incompetent.

Men, on the other hand, appear dominant in most of the ads portraying men and women. Women are usually shorter in relation to men, often sitting or lying down while men stand. Women cling to men and look adoringly at them, usually smiling, while men are in control of the action and look aloofly off into space or into the camera. Women are often grabbed, tossed, or otherwise treated like childlike objects to be played with by a dominant adult male (Goffman, 1979).

Much of advertising relies on sexual appeals. It is especially here that women are placed in a disadvantaged position relative to men. These advertisements, regardless of whether they target men or women, portray women as scantily clothed sex objects, even though the ad may have nothing to do with sex. For men, the implication appears to be that the woman shown is the man's reward for using the product; for women, it may be one of identification (i.e., the woman who uses the advertised product will succeed in appealing to men). Although recent decades have brought some improvement in the roles in which women in advertisements are portrayed (from family roles to incorporating occupational roles), these women continue to be depicted as concerned with personal beauty, household, and family, whereas the men are shown as cool, unemotional, and dominant (Courtney & Whipple, 1985). Recent findings suggest that television advertisements even today display

a trend towards females as sexual objects or nurturers (M. Hallak, personal communication, July 16, 2003).

School

School is a prime place for children to learn key skills and attain knowledge about the world. Children are "socialized" in schools and made aware of society's future expectations of them as citizens (UNICEF, 2003). Schools can also have a great impact on children's ideas about gender roles. In elementary schools, students are often separated by sex for both formal and informal events, such as lines for an assembly or separate places for girls and boys to hang up their coats (Delamont, 1990). In addition, school reading textbooks portray masculine and feminine stereotypes. Males are usually depicted as being more aggressive, argumentative, and competitive (Evans, 2000). A function of schooling is to socialize children into the world of adulthood by teaching them appropriate behavior, and this unfortunately can often include stereotypic gender-appropriate behavior. Girls and boys have very different experiences within the classroom. See, for example, Box 5.3.

According to Alton-Lee, Nuthall, and Patrick (1993), pronounced gender bias exists in several so-

---

Box 5.3

Gender Bias in School

There is a direct link between high school courses chosen by girls and their subsequent career choices. Typically girls opt for vocational classes in home economics, secretarial work, and health care. Boys tend to select courses that teach skilled crafts, such as woodworking and auto repair. When girls attempt to cross the gender barrier in their educational selections, they are met with many challenges. For example, note the difficulties experienced by this Vietnamese American high school student:

I took a full-year shop class in high school. I was the only girl in the class, that is, the only girl by the end of the year. There was another girl, at the be-

ginning, but the two of us were—well, I wouldn't exactly say harassed, but it's true. After just a few days, the other girl transferred out of the course. I'm quite stubborn, so I stayed in the course the entire year. The boys literally pushed me around, right into tables and chairs. They pulled my hair, made sexual comments, touched me, told sexist jokes. And the thing was that I was better in the shop class than almost any guy. This only caused the boys to get more aggressive and troublesome. . . .Throughout the entire year no teacher or administrator ever stopped the boys from behaving this way. (quoted in Sadker & Sadker, 1994)

Source: From *Race, Class, and Gender in a Diverse Society,* by D. Kendall, 1997, Boston: Allyn and Bacon.

cial studies units. The few women mentioned in these units are characteristically marginalized or rendered invisible. Alton-Lee, Nuthall, and Patrick also found that teachers were more likely to call on boys in class and criticize girls' responses to questions. Although their research was conducted in New Zealand, strong gender bias has also been demonstrated in school children in the Philippines, Guatemala, and the United States (Gibbons et al., 1993). In the United States, the educational system has been found to track girls toward traditional, sex-segregated jobs and away from areas of study that lead to careers in science and technology (American Association of University Women, 1992). Furthermore, despite progress over the years, fewer girls than boys enroll in school and once enrolled, girls do not have as much success in their studies as boys do. In general, fewer girls than boys finish their basic education (UNICEF, 2003).

Recently, the issue of whether single-sex schools or single-sex classrooms in coed schools would better serve to educate females has been the subject of considerable debate. In a study done by the American Association of University Women analyzing the value of single-sex education, girls did not attain measurably better skills in math and science. However, one study has pointed out that because girls tend to surpass boys in the arts and humanities, in coed schools where there is competition between boys and girls, pressure to conform to educational typecasts becomes difficult to defy (James, 2001). Furthermore, many girls did report having greater confidence and better attitudes about these subjects, which are traditionally male areas of dominance (*New York Times,* March 12, 1998). Another American study found that girls attending single-sex schools had higher real career aspirations than did girls and boys at coed schools (Watson, 2002).

In New Zealand, classroom dynamics tend to reflect a subtle negativity toward women. Social studies curricula overwhelmingly acknowledge the contributions of men and characteristically marginalize or derogate those of women. Thus, a message is conveyed about relative cultural devaluing of women, which in turn affects the children's attitudes toward them. Teachers were observed to favor the participation of male children in class and evaluate the contributions of the females more harshly. The classroom arrangement in itself relegated the girls to the back of the classroom, while the boys sat in a semicircle in close proximity to the teacher (Alton-Lee, Nuthall, & Patrick, 1993).

Teachers in the United States tend to allow girls to work independently as they attend to the boys in the classroom. Whereas boys demand attention from the teachers, girls learn to quietly wait their turn. Teachers watch boys carefully and are quick to reprimand their misbehavior in public, while girls who misbehave are usually rebuked quietly as if to avoid embarrassing them (Serbin, O'Leary, Kent, & Tonick, 1973). Many boys enjoy the public attention they receive for behaving badly, which serves as a reinforcer for misbehavior. Girls, on the other hand, do not receive this reinforcer and therefore, tend to act out less than boys do. As such, typical female schoolchildren take on a more passive stance, while typical male children learn to behave assertively.

The extent to which girls and boys are differentially treated by their teachers is also affected by ethnicity and social class. Teachers pay more attention to children from middle- and upper-middle-class families than those from working-class families, and White children are expected to be higher achievers than children of color (Alvidrez & Weinstein, 1993; Sadker, Sadker, & Klein, 1991). Within each gender, White middle-class children receive more attention on the whole than do ethnic minority lower-class children.

Schools also provide children with a sadly representative view of the status of employed women. An overwhelming majority of elementary school teachers are female, whereas barely half of high school teachers are female (U.S. Department of Commerce, 1990). Often, high school science and math courses are taught by males while English and foreign language courses are taught by females. Principals and superintendents, the major authority figures in the schools, are usually male. Research has demonstrated that this can affect children's perspective on gender roles; first graders in schools with female principals were found more likely to say that either women or men could be school principals than were children in schools with male principals (Paradise & Wall, 1986).

Peers

The peer group may be the most powerful socializing agent in an adolescent's life. Most teenage boys and girls are more anxious to earn the approval and acceptance of their peers than that of their families. Therefore, the peer group will have a profound influence on gender-role conceptions at this stage of life. However, the pervasive influence of the peer group begins before adolescence; once children begin school, whatever nonsexist upbringing they have had is subject to interference from their classmates' attitudes (Katz, 1979). Peers abet gender typing by encouraging segregation of girls and boys, expressing prejudice toward members of the other sex, and treating girls and boys differently.

As we have noted, at a young age children show strong preferences for members of their own sex when selecting playmates. Students of various ages who were asked to rate certain traits as typical of girls or boys tended to assign more favorable traits to their own sex and more undesirable traits to the other sex (Etaugh, Levine, & Mennella, 1984). In addition, physically attractive female children receive more positive attention from their peers than do physically unattractive female children, whereas physical attractiveness is not a factor in the treatment that boys receive from their peers (Smith, 1985). Clearly, girls are taught from an early age that their level of physical attractiveness affects their treatment by their peers, while this standard does not exist for boys.

In adolescence, many of the peer expectations of gender behavior learned in childhood are reinforced and may take on new definitions. Adolescent boys emphasize toughness as a masculine attribute, idealizing a strong, heavy, athletic body build, participation in sports, and even violence as an extension of competitive sports. "Coolness" is also a valued trait, requiring that males express little or no emotion. Adolescent males often experience homophobia and are therefore afraid to express emotions to other men for fear of appearing effeminate. A third ideal for adolescent boys is being good at something, preferably sports. This extends to expressing high achievement motivation in terms of a future career, although academic success is not necessarily part of this equation. Other areas fall into this category as well, such as being a good driver and/or being sexually competent.

Female adolescents are less likely than male adolescents to gain self-esteem from concrete achievements that are within their control. They tend to emphasize physical appearance, often preoccupying themselves with their weight to the point of anorexia or

---

Box 5.4

Peer Pressure in Adolescence

During adolescence females adopt strict gender roles as an attempt to fit in with a particular group. Peer cliques serve an important function in allowing an individual to feel acceptance. Often adolescents who are different from a peer group will be rejected, causing feelings of isolation, self-doubt, and depression. The following statements highlight the significance of establishing a peer group:

Unless you dress like everyone else, you are considered a neb.

You have to dress cool and act and behave accordingly; otherwise you are seen as weird.

Fitting in with my friends is important. Sometimes I don't feel like I belong and that makes me crazy.

The best thing about going to school is being with my friends and feeling like I am part of a group, where I matter.

Source: "Adolescent Females' Perception of Autonomy and Control," by J. Kaufman, 1998, in *Females and Autonomy: A Life-Span Perspective* (pp. 43–72), edited by M. B. Nadien, and F. L. Denmark. Boston: Allyn and Bacon.

bulimia (see Chapter 13). Sometimes, young women associate prettiness with being worthy as a person and will therefore feel unworthy if they consider themselves less than attractive. Girls also base a good deal of their self-esteem on their popularity and interpersonal relationships (see Box 5.4). In terms of the future, although girls have become more career oriented, they continue to juggle their career expectations with their expectations of having a family. Whereas some girls anticipate adjusting their career plans for the sake of having children, many girls wish to have it all. In a 1998 survey, the issues that preoccupied a sample of 733 girls were not the traditional concerns of marriage and children but rather their future careers and financial responsibilities (APA Monitor, October, 1998).

For adolescents who are physically disabled or are living with chronic disease, the challenges of this developmental period are certainly exacerbated. Teenagers of both sexes are inundated with images heralding physical beauty and fitness. More studies are needed that explore how these youths' social and emotional development are impacted. It is important to address whether girls and boys respond differently to their medical condition and, as a corollary, whether and how they are treated differently by peers and caregivers.

Peers and significant adults in these children's lives would do well to encourage and support interests and endeavors that reflect a range of values and abilities. It is especially important that these youth hear from important others that physical appearance and abilities are merely part of what is interesting and special in each individual. As we know, many disabled individuals have healthy, accomplished, and fulfilling lives.

In sum, many socializing forces affect the development of gender typing in children that may pave the way for a gender-discriminate adult world.

PUBERTY AND ADOLESCENCE

As children move toward their teenage years, both biological and social differences between girls and boys appear to increase. Biologically, hormonal processes catalyze internal and external bodily changes during the preteen and teenage years. These changes have social ramifications as well. Both girls and boys show

trends in the direction of gender-role intensification from grades seven through nine, when *not* acting like the other sex becomes more important (Hill & Lynch, 1983; Simmons & Blyth, 1987). This finding has not changed even though the times have; gender-role stereotyping among girls and boys has not decreased significantly in the decades following the onset of the feminist movement (Lewin & Tragos, 1987).

Young lesbians and gay male adolescents face many added challenges to the normal crises of adolescence. Most are not privy to the appropriate information regarding their sexual and emotional development. They also face prejudice and intolerance and possibly rejection from parents and their uninformed peers (Greene, 1994b). As such, they often fail to seek out support at this developmental period—when they are most in need (Hersch, 1991). As you read the rest of this section, these issues should be kept in mind because, for all the reasons mentioned here and more, adolescence may be an even more intense developmental period for the lesbian or gay adolescent.

Puberty is the period of the most rapid physical growth that humans experience, excluding prenatal and early postnatal life. Not only do children's bodies change at puberty, but their cognitive capabilities expand, and their relationships with family members change. Puberty involves physical events such as the growth spurt, changes in body composition, and the development of secondary sex characteristics. **Adolescence,** on the other hand, refers to social and psychological events and is defined by society as the period between childhood and maturity. (See Chapter 4 for fuller discussion of puberty.)

The timing of puberty, which differs for girls and boys, influences much of an adolescent's social development. On average, girls begin and end puberty approximately two years before boys do. Within this average, however, there are variations.

For the girl who begins to mature sexually earlier than her classmates, there are several disadvantages. For one, it has been suggested that fourth and fifth graders are disturbed about the loss of their childish bodies, choosing to camouflage breast development with sloppy big shirts and sweaters (Delaney, Lupton, & Toth, 1988). This self-consciousness is probably compounded for the girl who is one of the first of her peers to develop breasts (Lerner & Olson, 1997). In addition, while breasts are viewed as a prerequisite for physical attractiveness in a woman, women are usually dissatisfied with their breasts. For an early developing girl, the "imperfection" of her breasts is likely to serve as a source of severe self-consciousness.

Early maturing girls usually weigh more and are slightly shorter than their late maturing peers, even once pubertal growth is complete for both (Brooks-Gunn, 1987; Patlak, 1997). Perhaps this is a factor in early maturing girls' poorer body images and greater dieting concerns relative to late maturers (Attie & Brooks-Gunn, 1989).

In addition, early maturing girls have been found to date more than late maturing girls in middle and junior high school (Brooks-Gunn, 1988). They appear to be more involved with boys (Crockett & Petersen, 1987) and may engage in "adult behavior" such as smoking, drinking, and engaging in sexual intercourse at an earlier age (Magnusson, Strattin, & Allen, 1985; Patlak, 1997). This may be a function of associating with chronologically older friends. Early maturing girls are more likely to be asked out by older boys, which may give them the message that their physical appearance is their major asset. This may take a toll on their self-esteem (Simmons, Blyth, Van Cleave, & Bush, 1979) and could be related to the poorer academic performance of early maturing girls (Simmons & Blyth, 1987). Early dating also takes a toll on girls' friendships with other girls (Katz, 1997), which may explain why girls tend to choose best friends who are at the same level of physical maturation as themselves (Brooks-Gunn, Samelson, Warren, & Fox, 1986).

Early maturing boys, on the other hand, appear to be at an advantage. Boys who mature early tend to perceive themselves more positively than boys who are either on time or late (Lerner & Olson, 1997). A boy who reaches puberty early is likely to have a size advantage over his peers and to be successful in sports, a major key to social status for boys. Early maturation for boys is also associated with greater independence and decision making.

However, like their female counterparts, early maturing boys are more likely to get involved with older friends and to engage in activities for which they are not psychologically prepared. As a result,

they have a higher rate of school problems, substance abuse, and delinquency. Boys who have a few extra years of childhood have more time to develop emotionally. In addition to being just as successful in adulthood as their early maturing peers, late maturing boys also seem to be more creative and to enjoy life more (Steinberg, 1993).

Menarche

For many girls, **menarche,** or the onset of the menstrual period, signals the beginning of womanhood. As such, it is a pivotal event in female puberty. Our society conveys mixed messages to girls about menarche, viewing it as both a positive and a negative event. Adolescent girls themselves feel ambivalent about menarche, expressing feelings of both happiness and fright (Petersen, 1983). The way menstruation is presented can influence the way girls react to the onset of their menstrual cycles. Negative expectations about menstruation can cause women to concentrate more on the unpleasant symptoms associated with it. In spite of some girls' and women's negative outlooks regarding menstruation, other females experience their menstrual periods as "self-affirming, creative and pleasurable" (Boston Women's Health Book Collective, 1998).

Menarche appears to focus the adolescent girl's attention on her body (Koff, Rierdan, & Silverstone, 1978). In addition, postmenarcheal girls report thinking more about dating, marriage, and having children (Brooks-Gunn & Warren, 1988). Some girls feel that menarche means giving up the freedom of childhood (Peterson, 1983).

Younger and premenstrual girls appear to have very negative expectations about menstruation, expecting more severe symptomatology than do their postmenarcheal counterparts (Brooks-Gunn & Ruble, 1983). In general, adolescent girls view menstruation more negatively than their mothers do (Stoltzman, 1986). Girls will often not tell their friends that they have begun to menstruate for several months, even though menarche is a topic of discussion among them. They also appear to get more information about menstruation from the media and their peers than from their mothers. This makes it challenging, but even more important, for mothers to prepare their daughters adequately for menstruation. In fact, girls who are adequately prepared for these events have been found to experience less symptomatology (Brooks-Gunn & Ruble, 1983).

Some doctors and researchers consider **seme-narche** (also called *spermarche*), the boy's first ejaculation, to be the marker of sexual maturity that is analogous to menarche in girls (Stein & Reiser, 1994). Like girls learning about menarche, boys get much of their information about this milestone from the media rather than from their fathers (Brooks-Gunn & Matthews, 1979). Another aspect of seme-narche, which is paralleled by girls' reaction to menarche, is boys' reluctance to discuss the event with others (Gaddis & Brooks-Gunn, 1985).

While girls gain body fat during puberty, boys gain muscle. Both of these are normal physical changes, but girls tend to view their increase in fat as making them unattractive, while boys are proud of their changing bodies (Lerner & Olson, 1997). Girls tend to be less satisfied with their weight than boys are in general, and perceiving oneself as underweight was associated with the greatest amount of satisfaction for girls.

Social class tends to interact with girls' feelings about their weight. Young women from higher social classes are more likely to wish to be thinner, although the majority of young women in every social class wish they were thinner (Dornbusch, Gross, Duncan, & Ritter, 1987). Interestingly, Black adolescent girls appear more well adjusted than White adolescent girls with regard to body image (Freiberg, 1991; Ingrassia, 1995).

Parent–Child Relations

Parent–child relations change during puberty. For girls, for example, menarche seems to cause parents to view them as more mature (Danza, 1983) whether menarche is early or late. In the first six months after menarche, however, daughters report more parental control (Hill & Holmbeck, 1987).

Mother–daughter interactions change both qualitatively and quantitatively as puberty progresses. Mother–daughter conflict is pronounced during early puberty (Brooks-Gunn & Zahaykevich, 1989). Pre-menarcheal girls use more aggressive, oppositional,

and critical speech with their mothers. Postmenar-cheal girls, on the other hand, use more passive communication styles, such as indifference and denial (Zahaykevich, Sirey, & Brooks-Gunn, unpublished manuscript). Mothers of premenarcheal girls tended to use more dogmatic techniques (such as reference to a fixed external rule system) to influence their daughters, while mothers of postmenarcheal girls used more projective methods (such as requiring the girls to put themselves in their mother's place). This may foster mother–daughter conflict, because young adolescent girls find it more difficult to take their parents' perspective (Smetana, 1988).

Some fathers are more reserved with their adolescent daughters, who behave more assertively or brusquely once they have reached menarche (Hill, 1988). They are reluctant to discuss body changes or sexuality with their daughters, and girls, in turn, are embarrassed by these topics in front of their fathers (Brooks-Gunn & Zahaykevich, 1989). This may be a reflection of the incest taboo, with fathers attempting to distance themselves from their sexually maturing daughters. And perhaps some fathers are less emotionally invested in their daughters to begin with and are therefore more willing to let go as the child moves into adolescence.

For boys, relationships with their parents change as well. Mothers report the highest levels of opposition from their sons (Hill & Holmbeck, 1987). Mothers appear to lose influence over their sons during adolescence (Steinberg, 1981) and usually end up giving in to them during arguments (Welsh & Powers, 1991). The addition of a father figure provides increased monitoring, supervision, and support (Hetherington, 1989; Zimiles & Lee, 1991). This is probably connected to the fact that teenage sons of divorced mothers tend to do better in school when the mother remarries.

Fathers also yield to sons in some cases, possibly out of a desire to promote independence. However, as a rule, fathers have been found to become more controlling and competitive as their sons enter puberty, and the sons often yield to their fathers. Perhaps their sons' budding adulthood and strength is threatening to the fathers, who are concurrently reaching middle age and possibly feeling the onset of physical decline.

In general, however, parents of adolescents give boys more independence and autonomy than they give to girls. They are apparently worrying more over the possibility that their daughter will become pregnant than over the equally salient possibility that their son will impregnate someone else's daughter (Meyer, 1991). Unfortunately, both girls and boys are short-changed by this discrepancy. Adolescent boys suffer when parents give them too little discipline, attention, and support, rationalizing that boys need to learn to stand on their own feet. Girls, on the other hand, are likely to be excessively restricted (Dubow, Huesmann, & Eron, 1987; Leaper et al., 1989; Lempers, Clark-Lempers, & Simons, 1989; Vaughn, Block, & Block, 1988). When it comes to the possibility of contracting HIV/AIDs, middle-class parents of both daughters and sons do warn their children about the dangers of contracting the disease if they engage in unprotected sex (B. Mowder, personal communication, July 30, 2003). Parental support serves different roles in relation to peer influence and alcohol consumption and yields highly traditional results. Parenting serves to protect girls by fostering qualities that function to resist peer group pressure. Alternatively, for boys, increased parental support and discipline are viewed as threats to independence and thus encouraged rather than hindered boys' alcohol use (Marshall, 2000).

Peers

In adolescence, the peer group begins to take on increasing importance while the influence of the family diminishes. Intimate friendships are formed earlier for teenage girls than boys. These friendships are of central importance to girls, who will cultivate them by sharing secrets, asking for the friend's advice, complimenting the friend's popularity, and avoiding doing anything that would indicate they feel superior to their friends (Buhrmester & Furman, 1987; Savin-Williams, 1979). Girls' friendships in adolescence provide them with emotional support as they cope with self-consciousness, change, and other adjustments. Girls who mature early and start dating ahead of their peers are likely to miss out on some of the benefits of friendships with other girls (Miller, 1993; Steinberg, 1993).

Although girls' friendships are stereotyped as being more valued by them than boys' friendships are by their male counterparts, evidence suggests otherwise. Boys have a strong capacity and need for same-sex friendships (Blyth & Foster-Clark, 1987); they may simply be more cautious about admitting that their friends are important to them (Berndt, 1992). This could be a function of societal gender expectations associating masculinity with autonomy.

As in childhood, boys' peer groups exhibit themes of status and dominance, especially in junior high school when the transition to a new school takes place. Girls as a group appear to be much more permanently affected than boys are by school transitions during pubertal years. The shift from elementary school to junior high or middle school and then to high school has a strong detrimental impact on girls' self-esteem (Simmons & Blyth, 1987).

A possible explanation for the effects of school transition on girls' self-esteem is the shift in educational methods from elementary to secondary school. As children mature into adolescence, classes gradually shift from lectures and tests to seminars. In the former, quiet, conscientious work (i.e., taking notes and studying) ensures success; in the latter, confidence, assertiveness, and a willingness to take risks (i.e., participation in class discussion) prevails. Therefore, the type of academic work for which girls have been traditionally rewarded becomes less valued (Huston & Alvarez, 1990).

In sum, it appears that although boys may be subject to much turmoil in adolescence, girls are far more vulnerable emotionally. Their self-esteem is taxed by self-consciousness, poor body image, academic adjustments, and other changes. However, as one of the authors has pointed out, "Yet although adolescence represents an often difficult period in a young woman's life, for many teens, this is also a time of exploration, freedom to try new things, growing independence, and self-awareness. During this period, the adolescent girl begins to form her own unique identity" (Denmark, 1999, p. 337). In addition, they must deal with menarche and their mixed feelings regarding this milestone. It is interesting to note that Black girls appear to be better adjusted than White girls with regard to body image, and that girls of higher socioeconomic status have more difficulty dealing with weight issues. This attests to the significant influence of culture, ethnicity, and class.

ETHNICITY, RACE, CULTURE, AND CLASS EFFECTS ON GENDER DEVELOPMENT

Chapter 3 looked at culture, race, ethnicity, and class. In this chapter we are reviewing some of the effects of these variables on gender development. Research literature suggests that race, class, and ethnicity all affect the study of child development and gender (Binion, 1990). However, studies of gender that take these variables into account have been rare. A complete understanding of the factors influencing developmental processes, including gender role development, cannot be achieved without considering the effects of ethnicity and/or social class (Reid & Paludi, 1993).

Gender typing varies across race and ethnicity. For example, African American children appear to experience less gender stereotyping in their upbringing. Traditionally, African American women have worked outside the home and display independence and assertiveness in addition to nurturance. African American men, on the other hand, have often been more nurturing and expressive than their White counterparts (Bardwell, Cochran, & Walker, 1986). African American children report that they see both parents as providing instrumental (provider) and expressive functions. This would suggest that African American children are more immune to society's gender typing.

In school, both White and African American boys experience a conflict between their definition of masculinity and being a good student; however, this conflict is greater for African American boys (Reed, 1988). On the other hand, African American girls are probably free of some of the difficulties experienced by their White counterparts in this area. African American girls, having been encouraged by their community to be self-sufficient and assertive, are likely to be more independent in the school setting. As a result, although girls generally get less attention in the classroom, this lack of attention may not hurt African American girls' self-image as much as it does that of their White counterparts (Ogbu, 1982).

Some African American caregivers, particularly mothers, are very protective of their male children. This can create unique gender-role patterns that are not prevalent in other cultures. For example, older children in many African American families are responsible for caring for their younger siblings. Although this is particularly true of girls, the role flexibility in African American families allows for boys to fulfill this function as well or instead.

In Hispanic cultures, girls receive conflicting messages about their identity from an early age. On the one hand, women are considered morally and spiritually superior to men; yet, they are expected to accept male authority. This is reinforced by the concept of **marianismo,** which considers women morally and spiritually superior to men and, therefore, capable of enduring male-inflicted suffering (Stevens, 1973).

Both girls and boys in Hispanic cultures tend to be close to their mothers and feel alienated from their authoritarian or uninvolved fathers. The mother's relationship with the son tends to be more dependent, sometimes to the point where the son protects his mother from his father. The mother's relationship with the daughter, on the other hand, is of a more reciprocal nature; mothers teach their daughters how to be good women and fulfill their eventual roles of wife and mother (Stevens, 1973).

In American Indian culture, girls' education traditionally focused on domestic tasks and responsibilities once puberty commenced. However, in modern times, certain tribes teach community values to children without stressing sex differences. American Indian girls can participate in active sports enjoyed by their male counterparts (Schlegal, 1973).

Asian American cultures vary in terms of their views of females. Many Asian cultures, particularly those built on Confucian philosophy, are particularly oppressive toward women. Girls are raised to be deferent to family, community, and the patriarchs. However, Filipino culture ascribes to a more egalitarian distribution of power between females and males. Japanese parents' attitudes and behavior toward their child differ according to the sex of the child. Girls in Japan are expected to conform to the traditional female gender role; males, on the other hand, who are not as strictly disciplined, are not constrained to conform to the traditional male role (Sukemune, Shiraishi, Shirakawa, & Matsumi, 1993). Although traditional Chinese society has a similar double standard for girls and boys, Hong Kong has juxtaposed these ideas with more modern and Westernized ideas of child rearing (Yu, 1993). Korea, as a Confucian society, tends to favor men (Kim, 1993).

These diverse parenting styles indicate that Asian American children's ideas of gender will differ according to their (or their parents') country of origin. In general, however, it is clear that even among Confucian-based societies, increasing pressures to modernize and Westernize have mitigated proscriptions against women to some degree. This has had an effect on Asian American children's upbringing.

In Jamaican culture, gender roles are fairly stereotyped and rigid. Although girls are expected to embody traits such as obedience, femininity, and attractiveness, they are also required to be bright and educated. Yet, they must remain inferior to men in these areas. As such, Jamaican girls are exposed to a double standard whereby their education is strongly encouraged as a means to economic stability, but discourages remaining in school "too long" (Allen, 1988). Jamaican boys, on the other hand, are expected to be adventurous and less responsive to discipline. Masculinity is verified by the man's ability to father children and to earn a decent living. Thus, particularly in the lower classes, Jamaican boys are geared toward choosing employment that will enable them to support a family. Unfortunately, father absence is common, and boys are often socialized by their mothers. As a result, they are without an appropriate model of how to relate as a father and a husband. This deficit may result in a sense of inadequacy that negatively impacts their own child-rearing endeavors later on (Allen, 1988).

Within the U.S. classroom, girls of different racial backgrounds show a relative preference for same-race, same-sex playmates and a greater relative avoidance of White boys than of African or Asian American boys. Boys of various races showed a relative preference for White race, same-sex playmates and least relative avoidance of same-race girls. This might be explained by White boys being perceived as

having higher status and same-race children being perceived as more attractive (Fishbein & Imai, 1993). It is interesting to note that classroom racial minority status (i.e., being in a classroom in which most classmates are of a different race) was associated with peer rejection of girls but not of boys (Kistner, Metzler, Gatlin, & Risi, 1993). This suggests that girls are more victimized by their peers' racism than are boys.

Socioeconomic status is another variable that can affect gender typing. For example, division between the sexes is more rigidly defined in the working class than it is in the middle class. Women expect men to provide a decent living for their families, while the home is considered the woman's responsibility, in spite of the fact that economic necessity has forced a large percentage of working-class women to seek employment (Rubin, 1980). Therefore, one might expect children from working-class homes to form more rigid gender stereotypes than do children from middle-class homes.

This is consistent with the fact that, although studies show that middle-class children with externally employed mothers are less gender role stereotyped than those whose mothers are primarily housewives, these results are mixed for working-class children (Cordua, McGraw, & Drabman, 1979; Gold & Andres, 1978; Marantz & Mansfield, 1977; Meyer, 1980). It is possible that middle-class mothers tend to be employed by choice in jobs they find satisfactory, whereas working-class mothers are employed out of economic necessity and express less job satisfaction. Therefore, middle-class children are more amenable to the idea of women working than are working-class children. More information about the effects of maternal employment on children can be found in Chapter 7.

In a study of temper tantrum prevalence, boys who threw tantrums were more likely to be of an upper social class, whereas their female counterparts were more likely to be of a lower social class (Bhatia et al., 1990). In keeping with general behavioral theory, this would suggest that boys' tantrums are reinforced among upper-class families whereas girls' tantrums are reinforced among lower-class families. The ramifications of this for gender upbringing among those of different socioeconomic status would be of interest for future study.

In preschool, girls appear to be more aware of social class cues than are boys (Ramsey, 1991). This may parallel the finding already cited that girls who are the racial minority are more likely to be rejected by their peers than are boys who are the racial minority. Perhaps this can be explained by girls' emphasis on popularity and interpersonal relations as validating their self-worth and femininity. Girls might be afraid to make friendships that could jeopardize their social status and as such are far more sensitive to both social class and racial cues when choosing friends than are boys.

In general, little research exists that examines the interaction of race and class with gender. This area needs much study, and students of different demographic backgrounds are urged to devote their research to this highly important topic.

SUMMARY

Psychological theories of gender-role development include the psychoanalytic, social learning, and cognitive-developmental perspectives. Freud's psychoanalytic views emphasize intrapsychic forces and conflicts that result in children's identification with their same-sex parents. Social learning theory, on the other hand, focuses on external, environmental influences. The cognitive-developmental perspective discusses the role of the child in his or her own socialization.

While classic theoreticians assumed that girls were only capable of inferior moral development relative to boys, recent researchers such as Gilligan have suggested otherwise. Gilligan claims that girls' morality is merely different, not inferior, and studies suggest that this is based more on differential experiences than on innate personality differences.

Children's internalized images of gender play an important role in such areas as popularity in elementary school, conceptions of personal power, self-esteem, and motivation and personal goals for adolescents. Images of gender vary across cultures and are reinforced by the child's surrounding environment.

Gender schema theory suggests that children create knowledge structures that organize gender-related information in memory and are used to evaluate new information according to its gender. Children's gender schemas may be more or less flexible, and this flexibility or rigidity will affect their attitudes toward members of both sexes. Attitudes toward gender tend to be differentiated among children across cultures, with biases that usually favor men but sometimes favor women.

Parenting plays a significant role in childhood gender socialization. In general, parents tend to foster boys' autonomy and girls' dependence. Single-parent homes have their own set of ramifications for children's gender-role attitudes, however. Fathers tend to reinforce gender-typed behavior more than mothers do, so the absence of the father can result in more androgynous behavior. Children living with their fathers tend to have a more balanced experience in terms of male and female adult figures. Even in intact marriages, mothers and fathers parent differently.

Socializing forces that influence gender-role development after birth include language, play, media, school, and peers. Socialization into gender roles of girls and boys is also mediated by race and social class. However, far too few studies exist in this area. This topic would be an exciting one for future research.

KEY TERMS

Adolescence (p. 173)
Conventional reasoning (p. 155)
Gender identity disorder (p. 157)
Gender schema theory (p. 159)
Linguistic sexism (p. 166)

Marianismo (p. 177)
Menarche (p. 174)
Morality of constraint (p. 154)
Morality of cooperation (p. 154)
Postconventional reasoning (p. 155)

Preconventional reasoning (p. 155)
Puberty (p. 173)
Semenarche (p. 175)

DISCUSSION QUESTIONS

1. How are gender roles constructed for boys and girls before birth? What is the suggested connection between prenatal hormones, particularly the presence or absence of androgens in the womb, and the personality traits of boys and girls?

2. Compare the moral development of girls and boys based on the theories of Freud, Kohlberg, and Gilligan. Do you believe that moral reasoning lies on a continuum from lowest to highest? How does Gilligan's theory incorporate the experiences of girls into Kohlberg's male-based paradigm?

3. List the qualities and characteristics that you associate with femininity and masculinity. Compare the list of feminine items with the list of masculine items. Which list contains more positive traits? Which of these qualities do you personally embrace and which qualities do you reject? Why?

4. What role do cultural values and expectations play in developing gender attitudes in children? Identify the predominant roles of women and men prescribed by your own culture. How do these gender stereotypes resonate with the choices you have made?

5. Describe the differences between men and women as parents. How do fathers perpetuate gender stereotyping of their children? How does the match or mismatch between the sex of the parent and the sex of the child influence the type of parent–child interactions that occur?

6. How does language contribute to the differentiation of males and females? Do you feel the adoption of gender-neutral language empowers women?

7. Spend a few hours viewing television programs and commercials. How are women and men portrayed differently? List all the innuendoes you see and hear that denigrate women. Translate all of them into insults aimed at people with disabilities. Would people with disabilities allow that? Would the FCC allow that? Would you allow this if you were a person with a disability?

8. Girls and boys have been shown to adopt strict gender-role orientation during adolescence. To what extent is their adherence to traditional gender roles during adolescence due to the physical changes of puberty? What social forces operate during adolescence to explain this phenomenon?

9. Do you feel your gender-role development has been strongly influenced by your race and class? Can you think of experiences in which being a female transcends racial, ethnic, and class lines, and times when the reverse is true?

FURTHER READINGS

Crosby, F. (1991). *Juggling: The unexpected advantages of balancing career and home for women and their families.* New York: Free Press.

Johnson, N. G., Roberts, M. C., & Worrell, J. (1999). *Beyond appearance: A new look at adolescent girls.* Washington, DC: American Psychological Association.

Pipher, M. (1994). *Reviving Ophelia: Saving the selves of adolescent girls.* New York: Grosset/Putman.

Reid, P. T., & Paludi, M. A. (1993). Developmental psychology of women: Conception to adolescence. In

F. L. Denmark & M. A. Paludi (Eds.), *Psychology of women: A handbook of issues and theories* (pp. 191–212). Westport, CT: Greenwood Press.

Sadker, M., & Sadker, D. (1994). *Failing at fairness: How America's schools cheat girls.* New York: Charles Schribner's Sons.

Thompson, B. W. (1994). Childhood lessons: Culture, race, class, and sexuality. In *A Hunger so wide and so deep: American women speak out on eating problems* (pp. 27–45). Minneapolis: University of Minnesota Press.

CHAPTER 6

ABILITY AND ACHIEVEMENT

It is about as meaningful to ask "Which is the smarter sex?" or "Which has the better brain?" as to ask "Which has the better genitals?"
—Diane Halpern

Over the past 150 years, the most famous scientists of Europe have propagated scientific findings about sex and race. Virtually every claim that biological difference explains social inequality has turned out to be bogus. But hope springs eternal.
—Anne Fausto-Sterling

Although it is true that boys as well as girls benefit from an education, it seems that educating girls actually produces a greater return; in many parts of the world, it is the woman's schooling that is the crucial factor in lifting her family out of poverty. . . . Yet despite the long-term benefits of educating girls, parents in many parts of the world prefer to invest in educating their sons.
—Neft and Levine

It would be difficult to find a research area [than gender differences in cognitive ability] more characterized by shoddy work, overgeneralization, hasty conclusions, and unsupported speculations.
—Julia Sherman, as cited in Fausto-Sterling

Remember: No one can make you feel inferior without your consent.
—Eleanor Roosevelt

ISSUES IN COMPARING MALES' AND FEMALES' COGNITIVE ABILITIES

The History of Sex Comparisons in Cognitive Ability

UNDERSTANDING THE MEANING OF DIFFERENCE

Sex and the Brain

Sex differences in intellectual abilities and achievements have preoccupied scientists in many disciplines for decades. To this day, few sex differences are more fraught with political minefields and emotional rhetoric than those involving cognitive abilities. For many people, there is much at stake in the answer to these questions: Who is smarter: women or men? Are there sex differences in intelligence? If so, to what degree and for what reasons? The answers may have serious implications for males' and females' educational opportunities, academic achievement, career choices, occupational status, and lifelong earnings—for their standing as people in a society. This chapter reviews the evidence arising from studies of sex comparisons in cognitive abilities, as well as gender issues in education, literacy, and overall achievement. First we will review the history of sex comparisons in cognition and then explore the meaning and complexity of differences in cognitive areas. Then we will consider the implications of difference for academic achievement and attributions, motivations, and expectations for success and failure in achievement-related areas. Finally, we will explore special issues in ability and education wherein gender matters.

ISSUES IN COMPARING MALES' AND FEMALES' COGNITIVE ABILITIES

In Western society, in which we attach great weight to mental abilities, asking which group of people is smarter is tantamount to asking which group is better. Behind this question is the lurking suspicion, if not the outright assumption, that such differences, if they exist, are biological in origin, immutable, and socially significant. As Fausto-Sterling (1992b) has observed, at the crux of this question also lie important practical decisions about how to teach reading and mathematics, whether girls and boys should attend different schools, make different job and career choices, and about how much women and men are worth in the job market. The disciplines of psychology, education, sociology, and biology have all contributed to the scholarship on this issue. There have been thousands of empirical studies on sex differences in intelligence and thousands more commentaries explaining, refuting, and complicating the existence of such differences. The media and the public show a similar fascination with sex differences in this area, and it is not at all uncommon for a study trumpeting sex differences in brain functioning or cognition to make the front page of a newspaper or magazine, whereas a study of sex similarities or declining differences is more likely to be buried in the body of the text. This fascination with difference is rooted in the histories of intelligence testing and the study of sex comparisons in the United States that show evidence of a more general preoccupation with finding and explaining individual and group differences.

The History of Sex Comparisons in Cognitive Ability

The study of cognitive differences in intelligence has a long history in psychology, driven largely by the presumed lack of women of recognized genius or high achievement in the earliest part of the twentieth century. In 1903, James McKeen Catell, a psychology professor at Columbia University and then-editor of *Science,* the official journal of the American Association for the Advancement of Science and leading scientific journal in the English language, studied the lives of eminent individuals and noted that few were women. He found a dearth of high-achieving women throughout the ages and only a tiny proportion of women among the top thousand scientists (Fausto-Sterling, 1992b). Catell erroneously stated that because there was not any social prejudice against women in science, he found it "difficult to avoid the conclusion that there is an innate sexual disqualification" (Catell, 1903). Catell's colleague at Columbia, the leading educational psychologist Edward L. Thorndike, who championed the use of statistics in educational research, was also impressed by the rarity of female geniuses. Thorndike concluded that it made little sense to squander educational resources trying to bring women into the ranks of the intellectual elite and that women were better off studying to become nurses and teachers where the "average level is essential" (Thorndike, cited in Seller, 1981). Profiled in Chapter 1, G. Stanley Hall, the father of child psychology and the first president of the American Psychological Association, argued against coeducation at the American Academy of Medicine in 1906 on similar grounds:

> It (coeducation) violates a custom so universal that it seems to express a fundamental human instinct. . . . girls . . . are attracted to common knowledge which all share, to the conventional, are more influenced by fashions, more imitative and lack the boys' intense desire to know, be, do something distinctive that develops and emphasizes his individuality. To be thrown on their own personal resources in sports, in the classroom, in nature study and elementary laboratory brings out the best in a boy, but either confuses or strains a girl. (Hall, 1906, pp. 1–2)

Thus, three giants of psychology in its earliest days, Catell, Thorndike, and Hall, saw the differences between female and male intellectual achievement as rooted in biology, rather than in different socialization practices or severely limited educational, occupational, and social opportunities for women (Fausto-Sterling, 1992b). They also believed that men were, by nature, more *variable* than women on a number of characteristics. This variability presumably explained why, despite the fact that the mean (average) intelligence levels of men and women were the same, more men than women appeared at the highest levels of intelligence. According to the *variability hypothesis,* also discussed in Chapter 1, for biological reasons that are seldom made clear, males appear more frequently at both the lowest and highest levels of intelligence, with women clustered around the middle range.

The work of these men on the study of sex differences in all kinds of traits, including intelligence, has had a profound and lasting impact on psychology. Indeed, as we noted in Chapter 1, pioneers in the first generation of women in psychology frequently devoted large portions of their careers to attempting to discredit notions such as the variability hypothesis that in effect represent women as more ordinary and limited than men (Montague & Hollingworth, 1914). But versions of this hypothesis survive to this day, as we will see shortly.

The history of the study of cognitive sex differences closely parallels the history of the study of other presumed sex differences in personality, aptitude, and achievement, in which characteristics that are presumed to be more common among males are valued precisely because they are male. An enduring belief in male superiority on important traits has led most researchers to seek explanations, preferably biological and thus "natural," that have been widely used to justify the continuing unequal positions of women and men in society.

UNDERSTANDING THE MEANING OF DIFFERENCE

Before weighing the evidence for the what and where of sex differences in cognition, it might be useful to consider whether and how females' and males' brains are different. Further, we will examine how statisticians and psychologists find and interpret group differences, and what are the theoretical and social significances of group differences in cognition. In the following sections, we will discuss biological factors, methodological and statistical issues, and the meaning of cognitive differences in turn.

Sex and the Brain

The particular biological mechanisms by which men were thought to be superior to women have changed over time as each has been discarded for lack of scientific evidence and as technological advances have offered new possibilities. At various times, the seat of male superiority has been thought to be the size of the male brain, which is on the average larger than the female brain. As Fausto-Sterling (1992b) explains, this explanation ran afoul of the "elephant problem": If brain size is the key to intelligence, then elephants and whales ought to rule the earth. Attempts to correct for this problem by dividing brain size by body size resulted in females coming out ahead of males, and thus this line of explanation and research was subsequently abandoned. Interestingly, however, in what we will see is a theme of much biological research on sex differences in cognition, old ideas die hard and often resurface with modern twists.

A much discussed front-page finding in 1997 was that men have about 5 billion more brain cells than women (although men's brain cells die faster!) (Angier, 1999). Other supposed female deficiencies in the brain include a smaller surface area of the corpus callosum (a mass of nerve fibers that connects the left and right halves of the brain) than men have, in particular a smaller splenium (a large subsection of the corpus callosum) and fewer complexities of the convolutions of the brain. Both of these hypotheses have been largely discredited. For example, a review and meta-analysis of studies in this area conclude that men may have a larger corpus callosum than women, but there are no sex differences in the size or shape of the splenium (Bishop & Wahlsten, 1997). In fact, there is evidence that the size of the corpus callosum changes over the course of people's lifetimes, with it increasing for women into their fifties and peaking in men in their thirties (Cowell, Allen, Zalatimo, & Denenberg, 1992). Those who see the corpus callosum as the site of sex differences in cognition have generally not attempted to incorporate complex findings such as these.

More recently, attention has been paid to the topic of hemispheric differentiation or **lateralization.** Functionally, humans have two brains, with the left hemisphere appearing to specialize in language analysis, computation, and sequential tasks and the right side hosting artistic abilities and an emotional, nonanalytic approach to the world. Not long after the discovery by neurobiologist Roger Sperry that the supposedly symmetrical brain had different capabilities, some scientists have been using the asymmetrical brain to explain the different patterns of female and male abilities. Jere Levy, a student of Roger Sperry's, hypothesized that the most efficiently functioning brains have the most complete lateralization: the most complete hemispheric division of labor (Levy, 1969). According to the lateralization hypothesis, men and women appear to have different patterns of lateralization; that is, men have more highly specialized (more so-called "efficient") brains, with the left side active in solving verbal problems and the right side in spatial ones. In the popular culture, there are references to women being "left brained" and men "right brained." Some studies do suggest that there is more hemispheric specialization in males than females, but findings are inconsistent and the size of the sex difference appears to be very small, with most males indistinguishable from most females.

Although a great deal of research has been done in this area, there is still no strong supporting evidence that the brains of males are more lateralized in general than those of females. A meta-analysis of more than 250 studies in this area shows that sex differences in lateralization are close to zero (Voyer, 1996). There is some evidence, however, that the brains of females and males may differ in organization in some specific abilities; for example, the location of speech areas in the brains of females may be different from that of males (Kimura, 1987), but, again, there are broad variations across the sexes.

Brain organization is clearly involved in cognitive ability, but the mechanisms that could mediate any sex differences in cognitive areas have not been well elucidated. There is still little to no evidence of a clear relationship between hemispheric lateralization and sex differences in cognition. The origins, meanings, and size of this sex difference are still hotly debated, and, at present, it is reasonable to question why brain lateralization is so often framed in such positive terms. For example, the fact that women recover language abilities after a stroke significantly more quickly than men may be due in part to the kinds of differences in the brain that we are discussing here—lesser lateralization or "specialization" of the brain, size differences in the corpus callosum—or other sex differences, including hormonal differences between women and men. But, as we have repeatedly witnessed, sex differences in anatomy are routinely used to explain presumed male rather than female "superiority," and areas of so-called male superiorities are prized more highly than areas in which females appear to excel.

Many recent investigations of the effects of biological factors on sex differences in cognition have focused on the role of sex hormones. After all, it is through the sex hormones that chromosomal differences between the sexes have their effect. Thus, the action of sex hormones is responsible for differentiating the sexes from before birth. And although both females and males have female and male hormones, the sex differences in the distribution of sex hormones (androgens, estrogens, and progestins), unlike other sex differences, are actually quite large. We know, for example, that testosterone differences between males and females of college age may be as large as 10 to 1, with no overlap between females and males (Udry & Talbert, 1988). As we consider all biological evidence for sex differences, including research on sex hormones, it is crucial to keep in mind that most studies in these areas are correlational in nature, meaning that they cannot and do not prove a causal role for factors such as hormones. Such studies merely suggest an association between two factors that may be due to other factors not studied.

The work of Doreen Kimura and her associates suggests a role for *prenatal* sex hormones on brain organization (Kimura & Hampson, 1994). According to Kimura and Hampson, androgens (male hormones present to a greater degree in males than females) organize the male brain in ways that boost some forms of spatial ability throughout the entire life span. Furthermore, in adult men, seasonal and diurnal (daily) fluctuations of testosterone are associated with

changes in scores on tests of spatial ability on which men excel, but not on tests of abilities in which females excel, such as verbal fluency and verbal memory, or on tests of sex-neutral abilities. In women undergoing natural fluctuations of the menstrual cycle, high-estrogen periods are associated with enhanced performance on tasks in which females excel, such as fine motor skills and articulatory fluency, whereas low-estrogen periods correspond to enhanced performance in tests of spatial ability. Kimura and Hampson see these sex differences in evolutionary psychology terms and have invoked the different adaptive challenges that our female and male ancestors faced to explain sex differences in abilities.

As we will see shortly, the largest single cognitive sex difference appears in the general area of spatial abilities and is known as spatial or mental rotation—the ability to rotate an object mentally in space and accurately predict its orientation and appearance. This particular ability appears to vary in adults with hormonal fluctuations, although in complex and surprising ways. For example, in the United States and Canada, males have higher levels of testosterone in the fall than the spring and lower scores on mental rotation tests in the fall than the spring. Similarly, men have higher testosterone levels in the mornings than later in the day, and lower mental rotation scores in the morning than at other times. Thus, at least for mental rotation, higher testosterone is linked in men to poorer performance. On the other hand, females with above average testosterone levels do relatively well on mental rotation tasks relative to other females, and females with high estrogen levels do relatively poorly on such tasks (Hampson, 1990; Kimura, 1996). This has led some to conclude that, for both women and men, there are curvilinear relationships between hormonal levels and spatial performance (Hampson, 1990).

More evidence for the role of sex hormones in ability comes from people who are born with a rare genetic disorder that creates extremely high levels of androgens in utero. This disorder, *congenital adrenal hyperplasia,* known as CAH, leads to very high levels of circulating androgens in both affected boys and girls, and in girls to masculinization of genitals and other features. CAH girls behave in childhood much like normal boys, with higher activity levels and more interest in masculine toys and activities than most girls. Interestingly, CAH girls score higher than normal girls in spatial tasks such as mental rotation, but somewhat worse than normal girls in quantitative tasks (Collaer & Hines, 1995). This suggests not only that hormones may play a role in spatial ability but also that spatial and mathematical performance are independent of each other (Valian, 1998).

Experimental studies in which the effects of hormones are systematically manipulated and causal inferences can be made are relatively rare in humans because of the ethical and practical issues involved in manipulating such variables. But experimental studies with humans in which hormone levels were manipulated support the argument that female and male sex hormones may play a role in cognitive ability. For example, when normal aging men were given testosterone to enhance their sexual functioning, they also showed improved performance on visual–spatial tasks (Janowsky, Oviatt, & Orwoll, 1994). And when female-to-male transsexuals were administered high levels of testosterone in preparation for sex-change procedures, they experienced a dramatic improvement in their visual–spatial ability and a correspondingly dramatic impairment in their verbal fluency (Van Goozen, Cohen-Kettenis, Gooren, Frijda, & Van de Poll, 1995). The evidence in favor of hormonally induced increases and decreases in mathematical ability is less compelling. Experimental studies in which the presumed causal variables are manipulated rather than measured provide better evidence than correlational studies for a causal link between hormones and cognitive function. But such studies are uncommon, often involve specialized groups, and are frequently open to alternative explanations.

Recent experimental work with animals suggests that female hormones such as estrogen can preserve and even improve some of the brain's highest mental functions. Investigators have found that estrogen may have a therapeutic effect in the prevention and possible treatment of Alzheimer's disease (Wise et al., 2001). Apparently, estrogen protects nerve cells and may have diverse positive effects on learning and memory throughout the life span (Bisagno, Bowman, & Luine, 2003; Luine, Rentas, Sterback, & Beck,

1996; Luine & Rodriguez, 1994; Sherwin, 1998; Wickelgren, 1997).

As we have seen, the history of research on cognitive sex differences is replete with the practice of locating an anatomical difference—any difference—between female and male brains and attributing important functional disparities between the sexes to this difference, with or without scientific justification. It is true that sex differences in brain anatomy and function have been noted in many areas, including lateral asymmetry and anterior and posterior organization. The search for biological bases of sex differences in cognition has only heated up in recent years, along with improvements in computer technology such as positron emission tomography (PET) scans and magnetic resonance imagery (MRI), which enable us to better "see" the brain. Indeed, some studies have detected somewhat different patterns of brain activity among males and females when problem solving (Shaywitz et al., 1995).

But, to date, none of these biological differences or differences in patterns of activation has been conclusively related to the few, small differences in cognitive function that have been reliably observed. Moreover, the profound sexism that has pervaded the long search for biological explanations should render us cautious in interpreting research findings in this area. Because biological explanations sound more scientific than social or cultural ones, they are accorded more respect than other explanations. In fact, some people confuse biological explanations with scientific ones. But what renders a study scientific is not simply its subject matter, whether it is chromosomes or cognition, but rather the quality of the methods it uses.

Finally, even if some biological sex differences were conclusively related to some behavioral or cognitive tendency, as hormonal differences appear to be directly related to some sex differences in libido or aggression, it would be a mistake to conclude that biology is destiny. As cognitive psychologist Virginia Valian points out, "Biology leaves us a lot of room to maneuver" (Valian, 1998, p. 67). Valian goes on to say

In a way, it is odd that we should interpret sex differences as immutable, when we do not accept biology

as destiny in other aspects of human existence. For example, biology sets limits on the human life span, but we need not and do not for that reason accept a short average life span as our fate. As a society, we put forth great efforts to understand the mechanisms of health and to cure disease and illness. . . . Although we agree that no one can live forever, we successfully invest tremendous resources in trying to live longer. . . . I propose that we adopt the same attitude toward biological sex differences. . . . Biological sex differences arise through the actions of sex hormones operating in our physical and social environments. . . . We have good evidence from cultural, situational, and temporal differences that the (sex) differences are not immutable. (pp. 67–68)

Making Comparisons and Evaluating Differences

As we will see, there are many cognitive areas in which the sexes, on average, differ, and many in which there are no differences. Some differences favor women and others men, although, overall, sex differences in cognition are typically quite small. Moreover, sex differences that emerge in a given study are the function of many features of a study and may not reflect "true" differences in female and male cognitive abilities. These are discussed in the following sections on research methods and statistical issues.

Methodological Issues: Samples, Tests, and Context.
Samples.   It is increasingly clear from the thousands of studies of sex differences that the existence and size of cognitive sex differences depend on various, easily overlooked, features of the study. One critical feature appears to be how the samples of females and males were obtained. Many studies comparing females and males use convenience samples that are not representative of males and females and from which generalizations should not be made. Moreover, most gender comparisons are made of college students, who are certainly not representative of the general female and male populations on many dimensions, most notably age. Indeed, age of respondents matters a great deal in sex comparisons, as some sex differences appear early in life, others not until adolescence, and still others later in life (Halpern, 1997).

The fact is, however they are sampled, girls and boys and women and men are regarded by research methodologists as *nonequivalent groups,* and comparisons between them are fraught with difficulties. Females and males are nonequivalent precisely because they differ on so many uncontrolled dimensions—on the biological level, in genes, brains, and hormones, among others; on the psychological level, in life experiences of all types, attitudes, beliefs, emotions, and expectation levels, among others; and on the social level, in opportunities, discriminations, and stereotypes, among others. Thus it is virtually impossible to determine which of the many variables that are confounded or correlated with biological sex is responsible for a sex difference if one emerges. For example, if girls perform worse than boys on a test of visual–spatial ability, is it because their brains are different, their hormones are different, they have less experience with this kind of stimuli, or they have low expectations or high anxiety as a result of being told that girls struggle with these kinds of tests?

Scientists are people first, and just like people everywhere, scientists often have psychological, social, or political preferences for different levels of explanation of sex differences. Some scientists habitually favor biologically based explanations, such as evolutionary psychology theories, and others favoring more environmentally or socially based explanations, such as developmental or social role theories. More often than not, both biological and social–environmental theories predict similar findings, and neither type of explanation can easily be ruled out based on the evidence in any given study. We need to evaluate whether there is sound scientific evidence to support both the existence of and the explanation for the difference. Even when biological differences are found, we need not accord them the special status of being more fundamental or important than other factors, as we sometimes unintentionally do when we speak of environmental or social factors "moderating" or "influencing" biological effects (Valian, 1998). As Valian states, it would be equally wrong in these cases to assign the prime effect to the environment. Within behavioral, cognitive, and affective domains, biological and environmental–social forces act together or "coact" to produce effects (p. 69).

Tests.   Another crucial variable is the type of test or task used to measure cognitive differences. Increasingly, contemporary scholars are rejecting the old taxonomy that divides experimental results neatly into the areas of verbal, mathematical, and visual–spatial ability (Halpern, 1997). This is so because abilities are not unitary constructs, and this categorization scheme has not proved useful in organizing sex-related findings. As we will see, females excel at some visual–spatial tasks and not others, whereas males excel at some verbal tasks and not others. There is no one, ultimate verbal or mathematical test or task that fully represents the essence of verbal or mathematical ability.

Context.   Until recently, the importance of context surrounding the administration of the test was often overlooked. People do not come into testing situations "tabula rasa" (blank slates); they are profoundly affected by their values, beliefs, and expectations about the test and the meaning of their performance. As Eccles (1987) noted, the attributions people make for their successes and failures, their expectations for succeeding, their strategies for test taking, and their experience with tests all combine to affect their motivation and performance. Females and males are well aware of the different stereotypes that society holds about female and male abilities, and many people feel that "girls can't do math." Social psychologists Steele and Aronson have demonstrated the unconscious and powerful influences of negative stereotypes on vulnerable groups (Steele & Aronson, 1995). Claude Steele has coined the term **stereotype threat** to refer to the risk that targets of negative stereotypes feel about personally confirming negative stereotypes about their group. Steele posits that a negative stereotype about one's group, regardless of whether one internalizes the stereotype, can be activated in certain situations and can lead to self-doubt and concern about confirming the stereotype, which in turn damages performance. Steele (1997) found that, under instructional sets in which women felt that their mathematical ability was being tested, women performed more poorly than when the test was presented to women in a less threatening manner. How people interpret the meaning of the test and their scores on it appears to be quite relevant to their performance.

Some Basic Statistical Issues

Distributions.   Before we consider the vast and complex research on sex differences in cognition, it is crucial that we understand what the word *difference* means—and what it does not. Scores on tests are often represented in **frequency distributions,** which are graphs of how participants in a sample score on a test. Distributions vary in their shapes and means and the amount of variability of the scores. Most psychological traits, including intelligence and its many components, are **normally distributed,** with most scores clustered around the group mean (average) and successively fewer scores as you move to the extremes in either direction (see Figure 6.1a).

Research shows that when most people think about group differences in any trait, they tend to exaggerate the size of that difference and to imagine essentially **nonoverlapping distributions,** as we see in Figure 6.1b, where virtually all members of group B score higher than virtually all members of group A (Fausto-Sterling, 1995b). The fact is, with almost all group differences involving human traits, the frequency distributions are largely overlapping, with most members of the different groups being indistinguishable from each other, as we see in Figure 6.1c. The frequency distributions of female and male cognitive traits vary in their degree of overlap, but all of them look more like Figure 6.1c than Figure 6.1b. On virtually all psychological traits—certainly on intelligence—females and males are much more alike than they are different.

We have previously noted that a theme in the thinking of Cattell and Thorndike, which continues in various guises to this day, is that men are more variable in their cognitive abilities than women are—that while the mean measured IQ of women and men is about the same, the distribution or variation in scores is greater for men than for women. Obviously, it is possible to arrive at the same mean for two distributions despite very different patterns of scores: The mean of the following scores: 100, 100, 100, 100, and 100 is 100, and so is the mean of this distribution: 90, 110, 80, 120, and 100. In Figure 6.1d, you can see that the two distributions have the same mean of 100, but quite different variability, with distribution A showing considerably more vari-

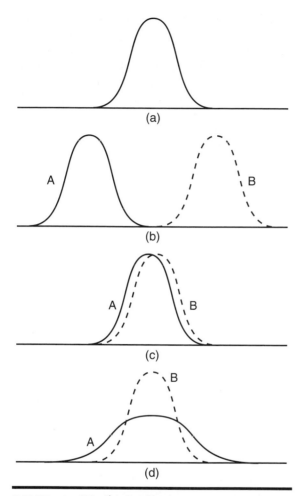

FIGURE 6.1   Distribution Curves

Line Graph (a) presents a normal distribution curve. Line graphs (b) through (d) present three combinations: (b) two frequency distributions with no overlap, a very uncommon outcome when comparing groups; (c) two frequency distributions with a high degree of overlap, typical of most distributions of male and female traits of all kinds; and (d) two frequency distributions of scores with the same mean but very different variability.

ability than distribution B. A bit later, in the conclusion of this section, we will review the contemporary evidence concerning whether male scores on cognitive skills are in fact more variable than female scores.

Statistically Significant Differences.   When cognitive differences between women and men are evaluated, the findings are typically reported in terms of the mean differences and, less often, the variability of the distributions, or the percentage of very high scorers. Mean differences are held to be either *significant,* meaning reliable and not due to chance, or *not significant,* meaning possibly due to chance alone. If the differences are statistically significant and the study meets methodological criteria, the investigator has a potentially publishable study and a potentially "sexy" finding: People pay attention to sex differences on important traits. If a difference does not achieve statistical significance, the study is far less likely to be published, despite the importance of the research topic or question or strength of its methodology. The finding of no difference will probably disappear into the investigator's file drawer.

Many people outside (and inside) of psychology are confused about the meaning of **statistically significant differences.** They often act as though the term *significant* means more than it does. Whether statistically significant differences are achieved depends, among other things, on the size of the samples, with larger samples having a much greater chance of yielding significant findings than smaller ones. For example, a mean difference of 6 IQ points is unlikely to be significant if the scores of six women and six men are compared, but highly likely to be significant if the scores of 6,000 women and 6,000 men are compared. The variability among scores is another consideration, with larger mean differences needed to achieve statistical significance the more variable the samples. Also, the mere fact of statistically significant differences says nothing about the size of the difference. A very tiny difference of just a few points on a 200-point scale may emerge as statistically significant, given other features of the study. Throughout this chapter, we will sometimes refer to a newer statistic known as the **effect size** (Cohen's *d*), which gives us a better sense than statistically significant differences of how large a difference exists between groups (Cohen, 1969). Sometimes statistically significant findings are too tiny, however reliable, to make a practical difference in the real world. For example, as we will see, there are many studies that show a slight advantage for women and girls over men and boys on some verbal tasks. But in most (not all) cases, the differences are so small that most investigators and educators do not find it useful to speak of a female–male difference in verbal ability. In any case, it is important to remember that statistical significance is contingent on many factors and must not be confused with practical (or social) significance. Relatedly, keep in mind that measures of variability and percentage of high scores depend critically on *which* women and men are in the study, that is, how the sample was constituted, as noted previously.

Meta-Analysis.   Would you drastically change your diet or begin taking a new drug on the basis of the results of a single study? Probably not, because you are undoubtedly aware that the results of multiple studies in a given area are often inconsistent. On virtually all important topics in psychology, there are literally thousands of studies of an effect or phenomenon, and the results, taken together, are often inconclusive. This opens the door for much mischief, as some people selectively choose to cite only those findings that support their position and conveniently ignore the rest. But thanks to a statistical technique called **meta-analysis,** we are now able to combine the results of different studies of the same research question. For each study included in the meta-analysis, the researcher computes the effect size noted above, Cohen's *d,* which not only measures the size of the difference between females and males but also indicates the direction of the difference (which group scored higher or lower). The statistic *d* is comparable across studies and can be averaged across studies to tell us how large the average sex difference is and which group it favors. What often emerges from meta-analytic reviews is a clearer and fairer portrait of the state of knowledge in a given research area. Thanks to pioneers, such as Janet Hyde, in the application of meta-analysis to the study of sex and gender issues, we are now able to summarize vast literatures on sex differences on various dimensions, and we will cite the findings of meta-analyses wherever possible (see Hyde, 1984; Hyde, Fennema, & Lamon, 1990).

Meaning Is in the Eye of the Beholder.   All scientific work takes place in a particular historical, cultural, and social context that both gives it special meaning and limits its generalizability to populations, settings, and times not studied. Scientific "facts" are always laden with the insights and blind spots of the times. It is deceptively easy to see the blatant sexism and racism in early research on sex and race differences, for example, but harder to identify the biases and shortcomings that currently shape intellectual trends. But we can be sure that, when we study variables such as gender, race, and class, for example, personal values and social pressures are at work.

Finally, we need to remember that a mind—male or female—is a tough thing to change (Halpern, 1997). Most of us have been observing and making judgments about the abilities of females and males all of our lives. Many of us have already formulated strong opinions about the origins, nature, and extent of sex differences. Such opinions are not easily changed by scientific evidence. Indeed, people tend to dismiss findings and reinterpret conclusions when they do not support their preexisting views (Lord, Ross, & Lepper, 1979; Valian, 1998). Altering the information rather than changing one's model of the world is especially likely with "hot-button" topics such as sex, race, and other group differences.

The What, Where, When, and Size of Sex Differences in Cognition

Overall Intelligence.   There are no overall sex differences in general or global intelligence (Fausto-Sterling, 1992b; Maccoby & Jacklin, 1974). As important as this statement appears to be, it is less than meets the eye, because the makers of IQ tests have discarded items on which females and males reliably differ. As some investigators have noted, saying that there are no gender differences in intelligence essentially means that the test constructors succeeded in their quest to eliminate sex differences (e.g., Hyde, Fennema, & Lamon, 1990). Nonetheless, it is clear that it is in *patterns of specific abilities,* rather than overall intelligence, that sex emerges as an interesting variable.

Sex Comparisons on Verbal, Mathematical, and Visual–Spatial Abilities. In Maccoby and Jacklin's (1974) famous early study of sex comparisons, they considered numerous possible dimensions on which females and males were thought to differ and concluded that the sexes differed reliably on only four. Three of those four dimensions were the cognitive areas of verbal, mathematical, and visual–spatial abilities (the fourth was in the noncognitive area of aggression). It is now part of general lore that females excel in verbal ability and males in mathematical and visual–spatial abilities. However, the real picture is considerably more complicated than that. In fact, the old taxonomy that divided abilities into the tripartite system of verbal, mathematical, and visual–spatial abilities has dissolved in the light of research showing that different cognitive processes underlie abilities within each of these domains. Some of the same cognitive processes underlie abilities across these different domains (Halpern, 1997). In other words, verbal, mathematical and visual–spatial abilities are each made up of very different kinds of tasks, and lumping the areas together is misleading. Research suggests that females reliably excel at some mathematical and visual–spatial tasks, just as males reliably excel at some verbal tasks.

As we see in Table 6.1, tests and tasks on which females obtain higher average scores than males are highly diverse and cross all three domains of abilities, including mathematical calculations, perceptual speed, memory for spatial location, reading comprehension, writing, and speech articulation. Similarly, tests and tasks on which males excel cover all domains, including tasks that require transformations in visual working (short-term) memory, such as mental rotation, in which a figure is manipulated in space and requires correct identification from another angle; mechanical reasoning; verbal analogies; and motor tasks that involve aiming.

We can see that it is not accurate to make sweeping statements about broad areas of female and male abilities. Indeed, that practice merely reinforces pernicious stereotypes about the sexes. "Math may be tough" as Barbie famously "said" in her first utterance, but in fact, it is not any harder for the average

female than for the average male. We summarize the latest information on verbal, mathematical, and visual–spatial abilities in the section that follows.

Verbal Abilities. In most areas of verbal ability, the sex differences are small and appear to be disappearing over time. Probably the largest remaining sex differences are in the areas of verbal fluency and writing ability, both of which strongly favor females and show up throughout the life span. There are also small to moderate advantages for females in reading comprehension, with Cohen's ds ranging from 0.18 to 0.30 (Hedges & Nowell, 1995). There is a slight male advantage in verbal analogies that emerges after adolescence (Halpern, 1997). But, overall, the sexes are far more similar in level of verbal skills than they are different, with similar mean scores and similar variances on most verbal tasks, with the important exceptions of writing and fluency.

Mathematical Abilities. The results of meta-analyses of mathematical skills generally suggest a very small overall advantage for males in average mathematical ability with Cohen's ds ranging from about 0.05 to 0.19 (Hedges & Nowell, 1995; Hyde, Fennema, & Lamon, 1990). But the size of sex difference varies with the level of difficulty of the particular types of mathematical tests, ranging from the least difficult computational tasks, through understanding of mathematical concepts, to the most difficult: problem solving. Girls show an early advantage over boys in mathematical computation in grade school and middle school, but this advantage evaporates by high school. The sexes are virtually indistinguishable on understanding of mathematical concepts throughout school. But in the area of problem solving, the sexes are similar throughout elementary and middle school, and a moderate difference favoring males emerges in high school ($d = 0.29$) and persists in college ($d = 0.32$). Males score consistently higher than females in word problems, graph interpretation, and estimation problems—problems that require the solver to apply mathematical knowledge (Lummis & Stevenson, 1990). Some researchers report that the sex difference in mathematics has declined over time (Feingold, 1988; Hyde, Fennema, Ryan, Frost, &

TABLE 6.1   Cognitive Tests and Tasks That Usually Show Sex Differences

TYPE OF TEST/TASK	EXAMPLE

Tasks and Tests on Which Women Obtain Higher Average Scores

TYPE OF TEST/TASK	EXAMPLE
Tasks that require rapid access to and use of phonological, semantic, and other information in long-term memory	Verbal fluency—phonological retrieval (Hines, 1990) Synonym generation—meaning retrieval (Halpern & Wright, 1996) Associative memory (Birenbaum, Kelly, & Levi-Keren, 1994) Memory battery—multiple tests (Stumpf & Jackson, 1994) Spelling and anagrams (Stanley, Benbow, Brody, Dauber, & Lupkowski, 1992) Mathematical calculations (Hyde, Fennema, & Lamon, 1990) Memory for spatial location (Eals & Silverman, 1994) Memory for odors (Lehrner, 1993)
Knowledge areas	Literature (Stanley, 1993) Foreign languages (Stanley, 1993)
Production and comprehension of complex prose	Reading comprehension (Hedges & Nowell, 1995; Mullis et al., 1993) Writing (U.S. Department of Education, 1997)
Fine motor tasks	Mirror tracing—novel, complex figures (O'Boyle & Hoff, 1987) Pegboard tasks (Hall & Kimura, 1995) Matching and coding tasks (Gouchie & Kimura, 1991)
Perceptual speed	Multiple speeded tasks (Born, Bleichrodt, & van der Flier, 1987) "Finding As"—an embedded-letters test (Kimura & Hampson, 1994)
Decoding nonverbal communication	(Hall, 1985)
Perceptual thresholds (large, varied literature with multiple modalities)	Touch—lower thresholds (Ippolitov, 1973; Wolff, 1969) Taste—lower thresholds (Nisbett & Gurwitz, 1970) Hearing—males have greater hearing loss with age (Schaie, 1987) Odor—lower thresholds (Koelega & Koster, 1974)
Higher grades in school (all or most subjects)	(Stricken, Rock, & Burton, 1993)
Speech articulation	Tongue twisters (Kimura & Hampson, 1994)

Hopp, 1990), whereas other researchers claim that the sex difference in mathematical ability has remained relatively constant over time (Halpern, 1997; Hedges & Nowell, 1995). We will return shortly to the issue of what changes over time in sex differences might mean.

One critical issue in sex comparisons of mathematical ability has to do with the relative numbers of females and males in the very highest ability levels. It is well established that average sex differences in mathematical ability are modest, but it appears that many more males than females score in the mathe-

matically gifted categories, with ratios ranging from 3:1 to 8:1 in favor of males. Males consistently score better than females on the Mathematics SAT (SAT-M) (Hyde et al., 1990). One of the reasons for this is that more females than males today take these tests and go on to college, meaning that a less select group of females than males is taking the test. Nonetheless, this does not account for all of the sex differences in scores. These findings are of concern because achievement in math and science generally requires high scores on these kinds of standardized tests.

TABLE 6.1   Continued

TYPE OF TEST/TASK	EXAMPLE

Tasks and Tests on Which Men Obtain Higher Average Scores

Tasks that require transformations in visual working memory	Mental rotation (Halpern & Wright, 1996; Voyer, Voyer, & Bryden, 1995) Piaget Water Level Test (Robert & Ohlmann, 1994; Vasta, Knott, & Gaze, 1996)
Tasks that involve moving objects	Dynamic spatiotemporal tasks (Law, Pelligrino, & Hunt, 1993)
Motor tasks that involve aiming	Accuracy in throwing balls or darts (Hall & Kimura, 1995)
Knowledge areas	General knowledge (Feingold, 1993; Wechsler Adult Intelligence Scale [Wechsler, 1991]) Geography knowledge (Beller & Gafni, 1996) Math and science knowledge (Stanley, 1993; U.S. Department of Education, 1996)
Tests of fluid reasoning (especially in math and science domains)	Proportional reasoning tasks (Meehan, 1984) Scholastic Assessment Test—Mathematics Graduate Record Examination—Quantitative (Willingham & Cole, 1997) Mechanical reasoning (Stanley et al., 1992) Verbal analogies (Lim, 1994) Scientific reasoning (Hedges & Nowell, 1995)

Source: From "Sex Differences in Intelligence: Implications for Education," by D. F. Halpern, 1997, *American Psychologist, 52*(10), p. 1102. Copyright © 1997 by the American Psychological Association. Adapted with permission.

Males are also overrepresented at the low-ability end of many distributions, including the following examples: mental retardation (some types; Vandenberg, 1987), a majority of attention-deficit disorders (American Psychiatric Association, 1994), delayed speech (Hier, Atkins, & Perlo, 1980), dyslexia (even allowing for possible referral bias; DeFries & Gillis, 1993), stuttering (Yairi & Ambrose, 1992), and learning disabilities and emotional disturbances (Henning-Stout & Close-Conoley, 1992). In addition, males are generally more variable (Hedges & Nowell, 1995). References provided are examples of relevant research. The literature is too large to attempt a complete reference list here.

There is evidence, for example, from occupational surveys in Project Talent that people who have careers in science and engineering are overwhelmingly more likely to have scored in the ninetieth percentile on mathematics tests in high school (Wise, Steel, & MacDonald, 1979).

Another important issue that emerges repeatedly in the literature is the relationship between mathematics performance on standardized tests and amount of mathematics studied in school. The single best predictor of standardized test performance in mathematics is the number of mathematics courses previously taken. When course taking is controlled, that is, when the number of math courses is equal for females and males, the sex difference is reduced (Crawford & Chaffin, 1997), but it is not eliminated. As time goes on, the sexes have become more equal in their enrollments in mathematics courses, with girls taking courses in algebra and geometry nearly as often as boys, although girls still tend to avoid calculus and other advanced math courses (Sadker & Sadker, 1994). As Crawford and Chaffin

(1997) note, however, we must keep in mind that, even when boys and girls take the same courses, they experience different worlds in the classroom, with boys, particularly White boys, receiving more encouragement from teachers than do other groups. Moreover, boys are more likely than girls to participate in activities such as chess, mathematics, and computer clubs and to attend science and computer camps in the summer. These activities supplement and enrich boys' experience with classroom mathematics in ways that encourage achievement, whereas the lack of these activities undermines girls' performance, self-confidence, and future possibilities. This said, the evidence suggests that differences in preparation do not explain all of the sex differences in mathematics performance on standardized tests. Increasingly, evidence from cognitive psychology suggests that females and males do not approach mathematics problems in the same way, and that these different strategies may account for some of the sex difference (Valian, 1998).

Visual–Spatial Abilities. Of all the areas of cognitive sex comparisons, it is in the area of **visual–spatial ability** that some of the largest and most persistent sex differences emerge. Meta-analytic studies of sex differences in these areas have revealed three broad classes of visual–spatial tasks (Linn & Petersen, 1985). One is *spatial visualization,* which involves finding a figure that has been embedded (hidden) in distracting stimuli. On this task, there is a very slight, near-zero sex difference favoring males ($d = +.13$). In *spatial perception,* which requires one to locate a true vertical or horizontal line in the midst of distracting information, males enjoy a moderate advantage ($d = +0.44$). It is on *mental rotation* tasks, which ask the test taker to mentally turn a figure in space so that it can be correctly identified from a different angle, that males enjoy a relatively large advantage ($d = +0.73$). Examples of some of these items are presented in Figure 6.2.

As we can see, with visual–spatial abilities as with other domains, the size of sex differences depends critically on the particular tests and tasks in question. There are some other visual–spatial tasks on which females excel, for example, memory for

SPATIAL VISUALIZATION
Is figure (a) part of figure (b)?

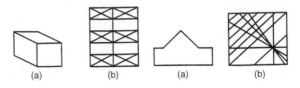

SPATIAL PERCEPTION
Which of the following four tilted glasses has a horizontal water line?

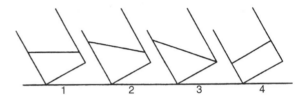

MENTAL ROTATION
Which two of the four choices below show the standard in a different orientation?

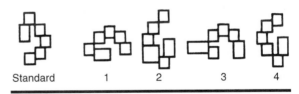

FIGURE 6.2   Test of Visual–Spatial Abilities
Source: Adapted from Yoder, 1999, and Rollins, 1996.

spatial location (Silverman & Eals, 1992). It is also true that for most visual–spatial tasks only a small percentage of the variation in scores can be accounted for by sex; the other 95 percent of the variation is due to individual differences having nothing to do with being female or male. Nonetheless, as with mathematical abilities, the highest scorers on visual–spatial tasks are disproportionately male.

As Hyde (1981) has noted, many, if not most, occupations do not require especially high levels of visual–spatial ability, but in some occupations, for example, engineering and architecture, these types of skills are very important. Still, sex differences in visual–spatial test scores do not account for the huge disparities in the numbers of females and males who are engineers or architects. If the only factor standing in the way of an engineering career for women were visual–spatial ability, we would still expect to find about one-third of engineering positions filled by women. But only about 10 percent of all U.S. engineers are women (Bureau of Labor Statistics, 2001); women who are equivalent to men on standardized tests drop out of engineering programs in greater numbers than men, and women who succeed in becoming engineers fare much worse on the job than men (Robinson & McIlwee, 1989). Clearly, factors other than visual–spatial ability are depressing the numbers of women in areas such as engineering, architecture, and mathematics.

Other Cognitive Abilities. Sex comparisons have been made on other cognitive abilities that do not fall neatly into the categories of verbal, mathematical, and visual–spatial abilities. As Table 6.1 suggests, females excel at fine motor tasks and tests of perceptual speed, perceptual thresholds, and speech articulation. Males excel at tasks that involve moving objects, motor tasks that involve aiming, tests of mechanical reasoning, and tests of *fluid reasoning* (Halpern, 1997).

Conclusions. In all domains of cognitive ability, women and men are more similar than they are different, and this is especially true of the vast majority (95 percent) of women and men who are somewhere in the middle of the distributions of scores. The largest sex differences appear to be in the areas of verbal fluency and writing, favoring females, and in some visual–spatial abilities, favoring males. The average effect size (Cohen's *d*) in these areas, about one standard deviation, is of a magnitude that can be said to have social or practical significance. That is, group differences of this size may have real-world consequences in the form of noticeably different proportions of females and males exhibiting a skill or scoring above a cutoff score for scholastic and occupational opportunities. In most other areas, cognitive sex differences, however statistically significant or reliable, are so small as to be virtually meaningless.

In part because of feminist scholarship and critique of existing research on sex differences in cognition, research on sex comparisons is today more sophisticated and methodologically sound than ever before. But sexism remains a serious problem in this research. Why is it, for instance, that the literature on the female advantage in verbal fluency or perceptual speed is so much smaller than the literature on the male advantage in visual–spatial ability? We need to question why scholars seem much more likely to value and attempt to explain male rather than female excellence. Are some abilities valued more in society precisely because they are "male" and others devalued precisely because they are "female"? It is by now well known that spatial abilities, like most other abilities, involve skills that can be taught (Newcombe, Mathason, & Terlecki, 2002; Vasta, Knott, & Gaze, 1996). If visual–spatial ability is as important as some believe, and if girls are at such a serious disadvantage in this arena relative to boys, why are there so few curricular programs to develop this skill in girls? Certainly, there are plenty of reading and language remediation programs for students, predominantly males, who are struggling in those areas.

Finally, we should be aware, and wary, of modern incarnations of biological explanations for cognitive sex differences favoring males. One of these is the still robust variability hypotheses, which posits that males are "generally more variable" than females. As noted earlier, saying that males are more variable suggests that they are more special, more promising, and less ordinary than females. In fact, the variability hypothesis has an undistinguished history rooted in questionable science and blatant sexism. The variability hypothesis to this day is inconsistently studied, found, reported, and interpreted, raising questions as to why variability is studied more often with some traits than with others, and what being "more variable" means. In the domain of cognitive abilities, variability has been invoked to explain the high-level performance of some males on standardized tests of mathematical and visual–spatial ability. Clearly, the connotation appears to be that high variability is in itself good, that variability is somehow biologically based, and that it is more characteristic of males than females, even in the absence of any scientific evidence.

But perhaps the latest and most compelling of the biological explanations are the evolutionary psychology theories of sexual selection to explain cognitive sex differences, particularly sex differences in visual–spatial ability. According to these theories, the division of labor based on sex required early men to roam large areas and kill animals, which in turn required cognitive and motor skills such as mental rotation and aiming missiles. Early women, on the other hand, were mainly preoccupied with pregnancy, nursing, child care, and gathering fruits and vegetables, which presumably did not call for nuanced spatial skills. Evolutionary psychology explanations, while seemingly compelling, are untestable, explain everything after the fact, and ignore large bodies of data that do not conform to that explanatory framework. For example, such explanations routinely fail to note that women have always engaged in spatial tasks and have played significant roles in hunting (Smuts, 1995). Box 6.1 summarizes the practical implications of the cognitive sex differences we have discussed.

GENDER ISSUES IN ACADEMIC ACHIEVEMENT AND THE EXPERIENCE OF SCHOOL

Education around the World

Education is probably the single most important factor in improving the lives of women and men. Although both boys and girls obviously benefit from an education, it appears that educating girls actually produces a greater return; in many parts of the world, it is the female's level of education that is the critical factor in lifting the family out of poverty (Neft & Levine, 1997). Throughout the world, it is generally the case that the more education a woman has, the brighter the future for her and her children. Educated women are more likely to use birth control, have smaller families with children spaced farther apart, and experience fewer complications of pregnancy. Educated women not only are better able to obtain a paying job but also are more likely to take good physical care of their children, educate them, and share their knowledge with them and community members. Yet despite the well-documented benefits of educating females, parents in many parts of the world, and some parents in the United States, prefer to invest in educating their sons rather than their daughters, keeping their daughters home to help with the household

chores and care for younger siblings. About two-thirds of all students who leave school before completing their first four years are girls, with the sex difference much larger in developing countries. Religious laws and customs also affect girls' access to education: In some Muslim societies, for example, girls are kept out of school because their parents do not want them taught by male teachers or sitting in classrooms with boys (Neft & Levine, 1997).

Whereas girls are severely disadvantaged educationally in the developing world, particularly in sub-Saharan Africa and parts of Asia, girls now stay in school longer than boys in most of the developed world. Over the past few decades, some countries have witnessed dramatic increases in the number of girls remaining in school through high school and college. In the United States, for example, 75 percent of girls now finish high school, compared to just 53 percent as recently as 1970. Astonishingly, in 2002, 57 percent of all bachelor's degrees awarded in the United States were earned by women (Hacker, 2003). Similarly, in many other developed countries women now outnumber their male classmates in colleges and universities. In fact, among developed nations, only in Switzerland and Japan, in which women account for 36 and 40 percent of the student body, respectively, do more men than women go to college (Neft & Levine, 1997). Women overtaking men in overall educational achievement in the United States and much of the West is a striking cultural development with a host of possible implications. Curiously, this trend has, until very recently, gone largely unremarked in the media. When it is discussed, it is often with alarm, questioning whether there is a "war against boys" in current U.S. and British societies (Sommers, 2000), whether there will be enough males to fill top positions, and just who there will be for these highly literate, college-educated young women to partner with, given past trends for women to "marry up" (see Chapter 9). Chapter 5 contains further information about the role of education in development.

Gender in the Classroom

Over the past 25 years, much research attention has been paid to gender in the classroom. We will briefly

Box 6.1

Some Practical Implications of Cognitive Sex Differences

Psychologist Diane Halpern (1997) has extensively reviewed the vast literatures on cognitive sex differences and offers the following guidelines in drawing conclusions from this complex research.

1. Just because there are average differences in some cognitive abilities between females and males does not mean that one group is smarter or better than the other. Sex differences depend on numerous features of the study, including the particular test or task, the instructions, and the sample of males and females. They are not necessarily permanent. Do not misuse the data to advance a social or political agenda.

2. Research findings are based on group averages, and no one is average. The results cannot be generalized to any one individual. Group membership must not be permitted to make inferences about individuals or to limit talent development.

3. Beliefs about group differences, even without conscious awareness, exert powerful effects on thoughts and behaviors. Research suggests that people hold stereotypes about females' and males' abilities, and that these stereotypes have negative effects on females' and males' performance. Research shows that instructions and other contextual factors affect performance and can exacerbate sex differences.

4. Be mindful that the hormone-like chemicals that are polluting our environment, particularly pesticides that mimic the action of sex hormones, may alter the intelligence of humans exposed to them, a hypothesis that remains untested.

5. Research on human cognition needs support. Research on the effects of estrogen and testosterone replacement therapy offer great hope to an aging society.

6. There are many implications of the fact that boys mature later than girls, and teachers should consider this when making assignments to low-ability groups in the primary grades, especially in reading.

7. We have remedial instruction in reading and mathematics, but spatial reasoning, in which boys far outperform girls, is virtually never taught in school, despite research suggesting that it is a skill that can be improved with training. All children need opportunities to develop these skills.

8. Most standardized tests used for admission to college, graduate, and professional schools and for scholarships underpredict or underestimate female performance and overpredict or overestimate male performance. Multiple measures of abilities must be used in decision making, including course grades and tests of writing.

9. There are no cognitive reasons to support sex-segregated schools, but there may be social reasons to support sex-segregated education. It is by now well documented that girls and boys have different experiences in schools. We need further research on the effects of sex-segregated learning environments.

10. Interpret all research results in the area of cognitive sex differences with a healthy skepticism and make sure that all conclusions are data based. People frequently have social and political preferences for different explanations. Be especially wary of simple-minded conclusions such as "It's all in the hormones" or "It's all in the mother's attitude." No one study will settle controversial issues raised by this research, and no one explanation for differences is likely at this point to account for the complex patterns of findings in this area.

Source: From "Sex Difference in Intelligence: Implications for Education," by D. F. Halpern, 1997, *American Psychologist, 52*(10), pp. 1097–1099.

review the research on how girls and boys perform in school, how teachers respond to girls and boys, and the potential effects of sexism in schools, from grade school to college.

Grades. Research is consistent in showing that girls get better grades than boys in all or virtually all subjects, including mathematics, throughout school (Stricken, Rock, & Burton, 1993). Many possible reasons have been put forth to explain why males do better on standardized tests and females do better in course grades or, alternatively, why standardized test scores *underpredict* (underestimate) later course grades for females but not for males. This means that girls, but not boys, consistently get better grades than their standardized scores would predict. Up until very recently, the kinds of tests on which females excel—written or essay tests—were rarely used by major crafters of tests, such as the Educational Testing Service (ETS), the organization that brings us the SAT and GRE tests. In the late 1990s, ETS incorporated a writing component into its exams. Newer changes in the structure of the exam, under preparation as this text was going to print, might further eliminate some of the advantage for boys. The new SAT will require an entire section devoted to writing, which will include an essay and questions about grammar and will eliminate verbal analogies, the section of verbal exams in which males tend to have a slight edge. The new math section will include, for the first time, Algebra II class material, and certain classes of applied math problems will be eliminated (Cloud, 2003). Of course, it remains to be seen what effects these changes, set to go into effect in 2005, will have on the relative scores of females and males.

It has also been suggested that grades reflect other sorts of behaviors besides cognitive ability, for example, studiousness and neatness, which are unrelated to cognition (Bridgeman & Moran, 1996). Finally, it is possible that there is a grading bias against boys. In any case, the fact that girls outperform boys in virtually all subjects suggests that they are learning in school at least as well as boys are and that factors other than ability to learn are keeping girls from entering some fields.

Teacher Expectations and Behavior. Research consistently shows that, from preschool through college and graduate and professional school, teachers, both female and male, give boys and men more attention than girls and women, although there is evidence that some differential treatment is starting to fade (Kleinfield, 1998). In elementary school, teachers check boys' work more often, call on them more often, and praise, criticize, and punish them more

often than they do girls (Brophy, 1985; Harris, 1997; Sadker & Sadker, 1994). This is in part because boys "demand more attention" from teachers than girls do in the form of presenting more behavior problems, challenging the teacher's authority or information, and asserting themselves by asking questions without raising their hands. As we read in Chapter 5, there is evidence of sexism in the classroom, with teachers treating girls and boys differently, for example, by directing more questions to boys than girls and asking boys higher-level questions than girls (Barba & Cardinale, 1991). The fact that teachers seem to spend more time on boys than girls is usually interpreted to mean that boys need and demand more attention by virtue of their disruptive behaviors. But this may also suggest that boys are less susceptible to teachers' influence than girls, and teachers may need to work harder to get boys' attention (Valian, 1998). This explanation is consistent with evidence that, for boys, attention and approval of their male peers is more important than the responses of either teachers or female peers (Fagot, 1985).

We have long known that teachers' attitudes toward their students affect students' performances and attitudes toward learning and their sense of themselves and their futures. Robert Rosenthal's classic Pygmalion studies illustrated that when teachers were told that certain of their students, randomly designated, had higher IQs than others, those students designated with high IQs did better at the end of the term than students who were said to have low IQs. Thus, teachers' expectations became self-fulfilling prophecies (Rosenthal & Jacobson, 1968). Studies of teachers' attributions for boys and girls have found that teachers are more likely to attribute boys' academic successes to ability and girls' successes to hard work (Hunter College Women's Studies Collective, 1995), and that teachers have overall higher expectations of boys than girls, despite girls' higher grades (Sadker & Sadker, 1994), especially in math and the sciences. There are some exceptions to this trend, however: Teachers generally have higher expectations for the performance of African American girls than boys (Ross & Jackson, 1991).

It would be unfair to characterize most teachers as sexist or blame teachers for reproducing gender inequities that are created by the larger society. And despite the fact that there are not large sex differences in how female and male teachers treat students, female college professors tend to be less traditional in the classroom and to use styles and techniques from which women—and men—students benefit. For example, female professors are less likely to be authoritarian in the classroom and more likely to encourage cooperation, discussion, and group work. There is also evidence that college women participate more equally with their male peers in college classes that women, rather than men, teach (Basow, 2004; Crawford & McLeod, 1990).

Sexism and gender inequities in the classroom are not limited to teachers' treatment of boys and girls. A report called "Women on Words and Images," published in 1974, analyzed 134 elementary school readers with 2,760 stories and found that stories in which boys were the center of attention outnumbered stories about girls by a ratio of 5:2. Stories about male adults outnumbered stories about female adults by 3:1. Male and female characters in animal stories appeared in a ratio of 2:1 and in folk and fantasy tales, 4:1. There were 147 role possibilities for male characters compared with 25 for girls (Hunter College Women's Studies Collective, 1995). Other examinations of gender-role stereotyping show a trend for girls to be portrayed as more active than they had been previously, but, overall, girls are still portrayed as less active and competitive than boys and boys as less nurturing and dependent than girls (Kimball, 1995; Kortenhaus & Demarest, 1993).

Similarly, school textbooks, especially in math and science, are full of sexist references. To this day, boys and men are more likely to be portrayed in active roles and exciting occupations, with women portrayed as less active and successful (Federbush, 1974; Marx & Roman, 2002). Only recently have nonsexist language and sex-fair portrayals become widespread in grade school textbooks (Hunter College Women's Studies Collective, 1995).

The situation does not improve markedly for girls as they climb the academic ladder. As noted in Chapter 5, a well-known study entitled "How Schools Shortchange Girls," supported by the American Association of University Women (AAUW, 1992), cited the unequal treatment that girls receive in high school in a wide range of areas, including curricula, materials used in classrooms, testing, and teacher attention. Despite these disadvantages, high school girls get better grades than boys in all subjects, including math and science, they like school better, and they drop out less frequently than boys. During high school, girls outnumber boys in all extracurricular activities except sports and hobby clubs. Almost twice as many girls as boys participate in student government, band and orchestra, and drama and service clubs. More girls than boys work on the yearbook and school newspapers and are members of honor and service societies. More boys than girls still participate in sports, but the gap is narrowing (Giuliano, Popp, & Knight, 2000).

Despite the gains made by girls in recent years, it remains the case that both overt and subtle factors affect adolescents in high school in ways that reinforce stereotypical choices in course selection and career preparation. Boys are much more likely than girls to belong to chess clubs, be members of math teams and clubs, and attend computer summer camps (Halpern, 2000). College-bound boys are 10 percent more likely than college-bound girls to take four years of high school math and much more likely to take high school science courses, particularly physics (Catsambis, 1999). High school counselors in particular have been found to steer adolescents in gender-biased directions. At the highest levels of academic achievement, boys are encouraged to seek the most prestigious and highest paying careers, and in vocational training, boys more than girls are guided toward higher-paying skilled craft jobs (Hoffman, 1972; Hunter College Women's Studies Collective, 1995).

On the college level, reports have described the classroom climate as "chilly" for women (Basow, 2004; Hall & Sandler, 1982). Several patterns of behavior that harm women in the college classroom have been identified, including disparaging comments about women generally, seductive behavior toward women, calling more on male than female students, offering men more and better choice research opportunities, and ignoring the women in the class (Hall & Sandler, 1982). Women's ideas are often credited to others (Basow, 2004). Women are conspicuously absent even in college textbooks (Ferre & Hall, 1990). Even when women's contributions are cited, their gender often goes unremarked and they are taken for men, or they are presented as hand-maidens to their male colleagues, sometimes their husbands. Even two-time Nobel prize–winning scientist Marie Curie has been characterized in print as her husband's "helpmate" (Basow, 1992, p. 150).

As we noted earlier, women now receive more undergraduate degrees than men, but they still do not receive an equal number of professional and doctoral degrees, especially in the sciences and engineering, and those who receive these advanced degrees do so in an atmosphere that is less supportive and hospitable than it is for men. The higher up one climbs in the academic ladder, the fewer women and more men one encounters as professors, mentors, administrators, and gatekeepers, and the more likely one is to encounter the chill in the academic climate. As Basow (2004) notes, this chill makes female college students feel like imposters in the halls of academia, contributes to their drop in self-esteem, and affects their choices of classes, majors, and careers.

Achievement Motivation

Despite the facts that girls and women do better than boys and men in school, and are graduating from high school and college in greater proportions than men, women still enjoy considerably less occupational success than men. Psychologists, among others, have taken pains to explain why there is a gap between women's cognitive ability and their career achievement. There are many possible candidates. For one thing, as we have just seen, there has been and continues to be discrimination against women throughout all levels of schooling, including professional schools. At the end of the nineteenth century, for instance, almost all women physicians were affiliated with women's institutions, because men's medical schools would not admit them. Quotas restricting entry of women (and Jews and men of color) into medicine persisted well into this century. Similarly, a struggle was necessary in nearly all the states in which women sought to become lawyers (Hunter College Women's Studies Collective, 1995).

Another possible explanation for women's lower levels of professional accomplishment may reside in their **achievement motivation.** As defined by the originator of this construct, David McClelland, achievement motivation is the desire to accomplish something of importance due to one's own efforts, the desire to excel at what one does (McClelland, Atkinson, Clark, & Lowell, 1953). McClelland and his colleagues tested achievement motivation using a projective technique that asked people to write a story about an ambiguous set of pictures that was designed to elicit achievement themes. They found that, under competitive conditions, men but not women showed an increase in achievement motivation. They concluded that women did not have the motivation to achieve and continued their program of research using only men.

Matina Horner revived interest in studying achievement motivation in women with a different kind of projective test (Horner, 1969). She asked her respondents to compose a story following this lead sentence, which differed only in the sex of the target person: "After first term finals, Anne (John) found herself (himself) at the top of her (his) medical school class." Female respondents wrote about Anne; males about John. Horner found that more than 90 percent of the men wrote happy stories about John that indicated satisfaction, dedication, and continued success for the character. But 65 percent of the female respondents wrote strange and conflicted stories about Anne that were full of negative imagery suggesting the belief that high academic success in women was associated with physical unattractiveness, social rejection, concerns about adequacy as a woman, and denial that Anne achieved her success. Horner dubbed her findings women's "fear of success," and the concept caught fire in psychology.

Subsequent research on **fear of success** has not consistently supported the notion that there are large gender differences in the motive to avoid success. Michele Paludi (1984) reviewed 64 studies on the fear of success and found about the same incidence of this fear in men as in women. Cherry and Deaux (1978) further refined our understanding of this construct by replicating the original Horner study (1969) with a new variable: how gender appropriate the occupation is for the target individual. They asked students to complete sentences about Anne and John, who were at the top of their classes in either medical or nursing school. They found high fear of success stories written about Anne in the medical school story and John in the nursing school story, suggesting that men and women may fear the negative consequences of deviating from societal norms that specify what is permissible for each gender. Meanwhile, despite a conspicuous lack of empirical support, research on fear of success as a personality defect in women continues to the present (Piedmont, 1995).

Some people have suggested that the key to explaining the achievement gap between men and women lies with their different motives to succeed: Men achieve because of their desire to excel; women because of a desire to affiliate or win others' approval (Hoffman, 1972). There is not much evidence to support the notion that men and women achieve for different reasons—indeed, research suggests the opposite. Women and men want the same things from their jobs (Valian, 1998). But gender-role socialization and the internalized norm standards by which men and women judge themselves suggest that there may be different expressions of achievement motives for men and women. Societal norms for being a successful woman have always involved being a nurturant, devoted wife and mother, a socially adept and physically attractive person. Being a successful man in our society does not require excellence in so many disparate domains, but clearly requires success on the job. Attempting to fulfill all of these roles pulls women in different directions and makes it more difficult to compete successfully with men in graduate and professional schools and in their occupations. As we note further in Chapter 9, there is ample evidence that high-achieving women often put their careers on hold to support their husbands' careers and begin families. For example, when graduate students marry each other, the woman is likely to undertake most of the household tasks and, once they become mothers, many women graduate students are unable to continue their studies, citing such reasons for dropping out as the emotional strain involved, pressure from husbands, and a belief that their professors did not take them seriously enough (Hunter College Wom-

en's Studies Collective, 1995). Relatedly, it is much more socially acceptable for women not to aim high and succeed in a profession, and much more stigmatizing for men to aim low, quit, or fail than women.

Women's achievement may take different forms throughout the life span, with some women becoming quite ambitious for their husbands and children while their families are young and pursuing their personal ambitions by returning to school or entering the workforce as their family obligations ease. We will discuss issues relating to returning or *reentry* women shortly. See Box 6.2 on women's and men's career patterns in science for a glimpse into some of the factors affecting the paths of elite women and men in science.

In conclusion, women and men are not very different in their overall fear of success or motive to achieve, although we need further research on the conditions that activate these motives in men and women. In any case, it is unlikely that these factors account for the large differences in occupational achievement between men and women.

Attributions for Success and Failure and Expectations for Performance

"I got an A." "She gave me a D."

We bet that at some point in your college careers you have heard students talking about their grades this way: taking responsibility for a positive outcome and distancing themselves from a negative one. Social psychologists have found that we make judgments all the time about the likely causes of outcomes in our lives and that these judgments have implications for how we feel and behave in the future. These judgments about the causes of our own and other people's behaviors are called **attributions** (Heider, 1958). Attribution theory has become one of the most influential of social psychological theories since it was introduced a half century ago. Some social psychologists have suggested that females and males make different attributions about their successes and failures in achievement situations and that females' patterns of attributions hurt their performance.

Psychologists have identified three dimensions of attributions about causality in achievement situations

BOX 6.2

Achievement Patterns of Women and Men in Science

The impetus for much of the work in cognitive sex differences was the observation that women were severely underrepresented in the ranks of great scientists. Women have clearly made progress in science over the course of this century, with more women than ever before listed as members of the prestigious National Academy of Sciences, the main scientific advisory group to the government. The number and percentage of women recipients of the Nobel Prize for science have slowly increased over the past 30 years. Since its inception in 1901, the Nobel Prize has been bestowed on more than 650 recipients in the areas of science, economics, literature, peace, but as of 1996, only 28—about 4 percent—of all recipients were women, and less than half of women's awards were in science (Neft & Levine, 1997). The position of women in science today is a blend of undeniable progress and unfulfilled promise (Sonnert & Holton, 1996). Despite clear gains over the past quarter century, a big gender gap in scientific achievement persists.

A large-scale study called Project Access researched the degree of gender disparity in career outcomes in science and examined possible causes for the gender differences (Sonnert & Holton, 1996). Project Access focused exclusively on an elite group of male and female scientists who had received prestigious postdoctoral fellowships in the areas of the biological, physical, and social sciences, engineering, and mathematics. About 700 scientists of different ages and stages of professional development participated in this study of career patterns.

As you would expect, the study found great variation in responses within each sex. But some clear sex differences emerged. For example, in most scientific areas, women's academic rank fell below that of men's, even after controlling for academic productivity (usually measured in terms of number of scientific articles). In fact, women published less than men, although their work was cited by other scientists more often, one clear indicator of scientific impact.

Other sex differences pointed to some of the obstacles that women face in science. Almost three quarters of the women reported experiencing sex discrimination in science, compared with 13 percent of the men who reported reverse discrimination based on their sex. This discrimination included not only sexual harassment by colleagues but also exclusion from collaborating on research projects as equal or senior partners and marginalization at scientific conferences. Many more women than men stated that their mentors treated them as subordinates rather than peers.

Sex differences in socialization and resultant gender differences in style may contribute to some of the differences in outcomes that were observed. Male scientists in the study expressed much more confidence in their scientific ability than women did, and men emerged as more combative, competitive, and self-promoting than comparable women. The competitive and aggressive style of male scientists is frequently noted by others in science. Relatedly, women were more likely than men to shun hypercompetitive areas in science and were more likely than men to carve out small niche areas to probe. There was no evidence in this study to suggest that women "did science" fundamentally differently from men; if anything they were more meticulous and perfectionistic in using traditional research methods.

The authors explained the differences in the ways that men and women approach science in terms of different socialization patterns of males and females and structural features of the scientific establishment. Women are taught from girlhood not to promote themselves or their ideas too forcefully, to back down when challenged, and to be conciliators and compromisers in groups of people. But beyond these gender-role explanations, we cannot ignore that gender differences in achievement in science also arise from a collegial environment that is hostile to women—putting them under the magnifying glass and denying them opportunities (Sonnert & Holton, 1996). Finally, while Sonnert & Holton did not find a negative effect of being married or having children on achievement in science for women or men in this elite sample, they did find that female scientists were far more likely to choose opportunities to be with their spouse than were male scientists, and thus women sacrificed high-powered scientific careers for their families far more than men did.

In her influential book *Why So Slow? The Advancement of Women,* Virginia Valian (1998) reviewed the results of hundreds of studies on the status of women in the professions, science, and the academy, and amplified these findings: Women start out on roughly equal footing, but over time their careers diverge, with men getting more promotions and raises. In science and academia, even when productivity in the form of publications is held constant, men advance more quickly than women. Although men publish more papers than women, women's work is cited more often by other scientists—a sign that their work is regarded as valuable. Valian, along with Sonnert and Holton (1996), found that women emphasize quality over quantity in research. She made the point that gender bias in science and academia is mild and subtle, but over time it profoundly affects women's outcomes.

(Weiner, 1986). The first is whether the cause is internal to the individual, something the individual is or does, or external, something that happens to the person. The second is whether the cause is stable, an enduring characteristic of the person or situation, or unstable, a condition or situation that can be changed. The third is whether the cause is controllable by the individual or uncontrollable. According to Weiner (1986), success and failure in achievement situations can generally be attributed to one of four causes: a person's ability, effort made, task difficulty, or luck. These causes all differ in how internal, stable, and controllable they are. Generally, ability and effort are considered internal factors, and luck and task difficulty, external factors. Task difficulty and ability are regarded as stable, whereas effort and luck are unstable. Effort is seen as controllable, but ability level, luck, and task difficulty are usually not. There are exceptions to this neat division; for example, sometimes people can control task difficulty by choosing or avoiding demanding courses, curricula, or institutions. And, with enough practice, we can often change our level of ability in many areas.

Early research in the 1970s comparing the kinds of attributions that men and women make for success and failure found an interesting and disturbing pattern of results: Men tended to attribute their successes to their ability, whereas women tended to attribute their successes to luck. In an interesting observational study, Kay Deaux and her colleagues noticed that, at amusement parks, men more often played games of skill such as tossing a ring around a bottle, whereas women tended to play games of luck, such as bingo (Deaux, White, & Farris, 1975). They then designed a laboratory study to test under controlled conditions the notion that men more than women prefer tests of skill. They found that 75 percent of the men chose a game of skill over a game of luck, compared with 35 percent of the women. The problems with this sex difference are clear: Attributing your success to your ability, an internal and stable characteristic, means that you may be more likely to pursue challenges in this area in the future, to say to yourself, for example, "I'm good at math; maybe I'll be a math major." But if you attribute your success to luck, an external and unstable factor, you may not wish to press that luck by taking any more math classes. The gendered pattern of attributions is replicated when people are judging others as well as themselves. Deaux and Emswiller (1974) found that when people are judging the performance of others they attribute men's successes to their abilities and women's to good luck or some other unstable, uncontrollable factor. As Virginia Valian (1998) notes, "Normal cause-and-effect relationships hold more often for men than for women; men live in a more lawful world" (p. 183).

In the 1980s, meta-analytic reviews of the studies on sex differences in attributions show essentially no differences in how people make attributions for successes and failures (Frieze, Whitley, Hanusa, & McHugh, 1982). Since then, however, research on sex comparisons has complicated the picture. Sex differences in attributions have appeared inconsistently, taking on a "now you see them, now you don't" look (see Mednick & Thomas, 1993, and Swim & Sanna, 1996, for extensive reviews). For example, it has been found that, when men and women score high in instrumentality, women make ability attributions at the same rate as men. More recently, Hill and Augoustinos (1997) failed to find the traditional pattern of female-derogating, male-favoring attributions for achievement in Australian college students. They explained their findings in terms of attitudinal, political, and social changes in the latter part of the twentieth century and noted the possibility that contemporary sexism is more subtle and expressed in more socially acceptable ways. Ongoing research is looking at the personal and situational factors that affect how women and men make attributions, for example, age and level of achievement of respondents and type of task.

Research on attributions for success and failure may show inconsistent gender patterns, but research on sex differences in expectations for success paints a clearer portrait. In elementary school and especially in the earliest grades, girls are more likely than boys to see themselves as smart and express confidence about their abilities to succeed, although boys already begin predicting that they will do better on certain tests, such as mathematical tests, in the earliest grades. By eighth grade, however, girls start to lose their confidence and come to perceive themselves as increasingly less intelligent and less likely to succeed. By high school and throughout college, girls have less confidence in their abilities to succeed than boys. In college, females asked to estimate their college grades predict lower grades than males do, even though their grades still tend to be higher than males' (Crandall, 1969; Valian, 1998). This tendency to underestimate their performance occurs especially on tasks and tests considered masculine, such as mathematics, visual–spatial ability, and unfamiliar tasks (Beyer, 1990). This trend is especially disturbing because research in psychology consistently shows that people who expect success are more likely to achieve it, and that low expectations are a drag on performance (Crandall, 1978).

Teachers' and parents' expectations for girls' achievements in mathematics and science decline as girls progress through high school, and may account in part for girls dropping out of the most challenging curricula in those areas. In turn, girls' and women's lowered expectations for success may indeed explain why they achieve less than their male counterparts. We need further research on the situational factors that affect expectations for success for men and women. We already know that instructions sets that stress competition lower women's expectations for success (House, 1974) and that evaluative feedback that offers an accurate assessment of their performance is particularly helpful to women (Roberts, 1991). Roberts points out that, because of socializa-

tion factors that encourage competition among boys and men and provide frequent evaluative feedback to them, boys and men are at an advantage relative to girls and women in receiving regular information about their abilities. As opportunities to compete and obtain feedback increase for girls, their expectation for success may also increase.

SPECIAL TOPICS IN ABILITY AND ACHIEVEMENT

Gender and Computers

At the same time that the gender gap is closing in on so many important areas in education, it is large and growing in a key area—technology, specifically computers. The late 1990s witnessed a puzzling drop of enrollment in higher-skill computer classes and in the numbers of bachelor's and master's degrees awarded in computer science for both women and men. But enrollment of women in computer classes and degrees in computer science awarded to women are dropping much faster than is the case for men. Thus, women are becoming a progressively smaller proportion of people in academic computer science and the computing industry. For example, in the early 1980s, 37 percent of graduates with computer science degrees were women, whereas in 1995 only 28 percent were women (Neft & Levine, 1997). There is mounting evidence that many women expressing early interest in computing careers drop out of the academic pipeline and pursue other careers. This information comes at a time when many scholars are also noting that girls from grade school to high school are also losing interest in computing.

We live in an age of high technology in which facility with computers and the Internet is helpful in virtually all disciplines and occupations and essential in others. Many people are concerned that we have created a hypermasculine "computer culture" that is hostile to girls and women and discourages their entry into certain career paths. Why has the use of computers become so gendered, and how can society foster more and better computer use among girls?

Some scholars argue that the lack of a formal computer science curriculum in most middle and high schools and the lack of required courses in computers at these levels are problematic in computer classrooms. The most aggressive students, typically boys, monopolize the machines. Leslie Klein, instructor of information systems at Pace University in New York City and computer teacher of middle school children, described the typical computer classes this way: "The computers are always consumed by the boys who rush in, desperate to continue where they left off the day before in Oregon Trail, Karateka, or Carmen San Diego. An occasional girl wanders in, but would practically need interference from the heavens to gain access to these monopolized computers" (Klein, 1990, p. 36). She adds that boys are more likely to use pirated software, whereas girls follow the school rules and subsequently have fewer and less interesting programs with which to work.

Others have pointed to sexist educational software as a cause for different computer use by boys and girls and men and women. In their book on sex bias in educational software, Huff and Cooper (1987) presented evidence to suggest that software designers virtually always use male as the "default" value of student and design gamelike programs featuring missiles, violence, and other metaphors and fantasies that are very exciting for boys but anxiety-producing and unappealing to girls. Less sexist software that is as attractive and interesting to girls as current software is to boys would increase girls' and women's interest in computers. As late as 1999, however, companies that tried to market computer games for girls that depict girls in nonstereotypic ways struggled to succeed (Harmon, 1999). In 1998, six of the top ten computer games for girls had Barbie themes, and the other four featured Madeline, the French heroine of children's books. Nonetheless, there is some recent evidence that girls' attitudes about technology and the software industry's attitudes about girls and technology are becoming more progressive (Harmon, 1999; Rothstein, 1997).

Relatedly, observers note that males and females use computers differently, with males more likely to see them as toys and females more likely to see them as tools for solving problems and doing tasks. Obviously, a competitive nation cannot afford to foster the notion that technology is a largely male domain. Developing and marketing more software aimed at helping females accomplish their academic, career, social, and personal goals would be a step in the direction of increasing computer use among females. Unfortunately, psychologists have been slow to study the effects of technology on learning, communication, and gender.

Issues in Evaluating Single-Sex and Coeducational Institutions

Do girls and boys and women and men learn better in schools and classes that are separated by sex? This question has captivated scholars in recent years (AAUW, 1998). It seems like a simple one, but in fact it has many complicated answers. For one thing, we need to consider college women and men separately from students in grades K through 12. During the 1960s and 1970s, most women's colleges either closed or became coeducational, seemingly ending a long and distinguished tradition in the United States of single-sex education for women. Around the same time, most remaining single-sex colleges for men, with the important exception of military academies, threw open their doors to women, who indeed now predominate on most college campuses. But recently there has been renewed interest in single-sex education, particularly for women, and single-sex women's schools are experiencing a surge in applications (AAUW, 1998). How do women benefit from single-sex schools? Are there disadvantages to women of single-sex schools?

Early studies on the effects of single-sex colleges for women appeared to show that such schools produced a disproportionate number of high-achieving women (Tidball, 1973). Tidball investigated the college backgrounds of women whose achievements were listed in *Who's Who of American Women* and whose college experience occurred between 1910 and 1960. She found that women's colleges produced more high-achieving women than did coeducational institutions in each of the five decades and attributed this to the greater number of women faculty and administrators who serve as role models in women's schools. At the turn of the century, even though women's colleges produce less than 5 percent of all female college graduates, 25 percent of all women who are on the boards of Fortune 500 companies and 50 percent of the women in Congress were graduated from women's colleges (Wood, 2001). It is also the case, as Rice and Hemmings (1988) noted, that the kinds of women who applied to women's colleges before the 1970s were a self-selected and special group—brighter, better prepared, and more socially and economically advantaged than female students who went to coeducational schools. Today, with so many options for top female students, it is not necessarily true that the most high-achieving women attend women's colleges. Still, it remains the case that in women-only colleges women experience fewer distractions, have more opportunities, and gain self-confidence to further develop themselves, especially to exercise leadership (AAUW, 1998).

The American Association of University Women (AAUW) Educational Foundation recently commissioned a major study of the broad effects of single-sex classes and schools on students in grades K through 12. This study found many shortcomings in the existing research on single-sex classes and schools, but found evidence for the value of such schools in helping girls to establish comfortable places to explore the world and to consider issues of gender identity, especially during early adolescence. A more recent study compared the effects of sex-segregated and coeducational high schools on boys and girls. Evidence for the effects of such classes and schools on academic achievement is mixed, with some studies showing clear advantages for single-sex settings and some not (AAUW, 1998).

One particularly large and complex study investigated how socialization to gender operates in three types of independent high schools: girls' schools, boys' schools, and coeducational schools (Lee, Marks, & Byrd, 1994). Observational data were collected in 86 classrooms in 21 schools. These investigators found similar amounts of sexism in all three types of schools, although the forms of sexism varied, with gender domination (either boys dominating discussions or teachers recognizing boys more often than girls) overwhelmingly more common in coeducational schools and sex-role stereotyping more common in single-sex schools. Explicitly sexual incidents, for instance, sexually objectifying the other sex, were found only in boys' schools. The severest forms of sexism overall were found in boys' schools. Within coeducational schools, chemistry classes were the sites of the most frequent and blatant forms of sexism: male domination of discussions and teachers favoring boys and humiliating girls. The authors concluded that, although girls' schools were the most gender fair of all three types of schools, they also perpetuated a pernicious form of sexism: academic dependence and nonrigorous instruction in some areas, including chemistry. There is other evidence that single-sex settings have more positive outcomes for high school girls than boys.

The spotlight has been placed on single-sex schools at all levels in the past few years. We have witnessed dramatic, less-than-successful attempts to integrate all male preserves such as the Citadel and Virginia Military Academy. In inner cities, educators are struggling to solve problems of learning and discipline by attempting single-sex public education for boys and girls. Given the reality that most students attend schools with both females and males, we need to focus on how coeducation can be made more gender equitable for the ultimate good of both females and males. At the same time, evidence suggests that we need more and better information on how to preserve and improve a single-sex option for students who want and might benefit from such a choice. Clearly, we need further research on how to develop the aspirations and goals of adolescent girls in coeducational institutions. For example, we have seen how, within coeducational schools, the presence of adult women in positions of leadership and the formation of a committee to monitor gender equity may be advisable (Lee & Marks, 1990). Although sex-segregated schools are prohibited by law (Title IX) in public schools, providing sex-segregated math, science, and computer classes may have merit under some circumstances.

Finally, we need to look beyond test scores as outcome measures in this research and instead look at measures of leadership, confidence, feelings of community, empowerment, and a sense of what is possible. We are just beginning to understand the complex effects of single-sex and coeducational schools on males and females at the primary, secondary, and college levels.

Diversity Issues in Education

There is no one female or male student; males and females come in different ages, ethnicities, social classes, and other demographic categories. There has been a great deal of research in recent years on how ethnicity, class, and other factors vary with measured cognitive ability and academic achievement. It is crucial to note here that failure to take these variables into account impedes our understanding of achievement and shortchanges women and underserved minorities.

College educations and professional careers are at odds with traditional concepts of women's family roles in many cultures. Among African American females, for example, achieving in school is highly compatible with the notion that women pass on their advantages to their children. African American women experience less conflict in combining roles of family and career than do White or Latina women, and African American girls and women outperform African American boys and men in all levels of schooling. Asian Americans, especially those from China and Japan, are exceptionally high achieving in the United States. Until recently, Asian American women lagged somewhat behind Asian American men in their academic achievement, but the evidence is that they are catching up fast. Still, it is the case that many Asian cultures remain traditional, with prescribed roles for women that require them to subjugate their career goals to family roles. Latinas are lagging behind other racial and ethnic groups of girls in several key measures of academic attainment, although they perform better than their male peers on many measures. A full discussion of these ethnic and diversity issues is beyond the scope of this chapter, but see Chapter 3 for additional perspectives on diversity issues.

The past two decades have witnessed large numbers of women, called reentry or returning women, who finish their education after many years outside of school, usually to raise families. Increasingly, these women are self-supporting (Hunter College Women's Studies Collective, 1995). Able to focus on their personal goals, often for the first time in their lives, many reentry women are especially strong students. The point is that cultural factors interact with gender and other factors to produce striking effects among different kinds of women.

There is disturbing evidence that some women, particularly disadvantaged women, believe that they must hide who they are in order to succeed. A fascinating qualitative study explored the educational experiences of women who were academic high achievers and were disadvantaged as children (Le Page-Lees, 1997). In this study, disadvantage was described as having all three of the following characteristics: coming from a poor family, being a first-generation college student, and experiencing at least one type of familial dysfunction or traumatic childhood stress. The article described how participants managed their disadvantage in a system that rewards silence about such matters. It explored whether there needs to be a separation between the personal and the professional for people who are disadvantaged and how a connection between education and life experiences can be forged. Investigations such as this point up the need to consider social class and other background factors in understanding achievement.

Violence: A Developing Issue in Our Schools

The surge of violence in our schools has created a climate in which children and adolescents have been physically threatened and harmed as well as emotionally traumatized. Events such as the mass murders at Columbine High School and physical attacks on gay teens in the late 1990s induced many scientists and laypeople alike to look at what causes teens to commit senseless and brutal acts of violence. Gender matters in these cases for several reasons. The perpetrators are overwhelmingly, although not exclusively, young males. School is made particularly unpleasant and dangerous for those who do not conform to rigid notions of gender stereotypes: gay youth and girls who are lesbians, intersexed and transgendered teens, and boys perceived as sissies. In fact, sexual harassment of all kinds is about as common in U.S.

high schools as it is anywhere, with some surveys showing that four out of five students in grades 8 to 11 reporting that they have been the target of unwelcome sexual advances while at school or a school function (AAUW, 1992).

There is much about the male gender role that is implicated in violence in our schools. Unlike girls, boys learn early from parents and teachers that confrontational physical aggression is tolerated, even encouraged, in some circumstances. And there is ample evidence that, for boys, the reference group that is important to impress is their male peers, not adult authority figures. Aggression and violence often bring boys social recognition and respect from peers, among other, more tangible benefits (Campbell, 1993).

The victims and witnesses of violent acts often suffer a range of psychological consequences after such incidents, including posttraumatic stress disorder (PTSD) (described more fully in Chapter 12 and Chapter 13), which includes a variety of symptoms such as anxiety, loss of appetite, sleep disturbance, and nightmares. Gay and lesbian teens are more likely to drop out of high school, abuse drugs and alcohol, and attempt suicide than are other students (Lock & Steiner, 1999). Violence and its emotional consequences not only are severe problems in and of themselves but also profoundly affect students' ability to achieve in school.

The disturbing increase in the number of violent incidents in schools challenges us to consider a broad range of noncognitive factors affecting the learning and development of students.

SUMMARY

There are no easy answers to questions such as: Who's smarter, men or women? In fact, women and men are more alike than they are different, and any differences that exist between men and women are subtle variations in the patterns of abilities. Indeed, what we call sex differences are better regarded as gender differences because we do not know what biological, psychological, social, or cultural factors are at the root of these variations. What we do know is that many of these differences are disappearing with time and are affected by practice.

Many noncognitive factors have been studied in an attempt to understand girls' and womens' achievement and, in particular, the achievement gap between women and men. Some of these include achievement motivation, fear of success, attributions for success and failure, and expectations for success. Research evidence for sex differences in these areas is generally inconsistent with the exception of expectations: Girls and women expect to do less well than boys and men, and girls and women tend to underestimate their performance on many different kinds of tasks. Given the importance of expectations for performing well, we need to find ways to raise the confidence level of girls and women, and research is pointing to the importance of factors such as specific, accurate feedback about performance.

There are fascinating issues that currently concern scholars who are interested in gender and achievement. These include computers in the classroom, sex-segregated versus coeducational schooling, diversity issues, and violence in our schools. We need to consider how gender equity can be achieved in testing and education, and beyond.

KEY TERMS

Achievement motivation (p. 200)
Attributions (p. 201)
Effect size (p. 189)
Fear of success (p. 200)
Frequency distribution (p. 188)

Lateralization (p. 184)
Meta-analysis (p. 190)
Nonoverlapping distributions (p. 188)
Normal distribution (p. 188)

Statistically significant differences (p. 189)
Stereotype threat (p. 188)
Visual–spatial ability (p. 194)

DISCUSSION QUESTIONS

1. Let us imagine that the cognitive differences that are currently understood to exist between women and men were found to be innate. What would be the practical implications of such a finding? What would change about the educational and career opportunities and outcomes for women and men?

2. Ask your friends about their understandings of cognitive sex differences. In what areas do they see differences? How large do they think they are? How do they explain them?

3. What are some of the sex differences and similarities in the ways girls and boys and women and men use computers? Consider word processing, programming, email, Internet use, computer games, and so on. What are some of the implications of the ways females and males use computers?

4. What are some of the advantages and disadvantages of single-sex schools? Do these differ for females and males? Why or why not?

5. Ask your female friends about their experiences with math and science in school. Were they encouraged or discouraged to pursue these areas? To what do they attribute their successes and failures in math and science (talent, effort, luck, difficulty of the material)?

6. Females now outnumber males in higher education. Why do you think this is so, and what are the implications of this trend?

FURTHER READINGS

Caplan, P. J., Crawford, M., Hyde, J. S., & Richardson, J. T. E. (Eds.). (1997). *Gender differences in human cognition.* New York: Oxford University Press.

Fausto-Sterling, A. (1992). *Myths of gender: Biological theories about women and men* (2nd ed.). New York: Basic Books.

Halpern, D. F. (2000). *Sex differences in cognitive abilities* (3rd ed.). Mahwah, NJ: Erlbaum.

Hare-Mustin, R. T., & Maracek, J. (Eds.). (1990). *Making a difference.* New Haven, CT: Yale University Press.

Valian, V. (1998). *Why so slow? The advancement of women.* Cambridge, MA: MIT Press.

CHAPTER 7

THE WORLD OF WORK

Women constitute half the world's population, perform nearly two-thirds of its work hours, receive one-tenth of the world's income and own less than one-hundredth of the world's property.
—United Nations report

When we abolish the slavery of half of humanity, together with the whole system of hypocrisy that it implies, then the "division" of humanity will reveal its genuine significance and the human couple will find its true form.
—Simone deBeauvoir

Somewhere out in this audience may even be someone who will one day follow in my footsteps, and preside over the White House as the President's spouse. I wish him well.
—Barbara Pierce Bush; remarks at Wellesley College commencement

Nobody objects to a woman being a good writer or sculptor or geneticist if at the same time she manages to be a good wife, good mother, good looking, good tempered, well groomed and unaggressive.
—Leslie McIntyre

People think at the end of the day that a man is the only answer [to fulfillment]. Actually a job is better for me.
—Princess Diana

Because I am a woman, I must make unusual efforts to succeed. If I fail, one will say, "She doesn't have what it takes." They will say, "women don't have what it takes."
—Clare Boothe Luce

This chapter discusses the changing role of women in the workplace. We will explore and critically examine the myths that prevail regarding women's alleged limitations and discuss how these myths have shaped societal attitudes regarding women. Gender-based segregation within the workplace will be examined, with specific examples from both the white- and blue-collar worlds, describing experiences of women in both traditional and nontraditional occupations. Women experience a variety of discriminatory practices in the workplace based on sex, race, class, and sexual orientation. Yet women do more than simply survive in the workplace. They and their families thrive on the economic advantages that work provides to women and their families. This chapter considers women's multiple roles, suggesting ways in which women (and men) can attempt to deal effectively with the often conflicting demands of their personal and professional lives. Examples of sex discrimination, both in hiring practices and on the job, are explored, along with other obstacles (both overt and covert) that impede the progress of women in the workforce. Finally, this chapter deals with the exploitation of women and the very human need of women to have access to meaningful work outside the home as a part of their lives.

THE CHANGING ROLE OF WOMEN IN THE WORLD OF WORK

According to one estimate, approximately 60 percent of all women presently work outside the home and comprise 45.3 percent of the U.S. labor force (Hunter College Women's Studies Collective, 1995). These figures reflect a steady increase in working women over the past several decades. However, these proportions represent a major increase in the labor force participation rate of White women and a lesser increase in the rate among African American women (Higginbotham, 1997). African American women's work experience outside their homes is uniquely rooted in slavery (Jones, 1985), and their participation in paid employment is long established (Davis, 1981). Table 7.1 shows women's occupational and labor participation rate by ethnic category.

Not only are women working in more significant numbers than ever before, but they are also taking on far more significant roles within the workforce, training for and assuming positions of leadership in the worlds of business, medicine, and other realms that were once considered exclusively male (Iglitzen & Ross, 1986; United Nations, 1991). Just as women were once considered bad business risks and/or not worth training for executive positions, because it was assumed that the responsibilities of home and family would soon usurp their loyalty to their professions, today's antidiscrimination legislation has declared such thinking both archaic and illegal. Moreover, the trend toward allowing women (and men) more generous maternity (paternity) leave and providing on-site day care has opened doors for working mothers, whose numbers have increased tremendously since 1940 (Russo & Denmark, 1984). President Clinton's Family and Medical Leave Act has secured workers up to a total of 12 workweeks of unpaid leave during any 12-month period for one or more of the following reasons: for the birth and care of the newborn child of the employee; for placement with the employee of a son or daughter for adoption or foster care; to care for an immediate family member (spouse, child, or parent) with a serious health condition; or to take medical leave when the employee is unable to work because of a serious health condition (U.S. Department of Labor, 2003). This law has also helped to secure the future for women who wish to pursue meaningful, productive, lifelong careers.

According to an article in the *New York Times,* Norway has implemented a new policy to assist working mothers. Working mothers are being given two hours off during the workday each day to breast-feed their child at home or in the office. Norwegian law also allows women to breastfeed in public places, such as buses, parks, cafés, and stores. Currently, 99 percent of mothers in Norway breast-feed their children. Unlike the United States and Great Britain, Norway and Sweden are both countries that have had great success in encouraging mothers to breast-feed and promoting the benefits of breast milk. Additionally, Norwegian mothers are provided with a 10-month maternity leave at full pay or a 12-month leave at 80 percent pay. This makes it more practical for mothers to breast-feed their babies, as opposed to in the United States, where often maternity leave is allowed for only 4 to 6 weeks. Mothers in the United States may feel too harried and rushed, and choose not to breast-feed simply because it is impractical for them due to the demands of their employment (Alvarez, 2003).

Before proceeding to the next section, take a moment to answer the questions in Box 7.1. See how your own experience concurs with the answers.

MYTHS OF THE WORKPLACE

The myths that abound regarding women in the workplace tend to echo society's beliefs regarding the limitations of women and how these so-called limitations should dictate the positions to which they aspire. In academia, for example, women are seen as capable of taking on positions that are interactive, responsive, supportive, and labor intensive, such as teaching large introductory classes that call for an enormous amount of preparation, paperwork, and student contact. Men, on the other hand, are perceived as capable of doing work that is described as solitary, dominating, controlling, and unilateral, such as research (Fowlkes, 1987). Their work is objective and dispassionate. Thus, just as housewives are expected to play enabling roles in home and family while their husbands assume jobs that remove them from family life, teachers, usually women, are expected to play featured roles on campus, motivating students to succeed in both curricular and extracurricular activities, while highly paid researchers, usually men, tend to remove themselves from contact with students. Just as housewives and mothers are lauded with great sentimentality for efforts on behalf of others that go largely unpaid, so too are teachers more readily compensated sentimentally than financially.

Similarly, women living on a kibbutz in Israel, where egalitarianism among the sexes is a philosophical ideal, tend to associate continuing education and pursuing a career with masculinity. Some Israeli women, according to a study by Lobel, Agami-Rozenblatt, and Bempechat (1993), are likely to aspire only to

TABLE 7.1 Women's Occupational and Labor Participation Rate by Ethnic Category

CHARACTERISTIC	TOTAL UNITED STATES	WHITE AMERICAN	AFRICAN AMERICAN[a]	ASIAN AMERICAN[a]	HISPANIC	MEXICAN AMERICAN	PUERTO RICAN	CUBAN AMERICAN
Total Females 16+	100,654	77,270	11,684	2,550	7,842	4,726	883	480
In civilian labor force[b]	57,558	44,682	6,803	1,502	4,072	2,348	408	232
% in civilian labor force	57.2	57.8	58.2	58.9	51.9	51.6	46.2	48.4
Employed females	53,997	42,456	6,119	1,439	3,617	2,168	363	216
Percent unemployed	7.3	6.2	5.0	10.0	4.2	11.1	11.1	11.0
Occupation (%)								
Managerial/professional	28.8	30.9	18.8	27.9	15.4	13.6	18.5	18.4
Technical/sales/administrative support	42.8	43.9	39.7	43.3	40.9	40.7	48.4	49.0
Service	18.0	16.0	27.0	15.7	24.6	24.9	19.9	20.1
Farming/forestry/fishing	0.8	0.9	0.3	0.2	1.8	2.8	—	—
Precision production/craft/repair	1.9	1.7	2.3	3.0	2.5	2.8	2.4	2.0
Operators/fabricators/laborers	7.7	6.6	12.0	10.0	14.8	15.2	10.8	10.6
Females with earnings	62,050	48,613	10,944	1,606	4,240	2,542	424	251
Less than $10,000	37.9	37.0	54.0	36.0	32.7	49.6	35.9	33.3
$10,000–19,999	—	—	24.1	29.3	—	—	—	—
$10,000–24,000	37.9	37.7	—	—	38.1	36.7	42.3	42.0
$20,000–29,000	—	—	11.6	17.2	—	—	—	—
$25,000–49,000	21.1	22.0	—	—	14.5	12.7	20.8	23.7
$30,000–39,000	—	—	—	8.7	—	—	—	—
$30,000 or more	—	—	7.3	—	—	—	—	—
$40,000–49,000	—	—	—	4.8	—	—	—	—
$50,000 or more	3.1	3.3	—	4.0	1.4	1.0	1.0	0.9
Median earnings ($)	13,675	14,241	9,623	14,122	10,813	10,098	14,200	14,117
Mean earnings ($)	16,745	17,141	—	—	13,587	12,588	15,656	16,456

Source: For total United States, Whites, Hispanics, Mexican Americans, Puerto Ricans, and Cuban Americans, U.S. Census Bureau (1993d, 1994c); for African Americans, U.S. Census Bureau (1991, 1993c); for Asian Americans, U.S. Census Bureau (1992).

[a]Includes Hispanic origin.

[b]All numbers are in thousands.

True or False? Test Your Ideas about Women and Work

1. ___ T ___ F Most women in the United States seek employment in order to earn money for little luxuries that their families could not afford with one income.

2. ___ T ___ F There is clear evidence that a woman is more likely to be employed if her mother was employed.

3. ___ T ___ F High school career counselors have different aspirations for female and male students.

4. ___ T ___ F Women earn less than men on the average, but the difference between their salaries can be attributed to the fact that men have more experience, work more hours, and so forth.

5. ___ T ___ F American women spend about the same amount of time on housework now as in the 1920s.

6. ___ T ___ F Men and women in the same profession, such as business administration, are fairly similar in their personality characteristics.

7. ___ T ___ F The best explanation for the absence of women in nontraditional fields is that they lack the appropriate personality characteristics and skills.

8. ___ T ___ F When women are employed, their husbands perform substantially more household chores than when women are not employed.

9. ___ T ___ F Children of employed women have normal intellectual development, but they are often socially maladjusted.

10. ___ T ___ F Role strain, which women experience when they combine employment and home responsibilities, often leads to poor mental health.

Answers: (1) F; (2) T; (3) T; (4) F; (5) F; (6) T; (7) F; (8) F; (9) F; (10) F.

"women's" occupations, such as teaching and social work, nurturing roles that are extensions of motherhood. Nonetheless, despite their tendency to choose "feminine" jobs, these women consider themselves more masculine than their less educated counterparts on the kibbutz, who perform such traditionally feminine tasks as cooking, cleaning, and tending children. This attitude is entirely consistent with our own society's image of a corporate woman as less than feminine, as though ambition, assertiveness, and self-reliance were sex-related traits. Indeed, whether a woman breaks with society's norms by continuing her education, or by becoming an engineer or astronaut, chances are that society, and the woman herself, will see her very nonconformity as a masculine trait.

CONTEMPORARY SOCIETAL ATTITUDES TOWARD WORKING WOMEN

Economic and Personal Outcomes

Despite the strides that women have made, social attitudes and expectations regarding women are slow to change. Economic reality notwithstanding, there are many critics of working women, just as there are receptive audiences for these harsh comments. Such criticism grows more intense if a woman is also a mother and more intense still if she is perceived as a woman who is working to realize her professional ambitions. Society's attitudes toward professional women play an important role in the way that grown women perceive themselves as workers and the way that adolescent women perceive themselves as prospective workers. See Box 7.2.

The perception of gender differences can have a profound impact on women's success in the workplace. Even though research demonstrates few gender differences in the leadership behaviors of men and women, men more often emerge as leaders because both men and women are still being perceived in stereotypical ways. In the literature, an effort has been made to understand why women have not made more progress through attaining leadership roles in their careers. It has been shown that self-efficacy, androgyny, and self-esteem are positive and direct pre-

Box 7.2_____

Discrimination Questionnaire

Discrimination has become a fact in society and permeates our lives. If we seriously examine almost any situation, we can usually find evidence of some unequal disadvantage. Please answer each of the following questions:

1. Overall, how much discrimination do you think *women* experience in the *United States?*
_____ None _____ Some _____ Moderate _____ A Great Deal

2. Overall, how much discrimination do you think *women* experience in *your community?*
_____ None _____ Some _____ Moderate _____ A Great Deal

3. Overall, how much discrimination do *you* experience?
_____ None _____ Some _____ Moderate _____ A Great Deal

Source: Adapted from "The Denial of Personal Disadvantage among You, Me, and All the Ostriches," by F. J. Crosby, et al., in *Gender and Thought: Pyschological Perspectives,* edited by M. Crawford and M. Gentry, 1989. New York: Springer-Verlag.

dictors of a transformational leadership style. In addition, the level of education that a man or woman has attained also affects her or his leadership style indirectly by impacting self-efficacy (Younger, 2002).

Cross-Cultural Perspectives

A 1993 study of Guatemalan, Filipino, and U.S. adolescents' images of women as office workers and homemakers (Gibbons et al., 1993) reveals that a great many pancultural similarities exist in the traits differentially attributed to women and men. Their findings corroborate earlier research by Williams and Best (1982, 1990); Offer, Ostrov, Howard, and Atkinson (1988); and Schlegel and Barry (1991), with Williams and Best and Offer and colleagues approaching the question from an **etic** (universal) and Schlegel and Barry an **emic** (culturally specific) perspective. Their conclusions, which support the notion of a *universal adolescent* (similar across cultures), are consistent with the report by Gibbons and her colleagues (1993).

Gibbons and her group worked with adolescents in Guatemala, the Philippines, and the United States. These three nationalities were chosen because they

represent three different continents, cultural traditions, and sets of conditions for women in the home and the workplace. The researchers approached adolescents within these groups and had them interpret drawings that were executed by other adolescents within their respective groups. These drawings depicted ideal women within both the home and workplace. The results demonstrated the greatest degree of individualism among U.S. respondents and the greatest degree of collectivism among Guatemalan respondents. Filipino respondents were intermediate in their collectivism–individualism scores.

Although a number of significant differences characterized responses in the three settings, a number of universal perceptions also emerged that attest to adolescents' views of women and work, a view that shapes the way adolescent females perceive themselves as they mature and the roles to which they intend to aspire as adults. The women who were cooking, for example, were seen by respondents from each of the three countries as mothers; that they were cooking for others and not preparing their own meals was a given. Thus, the adolescents in this study echo the widely held belief that women are more relational than men, a notion encountered in Pease's study

(1993), which reported the tendency to offer teaching positions to women, who are seen as nurturers and enablers, and research positions to men, who are considered better suited to this isolated task.

In all three samples, the women who were engaged in office work were perceived as hardworking and in pursuit of an end. In Guatemala this end was the betterment of self or family; in the United States and the Philippines this end was the realization of a dream. These responses are consistent with other responses that point to a very traditional view of women among Guatemalan youth and a more modern view of women among adolescents in the United States, with Filipino youth falling somewhere in between. The Guatemalan adolescents, who live in a male-dominated society and see women in the workforce as something of an innovation, tended to interpret the desire for women to work within the context of tradition; that is, their desire to work was viewed by participants as an extension of the women's desire to better their families. The U.S. respondents, however, tended to see working outside the home as a norm for women and a means through which they might realize personal ambitions; nevertheless, the U.S. respondents acknowledged that this has not always been the case.

THE PERSISTENCE OF DISCRIMINATION: CONTEMPORARY OCCUPATIONAL SEGREGATION

Just as gender schemas have shaped societal attitudes regarding women in the workplace, so have these perceptions shaped the roles that different women are permitted to play therein, a phenomenon called **occupational segregation** (Blau & Ferber, 1987). Occupational segregation occurs when specific occupations are overwhelmingly either female or male. Many researchers use a quantitative rule to determine whether an occupation is segregated, such as 70 percent. That is, if an occupation is more than 70 percent male, such as auto mechanics, then that occupation is considered to be segregated. Such segregation is observed at every level of employment, ranging from the most menial, entry-level positions in supermarkets or fast-food chains to the highest levels of corporate management.

It both reflects and perpetuates the social norms from which it springs.

The workplace, not unlike the home, is unofficially divided into women's work and men's work (Reskin & Hartmann, 1986). In fact, according to Reskin and Padavic (1994), full integration would require 53 percent of women (or men) workers to change their occupations. Studies indicate that, although the degree of occupational differentiation between the sexes dropped nearly 23 percent between 1940 and 1980, it decreased by only 3 percent between 1980 and 1988 (King, 1992). Many women continue to find themselves in female-dominated occupations, that is, jobs that offer lower pay, status, and responsibility than jobs in male-dominated fields (Tomkiewicz & Hughs, 1993). Reskin and Padavic (1994) point out that if the occupations of typist, office clerk, and stenographer were added to a job category with secretary, that one category would account for about 10 percent of all women workers! Additionally, Table 7.2 demonstrates what women would earn if they were paid for unpaid labor in the United States.

Denmark and her colleagues (1996) summarized work showing that women of color (African American, Latina, Asian American, and American Indian women) experience racial discrimination along with sex discrimination. Racism has placed African American women at the lowest rung of the labor market. A study of Latina professionals (Mexican American, Puerto Rican, Cuban, and women from other Latino groups) shows that 82 percent report some form of discrimination. Asian American women enjoy higher labor participation, education, and economic status than Latinas, but highly educated Asian American women are rarely rewarded equitably. American Indian women are the most economically disadvantaged group in the United States (Hunter College Women's Studies Collective, 3rd edition, in press).

Women with disabilities comprise another group vulnerable to workplace discrimination. Although the Civil Rights Act of 1964 explicitly prohibits this type of discrimination, the reality for these women does not always conform to the law. A study of women and men with disabilities highlighted the need for retraining programs and additional employer education

TABLE 7.2 What Women Would Earn if Women Were Paid for Unpaid Labor in the United States*

ROLE	NUMBER OF HOURS PER WEEK	HOURLY RATE	DOLLAR AMOUNT
Food preparer	18	8.72	$ 157
Cleaner	6	6.36	38
Washer	3	6.36	19
Ironer	3	6.36	19
Chauffeur	10	12.17	122
Social secretary	18	10.00	180
Psychologist	7	150.00	1050
Child care worker	51	7.65	390
Health care worker	1	9.17	9
Repairer	2	15.72	31
Total weekly earnings			$2,015

Source: Calculations are based on data from *Highlights of Women's Earnings in 2001,* by U.S. Department of Labor, Bureau of Labor Statistics, May 2002, Report 960.

workshops. Women with disabilities who were employed had a significantly better outlook on their health status than disabled women who were not employed (Kutner, 1984). This finding suggests the possibility that employment may improve the physical and psychological well-being of individuals with disabilities.

Although it has been about 40 years since the passage of the Equal Pay Act, men are favored as candidates for more prestigious jobs, and they also earn higher salaries than their female counterparts in the same jobs. For every dollar that men earn, women earn only 77 cents (U.S. Census Bureau Statistics, 2001). In a *Washington Post* article, Mann (1997) wrote, "With all of the educational and professional progress women have made in the last 20 years, the wage gap has proven the most intractable barrier to economic equality" (p. E3). Rosenberg, Perlstadt, and Philips's (1993) comment that women lawyers are at greater risk of discrimination within the private sector than they are within the public sector holds true for professional women across the board. Mann (1997) quotes Susan Bianchi-Sand, who addresses the problem of the information gap. Because salaries in the public sector are made public, less of a wage gap exists there. "It's time to close the wage gap," she proclaims. "We don't fully value women's work" (p. E3). Figure 7.1 humorously depicts the wage gap that persists between women's and men's work.

If major inequalities still persist for women, for example, crowding women into fewer "acceptable" occupations than men, there will be some differences among women when considering race and ethnicity. Table 7.1 also demonstrates that White women are far more likely to be employed as managers and professionals than any other group except Asian American women. Service jobs, which are among the poorest paying, are disproportionately held by African American women.

Some would argue that a certain degree of occupational segregation may be appropriate. Tomkiewicz and Hughs (1993), who studied the differences between those women who choose business administration and those who choose administrative services, concluded that it would not be wise to "impetuously" integrate women into higher-echelon jobs in business. Tomkiewicz and Hughs set out to understand why it is that more women who attend business schools choose to prepare for careers in administrative services, training for careers that the U.S. Bureau of Labor Statistics classifies as "administrative support" (e.g., office supervision), rather than opting for the study of business

" OH! THAT EXPLAINS THE
DIFFERENCE IN OUR WAGES "

FIGURE 7.1   The Wage Gap

administration, which would prepare them for career opportunities that the U.S. Bureau of Labor Statistics classifies as "executive, administrators, and managerial." This is a puzzling phenomenon in light of the fact that the latter careers yield greater prestige and higher earning power, while both types of fields call for equivalent amounts of training and expense.

Their study reveals that the women who pursued the respective study tracks differed in their attitudes toward feminism. Not surprisingly, those who chose the administrative service track that prepared them for occupations that have traditionally been held by women were less profeminist than those who chose the business administration track, which prepared them for executive and managerial positions. Also, the female administrative service majors differed from their counterparts in business administration in their attitude toward management. The former were

significantly more amenable toward unionization and strike activity than the latter. This would indicate a labor (as opposed to management) orientation on their part. Thus, Tomkiewicz and Hughs (1993) conclude that the more traditional women cannot be considered equivalent to their feminist counterparts in the business administration program. The major thrust of this research was that, even when women share many occupational characteristics and pursuits, they were not necessarily homogenous. One should bear in mind that when "women" are mentioned, we refer to a highly varied category of individuals who do not necessarily share common values, aspirations, or goals. If we discuss women as if they are a unified group, we may, in fact, be contributing to some stereotype of women that is less complex and nuanced than it should be (see Chapter 1).

To conclude, many researchers point to the fact that much, if not most, occupational segregation does not have a logical or scientific basis. Even as early as 1978, Krefting, Berger, and Wallace noted that sex imbalances in a particular trade may well be self-perpetuating. Often an employer favors a particular sex when interviewing candidates merely because that sex dominates the field. Men's work is not necessarily work that men perform better than women; men's work is nothing more than work that has been traditionally performed by men.

Affirmative Action

The Equal Employment Opportunity Commission (EEOC) was created to administer Title VII, enacted in 1964, which outlawed job discrimination on the basis of sex, age, and race in hiring and promotion. The term *affirmative action* is a legal expression with historical grounding in the labor laws of the first part of the twentieth century. "In general, affirmative action consists of extra steps taken to ensure that a legally required result is actually produced" (Lindgren & Taub, 1993). Affirmative action emerged as the result of a set of presidential executive orders in the 1960s and 1970s (Reskin & Padavic, 1994). Initially, affirmative action was meant to change the employment practices of contractors who did business with the federal government so that White women and minority women and men would have the equal access that White males have traditionally enjoyed. As Reskin and Padavic point out, because all taxpayers meet the requirements for government contracts, all taxpayers should have a chance at obtaining the jobs that result.

Affirmative action has been recommended as a means by which to correct job-related gender inequities at the hiring level. A *USA Today*/CNN/Gallup Poll, taken in March 1995 showed that 55 percent of women favor affirmative action programs both for women and for minorities. A *Los Angeles Times* poll indicated that while 52 percent of Americans supported affirmative action for minorities, 60 percent supported affirmative action for women. However, Jeffe (1995) reports that women cannot be expected to represent a united front regarding affirmative action. Unlike sexual harassment, which women oppose in a single voice, affirmative action evokes some ambivalence. Not all women, Jeffe claims, care to break through the **glass ceiling;** some do not aspire to CEO positions. Affirmative action threatens them because they fear for their husbands' or sons' professional positions. Interestingly, this filial regard on the part of mothers corresponds to similar emotions expressed by men in the business world. According to the *New York Times* (Barringer, 1992), men advocate day-care and parental leave reforms in the interests of their daughters whom they have educated and prepared for productive professional lives.

The Need for Two Incomes: Contemporary Trends

The growing presence of women in the workforce reflects not only personal ambition but also the economic realities of the present time. No longer can the ideals of the 1940s and 1950s—large, single-family dwellings, multiple cars, and so on—be maintained on a single income. Indeed, at nearly every social and economic level we find a need for two incomes in order to sustain a desirable standard of living. The cost of living rose dramatically in the latter half of the twentieth century, but income levels did not keep pace. Thus, the percentage of working mothers with children younger than one year old has risen from 31 percent in 1976 to 55 percent in 2002. Overall,

women with young children are increasingly found working outside the home. Figure 7.2 shows that in families in which there is a spouse and a child under 6, women in 1996 were three times more likely to work outside the home than similar women in 1960. As of 2000, 70.5 percent of all single mothers with children under 6 were in the work force, and 62.8 percent of married women with children under 6 were in the work force. For those women with children between the ages of 6 and 17, 79.7 percent of single mothers and 77.2 percent of married mothers were in the work force (U.S. Census Bureau, Statistical Abstract of the United States, 2001). These women are driven by economic need, as well as by changing attitudes toward self-fulfillment (Eckholm, 1992). In fact, the dual-earner model, a pattern in which both partners work outside the home for income, now dominates. In 1997, 60 percent of married couples were two-earner couples, a dramatic increase from 1970 when only 36 percent of couples were dual earners (Jacobs, 1998). Labor force participation rates among married women have amplified in recent decades, increasing from 35 percent in 1966 to 61 percent in 1994 (Winkler, 1998). This increase was even more dramatic for married women with children under 3 years old within this time period, rising from 21 percent to 60 percent (Winkler, 1998). The Bureau of Labor Statistics predicts that by the year 2008, women will comprise 48 percent of the labor force (Jalilvand, 2000). Two incomes per family mean not only greater economic stability, especially during job losses and illness, but also the potential for a family lifestyle that models cooperation among all its members in maintaining a household (Barnett & Rivers, 1996).

Just as families are increasingly voting for the economic and psychological rewards associated with all its members working, employment relations in the United States are rapidly changing. The dominant twentieth-century model of employment encouraged long-term attachment to an organization and provided career ladders for promotion. But these rules are being tested and, in many instances, rewritten (Barker & Christensen, 1998; Spalter-Roth et al., 1997). The rise of the **contingent** (or "nonstandard") **worker,** an individual who is working part time as a "temp" or

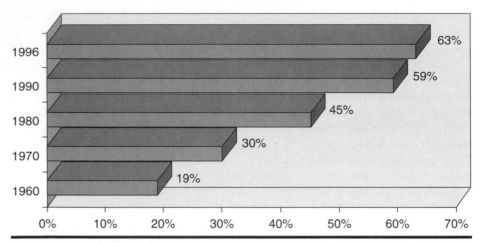

FIGURE 7.2 Women in the Workforce with Young Children
Source: Department of Labor.

on a per diem basis, does not resemble the permanent and full-time employment pattern we frequently associate with work. Furthermore, the rapid advance of technology and corporate downsizing have threatened the security of white- and blue-collar workers alike. These multiple trends—changing employment relations, downsizing, and new technologies—plus the need for two incomes in many families, create a dilemma for many workers. On one hand, the rainy day looms as a very real prospect for all workers, female and male alike. Thus, workers are wise to hold on to their jobs and whatever seniority and security these positions offer. On the other hand, many workers question whether employers are committed to long-term employment relations, given the evidence of corporate downsizing and the rise in the use of temporary hires (Bennett, 1989; Uchitelle, 1996). Therefore, both women *and* men need to continuously develop their skills and abilities and seek new ones so that they can negotiate a changing landscape of employment expectations and opportunities over the course of their lives.

Given these changes, one can well understand women as a vital and vibrant part of the workforce continuing into the twenty-first century. This emergence has not occurred without a significant amount of controversy and stress, and the many issues that women face—the "double shift" of working a shift at work and another shift at home, family members' lack of contributions, and employer discrimination—have yet to be resolved for all women.

SEX SEGREGATION: A MATTER OF ASPIRATION, DISCRIMINATION, OR CHOICE?

What came first, the need for "manly" traits to implement men's work, or the predominance of men in that field, dating back to a time when women did not work outside the home? This chapter discusses a number of job-related gender inequities affecting pay and prestige. Gottfredson (1981) attributes these inequities and other aspects of occupational segregation to differences in career aspirations of women and men. That is, women and men are in different careers because of preference, not discrimination. An early review of the research, however, indicated that sex discrimination in hiring plays a more important role than any differences that may exist in aspiration (Safilos-Rothschild, 1979). A more recent review has confirmed this pattern (Valian, 1998).

Sex Discrimination in Hiring

Masculine Chauvinists. Peter Glick (1991) argues that those who wish to explain the difference in prestige and salary between women's and men's jobs and the existence of sex discrimination in hiring fall into two camps: those who stress gender-typed personality traits associated with a particular job and those who suggest that sex discrimination in hiring exists regardless of the traits that applicants are thought to possess. Glick calls the former theorists *masculine chauvinists,* individuals who value prototypically masculine personality traits over feminine ones. He cites Eagly (1987), who suggests that masculine traits tend to be instrumental or agentic and are therefore the kind of traits required in most jobs, whereas feminine traits cluster around the home-oriented trait of nurturance. Thus, jobs associated with masculine traits will naturally bestow greater prestige on those who perform them and demand higher pay.

Glick adds that, although particular jobs may seem to call for masculine traits, women may still be hired to fulfill them. Nonetheless, those who discriminate because of preconceived notions regarding gender traits will tend to favor applicants whose "biological sex" seems to predict success in a particular role. Women are favored for positions such as administrative assistants—positions that offer neither high pay nor prestige—whereas men are favored for executive positions. It may be, Glick points out, that because society as a whole seems to value masculine traits over feminine traits, lower prestige and pay are accorded those occupations that call for feminine traits.

Leidner (1991) argues that traditionally masculine and feminine traits take on flexible definitions within the context of the workplace. That is, the skills that are required to perform one job (for instance, a job dominated by men) may not be different from those skills that are needed to perform a different job (one dominated by women). But these same skills may be socially constructed to be vastly different. For example, the skills needed to perform effectively as an insurance agent, in a field that is dominated by men, do not differ substantively from those required to work at the window of a fast-food restaurant, a female-dominated area. Like all interactive jobs that rely on forming relationships between people, both of these jobs are often scripted, both call for achieving a tone of friendliness and urgency, and both require tact when dealing with difficult people.

Male Chauvinism. *Male chauvinism* is the preference for hiring men over women regardless of the gender traits that are required by the job. This notion states that men are more highly valued than women. Therefore, those jobs that attract a large proportion of men will be more highly valued and will offer both higher prestige and more pay. Finally, jobs may be defined as man's work or woman's work simply by the existing ratio of men to women in the field. Krefting, Berger, and Wallace (1978) purport that once a job is dominated by one sex, that job takes on a male or female identity. Thus, if one has been accustomed to seeing men driving buses, then one would not expect a woman to perform this job successfully; if one is accustomed to seeing women teaching preschool, one would not expect a man to function effectively in that role. This reality makes it difficult to distinguish whether discrimination in hiring is based on a preference for masculine or feminine traits or is simply a reflection of the status quo. There is every reason to believe that the root of discrimination consists of a complex combination of these factors.

Job Prestige: A Matter of Sex Typing

Glick's 1991 study of trait-based and sex-based discrimination demonstrated that masculine traits are more highly valued than feminine traits in the workplace. The best predictor of job *prestige* is the degree to which that job is associated with masculine traits. Although feminine traits are not without value, they do not carry the importance of masculine traits. Glick notes that the tendency to pay men higher salaries, while it may have originated because men were assumed to be the primary breadwinners in the family, continues even when they are *not* sole breadwinners. Men, the study shows, receive more pay not for any perceived masculine traits, but simply because they are men.

Along with gender trait discrimination, women must also deal with discrimination based on appearance. Attractive women have been evaluated more favorably for feminine jobs, but not for masculine jobs. Attractive men, on the other hand, are generally evaluated more favorably for both types of jobs (Cash, Gillen, & Burns, 1977). Thus, even when applying for feminine jobs, attractive women lose their edge when competing against attractive men, and their appearance does not help them at all if they are competing for jobs that are not female dominated. The notion of discrimination based on appearance is part of **Heilman's lack of fit model** (1983), which postulates that gender biases stem largely from an incongruity between an applicant's perceived attributes and the requirements of the position.

To conclude this section, it should be noted that the devaluation of women's work is a truism that holds up both historically and universally. Women's work, whether paid or unpaid, skilled or unskilled, is both underpaid and undervalued, regardless of where on the planet it is being done. This attitude is slow to change, although some progress has been made, as noted previously when comparing the responses of students in the United States, Philippines, and Guatemala to drawings of women at work. In addition, in his study of sex differences in work values and personality characteristics among Indian executives, Singh (1994) discovered that, compared to men, women seemed "more interested in making money, more involved in their work, more enthusiastic, more socially bold, more opinionated, and somewhat more tense" (p. 700). They also seemed to derive more satisfaction from performing well at their jobs. These differences are also echoed, to some extent, in the United States (see Jeffe, 1995). The gender gap, however, seems to be closing regarding professional ambition as more women climb the corporate ladder—but not without some ambivalence on the part of women.

TURNING THE TIDE: ISSUES OF COMPETENCY, ACCESS, AND SOCIALIZATION

Despite the barriers of occupational segregation and discrimination in hiring and pay, women continue to press forward and advance at most levels in the workplace. Is this advance due to a change in attitudes toward women and the jobs they are suited for? Is it due to women's continued success in higher education? If stereotyping does remain, how pervasive and damaging is it to women as they continue to make inroads

in domains that were once male? An examination of how women's success is characterized and how women are faring in nontraditional professional schools provides both some encouraging and some discouraging insights.

Aversive Sexism

In 1978, Cherry and Deaux studied a group of undergraduate women and men, having each of them write a story about a female (Anne) or male (John) target who was at the top of her or his class in medical school or nursing school. The ensuing stories indicated that women and men alike evaluated both targets negatively when they excelled in nontraditional occupations, that is, women in medical school or men in nursing school. Yoder and Schleicher (1996) sought to replicate this study, allowing for the changes in attitudes that have evolved since 1978, such as the fact that attitudes and stereotypes regarding both women's and men's work have changed with the introduction of greater numbers of women into the workforce (Kelley & Streeter, 1992). In addition, they noted, the sex composition of medical schools has changed in the past two decades, with women in the early 1990s constituting 33 percent of the student body (Reis & Stone, 1992), as opposed to a mere 13 percent in the mid-1970s (Taeuber, 1991). Enrollment in nursing schools has remained stable, with women constituting 95.4 percent in 1974–1975 (*Digest of Educational Statistics,* 1976), and 94.7 percent in 1988–1989 (*Digest of Educational Statistics,* 1992). For this reason, Yoder and Schleicher (1996) added a number of options for Anne and John, including electrical engineering school, in which the gender composition (8.5 percent women) parallels that of medical school in 1978. Their results support those of Cherry and Deaux—eighteen years later, occupational gender stereotypes still existed.

Although one might predict that, given today's more egalitarian ideals, the study would indicate a substantial diminution of occupational gender stereotypes, this is not entirely the case. Overt attitudes may have changed, but more subtle forms of stereotyping persist. Dovidio and Gaertner (1986) discuss **aver-**

sive racism, a process in which covert forms of discrimination prevail even among those who loudly proclaim their egalitarianism. Yoder and Schleicher's review and research also attest to aversive sexism that is still alive and well within the working world. Citing studies performed in the mid-1970s (Hagen & Kahn, 1975) and mid-1980s (Hodson & Pryor, 1984), which indicate that successful women are rejected socially and professionally, Yoder and Schleicher suggest that successful women suffer work-related costs as well as personal costs in today's workplace. Furthermore, studies that focus on the attributions that underlie women's successes show that these are seldom perceived as stable dispositional traits, such as ability (Deaux & Emswiller, 1974; Feather & Simon, 1975; Weiner, 1974). Instead, their successes are generally ascribed to good luck (Deaux & Emswiller, 1974), easy tasks (Feather & Simon, 1975), or hard work (Feldman-Summers & Kiesler, 1974; Yarkin, Town, & Wallston, 1982). In many cases, women's achievements are viewed as having been enabled by their male colleagues. Finally, a study by Greenhaus and Parasuraman (1993) reveals that the effective performance of most highly successful women managers is less likely to be attributed to ability than is the performance of their male counterparts. Egalitarianism notwithstanding, aversive sexism and the double standards that nourish it are very real factors in today's workplace.

For all that, though one can applaud the fact that overt stereotyping regarding women and men in nontraditional occupations has been reduced, it is clear that the road to gender equality has yet to be paved. Although demographics reflect a change in gender balance within the world of medicine, such occupations as day care, electrical engineering, and nursing remain skewed. Moreover, the aversive sexism that shapes attitudes toward individuals in nontraditional occupations seems to be especially severe for women targets (Yoder & Schleicher, 1996). Women, it would seem, are less territorial about their traditional occupations than are their male counterparts. Perhaps one may ascribe this lack of territorialism to Leidner's (1991) belief that women do not offer proof of their femininity by citing their job, regardless of the nature

of their work, because adult female identity is not usually viewed as something that is attained through paid work. Men, on the other hand, have traditionally believed that the performance of manly work supports their male identity. Thus, as Williams (1989) discovered, women nurses do not feel threatened by men who join their ranks, whereas male marines attempt to exclude women from the corps. Moreover, although male nurses attempted to assert their masculinity by distinguishing their work from that of their female counterparts, female marines felt no such need. That women do not invest their feminine identity in their occupation tends to hold true for working women across the board, at least in the United States.

Discrimination against Lesbian Women

While much has been written on the career development of heterosexual women, less attention has been paid to the experiences of lesbians in the workplace (Morgan & Brown, 1993). Many women enter educational and career paths that were originally based on the "male-as-normative" model of development. But does this model apply to all women, including women with a same-sex orientation? At least two different perspectives prevail on the issue of the career development of lesbians, and these perspectives are not always exclusive of one another.

The first position is that lesbian women experience vastly different workplaces, different from and more hostile than heterosexual women face. Lesbian women's needs in terms of their work experiences should not be "subsumed under the study of the general female population" (Morgan & Brown, 1993, p. 267). Like other women, lesbian women earn 77 percent of what men earn, but unlike some heterosexual women, they do not live with a male wage earner who usually earns substantially more. Lesbian women may experience discrimination based on their sexual orientation. Heterosexism and homophobia may influence hiring, promotion, and firing. Yet, Morgan and Brown also indicate that little empirical data on lesbian workers are available, and even the available data are based on nonrandom samples of lesbians who were willing to identify themselves.

Janis Bohan (1996), another scholar long involved in the psychology of lesbian, gay, and bisexual issues, has reviewed the literature on gender and sexual orientation. She concluded, in contrast to Morgan and Brown, that

> *Gender is a more significant determinant of behavior and experience than is sexual orientation. Gender role socialization appears to result in gay men's being more like straight men and lesbians more like straight women than gays and lesbians are like each other. We have seen this in the research on developmental tasks, on relationships, on sexuality, on the nature of community. . . . It is a profound commentary on the oppressive nature of heterosexuality and the gender roles that undergird it that people would choose an identity that is so pervasively denigrated rather than accede to heterosexist norms. . . . In all these areas, the profound impact of gender is highlighted, and new directions for psychology emerge from the shadows. It is not sexual orientation per se that represents so great a challenge to established systems, but the coercive weight of socially constructed notions of gender. It is toward this coercion that psychology might well direct its energies, for it appears that gender rather than sexual orientation is the culprit. . . . It appears that in all this, sexual orientation is fundamentally a vehicle for incursions of gender. (pp. 233–234)*

Research is needed to probe and explore the issues of workplace discrimination based on sexual orientation.

Becoming "Gentlemen": The Tolerance of Inequities in the Legal Profession

Whereas research shows that most women may not perceive *themselves* as more or less feminine because of the demands of their occupations, social stigma targeting working women persists. Citing a survey conducted by Shaffer and Wegley (1974), Yoder and Schleicher (1996) report that women and men rated a target woman as least attractive as a work partner when she combined competence with high career orientation and "masculine" preferences. This research indicated that social stigma and negative stereotyping played a far greater role in the perpetuation of occupational segregation than did personal identity issues. Certain occupations may be

especially hostile to women because they have a long history of male incumbency and, to be successful in these occupations, a woman needs to demonstrate both a high career commitment and behavior that is stereotypically associated with men. One such profession is law.

Rosenberg, Perlstadt, and Phillips (1993) undertook a study of women lawyers and the discrimination, disparagement, and harassment that they experienced at work. Their study bears out the patterns that we have discussed previously and is relevant to this chapter's discussions of women in various workplaces, ranging from higher education, to fast-food restaurants, to coal mines. Compared with male colleagues, women lawyers tend to occupy lower-status positions. In private practice they are concentrated in lower-paying specialties (Heinz & Laumman, 1982) and are less likely to be made partners than their male counterparts (Curran 1986). Although salaries start out the same, a discrepancy grows over years of employment, such that women earn approximately two-thirds the salary of men (Chambers, 1989; Hagan, Zatz, Arnold, & Kay, 1991).

Studies suggest that, although hiring practices have grown less unfair, women lawyers continue to face on-the-job discrimination (Acker, 1990). Rosenberg et al. (1993) suggest that women lawyers may be less than forthcoming about reporting instances of sexual harassment for fear of rocking the boat and appearing to take a too staunchly feminist position, one that would jeopardize their relations with their colleagues and superiors. They consider themselves newcomers to the playing field and feel an overwhelming pressure to conform to professional norms and defer to authority. It is easy to see how this pressure can inhibit their ability to see discrimination for what it is. But when does this pressure begin? To what values are female attorneys conforming?

In 1994, Lani Guinier, Michelle Fine, and their colleagues conducted a comprehensive study of women's experiences at an Ivy League law school, the University of Pennsylvania (Guinier, Fine, Balin, Bartow, & Stachel, 1994). Guinier, herself a law professor at the law school, and her colleagues paint a disturbing picture in which female law students were excluded from the formal educational structure of the school and also excluded from the informal educational environment.

Within the formal structure of the institution, alienation and a decline in academic performance were linked. For example, although both women and men had exactly the same credentials on admission to the law school (college GPA and LSAT scores), men received better grades by the end of their first year. Importantly, men retained this advantage, as male–female differences in GPA were consistent across the three years of school. These disproportionate low rankings for women have far-reaching effects ranging from nonelection to the school's *Law Review* and moot court to lower employment status offers at graduation. If women and men are so similar in capabilities on entering a law school, why are women performing so poorly?

Guinier and her colleagues uncovered a series of problems that women encountered in the formal education system. First, law professors, who are primarily male at this law school, prefer the Socratic method of teaching in the classroom—the use of a particularly challenging form of questioning. Many legal educators assume that learning is most effective when accompanied by stress and pressure. However, many women reported being uncomfortable and anxious with this method and the hierarchy implicit in many law classrooms. "Many students, especially women, have simply not been socialized to thrive in the type of ritualized combat that comprises much of the legal educational method" (Guinier et al., 1994, p. 62). Students perceived that White men are encouraged to perform in the classroom much more than are women and students of color. Many students, primarily women, withdraw from the classroom, choosing silence. This silence, however, was also imposed on women vis-à-vis a type of peer hazing to which the first-year women were subjected. Women who spoke up in class reported being laughed at, being called "man-hating lesbians" (the latter from a woman who was married), and hissed at within and outside the classroom.

Given the chilly quality of the classroom, it is not surprising that women begin to withdraw from or not be encouraged to participate in the school's informal educational structure. Guinier and her colleagues believe, as most educators do, that a substantial amount of learning takes place informally out of the classroom. In their study, they found that male students reported being more comfortable interacting with faculty outside the classroom than did female students, who tried to determine by indirect cues whether a professor would be open or friendly to them. Women reported that the hazing that took place within the school forced them to seek intellectual and emotional support from female peers, not their professors. Thus, it was not surprising that when awards were granted at graduation, the basis of which is often subjective, a mostly male faculty bestowed a disproportionate number of awards on their male students. Women reported feeling incompetent in "thinking like a lawyer," and this led to a lower sense of self-esteem, a feeling that one's place is at the bottom of the hierarchy.

The studies conducted by Guinier et al. (1994) and Rosenberg et al. (1993) demonstrated that, ironically enough, the very legal and social developments that have created opportunities for women have reinforced patterns of gender stratification and inequality, indirectly and directly. Women who study law face disparagement, risk harassment, and are compelled to deal with situations in which their ideas are roadblocked, their advancement impeded, and their identities "zippered" as they learn to enact a lawyer's role, or "become gentlemen."

It should come as no surprise that **tokenism** is widely practiced among lawyers, who well know the consequences of exercising overt discrimination. No less predictable are the results of Rosenberg et al.'s (1993) study, which indicate that women who occupy token positions in law firms are more frequently the objects of discrimination and harassment than are their counterparts in firms in which women are employed in greater numbers. Women who seek employment in the private sector are at greater risk of discrimination, both in hiring and on the job, than those in the public sector, where they are protected somewhat by rules and regulations governing fair hiring. Nonetheless, Curran (1986) notes that women are being recruited into the private sector in greater numbers than before. The question for many women remains: How far up the career ladder can I go?

THE GLASS CEILING

Occupational segregation is not only manifested in the types of employment readily available to women; it also plays a role in the level of advancement to which they may aspire, the so-called "glass ceiling" that prevents women from rising beyond a given point in a particular corporate ladder. The Glass Ceiling Commission, set up by the federal government in 1991, reported in 1995 that, while the federal workforce was 57 percent female, women held a mere 5 percent of senior management jobs (Stead, 1996). Results from a large Swedish longitudinal study indicate that quite often men who work in typically female-dominated occupations have a significantly better chance of internal promotion. This phenomenon is referred to as the glass elevator, because underreported men are thrown into an upwardly mobile internal career path at a great speed that their female colleagues can scarcely enjoy (Hultin, 2003). Attempts to ameliorate imbalances are often perceived as a threat to men, who feel that any change in the status quo reflects an unfair bias favoring women (Orenstein, 1995). This perception reflects an entitlement that men have claimed and that, until recently, women have conceded. In an interview reported in *USA Today* (Cauchon, 1991), Katharine Graham, then chair and CEO of the *Washington Post,* admitted that she did not consider herself equal to her male colleagues in the boardroom when she inherited her position from her husband a quarter-century ago. "I was brought up in the old-fashioned world," she told Dennis Cauchon. "We were as much of a problem as the men. We did not view ourselves as equals. . . . When the women's movement started, it had a lot to tell me as well as men" (p. 9A).

It seems that much remains to be told, not only to women and men, but to girls and boys as well. Orenstein (1995) tells of a particular grade-school teacher who, in an attempt to correct an imbalance, consciously called on the girls in her class exactly as often as she called on the boys, keeping track in her roll book. The boys began to complain that the girls

were called on more frequently than they, when in reality the teacher had simply begun to give girls equal time. It is clear that work must begin from the ground floor up if society hopes to shatter the glass ceiling for good.

Just as the glass ceiling has inhibited the professional growth of women within the corporate world, it also serves to suppress them within the blue-collar workforce in workplaces that have traditionally been dominated by men. Reskin (1993) reports that, among the women who entered nontraditional blue-collar occupations some two decades ago, many have remained in entry-level positions. Antidiscrimination regulations notwithstanding, men still dominate the channels of upward mobility and hold higher-salaried positions of authority.

In her study of gender relations and the division of labor in coal mines, Tallichet (1995, p. 698) cites Reskin and Roos (1987, p. 9), who contend that **gendered division of labor** is "grounded in stereotypes of innate sex differences in traits and abilities" and that through "various social control mechanisms" these divisions continue to function. Women are perceived as posing a threat to the privileges that men feel entitled to enjoy by virtue of their masculinity. For this reason, men will stress women's alleged incapability of performing "man's work." If women are allowed, grudgingly, to participate in this work, they are expected to remain "in their place," occupying subordinate positions and deferring to the men in charge. Thus, men are able to tolerate women who work in male settings provided they continue to perform "women's jobs" and do not attempt to take on traditionally male roles. As we have already noted, the reverse does not hold true when men occupy women's professional territory.

Kanter (1977a, 1977b) documented that women's presence in workplaces from which they had been barred led to men's exaggeration of the differences between them. This results in what Enarson (1984) calls "sexualization of the workplace." What should be an asexual, professional domain suddenly takes on a dimension of sexuality, with the introduction of sexual harassment and bribery, particularly on the part of foremen and others who wield power, as well as an increase of gender-based jokes and profanity in an attempt to "separate the men from the boys" or rather, the boys from the women (Enarson 1984; Gruber & Bjorn, 1982; Swerdlow, 1989). Enarson adds that these behaviors can be considered abusive and that they reflect "a cultural tradition which sexualizes, objectifies, and diminishes women" (1984, p. 109).

It is this objectification of women that lays the groundwork for discrimination and occupational segregation in the coal mines, according to Tallichet (1995). Women are expected to assume "womanly" roles and so are assigned low-level tasks, requiring little skill, if any. Their successful completion of these tasks tends to reinforce their employers' (male) opinion that they have been well assigned, rather than suggesting that they might be capable of rising to greater challenges. Thus, as Schur points out (1984), objectification and work-related trivialization are mutually reinforcing processes. The trivialization that women experience is, to an extent, self-perpetuating as well, because many women will fatalistically accept the boundaries that men have placed on them, their self-esteem having been eroded by their treatment on the job. Not unlike Katharine Graham, whom we quoted previously, the blue-collar female worker stands to learn a great deal from the women's movement and *must* do so if she hopes to realize her potential as a worker. As one woman miner in Tallichet's survey said, "For the past ten years I felt like I was the underdog, that I shouldn't be stepping on their toes. *I haven't felt like I was a person. . . .* If there was a top-paying job, if I thought I could do it, most of the time I'd say let him do it" (Tallichet, 1995, p. 708, emphasis added).

Just as women's positions in the white-collar world mirror their traditional roles in society, with women serving as teachers but not researchers, pediatricians but not cardiologists, so, too, the women in the blue-collar world are expected to perform tasks that correspond to their duties at home, chores that service and support men. Tallichet (1995) quotes a female miner who complained that her job consisted of carrying cinder blocks and rock dust behind the male miners, "cleaning up after them." Another said that no matter what section she was assigned, she was expected to clean the "dinner hole."

Tallichet (1995) points out that women miners who wish to advance in what has long been a male-defined workplace have, on an individual level, maintained a continued effort to demonstrate their competency in spite of the obstacles set before them. Laudable though these efforts may be, they cannot adequately address what is a collective problem. As long as sexualization of the workplace is tacitly promoted or tolerated at the managerial level, advancement of women miners will continue to be unnecessarily difficult.

According to an article by Spencer (2003), many women are beginning to take the initiative to make career changes later in life. As they reach midlife, women may seek out jobs that are more suited to their interest or lifestyle. As women reach this stage of their lives, they begin to feel that they are running out of time to do the things that they truly enjoy. In addition, they are no longer overwhelmed with pressure to follow the career path that their parents wanted for them. There are several reasons for the decision to make these career changes later in life. These include the need to care for children, being laid off, or hitting the glass ceiling in their current place of employment. Engaging in a dramatic career shift, such as a change from an attorney to a photographer, can increase a woman's satisfaction with her life and reduce her stress level, as well as provide unexpected financial rewards.

Whether they choose to work or they are compelled to do so for financial reasons, whether they are single or married, whether they do or do not have children, all women confront a variety of obstacles in the workplace. Women in the military complain about a **brass ceiling,** restrictions placed on combat, which prevents their advancement. Still, opportunities for women in the military have increased both in number and in variety. For instance, Kathleen McGrath, a mother of two children, recently sailed to the Persian Gulf region in order to attempt to catch oil smugglers breaking the United Nations restrictions against Iraq. McGrath is the first female commander of a navy warship, and her mission highlights the steady progress of women in the navy, as well as the armed forces, that started in 1948 with the enactment of the Women's Armed Services Act (Brown, 2003). Although women in nontraditional occupations feel that they have too few female mentors and complain of loneliness on the job, they express overall happiness with the range of opportunities offered.

Obviously, biased institutional policies and practices need to change for women to advance. Additionally, it is important for women to form alliances. Only when they understand that they need not accept the notion that they are subordinates or intruders in a man's world will women succeed in effecting positive change (Tallichet, 1995). This is true whether they are in mines, on military bases, or in office suites high atop Wall Street.

DENIAL OF PERSONAL DISADVANTAGE

Given the preceding findings, one could expect that women are especially resentful of limited career choices and opportunities. Research by Faye Crosby, however, indicates otherwise. Crosby and colleagues have conducted a number of studies (Crosby, 1982, 1984; Crosby, Clayton, Alkinis, & Hemker, 1986; Crosby, Pufall, Snyder, O'Connell, & Whalen, 1989) that asked women and men to consider the issue of discrimination as it affects women in general and, more specifically, their personal experiences of discrimination. Reasoning that movement toward gender equality has been slow and fitful, Crosby was the first to document and investigate a very durable finding: Individuals acknowledge that others can be disadvantaged, but deny that they *themselves* have been the victims of discrimination. In other words, although women will acknowledge that, in general, women experience disadvantages, they consider themselves to be personally privileged, or exempt, from similar disadvantages. Crosby has termed this an **ostrich effect,** by which sex bias is acknowledged to operate in society, "but not for me."

Crosby has speculated on some of the reasons for the durability of this particular form of denial. First, it is difficult, if not impossible, to constantly confront bias and prejudice on a minute-to-minute and day-to-day basis. Few individuals are capable of sustaining the resentment that would result from such constant

vigilance, never mind the poor mental health that can emerge from chronic dissatisfaction. Living the "personal is political" may not always be possible or optimal. Another reason for the observed denial is that individuals do not always have aggregate data with which to compare their situations with others. For example, most workers in nonunion settings do not know what others are earning. A manager may be pleased with her salary of $40,000, knowing that two other managers, Fred and Juanita, make slightly less. What she does *not* know is that her information is anecdotal, not systematic. If she has all the data for her firm, she might learn that Fred and Juanita are the exception and that she earns substantially less than the average earnings of male managers with comparable skills and experience.

The lesson from these investigations is perhaps best summarized by Crosby and her colleagues: "We must not measure the need for social reform by how upset people feel with their personal situations in life. Karl Marx was right about false consciousness: those who are oppressed or disadvantaged rarely have a well-developed sense of their own disadvantage" (Crosby et al., 1989, p. 94).

COPING WITH STRESS

Even though a woman may not categorize herself as one who is discriminated against, she may still experience a substantial amount of stress. (For a full discussion of stress and mental health, see Chapter 13.) Some of this stress may be due to her working conditions, whereas other stress may arise due to home-related conflicts. Traditional occupations for women, such as sewing machine operators, maids and cleaners, and cashiers, produce stress because they are routine and low-paying "women's work" (Epstein, 1986). Women who choose to pursue nontraditional professions also expose themselves to a great degree of pressure. Much of this pressure relates to the external factors discussed earlier, such as the continuing need to prove competency, the need to combat (or tolerate) sexual harassment, and the frustration that comes with being the object of discrimination, to name a few. Working women who also manage homes and families cope with many pressures that are part of those roles as well.

Internal versus External Stress

Research supports the notion that women and men react differently to stressors, with women reporting more symptoms than men (Gerdes, 1995). Men apparently predominate when it comes to substance abuse disorders and personality disorders, whereas women are predominately diagnosed with more anxiety and affective disorders, particularly depression (Thoits, 1987b). Women also consistently demonstrate higher levels of anxiety, depressed mood, and demoralization (Thoits, 1987b). Although some believe that this difference may be attributed to their differing *exposure* to stressors within their social roles (Barnett & Baruch, 1987; Gore & Mangione, 1983), others hypothesize that the two groups differ in their *vulnerability* to stressors (Newmann, 1986; Thoits, 1987a).

As Gerdes (1995) notes, the research regarding work-related stress has, until recently, concentrated on specifying the dangers of work for men. If one were to accept that women are more vulnerable to stress than men, one would expect to find women's mental health at risk when they enter the workforce. This hypothesis, which was put forth in 1976 by Waldron, has not been supported. In fact, research indicates that women who are employed outside the home demonstrate better physical and psychological health than their nonemployed counterparts (Aneshensel, Frerichs, & Clark, 1981; Baruch, Beiner, & Barnett, 1987; Thoits, 1987b). Moreover, studies by Los Cocco and Spitze (1990) and Barnett, Marshal, Raudenbush, and Brennan (1983) show that relationships between job experiences and distress are similar for women and men. As a result of work-related stress, both men and women may develop cardiovascular disease, musculoskeletal disorders, psychological disorders, such as depression and burnout, workplace injury, suicide, cancer, ulcers, and impaired immune functioning (National Institute for Occupational Safety and Health [NIOSH], 1999). According to data from the Bureau of Labor Statistics, workers who must take off time from work as a result of work-related stress, anxiety, or a related disorder will be absent from work for approximately 20 days (NIOSH, 1999).

Nonetheless, a study conducted at Bucknell University (Gerdes, 1995) in which nontraditional women and traditional women were observed showed that, although men and traditional women differed in their *responses* to stress on the job, no significant difference was found between women with traditional aspirations and women with nontraditional aspirations. Female students were more susceptible than their male counterparts to psychosomatic symptoms, physical illnesses, psychological disorders, and anxiety. The women preparing for traditionally male professions reported more chronic stress than men, whereas women preparing for traditionally female professions did not. However, the symptoms that they demonstrated did not differ qualitatively.

Some differences were observed among the two groups of women regarding the relationship between stressor and symptom. Although the two groups did not differ when exposed to average levels of stress, nontraditional women reported higher levels of anxiety, depressed mood, and physical illness when exposed to higher levels of stress. Also, nonwork stress (home events) predicted greater anxiety for nontraditional women. Gerdes (1995) suggests that women who seek to compete in male-dominated fields are more threatened by home events because of the potential conflict between family and professional demands.

Gerdes's (1995) study concludes that, at a high level of work stress, nontraditional women report more job tension than both men in the same fields and traditional women. She suggests that these greater vulnerabilities may be attributed to such factors as personality, coping styles, choice of career, or gender. Finally, she notes, one must also consider the social pressures and discrimination that loom ahead of those women who choose nonnormative careers.

NIOSH suggests that, although both men and women experience work-related stress, in many respects, the risks are greater for female than for male workers. Women are increasingly moving to occupations once held solely by men, such as the construction trades. In such cases, physiological differences between men and women may result in occupational hazards, because they may be operating equipment designed for male workers of larger builds. Furthermore, they may experience other gender-specific work stress factors such as sex discrimination, balancing work and family demands, and barriers to career and financial advancement (Blosser, 2000).

Sexual Harassment

The term *sexual harassment* did not even exist until 1976, when it was used in connection with a legal suit filed by Carmita Wood, the first woman to seek unemployment compensation after leaving a job in which her boss made sexual advances toward her (Fitzgerald, 1996). As Catherine MacKinnon, law professor and leading advocate for women's rights, noted, "The unnamed should not be taken for the nonexistent" (MacKinnon, 1979, p. 28).

Sexual harassment refers to the making of unwanted and offensive sexual advances or of sexually offensive remarks or acts, especially by one in a superior or supervisory position. Furthermore, it is considered sexual harassment when continued employment, promotion, or unsatisfactory evaluation is contingent on acquiescence to such offensive or inappropriate behavior (*American Heritage Dictionary,* 2000). Studies imply that anywhere between 40 and 70 percent of women and 10 and 20 percent of men have been subjected to sexual harassment in the workplace. Moreover, the Equal Employment Opportunity Commission (EEOC) in 2003 reports that the number of sexual harassment cases has more than tripled in the past few years, with about 15,000 cases presented to the EEOC every year.

In the workplace, a few predictors of sexual harassment have emerged. For instance, research suggests that men who harass women tend to be older than their victims and less attractive than women who harass men (Hemming, 1985; Tangri, Burt, & Johnson, 1982). Moreover, women are more often harassed by men of equal or greater power, whereas men report the greatest amount of unwanted sexual attention from less powerful women (Bingham &

Scherer, 1993). In several studies, peers have emerged as the most frequent source of harassment, followed by supervisors, subordinates, and clients (Lafontaine & Tredeau, 1986).

In the study of attorneys by Rosenberg et al. (1993), it was found that, although as a rule younger women tend to be victims of harassment more often than older women, the numbers change when working in the private sector. There, older and younger women alike were subject to harassment. However, whereas a woman's marital status did not seem to affect the likeliness of harassment overall, married women suffered less harassment in the private sector than did single women. Rosenberg et al. suggest that this indicates that the harassment is based not so much on sexuality as on an aggressive need on the part of the men involved to demonstrate dominance. For this reason, married women would be protected by the fact that harassers perceive that other men have established a claim upon them.

Surprisingly, women who define themselves as "careerist" rather than feminist in orientation may be more vulnerable to sexual harassment and disparagement. Because they claim to believe in the system and consider the schedule of promotions within their firms to be based in meritocracy, they are less likely to complain about discrimination. To do so might indicate that they are bad sports. As a result, they will go along with whatever behavior seems normative, even if this behavior is disparaging and/or discriminatory in nature. Feminists, on the other hand, put forth a clear message that they will not stand for sexual games of any sort. Although their stridency may not win them a great many fans among potential harassers, it may well save them the discomfort of having to put up with them.

Various contextual or situational factors have been explored in connection with the incidence of harassment. One major variable to be studied is the sex-ratio or gender composition of the occupation. Generally, sexual harassment is more common in male-dominated occupations such as firefighting and construction work and in female-dominated occupations such as nursing and secretarial work than in sex-integrated occupations in which there is an approximately equal number of women and men (Konrad & Gutek, 1986). Even before women enter the workplace, they are likely to meet with such disagreeable challenges as sexual harassment while training for eventual employment in male-dominated areas. On March 11, 1997, *USA Today* reported that the Citadel dismissed a male cadet and punished nine others who hazed, harassed, and assaulted two female cadets (Kanamine, 1997). The article pointed out that this behavior was part of a broader treatment of women in the military, noting that a recent sexual harassment scandal has brought "a torrent of complaints" from young female recruits who claim that they have been treated unfairly and subjected to sexual harassment, bribery, and other forms of sexualization of the workplace.

Several investigators have attempted to explain why sexual harassment occurs at work. Tangri, Burt, and Johnson (1982) offered three explanatory models: the *natural biological model,* which stresses males' greater sex drive; the *organizational model,* which sees harassment as the abuse of power in formal hierarchies; and the *sociocultural model,* which views harassment as the result of gender inequalities throughout society.

Based on their three models of sexual harassment, Tangri et al. (1982) made predictions and tested them using data from the U.S. Merit Systems Protection Board (1981). Whereas none of the models received clear-cut empirical support, stronger support was found for the organizational and sociocultural models, both of which conceptualize sexual harassment as an abuse of power, than for the natural biological model (Saal, Johnson, & Weber, 1989).

In their explanatory model, Terpstra and Baker (1986) identified three *causal factors* in sexual harassment: gender, power, and perceptions of work climate. They predicted and found that women were more likely to be harassed than men, that people with less institutional power were more likely to be harassed than people with more institutional power, and that sexual harassment was more common in organizations that were perceived as tolerant of harassment. Other tests of their model have generally garnered some support (Bingham & Scherer, 1993).

Another model attempting to explain sexual harassment was proposed by Gutek and her associates

(Gutek, 1985; Gutek & Morasch, 1982). They proposed that sexual harassment of women at work was a product of sex-role spillover. *Sex-role spillover* is the carryover into the workplace (or academy) of gender-based expectations for behavior. Several aspects of the female gender role are often carried over to work. One is the "stroking function" of women, in which women are expected to be more nurturant, supportive, sympathetic, or complimentary than men in the same work roles. According to Gutek and Morasch (1982), "Projecting a sexual image and being a sex object are also aspects of the female sex role: sex-role spillover occurs when women, more than men in the same work-roles, are expected to be sex objects or are expected to project sexuality through their behavior, appearance, or dress" (p. 58).

Gutek and Morasch (1982) claim that sex-role spillover is a potential cause of sexual harassment when the sex ratio is skewed in either direction, that is, when women are in male-dominated or female-dominated occupations. There is some empirical support for Gutek's model, just as there is for the other models discussed. It is important to note that these models are not contradictory and in many cases make identical predictions about the conditions under which harassment is most likely to occur.

All the models reviewed so far are helpful in explaining sexual harassment, but no one model entirely explains why sexual harassment exists. Most recent conceptual frameworks see sexual harassment in all its forms in the workplace, academia, and public sphere as being rooted in the combination of sexual interest and unequal power between the sexes. Whereas power is often defined as one's position within an organization, power may stem from any of several sources other than formal authority, such as work-group alliances, personal characteristics such as physical size, and control of valued resources (Bingham & Scherer, 1993). In this way, sexual harassment is used as a tactic of social control, a means of keeping women in their place, especially in work and school settings that are traditional male preserves, such as the firehouse or military academy.

Relatively few studies have examined the relationship between occupation and harassment. Tangri et al. (1982) found no overall differences in level of harassment between or within white- and blue-collar jobs. Lafontaine and Tredeau (1986) found higher levels of reported harassment in management and engineering than in professional careers in the sciences, computers, higher education, and public administration.

Organizational climate with regard to sexual harassment—the perception that workers have about how organizations respond to sexual harassment—has received some research attention. Working environments differ in the degree to which sexual harassment is a problem, and employees frequently describe their workplace in terms of tolerance of sexual harassment (Bingham & Scherer, 1993; Booth-Butterfield, 1986). Some research supports the idea that perceived organizational climate is related to the prevalence of sexual harassment (Bingham & Scherer, 1993). For example, Lafontaine and Tredeau (1986) found that the percentage of women reporting sexual harassment was higher among those who rated their company low on the equal-opportunity scale than among those who rated their company high on this scale. More research is needed on the effects of organizational climate on sexual harassment.

Coping Strategies

Along with the social pressures faced by working women, one must take into account the inner conflicts that they face, particularly those represented by combining their roles at work with their life roles. Kibria, Barnett, Baruch, Marshall, and Pleck (1990) reported that the quality of the homemaking role has important associations with the psychological well-being of women. Women who devote themselves exclusively to homemaking often feel socially isolated and suffer from low self-esteem related to the low social status of homemaking (Berk & Berk, 1979; Bose, 1985; Lopata, 1971; Nilson, 1978). Kibria and colleagues, however, discovered that women who combined their homemaking with outside employment derived greater satisfaction from their roles within the home. Thus, they conclude, one can compensate for the negative aspects of a particular role by engaging in another that provides stimulation or gratification.

According to Amatea and Fong-Beyette (1987), most professional women employ *problem-focused* coping methods when dealing with conflicts between their work and life roles. The methods they choose include reactive role behavior (i.e., working harder to meet all demands, attempting to meet all demands in a beleaguered way), external role redefinition (i.e., delegating tasks to others), increased planful role behavior (i.e., trying to work more efficiently in order to meet all demands), and internal role definition (i.e., purposefully modifying standards and overlooking certain role demands).

Professional women use *emotion-focused* coping methods less frequently, usually when stressors are health related rather than work related. They are more likely to take an active role in solving problems related to parenting and a more passive role when dealing with demands of self and spouse or lover. Varying coping devices meet with varying degrees of success, with the most consistent rates of success attributed to social support strategies that involve others in the solution of personal problems.

McLaughlin, Cormier, and Cormier (1988) conclude that women who cope most successfully with stress are those who take an active approach to their problems. Too many women are prepared to accept stressors as the price they must pay for the opportunities that have now come their way. This acceptance, they point out, acts as yet another stressor. Denmark, Novick, and Pinto (1996) advocate "reframing" problems, a three-part process consisting of changing the standards by which a woman measures herself, viewing problems as solvable rather than inevitable, and seeing problems as part of a particular situation, rather than an indication of a personal deficit.

As early as 1982, Carol Gilligan has emphasized that woman must begin to develop self-interest, recognizing their personal validity and nurturing themselves along with the many others with whose care they are involved. This form of self-centeredness should not be perceived as a character flaw; rather it is a necessary survival skill worthy of cultivation. They should seek out support groups and enlist the encouragement of bosses, mentors, professional counselors and therapists, as the dictates of particular situations require. The National Institute for Occupational Safety and Health (NIOSH) suggests three strategies for managing work-related stress: finding a balance between work and family and personal life, establishing a support network of friends and coworkers, and maintaining a relaxed and positive outlook (NIOSH, 1999).

Multiple Roles: Myths and Realities

When considering the stressors that affect working women, one cannot overlook female workers with family obligations. The induction of women into the workforce and their ascension up the career ladder has given rise to a new character in popular mythology, the "Super Mom." Her life runs like a well-oiled machine. She comes to work each day, meticulously groomed and dressed, having shipped her 2.5 children off to school no less well dressed, carrying nutritious lunches that she prepared the night before. She projects a totally professional image from 9 to 5—working overtime, if necessary—and somehow arrives home with the energy to prepare dinner and deal with the children's homework, the careful delegation and implementation of household chores, which she shares with her Super Dad husband, the soothing of hurts and minor traumas that may have plagued her perfect children, the reading of bedtime stories and singing of lullabies, preparation for tomorrow's work as a high-power executive, and the next chapter in her vibrant and exciting sex life. The only problem here is that our Super Mom is no less a mythological character than Athena, Venus, and Juno—all of whose qualities she is alleged to possess.

In reality, women who manage career and family do so only if they have strong support systems. Even older school-aged children must be cared for after school hours, and mothers must have effective backup plans for when their children are ill. The notion of dividing household chores equally does not hold up in reality. In fact, according to Coltrane (1997), overall, men perform five to eight hours of household chores a week, or about one-third of what their spouses perform. Similar findings have been reported for dual-earner African American families (Hossain & Roopnarine, 1993). Even among young dual-career couples, people in their twenties and early thirties

with no children, the men spent only half as much time as the women doing housework (Denmark, Shaw, & Ciali, 1985). Moreover, the onus of responsibility for child care and household chores falls on the woman, regardless of any arrangements that she and her spouse may have made to the contrary. Roxanna Diaz, a Miami-based social worker, notes that if her husband does 50 percent of the child care "that's a lot more than is expected of him. . . . If I do 50 percent, it's a lot less than is expected of me" (Stead, 1996).

Overall, women retain the responsibility for arranging and supervising labor-inducing services, such as child care and cleaners (Hochschild, 1997), responsibilities that are time consuming. An acquaintance of one of the authors of this volume, a woman in her sixties who combined a career as a teacher with duties in the home at a time when this was all but unheard of, admits that she considered herself obliged to serve meals no less varied, healthful, and attractive than her stay-at-home friends, in spite of the hours spent teaching, preparing her work, and grading papers. To her mind, greater demands are being made of women. They have not so much exchanged their household chores for professional duties as they have increased their burden by adding professional duties to the long list of household chores from which they have not been exempt. This woman's critique notwithstanding, the number of mothers in the workforce has increased more than ten times since 1940 (Russo & Denmark, 1984) to include 62 percent of all mothers (Bianchi, 1995). By 1996, six out of ten mothers with children under age 6 were in the labor force.

This raises an issue of some controversy: Do children of working mothers suffer at the expense of their mothers' careers? According to Eyer (1994), there is no scientific evidence that women shortchange their infants and toddlers by working outside the home. Not only are the negative effects of day care questionable at best, but studies usually show that working mothers spend close to the same amount of time with their children as do the so-called stay-at-home mothers (Eyer, 1994).

One might expect that the stressful demands of job and family would be difficult for a mother to juggle and that she would experience overload. Were this the case, the toll on the mother's mental health would make it difficult for her to be an adequate, let alone good, mother. Fortunately, a review of the literature concludes to the contrary that the effects of multiple roles on women's mental health vary, and that for many women, working actually has a positive impact on self-esteem and life satisfaction (Denmark, et al., 1996; Hyde, Klein, Essex, & Clark, 1995). We have already seen that women employed outside the home, whose interests are varied, derive more satisfaction from the routine chores of homemaking than their nonemployed counterparts (Kibria, Barnett, Baruch, Marshall, & Pleck, 1990).

The population of women with children under 3 years of age who are in the workforce has been growing steadily in recent years, reaching 66 percent in 2000 (U.S. Department of Labor, 2000). The wisdom of the mother's decision to leave her infant or toddler to go to work is not uncontested; in fact, the subject has evoked such controversy as to inspire several federal studies. One such study, coordinated by Sarah Friedman, of the National Institute of Child Health and Human Development, involved 1,364 children from the time that they were 6 months old through age 3. The results, published in *USA Today* (Elias, 1997, pp. 1A, 11A), indicated that language and cognitive development and the relationship with mother are linked more directly to family qualities and the child's temperament than to whether that child has been in day care. Nonetheless, the quality and quantity of care are important factors. The study also demonstrated that children who received higher-quality care had better language development and more positive social skills. However, if the mother's working hours were such that she spent very little time with the child, the less socially engaged the pair was likely to be and the less sensitively the mother related to the child. This failure to bond adequately at an early age is likely to be a harbinger of greater problems to come.

So, working mothers face a double dilemma. Not only must they secure day care of high quality, but they must also determine how many hours of day care are advisable so as not to jeopardize the bonding process and their relationships to their children. At the same time, their own mental health is likely to be

more secure if they do participate in some work outside the home. The result is often a juggling act.

We have already noted that women in multiple roles exhibit greater levels of self-esteem than those who identify themselves as homemakers and do not work, either for pay or as volunteers, outside the home. This is true of working women even after they have retired. Studies show that women who identify themselves as retirees as well as homemakers demonstrate greater levels of self-esteem than those who identify themselves only as homemakers (Adelmann 1993). Lower rates of depression and higher self-esteem were noted among older women who kept busy with do-it-yourself projects and volunteer activities that provided concrete and social rewards, as well as a sense of personal accomplishment. Traditional household chores, on the other hand, were not related to self-esteem. Child care was negatively related to self-esteem. Adelmann points out, however, that this refers to primary care for a child living in the home, not the typical care associated with being a grandparent. In conclusion, we find that traditional women's work to the exclusion of work that provides intellectual and social stimulation is not enough to generate self-esteem and promote good mental health at any phase of a woman's life.

THE TIME BIND

Many individuals still think of home as a sanctuary from the hubbub of day-to-day life. In this view, home is an escape from the pressures of modern life and provides an individual with opportunities for privacy, leisure, and pleasure from interaction with household members. But is this home-as-sanctuary model true today, and if so, for whom? Increasing levels of education and career attainment result in, supposedly, the benefits of job security and enough affluence to enjoy travel and other activities. However, companies have increasingly downsized their workforce. At the same time, they have implemented empowerment programs, such as quality circles, in which employees are expected to be serious players and demonstrate their commitment to a firm through long hours. These same firms have also initiated family-friendly policies that permit workers to re-

THE WORLD OF WORK

quest job sharing, part-time schedules, or reduced workload. In this section, we will consider the competition workers feel between family obligations, career commitments, and the issue of *time*—whose is it and how should it be used—in the modern workplace.

Part-Time Work and Flextime

Thirty years ago, it was commonplace for women to reduce or resign their jobs during their childbearing years. Today, however, women's work patterns more closely resemble men's patterns of continuous workforce attachment (Spalter-Roth et al., 1997). Women want and need full-time permanent work. According to Moen (1992), women recognize the disruptive effects of discontinuous jobs and careers in terms of earnings, job stability, and advancement. However, as noted earlier, men have not stepped forward to assume an equal share of household responsibilities when their spouses work. At the same time, many women recognize and appreciate the social benefits and psychological rewards associated with paid employment. The dilemma for women is how to juggle these activities, a feat even more onerous when a couple is not "collaborative" (Barnett & Rivers, 1996) in sharing the workload at home. For some women, nonstandard work arrangements, such as part-time, temporary, on-call, home-based work or independent contracting and self-employment, promise reconciliation between home and work. A key research question, however, is whether these actually help in managing work and family. Research indicates that some women may be swapping one set of problems for another when they enter these arrangements.

Barker (1993) was concerned that women who selected part-time work, no matter what their occupational status (i.e., attorneys, bankers, nurses, professors, or clerks), were penalized in the workplace. Many women select part-time employment to cope with child-care and home-related activities. Yet, a part-time work status, in distinction to the male normative work status of a full-time work schedule, is not neutral. For example, the social history of part-time work demonstrated that it was relegated to immigrants, freed slaves, and women because they were deemed by employers as "inferior" (Morse, 1969).

Yet contemporary occupations have also historically varied in their traditions regarding the availability of part-time work. Therefore, Barker examined women working full and part time in male- and female-dominated professions (primarily attorneys and nurses) and clerical occupations.

Within occupations, Barker found that part-time women workers consistently reported less inclusion than full-time colleagues. Greater inclusion in the workplace was most often associated with those in the professions. The feelings of exclusion were greatest for those in clerical occupations. In general, part-time workers were more apt to report that they were unlikely to be promoted, felt they were off track, and were perceived by others to be less committed than they really felt they were. However, Barker found that both full- and part-time groups uniformly reported that they worked because it brought personal satisfaction.

Finally, in terms of the juggling of work and family responsibilities, Barker wanted to know whether women working part time would report lower role conflict and overload than would full-time working women. She found that part-time work did not contribute to lower role conflict or overload. Occupation did, however, predict role conflict. Women working in female-dominated professions reported lower amounts of role conflict than women working in male-dominated professions. Control over work schedule appeared to be more important than the actual work itself. Single mothers can face an even more dramatic home workload in addition to being the sole income provider for their families. These women cannot consider leaving the workforce for even a brief period, nor can they freely choose alternative work arrangements that reduce earnings or are inherently unstable, such as temporary or seasonal work.

Perhaps the most important consideration for women thinking about nonstandard work versus regular arrangements has to do with earnings and benefits. Nonstandard workers receive fewer benefits than do workers in regularized employment. Only 23 percent of women and 16 percent of men in nonstandard arrangements receive health and pension benefits compared with 80 percent of full-time women and men workers (Kalleberg & VanBuren, 1996). Considering that women live longer than men, the absence of pension benefits in most nonstandard jobs points to a long-term vulnerability that women bear in coping with work–family conflicts. When women opt out of the workplace, they do not contribute to separate social security benefits, and when women work part time, their social security benefits on retirement may be much less than if they had worked full time (DuRivage, 1992). The message is clear that women *pay* in multiple ways for coping with work–family responsibilities.

Maternal and Paternal Leave

Many couples who hope to combine dual careers with raising children will decide to engage in some form of a reduced work schedule, at least while their children are small. There is, however, no reason to assume that it is the woman who will have to cut back on her career. Many individual decisions need to be carefully weighed before and after a child enters a dual-career working couple's life. Options such as on-site day care, job sharing, working in the home, and flextime enable more parents to combine child rearing and career. Many couples find that through careful time management, judicious use of nannies and housekeepers, and compartmentalization of their work and home lives they are able to enjoy the economic and psychological benefits that come with pursuing a meaningful career along with the intense emotional satisfaction that comes from raising children.

A related issue of debate to the problem of combining career and family is the amount of postpartum parental leave to which mothers (and fathers) are entitled. The notion of parental leave is relatively new in the United States. Until recently, postpartum leave was confined to mothers and was generally aimed at allowing women to recover from childbirth (Hyde & Essex, 1991). However, recovery from childbirth should not be viewed as physical recovery alone. As Hyde, Klein, Essex, and Clark (1995) point out, when an employed woman takes on the role of mother, she can be expected to experience physiological and psychological stress and distress. Adding this role may

well overload her system, according to the **scarcity hypothesis,** which states that human beings have a set amount of time and energy (Goode, 1974).

Parental leave takes into account more than a woman's recovery from childbirth; it refers to time allowed to either parent for child rearing. In January 1993, then-President Clinton signed the Family and Medical Leave Act, providing for up to 12 weeks of parental leave with job security following birth or adoption of a child. Although this has apparently been in an effort to consider the needs of the infant, Hyde et al. (1995) maintain that the emotional needs of mothers must also be addressed. Their study found that short parental leave is a risk factor for psychological distress when combined with other factors such as unfulfilling work or a rocky marriage. Another finding was that women employed full time display increased anxiety, emphasizing the importance of workplace policies that permit part-time work, job sharing, and incremental (rather than immediate) return to work for women during the first postpartum year. A more recent study, reported next, however, focuses on the failure of many parents, both women and men, to pursue flexible workplace policies.

Evading the Time Bind

In a study of one of two major corporations with such family policies, Hochschild (1997) found that most workers did not avail themselves of progressive workplace policies even when they had supervisors who were flexible, because the firm still managed to pressure its employees to be more work centered. The result was that parents experienced a time crisis. She wondered why parents were not engaged in a "culture of resistance" (p. 34), fighting for more time with their families and less time at work. Rather than asking for shorter hours, for example, parents found ways to avoid or deny the problem existed. Hochschild described a cultural reversal under way in which the workplace and the home traded roles, with work serving as a retreat from pressures at home. In one organization, Hochschild reported a number of disturbing findings in her survey of mostly middle- or upper-middle-class parents in their thirties: eighty-nine percent considered themselves workaholics,

89 percent reported experiencing a problem termed *time famine* or lack of sufficient time, and half of those who reported a time famine also reported feeling guilt about not spending enough time with their children. Only 9 percent reported that they felt they could balance work and family.

Hochschild then wondered whether these working parents were tolerating their situation because they found work more rewarding than family life. She asked, "Does it sometimes feel to you like home is a workplace? Eighty-five percent said yes. She also asked, "Is it sometimes true that work feels like home should feel?" and 25 percent answered, "very often," or "quite often," and 33 percent answered, "occasionally." The remainder, 37 percent, responded, "very rarely." Hochschild concluded that in her study of employees "working parents feel more at home at work because they come to expect that emotional support will be more readily available there" (p. 200). At one firm, 49 percent of the workers reported being more relaxed at work than at home. For these workers, the shortened family hours burdened them with the sort of stress that once characterized the workplace. Hochschild says that more and more workers practice "emotional asceticism" as a coping device, denying themselves the fun and support that normal family relations provide. This perpetuates the growing phenomenon of *workaholism.* Indeed, studies show that women who are workaholics, devoting 50 hours or more each week to their professions, are more likely than men to pay for this behavior with divorce and fewer deep, personal relationships. Some 35 percent of these women never marry, as compared to 9 percent of their male counterparts. Their devotion is not always rewarded with greater prestige or higher salaries (Elias, 1984).

As more and more women enter the workforce, few can envision a return to the time when women were primarily in the home. Yet, women's emergence in the workplace occurred without a challenge to the normative working week—35 to 40 or more hours—that dominated the model of full-time work in the twentieth century. Despite the coping strategies that women develop, some investigators forecast tremendous personal costs due to time famine. Writers such as Hochschild (1997) foresee that time famine will continue to accrue and perhaps worsen unless society engages in a debate on the organization of work, including flexibility, and the competition between the emotional investment in personal relationships and America's "love affair with capitalism" (p. 249).

Many husbands alleviate their wives' stress about taking long-term leave from work by choosing to stay at home and raise their children. A 20-year study demonstrated a growing trend in which many mothers are working while fathers are staying home to care for children (Stay-at-Home Dads, 1998). According to the U.S. Census Bureau, in June 2003, 336,000 children under the age of 15 reported that they had fathers who stayed at home to take care of them. These children all lived in two-parent homes, and their mothers worked outside of the home (U.S. Census Bureau, 2003). This is now the fastest-growing family arrangement, with an estimated 2 million stay-at-home dads in the United States. This number has quadrupled since 1986. Several reasons for this pattern include desire not to put children in day care, larger income for wives, a desire for mothers to work, and the fathers' greater desire to stay home (Fisher, 2000).

CONCLUSION: LOOKING BACK WHILE LOOKING AHEAD

We have seen that exploitation of women continues, not only on the job, but in the home as well. The tasks that have traditionally defined women's roles culturally and socially continue to define their activities within the workforce. They are seldom credited with their accomplishments within the home, but quickly and harshly condemned for falling short of their duties as mothers. One has but to recall prosecutor Marcia Clark's experiences when prosecuting former football star O. J. Simpson in the mid-1990s for an example of the cruel judgmentalism that threatens a successful, high-profile woman. Her professionalism was called into question when she responded to her children's needs, and her competence as a mother was called into question when she demonstrated an appropriate level of commitment to her profession. The defense attorney, Johnnie Cochran, was held to no such personal standard.

Good news for women comes not only from the United States, where such women as Katharine Graham, former publisher and owner of the *Washington Post,* and Sheila Widnall, former secretary of the navy, have blazed trails for women within the worlds of journalism and the military, respectively. Additionally, Madeline Albright was the first woman to serve as U.S. Secretary of State and U.S. Congress member Nancy Pelosi became the first woman to hold the position of whip in the Congress. Good news also comes from South Africa, where Mamphela Ramphela served at the first Black president of the University of Cape Town. The progress that women have made across the world should not obscure the work that remains to be done. For example, when compared with women in the United States and Europe, Japanese women suffer far greater obstacles to equal opportunity. "Thus, even though nearly 40 percent of the Japanese work force consists of women, most of them work in insecure jobs without benefits accorded to men" (Sukemune, Shiraishi, Shirakawa, & Matsumi, 1993, p. 180). Feminist researchers in Japan believe that there is a lack of fundamental re-spect for women's human rights in Japanese society. Japanese women are far less likely to be elected to policy-making arenas, such as parliament, or have distinguished positions in the public sector, such as posts in government. As access to all levels of society is impeded, so too is Japanese women's progress in the workplace.

The workplace has traditionally been considered a man's world. Men carried out important tasks; men made important decisions; the mundane and routine stuff of life was the domain of women, their sole domain. The emerging role of women in the workforce has shattered the long cherished myth of male entitlement, not without resentment on the part of men and not without suffering on the part of women. Occupational segregation, unequal pay, unequal distributions of work and family obligations, and sexual harassment—all of these testify to the challenges to which women must continue to rise so that collectively they will eventually realize their considerable worth, not only within the home but also within the world of work.

SUMMARY

Women have always worked but in the past few decades, increasing numbers of women are working outside the home in paid employment. Economic forces are the primary reason for women's increasing profile in the workplace. Yet, myths regarding women's role in the workplace—such as their lack of physical prowess and negative concomitants of the menstrual cycle—are referred to in stereotypes regarding the limitations of women workers. Some of the more intense criticism of women concerns their dual roles as mother and worker. Unfortunately, society's ambivalence toward women workers impacts women's views of themselves as workers and mothers.

Occupational segregation within industrial societies continues at overwhelming rates. "Women's work" and "men's work" remain divided, with women crowded into fewer and lower-paying jobs than men. Women receive 77 cents for each dollar that men earn. Furthermore, women of color experience additional discrimination due to race and ethnicity, with fewer African American women and Hispanic women working as managers and professionals than White women. Studies of the differences in political views of women with different career histories points to fears regarding integration of women in high-level positions. Some women may have "feminist" viewpoints, which threaten traditional managerial or corporate perspectives. Women are not a homogenous group, and that is especially true when querying women about their perspectives on workplace justice, such as affirmative action.

Post–World War II ideals were the foundation of many boomers born during the 1950s. These ideals collided with the economic realities that greeted their generation: stagnant wages and downsizing. Many women raised during the rhetoric of the 1960s and 1970s women's liberation movement sought outside employment. A major revolution accompanied the rise of women in the workplace. Women sought empowerment through education and work, and many families benefited. Yet, even as many women were seeking a collaborative couple approach to work, contingent work in the United States began to erode prior gains for many workers, men included. The collaboration between the sexes that is needed at home to nurture family members is still not apparent in the workplace, as the distribution of women in jobs that pay well falls far short of that of men. In fact, researchers note that what is perceived to be a necessary trait for a job is based on highly stereotypical assessments of both the job and gender. Skills that are required to perform one job (e.g., appliance sales*man*) may not be different from those required to perform a job dominated by women (e.g., cosmetics sales*woman*). Yet many employers simply hire men for jobs, because men are preferred by the employer. Furthermore, if a job attracts more women, incumbents begin to fear that womanly traits will characterize a job, demeaning men's skills and masculinity. Extensive research demonstrates that men are paid more simply because they are men, not because of special masculine traits. The endurance to keyboard all day at a computer is considered equal to the endurance and physicality required to be a truck driver. Unfortunately, however, so-called women's work has been traditionally devalued, regardless of the cultural or social context.

Whereas once certain individuals would have easily reported that women's "proper" work was in the home, these individuals now suppress such comments. It is not that they want to be "politically correct" as much as they don't want to reveal their deeply held sexist or racist beliefs and therefore be "incorrect." Aversive sexism, a covert form of discrimination, continues unabated in the arena of workplace discrimination. Women not only experience a work-related penalty (salary) but a personal cost (stress) from discrimination. Enforced heterosexuality in the workplace extracts a penalty from lesbian women workers although preliminary evidence supports the notion that the primary discrimination they face is gender based, not due to sexual orientation. The very legal and social development that created

opportunities for women has reinforced patterns of gender inequality. Such inequality in the workplace results in an unearned male privilege that men take for granted and women concede. When women do not conform to the stereotypes that define working women, they may experience a "penalty" and need to be "put in their place" through sexual harassment or bribery. The effect is to confer special privileges and status upon male workers, such as those in the mines or in military schools. Women who describe themselves as careerist tend to believe in the meritocracy of the workplace and are less likely to interpret sexual aggression as a function of male social dominance, which intends to discriminate against women.

Although many people do not want to recognize their own disadvantages vis-à-vis others, women in nontraditional professions expose themselves to greater health risks. Women in both traditional and nontraditional jobs do have similar responses to stress, however. Married women are less subjected to sexual harassment in private firms than are single women. Women who cope most successfully with their stress are those who take an active approach to their problems—Super Moms excluded. Women who manage careers and family successfully do so only if they have strong support systems. However, even women who think they have good family support systems would be surprised to learn that male spouses, on average, perform less than half of the housework that women perform. Yet, given the obstacles women face at work and at home, children of working moms are no different psychologically than children of nonworking moms, perhaps due to the higher self-esteem that women in multiple roles exhibit.

Employment arrangements, such as nonstandard or "contingent" work, may ameliorate some work–family conflicts, but part-time work is not possible for single mothers who need income to support their families. Nonstandard work is less likely to offer benefits, such as health care or pensions, and such employment may impact women in retirement. Alternatively, some parents choose to work full time and withdraw from the home, practicing an emotional asceticism as they live a workaholic lifestyle.

Despite the multiple problems and issues that women confront in the workplace and the challenges of balancing work and family, women continue to enter and stay in the workforce over the course of their lives. Movement to a more progressive society may be perceived as occurring at a glacial rate.

Women continue, however, to press for greater equality in the home and workplace, and change is occurring, however slow it appears.

KEY TERMS

Aversive racism (p. 222)
Brass ceiling (p. 227)
Contingent worker (p. 219)
Emic (p. 215)

Etic (p. 215)
Gendered division of labor (p. 226)
Glass ceiling (p. 219)
Heilman's lack of fit model (p. 222)

Occupational segregation (p. 216)
Ostrich effect (p. 228)
Scarcity hypothesis (p. 236)
Tokenism (p. 235)

DISCUSSION QUESTIONS

1. Researchers have found that boys travel farther from home without an adult and are more familiar with and are more manipulative of their environment than girls. How might these early different relations with the environment later influence one's relationship to it in terms of jobs and career?

2. In order to facilitate one's awareness of career options and eliminate the consequences of occupational sex typing, some researchers suggest that the socialization process of young girls must be changed. How might this occur? What may be the long-term effects of the change?

3. Considering occupational segregation, what are the similarities and differences among White women, Black women, and Asian women?

4. What are the paradoxes for women working part time? For which women is part-time work an entitlement? For whom is it a privilege? If part-time work is not a permanent solution to work–family conflicts, what is a solution, taking into account the emerging growth of contingent work?

5. What are the paradoxical effects of attractiveness for women in the workplace? Do you think that this paradox is true for all jobs, some jobs, and/or certain jobs? What characteristics of a setting have to be present in order for Heilman's results to be generalizable? Consult research articles to support your position.

6. Would you choose to enter an extremely male-dominated field? Why or why not? What would be the pluses and minuses after reading this chapter? Ask a 5-year-old girl what she intends to do with her life. How does she explain her choices?

7. Women today have a variety of career options from which they can choose. Ask an elderly aunt or grandmother what she would do if she had to do it all over again. Why would she make that particular choice? Was her choice in congruence with your expectations? Why or why not?

8. What are the consequences for men who stay home and take care of the children while their wives are at work?

9. What are the emotional costs for husbands who earn less than their wives?

FURTHER READINGS_____

Barker, K., & Christensen, K. (Eds.) (1998). *Contingent work: American employment relations in transition.* Ithaca, NY: ILR/Cornell University Press.

Barnett, R. C., & Rivers, C. (1996). *She works/He works: How two-income families are happier, healthier, and better off.* San Francisco: Harper San Francisco.

Franz, C. E., & Stewart, A. J. (1994). *Women creating lives: Identities, resilience, and resistance.* Boulder, CO: Westview Press.

Morgan, K. S., & Brown, L. S. (1993). Lesbian career development, work behavior, and vocational counseling. In L. D. Garnets and D.C. Kimmel (Eds.), *Psychological perspectives on lesbian and gay male experiences* (pp. 267–286). New York: Columbia University Press.

Nelson, D. L., & Burke, R. J. (2002). *Gender, work stress, and health.* Washington, D.C.: American Psychological Association.

Schein, V. E. (1995). *Working from the margins: Voices of mothers in poverty.* Ithaca, NY: ILR Press.

CHAPTER 8

SEXUALITY

The most intense way we relate to another person is sexually. . . . Sex is not simply a matter of frictional force. The excitement comes largely in how we interpret the situation and how we perceive the connection to the other. . . . What is exciting is interpersonal; how the other views you, what attitude the actions evidence.

—Robert Nozick

Sex is not, of course, the only biological activity to be overloaded with social meaning; both eating and defecating spring to mind. However, it does appear to be the primary and principal act in most human societies.

—Tamsin Wilson

Female sexuality is turned inside out from birth, so "beauty" can take its place, keeping women's eyes lowered to their own bodies, glancing up only to check their reflections in the eyes of men.

—Naomi Wolf

Perhaps the best we can do in a bad situation is to speak the truth of both sides of the reality that we live in by speaking the truths about female sexual desire—both the pleasures and the dangers—and voicing the real experiences that girls and women have in their bodies.

—Deborah Tolman

There is no one right pattern of sexual response. What works, what feels good, what makes us feel more alive in ourselves and connected with our partners is what counts.

—Our Bodies, Ourselves

SEXUALITY IN A SOCIAL CONTEXT

The Double Standard: A Historical Perspective

Socialization in the Double Standard
Sex, Race, Ethnicity, Religion, and Class

It is hard to imagine a topic in which gender matters more than sexuality. Gender surely influences people's patterns of sexual desire and arousal, their responses to sexual imagery, and their sexual attitudes and practices. As we will see in this chapter, sexual behavior is a response to a complex mix of sociocultural, psychological, and biological forces and cannot be adequately understood in terms of any one force alone.

In this chapter, we consider physical aspects of sexuality, research on the nature and extent of various sexual behaviors, sexual orientation, sexual fantasy, responses to sexual imagery, sexuality among those with disabilities, sexual dysfunction, and contraceptive use. But we begin with a discussion of how female sexuality has been socially constructed—how social realities affect how we identify, describe, classify, and ultimately experience sexuality.

SEXUALITY IN A SOCIAL CONTEXT

We take a social constructionist perspective on sexuality that focuses on the historical and cultural contexts in which sexuality is learned and practiced. This view suggests that all societies organize sexual desires, behaviors, and identities into approved or encouraged, tolerated, and tabooed patterns (Lorber, 1994). These patterns are internalized by individual members of societies, who often come to view them as natural and inevitable, even biological, in origin.

Both female and male sexuality are shaped by society and culture. To be sure, societal messages to males about sex are value laden and conflicting, and may pose many emotional and sexual difficulties for them (Kil-

martin, 1994). But in most societies throughout history, sexuality is made problematic for females in ways that it is not for males (Gagnon, 1977; Gagnon & Simon, 1973). Some of these problems are due to the biological fact that sexual intercourse is far more consequential for females than males, because females alone bear children. But others result from the social reality that, throughout history, males have defined sexuality, including female sexuality, from their own perspective. Because of their historically greater physical, social, and economic power, men have been in positions to define when, how, with whom, and under what circumstances sex is appropriate, and they have often done so in ways that are disadvantageous to women. For example, the very definition of what constitutes "having sex" reveals a deeply androcentric (male-centered) and heterosexist bias (see Box 8.1). In Western societies, having sex usually refers exclusively to vaginal intercourse, involving male penetration and ejaculation. Hugging, touching, and kissing (which for some women are more stimulating than vaginal intercourse) do not count as having sex in this formulation. If they are considered at all, it is as *foreplay,* a preliminary, secondary, and ultimately dispensable set of activities.

As we shall see, females and males have been seen by scientists and laypeople alike as representing very different modes of sexual behavior, attitudes, and feelings, with females generally seen as less sexual and more variable in their sexual desire, behavior, and responses than men. In many textbooks on the psychology of women, there are no chapters devoted exclusively to female sexuality, although there are often chapters on the sexual victimization of

BOX 8.1

Heterosexist Bias in the Study of Sexuality and Intimacy

Defining sex as vaginal intercourse reveals a heterosexist as well as androcentric bias. Many authors have challenged what they perceive is a deep and widespread heterosexist bias in the literatures of sexuality and intimate relationships, a bias that has contributed to gender inequality. Adrienne Rich (1980) forcefully criticized heterosexist bias in the social sciences in her influential and provocative essay "Compulsory Sexuality and Lesbian Existence." In this essay, she takes on the notions that women are "innately sexually oriented toward men" and that lesbian experiences are deviant, abhorrent, or insignificant. She argues that heterosexuality has been forcibly imposed on women, as a means of assuring male rights of physical, economic, and emotional access. According to Rich,

> Women have married because it was necessary, in order to survive economically, in order to have children who would not suffer economic deprivation or social ostracism, in order to remain respectable, in order to do what was expected of women because coming out of "abnormal" childhoods they wanted to feel "normal" and because heterosexual romance has been represented as the

great female adventure, duty, and fulfillment. (p. 82)

Rich challenges feminists to examine heterosexuality as an institution maintained by a variety of forces, including physical violence, and to question the extent to which it represents a choice or preference for women. One of the many ways that heterosexuality is made compulsory for women, according to Rich, is the "rendering invisible of the lesbian possibility" (p. 78). Just as African American women have historically been deprived of a political existence through inclusion in the discourse on African American men (hooks, 1981), lesbian existence has often been yoked with, and eclipsed by, the gay male experience. Gay males receive much more attention from science and society than do lesbians. Rich recognizes the shared experiences and common causes of gay men and lesbians, but insists on the acknowledgment of the differences between them, including men's economic and cultural privilege relative to women. Rich's analysis invites us to revisit the assumption that certain forms of sexual behavior are more "natural" than others and to consider, for example, whether we should question the causes and meanings of heterosexuality as well as homosexuality.

---

women (rape, incest, sexual harassment) and/or reproductive issues (pregnancy, menstruation, contraception, and sexually transmitted diseases)—the complications that sex presents for women.

We see the distinctions in the constructions of female and male sexuality quite clearly in the *double standard* by which the sexual feelings and behaviors of women and men are judged differently. We will discuss the double standard at length, because it is the lens through which virtually all aspects of female and male sexuality are seen and distorted. The double standard has several related strands, including the Madonna–whore dichotomy, the prizing of female virginity and fidelity, the differential socialization of girls and boys, and the relationship between physical attractiveness and sexuality in females. We will consider how such variables as race, class, and ethnicity

affect sexuality. We will discuss these topics in turn, focusing on how they contribute to profound ambivalence about female sexuality among females and males alike.

The Double Standard: A Historical Perspective

It is important to note that the widespread notion that women are less sexual than men has not always prevailed. Several of the ancient myths and images of women discussed in Chapter 2 depicted women as sexually desiring as well as desirable. In some preliterate societies, women's capacity for multiple orgasms so threatened men that they physically confined women to control their sexuality (Lorber, 1994). In Europe from the sixteenth through the eighteenth centuries, it was believed that women's orgasms were as necessary for conception as men's (McLaren, 1984).

We can trace modern sexual norms in the United States and Europe to the Victorian era in Great Britain, roughly during the middle and later parts of the nineteenth century. Queen Victoria, whose name has become virtually synonymous with sexual repression, ruled England from 1837 until her death in 1901. During this time, science and medicine bolstered the prevailing Judeo-Christian ethic in actively discouraging the pursuit of sexual pleasure. Sexual intercourse was seen as physically and spiritually harmful to women, and good women were thought to lack interest in sex. Men, whose sexual passions were never questioned, were cautioned to be gentle and restrained sexually with their virtuous wives. Apparently, many thought that they were doing their wives a favor by indulging their lustful feelings with the "other kind of women"—readily available prostitutes (Wade & Tavris, 1994). One estimate holds that there may have been as many as one prostitute for every 12 London men (Tannahill, 1982). Women were depicted in medical textbooks at that time as rarely interested in sex and often frigid and sexually dysfunctional. William Acton, an influential English physician, observed in 1857 "that the majority of women (happily for society) are not much troubled with sexual feeling of any kind" (Acton, as cited in Rathus, Nevid, & Fichner-Rathus, 2002, p. 16). The double standard of sexual behavior and desire, a historic feature of Western civilization, was reinforced with religious, medical, and even legal backing.

During the early twentieth century, several forces acted to change sexual attitudes and behavior in the United States and Europe. Two world wars caused tremendous social upheaval, and with this, more sexual permissiveness. The revolutionary writings of Sigmund Freud (1856–1939) put sexuality squarely at the center of personality development. Freud thought that the sex drive was the principal motivating force in life. Freud not only recognized female sexuality but also saw a link between taboos on women's sexual expression and constraints on their thinking and life options (Wade & Tavris, 1994). The 1960s saw more dramatic changes in scientific, economic, political, and social life in the United States.

Scientific advances in birth control and sexually transmitted disease control removed many barriers to sexual activity. The economy was booming and commercialism was spreading. The profoundly divisive Vietnam War moved young people in particular to rebel against the war, the government, and the commercialism of the times. The media in all forms became more open to sexual topics and more sexually explicit. These forces all contributed to the *sexual revolution* of the 1960s and 1970s in sexual attitudes and behaviors. During this time of relative economic affluence, political liberalism, and increased social permissiveness, traditional prohibitions against casual sex collapsed, to the point where, in 1987, nearly 52 percent of students entering college surveyed approved of casual sexual encounters (Durex, 2001).

Throughout the 1980s and 1990s, growing political conservatism and awareness of the threat of AIDS and other sexually transmitted diseases brought with them a return to more conventional sexual behavior at least among some groups (Centers for Disease Control [CDC], 1990). But some aspects of the sexual revolution have endured: a greater willingness to discuss sex openly; increasing tolerance of premarital sex, especially among younger teens; and the liberation of female sexuality, bringing female levels of premarital and even extramarital sexual behavior closer to that of males (Rathus et al., 2002). But even with the general decline of sexual repressiveness for men and women and increasing equality between the sexes, evidence abounds that the double standard of sexual behavior is still alive and well.

The Madonna–Whore Dichotomy. Perhaps nowhere is the double standard more stark than in the way in which women are divided into *Madonnas,* sexually chaste, desirable, but not desirous women who "just say no" to sex, and *whores,* sexually wanton, promiscuous women who like sex and have many sexual partners (or just one under the wrong circumstances). These conflicting representations of women date back at least to the Middle Ages, the period in Western history from about 476 to 1450. The Roman Catholic Church, which dominated medieval Europe, regarded women as tainted by the sin of Eve, the seductress who used her sexuality to tempt men to their downfall. In the Eastern Church of Constantinople, the cult of the Virgin Mary flourished, which depicted Mary as the ideal image of womanhood: chaste, loving, pious, and saintly.

The schism between the Madonna and the whore suggests a profound rejection of female sexuality in Western thought. In this dichotomy there is no middle ground, no way for a woman to engage in sex, especially outside of a committed love relationship, and still be a "good woman." Many writers have noted the large number of derogatory slang terms for women who like or have sex too much: *sluts, tramps, nymphos,* and *bimbos,* to name a few. In both everyday and scientific usage, sexual women are often regarded as promiscuous, sex addicted, or nymphomaniacs, terms that imply moral turpitude, abnormality, even illness. There are certainly terms with negative connotations for men who are in some way sexually "transgressive," including lech, philanderer, dirty old man, and libertine. But none of these is as stigmatizing or invalidating as comparable terms for women. Indeed, such men are often admired and praised with names such as *Romeo, stud, playboy, stallion,* and *player.* According to sexuality expert Deborah Tolman, the threat of being labeled a slut still looms large for adolescent girls. In *Dilemmas of Desire,* Tolman (2002) wrote

> *The so-called Madonna–whore split is surprisingly alive and well in the public imagination and in the lives of adolescent girls; even girls who do feel entitled to their own sexuality negotiate this label. One fifteen year old girl writing on a teen website described herself as "unashamed about being sexual," recognizing that such behavior by a girl is still frowned upon: "I am a slut . . . to some people it's someone who sleeps around, and to others it's someone who is open about her sexuality. Either way, I guess that's me."* (p. 11)

Prizing of Female Virginity and Fidelity. Throughout most of the history of Western civilization, women have been regarded as the property of men. A female belonged first to her father and later to her husband. She was an item of exchange among men, valued chiefly for her worth as a sex object and reproducer. The influential anthropologist Levi-Strauss (1969) suggests that the institution of marriage arose through the reciprocal exchange of women by tribal leaders to enlarge and strengthen kinship systems. The practice of trading women for other valued objects and influence has been credited for spawning the "ideology of virginity"—the notion that a woman is more valuable as a bride if she has never belonged to another man.

Virginity before marriage has been highly prized, but only for females. We can find evidence for this valuation in disparate times, places, and peoples in myths, proverbs, and ancient and modern history. In Christianity, the virginity of Mary, the mother of God and central female figure, is an article of faith. In most European countries until modern times, a family's honor depended on the virginity of its unmarried females, and death was preferable to dishonor.

Psychologist David Buss conducted a major survey of over 10,000 participants from 37 cultures on six continents about the characteristics they sought in mates (Buss, 1989, 1994). He found that the value that people currently place on chastity in prospective mates ranges from "indispensable" in China to "irrelevant" in Sweden and the Netherlands. In 62 percent of the 37 cultures, males valued chastity in mates more than did females, and there was no culture in which the reverse was true.

Today, a woman's virginity can enhance her value in institutions ranging from marriage to prostitution. The long-standing African practice of female genital mutilation exists in large part to insure virginity and improve marriageability (Toubia, 1993). The worth of virgins can be seen in the burgeoning sex trades of Asian countries such as India, where virgins command three times the price of sexually experienced girls and women in part because of a common belief that sex with a virgin cures venereal diseases (Serril, 1993).

If virginity before marriage has been (and in many cultures still is) valued in females, female fidelity after marriage can be a matter of life or death. Throughout most of history and in almost all cultures, adultery has been tolerated in men but punished—sometimes by death—in women. Suzanne Frayser, an anthropologist, has studied sexual behavior in 62 different cultures. She found that, in 26 percent of the cultures, the husband alone is permitted sex outside of marriage, whereas there is no society in which only the wife is permitted extramarital sex (Frayser, 1985). More than half of the 48 societies for which data were available allowed the husband to kill his unfaithful wife. In modern societies, the price of even suspected infidelity for women is too often battering or death.

Although precise figures are impossible to determine and the gap between women and men has narrowed over recent years, almost all surveys of extramarital sexual behavior suggest that men are more likely to be unfaithful in marriage than women (Kinsey, Pomeroy, & Martin, 1948; Kinsey, Pomeroy, Martin, & Gephard, 1953; Laumann, Gagnon, Michael, & Michaels, 1994). There is also evidence to suggest that men feel more approving of extramarital sex than women and feel more justified in engaging in it and less guilty and remorseful about it (Glass & Wright, 1992; Lamanna & Riedmann, 1997; Margolin, 1989; Townsend, 1995). Men's permissiveness with respect to their own extramarital behavior does not extend to their wives. In U.S. surveys, men place fidelity as the number-one desired characteristic in a potential spouse. This finding has been replicated in other Western societies such as Germany and the Netherlands (Buss, 1994). Women's attitudes toward extramarital sex are more conservative and reflect an acute awareness of the double standard. Both faithful and unfaithful wives believe that infidelity is morally wrong, and most wives believe that adulterous wives are judged more harshly than adulterous husbands (Glass & Wright, 1992; Sprecher, Regan, & McKinney, 1998).

Both evolutionary and learning theories have been advanced to explain why males seek to control female sexuality both before and after marriage. Social learning theories tend to focus on differing sexual socialization of girls and boys (to be discussed later), greater taboos and societal sanctions against adultery for women than for men, and historically fewer opportunities for women, especially homemakers, to have outside relationships. Evolutionary psychologists argue that female monogamy is central to males because, unlike females, males can never be certain that they are the biological fathers of their children. They point out that because males do not want to rear and support someone else's children, it is essential to them that their female mates do not stray. Whatever the explanation offered for the greater importance of female fidelity, there can be little question that males have sought to control the sexual behavior of females through the premiums placed on female chastity: virginity before marriage and fidelity after it.

Socialization in the Double Standard

Girls face the trials of exploring their sexuality in the shadow of realistic fears of pregnancy, interpersonal violence, and sexually transmitted diseases. Rates of adolescent pregnancy are declining in the United States, but they are still higher in the United States than in virtually any other developed country (Brody, 1998; Jones, 1985; Singh & Darroch, 1999), and about 10 percent of American girls aged 15 to 19 become pregnant each year (CDC, 2000a). Girls and young women are more likely to be victims of rape than any other age group (Koss, Heise, & Russo, 1994), with young women aged 16 to 24 two to three times more likely to be raped than other women (National Crime Victimization Survey, 1995). Females are much more likely—perhaps up to 15 times more likely—than males to contract AIDS through heterosexual sexual intercourse (Rodin & Ickovics, 1990). Young women, especially young women of color, are becoming the fastest growing segment of people infected with HIV (CDC 2000b, 2002; Ickovics & Rodin, 1992). Realistic fears of violence, victimization, pregnancy, and sexually transmitted diseases take on important social and psychological overlays through the processes by which girls and boys learn about sex.

From early childhood, traditional socialization encourages very different goals and roles for females and males in sexual relationships (Allgeier & McCormick, 1983; Lottes & Kuriloff, 1994). Compared to little boys, the names that little girls have for their sex organs are often vague (e.g., "down there" and "private parts") and are unlikely to inspire pride. During adolescence, boys are socialized to enjoy their sexuality, initiate sexual relations, and take pride in their sexual development, prowess, and experience. Girls, on the other hand, receive more complex, ambivalent, even negative messages about sex. Most girls learn to view the physical changes that occur during adolescence, and the attention that these changes bring from boys and men, with a mixture of pride, excitement, fear, and mistrust. The message that "good girls" don't want or have sex is not lost on girls, as research with diverse populations of girls and young women shows. In her interview study of 52 young women aged 16 to 24, Woodhouse (1982) found that many feared being seen as sexually promiscuous by their boyfriends. These girls equated femininity with the absence of sexual behavior, understanding that they were expected to display sexuality but "not use it directly." More recently, Tolman (1992, 2002) reports similar findings with samples of urban and suburban adolescent girls from middle to low socioeconomic classes.

With a different population of adolescents, Mc-Cormick (1987) found that having sex was a male goal, whereas avoiding sex was a female goal. Subsequent studies have found that a young woman described as sexually experienced received less positive evaluations than a less experienced woman (Garcia, 1986), and that promiscuity is shameful only for women (Mundy, 2000; Preston & Stanley, 1987). In a survey of high socioeconomic status students enrolled in an elite private college, where the likelihood of sexual equality is relatively high, men reported more permissive sexual socialization than women from both parents and peers (Lottes & Kuriloff, 1994). Combining the results of many studies of gender differences in sexual attitudes using meta-analytic techniques (explained in Chapter 6), Oliver and Hyde (1993) found greater acceptance by males than females of all categories of sexual behavior, including casual premarital sex, sexual permissiveness, premarital sex in a committed relationship, and extramarital sex. Even today, 40 years after the much-vaunted sexual revolution, there is strong evidence of differential sexual socialization of females and males.

The Missing Discourse of Desire

> When I searched the literature to find out what psychologists knew about adolescent girls' sexual desire, I found that no one had asked about it. (Tolman, 2002, p. 9)

Where is the good news for girls about sex in a society that tells them that sex, at least for them, is bad? Michelle Fine posed this and other related questions in a groundbreaking article in which she identified the "missing discourse of desire" in discussions of female, especially adolescent female, sexuality (Fine, 1988). Fine describes the extent to which schools, parents, and religious institutions unwittingly conspire to scare girls and young women away from sex by equating sexuality entirely with negative outcomes—violence, victimization, pregnancy, disease, immorality, and low-class behavior. What females hear most often from authority figures is that all males are out to take advantage of them sexually, with dire social, psychological, and physical consequences. It is their job to put the brakes on boys' behavior and, better yet, to gain their love and respect. This is a heady assignment for girls and young women, and it is hardly surprising that there is so little room for desire in the discourse on female sexuality.

Although sex is consistently portrayed negatively to girls, it obviously does not prevent them from having sex (Lauritsen & Swicegood, 1997; Zeman, 1990), with current estimates suggesting that about 37 percent of females have sex before age 16, and 65 percent by age 19 (Tolman, 2002). But many girls experience a wide gulf between their sexual desire, intimacy needs, peer and media influences, and actual experience of sex on the one hand, and the profoundly negative messages about sex from authority figures on the other hand. According to Fine (1988), messages that acknowledge female desire and the attractions of sexual relationships while warning of realistic dangers might be more successful.

Sexual Scripts. What happens to female sexual desire when it is shrouded in so many social, psychological, and physical dangers? From all directions, and in many different ways, girls learn that the only way to have sex and still be a "good girl" is to fall in love and enter the romance and marriage market. Surveys over the past 20 years consistently suggest that a majority of men and women endorse premarital sex in the context of long-term relationships or when the partners are described as being "in love" (Michael, Gagnon, Laumann, & Kolata, 1994; Oliver & Hyde, 1993). Many adolescents report engaging in intercourse because of feelings of love (Browning, Hatfield, Kessler, & Levine, 2000), but affection for partner is cited as the prime motive of first intercourse for nearly twice the percentage of women (48 percent) as men (25 percent) (Michael et al., 1994). The message to girls is that sex and love are inextricably intertwined, and love makes sex right. Debold, Wilson, and Malave (1993) write (p. 72):

> Good girls have sex when it is "true love." As many girls and women come to find out, this is one of the biggest manipulations that boys and men figure out. "Tell them that you love them and you can do anything."

Many boys hear a distinctly different message, that is, that sex and love are contradictory, so that they cannot love someone with whom they are sexual and cannot be sexual with someone they love (Kilmartin, 1994). We recognize this as a by-product of the Madonna–whore dichotomy discussed earlier. Many studies have shown that men are considerably more comfortable than women in viewing sex as a purely physical release or adventure, unconnected to relationships (Carrol, Volk, & Hyde, 1985).

In 1977, Laws and Schwartz coined the term *sexual scripts* to denote the unspoken, informal, but nonetheless critical rules and guidelines that women and men follow in their interactions with each other. The rules are backed by substantial social rewards for following the scripts and punishments for failing to follow them. In Western societies, at least for the dominant (White) subculture, women gain power and status through attracting and marrying men of higher socioeconomic status. Her lures, or "weapons of weakness," are her innocence (expressed by her virginity, sincerity, and reasonableness), youth, and beauty (Debold et al., 1993). These scripts are taught literally from infancy by countless fairy tales and the cartoons and images they inspire, and are reinforced later in the soap operas, romantic movies, and romance novels that are marketed so successfully to adolescent and adult women.

Nowhere are sexual scripts so transparent as in romance novels, whose authors literally follow a formula that permits few variations (Debold et al., 1993). Romance novels account for almost 40 percent of all mass-market paperback sales. The leading romance pubisher, Harlequin Enterprises, sold more than 160 million books worldwide in 2003 alone.

Harlequin books are sold in more than 100 international markets and have been translated into more than twenty-three languages around the world. It is estimated that more than 50 million people read Harlequin books, virtually all of them women (http://www.eHarlequin.com). Interestingly, girls' and women's "real" thoughts and feelings are not part of the scripts for romance novels (Tolman, 2002).

Sexual scripts specify that men choose whom they will ask for dates and initiate sexual contact, and women act as gatekeepers who accept or reject dates and forbid or permit sexual activity. If women forbid sex, men are encouraged to press their case and not take no for an answer, to overwhelm or ravish women. If sexual activity is permitted, men are scripted to take active, even aggressive stances, whereas women are scripted to be passive, submissive, receptive, and, at most, "responsive."

Sexual Objects and Sexual Subjects

> Beauty pornography . . . claims that women's "beauty" is our sexuality when the truth goes the other way around. (Wolf, 1991, p. 136)

A gendered perspective on sexuality suggests that we consider physical attractiveness and body image in conjunction with female sexuality. Research consistently shows that physical attractiveness is a major determinant of interpersonal and sexual attraction (Rathus et al., 2002). Research also suggests that, unlike most men, many women bring to their sexual relationships strikingly negative feelings about their looks generally and their bodies particularly (Debold et al., 1993; Wolf, 1991). Appraisals of female beauty, her own and others', play an important role in a woman's sexual desire, expression, and behavior, and can profoundly affect her self-esteem and self-confidence.

A vital, nearly invariant part of sexual scripts in Western societies is that interesting, wonderful adventures and opportunities for romance and riches happen only to young, beautiful women. Through myths and fairy tales, movies and romance novels, even great works of literature, girls and women learn that heroes risk their lives only for beautiful women, and men learn that beautiful women will be their rewards for bravery and success (Debold et al., 1993).

Several lines of research consistently show that men value physical attractiveness in potential mates more than women do (Coombs & Kenkel, 1996; Hatfield & Sprecher, 1986). Attractiveness matters more to men in evaluating a prospective date, and especially a prospective sexual partner, than it does to women (Nevid, 1984). An interesting way of comparing the relative importance of physical beauty for men and women is to examine what qualities they seek and offer in personal advertisements. Personal advertisements are a particularly valuable source of information for researchers because, in them, advertisers make very explicit the qualities about themselves that they think others will find attractive, and the characteristics about others that are most important to them. In almost all studies of personal advertisements, across time, geographic location, and social class of advertisers, researchers have found that, regardless of sexual orientation, men are more likely than women to seek physical attractiveness in their partners, and women are more likely than men to offer physical attractiveness to their partners (Deaux & Hanna, 1984; Harrison & Saeed, 1977).

From an evolutionary psychology perspective, Buss's large-scale cross-cultural study of mating preferences and selection looked at gender differences in sexual attraction (Buss, 1994). Buss and other evolutionary psychologists believe that how people select sexual partners is of great scientific importance because it reveals ancient, ancestral selection pressures on men and women. It also affects other components of the mating system, such as how women and men compete within their own sex for access to attractive mates. Buss found that in each of the 37 cultures studied, men placed a greater premium on physical attractiveness than did women. He concluded that "Contrary to thinking in the social sciences, it is now known that our desires in a mate are neither arbitrary nor infinitely variable across cultures" (p. 40). In other words, Buss (and other evolutionary psychologists) believe that gender differences in mate selection leading males to prefer beautiful females are natural and biologically determined rather than learned and culturally determined.

Buss's research has spawned a number of studies from an evolutionary psychology perspective on what specific female characteristics men desire. Singh (1993) found that men particularly prize a low waist-to-hip ratio, which is regarded as a key indicator of fertility, and symmetrical body features, which are interpreted as a sign of good health. Other studies have found that facial features such as clear, smooth skin, clear eyes, lustrous hair, full lips, and an absence of sores or lesions are widely seen as attractive in females (Symons, 1979). Perrett (1994), studying British and Japanese men, found that female faces characterized by large eyes, high cheekbones, full lips, and narrow jaws were ranked as most attractive. Evolutionary psychologists argue that these preferences are tied to disease resistance, health, fertility, and youth. It is important to note, however, that some evolutionary psychology predictions about preferences for physical characteristics have not been borne out. For instance, the hypotheses that people would find most appealing those faces that displayed gender-appropriate characteristics was not supported in recent research. Whereas it was predicted that men with traditional hallmarks of male dominance such as a big jaw, square face, and heavy brow would favorably impress men and women, people of both sexes preferred feminine facial features in men as well as women (Angier, 1998). Generally, research findings on sex differences in preferences for various facial and body features have been more complicated than evolutionary psychology predicted, and the significance of these findings for the claims of evolutionary psychology remains unclear. Despite sex differences in certain preferences, both men and women value some physical characteristics such as good teeth and firm muscle tone, and both report that they place greater emphasis on a prospective partner's personality and values than physical characteristics, especially in long-term relationships.

Whatever the source of male preferences for various physical attributes in females, females from childhood onward are bombarded with the message that their power and worth lie in their physical attractiveness, and that they need to invest time and money in improving their looks. And they do not have to look hard to see how female beauty is defined. Media images have never been so available or explicit, and the standards of beauty they promote have never been so high. Current images of beautiful female bodies, for instance, portray women as thin, tall, athletically fit, with large breasts, a constellation of characteristics that is rare in any one individual. Today's women have omnipresent, graphic images of perfection against which to measure themselves and find themselves wanting. It is hard to overestimate the various effects of these standards on female sexuality, as we will see when we consider the cases of women with physical disabilities.

Sex, Race, Ethnicity, Religion, and Class

If sexuality is socially constructed, as we argue throughout this chapter, we would expect to see a wide variety of sexual beliefs, attitudes, and practices around the world and within the United States, which is a nation of hundreds of different ethnic and religious groups. Indeed, there has been an explosion of recent research documenting a rich variety of sexual expression throughout the world and in the United States. This research confirms that there is no one female or male sexuality. People come in different ethnicities, religions, and social classes, and these variables interact with gender and each other to affect how sexuality is experienced and expressed.

Much recent research has focused on race in the study of sexual behavior and outcomes in the United States (Laumann et el., 1994; Wyatt, 1994). Our society has long been preoccupied with race as it is defined in the popular culture and has had an abiding interest in emphasizing racial differences in sexual practices. Historically, studies have compared African and European sexual practices (cf. Laumann et al., 1994; Wyatt, Vontross, cited in Wyatt, 1994) and, more recently, Asian, African, and U.S. sexual practices (Chan, 1990). Because of widespread racial myths and stereotypes, along with real subcultural differences among broadly defined racial groups, many researchers have found it worthwhile to explore race as a variable in research on sexuality.

Recent studies of sexuality and ethnicity suggest that Asian American and Hispanic American teenagers are more sexually conservative than either their White (non-Hispanic) or African American counterparts. Among Chinese American college students at the University of California at Berkeley, Huang and Uba (1992) found that only 40 percent reported engaging in premarital intercourse. Research suggests that Mexican American women also initiate sexual intercourse later than their White (non-Hispanic) and African American peers (Slonim-Nevo, 1992) and that Mexican American male and female college students report having sex less frequently and with fewer partners than comparable Anglo students.

Race is a troublesome variable in sexuality research, as it is in so many other areas, in part because racial biases and stereotypes often affect the research questions asked and the findings reported. African American females and males are often stereotyped as being "more sexual" and "promiscuous" than White males and females, even by African Americans (Wyatt, 1994), despite the lack of good research evidence to support these stereotypes. For instance, research suggests that White women are more likely than minority women to reject religious teachings about contraception and adopt a recreational rather than procreational model of sex, to plan sexual activity in advance, and to engage in a wider variety of sexual practices (Laumann et al., 1994; Wyatt, 1994). White women also report having sex more often than minority women (Laumann et al., 1994). Clearly, what constitutes promiscuity is in the eye of the beholder, and promiscuity is a value-laden, problematic term to use in characterizing groups.

In considering race differences in sexual behavior, it is critical to note that race is usually correlated (or confounded) with other major variables, most notably social class indicators, such as education level, occupation, and income. In the United States, most racial minorities are disproportionately poor. Wyatt (1994) notes that the differences in the ages of first sexual intercourse between White and African American girls disappear when social class is taken into account. The best-known study of the reproductive and health behaviors of American Indians, the Billings (Montana) Indian Health Service Study (Warren et al., 1990), found reproductive patterns among American Indian women that parallel findings among poor, urban African American women: early age of first intercourse, relatively high levels of teen pregnancies and unplanned pregnancies, and low contraceptive use. Racial differences in unintended pregnancies, sexually transmitted diseases, and abortions may be more properly attributed to social class, life experiences, religious beliefs, and ethnic–cultural values than to race. For instance, it is Catholic doctrine that the purpose of sex is procreation, and contraceptive use for any reason is itself sinful. Low rates of contraceptive use among Hispanic and African American girls relative to White girls may be due not to lack of knowledge or concern about birth control, but rather to traditional religious beliefs and conservative value systems.

Moreover, when racial differences in sexual behaviors or outcomes are found, the assumption may be that there is something inherent in racial group membership that causes those behaviors or outcomes. Often, little consideration is given to how or why gross racial categorizations, which identify a superficial common dimension of people who vary along many other dimensions, can explain something as complex as sexuality. Finally, a focus on racial differences inevitably risks exaggerating the differences and downplaying the similarities among people of different races, and may erroneously suggest that the races are more different in their sexuality than they are similar. In fact, within-group variation is much larger than between-group variation. Moreover, recent surveys suggest that the races and ethnic groups in the United States are much more similar than different in their sexual behavior and are becoming more similar over time.

SCIENCE STUDIES SEXUAL BEHAVIOR

Until the middle of the twentieth century, sexual behavior was considered an inappropriate topic for scientific study, and there was little research into the nature and extent of human sexuality. Since the landmark publication of Alfred Kinsey's first survey of sexual behavior entitled *Sexual Behavior in the Human Male* in 1948, followed by *Sexual Behavior in the Human Female* in 1953, the study of sexual behavior has become respectable and indeed quite popular in recent years.

Researchers in human behavior use the same panoply of research methods that all scientists use.

As in all areas of research, the choice of research methods depends on the research question and hypothesis (if any). Much of the research in human sexual behavior to date has focused on one of two areas: (1) determining the prevalence of various sexual practices and desires among different groups and (2) studying patterns of sexual arousal. Prevalence has most often been studied in the field by means of the survey, and arousal in the laboratory by means of physiological measures. We will consider the prevalence issue first.

Sex by the Numbers: Sex Lives in the United States from World War II to the Present

The first major survey of sexual behavior was conducted from 1938 to 1949 by Alfred C. Kinsey, a biologist. Kinsey and his colleagues interviewed 5,300 males and 5,940 females about their sexual behavior, including premarital and extramarital sex, masturbation, responses to erotica, incidence of orgasm, and homosexual activity. Kinsey's was not a "scientific survey," meaning that there was no attempt to gain a sample that was truly random or representative of the people in the United States as a whole. He recruited what is known as a convenience sample—volunteer members of a variety of organizations and institutions (such as college fraternities and sororities, boardinghouses, and prisons) who were willing to discuss their sex lives in detail. Certain groups of people, such as the elderly, ethnic and religious minorities, and those living in rural areas, were underrepresented. People who were especially sexually permissive and adventurous may have been overrepresented. In addition, Kinsey's respondents, both females and males, were all interviewed by male interviewers. Women and other subgroups may not have felt comfortable reporting certain kinds of information to male interviewers.

It is generally accepted today that Kinsey's survey methods were quite flawed. Nonetheless, Kinsey's was a heroic first effort to understand human sexuality, and his surveys had several methodological strengths. For instance, he was sensitive to research concerns such as reliability and validity of reports. Although his sample was not representative of the U.S. population, it was broad based and in-cluded many people of different ages, socioeconomic groups, and geographic localities.

What did Kinsey find? The Kinsey studies shocked America in the mid-twentieth century by de-scribing a sexually permissive society in which mas-turbation and homosexual acts were far more common, and fidelity in marriage less common, than most people believed. With a few notable exceptions, Kinsey's results have been supported by several more recent surveys using different populations and meth-ods conducted by university researchers, research or-ganizations such as the *Playboy* Foundation, and such magazines as *Redbook* and *Cosmopolitan.*

The first large-scale *scientific* survey of sexual behavior in the United States was published by Uni-versity of Chicago scientists Laumann, Gagnon, Michael, and Michaels in 1994. This landmark sur-vey, in which all respondents were both personally interviewed and administered questionnaires, is the first major survey of the sexual practices of adults in the United States to use a form of probability or ran-dom sampling. Probability samples are ones in which every individual (within certain stated restrictions) has an equal chance of being selected to participate. The significance of this is that we can often general-ize from studies that correctly use probability sam-ples to the public at large depending on the response rate. Almost 80 percent of all people contacted agreed to be interviewed and fill out the questionnaires, a re-markably high return rate for any kind of survey, par-ticularly one that measures private behavior such as sexual practices.

With some important exceptions, this study of 3,432 people between the ages of 18 and 59 paints a picture of a far more sexually conservative America than Kinsey, *Playboy,* and most other earlier surveys (Laumann et al., 1994). What do sex surveys from Kinsey et al. to Laumann et al. and beyond suggest about sexual behavior in the United States from the mid-twentieth century to the present?

Overall, surveys of sex in the United States show a trend over the past 50 years toward a higher inci-dence of all kinds of heterosexual activity, in virtu-ally all age groups studied, especially younger ones, and a greater variety of sexual activity. With only minor variations across race and ethnicity, religious affiliation, and level of education, U.S. adults be-tween the ages of 18 and 59 fall into three groups: About one-third have sex at least twice a week, one-third a few times a month, and one-third a few times a year or not at all.

Sex before marriage, once uncommon in fe-males, has become the norm for both sexes, and atti-tudes toward premarital sex are generally permissive. Still, as measured by the number of sex partners women and men have over a lifetime, sex has not be-come much more casual or "promiscuous." The av-erage woman in the United States reports two sexual partners over a lifetime and the average man, six. Overwhelmingly, Americans' favorite sex act is vagi-nal intercourse, with 96 percent reporting this as "very or somewhat appealing." Watching one's part-ner undress is rated second, and oral sex is listed as a distant third (Laumann et al., 1994). The trend is also toward more permissive attitudes about homosexual-ity, but not a greater incidence of homosexual activity itself. In fact, recent surveys have failed to support Kinsey's frequently repeated finding that one in ten men is homosexual. The general increase in sexually permissive attitudes apparently does not extend to ex-tramarital sex, with most Americans strongly disap-proving of extramarital sex, although it may be particularly difficult to measure the incidence of this almost universally disapproved behavior. Estimates of the incidence of extramarital sex vary widely from survey to survey and are regarded as particularly sus-pect in surveys of sexual behaviors.

Sex In and Out of Marriage

Premarital Sex. Perhaps nowhere is the sexual rev-olution of the 1970s more obvious than in the in-creased rates of premarital sexual intercourse, especially for girls and women, from the time of Kin-sey's work to the present. Kinsey found that 77 per-cent of single men but only 20 percent of single women had experienced intercourse by age 20. Among those still single at age 25, 83 percent of men and 33 percent of women had engaged in sex. In the early 1970s, the *Playboy* survey found that among people under 25, 95 percent of men and 81 percent of women reported having premarital coitus, a striking increase for women (Hunt, 1974). Rates of premarital sex have continued to climb since the *Playboy* survey (Janus & Janus, 1993), although there is some evidence that sexual activity has begun to decline among unmarried women on college campuses in response to fears of AIDS and increased political conservatism.

Not only has premarital sex become the norm for men and women in the United States, but people are also having sex at younger ages. At the time of the Kinsey surveys, only 7 percent of White females had sex by age 16; in 1988, Zeman found that 27 percent of females had sex by age 15 (Zeman, 1990); and more recent estimates are that between 50 and 65 percent of females have sex by age 16 (Rathus et al., 2002; Tolman, 2002). Estimates of the average age of first intercourse today are put at 16 for girls and 15.5 for boys (U.S. Department of Health and Human Services, 1992). Some surveys suggest that African American adolescents begin having intercourse about two years before White adolescents (Brooks-Gunn & Furstenberg, 1989; Laumann et al., 1994).

Several investigators have recently tried to identify some of the factors associated with premarital sexual intercourse, especially among young teens. At the turn of the century, surveys reveal that about half of all high school students are sexually active (CDC, 2000b; Gates & Sonenstein, 2000), with African American boys (78 percent) more likely than European American (50 percent) or Latino American (58 percent) boys to have engaged in sexual intercourse. Premarital intercourse is motivated by many factors, including the activation of sexual arousal by sex hormones. There is evidence that physically mature teens whose secondary sexual characteristics develop early begin dating and having sex sooner (Belgrave, van Oss, Marian, & Chambers, 2000). We have already discussed the importance of feelings of love and affection, especially for females. Other factors associated with premarital sex are conformity to peers, seeking peer recognition, the desire to please one's partner, and the desire to dominate someone (Browning et al., 2000).

One consistent finding is that adolescents whose parents are separated or divorced engage in sex earlier than their peers from homes with both parents present (Belgrave et al., 2000; Coles & Stokes, 1985). Other factors associated with early sexuality among adolescents are poor academic performance and low education and career aspirations, father absence, and permissive attitudes in the family about sexuality (Keith et al., 1991). New studies show that the quality of the relationships between adolescents and their parents is important, with parents who communicate their values and expectations and show interest in their children's lives more likely to have children who show sexual restraint (Belgrave et al., 2000).

Marital Sex.   Sexuality in marriage has itself undergone something of a transformation since the Kinsey surveys of the 1940s and 1950s. In general, recent research evidence suggests that the frequency, duration, and varieties of sexual activity have all increased in marriage. For example, Kinsey reported that married couples between the ages of 16 and 25 had the most frequent sex (2.45 times per week), with the frequency of relations steadily declining to the oldest category of respondents, between ages 55 and 60 (0.50 times per week). In 1974, the *Playboy* survey estimated frequency among the youngest group at 3.25 times per week, with those 55 and older reporting having sex once per week (Hunt, 1974). Regardless of the couple's age, the frequency of sexual intercourse appears to decline with the number of years married (Blumstein & Schwartz, 1990).

Sex in marriage is rated as highly pleasurable by men and women. The *Playboy* survey found that, depending on age, from 94 to 99 percent of men rate marital coitus as very or mostly pleasurable (Hunt, 1974), with ratings dropping off very little with age. Using reported incidence of orgasm as a measure of sexual satisfaction in marriage, satisfaction has increased from the time of Kinsey's survey to the present, with more married women now reporting always having orgasms during coitus and fewer women now reporting never having orgasms during coitus (Ren, 2004).

One of the most dramatic changes in marital sex from the Kinsey to the *Playboy* surveys was in the duration of marital coitus, from about two minutes (Kinsey) to ten to thirteen minutes (*Playboy*). Women are more likely to experience orgasm during marriage than during premarital sexual activity. In the *Redbook* survey (Tavris & Sadd, 1977), over one-third of unmarried female respondents said that they never had orgasms during premarital intercourse, about a third reported achieving orgasms most of the time, and less than 7 percent said that they experienced orgasm all of the time. Among married women, only 7 percent reported never experiencing orgasm during coitus, 48 percent reported achieving orgasm most of the time, and 15 percent reported experiencing orgasm all of the time.

The increased sexual interest and pleasure that couples, especially women, apparently find in marriage has been variously attributed to better birth control methods, more information about how to obtain sexual satisfaction, and freer attitudes about sex, especially about women's sexual expression (Hunt, 1974). Married couples are more sophisticated about the importance of variety and on exchanging sexual pleasure. Sexual pleasure in marriage consistently correlates positively with overall marital satisfaction, with wives' open communication about sexual needs and feelings, and with wives taking an active role in sex (McCarthy, 2003; Ren, 2004; Tavris & Sadd, 1977).

Extramarital Sex. Unquestionably, one of Kinsey's most surprising and provocative findings was that over 50 percent of all married men and about 26 percent of all married women reported engaging in sexual intercourse at least once outside of marriage (Kinsey et al., 1948, 1953). Most of the more recent surveys in the United States suggest that the rates of extramarital sex are not as high as Kinsey indicated. In fact, according to most survey results, extramarital sex may be the type of sexual behavior that has been least affected by the sexual revolution. In the Laumann et al. study (1994), nearly 75 percent of married men and 85 percent of married women reported that they have never been unfaithful. These figures are comparable to those obtained with probability samples in surveys in the late 1980s by the National Opinion Research Center (NORC), which reported that 96 percent of the married respondents were faithful in the preceding year, suggesting that married men and women in the United States have particularly

high rates of monogamy (Laumann et al., 1994). Blumstein and Schwartz (1990) found that among married couples, 11 percent of husbands and 9 percent of wives reported at least one extramarital relationship within the past year.

Magazine surveys, which use convenience samples of interested readers, tend to show somewhat higher levels of nonmonogamy among women. For example, in the *Redbook* magazine sample, which polled 100,000 married women, 29 percent admitted having at least one extramarital experience (Tavris & Sadd, 1977). It is important to keep in mind that regular readers of most magazines such as *Playboy* and *Redbook* are often younger, better educated, and more affluent than the general population, and may have more liberal attitudes toward sex. Moreover, volunteer respondents to a magazine sex survey may be more sexually permissive and adventurous than a random sample of respondents. It is also worth noting that, unlike premarital and marital sex, extramarital sex is still considered highly undesirable behavior, especially for women. Given the strong taboos against extramarital sex, it is unclear to what extent women (and men) truthfully answer even anonymous, confidential survey questions about infidelity. Most investigators in this area caution that actual rates of extramarital sexual intercourse are probably underreported by men and women to an unknown extent.

Taken together, what the surveys suggest about extramarital sex in the United States is that it is relatively uncommon and that, unlike premarital and marital sex, it has not increased among most groups since Kinsey's time. The one exception may be younger married women, especially those employed outside the home, whose rates of infidelity may be approaching those of men. Although no statistics are available on the topic, there are indications that there is an increase in "starter marriages" among young women and men under age 30 who have jobs outside the home, no children, and little joint property. After a few years, there are extramarital relationships and divorce (Kelly, 2004). Nonetheless, all surveys show that extramarital sexual activity is still more common among men than women, and, as we noted in the section on the double standard, it is more accepted for men by both men and women. In Kinsey's survey, despite the fact that twice as many men admitted being unfaithful, women's infidelity was more likely to be cited as the reason for divorce. Among divorced respondents in that survey, 27 percent of women compared to 51 percent of men reported that their spouses' infidelity was grounds for the divorce. More recent surveys also show that a wife's affair can be an unforgivable blow to a husband's pride or ego (Alterman, 1997).

What are the factors related to extramarital activity? People who are unfaithful report being less committed to and less satisfied with their marriages. They are also more likely to have friends who have had affairs (Nevid et al., 1995). Among women, extramarital activity is related to employment outside the home (Tavris & Sadd, 1977). People engaged in extramarital sex have offered many reasons for their affairs. Some report that they are not fulfilled by their sexual relations, and others cite boredom, curiosity, or strong attraction to another. For others, nonsexual motivations such as retaliation for past injustice or hostility are given (Nevid et al., 1995). Men and women offer somewhat different reasons for engaging in extramarital sex. Men (75 percent) are more likely than women (55 percent) to offer a desire for sexual excitement as a justification for the affair, whereas women (77 percent) are more likely than men (43 percent) to offer "falling in love" as a reason for extramarital sex (Glass & Wright, 1992). It is possible that men and women offer different reasons for their affairs not because they actually have different motivations, but rather because they have been socialized to explain their actions differently. It is more socially acceptable for men to cite sexual motives and for women to invoke romantic love to justify sexual relations.

Sexual Orientation

Sexual orientation is usually defined as the focus of one's sexual and romantic desires and behaviors toward members of the other sex, one's own sex, or both. The past two decades have seen a surge of scholarly interest into the basic questions of sexual orientation and sexual identity, probing the nature, extent, and causes of straight, gay, and bisexual sexual

orientation. For example, is sexual orientation learned, or is it inborn? Once established, can it be changed? What defines sexual orientation: behavior and/or desire? Do people fall into discrete categories that differ qualitatively from each other? Or is sexual orientation on a continuum, with people possessing degrees of "straightness" and "gayness"? What proportions of men and women fall into each category? Are certain orientations healthier than others?

Obviously, complete discussions of these issues go beyond the scope of this chapter. But one's sexual identity and orientation are such central parts of one's self-concept that they merit some treatment here. We explore the position that sexual orientation and sexual identity, like all of sexuality, are socially constructed. To say that sexual orientation is socially constructed is not to deny a role for biological factors in influencing sexuality, and we will discuss biological perspectives and research in this section. All it means in this context is that defining heterosexuality, homosexuality, and bisexuality is itself complex because the definitions vary over historical periods, cultures, communities, and situations. Sexual acts that in some cultures and at some times will be labeled homosexual will not be labeled as such in other cultures and at other times. For example, there is an initiation rite among Sambians of the New Guinea highlands in which adolescent boys perform fellatio on the adult men of the village, because of a belief that young boys grow into adulthood only through the ingestion of semen (Money, 1990). Would it be correct to regard these as homosexual acts? Heterosexual men who have been separated from women for long periods of time, as in prison, sometimes engage in sex with men. Have these men "turned gay"? If a woman has sex with men but fantasizes about having sex with women, what is her sexual orientation? Among some ethnic groups, men who are the insertive partners in sexual intercourse with other men do not identify themselves as homosexual. Does it matter how people identify themselves? What does it mean to call oneself a "political lesbian"? As these examples suggest, the relationship among sexual attractions or desires, sexual behaviors or acts, and sexual self-identity are variable and complex. The chief advantage of a constructionist perspective on sexual orientation is the new questions it encourages us to ask.

Before reviewing the research and perspectives on sexual orientation, we need to define key terms, and make clear how we will use them. Following Rathus, Nevid, and Fichner-Rathus (2002), we define *heterosexual orientation* as erotic attraction to, and preference for developing romantic and sexual relationships with, members of the other sex; and *homosexual orientation* as erotic attraction to, and preference for developing romantic and sexual relationships with members of one's own sex. The prefix comes from the Greek *homos,* which means "same," not the Latin *homo,* which means "man." We will use the term *homosexual* sparingly, because it bears a social stigma that many gay people now find offensive. Instead, we will refer to males who have sex with males as gay, and women who have sex with women as lesbians or gay women. *Bisexuality* is a term that refers to an orientation in which one is erotically attracted to, and interested in developing sexual relationships with, both females and males (Rathus et al., 2002).

Most surveys that have probed sexual orientation have grappled at least to some extent with these issues of definition and self-identity. Not surprisingly, the first to do so was Kinsey, who yet again shocked the nation with explosive findings on sexual behavior from his surveys of women and men. He found that, among males between the ages of 20 and 35, 18 to 42 percent had at least some same-sex sexual experience. Between 3 and 16 percent of males in this age group had exclusively male–male sexual experiences (Kinsey et al., 1948). For women, the figures were somewhat lower, with 11 to 20 percent of the women between the ages of 20 and 35 reporting at least some female–female sexual experience, and 2 to 3 percent of females in this age category reporting exclusively female–female experiences (Kinsey et al., 1953). It has long been suspected that biases in Kinsey's samples, especially of men, accounted in part for the strikingly high level of homosexuality. For example, in Kinsey's survey, a higher proportion of male prisoners than exist in the general population served as respondents. But even correcting for this bias, the proportion of homosexuality reported by Kinsey was considered startling.

Prevelance of Gay, Lesbian, and Bisexual Sexual Orientation.   In his surveys, Kinsey and his associates went against the prevailing views of the day, that homosexuality and heterosexuality were discrete categories, by measuring sexual orientation on a seven-point continuum, with heterosexual and homosexual at the poles. He also recognized that how people were defined depended on what particular questions were asked. For example, asking people if they had ever reached orgasm with a member of the same sex might exaggerate levels of homosexuality, because many more people have a few same-sex encounters in adolescence than identify as homosexual in adulthood.

More recent surveys in the 1990s, including one by the Kinsey Institute, tend to report lower incidence of same-sex sexual behavior among both females and males, especially if single or sporadic episodes of adolescent experimentation are excluded. Several large-scale studies of sexual orientation in the United States, Britain, and France put the estimates of adult male homosexuality in the range of 1 to 4.1 percent (Barringer, 1993; Billy, Tanfer, Grady, & Keplinger, 1993). The researchers in the Laumann et al. study (1994) divided their questions about sexual orientation into the three basic underlying dimensions that we have already discussed: sexual behavior, sexual desire, and sexual identity. Over 4 percent of the women and 9 percent of the men reported engaging in some type of sexual activity with a member of the same sex. When asked about sexual attraction to same-sex others and the appeal of sex with a same-sex partner, about 5 percent of men and women reported some same-sex attraction and finding the idea of sex with a same-sex partner somewhat appealing. But less than 3 percent of the men and 1.5 percent of the women surveyed reported some level of homosexual or bisexual identity. Clearly, these numbers are well below Kinsey's figures. But they do suggest that estimates of gay and bisexual orientation depend, among other things, on whether behavior, desire, or self-identity is explored. And depending on how bisexual is defined, there are at least between 1.5 million and 7.5 million bisexual people over the age of 18 in the United States, that is, between 1 and 4 percent of the adult population.

Bisexuality.   Research suggests that **bisexuality** may be understudied and underreported in surveys (Garber, 1995; Weinberg, Williams, & Pryor, 1994). In part, this is because bisexuality is particularly complex and fluid, with sexual orientations changing over time and attraction to both sexes often unequal. Furthermore, people may be reluctant to embrace the label of bisexuality in surveys because bisexual individuals have often been rejected and stereotyped by both gay and straight people. Bisexuals are seen by some as straight people who are indulging their taste for the exotic and forbidden, and by others as gay people without the courage to reveal their sexuality openly. Since the AIDS epidemic, the term *bisexual* is used more often and has taken on special meaning because bisexuals are seen by many as the conduits by which AIDS can spread, particularly from gay men to heterosexuals. This concern on the part of society, and the scapegoating of bisexuals in its wake, has had the effect of politically mobilizing bisexuals, resulting in new visibility and new, more positive images.

The new scholarship on bisexuality takes a more affirmative approach to this sexual orientation (Klesse, 2003). Ronald Fox (1996) attributes this willingness to acknowledge bisexuality as a valid sexual orientation to the elimination of homosexuality as a clinical diagnostic category by the psychiatric and psychological communities. This has led to the development of lesbian and gay identity theory, a critical reexamination of the dichotomous model of sexual orientation, and the articulation of a multidimensional model of sexual orientation.

Causes of Sexual Orientation.   As the tongue-in-cheek questionnaire in Box 8.2 suggests, researchers and laypeople alike often speculate about what causes homosexuality, but very few ask what causes heterosexuality. Perhaps a better question than either of these asks what factors influence sexual orientation. Most researchers today believe that sexual orientation is determined by a complex interplay of biological, psychological, and social factors, not by any one factor alone (Rathus et al., 2002).

Biological Perspectives.   Is sexual orientation an inherited trait like eye color or height? Is it affected by sex hormones? Are the brains of gay and straight people organized differently? These are some of the key questions that have dominated research in the quest for biological factors in sexual orientation.

There is growing evidence for a genetic influence in sexual orientation. Some of this comes from research on families, specifically twins. One study looked at the sexual orientation of relatives of a convenience sample of 51 predominantly gay men and found that 22 percent of the brothers of these men were either gay or bisexual (Pillard & Weinrich, 1986). This is about four times the proportion expected in the general population. Of course, families share environments as well as genes, and a study of family patterns of sexual orientation cannot be conclusive. Twin studies provide better evidence for the role of genes, especially studies that compare the *concordance (similarity) rates* for a given trait, such as sexual orientation, between *identical* or *monozygotic* twins, who develop from the same fertilized ovum, and *fraternal* or *dizygotic* twins, who develop from different fertilized ova (Bailey & Pillard, 1991; Dawood, Pillard, Horvath, Revelle, & Bailey, 2000). Several studies have identified gay men with identical or fraternal twins to compare concordance rates among the different kinds of twins. One study reported a 52 percent concordance rate among identical twins compared with 22 percent concordance for fraternal twins (Bailey & Pillard, 1991). A more recent study replicated these results (Dawood et al., 2000). Another study was conducted with 147 lesbians and their sisters. Of the 71 lesbians who had identical twins, 48 percent of the twins were also lesbian, and of those whose sisters were fraternal twins, 16 percent of the sisters were lesbian (Kelly, 2004).

Is there a particular gene that is linked with sexual orientation? Researchers have found some evidence associating a region on the X sex chromosome to a gay male sexual orientation (Rathus et al., 2002). Bailey et al. (1999) discovered that gay males were more likely to have gay male relatives on their mothers' side than we would expect by chance alone. Subsequent examination of the X sex chromosome that males inherit from their mothers revealed identical

Box 8.2

The Heterosexuality Questionnaire

The purpose of this questionnaire is to examine the manner in which heterosexual norms and assumptions affect how gay men and lesbians are studied and represented. You may recognize these items from the questionnaire as parodies of the ones that gay men and lesbians are asked all the time about their sexual orientation and lives.

THE HETEROSEXUAL QUESTIONNAIRE

Instructions: Heterosexism is a form of bias in which heterosexual norms are used in studies of homosexual relationships. Gay men and lesbians are seen as deviating from a heterosexual norm, and this often leads to marginalization and pathologizing of their behavior.

Read the questionnaire below with this definition in mind. Then respond to the questions that follow.

1. What do you think caused your heterosexuality?
2. When and how did you first find out that you were heterosexual?
3. Is it possible that your heterosexuality is just a phase you may grow out of?
4. Is it possible that your heterosexuality stems from a neurotic fear of others of the same sex?
5. If you have never slept with a person of the same sex, is it possible that all you need is a good gay lover?
6. Do your parents know that you are straight? Do your friends and/or roommate(s) know? How did they react?
7. Why do you insist on flaunting your heterosexuality? Can't you just be who you are and keep it quiet?

8. Why do heterosexuals place so much emphasis on sex?
9. Why do heterosexuals feel compelled to seduce others into their lifestyle?
10. A disproportionate majority of child molesters are heterosexual. Do you consider it safe to expose children to heterosexual teachers?
11. Just what do men and women *do* in bed together? How can they truly know how to please each other, being so anatomically different?
12. With all the societal support marriage receives, the divorce rate is spiraling. Why are there so few stable relationships among heterosexuals?
13. Statistics show that lesbians have the lowest incidence of sexually transmitted diseases. Is it really safe for a woman to maintain a heterosexual lifestyle and run the risk of disease and pregnancy?
14. How can you become a whole person if you limit yourself to compulsive, exclusive heterosexuality?
15. Considering the menace of overpopulation, how could the human race survive if everyone were heterosexual?
16. Could you trust a heterosexual therapist to be objective? Don't you feel she or he might be inclined to influence you in the direction of her or his own leanings?
17. There seem to be very few happy heterosexuals. Techniques have been developed that might enable you to change if you really want to. Have you considered trying aversion therapy?
18. Would you want your child to be heterosexual, knowing the problems that she or he would face?

Source: From *Sex and Gender: Student Projects and Exercises* (pp. 35–36), by C. A. Rickabaugh, 1998, New York: McGraw-Hill. Reprinted with permission from the publisher.

DNA markers on the end tip of the X chromosome, implicating this chromosomal region as possessing genes that may predispose men to a gay sexual orientation. Taken together, these studies suggest that that same-sex sexual orientation is not 100 percent dependent on genes by any means, but that there is likely some degree of *heritability* or dependence on genes passed from one generation to another. Pre-

cisely what is inherited is not clear. It may be sexual attraction or gender nonconformity.

Another area of research influenced by a biological perspective looks to the possible role of sex hormones in affecting sexual orientation. The most promising line of research in this area was inspired by studies with animals that suggested a role for prenatal hormones in influencing sexual orientation.

When pregnant rats were given drugs that block the effects of testosterone at a critical period when their fetus's brains were becoming sexually differentiated, their male offspring showed female mating patterns. Obviously, prenatal sex hormones cannot be experimentally manipulated in humans, but there is some evidence from naturalistic observation to suggest that prenatal hormones may play a role in human sexual orientation as well. For example, women whose mothers took DES, a synthetic estrogen, while their mothers were pregnant with them, were more likely to report a lesbian or bisexual sexual orientation than would be expected by chance alone (Collaer & Hines, 1995). The role of prenatal sex hormones in sexual orientation remains an unsettled issue.

Another area of biological research questions whether there are differences in brain anatomy between gay and straight people. Much of this research centers on the hypothalamus, which is influenced by hormones and known to play a role in determining sexual behavior among mammals. In 1991, neurobiologist Simon LeVay made headlines the world over with his discovery that a segment of the hypothalamus was less than half the size in gay men as in straight men, and that gay men and women were much more similar than different on this trait. LeVay's sample size was small and nonrepresentative: His samples were derived from autopsies of gay men and straight men and women who had died of AIDS. Subsequent research has found some more anatomical differences in brain structure between gay and straight men, although none of differences is known to have any direct bearing on sexual orientation, and the implications of the differences remain unclear (cf. LeVay, 1996). These findings need further confirmation and expansion.

Although it is clear that biological factors are not determinate, they appear to have a place in understanding sexual orientation. There is evidence that biological perspectives on same-sex sexual orientation have gained force in recent years, both in academia and in the mind of the American public. Intriguingly, nationwide polls that ask the public to name the causes of homosexuality have shown a steady increase in the percentage of people who believe that gay people are "born with" their sexual orientation, from a low of 13 percent in 1977 to 18 percent in 1989 to 31 percent in 1998 (Rathus et al., 2002).

Psychological Perspectives. Psychological approaches to the origins of sexual orientation look to family patterns, early experiences, and environmental factors as possible explanations. An important class of psychological theories of sexual orientation are psychoanalytic theories. Freud believed that infants' sexuality is undifferentiated and that children are open to all forms of sexual stimulation, a condition he called *polymorphously perverse* (Rathus et al., 2002). Freud posited the existence of a "bisexual disposition which we maintain to be characteristic of human beings" (Freud, 1931, p. 255), a disposition that he believed manifested itself more commonly in females than males. Thus, in Freud's view, we all have the potential to be heterosexual, homosexual, or bisexual in our sexual orientation.

Under the normal course of development, a child is expected to develop a heterosexual orientation. According to Freud, gay sexual orientation is the result of problematic psychosexual development born of a family pattern that features an overbearing, possessive mother and a distant and hostile father. Freud believed that the family dynamic in the lives of homosexual men does not foster successful resolution of the Oedipus complex in which the male child displaces his erotic attachment to his mother and identifies with his father. Instead, the boy raised in such a family identifies with his mother and even transforms himself into her, resulting in erotic attraction to men. Further, Freud believed that homosexual men experienced *unresolved castration anxiety* in which they unconsciously associate the vagina with teeth or other sharp instruments and are unable to perform sexually with women.

Characteristically, Freud's view of female homosexuality is less well developed than his view of male homosexuality. Essentially, he theorized that little girls become envious of boys' penises when they discover they do not have penises of their own. In Freud's view, if a girl fails to resolve her *penis envy* by supplanting her desire for a penis with the desire to marry a man and bear male children—the ultimate penis substitute—she will develop a lesbian sexual orientation.

Generally, psychoanalytic theories of sexual orientation tend to focus on the family dynamics in "causing" gay, especially gay male, sexual orientation. The pattern supposedly fostering lesbian development is a rejecting, unconcerned mother and a distant or even absent father. Is there empirical evidence for the family dynamic that Freud implicates? Of course it is difficult to find evidence of unconscious motives. Some retrospective interview studies, such as those of psychoanalyst Irving Bieber with gay men (Bieber et al., 1962) and of psychiatrist Charlotte Wolff in a rare early study of lesbians (Wolff, 1971), have been interpreted as supporting such theories. But these studies are fraught with methodological problems, and evidence for this view is generally not strong. It cannot be determined, for example, whether a son's sexual orientation alienated the father, or whether the father's hostile behavior engendered gay sexual orientation. Moreover, gay men and lesbians come from a variety of family backgrounds exhibiting many different kinds of patterns (Isay, 1990).

Learning theories have traditionally focused on the role of reinforcement in the development of sexual orientation, especially the important determining role of pleasurable early experiences with the same or the other sex. But many people have early pleasurable experiences with the same sex and go on to have heterosexual sexual orientations. Moreover, many gay people report that they were aware of their attraction to same-sex others before their first sexual encounter. Although learning may play some role in the development of gay sexual orientation, learning theorists have not identified the specific experiences that might lead to gay or straight sexual orientations (Rathus et al., 2002).

Social psychologist Darryl Bem has offered a provocative developmental explanation for same- and other-sex sexual orientation in a gender-polarizing society such as ours, based on the importance of both biological and experiential variables. Bem's (1996) theory proposes a developmental sequence that begins with genes and prenatal hormones, which do not cause sexual orientation per se but childhood temperaments, such as aggression or activity level, that are relevant to gender conformity or nonconformity.

The child's temperament predisposes him or her to enjoy some activities more than others, to prefer gender-conforming or gender-nonconforming activities, and same-sex or other-sex playmates. Gender-conforming children will feel different from other-sex peers, whereas gender-nonconforming children will feel different from same sex-peers. These feelings of dissimilarity or unfamiliarity produce heightened autonomic arousal, which is then transformed in later years into erotic–romantic attraction. In this way, "the exotic becomes erotic." Bem's hypothesis, that a mediating personality variable might account for the observed correlations between biological variables and sexual orientation, is intriguing. It is consistent with some of the existing evidence generated by both the biological theorists, who can point to empirical links between biology and sexual orientation, and the social constructionists who can point to historical and anthropological research suggesting that sexual orientation is a culture-bound notion. It is as yet unclear whether the theory will generate new research that supports its predictions, but it has already come under fire for failing to clearly define key terms such as exoticism, to present new data to support the theory, and to consider evidence that does not support the theory. Moreover, Bem's claim that his theory applies equally to both sexes has been questioned. It has been argued that the theory particularly neglects and misrepresents women's experiences (Peplau, Garnets, Spalding, Conley, & Veniegas, 1998).

Social Perspectives. Sociological theories of sexual orientation emphasize how social structures and forces in society influence our sexual desire and behavior. Conceptions and definitions of heterosexuality, homosexuality, and bisexuality are the products of particular cultures and have been shown to vary widely across different cultural groups and shape their behavior. In exploring the social origins of same-sex attraction, sociologist Reiss (1986) suggests that the power and dominance hierarchies in society influence patterns of sexual orientation. In this view, male-dominant societies with highly rigid gender roles should show the greatest prevalence of gay sexual orientation. For a variety of reasons, some young boys may find it difficult to observe, learn, and/or embrace such a narrow, highly defined role. In such societies, there will always be a certain number of males who either do not like such roles or cannot completely conform to them, and will reject aspects of the role, including heterosexual behavior. Societies with less rigid roles are more flexible and indulgent about the expression of different types of sexuality (Hyde, 1996; Reiss, 1986).

One pertinent psychologist expresses her views on the origins and meanings of sexual orientation in Box 8.3.

In short, from what we now know from several lines of research, it does not appear that there is a single cause of sexual orientation—gay or straight. Sexual orientation, comprising as it does a complex array of desires, behaviors, identities, and commitments, is an unlikely candidate for a simple explanation. For example, one study of bisexual individuals suggests that different components of an individual's sexual orientation need not coincide: For example, some bisexual respondents reported that they were more erotically attracted to one sex and more romantically attracted to the other (Weinberg, Williams, & Pryor, 1994). Moreover, there is some evidence that gay male sexual orientation may be more fixed and stable from an early age than lesbian sexual orientation (Tolman & Diamond, 2002). There is a growing realization that as research into the origins of sexual orientation continues, there will be more evidence for a multifactorial model of sexual orientation. There is not one kind of lesbian or gay man, or straight woman or man, or bisexual woman or man, and the complexity and variability of our sexual orientations need to be better reflected in research.

Box 8.3

Sexual Orientation: Fixed or Fluid?

VIEW FROM MARYKA K. BIAGGIO

Of course public debate has raged in recent years, driven largely by contentions of the religious right that homosexuality is an immoral behavior that an individual can choose not to engage in. On the other hand, gay/lesbian/bisexual rights activists have claimed that sexual orientation is not a choice, and persons of diverse sexual orientations should not be condemned or denied civil rights on the basis of their orientation. Thus, in the public arena, the debate has revolved around the question of choice.

In my opinion we don't fully understand the forces that shape sexual orientation, though they are undoubtedly complex. Questions about the fixedness or fluidity have not been given much scientific consideration, but it appears that for some individuals sexual orientation is somewhat fluid. There appears to be some gender difference here, with sexual orientation being somewhat more fluid among some women than among men in general. Some have suggested that this means that biological variables may play a more important role in the etiology of sexual orientation for men than for women. This is not necessarily the case. We know that gender roles are generally more fixed for males than for females, and that females are afforded more flexibility in terms of gender-role behavior than are males. In fact, for developing males, there is more negative social judgment for gender-inappropriate behavior than there is for females. It is possible that some of the same mechanisms at work for gender-role development also impact the development of sexual orientation, and this could explain the apparent gender difference in fluidity of sexual orientation.

Many questions remain: Is it possible that there are multiple paths to diverse sexual orientations, and that individuals may vary greatly in the fluidity of their sexual orientation? Might there be clear gender differences in how sexual orientation develops and is expressed? How can we explain the phenomenon of women who have led heterosexual lives electing in their later years to adopt a lesbian or bisexual orientation? What, if any, is the relationship between scientific questions, such as whether or not sexual object preference is a choice, and the social treatment of diverse individuals?

Source: Printed by permission of Maryka K. Biaggio. Piece previously published in *Engendering Psychology,* 1st edition, p. 247.

Sexual Practices

In this section, we consider the role of sex and gender in the appeal and practice of various sex acts. A summary of the percentages of respondents reporting various sexual activities in three prominent sex surveys spanning over 50 years is presented in Table 8.1.

Masturbation. The word **masturbation** comes from the Latin *masturbari,* which combines the roots for "hand" and "to defile" (Rathus et al., 2002). Masturbation is solitary sexual activity, practiced by means of manual stimulation of the genitals, with or without the aid of artificial stimulation. Masturbation, like all forms of nonprocreational sex, was denounced by Jews and Christians, at least in part because it did not lead to an increase in their numbers at a time when fecundity was an issue of survival of communities. The ancient notion that masturbation is defiling oneself through one's hand and warrants condemnation on moral, religious, and medical grounds persisted until very recently. Even today, masturbation is considered such a sensitive issue that all information in the Laumann et al. (1994) study pertaining to masturbation was gathered using a self-administered questionnaire, with no questions about masturbation asked during the face-to-face interviews. In 1994, Surgeon General Jocelyn Elders was forced to resign

after the uproar that attended her suggestion that sex education in the schools should aim to destroy the myths and guilt associated with masturbation in adolescents. Her endorsement of masturbation as a technique that can provide sexual satisfaction without the risk of pregnancy and sexually transmitted diseases was widely regarded as irresponsible.

Despite these condemnations of masturbation and the guilt that half of all men and women report feeling about masturbating, survey results show that most people have masturbated at some point in their lives. Laumann et al. (1994) state, "Masturbation has the peculiar status of being both highly stigmatized and fairly commonplace" (p. 87). All studies show that more men masturbate than women (e.g., Hunt, 1974; Kinsey et al., 1948, 1953; Laumann et al., 1994), that men begin masturbating at younger ages than women (Leitenberg & Henning, 1995), that men masturbate more frequently than women (Leitenberg & Henning, 1995), and that men are more likely to experience orgasm while masturbating than women (e.g., Kinsey et al., 1948, 1953). In their meta-analysis of sex differences in a wide variety of sexual practices and attitudes, Oliver and Hyde (1993) found that the largest sex difference of all sexual practices was in the incidence of masturbation, with males much more likely to masturbate than females. We do not know why sex

TABLE 8.1 Percentage of Participants Reporting Sexual Activities in Three Sex Surveys

SEXUAL ACTIVITY	KINSEY SURVEYS (1948, 1953)		PLAYBOY FOUNDATION SURVEY (1974)		NATIONAL OPINION RESEARCH COUNCIL (1994)	
	Men	*Women*	*Men*	*Women*	*Men*	*Women*
Masturbation to orgasm	92.0%	58.0%	94.0%	63.0%	—	—
Masturbation before age 13	45.0	14.0	63.0	33.0	—	—
Masturbation during marriage	40.0	30.0	72.0	68.0	57.0%	37.0%
At least one homosexual experience	37.0	28.0	—	—	7.1	3.8
Primarily homosexual orientation	13.0	7.0	2.0	1.0	4.1	2.2
Premarital intercourse	71.0	33.0	97.0	67.0	93.0	79.0
Extramarital sex	50.0	26.0	41.0	18.0	<25.0	<10.0
Sexual abuse during childhood	10.0	25.0	—	—	12.0	17.0

Source: From *Gender: Psychological Perspectives,* 2e by L. Brannon, 1999, Boston: Allyn & Bacon. Copyright © 1999 by Pearson Education. Adapted by permission of the publisher.

differences are so pronounced in these areas. Women's lower rates of masturbation have variously been explained in terms of their lower sex drive and greater tendency to tie sex to love relationships, and the socialization pressures that teach women not to explore their own bodies and that sex for its own sake is not really acceptable for women. Alternatively, it is possible that women do not report masturbation because it is stigmatizing.

Research shows that masturbation is strongly related to level of education, with more educated women and men reporting higher levels of masturbation. Race, decade of birth, and age are three other factors related to masturbation. Whites tend to masturbate more than other groups (Laumann et al., 1994). There is a decade-of-birth effect for masturbation as well, especially for women, with those born more recently more likely to report masturbating (Oliver & Hyde, 1993). Masturbation tends to decline with age for both men and women, although it increases when people lose partners through death and divorce (Hegeler & Mortensen, 1977).

It is commonly assumed that people who have stable sexual relationships with available partners seldom masturbate. However, research since the time of Kinsey has failed to support this assumption. Although married people masturbate less frequently than their single counterparts, most married people, especially when young, masturbate at least occasionally (Tavris & Sadd, 1977). Unmarried, cohabiting men and women masturbate quite frequently (Laumann et al., 1994). This research has gone a long way toward dispelling the unfortunate myth that people who masturbate are lonely, sex-starved individuals incapable of maintaining stable intimate relationships with others.

Indeed, masturbation is emerging from recent research and clinical practice with a new, more benign image. It is now understood that people masturbate for many different reasons, ranging from achieving tension release in order to go to sleep to attaining self-knowledge (Dodson, 1987). We now know that women experience orgasms more reliably through masturbation than through sexual intercourse and that the experience of masturbating serves as a means for women to explore their bodies

and learn more about what arouses them (Dodson, 1987; Masters & Johnson, 1966). Masturbation does not supplant or eclipse partnered sex for women (or men); if anything, people who masturbate are more sexual and sexually aroused during sex with others. In fact, many sex therapists recommend directed masturbation programs as the treatment of choice for women who have trouble reaching orgasms with their partners.

Sex with Partners. Obviously, there is an almost infinite number of possible sexual expressions between two people. It is important to keep in mind that the very definition of what constitutes a sex act is socially constructed. The impeachment trial of President Clinton in 1999 began a public debate in the United States about what counts as sex. That same year, a highly publicized survey of college students' attitudes about what constitutes sex was published (Sanders & Reinisch, 1999). Results showed that 59 percent of respondents indicated that oral sex was not having "had sex," and 19 percent said that anal sex was not having "had sex." These findings support the view that, at least at the present time in the United States, there are widely divergent opinions about what "having sex" is.

Kissing is completely absent in some cultures as an act with erotic overtones. In other cultures, it is practiced very differently from the way it is in Western countries and takes the form of partners sucking each others' lips and tongues (Rathus et al., 2002). In our own culture, where kissing is almost universally practiced, kissing techniques vary widely, and many forms of kissing are loving without being erotic.

Kissing can be regarded as a type of foreplay. Like kissing, **foreplay,** the general name given for a variety of acts that are intended to be sexually arousing and a prelude for later intercourse, is also present in some cultures such as ours, and absent in others (Frayser, 1985). The kinds of acts that are construed as erotic and therefore part of foreplay differ among and within cultures. Some acts, such as kissing and breast stimulation, may be considered foreplay in some circumstances by some people, but are considered ends in themselves by others.

Interestingly, the kinds of sexual acts in which there are cultural differences in frequency and appeal are the ones in which we find sex differences as well. Masters and Johnson (1979) discussed sex differences in preferences during foreplay, noting, for example, that women are less genitally oriented than men, and tend to favor relatively long periods of foreplay, with overall body kissing and caressing before direct manual, oral, or genital contact is made. Men, who are more quickly aroused than women, are more likely to desire direct genital stimulation early in foreplay. Surprisingly, watching a partner undress, a behavior not ordinarily considered a sex act at all (and not typically measured by researchers even as a form of foreplay), has emerged as the second most sexually appealing act to both sexes (Laumann et al., 1994). Interestingly, this is one of the few forms of foreplay rated more appealing by men than women.

As noted earlier, only vaginal intercourse is rated more appealing by heterosexuals than watching a partner undress. Oral–genital sexual activity, called **fellatio** when performed on men and **cunnilingus** when performed on women, was rated the third most appealing sexual activity. It appears that the prevalence of oral sex has increased dramatically from Kinsey's time to the present. Kinsey found that the educational level of respondents was a major predictor of whether they had engaged in oral sex, with 60 percent of married college educated couples, 20 percent of those with a high school education, and 10 percent of those with a grade-school education reporting this activity. Age is another factor related to the incidence of oral sex, with younger people more likely to give and receive oral sex than older people. This may be as much a *decade-of-birth* or *cohort effect* as an age effect. That means that it may be the particular times in which people live rather than their ages that is the important variable here. In more recent generations, oral sex has become a regular part of many couples' sexual repertoire. In the Laumann et al. (1994) survey, 75 percent of the men and women surveyed reported experiencing oral sex in their lifetimes, but only about 25 percent reported it as a "current activity."

Apparently, anal sex is not widely practiced among heterosexual couples. About one-quarter of all heterosexual men and one-fifth of all heterosexual women reported ever having had anal sex. Only 2 percent of men and 1 percent of women reported engaging in anal sex in their last sexual encounter (Laumann et al., 1994).

Many heterosexual people express puzzlement about how gay men and lesbians, particularly lesbians, "have sex." With the obvious exception of vaginal intercourse, gay and lesbian couples have as many modes of sexual expression as heterosexual couples. Sexual activities such as hugging, kissing, caressing each others' bodies, oral and manual stimulation of the breasts, and mutual genital stimulation are common in all couples, regardless of sexual orientation. Whereas the types of activities engaged in by heterosexual and gay couples tend to be more similar than different, the frequency of various sexual practices certainly differs between heterosexual and gay and lesbian couples. Mutual genital stimulation is a very common sexual technique among gay men and lesbians and may be the single most common technique among lesbians (Bell & Weinberg, 1978). Active and passive oral sex is also a common activity among both gay men and women, characterizing over 80 percent of gay-identified respondents in Laumann et al.'s (1994) survey.

The incidence of anal sex among gay men is significantly higher than in the heterosexual population, with about 75 to 82 percent of gay-identified men reporting engaging in this activity at least once since puberty (Laumann et al., 1994). Most men who practice anal sex alternate between the insertive and receptive roles at various times. The frequency of anal sex, which has been associated with the spread of AIDS/HIV infection, declined among gay men throughout the 1990s, though recent research suggests that it may again be on the rise. For example, Halkitis, Parsons, and Wilton (2003) report an increase among gay men in a particular form of anal sex, *barebacking,* in which people deliberately seek out unprotected anal sex (Catania et al., 1991; Centers for Disease Control, 1990).

Aside from oral and manual genital stimulation, lesbian couples commonly engage in "humping" or genital apposition, whereby partners position themselves so as to rub their genitals together (Masters & Johnson, 1979). Lesbian women, like heterosexual women, tend to be less genitally oriented and focused on achieving orgasms than are gay or heterosexual men. More than heterosexual lovemaking, lesbian lovemaking, especially in its early stages, involves hugging, caressing, kissing, and other forms of non-genital contact before direct stimulation of the breasts and genitals. Lesbian sexuality, like so many other aspects of lesbians' lives, has received far less research attention than gay male sexuality or heterosexuality. Even the ambitious Laumann et al. (1994) survey studied too few of the sexual activities in which lesbians engage (construing homosexual behavior in male-centered terms of masturbation, oral sex, and anal sex) and located too few lesbian-identified women to present a picture of what lesbian sex looks like.

Human Sexual Response

The groundbreaking laboratory research of William Masters and Virginia Johnson in the 1960s has been indispensable in understanding the *sexual response cycle,* the series of bodily changes that occur as females and males become increasingly sexually aroused. Masters and Johnson (1966) measured and photographed the physiological responses of 382 women and 312 men. Single respondents participated in studies that did not involve intercourse, such as various forms of autoerotic behavior, whereas married couples engaged in intercourse. They developed specially designed machinery, such as a transparent artificial penis containing photographic equipment, to measure female sexual response. One of the most important products of their research is the finding that the sexual responses of men and women are surprisingly similar, with men and women passing through the same four stages of physiological responsiveness: excitement, plateau, orgasm, and resolution. The stages of sexual arousal are depicted in Figure 8.1.

Four Stages of Sexual Arousal

Excitement Phase.   In men and women, sexual feelings can be aroused by a variety of stimuli, from internal stimuli such as fantasies or memories to external stimuli such as reading erotic material or the caress of a lover. In the early stages of arousal, in-

creased blood flow to the sexual organs, known as **vasocongestion,** occurs. This causes a penile erection in the male and a "sweating" reaction in the female, in which fluid seeps from the vaginal wall and lubricates the vagina. Vaginal lips and the clitoris, which is densely packed with nerve endings and highly sensitive, begin to swell. At the same time, muscles throughout the body contract, which is known as **myotonia.** For example, the nipples of both women and men may become erect. Breathing, heart rate, and pulse all may increase.

Plateau Phase.   A plateau is an elevated but level plane, and the plateau phase refers to a time when vasocongestion and myotonia reach a peak level and men and women are highly sexually aroused. In men, the testes become elevated, and Cowper's glands, which are located at the tip of the penis, may secrete a few droplets of clear fluid. In women, the outer third of the vagina becomes engorged with blood and the vaginal opening narrows, thus grasping the penis more tightly if this occurs during intercourse. Other physiological changes in the female are the elevation of the uterus and the retraction and shortening of the now extremely sensitive clitoris.

Orgasmic Phase.   Orgasm in the male consists of two stages of involuntary muscular contractions. The first stage causes seminal fluid to collect in the urethral bulb at the base of the penis. In the second stage, five to eight contractions of muscles surrounding the urethra and urethral bulb propel the seminal fluid through the urethra and out of the body. The contractions tend to occur at intervals of 0.8 seconds, with the first few contractions faster and more intense.

In women, orgasm is a series of anywhere between 3 to 18 involuntary rhythmic contractions of the vagina and uterus and, in some women, of the rectal and urethral sphincter muscles as well. The first few contractions occur at a faster pace, in about 0.8-second intervals, with later contractions occurring at a more variable pace.

Women generally reach orgasm more slowly than men, because a greater level of vasocongestion is required in women for orgasm to occur. In both men and women, orgasm is accompanied by peak levels of blood pressure, heart rate, and respiration. Subjectively,

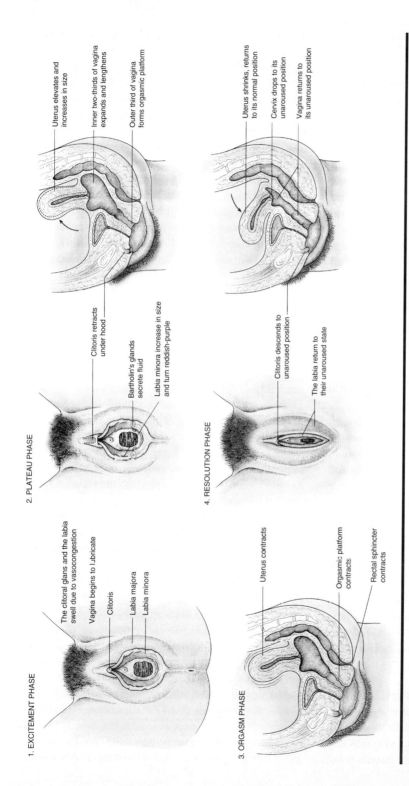

FIGURE 8.1 Female Genitals during the Phases of the Sexual Response Cycle

Source: From *Human Sexuality in a World of Diversity* (3e, pp. 150–151), by S. A. Rathus, J. S. Nevid, and L. Fichner-Rathus, 2002, Boston: Allyn and Bacon. Copyright © 2002 by Pearson Education. Reprinted by permission of the publisher.

1. EXCITEMENT PHASE

The clitoral glans and the labia swell due to vasocongestion

Vagina begins to lubricate

Clitoris

Labia majora

Labia minora

2. PLATEAU PHASE

Uterus elevates and increases in size

Inner two-thirds of vagina expands and lengthens

Outer third of vagina forms orgasmic platform

Clitoris retracts under hood

Bartholin's glands secrete fluid

Labia minora increase in size and turn reddish-purple

3. ORGASM PHASE

Uterus contracts

Orgasmic platform contracts

Rectal sphincter contracts

4. RESOLUTION PHASE

Uterus shrinks, returns to its normal position

Cervix drops to its unaroused position

Vagina returns to its unaroused position

Clitoris descends to unaroused position

The labia return to their unaroused state

it is also associated with feelings of sexual pleasure and release of sexual tension.

Resolution Phase.   This phase describes the body's return to its prearousal state. After orgasm, blood is released from the engorged blood vessels in the penis and vagina. In the male, the swelling of the penis diminishes and the erection is either partially or totally lost. Some men are capable of continued intercourse after ejaculating. Following orgasm in the female, the clitoris emerges from its retracted position and begins to lose its erection. Decongestion of the female organs proceeds at a slower rate than that of male organs, and in the presence of continued stimulation, females may become rearoused and may experience multiple orgasms within a short period of time. Most men, on the other hand, experience a refractory period during which they are physiologically unable to experience erection and orgasm. The duration of the **refractory period** varies with a man's age, physical health, and various psychological factors, and can last anywhere from a few minutes to 24 hours. Some men report varied patterns of multiple orgasms with little or no loss of erection between orgasms (Dunn & Trost, 1989).

Masters and Johnson's model of sexual response has not been immune from criticism, nor is it the only model of sexual responsiveness. Some have criticized this model because of the total absence of cognitive and affective or emotional factors in sexual response. An alternative model of sexual response that considers such factors was developed by the late Helen Singer Kaplan, a clinician who worked with people with sexual dysfunctions. She proposed three independent stages of response: desire, excitement, and orgasm (Kaplan, 1979, 1987). By putting a spotlight on sexual desire or interest as a separate phase of sexual response, Kaplan identified one of the most common problems that people have with regard to sexual responsiveness.

Factors Related to Orgasm.   One by-product of the sexual revolution and women's movement of the 1970s was the recognition of female sexual potential, and particularly, the focus on women's orgasms as a topic of interest. It has been noted that female sexuality is more variable than that of males, and one of the areas that best exemplifies this variability is the experience of orgasm. Some adult women have never experienced an orgasm, whereas others regularly have several orgasms in a single sexual encounter. Some women reliably experience orgasms under certain circumstances (e.g., when masturbating with a vibrator or receiving oral sex) and seldom have them under other conditions (e.g., when having vaginal intercourse). Some women's orgasms consist of 3 to 5 contractions; others' orgasms involve 12 to 15 contractions. The male experience of orgasm appears to be less variable with respect to the percentage of those who have reached orgasm, the likelihood of achieving orgasm during any given sex act, the number of orgasms achieved during a single sexual encounter, and the number of contractions during an orgasm.

Generally, males reach orgasm more consistently than females. The Laumann et al. (1994) study found that about three-quarters of the men reported always having an orgasm during sex with their primary partner compared to about one-quarter of the women. These percentages did nor vary much with age, marital status, education, or religion.

What are the factors associated with experiencing orgasm in women? It appears that the variability in orgasmic capacity in women is not related to differences in physiological capacity, but rather to their amount of sexual experience, opportunities for sexual expression, and sexual values, beliefs and practices. Research suggests that orgasmic capacity is correlated with age, with many women reaching their peak in their thirties and forties (Kinsey et al., 1953), and with level of intimacy, with more women achieving orgasm in the context of committed relationships, especially marriage, than in casual sexual relationships (Laumann et al., 1994). Women who reach orgasm have also been found to be better able to communicate with a partner regarding the need for direct clitoral stimulation and to have greater sex knowledge, less sex guilt, and less negative attitudes about masturbation (Kelly, Strassberg, & Kircher, 1990).

Like female sexuality generally, the female orgasm has long been a topic of controversy. Among the issues debated are whether there are two (or three!) kinds of female orgasms and whether one is superior to the other(s) (Singer & Singer, 1972); whether there exists in the vagina a **G-spot**, short for **Grafenberg spot,** that, when stimulated, produces a distinct and powerful form of orgasm, accompanied by vaginal ejaculations (see Box 8.4); and whether women's orgasmic capacity (in terms of number and intensity) is more likely to be realized during masturbation than vaginal intercourse. Some people wonder whether women who do not have orgasms at all suffer from a "sexual dysfunction" or whether women who have just one orgasm during a sexual act are missing out and should be seeking more.

Clitoral versus Vaginal Orgasms.   No less a figure in twentieth-century Western thought than Sigmund Freud argued that females can experience two distinct orgasms, the clitoral orgasm and the vaginal orgasm. According to Freud, orgasms due to oral or manual clitoral stimulation are immature, representing fixation at the phallic stage of development, and are inferior to the vaginal orgasm, which results from deep penile thrusting. Freud's view, supported by psychoanalysts and psychiatrists over decades, has had the effect of glorifying the vaginal orgasm and making

women who require direct clitoral stimulation feel that they are sexually inadequate. Research conducted by Masters and Johnson (1966) showed that, physiologically speaking, there is only one kind of orgasm. In fact, all female orgasms require some clitoral stimulation, however indirect. The clitoris is the only sex organ whose sole function is sexual pleasure; it develops from the same fetal tissue as the penis and, like its male counterpart, is richly endowed with nerve endings that are exquisitely sensitive.

Is there evidence then for the vaginal orgasm? Research is inconclusive, and researchers remain divided on this issue. Women in other cultures who have had their clitorises entirely removed in the procedures of clitoridectomies or infibulations (a procedure that is even more mutilating, involving not only the complete removal of the clitoris, but also the removal of the inner and outer lips of the vagina) still report experiencing orgasms during vaginal intercourse (Toubia, 1993). (See Chapters 3, 12, and 14 for more information on female genital mutilation.) The vagina, which has the important reproductive function of serving as the birth canal, contains relatively few nerve endings and is more sensitive to pressure than touch. It may be that deep penile thrusting that distends the vagina may cause sexual pleasure to the point of orgasm.

Multiple Orgasms.   Another of Kinsey's most exciting and controversial findings had to do not with the nature of the female orgasm, and its vaginal or clitoral origins, but the extent of the female orgasm. It was Kinsey who first noted that a small percentage of women (14 percent) reported regularly experiencing multiple orgasms (Kinsey et al., 1953). This finding was met with much skepticism, and many of those who accepted the results derogated the women who reported multiple orgasms, regarding them as nymphomaniacs (Rathus et al., 2002). Masters and Johnson's (1966) laboratory research later confirmed that many women do indeed experience multiple orgasms, which they defined as the occurrence of one or more orgasms after the first within a short period of time, before the body returns to the prearoused state. In fact, Masters and Johnson found that most women were capable of experiencing multiple orgasms if they continued to

Box 8.4

The G-Spot

In 1950, a gynecologist named Ernest Grafenberg identified what he believed was a highly sensitive spot in the vagina, situated about two-thirds of the way up the vagina toward the cervix, along the front or anterior wall. According to Grafenberg and others (e.g., Perry & Whipple, 1981), women in whom this area is sufficiently stimulated by stroking experience unusually intense and pleasurable orgasms, which may be accompanied by a gush of milky discharge, similar to the release of semen in men. There is considerable controversy about whether the G-spot exists, because it cannot be seen and apparently requires continued stimulation to be felt. Moreover, the nature and source of the ejaculate remain mysterious. More research is needed on the nature of the female orgasm and the possibilities inherent therein.

receive stimulation in the resolution phase of the response cycle. In their laboratory, some women had between 5 and 20 orgasms during masturbation, and even more with a vibrator, where fatigue is less of an issue. According to Masters and Johnson it is not possible for men to experience multiple orgasms; a refractory period, however short, is necessary after each orgasm. However, more recent evidence suggests that some men do not enter a refractory period and apparently are capable of multiple orgasms. These can take the form of one or two dry orgasms—orgasms without ejaculation—followed by orgasm with ejaculation, or several dry orgasms following ejaculation (Dunn & Trost, 1989).

Although women can experience multiple orgasms through masturbation, petting, and coitus, masturbation, especially with a vibrator, tends to be the most reliable method of achieving multiple orgasms (as it is the most likely method for achieving any orgasms for women). Further, Masters and Johnson (1966) found that for both men and women, orgasms achieved through masturbation are more physiologically intense than orgasms obtained through sexual intercourse. However, they note that physiological intensity is not the same thing as subjective pleasure, and that most men and women greatly prefer sex with a partner to the solitary act of masturbation.

What are the factors correlated with the experience of multiple orgasms in women? There is not yet a great deal of research on this issue. One survey of female nurses found that 43 percent reported having multiple orgasms (Denney, Field, & Quadagno, 1984). Compared to those who had single orgasms, multiorgasmic women began masturbating earlier, were more likely to use sexual fantasy and erotic material, to give and receive oral sex, and to have sex partners who stimulated their breasts. Multiorgasmic women had less sex guilt and seemed overall to be less constrained by society's constructions of female sexuality.

Orgasms and Sexual Dysfunction. One unfortunate and unintended consequence of the tremendous amount of scientific attention devoted to the female orgasm in recent years is that many women have come to feel sexually inadequate. Especially vulnerable are women who have never had orgasms, those who experienced them only during masturbation, and those who have never experienced multiple orgasms. For these women, females' legendary biological capacity for multiple orgasms sometimes becomes a burden and a reproach.

The fact is that many women are not orgasmic not because they are dysfunctional, but because they have never received the type and amount of stimulation that arouse them to the point of orgasm. As we have noted throughout this chapter, female sexuality is poorly understood by both women and men. Moreover, many women are socialized to be passive and accepting during sex and not to verbalize their own needs and desires. After a long history of not experiencing orgasms, some women understandably develop anxiety and negative attitudes about sex. Concerning the number of orgasms, many women are happy to have just one in a sexual encounter.

Sexual Dysfunction

The most authoritative system of classification of **sexual dysfunction** comes from the American Psychiatric Association's *Diagnostic and Statistical Manual of Mental Disorders* (the DSM, described more fully in Chapter 13). In the latest (fourth, text revision) edition, the DSM-IV-TR identifies four types of sexual dysfunctions: disorders of desire, arousal, orgasmic capacity, and pain.

Women are more likely than men to have a lack of sexual desire, although the image of men as always desirous of sex is by no means accurate. Biological and psychological factors both contribute to a lack of desire. Problems of sexual arousal have been labeled impotence in men and frigidity in women, though both of those terms are pejorative and stigmatizing and are avoided by professionals today. Lack of sexual arousal in men is now called *male erectile disorder* and is described as the inability to achieve or maintain an erection due to physical or psychological causes. This disorder in men increases with age and is associated with fatigue, alcohol, and anxiety. Sexual arousal problems in women are characterized by difficulties becoming sexually excited and vaginally lubricated in response to sexual stimulation.

They are more often due to psychological than physical factors (Rathus et al., 2002).

Male orgasmic disorder is also known as *delayed ejaculation.* In most cases, the problem is limited to coitus, and affected men are capable of ejaculating during manual stimulation or oral sex. This disorder may be caused by neurological problems such as multiple sclerosis or may be a side effect of certain drugs. A second type of orgasmic disorder affecting men is *premature ejaculation*—ejaculating too rapidly to permit themselves and their partners from enjoying sex to its fullest. However, there is no generally agreed-on definition of what "premature" is and whether the focus should be on the length of coitus rather than the satisfaction of the couple. Women with orgasmic dysfunction are unable to reach orgasm even after what is considered an adequate amount of sexual stimulation. Some women are unable to reach orgasm during coitus, but experience orgasms during masturbation or oral sex. Women who do not experience orgasms by any means are called *anorgasmic* or *preorgasmic.*

For some people, coitus is not pleasurable, but painful. The term for painful intercourse is *dyspareunia,* and it can affect women or men. Pain during intercourse can be present for many reasons, physical, psychological, or an interaction of the two. It is more common in women than men. The most common reasons for painful intercourse in women include inadequate lubrication, vaginal infections, and sexually transmitted diseases. Another pain disorder, and one that exclusively affects women, is *vaginismus,* the involuntary contraction of the pelvic muscles that occurs reflexively during intercourse. Vaginismus does not have a physical origin, but is psychologically caused. Many women with this disorder have histories of rape, sexual abuse, or botched abortions that resulted in vaginal trauma (LoPiccolo & Stock, 1986).

It was once commonly believed that most sexual dysfunctions had organic or physical causes, but this is no longer the case. Certainly, many sexual dysfunctions, particularly of men, are due to poor health, specific medical conditions, prescription and illicit drugs, and complications from surgical procedures. But now it is widely understood that many sexual disorders have psychological causes ranging from anger and depression to lack of sexual knowledge and problems in a relationship. Today, there are treatment approaches to sexual dysfunctions. They include behavioral and psychological sex therapies that aim to change self-defeating behaviors, teach sexual skills, improve sexual communication, and reduce performance anxiety. Biological treatments have received a great deal of scientific and media attention in recent years. Viagra is helpful in most cases of erectile dysfunction, and many similar products are emerging. Biological treatments are also being developed for premature ejaculation and female orgasmic dysfunction (Rathus et al., 2002).

Sexual Fantasy

By **sexual fantasy,** we mean any mental imagery that people find sexually arousing. Until recently, the study of sexual fantasy has been regarded as frivolous and barely scientifically respectable. After all, descriptions of people's fantasies are titillating, and collections of fantasies in books and magazines have an obvious erotic function. However, the last two decades have witnessed an explosion of scientific research on this topic, because it is increasingly recognized that fantasy is a central aspect of human sexual behavior. In an important review of the work in this area, Leitenberg and Henning (1995) note:

> *Certainly it is by now a truism that one's brain is at least as important a sexual organ as one's genitals. What humans think about can either enhance or inhibit sexual responsivity to any form of sensory stimulation, and, in the absence of any physical stimulation, sexual fantasy alone is arousing. (p. 469)*

Leitenberg and Henning (1995) also consider sexual fantasies potentially important for many other reasons. For instance, they are almost universally experienced. They may affect future sexual behavior as well as reflect past sexual experience. Unlike sexual behavior, sexual fantasies are relatively unconstrained by societal and legal restrictions, and thus may be more revealing of people's sexual desires than their behaviors are. Some researchers find that fantasies may play a significant role in the commission of sexual offenses such as child sexual abuse (Hall, Shondrick, & Hirschman, 1993). From our perspective, they are also interesting for what they reveal about women, men, and gender differences.

Sexual fantasies have been studied in terms of the context in which they occur, their frequency, and their content. The three contexts in which fantasies are typically assessed are during masturbation, during intercourse, and during nonsexual activity. Research consistently shows that most people have sexual fantasies while they masturbate, with men significantly more likely than women to fantasize during masturbation. Studies of gender differences in sexual fantasies during intercourse present a somewhat different picture. Again, studies find high levels of fantasizing during intercourse, with many studies reporting about 90 percent of all respondents expressing such fantasies (Knafo & Jaffe, 1984; Price & Miller, 1984). But there are no consistent sex differences in sexual fantasies during intercourse; women are as likely to fantasize during intercourse as men are. Sex differences reemerge in the incidence of fantasies during nonsexual activity. Laumann et al. (1994) found that 54 percent of men compared with 19 percent of women thought about sex every day or several times a day. Cameron and Biber (1973) also found that men thought about sex more often than women in all age groupings. Men also report having a greater number of different kinds of sexual fantasies than women.

Interesting sex differences have also been found in the content of sexual fantasies. In fantasy, men more than women imagine *doing something sexual to a partner* and women more than men imagine *something sexual being done to them*. Women are more likely than men to fantasize about someone they are currently or have been involved with and to focus on personal and emotional aspects of the partner and their own and the partners' physical and emotional reactions. Men's fantasies are more impersonal and sexually graphic, with a focus on visual images and body parts, specifically genital features of their imagined partners. Men are more likely than women to fantasize having sex with multiple partners, including partners whom they desire but have never had a relationship with. Finally and perhaps most contro-

versially, women are more likely than men to have submission fantasies, whereas men are more likely than women to have dominance fantasies (Leitenberg & Henning, 1995).

In all of the literature on sexual fantasy, the finding that women commonly (but by no means universally) have fantasies of being overpowered or forced to have sex, is probably the most controversial. This appears to reinforce the pernicious "rape myth" that women want to be raped and enjoy being raped. As Leitenberg and Henning (1995) show, nothing could be further from the truth. Women who have these fantasies emphasize that they have no wish to be raped in reality. Moreover, in women's submission fantasies, women and not men are in perfect control of the situation, the imagined violence is very little, the women know that they are safe, and they do not experience any physical pain. In the typical rape fantasy, the woman perceives herself to be so sexually desirable that the man cannot resist her and so ravishes her. One of the most common explanations of submission fantasies is that they are actually fantasies of a woman's sexual attractiveness and desirability—her sexual power over men, rather than her weakness with respect to them (Hariton & Singer, 1974). It has also been suggested that, in a society that restricts female sexuality, submission fantasies allow a woman to feel blameless for engaging in sex, especially in sexual acts that are socially unacceptable or prohibited (e.g., anal sex, sex with a spouse's best friend, etc.) (Leitenberg & Henning, 1995).

Psychologists have attempted to account for overall sex differences in the incidence, frequency, and content of sexual fantasy with explanations based on learning theories, evolutionary psychology theories (Udry, Billy, Morris, Groff, & Raj, 1985), and sociocultural theories (Wincze, Hoon, & Hoon, 1977).

Research on sexual fantasies may illuminate sex differences in responses to pornography. (For further discussion of pornography, see Chapter 12). Like men, women become physiologically aroused by watching X-rated videos, but it is well known that many women have negative reactions to such videos and do not seek them out (Wincze et al., 1977). Men are overwhelmingly the primary consumers of X-rated videos and all other forms of hard-core pornography, whereas women are overwhelmingly the primary consumers of romance novels. According to Leitenberg and Henning (1995), that is precisely because the videos and novels capture the essence of the male and female sexual fantasies, respectively:

> *If one examines the typical X-rated movie, one immediately sees naked bodies engaged in sexual activity without much story line, gradual build-up, affectional–emotional ties, and so forth. The fantasy being portrayed is primarily the male fantasy of multiple female sexual partners ever ready for sexual activity of any kind without any chance of the man being rejected. On the other hand, the primary fantasy of the typical romance novel is a woman who inflames the passion and lifelong love of a desirable man under difficult circumstances. . . . The sex, however fervent, is subsidiary to the love story. (p. 484)*

Sexuality among People with Disabilities

For too long, the sexuality of people with disabilities, especially women, has been ignored or dismissed by science and society. The underlying assumption appeared to be that "disability is not sexy"—that people with disabilities, especially women, were not sexually desiring or desirable. What research exists is largely done on males, and successful sex is defined in male terms, such as intromission and sustained erection. In women with spinal cord injury, their reproductive capacity to sustain pregnancies and deliver babies has been studied more than their sexual capacity, possibly because of the underlying belief that women play a passive role in sexual relations (Fitting, Salisbury, Davies, & Mayelin, 1978). The women's movement of the 1970s and the more recent political organization of people with disabilities in the 1980s and 1990s have begun to focus much needed scientific and clinical attention on the sexuality of women with disabilities.

The sketchy portrait that emerges from studies of sexuality and disability is interesting indeed. In important early calls for attention to concerns of women with disabilities, Fine and Asch (1981, 1988) note that men with disabilities are much more likely to marry than are women with disabilities, and women who are already married at the time they are disabled are more likely to get divorced than men who become disabled. A study of sexuality of women with spinal cord injuries found that less than 10 percent of the women who had a sexual relationship prior to injury maintained that relationship postinjury (Fitting et al., 1978). Several investigators report that physical disability renders a woman more vulnerable to abuse of all kinds (Nosek et al., 1994). These findings are sobering, suggesting that women with disabilities are strongly devalued by others as sexual beings, and treated to what Fine and Asch (1981) refer to as "sexism without the pedestal" (p. 233). Fortunately, these findings do not make up the whole picture.

While the onset of a disability may break up preexisting sexual relationships, there is evidence from at least one study that most women with spinal cord injuries began new intimate relationships after injury and described their sexual relationships as very enjoyable. Some women continued to have orgasms after their injuries (although the orgasms were experienced differently). Importantly, all women involved in a sexual relationship after becoming disabled perceived themselves as very or somewhat attractive (Fitting et al., 1978). A more recent study of women with mobility impairments found that after injury women felt that their bodies were only half as attractive as before, despite the fact that while physical function had decreased, overall physical appearance had not changed markedly. Sexual self-esteem was lower among women whose disabilities occurred later in life. Sex and even orgasm (for about 50 percent of respondents) remained possible and enjoyable, but both were more difficult and occurred less frequently (Mona, Gardos, & Brown, 1994). One interesting finding of this study is that women surveyed did not expand their repertoire of sexual behavior after their injuries, but continued to express themselves sexually as they always had. Perhaps more intimacy and pleasure for these women and their partners would be possible with open communication, education and counseling, and sexual experimentation.

Increasingly, it is understood that people with disabilities have the same needs, feelings, and desires as people without disabilities. Margaret Nosek and her colleagues suggest that sexual wellness, for all people, including those with disabilities, involves a positive self-concept—seeing oneself as sexually valuable; having knowledge about sexuality; enjoying positive, productive relations; coping with barriers to sexuality; and maintaining the best possible general and sexual health (Nosek et al., 1994).

There are now many organizations, books, and educational materials available for people with disabilities who wish to explore their sexual options. In the landmark sex manual *More Joy of Sex,* published over 30 years ago, Alex Comfort (1974) had these inspiring words for people with disabilities and they resonate still:

> *Minor disability may only limit your choice of positions, etc. Major disability will mean that you may have to carve out a whole special form of sex for yourself. Virtually nobody is too disabled to have some pleasure from sexuality—with a partner if you can, without one if you must. Generations of disabled people have been hocused out of this by other people's embarrassment, the pattern of institutions, and the desire of society to suppress any sexual expression which was suppressible. . . . Your big problem, after that of getting well people to treat you as a person, will be in getting it through their heads that you have the same needs as they have. . . . Above all, get rid of the idea that nobody can love, or have pleasure with, a disabled person. Thousands can and do. . . . (p. 202)*

Birth Control and Safe(r) Sex

It is a fact of life that sex is far more consequential for women than it is for men, and this is mainly (but not only) because women bear children. Few events have the potential of changing women's lives as much as bearing and rearing children. Given these realities, it is hard to overestimate the effects of readily available, relatively safe, and effective forms of birth control on the sexual revolution in the 1960s and 1970s. For many women, the ability to control their fertility is fundamental to their sense of themselves as free, autonomous, and sexual people. Many of the changes in women's sexual behavior that we have noted from the time of Kinsey's surveys to the present are directly attributable to the widespread use of birth control methods over the past 40 years. At the same time,

birth control remains a highly charged issue in the United States and elsewhere. Artificial means of controlling birth are vigorously opposed by the Catholic Church and orthodox Jewish groups, among others. However, they are even more vigorously *promoted* among women in China, where the "one child per family" policy is enforced in some cases by involuntary sterilization, the public tracking of menstrual cycles, and even more draconian measures.

Reproductive health and birth control are political as well as physical and mental health issues. Decisions about birth control do not take place in a political or social vacuum. Reproductive research and services are sometimes as responsive to perceived needs of society, such as the desire to reduce the welfare budget, as they are to women's needs and realities. It cannot be assumed, for example, that every woman wants to use birth control or that every woman is able to use birth control when she wants to. Models of birth or sexually transmitted disease (STD) control that fail to take social and psychological factors into account may be doomed to failure.

This section considers those social and psychological factors that enter into contraceptive use and discusses some of the variables that predict contraceptive use. We also consider when and how people try to prevent the spread of STDs. Since the onset of the AIDS epidemic in the 1980s, there has been increased attention to and practice of safe(r) sex. Obviously, birth control and STD control are not the same thing: Some methods of birth control offer protection against STDs and others do not. For further discussion of STDs, including treatment and prevention, see Chapter 14.

Contraceptive Use. Throughout the world, most men and women appear to assume that women, who have much more at stake than men in preventing pregnancy, bear the responsibility for birth control. This places an enormous burden on women, in part because there is no such thing as a perfect contraceptive and in part because sexual pressures from men can make it difficult for women to control their fertility.

Rathus et al. (2002) have listed a number of factors that affect the use of **contraceptives.** For example, contraceptives differ considerably in how convenient they are to use. Generally, a technique or device is more convenient if it does not have to be purchased in advance and does not require a visit to the doctor or a prescription. Cost is another factor affecting use. Some contraceptives are relatively cheap, such as condoms, whereas others, such as intrauterine devices (IUDs), may cost several hundred dollars. Safety (or perceived safety) is an important variable in determining contraceptive use. The use of the birth control pill and IUDs has fallen off among some women because of side effects: weight gain, headaches, and dizziness in the case of the pill (Shapiro, 1988) and perforation of the uterine or cervical walls with IUDs (Reinisch, 1990). Reversibility, that is, the ease with which fertility can be regained, is a critical factor; as most methods are reversible, but others, notably sterilization, are not. Obviously, effectiveness and perceived effectiveness are important predictors of contraceptive use, and techniques vary widely in effectiveness.

Most pregnancies in the United States are unplanned, and most techniques are not used consistently and correctly. Much of the research on the effectiveness of different techniques compare failure rates with perfect (correct and consistent) use to failure rates with typical (less than perfect) use and find the latter considerably higher. Approximate failure rates of various methods of birth control are presented in Table 8.2. For example, overall, spermicides have a failure rate of 6 percent when used perfectly and a very high failure rate of 26 percent when used typically. Condoms have a relatively low failure rate of 3 percent when used perfectly, and a considerably higher rate of failure of 12 percent with typical use (Rathus et al., 2002).

Contraceptives differ widely as to whether they offer protection against STDs, and this is another factor affecting their use. The resurgence of the popularity of condoms in recent years can be directly traced to the protection they offer against AIDS and other STDs. Many adolescents who use condoms do so more to protect themselves against AIDS than against unwanted pregnancies (Lewin, 1991).

Other more psychological variables come into play in choosing contraceptive methods. Some methods require more sharing of responsibility between partners than others, and for some couples this sharing is a positive feature, whereas for others it is not. The use of the pill and the IUD requires no sharing of responsibility, whereas alternating the use of condoms and a diaphragm involves both partners. Some men like to use condoms because they have some control over the likelihood of impregnating their partners and contracting STDs from them. Other men believe that it is the women's responsibility alone to control fertility and do not wish to use condoms. The perceived effects of a birth-control method on one's own and one's partner's sexual pleasure are understudied variables in birth-control research, but they are potentially very important variables. It is well documented that women have more positive attitudes about condom use than men do and that more men than women report that condoms diminish their sexual pleasure (Campbell, Peplau, & DeBro, 1992). The perception that condoms reduce male pleasure is one of the reasons that some men refuse to wear condoms, and some women are reluctant to ask their male partners to use them. The use of condoms also requires that the couple interrupt lovemaking long enough for the man to put on the condom. Some people find that this interruption "breaks the mood" or reduces spontaneity and passion.

Different contraceptive techniques vary in how morally acceptable they are to potential users. The *rhythm method,* whereby the couple has sexual intercourse during the times in a woman's menstrual cycle when she is unlikely to be fertile, does not involve artificial means and is the one method of birth control that is sanctioned by the Catholic Church. Women who are opposed to abortion may find that oral contraceptives that prevent fertilization from taking place are acceptable, whereas those methods that allow fertilization to occur but prevent implantation of the fertilized ovum in the uterus are not. Methods of birth control that involve planning ahead, such as taking the pill or having an IUD inserted, require that a girl or woman admits to herself (and her physician) that she is having or intends to have sex. Many adolescents and young women find it difficult to admit this to themselves or others, because they feel, or others have told them, that it is wrong to have sex.

TABLE 8.2   Failure Rates of Various Methods of Birth Control

| METHOD | % OF WOMEN EXPERIENCING AN ACCIDENTAL PREGNANCY WITHIN THE FIRST YEAR OF USE | | % OF WOMEN CONTINUING USE AT ONE YEAR[3] | REVERSIBILITY | PROTECTION AGAINST SEXUALLY TRANSMITTED INFECTIONS (STIS) |
	Typical Use[1]	Perfect Use[2]			
Chance[4]	85	85		yes (unless fertility has been impaired by exposure to an STI)	no
Spermicides[5]	26	6	43	yes	no
Periodic abstinence	20		67	yes	no
Calendar		9			
Ovulation method		3			
Sympto-thermal[6]		2			
Post-ovulation		1			
Withdrawal	19	4		yes	no
Cervical cap[7]					
Parous women[9]	40	30	45	yes	some
Nulliparous[10] women	20	9	58	yes	some
Diaphragm	20	6	58	yes	some

Sources: From Spencer A. Rathus, Jeffrey S. Nevid, Lois Fichner-Rathus, *Human Sexuality in a World of Diversity* (4e), © 2002. Published by Allyn and Bacon, Boston, MA. Copyright © 2002 by Pearson Education. Adapted by permission of the publisher. For failure rates and percentages of women discontinuing use, adapted from Hatcher et al. (1994, 1998). Information on reversibility and protection against STIs added.

[1]Among typical couples who initiate use of a method (not necessarily for the first time), the percentage who experience an accidental pregnancy during the first year if they do not stop use for any other reason.

[2]Among couples who initiate use of a method (not necessarily for the first time), and who use it perfectly (both consistently and correctly), the percentage who experience an accidental pregnancy during the first year if they do not stop use for any other reason.

[3]Among couples attempting to avoid pregnancy, the percentage who continue to use a method for one year.

Most of the research on the characteristics of different contraceptive users has focused on teenage girls and young women. Many people find the focus on girls and women to the virtual exclusion of boys and men to be deeply sexist and misguided (Amaro, 1995). Scientific researchers, like society generally, tend to ignore how gender, women's social status, and women's roles affect contraceptive behavior and women's ability to control their fertility, and we will consider these factors shortly. Females' role in contraceptive use is exaggerated by science and society not because they are in fact more responsible for birth control, but rather because they are the ones who become pregnant.

TABLE 8.2   Continued

| METHOD | % OF WOMEN EXPERIENCING AN ACCIDENTAL PREGNANCY WITHIN THE FIRST YEAR OF USE | | % OF WOMEN CONTINUING USE AT ONE YEAR[3] | REVERSIBILITY | PROTECTION AGAINST SEXUALLY TRANSMITTED INFECTIONS (STIS) |
	Typical Use[1]	Perfect Use[2]			
Condom alone					
Female (Reality)	21	3	56	yes	yes
Male	14	3	63	yes	yes
Pill	3		72	yes	no, but may reduce risk of PID[8]
Progestin only		0.5			
Combined		0.1			
IUD					
Progestasert	2.0	1.5	81	yes, except if fertility is impaired	no, and may increase the risk of PID
ParaGard Copper T 380A	0.8	0.6	78		
Depo-Provera	0.3	0.3	70	yes	no
Norplant (6 capsules)	0.05	0.05	85	yes	no
Female sterilization	0.5	0.5	100	questionable	no
Male sterilization	0.15	0.10	100	questionable	no

[4]The percentages failing in columns (2) and (3) are based on data from populations where contraception is not used and from women who cease using contraception in order to become pregnant. Among such populations, about 89% become pregnant within one year. This estimate was lowered slightly (to 85%) to represent the percentage who would become pregnant within one year among women now relying on reversible methods of contraception if they abandoned contraception altogether.

[5]Foams, creams, gels, vaginal suppositories, and vaginal film.

[6]Cervical mucus (ovulation) method supplemented by calendar in the pre-ovulatory period and basal body temperature in the post-ovulatory period.

[7]With spermicidal cream or jelly.

[8]Pelvic inflammatory disease.

[9]Women who have borne children.

[10]Women who have not borne children.

About 800,000 adolescent girls in the United States become pregnant each year, and 90 percent of those pregnancies are unplanned (Rathus et al., 2002). While overall rates of teen pregnancy are declining, rates of pregnancies to unmarried adolescents have been increasing in recent years. Today, 79 percent of adolescent mothers are unmarried, compared with just 15 percent in 1960 (Centers for Disease Control & Prevention, 2004). The consequences of these unplanned pregnancies for the teenagers and their babies, families, communities, and society can be disastrous. Babies born to teenage mothers are at greater risk of physical, emotional, and intellectual problems and are much more likely to live in poverty and to suffer maternal abuse and neglect.

In the United States, the percentage of sexually active teenage girls is no different from the percentage of sexually active girls in other developed countries, but U.S. rates of adolescent pregnancy, while declining steadily, are still two and five times higher than those of the rest of the industrialized world (Rathus et al., 2002). It is difficult to explain why U.S. teens are at such a high risk of pregnancy compared to their peers in other countries, although some investigators point to the profound ambivalence toward teen sexuality in the United States, as manifested in the lack of sex education in the schools, poor access to services that provide cheap or free contraceptives, and relatively low use of birth-control pills, a highly effective form of birth control, among young women in the United States (Hess, Markson, & Stein, 1993). The United States is also home to one of the Western world's strongest antiabortion movements, which not only has affected girls' acceptance of and access to abortions but also has affected attitudes about and impeded access to other family planning services, including birth control.

We cannot overlook the fact that, although most teenage pregnancies are unplanned and unwanted, some teens want to become pregnant or become mothers. Some believe that becoming pregnant will cement a shaky relationship or win independence from their parents. Others believe that having a baby is the best of a limited set of options they perceive for themselves (Nevid et al., 1995). Many conceptual models that have recently been developed to explain contraceptive use ignore the fact that in some ethnic groups women use a model of sexuality that is based not on recreation but procreation, in which sex includes a possible, even likely, outcome of conception and pregnancy. When the intent of sex is conception, a couple will obviously not use a condom, even though the condom also protects against STDs (Wyatt, 1994).

Finally, it is clear that many girls and women resent being made increasingly responsible for ensuring birth control. This may be especially true for Women of Color, who are frequently criticized by society for their high rates of teen pregnancies and who are the regular targets of birth-control efforts. Up until recently, there were few programs attempting to encourage teenage boys who are sexually involved with teenage girls to take responsibility for unintended pregnancies. Women's socialization encourages them to let men take the initiative on matters pertaining to sex, including contraceptive use. The assumptions that women do all or most of the sexual and contraceptive decision making in relationships, that women make decisions about sex or contraception independent of their partners, and that women talk to partners in advance about the sexual practices in which they will engage do not correspond with reality for most women, especially for poor women of color. Recent research and practice are aimed at increasing responsible sexual and contraceptive practices among men as well as women, and at understanding, rather than controlling, contraceptive use in diverse populations.

There is evidence that this is working. The U.S. birthrate among women aged 15 to 19 is now at the lowest level it has been in the last half century (Centers for Disease Control and Prevention; the Alan Guttmacher Institute, Child Trends Databank as cited in *The New York Times,* March 7, 2004). The most recent reports suggest that both abstinence and condom use are increasing among teens, particularly among teenage boys from poor minority communities. It is not entirely clear what is behind the finding of "less sex, more protection, fewer pregnancies" (p. 36), though experts believe that young people, boys and girls alike, may be distilling new, hopeful codes of conduct from a blend of sex education, popular culture, and family experiences. Possible reasons for the turnaround include the fear of AIDS and the impact of AIDS prevention education. They also include the more widespread use of injectable forms of birth control. Further, changes in welfare policy and crackdowns on fathers for child support, the rise of a more religious and conservative generation of teenagers, more economic opportunity for young people, and an array of new youth programs stressing both abstinence and contraception may also contribute. Some of the most heartening news is that efforts to postpone parenthood will increasingly target boys and young men as well as girls and young women.

Safe(r) Sex.   Ever since it was recognized in the mid-1980s that *acquired immunodeficiency syndrome* (AIDS) can be a sexually transmitted disease, the terms **safe sex** and **safer sex** have become commonplace in the discourse of our society. As most sexually active Americans know, the terms refer to sexual practices that eliminate or substantially reduce the chances that human immunodeficiency virus (HIV) will be transmitted from an infected to an uninfected individual. Some sexual practices are far more efficient transmitters of HIV than others. For example, the chances that HIV will spread through oral sex is quite low, whereas the likelihood that HIV will spread through unprotected anal sex is relatively high.

As we will discuss further in Chapter 14, in the United States, AIDS is a disease that predominantly affects intravenous drug users and men who have sex with men. But recent research suggests that heterosexual transmission accounts for the largest proportionate increase in AIDS cases (Kelly, 2004). Heterosexual transmission occurs mainly through unprotected vaginal intercourse without a condom. (Unprotected anal intercourse is another, less common route among heterosexuals and the major route of transmission among gay men.) While it is possible for men to contract HIV through vaginal intercourse, presumably through vaginal secretions that contain the virus, it is much more likely that women will contract the virus from men than men from women. This is apparently because more of the virus is contained in men's ejaculate than in women's vaginal secretions. Thus, unprotected vaginal intercourse puts women at considerably higher risk of HIV infection than men.

After abstinence, condom use is the most effective means of protecting oneself and one's partner from sexually transmitted HIV. While condom use has increased in recent years in response to the AIDS epidemic, condom use among sexually active adolescents and adults is alarmingly low. Most sexually active people do not use condoms consistently. A survey of condom use among sexually active college students found that only 20 percent reported using condoms all the time (Rathus et al., 2002), although more recent surveys seem to show increased condom use among young people at the turn of the century

(Santelli et al., 2000). In a national survey of HIV risk factors among the general population, Catania et al. (1992) found that only 17 percent of those with multiple sex partners, 13 percent of those with high-risk partners, and 11 percent of untested transfusion recipients used condoms all the time. This study also found that Hispanic women were the least likely group to report using condoms. In a survey of adolescent and adult residents in a high-risk urban area of Philadelphia, one-third of respondents reported using condoms all the time, one-third some of the time, and one-third never used condoms (Geringer et al., 1993). In this study, women were more likely than men to identify themselves as responsible for condom use decisions, but were less likely than men to use a condom with a new partner. Heterosexual couples often do not consistently use condoms even when one partner, usually the man, is known to be infected with HIV (Lollis, Johnson, Antoni, & Hinkle, 1996).

Recent surveys suggest that knowledge about AIDS in the general population is increasing rapidly. The vast majority of Americans now know that AIDS can be transmitted through heterosexual intercourse (Geringer et al., 1993). Despite massive educational efforts by the media and other sources to inform people about how AIDS is transmitted and to encourage condom use to prevent the spread of AIDS, many people continue to engage in unprotected sex. Why do so many heterosexual people consistently fail to protect themselves against AIDS/HIV? Many reasons have been suggested for the high prevalence of risky sex in all age groups, but especially in young people. For one thing, sex is not primarily a future-oriented, cognitive experience for most people, involving purposeful planning and thinking about consequences before it occurs. For many people, especially those who are poor, sexual encounters are not anticipated, nor are the consequences of unprotected sexual encounters (Wyatt, 1994). The act of having sex is highly complex, affected by various thoughts and feelings, diverse personal histories, cultural backgrounds, fleeting circumstances, relationship characteristics, and the like. It is naïve to think that simple information about transmission patterns will greatly influence such a complex, multidetermined behavior or that concerns about the threat of AIDS are uppermost in people's minds when they contemplate—or are confronted with—sexual situations.

Other factors identified by researchers as predictive of risky sex include perceived low risk of infection among heterosexual individuals and the belief that one can identify high-risk individuals by the way they look and act. People sometimes form informal personal theories, known as *implicit personality theories* that they use to categorize others as safe or unsafe. Once people have established a stable relationship with someone, they are more likely to regard that person as safe and to stop using condoms with them. Many of us subscribe to the myth of personal invulnerability: the false belief that AIDS happens to "other people" (Rathus et al., 1997). Tragically, research shows that some minority populations who are at highest risk for AIDS/HIV infection are most likely to report believing that they have "no chance at all" of contracting AIDS (Amaro, 1988; Rodin & Ickovics, 1990).

Just as with the topic of general contraceptive use in avoiding unwanted pregnancies, far too little attention from science and society has been given to men's roles in low and inconsistent condom use. Several dilemmas are at the heart of this issue. Even though it is men and not women who must wear condoms, women are the targets of condom use programs. It tends to be men and not women who resist condom use, and they resist on several grounds. For some adolescent boys with traditional attitudes toward masculinity, pregnancy among female partners validates masculinity (Pleck, Sonenstein, & Ku, 1993). Condom use seems too premeditated, clinical,

or "unnatural" to some men, especially poor men and men of color, and robs them of their masculinity (Amaro, 1995). Some men interpret the request to use a condom as a sign that they are regarded as diseased or unclean or that their women have had other sexual partners. Others believe that a woman's preference for condom use signals that she is not very committed to the relationship. Finally, many men believe that condom use reduces their sexual pleasure.

Unlike the birth-control pill, IUD, diaphragm, and many other contraceptive techniques, the use of a condom requires male cooperation. Women generally do not have equal power with men in their relationships. Many women, whether because of financial dependence, cultural tradition, fear of violence, rejection, or abandonment, do not perceive that they are in positions to insist on condom use (Amaro, 1995). Exhorting women to assure using condoms more consistently, like educating people about how AIDS is transmitted, does not go far enough in promoting safe(r) sex. Just as we need to increase boys' and men's responsibility for contraception, we also need research and prevention efforts designed to increase their responsibility for safe(r) sex. As things currently stand, women have even less control over condom use than over the use of other contraceptives, and this situation will not change until women have a contraceptive of their own that prevents STDs as well as conception. The goal of maximizing the sexual health of our diverse population will not be easily attained. It requires, for example, that we understand the underlying social conditions that facilitate STDs and work for improvements that seek to change unjust aspects of society that cause these conditions (Amaro, 1995).

SUMMARY

In this chapter, we have attempted to show how female and male sexuality is strongly influenced by historical, cultural, and social forces. This social constructionist perspective challenges the belief that any one form of sexuality or any one sexual behavior is solely determined by biological mechanisms. Sexuality and sexual behaviors have been and continue

to be subject to social and situational factors, and thus can change.

In the first part of the chapter, we use the double standard of sexuality as the lens through which to view gender differences in a variety of sexual behaviors. We discuss how gender differences develop and are maintained through socialization in the double standard. We explore how racist, ethnocentric, and heterosexist biases can affect our judgments of sexual behavior.

In the second section of the chapter we review scientific research on sexuality, from the groundbreaking work of Kinsey and Masters and Johnson to the present. Issues and methods of research in sexuality are presented, and research on sexual practices is summarized. The human sexual response is described.

In the final section of the chapter, selected topics in human sexuality are treated. We describe common sexual dysfunctions and question possible sexist biases in the use of that term. We discuss recent research and thinking about sexual orientation and consider how culture and society construct categories of heterosexual, homosexual, and bisexual. We review the rapidly growing literature on sexual fantasy and consider various theories about gender differences in this area. Sexuality among people with disabilities, a grossly understudied area of research, is briefly discussed. Finally, we present current research and thinking in the important areas of contraceptive use and safe(r) sex practices, exploring the critical role of gender in these areas.

In conclusion, sexuality generally and female sexuality particularly remain understudied and poorly understood. As we have seen, gender inequalities abound, and 30 years after the sexual revolution, sex remains far more problematic for females than males. Fortunately, science and society have begun to acknowledge some of the biases and gaps that have hampered their efforts. There is increased recognition that sex and sexuality always occur in a context and must be described and studied with that awareness.

KEY TERMS

Bisexuality (p. 288)
Contraceptives (p. 274)
Cunnilingus (p. 265)
Fellatio (p. 265)
Foreplay (p. 264)

Grafenberg or G-spot (p. 269)
Masturbation (p. 263)
Myotonia (p. 266)
Refractory period (p. 268)
Safe(r) sex (p. 279)

Sexual dysfunction (p. 270)
Sexual fantasy (p. 271)
Sexual orientation (p. 256)
Vasocongestion (p. 266)

DISCUSSION QUESTIONS

1. Think about your first conversations with your parents about your sexuality. What were their issues and concerns? Did they attend to the positive as well as negative aspects of sexuality?

2. List some of the terms we use to indicate sexual activity. Many of these terms indicate harm and hostility. Why do you think this is so? In describing heterosexual intercourse, the man is usually the grammatical subject and the woman the grammatical object. What does this convey about sex between a woman and a man?

3. What "counts" as having sex? To what extent are genital contact, penetration, and orgasm important to your definitions of sex?

4. Men typically report many more sexual partners in their lives than women do. What are the possible explanations for that finding?

5. Some people regard masturbation as a dirty little secret—tolerable only among teens, the very old, and the lonely. Why are there so many taboos about masturbation?

6. One of the largest, most consistent sex differences has to do with prevalence of masturbation, with many more men reporting having masturbated than women. Why do you think this is so?

7. Women are far less likely than men to experience orgasm during vaginal intercourse, and some women fake orgasms during vaginal sex. What are the implications of these facts for how men and women think about intercourse?

8. Bisexuality is becoming more visible in our culture. Some people say that we are in a "bisexual moment," in which more and more people are being experimental about their sexuality, but others doubt that bisexuality really exists. What do you think, and why? To what extent do you think that sexual orientation is shaped by culture and fluid in the sense that it can change throughout a lifetime?

9. Many women and men report sexual fantasies that are not "politically correct"; that is, they represent such themes as overpowering or being overpowered by others, multiple partners, and so on. What does this reveal, if anything, about the nature of women and men, and about our culture?

10. Research suggests that more men than women want to avoid using condoms during vaginal intercourse. What are some of the strategies that men use to avoid wearing condoms? How can women deal with these strategies? What are some of the strategies that women can use to persuade men to wear condoms?

11. If you use contraceptives, what factors are important to you in choosing them? What advice would you give to a female friend who was considering her options? A male friend?

12. Despite the fact that most people know that STDs such as AIDS are spread through unprotected sex, most people continue to have unprotected sex. Why do you think this is so?

FURTHER READINGS

Califia, P. (1997). *Sex changes: The politics of transgenderism.* San Francisco: Cleis Press.

DeVillers, L. (1997). *Love skills: More fun than you've ever had with sex, intimacy, and communication.* San Luis Obispo, CA: Impact.

Dodson, B. (1987). *Sex for one: The joy of selfloving.* New York: Crown.

Fine, M. (1988). Sexuality, schooling, and adolescent females: The missing discourse of desire. *Harvard Educational Review, 58,* 29–53.

Oliver, M. B., & Hyde, J. S. (1993). Gender differences in sexuality: A meta-analysis. *Psychological Bulletin, 114,* 29–51.

Rich, A. (1980). Compulsory sexuality and lesbian existence. *Signs: Journal of Women in Culture, 5,* 647–650.

Tasker, F. L., & Golumbok, S. (1997). *Growing up in a lesbian family.* New York: Guilford Press.

Tolman, D. L. (2002). *Dilemmas of desire.* Cambridge, MA: Harvard University Press.

Wolf, N. (1991). *The beauty myth: How images of beauty are used against women.* New York: William Morrow.

CHAPTER 9

INTIMATE RELATIONSHIPS: WOMEN AS LOVERS, SPOUSES, FAMILY, AND FRIENDS

Genuine love ought to be founded on the mutual recognition of two liberties; the lovers would then experience themselves both as self and as other: neither would be mutilated, together they would manifest values and aims in the world.

—Simone de Beauvoir

The inarticulateness of love is not its flaw but its essence; not its lack of insight but its insight. If we could ascribe our feelings to the attractiveness or virtue of the loved one, our love would be attached to this attractiveness or that virtue rather than to the love object itself. Love is precisely the sense that we are acting far beyond the call of any particular external qualities, that we are creating or generating value from deep within ourselves.

—Philip Brickman

The more connections you and your lover make, not just between your bodies, but between your minds, your hearts, and your souls, the more you will strengthen the fabric of your relationship, and the more real moments you will experience together.

—Barbara De Angelis

The idea of there being more than one body's worth of substance, will, and wit lined up behind one's projects has its appeal. As one woman said, after going through the reasons, "My God, who wouldn't want a wife?"

—Marilyn Frye

Every family is a normal family—no matter whether it has one parent, two or no children at all. A family can be made up of any combination of

people, heterosexual or homosexual, who share their lives in an intimate (not necessarily sexual) way. . . . Wherever there is lasting love, there is a family.
—Shere Hite

Love is like pi—natural, irrational, and very important.
—Lisa Hoffman

And in the end, the love you take, is equal to the love you make.
—John Lennon and Paul McCartney

Only connect.
—E. M. Forster

For most people, the personal relationships they have with others—being parents, grandparents, lovers, spouses, children, and close friends—represent their most cherished identities, their strongest feelings, and their deepest commitments. You might think that, given their obvious importance, intimate relationships have long been a major focus of psychological research. But in fact, as we shall see, scientific research in many types of intimate relationships is sparse indeed. Until recently, psychology has ceded the study of many of these relationships to sociology and social work. Within psychology, intimate relationships have often been studied in a clinical context, involving couples and families that are distressed or troubled. And, for the most part, research on intimate relationships in the United States has taken place with the White middle class. As we have seen throughout this book, such research may not be generalizable to a broader range of people.

There are probably several reasons for mainstream psychology's relative lack of interest in intimate relationships. These include psychology's long-standing bias against probing topics associated with relational as opposed to individual processes, "feminine" interests as compared with "masculine" ones, and the home and personal sphere relative to work and the public sphere. But psychology's late entry into the study of intimate relationships also reflects how difficult it can be to study close personal relationships scientifically. By their very nature, such relationships are long term, dynamic and everchanging, and intensely complex and private. For ethical and practical reasons, they resist most forms of experimental and laboratory study. Research on intimate relationships relies heavily on self-report surveys and is vulnerable to the kinds of problems inherent in such data; for example, people misremembering information or trying to "look good."

The last two decades have witnessed an explosion of psychological research in personal relationships. Most treatments of close personal relationships in gender texts concentrate on only love and marital relationships, with occasional portrayals of motherhood. The present chapter brings together research from psychology and numerous related areas to represent the rich variety of intimate relationships that men and women have: romantic love, dating, and marriage relationships, to be sure, but also other vital relationships such as cohabitation, friendships, and caretaking. First, we will discuss dating and marital

relationships, with a focus on heterosexual couples. Next, we will consider gay marriage. We will also consider conflict in marriage, cohabiting, and relationship dissolution and divorce.

Family relationships, with a particular focus on what it means to be a female in a family, comprise our next major section. In our final section, we consider the research on other important personal relationships in the lives of women and men that are too often overlooked in treatments of intimacy: friendships and caretaking relationships. Throughout our discussion on close relationships, we braid together issues of race, ethnicity, culture, and social class and call for more and better research on the diverse experiences of women and men in intimate relationships.

LOVE

Who Dates Whom, and Why?

Who dates whom? Why do people date? What are the implications of dating patterns for sexual and marital relationships?

Theories about becoming a couple or *pair bonding* in dating, romantic, and sexual relationships can be classified into four basic categories. The first focuses on the importance of *physical attraction* on the partnering process (Feingold, 1991). Physical attractiveness is a key determinant of interpersonal attraction to both sexes, although, as we will discuss shortly, there are important sex differences between women and men in the relative importance of physical attractiveness. Some of the work on the importance of attractiveness attempts to explain the consistent finding, among both dating and married couples, that the physical attractiveness of partners is moderately positively correlated (about 0.50) (Laumann et al., 1994): We tend to date people who are roughly as attractive as we are. As Laumann et al. explain, this finding may indicate that people intentionally choose partners similar in attractiveness to themselves. Alternatively, as Kalick and Hamilton (1986) suggest, this finding may also result from people choosing the most attractive partner available, with those who are most attractive choosing each other early on and dropping out of the market.

As we have discussed in Chapter 8, both evolutionary and social learning theories predict sex differences in the importance placed on physical attractiveness in prospective mates by women and men. In an influential survey of the characteristics considered important in prospective partners for sexual and meaningful relationships, Nevid (1984) found that men were much more likely than women to emphasize physical attributes such as figure and facial features for both short- and long-term relationships, especially for short-term sexual relationships. Women reported valuing warmth, assertiveness, wit, ambition, and earning power more than physical traits. But both men and women rated attributes of personality and character as more important than physical characteristics when considering what was important in long-term, meaningful relationships, and the single most important trait overall was honesty.

This is not to say that women are uninterested in men's physical attributes. For example, both women and men perceive short stature as a liability, but women consider tallness a more important attribute in a prospective mate than men do (Jackson & Ervin, 1992). Both women and men find slenderness in potential partners attractive, although slenderness is particularly valued for females (Rozin & Fallon, 1988).

Nevid's findings have been replicated many times and in a variety of contexts. Rathus, Nevid, and Fichner-Rathus (2002) summarize the literature on the importance of physical attractiveness for both sexes this way:

> *Although personal qualities may assume more prominent roles in determining partner preferences in long-term relationships, physical appeal probably plays a "filtering role." Unless a prospective date meets minimal physical standards, we might not look beneath the surface for "more meaningful" traits. (p. 212)*

A second approach to understanding how people select partners focuses on the importance of *similarity* in certain social attributes, such as race, religion, age, and education level. There are several reasons why people may seek similar others or "matches." People may be better able to communicate with those with whom they share cultural backgrounds, tastes, interests, and attitudes. They may view interactions with similar others as more validating and gratifying (DiMaggio & Mohr, 1985). Moreover, people may be stigmatized and punished by friends, family, and the larger society for dating outside of their ethnic, racial, religious, and class groups. Expectations of disapproval by others can serve as a powerful disincentive for romantic involvement with people outside of one's group (Cappella & Palmer, 1990; Parks, Stan, & Eggert, 1983). In fact, recent evidence indicates that even among sexual partners who are unmarried and noncohabiting, there is a strong tendency for people to seek out similar others, especially with respect to race and ethnicity, and for certain groups—Catholics and evangelical Protestants, for example—religion as well. Here again there is a sex difference, with attitudinal similarity being a more important factor in attraction for women than for men (Feingold, 1991).

The third approach to explaining how romantic partnerships are formed construes relationships as a *form of exchange,* in which people pursue those partnerships in which they can strike the best deal for themselves and get the greatest return on their assets. Exchange theory neatly explains the traditional pattern of a woman when selecting a prospective husband, exchanging her attractiveness and homemaking skills for a man's earning potential. Thus, exchange theory stands as one explanation for the consistent research finding that women tend to marry men who are more educated than they are, even after taking into account sex differences in educational attainment (Laumann et al., 1994). Exchange theory is often invoked to explain the consistent patterns of seeking and offering traits found in studies of personal advertisements, in which heterosexual men offer financial security in exchange for women's youth and beauty, and vice versa (Davis, 1990; Deaux & Hanna, 1984). (See Box 9.1.) A key motive for seeking matches seems to be fear of rejection by more attractive partners. So strong is the notion of exchange in relationships that when people see a couple who are mismatched on a salient characteristic, such as physical attractiveness, they often assume that the less attractive partner has compensating features that even out the exchange. Thus, Bar-Tal and Saxe (1976) found that people judging mismatched pairs in which

Box 9.1

Desperately Seeking . . . or Not . . .

Much information as to what women and men seek in a partner is revealed in a look at personal advertisements. Personals written by women and men are surprisingly similar, and both women and men tend to request a partner who is sensitive, warm, or romantic. However, men are more likely to seek physical attractiveness in a partner (Koestner & Wheeler, 1988). This is consistent with findings that men seeking partners are more motivated by the possibility of sexual activity (Peplau, Rubin, & Hill, 1977; Roscoe, Diana, & Brooks, 1987). Men are also more likely than women to describe their own financial status in an ad, whereas women are more likely to include financial status of a possible partner among their specifications (Goode, 1996; Koestner & Wheeler, 1988). In a study examining mate preferences at various stages of relational in-

volvement, it was established that men favored mates higher in physical attractiveness than themselves. Alternatively, women preferred mates who surpassed them in income, education, self-confidence, intelligence, dominance, and social position (Buunk, 2002). Results from a study investigating mate selection in Taiwan demonstrated that females emphasized the earning potential of a spouse more than males did, whereas males focused more on youthfulness and physical attractiveness. Furthermore, the study revealed that in terms of the Big Five (the Big Five personality factors—openness, conscientiousness, extraversion, agreeableness, neuroticism), females valued conscientiousness most in men, whereas men valued agreeableness most in women (Chuang, 2002). The following personal ads have been modified from a newspaper in a large metropolitan area.

WOMEN

Sexy and Strikingly Attractive Woman, 33, two children. Affectionate, funny, vivacious. Interests include opera, art museums, literature. Seeks single man, 35–45, financially secure, professional, to share romantic possibilities.

Head-Turning Blonde Cute, shapely young lady, 20s, enjoy fitness and the arts. My man is educated, generous, stylish, and very accomplished CEO, investment banker, or lawyer in his 30s or 40s. We will enjoy friendship and romance together, and possibly children.

MEN

Self-Made Millionaire Male, 48, Harvard MBA, successful entrepreneur. Interested in mountain biking, travel, dining out, and exercise. Seeks attractive, slim (110 lb or less), physically fit female with good sense of humor and common interests.

Manhattan MD 36, 6′, 200 lb, good-looking athletic male. Loves being spontaneous, the outdoors, good books, and good company. Seeks bright, beautiful, blond female in her 20s without kids. Missing that special person to share life with.

the woman was much more physically attractive than the man ascribed greater wealth, success, or intelligence to the man.

Finally, the principle of reciprocity has been advanced to explain interpersonal attraction. When we feel liked, admired, or loved, we tend to return those feelings. There is a wealth of data in social psychology suggesting that we like people who like us, that we are kind and warm and trusting with people when we believe that they like us, and that one of the most

efficient ways of inducing others to like us is to let them know that we like them. The power of reciprocal liking may play a large role in the initiation and maintenance of love relationships. Knowing that someone is attracted to us can help move us from a neutral to a more positive stance toward someone. And reciprocating loving words or actions can stoke sparks into flames (Rathus et al., 2002).

One might expect a woman or man seeking a romantic partner to want a strongly gender-typed individual. This will depend on how strongly one identifies with one's own traditional gender role, however. "Hyperfeminine" women tend to prefer "macho" men who approach sexuality more aggressively. This may be due to the idea that hyperfeminine women deem that their success is established by maintaining romantic relationships with men and that their sexuality can be used to sustain these relationships. Conversely, women who were less hyperfeminine did not express this preference (Maybach & Gold, 1994). Whereas nontraditional college-aged men preferred androgynous females, traditional college-aged men expressed an equal preference for androgynous and stereotypically feminine females (Orlofsky, 1982). With regard to expressiveness in relationships, one study showed that male undergraduates preferred more androgynous partners first and highly expressive female types second when given the option (Greene, 1994b).

As interesting as the theories of interpersonal attraction may be, none fully explains attraction, let alone something as elusive as love. They tend to exaggerate the extent of individual choice and ignore the actual social processes by which real-world relationships are initiated and maintained. We do not pick people off a shelf as we do sweaters. Instead of selecting partners from the world at large according to our own criteria, we are limited to those with whom we come in contact. The findings of Laumann et al.'s survey (1994) suggest that in the case of dating relationships that end in marriage, almost 50 percent of people report meeting their partners through friends and family members, with another third reporting self-introductions as the source of contact. In the case of short-term sexual relationships, family members were much less likely to introduce the couple, and self-introductions accounted for almost half of all cases. Thus, relationships that lead to marriages, cohabitations, and other long-term partnerships are more likely to begin at school, work, and places of worship, whereas those that end in short-term sexual pairings more often begin at private parties and bars. These and other survey findings raise more questions than they answer about how people meet and fall in love. But they do suggest that our choices of dating and sexual partners are actually

quite constrained, and the social context in which an introduction occurs is an important predictor of the course of a romantic relationship.

What's Love Got to Do with It?

Romantic Love as the Basis of Relationships.   Our culture recognizes many kinds or styles of love, but the notion of romantic love, distinct from companionate love or lust, is a powerful one in Western culture. For all of our familiarity with the concept, **romantic love** is difficult to define. It is generally understood as strong physiological or sexual arousal paired with an idealized image of the beloved. Although most societies throughout history show evidence for the existence of romantic love, its centrality in Western culture, particularly contemporary Western culture, is hard to overestimate (Brehm, Miller, Perlman, & Campbell, 2002). In one survey, over 80 percent of U.S. college women and men report believing that being in love is a prerequisite for marriage (Berscheid, 1988). In a more recent cross-cultural survey, less than 4 percent of U.S. college students said that they would marry a person they did not love even if she or he had all of the other attributes they desired, whereas nearly 50 percent of the students from India and Pakistan said that they would marry such a person, as did nearly 20 percent of the Thai college students (Hatfield & Rapson, 1996). In traditional Chinese culture, feelings of love and compatibility are less important than pleasing one's parents in choosing a spouse (Pimental, 2000).

Not only is love the basis for marriage in our culture, but it also justifies extramarital affairs in the eyes of both women and men, and the lack or loss of love is seen as just cause for divorce (Glass & Wright, 1992). Romantic love provides the theme for much of our great art and literature and for most forms of popular entertainment. Concepts of romantic love are introduced to young children in Western countries by means of fairy tales, myths, and legends that explain and give meaning to human experience. Cinderella, Sleeping Beauty, Beauty and the Beast, and numerous other fairy tales are powerful showcases for romance stories. Later, in adolescence and adulthood, countless books, songs, movies, and advertisements embody romantic notions of heterosexual relationships. Indeed, "love makes the world go 'round."

Romantic love is a powerful concept for both men and women. Over 95 percent of both U.S. women and men, for example, report in nationwide surveys that romantic love is important to them (Janus & Janus, 1993). And, as we shall see, the question of which sex is the more "romantic" is far from settled and depends on specific definitions and various components of romance, as well as the stage of the relationship (Rathus et al., 2002). But romantic love is a very gendered concept in the sense that it has quite different meanings and consequences for girls and boys, women and men.

> For men, the cultural story-to-live-by is the hero legend. For women, it is the romance story. . . . On entering adult society, men must sacrifice intimacy, emotional vulnerability, and community. Women must sacrifice their public life, voice, and power, as well as their trust in other women. As children, we take in these stories as important prescriptions for our lives. Eager to learn how to live in the world, children grab hold of these stories as guides and as a balm that soothes the pain of the sacrifices made to fit into Western culture. (Debold, Wilson, & Malave, 1993, p. 66)

The representations of boys and girls in the "stories we live by" differ sharply. Boys and men are invariably the heroes of myth and legend. Theirs is the world of action and adventure. For their sacrifices, courage, daring, and lack of emotional connectedness, they are rewarded with "the run of the place"— entitlement to act as they please in the public world and in their private worlds to have access to and power over the most beautiful and virtuous women. As Debold et al. (1993) point out, women fit into only one chapter of the hero story: the romance story. As long as women are young, pretty, sweet, and innocent enough, they are the heroes' reward for bravery and sacrifice. The romance story in its various guises encourages girls and women to put their ambitions and hopes into the narrow search for the perfect relationship. In this way, they learn to look outside themselves—to boys and men and, later, their children—for their deepest fulfillment, to confuse sexual desire with love, and to equate finding a

mate with securing a rosy economic future: "living happily ever after." The romance story even encourages women to view relationship violence, extreme jealousy and possessiveness, and other oppressive aspects of gender relations, as more tolerable. It should not be surprising that the romance story—the notion that love defines a woman's existence—has profound effects on heterosexual dating, cohabiting, and marital relationships.

Several scholars have remarked on how society writes the script for girls and boys and young women and men in their dating behavior. For example, it falls to males to ask for the date, arrange the transportation, plan the activities, pay for the date, and initiate any sexual activity. Girls and women are the gatekeepers of activities: They respond to male initiatives. Although gender-associated beliefs have become less conventional, it has been shown that the initial dating practices of college students remain traditional. Laner (2000) found that traditional scripts for women and men are well known to today's college students, which makes the arrangements of first dates very predictable. In addition, advice from current dating guides emphasizes "appropriate behaviors" for both women and men. Lest readers think that dating scripts have changed much since the sexual revolution, they should read *The Rules,* a mid-1990s restatement of the traditional dating script (Box 9.2).

One might expect, intuitively, that because lesbians are not in romantic relationships with men, the importance of standard appearance is lessened. This is not always the case, however; lesbians are often reared by and work with heterosexuals and are thus socialized to place a high premium on their physical appearance. The pressures on women to be beautiful are many (Rothblum, 1994). So although lesbians may not be competing for men's attentions, the fact that they are often not "out" means that they face many of the pressures to present themselves in ways that are appealing to men (Rothblum, 1994).

Falling in Love

If women are culturally scripted to be the more romantic ones in a heterosexual relationship, are they more likely to fall in love than men and to hold

BOX 9.2

Do You Follow *The Rules?*

Don't meet him halfway or go Dutch on a date.

Don't open up too fast.

Don't call him and rarely return his calls.

Don't expect a man to change or try to change him.

So begins a best-selling book in the mid-1990s, *The Rules: Time-Tested Secrets for Capturing the Heart of Mr. Right,* by Ellen Fein and Sherrie Schneider (Fein & Schneider, 1995). *The Rules* are 35 prescriptions for attracting and marrying the right kind of man. As the authors admit, *The Rules* may sound familiar—indeed, you may have heard them from your grandmothers— but, according to the authors, that does not mean that they are ineffective in helping to form committed relationships in the modern age. *The Rules* operate on the principle that women are more desirable when they play "hard to get." Thus, women are cautioned not to accept dates for Saturday after Wednesday, to end phone calls and dates first, to be mysterious, aloof, and unavailable. This notion that we value people and

things more when we "suffer" for them is a basic tenet of cognitive dissonance theory (Festinger, 1957) in social psychology. Cognitive dissonance theory holds that we act to reduce the discomfort (dissonance) we feel when two of our thoughts (cognitions) are inconsistent by changing one of our thoughts. When someone acts in a cool way toward us, or is hard to attract, we often come to feel that they must be worth the trouble. Evolutionary theory is another theoretical pillar of *The Rules,* because it suggests that it is in men's deepest biological interest to pursue many women, whereas it is in women's interest to be coy and selective.

The Rules caused quite a stir when it was published, with some feminist thinkers protesting their sexist assumptions. And it inspired other critiques, parodies, and sequels, for example, *The Sistah's Rules: Secrets for Meeting, Getting, and Keeping a Good Black Man* (Millner, 1997) and *The Real Rules: How to Find the Right Man for the Real You* (De'Angelis, 1997). The authors wrote a sequel to the book in 1997 entitled *The Rules 2: More Rules to Live and Love By* (Fein & Schneider, 1997).

romantic notions about true love overcoming obstacles and lasting forever? It depends. At least in the early stages of dating, men are quicker to fall in love and express more attraction to and passion for their partners (Hatfield & Sprecher, 1986; Hill, Peplau, & Rubin, 1981). Moreover, men are more likely than women to subscribe to romantic ideals such as the idea that true love lasts forever and can overcome obstacles such as race and class. However, some evidence exists that these sex differences level off as the relationship progresses (Hatfield & Sprecher, 1986), and, in fact, women may become more emotionally involved than men over time. Women report more emotional reactions to falling in love, such as the inability to concentrate, than men do (Peplau & Gordon, 1985). In a nationwide survey, slightly more single men than women described themselves as romantic, whereas among married respondents, more women than men self-identified as romantic (Janus

& Janus, 1993). Women are more likely than men to initiate breakups, and men are more likely than women to report depression after breakups.

How can we explain these disparate findings about women's and men's romanticism? Peplau and Gordon (1985) offer some possible reasons. Men, more than women, depend on physical attributes in forming attractions, and these can be quickly determined. Women may be more cautious in falling in love because they have to take a more pragmatic orientation to relationships. Traditionally, in choosing a mate, a woman was also choosing her social class and other life circumstances. That may be less true today than it was in the past, but even today, women have more at stake in sexual relationships than men do and may feel more pressure to define their feelings as love, at least after the relationship has become sexual. Moreover, women are permitted the expression of a wider range of most emotions than men, and it is more socially acceptable for women than men to disclose the emotional symptoms of love.

Some psychologists have offered theories of different styles or components of love. Thus, Hendrick and Hendrick (1986) developed a love-attitude scale that measures six distinct styles of love: romantic, game playing, friendship, logical, possessive/excited, and selfless love. They have found that, at least among college students, most people in love experience several of these styles simultaneously. However, women and men differ somewhat in their dominant styles of love. College men more often reported romantic (idealized) and game-playing (uncommitted) styles, whereas college women more often reported friendly, logical (practical), and committed styles. Another theory of love offered by Robert Sternberg (1988) suggests that love consists of three components: passion, intimacy, and decision/commitment. He predicts that different combinations of these three components result in different kinds of love. For example, he defines romantic love as an experience characterized by passion and intimacy, but without the decision/commitment component. Consummate love, on the other hand, is the complete measure of love and involves the combination of all three components. Partners are well suited to each other to the extent that their "triangles" are congruent. Sternberg has developed a scale to measure the three components of love (see Box 9.3). How useful are these theories in explaining romantic love? Research evidence in support of these theories to date is somewhat mixed, and it is clear that we need more study of ongoing love relationships.

Communication and Conflict in Relationships

Once the relationship between a woman and a man has progressed, more gender differences become apparent. For example, although the actual amount of self-disclosure that takes place is about equal, women *prefer* to reveal more personal information than men do (Cozby, 1973; Morton, 1978). This phenomenon may be culture bound, however; studies of Chinese Americans do not find these gender differences in self-disclosure (Wheeler, Reis, & Bond, 1989). Interestingly, both women and men are more comfortable

revealing themselves to a woman than to a man (Derlega, Winstead, Wong, & Hunter, 1985).

When conflicts arise, women and men tend to communicate differently. Consistent with traditional gender roles, men urge women to "calm down," whereas women wish men would "warm up," a situation that can eventually jeopardize the couple's relationship if it becomes a regular pattern (Levenson & Gottman, 1985). Women and men's modes of verbal expression reflect this (Tannen, 1990). In order to be satisfied with the relationship, couples need the ability to appreciate the other partner's perspective (Long & Andrews, 1990). Conflict has the potential to break up a relationship but can also strengthen it and increase the partners' commitment to each other. Withdrawal during arguments in relationships (by either or both partners) is linked with negativity and a lack of positive bonds in relationships.

Lesbian relationships progress along similar developmental lines, with the initial idealizing period, in which only the partner's positive qualities are perceived. With same-sex couples, however, this idealizing period may persist as many women may fantasize that their gender similarities preclude any differences that may exist (Greene, 1994b). This idealized period is followed by the introduction of reality-based concerns such as finding ways of dealing with conflict and power struggles (Kurdek, 1994). Lack of support from the larger society means that lesbians in unsatisfactory relationships have fewer resources available when they need them the most (Greene, 1994b). Finally, lesbian couples settle into trust-based relationships in which each party balances autonomy yearnings with her commitment to the relationship (McWhirter & Mattison, 1984, cited in Kurdek, 1994).

MARRIAGE

Despite regular laments about the decline of the family in recent years, adults in the United States and elsewhere overwhelmingly continue to form long-term social and sexual relationships. Most recent statistics suggest that by age 30 almost 85 percent of U.S. women and 70 percent of U.S. men have formed a stable two-person partnership, either through marriage

BOX 9.3

Sternberg's Triangular Love Scale

According to psychologist Robert Sternberg (1988), all kinds of love relationships can be conceptualized as a mix of three elements: intimacy, passion, and commitment. He represents his model as a triangle with intimacy, passion, and commitment as the vertices of the triangle, with the shape of the triangle determined by the way the elements are balanced. Different kinds of love involve varying degrees of these elements. For example, maternal love is a mixture of commitment and intimacy, whereas romantic love consists of passion and intimacy. What Sternberg calls consummate love, the highest and most desired form of love, is represented as an equilateral triangle, the "perfect balance" of all three elements.

How do you know the combination of elements that describes your love relationship? Take Sternberg's *Triangular Love Scale* and consult the scoring key.

TRIANGULAR LOVE SCALE

Instructions: To complete the following scale, fill in the blank spaces with the name of one person you love or care about deeply. Then rate your agreement with each of the items by using a nine-point scale in which 1 = "not at all," 5 = "moderately," and 9 = "extremely." Use a point in between to indicate intermediate levels of agreement between these values.

Intimacy Component

_____ 1. I am actively supportive of _____'s well-being.
_____ 2. I have a warm relationship with _____.
_____ 3. I am able to count on _____ in times of need.
_____ 4. _____ is able to count on me in times of need.
_____ 5. I am willing to share myself and my possessions with _____.
_____ 6. I receive considerable emotional support from _____.
_____ 7. I give considerable emotional support to _____.
_____ 8. I communicate well with _____.
_____ 9. I value _____ greatly in my life.
_____ 10. I feel close to _____.

_____ 11. I have a comfortable relationship with _____.
_____ 12. I feel that I really understand _____.
_____ 13. I feel that _____ really understands me.
_____ 14. I feel that I can really trust _____.
_____ 15. I share deeply personal information about myself with _____.

Passion Component

_____ 16. Just seeing _____ excites me.
_____ 17. I find myself thinking about _____ frequently during the day.
_____ 18. My relationship with _____ is very romantic.
_____ 19. I find _____ to be very personally attractive.
_____ 20. I idealize _____.
_____ 21. I cannot imagine another person making me as happy as _____ does.
_____ 22. I would rather be with _____ than anyone else.
_____ 23. There is nothing more important to me than my relationship with _____.
_____ 24. I especially like physical contact with _____.
_____ 25. There is something almost "magical" about my relationship with _____.
_____ 26. I adore _____.
_____ 27. I cannot imagine life without _____.
_____ 28. My relationship with _____ is passionate.
_____ 29. When I see romantic movies and read romantic books I think of _____.
_____ 30. I fantasize about _____.

Decision/Commitment Component

_____ 31. I know that I care about _____.
_____ 32. I am committed to maintaining my relationship with _____.
_____ 33. Because of my commitment to _____, I wouldn't let other people come between us.
_____ 34. I have confidence in the stability of my relationship with _____.
_____ 35. I could not let anything get in the way of my commitment to _____.
_____ 36. I expect my love for _____ to last for the rest of my life.

_____ 37. I will always feel a strong responsibility for _____.

_____ 38. I view my commitment to _____ as a solid one.

_____ 39. I cannot imagine ending my relationship with _____.

_____ 40. I am certain of my love for _____.

_____ 41. I view my relationship with _____ as permanent.

_____ 42. I view my relationship with _____ as a good decision.

_____ 43. I feel a sense of responsibility toward _____.

_____ 44. I plan to continue my relationship with _____.

_____ 45. Even when _____ is hard to deal with, I remain committed to our relationship.

Source: From "Triangulating Love," by R. J. Sternberg, in *The Psychology of Love* (pp. 119–138), edited by R. J. Sternberg and M. L. Barnes, 1988. New Haven, CT: Yale University Press. Copyright 1988 by Robert Sternberg. Reprinted with permission.

---

or cohabitation (Laumann et al., 1994; Barber & Axinn, 1998). By the time they turn 40, 93 percent of women and 90 percent of men in the United States marry at least once (Kammeyer, 1990). Nonetheless, as several scholars have recently noted, the U.S. family has changed more in the last 50 years than in the previous 250. Many of these changes are attributable to changing patterns of marriage and divorce, particularly since World War II, and the sexual revolution of the 1960s and 1970s (Blumstein & Schwartz, 1983). Since the 1960s, we have witnessed a fall in the rate of marriage and a rise in the average age of first marriage, an increase in the rate of divorce, a decrease in fertility, and an increase in the rate of cohabitation. These social trends have enormous implications for the meaning of marriage and family today.

As we have noted, both women and men ascribe to our society's notions of romantic love and say that they marry for love. But marriage generally and the wedding day in particular are idealized for women in ways that they are not for men. In the cultural "story-to-live-by," the wedding day is the goal, the mark of success, and the end of story for girls. Like the princess of myth and fairy tale, great emphasis is placed on brides and brides-to-be in our society, as in most others as well, with grooms playing decidedly subordinate roles. It is to brides that all attention is turned. Advertisers pitch their appeals to brides in the many successful magazines targeted specifically to them. (A magazine aimed at grooms in the early 1990s produced a single, obviously unsuccessful,

issue.) Indeed, in most households of all social classes, the wedding validates an enormous expenditure by the bride and her family that is rarely exceeded by any other purchase over a lifetime except a house and, for many, a college education.

As Debold et al. (1993) note, few stories are ever written about the princess after the wedding day. They write:

Reading between the lines of other stories, we can sketch out her "happily ever after": The princess gets pregnant and hopes for sons. As long as she is faithful and bears sons, she is considered to be a good wife. We don't hear whether or not she's a good mother, unless something goes wrong with her children. She's safe and cared for in the castle. Occasionally, something might be written about the good deeds she performed, acts of charity and the like. But by and large, she's not heard from again. (p. 64)

Why Do People Marry?

In the United States today, as in the past, romantic love is the basis of marriage. As Blumstein and Schwartz (1983) note in the introduction to their volume on the U.S. couple:

Marry someone handsome and wealthy and you will be congratulated, but say that you are not in love with that person and your cynicism will earn you the censure of all around you. At the same time it is clear that people accrue great benefits by the marriages they contract. "Marrying up" is applauded as long as one

does not consciously admit to having made this the
foundation for choosing a mate. We, as a people, still
firmly believe that arranged marriages and marriages
of convenience, are un-American. (p. 28)

It is often noted that marriage is both a personal relationship with individualized characteristics and a universal institution that is highly culturally scripted. On the personal level, marriages serve deep emotional needs for sex, companionship, intimacy, and security, and strong practical needs for tangible benefits such as financial support, housekeeping, and child care. On the cultural or societal level, marriages serve many critical functions as well, including the legitimization and restriction of sexual relationships and the provision of economic responsibility for children, the maintenance of stable family life, and the orderly transmission of property and wealth from one generation to another (Rathus et al., 2002). Of course, it is often noted that most married people most of the time do not conceive of themselves as "living in an institution" subject to laws about their marital rights and responsibilities, but rather as making a unique relationship as they go along. The culturally scripted, prescribed nature of marriage tends to come to the fore during relatively unusual circumstances, as when we need medical or legal assistance, for instance, during marital separations, divorces, serious injuries, and deaths. Marriage, with its substantial privileges, is not legally permissible for people seeking same-sex unions. But, as we write in 2004, laws regarding gay marriage are changing rapidly. And, as we shall see shortly, the institution of marriage prescribes certain roles for husbands and wives.

When Marriage Takes Place, Who Marries, and Who Marries Whom?

When Does Marriage Take Place?   As noted earlier, most people in the United States, as in Western nations generally, do get married: Recent trends suggest that between 70 and 80 percent of people in the United States will eventually marry at least once (Rathus et al., 2002). These high percentages suggest the durability of marriage as an institution at the same time that they mask important changes in how and

when people enter marriage and large differences in the rates of marriage of people of different races and ethnicities. For example, in 1963, 83 percent of American women aged 25 to 55 were married, compared with about 65 percent today (Edwards, 2000).

Throughout the West, there has been a dramatic increase in the age of first marriage among men and women in the last 35 years, so that singlehood, not marriage, is now the most common lifestyle for people in their early twenties. The percentage of single people in their late twenties and early thirties has more than doubled since 1970 (Edwards, 2000). The median age of first marriage for women is 25 years, and for men, 26.7 years, up more than 3 years for men and 4 years for women since 1970 (U.S. Census Bureau, 1998c). Canadian women and men marry at later ages than their U.S. counterparts (Statistics Canada, 2000). Several factors may explain this shift. Men and especially women are attending college in increasing numbers, and the pursuit of education has traditionally postponed marriage. Women's increased career opportunities and financial independence allow them to be self-sufficient, and the need to "find a man to take care of you" financially is obsolete. Today's more permissive attitudes make sex more available for the single woman or man, and allow couples to postpone commitment by living together without officially marrying. In recent years, over 50 percent of all people reported living with a partner before marrying, compared with only 11 percent in 1970 (Smock, 2000). In addition, the availability of contraceptives, as well as the growing awareness and acceptance of single motherhood as an option, decrease the likelihood of an unexpected pregnancy forcing a "shotgun wedding." Relatively stagnant wages and high unemployment along with high prices for housing have made it hard for young couples to have formal weddings, set up housekeeping, and start families. Finally, knowledge of the increase in the divorce rate may also play a role, causing young women and men to think twice before accepting the risks involved with marriage.

In the United States, race and ethnicity are important predictors of marriage rates. It is a consistent research finding, for example, that African American women are less likely than White women to marry. There are several possible reasons for this racial disparity, many rooted in economic conditions related to racism and discrimination in the United States. It is often noted that there is a shortage of "marriageable" African American men for African American women to marry, contributing to what has been called a "marriage squeeze" for African American women. This shortage is due largely to structural factors such as relatively high rates of migration, incarceration, unemployment, poverty, and interracial marriage among African American men in the United States (McLauglin & Lichter, 1997), and to patterns of educational attainment among Blacks in which women are more highly educated than men, reversing the usual sex difference in educational levels. (Increasingly, women of all ethnic groups are becoming more educated than men, as we discuss in Chapter 6). Traditionally, marriage has not afforded Black women the same economic and social benefits that it has conferred on White women. Moreover, having children and primary romantic relationships outside marriage has not carried with it the same stigma in African American communities that it has, at least until recently, in White communities. This suggests that the relatively low rate of marriages among African American couples is not rooted in lack of interest in forming nuclear families, but rather in the nexus of political, economic, and social forces that make it difficult to support families adequately. Marriage rates for Asian and Latina women are comparable to rates for White women (U.S. Census Bureau, 2000).

What are some of the implications of these new trends? For example, are single people happier than married people? According to a study by Wu and Demaris (1996), they are not. Unmarried women and men and married women report higher depressive symptoms than do married men. However, married women were found to be happier than unmarried women. Clearly, although singles may be put off from marriage by the rising divorce rate, this decision is not necessarily optimal for their happiness. This is not to suggest that marriage is the cause of happiness. It was once believed that never-married individuals had lower self-esteem than married individuals. However, a recent study indicated higher self-esteem

scores for never-married individuals, which may reflect the idea that not marrying has become more socially acceptable. In addition, research shows that social support from friends and family not only facilitates adjustment to a single way of life but also contributes to this adjustment by strengthening and endorsing positive self-esteem (Fahrenkamp, 2001). Men and women choosing to remain single are experiencing a great deal more happiness than they have in the past. It is important for society to recognize that remaining single can be a healthy life option for many people and that an unmarried status is acceptable (Barile, 2001).

Staying single longer has ramifications for gender-role behavior. Women who stay single longer are more able to grow as individuals and move ahead in their careers, acquiring more education and greater financial independence. These women are likely to be more assertive and to possess means of finding fulfillment outside of marriage. Men who have lived alone, on the other hand, are likely to be more domestic and to have developed friendships with other women and men, which might have been precluded by marriage. This may account for part of the general shift in society from prescribed gender-role identities to more androgynous modes of being (Vannoy, 1991).

Who Marries, and Who Marries Whom? It should come as no surprise that people marry others similar to themselves on important characteristics. After all, people are attracted to and date similar others. Given the obvious importance of practical matters in a lifelong partnership, there are several key categories within which people seek others like themselves.

The notion of like marrying similar others, called **homogamy,** extends to physical and psychological characteristics, but is especially dramatic with respect to demographic characteristics. In over 99 percent of cases, people marry within their own race (U. S. Census Bureau, 1998b), although intermarriage rates vary within different ethnic groups and by sex. For instance, Asians, especially Asian women, have relatively high rates of intermarriage, whereas White men have relatively low rates. Black men are more likely to marry outside their race than are Black women, and Hispanic women are more likely to intermarry than are Hispanic men (Laumann et al., 1994; U.S. Census Bureau, 1998b). Over 90 percent of the people in the United States marry within their own religion, although, again, rates vary within subgroups (Berger, 1988; Laumann et al., 1994). In our culture as in other Western cultures, people tend to marry others within their social class and general geographic location (Ember & Ember, 1990). We also tend to marry people within our age range, at least for first marriages. On the average, men tend to be two to five years older than their wives in the first marriage (Buss, 1988). In later marriages, the age gap between men and women widens.

Aside from demographic characteristics, we marry people who resemble us in height, personality traits, attitudes, intelligence, overall physical attractiveness, and even specific physical characteristics such as the thickness of the lips. Opposites may attract, but in dating and especially marriage patterns, birds of a feather flock together. There are exceptions to this rule, of course, and one of the most common is known as the **marriage gradient.** This refers to the tendency for men to *marry down* in age and social and economic class, and for women to *marry up* on these factors. Thus, it is not uncommon to see a male boss marry his female secretary, but the opposite scenario is less likely. As we have seen, the marriage gradient is well explained by **exchange theory,** which suggests that men exchange their socioeconomic resources for women's youth and physical attractiveness.

Why do we seek similarity so pervasively in our marital relationships? People who are similar to us in background, experience, and general appearance are more likely than others to share our interests, values, attitudes, and goals. Indeed, happily married couples frequently cite these areas of similarity as the reason for the success of their marriages (Lauer, 1985). Couples who are similar to each other may experience less conflict over the kinds of things that couples fight about: rearing children, religion, and money, to name a few. We should not assume, however, that similarity guarantees happiness or that dissimilar couples are doomed to be unhappy. Dissimilar couples can and do work to resolve the issues that divide them, developing shared interests and goals and creating in their

households respect for diversity and richness of experience. Increasingly, people, especially young people, are crossing the borders of race, ethnicity, and religion in their formation of love relationships. For example, Knox and his colleagues have found that college students are increasingly dating people of other races, with about one-quarter having already done so, and nearly half of all students expressing a willingness to become involved in an interracial relationship (Knox et al., 1997). Given these trends, marriage across frontiers is bound to increase. Indeed, there is evidence that this is already happening across the variables of religion and ethnicity. Recent evidence suggests that intermarriage is most acceptable among college-educated, middle-class people, and that in most interracial marriages, the educational level of the two parties is simliar (Jacobs & Labov, 2002).

Types of Marriages

The social institution of marriage evolves with the times and has changed perceptibly in recent years. In the past, when traditional gender roles were more prominent, marriages were symbiotic in the sense that women provided expressiveness and men provided instrumentality. In this way, each needed the other in order to experience the full spectrum of human emotions. With the advent of women in the workplace, however, both partners now play an instrumental role. As such, a more ideal framework for contemporary marriage would be the mutual marriage, whereby each spouse provides both instrumentality and nurturance (Vannoy, 1991). As we have noted, marriages have universal and unique elements that make them at once like all other marriages and like no other marriages. Obviously, marriages can also be classified into particular types. One common way to classify marriages is according to how conventional or traditional they are, based on the division of power in the marriage, how wives' and husbands' roles are defined, and the quality of the relationship between the spouses (Brown & Amatea, 2000; Peplau & Gordon, 1985; Scanzoni & Scanzoni, 1976).

In **traditional marriages,** the husband is the dominant partner and the wife submissive. The husband is better educated than his wife, his source of income is the sole source of money for the family, and his career dictates where the family lives. The roles for the husband and wife are specific and rigid: For instance, the husband initiates sexual activity and makes major purchasing decisions, whereas the wife takes care of the children and the house. In traditional marriages, the couple does not live together before marriage, and the wife takes on the husband's last name. The emphasis in such relationships is on ritual traditional roles rather than friendship and shared interests. Husbands' friends are male peers; wives' are other women. Husbands and wives do not often socialize or share leisure interests together.

Traditional marriages have been in decline over the past three decades, largely because of economic conditions, which have meant that most women must work to help support the family, and the women's movement of the 1970s, which challenged traditional roles for women. But traditional marriages as defined by a working-for-pay husband and a stay-at-home wife are by no means a thing of the past. According to surveys, the percentage of households in which women stay at home while their husbands support the family stands at about 16 percent (Hochschild, 1989; Jacobs & Gerson, 2001). This situation, while increasingly uncommon, continues to represent the ideal family scenario for some couples. The form of traditional marriage varies by class and ethnicity, although the stereotype of this type of marriage is probably a working-class couple with fixed views of gender roles. But traditional marriages are found in every social class and among all ethnic groups.

Modern marriages have been characterized as "senior partner–junior partner" relationships (Brown & Amatea, 2000). This captures the notion that the wives and husbands are almost equals in most respects, but in important matters, such as whose career will be given priority or who will make a major family decision, the husband's will predominates. Marital roles are not so rigidly prescribed in modern marriages: Wives often do work outside the home, but their income is less central to the household and their careers are often interrupted for child rearing. The emphasis in relationships is on companionship and sharing leisure activities; husbands and wives in modern marriages often describe themselves as "best friends."

Many marriages of dual-career couples today can probably be characterized as modern marriages and, at a glance, they appear reasonably equal and fair. But, as we will soon see, studies of dual-earner couples find that, even when women work full time outside of the home, husbands do not adjust their work around the house or with the children accordingly (Hochschild, 1989; Jacobs & Gerson, 2001).

Finally, in **egalitarian marriages** the husband and wife are partners in the truest sense of the term. Neither spouse is dominant or submissive; education is considered equally important for both spouses; the breadwinning role is shared, and the career of either spouse may determine the location of the family residence. The parents share child-rearing chores, and both spouses have flexible roles. Egalitarian couples may live together before marriage, and the wife may choose to keep her maiden name. The emphasis in this kind of marriage, like the modern marriage, is on companionship and sharing. Egalitarianism in marriage is more highly valued today than ever before, especially by women, but behavioral equality is hard to come by and rare to this day (Steil, 1997).

Division of Labor

One of the main areas in which egalitarianism eludes most couples is in the division of household labor. As we have stated earlier, a majority of women, even those with young children, now work outside of the home for pay. What are the effects of wives' working for wages on the division of household labor? Research consistently shows that working wives' reported contributions to the household decline when they are employed outside the home. And the contributions of professional and managerial women decline more rapidly than those of women who work in less prestigious careers (Berardo, Shehan, & Leslie, 1987). But most husbands spend only marginally more time on housework than they had before their wives worked. If the couple cannot afford to hire outside help, this means that housework gets done more efficiently, less elaborately, or not at all (Baxter, 1992). Berardo, Shehan, and Leslie (1987) found that dual-earner wives devote less than half the hours on household chores than do full-time housewives, but they continue to spend nearly triple the amount of time that their husbands spend on household tasks. Husbands of working wives are doing more than they used to around the house, with some recent estimates as high as 33 percent of household chores done by men (Bianchi et al., 2000). Yet only about 10 percent of men do as much work around the house as women do. Burn (1996) found that husbands' understanding of their household responsibilities did not really change when their wives became employed outside of the home. Employed wives are still primarily responsible for the care of the house and the children, which means that many of them put in "second shifts" at home after working full time outside the home (Hochschild, 1989).

Generally speaking, the balance of power in a marital relationship affects the division of household labor, although some of the evidence for this is not entirely consistent and defies easy explanation. For example, husbands do more around the house when their wives' earnings approach their own, but, surprisingly, do less around the house when wives earn more than they do. Remarried men do proportionately more work around the house than first-married men (Ishii-Kuntz & Coltrane, 1992). Less surprisingly, men do more around the house when both wives and husbands hold egalitarian beliefs.

A number of other factors complicate the picture of how women and men divide their housework. Women and men tend to do different kinds of tasks around the house, with women's tasks more frequent, inflexible, time consuming, constraining, and menial than men's. Women's tasks include meal preparation and cleanup, heavy and light housework, laundry, grocery shopping, and child care. Men's tasks, on the other hand, include yard work, car maintenance, and financial management, which are less time intensive, regular, and often afford considerably more autonomy and flexibility (Biernat & Wortman, 1991).

Thus, despite the reevaluation and redefinition of gender roles over the past three decades, very few couples can be described as egalitarian at the present time, especially after the birth of children. But even with strikingly unequal division of domestic labor in most households, many women perceive their marital relationships as fair and equal. Researchers in recent years have struggled to understand how and why women maintain these perceptions of fairness in the face of continued unequal division of labor. Many have concluded that people are strongly motivated to think of their relationships as fair and equal. In fact, couples generally overestimate the extent to which their relationships are truly egalitarian (e.g., Press & Townsley, 1998). We know from social psychology that people generally are motivated to believe in a "just world" in which people get what they deserve and deserve what they get (Lerner, 1980), and are not quick to perceive injustice. Injustice may be particularly hard to acknowledge in love relationships, in which ordinary rules of fairness are often not applied, especially for women who are socialized to sacrifice for love (Valian, 1998).

Some have suggested that women feel less entitled than men to value their own labor (Crosby, 1982). Women may describe the division of household labor as fair even when it is not because they feel that their husband's time is more valuable than their own. Other researchers note that men who help around the house are credited for crossing traditional gender lines, doing "women's work," and their behavior is more salient and more likely to be taken into account and credited (Thompson, 1991). Furthermore, research has found that women tend to compare their husbands' household contribution with that of men who do even less, which permits them to think of their situation as fair even when it remains unequal (Burn, 1996). What these various explanations have in common is the importance of gender-role attitudes and the unequal power relations between women and men in the development and maintenance of perceptions of fairness. The fact that women accept as fair unequal divisions of household labor does not mean that they are satisfied with this state of affairs. Division of labor is a major source of conflict and resentment in married couples. Furthermore, the mental and physical health consequences of the unequal division of labor for women may be profound, as we will see in the following section.

What can be done to reduce the inequity in the division of household labor? Burn (1996) offers a number of worthwhile suggestions. One is to reduce the gap in earnings between women and men, because this would eliminate the rationalization that women need to do more at home to offset their smaller financial contributions to the household. Another suggestion, one that is apparently already well under way, is that women should consider changing their standards for cleaning house, entertaining, and maintaining the family's social life. Burn further recommends that parents teach their male children how to perform household tasks, just as men should allow themselves to be tutored by women. Finally and importantly, Burn cautions that women need to be clear, direct, and straightforward in their requests for men's participation in work around the house. She notes that women are often ambivalent about asking men to do more, and they couch their requests for help in indirect terms that are easily misconstrued or dismissed: "They may, for example, say something like 'Boy, this laundry really piles up quickly. I'm having a hard time staying on top of it,' when what they really mean is, 'Please do a couple of loads of laundry this week'" (pp. 172–173).

Happiness and Psychological Well-Being in Marriage

Many writers and researchers have noted a central irony surrounding gender, marital happiness, and psychological well-being. Women are the ones typically thought of as seeking marriage and commitment, defining themselves in terms of their marital and family relationships, and fulfilling their deepest emotional needs through those relationships. But in fact it is men who appear to reap more varied and substantial benefits of married life. As sociologist Bernard (1972) noted, there are two marriages in every relationship—his and hers—and his is better.

The literature on the relationship between marriage and psychological health and happiness for women and men is inconsistent. Early studies showed that married women have more psychological problems than married men, whereas single women have fewer psychological problems than single men (Bernard, 1972). More recent studies seem to show that marriage "works for women, too." Still, it appears that married men are less depressed and more

satisfied with their relationships than are married women (Fowers, 1991; Steil & Turetsky, 1987). These sex differences emerge most clearly in dissatisfied marriages. One study of long-term marriage found that wives had poorer physical and psychological health than husbands in dissatisfied marriages, but not in satisfied marriages (Levenson, Carstensen, & Gottman, 1993). Recent research suggests that marriage brings considerable benefits to both men and women. Specifically, marriage changes people's behavior in ways that favor physical and mental health: It is associated with much lower illegal drug use, more active sex lives, less violence in the home, and better health care and higher incomes. Married men and women live longer than single people. The benefits of marriage for men and women hold up all over the world (Stack & Eshleman, 1998). But married women more often than married men make sacrifices for the sakes of their marriages and families that depress marital happiness for women. One important sacrifice women make is taking on the drudgery of housework. Another is the relinquishing of important decision making. In most marriages, women make the relatively unimportant day-to-day decisions regarding the home and the family's social life, whereas men make decisions about where to live, what home to buy, and what investments to make. Women are more likely than men to relocate for their spouses' employment and become, literally, the "trailing spouse."

The question of why married women are less happy, less psychologically well adjusted, even less physically healthy than married men has intrigued many scholars and inspired a great deal of research in recent years. There are probably many reasons underlying the sex difference in marital satisfaction and well-being. The key to understanding this difference may lie in examining satisfaction levels in different kinds of marriages that we discussed earlier. For example, research has found that employed men exhibit the highest levels of psychological adjustment, employed women an intermediate level, and full-time housekeepers the lowest levels of adjustment (Kaslow, Hansson, & Lundblad, 1994; Steil & Turetsky, 1987). Although there are several possible interpretations of this finding, one suggestion is that something about being "just a housewife" contributes to unhappiness and dissatisfaction in women. Even for people who enjoy keeping house, housework is frequently boring, repetitive, and physically demanding. It often involves serving other people and taking their needs, tastes, and perspectives into account. It receives practically no recognition or respect from people outside the home and, all too frequently, little from those within the home who benefit from it most directly. It is unpaid and never-ending. Historically, housework is the work of women and the poor, people with little power and status.

For the growing legions of married women who work both outside and inside the home, **role overload** is a common problem (Benin & Agostinelli, 1988), especially if they have children. According to Vanessa McLean (2002), depression will be the most significant cause of disability in women internationally in the year 2020, and stress will play a contributing role. The work–home role conflict for women will continue to supply a significant amount of this stress (McLean, 2002). Unequal power and status seem to underlie much of marital unhappiness in women.

A sizable minority of women, between 25 and 35 percent, are dissatisfied with the amount of work that their spouses do around the house and report feeling overburdened and resentful as a result (McHale & Crouter, 1992). It is important to emphasize that wives' employment outside the home brings with it many benefits to mental health and does not undermine happy marriages. Rather, it jeopardizes unhappy marriages (Schoen et al., 2002).

The general mental health benefits of working outside of the home for women (discussed more fully in Chapter 7) are greatest when their husbands share more equitably in household tasks. One early study found that employment was associated with greater psychological well-being for wives only if their husbands shared household tasks (Krause & Markides, 1985). Similarly, another study found that wives whose husbands shared in child-care responsibilities reported lower levels of depression than wives whose husbands did not (Ross & Mirowsky, 1988). This problem is difficult to resolve, even for men who

want equitable relationships with their wives. Benin and Angostinelli (1988) reported that women and men both wanted equitable relationships, but women wanted to achieve this via more help from men and men wanted to achieve it by both members of the couple spending fewer hours doing housework. Recent research continues to suggest that husbands' participation in household chores increases their wives' satisfaction in marriage but decreases husbands' marital satisfaction (Amato, Johnson, Booth, & Rogers, 2003). Box 9.4 illustrates how marital roles are changing for women in other cultures.

The unequal division of household labor, a clear sign of power imbalance due to gender-role inequality, stands as one strong possible explanation for women's greater dissatisfaction and psychological distress in marriage. The responsibilities of child care, especially the care of young children, no matter how rewarding, are wearing for women and also depress marital satisfaction (Belsky & Rovine, 1990). But research reveals many other possible explanations as well. Perceptions of social support by one's spouse is strongly related to marital satisfaction and well-being, and wives tend to be more supportive, caring, and communicative than husbands (White, Speisman, Jackson, Bartis, & Costos, 1986). Women have been found to be more sensitive to problems in a relationship than men are, and this may be a source of greater marital dissatisfaction.

Men are increasingly forced to deal with definitions of masculinity that stress egalitarianism and flexibility, and must find ways to define their role that goes beyond providing financially for their families (Lee & Owens, 2002). Some men may struggle with engaging in family work and household chores because they view it as a threat to their masculinity and associate it with "women's work" (Arrighi, 2000).

Although it is interesting to ponder sex differences in marital satisfaction and well-being, it is important to note that many factors that predict happiness in wives are associated with happiness in husbands as well. These include high level of education, lack of financial problems, long acquaintanceship prior to marriage, equality in decision making, nontraditional attitudes regarding gender, good communication and conflict resolution skills, and en-

Box 9.4

Evolving Marital Customs in Other Cultures

Some marriage customs are starting to change from a traditional form to a modern one. For example, in the People's Republic of China the marriage law was passed in 1980. This marriage law abolished the feudal marriage system, which deprived women of the right to choose their spouses. This law has established a democratic marriage system, one that gives women free choice of partners, and mandates monogamy and equal rights for both sexes. It also protects the lawful interest of women and children and outlaws bigamy, concubinage, child betrothal, interference in a widow's remarriage, and the extraction of money or gifts in connection with marriage (Yu & Carpenter, 1991).

Among the changes in Taiwan today are those that permit women to retain their family names after marriage. Women are also allowed to inherit property and to retain property and income in their own name. But in order for a woman to gain ownership of any property, a special contract must be drawn up. If this contract is not drawn up, all property acquired before and during the marriage will go to the husband (Yu & Carpenter, 1991). On the other hand, women are held responsible for their husbands' debts (Diamond, 1973).

Source: From "Autonomy in a Cross-Cultural Perspective," by L. L. Adler, in *Females and Autonomy: A Life-Span Perspective* (p. 14), edited by M. B. Nadien and F. L. Denmark, 1999. Boston: Allyn & Bacon. Reprinted with permission of Lenore Loeb Adler, Ph.D.

couragement for the custom of lifelong marriage (Amato et al., 2003; Antill, 1983; Birchler, Fals-Stewart, & Herson, 1996). Intriguingly, physical attractiveness in a partner is negatively correlated with relationship satisfaction (Howard, Blumstein, & Schwartz, 1987).

Regardless of whether the partners are satisfied, the rising divorce rate may overshadow the fact that many marriages last for decades. Schlesinger (1982) found several common factors among couples with enduring marriages. The top ten factors cited by husbands and wives were mutual respect, mutual trust, loyalty, loving each other, depending on each other, considering each other's needs, providing each other with emotional support, commitment to making the marriage last, fidelity, and give and take. Wives, more than husbands, added recognizing one's own needs, positive relationships with children, sharing feelings and emotions, similar goals in life, and a sense of humor. Financial security was also rated high among factors said to contribute to a marriage's staying power. A recent Chilean study indicated a positive correlation between contentment with marriage and happiness during childhood. Nevertheless, the most

important factors associated with happy marriages for these Chilean individuals in both satisfying and unsatisfying relationships were love, trust, and loyalty (Roizblatt, 1999).

Lazarus suggests that temperamental compatibility may contribute more to lasting marriages than congruent interests. He believes that although hard work pays off for some marriages, most lasting marriages do not require it, because well-matched couples are able to resolve or drop conflicts quickly and easily (Lazarus, 2000). Recently, it was found that the rising age at first marriage and increased education are functioning to decrease the rate of marital dissolution (Heaton, 2002). Furthermore, college graduates are more likely to marry and less likely to separate than their less educated peers (U.S. Census Bureau, 2002).

Gay Marriage. At the time of this writing, there is a national firestorm over gay marriage in the United States. In early 2004, in cities across the United States from San Francisco, California to New Paltz, New York, gay and lesbian couples have been streaming into city halls seeking and receiving marriage licenses and exchanging wedding vows, although the legal status of those marriages has yet to be determined in the courts.

As of early 2004, gay men and lesbians cannot legally marry in the United States. In 1996 the U.S. government passed the Defense of Marriage Act, which banned federal recognition of same-sex marriage, and allowed the states to decide on their own whether to recognize such marriages performed in other jurisdictions. To date, thirty-eight states have passed state versions of the Defense of Marriage Act. Civil unions that allow same-sex couples the rights and benefits of marriage are currently legal in only one state—Vermont. California's State Assembly recently passed a domestic partnership law to provide similar benefits, but it stops short of allowing gays to marry. In Massachusetts, in a 4–3 ruling, the State Supreme Judicial Court cleared the way for lesbian and gay couples in the state to marry, ruling that government attorneys failed to identify any constitutionally adequate reason to deny them the right. The Massachusetts legislature was granted until May 2004 to rewrite the state's marriage laws for the benefit of gay couples. At the same time, President George W. Bush, in an election year, came out in favor of a constitutional amendment banning gay marriage in the United States.

Increasingly, the rights of same-sex couples to marry or join together in civil unions are being recognized throughout the world. In 2001, the Netherlands became the first country to legalize same-sex marriages. Belgium followed suit in 2003, as did two Canadian provinces, Ontario and British Columbia, leading scores of gay and lesbian couples in the United States to cross the border to tie the knot. In Brazil, longstanding gay and lesbian couples can inherit from each other and claim each other as dependants on tax returns. In the Argentine province Rio Negro and the capital city of Buenos Aires, laws now allow registered gay couples to qualify for family welfare payments. Many countries, including Norway, Sweden, Denmark and its province Greenland, have registered partnership laws that extend many benefits of marriage to unmarried couples, both gay and straight. Germany has also expanded rights for cohabitating couples. France in 1998 approved the Pacte Civil de Solidarite—an intermediate step between casual cohabitation and formal marriage that provides a variety of tax and health benefits (Kantrowitz, 2004).

Social science research suggests that most gay people strongly favor the right of gay people to marry legally whether or not they believe that it is right for them. Straight people are largely mixed in their feelings about extending the rights and privileges of marriage to gay couples. Meanwhile, acceptance of lesbian and gay couples and support for recognition of their relationships is growing in the general population. For example, in one recent USA TODAY/CNN/Gallup poll, a majority of adults in the United States favored legalizing civil unions for gay couples as an alternative to same-sex marriage (Cauchon, 2004). The poll found that 54 percent support civil unions, which provide some of the legal benefits of marriage, and 42 percent oppose them. That is a change from July 2003, when respondents opposed civil unions by 57 percent to 40 percent. This shift in attitudes in such a short period of time is significant, and stands as one indicator of the volatility of the issue.

The push by gay activists to gain equal rights in marriage was initially motivated by the desire to obtain the legal benefits of being a spouse, such as health insurance and inheritance rights. But many gay people say that it is equally important to make a public statement of affection and commitment—a view of marriage that crosses political and social boundaries. Many lesbians and gay men say that by denying gay people the right to marry, society refuses to recognize the magnitude and importance of their love for each other and undermines the stability and respectability of their relationships. Moreover, married people enjoy many rights and benefits that unmarried couples, even those in domestic partnerships, do not have. Halvorsen (1998) has documented many of the benefits denied same-sex couples: reducing their tax liability by filing joint tax returns, Social Security and other retirement funds for surviving spouses and dependents; health, life, and disability insurance and other spousal benefits from employers; automatic inheritance and rights of survivorship; immunity from subpoenas requiring testimony against a spouse; next-of-kin status in medical and legal decisions; and numerous others. Obviously, these benefits are of enormous practical and tangible importance in and of themselves, but they also serve to reinforce the personal aspects of relationships.

Aside from the illegal status of gay marriages, the major religions practiced in the United States also forbid gay marriage. But, increasingly, some ministers and rabbis are performing formal marriage ceremonies for same-sex couples. While these marriages are not recognized by the state or by mainstream Christianity or Judaism, they are often seen by gay people as an important step in the process of becoming recognized for their love and commitment. As one lesbian woman, Dr. Kerryn Phelps, said in connection with her 1998 marriage to Jackie Stricker, "No group in any society should be grateful for crumbs from the table masquerading as grand gestures. I feel robbed of the language of being married, of being the daughter-in-law, the wife, the aunt, the stepmother." And when the law says "You can't," the sweetest words are "I do" (Kantrowitz, 2004, pg. 2).

Conflict in Marriage

Even under the best of circumstances, blending two lives is difficult. On a daily basis, married couples need to make decisions for themselves, each other, and others, leaving much room for disagreement and conflict. Moreover, the ideology of and societal support for marriage enable a marital relationship to absorb a great deal of conflict and negativity without collapsing. This permanence and security affords couples great latitude to express unhappiness.

In their landmark study of U.S. couples, Blumstein and Schwartz (1983) intensively interviewed heterosexual married and cohabiting couples and gay and lesbian couples about three major areas of life that concern couples today: money, work, and sex. This survey was not scientific; that is, like most surveys of its type, its sample was not randomly drawn from the population, and its respondents were volunteers and not necessarily representative of the four types of couples. But the researchers made a strong effort to include a diverse sample of respondents in all categories and reduce selection biases. And it is one of the few studies that compares heterosexual

married and cohabiting partners and lesbian and gay male partners on a number of dimensions. Unlike many studies of relationships, it explored relationship processes. We will draw from this important study throughout the sections on marital, cohabiting, and lesbian and gay relationships, updating information where relevant.

A central finding of this study, which has been upheld in subsequent investigations, is that most conflict in marriage is centered on money (both the amount of money available and the management of money), working lives, especially women working outside of the home, and sex, both within and outside of the relationship. We will briefly consider the nature of marital conflict in each of these three domains.

Unlike the cohabiting heterosexual and gay and lesbian couples we will discuss shortly, married people operate within an institution that offers guidelines for money acquisition and management. In traditional marriages, the husband makes (at least most of) the money and makes decisions about major expenditures, whereas the wife makes day-to-day household purchases. It is assumed that the couple shares everything, despite different levels of contributions or individual attitudes about sharing. But Blumstein and Schwartz (1983) found that married couples fought more about money than did other kinds of couples and more about money management than about income per se. Typical conflicts arise when a husband does not respect a wife's ability as a household manager or when one partner feels that the other is spending improperly on herself or himself. When the wife works outside of the home, too, she expects to exercise more control over financial decisions, and this may be another source of conflict. With married couples as with other kinds of couples, partners who feel that they have equal control over how money is spent experience less conflict than those who do not feel that they are participating equally in financial decisions.

Because of profound changes in the participation of women in the workforce, the inability of one paycheck to support a family in an increasing proportion of families, and recent trends in the U.S. economy that have made employment for men and women less secure than it used to be, work has emerged as a major source of conflict in marriage. Couples disagree a great deal about whether wives should work full time outside the home. There is sometimes disagreement about whether wives should work outside the home at all, especially wives who are the mothers of young children. When such disagreement occurs, it is usually because wives want to work and husbands want wives to stay home. Many men—and women—feel that a wife's first duty is to her home and children. Indeed, regardless of their level of education or the importance of their income to their family, many women who work outside the home describe frequent feelings of guilt and anxiety about the home and children that working men do not report (Forster 2001; Finkel & Olswang, 1996). As we have seen, when women work outside the home, especially when they work full time, the balance of power within their relationship shifts toward equality. Women and men have both been socialized to appreciate the skills and discipline, the stresses and competitions involved in work outside the home. And in this as in many other societies, money is power and the ability to earn it confers respect. Married couples who disagree about the wife's right to work are less happy than couples who do not.

Even among couples who agree about a woman's right to work as she wishes, work may be a significant cause of conflict. Working wives still bear the brunt of the responsibility for housework and child care no matter how much they earn, although in affluent households hired help relieves some of this burden. Unlike the case of *Mr. Mom* in the movies, in which an initially reluctant househusband becomes a Super Dad in short order, in the cases of real-life husbands who do a lot of housework, there is often a great deal of resentment and marital conflict (Steil, 1997). And when wives work, couples fight more about how the children are being reared (Blumstein & Schwartz, 1983). Nonetheless, for wives, a good marital relationship and a good job can be mutually enhancing. With work, women gain status in the household and have a stronger voice in all decisions than they would have had otherwise. Relationships in which partners share power and control, and compromise and negotiate, are happier and more stable in the long run (Gottman, Coan, Carrere, & Swanson, 1998).

Sex inside and outside of the marital relationship poses rich possibilities for conflict. Couples may fight over how and how often they have sex with each other and may experience conflict over real or suspected extramarital relationships. The quality and quantity of a couple's sex life is important to the overall well-being of the couple. Married people who reported infrequent sex experienced dissatisfaction with their entire relationship. Obviously, it is hard to disentangle whether a poor sexual relationship leads to problems in other domains in a marriage, or troubles in nonsexual aspects of a marriage sour the sexual relationship, and certainly the causal arrow can point both ways. But Blumstein and Schwartz (1983) concluded from their survey that the more likely causal path is that conflicts in other areas of the relationship, particularly conflicts over housekeeping, income, and expenditures, spill over to the sexual relationship. They note,

> It is hard to know whether an unsatisfactory relationship leads to less frequent sexual activity and reduced sexual pleasure or whether the problems begin in the bedroom and eventually corrode the entire relationship. From our vantage point it looks as if other problems come into the bedroom and make it less likely that the couple will want to have sex together. The low frequency then becomes a source of dissatisfaction in and of itself. (p. 201)

Dissatisfaction with marital sex and fighting about sex, but not frequency of sexual relations, are associated with breaking up.

Couples have strains over issues surrounding initiating and refusing sex. Generally, in most marriages, husbands initiate sex more often than wives and wives refuse sex more often than husbands. Equality in sexual initiation and refusal is related to a happier sex life (Rathus et al., 1997).

Physical attractiveness, especially of wives, continues to exert an influence on couples' sex lives throughout the marriage. Some people view a partner's weight gain or other physical changes in marriage as signaling a loss of interest in sex, or a lack of respect for the relationship. Even when beauty is not especially important to people, the couple is more likely to prosper if both partners are about equally attractive. If one partner becomes much more or less attractive than the other, the balance of power in the relationship shifts perceptibly.

As we note in Chapter 8, it is difficult to establish the frequency of nonmonogamy, or extramarital relationships. But whether it actually occurs, nonmonogamy occupies a big place in people's imaginations. Many studies suggest that monogamy in marriage is a strongly held moral ideal even when people do not live up to it (Nevid et al., 1995). Many married people are jealous or possessive of their spouses and wonder and worry about their partners' straying. And many married people are at least occasionally tempted to have an affair. People offer several motives for having affairs, including retaliation and hostility toward a spouse, a need for sexual excitement and variety, the desire to boost one's self-esteem or prove that one is still attractive to others, and a need for emotional closeness that is missing in the marriage (Glass & Wright, 1992). Men are more likely than women to have extramarital affairs, and they have more extramarital partners than women do, but married women have more emotional attachments to other men than married men have to other women. In general, the more powerful person in the marriage (often, but not always, the man) is more likely to have an affair than the less powerful partner.

Interestingly, research suggests that married people who have extramarital affairs do not have less sex or lesser quality sex within their marriages and are not less happy with their marital relationships than people who do not have affairs. But people who have affairs are less certain that their marriages will last than other people. Thus, they may be less committed to the future of their marriages. Couples in which a partner has had extramarital affairs are in fact more likely to break up than are other couples. Infidelity, whether verified or merely suspected, is the most common cause of marital breakups throughout the world (Beitzig, 1989).

Finally, it is important to keep in mind that marital conflict is common, and it does not, in and of itself, spell trouble for the marriage. It appears to be less important what couples disagree about than how they express disagreement. Couples who express strong disagreement and anger with affection, warmth, respect, and humor tend to survive. It is harder for couples to survive long-standing control and power imbalances, however (Gottman, et al., 1998). Today, about half of all marriages end in divorce, which is discussed more fully later in this chapter.

COHABITATION

The term **cohabitation** refers to unmarried people who live together. Over the past three decades, cohabitation has been increasing greatly in popularity, visibility, and acceptance. The Census Bureau of the U.S. government keeps statistics on the number of unmarried people of different sexes who share the same household (though not necessarily the same bed) and found that this number increased 80 percent, from 1.6 million couples in 1980 to 2.9 million in 1990 to 5 million in 2000 (Smock, 2000). The number of unmarried heterosexual couples cohabiting in the United States has quadrupled in the past 25 years.

The dramatic increase in cohabitation over the past quarter century has caused many people to worry that cohabitation is a dangerous new form of relationship that will replace marriage. But, as we noted earlier, there is insufficient evidence to date that marriage is being supplanted by cohabitation, despite recently declining marriage rates and the rise in the average age of marriages. At least up until now, about half of all cohabitations have ended within a year, and another 40 percent end in formal marriage (Laumann et al., 1994). At this time, it is not clear whether higher levels of cohabitation simply mean more trial marriages, leading to either formal marriages or breakups, or more people adopting cohabitation as a permanent lifestyle.

Kammeyer (1990) has distinguished three styles of cohabitation: (1) part-time or limited cohabitation, (2) premarital cohabitation, and (3) substitute marriage. In the first type, limited cohabitation, a dating couple progressively finds itself spending more and more time at one partner's residence until eventually the couple is practically living together. In this case, a conscious decision to live together is never made. Rather, the couple drifts into cohabitation. In premarital cohabitation, the couple expects to get married but lives together first. One variation of this arrangement is the trial marriage, in which living together is a test of their compatibility or commitment. Finally, in the type of cohabitation that is substitute marriage, the couple makes a long-term commitment to each other but, for one of a variety of reasons, does not expect ever to marry. For example, a widow may not wish to sacrifice her deceased husband's pension, social security payments, or welfare eligibility to a new marriage. Some older adults choose to cohabit because their grown children oppose their marriage. Alternatively, a person who has experienced a very messy divorce may be reluctant to enter another marriage.

Who Cohabits?

Typical images of cohabiting couples include liberal college students and well-to-do professional people. It is true that most cohabitors are younger than 35. Cohabitation is much more likely among younger people than older people, although it is not clear whether this represents an age effect (as people grow older, they are less inclined to cohabit) or a cohort effect (people born more recently are more likely to cohabit than are people in previous generations). But, contrary to stereotype, most cohabitors are not particularly well educated or well off financially. And the cohabitation rate is about twice as high among African American people as White people (Nevid et al., 1995). Taken together, this information suggests that people may cohabit at least in part because they cannot financially afford to be married, with all that being married entails in modern-day society.

There are a few other variables that predict cohabitation. People whose parents were divorced before they turned 14 and who had sexual partners before age 18 are more likely to cohabit than are other people. Church attendance is negatively correlated with cohabitation rates (Laumann et al., 1994). Cohabitors are generally less traditional and more committed to personal independence than are noncohabitors (Bumpass, 1995). But as cohabiting becomes more common, these predictors may change.

In more than half of all marriages since 1990, the couple has lived together before getting married (Smock, 2000).

Money, Work, and Sex among Cohabiting Couples

One of the most comprehensive studies of cohabiting couples was Blumstein and Schwartz's (1983) survey of U.S. couples. As previously noted, they compared cohabiting couples with heterosexual married couples and lesbian and gay couples on attitudes and behaviors related to money, work, and sex. Overall, they found that cohabiting couples were much more likely to use money to achieve equality in their relationships. That is, for cohabiting couples, unlike married couples, the impact of income differences on the balance of power in relationships is substantial. The male is not cast as the provider and the female as homemaker. Cohabitors believe strongly in each partner's contributing her or his share. The partner with the larger income exerts more control over financial matters and even recreational activities. Because the relationship is not regarded as permanent, questions of trust and pooling assets are tricky ones for cohabiting couples, who often consciously design their relationships to avoid the economic entanglements of marriage. Blumstein and Schwartz (1983) found that cohabiting couples shy away from pooling if they doubt the durability of their relationship and are far less dependent on each other in financial matters. In this way, for better or worse, they prevent themselves from forging a bond that could sustain them through troubled periods.

As a group, cohabitors more than married people feel that both partners should work outside the home. This is especially true of female cohabitors, who are more concerned than married women about the power that working outside the home and earning an income provides. More than married couples, cohabiting couples feel strongly about having time away from their partners. They are more likely to see friends and enjoy other recreational activities separately. They are more independent than married couples in their expenditure of time as well as money, and these factors direct their energies away from the relationship (Nock, 1995).

Cohabiting is generally seen as a "sexier" relationship than formal marriage. No matter how long they are together, cohabiting couples report having more sex than married couples. The institution of marriage acts to preserve a married couple's relationship even when sex occurs infrequently. Cohabitors do not enjoy the protection of the institution, so sex functions differently in cohabiting than in married relationships. Sex becomes a more important bond for cohabitors than for married people. Still, cohabitors are less likely to be monogamous than are wives and husbands, and that is especially true for males.

Which Cohabitors Marry?

Only about 40 percent of cohabitors eventually marry. Blumstein and Schwartz (1983) found that the cohabitors in their study who married were very different from those who did not. First of all, they were more traditional in their attitudes about gender roles and relationships. They were possessive about each other and wanted to spend more time with each other. They were more likely to pool their resources from the very beginning. They tended to see each other in flattering ways; for instance, male cohabitors saw their partners as sexy. Both male and female partners saw the other as ambitious and successful.

It should not be surprising that cohabiting couples are much more likely than married couples to break up. After all, as we have argued, they have fewer ties that bind them during the inevitable tough periods of any long-standing relationship. What may be more surprising is that cohabitors who eventually marry are significantly more likely to break up than are people who did not live together prior to marriage. A recent study in the United States showed that 40 percent of cohabitors who married later got divorced (Smock, 2000), and a similar study in Sweden found that the divorce rate among women who cohabited before marriage was 80 percent higher than the rate for women who did not cohabit before marriage (Bennett, Blanc, & Bloom, 1988). Researchers generally explain this finding by pointing to the selection factors that lead some people to marry and some people to cohabit in the first place. As we have stated, cohabitors are more concerned than others with personal independence and autonomy, and

are less religious and conventional than people who marry. Thus, it may be the values and attitudes of cohabitors, rather than the fact of cohabitation itself, that lead to marital dissolution (Nevid et al., 1995). In any case, cohabiting before marriage does not appear to strengthen the marital bond.

In conclusion, it seems that cohabiting is not yet an institution that takes a predictable form. Despite some signs that this may be changing, cohabiting is still an unstable way of life, not supported by society in any of the usual ways. For example, other than the old expression *common-law marriage,* there are few generally accepted terms for people who live together before marriage. Rules of law and etiquette designed for married couples do not always apply to cohabiting couples. Families and other communities frequently do not know how to treat cohabiting partners. The lack of societal support for cohabitation makes staying together through difficult times a daunting challenge for these couples. There is, however, increasing evidence that cohabitation has become much more socially acceptable, with many fewer references these days to "living in sin" and "shacking up" than there once were (Rathus et al., 2002).

Lesbian and Gay Couples

Most work on romantic relationships has been done with heterosexual couples. For a variety of reasons, information about heterosexual couples cannot be generalized indiscriminately to lesbian and gay couples. Scientific information about same-sex couples is limited to date, but the past decade has witnessed new interest in psychology in studying lesbian and gay couples. Despite the many serious gaps in our knowledge, some research findings appear to be consistent across studies, and new theoretical models are being developed that provide a framework for understanding and generating research (D'Augelli & Garnetts, 1995; Kurdek, 1994).

Lesbian and gay couples differ importantly from heterosexual couples in at least three ways. First, given that females and males are socialized so differently in most societies, the fact that lesbian and gay couples are composed of two people of the same sex may well have profound effects on attitudes, feelings, and behaviors within relationships. Second, unlike heterosexual relationships, lesbian and gay relationships develop without the support of economic and social institutions and often without the support of families and communities of origin. Finally, Kurdek (1994) argues that because sexual activity in same-sex relationships does not have procreative intent, issues such as monogamy and fidelity may play out differently in lesbian and gay relationships than they do in heterosexual relationships.

Stereotypes about Lesbian and Gay Couples. Lesbians and gay men grow up in a heterosexist world that stereotypes them or renders them invisible. By and large, this world does not provide role models to guide their relational behavior or safe spaces for them to get to know themselves and others. Peplau (1991) notes a variety of commonly held and uniformly negative stereotypes about lesbian and gay couples. These include the notions that lesbians and gay men are incapable of forming lasting relationships and that their relationships are inferior imitations of heterosexual relationships. Other pervasive stereotypes are that lesbians and gay men do not like children, pose a sexual threat to children, do not make good parents, and adversely affect their own children's development. Despite increasingly tolerant attitudes toward lesbians and gays, many people in the United States still believe that sex between adults of the same sex is always wrong, and consider gay men and lesbians to be immoral, unhappy, and harmful to others (Rathus et al., 2002; Rothblum, 1994). Gay men are often portrayed as "sex machines," overly concerned with physical appearance, whereas lesbians are depicted as physically unattractive women who do not like men (Rothblum, 1994). Obviously, it is not easy to develop a sense of oneself as a worthwhile person and maintain caring and rewarding relationships in light of such pejorative portraits. In fact, given the many obstacles placed in the way of gay and lesbian youth and adults, D'Augelli (1994) has suggested a model of lesbian and gay development that takes as its premise the idea that lesbians and gay men lead exceptional lives:

Women and men who express their needs for closeness and intimacy more consistently with people of the same gender have evolved within their own life histories and have departed from heterosexual socialization patterns. Continued growth and personal fulfillment as a lesbian or gay man in our culture at this time demands unusual competencies and special strengths. By starting with the assumption of exceptionality, efforts can be made to discover these adaptive coping talents. (p. 120)

Despite profoundly negative images and stereotypes and lack of social support, lesbians and gay men do indeed shape their own development and form successful relationships. Peplau and Cochran (1990) found that between 40 and 60 percent of gay males and between 45 and 80 percent of lesbians are involved in steady relationships, and many lesbian and gay couples form lifelong relationships. Moreover, they found that reports of relationship satisfaction and love among lesbian and gay couples is similar to that found among heterosexual couples who are matched on age and other relevant characteristics. More recently, Patterson (2000) found that lesbians report the same level of relationship satisfaction that heterosexual couples do.

These core similarities are not to suggest that there are no differences between heterosexual and same-sex couples. As D'Augelli (1994) notes, because of historical need, over time distinctive social institutions have evolved to structure the socialization and intimate relationships of lesbians and gay men. The primary meeting place for urban gay men has been the gay bar and, to a lesser degree, the gay bathhouses that have largely disappeared since the onset of the AIDS era. On the other hand, lesbian socialization often takes place in small, private, informal groups or in women's communities. According to D'Augelli (1994), these very different contexts have shaped highly distinct behaviors and stereotypes: the gay man as "sex machine" and the lesbian as "relationship bound" (p. 127). In recent years, the number and variety of social opportunities have increased for both gay men and lesbians, with more nonsexual options for gay men and more expressive options for lesbians. Young gay men and women who are coming of age today will have a different developmental history and be socialized under different circumstances than earlier gay and lesbian cohorts. In D'Augelli's

(1994) words, they will be "different persons" (p. 127).

How Money, Work, and Sex Are Negotiated among Lesbian and Gay Couples.

As we noted earlier, Blumstein and Schwartz's (1983) major study of U.S. couples included volunteer samples of gay men and lesbians as well as heterosexual married and cohabiting couples. Although the sample was not randomly selected or scientific, and generalizations across all lesbian and gay couples cannot be made, it nonetheless gives us a glimpse of how major issues are negotiated in same-sex relationships.

Concerning the earning and expenditure of money, Blumstein and Schwartz found that money establishes the balance of power in all relationships except among lesbians. Because women in this society are not socialized to judge their own worth by their income, they tend not to judge their female partners by this standard. Gay men, on the other hand, gain significant control and power advantages over their partners when they earn substantially more than them. Because earning power is a central part of a man's identity, having more money gives a man symbolic and real advantages. More recent research suggests that, while lesbians are indeed relatively egalitarian with respect to control and power when compared to other kinds of couples, when there is an imbalance, the partner who has more education and a higher income tends to exert more power within the relationship (Patterson, 2000). For all kinds of couples, partners who feel that they have equal power and control over how the money is spent have a more tranquil and happy relationship.

Lesbian and gay couples, like an increasing proportion of married couples, have to deal with the stresses of making a living, dealing with competition, allocating housework, and finding time to be together. The great majority of same-sex couples believe that both partners should work, and in most same-sex couples, both partners do work outside of the home. Lesbian couples are more likely than other couples to share household chores (Kurdek, 1993) and to value equality of power (Patterson, 2000). Gay men tend to be more competitive with each other about work than lesbians, probably because of the meaning of work to

men's self-esteem (Blumstein & Schwartz, 1983). Interestingly, same-sex couples appear to enjoy an advantage over heterosexual couples when it comes to juggling the conflicting demands of work and home. Same-sex couples conserve more time than heterosexual couples because they share similar lives and interests by virtue of their gender roles.

In exploring the sex lives of lesbians and gay men, Blumstein & Schwartz (1983) uncovered large and important differences between these couples in the frequency and variety of sexual expression. They found that gay men have sex more often in the early part of their relationship than any other type of couple, but after ten years have sex together less often than married couples. Sex with other men tends to balance the declining sex with the partner. Lesbian couples have sex less often than any other couples, and they do not have much compensating sex outside of the relationship. Taken together with their data on heterosexual couples, these findings suggest some generalizations about men as a group and women as a group, regardless of sexual orientation. That is, they found that husbands and male cohabitors were more like gay men in their sexual behavior and attitudes than they were like wives and female cohabitors, and wives and female cohabitors were more like lesbians than they were like husbands and male cohabitors. Regardless of sexual orientation, men generally are more likely to value physical attractiveness in their partners, to pursue sex within the relationship, and to be nonmonogamous than women are. Regardless of sexual orientation, women generally are more likely to link love and sex than men are. Thus, gender per se matters in shaping a person's sexual opportunities and choices.

The finding in some studies that lesbians do not have as much sex in their relationships as other couples should not be taken to mean that sex is unimportant or unsatisfying in lesbian relationships. For example, in one study, 70 percent of lesbian women reported experiencing orgasms within the context of their relationships (Peplau et al., 1977; Peplau, Padesky, & Hamilton, 1982), a figure comparable to that for married women. Other issues that arose with respect to same-sex couples concern sexual competitiveness for the admiration of others, and working out a sensitive ratio of initiating and refusing sex. These and several other issues relevant to gay and lesbian relationships need further research. For example, some theorists have suggested that gay men and lesbians have a tendency to idealize romantic relationships, believing that gender similarity precludes conflicts. If lesbian and gay couples are "out," their relationship may be challenged or ridiculed, and if they are not out, they may suffer the strains of secrecy, deception, and lack of acknowledgment (Greene, 1994b). Relationships in which lesbians and gay men are involved with people who self-identify or are seen by others as bisexual also need further study.

DIVORCE

Obviously, conflict in committed relationships sometimes ends in divorce. In the United States, the divorce rate was low and rather constant throughout the 1950s and early 1960s. It started rising dramatically around 1966, doubled over the next decade, and then leveled off at the higher rate, with a very slight decline more recently. Today, about half of all marriages end in divorce, with about half of those ending in divorce breaking up within the first seven years (U.S. Census Bureau, 2002). According to the Census Bureau, first marriages that end in divorce typically last between seven and eight years (U.S. Census Bureau, 2002). The United States has the highest divorce rate of any industrialized country. In 1997, there were 2.4 million marriages and 1.2 million divorces in the United States, meaning that there were about 3,200 divorces a day (U.S. Census Bureau, 1999a). One recent census report reveals that 19.3 million adults, or 10 percent of the adult population, were divorced at the time of the survey (U.S. Census Bureau, 1999a).

Half of those individuals who remarry after a divorce from a first marriage do so within approximately three years (U.S. Census Bureau, 2002). In addition, one study suggests that those who initiate divorce tend to enter into subsequent relationships sooner than noninitiators, although this likelihood diminishes significantly after three years of separation.

Nonetheless, remarriages are even more likely than first marriages to end in divorce (Lown & Dolan, 1988).

Why has the divorce rate risen so sharply in this country over the past 40 years? Many explanations have been offered for this trend, including relaxation of legal restrictions on divorce, especially the introduction of the no-fault divorce. No-fault divorce was first instituted in California in 1970 and was followed by a 46 percent increase in the number of divorces within three years (Wheeler, 1974). It quickly spread to the other 49 states. Prior to no-fault divorce, the only legal grounds for divorce were adultery, extreme cruelty, and desertion. Now, no charge of marital misconduct is necessary for petition of divorce, and the most frequently cited reason for divorce in recent years is lack of communication and understanding, rather than adultery or other "misconduct" (Carrere, Buehlman, Gottman, Coan, & Ruckstuhl, 2000; Kitson & Sussman, 1982). Since the introduction of no-fault divorce, about 90 percent of divorces are *uncontested;* that is, there is no dispute about the existence of grounds.

Other reasons for the rising divorce rate include the rise in women's incomes, which makes leaving bad marriages more feasible, higher expectations for marital relationships, less tolerance for unsatisfying relationships, and a decrease in the stigma attached to divorce.

What Risk Factors Are Associated with Divorce?

Social scientists have identified a variety of demographic, personality, and relationship characteristics related to divorce. As we review these factors, it is important to keep in mind that they are merely associated (correlated) with divorce rates; they do not necessarily *cause* divorces.

Several demographic attributes are associated with higher levels of divorce. These include the age of marriage, with younger couples more likely to divorce than couples who were older at the time of marriage. In addition, less educated people are more likely to divorce than more educated ones, although among the very highest levels of educated women (women who attend graduate and professional schools) divorce is relatively common. Catholics and certain denominations of Protestants are less likely to divorce than other people. People who grew up in households in which the parents lived together until the children were at least 14 years old are less likely to divorce than those from families in which divorce occurred sooner. People who are of the same religion, race–ethnicity, educational level, and age level (within three years of each other) are less likely to be divorced than people who differ from their partners on these important dimensions (Laumann et al., 1994; Kelly, 2004).

Other demographic variables that predict divorce rates are race and socioeconomic class, which are confounded, meaning they occur together so that one cannot tease apart the effects of either alone. African Americans are about twice as likely as White people to get divorced, but this is largely because they tend to be more often in lower socioeconomic classes, which have higher divorce rates (Laumann et al., 1994; Price & McKenry, 1988).

Other risk factors for divorce include having sex before age 18, having children prior to marriage, and cohabiting before marriage. Regular church attendance is associated with a low rate of divorce (Laumann et al., 1994). Wives who hold nontraditional jobs for women such as engineer and architect are more likely to get divorced than women who hold traditional jobs (Philliber & Hiller, 1983).

Some studies have looked at attitudinal and personality correlates of conflict in marriage and divorce. Different expectations about women's work outside of the home and the division of labor within the home predict marital strife and divorce (Blumstein & Schwartz, 1983). Although the evidence for this is not completely consistent, several studies suggest that women who hold nontraditional gender-role attitudes are more likely to get divorced. Other predictors of divorce today include the husbands' criticisms, stonewalling, contempt, and defensiveness (Carrere et al., 2000).

The Social and Psychological Costs of Divorce

Even when the decision to end a marital relationship is mutual, there are almost always feelings of pro-

found disappointment by both parties. In some religions, notably the Roman Catholic faith, divorce is a sin leading to excommunication from the sacraments. Many people view divorce as a great personal failure. Research consistently shows that divorce is a highly complex social and personal phenomenon and one of life's chief stressors, akin to experiencing the death of a spouse or other loved one.

Divorce is complex because it is multifaceted: There are many legal, personal, and community aspects to divorce, all of which have potential to cause enormous stress. Legally, money and property must be divided, and different states have different laws. If there are children, custody, visitation, and support arrangements must be made. On a personal basis, people, especially women, commonly struggle with feelings of guilt, anger, hostility, regret, sadness, and loneliness. Many people report continuing feelings of attachment to their ex-spouses and a long struggle to regain individual autonomy (Bohannan, 1970). Better adjustment to divorce is positively related to high financial status, steadily dating someone, remarriage, an approving outlook toward divorce prior to marital dissolution, being the initiator of divorce, and being younger. Surprisingly, other than being unemployed, stressors such as decreases in standards of living, losing friends, and moving exerted little influence on divorce adjustment (Wang, 2000). On a positive note, one study reported that postdivorce mothers' feelings of loss and guilt were replaced, over time, by feelings of greater personal contentment, better parent–child relationships, and more gratifying lives. Focusing on the benefits of divorce provided a means for dealing with the negative consequences of divorce (Arditti, 1995).

Divorce affects people's social lives and relationship to the community in countless ways, particularly for women. Many women report a loss of friends and social activities when they are no longer part of a couple. This may have serious consequences for women as the divorce rate continues to increase. According to Carolyn Liebler (2002), people have always depended on friends, neighbors, and colleagues, in addition to family members, for support. Unfortunately, residential mobility has continued to increase along with the divorce rate, taking people away from their relatives. Thus, women may be left with very little social support, feeling deserted. Demographic and other factors make single men—especially single older men—more socially valuable than single women, and many divorced men find themselves highly prized in their social circles. Indeed, divorced men are significantly more likely than divorced women to remarry (Ozawa & Yoon, 2002), especially in older age groups.

For divorced lesbian women who wish to pursue a lesbian life after divorce, a significant concern is the fear that if their gay identity is divulged, they will lose the right to raise their biological children (Greene, 1994b). This fear is pervasive and, says Greene, justifiable, given the courts' history of denying or restricting lesbian women and gay men custody in divorce settlements. In their review of the literature in this area, Patterson and Redding (1996) find that despite popular stereotypes, children raised by parents who are lesbian or gay have positive developmental outcomes, as positive as children raised by heterosexual parents. That is, their parents are just as likely to provide an environment conducive to healthy development as are heterosexual parents. Thus, sexual orientation alone should not be the deciding factor in whether to grant custody (Patterson & Redding, 1996).

Another problem that disproportionately affects women is the economic crunch that often accompanies divorce. When a couple breaks up, legal expenses mount, two households are formed, and resources are often strained to the limit. Women, especially mothers of young children, do not usually make as much money as men. Women who have stayed home to raise their children often find that they cannot compete in the marketplace with younger, better trained, more mobile and flexible employees. Women benefit more financially from remarriage than men do (Ozawa & Yoon, 2002). Divorced fathers may find that it is difficult for them to pay child support and alimony, if awarded, while setting up a new household and adopting a new lifestyle.

Research on the effects of divorce on children is deeply flawed, because it is difficult to disentangle the effects of divorce per se from those of growing up in a household in which there is serious marital strife.

We know that approximately 85 percent of single-parent children live with their mothers (U.S. Census Bureau, 1998b). Most large-scale studies on the effects of divorce on children do not survey the children before the divorce occurs and do not compare these children with matched control groups of children who live in households with marital problems. Although the evidence to date is far from conclusive, it suggests that most children have problems adjusting for at least the first year following the divorce. These problems include plummeting grades and behavior problems at school, especially for boys, and increased anxiety and dependence (Hetherington, Cox, & Cox, 1982). Regrettably, adjustment problems may endure throughout early adulthood. Wallerstein and her associates have found that 40 percent of children of divorce show evidence of academic underachievement, decreased self-worth, and anger even ten years after the divorce (Wallerstein & Kelly, 1980; Wallerstein & Lewis, 1998).

Moreover, people whose parents divorce have more difficulty than others in trusting romantic partners and forming commitments in adulthood and are themselves more likely to get divorced than are people whose parents did not divorce (Wallerstein & Blakeslee, 1989; Wallerstein & Kelly, 1980). Other research by Wallerstein ties higher rates of alcoholism and other substance abuse to children of divorced parents (Wallerstein, 1997). For example, in one study, it was found that children whose parents had divorced recently were more likely to drink alcohol in larger quantities more frequently and were more likely to be under the influence of alcohol while at school (Jeynes, 2001). An additional study showed that children whose parents had recently divorced and who were from single-parent families were more likely than children from families in which there was no divorce to have consumed illegal drugs in the previous 12 months, to have used marijuana and cocaine frequently throughout their lifetimes, and to have used marijuana while at school (Jeynes, 2001). A longitudinal study by Wallerstein and Lewis (1998) showed that 25 years after divorce, children of divorced parents remembered their adolescence as a time characterized by early sexual activity and experimentation with drugs or alcohol. Thus, as much as divorce is a personal problem, it is also a problem for society.

Few people would deny that divorce is a painful and unfortunate event, or that children are better off when reared by both parents. Virtually everyone would prefer a loving and solid marriage to a divorce, and two caring, cooperative adults in the home sharing parenting responsibilities to a single parent struggling alone. But this is not what the choice is for people in bad marriages. Most people contemplating divorce are not throwing away good relationships for selfish and frivolous reasons. Only about 20 percent of divorced people believe that the divorce was a mistake five years later (Wallerstein & Kelly, 1980). Many people experience some positive feelings after divorce, including enhanced senses of autonomy, independence, strength, and courage. Most people eventually start dating again, and between 70 and 80 percent remarry (Glick & Lin, 1986; Kelly, 2004). When parents cooperate with each other after the divorce, contribute fairly to the support of children, and continue to play active roles in their children's lives, there is evidence that children's adjustment to the divorce is eased considerably.

As discussed, there are several factors that impact the staying power of a marriage. The decisions about whether to have children, how to raise them, and other issues can place a financial, physical, and emotional burden on couples. The quality of marriage has been found to decrease somewhat once there are children and to increase after the children have left the house (Rollins, 1989). In Chapter 10, we will consider issues relating to parenting. In the next section, we will explore women's experiences of being family and friends.

TAKING CARE: WOMEN'S OTHER RELATIONSHIPS

Obviously, women have many key relationships in their lives other than those with lovers and spouses. These relationships are central to most women's sense of well-being and happiness. Until recently, psychology had almost completely overlooked the study of women, gender, and close relationships out-side of romantic and parental bonds, but interest in these areas is rapidly expanding.

Women are widely seen as the relationship experts. Certainly, gender stereotypes suggest that women are more socially skilled, agreeable, emotionally sensitive, expressive, and concerned with personal relationships than men are (Eagly, 1987). Research consistently shows that women are more likely to seek and receive social support from others than men are and that women have more extensive, effective, and satisfying social support networks than men have (Barbee et al., 1993). In families, generally middle-aged women carry out most of the caregiving and support functions needed by younger and older members, including in-laws. It is often noted that families are linked through their female members, who have closer ties with each other than with male family members. Middle-aged and older women are more likely than men or younger women to worry about other family members and to experience more family-related conflicts and stresses (Etaugh, 1993a, 1993b; Green & Russo, 1993). Overwhelmingly, the direct care of the sick and elderly in our society, as in others, is in the hands of women. By virtue of their gender role, cultural expectations, and social power, women are the caregivers of society. This role can obviously be enormously demanding and debilitating, as the substantial literature on caregiver burden suggests (Etaugh, 1993a, 1993b; Denmark, 2003; Green & Russo, 1993). But it is also a role that many women cherish, and new research is uncovering some of the rewards of, for instance, daughters caring for their elderly mothers.

Grandmothering, discussed more fully in Chapter 11, is a central identity for many women and a critical function in many families. Psychologists are only now beginning to study grandmothering in a systematic way. New theoretical work in evolutionary psychology puts the spotlight on grandmothering (Lee, cited in Wade, 2003). Lee suggests that humans generally and females particularly live so long beyond their prime reproductive years because grandmothers are so important to the survival of their grandchildren. As little as we know about grandmothers, we know even less about women as sisters, daughters, daughters-in-law, mothers-in-law, and aunts.

Indeed, given their importance in the lives of women, all of the roles women play in families need and deserve more research. We will now consider women as daughters and sisters.

Women as Daughters and Sisters

It is well established that, the world over, couples prefer to have sons than daughters, particularly for first children, and sons are treated better than daughters in countless ways. This includes everything from the selective destruction of female fetuses and babies to the better feeding, health care, and education of boys than girls. The devaluation of girls occurs for many reasons, but is historically rooted in values favoring the accumulation of wealth and property, the forging of political alliances, the perpetuation of the family line, and the relative importance of warriors compared to mothers (Hunter College Women's Studies Collective, in press).

Of course, daughters have always had intrinsic value to families, because only daughters can produce future generations. Daughters also do vital domestic work in the home, including taking care of younger siblings, and, where child labor is common, work outside the home for pay. In many societies, including our own, to this day, daughters are viewed as critical to ensuring the well-being and security of their aged parents and parents-in-law. Changes in social, economic, military, and political forces over the centuries have improved the status of women in many cultures and reduced many of the most dramatic inequities between daughters and sons. Nonetheless, it is still the case that sons are more highly valued than daughters, even in modern societies such as ours, in which many of the structural factors favoring boys and men no longer exist, and in which the dominant social norms discourage expressing favoritism concerning the sex of future offspring. One way we know this is that couples tend to continue having children until they have a son and couples who seek to use sex selection techniques in planning their families overwhelmingly prefer males to females (Hunter College Women's Studies Colelctive, in press). It is against this backdrop of devaluation that daughters today are born and reared.

Much of the psychological work on being a daughter comes from the psychoanalytic tradition. Psychoanalyst Nancy Chodorow presents a developmental theory in which she reasons that all infants experience the mother as the first "other," and that the chief developmental challenge to both girls and boys is to forge a separate identity from this other. Because the mother and daughter are of the same sex, daughters and mothers are closer and daughters have both a more difficult time separating psychologically from the mother and an easier time learning their possible roles and gender-appropriate behavior (Chodorow, 1978). In traditional societies in which girls' roles are highly scripted, options are limited and futures predictable, there is little cause for stress and conflict between mothers and daughters as daughters mature. But in modern societies in which these conditions do not pertain, opportunity for strife between mothers and daughters is rife, and conflict, especially during adolescence, is seen as normal and inevitable. Modern daughters in this second stage are seen as striving for autonomy and independence at the same time that they maintain closeness with the mother. Mothers are seen as restricting girls' mobility and independence. When daughters reach adulthood and become mothers themselves, the mother–daughter relationship enters a third phase of renewed relations and harmony as daughters seek the advice and support of their mothers, and mothers seek closeness with their daughters' children (Hunter College Women's Studies Collective, in press). The relationship of mothers to the children of their daughters is widely understood to be closer than the relationship of mothers to the children of their sons.

This psychoanalytic model has been criticized for representing White middle-class development better than pathways among peoples of other social classes and ethnic and race groups. For many of these groups, beset with problems of racism and poverty, mothers have to work long hours outside the home, and other female figures, including grandmothers, aunts, siblings, and neighbors, loom large in daughters' development.

Accounts of mothers and daughters depict mothers as both the greatest champions of their daughters' independence, opportunities, and options, and the most vocal critics of their daughters' choices and circumstances. Many contemporary scholars have written of the complexity, ambivalence, and tension in this relationship (Glasman, 2002). It is clear that the mother–daughter relationship is among the richest and closest of all human relationships and that mothers provide daughters a framework through which they evaluate themselves and their experiences throughout their lifetimes.

The father–daughter relationship is also complex and multifaceted. Father–daughter relationships have not been given a great deal of attention in the psychological literature. But it is well documented that fathers, more than mothers, express preferences for sons and spend more time with sons than daughters. Fathers treat daughters, from infancy on, in a more sex-typed manner than mothers do. Recent demographic and economic data show that, in some fundamental sense, men do not value daughters as much as they value sons. Men are 25 percent more likely to marry the unmarried mother of their child if that child is a boy than a girl. The likelihood that a marriage will survive increases by about 7 percent if the couple has a son than if it has only daughters (Morin, 2002/2004). Men work much harder after the birth of a son than a daughter. For example, if the first child is a daughter, the father works 54 more hours a year, but if it is a son, 118 more hours (Morin, 2002/2004). Sadly, the context in which father–daughter relationships are most often studied in psychology is incest. Father–daughter incest is the most commonly reported type of incest in the United States, and its effects are among the most devastating (see Chapter 12).

These facts paint a dismal picture of father–daughter relationships. But it is also known from the earliest days of the women's movement that daughters who are very accomplished in business, science, academia, and art have often had exceptionally close, supportive relationships with their fathers and cite those relationships in explaining their successes. There is heartening recent empirical evidence that the experience of having and rearing daughters changes men in ways that render them more supportive of the advancement of women. Warner and Steel (1999) have found that men with only daughters endorse gender equity policies in the workplace more than do childless men or men with both daughters and sons, and much more than do men with sons only.

There is little doubt that fathers' attitudes toward their daughters can profoundly affect the daughters' educational and occupational prospects, as well as their later relationships with men.

The relationships of siblings are studied even less frequently than parent–child relationships and are seldom studied at all in psychology. Yet we know that the roles and relationships of sisters are among the strongest of family ties. Older sisters often run the households like "little mommies" to their younger siblings. As they mature and leave the family home, they may still function as family leaders, providing places for younger siblings to live, and seeking opportunities for them to find work and love relationships. This is particularly the case with immigrant families, in which older sisters who migrate provide a base for following opportunities (Hunter College Women's Studies Collective, in press). Still, in most cases, it is the males in the households whose ambitions are fostered, and historically, many sisters have accepted secondhand status within their own households, regardless of their talents and drives relative to their brothers. For example, when resources are scarce, as they have been for most people at most points in history, and when only one child in a household can be afforded the opportunity to travel or attend college or private school, that child is much more likely to be a male than a female child. Birth order, age distribution, and household size are important variables to take into account when considering the roles of sisters and brothers, with firstborn children often bearing both more responsibilities and more privileges than others.

The bonds of sisterhood often last a lifetime. Despite rivalries, competitions, and jealousies, sisters are close, loving, and useful to each other throughout their lives. In old age, it is not uncommon for divorced, maiden, or widowed sisters to live together. In fact, after wives and husbands, sisters living together are the most common household constellation among older adults sharing a home.

Psychologists have done so little work on what it means to have or be a daughter or sister that most psychology of women and gender texts do not even discuss these topics, let alone treat them in depth. There is clearly a need for more research on girls and women as daughters and sisters.

Friendships

Friends who share our interests, help us in time of need, enjoy our company, and value our opinions greatly enrich our lives (Veniegas & Peplau, 1997). For many groups of people today, friends have replaced family as their most cherished and reliable support networks. However, friendships are complicated relationships, varying in depth, closeness, and conflict. Like all other intimate relationships, they are poorly understood but increasingly the focus of empirical research.

People have long noticed sex differences in friendship patterns. For one thing, at least until recently, our closest friends tend to be people of our own sex. Male friendships tend to be based on shared interests, whereas female friendships are more often based on disclosure (Reis, Senchak, & Solomon, 1985). Not so long ago, male friendships, sometimes called *male bonding,* were extolled in literature, television, and film as more noble, loyal, and deep than female friendships, which, when they were portrayed at all, were depicted as shallow, trivial, and competitive. But today, *Butch Cassidy and the Sundance Kid* has given way to *Thelma and Louise, Waiting to Exhale* and *Divine Secrets of the Ya-Ya Sisterhood.* Many factors have combined to change the view of what friendship is and might be and the valuation of male and female friendships. For instance, with the feminist revolution came a more positive reassessment of female qualities such as expressivity and nurturance. Empirical research in psychology over the past 30 years has consistently documented the positive effects of social support and self-disclosure on physical and mental health and, alternatively, the negative effects of "keeping things in" and suppressing emotions. Moreover, women's greater willingness to talk about their feelings and ask for help means that they are more likely to get the help that they need than men are.

Research on diverse samples of people consistently finds sex differences in the quality of same-sex friendships, regardless of how quality is measured: Women rate their friendships higher than do men on meaningfulness, intimacy, nurturance, enjoyment, and satisfaction (Veniegas & Peplau, 1997). Although we do not yet understand why women's friendships appear to be closer, more meaningful, and more satisfying, several possible explanations have been offered (Kilmartin, 1994). Many of these are rooted in aspects of the masculine gender role that inhibit the formation of close relationships between men. For instance, men are socialized to believe that other men are competitors and that the establishment of intimacy rests on revealing one's weaknesses. This leads to an atmosphere of distrust among men. The gender-role demand for independence also inhibits self-disclosure in men because it keeps them from asking for help or comfort. According to Kilmartin (1994), homophobia is probably the greatest barrier to friendships between men. Some men may have difficulty making a clear distinction between sexual and nonsexuality intimacy and may be concerned that getting close to another man is tantamount to being sexual with him.

It is true that the style of intimacy associated with female friendships has many benefits and the style associated with male friendships some drawbacks. But it would be a mistake to exaggerate the differences between male and female friendships or to disparage the different forms that friendships might take. There are some aspects of male friendships that may be beneficial to all people, and some features of female friendships that are not always desirable. For example, shared interests and activities and instrumental acts of helping others, mainstays of male friendships, are generally valuable to all people. On the other hand, talking or ruminating about problems in the absence of direct action to change circumstances can keep women stuck in bad jobs and relationships. Finally, women's and men's friendships are more alike than they are different (Veniegas & Peplau, 1997) and may become more similar if girls and boys are socialized less differently in the future.

Although they are not nearly as common as same-sex friendships, cross-sex friendships are vital sources of satisfaction for a growing number of adults. Men as well as women seek out women with whom to talk about their feelings, and, like women, men report feeling more emotional closeness to female than male friends (Wheeler, Reis, & Nezlek, 1983). Cross-sex friendships are complicated by the fact that men and women have different interactional styles (Tannen, 1990), with men generally less egalitarian and more directive than women in their communications, which some women find aversive (Kilmartin, 1994). Cross-sex friendships are sometimes made difficult because of sexual tension (Dion & Dion, 2001). Studies show that men are more likely to sexualize a relationship than are women, and to perceive sexual interest or flirtation where women see only friendliness (Abbey, 1982; Kaplan & Keys, 1997 in Dion & Dion, 2001). The movie *When Harry Met Sally* humorously captures the dilemma, when Harry says to Sally, "No man can be friends with a woman . . . [because] he always wants to have sex with her" (as cited in Dion & Dion, 2001, p. 263). Kaplan and Keyes surveyed college students about cross-sex friendships and found that more men (57 percent) than women (32 percent) reported feeling moderate to high levels of sexual attraction toward their closest, other-sex "platonic" friend. More cross-sex friendships are found in young adulthood than in any other developmental period. In later adulthood, especially after marriage, it is difficult to maintain these relationships, partly because of concern by spouses and others about the sexual possibilities in the friendship (Kilmartin, 1994). Of course, the fact that cross-sex relationships have been inhibited in the past does not mean that they will be uncommon in the future. As traditional gender roles break down, there may be more possibilities for rich, egalitarian relationships between men and women.

SUMMARY

In this chapter we have considered the major topics explored by social scientists in attempting to understand intimate relationships in their richness and complexity. As you can see, psychologists have raised and attempted to answer some interesting questions but have barely scratched the surface of these intriguing topics. What is clear from this chapter is that intimate relationships are particularly important to women; that men, women, and children depend critically on women for social support; and that most problems that people face in their relationships may be improved substantially with social support. We need to shine a spotlight on new relationships that women are forging with other women as mentors of other women. We may need new lines of inquiry to capture the changing nature of relationships in the context of continually evolving social structures, gender roles, attitudes, beliefs, behaviors, and values. And we are challenged with the task of illuminating those factors that cause problems for women and men in their most important relationships, that contribute to distress and conflict, and that stand in the way of contentment and fulfillment.

KEY TERMS

Cohabitation (p. 305)

Egalitarian marriages (p. 297)

Exchange theory (p. 296)

Homogamy (p. 295)

Marriage gradient (p. 296)

Modern marriages (p. 297)

Role overload (p. 300)

Romantic love (p. 288)

Traditional marriages (p. 296)

DISCUSSION QUESTIONS

1. How does it make you feel to read *The Rules*? Do you believe that behaving according to *The Rules* "works" for women in establishing long-standing, committed relationships?

2. Do you think that romantic love is a good basis for marriage or lifelong commitment? Why or why not? Compare it with an alternative, for example, arranged marriages.

3. Should heterosexual women pay their own way on dates? Why or why not? Have you ever felt obligated to someone who was paying your way? What does it mean for a man to pay for a date?

4. Is there any reason to think that same-sex couples cannot achieve the same levels of love and commitment that heterosexual couples do? What is your position on gay marriage? Why do you support or oppose it?

5. Do you think that there should be two forms of marriage: one for childless couples, which is relatively easy to dissolve, and another for couples with children, which is more difficult to dissolve than marriages today?

6. How are dating and marriage possible under conditions of economic scarcity?

7. Discuss the relationship of power to the household division of labor. How was labor divided in the house in which you were reared, and how would you like it divided in your household?

8. To whom do you feel closest in your family? Describe this relationship, with a focus on the joys and tensions in this relationship. How do gender issues affect this relationship?

9. Think of your closest friendships. Do any of them cross race or ethnicity? If so, are there any special issues that have arisen in these friendships? How do you and your friend(s) resolve those issues?

FURTHER READINGS

Adelman, M. R. (Ed.). (2000). *Midlife lesbian relationships: Friends, lovers, children, and parents.* Binghamton, NY: Haworth Press.

Brehm, S. S., Miller, R. S., Perlman, D., & Campbell, S. M. (2002). *Intimate relationships.* Boston: McGraw-Hill.

D'Augelli, A. R., & Patterson, C. J. (Eds.). (2001). *Lesbian, gay, and bisexual identities and youth.* New York: Oxford University Press.

Debold, E., Wilson, M., & Malave, I. (1993). *Mother–daughter revolution: From betrayal to power.* Reading, MA: Addison-Wesley.

Goss, R., & Strongheart, A. (1997). *Our families, our values.*

Gottman, J. (1999). *Marriage clinic: A scientifically based marital therapy.* New York: W. W. Norton.

Hetherington, E. M., & Kelly, J. (2001). *For better or for worse: Divorce reconsidered.* New York: W. W. Norton.

CHAPTER 10

PARENTING AND REPRODUCTIVE ISSUES

And then I realized what the first word must have been: ma, the sound of a baby smacking its lips in search of her mother's breast. For a long time, that was the only word the baby needed. Ma, ma, ma. Then the mother decided that was her name and she began to speak too. She taught the baby to be careful: sky, fire, tiger. A mother is always the beginning. She is how things begin.

—Amy Tan

Mothering, like everything else in life, is best learned by doing. I think that the mothering women have done has taught many of us skills of listening to what is said and to what is not said. I think in mothering we hone our empathic abilities, learn to understand the vulnerability in others without profiting from it. I think that the experience of mothering teaches people how to be more emotionally and intellectually nurturant, how to take care of each other. It is not the only way to learn that lesson, but it is hard to mother and not learn it.

—Barbara Katz Rothman

There is no question that the dominant society has said, men will do the important work; women will tend to the "lesser task" of helping other human beings to develop. At the outset, this dichotomy means that our major societal institutions are not founded on the tenet of helping others to develop. All people need development at all stages, but it is made to appear as if only children do. This casts both women and children under a pall, with many psychological consequences for children of both sexes. The person most intimately involved in their development is seen as a lesser figure performing a lesser task, even though she is of preeminent importance to them.

—Jean Baker Miller

I have never sat down to write about abortion without feeling, at least for a moment, the complexities sweep over me like a fit of faintness: the

*complete life of the woman and the burgeoning life of the child, the
primitive development of the embryo and the potential traits of the baby,
the joy a pregnancy often brings and the despair it sometimes carries
with it.*
—Anna Quindlen

*Making the decision to have a child—it's momentous. It is to decide
forever to have your heart walking around outside your body.*
—Elizabeth Stone

Parental love and commitment can attain a peak of intensity that has become proverbial. The bonds that tie parent to child are widely understood to be the strongest and most enduring of most people's lives. For parents, especially mothers, in modern-day Western society, the costs, sacrifices, and inconveniences of rearing children are profound and far outweigh any material benefits that people can reasonably hope to realize through having offspring. The evidence that people appreciate this is that many fewer people today are choosing to have children at all, and most others are having many fewer than they might. Nonetheless, most adults become parents, and those who cannot easily conceive children frequently endure remarkable hardships to become parents.

Why do so many people, particularly women, "choose" sleepless nights; drastically reduced flexibility and freedom in career choices and social life; the financial and emotional burdens of care, feeding, housing, and education; and the general and continuing costs of socializing unwilling recruits to civilization (Brickman, Janoff-Bulman, & Rabinowitz, 1987)? Psychologists have long sought to explain the ferocity of parental love, the reasons that people want children so much, and, because parenting is perhaps the most gendered of all human endeavors, the different meanings and significance of motherhood and fatherhood for women and men. In this chapter, we will consider why people become parents, the special meanings of motherhood, the experiences of pregnancy and giving birth, fatherhood, infertility, and abortion.

WHY DO PEOPLE BECOME PARENTS?

Not surprisingly, there are a variety of biological, psychological, and social explanations for the complex behaviors involved in wanting and having children. Before briefly reviewing them, it is important to note that such explanations seemed quite unnecessary when children had greater economic value than they do now. Romanticized views of parenthood, particularly motherhood, and of children are quite modern notions. Throughout most of human history, children were far less costly and more materially valuable to their families as workers and sources of support in old age than they are today. In eras when children had greater material value to parents, parents took a more instrumental or pragmatic orientation toward their children (Aries, 1962; Shorter, 1975). By drastically reducing the economic value of children, other explanations for wanting children stand out in sharp relief.

On the one hand, the answer to the question of why women and men want to be parents may seem quite obvious: In order for the species to survive, it is necessary for women and men to procreate. Theories of evolution help us understand that the pleasure involved in sexual reproduction is in service of this necessity on the species level. But, although it is to the obvious benefit of the species that men and women have offspring, it is not obviously beneficial (at least in modern-day Western societies) for individual women and men to reproduce. Indeed, as we noted, when one considers the potential costs to one's freedom, social and career options, emotional and financial independence, and physical health and safety, especially for women, the decision to have children hardly seems rational. Major theories of behavior, such as evolutionary psychology, suggest that it is the largely irrational and unconscious desire to pass on one's genes through having children that is the central motivator of all human action (Buss & Kendrick, 1998). In these theories, the desire to become parents is instinctual for both sexes, but especially for women, giving rise to the frequently invoked notion of the *maternal instinct* (Bernard, 1972).

There is little dispute that women are more likely than men to nurture children and appear more skilled at it. The question is whether such nurturance is the expression of an innate biological drive or a learned behavior. The idea that women are biologically programmed to be more nurturant than men is an extension of the observation that femaleness in humans and other mammals is defined by the manner of reproduction: gestation and nourishment in the womb followed by nursing infants after birth.

In her social history of parenting, Lorber (1994) notes that, while it makes evolutionary sense for a mother to bond with her newborn, whether she actually does has always depended on the social worth of both the mother and the child. Lorber reviews the historical evidence, which suggests that the strong emotional bond that we take for granted as part of parenting is a luxury that many women and men throughout history could not afford. The abandonment, neglect, and murder of infants have always been prevalent among parents of children who had too many to feed or too many of one sex (virtually always female) or whose children were called "illegitimate." In early modern Europe, 10 to 40 percent of the children registered as born were abandoned, even in prosperous times (Boswell, 1988). In England, infant mortality rates were not recorded until 1875, and registration of births was not compulsory until 1907. In fact, as Lorber notes, the lines between stillbirths, accidental deaths, neglect, and infanticide have never been clear, and how an infant's death is classified, today as in the past, depends to some extent on society's judgment of the mother's social and moral "worth."

Today, news stories about discarded newborns, some alive, some dead, rivet the nation's attention. These incidents signal to some a lack of morality and humanity in the modern world. The abandonment, neglect, and murder of infants, by mothers and fathers alike, are not new signs of troubled times. In fact, they were once much more common in the West than they are today. In any case, history relates that the social and emotional value of children to parents is not fixed biologically, but fluctuates widely from time to time and place to place, and with it the fortunes of children. In fact, there is little evidence to date to suggest the existence of a biological instinct to parent and, more specifically, to mother.

Closely related to the biological–evolutionary theories about parenting are the psychoanalytical theories positing an innate psychological need on the part of women to have children. Certainly the most famous or infamous of these is Freud's, postulating that women want to bear a child, preferably a male child, as a penis substitute (Freud, 1925/1961). In fact, research suggests that, despite clear societal preferences for boys and, frequently, their own husbands' preference for sons, most U.S. women do not prefer sons to daughters before their children are born (Steinbacher & Gilroy, 1996). Moreover, there is no evidence that women seek fulfillment through their sons more than their daughters. (More information about sex preferences and sex selection of offspring is presented in Box 10.1.) In fact, research suggests that mothers' relationships with their daughters occupy a more central place in their lives

than their relationships with sons throughout the life span (Forcey, 1987). As the old adage states, "Your son's your son till he picks a wife; your daughter's your daughter for the rest of your life."

In a more recent formulation that combines psychoanalytic theory with a feminist orientation, Chodorow (1978) has suggested that women's nurturing orientation derives from girls' early childhood experiences of closeness to their mothers. According to Chodorow, little girls, unlike little boys, do not have to distance themselves from their beloved pri-

Box 10.1

Sex Selection

People from earliest times have expressed great interest in the sex composition of their offspring. There are many old wives' tales about how to improve the chances that one will conceive a child of one sex or the other by eating certain foods, or having sex in certain positions or at certain times during a woman's menstrual cycle. Modern technology now offers us several approaches to select the sex of an infant, and many people around the world are very interested in these developments. The prevailing view in the United States at the present time is that people should have the right to make choices about issues of concern to them, and over half of all U.S. geneticists have expressed a willingness either to perform prenatal tests to determine the sex of the fetus or to refer patients to someone who will (Kelly, 2004).

There are sound medical reasons for couples to be interested in sex selection; for example, there are sex-linked diseases from which one can seek to spare one's offspring if one could select by sex. But many people are concerned that sex selection procedures, should they become reliable, will overwhelmingly be used by people who are interested in engineering the sex composition of their families because they prefer males. That will almost certainly lead to a great oversupply of boys around the world.

In the United States, where the preferences for boys are less extreme than in some other parts of the world, sex selection techniques may be used to ensure that the first child is a boy. With what we know about the effects of birth order on achievement, for example, a trend for first children to be boys will increase advantages for males throughout society.

Sex selection techniques are not yet highly reliable, although some sperm separation procedures that sort X- and Y-bearing sperm by weight are very promising. These procedures take advantage of the fact that the X chromosome carries more genetic material than does the Y chromosome. In the one procedure, sperm bearing the larger and heavier X chromosomes are separated from the Y chromosomes before artificial insemination. The success rate for parents who wish to conceive a girl can be as high as 90 percent and for those who wish to conceive a boy, about 75 percent. Such procedures now cost about $3,000 (Rhode, 2003). As the cost of such procedures declines and their reliability increases, sex selection procedures are likely to become more popular.

Right now, the most reliable way of ensuring the sex of offspring is selective abortion. Techniques such as chorionic villi sampling and amniocentesis can identify the sex of a fetus within a few weeks after conception by identifying the sex chromosomes in fetal cells (Kelly, 2004). Later in gestation, widely available ultrasound scans also reveal the sex of the fetus. The use of ultrasound scans throughout the world has led to the abortion of millions of female fetuses, particularly in India and China, where the sex ratios in some provinces now approach 3 girls for every 4 boys. The use of ultrasound techniques to abort female fetuses is increasing rapidly in South Korea, Bangladesh, and Pakistan. Such extreme sex ratios may well require new partnering and family arrangements when these cohorts of girls and boys reach marriageable ages.

mary caregiver in order to identify with a powerful same-sex adult. Thus, girls' development emphasizes relatedness and connectedness with others, whereas boys' requires separation from others, rejection of things feminine, and mastery of the outside world. In this formulation, having babies satisfies women's deep-seated relational needs.

But the emotional closeness between most (but by no means all) mothers and their children is at least as likely to be the *effect* as the *cause* of the fact that women are the primary caregivers of children in most societies. Studies suggest that becoming a mother changes women in the direction of becoming more mature, responsible, tolerant, warm, and vulnerable—more feminine (Helson, Mitchell, & Moane, 1984; Hrdy, 1997). Further, when fathers are the primary caregivers, they experience more intimacy with their children and exhibit more stereotypically female characteristics, such as nurturance and expressivity, than do traditional fathers (Kilmartin, 1994; Risman, 1987; Silverstein, 1996). In short, when men must mother, they behave more like mothers.

Until recently, women often became mothers simply because they had little or no control over their sexual and reproductive lives or few other ways to feel valued in their communities and function as respectable adults. With advances in reproductive technologies and increases in women's rights and life options, many women in industrialized societies have more choices, and an increasing proportion of them are choosing not to have children at all, or to have many fewer than women typically had just one or two generations ago (Kelly, 2004). Indeed, the birthrate in the United States is plummeting on a yearly basis and is at a historical low. The U.S. birthrate was 13.9 per 1,000 people in 2002, compared with 14.1 in 2001, and 16.7 as recently as 1990 (Associated Press, 2003). Moreover, this trend is not merely confined to the United States, but can be seen in Europe, Japan, and some developing countries. Recently Italy has become the first country in history where there are more people over the age of 60 than under the age of 20, and the birthrate in Italy is the lowest in the world (The Baby Bust: A Special Report: Population Implosion Worries a Graying Europe, 1998). And, as we shall see, there is very little evidence to suggest that women who do not have children are less happy or fulfilled than those who do. In fact, there is evidence to suggest the opposite: Women without children are somewhat happier than those with children (Ratner, 2000), although research results are somewhat inconsistent on this topic. These findings suggest that factors beyond innate biological and psychological forces support motherhood.

Many surveys have been conducted asking people, often college students, why they want to be parents. In one study of college students, the most frequently endorsed motives for having children, in descending order, were the desires to expand oneself and have someone to follow one, to achieve adult status or social identity, to provide a family for oneself, to experience the fun and stimulation of children, and to be able to influence or control someone (Gormly, Gormly, & Weiss, 1987; McMahon, 1995). The only significant sex difference emerged in the rating of one item, to achieve adult status or social identity, which was much more frequently endorsed by women than men. Another study of undergraduates compared motivations for having children in 1977 and in 1986 (Morahan-Martin, 1991). This study found an increase in emphasis on positive factors cited by both sexes over time, with a corresponding decrease in emphasis on the negative aspects of parenting. There were, however, sex differences in the rated importance of traditional reasons for having children, with men more likely than women to cite reasons such as continuity, tradition, security, and role motivations.

Responses to such surveys are interesting in and of themselves, not so much because they reveal people's actual needs and motives, but because they reflect the culture's constructions of parenthood. Psychologists have long known that the processes that govern people's actions and the processes that govern how they explain their actions to themselves and others are quite distinct. People are especially unlikely to invoke unconscious motives, such as a desire to pass on one's genes or fulfill one's deep-seated emotional need for closeness, or socially undesirable motives, such as a desire to produce an heir and inherit money or raise one's status in the family, in a straightforward survey.

THE MOTHERHOOD MANDATE

There may be little direct evidence for a biological imperative to have children, but there can be little doubt of a social imperative. Russo has labeled the enormous social pressure to have and raise children as the **motherhood mandate** (Russo, 1976). This mandate refers to the pervasive belief that in order to be a real and complete woman, a woman must have children, preferably more than one, and raise them successfully. No other accomplishment by a woman, no matter how unusual or significant, can compensate for the failure to mother. Speaking for generations of women, First Lady Jacqueline Kennedy once remarked that: "There is no more important job for a woman than to be a good mother. If a woman bungles that, then it doesn't much matter what else she does."

Training in the **motherhood mystique** starts early for girls, who are given baby dolls as toys and praise for expressing the desire to be mommies when they grow up. In contrast, boys who play with dolls, especially baby dolls, are often the source of great concern for parents. In the uncommon event that boys claim ambitions to be daddies, they are likely to be asked what else they want to be, with the clear implication that being a daddy is not enough of an ambition for a boy. But being a mother is supposed to be the major preoccupation of adult women, and this mandate is enforced, like most successful societal imperatives, by idealization of the role on the one hand and stigmas and punishments attached to failing to fulfill the role properly on the other hand. We will now discuss how motherhood is alternatively romanticized, regulated, and devalued in modern Western society.

THE MOTHERHOOD MYSTIQUE

The word *mother* simply denotes a woman who has borne (or raised) a child, but few words in the English language connote greater depth of positive feeling. Phrases ranging from "motherhood and apple pie" to "a face that only a mother could love" suggest the unquestioned good that is motherhood and its incomparable potential for unconditional love. As sellers of greeting cards, telephone operators, and restaurateurs know all too well, Father's Day is not a close second to Mother's Day in the sentiment—or business—it in-

vokes. A spate of recent books and articles by Arlie Russell Hochschild (who coined the term *second shift*), Felice N. Schwartz (who popularized the term *mommy track*), Joan Williams (author of *Unbending Gender*), Sylvia Ann Hewlett (author of *Creating a Life*), and Lisa Belkin (*New York Times* columnist) features the modern incarnation of the motherhood mystique. In different ways, these contemporary authors all write about how the workplace has failed women, and how women, especially elite, educated women, are rejecting the workplace in favor of staying at home and rearing children (Belkin, 2003).

The images of motherhood that we cull from religion, myth, fairy tale, and the mainstream media are stunningly similar and idealized portraits of young, well-groomed, usually slim, and conventionally beautiful women. They are virtually always heterosexual, married to the fathers of the children, White, and middle class. In personality and orientation to their children they are usually gentle, patient, loving, devoted, and self-sacrificing. They are basically asexual; in fact, they have few personal needs and desires of any kind and certainly not negative proclivities. These qualities are reified by the Latin American mestizo cultures in an ideal known as *marianismo,* based on the qualities symbolized by the figure of the Virgin Mary. According to Stevens (1993), *marianismo* is a ubiquitous stereotype prescribed for all social classes. Among the characteristics of this ideal are "semi-divinity, moral superiority, and spiritual strength. This spiritual strength engenders abnegation, that is, an infinite capacity for humility and sacrifice. No self-denial is too great for the Latin American woman, no limit can be divined to her vast store of patience with the men of her world" (p. 485).

Recently, scholars have studied so-called "myths of motherhood"—how the ideology of patriarchal cultures supports and maintains women in the incredibly demanding, low-status, uncompensated work of mothering—and how they affect real mothers' feelings and behaviors (Weseen, 2000). These myths include the seemingly natural and commonsense notions that only women can be loving and nurturing enough to raise a child; that men are vocationally superior to women; that good parenting requires that one parent, virtually always the woman, regularly subordinate personal goals to the children's and family's needs;

that motherhood is uniquely joyous and fulfilling for women; that a good mother is invariably kind, unselfish, and loving; and that motherhood is the ultimate way for women to gain esteem and support as adults. Research has largely dispelled each of these myths, and these myths hurt women, because when women and their families do not live up to them, they frequently feel that they have failed as mothers and thus as women and as people (Hunter College Women's Studies Collective, in press; Weseen, 2000). Yet they persist in the minds of women and men. Why?

Feminist analyses of mothering have pointed to the ways in which such myths, widely held to as sacred and beyond question, control and constrain the behavior of women in ways that support patriarchy and the prerogatives and privileges of men. Polatnick (1993) has reviewed the many ways in which "breadwinning beats childrearing." These include, first and foremost, the ability to achieve in the workplace as the major source of money and social status in Western societies. As we saw in Chapter 9, breadwinning power translates into power within the family, with studies showing that the more money a man (or woman) makes, the greater the decision-making power in the family. With the ability to make money comes the right to exercise control over its use and a corresponding lack of dependence on others. However it idealizes motherhood, society continues to attach greater value to the role of wage earner than parent, and earning wages legitimizes power wielding inside and outside of the family.

Feminist analysts point out that, in working outside the home, one accrues many tangible and intangible benefits that can affect the balance of power within relationships. To name a few, wage earners gain organizational experience; social contacts, including contacts with potential sexual and romantic interests; knowledge of the world; and feelings of independence and confidence. Aside from wanting and benefiting from the increased power due to their wage earning, men gain from women staying home in countless other ways as well. When women are home, they are not competitors for jobs, and this ensures continued male domination in the occupational world. While women are consumed by domestic duties, men are building careers and consolidating resources in the outside world. By the time women

complete their full-time child-rearing tenure, most women cannot catch up occupationally and recoup their losses (Polatnick, 1993). All the while, women who stay at home minister to husbands' everyday needs of laundry, cooking, cleaning, and keeping the social calendar, just as they do to their children's, thus making husbands' careers and lifestyles possible.

This brings us to the issue of the nature of many child-rearing tasks themselves. Not only are these tasks not a significant source of power, money, or prestige in the larger society, but they are also inherently onerous. They involve tremendous responsibility, constant demands, deprivation from other identities, isolation from other adults, disappointment with unhelpful spouses, and guilt about not measuring up to the ideal. They do not confer power on people, and people with power do not perform them. We know that few men do these tasks with or without pay, and women do not perform them for pay when they have other options. Whatever rewards there are in mothering—and as mothers, the three authors know them well—the fact is that child rearing is not regarded as a desirable job for those who are not the mothers of the children. Hollingworth made this point as early as 1916, in her groundbreaking and myth-exploding early study of mothering, in which she cited the long years of exacting labor and self-sacrifice, and also the

> drudgery, the monotonous labor, and other disagreeable features of childbearing are minimized by "the social guardians." On the other hand, the joys and compensations of motherhood are magnified and presented to consciousness on every hand. Thus, the tendency is to create an illusion whereby motherhood will appear to consist of compensations only, and thus come to be desired by those for whom the illusion is intended. (Hollingworth, 1916, pp. 20–21)

ENFORCING MOTHERHOOD

The motherhood mystique is invaluable in maintaining the status quo, which so clearly benefits men at the expense of women. But it is not through rewards alone that society supports motherhood. The flip side of idealization of motherhood is punishment and devaluation of "bad" women: women who do not mother or mother differently from the cultural ideal.

In this section, we will consider how society constructs women who have no children by choice or who are lesbian mothers, single mothers, noncustodial mothers, mothers on welfare, or simply mothers who work too long or at dangerous jobs.

Women Who Choose to Remain Child-Free

Most recent surveys show that, overwhelmingly, women still expect to become mothers. One survey of undergraduates found that less than 3 percent wished to be child-free (Baber & Allen, 1992). When child-free couples are asked why they do not want children, they frequently cite the cost of rearing a child today, the fear that they will not be good parents, and concerns about interference with flexible lifestyles and vocational and educational plans (Cowan & Cowan, 1992; Ireland, 1993). Research on women who do not have children shows that they are often White, urban, well educated, and professional (DeVellis, Wallston & Acker, 1984; Kelly, 2004), suggesting the importance of career considerations in remaining child-free. In fact, nearly 40 percent of women in certain professions such as academia forego childbearing altogether (Rabinowitz, 2003). Yet, in contrast, professional men often have families with two or more children and do not have to choose between having careers and families. In some cases, women choose not to have children because they themselves had unhappy childhoods or distant relationships with their parents and do not wish to repeat these patterns (Houseknecht, 1979). But increasingly, women are choosing not to have children for more positive reasons, and the number of such women is growing. The number of childless married, divorced, or widowed women without children *by choice* has more than doubled in the United States since the 1970s, hovering around 25 percent (Kelly, 2004).

Even today, however, a stigma is attached to women who do not have children, whether by choice or not. The terms applied to child-free women, *childless* and *barren,* reflect this negative bias. Married women without children are seen as more selfish, unhappy, and neurotic than other women (Kelly, 2004; Petersen, 1983). People wonder why they did not have children, suspect that they do not like children,

frequently ask them about the decision not to have a child, and question whether they feel that they are missing something essential in life—questions that arise far less frequently with men. Research consistently shows that women without children are, at least in early adulthood, basically happier, more satisfied with their marital relationships, less conflicted, and more successful in their careers than women with children. Only widows between the ages of 60 and 75 with children report being more happy and less lonely than comparable women without children, but the differences between groups was quite small (Beckman & Houser, 1982). Of course, these correlational findings do not suggest that children cause unhappiness in women, and most women who have children are very happy with their choice and report that they would make the same choice again. Some more recent studies suggest that there are no overall differences in happiness and fulfillment between childless women and women who have children (Mueller & Yoder, 1997). But these findings, taken together, explode the myth of the miserable barren woman.

Mothers Who Fall Short of the "Ideal"

Given the narrow stereotype of the ideal mother, it is not surprising that so many women fall short of the ideal and incur society's disapproval and even rejection and punishment. Lesbian mothers risk losing their children in custody battles, despite the fact that research consistently shows that the children of lesbians are indistinguishable from the children of heterosexual mothers on numerous psychological and behavioral characteristics (Flaks, Ficher, Masterpasqua, & Joseph, 1995; Hoeffer, 1981). Stepmothers are among the most hateful and hated characters of myth and fairy tale, so much that one of our daughters, at age 5, on seeing an attractive and pleasant stepmother (author Judy Blume!) interviewed on television, marveled that a stepmother could be pretty and nice. The image of stepmothers so prevalent in our culture may contribute to the resistance and resentment that some stepchildren feel toward stepmothers.

Single mothers, especially those who are sexually active, are frequently seen as "loose," immoral, and unfit, whereas the fathers of those children frequently escape our gaze altogether, even if they shun all responsibility for their families. Society is especially disapproving of the single "welfare mother," who is often depicted as using her fertility to enrich herself while defrauding the taxpaying public. We have only to consider how seldom we hear the devalued terms *single father, unwed father,* and *welfare father,* to realize how harshly society judges women by their mothering.

Stereotyped depictions of African American mothers have been particularly pernicious and harmful throughout history. According to African American feminist Patricia Hill Collins, African American women are hindered in U.S. society by evolving but unrelentingly negative stereotypes about their mothering. These begin with the stereotypical "Mammy," a goodhearted, faithful domestic servant who nurtures and cares for White children to the point of neglect of her own family. Next is the sexually aggressive and promiscuous "Jezebel" stereotype, not directly focused on mothers, which nonetheless portrays African American women as inferior to other mothers due to sexual preoccupation and lack of responsibility. The third stereotypical image was created in the 1960s, that of the "matriarch," a strong, powerful, but negative image that holds African American women responsible for driving fathers out of the home, necessitating that they go on welfare or leave their children with others in order to make a living. The 1960s brought the institutionalization of the image of the "welfare mother," which depicts the fertility of African American women as both a drain and a danger to the larger society. More recently, the stereotype of the Superwoman or "Super/Essence woman" has emerged. This more positive image requires that African American women do it all—support the family and rear the children—and do it well, although any such ideal is obviously hard to live by and sets up expectations that are impossible to fulfill (Collins, 1990). Of course, these stereotypes fail to acknowledge how profoundly institutional racism has constrained the options of African American mothers.

There seems to be no end of ways that women can fail at mothering. Women who have only one child are frequently criticized for that choice (Russo, 1976), and women who have "too many" children are seen as foolish and irresponsible. Mothers who

"lose their children"—who do not seek or obtain custody of their children in divorce proceedings, for example—are viewed as stunning failures, often stemming from a lack of understanding about how mothers become noncustodial and from the common belief that only mothers can be good parents (Grief, 1979; Silverstein, 1996). Mothers whose jobs are demanding are frequently blamed for their absence from home, their use of day care or baby-sitters, and their concentration on their careers, in a way that fathers almost never are. Mothers whose jobs are possibly dangerous, for example, police officers or soldiers, are often viewed as irresponsible and self-indulgent parents for risking their lives, whereas fathers who have such jobs are viewed differently, even heroically. Christa McAulliffe, the teacher who was aboard the space shuttle *Challenger* when it exploded in the disaster of 1986, was roundly criticized before and after her death for putting her interests in being part of history ahead of those of her children, but the male astronauts who were fathers were not similarly judged. Mothers who smoke, drink, or use other drugs, especially while they are pregnant or breast-feeding, face extremely harsh disapproval, criminal prosecution, and even the loss of their children in some cases.

Along with blaming women for mothering that diverges from the ideal, mothers have traditionally been blamed for all kinds of problems in their children and the family generally. This pattern of mother blaming in psychology dates back at least to Freud, in whose theory of psychosexual development all mothers walk a tightrope between overindulging and underindulging the child at each stage of development, leading to lifelong unresolved problems for the child. A content analysis of articles published in mental health journals, across the disciplines of psychoanalysis, psychiatry, psychology, and social work, found strong evidence of a tendency to blame mothers for the myriad problems of clients, ranging from arson to frigidity to minimal brain damage (Caplan & Hall-McCorquodale, 1985). Except when fathers clearly physically or sexually abuse their children, fathers are strangely immune from blame for their children's physical, psychological, and social problems, and even in cases of fathers assaulting their children, mothers are still blamed for not better protecting their children from their fathers! The point is that, given how motherhood has historically been constructed, all mothers fall short of the "ideal mother" to which they have been socialized from birth to aspire. Mothers are made to feel guilty and inadequate for that failure and are blamed by society for "deficiencies" in themselves and their children.

THE EXPERIENCE OF MOTHERING

Pregnancy

Most women who become mothers do so as a result of sexual intercourse and biological pregnancy (as described in Chapter 4), although there are increasing options for would-be parents (see Box 10.2). We are about to describe pregnancy for the many women who wanted and planned for this event. This should not obscure the fact that by recent estimates 57 percent of all births in the United States are not planned (Kelly, 2004), though in many cases the woman adjusts and warms to the idea of having a child throughout the pregnancy. Obviously, unwanted pregnancies are sources of fear and hopelessness for many women, particularly unmarried teens.

For many women, the lived experience of mothering begins with the recognition that they are expecting a child. For some women, the first sign of pregnancy is a missed period, but this form of diagnosis is not fully reliable. Today, pregnancy can be reliably determined in minutes by tests that directly test the amount of human chorionic gonadotropin (HCG) in the urine. Such tests are reliable after the third week of pregnancy. Home pregnancy tests can be reliable after a missed period.

Pregnancy is a period of enormous change. Being pregnant creates a critical new relationship in one's life, and the announcement or recognition that a woman is pregnant changes her relationships to the

---

Box 10.2

Alternate Ways of Conception

In vitro fertilization (IVF): Fertility drugs stimulate ripening of the ova. Ripe ova are surgically removed from the ovary and placed in a laboratory dish with the father's sperm. Fertilized ova are then injected into the mother's uterus.

Donor IVF: A variant of IVF in which the ovum is taken from another woman.

Gamete intrafallopian transfer (GIFT): Sperm and ova are inserted together into the Fallopian tube, and conception occurs in the tube.

Zygote intrafallopian transfer (ZIFT): A combination of IVF and GIFT, sperm and ova are combined in a laboratory dish. After fertilization, the zygote is placed in the mother's Fallopian tube to begin its journey to implantation. This offers the advantage that one can know that fertilization has occurred before insertion.

Embryonic transfer: For women who do not produce ova of their own, a woman volunteer is artificially inseminated by the male partner of the infertile woman. Five days later, the embryo is removed from the volunteer and inserted into the uterus of the mother to be.

Intracytoplasmic sperm injection (ICSI): ICSI has been used when the man has too few sperm for IVF or IVF fails. In this method, a single sperm is injected into an ovum. This has enabled many pregnancies but may be associated with a higher than normal incidence of birth defects.

Surrogate motherhood: A surrogate mother is artificially inseminated by the partner of the infertile woman and carries the baby to term.

Adoption: Despite all of the recent attention given to problems with adoption, most adoptions in the United States result in loving families. Most people in the United States find it easiest to adopt children from other countries, children with special needs, and older children.

Source: From *Human Sexuality in a World of Diversity* (5th ed.), by S. A. Rathus, J. S. Nevid, & L. Fichner-Rahus, 2002, Boston: Allyn and Bacon.

important people in her life, her community, and the larger society. All cultures mark pregnancy as a special event and shape individual women's attitudes and behaviors toward it (Seegmiller, 1993).

Seegmiller (1993) has extensively reviewed the vast literature on the experience of pregnancy. She notes that women receive information about pregnancy from a variety of sources that affect their views about their own pregnancy throughout their entire lives. With pregnancy, women often enter into a "society of women" through which the folklore, prescriptions, and taboos of pregnancy are communicated both transgenerationally and among peers. Folklore touches on virtually all aspects of pregnancy. We are all familiar with some of the ways in which people in our culture predict the sex of the fetus using signs such as heart rate, the amount of fetal kicking, how a women's weight is distributed, or whether the woman is carrying the fetus high or low. Prescriptive actions are recommended to ensure easy or successful pregnancy and birth. For instance, some Puerto Rican and Mexican women drink certain teas to prevent morning sickness, whereas Anglo women ingest saltines or Benedictine for the same purpose. Taboos, usually surrounding food but often about action and sex, derive from fears of causing harm to the mother, fetus, or others. In her fieldwork among Jamaican women, Kitzinger (1978) found many rules for pregnant women: Do not cork bottles or one will not "open up" and have an easy birth; avoid looking at disabled or ugly people or things lest the baby will be similarly marked. In the United States today, many women are fearful that baby showers and baby gifts before the birth may jinx the baby's chances of survival or that sex during pregnancy will harm the fetus (Brown, 1981).

Most researchers of pregnancy have identified a series of stages as the major tasks of pregnancy. In the first stage, the woman adjusts to being pregnant, becoming more preoccupied with herself as she becomes aware of and focused on the subtle changes occurring in her body. The next stage is incorporating (feeling that the fetus is a part of one) and accepting the fetus, which is facilitated by becoming visibly pregnant or experiencing ultrasound procedures and hearing the heartbeat. Forming an attachment to the fetus, the third stage, often begins with sensing fetal movement

or "quickening" in the second trimester. It is around this time that many women begin talking to the fetus, with references to "we." This is when the woman tends to bring her partner further into the pregnancy by encouraging the partner to talk to and about the fetus, feel the fetal movements, and attend prenatal classes (Sherwin, 1987). During this period of attachment to the fetus and with increasing identity as a mother-to-be, a woman becomes more concerned with her relationship with her own mother, reconciling differences, drawing closer, and forming a new relationship based on shared identities and experiences. The final stage, during the third trimester, is marked by differentiating and separating from the fetus and internalizing the identity of "mother." It is then that the woman often names the fetus and engages in "nesting behaviors" (e.g., decorating the baby's room, buying clothes for the baby, cleaning the house). In the last trimester, the woman's body size is a constant reminder that the baby will soon separate. Most women focus closely on the delivery date in the last trimester and are eager to give birth. The culmination of this process is a new sense of one's self, the baby, one's own mother, and one's partner (Seegmiller, 1993).

Obviously, the development and intensity of attachment to the fetus vary widely from woman to woman and depend on many factors. A consistent finding is that a woman's relationship to her fetus is associated with her feelings about her own mother, particularly her early experience of having been mothered. Women who have positive experiences of being mothered—who view their own mothers as warm, empathic, and satisfied with their maternal role—have an easier time adjusting to pregnancy and show greater ego strength and less anxiety during pregnancy (Liefer, 1977). There are many other physical, psychological, and social factors associated with adjustment to pregnancy. Some of these concern the pregnancy itself: whether the pregnancy was wanted and planned, whether the pregnancy is easy or difficult physically, the woman's reactions to the physical changes of pregnancy, especially weight gain, and expectations and hopes about the sex of the baby (Seegmiller, 1993). Personality factors such as strong coping ability and ego strength, high self-concept and level of growth motivation, nurturance, and independence are associated with positive experiences of pregnancy.

Social, relationship, and other contextual variables have also been correlated with adjustment to pregnancy. The amount and quality of social support that a pregnant woman receives are critical determinants of the lived experience of pregnancy. Strong social support from one's partner and others can buffer the inevitable stresses and anxieties of pregnancy. Increased social support has been cited as one reason that first pregnancies are experienced more positively than subsequent ones. The finding that women of low socioeconomic classes do not show poorer adjustment to pregnancy than more privileged women, despite suffering a greater incidence of physical problems during pregnancy, birth, and the neonatal period, has been linked to the beneficial effects of social support (Seegmiller, 1993). Women of color, who comprise a disproportionate share of the poor in the U.S., tend to have more extensive and reliable networks of social support for pregnant women than do other women (Collins, 1990; Stack, 1974).

Pregnancy changes women's relationships to individuals and communities. We have discussed its potential to change women's relationships with their mothers, often, but by no means always, for the better. For many women, their first pregnancy is a time of increased sharing, more open affection, and recognition and acceptance of their adult status. For some, however, the mother–daughter relationship degenerates when the mother fails to accept the daughter as an adult and attempts to control the daughter or to prove that she is a better mother (Seegmiller, 1993).

Women's relationships with their partners affect and are affected by their pregnancies. Most studies of women's relationships with their partners during pregnancy are of married heterosexual couples, and the results may not be generalizable to other kinds of partnerships. These studies tend to show that the pregnancy is associated with decreased relationship satisfaction, especially for husbands (Leifer, 1977). But some studies show that pregnancy is associated with more relationship satisfaction and closeness when the couple perceives the pregnancy as a common goal (Seegmiller, 1993). Men, like women, vary greatly in how much they look forward to becoming parents, and their response to pregnancy will vary accordingly.

Fathers-to-be who are financially or emotionally unprepared may feel trapped by the pregnancy. Occasionally, an expectant father actually experiences some of the symptoms of pregnancy, known as *sympathetic pregnancy* (Rathus et al., 2002).

Women's experiences of pregnancy vary enormously. Some women describe pregnancy as one of the happiest and most hopeful times in their lives, whereas others describe it as a time of constant sickness, stress, and anxiety. Factors such as cultural and family background, psychological make-up, physical circumstances, and social and relational contexts interact to produce different reactions in every woman (Seegmiller, 1993; Unger, 1979). Of course, it is important to remember that not every woman who becomes a mother does so intentionally, in the context of a sexual relationship, or even by becoming pregnant. Some women who become pregnant choose to terminate their pregnancies via abortion, as we will discuss later.

Pregnancy, like motherhood generally, remains an understudied phenomenon by psychologists, despite the fact that most women consider their pregnancies to be among the most significant events in their lives. We do not yet have sufficient research on the topics covered here, let alone psychological responses to the use of new reproductive technologies and the process of adoption, although these are becoming vital areas of research.

Giving Birth

The experience of giving birth, like the experience of pregnancy, is one of the central events in a mother's life and is undervalued and understudied in psychology. This is largely because giving birth in the United States has been treated as a medical event that was, until recently, primarily managed by men to a degree unparalleled in the world. The medicalization of childbirth in the United States and, to a lesser extent, elsewhere in the industrialized West, inevitably colors how women perceive themselves, their babies, and the experience of childbirth.

A brief history of the medical management of childbirth reveals a struggle between male and female practitioners. In the preindustrial United States, babies were delivered by midwives and community women. When complications arose, women called on barber–surgeons, usually male, who used forceps-like instruments and hooks to extract babies. A formal training period was deemed necessary for the surgical removal of babies, and the subspecialty of obstetrics, the first subspecialty to be taught in medical schools in the United States, was born. During the Victorian era, male doctors gained control of childbirth in the middle and upper classes, aided by new prosperity and increased respect for education, science, and technology among these social classes. Once entrenched, obstetricians waged an aggressive campaign against midwives, stereotyping them as ignorant, dirty, and irresponsible. As medical boards and state legislators suppressed **midwifery,** women had little recourse but to turn to doctors and hospitals for childbirth. In 1900, 5 percent of babies were born in hospitals; by 1935, 75 percent; and by 1970, 95 percent (Boston Women's Health Book Collective, 1992; Ehrenreich & English, 1979).

Childbirth has always involved a natural fear of things going wrong, the unknown, pain, and the risk of death of the mother and baby. But insensitive medical attitudes and practices may foster doubts and intensify fears of something going wrong. At its worst, the hospital experience for women about to give birth may be frightening and isolating, as the following quote illustrates:

> Hospitals reduce labor and birth to a medical, debilitating event. As healthy strong women, we enter these places for sick people and our strength is systematically depleted. Often we are put into wheelchairs. Our personal effects are taken away. We are cut off from our friends and the people closest to us, isolated among strangers and made dependent and anonymous. . . . (Boston Women's Health Book Collective, 1992, p. 438)

At their worst, hospital deliveries feature little continuity of care, with unfamiliar doctors and nurses hovering over the pregnant women for short periods of time. There may be no one with the laboring women for some periods of time. Women are often wheeled from room to room as they progress through labor. By the time a woman gives birth vaginally, she is on her back with her feet in stirrups, often drugged, and isolated from all familiar faces except possibly, in recent years, her partner. Many scholars have noted

that such a position is unnatural for childbirth because it defies gravity. Increasingly, women do not deliver babies vaginally, but have **cesarean sections** in which babies are surgically removed. In 1968, the average rate of cesarean section in the United States was 5 percent, and by 1987 it had risen to 25 percent, though it has started to decline in recent years, and now stands at about 22 percent (Associated Press, 2000). This high rate of C-sections, the highest in the world, has been attributed to several factors, including physicians' practice of defensive medicine, having had a previous delivery by cesarean section, trends in obstetrical training, changing indications for cesarean section, and economic incentives for surgery.

It is important to note that cesarean sections are sometimes medically necessary. Advances in reproductive technology have enabled many women who could not conceive or carry a fetus to term, including older women who wish to become mothers, to have successful pregnancies. With the increase in the number of high-risk pregnancies in both these groups, there may be greater need for careful medical management, including cesarean sections. C-sections are also indicated when the mother's pelvis is small or misshapen, the mother is tired or weak, the mother has herpes or HIV, or the baby presents in a breech (feet down) or transverse (lying crossways) position. C-sections do appear to be less stressful for the baby (Rathus et al., 2002).

An increasing number of women are choosing more natural ways of giving birth at home, in birth centers, and even in hospitals. Over the past 30 years, women have made substantial gains in their efforts to exert control over one of the central events of their lives. More partners attend childbirth classes and are present at births, and more births are attended by mothers, sisters, friends, and other children. And more women are using midwives. This excerpt from Rathus et al. (2002) captures the array of choices, from *water births* (whereby the woman labors in a bathtub and delivers underwater) to *doulas* (minimally trained assistants who offer comfort and support), confronting today's mother to be:

> Women have never had so many choices in childbirth. They have the option to labor in a pool of warm water or at home in bed, in a cozy hospital "birthing suite" or in a traditional hospital room. They can choose between

an obstetrician or midwife—or both. How about some aromatherapy or acupuncture, yoga, or Yanni to help ease the pain and discomfort? Whatever your desire, those in the baby-delivery business want to make sure that your "birth experience" is all that it can be. (p. 360)

The Postpartum Experience

Postpartum literally means "after birth" and denotes a period of time ranging from the first days to the first year following delivery, when women are adjusting to what it means to be the mother of a baby. It is sometimes divided into three phases: the first phase, during which women make the transition from pregnancy to motherhood; the second phase, during which the focus is on learning what it means to have a baby in their lives; and the final phase, when women begin to face some of the long-term issues that motherhood poses for them (Boston Women's Health Book Collective, 1992). As we review these phases, it is important to keep in mind that the **postpartum experience** varies widely from woman to woman depending on the physical, psychological, and social landscape of her life.

The first phase, transition to parenthood, is a time of tremendous physical and emotional upheavals for many women. Depending on the circumstances of the birth, women may feel exhilarated and jubilant, proud of giving birth and of their new "issue." But they may also feel disappointed or ambivalent about many aspects of the birth, ranging from their experience of labor or delivery to the responses of their partner to the health, sex, or appearance of the baby. Around three days after birth, many women experience "the baby blues," a brief period of inexplicable sadness, seldom lasting more than a week, which is believed to be a normal response to hormonal and psychological changes that attend childbirth (Morris, 2000). A small percentage of women experience a full-blown depression that is incapacitating, described more fully in Chapter 13. Hormonal shifts are at least partly responsible for these reactions, which often appear just as mothers' milk comes in. But many women are also saddened by frustrations with breast-feeding, problems with

the newborn, fear of the awesome responsibility of motherhood, or sheer physical exhaustion.

During the second postpartum phase, from a week to about six months after birth, women learn to adjust to life with their baby. This period, especially the early part, is often experienced as fragmented and disorganized. Probably the most common stressor is fatigue, caused by nights of interrupted sleep and the experience of being on 24-hour call. Some mothers experience loss of interest in sex and physical discomfort. Others struggle to cope with the monotony of long hours spent alone with an infant and isolated from the society of adults. In this stage some mothers experience postpartum depression that is more serious and longer-lived than the baby blues experienced right after birth. Almost one in three women experience some mild form of recurring depression after they give birth, and up to two in a thousand women experience such debilitating depression that they require hospitalization.

Just a few decades ago, women who experienced postpartum depression were seen as mentally ill or unconsciously rejecting the responsibilities of motherhood. Today, the causes of postpartum depression are not completely understood, but two types of stressors may be involved. Physical-stress theories cite the dramatic reduction in estrogen and progesterone in causing depression. Oakley (1980) studied postpartum mothers living in London and found that the likelihood of postpartum depression increased with low levels of help with child care from the partner, unrealistic views of motherhood, few interests outside of child rearing, high levels of isolation, low levels of social support, and low levels of control over what happened during pregnancy and childbirth. Other studies have shown that those most likely to suffer from postpartum depression are having a first baby, have had previous bouts with postpartum depression, have experienced a move or change of lifestyle that has separated a woman from her family, or have a family history of death of a parent during childhood or childhood experiences of desertion, abuse, or traumatic divorce (Gitlin & Pasnau, 1989; Gordon & Gordon, 1967). If the new baby is premature or ill, has to remain in the hospital after the mother's discharge, or has ongoing health problems, postpartum depression is more likely. Often overlooked in studies of postpartum depression is infant temperament. Individual differences in behavior are present from early infancy, and mothers whose infants are irritable, unadaptable, and difficult to console are in fact more likely to be depressed (Hopkins, Campbell, & Marcus, 1987).

For many new mothers the experience of fatigue, loneliness, and loss of self during this period is outweighed by the wonderful aspects of mothering a new baby: the pleasures of holding and kissing the baby and watching the baby develop intellectually and emotionally and become more responsive each day. Many mothers are overwhelmed by the intensity of their feelings of love, connectedness, and protectiveness.

In the third and final postpartum phase, the period between 6 and 12 months, some of the chaos and uncertainty subsides, and mothers feel more relaxed, energetic, and confident. By now, most babies begin to sleep through the night, eat solid food, and take predictable naps. With the welcome routine, however, some troubling long-term issues may come to the fore. With the birth of the baby, mothers' lives are irrevocably changed. Some women struggle with changes in their bodies that are not easily reversible; others mourn other losses: of their sense of self and their former interests and activities. Still others worry that they are not as effective at or satisfied with being a mother as they expected to be. If women live with partners, these relationships are changed. Studies of married couples consistently show that relationship satisfaction declines sharply with the birth of the first child (Etaugh, 1993b; Hackel & Ruble, 1992). Partners may resent that the sexual relationships change as women have less time, energy, and privacy. Women are often disappointed in the share of housework and child care taken on by their partners and are surprised at how easily they have slipped into traditional gender roles now that their daily lives differ so much from their partners' in their routines, social opportunities, tasks, and rewards. As difficult as it is to renegotiate relationships after the birth of a baby, women without partners experience even more difficulties and more depression than women with partners (Gitlin & Pasnau, 1989; Hopkins et al., 1987). Feelings of fatigue,

isolation, and loneliness are especially high in single mothers during the postpartum period.

An increasing proportion of women face the prospect of working full or part time during the postpartum period. Working while one has very young children is complicated practically and emotionally:

We have to find child care and juggle the double demands of home and workplace. We love and miss our children; we are afraid of being replaced in their affections; we want to know that other caregivers will care deeply, too. These kinds of anxieties and questions are normal signs of caring. However the deep doubts and guilt that many of us feel in making and carrying out the decision to work are not a necessary part of being a working mother. These doubts are our response to being raised as females in a culture that insists that nurturing, and especially child care, is "women's work." (Boston Women's Health Book Collective, 1992, p. 492)

Over 60 percent of U.S. women with preschool-age children are now in the workplace, a percentage that has increased steadily in recent years. Yet the United States remains the only major industrialized country not to have governmental policies and institutions that recognize parents' need for high-quality child-care options. In the United States, a parent is entitled to 12 weeks of *unpaid* leave for the birth and care of a newborn, whereas Japan grants 14 weeks of maternity leave at 60 percent pay, and in Sweden, 450 days of parental leave are granted: 360 days at 75 percent and 90 days at a flat rate (Hunter College Women's Studies Collective, in press). Many U.S. parents do not avail themselves of the meager leave benefit, both because they cannot afford to and because taking the leave may stigmatize them as being less than serious about their jobs.

Because men have been spared the stresses involved in trying to make a living and caring for families at the same time, they are not, by and large, highly motivated to transform the workplace to provide supports for working parents (Silverstein, 1996). We might question whether motherhood necessarily means constant child care and how we might restructure society—its policies and practices—to help to support children and those who care for them. Combining motherhood and work is discussed more fully in Chapters 7 and 9.

Motherhood beyond the First Year

Like pregnancy, childbirth, and the postpartum period, motherhood through the life span is little studied by psychologists. There is a renewed empirical interest in the study of motherhood, largely fueled by the influx of women in psychology, and much of it concerns how women combine child care and work (a major preoccupation for psychologists who are mothers!). Motherhood, like other major life experiences, remains difficult to study because it is embedded in psychological and social variables such as social class and ethnicity, which are themselves large and complex. There is no "all-purpose mothering experience": Mothers come in different social classes, races, and ethnicities, with different family backgrounds and family constellations, and different personalities and social realities. As children age and families take different shapes, women's experiences of mothering diverge all the more. This makes it difficult to generalize about the experience. We will briefly discuss two of the themes that emerge in research and writing about mothers.

Motherhood as the Central Identity and Commitment of Women's Lives. As Rich (1976) aptly noted, motherhood is both an institution and a relationship. Despite the constraints and commonalities of the stereotypes about motherhood, there is no one way to mother, no simple set of stages through which all women progress, no classic patterns of problems and solutions for all mothers. What most mothers share is the reality that having children has changed their lives forever and that being a mother is one of their most central identities. It is also their largest and most cherished commitment: Mothers report overwhelmingly that if they could relive their lives they would have children again (Yankelovich, 1981). Despite the substantial costs of mothering so often noted in this chapter, most mothers find the positive aspects of mothering far more intense and compelling, and yet much harder to describe, than the negative aspects, which are plentiful and easily listed. When people name the advantages of mothering—that it is challenging; confers adult status; can be a source of fun, pleasure, and pride; carries on the family line, and the like (Gormly, Gormly, & Weiss, 1987; McMahon, 1995)—the list often seems trite and beside the point. Like other ultimate values, for example, romantic love and religious faith, maternal love is difficult to explain and justify in rational terms, by appealing to external qualities of the child or rewards such as fun, challenge, or societal respect. Indeed, maternal commitment is precisely the sense of acting beyond the call of any particular external qualities or rewards, and the profound rewards of maternal commitment come through the simple acts of loving and caring.

Motherhood Is Constantly Changing as Both Mother and Child Develop over Time. It seems obvious that the experience of mothering is quite different with babies than it is with elementary school-age children, adolescents, and adult children. As children age, they become less physically demanding, and this frees mothers from the fatigue and isolation that mark the earlier postpartum period. School-age children are frequently seen as "easiest" on mothers, although mothers continue to be constrained by school schedules and the round of after-school activities—soccer, scouts, dancing, or piano lessons—that figure prominently in the lives of many middle- and upper-class children today and keep many women from pursuing careers or full-time jobs. Rearing adolescents is widely seen as the most difficult period of motherhood after rearing infants. As the old saying goes, "Little children, little problems; big children, big problems." Adolescence is a particularly difficult time for the mothers of daughters, who often rebel by asserting themselves or withdrawing as a way of detaching from their mothers (Fischer, 1987). But mothers are closer to their adult daughters than their adult sons, with the turning point often being when the daughter herself becomes a mother. And daughters play a key role when mothers become elderly and the daughters are often the ones to become caregivers (Walker, Pratt, & Wood, 1993). Strong emotional relationships between mothers and children last a lifetime, enduring profound changes in circumstances. More research is needed on the experience of mothering—how mothering changes women and how women change as mothers—over the life span.

Mothering under Difficult Circumstances

It has been a theme of this section that under the best of circumstances mothering is difficult work, but it is especially taxing under the less than best conditions in which virtually all of us find ourselves. As we have noted, mothering can take place only in a context. When the family is poor or children (or parents) are seriously ill, mothering is complicated still further. Nearly one in five children in the United States lives in poverty today. The poverty rate for children in single-parent (mostly mother-headed) households is 50 percent, a figure that has changed little in more than 30 years (Schatz & Bane, 1991; Hunter College Women's Studies Collective, in press). Those of us who were reared or are rearing children in middle-class households can only imagine the bleakness and terror of living in substandard housing in unsafe neighborhoods, being unable to afford nutritious food, having inadequate access to decent medical care and educational systems, being hassled by creditors, or humiliated and disrespected by teachers and social service workers. In a consumer society such as ours, in which all children are bombarded by images of great wealth and glamor, it is heartbreaking to have to say constantly to your children, "no," to deny them the products, experiences, and opportunities that so many other children enjoy (Lott, 1991). It is especially difficult for mothers to be competent and nurturant when, being poor, they themselves are more likely to be ill, poorly educated, single, or to have a history of abuse or neglect. From the 1980s to the present, under varieties of leadership, the United States has basically espoused a moral model of poverty that justifies reducing aid to the poor via tightening welfare eligibility and cutting benefits. The harsh and sweeping welfare policy changes of the mid-1990s have not been helpful to poor women and children, raising questions about how a wealthy nation such as the United States can tolerate such a high percentage of poor children.

Mothers of children who are chronically ill or have disabilities also face special challenges that deserve more research and societal attention than they currently receive. A society that worships the healthy, able-bodied, and good looking and renders others invisible makes it difficult indeed to rear children who do not conform to the ideal. Mothers rear children who are ill or have disabilities in a context that subscribes to the notions that health and vigor are moral virtues for everyone, and that the body can be controlled if only one tries hard enough. We also live in a society that prizes individual solutions for problems and holds that individual families are responsible for providing all the resources that children who are ill or have disabilities need, often at enormous personal sacrifice (Wendell, 1993). Moreover, in the United States, the only major industrialized society without some kind of national health care policy, families without Medicaid or an excellent private insurance plan quickly spend all of their money trying to secure adequate medical help for their children.

Children who are sick or have disabilities often require more care and resources than other children, and this strains the entire family physically and emotionally, as well as financially. Mothers may feel guilty that their healthier children are burdened and neglected because of the attention devoted to the child who is ill or has disabilities. Fathers frequently work overtime or take extra jobs to make ends meet. Parents and children could be significantly helped by policies—and a construction of illness and disability—that did not impoverish, isolate, shame, and blame families for children's problems. We now understand that some of what is ill or disabling about a physical condition is a consequence of social arrangements and attitudes. These can be changed in ways that can support families in their struggles and enable affected children to participate more fully and productively in society.

FATHERHOOD

Fatherhood is a central commitment and identity to many men, our fathers, husbands, and many friends among them. Yet there is a long tradition of ignoring the father's role in parenting. In the first edition of *Dr. Spock's Baby Book,* Spock devoted only nine pages to fathering. Many current textbooks on men do not feature chapters or even separate sections on fatherhood but, sadly, do have sections on "father absence" (Kilmartin, 1994). The fact is that fatherhood is only recently getting the attention it deserves from psychologists and others. There are many reasons for the relative absence of fatherhood as a topic for study in psychology. One is surely the androcentric (male-centered) bias within psychology that devalues the study of all relationships, especially family relationships. Another is the implicit belief (and, at least in the past, too often the reality) that for many men being a father was a less central identity than others, for instance, being a worker. As Silverstein (1996) notes, "late 20th century fatherhood ideology continues to reflect the belief that active participation by mothers in the daily care of children is obligatory, whereas nurturing and caretaking by fathers is discretionary" (p. 11). This ideology generally rendered fathers invisible, with the curious exception of when they *were* invisible, that is, absent from the family. Father absence is blamed for a grab bag of pathologies in children, especially African American children, even though *why* father absence is so problematic is rarely addressed. Still others see the new emphasis on fatherhood at this point in history as a ploy to reassert the essential significance of men's paternal rights at a time when men's power and control over women are declining (Silverstein, 1996). With the rise of the new discipline of men's studies, in which men are studied *as men* rather than as exemplars of all humanity, fatherhood is finally attracting scholarly attention.

Much of the psychological research on fatherhood can be organized around a few themes: (1) Must mothers be the primary parent? Can fathers nurture? Can fathers mother? (2) Does father absence really matter? and (3) How much do and how can fathers participate in child care? We will very briefly consider the empirical research on each general question.

To the question of whether fathers *can* nurture children in ways similar to mothers, the answer appears to be yes. In her excellent review of fathering, Silverstein (1996) notes that, historically, fathers were responsible for the religious, moral, and vocational education of their children. The introduction of mandatory formal education, along with industrialization and the separation of home life and work life, contributed to the demise of fathers as teachers and moral leaders in the family. Early research suggest-

ing that fathers and mothers parent differently is being reevaluated. As Silverstein notes, despite cultural beliefs to the contrary, research findings with humans and animals do not suggest sex differences in the ability to care for infants. Rather, the extent to which fathers in human and other mammalian species actively care for infants depends on a complex array of ecological, demographic, and temperamental variables. When fathers are thrust into the primary caretaking role, they act like mothers.

The question of whether fathers freely choose to nurture their children is another matter. Studies on the amount of time fathers spend in direct interaction with their children each day averages between 12 and 26 minutes (Silverstein, 1996). Lamb (1987) found that mothers continue to shoulder about 90 percent of the care of young children. Hyde, Essex, and Horton (1993) found that the way that fathers increase their contributions to their young families is by working harder on the job, not by spending more time with the children. Despite the media attention in recent years on the "nurturant" father, paternal involvement in child rearing has not changed so much in the past 30 years. Even in countries that are more supportive of parental child care than the United States, for example, Sweden, fathers do not appear to take on significantly more of the child-rearing duties than fathers in the United States (Silverstein, 1996).

How important is involved fathering anyway? Is father absence a devastating blow to the children? In her review of the relevant literature, Silverstein concluded that the active involvement of responsible, nonabusive fathers was indeed beneficial to the entire family in several domains. Active father involvement in the household is one of the major determinants of decreasing stress for working mothers (Hoffman, 1989) and contributes to fathers' sense of competence, self-confidence, and self-esteem as fathers. The bulk of the research suggests that neither a male nor female parent is necessary for positive developmental outcomes or gender identity formation. What is needed is loving and caring *adults,* rather than mothers or fathers *per se.* Silverstein (1996) argues that the many studies consistently showing that children who grow up in mother-headed households fare more poorly than children who are reared by both biological parents cannot be adequately explained by father absence. The general pattern of findings suggests that father absence is confounded with numerous other variables. With two loving and responsible adults in the home, the family experiences a higher income, an additional attachment figure and role model, more adult supervision, and some relief for the primary caretaker.

Women now contribute a substantial amount to the family income in over half of the households in the United States. They are in the workplace to stay. Overwhelmingly, men and women continue to want to have children. It seems that, as we move through the twenty-first century, mothering and fathering will increasingly involve both earning money and nurturing children. As a society we need to figure out how the workplace can be reorganized to accommodate the new realities (Silverstein, 1996; Hewlett, 2002). Moreover, research suggests that we need to acknowledge and reinforce men's capacity to nurture. Finally, there is much research yet to be done on fathering. We do not know enough about how fathering differs for boys and girls, although research suggests that fathers are involved more with their sons than with their daughters (Crouter, McHale, & Bartko, 1993). We have too little information on fathers of color, although new research is exploding some myths about irresponsible young African American fathers. For example, McAdoo, cited in Silverstein (1996), found that many poor and working-class African American men who do not live with their families do play a role in their children's lives. McAdoo also cited data suggesting that young African American teen fathers were more likely to contribute to their children's support than White teen fathers. We need more information on gay fathers. Also, we need further work on how fathering changes men and their constructions of masculinity, and how we might strengthen the identity and commitment of fatherhood.

INFERTILITY

Infertility is defined as the failure to conceive after one year of vaginal intercourse without the use of contraceptives (Benson, 1983; Kelly, 2004). In the United States, there is evidence that infertility is on the rise. Although there is no direct evidence for the cause of this trend, environmental pollutants, sexually transmitted diseases, and the advanced age of couples wanting to conceive all stand as possible explanations. Approximately 15 percent of couples in which the woman is of childbearing age are infertile: about 20 percent of all couples without children (Kelly, 2004). About 50 to 60 percent of infertile couples eventually conceive, but the remaining 40 to 50 percent will remain infertile (Abbey, Andrews, & Halman, 1991). In about 20 percent of the cases, fertility problems are found in both partners. In the 80 percent of the cases in which infertility is due to one individual, about 40 percent of the time it is the woman, and in 30 percent of the cases, the man. In 10 to 20 percent of the cases, the cause is unclear (Hatcher et al., 1998). In males, major causes of infertility reflect abnormalities such as low sperm count, malformed sperm, low sperm motility, chronic diseases such as diabetes, sexually transmitted diseases (STDs), and injury to the testes. In females, major causes of infertility are irregular ovulation, including failure to ovulate; obstructions and malformations of the reproductive tract, some of which are caused by STDs or intrauterine devices (IUDs); endometriosis; and declining hormone levels that occur with aging (Rathus et al., 2002). (STDs are discussed further in Chapter 14.) Among women, smoking tobacco is associated with taking a long time to conceive (Bolumar, 1996). Regardless of which member of the couple has the physical problems that cause infertility, most of the tests and treatments focus on the woman's body and require her to take an active role (Abbey et al., 1991; Kelly, 2004).

Infertility is almost always unexpected and is experienced by most people as a life crisis. Many investigators have documented the negative psychological, behavioral, and social effects of infertility. These include depression, anxiety, guilt, anger, frustration, and helplessness. Infertile individuals report feeling like defective or failed men or women, with predictably poor effects on self-esteem and body image (Menning, 1977).

Infertility can strain a marital relationship. The infertile member of the couple may even suggest that it is understandable if the other partner leaves the relationship (Andrews, 1984), despite how devoted to each other they are. As people are unlikely to confide this particular problem to others, the two partners are often each other's only source of emotional support, and this further isolates them. When couples are experiencing trouble conceiving, sex can become a chore rather than a joy as it becomes routinized and prescribed.

There are consistent sex differences in response to infertility, with women experiencing much more negative affect than men. One study found that half of the infertile women, compared to only 15 percent of infertile men, described their infertility as one of the most upsetting experiences of their lives (Freeman, Boxer, Rickels, Tureck, & Mastroianni, 1985). Infertile women perceive having children as more important than their husbands do (Abbey et al., 1991). Women's greater infertility-related stress and depression probably have several causes, chief among them the centrality of the parenting role and identity for women, and the fact that other people typically regard infertility as being the "woman's fault," thus stigmatizing the woman. Women tend to cope more actively with the infertility, take more responsibility for it, and work harder to control or reverse it. Infertile men experience a somewhat different set of problems. They sense that their wives experience the prospect of not having children more negatively than they do, and they struggle to cope with their wives' distress (Abbey et al., 1991). There is evidence that men are more distressed by infertility if they believe that it is not "their fault" (Keye, 1999).

Recent research on infertility suggests that it may not be as distressing to couples as was once thought. For one thing, as we see in Box 10.2, there is much more open discussion of the problem in society, and many more real options are available to infertile couples today than every before. For another, working together on the problem brings many couples closer (Burns, 1999). However, the reproductive technologies presented in Box 10.2 are often expensive and not always effective. This can increase the pressure and stress for infertile couples.

ABORTION

Many women who become pregnant choose—or are coerced—not to become mothers. Reliable figures on the number of *induced (intentional) abortions* per-

formed each year are not available, but estimates are that about 1.5 million abortions are performed each year in the United States. As we have stated, about half of all pregnancies in the United States are unplanned, and about half of those end in abortion (Alan Guttmacher Institute, 2002).

There are between 45 million and 50 million induced abortions annually worldwide (Neft & Levine, 1997). Of the 50 million abortions, about 20 million are illegal, with most of these performed in developing countries. In some countries, especially those with highly restrictive abortion laws, illegal abortions may terminate as many as one quarter of all pregnancies (Neft & Levine, 1997). Illegal abortions are much more likely to be unsafe than are legal ones and may result in a host of problems, including infections, infertility, and death.

About 38 percent of the world's population live in countries where abortion is available on request. These include the United States, Canada, China, and Russia. Another 46 percent live in countries where abortion is available under certain circumstances. These include countries such as Argentina, Brazil, and Mexico, where abortion is still quite restricted, and countries such as Australia, France, and Italy, where there are many more permissible grounds for abortion. Grounds for abortion, aside from saving the life of the woman, are preserving her physical and or mental health, conditions of rape or incest, and fetal impairment. Finally, the remaining 16 percent of the world's population lives in countries where abortion is legal only to save the woman's life. The great majority of these countries is overwhelmingly Islamic or Roman Catholic, because these religions strictly forbid abortions. Ireland, a very Catholic country, is the only developed country in the world where abortion is permitted only to save the woman's life. Only a handful of countries, most notably Chile, does not permit abortion under any circumstances at all (Neft & Levine, 1997).

Within the United States, African American women are about three times and Latina women two and a half times more likely than European American women to have an abortion (Alan Guttmacher Institute, 2002). About half of all women who have abortions are under 25 years of age, with another quarter between the ages of 15 and 19. Approximately 88 percent of all abortions occur in the first 12 weeks of pregnancy (Alan Guttmacher Institute, 2002). Contrary to stereotypes, almost half of the women having abortions are already mothers with significant family responsibilities (Henshaw & Silverman, 1988; Neft & Levine, 1997).

Just as policies about abortion vary enormously throughout the world, attitudes about abortion differ widely among individuals within societies. In 1973, the U.S. Supreme Court legalized abortion nationwide in the landmark *Roe v. Wade* decision, which held that a woman's right to an abortion was protected under the right to privacy guaranteed by the Constitution. Abortion remains one of the most controversial of all social issues in the United States, with a capacity to divide families and other social groups like few other topics. In the United States, there is a strong right-to-life (prolife) movement, which takes the position that human life begins at conception, and abortion is the murder of an unborn child. People endorsing this position sometimes favor permitting abortion to save the woman's life or when the pregnancy results from rape or incest. There is also an active prochoice movement, which contends that abortion is a matter of personal choice, and that the government has no right to make laws restricting access to abortions. Other countries where abortion is still a contentious issue include Canada, France, Germany, and Ireland (Neft & Levine, 1997).

Most people in the United States today favor a woman's right to have an abortion, within limits. There appears to be a consensus emerging in the United States, with the majority seeming to think that abortion is an important right, even though many disapprove of it personally and believe that it should not be undertaken lightly (Rathus et al., 2002). At the present time, there is substantial disapproval in the United States of so-called "partial birth" (late-term) abortions, with some objecting to the timing of the abortion (second trimester), and others to the method of disposing of the fetus (Hitt, 1998). One of the results of the heated controversy over abortion in the United States is a steep decline in the number of doctors who perform abortions, with only about 33 percent of obstetricians today willing to do them (Hitt, 1998).

Not every woman who has an abortion freely chooses this outcome. In China, where the government has instituted a policy of one child per family, some woman are coerced into aborting fetuses by agents of the government if they have already borne a child. Others feel enormous pressure from their husbands or others to bear a son and abort female fetuses.

In countries such as the United States, individual women may also be coerced by others—parents, lovers, husbands—to have abortions that they do not want. But more often, U.S. women choose to have abortions for many reasons. Some women become pregnant because their birth control fails. Others become pregnant and want a child, but find that their personal or social circumstances would make rearing a child very difficult. Others find out through prenatal screening that their fetus has serious problems. Still other women become pregnant because of rape, incest, or other forms of sexual coercion. Increasingly around the globe, people are encouraging abortion for reasons of sex selection.

But even when a woman wishes to end her pregnancy, she does so against a backdrop of moral, social, and political forces that deeply affect the decision to have an abortion and the experience of abortion. Some women, including many but not all Catholics, Muslims, and Orthodox Jews, believe that abortion is murder. Even those who do not see abortion unequivocally as murder often experience a spiritual quandary about taking away the potential for human life. Indeed, few people are "pro-abortion." For other women, it is compulsory pregnancy and enforced motherhood that are morally wrong (Boston Women's Health Book Collective, 1992). Some people view abortion as a tool of population control, especially as a way of eliminating Third World peoples. Within the United States, some women of color are skeptical about the possibly racist motives of the prochoice movement and link abortion to genocide. At the same time, some women of color choose to have abortions, and many advocates for women of color argue that accessible, affordable, safe, and legal abortions are essential for these as for all women. In recent years, there has been a spate of illegal and increasingly violent acts against abortion clinics and providers, and many people are increasingly concerned about the erosion of women's access to abortions because of these trends: less judicial support for legal abortion, new restrictions such as parental consent and notification laws in many states, reinstating spousal consent laws, prohibitions against the use of public facilities and federal funds for abortion services, including providing information and making referrals about abortions (Boston Women's Health Book Collective, 1992).

Given the social context in which abortions take place, what are the effects of having an abortion on women's mental health? It is commonly believed that abortion causes severe guilt and depression, and some opponents of abortion have offered this perception in the ongoing debate. But a vast literature on the effects of abortion reveals that to be a myth (Adler et al., 1990; Russo, 2004; Russo & Green, 1993; Schwartz, 1986). Schwartz (1986) reviewed thirty-two scientifically sound studies on the psychological consequences of abortions and found that psychiatric problems were rare in women, on the order of 1 or 2 percent. When they did occur, they were related to preexisting psychiatric problems and pressure to have an abortion against one's own judgment. A review of well-controlled empirical studies documented relatively minor risks to women's psychological well-being due to abortion (Adler et al., 1990). This review found that the predominant response to abortion is relief. Although some feelings of guilt, depression, and regret may be experienced after the procedure, those feelings are usually mild and transitory (Russo & Green, 1993). When compared with other significant reproductive-related events, such as childbirth and miscarriage, abortion held no greater risk for depression (Wilmoth & Adelstein, 1988). Repeatedly, studies show that most women respond well to abortions. The predictors of negative responses to abortions are history of emotional disturbance, not expecting to cope well with the abortion, feeling coerced to have the abortion, difficulty in deciding to have the abortion, abortion in the second trimester of pregnancy, and limited or no social support (Adler et al., 1990; Russo & Green, 1993).

Research on responses to abortion has been plagued with a number of problems, including its emphasis on finding negative outcomes to abortions, and its reliance on clinical samples; that is, women who are experiencing some kind of psychological distress. Even with these negative biases, however, research has failed to link abortions with psychiatric or other serious disturbances of any kind. Unwanted pregnancy and its resolution are unquestionably distressing for many women, but most women who seek abortions are relieved to have had access to the procedure and do not regret the experience (Russo & Green, 1993), especially if abortion occurs in the first trimester (Russo, 2004). Adoption, often proposed as an alternative to abortion for the resolution of an unwanted pregnancy, poses psychological difficulties for many women, who show evidence of distress even decades after the adoption, and who frequently initiate searches for their surrendered children (Russo & Green, 1993). Clearly, we need more research on how women make pregnancy-related decisions, and on the psychosocial outcomes of those choices, given their importance in the lives of so many individuals.

SUMMARY

The experiences of wanting, having, and rearing children are among the most personally and societally important in the human repertoire. In one way or another, psychological theories from psychoanalysis to evolutionary psychology have put mating and parenting at their very core. Despite the obvious importance of parenting and being parented, psychologists have tended to study parenting generally and mothering particularly, in narrow, largely negative ways. When aspects of mothering are the focus of research, the spotlight is often turned on problematic aspects: teen pregnancy, postpartum depression, and how problems with the child reflect maternal inadequacies. Characterizations of mothers who are poor or members of ethnic minorities are particularly judgmental and harsh.

When reproductive issues such as infertility and abortion are studied, too often the assumption is that women who are affected by these experiences are scarred for life, when, in fact, research evidence points to women's resilience and resourcefulness in coping with these issues. The psychological richness of the experiences of pregnancy and giving birth has barely been mined. We need more research on effective strategies for enhancing women's mental health through these life-altering events, and on societal supports for motherhood, fatherhood, and families. Meanwhile, research on new reproductive technologies is providing some solutions to problems such as infertility and challenging the world with new options, such as the promise of sex selection of offspring. Psychologists can and do directly address many of the questions posed by these developments, and we need to step up our efforts to play a constructive role in the public discourse on parenting and reproductive issues.

KEY TERMS

Cesarean section (p. 331)
Infertility (p. 337)

Midwifery (p. 331)
Motherhood mandate (p. 324)

Motherhood mystique (p. 324)
Postpartum experience (p. 332)

DISCUSSION QUESTIONS

1. What are the stereotypes about women who are mothers, and how do they vary among ethnic, cultural, and social class groups?

2. Many single women today are opting to have children and rear them themselves. Based on what you have learned, what problems will these women face, and how can psychologists assist society in supporting these families?

3. Infertility is apparently on the rise in some areas of the world. What are the possible causes of this troublesome trend, and what are the implications for societies in which this trend is apparent?

4. In the United States, sex selection is likely to be used to increase the chances that first children are male and that each family has at least one male child and one child of each sex. What are the implications of this for U.S. society? What do you think about such trends?

5. Abortion rights are imperiled in the United States, with most adults in the United States seemingly conflicted about some aspect of abortion. Where do you stand on abortion? How can psychology contribute to the national debate on abortion?

6. Do you feel that fatherhood is as important as motherhood? If not, can it be? What changes would need to be made for this to be so?

FURTHER READINGS

Davis-Floyd, R., & Dumit, J. (Eds.). (1998). *Cyborg babies: From techno-sex to techno-tots.* New York: Routledge.

Lerner, H. (1998). *The mother dance: How children change your life.* New York: HarperCollins.

Marsiglio, W. (1998). *Procreative man.* New York: New York University Press.

Reiss, M. J., & Straughan, R. (1996). *Improving nature? The science and ethics of genetic engineering.* New York: Cambridge University Press.

Villani, S. L. (1997). *Motherhood at the crossroads: Meeting the challenge of a changing role.* New York: Plenum Press.

Wolf, N. (2001). *Misconceptions.* New York: Doubleday.

CHAPTER 11

GROWING OLDER

I have enjoyed greatly the second blooming that comes when you finish the life of the emotions and of personal relations; and suddenly you find—at the age of fifty, say—that a whole new life has opened before you, filled with things you can think about, study, or read about. . . . It is as if a fresh sap of ideas and thoughts was rising in you.
—Agatha Christie

The older I get, the greater power I seem to have to help the world; I am like a snowball—the further I am rolled the more I gain.
—Susan B. Anthony

I've been in the twilight of my career longer than most people have had their career.
—Martina Navratilova

If we could sell our experiences for what they cost us, we'd be millionaires.
—Abigail Van Buren

I believe the second half of one's life is meant to be better than the first half. The first half is finding out how you do it. And the second half is enjoying it.
—Frances Lear

Age ain't nothin' but a number. But age is other things too. It is wisdom, if one has lived one's life properly. It is experience and knowledge. And it is getting to know all the ways the world turns, so that if you cannot turn the world the way you want, you can at least get out of the way so you won't get run over.
—Miriam Makeba

It is not how old you are, but how you are old.
—Marie Dressler

How old would you be if you didn't know how old you were?
—Satchel Paige

When people say to me, "Why don't you act your age?" I say, "I've never been this age before, so I don't know how to act."
—Darrell Feit

This chapter will deal with the phenomena of midlife and aging. As the years of young adulthood pass, individuals suddenly find themselves at another transitional point of life—midlife. Women and men are confronted with the social stigmas of aging. A number of these stigmas are found to have surprisingly little validity when examined against the actual events in question. Menopause, once viewed as an earth-shattering end to a woman's youth and purpose, can actually be a positive event. The empty nest syndrome, when children leave home, rather than being a depressing period of purposelessness for middle-aged women, provides many of them with the opportunity to discover new talents and interests as reentry women. These women, bravely returning to school or work, are increasing in number.

As the aging process continues, new difficulties arise for women and men, such as retirement, spousal bereavement, and psychological and cognitive changes. Yet, just as in the middle years, some events of later adulthood are unfairly stigmatized. Spousal bereavement, while certainly an unfortunate and sometimes tragic experience, may provide older people with the opportunity to form new social circles, especially if relieved of caring for an ill spouse or partner. Retirement not only is the end of a career but also may be the beginning of an exciting new period as older people find themselves with more free time to engage in new pursuits and enjoy their grandchildren, another satisfying transition.

In addition, older members of the population may feel freer and less bound to conform to traditional gender-role expectations. Older women may "come into their own" and be more assertive and outspoken, and older men may discover a gentler, more affiliative side to their personalities. Whether this is the result of their no longer being bound by traditional gender roles or not, the change is a positive one that seems to be correlated with growing older.

One may not be able to escape the almost inevitable physical and/or cognitive decline brought upon by increasing age. Yet, many older people enjoy life in a way they never have before this point. They no longer feel the pressures of earning money and raising a family, and are able to relax and do things they have always wanted to do.

This chapter should provide the reader with a comprehensive overview of the developmental changes of middle and later adulthood. Many of the myths surrounding aging should be dispelled by the information contained herein, in particular, those myths that are gender biased and present women or men in an unfair light.

LIFE-SPAN DEVELOPMENT

We begin our discussion of growing older by looking at two views of life-span development.

Erik Erikson

Psychologist Erik Erikson placed a great emphasis on the notion that development continues far beyond childhood. In fact, he was the first to suggest a comprehensive life-span theory of development in any domain (Foos & Clark, 2000). Erik Erikson's theory of life-span development brought increased realization that important cognitive and psychosocial changes occur not only in childhood but throughout the adult years as well. His paradigm of psychosocial development is comprised of eight stages that begin in infancy (Trust versus Mistrust) and culminate in late adulthood (Integrity versus Despair). According to Erikson, the establishment of love relationships is a key facet in early adulthood, and the major task of young adults is to resolve the conflict between intimacy and isolation. Erikson maintained that the development of the capacity for intimacy depended on the successful formation of a stable psychosocial identity in adolescence. Furthermore, Erikson posited that autonomy is a fundamental part of development throughout the life span, from childhood through old age. This is crucial,

because in old age, individuals may experience a loss of personal control or independence, which may be undermined by the deterioration of physical health and sensorimotor functioning (Nadien & Denmark, 1999). According to Erikson, the main task of middle adulthood is the resolution of the conflict between generativity versus stagnation. During this stage, adults must take an active interest in guiding younger generations or they risk becoming preoccupied with themselves and self-absorbed. Successful middle age involves being productive workers, spouses, parents, mentors, and guides for new generations of family members, students, and apprentices.

Finally, Erikson claimed that the main psychosocial task of late adulthood is to resolve the crisis of integrity versus despair. Reflecting on their lives, older adults struggle to find meaning in their lives. Integrity results from looking back on one's life as important and successful, whereas despair arises from regret, meaninglessness, and social isolation. Integrity may serve to overcome feelings of despondency, which may result from the realization of deteriorating physical and mental capabilities (Nadien & Denmark, 1999). Thus, even in the face of decline, individuals may look back on life without feelings of regret and experience a sense of fulfillment. (See Table 11.2 on p. 364 for a complete listing of Erikson's psychosocial stages, from infancy through adulthood.)

Carol Gilligan

Psychologist Carol Gilligan (1982) has criticized Erikson's theory because it describes the developmental trajectory of males better than that of females. Because Gilligan contends that female development emphasizes attachment to others and interdependence, many females must first achieve intimacy prior to the development of stable identity. Erikson's placement of identity formation prior to the development of deep relationships in his sequence of psychosocial development reflects the traditional pathway of male development in which independence is highlighted as the primary goal.

As the years pass, new issues and adjustments arise for both couples and single parents. The fortieth birthday approaches and adults suddenly find themselves in the period known as *middle age*. This era of life is stigmatized, often unfairly, as one of crisis and negative changes. In the coming section, we will review the changes wrought for women and men by midlife, as well as the contrast between expectations and reality for adults entering this period of life.

MIDLIFE

This section of the chapter will discuss a rarely emphasized but important area of gender—women and men as they grow older. It will cover such areas as the double standards of aging, midlife crisis, menopause, midlife relationships, and reentry women. With increased medical awareness in the United States comes increased longevity, a trend that is sometimes referred to as the **graying of America.** With these advances comes a shifting definition of what middle age is and when it begins. (See the section A Traumatic Transition? for additional discussion of this topic.) Until recently, older adults as a minority were frequently neglected in research. However, the proportion of older people in our population is increasing, and as such, the body of knowledge pertaining to them is inadequate. Psychologists examining gender as a variable that influences the human experience are well advised to study its interaction with aging. Aging affects women and men differently in its various realms, including the physical, economic, and the socioemotional domains. In addition, middle-aged women and men are viewed differently by our society, a topic that the next section explores.

Double Standards of Aging

Different standards of aging are applied to women and men, that is, a **double standard of aging.** Our youth-oriented society stigmatizes aging in general, particularly for women. One study found that 57 percent of monitored television ads promised "youth, youthful appearance, or the energy to act youthful." By contrast, seniors in the same ads were shown dealing with backaches, loose dentures, and constipation (Richmond-Abbott, 1992). Interestingly, however, ageist stereotypes of women and men emerge before old age: Essentially, they originate in the middle years. Middle-aged women, whose primary duties

have been child rearing and child launching, are considered to be at the "tail end" of responsibilities and accomplishments. Middle-aged men, on the other hand, are supposed to be at the "prime of life," having built their careers in their youth and now holding top jobs and accomplishing much. For this reason, a thorough examination of the aging process and gender must begin with a look at the middle years.

Women suffer more from losing the beauty that is associated with youth. As women age, they are perceived as less physically attractive and desirable and their reproductive and nurturant functions are no longer relevant. Women's most socially valued qualities, that is, the ability to provide sex and attractive companionship and to have children and nurture them, are expressed in the context of youth. This stereotype holds true for aging lesbians as well. According to Sarah Pearlman (1993), although lesbians are not actively competing for men's attention, as middle age approaches, they may experience some ambivalence about no longer being acknowledged as sexual beings by men. This loss in self-esteem is furthered by their often unrequited attraction to younger women (Pearlman, 1993).

On the other hand, the wrinkles and extra flab viewed as revolting on the female body are euphemized and even glorified for men by terms such as *character lines* or *adding distinction.* Neither youth nor beauty is associated with successful mate selection for females (Perlini, 2001). Alternatively, "masculinity" is identified with competence, autonomy, and self-control—qualities that the disappearance of youth does not threaten. As a result, men may be viewed as more distinguished and attractive with age (Bazzini, McIntosh, Smith, Cook, & Harris, 1997). Unfortunately, women are not traditionally encouraged to develop those qualities that often improve with age, such as intellectual competence and earning capacity. Thus, the same wrinkles and gray hair that may enhance the perceived status and attractiveness of an older man may be seen as diminishing the attractiveness and desirability of an older woman (Etaugh, 1993). Overall, there are numerous common myths about aging for both women and men that prevail regardless of their lack of accuracy. See Box 11.1 for a list of some of these myths (Denmark, 2002).

Box 11.1

The Myths of Aging

1. Increasing age brings about greater psychological distress.
2. Older adults are more depressed than younger adults.
3. As individuals reach old age, they become preoccupied with memories of their childhood and youth.
4. Older adults are less satisfied with their lives than younger adults.
5. Older adults are alienated from the members of their families.
6. Because older adults generally do not reside with their children, they rarely see them.
7. Increasing age brings about a decline in sexual desire and interest.
8. Older adults are not physically capable of engaging in sexual intercourse.
9. Older adults are very isolated from their communities.
10. Social contacts decrease with increasing age.
11. Older women focus mainly on keeping their families together.
12. Older women suffer from poor physical health.
13. Married couples may legally engage in any sexual activity they mutually agree on.

All of these statements are false. With reference to number 13, in many states in America legal statutes prohibit couples from certain sexual acts. For example, in Georgia, the only sexual position that is considered legal is when a male occupies a dominant position and a female occupies a subordinate position. These laws are generally not enforced because the violations occur in private homes and therefore go undetected.

Source: From *Myths of Aging,* by F. L. Denmark, 2002, *Eye on Psi Chi, 7*(1), pp. 14–21.

The Media

Movies. The Academy Awards provide another example of where double standards prevail. Markson and Taylor (1993) found that women over the age of 39 have accounted for only 27 percent of all winners for Best Actress since 1927, while their male counterparts have accounted for 67 percent of the Best Actor awards. It is apparent that female film actresses, considered "older" by the time they are 35, find their careers winding down at the same time that male actors' film careers pick up. The biased images provided to movie viewers with this double standard are noteworthy. Where does the media provide positive role models for aging women?

Television. Even television shows apparently designed to portray older women in a better light fall prey to stereotyping. *The Golden Girls* was a popular television series featuring three bright, attractive, and articulate women over 50 years of age. In spite of these women's *joie de vivre* and spunk, they were still depicted as preoccupied with finding men and maintaining relationships with them. A study examining the depiction of women in twenty-first–century soap operas on television reported that only 13.7 percent of the characters presented were women over 51 years old. Thus, a significantly larger proportion of younger women were portrayed on television than in real life (Wiergacz & Lucas, 2003).

Magazines and Advertisements. Other forms of media reflect negative stereotypes of older people as well. The media often portray older people as frail, weak, unattractive, and useless (Williams, 1998). One study examining the depiction of older adults in *Time* and *Newsweek* magazines indicated that older adults, particularly older women, were rarely presented. Furthermore, when presented, women's roles were frequently submissive or dependent (McConatha, 1999). Another study indicated that in comparing U.S. magazines between 1956 and 1996, the percentage of ads representing older women had decreased overall. Moreover, for the ads that still depict older women, the percent of ads portraying negative stereotypes has continued to increase, while the percent of ads portraying positive stereotypes has continued to decrease (Miller, 1999). Many popular magazines, such as *Vanity Fair, Vogue,* and *Ladies' Home Journal,* communicate the same messages: Older women are for the most part invisible. Betty Friedan (1993) investigated the illustrations in these three magazines and found only a dozen photos of women over 60 years old out of approximately 400 photos. Conversely, ads that do represent women portray them as older than they actually are in order to increase cosmetic sales. These ads provide the means for older women to conceal signs of aging (Freedman, 1986; Friedan, 1993). For instance, certain lotions are said to prevent or remove wrinkles, suggesting that wrinkles are a negative or unpleasant sign of aging. Finally, a study evaluating stereotypes of older women in narrative jokes found that women were typically portrayed as unattractive, unappeasable, disinterested, forgetful, in poor health, and innocent, as in childhood (Bowd, 2003).

Cultural Values and Ageism

Cultural values influence the way in which older women and men perceive their bodies. A study of gender and body image perception among senior citizens showed that older men assessed by the Draw A Person technique drew figures that were larger, taller, and more centered than those of women, suggesting more positive self-image on the part of the men (Janelli, 1993).

Surprisingly, life expectancies in the United States for women and men are not as high as those in many developed countries. Although life expectancy has increased in the United States, it remains lower than that in other developed countries (see Table 11.1). In general, women tend to live longer than men and comprise the majority of the elderly population. According to the National Center for Health Statistics, in 2001 life expectancy for women in the United States was 79.8 years old, while for men, it was 74.4 years (Anas et al., 2003).

Nevertheless, older women are subject to **ageism** more often than older men. Ageism refers to discrimination against middle-aged and elderly individuals. Older men are usually cared for by women, and so the impact of ageism on older men is often buffered by

their female caretakers. Women, on the other hand, have no such buffer (Kimmel, 1988). The fact that jokes about elderly people poke fun at old women three times as often as old men attests to this (Palmore, 1971). Older women are frequently deemed neurotic and whiny when mentioning physical ailments, whereas men are considered tough and courageous. This double standard continues to exist despite the tendency for older women to have higher rates of long-term illness than older men (Etaugh, 1993).

Age and Partner Choice

Another area in which the double standard is evident is that of choosing a partner. While it is socially acceptable for men to marry women as much as 20 years younger than themselves, older women–younger men combinations are relatively rare, yet are increasing (Bell, 1989). In the year 2000, 12 percent of married women were 2 or more years older than their spouses (U.S. Census Bureau, 2001). Numerous female celebrities have openly dated men between 10 and 15 years younger than themselves. For instance, successful actress Demi Moore has dated Ashton Kutcher, a popular actor about 15 years younger than herself. Cameron Diaz, a popular actress, has dated Justin Timberlake, a singer approximately 10 years younger than herself. These celebrity couples have attracted significant attention from the media, because a large majority of Americans seem to disapprove of these relationships due to the substantial age gaps. Many have even gone so far as to say that Demi Moore was experiencing a midlife crisis. On the contrary, male celebrities dating or married to women 10 to 15 years younger, such as Michael Douglas and Catherine Zeta Jones, received significantly less attention. The stigma of aging is so much greater for women than for men that in the official membership directory of the American Psychological Association, women are ten times as likely as men not to list their age (Bell, 1989).

Language

Language is also an important area of a double standard for aging women and men. Metaphors about women's aging emphasize loss, such as vaginal

TABLE 11.1 Life Expectancy for Males and Females from Selected Nations of the World

			ESTIMATED LIFE EXPECTANCY FOR FEMALES		ESTIMATED LIFE EXPECTANCY FOR MALES	
			2000–2005	*2040–2050*	*2000–2005*	*2040–2050*
Less Developed Regions	Africa	Burkina Faso	46.2	65.7	45.2	64.2
		Morocco	70.5	80.3	66.8	75.6
		Zimbabwe	32.6	44.2	33.7	47.3
	Asia	Afghanistan	43.3	64.0	43.0	61.0
		China	73.3	79.7	68.9	73.9
		Japan*	85.1	92.5	77.9	83.7
		Turkey	73.2	81.0	68.0	76.0
	Latin America and the Caribbean	Cuba	78.7	83.5	74.8	78.5
		Bolivia	66.0	79.0	61.8	74.0
		Guadeloupe	81.7	86.0	74.8	80.1
		Haiti	50.0	69.2	49.0	67.4
		Uruguay	78.9	84.6	71.6	78.1
More Developed Regions	Europe	Germany	81.2	86.3	75.2	80.6
		Hungary	76.0	82.4	67.7	76.0
		Switzerland	82.3	86.0	75.9	79.9
	North America	Canada	81.9	85.7	76.7	80.8
		Mexico	76.4	82.7	70.4	76.5
		USA	79.9	84.1	74.3	79.2
	Oceania	Guam	77.0	82.9	72.4	77.9
		New Zealand	80.7	84.7	75.8	79.8
		Solomon Islands	70.7	80.5	67.9	76.2

*Japan is the only nation in this region that is considered a more developed country.

Source: All data have been retrieved from *The World Population Prospects, 2001,* a publication of the United Nations.

atrophy and degenerative changes (Kitzinger, 1983). As a result, many women view midlife changes pessimistically, seeing them as inescapable and debilitating (Ussher, 1989). Men's age-related changes are not described in a parallel fashion, and men who receive hormone therapy (e.g., testosterone) are described as attempting to increase libido rather than preserve their youth (Reitz, 1981).

Pfizer introduced a drug called **Viagra** (sildenafil citrate) to the market in 1998. Viagra is considered a solution to male impotence. The drug works by enhancing the effect of nitric oxide, which increases blood flow to a man's penis, which, in turn, increases sexual drive. Viagra has been reported to be effective for 80 percent of men. Although the FDA has not approved Viagra yet for women, it may ultimately help women with sexual issues caused by impaired blood flow (McAnulty & Burnette, 2004). A testosterone patch for women, to increase sexual desire, is currently being tested. Viagra has been known to provide relief to many stable marriages, and yet at the same time, for some marriages, Viagra may bring issues of infidelity to the surface. Restored sexual function may cause a man to search for other sexual partners if he feels rejected by his significant other or if his partner is unenthusiastic (Rathus et al., 2002).

A Traumatic Transition?

As stated earlier and depending on the writer, middle age might be pinpointed as being anywhere from the age of 35 to 65 (Barbanel, 1990). However, many people place the start of the aging process at approximately the ages of 40 to 50, or *midlife.* This stage of life involves many personal and social changes, which affect women and men in different ways. Women in particular are affected by adjustments required of them in the middle years, such as caring for elderly parents, death of parents, illness or death of a spouse, unemployment, children leaving home, midlife crisis of a spouse, divorce or separation, and moving (Rollins, 1996). According to Laura Barbanel (1990), members of this cohort comprise the **dominant generation.** This generation, also called the **sandwich generation,** is responsible for caring for both the young and the the old.

As they move through midlife, both women and men begin to lose their physical vitality, but only women are viewed as diminishing in sex appeal. Although both women and men fear the changes wrought by this stage in life, men appear to fear dying in particular, whereas women fear the general aging process (Barbanel, 1990).

Middle age for women, according to Pearlman (1993), might be construed as a developmental crisis, with the potential to disrupt one's sense of self and create feelings of heightened vulnerability, shame, and severe loss of self-esteem. Pearlman describes a developmental transition called **late midlife astonishment.** Typically beginning in a woman's fifties, this passage is marked by a sudden cognizance of the onset and stigma of aging. It is characterized by feelings of amazement and despair at the changes wrought by and/or occurring with increasing age, such as diminished physical and sexual attractiveness and other losses.

Thus, the fiftieth birthday for women may precipitate an emotional crisis. This crisis is usually worked through eventually once the woman has been in her sixth decade for a few years (Niemela & Lento, 1993). In a comparison of women aged 49 to 51 and 52 to 55, the older women were found to be better adjusted and were experiencing their lives and relationships more

positively. In addition, they were less concerned about health and the prospect of illness and were more accepting of death (Niemela & Lento, 1993).

Some women in their forties and fifties may be starting a family, returning to school, beginning new love relationships, or peaking in their careers (Gilbert, 1993). In fact, many U.S. women actually view the early fifties as a new prime of life. Some aspects of this age period reported by informants include empty nests, better health, higher income, and more concern for parents. Women in their early fifties showed confidence, involvement, security, and breadth of personality (Mitchell & Helson, 1990).

Despite this, middle-aged women are often viewed negatively and ridiculed by society. Clearly, cultural myths about these women are far removed from the realities of women's lives and experience. Specifically, two major areas of women's midlife experience subject to much stereotyping are menopause and the empty nest syndrome.

Menopause

Although the **climacteric** is the appropriate term for the entire aging process between the ages of 45 and 65, menopause is considered the pivotal event in women's aging and is therefore the more discussed topic. In fact, an examination of articles listed on Psych Lit and Medline (electronic databases) revealed that only a small percentage of articles written about women at midlife did *not* discuss menopause (Rostovsky & Travis, 1996). **Menopause** is the cessation of the menstrual period, occurring in most women between the ages of 45 and 55. It is defined as having occurred when a woman has not menstruated for one year. See Chapter 4 for details on the biological aspect of menopause.

Menopause is viewed as bringing with it both physically distressing symptoms and psychological discomforts. Some of these symptoms include profuse sweating, headaches, increased weight, insomnia, aches and pains, dryness and thinning of the vaginal walls, irritability, osteoporosis, and hot flashes (Dan & Bernhard, 1989; Weidiger, 1975). Hot flashes are the best known of menopausal symptoms, and most women experience the same progression. However, women experience the symptoms in varying degrees. During a hot flash, the blood vessels in the woman's skin dilate and her skin conductance increases, so that she feels extremely hot (Israel, Poland, Reame, & Warner, 1980). For many years, women were told that the hot flashes they complained of were "all in their heads" (Kronenberg, 1990, p. 52). In general, these physical changes occur together with falling estrogen levels; yet, it is unclear whether the drop in estrogen actually causes these changes (DeLorey, 1984). It is important to remember that the woman's social context will affect her experience of menopause. Thus, personality, life events, and culture will all have an effect (Dan & Bernhard, 1989).

Menopause's physical ramifications are exaggerated by medical personnel. Physicians tend to view all types of women's health problems as connected with female hormones when, in fact, problems occurring around menopause are more often a function of the aging process (Dan & Bernhard, 1989). In addition, physicians' and nurses' experience with menopausal women tends to be limited to those whom they have treated for excessively severe symptoms. Women who seek treatment for menopausal symptoms tend to view menopause more negatively (Ussher, 1989). The vast majority of articles on menopause in medical and/or psychological literature promote the image of a deficiency disease that will be troublesome for most women. These articles are often replete with methodological flaws (Rostovsky & Travis, 1996). Such factors may help explain medical personnel's tendency to view menopausal symptoms as more severe and pathological than menopausal women see them (McElmurry & Huddleston, 1987).

Negative Stigmatizing.   Menopause is also mistakenly connected with vague illnesses (Bush, 1990) and with emotional disturbance (Busch, Zonderman, & Costa, 1994). The menopausal woman is stereotypically perceived in Western culture as ailing and in need of medication (hormones and tranquilizers), emotionally unstable, and having lost her purpose in life. Her discomfort is depicted as unique to her stage in life even though symptoms from hot flashes to cessation of menstruation can happen at any stage in a woman's life and be attributed to factors other than menopause,

such as surgical removal of the ovaries in premenopausal women (Kaufert, 1982; Neugarten & Kraines, 1965). Although menopause is a biological phenomenon, social and cultural beliefs and attitudes toward menopause have structured women's responses to it as well as society's attitudes. As such, stereotypes are easily formed and individual variation summarily dismissed or ignored (Rostovsky & Travis, 1996).

This negative stigmatizing of menopausal women is part of many cultural traditions in which older women have been portrayed as sorceresses or witches in anthropological literature (Evans-Pritchard, 1937; Fortes, 1962; Harper, 1969). Base motivations were ascribed to these women such as the "evil eye" or witchcraft (Fuller, 1961). The idea of fertility representing good power and, conversely, infertility representing malevolent power, has been a pervasive one (Kincaid-Elders, 1982), which might explain this view of menopausal women. Anthropological research demonstrates that this notion exists today across several cultures. Cultural images of menopause stress deterioration, decline, regression, and decay (Van Keep, 1976). This would impact on menopausal women's self-image.

In fact, Mansfield and Voda (1993) conducted a survey of middle-aged women and found that most of the perceived benefits of menopause were not benefits in and of themselves, but rather represented cessation of current, unpleasant conditions (i.e., termination of the menstrual period and its various difficulties). Many participants in this survey expressed fears of becoming a "typically . . . bitchy menopausal lady," which may be a reflection of society's negative stereotypes of the aging woman. It is telling that the majority of the women surveyed obtained their information about menopause from friends and from the media (including television sitcoms) rather than from medical sources. Overall, women's views of menopause in this study lacked any sense of achievement or attained status associated with being menopausal. The negativity surrounding menopause may have unfortunate implications for women's adjustment to this transition (Mansfield & Voda, 1993).

A More Balanced View.   Negative stigmatizing of the changes wrought by menopause is very likely culture bound and based in accepted societal custom rather than in fact. Among the Giriama of Kenya, for example, postmenopausal women are custodians of the central ritual objects of a female cult that is believed to enable reproductive health. The Giriama see the life course as a continuum of hot or cool states, and focus on maintaining harmony and social order. Because of its creative potential, the entire fertile period of women's lives is considered one of *heat.* The *cool* aspect of the elderly woman's postfertile state makes them ideal for counteracting the heat created through the required rituals (Udvardy, 1992). The Winnebagos, a group of American Indians, view menopausal women positively as well, perceiving them as being "just like a man" (Comas-Diaz & Greene, 1994). An increase in women's status following menopause is common to several non-Western societies (Brown, 1982). This may explain findings that suggest that women in non-Western societies seem to suffer fewer physiological and emotional difficulties during menopause than do Western women (Kaiser, 1990).

Even in the United States, however, where menopause is believed to be a difficult, troublesome, confusing, and depressing period, psychologists and sociologists state otherwise. On the contrary, many women are happy and relieved to reach the finish of the reproductive stage in their lives marked by menopause. In a physical sense, menopause actually presents few problems for women and is frequently viewed as a "nonevent," or even as a positive body change by women after the fact (Gilbert, 1993). Clearly, menopause is not the crippling life event as it once was portrayed. In fact, three out of four women undergo little or no physical distress due to menopause (National Institutes of Health/National Institute on Aging, 1993). The most widespread symptom of menopause is hot flashes, yet the intensity of this symptom varies between individuals. Some women never experience them, while others experience them incessantly. Nevertheless, the experience of hot flashes may be alleviated with utilization of estrogen therapy (Avis, 1999). Other potential symptoms consist of vaginal dryness, burning, itching, urinary troubles, and vaginal infections. Some of these symptoms may cause pain during intercourse. Other physical problems associated with menopause are joint or muscle pain, headache, insom-

nia, fatigue, dizziness, weight gain, and constipation. However, these symptoms may be related only indirectly (Avis, 1999; te Velde & Van Leusden, 1994).

Older women who have already experienced menopause view it more positively than do younger women who have not yet reached the age of menopause (Avis, 1999). Apparently, dramatic myths about menopause are more pervasive than the anticlimactic reality. However, a small but significant minority of women actually experience emotional difficulties during menopause. This may be correlated with low self-esteem and life satisfaction before menopause (Bart & Grossman, 1978). These and other women's menopause-related troubles may actually be a function of psychological factors rather than biological events at their stage in life (Greene & Cooke, 1980). In support of this hypothesis, one cross-cultural study found that women in cultures with fewer positive roles (or more demeaning roles) available for them experienced menopause more negatively (Griffen, 1979). Psychological symptoms such as anxiety and depression were more strongly associated with current life events and difficulties, specifically in family life, than with stage of menopause (Hardy & Kuh, 2002). A study conducted in London found that women who intended to pursue the use of hormone replacement therapy (HRT) to alleviate symptoms associated with menopause reported lower self-esteem, higher levels of depressed mood, anxiety, and negative attitudes toward menopause when compared with women not intending to pursue the use of HRT. This suggests the possibility that some women may be seeking HRT to ease preexisting emotional difficulties (Hunter & Liao, 1994).

Psychologically, adolescence appears to be a more difficult adjustment for women than menopause. Menopausal women and adolescents reported the highest level of symptomatology, with adolescents reporting more psychological symptoms and menopausal women reporting more physical ones. It is interesting to note that postmenopausal women reported the lowest level of symptoms, suggesting that once this milestone has passed, women's well-being improves and exceeds their state at any other time of life (Neugarten & Kraines, 1965). Most women in the United States who have passed through menopause view this change in a positive manner. They consider menopause an indication of a shift into the second half of adult life, a time for changing roles, increased autonomy, and personal development (Avis, 1999).

Estrogen Replacement. The physical symptoms of menopause can be ameliorated by taking replacement estrogen. However, it has been suggested that estrogen replacement therapy may increase a woman's risk of developing uterine or breast cancer, blood clots, liver tumors, and other problems (see Adami, 1992; Persson et al., 1989; Satyaswaroop, Zaino, & Mortel, 1983). On the other hand, estrogen therapy may significantly reduce the risks of cardiovascular disease and osteoporosis (Ettinger, 1993; Lindsay, 1993; Seed, 1994). Recently, it has been suggested that estrogen replacement therapy may also serve to maintain cognitive functioning in postmenopausal women, thus protecting against age-related cognitive degeneration (i.e., memory) (Tivis, 2001). For instance, estrogen may lower the risk of developing dementia and Alzheimer's disease (Morrison, 2000). However, there is evidence that rather than remediating the symptoms, estrogen therapy merely postpones them: Hot flashes return when estrogen is stopped. Some menopausal symptoms may be relieved with nonestrogen treatments, such as creams or jellies for vaginal dryness, or a high-calcium diet, exercise, and avoidance of cigarette smoking and heavy drinking to prevent osteoporosis. Finally, women who are in good physical shape experience fewer symptoms (Wilbur, Dan,

Hedricks, & Holm, 1990). Results from a study at the National Institutes of Health, called the Women's Health Initiative (2002), depict the proportion of particular medical conditions expected to surface yearly in a group of 10,000 women taking estrogen plus progestin pills as opposed to a placebo (see Box 11.2). Due to the small but significant number of women who had an increase in heart attacks, strokes, and breast cancer, the study was halted. However, a number of researchers and physicians believe this study was limited, and its results led to an overreaction. A new investigation is being planned to fill in the gaps left by the Women's Health Initiative study (Mathews & Hensley, 2003). A large-scale NIH study of women taking estrogen alone was halted in early 2004 when preliminary findings indicated an increased risk of stroke as well as a slight increase in risk of developing dementia or mild cognitive impairment (Rabin, 2004).

Men at Midlife

Middle-aged men experience negative stereotyping about their declining health, strength, power, and sexual potency. A gradual drop in libido is actually a common change among middle-aged men (Davidson, 1989). For men, the middle years often bring the first markers of inevitable physical decline (e.g., minor hearing loss, eyeglasses, graying or receding hair). Men's testosterone level and sperm production gradually decrease from the age of about 30 onward. For men over 40, enlargement of the prostate gland is a

---

Box 11.2_____

Women's Health Initiative Study: Results of Estrogen and Progestin

	ESTROGEN AND PROGESTIN	PLACEBO
Heart attack	37 women	30 women
Stroke	29	21
Breast cancer	38	30
Colorectal cancer	10	16
Hip fractures	10	15

Source: From "Hormone-Therapy Debate Grows," by A. W. Mathews and S. Hensley, October 8, 2003, *The Wall Street Journal,* Health & Family, Section D7.

common change. This enlargement causes urinary problems and may be related to changes in hormone levels, but can be treated by medication and/or surgery.

Yet, age-related changes taking place for men in their middle years appear to be more connected with changes in family status, social position, career, or health than with physiological processes. Some of these changes might include changes in workplace status (e.g., becoming a mentor or senior partner) or children moving out of the house. Men at midlife may become aware that they will never achieve their ambitions of earlier years and may feel disappointment or the need to redefine their goals. For some men, youth-oriented masculine traits define their gender identity, and these changes force them to rethink this definition (Rybarczyk, 1994). Men may feel less confident in their masculinity as they shift their identities away from work-related achievements and become more dependent on their spouses to fill the void that a career once filled (Biladeau, 2003).

Empty Nest Syndrome

The **empty nest syndrome** results from the departure of children from the home, which has been said to leave middle-aged women feeling lonely and deserted (Mantecon, 1993). Pauline Bart, in 1971, coined this phrase to indicate that the departure of children may have an extremely profound influence on women without careers, whose identities were centered on motherhood. The percentage of children actually leaving the home to go away to college has steadily increased through the years. By 2008, it is expected that 3.2 million children in the United States will graduate from high school, the largest quantity to date (Kantrowitz & Springen, 2003). Most likely, the majority of these graduates will leave for college, and many of them will choose schools far away from home. Therefore, many parents not only have to deal with the fact that their children are out of the home for the first time, but in addition, it is difficult to visit and communicate with them.

The point at which the empty nest is experienced is relative—not all parents feel it when their children leave for college. Some women actually feel it when their youngest child reaches adulthood, while others may feel it when their youngest child enters kindergarten (Black & Hill, 1984). Just as the starting point of the empty nest syndrome varies from person to person, so too do its effects. Midlife women who work can enjoy benefits such as a sense of self independent of one's family, professional development, financial autonomy, intellectual stimulation, and an expanded social group. These women may associate an empty nest with a sense of relief. Many couples report greater marital satisfaction after the children have left the house (Rollins, 1989).

A review of the literature (Troll, 1989) suggests that many mothers (and fathers) view their children's departure as a positive event, albeit with mixed emotions. The empty nest catalyzed a crisis mainly for those women whose lives revolved around their children to the exclusion of a career. This may suggest that in today's day and age, with more than half of American women working and building their own careers, the empty nest syndrome is becoming less and less common. Nonetheless, for some, the empty nest syndrome still exists. For divorced women, separation anxiety may be magnified when their children leave for college, because nobody is left at home to talk to. Some married couples may experience difficulties as well. They may find that without children at home, they have fewer topics of conversation and thus more uncomfortable periods of silence. The empty nest can be a very stressful adjustment in marriage (Kantrowitz & Springen, 2003).

Midlife Relationships

Couples may undergo several changes during midlife. As relationships mature, tender feelings of affection and loyalty tend to replace passion and sexual intimacy as a main focus (Reedy, Birren, & Schaie, 1981). Some marriages, which were more turbulent in early adulthood, turn out to be better adjusted during middle adulthood (Rollins, 1989). One explanation for this might be that as marital partners grow older, many of their earlier incompatibilities brought about by differences in religion, ethnicity, social class, levels of education, family backgrounds, and personality patterns have been either eliminated or adjusted to and did not lead to the breakup of the marriage (Golan, 1986). (See Chapter 9 for further information.)

Friendships change for both men and women who have reached midlife. Whereas younger men tend to undervalue empathy and altruism in friendship, middle-aged men appear to be more concerned and thoughtful about friendship. Middle-aged women seem to be more tolerant and less confrontational than younger women. Both women and men were found to describe themselves as eager to hold on to their friends. Gender-typed behavior exists in this realm, however; men tend to be negative about too much dependency in friendships and express an instrumental concept of need (i.e., concrete assistance) in contrast to women's more expressive emphasis (i.e., the need to talk, share, and be comforted) (Fox, Gibbs, & Auerbach, 1985). It has been reported that as men age, there is a decrease in their pursuit of new friends, in the intimacy of their interactions with friends, and in involvement in activities outside of their families. For women, on the other hand, there is no change in these measures of friendship (Field, 1999).

One change of middle adulthood for both men and women is that of their children becoming adults and replacing their parents as the "present generation." When children and their parents are both within the adult age range, their relationships undergo an adjustment. As the middle generation maintains contact with both their older parents and their growing children, similarities and differences across generations may be apparent. Gender roles, however, is one area in which parent–child similarity is most noticeable (Elder, Caspi, & Downey, 1986).

Middle-aged women are often forced to deal with a conflict between both the needs of their aging parents and those of their husbands, children, and employers. As daughters, middle-aged women serve as the primary source of caregiving for their frequently widowed mothers. However, many of these women do not experience this as a conflict on a regular basis, and those who do often have poorer relationships with their mothers (Walker, Pratt, & Wood, 1993).

Middle-aged women who are expected to tend to their elderly parents as well as to their children are often forced to cut back on their own private time in order to fulfill their responsibilities. They belong to the so-called *sandwich generation*. In addition to providing physical assistance, both men and women also attempt to advise both their parents and their children, although men focus more on their children. Clearly, in spite of the much-touted generation gap, adult parents and children maintain contact (Troll, 1989).

Another challenge faced by middle-aged mothers, but seldom addressed in the literature, is the conflict that arises when a daughter is a lesbian or a son is gay. Mothers often have a difficult time reconciling that their daughters' and sons' lifestyles are not in keeping with society's norms and may resort to self-blame in keeping with society's tendency to blame mothers for their children's outcomes (Pearlman, 1992).

Surprisingly, middle-aged women are not caught between their parents and their children as often as one might expect. The majority of older people are in good health, suggesting that they are not forced to rely on their daughters. In addition, ages of women with elderly parents vary—a 65-year-old woman may still have a living parent to whom she is tending (Stueve & O'Donnell, 1984), while her daughter is in her late thirties or early forties. Research is needed to examine the actual dynamics of intergenerational relationships.

Midlife Crisis

In the 1970s, society became fascinated with the idea of a male *midlife crisis*. Popular opinion maintained that this crisis is universal and an automatic stage for men who have reached a certain age. So-called "normal" men who have reached age 40 were expected to be making drastic changes in their lives (Rybarczyk, 1994) and experiencing intense emotional turmoil and despair (Levinson, Darrow, Klein, Levinson, & McKee, 1978). Middle-aged men were stereotyped as having heart attacks, which frighten them with the prospect of their mortality. The stereotype suggests that in reaction to this, they abandon their families and marry **trophy wives,** that is, highly attractive women who are far younger than they are. The image of men going through midlife crises also includes aging men buying sports cars, dressing in clothes usually worn by younger men, and flirting with women half their age. Donald Trump's second marriage to Marla Maples was viewed by many as a classic example of male midlife crisis.

Midlife crisis was originally described in a psychoanalytic framework as being a function of a midlife man's awareness of his mortality. During this time, the middle-aged man experiences a struggle between his life instinct of Eros and his pull toward destruction and death, or Thanatos. He equates his loss of youth with loss of life and experiences inevitable psychic angst (Jaques, 1965). Subsequent theoreticians of various orientations support the idea of a crisis surrounding the middle-age transition (Pearlman, 1993; Yalom, 1980).

In reality, empirical research fails to support the idea that this crisis is universal and age related. Research does show that men in their forties have higher depression scores and greater frequency of alcohol and drug use than other adult men; however, they are similar to other men in experiencing anxiety, life satisfaction, and happiness (Tamir, 1982). Midlife crisis is actually viewed as a myth by one researcher based on his survey of the literature (Kruger, 1994). If it does exist for a man, it appears to be related to career and/or family life rather than the aging process (e.g., children moving from home and leaving their parents alone together for the first time in years; women returning to work or school and developing new interests, thus forcing adjustments in the couple's relationship). Men can usually adapt to it without making vast changes in several areas of their lives (Rybarczyk, 1994).

Midlife crisis is a social construction, according to Markson and Gognalons-Nicolet (1990). Their research on French, Swiss, and American samples concludes that cultural and historical factors influence one's conceptualization of midlife crisis. While certain midlife events such as the departure of children and concern about elderly parents are common to all industrialized nations, reactions to these events might be altered by factors such as age cohort and age structure of the population (Markson & Gognalons-Nicolet, 1990).

Reentry Women

An increasing number of women are returning to college or work or beginning college for the first time in middle or older adulthood after years of devoting their lives exclusively to their families. Several possible reasons for this have been suggested, such as reduction in family responsibilities or divorce. In fact, divorced women are overrepresented among adult students and are also more dedicated as students and/or workers (Alington & Troll, 1984).

Middle-aged women who have chosen this course of action, known as **reentry women,** face a number of problems. Those entering or reentering college must deal with feeling unable to relate to their much younger classmates, convincing their colleges to accept their transfer credits from several years earlier, and, in particular, institutional barriers such as lack of evening courses or minimum course load requirements (Schlossberg, 1984). In addition, reentry women must make a successful transition from housekeeper to college student or worker. Men, and perhaps younger women, experience this transition in a more traditional way (i.e., high school to college to graduate school to career) than do these women, who transform their roles later on in their adult lives. As such, reentry women are at a disadvantage because mentors are less likely to want to invest in the women's careers and they may be socially isolated from their younger colleagues.

While women going back to school in their middle or later years are commonly viewed as attempting to occupy their newfound leisure time, many women choose to continue their education at this point, perhaps as a result of divorce or widowhood. Women's economic, social, and personal resources are more vulnerable than those of men in the later years as a function of gender-related limitations (such as lower salary and fewer job opportunities) experienced across their life spans. Some women may confront this bias on returning to school in later life (Harold, 1992).

In spite of such obstacles, reentry women do extraordinarily well. In college, they work hard and participate actively in their education. They participate fully in the workplace, in politics, and in organized efforts for social change. In fact, activism on the part of older people is a topic that has been underresearched, but has much significance. The elderly have been instrumental in forming organizations to improve their position, such as the Gray Panthers, the Older Women's League, Senior Action in a Gay Environment

(SAGE) for older gay men and lesbians (MacDonald & Rich, 1983), and others. Several older women have also become active in other social causes, and many view their efforts as connected to feminism (Garland, 1988).

Life begins at 40 or 50 for many women, and it is not uncommon for women at midlife and even later to discover new talents and interests and employ them successfully (Alington & Troll, 1984). In addition, women who attend college at an older age were found to be more assertive, and as such, expected and received more spousal support (De Groot, 1980). This would bode well for their success.

The population of reentry women is likely to increase, as life spans grow longer and good health care continues. In fact, women in their early fifties gave a higher rating to their lives than either older or younger women (Mitchell & Helson, 1990), attesting to the possibilities and opportunities arising during midlife.

LATER LIFE

It is important to remember that research on women who are older today applies to women who grew up several decades ago, before the women's movement. Research on middle-aged or older women in the future may yield dissimilar findings, because women who are growing up today are exposed to and shaped by very different social norms. As such, currently available research may not be applicable to midlife or older women of the twenty-first century (Grambs, 1989). A person's **cohort,** or group of people born within the same year or years, provides a more accurate prediction of her or his ideals and actions than does her or his chronological age.

The middle and later years are commonly stigmatized as a depressing era of decreasing physical well-being and life satisfaction. Yet, these years can actually be a happier, productive, and more contented time than the much-glorified era of early adulthood. Some women have accomplished great things at advanced ages (see Box 11.3). Older women in particular are falsely stigmatized as being unhappy with their lot in life, although no conclusive evidence points to systematic gender differences in later life satisfaction. In several studies, older women proved to be just as satisfied as their same-age male and younger female

---

Box 11.3

Extraordinary Older Women

Maggie Kuhn was 64 years old in 1970 when she organized the Gray Panthers, a network of highly vocal individuals in the United States who were dedicated to fighting ageism.

Margaret Mead was 73 years old when she returned to New Guinea 48 years after her first voyage.

Grandma Moses began painting at 88 years old. At 100, she illustrated an edition of *The Night before Christmas.* She died at 101.

Anthropologist Ruby Rohrlich at the age of 86 published an anthology, *Resisting the Holocaust,* in 1998.

---

counterparts (e.g., Liang, 1982). Individual factors such as health, finances, and family relationships pertain more directly to individual differences in life satisfaction than does gender. In fact, midlife is a time of self-discovery for older women, as they pick up new interests and redefine their self-image.

For non-White elderly women in America, aging is a unique experience. On the one hand, they are forced to contend with the quadruple burden of being old, poor, female, and of minority status. Black and Hispanic women are worse off economically than White women, and the majority of elderly Black women are in "poor" or "nearly poor" categories (Grambs, 1989). On the other hand, women from minority groups are often equipped with adaptive advantages for dealing with aging. For example, in African American culture, grandmothers play a significant role in child rearing, and as such, women's importance and status within the family is enhanced with age (Comas-Diaz & Greene, 1994). Despite the fact that African Americans are significantly more disadvantaged socioeconomically than are Whites, and that African Americans perceive their health as worse than Whites do, African Americans express significantly more contentment with their lives than do Whites (Johnson, 1994).

In American Indian societies, older women's age and wisdom are revered, and their knowledge of tribal history, herbal medicine, and sacred matters are valued. Despite living in poverty in large numbers

(LaFromboise, Berman, & Sohi, 1994), in general, American Indian women report more satisfaction with their lives and greater enjoyment in spending time with old people than do their European American counterparts (Comas-Diaz & Greene, 1994).

In comparison with men, however, women may have less positive attitudes toward aging. A cross-cultural study comparing both Swedes and Turks found that in both cultures, women were more negative about aging and expressed higher feelings of personal loneliness (Imamoglu, Kuller, Imamoglu, & Kuller, 1993). Negative stereotypes of older women in the United States presented by the media (as discussed earlier) suggest that this is probably the case in the United States as well.

The gradual changes, which begin in the middle years, become increasingly apparent as the aging process continues, and new changes take place as well. In terms of activities of daily living, dependence and mobility impairment have been found to increase in prevalence with old age, while functioning decreases (Strawbridge, Kaplan, Camacho, & Cohen, 1992). Older people must also contend with pivotal life events such as retirement and spousal bereavement. As is true of midlife, much of one's personal well-being in later life depends on one's perspective, an important aspect being one's feeling of autonomy and personal control. Perception of personal control is an important factor in one's psychological well-being and one especially relevant to the elderly. One's locus of control (i.e., degree of internality) may significantly affect life adjustment throughout the life span and influence the ability to cope with changing life circumstances that occur in later life such as retirement (Hollis, 1994).

Although much of the research with older adults has been conducted with heterosexual elders, Reid (1995) speculates that the unique challenges faced by aging lesbians and gay men enable them to more successfully negotiate this developmental stage. However, for the aging lesbian, her sense of well-being and ability to accept all aspects of her self and reality depend in large part on the social context in which her lesbianism is framed. Many of these women are unable to publicly or personally acknowledge their lesbian identity because the environment has not allowed for public discourse. Thus, they are often in-visible to the larger society (Thorpe, 1989). Shenk and Fullmer (1996) found that when public acknowledgment is not available, the older lesbian is often unable to acknowledge that aspect of her identity.

The normal changes of aging can include physical disabilities and medical experiences (Cole & Cole, 1993). For example, visual and reflex impairments may prevent elderly people from driving, resulting in increasing dependence on others. (Additional physical health issues pertaining to women and men will be discussed in Chapter 14.) These and other setbacks experienced by aging people on physical, mental, and social fronts can result in a decreased sense of personal control over one's life. These life experiences can blur gender roles, impede sexual creativity, and/or have a desexualizing effect on self-esteem and libido (Cole & Cole, 1993). Negative stereotypes of old age, when internalized, can also perpetuate a self-percept of helplessness.

A decline in functional capacity, possibly resulting from physical disabilities, has been found to greatly increase the likelihood that an elderly person would move in with others or become institutionalized. Women who suffered declines in functional capacity were found to be somewhat less likely to live alone two years later than were their male counterparts. African Americans who suffered declines were more likely than their White counterparts to continue living alone (Worobey & Angel, 1990).

While men are more likely to have acute and fatal diseases, women are more likely to suffer from functional impairment due to chronic diseases (Barer, 1994). As such, women experience disability and the use of personal assistance to a greater extent than do men. For men, reliance on others or on devices for assistance is associated with feelings of reduced well-being. Reliance on devices brings about the same feeling for women. For women, the use of devices may also be accompanied by feelings of frustration, embarrassment, and stigma rather than increased independence. Yet, reliance on personal assistance does not evoke these responses in women according to Penning and Strain (1994).

Another study (Stoller & Cutler, 1992) found no gender differences in the source of paid help providing assistance for activities of daily living. In addition, husband caregivers were more likely to incorporate extra-household assistance than were wife caregivers. This may be a function of women's feeling more comfortable in the caregiving, nurturing role than do men. The association of women and domesticity includes older women as well (Eagly & Mladinic, 1998), which probably results in the disparity between men's and women's self-perceptions as caregivers. It is interesting to note, however, that this view of older women implies an expectation that women devote themselves to others consistently (Eagly & Mladinic, 1998).

After the age of 80, death rates for males are higher but surviving females appear to decline more than do surviving males. Females tend to survive longer with incident disability than do males (Strawbridge et al., 1992). For this reason, in addition to the fact that many women marry men older than themselves, older women are widowed far more often than older men. One-half of the women over the age of 65 are widows and 70 percent of these women live alone (U.S. Census Bureau, 1997). Specifically, among Americans between the ages of 65 and 69, there are 119 women for every 100 men. This ratio becomes more discrepant with age. By the ages of 85 to 89, there are 220 women for every 100 men, and by 95 years of age, there are 384 women for every 100 men. (Costello & Stone, 2001). Thus, older women are more likely to live alone. For women who are 85 and older, 62 percent live alone (Fields & Casper, 2001). Within the elderly population, a high proportion of women were found to be unmarried, living alone, functionally impaired, and financially limited. Men, in contrast, had fewer decrements, were more independent, and exercised more control over their environment (Barer, 1994).

Retirement

Like spousal bereavement, retirement is also traditionally viewed as an emotional trauma for aging people. Thus, many individuals are reluctant to retire. According to the U.S. Census Bureau, one in eight individuals aged 65 and over (4.5 million) were either working or looking for work in 2002. Of these individuals, 57 percent were men and 44 percent were women. Furthermore, about one-half of

married-couple households with at least one individual over 65 years old had annual incomes of $35,000 or more in 2001 (U.S. Census Bureau, 2003). However, since the 1970s, studies have shown that most women and men look forward to retirement; retirement is far from the emotional trauma it has been believed to be (Palmore, Burchett, Fillenbaum, George, & Wallman, 1985). Apparently, retirement and widowhood have a much more multifaceted meaning to people than we might think, symbolizing not only leaving something but also entering a new stage of life.

Retirement can contribute to psychological difficulties though, particularly for the man whose identity is wrapped up in his work role. Men often experience themselves and their status as an extension of their occupational success, because a man's work role is closely tied to his job as the family provider. Once it is gone, a man sometimes experiences a loss in status and a loss of relationships and contacts with former friends and associates. He must often develop a new identity, with new relationships, particularly with his wife and family, which may require him to be more intimate and vulnerable. Leisure time is yet another new experience that is often quite difficult to adjust to, particularly for the man whose life has been his work (Denmark, Nielson, & Scholl, 1993).

Women who have chosen to work, whether out of financial need or commitment to their jobs, may find it more difficult to stop working. In addition, retired women are more likely than retired men to report that their incomes are inadequate. This reflects the fact that women's retirement income typically is only about one-half that of men's. Women's concentration in low-paying jobs and their often interrupted or delayed work careers, can result in smaller retirement benefits. In addition, women are less likely to receive pensions than are men as a function of women's lesser years in the workforce and lesser affiliation with unions, segregation in low-wage occupations, and discrimination involving training, promotion, and raises. Preretirement planning could help alleviate some of women's serious financial problems (Rollins, 1996).

The vignette in Box 11.4 illustrates the complex decisions faced by women who feel torn between early retirement and remaining at work.

BOX 11.4_____

Early Retirement

Imagine Alice, a healthy 62-year-old, faced with the possibility of early retirement from her position in a large communications firm. Her career has been successful and she has received many steady pay increases. However, she has not been promoted to a higher position in the last twelve years. She feels that the company is waiting for her to announce her retirement so they can fill her position with a younger employee. The firm is offering a desirable early retirement package that is starting to look tempting to Alice. Also, the company recently paid for Alice and other employees in their late fifties and early sixties to attend a retirement seminar. She attended several seminars led by psychologists that emphasized the benefits of early retirement. One psychologist noted, "Early retirement will leave you free to pursue your interests while you still have your health." The sessions were compelling and offered some interesting views on early retirement. What should Alice do?

Alice derives immense satisfaction and pleasure from her job. She is competent to handle the demands of her job and makes valuable contributions to the firm (although she feels these efforts are not always appreciated). Alice feels she is just as sharp as the younger employees in her department. In fact, her experience and expertise in communications have proved invaluable on many occasions when critical decisions were made. Aside from slight arthritis, Alice is in perfect physical condition. She has not missed a single day of work in ten years. Why should Alice retire early?

On the positive side, retired women, particularly those without husbands, are more involved with friends and neighbors than are retired men or lifelong housewives. For both women and men, a high level of life satisfaction in retirement is generally associated with having good health, adequate income, a high activity level (Etaugh, 1993), and, specifically for widows, support networks (Hong & Duff, 1994). However, although older females did not necessarily express less life satisfaction than elderly males when surveyed, the interviewed female retirees appeared to be significantly less well adjusted psychosocially than their male counterparts (Hollis, 1994).

Adelmann (1993) found that women who described themselves as both retired and homemakers had higher self-esteem and lower depression than did women who identified themselves with a single role. Lower depression for older women was also associated with higher levels of education, marriage, good health, age, and engagement in hours of do-it-yourself activities. Higher self-esteem for older women was associated with age, education, health, do-it-yourself activity, and volunteer activity. On the whole, it appears that involvement in a number of activities and roles is beneficial for older women.

Reactions to retirement vary across cultures. One study (Yee, 1990) highlights the importance of care-ful cross-cultural research in the area of aging. In this study of American Indian, Native Alaskan Eskimo, Asian, and Pacific Islander, African American, and Hispanic families, it was concluded that there is diversity within each minority group and that the subgroups in each ethnic category share more similar life experiences with each other than with White, middle-class families.

Although men are stereotypically viewed as becoming less productive as they lose or surrender their competitive and aggressive "instincts," older men have actually made significant achievements in our culture. Many U.S. men continue to hold powerful positions well past the age of 65, sometimes hitting career peaks in "old age." These men continue to base their self-esteem on the success ethic (i.e., you are what you produce or achieve) and are not daunted by their advancing age in this respect (Rybarczyk, 1994).

Spousal Bereavement

Spousal bereavement is a change that profoundly affects older people, especially women. A husband's pension usually ends with his death, and the couple's savings may have been exhausted during his final illness. In addition to the financial burden and emotional hardship incurred by this event, many widows *may* endure diminished social status and increased isolation. This occurs whether the spouse's death lessens or ends interaction with his family (Lopata, 1973) or whether the widow is dropped from her network of married friends, a condition that occurs when married friends view her continued presence as a threat to them or to their network's gender balance (Babchuk & Anderson, 1989). Overall, however, it has been found that the degree of social participation usually increases directly following the loss of a spouse due to an increase in support from friends and relatives. Many older adults attempt to cope with the loss of a spouse by maintaining constancy in their degree of social participation. It is important to note, however, that not all widowed persons have access to the same resources to maintain a comfortable level of social contact (Utz, Carr, & Nesse, 2002).

Although it was once thought to be a pivotal tragedy of old age, more recent studies of spousal bereavement in the elderly have confirmed that older people tolerate this so-called worst life event surprisingly well, showing few intense symptoms even in the first few months after a spouse's death (Breckenridge, Gallagher, Thompson, & Peterson, 1986, cited in Belsky, 1992). This applies to both men and women. In fact, for a sample of middle-class women, widowhood was seen as a mixed experience—not just as a trauma, but as a chance for self-expansion, even, in part, a positive event!

However, spousal bereavement and the death of friends may make loneliness a central part of an older person's existence. Research suggests that loneliness expressed by older persons is related to gender, health status, and economic condition; needs for affection and security and desire to be part of a social network; and the existence of a set of friends (Mullins & Mushel, 1992). In a study of gender effects on elderly lifestyles, Arber and Ginn (1994) found that although elderly women's opportunities for making and maintaining friendships are constrained by their having fewer material and health resources than elderly men have, the relationship skills that women acquire earlier in life are an asset. Women are less likely than men to have relied entirely on their spouse for friendship, and women seem more adaptable to changed circumstances.

For lone elderly women, friendships act as a buffer, alleviating effects of their considerable disadvantage in material and health resources. Mental health among the elderly in general is facilitated by regular social interactions (O'Connor, 1992). Although old age is a time of losing friendships through death, the majority of elderly women make new friends (Rollins, 1996). Men, on the other hand, are less likely than women to have close friends and confide intimate matters to them (Grambs, 1989; Lewittes, 1988). Although both women and men are vulnerable to ailments and illnesses when they experience the loss of a spouse, research shows that widowers have more extreme negative consequences than do widows. In general, it is important to understand the grieving process in order to provide better support for both men and women experiencing spousal bereavement (Stroebe, 1998).

One study demonstrated that although older adults who were never married and are childless benefited most from contacts with siblings, friends, and neighbors, divorced and widowed adults were more likely to profit from contact with adult children. In addition, gender differences were found in the degree of loneliness among unmarried older persons. Unmarried men reported higher levels of loneliness than did unmarried women (Pinquart, 2003). Friendships, unlike family members, are voluntarily chosen and based on common interests. Friends are also viewed as desiring to help out in order to contribute to the friend's welfare, whereas family members might feel obligated to do so (Arling, 1976a).

Among older adults, it has been found that for both females and males there is less of a chance that there will be a decrease in cognitive functioning among those with a higher degree of visual contact with friends and relatives (Zunzunegui, Alvarado, & Del Ser, 2003). Even women who are physically limited can maintain and widen their social networks via the telephone (Hochschild, 1978). More recently, older individuals have begun to take advantage of the use of computers and the Internet in order to gain more personal control over their lives through participating with others in an electronic community. The use of computers as a way to connect with others and gain access to information has been reported to enrich the lives and expand the worldviews of older persons, therefore having an impact on their mental health and quality of life (McMellon, & Schiffman,

2002). In addition to the social connection that the use of computers can provide, they also can make lifestyles easier for older persons through at-home shopping, banking, and bill paying (Ogozalek, 1991).

It is interesting to note that Black widows are even more likely than are White widows to be actively involved with friends and neighbors (Arling, 1976b). In addition, their families provide them with more social support (Jackson, 1988). A review of the literature suggests that older women maintain a support system of friends, become more knowledgeable regarding finances, and seek professional help for physical and psychological problems. Advice to older men includes lessening dependence on their wives for companionship, making social contacts, and participating in community and other activities. Suggestions for therapeutic intervention with both aging women and men include helping elderly women deal with problems related to sexuality and relationships with adult children, and helping elderly men find ways to replace lost status, activities, and contacts (Jacobs, 1994).

Research is needed to examine racial and class differences in the impact of spousal bereavement. Marriage appears to be relatively less central to Black women's existence; Black women appear to be more independent than White women in this respect (Brown & Gary, 1985). This may be a function of poorer health among Black males, which causes Black women to rely less on male support in later life (Spurlock, 1984).

Sexual orientation may also have an effect on one's reaction to losing one's partner in life. Lesbians, whose relationships with their partners may not be publicly acknowledged, might not receive the same social support provided to widows. Even people who are aware of the relationship might not understand the depth of the loss involved (see Doress et al., 1987). In addition, lesbians who have lost their partners may suffer the same economic repercussions as widows, but without the same legal financial provisions.

Grandparenting

Becoming a grandparent is a common role change among aging people. For most women, becoming a grandmother is a positive event, because it does not bring with it the stress that motherhood entailed. This is especially true today in the United States as grandmothers are taking less responsibility for child care (Doress et al., 1987). Yet economic factors may necessitate the grandmother's becoming a baby-sitter for her grandchildren, because her children may live with her (Long & Porter, 1984). In some cultures, if the child's parents become ill or die, it may even fall to the grandmother to raise the child.

In New York alone, it has been projected that there will be over 100,000 orphans by early in the twenty-first century due to HIV/AIDS. Such situations compel grandparents to postpone their plans and raise their grandchildren instead (AARP, 2001). Many grandparents, however, derive enjoyment and gratification from helping to raise their grandchildren and take their responsibilities very seriously. According to results from a study done by the AARP, a substantial majority of the grandparents interviewed (83 percent) believed it was their duty to instill values in their grandchildren. They also believed they were responsible for teaching the children spirituality and religion, informing them about their family history, disciplining them when required, and assisting with schoolwork. Furthermore, approximately 70 percent of the individuals interviewed managed to meet with their grandchildren at least every week or two (Lanzito, 2002). Some grandparents actually live with their grandchildren or live very close to them so they can spend time with them (as well as their own children) on a regular basis. Following parents, grandparents typically take on the preponderance of child-care duties for preschool children. In fact, of the 19.6 million preschoolers in the United States, grandparents take care of about 21 percent of these children (Healy et al., 2002). Although it is more time consuming, taking care of grandchildren can be a very positive change for many older individuals. In an article from the *Washington Post,* one grandmother moved next door to her grandchildren when her husband died and consequently felt less lonely. She regarded living next door to her grandchildren as a rewarding experience and as a new and valuable opportunity to form intimate bonds with them before they grew up (Salant, 2003). Research shows that spending time with grandparents is beneficial for children, because they gain the benefit of having additional caring adults in their lives (Peterson, 2002). When grandparents divorce, however, they often communicate with their grand-children less frequently and do not feel as close to them. As a result, the role of grandparent becomes less significant in their lives. Unfortunately, it is anticipated that the costs of divorce among grandparents will magnify in next 10 to 20 years, because those who are divorcing currently will become grandparents at that point in time (Peterson, 2002).

Gender-Role Flexibility in Aging

An interesting phenomenon among older couples is the idea that the sexes become more like each other or even trade personality traits as they age. This was a basic finding in the Kansas City Studies of Adult Life (Neugarten et al., 1968); that is, the idea that women become more assertive and men softer and less stereo-typically masculine in the second half of adult life. Similarly, Fischer and Narus (1981) found that older women view themselves as more autonomous and competent than do younger women, and older men view themselves as more communal and expressive than do younger men. These self-descriptions run counter to gender stereotypes. Although other studies find an increase in the numbers of feminine women and masculine men in those aged 61 and older (Hyde, Krajnik, & Skuldt-Niederberger, 1991), possible gender-role flexibility of aging bears investigation.

A possible explanation for this flexibility is that earlier in life the more androgynous people may have had to suppress their real selves in order to conform to what Gutmann (1987) would call the **parental imperative;** that is, parental roles force female and male adults into relatively powerful or less powerful positions consistent with their respective gender roles. The onset of the postparental era at around age 50 may have provided them with the opportunity to express their true personalities.

However, the results of a study on older people in the Israeli kibbutz setting (Friedman, Tzukerman, Wienberg, & Todd, 1992) countered the parental imperative as an explanation for this shift in gender roles. Although parenthood did increase the power of the male and decrease the power of the female as Gutmann argued, this was true only among urban families. Kibbutz couples experienced the reverse,

whereas parental status actually increased power for the female and decreased power for the male. Apparently, the parental imperative described by Gutmann (1987) is affected by culture in terms of its ramifications, not biology as Gutmann suggested. Furthermore, older women were found to use traditionally feminine power strategies, such as indirect power or manipulation, personal resources (e.g., friendliness and emotional support as opposed to concrete resources such as money or strength), and helplessness (Johnson, 1976). Yet, their behavior was evaluated as more powerful than the same behavior in younger women. Thus, it is not the behaviors but rather people's evaluation of the behaviors that changes across the life span (Friedman et al., 1992).

A possible explanation for observed shifts in gender-typed behavior among older people is that as men age, the social roles available to them change. Men may engage in more domestic activities once retirement affords them with the free time to do so. The gender-role expectations for older males may be less rigid, causing older men to feel freer to engage in less gender-stereotypical behaviors. They may view themselves as equally masculine but have less concern about maintaining outward appearances (Rybarczyk, 1994).

Although the shift in gender-typed behavior may occur in the realm of personality, it does not necessarily extend to choice of activities. On the contrary, older women of various ethnic groups have been found to engage more in traditionally female gender-typed activities such as housework and cooking. While older men engage more in hunting, farming, or working to support themselves, this difference was not significant (Harris, Begay, & Page, 1989). This lends some basis to the common stereotype of older women as nurturing, cheerful grandmother types (Brewer, Dull, & Lui, 1981). Typical older women are viewed as less self-centered, more nurturant, and more sensitive than typical older men (Canetto, Kaminski, & Felicio, 1995), possibly as a function of this stereotype.

Cognitive Changes

You have already learned about cognition in Chapter 6. One of the most greatly feared aspects of growing older for both women and men is the decline in cognitive ability, which often accompanies aging. For example, significant changes in everyday memory, memory capacity, processing speed, and depression have been found to occur with age (see Chapter 6 concerning women and men's cognitive abilities). Sex differences have been found as well, with older and aged males showing a decrease in memory problems and females showing an increase in memory problems (Agrawal & Kumar, 1992). However, a longitudinal study of female and male senior citizens tested twice over three years found that, on retesting, females were better at prose recall and list recognition performance than were men (Zelinski, Gilewski, & Schaie, 1993).

Memory decline actually begins in middle adulthood, when it is more common with long-term than with short-term memory (Craik, 1977). Memory is also likely to decline at this stage if memory strategies such as organization and imagery are not used (Smith, 1977). In addition, memory for recently acquired information or infrequently used information begins to worsen in the middle years (Riege & Inman, 1981). Finally, in the middle years, recognition is better than recall (Mandler, 1980). A study conducted by Naveh-Benjamin and colleagues (2002) investigated age-related differences in cued recall at the stages of encoding information as well as retrieving it. It was found that younger adults benefited significantly from support only at the level of encoding, whereas older adults needed support at both encoding and retrieval (Naveh-Benjamin, 2002). Not all cognitive changes for older persons are negative. Thus, according to a study by Michael Wesner (2001), although older adults had slower reaction times in performing a visual search task, they required less contrast to detect a target from distracters than did young adults. Although there is a significant amount of evidence demonstrating that changes in the ability to consciously learn and retain new information is associated with the normal aging process, there is still an unclear boundary between normal aging and the early stages of Alzheimer's disease (Albert, 2001).

Intellectual decline in the later adult years is a subject of much debate and controversy. Although some maintain that the aging process results in cognitive deterioration universally (Wechsler, 1972), others argue that some abilities decline while others do not. For example, Horn and Donaldson (1980) agree that *fluid intelligence* (i.e., one's ability to reason abstractly) declines steadily from middle adulthood, but *crystallized intelligence* (i.e., one's accumulated information and verbal skills) actually increases with age. On the other hand, Schaie (1994) found that mental abilities do not decline until the age of 74, and when age changes and perceptual speed are removed, the actual decrement is significantly reduced.

However, the speed of processing information has clearly been found to decline in late adulthood (Sternberg & McGrane, 1993). Other cognitive changes supported by the research include decreased ability to retrieve information from memory (Sternberg & McGrane, 1993) and to efficiently use mental information in memory (Baltes, Smith, & Staudinger, 1992).

Do age-related cognitive changes differ according to sex? Recent magnetic resonance imaging (MRI) data suggest that men show more rapid age-associated atrophy of the left hemisphere than do women. However, data suggest that this does not translate into differential functional decline in simulated everyday verbal memory (Larrabee & Crook, 1993). In a study of memory for visual–spatial arrays in young and older adults, absolute errors increased with age. This is consistent with decreased anterograde memory and visuospatial skills in older people. The writers speculate that "components of the complex mechanisms underlying visuospatial processing may be differently affected by gender" (Jue et al., 1992, p. 236), because older women outperformed older men on a spatial array memory test, and the reverse was true when the groups were tested on the judgment of line orientation.

Age-related cognitive decline has emotional effects as well. Fuhrer, Antonucci, and Dartigues (1992) examined the co-occurrence of depressive symptomatology and cognitive impairment in female and male older adults. Co-occurrence was found to be associated with age, little or no education (women were at a higher risk than men when this predictor was involved), functional impairment, and dissatisfaction with social support (for the latter two factors, men were at a higher risk than women). Women over the age of 85 were at an increased risk, and marital status was associated with co-occurrence for men but not for women.

TABLE 11.2   Erikson's Stages of Psychosocial Development

PSYCHOSOCIAL STAGE	TASK
1: Trust vs. Mistrust	If their needs are consistently met, infants learn to trust their environment. The failure to meet an infant's needs results in the development of mistrust.
2: Autonomy vs. Shame and Doubt	Toddlers who learn to regulate their bodily functions gain a sense of independence and autonomy. Toddlers who fail to achieve control over their bodies experience shame and doubt.
3: Initiative vs. Guilt	As preschoolers experiment with their developing physical and mental skills, they must learn to control their impulses.
4: Industry vs. Inferiority	Children aged 6 to 11 years learn to take pride in their emerging skills and abilities. Negative comparisons with other children often lead to feelings of inferiority.
5: Identity vs. Role Confusion	Adolescents combine their various roles to form one coherent self-identity. The failure to integrate different aspects of the self leads to role confusion.
6: Intimacy vs. Isolation	Young adults develop the capacity to form intimate relationships with others. Failure to develop interpersonal attachments leads to social and emotional isolation.
7: Generativity vs. Stagnation	During middle adulthood, individuals take an interest in fostering the development of younger generations. Preoccupation with one's own needs leads to stagnation and self-absorption.
8: Integrity vs. Despair	During late adulthood, individuals reflect on their lives, searching for meaning. If they find meaning in their lives, they experience integrity. If they fail to glean meaning from their lives, they experience despair.

SUMMARY

Clearly, development for both genders does not end with the onset of middle adulthood. Nevertheless, older adults face a double standard as they approach midlife. For instance, the media tend to disregard older women or portray them in a negative fashion. Men are most often viewed as being in their prime and reaping the benefits of career building in young adulthood. Women, on the other hand, face ageism that is perpetuated by a society that disparages the physical changes that come with growing older (e.g., menopause, graying, wrinkles) and are viewed as worthless as their children have left the home and assumed independent lives. Many of these women, however, are responsible for providing emotional support for their adolescent and adult children and their own aging parents. Moreover, many older women and men take on a significant role in raising and caring for their grandchildren. Other women go back to school or reenter the workforce if they are not already active in a career.

Both genders experience cognitive and physical decline as they approach retirement age. These changes may correlate function impairment with psychological difficulties as those suffering struggle to adjust to decline in abilities. This decline may be more evident in women; they live longer than their male counterparts and may require more social support. Close family members and friendships may help buffer some of the unpleasant outcomes of aging and make later life a more positive and productive experience. Even in the face of physical difficulties, older women can accomplish great things.

KEY TERMS

Ageism (p. 347)
Climacteric (p. 349)
Cohort (p. 356)
Dominant generation (p. 349)
Double standard of aging (p. 345)

Empty nest syndrome (p. 353)
Graying of America (p. 345)
Late midlife astonishment (p. 349)
Menopause (p. 349)
Parental imperative (p. 362)

Reentry women (p. 355)
Sandwich generation (p. 349)
Trophy wives (p. 354)
Viagra (p. 348)

DISCUSSION QUESTIONS

1. What are some of the advantages of combining marriage with a career? What are some of the disadvantages? Are these the same for women and men? If not, what are the differences?

2. What are the physical and psychological changes that occur during midlife for women and men? How do changes in physical appearance during midlife impact women and men differently? What are your own beliefs regarding aging women and men?

3. How do women's responsibilities change as they grow older? What options open up for women? What additional tasks are relegated to women? In your opinion, do women gain or lose options in society as they age?

4. It has been shown that, on average, women live longer lives than men do. What are the positive and negative consequences of longevity?

5. Is the empty nest syndrome a positive or negative experience for women? How do men experience the departure of their children from the home?

6. How important are grandparents in the lives of their grandchildren?

FURTHER READINGS

Babladelis, G. (1999). Autonomy in the middle years. In M. B. Nadien & F. L. Denmark (Eds.), *Females and autonomy: A life-span perspective* (pp. 101–129). Boston: Allyn and Bacon.

Etaugh, C. (1993). Women in the middle and later years. In F. L. Denmark & M. A. Paludi (Eds.), *Psychology of women: A handbook of issues and theories* (pp. 213–246). Westport, CT: Greenwood Press.

Nadien, M. B., & Denmark, F. L. (1999). Aging women: Stability or change in perceptions of personal control. In M. B. Nadien & F. L. Denmark (Eds.), *Females and autonomy: A life-span perspective* (pp. 130–154). Boston: Allyn and Bacon.

United Nations Political Declaration and Madrid International Plan of Action on Aging. (2003). New York: Department of Public Information.

Wilcox, S., Evenson, K. R., Aragaki, A., Wassertheil-Smoller, S., Mouton, C. P., & Lee Loevinger, B. (2003). The effects of widowhood on physical and mental health, health behaviors, and health outcomes: The women's health initiative. *Health Psychology, 22*(5), 513–522.

CHAPTER 12

GENDER, VIOLENCE, AND EXPLOITATION

A dog, a wife and a cherry tree, the more ye beat them the better they be.
—Anonymous

It pays men to be aggressive, hasty, fickle, and undiscriminating. In theory, it is more profitable for females to be coy, to hold back until they can identify the male with the best genes. . . . Human beings obey this biological principle faithfully.
—E. O. Wilson

Alone and in isolation, the person who has been hit must struggle to regain broken trust—to forge some strategy of recovery. Individuals are often able to process an experience of being hit mentally that may not be processed emotionally. Many women I talked with felt that even after the incident was long forgotten, their bodies remained troubled.
—bell hooks

This is my weapon
This is my gun (points to groin).
This one's for killing
This one's for fun.
—Old Marine Corps chant

Among the more than 600 families surveyed in Southern Asia, 51 percent reported having killed a baby girl during her first week of life.
—N. Neft and A. D. Levine

Women want to be free to choose from the same range of options that men take for granted. In our quest for equal pay, equal access to education and opportunities, we have made great strides. But until

women can move freely in their homes, on the streets, in the workplace
without the fear of violence, there can be no real freedom.
—Anita Roddick

THE NATURE AND SCOPE OF GENDERED VIOLENCE AND EXPLOITATION

Wherever they occur, from the family to the workplace to the street, experiences of violence and exploitation define and limit women in sexual and gender-specific terms. Sexist responses to women, ranging from put-down humor and insults to physical abuse and murder, are shockingly common in U.S. society and around the world. Why are women so often violated, exploited, and devalued? No doubt the answer is complex and multifaceted, involving biological, psychological, social, and cultural factors. But it seems likely that the most important causes of violence and exploitation of women by men lie in gender inequality: women's lack of power relative to men. Whenever people are categorized into groups such as female and male, and one group has more power than the other, as men have more power than women, differences between groups are usually transformed into disadvantages for the less powerful group. We have seen these disadvantages in the many negative stereotypes and hurtful myths that exist about girls and women. These myths and stereotypes devalue women in their own and others' eyes. They make it more likely that women will construct identities, personalities, and sexualities around deference to men, and this in turn makes it more likely that women will be mistreated and abused by men (Bem, 1994).

This chapter addresses central questions of how gender inequality creates interpersonal and social conditions conducive to exploitation of, and violence against, women and girls. The intersection of gender and violence is a particularly problematic area for a number of reasons. As we consider the many different forms that gendered abuse may take, we confront several hard questions. Chief among them is what it is that constitutes violence and exploitation. For example, few people would deny that incest, sexual assault, and the rape of a stranger constitute clear-cut examples of the abuse of women. But more people have difficulty classifying sexual harassment, date rape, and spousal and parental abuse as serious problems for women. There is lively debate and widespread disagreement about whether and how pornography and prostitution harm women. And scholars and advocates for women everywhere grapple with the question of how best to conceptualize and respond to social, religious, and cultural differences in values, policies, and practices that affect girls and women differently than boys and men. Where possible, we will discuss the gender, ethnic, cultural, and social class variations in the perceptions of different practices and behaviors as violent or exploitative.

Men as well as women are targets of violence and exploitation. In fact, men are more often the targets of most forms of violence than are women (Kilmartin, 1994). Heterosexual men are sometimes the victims of sexual assault, as in cases of prison rape. Although the perpetrators of violence against men are overwhelmingly other men, women sometimes abuse and murder men. Violence against and exploitation of heterosexual men and boys are obviously serious problems, but they will not be treated extensively in this chapter because they are not regarded as cases of *gendered* abuse. That is, heterosexual men are privileged in society relative to other groups and are not abused and exploited because of their lack of power or status as a social group.

The most common and salient forms of gendered violence and exploitation are the abuses of women and girls by men, but these are not the only forms. This chapter also discusses the abuse of lesbians and gay men as in gay bashing, gay baiting, domestic abuse among lesbians and gay males, and other acts of violence and intimidation against people rendered vulnerable because of their gender or sexuality.

This chapter considers the following classes of behaviors as instances of gendered violence or exploitation: sexual harassment, rape, partner abuse, child sexual abuse, pornography, prostitution, anti-gay violence, female infanticide, female genital mutilation (FGM), and elder abuse. While some scholars attempt to order forms of violence against women on a continuum of severity of abuse, we do not do so. We wish to emphasize that all forms of abuse and exploitation engender a range of consequences in women, depending on a variety of background, situational, and personality factors. Moreover, in this chapter, the term *sexual assault* is not used synonymously with rape. We define sexual assault more broadly, to include any physical attack on the sexual parts of a woman's body—pinching, grabbing, and the like. So defined, sexual assault can occur in any form of violence against women. For each form of violence and exploitation, we will address issues of definition and prevalence, explore its social and cultural significance, review relevant theories and research about its origins and consequences, and discuss a range of potentially helpful individual and social responses to the problem.

SEXUAL HARASSMENT

Few forms of gendered abuse have posed more problems of definition for laypeople and psychologists alike than sexual harassment. The term **sexual harassment** did not even exist until 1976, when it was used in connection with a legal suit filed by Carmita Wood, the first woman to seek unemployment compensation after leaving a job in which her boss made sexual advances toward her (Fitzgerald, 1996). As Catherine MacKinnon, law professor and leading advocate for women's rights, noted in 1979, "The unnamed should not be taken for the nonexistent" (p. 28). Sexual harassment has been a fixture of women's lives in the street, the workplace, and the academy for as long as women have appeared there. After the naming of sexual harassment in the mid-1970s, the closely watched confirmation hearings of Clarence Thomas in 1991, in which accusations of sexual harassment were made by Anita Hill against then U.S. Supreme Court Justice nominee Thomas, put the spotlight on a social problem of enormous proportions. The U.S. Navy Tailhook scandal and the resignation of U.S. Senator Robert Packwood after multiple accusations of sexual harassment by aides further increased awareness of sexual harassment, as have, more recently, Paula Jones' sexual harassment charges against then-Governor Bill Clinton and charges of sexual harassment (among other gender inequities) in the U.S. Air Force. The last 30 years have witnessed an explosion of interest, research, and litigation in sexual harassment. In this chapter, we deal with issues relating to all forms of harassment wherever they occur, but topics particularly relevant to workplace harassment are covered more extensively in Chapter 7.

Definitions and Prevalence

There is no widely agreed-upon definition of sexual harassment that is both broad enough to encompass the variety of experiences to which the construct refers and yet specific enough to be of practical use in identifying harassment (Fitzgerald, 1996). Basically, definitions of harassment can be classified into two categories: (1) general or theoretical statements that focus on the nature of the behavior and often the status of the individuals involved, and (2) those that list specific classes of behaviors that constitute harassment.

In the first category are most legal and regulatory definitions and some theoretical statements on harassment offered by psychologists. Catherine Mac-Kinnon's early definition has been most influential: "Sexual harassment . . . refers to the unwanted imposition of sexual requirements in the context of a relationship of unequal power" (1979, p. 1). The Equal Employment Opportunity Commission (EEOC) defined harassment as unwelcome sexual advances, requests for sexual favors, and other verbal or physical conduct of a sexual nature when (1) such behavior is made explicitly or implicitly a term or condition of employment, (2) submission to such terms is used as

the basis for employment decisions affecting the individual, or (3) verbal or physical conduct of a sexual nature has the purpose or effect of creating an intimidating, hostile, or offensive work environment. In an academic setting, sexual harassment has been defined as "the use of authority to emphasize the sexuality or sexual identity of the student in a manner which prevents or impairs that student's full enjoyment of educational benefits, climate, or opportunities" (Till, 1980, p. 7).

The second category of definitions of harassment is much more concrete and focuses on the specific classes of behaviors that constitute harassment (Fitzgerald, 1996). One particularly thorough catalog, included as Box 12.1, classified the responses of a national sample of college women into five general classes of harassing behaviors (Till, 1980). Till's work made the crucial points that sexual harassment can be verbal as well as physical, comprise sexist as well as sexual behaviors, and is behavior that is experienced as unwelcome by the target.

Whichever type of definition of harassment is used, problems arise that affect issues of measurement, incidence, and theories of harassment. One problematic feature of defining harassment lies in whether the conduct occurs in the context of unequal power relations between the victim and perpetrator. According to many legal and theoretical definitions, in order to be labeled harassment, the sexist or sexualized behavior must take place when people have uneven power; that is, when the harasser has power over the victim's outcomes and can use that power to reward or punish, as a teacher can punish a student or a boss an employee. Can someone be sexually harassed by a peer or even a subordinate? Most scholars today take the view that people can be harassed by peers and, indeed, that this form of harassment is very common (Gutek & Done, 2001; Hughes & Sandler, 1988). In societies in which men are pervasively privileged, where they have more freedom, autonomy, authority, credibility, education, money, status, and the like, men in general have greater power than women and sometimes abuse that power.

Another key issue to keep in mind is that sexual harassment is not simply a behavior of interest to scholars; like rape and many other issues we will discuss in this chapter, it is also illegal. This means that

Box 12.1_____

Categories of Sexual Harassment

1. Generalized sexist remarks and behavior. This behavior, sometimes called **gender harassment,** is not necessarily designed to obtain sexual favors, but to convey insulting, degrading, or sexist attitudes about women.

2. Inappropriate and offensive, but essentially sanction-free sexual advances. This category, sometimes called **seductive behavior,** includes unwanted sexual advances for which there is no penalty attached to a woman's noncompliance.

3. Sexual bribery. This is the solicitation of sexual activity by the promise of reward.

4. Sexual coercion. This is the solicitation of sexual activity by the threat of punishment. With category 3, this category is sometimes called *contingency* or **quid pro quo harassment.**

5. Sexual crimes and misdemeanors. This category includes gross sexual imposition, sexual assault, and rape.

Source: From *Sexual Harassment: A Report on the Sexual Harassment of Students,* by F. J. Till, 1980, Report of the National Advisory Council on Women's Educational Programs, U.S. Department of Justice.

_____

the EEOC and the Supreme Court, among other parties, are defining sexual harassment along with scholars from different disciplines, and that legal concerns are increasingly shaping a great deal of social science research (Gutek & Done, 2001). For example, there is now research examining the "reasonable person standard"—how would an objective, reasonable outsider view the situation?—with a "reasonable woman standard"—how would an objective reasonable outside woman view the situation? According to the law, sexual harassment must meet "subjective" as well as "objective" criteria: That is, the target of the harassment must experience the harassment as severe or pervasive, and reasonable people or reasonable women must find the harassment as severe or pervasive enough to meet a legal definition (Gutek & Done, 2001).

Probably the greatest difficulties in defining and labeling conduct as sexual harassment lie in the differing judgments people make about the meaning of behaviors. As we will see to some extent with date rape, pornography, and prostitution, there is great disagreement about the intentions of men and the harm done to women by various forms of sexual harassment. Individuals differ widely in their perceptions of sexist or sexualized conduct as harassing. Conduct that is extremely offensive to some people is not at all objectionable to others. Some scholars believe that, because all women are invariably op-

pressed by sexist and sexualized encounters in a society stratified by gender, all sexist and unwelcome sexualized behavior in settings such as the workplace should be regarded as harassing, regardless of the victim's judgment of it as problematic (Fitzgerald, 1996; Lafontaine & Tredeau, 1986). For others, the perceptions of the victim are particularly critical to the label of harassment: If the conduct in question is unwelcome, unsolicited, nonreciprocated, offensive, or repeated, then it is regarded as harassing.

More than most forms of violence against and exploitation of women, appraisals of sexual harassment depend on various personal and situational factors. Many variables shown to influence perceptions of sexual harassment have already been identified. None is more consistently related to perceptions of harassment than gender. In study after study, women have been more likely than men to view behaviors as harassing and offensive (Fitzgerald & Ormerod, 1991; Powell, 1986). This is probably because women, far more than men, have experienced unwanted sexual attention in their lives. We will discuss the implications of these consistent sex differences later.

Other variables influencing perceptions of harassment include status of the harasser. Behaviors initiated by supervisors or others with a substantial power advantage are more likely to be judged as harassment. The degree of coercion represented by the behavior is also important: Requests for sex linked to threat of punishment or promise of reward (quid pro quo) are viewed more negatively than sexist remarks or jokes (gender harassment) or seductive behavior. Whereas quid pro quo behaviors are virtually always seen by both women and men as sexual harassment, gender harassment and seductive behavior elicit considerably more disagreement (Fitzgerald, 1996). For example, in one survey of college students, only 30 percent of the male but 47 percent of the female students regarded sexist comments as sexual harassment (Adams, Kottke, & Padgitt, 1983). More recent studies in the United States (e.g., Fitzgerald & Ormerod, 1993) and in other cultures such as South Africa (Mayekiso & Bhana, 1997) consistently find sex differences in appraisals of harassment.

Other definitional challenges have to do with distinguishing sexual harassment from unreciprocated sexual interest and seemingly consensual unions, and distinguishing "merely" boorish behaviors from harassment. Time has emerged as a key variable in a determination of harassment. A single incident, depending on its nature, is much less likely to be regarded as harassing than is a pattern of behavior.

These definitions of sexual harassment raise some important questions with theoretical and practical significance. Is it possible for women to harass men? What about consensual sexual relationships between supervisors and subordinates? Isn't it possible for people with unequal power within an organizational setting to enter into loving, mutually satisfying, long-lasting relationships devoid of coercion and exploitation?

In the early 1990s, Michael Crichton wrote *Disclosure,* a best-selling novel that was made into a major motion picture starring Michael Douglas and Demi Moore, about a woman who harassed a male coworker. In fact, some males are harassed at work, at school, and in the street. Surveys of harassment find that, depending on the definition used, between 9 and 35 percent of all men report experiencing sexual harassment on the job (compared to about 35 to 50 percent of women) (U.S. Merit Systems Protection Board, 1981, 1988, 1995). In about one-fifth of the cases, men are harassed by other men. The forms of sexual harassment that men report are different than

the forms of harassment experienced by women, with men complaining most about lewd comments and attempts to enforce behaviors consistent with the male gender role, and women most often reporting sexist and negative remarks and unwanted sexual attention.

Research suggests that many of the behaviors that women find offensive are not considered offensive to men when the initiators are women. And, as we have seen, women are not socialized to initiate sexual relationships in most societies. Indeed, sexually aggressive women are often stigmatized and punished. Moreover, women are much less likely to hold the organizational power that would permit them to offer rewards and punishments to men in exchange for sexual relationships (Fitzgerald & Weitzman, 1990). Women sometimes do make unwanted sexual overtures to men, and these may be inconvenient, worrisome, or even painful to some men. But research evidence suggests that men suffer significantly less harm from sexual harassment than do women (Bingham & Scherer, 1993; DuBois, Knapp, Faley, & Kustis, 1998). Given the relative power and threat of women and men in most societies, such unwanted overtures are often viewed by targets and scholars alike as private hassles rather than sexual harassment (Dziech & Weiner, 1990), because men generally have the power to control the problem. An important exception to this is same-sex sexual harassment of men, reported by men as the most distressing and negative kind of sexual harassment (DuBois et al., 1998; Stockdale, Visio, & Batra, 1999).

The issue of seemingly consensual sexual relationships between people in the context of unequal power remains a problematic and controversial issue for scholars who study sexual harassment. In fact, many people who enter into sexual relationships in which there is unequal formal power are convinced that there is equal power within the relationship, that both parties are equally free to enter into or terminate the relationship, and that neither party is at risk to be harmed by the relationship. Bosses dating secretaries, professors falling in love with students, and employers marrying housekeepers or nannies are common story lines in books, television programs, and movies, and are not uncommon scenarios in real life. Some of these couples do indeed end up living "happily ever after." So what is wrong with this picture?

On the one hand, some scholars have argued that to regard all consensual relationships between people of formally different statuses as inherently unethical or harassing limits the power, control, and freedom of all people, including the powerless (Hoffman, Clinebell, & Kilpatrick, 1997). In this line of thinking, why should secretaries or students not be "free" to have sexual relations with bosses or professors? On the other hand, others believe that "truly consensual relationships are probably not possible within the context of unequal power, and thus may be generally inappropriate" (Fitzgerald, 1996, p. 42). Fitzgerald, Weitzman, Gold, & Ormerod (1988) noted that while not always unethical, sexual relationships among people of unequal power within an organization are almost always unwise. As we will discuss, some of the evidence for this is that events that women do not initially label as harassing and coercive often come to be seen that way with time (Kidder, Lafleur, & Wells, 1995).

The prevalence of sexual harassment has been notoriously difficult to study because of the lack of a commonly accepted definition and, at least until recently, of any standardized survey instrument that could provide comparable results across studies (Fitzgerald, Shullman, et al., 1988; Fitzgerald et al., 1999). But since the early 1980s, the results of several large-scale studies in academia and the workplace suggest that sexual harassment is a widespread phenomenon. Probably the best-known study of the prevalence of sexual harassment is an early national survey using a random sample of almost 24,000 male and female employees working for the federal government (U.S. Merit Systems Protection Board, 1981). The response rate to this survey was a very high 83.8 percent. Forty-two percent of all women respondents reported that they had been the targets of sexual harassment within the previous two years. A wide range of harassing behaviors was reported, with repeated sexual remarks (33 percent) and unwanted physical touching (26 percent) the most common complaints. Subsequent studies by the U.S. Merit Systems Protection Board (USMSPB) find similar results (USMSPB 1981, 1988, 1995). Reviews of the literature on sexual harassment in the workplace put the median percentage of women who have *ever* experienced sexual harassment at work at about 44 percent (Gruber, 1990),

with the most common forms cited among the less severe forms—sexist or sexual comments, undue attention, or inappropriate body language.

The incidence of sexual harassment has been studied extensively in colleges and universities. The academy is an important place to study harassment because for many it is the repository of the best that society has to offer its members: It is an "ivory tower" or "safe haven" from the corruption of the workplace. Values are an important part of education, and colleges communicate values in many ways, including in the kinds of relationships between women and men and faculty and students that they promote on campus (Hughes & Sandler, 1988). Moreover, the relationship between a professor and a student is held by many to be a special one with unique ethical responsibilities. Sexualizing that relationship is regarded as a particularly problematic betrayal of trust.

In fact, most surveys of sexual harassment on college campuses show that levels of sexual harassment by both professsors and peers (other students) is shockingly high. In one survey of students in two large public universities, about 50 percent of the undergraduate women at one university and 76 percent of the undergraduate women at the second university reported experiencing at least one incident that meets the definition of sexual harassment (Fitzgerald, Shullman, et al., 1988). At both settings, the most frequently reported situations involved either gender harassment or seduction. Between 5 and 8 percent reported being propositioned and another 5 to 8 percent reported unwanted attempts by professors to touch or fondle them. Nearly 5 percent at both universities reported being subtly bribed by professors with some sort of award to engage in sexual activity. Despite the severity of many of these behaviors (touching, fondling, propositions, etc.), only 5 percent of the female sample believed that they had been sexually harassed. Other surveys of college students variously put the incidence of sexual harassment at between 15 and 50 percent, with higher estimates occurring when situations involving gender harassment are included in the survey (Dziech & Weiner, 1990; Paludi, 2004; Reilly, Lott, & Gallogly, 1986). As Paludi notes, as high as these estimates are, they are likely underreports, because most women still maintain a silence about sexual harassment on campus, in the United

States and around the world, and do not label behavior as harassing.

Street harassment—from whistling, to sexist and lewd remarks and verbal come-ons, to obscene gestures, to following, to men exposing themselves, or to grabbing and sexual assault—is often regarded as relatively trivial and has received far less research attention by psychologists and other social scientists than either workplace or academic harassment. But, in fact, street harassment may be more common than either of the other two types. A cross section of female respondents in New York City estimated that the average woman is harassed on the street about seven times a week, and male respondents guessed slightly larger numbers (Packer, 1986). Street harassment is not trivial, often restricting women's movements, autonomy, and sense of control, and sometimes causing great pain, fear, and humiliation.

Theories of the Origins of Sexual Harassment

As we have noted, recent surveys suggest that sexual harassment is probably one of the most common forms of abuse of women, with most women having experienced some forms of harassment at school, on the job, or on the street. Why do men harass women? There is relatively little literature that specifically addresses the origins of sexual harassment, but most theorists believe that we cannot understand sexual harassment without placing it within the context of gender inequality and discrimination.

Some models of sexual harassment trace a proclivity of sexual harassment to the conventional male gender role, especially the socialization of males to dominate and control others, to restrict emotional expression, to actively seek sex whenever possible, to avoid "feminine" behavior and feelings and define themselves in terms of achievement and success. Traditionally, males are not socialized to take an interpersonal orientation, to empathize with others or consider how others interpret an act. Sexual harassment is often a matter of whether the intended target feels uncomfortable, attacked, offended, or intimidated—what some people call the "eye of the beholder criterion." Kilmartin (1994) notes, "Many men are wondering, at what point does 'normal' flirting, sexual discussion, or complimenting cross the line into harass-

ment?" (p. 241). Kilmartin suggests that men harass women at least in part because their socialization offers them little experience in making judgments about what others, especially women, are thinking and feeling, and many men are unaware of their effects on women.

There is ample research suggesting that men and women do have different perceptions of some of the behaviors that constitute sexual harassment, especially the less severe forms of harassment. Generally, men are far less likely to view a behavior as harassing than women are. In the U.S. Merit Systems Protection Board studies (1981, 1988, 1995), women were more likely than men to regard sexual teasing, jokes, or remarks to be sexual harassment. Gutek (1996) also found that women who encounter sexual comments, looks, gestures, and unnecessary physical contact in the workplace are more likely than men to consider such behaviors sexual harassment. These findings are consistent with those of Abbey (1982) and Abbey and Melby (1986), which suggest that men tend to perceive women's friendly behavior as a sign of sexual interest or availability. Men may initiate some behaviors that they do not believe to be offensive but are viewed as harassing by some women. Differences in the ways men and women view social exchanges in the workplace are important components of any useful model of sexual harassment.

Using previous research, court cases, and legal defenses as their guide, Tangri, Burt, and Johnson (1982) proposed a theoretical framework of sexual harassment with three possible explanatory models, which has been refined and updated (Tangri & Hayes, 1997). One version of the *natural–biological model* suggests that women and men are naturally attracted to each other at work or in the academy, but that men simply have stronger sex drives than women and are thus more likely to initiate and maintain sexual behaviors. A more sophisticated version of the natural–biological model is an *evolutionary adaptation model,* which represents harassment as an evolved reproductive strategy used by men to ensure reproduction. The critical aspect of this model is the absence of discriminatory or harmful intent on the part of the male perpetrator. There are two versions of the *organizational model* as well. The earlier version focused on power relations and suggested that the hierarchical relations that exist within organizations create opportunities for sexual harassment. Various features of an organization, such as differential power, the numerical ratio of males to females, the norms of the organization, and the availability of formal or informal grievance procedures may all affect the incidence of sexual harassment. Another form of the organizational model is called the **sex-role spillover** theory, defined as the carryover into the workplace of gender-based expectations that are irrelevant or inappropriate to work. Finally, the *sociocultural model* describes sexual harassment as a result of the gender inequality that exists more generally throughout society. In this formulation, sexual harassment on the job is a mechanism for maintaining male dominance over women in the workplace and in the larger society.

In their excellent review of the research spawned by these models, Tangri and Hayes (1997) make the point that there is likely to be no one explanation for all of the behaviors we call sexual harassment, and each of the models appears to have some explanatory power for some forms of harassment. For example, the natural–biological model might explain some less severe forms of sexual harassment that most resemble courting behavior; the organizational model can explain harassment of subordinates, but fails to account for the fact that at least half of all sexual harassment is done by peers. Research on sex-role spillover theory suggests that the theory correctly predicts higher incidence of harassment in gender-stratified rather than gender-integrated workplaces. Sociocultural theories have also received support cross-culturally in studies that suggest that there is less sexual harassment in societies in which women and men are more equal.

Terpstra and Baker (1986) offer a different explanatory model that identifies three *causal factors* in sexual harassment: gender, power, and perceptions of work climate. They predicted and found that women are more likely to be harassed than men, that people with less institutional power are more likely to be harassed than people with more institutional power, and that sexual harassment is more common in organizations that are perceived as tolerant of harassment. Other tests of their model have generally garnered some support (Bingham & Scherer, 1993).

All of the models reviewed are helpful in explaining sexual harassment, but no one model entirely explains why sexual harassment exists. Most recent conceptual frameworks see sexual harassment in all its forms—in the workplace, academia, and the public sphere—as being rooted in some combination of sexual interest and unequal power between the sexes. This view recognizes that not all sexual harassment is meant to demean, control, or harm women, but that sexual harassment can be and often is used as a tactic of social control, a means of keeping women in their place, especially in work and school settings that have been traditional male preserves, such as the firehouse or military academy.

Research on Sexual Harassment: Who Harasses, and Who Is Harassed?

Theories on what causes and maintains sexual harassment have inspired a great deal of empirical research in the past three decades. Research strongly suggests that there are no typical harassers or victims of harassment, but certain individual and social characteristics are correlated with the incidence of sexual harassment. Although most harassers are men, most men are not harassers. Although many women report having been harassed in their lives, more than half of all women do not report having been harassed. An *individual difference approach* to the study of harassment asks who is likely to harass, and who is likely to be harassed.

Who Harasses? As we have stated, studies consistently find that men harass women far more often than women harass men (Bingham & Scherer, 1993; Gutek, 1985; U.S. Merit Systems Protection Board, 1981, 1988, 1995). Remarkably little empirical literature bears on the social and psychological characteristics of men who harass women. The reasons for this omission are obvious. How does one study sexual harassers? Men who harass women are understandably reluctant to volunteer as participants for research. They do not declare themselves publicly. They are not found in self-help groups because they do not judge their behavior to be symptomatic of a personal problem (Zalk, 1996). Unlike rapists or child abusers, they are not found in jails.

The little research that has been done on male harassers finds few reliable predictors of harassment. Attitudes consistent with the traditional male gender role have been associated with the likelihood of sexual harassment. Pryor (1987) found that men who see women as sex objects first and human beings (or coworkers) second are at risk for inflicting sexual harassment. Men who hold adversarial sexual beliefs— that sexual relationships are a matter of exploitation and manipulation—are more likely to harass (Rudman & Borgida, 1995), as are men who equate sex and power (Bargh, Raymond, Pryor, & Strack, 1995), and men with less self-control (Done, 2000). In these ways, as we will see, the characteristics of sexual harassers are similar to those of acquaintance rapists in that feelings of masculine inadequacy and misogyny appear to fuel the behavior (Kilmartin, 1994). The psychological dynamics of male harassers in the academy and profiles of different types of harassers have been explored in depth by Dziech and Weiner (1990) and Zalk (1996).

In the workplace, a few predictors of sexual harassment have emerged. For instance, research suggests that men who harass women tend to be older than their victims and less physically attractive than women who harass men (Hemming, 1985; Tangri et al., 1982). Moreover, women are more often harassed by men of equal or greater power, whereas men report the greatest amount of unwanted sexual attention from less powerful women (Bingham & Scherer, 1993). In several studies, male peers have emerged as the most frequent harassers, followed by supervisors, subordinates, and clients (Gutek & Done, 2001; Lafontaine & Tredeau, 1986). Susan Fiske and Peter Glick (Fiske & Glick, 1995; Glick & Fiske, 1996) have used their ambivalent sexism inventory to predict individual differences in harassers. The ambivalent sexism inventory is composed of two scales: hostile sexism and benevolent sexism. Hostile sexism is defined as generalized hostility toward women whereas benevolent sexism is defined as a subjectively positive, but sexist, view of women. Fiske and Glick have hypothesized that hostile, but not benevolent, sexism should predict willingness to harass, but results so far are mixed, as they are, by and large, for most individual difference predictors of sexual harassment.

Who Is Harassed?   The best predictor of being a victim of sexual harassment is gender: Women are more likely than men to be victims of harassment, to be victims of the more severe forms of harassment, and to suffer a variety of negative consequences of harassment.

Aside from gender, position of power within an organization has been studied in its relationship to sexual harassment. People are much less likely to be harassed if they are supervisors than if they are not. For all types of harassment behavior, lower-status service workers are more likely to be harassed than higher-status professionals (Fain & Anderton, 1987). Within academia, some studies show that graduate students are more likely to be sexually harassed by their professors than are faculty members or undergraduate students (Fitzgerald, Shullman, et al., 1988). Given that graduate students have more status than most undergraduates, this may seem surprising. But graduate students, who rely on their relationship with a particular mentor for guidance, success in the program, and career opportunities, have more at stake than undergraduates and are in fact more dependent and vulnerable than the typical undergraduate student.

The relationship between marital status and all types of sexual harassment has been explored. In the workplace, divorced, separated, and widowed women are most likely to be harassed and married women the least likely (Fain & Anderton, 1987; Lafontaine & Tredeau, 1986; U.S. Merit Systems Protection Board, 1981, 1988, 1995). Similar findings with respect to marital status have been found with students (Dziech & Weiner, 1990). One possible explanation for these findings is that, traditionally, women are perceived as the property of their husbands and are off limits to other men.

Age is another variable that is strongly associated with being sexually harassed: Younger women are more likely to experience sexual harassment than are older women (Dziech & Weiner, 1990; Fain & Anderton, 1987). Of course, age is correlated with other variables (marital status, power within an organization, less education, more conformity to societal standards of beauty) that may be related to the incidence of harassment.

Recent research has focused on the effects of a victim's race or ethnicity on the likelihood of being sexually harassed (DeFour, 1996; Murrell, 1996). Although evidence suggesting that women of color are more vulnerable to harassment than other women is far from consistent, there is cause for concern about this issue. Stereotypes demeaning minority women abound in our society, and some of them focus on the sexuality, sexual availability, and exotic allure of minority women (DeFour, 1996). Women of Color are also more marginalized and less powerful in our society than are White women. As Murrell has noted, we need to better understand different minority women's interpretations and definitions of harassment before we compare their experiences and perspectives with those of White women. Sexual harassment of Women of Color can be viewed not only as a form of sex discrimination but also as a form of race discrimination (DeFour, 1996; Murrell, 1996). Clearly, more research is needed on the interaction of race and ethnicity on sexual harassment.

Consequences of Sexual Harassment

A distressing portrait has emerged from research on the harmful effects of sexual harassment on its targets. The most obvious costs of sexual harassment are job and school related. Working women who are subject to harassment quit their jobs and show evidence of decreased morale and job satisfaction, greater absenteeism, poor job performance, and damaged interpersonal relationships at work (Equal Opportunity Employment Commission, 1999; Fitzgerald, 1993; Gutek, 1985, 1993; Gutek & Koss, 1993; U.S. Merit Systems Protection Board, 1981, 1988, 1995). As we saw in Chapter 7, there is strong and consistent evidence that the job-related consequences of sexual harassment for women are far more negative than those for men.

Similar negative consequences have been found among victims of sexual harassment on college campuses. The relatively subtle, sophisticated form of sexual harassment that occurs in an academic setting commonly engenders in student victims confusion, embarrassment, doubt, self-blame, and a desire to flee the situation rather than confront it (Rabinowitz,

1996; Till, 1980). Ninety percent of harassed female graduate students surveyed by Schneider (1987) reported negative reactions, with two-thirds worrying about actual and potential consequences to their careers. Dziech and Weiner (1990) conclude that sexual harassment often "forces a student to forfeit work, research, educational comfort, or even career. Professors withhold legitimate opportunities from those who resist, or students withdraw rather than pay certain prices" (p. 10). Women who have been harassed by their professors commonly stop coming to class, drop courses, change majors or educational programs, and even change their career goals as a result (Rabinowitz, 1996). Consequences tend to be more severe for graduate students, who have more invested in their career paths, and for women who have entered into what they believed were consensual sexual relationships, who may feel particularly compromised and betrayed (Rabinowitz, 1996).

Recent studies, including controlled laboratory studies, on the consequences of sexual harassment have looked at self-esteem and self-confidence. In one intriguing line of laboratory studies, a male confederate posing as an advertising executive praised the work of undergraduate women who drew designs for a perfume campaign. There were two conditions in the study, an experimental and a control group: In both conditions, the confederate praised the women for their work in identical terms, but in the experimental condition he mixed his praise with flirtatiousness and in the control condition he did not. Postexperimental ratings of creativity showed that women in the control group had significantly higher self-creativity ratings. This was interpreted to mean that women are less likely to interpret praise for their work as diagnostic or meaningful when the praise is mixed with flirting and other forms of sexualization (Heilman, 1994; Satterfield & Muehlenhard, 1997).

In addition to job- and school-related consequences, women who have experienced sexual harassment sometimes suffer consequences to their physical and emotional health. Psychological outcomes reported in the literature include anxiety, depression, irritability, headaches, sleep disturbances, gastrointestinal disorders, weight loss or gain, and sexual dysfunction (Fitzgerald, 1993; Fitzgerald,

Drasgow, Hulin, Gelfand, & Magley, 1997). In particularly severe cases, clinically significant depression or posttraumatic stress disorder (PTSD) may result, especially if the harassment is severe, frequent, and prolonged (Danseky & Kilpatrick, 1997). Of course, individual responses to academic and workplace sexual harassment vary as a function of the victims' personal style, the severity of the harassment, and the availability and quality of social support after the harassment (Paludi, 2004).

Personal and Societal Responses to Harassment

Personal Responses.   Women who experience sexual harassment are often faced with choices so aversive that they hardly qualify as choices at all. They may go along with their harassers and feel guilty and compromised, or resist and face a host of negative outcomes for their careers and feelings of well-being. They may report the harassment and be ostracized, transferred, demoted, or fired, or be silent and endure (Fitzgerald, 1993). Whatever choices women make and whatever the outcome of the harassment, sexual harassment frequently shatters women's assumptions about their world and changes their lives (Koss, 1990; Paludi, 2004).

In fact, there are relatively few empirical studies of how women cope with sexual harassment. A recent major study of men and women who experienced workplace harassment suggested that women and men generally responded similarly to harassment and that one of the most common responses, given by about half the respondents, was confronting the harasser directly and asking him or her to stop. For women, talking to friends and family about the problem was another common response. Consistent with findings from other studies, less than 5 percent of the respondents filed a formal complaint against the harasser (Bingham & Scherer, 1993; Paludi, 2004).

Many studies have concluded that few women who are sexually harassed file formal (or even informal) complaints. This leads some people to mistakenly believe that sexual harassment is not a common or serious problem for women. But studies that have examined women's explanations for not filing complaints have uncovered a variety of reasons for this phenomenon. Many women are reluctant to file complaints because they have sympathy and concern for their harassers and do not want to destroy their families and careers. Some offenders are thought by their victims to need psychological or educational help, not exposure or punishment. Some victims believe that they share some responsibility for the situation; that is, they sought or at least enjoyed the sexual attention they received. Others worry about not being believed in the first place, or, if they are believed, they fear social rejection for being the whistle-blower. Many people are concerned with loss of privacy if their complaint becomes known. A substantial proportion of people, including ethnic minority respondents, strongly distrust legal and other formal processes for the management of sexual harassment and attempt to deal with the problems privately (Murrell, 1996; Rowe, 1996).

Michelle Paludi (2004), an expert in sexual harassment, has recently offered specific recommendations to college women who believe that they have experienced sexual harassment. Although developed for harassment in academia, Paludi's guidelines for individuals will stand all targets of harassment in good stead, and they are adapted in Box 12.2.

Societal Responses.   The millions of women who suffer the many negative effects of sexual harassment every day are not the only victims of this problem. The costs of sexual harassment to organizations and institutions in terms of lost productivity, turnover, and retraining expenses are huge. Sexual harassment has become one of the most frequently litigated issues in employment law (Fitzgerald, 1993; Terpstra, 1986). The burden on society of physical and mental health care costs is substantial (Quina, 1996). Louise Fitzgerald (1993) has outlined a variety of responses to sexual harassment in the workplace and other institutions that a society might take. She calls for legislative initiatives to require employers to develop and promote clear policies against harassment. She also recommends legal reforms that remove caps on damage awards, enable women who quit jobs due to harassment to collect unemployment compensation, extend the statute of limitations for filing sexual harassment charges, and ensure that the legal system does not revictimize harassment victims.

Box 12.2

Individual Responses to Sexual Harassment

1. Don't blame yourself. It is not your fault.
2. Write down the description of the sexually harassing behaviors. Include dates, times, circumstances, people present, what happened, how you responded, and how you felt.
3. Talk with someone you trust about the incident(s)—a family member, a friend, an advisor, clergy, or a professor. Keep a record of this talk.
4. Read through your organization's policy statement and investigatory procedures. Learn how your confidentiality will be protected, and how your orga-

nization will deal with any potential retaliation against you for filing a complaint.
5. Contact your unit's, union's, or organization's representative who is responsible for investigating complaints of sexual harassment.
6. Consider participating in a support group.
7. Be good to yourself. Dealing with sexual harassment is emotionally and physically draining. Rest, eat well, get medical checkups, and spend time with family and friends.

Source: Adapted from Paludi, 2004, p. 350.

Finally, Fitzgerald notes that the only real solution to the critical problem of sexual harassment lies in primary prevention. Harassment grows out of women's inferior status in the workplace and academia and can be reduced by elevating that status. It has consistently been found that women who work in sex-integrated workplaces (where men and women work together in approximately equal numbers) experience less harassment than do women who work in either female- or male-dominated workplaces. Fitzgerald advocates the widespread adoption of such policies as helping women to move into jobs traditionally held by men, eliminating discrimination in hiring and training, and instituting family leave and child-care assistance programs. Sexual harassment specific to the workplace is discussed further in Chapter 7.

RAPE

As this chapter attests, violence against women can and does take many forms. But to many people, rape is practically synonymous with violence against women. There is no form of gendered violence that women fear more than rape (Brownmiller, 1975; Griffin, 1979). In its threat or actual occurrence, rape is unique in its ability to change women's lives.

As noted earlier, women are not the sole victims of rape. In the general U.S. population it has been estimated that 1 in 10,000 men is a victim of rape or

attempted rape every year, with the incidence of prison rape being much higher (Kilmartin, 1994; Struckman-Johnson, 1991). Rape of men by other men also occurs in fraternity and military settings (Funk, 1993). Contrary to popular belief, these experiences are emotionally devastating for men (Kilmartin, 1994). Nonetheless, throughout the world, rape is overwhelmingly a problem of male violence against women (Rozee, 2000).

Definitions and Prevalence

Like some other forms of gendered abuse, rape is notoriously difficult to define. Rape is a crime that occurs in a particular sociocultural context as well as an event with profound psychological consequences. Thus, there are legal definitions of rape that vary from state to state and across countries, and legal reforms continue to change the acts that define rape and the range of perpetrators (Estrich, 1987; Rozee, 2000). Many states, for example, include penetration by objects and fingers, as well as anal penetration, in their definitions of rape (Rozee, 2000). To further complicate the picture, it is now well known that many people have private definitions of rape that differ considerably from current legal definitions: Koss, Gidycz, and Wisniewski (1987) found that over 50 percent of the women who had experiences that met the legal definition of rape did not regard themselves as rape victims. The work of Mary Koss and her associates has succeeded in conceptualizing rape as a woman's health issue with long-term consequences for women's physical, psychological, and social circumstances (Koss, Heise, & Russo, 1994; Rozee & Koss, 2001).

Although definitions of rape continue to vary, they share the essential element that rape is the lack of choice to have sexual intercourse. More specifically, **rape** is defined as vaginal, oral, or anal penetration by an object or body part, against consent and through force or threat of bodily harm, or when the individual is unable to consent (Searles & Berger, 1987). Current categorizations of rape often distinguish among stranger rape, acquaintance rape (including friends, coworkers, dates, etc.), and marital rape. Gang rape can occur in each of these cases.

Some scholars have also differentiated *normative* and *nonnormative* rape (Rozee, 1993, 2000). According to Rozee, **normative rape** is supported or at least tolerated by society. It includes rape by intimates, especially husbands, for which traditional notions hold that the marriage contract represents tacit agreement by the woman to provide sexual services on demand. *Punitive rape* is a category of normative rape that involves raping women to punish them for gender-inappropriate behavior, that is, for behaving too much like men. Rape during times of war is another form of normative rape. Rape has been a frequent and particularly brutal weapon of war throughout history, including present times, as documented cases of widespread rape of Bosnian, Somalian, Rwandan, and Albanian women attest. According to Rozee (1993), *exchange rape,* the bartering of female sexuality for male advantages*; ceremonial rape,* such as deflowering rituals; and *status rape,* which occurs because of unequal power between high-status men and the women over whom they have control, are examples of normative rape. According to Rozee (2000) because the vast majority of rapes in the United States—between 80 and 98 percent—go unpunished, rape is normative in the United States.

Nonnormative rape, which is not supported or tolerated by society, includes the kinds of rapes that come to mind most readily and conform to the stereotypical notion of rape: the "surprise attack on a virtu-

ous women" (Koss et al., 1994). As Koss and colleagues point out, even in nonnormative rape, the wrongness of rape emanates not from the nature of the act against the woman, but from others' perceptions of her sexual history and standards, her behavior and attire around the time of the attack, her prior relationship with the attacker, and her marital status, among other things.

Finally, rape can be distinguished by whether it is *forcible* or *statutory. Forcible rape* is sexual intercourse with a nonconsenting person obtained by the use or threat of force. *Statutory rape* is intercourse with a person below the age of consent. Sexual intercourse with an underage person is considered statutory rape regardless of whether the underage person cooperates (Rathus et al., 2002). What constitutes the age of consent varies by state, but it usually involves having sex with a child between the ages of 12 and 16 (Lott, 1994).

Obviously, it is hard to estimate the prevalence of something that cannot be clearly defined and takes so many different forms. National crime statistics on rape are notoriously poor guides to rape prevalence for several reasons, starting with the fact that many reported sexual assaults are not classified as rapes. Additionally, the sexual assault of children is not typically regarded as rape, but as incest if the perpetrator is a father or stepfather and child abuse if the perpetrator is not a family member. The FBI also does not include marital, statutory, or attempted rape in its rape statistics (Rozee, 2000).

But beyond problems of definition and official classification, it is nearly impossible to estimate the prevalence of rape because women throughout the world resist reporting rapes to authorities. Koss et al. (1994), in an extensive review of the prevalence of rape worldwide, note that in community-based samples, less than 2 percent of rape victims in Korea and 12 percent of rape victims in the United States informed the police that they had been raped. Women not only resist reporting rapes to authorities but also usually resist telling anyone else about their victimization, especially if their attacker is someone they know. For a variety of reasons to be discussed later, most women in most societies are extremely reluctant to claim the dubious status of rape victim. This helps to explain why rape is the most seriously underreported of all major crimes in the United States and elsewhere.

Ethnographic (naturalistic observational) studies of nonindustrialized societies suggest that, depending on how it is defined, rape is found in between 42 and 90 percent of nonindustrialized societies (Koss et al., 1994). Rozee (1993) examined the incidence of rape in 35 nonindustrialized societies and found some form of rape in 97 percent of them. Sanday (1981) examined the prevalence of rape in 156 tribal societies. She categorized societies as "rape-prone" if the incidence of rape is high or normative rape is common. Societies were regarded as "rape-free" if rape was extremely rare and not tolerated by society. Using these definitions, she classified 18 percent of the societies as rape-prone and 47 percent as virtually rape-free. Sanday found that rape-prone societies were the products of sexist and violent cultures in which males and females were separated and unequal, and sex roles were highly differentiated. In rape-prone societies, men were encouraged to be aggressive generally and warfare was common, whereas in rape-free societies gender inequality was reduced, interpersonal violence was uncommon, and women's roles and contributions were valued (Sanday, 1981).

The United States has the highest reported rate of rape of any industrialized country in the world (Gordon & Riger, 1989; Lott, 1994; Rozee, 2000). Within the United States the prevalence of rape varies considerably by state, with Alaska suffering the highest rate and North Dakota the lowest (Baron & Straus, 1989). States with high rates of rape were found to have high levels of social disorganization (meaning high divorce rates, high percentages of female-headed households, and low rates of religious affiliation, among other things), high circulation of pornographic magazines, and high levels of gender inequality on economic and political measures (Baron & Straus, 1989). Rates of reported rape in the United States have declined precipitously since 1989. Indeed, they are down by half since 1993, though regional differences remain, and rates of rape and sexual assault are higher in the Midwest and West than in the Northeast and South (Rape, Abuse and Incest, and National Network, 2003).

Because of the certainty that rape is underreported to the authorities, researchers interested in rape prevalence have found it more useful to rely on scientifically sound, anonymous sample surveys than official statistics. The majority of U.S. studies estimate that between 14 and 30 percent of all adult women have experienced rape or attempted rape (Koss, 1993b). In studies of rape prevalence, college students have been the most extensively studied group of adult women, in part because of their availability, but also because they are in the age range of females who are most commonly sexually assaulted. In most recent methodologically strong surveys, women are not directly asked whether they have been raped, because, as noted previously, so few women regard themselves as rape victims. Rather, they are asked whether they have had specific sexual experiences involving threat or force, experiences that legally qualify as rape. One groundbreaking study using these types of questions was conducted by Mary Koss and her associates and was supported by the National Institute of Mental Health and *Ms.* magazine. They surveyed a random sample of over 6,000 college men and women at 32 different colleges and universities. They found that over 15 percent of the women had had experiences that met the legal definition of rape and another 12 percent had experienced attempted rape, since age 14 (Koss et al., 1987). Using samples of college women, other surveys in the United States, Canada, the United Kingdom, and other industrialized societies have found similar results (Koss et al., 1994). Taken together, these surveys reveal that rape and attempted rape are much more common than crime statistics and popular thinking suggest, that between 14 and 25 percent of women in the United States are raped in their lifetimes, and that sexual coercion and assault are an alarmingly frequent part of women's lives.

Who Is Raped?

Are some women more likely to be raped than others? Many studies have attempted to answer this question, with mixed results. Findings are inconsistent, suggesting generally that there is no typical rape victim and that no one is immune from rape. But a few patterns have emerged. Surveys of rape prevalence from seven different countries commissioned by the World Bank (1993) reveal that a high percentage of rape victims are young girls: Between 36 and 62 percent of rape victims were 15 years old or younger, and between 13 and 32 percent were 10 years old or younger (Koss et al., 1994). The National Crime Victimization Survey (1995) also found that young women were most vulnerable, with women ages 16 to 24 two to three times more likely to be raped. The most recent available statistics suggest that, within the United States, about 44 percent of rape victims are under 18, and 15 percent are under 12 (Rape, Abuse and Incest, and National Network, 2003). Aside from youth, history of sexual victimization in childhood, multiple sex partners, insecurities about relationships with men, and higher-than-average alcohol use by the victim have also been associated with a likelihood of being raped (Koss & Dinero, 1989; Rozee, 2004).

Some other characteristics of rape victims have been associated with rape, although some of the research is contradictory. For example, some surveys looking at class, ethnic, and cultural variables have found that African American women, especially poor women, are more likely than White women to be victims of stranger rape (Goodman, Koss, Fitzgerald, Russo, & Keita, 1993; Wyatt, 1992). But other surveys suggest that African American women report less rape when all forms of rape are considered than do White women (Koss & Dinero, 1989). Several explanations have been put forth to address this inconsistency. It is possible that African American women, because of strong cultural values of self-reliance and avoidance of personal exploitation, are more likely than White women to physically resist rape. There is research suggesting that African American women are indeed more likely to physically resist rape, and that resistance is an effective strategy (Rozee, 2004). It is also possible that African American women may be less likely to report an experience as rape. The latter is particularly likely if the rapist is known to them, or if the rape did not meet standards of what constitutes rape in their communities (Rozee, 2000). This research points to the importance of considering cultural and community standards and conditions in interpreting rape statistics.

Finally, people who in some way challenge the system may be targeted for rape as a form of punishment for their presumed "transgressions" (Rozee, 2001). The rape of lesbians, gay men, and transgendered people may be considered a punishment for their flouting of traditional gender norms. The 1999 Academy Award–winning movie, *Boys Don't Cry,* based on a true story, depicted a brutal rape of a young girl who was attempting to live her life as a boy.

Relationship of the Rapist and Rape Victim

Popular mythology has it that most women are raped by unknown assailants, loners, or psychopaths who are sexually frustrated and easily overcome by sexual enticement. Are most women raped by unknown assailants? Surveys of rape prevalence are consistent on this point as they are on few others: Most girls and women are raped by men whom they know—dates, acquaintances, and family members, including spouses. In the seven surveys sponsored by the World Bank (1993), between 60 and 78 percent of rape perpetrators were known to their victims. In the National Crime Victimization Survey (1995), 80 percent of reported rapes were committed by men known to the women. Because a woman is less likely to label an experience rape if she knows her assailant and is especially unlikely to report the rape to the authorities if the rapist is a friend, boss, or family member, we can only assume that the percentage of perpetrators known to the victim is even higher than these numbers suggest.

Men Who Rape

Who are the men who rape? There are many elements of patriarchal and violent societies that support and maintain the rape of women by men, but it is nonetheless a fact that most men do not rape women and that situational and interpersonal factors are important. Again, research findings are inconsistent in this area, and it is clear that there is no one kind of rapist. In fact, rapists vary widely in their personal and background characteristics. Most of what we know about rapists has been learned from surveys, interviews, and other studies of incarcerated rapists. Trends that have emerged in this literature suggest that most rapists are not mentally ill or retarded. Some rapists do report feeling socially inadequate and unable to find willing partners, and some are antisocial and have trouble with impulse control. Some have been sexually abused as children (Rathus et al., 2002). But most are not undersexed loners and have had active and ordinary sex lives as adolescents and adults. Many are married or in other committed relationships (Lorber, 1994). These findings are interesting and important because they suggest that rapists are not apparently abnormal or easily identifiable. It is also worth noting that incarcerated rapists are not representative of rapists generally. Most rapists are not caught and convicted, and studies of incarcerated rapists certainly underestimate acquaintance and marital rapists.

Anonymous surveys of college men suggest that men who rape are more hostile toward women, are more aroused by depictions of forced sex, and subscribe more strongly to false beliefs that condone rape than are men who do not rape. There is some survey evidence that sexually aggressive men are more likely to hold traditional sex-role attitudes, condone violence against women, and belong to peer groups, such as college fraternities and sports teams, that encourage sexist behaviors toward women (Koss et al., 1987; Malamuth, Sockloskie, Koss, & Tanaka, 1991). From surveys of self-identified aggressive men, Harney and Muelenhard (1991) identified the following characteristics of potential rapists: They hold traditional gender-role attitudes, are irresponsible, are hostile toward women, are sexually experienced, become aroused by depictions of rape, and view sex as a way to dominate women.

Categories of Rape

Date and Acquaintance Rape. As we have noted, the overwhelming majority of rape victims know their assailants. One of the subcategories of acquaintance rape that has received a great deal of research attention in the past decade is **date rape** or courtship rape—rape that occurs in the context of a dating or romantic relationship. In the early 1990s, the highly publicized courtroom trials of celebrities such as Mike Tyson and William Kennedy Smith, and in this decade, the case of Kobe Bryant, have brought the reality and complexity of date rape to the rapt attention of the U.S. public. According to one survey of college women, 10 to 20 percent of women have been forced to have sexual intercourse during a date (Tang, Critelli, & Porter, 1995).

For many people, date rape raises different issues than other forms of rape because, by virtue of having agreed to the "date," the woman has on some level expressed her interest in a man and consented to a relationship with him. If the sexual relationship somehow gets out of hand, in this view, the problem is one of misunderstanding, miscommunication, or mixed signals, rather than sexual assault.

Research on date rape has identified several variables associated with its occurrence, many arising from the different socializing messages that boys and girls hear about masculinity and femininity and the relationship between the sexes. Males are generally socialized to deny and control their emotions, with the important exceptions of sexual feelings, anger, and aggression. Like many societies, our society measures a man's worth by his deeds and results, rather than his feelings about himself and others. As Kilmartin (1994) notes, we admire men who "go after what they what" and "won't take no for an answer." As we have seen, boys are socialized to believe that when a girl says "maybe" she means "yes" and when she says "no" she means "maybe."

Socialization of girls and boys in our society rarely includes training about sexual communication. Poor sexual communication characterizes most dating relationships, especially among young people. Few young couples are comfortable discussing sex between them before it occurs, and most people are reduced to reading each others' unpracticed nonverbal signals under emotionally complex and ambiguous circumstances. This sets the stage for misunderstandings that can lead to unwanted sexual intercourse and rape. In fact, Blader and Marshall's (1989) research suggests that men who sexually assault acquaintances usually want consensual sex, but are not deterred by women's resistance, often because they think that the resistance is just an act or that the women will change their minds if they forcefully persist.

One factor that predicts date rape is males' permissive attitudes about rape, for instance, endorsement of the idea that rape is an unimportant issue in society (Gillen & Muncer, 1995). Another factor is male peer support for aggressive sexual behavior. DeKeseredy and Kelly (1995) found that support for sexual aggression by male peers was one of the most important predictors of sexual victimization of college women. Drinking by men, women, or both, consistently emerges as another precipitating factor in date rapes. In one study, 55 percent of the victims reported being drunk at the time of the sexual assault (Harrington & Leitenberg, 1994). In another study, drinking by men was associated with sexual violence (Fritner & Rubinson, 1993). Some men assume that women who frequent clubs or singles bars are expressing, at least tacitly, a willingness to have sex with men who show interest in them. Date rape is also associated with being parked in a man's car or going back to a man's residence (Rathus et al., 2002). Violence is more likely to occur in serious rather than casual dating relationships (White, Donat, & Bondurant, 2001).

Marital Rape. The very idea that a man could rape his wife is a relatively new one in our society. Traditionally, women became the property of their husbands when married, and husbands were seen as having a right to sexual favors from their wives. In the United States, it was not until 1977 that Oregon became the first state to criminalize marital rape, and, as of 1989, only 36 states specified that it was against the law to rape one's spouse (Pagelow, 1992). As late as 1992, marital rape was still legal in North Carolina and Oklahoma (Allison & Wrightsman, 1993), although now all states in the United States have laws prohibiting rape in marriage. Marital rape remains a problem in most countries.

The incidence of **marital rape** is even harder to estimate than other forms of rape because women are especially reluctant to label forced sex by their husbands as rape and to report marital rape to the authorities. As we will see again with women who are physically abused by their husbands, many women who are raped by their husbands feel that they have nowhere to go and no one to turn to when their own homes are not a safe place. Using survey methodology, Frieze (1983) estimated that between 10 and 14 percent of married women have experienced this

form of rape, and a U.S. congressional committee estimated that one in seven women is raped by her husband (Rathus et al., 2002; Resnick, Kilpatrick, Walsh, & Veronen, 1991).

Even more than acquaintance and date rape, marital rape is not often taken very seriously and is regarded by many people as much less brutalizing and less traumatic than stranger rape (Sullivan & Mosher, 1990). In fact, marital rape can be among the most severe forms of rape, embedded as it often is in a generally violent and otherwise troubled relationship. A rape is more likely when the husband associates sex with violence, has extramarital affairs, and is unreasonably jealous of his wife (Frieze, 1983). Women who are raped by their husbands are as fearful for their health and their lives as women who are raped by strangers (Koss, 1993b).

Just as with other forms of rape, motives for marital rape vary. Finkelhor and Yllo (1982) interviewed wives who had been raped by their husbands and identified three categories of marital rape. The first type is the "battering rape," committed by men who physically intimidate, beat, and rape their wives. Alcohol and drug use often accompany this form of rape. The second type is the "force only rape," wherein violence is limited to the sexual relationship, and the husband uses sex to dominate his wife. Finally, the third and least common form of marital rape is the "obsessive rape," wherein the husband, obsessed with pornography and relatively unusual sexual practices, forces his wife to engage in activities, such as anal intercourse or being bound, in which she is not interested. Marital rape sometimes occurs within a pattern of domestic violence that includes battery and intimidation, and sometimes is limited to the sexual relationship. Some men view sex as the best way to solve all marital disputes and believe that if they can force their wives into sex, then everything will be all right (Rathus et al., 2002).

Stranger Rape. Stranger rape is committed by an assailant (or assailants) who is not previously known to the rape victim. It is this form of rape that most people think of as "real rape," that most readily comes to mind when people think of rape, and that women most fear. In fact, only about 20 percent of all rapes are stranger rapes. The typical stranger rapist is an opportunist who preys on women who seem particularly vulnerable—those who live alone or are older, retarded, drunk, or asleep. After selecting a target, the stranger rapist seeks a safe time and place in which to commit the crime—a darkened street, an empty apartment, a deserted staircase, or the like (Nevid et al., 1995). More often than acquaintance rape, stranger rape is physically violent and involves a series of assaults by the same offender (Koss, Dinero, Seibel, & Cox, 1988). There is some evidence that rape by strangers is particularly psychologically traumatizing (Thornhill & Thornhill, 1991). Women who are raped by strangers are more likely than other rape victims to label the experience as rape and report the crime to the authorities.

Gang Rape.   Gang rapes involve two or more assailants and one rape victim. They are more frequent among strangers but can occur among acquaintances and even within stable relationships. They are distinguished by their particularly violent and brutal nature. Men who rape in gangs tend to be younger than other rapists and to have criminal records. Alcohol use and public drinking are common in cases of gang rape (Gidycz & Koss, 1990).

It is often noted that the exercise of power over women and feelings of anger and hostility toward women motivate gang rape. Social psychologists have identified a number of cognitive and behavioral processes that occur in groups that can contribute to the mistreatment of outsiders and poor decision making (O'Sullivan, 1995). One cognitive process that may facilitate gang rape is the *outgroup homogeneity effect,* whereby all people not in one's own group (i.e., females) are seen as fitting one stereotype (i.e., "sluts"). Outgroup homogeneity often occurs with another cognitive process, *ingroup superiority,* the belief that one's own group (i.e., males) is better than other groups and more worthy of rewards and privileges. Finally, *groupthink* is the process by which groups, particularly elite groups (such as sports teams), make faulty decisions because of an inflated belief in their own righteousness coupled with an exaggerated sense of other groups' unworthiness. It is easy to see how these cognitive processes can give men in groups the feeling of invulnerability and enti-

tlement, as well as disdain for women, that make it easier to victimize them (O'Sullivan, 1995).

These cognitive processes operate along with other factors to promote gang rape. People are often more aggressive in groups, in which they are relatively anonymous and undifferentiated, than they are singly. This is especially true under conditions of drinking, partying, "wilding," and other forms of excitement. Male socialization to be independent, unsentimental, tough, and success-oriented obviously contributes to group sexual aggression by men. In addition, male friendships often entail a combination of competition and camaraderie. Sexual success is an important arena for this competition, and it can be defined as having sexual access to a lot of women or getting women to do things that they do not want to do. Drinking and other forms of risk taking and breaking societal rules are also arenas for male competition and contribute to gang rape. On college campuses, the majority of gang rapes are perpetrated by fraternity men, followed by those who play team sports.

Cultural Significance of Rape and Sexual Assault

The notion of rape as a harm to or crime against a woman is a relatively recent phenomenon. For most of recorded history, rape, if it was regarded as a crime at all, was seen as a crime against a husband or father because of the damage and devaluation of his "property." Indeed, the only rapes that were considered crimes were the rapes of virgins. In both ancient Hebrew and Babylonian cultures, women who were raped, including married women and virgins, were routinely stoned to death because is was believed that they could have prevented the rape by crying out (Nevid et al., 1995). Today, violence against women is obviously not a problem of any one culture but is endemic throughout the world (see Box 12.3). Some scholars question whether rape is particularly "misogynist" or has a special status as a crime against women, as we see in this quote by philosopher Christina Hoff Sommers: "That most violence is male isn't news. But very little of it appears to be misogynist . . . Rape is just one variety of a crime against the person, and rape of women is just one subvariety" (1994, pp. 225–226). (Obviously, the authors of this text do not subscribe to this view.)

BOX 12.3_____

Violence against Women around the World

In their important book *Where Women Stand: An International Report on the Status of Women in 140 Countries, 1997–1998,* Naomi Neft and Ann D. Levine (1997) chronicle how domestic abuse, rape, and other forms of sexual assault are universal problems that cut across geographic, cultural, religious, ethnic, and class boundaries. They note the specific forms that violence against women takes in various parts of the world. The following are adaptations of their reports on three selected countries, India, Nigeria, and Brazil, on three different continents.

INDIA

In India as in much of Asia, there is widespread preference for sons over daughters, and the killing of baby girls is common in some parts of India, with as many as 10,000 baby girls killed every year. Despite the fact that Indian laws ban infanticide and impose penalties of life imprisonment or death, few cases are brought to trial, and those that are rarely end in convictions.

Wife abuse is another terrible problem in India, with the most dramatic forms being physical abuse, torture, and even murder of young brides whose husbands or in-laws are dissatisfied with their dowries. Dowries are the lavish gifts and large sums of money that the bride's family must transfer to the groom's family upon marriage to compensate for the fact that daughters cannot inherit property from their parents.

Suttee, the centuries-old custom by which the widow is burned alive on her husband's funeral pyre, has been illegal since 1829, but a resurgence of Hindu fundamentalism in the 1980s has led to renewed calls in India for the legalization of the practice. Meanwhile, widows in India have very low social status and are essentially treated like slaves.

NIGERIA

Though seldom reported, violence against women is common in Nigeria and cuts across all religious, ethnic, and regional boundaries.

The Nigerian penal code specifies that a husband can "correct" his wife as long as the correction does not leave a scar or require a stay of more than 21 days in the hospital. Women, especially those in polygamous marriages, commonly believe that physical abuse is a normal condition of marriage.

Although rape is illegal and punishable by life imprisonment, it is rarely reported in Nigeria.

Female genital mutilation is practiced throughout Nigeria, especially among Christians in the South and the Muslims in the North. Almost half of all women have undergone some form of the procedure, ranging in severity from removal of the clitoral hood (clitoridectomy) to complete removal of the clitoris and the labia with the edges stitched together, leaving only a small opening for the passage of urine (infibulation).

BRAZIL

Violence against women is a major problem in Brazil, where the law and criminal justice system reflect deeply held cultural beliefs that women are inferior to men. As a result, many of the laws protect the assailants and not the victims. Domestic violence is a serious problem for Brazilian women, with over half of all female homicide victims killed by current or former partners. Until 1991, a man could be pardoned for killing his wife if he even suspected that she had been unfaithful. Although this concept of "defense of honor" has been struck down, the courts are still reluctant to prosecute and convict men accused of assaulting their wives.

Rape is illegal and punishable by imprisonment in Brazil, but few rapists are brought to trial and convicted. If the rapist marries the victim, he is exonerated by law.

Why Do Men Rape Women? There is no simple answer to this question. Sociobiologists, who see all behavior as motivated to pass on one's genes, and evolutionary psychologists, who view brain "mechanisms" and behavioral tendencies as hard-wired in our genes, view rape as an extension of "normal" male sexual behavior (Thornhill & Palmer, 2000). According to evolutionary and sociobiological theories, males have stronger sex drives than women and are naturally more sexually aggressive. Sociobiological theory posits that evolution favors males who are always alert for new female partners and are visually stimulated by physical attributes of prospective partners. Sociobiological theory suggests that, under certain circumstances, such as sexual scarcity or absence of punishment, many more men would rape women. In fact, Malamuth (1981) found that 35 percent of the college men that he surveyed reported that they would force a woman to have sexual intercourse if they knew that they could get away with it. In another survey, 51 percent of the men admitted at least some likelihood of committing rape if they were sure that they would not be punished (Malamuth, Haber, & Feshback, 1980). Given that people generally strive to avoid expressing socially undesirable intentions even in anonymous surveys, it is possible that the percentage of men who hold this view is actually much higher. In fact, numerous studies suggest that young people, female and male, are likely to think that there are many conditions under which it is all right for men and boys to force sex on women and girls. These include circumstances when the woman asks the man out, when the man spends a lot of money on the woman, and when the woman has already been sexually intimate with the man or other men (Goodchilds, Zellman, Johnson, & Giarusso, 1988). In another study, a majority of young men reported a belief that it was all right to force sex on a woman if the couple were engaged or married (Lott, 1994).

Clearly, sociobiological and evolutionary theories view rape as a sexually motivated act and all men as potential rapists. Other psychological theories attempting to explain rape take issue with one or both of these propositions. Some challenge the view that sexual desire is the basic motivation for rape, and some look to individual pathology or social and cultural factors, rather that genetic and hormonal ones, to account for the prevalence of rape.

Sexual arousal and expression are obvious features of rape, but they are not necessarily the underlying causes of all or even most rapes. Groth and Birnbaum (1979), based on their clinical experience with more that 1,000 rapists, concluded that there were three categories of rapes: *anger rapes,* which are particularly forceful and degrading rapes motivated by anger and resentment toward women; *power rapes,* which are less vicious and motivated by desire to control and dominate women; and, finally, *sadistic rapes,* which are ritualized, humiliating, sometimes mutilating or murderous assaults that may be associated with individual pathologies. About 40 percent of rapes were categorized as anger rapes, 55 percent as power rapes, and 5 percent as sadistic rapes (Groth & Burgess, 1980). Other scholars contend that not all rapes are acts of aggression, control, or power and assign a larger role to sexual motivation in the commission of some sexual crimes (Hall & Hirschman, 1991; Leitenberg & Henning, 1995).

It seems clear that rape and sexual assault, like all human behavior generally, are complex and multiply determined by social, cultural, personal, and situational factors. Not all rapists are motivated by the same forces, and the extent to which sexual motives contribute to rape can be expected to vary considerably across individuals and categories of rape.

The importance of contextual and situational factors in supporting rape must not be underestimated. As noted above, it is well known that under circumstances that remove the usual constraints on sexual and aggressive behavior, rape can become commonplace. During wartime, for example, women are traditionally considered "spoils"—the reward for conquering a people. The rape of women by soldiers has a long tradition in the military histories of many countries. It is considered one of the most effective means of demoralizing the enemy (Funk, 1993). The world witnessed this use of rape in Bosnia, Rwanda, Kosovo, and the Congo. Cohesive male peer groups, such as gangs, sports teams, and fraternities, sometimes use rape as a means of initiation into or bonding with the group. Finally, many studies suggest that drinking by men, women, or both is often associated with rape (Harrington & Leitenberg, 1994). About three-quarters of acquaintance rapes involve alcohol consumption on the part of the victim, assailant, or both (Koss et al., 1987).

The introduction of so-called "date rape drugs," including Rohypnol (also known as "roofies" or "roaches") and GHB (gamma hydroxybutyrate), into social settings increases women's vulnerability to rape (McAnulty & Burnette, 2004). These odorless, colorless substances are easily slipped into women's drinks, and render them drowsy, disoriented, amnesic, and disinhibited. Thus, they are ideal rape drugs. To combat the effects of these drugs, some companies have developed products that help people identify whether their drinks contain these drugs (Villalon, 2002).

How Does the Existence of Rape Change Women and the Relationships between Men and Women?
Rape affects all of us, men and women, even those whose lives are not directly touched by it. Indeed, it is well known that women's fear of rape is disproportionate to their actual likelihood of being raped (Day, 1999). In a thoughtful article offering a male perspective on rape, Beneke pointed to what is missing when people contemplate rape statistics: the effects on women of the ubiquitous threat of rape (Beneke, 1993). In asking women how their lives would be different if rape were suddenly to end, he learned that the threat of rape is an "assault upon the meaning of the world" (p. 312). Beneke notes that the threat of rape alters the meaning and feel of the night for many women, transforming their cars into armored tanks and their apartments into fortresses. The threat of rape alters the meaning and feel of nature and women's ability to be alone in parks and wooded areas. It means that women need more money to buy security at the same time that it limits women's mobility and job options. Thus, the threat of rape seriously affects all women's freedom; it makes solitude and relaxation more difficult, inhibits women's expressiveness and freedom to be friendly, to make eye contact, and to dress the way they wish, among other things.

The threat of rape also makes women more dependent on men for protection. In this and other ways, the threat of rape benefits men as it diminishes women. It grants the night, the unknown, and the public sphere to men. It keeps women in a position of relative defensiveness and fear. It maintains male power and privilege by restricting women's freedom, independence, and opportunities. As Funk (1993) explains, the "rape culture" guarantees men an important position or role to play: that of protector of "his" women and "his" family. The more salient and constant the threat of rape is, the more justifiable male dominance over women is. According to Funk, "all

men benefit from rape and the constant threat of rape" (p. 32).

The Role of Rape Myths in Supporting the Rape Culture.
Of all the forces that support the existence of rape in societies like ours, **rape myths** are among the most subtle, pervasive, and important. Lonsway and Fitzgerald (1994) have defined rape myths as "attitudes and beliefs that are generally false but are widely and persistently held, and that serve to deny and justify male sexual aggression against women" (p. 134). Rape myths are best conceptualized as stereotypes that people have about behaviors, attitudes, and feelings surrounding rape. Some common myths include the notions that only certain kinds of women are raped, most women harbor an unconscious desire to be raped, women routinely lie about being raped, and women cannot be raped against their will.

Since rape myths were first named by Burt (1980) over two decades ago, there has been a virtual explosion of research on rape myths and their acceptance. The single most consistent finding in this area is that men are more likely to accept rape myths as true than are women (Davies & McCartney, 2003; Kassing & Prieto, 2003). People with traditional sex-role attitudes and negative attitudes toward women are also more likely to subscribe to rape myths. Finally, men who report greater likelihood of raping women consistently demonstrate higher rape myth acceptance (Lonsway & Fitzgerald, 1994). As these authors note, the extensive research in this area holds immense potential for understanding what causes, maintains, and justifies sexual assault in societies such as the United States, in which rape is common and rape myths are widely believed.

Rape, Denial, and Blame.
Two of the most consistently baffling and disheartening findings in all the rape literature concern how often women attempt to deny even to themselves that they have been raped and how often they are held responsible—by themselves and others—for being raped.

As mentioned earlier, Koss et al. (1987) found that over half of all women who had experiences that met legal definitions of rape did not regard themselves as rape victims, even in an anonymous survey. Koss and her associates explain this finding by suggesting that to admit that one is a victim is to adopt the stance of a "loser," especially in our society, which so clearly values winning and success. One's losses in the case of rape are often severe and may include one's reputation, privacy, peace of mind, autonomy, feelings of control, and assumptions about the world. Contrary to a common rape myth, few women falsely accuse men of rape or seek the label of rape victim.

Even when women can admit to themselves that they have been raped, they frequently do not share their experience with others, especially when the rapist is a family member, date, or other acquaintance (Thornhill & Thornhill, 1991). We can only speculate about why women who have been raped by people whom they know are so reluctant to come forward. Some women fear that the pain of accusation and possible trial is not worth the trouble. Others fear some form of retaliation or worry that they will harm the rapist or his family. But, clearly, many women fear that they will not be believed, and that in a society in which women are held responsible for exciting and controlling men's sexual urges, they will be blamed for the rape. Women of color and immigrants have additional reasons for not reporting rapes. Many African American women have learned the hard way not to trust authorities, who may make racist assumptions about them or their lives. As Wyatt (1992) has noted, in U.S. society, the rape of a Black woman is not taken as seriously as that of a White woman, and some people do not believe that Black women can be raped. Immigrant women may be similarly distrustful of the kind of treatment they will receive from the police, the health system, and the courts, and worried about the real dangers that confront them and their families if they interact with societal institutions.

Blaming the rape victim is part of a more general tendency people have to blame others for their misfortunes. According to Lerner's (1980) "just world hypothesis," we have a need to believe that people get what they deserve and deserve what they get. By believing that a rape victim somehow did something wrong to bring on her rape or that she is the type of person who deserves to be raped, people are able to maintain the position that this terrible fate will not befall them or the people that they love.

Studies of attributions of responsibility for date rapes consistently show that men, particularly traditional men who hold conventional sex-role attitudes, are more likely to assign responsibility to women for rape than women are (Bridges & McGrail, 1989). One study found that one in four men believe that rape is often provoked by the victim (Holcomb, Holcomb, Sondag, & Williams, 1991). Men have less empathy for rape victims than women do, are less supportive of rape victims, and are more lenient to rape perpetrators in courts of law (Kleinke & Meyer, 1990). There is ample evidence that some men do not take date rape seriously (Stacy, Prisbell, & Tollefsrud, 1992) and do not consider it "real" rape. Regrettably, society colludes in diminishing the seriousness of date rape in the rape myths that it perpetuates and the androcentric (male-centered) ways that rape law is written and enforced.

Effects of Rape and Sexual Assault on Women

Many studies attest to the fact that rape has significant emotional, behavioral, and health consequences for women. To date, most studies on the effects of rape have been conducted on Western women in peacetime who have experienced a single episode of rape (Koss at al., 1994). Thus, these findings may not be generalizable to women from other cultures, to women who are raped during times of war or other conflicts, or to women who have experienced multiple rapes.

Obviously, women differ in their responses to rape based on their family history, personality, experience of prior trauma, ethnicity, social class, and other variables. But some symptoms of psychological distress, including intrusive memories, attempts to avoid reminders of the trauma, depression, and anxiety, are experienced by almost everyone. In fact, these particular psychological effects are often conceptualized in North America as posttraumatic stress disorder (PTSD). In one study, 94 percent of rape victims exhibited the symptoms of PTSD an average of 12 days following sexual assault, and 46 percent met the criteria three months later (Rothbaum, Foa, Riggs, Murdock, & Walsh, 1992). For most rape victims, high levels of anxiety and depression gradually diminish over the course of the year following a rape, but fully 20 percent have continuing difficulties several years after the rape (Hanson, 1990). Burgess and Holmstrom (1974) have identified a particular form of PTSD called **rape trauma syndrome,** which is characterized by two phases. The first is an acute phase, usually lasting for several weeks, in which survivors exhibit severe disorganization in their lives and experience frequent bouts of crying and feelings of anger, shame, and fear. The second phase, long-term reorganization, may take several years. It is characterized by fears of recurrence, frightening dreams, and mistrust in interpersonal relationships.

Of course, not everyone experiences a variation of the rape trauma syndrome. Some women have a silent reaction to rape; that is, they tell no one about their experience, subtly avoid men or sexual situations, and quietly struggle with anxiety and loss of self-esteem, often for long periods of time. Others are somehow able to put the rape behind them with little outside assistance. Koss et al. (1994) suggest that what determines a woman's response to rape is not the actual event itself or her intrapsychic processes but rather an *interaction* between the two: her cognitive appraisal of the rape—her judgment of the experience arising from personal, cultural, and situational factors. In order to understand a woman's trauma and recovery process, one needs to know the personal meaning that the rape has for an individual woman. For instance, in societies in which virginity is highly prized and the stigma of rape is profound, the greatest concern of unmarried rape victims in the aftermath of rape is getting their hymens reconstructed (Koss et al., 1994).

Aside from psychological reactions, girls and women often experience physical and sexual health consequences of rape. Many chronic conditions, including premenstrual syndrome and gastrointestinal disorders, occur disproportionately among rape survivors. In the United States, early sexual abuse is associated with a range of high-risk sexual behaviors on the part of the victims, including unprotected sex and prostitution, and the use of alcohol and drugs. Koss and Heslet (1992) have found that sexually transmitted infections are the result of rape in anywhere from 4 to 30 percent of the cases. If left untreated, as these stigmatized infections often are, STIs can result in pelvic inflammatory disease and infertility, or facilitate the transmission of HIV. The global, cumulative cost of sexual violence in terms of additional burdens on the health care system and healthy, productive years of life lost is staggering and is comparable to the burdens posed by HIV, cancer, and cardiovascular disease (Koss et al., 1994).

Personal and Societal Responses to Rape

As we have repeatedly stated, the personal tragedy of rape occurs within personal, political, and sociocultural contexts. An effective response to rape requires that we respond to rape on many levels.

Personal Responses. On the personal level, there are many steps that individual women can take to lessen the probability that they will become victims of rape. *The New Our Bodies, Ourselves* (Boston Women's Health Book Collective, 1984) lists several tips for women who seek to protect themselves and other women from stranger rape, including these suggestions to avoid being raped in one's own home (p. 137):

> *Keep lights in all the entrances; keep the windows locked and in place, have strong locks on every door; be aware of places where men might hide; don't put your full name on the mailbox; know which neighbors you can trust in an emergency; find out who is at your door before opening; say, "I'll get the door, Bill" when going to the door.*

Over the past decade, research has begun to address the question of what kinds of behaviors are most effective for women who are attacked by rapists. Regrettably, findings are inconsistent concerning the best ways for women to respond, and no single response is uniformly more effective than others. For example, some research shows that some of the less forceful and provocative forms of resistance, including pleading, begging, or reasoning with the assailant, can be dangerous strategies that actually heighten the probability of injury. Vigorous resistance by women makes it less likely that a rape will be completed, but it also may make it more likely that women will be physically injured during the attack (Nevid et al., 1995). Tactics that work in certain situations may not in others. For example, running away may be highly effective when there is a single assailant and an exit route, but is less likely to succeed when there are multiple assailants and nowhere to go. It appears that effective self-defense must be built on multiple strategies and an accurate appraisal of the options based on an assessment of the rapist, the situation, and a woman's ability to resist. This said, recent research suggests that fighting back is more effective than not fighting back. Patricia Rozee, who has written extensively about rape, has usefully summarized research on the matter of rape resistance (see Box 12.4).

Researchers have offered strategies particularly tailored for avoiding date rape. For instance, Powell (1991) advises women to communicate their sexual limits to dates, meet new dates in public places, be firm in refusing sexual overtures, be wary of their own fears of displeasing their partners, pay attention to their gut-level feelings about men, and be especially cautious if they are in new environments or have recently broken off a relationship with someone whom they don't feel especially good about.

The personal responses that women make to reduce the threat of rape are perhaps best construed as forms of *rape deterrence,* not rape prevention. Rape deterrence strategies protect individual women who use them (although with no guarantees), but do not reduce the vulnerability of women as a group. No one can be vigilant or respond effectively all the time. To the extent that there are men who will commit acts of sexual assault, women as a group remain vulnerable to rape. Obviously, personal responses do not address the major causes of rape—men's motivation (Lonsway, 1996), and societal norms that tolerate rape (Rozee, 2000).

Societal Responses.   In recent years, there is increased recognition that personal responses to rape, however important, are not sufficient to combat what is a societal problem. To date, the most common societal responses to the problem of rape can be best characterized as environmental: installing better lighting or mirrors in elevators, trimming shrubbery for better visibility, and the like (Lonsway, 1996). But the past two decades have also witnessed a sharp increase in the number of education programs aimed at men, women, or both mostly on college campuses (see Box 12.5).

Scholars and advocates for women around the world are just beginning to unite around a global research agenda on sexual violence. This agenda calls for research into the sociocultural context of gender-based violence, the multiple consequences of rape for physical and mental health, the societal structures that promote rape, and the social networks through which people deal with sexual assault, as well as prevention and education efforts (Koss et al., 1994).

PARTNER ABUSE

Violence is a common feature in intimate relationships of all kinds. In this section, we focus on partner

---

BOX 12.4

Resisting Rape

Rape resistance studies show a consistent pattern of results.

1. Women who fight back and fight back immediately are less likely to be raped than women who do not fight back.
2. Women who fight back are not more likely to be injured than women who do not fight back.
3. Pleading, begging, crying, and reasoning are ineffective in preventing rape or physical injury.
4. Women who fight back experience fewer negative symptoms afterward and faster psychological recovery whether or not they have been raped.
5. Fighting back strengthens the physical evidence should the survivor decide to prosecute for rape or attempted rape.

Source: Adapted from "Sexual Victimization: Harassment and Rape," by P. D. Rozee, 2000, in *Issues in the Psychology of Women,* edited by M. K. Biaggio and M. Herson. New York: Kluwer Academic/Plenum Publishers.

BOX 12.5

Educational Programs to Combat Rape

Educational programs to combat rape differ considerably in their assumptions and strategies. Programs aimed at women often incorporate elements of self-defense, assertiveness training, sexual communication strategies, debunking of rape myths, and assessment of risky situations. Programs for men also attempt to decrease rape myth acceptance and improve sexual communication, often by educating men about how male socialization affects men's capacity for violence and intimacy. Several include components that attempt to increase empathy among men for rape victims. Rape prevention efforts designed for both women and men include many of these elements, along with general sex education and feminist reconceptualization of gender relations, often with a focus on common problems in cross-sex communication and dating expectations.

How well do such educational programs work in reducing rape? Evidence for their effectiveness is inconclusive to date. It appears that educational programs can reduce endorsement of rape-supporting attitudes among women and men, at least in the short run. But there is little evidence to date that such programs produce long-term attitude change or actually reduce sexual aggression and other rape-supportive behaviors (Lonsway, 1996).

Finally, rape prevention efforts aimed at men need to make clear the benefits *to men* of a rape-free society (Lonsway, 1996). Men as a group benefit in some ways from the existence of rape and the threat of rape. The payoffs for women of a rape-free society are obvious; the payoffs for men need to be articulated.

---

abuse—violence directed at spouses or lovers. It is clear from recent research that both women and men perpetrate violence in intimate relationships and that violence characterizes same-sex as well as heterosexual relationships.

Definitions and Prevalence

Like other forms of violence against women, partner abuse has only recently been widely regarded as a crime and a problem in society. Historically, a husband's authority over his wife extended to his right to hit her in order to keep her in line. Until quite recently, the criminal justice system in the United States viewed violence against women in intimate relationships as matters of "privacy" and "civil disturbances" not appropriate for criminal proceedings (Stahly, 1996). And like other forms of violence against women, partner abuse is hard to define. In all cases, hitting, punching, slapping, kicking, and shoving constitute abuse. Aborted attempts and threats to hurt a partner physically appear in most definitions. Many definitions of partner abuse contain elements of intimidation: controlling and limiting what a partner does, whom the partner sees, and where he or she

goes, and frightening a partner by smashing things or destroying property. Some definitions of partner abuse also include emotional and sexual abuse.

Obviously, variations in the definitions of abuse lead to differences in measurement and estimates of prevalence. But most estimates of partner abuse are based on some kind of physical violence. And these estimates suggest that nowhere is a women in greater danger of becoming a victim of male violence than in her own home. In the United States each year, depending on the definition of physical violence used, between 2 million and 6 million women are beaten by the men they live with, and about 4,000 U.S. women die each year as a direct consequence of spousal or partner abuse (U.S. Department of Justice, Bureau of Statistics, 1994, as cited in Stahly, 1996; Walker, 1979). Women physically assaulted by their husbands or boyfriends account for between 25 and 40 percent of all women who are murdered each year (Arias & Pape, 1994; Bachman & Saltzman, 1996; U.S. Department of Justice, Federal Bureau of Investigation, 1996). At any point in time, 40 percent of women treated in emergency rooms are victims of wife abuse (Dearwater et al., 1998; Stark & Flitcraft, 1988). The American Medical Association estimates that about one-quarter of the women in the United States will be abused by a current or former partner at some point in their lives (Lawson, 1992). Almost 30 percent of married couples in the United States report experiencing at least one physically violent episode during their marriage (McHugh & Bartoszek, 2000; Straus, Gelles, & Steinmetz, 1980). Given the private nature of abuse in the home, the stigma attached to domestic abuse, and the fear in which most victims live, the actual incidence of abuse may be much higher. More U.S. women suffer injury at the hands of their partners than as a result of rapes, muggings, and automobile accidents combined (Stahly, 1996, 2004). When estimates of violence include instances of psychological abuse, they are much higher.

Unlike rape, which is virtually always committed by men (against women or other men), partner abuse is perpetrated by both women and men. Research shows that women are about as likely as men to start a fight or hit their spouses or dating partners (Ingrassia & Beck, 1994; O'Leary et al., 1989; Steinmetz & Lucca, 1988). A study of couples seeking psychological treatment for problems connected with marital aggression found that 86 percent of aggressive couples reported reciprocal aggression, and only 14 percent reported unilateral aggression (Cascardi, Langhinrichsen, & Vivian, 1992). There is little question that some women in violent relationships are themselves violent. But research evidence suggests that violence by women usually occurs in response to their partners' attacks, either in retaliation or self-defense (Gelles & Straus, 1998). And violence by men is far more likely to result in serious injury to a partner than violence by women.

The term *battery* is often used as a synonym for partner abuse, and abused women are commonly called battered women. But, as hooks (1993b) notes, the term **battered women** is problematic. Although categories and labels can play an important role in drawing public attention to the seriousness of male violence against women in intimate relationships, labels such as "battered women" can also be stigmatizing and inadequate. hooks states:

Most importantly, the term "battered women" is used as though it constitutes a separate and unique cate-

gory of womanness, as though it is an identity, a mark that sets one apart rather than being simply a descriptive term. It is as though the experience of being repeatedly violently hit is the sole defining characteristic of a woman's identity and all other aspects of who she is and what her experience has been are submerged. (p. 207)

hooks asserts that categorizing women's identity with this label strips women of their dignity and renders them silent and ashamed. It keeps the focus on their stigmatized identity rather than on the behavior of the abuser.

Abuse in Lesbian Relationships. As several scholars have noted, there is widespread belief that same-sex couples do not experience violence in their relationships at the same rates as heterosexual couples, because power imbalances due to gender differences do not exist (Browning, Reynolds, & Dworkin, 1991; Patterson & Schwartz, 1994). Furthermore, there is a cultural myth that lesbians in particular, because of their socialization as women and commitment to egalitarian relationships, do not encounter domestic violence (Browning et al., 1991). Although precise estimates are impossible, research suggests otherwise: Levels of abuse in lesbian couples are comparable to those of heterosexual couples and actually exceed current estimates in gay male couples (McHugh & Bartoszek, 2000; Waterman, Dawson, & Bologna, 1989, cited in Patterson & Schwartz, 1994). How can we understand the surprisingly high rates of partner abuse among lesbian couples? Several explanations have been put forward. For one thing, women may be more sensitive to issues of abuse and more likely to label acts as abusive than men are. For another, the pressure of mutual dependence may itself be conducive to violence (Galvin & Brommel, 1991, cited in Patterson & Schwartz, 1994). That is, the high value that women place on making relationships work may render relationships involving women more tolerant of abuse than relationships involving men. It is also important to note that, simply because both members of a couple are of the same sex, we cannot assume that there are no power differences in the couple or that power differences between individuals are irrelevant to the abuse. We need further research on domestic abuse in same-sex couples and on the role that power plays in these relationships.

Theories of Partner Abuse

Is violence against women learned behavior? Are women masochists? Are all abusers of women substance abusers, psychotics, psychopaths, or just plain bullies? Are all men potential abusers of women? These are some of the questions that have preoccupied those who have sought to understand the phenomenon of partner abuse.

Basically, theories of partner abuse divide into three categories: (1) those that focus on the role of women in causing and maintaining abuse, (2) those who see violence against women as the result of individual pathology in some males, and (3) those that see physical violence against women as arising from societal structures in which there is significant gender inequality.

Many scholars who have studied abuse against women have noted the curious emphasis in both the scholarly literature and the media on the characteristics of female victims and the reasons why abused women stay in abusive relationships. As we have noted in other contexts, this focus on the victim rather than on the perpetrator suggests that the victim somehow causes her misfortune and deserves at least some of the blame for it. Within psychology, blaming women for physical violence against them can be traced back to Freud's theory of psychosexual development, in which Freud posits that *sadism* is an innate organizing feature of normal male development and *masochism* of normal female development (Shafter, 1992). Psychoanalyst Karen Horney asserted that social and cultural conditions rather than biological ones alone accounted for masochistic behavior in women. Contemporary psychoanalytic views discuss masochism in women as the outcome of the fear of separation or abandonment (Lego, 1992). However differently intrapsychic theories explain the origins of "female masochism," they all take the view that women have an unconscious need to be hurt and punished for their anatomic inferiority, sexual feelings, or other shortcomings.

Despite the long history of such theories, there is no empirical support for the notion that women are masochists, that they like being hurt by men, or that they stay in abusive relationships when they perceive that they have real alternatives. Women who are beaten by their husbands are less likely to initiate or enjoy sexual relations with them, less likely to regard their husbands as physically attractive, and more likely to report that they are staying in their relationships for financial reasons than are women who are not beaten by their husbands (Barnett & La Violette, 1993). Many women who stay in abusive relationships do so predominantly because they are afraid of leaving. Indeed, women are much more likely—about 70 percent more likely—to be hurt or killed at the point of leaving than at any other time in the relationship (Stahly, 2004).

A second class of theories about the origins of partner abuse takes the position that men who are violent against women are certain kinds of people: alcoholics and other drug abusers, psychotics, psychopaths, or just plain bullies. "Normal men" do not abuse their partners. In fact, as we discuss later, partner abuse is statistically associated with certain characteristics of males, just as it is also related to some female characteristics and certain features of the relationships between women and men. But research is consistent in showing that partner abuse cuts across all socioeconomic, ethnic, religious, and age categories. Although certain variables, particularly having witnessed or experienced abuse as a child, are good predictors of abusing a partner, there is no evidence that abusers are fundamentally different from normal men.

The third and final set of theories concerning the origins of partner abuse locates the sources of the problem of abuse in social and cultural factors that affect all men. These theories suggest that pervasive sexism and gender inequality in such institutions as marriage, formal religions, the economic and criminal justice systems, and the media support and maintain male violence. Historically, society has sanctioned a man's exercising his authority over his family by means of physical violence. The patriarchal tradition of treating women as property had granted men permission to do whatever they wanted with their wives. Research suggests that households in which there is domestic violence are more likely to be characterized by rigid, traditional divisions of labor by sex. Virtually all formal religions stress the primacy of the family and the virtues of remaining in marriage "for better or worse." Economic conditions in which men make almost 30 percent more money than women on average, render women, especially women with children, financially dependent and vulnerable. The law enforcement and criminal justice systems have long histories of treating domestic abuse cases as private, internal family matters instead of criminal offenses. Finally, male violence is glorified in cartoons, sports, Westerns, war, action movies, and "cop shows." These media depictions encourage modeling and provide vicarious reinforcement of violent male behavior in this society (Kilmartin, 1994).

Evidence supporting the sociocultural approach comes from research suggesting that domestic abuse thrives on patriarchal attitudes, rigid gender arrangements, and acceptance of male aggression. It is a problem in all sectors of society. Sociocultural analyses suggest that domestic abuse will remain a problem for women generally as long as gender inequality exists.

Research on Partner Abuse: Who Abuses Women, and Who Is Abused?

All three sets of theories about the origins of partner abuse have spawned research that focuses on the characteristics of men and women and the relationships and circumstances that are associated with partner abuse. It is important to bear in mind that because there are statistical correlations among groups of variables we cannot conclude that one set of variables causes another set of variables; in particular, the fact that some women are more likely than others to be victimized does not at all mean that those women somehow invite their own victimization.

Increasingly, researchers have turned their attention to the social and psychological characteristics of male abusers. Probably the best single predictor of abusing a partner is having witnessed or experienced abuse oneself. Depending on the study, between 63 and 81 percent of men who abused their partners either experienced abuse as victims in their childhood or witnessed their fathers beating their mothers (Ewing, 1993). Partner abuse is also associated with

low educational attainment and unemployment or low occupational status among males (Hotaling & Sugarman, 1986). Alcohol and illicit drug use also predict partner abuse. Most abusers tend to be young (under age 30) (Ingrassia & Beck, 1994).

The psychological profile that emerges from research on male abusers suggests that they tend to be overconforming to the traditional male gender role and the masculine culture of violence (Kilmartin, 1994). They have a high need for power and control over their partners. While their masculinity is tied to notions of dominance, they often do not have the economic status and resources to support a dominant stance (Lorber, 1994). Male abusers are more likely to have low self-esteem and show greater depression and emotional dependency than other men (Cascardi et al., 1992; Gondolf & Hanneken, 1987). In self-reports of reasons for spousal homicide, the most frequently cited justification given by men is sexual jealousy and/or the wife threatening to terminate the relationship (Cazenave & Zahn, 1992; Stahly, 2004).

Empirically, characteristics of male partners are better predictors of women's risk of being victimized than are characteristics of women themselves (Hotaling & Sugarman, 1986). But research suggests that some women are more likely to be abused by men than others. The most consistent risk factor for women is witnessing violence in their homes as children or adolescents (Hotaling & Sugarman, 1986). Women who are young, poor, and unemployed are also at risk for physical abuse by a partner. A history of alcohol and other drug use, dependency, isolation, and low self-esteem are predisposing factors (Marano, 1993). Pregnant women are particular targets of abuse (Browne, 1993). Obviously, not all abused women fit this profile, and no woman, regardless of social class and life circumstances, is immune from this problem.

There are also characteristics of couples or relationships that predict the incidence of physical abuse of women. As Lorber (1994) notes, paradoxically, abusive relationships often seem very romantic at first, because the man seems especially attentive. Over time, however, his interest appears increasingly possessive, controlling, and limiting. One study that compared women in violent and nonviolent relationships found that wives of abusive men were more likely than wives in nonviolent relationships to report that their husbands were jealous, did not trust them, and had them under surveillance (Barnett & La Violette, 1993). Violent men are more likely than other men to be preoccupied with their intimate relationships and to have few outside friends or interests. As a result, they may be particularly emotionally dependent on, and fearful of the loss of, their relationships and are more likely to misinterpret neutral situations as threatening (Marano, 1993). Other relationship characteristics associated with violence include the following: The female and male have different religious backgrounds, the female and male cohabitate without being married, the female or male uses violence against children in the home, and the total family income is below the poverty line (McHugh & Bartoszek, 2000).

Consequences for Abused Women

Women suffer numerous physical and psychological outcomes from partner abuse.

Physical Consequences of Abuse.   Epidemiological studies reveal that the kinds of aggressive acts that women report range from being slapped, punched, kicked, or thrown to being scalded, cut, bitten, choked, and smothered. Typical injuries range from bruises, black eyes, and broken bones to permanent problems, such as partial loss of vision or hearing and scars from burns or knife wounds (Browne, 1993). Research is consistent in showing that women sustain more injuries and more severe injuries from partner abuse than do men and that nearly half of all women in emergency rooms seek treatment because of partner abuse (Cascardi et al., 1992; O'Leary & Cascardi, 1998). In addition, women who experience male partner abuse are at risk for a variety of other health complaints, including headaches, back and limb problems, frequent colds, fainting and dizziness, stomach and gastrointestinal problems, gynecological problems, heart and blood-pressure problems, lung and breathing problems, and/or skin problems (Follingstad, Brennan, Hause, Polek, & Rutledge, 1991). Physical abuse and the many problems it causes can shorten people's lives. Recent research on the mortality of older people (mostly women) who have suffered abuse at the hands of family members suggests that abused people may not live as long as similar others who are not abused (Lacks, Williams, O'Brien, Pillemer, & Charlson, 1998).

As noted earlier, it is a stunning and sad fact that pregnant women are particularly at risk of being abused by their partners. In the 1985 National Family Violence Survey of a representative sample, 154 of every 1,000 pregnant women reported being assaulted by their partners during the first four months of pregnancy and 170 out of 1,000 during the last five months of pregnancy (Gelles & Straus, 1988). Assaults around the abdomen may have devastating consequences, including placental separation; rupture of the uterus, liver, or spleen; and premature labor (Browne, 1993).

Thousands of women are killed each year by their partners. As Browne (1993) notes, women are more likely to be killed by their partners than by all other categories of persons combined. Men are more likely—at least twice as likely—to murder their partners than women are (Browne, 1993). When women murder men, it is usually in self-defense or in response to threats or a long history of physical abuse. It is true that almost 40 percent of partner homicides are men killed by their female partners, but a critical point to keep in mind is that women kill men trying to defend themselves or leave an abusive relationship; men kill women who are trying to leave or have succeeded in doing so (Stahly, 2004). Women who murder their spouses are typically given more severe penalties than are men who murder their spouses (Browne, 1993). White and Kowalski (1994) note that a woman who murders her husband is likely to receive a sentence of 15 to 20 years, whereas a man who murders his wife is generally given only 2 to 6 years.

Despite the fact that male violence against women is more common, severe, and lethal than female violence against men, women do participate in and even initiate violence in their relationships. Recent research is looking more closely into women's violence against their partners. One study found that women may initiate violence in up to 25 percent of all cases (Hamberger, 1997). Female-initiated and mutual violence is more likely among younger women, and may be increasing. This topic requires more research and possibly a reconceptualization of gender issues in partner violence (McHugh & Bartoszek, 2000).

Psychological Consequences of Abuse. Women show a wide range of psychological effects of suffering physical abuse at the hands of a male partner. Because there are no truly representative surveys of the psychological responses of abused women and because so many abused women do not avail themselves of psychological treatments of any kind, it is extremely difficult to estimate the proportions of women who suffer various consequences.

Research suggests that abused women's psychological reactions to male violence closely follow the general pattern of responses that people have to a variety of traumatic events. Many of the psychological aftereffects of violence can be understood as conforming to the diagnostic construct of posttraumatic stress disorder (PTSD). (See also Chapter 13). During assaults, women's focus is on their own survival. They may react with a mixture of shock, denial, withdrawal, confusion, and fear (Browne, 1987). After the assaults, high levels of depression and anxiety are common (Browne, 1993). Other symptoms include chronic fatigue and tension, nightmares, and disturbed sleeping and eating patterns. After severe or chronic beatings, some women respond by abusing substances.

The severity and duration of the abuse are strongly related to women's psychological consequences. The more severe and repetitive the abuse is, the more likely the woman is to feel isolated and depressed and to consider committing suicide. As useful as the PTSD diagnosis is in characterizing the psychological consequences of violence as normal responses to abnormal events, it does not account for all the symptoms manifested by female victims of domestic abuse.

Personal and Societal Responses to Partner Abuse

Personal Responses to Partner Abuse: Why Don't Women Just Leave? When the issue of partner abuse is raised, the single most frequently asked question concerns why abused women stay in violent relationships. This question appears to locate the cause of the problem in the women who are abused. Instead, a more useful question concerns the social and psychological factors that constrain women from leaving.

Despite the popular portrayal of battered women as meek and passive, most women employ a variety of strategies to stop the violence or escape, especially early on in abusive relationships. They attempt to change the behavior that their partner criticizes, call the police for help, seek the counsel of clergy and family members, and turn to their doctors. These strategies, however reasonable, are often ineffective. Abusive partners find other things to criticize. The police may do little more than diffuse the current crisis. Clergy or family members may advise women to do whatever they can to "save their families," including being more submissive, accommodating, and accepting. Even medical doctors are limited in their responses to women and frequently treat the problem with tranquilizers, antidepressants, and sleeping pills. And many women do leave, at least temporarily, after beatings, only to be actively pursued by their partners with gifts and promises (and threats) and encouraged to go home by friends and family (Stahly, 1996). Studies consistently show that well over 40 percent of the women who seek aid from spouse abuse shelters return to live with their partners (Rusbult & Martz, 1995).

Over time, physical and psychological responses to abuse render many women depressed, dependent, helpless, and suggestible. Some abused women consider themselves failures because they have not succeeded in making happy homes. This makes it difficult for them to engage in long-range planning and take decisive action (Browne, 1993). Some investigators have found it useful to apply the "hostage syndrome" to the plight of abused women (Dutton & Painter, 1981). That is, when people feel that their survival depends on placating an unpredictable aggressor, a bond of sympathy and even affection develops. Studies of animal and human behavior suggest that intermittent punishment and reward appear to strengthen the power of attachment (Stahly, 1996). Abused women often love their abusers and are committed to their marriages or relationships. They may depend on the abuser for shelter and other necessities of life. They have long histories of being blamed by their partners for the violence they "provoke" and have learned to survive largely by seeing the world through their abusers' eyes. They find fault with themselves and make excuses for their partners.

Some psychologists are beginning to offer explanations for why women stay in violent relationships that go beyond women's personal dispositions (whether they precede or follow the onset of abuse). Rusbult and Martz (1995) use an *investment model* analysis to understand why women remain in abusive relationships that underscores the social and structural factors that constrain women from leaving. The investment model suggests that a woman's commitment level to the abusive relationship level depends on the availability and attractiveness of alternatives to the relationship and the size of her investment in the relationship. Rusbult and Martz (1995) predict that commitment to an abusive relationship should be greater among women who have been involved with their partners longer, among women who are married rather than cohabiting or dating, and among women with a greater number of children with their partners. Empirical research on abusive relationships supports the investment model and suggests that, to understand the dynamics of abusive relationships, we must address the nature of an abused woman's relationship with her partner.

In addition to psychological and social variables, we need to consider the external realities that many women confront in deciding whether to stay in or leave an abusive relationship. Behaviors such as failing to press charges against the abuser, which strike others as helpless or craven, may represent accurate and realistic evaluations of the abuser's potential for escalated violence and murder. The most likely time for a man to kill his partner is at the point when she leaves him or shortly afterward (Stahly, 2004; Walker, 1979). Normal psychological responses to assault may well cloud a woman's thinking and lead to poor decision making. But even the clearest, most rational appraisals of threat and danger may induce a woman to stay with a violent partner (Browne, 1993).

Societal Responses.   The problem of violence against women cannot be fully understood, let alone solved, by focusing exclusively on individual women and men (Goodman et al., 1993). A lasting solution to the problem can come only with social and cultural change. As Goodman et al. (1993) note, many authors find the roots of male violence against women in women's efforts to escape their subordinate roles in the family, workplace, academy, and the larger society.

A variety of community-based services exist for women who have been abused by their partners, many of them created by grassroots organizations and advocates for women (Goodman et al., 1993). These services include shelters for victims of violence and their children, crisis hot lines, support groups, and legal aid centers. As vital as these services are, they are underfunded and cannot meet the needs of all the women who need them. Evaluations of rape prevention programs have yielded mixed results. It is becoming apparent that one of the most promising avenues for sexual assault and rape prevention may be self-defense training, which is presently not an integral component of typical prevention programs (Sochting, Fairbrother, & Koch, 2004).

On a larger scale, psychologists should work together with other social scientists and policy makers to bring about a fundamental change in social attitudes and social institutions. Legislative efforts to treat gendered violence as civil rights violations, along with violence based on religion, ethnicity, disability, or race, exemplify how policy makers can attempt to shape society's attitudes toward women and reduce the social acceptability of abuse directed at them.

SEXUAL ABUSE OF CHILDREN

In the eyes of many people, child sexual abuse is among the most morally reprehensible of all acts. Indeed, it often has devastating effects on children that persist well into adulthood. It is a gendered crime in that most of the victims are girls and, overwhelmingly, most of the perpetrators are men.

Child sexual abuse was not even acknowledged as a serious social problem until the 1970s, when the women's movement and child protection legislation brought it to public attention. Feminists at this time noted that girls were vastly overrepresented as victims of child sexual abuse and that these problems were attributable to a patriarchal culture that exploited women and children (Cosentino & Collins, 1996).

Definitions and Prevalence

Sexual abuse of children is usually defined by researchers as any form of sexual contact that occurs before age 18, with a relative, a person at least five years older than the child, or someone who forces himself or herself on the child regardless of the age difference (Downs, Miller, Testa, & Panek, 1992). Sexual contact may range from invitations to perform a sexual act, to exhibitionism, fondling, and sexual touching, to anal or vaginal intercourse. By definition, any form of sexual contact between an adult and child is regarded as abusive, even if no threat is made or force used, and even if the child appears to consent or enjoy the sexual activity. Children are not capable of giving truly voluntary consent to have sex with adults. Voluntary sexual activity among children of similar ages is not considered child abuse (Rathus et al., 2002).

It is enormously difficult to estimate the prevalence of child abuse because the number of cases reported to authorities, fewer than 50,000 cases a year, is certainly a gross underestimation (Finkelhor & Hotaling, 1984). Most victims of child sexual abuse do not report their experiences because of feelings of guilt or shame, fear of retaliation or blame, or failure to label and remember their experiences as abusive. The closer the relationship between the child and the abuser, the less likely it is that the abuse will be reported to the police (Finkelhor, 1986). Surveys of adults that require people to reconstruct their childhood experiences, and thus are not highly reliable, have variously estimated the prevalence of child sexual abuse to be between 4 and 16 percent among boys, and between 16 and 30 percent among girls (Janus & Janus, 1993; Kohn, 1987).

Patterns of Child Sexual Abuse

Who Abuses Children?   There is virtual unanimity that most sexual abusers of both male and female children are male, with some estimates suggesting that 94 percent of young female victims and 84 percent of young male victims were molested by men (Finkelhor, 1984). Almost all *pedophiles*—people who have persistent or recurring sexual attraction to children—are male. Some people have sexual contact with children only under conditions of unusual stress or lack of other sexual outlets and are not regarded as pedophiles. Some pedophiles are responsible for large numbers of sexual assaults on children, with one study of 232 convicted pedophiles stating that they had molested an average of 76 children each (Abel et al., 1989).

There is currently increased research interest in women as perpetrators of child sexual abuse, with some researchers suggesting that it is more common than previously believed (Wakefield & Underwager, 1991). Female sexual abuse of children may be underreported for many reasons. Women can more easily than men mask sexually inappropriate contact through activities such as bathing or dressing children. However, as Finkelhor and Russell (1984) note, female sexual abuse of children in which women act alone is rare. In most reported cases of child sexual abuse in which female perpetrators are named, females were complying with male child abusers.

There is no consistent personality profile of the child molester. But it has long been known that a disproportionate number of males and females who sexually abuse children were themselves sexually abused as children (De Young, 1982; Muster, 1992). In this way, cycles of abuse may be perpetuated from generation to generation as children who are sexually victimized themselves become victimizers or partners of victimizers as adults (Nevid et al., 1995).

Contrary to the stereotype of the pathological stranger lurking in the schoolyard, the typical sexual abusers of children are people who are close to them—a relative, step-relative, family friend, babysitter, or other acquaintance. In one major study of child abusers, Gray (1993) found that noncustodial acquaintances made up the largest single group of abusers, with the victim's stepfather or mother's boyfriend the next largest group. Only about 20 percent of all child sexual abuse involves strangers (Waterman & Lusk, 1986). Sadly, the most notorious cases of sexual abuse of children in the United States to date have involved Catholic priests. A recent study commissioned by United States bishops, the first comprehensive study of the issue, reveals that about 4 percent of U.S. priests ministering from 1950 to 2002 have been accused of sexual abuse of a minor.

GENDER, VIOLENCE, AND EXPLOITATION

The study claimed that 4,392 clergymen—almost all priests—were accused of abusing 10,667 people, with 75 percent of the incidents taking place between 1960 and 1984. Eighty-one percent of the victims were male. Further, 22 percent of the victims were under 10 years old, 51 percent were 11 to 14 years old, and 27 percent were 15 to 17 years old. The report states: "Like in the general population, child sex abuse in the Catholic Church appears to be committed by men close to the children they allegedly abuse, many appear to use grooming tactics to entice children into complying with the abuse, and the abuse occurs in the home of the alleged abuser or victim" (Bono, 2004).

As Rathus et al. (2002) point out, sexual attraction to children may be more common than is generally believed, with anonymous surveys suggesting that about 20 percent of male college students admitting some sexual attraction to young children, and 7 percent stating that they would have sex with a young child if they had no fears of being caught and punished (Briere & Runtz, 1989).

Who Are the Victims of Child Sexual Abuse?   Approximately 80 percent of child sexual abuse victims are girls and 20 percent boys (Gray, 1993). The average age at which most children are first sexually abused ranges from 6 to 12 for girls and 7 to 10 years for boys (Knudsen, 1991). Girls are relatively more likely to be abused by acquaintances and family members, whereas boys are relatively more likely to be victimized by strangers and nonfamily members (Knudsen, 1991).

Context in Which Abuse Occurs.   Several other social variables have been found to be correlated with the incidence of child sexual abuse. Whereas children from all social classes are vulnerable to child sexual abuse, children from poorer, less cohesive families are more likely to encounter it than are children from stable, middle-class families (Finkelhor, 1984), although father–daughter incest may be as likely in middle-class as in lower-class homes. Abuse of children is more common in socially or geographically isolated environments, for example, rural areas, and in overcrowded living conditions (Finkelhor, 1979).

But no race, ethnic group, or economic class is immune from this problem.

Incest

Incest has been defined as sexual relations between people (of any age) who are so closely related (by blood) that sexual relations are prohibited and punishable by law (Nevid et al., 1995). The law may also proscribe sexual relations between family members who are not blood related—for instance, stepfathers and stepdaughters. Incest between adults and children by definition always constitutes child sexual abuse. As we have noted, incest is a highly gendered abuse: The typical pattern involves a male family member—father, stepfather, uncle, older brother—sexually abusing a young girl.

Sigmund Freud was the first to propose what is called **seduction theory,** the notion that women's neuroses were caused by child sexual abuse, based on his female patients' accounts of early sexual relationships with their fathers and other male family members. The idea that upper-middle-class Viennese men were molesting their daughters was so abhorrent to Freud's peers in the medical community that he later repudiated seduction theory. Freud then proposed that the sexual relationships described by his patients were in fact their disguised wishes and desires to have sexual relations with their father, which he termed the *Electra complex* (Masson, 1984). Many scholars feel that if Freud had held to his original view, the terrible secret of incest would have emerged much sooner.

The focus in this section is on father–daughter and stepfather–stepdaughter incest. These are not the most common forms of incest, although they are probably the best known and are recognized as the most traumatic. In fact, brother–sister incest is by far the most common, with almost 40 percent of college women in one sample and 21 percent of college men reporting some sexual contact with a sibling of the other sex in their childhoods (Finkelhor, 1979). Sibling incest is most likely to be harmful when it is recurrent or forced (Rathus et al., 2002). Siblings of the same sex rarely enter into sexual relationships. Mother–son incest is very uncommon, and mother–daughter incest is the most uncommon of all forms of incest.

Estimates of father–daughter incest are notoriously unreliable because parental abuse is the least likely form of abuse to be reported. Russell (1968), in a scientific survey of women in San Francisco, found that 16 percent of the women had been incestuously abused by age 18. Finkelhor (1979) put the estimate of father–daughter incest at 4 percent.

In its most typical form, father–daughter incest appears to emerge within a context of broader family dysfunction. Families in which incest occurs are characterized by alcoholism, strained marriages, and other forms of abuse (Waterman, 1986). They also tend to be socially isolated and rigidly religious (Storer, 1992). Marriages in incestuous households have been described as unequal relationships in which an authoritarian, punitive, and intimidating man dominates his passive, often incapacitated wife (Storer, 1992). Of course, incestuous families are not a homogeneous group, and no specific preexisting family patterns have been identified. The literature on father–daughter incest typically represents the father as religiously devout, under great stress, and sexually frustrated because of a withholding, unresponsive wife. Because of his strict religious beliefs, he does not seek sexual gratification in extramarital affairs, but rather looks within the family, usually to the oldest daughter, for the emotional and sexual support that he does not get from his wife. The daughter then becomes the "woman of the house," assuming many of the household responsibilities of her mother, who is often characterized as ill, alcoholic, mentally disabled, and so on (Waterman, 1986).

Traditional psychiatric analyses of the incestuous family frequently blame the mother in cases of father–daughter abuse, often portraying her as responsible for her husband's behavior by virtue of her incapacity, passivity, and refusal or inability to sexually satisfy her husband and protect her child. In fact, research on the mothers of daughters abused by their fathers suggests that in 75 percent of the cases the mothers did not know about the abuse, and in more than half the cases in which the mothers were aware of the abuse, they protected their daughters and rejected their husbands when the abuse became known (Myer, 1985). There is little evidence the mothers should be blamed for their husband's behavior.

In the classic case of father–daughter incest, some stressful event in a father's life, coupled with alcohol use, triggers the first episode. This particular type of abuse often begins with cuddling and non-sexual touching and then escalates to teasing sexual play, kissing, masturbation, genital contact, and, when the child reaches adolescence, even penetration (Nevid et al., 1995). The average age at which father–daughter incest begins is 10 years, and it usually lasts about three years. Father–daughter incest lasts far longer than other kinds of child sexual abuse. Few of these relationships involve violence and force because they often begin before the child can understand their meaning. Nonetheless, some form of coercion is usually present (Urbancic, 1987).

Consequences of Child Sexual Abuse

It is clear that incest victims must cope with multiple aspects of the experience: the physical and psychological trauma in the form of the actual sexual experiences, including violation of one's body, extended periods of fear, guilt, shame, and, in the case of incest, the loss of a trusted relationship with an emotionally significant person. Childhood sexual abuse often inflicts great psychological harm on its victims. It has many diverse, negative short- and long-term consequences for children.

Short-term effects, those occurring within two years of the abuse, include fear, anger and hostility, guilt, shame, depression, low self-esteem, physical and somatic complaints, sexual behavior disturbances, and poor social functioning (Browne & Finkelhor, 1986; Maltz & Holman, 1987). Abused children frequently either act out; that is, display aggressive, antisocial behavior in school, or withdraw, retreating into fantasy and isolation. Regressive behavior such as bed-wetting and thumb sucking also characterize some abused children.

Adolescents who have experienced incest tend to have many of these same problems, plus the additional problems of teenage pregnancy, promiscuity and sexually aggressive behavior, truancy, running away from home, and drug and alcohol abuse. Benward and Densen-Gerber (1975) found that 52 percent of the girls who were sexually abused by relatives left home by age 16. They stress that a history of incest should be considered in all cases of adolescent runaways.

Long-term effects have included depression; behavioral and social problems, such as prostitution, alcoholism, and substance abuse; emotional disorders; suicide; somatic disorders; problems in interpersonal relationships; sexual disturbances; and revictimization (Browne & Finkelhor, 1986; Downs, 1993). For some victims, the negative effects of the abuse increase with time. Tragically, one long-term effect of incest is that it is often repeated from generation to generation.

There is today great controversy about the validity of *repressed memories* of child sexual abuse: cases in which adults, usually in therapy, come to remember that they were abused as children. Some people have expressed great skepticism about the veracity of such memories, suggesting that they may be induced by therapists. Research suggests that it is certainly possible to induce false memories in people (Loftus, 1993). But research also shows that people are far more likely to shun victim status when it applies to them than to claim that status when it does not. Further research and debate will shed light on this controversial issue.

Obviously, individuals vary greatly in the severity and specific form of their responses to child sexual abuse. Researchers have found few consistent sex differences in response to abuse, with the most reliable difference being that boys more often than girls externalize their problems by becoming physically aggressive, whereas girls are more likely to internalize their problems by becoming depressed (Finkelhor, 1990). Older children are more likely to turn to substance abuse and premature sexual activity as ways of coping with abuse (Kendler et al., 2000).

Societal Responses to Child Sexual Abuse

Society is coming to recognize that childhood sexual abuse is a devastating and formative experience in the lives of countless women and men. As Cosentino and Collins (1996) note, significant progress has been made toward understanding some of the causes and effects of child sexual abuse, but we know too little about treatment of children and offenders. Given that research suggests that some victims are vulnerable to revictimization or to having children who are victim-

ized later, we need to focus efforts on the psychological processes underlying intergenerational transmission so that we can reduce further victimization.

Society must help parents and schools better protect children against the likelihood of abuse. Obviously, children cannot prevent their own victimization in many cases, but they can be encouraged to tell about their experiences. Tighter controls in the hiring of people who work with children are necessary, as are educational efforts to help professionals at all levels to recognize the signs of abuse. Programs aimed at helping people who are sexually attracted to children before they commit abusive acts are also badly needed.

PORNOGRAPHY

Few topics in this chapter are more complex and controversial than pornography. As we will see, its very definition is widely disputed. Some people distinguish pornography from *erotica*, arguing that pornography harms women through its depiction of male dominance and humiliation of women, whereas erotica, which portrays consensual and mutually satisfying sex among equals, is not harmful to women. Others argue that all sexually explicit material is inherently harmful to women. Pornography is opposed by some people on moral or religious grounds because of its graphic sexual content and the casualness with which it presents sexual activity, and by others because it degrades women because of its violent and misogynist content. Some researchers have linked pornography to misogynist and aggressive behavior, attitudes, and fantasies in men; others have not. There are constant legal challenges to the dissemination of pornographic material; complaints against its spread to new outlets, such as music, cable television, and cyberspace; and calls for its censorship. Meanwhile, the sale and rental of pornographic materials is at an all-time high; pornography is one of the most profitable industries in the world, exceeding even the music and movie industries, earning billions each year.

What is pornography, and what important distinctions need to be made among forms of pornography? How common is exposure to pornography? Who uses pornography and how and why is it used? What are the attitudinal and behavioral effects of pornography on men and women and on male–female relationships? What are some constructive personal and societal responses to pornography? These are some of the questions that we will treat in this section.

Definitions and Prevalence

Many psychologists, lawyers, politicians, and others have noted the difficulty of clearly defining pornography and erotica and distinguishing between the two. That so many people continue to struggle with these definitions and distinctions attests to the critical importance of differentiating explicit sexual content, on the one hand, from negative and harmful depictions of women, on the other.

The elusive term **pornography** comes from the classical Greek *pornographos,* meaning the writing (sketching) of harlots (Tong, 1982). Modern dictionaries tend to define pornography as materials specifically intended to arouse sexual desire. Generally, defining characteristics of pornography also include one or more of the following elements: Its primary intention is to produce sexual arousal; it is usually produced for commercial (as opposed to artistic or educational) purposes; it objectifies people by reducing its targets, typically women, but also gay men, children, and animals, to their genitals and other body parts; it appears to condone or even endorse sexual desires and behaviors that are demeaning to or abusive of its targets; and it sexualizes power inequalities among people through sexist, racist, and homophobic depictions. *Erotica* is often defined as what pornography is not: it is seen as artistic expression with no specific intent to arouse sexual responses; it depicts the body or sexual acts with respect, portraying consensual and mutually satisfying acts among equals; and it is free of sexism, racism, homophobia, and other forms of discrimination.

It is an often-repeated phrase that "one man's erotica is another man's pornography" (Russell, 1993), and indeed the distinctions between erotica and pornography can be problematic, especially when applied to particular cases. As Brod (1995) suggests, erotica and pornography are probably best seen as the poles of a continuum, with gray areas in between. Increasingly, however, there is recognition that the key to identifying sexually explicit material as porno-

graphic is its sexist or discriminatory stance toward its targets—its degrading or abusive portrayal of female sexuality.

In part because of the different definitions of pornography, the different ways questions are phrased, and the explosion of new outlets for pornographic material, such as the Internet and cable television, surveys of the use of pornography offer varying estimates of adult exposure. *The Hite Report on Male Sexuality* (Hite, 1981), a nonscientific survey, suggested that 89 percent of men report some involvement with pornography. A representative survey of 600 midwestern adults found that over 90 percent of the men and women had been exposed to pornographic magazines, over 90 percent having seen at least one sexually oriented R-rated film, and 69 percent of men and women having seen an X-rated film (Bryant & Brown, 1989). Before the emergence of the Internet as a major force in pornography, the readership of the six most popular pornographic magazines alone was as high as 52 million people per year (Russell, 1993). All the evidence suggests that exposure to pornography among women and men is on the rise, especially given the availability of pornography on the Internet, as we see in Box 12.6. In the new millennium, younger and younger people are surfing the Internet for sexual images, movies, and websites that allow viewers to see aspects of someone's intimate life, as well as information about local massage parlors, lap dancing, and escort services.

Cultural Significance of Pornography

On one level, the question of what makes pornography so popular among men and, increasingly, among women does not appear very complex. After all, people are sexually motivated, and yet societies throughout the world, historically and presently, have sought to restrict sexual expression. Even in relatively open societies such as the United States and other Western countries, willing sexual partners are not readily available for many people, even for those in otherwise close and loving relationships. According to some scholars, widespread conditions of sexual desire thwarted by typical conditions of sexual scarcity give rise to the overwhelming popularity of pornography (Steinberg, 1993). Although explanations of

BOX 12.6

Pornography on the Internet

The accessibility and anonymity of the Internet has contributed to a mind-boggling array of sex-related topics, from incest and pedophilia to bestiality and mutilation in a sexual context. Online porn or cybersex is one of the most profitable businesses on the Internet, accounting for sales that range from $370 million to $1 billion a year (McAnulty & Burnette, 2004). Every day, at least 4 million people use the more than 50,000 sexually explicit sites (Webb, 2001). Nearly 44 percent of college students admit having accessed pornography on the Internet (Goodson, McCormick, & Evans, 2001).

The majority of those who visit sexually explicit websites are males, and there are sex differences in how sexually oriented sites are used. Men are more likely than women to seek visual material, whereas women prefer sexy chat rooms (McAnulty & Burnette, 2004). Most people who access porn websites are occasional visitors, but almost 10 percent of the visitors are compulsive in their use of these websites, spending hours a week on porn sites, and reporting that Internet surfing has caused some problems in their lives (Cooper, Scherer, Boies, & Gordon, 1999).

the sources of the sex difference vary, it is generally agreed that the experience of high sexual drive coupled with sexual scarcity describes men better than women. To explain why a much greater proportion of pornography is geared toward heterosexual males than females, sociobiological and evolutionary psychology theorists appeal to the greater (inborn) sex drive of males. On the other hand, sociocultural theorists explain this imbalance in terms of the different socialization messages that men and women receive about sex, with boys and men taught to pursue sexual success ("scoring") and girls and women taught to limit sexual accessibility to a single highly desirable and committed partner.

Several investigators have noted the similarities between the content of commercial pornography and male sexual fantasies. As Leitenberg and Henning (1995) have noted, the fantasy being portrayed in most pornography is primarily the male fantasy of multiple female sexual partners always ready for sexual activity of any kind without any chance of the man being rejected. According to Steinberg (1993), pornographic images that address the scarcity of sex partners and male desire for appreciation and reciprocation of desire, specifically those that convey female lust and female expression of male desirability, account for over 75 percent of all pornography.

Thus, currently available pornography, created overwhelmingly by and for males and most specifically for male masturbation and fantasy enhance-

ment, casts a particularly male gaze on sexuality. It treats the sexes fundamentally differently and unequally. Women are more likely than men to be portrayed as victims of violence or aggression in pornography, as injured, tortured, bleeding, bruised, or hurt. Other forms of sexism are even more common. Women more often than men are depicted in scenarios of degradation, as inferior or debased. It is typical in pornography for male orgasm to be the mark of success—and end point—of a sexual encounter. Female orgasm is less commonly depicted and is rarely the point of sexual activity. Overwhelmingly, women featured in pornography are younger and more physically attractive than their male counterparts, more passive and sexually submissive. They are chiefly valued for these characteristics.

Effects of Pornography on Women and Men

Many social, political, and legal commentators who have written about pornography have pondered whether it is morally wrong or morally neutral and inherently harmful or not harmful to women. As scientists, psychologists empirically study the consequences of exposure to pornography on people's attitudes and behaviors.

Most of the psychological research on the effects of pornography to date has focused on its impact on the aggressive behavior of men against women. Malamuth, Donnerstein, and their associates have conducted a series of carefully controlled laboratory studies on the effects of exposure to pornographic movies on college men. They have found it useful to distinguish between *aggressive pornography* or *sexually violent mass media images,* in which victims are often portrayed as deriving pleasure from a sexual assault, on the one hand, and nonviolent sexually explicit material, on the other, and much of their research compares reactions to these two broad classes of materials. Research by Malamuth and his colleagues (Malamuth, 1981; Malamuth & Check, 1983; Malamuth & Donnerstein, 1982) consistently shows that college men show evidence of increased sexual arousal to video images of rape, particularly when the female victim exhibits signs of pleasure and arousal. Aggressive pornography in which the female victim shows a positive reaction while being raped tends to change men's attitudes toward rape: That is, it produces less sensitivity to the harm of rape, more acceptance of rape myths (such as the mistaken idea that most women secretly wish to be raped), and an increase in men's self-reported likelihood of committing rape (Donnerstein & Linz, 1993, 1995). More than half of the college men who had been exposed to violent pornography expressed some likelihood of raping a woman if they knew they would not be caught (Donnerstein, 1983; Malamuth, Haber, & Feshback, 1980). In an important series of laboratory studies, Donnerstein and his associates demonstrated that exposure to violent pornography actually increases aggression against women (measured by willingness to shock a female student) (Donnerstein & Berkowitz, 1982).

More recent studies have examined more varied effects of repeated or long-term exposure to sexually violent mass media portrayals. One major study exposed college men in experimental groups to ten hours (five films over five days) of films that differed in their levels of violence and sexual explicitness. One significant finding suggested that over the course of five days, men exposed to aggressive pornography rated the material as less degrading to women and more humorous and enjoyable. They expressed greater willingness to see this kind of material again. These men were also more likely than those in a control group (that saw no film) to rate a rape victim as

more worthless and her injury less severe. These kinds of effects were not found for men who were exposed to sexually explicit, nonviolent films (Linz, Donnerstein, & Penrod, 1984).

This research strongly suggests a potentially harmful effect of sexualized (and nonsexualized) aggression against women, but few harmful effects of merely sexually explicit material. In fact, more research attention is now being given to the possibly harmful effects of nonaggressive pornography. Zillman and Bryant (1982, 1984) have conducted some of the few studies of nonaggressive pornography that examine the effects of long-term exposure to material and the responses of women as well as men. They found that long-term exposure to nonaggressive pornography caused both undergraduate women and men to (1) express more tolerance of sexually violent pornography, (2) become less supportive of statements espousing sexual equality, and (3) become more lenient in assigning punishment to a rapist depicted in a newspaper account. Moreover, extensive exposure to nonaggressive pornography significantly increased men's sexual callousness toward women. Men's increased lack of sensitivity toward rape persisted for at least three weeks after exposure. It is important to note, however, that long-term exposure to nonviolent pornography did not increase, and in fact decreased, men's aggressive behavior (Donnerstein & Linz, 1993). The recent explosion of pornography on the Internet, with the attendant concerns of parents, policy makers, and other advocacy groups, adds urgency to this discussion.

Obviously, much research remains to be done on the effects of pornography. The critical question of whether pornography is a major cause of violence against women in the real world remains unanswered and hotly debated. The effects of long-term exposure of pornography in real-world settings need to be explored further. An increasing number of women are exposed to pornography and erotica, and there are too few studies of the effects of pornography on women and on couples. Some new studies suggest that a significant minority of women, about one third, are very distressed by their partners' use of pornography on the Internet, especially if it is hidden from them and perceived as heavy (e.g., Bridges,

Bergner, & Hesson-McInnis, 2003). One such woman wrote this about her husband's use of pornography:

> *"[My husband] was going online constantly without letting me know. I hated it. He watches [pornography] tapes without me too . . . and magazines . . . you name it. It makes me feel really fat and ugly and like he'd rather masturbate to those images than have the real thing sometimes . . . I find it degrading to think that he's turned on by those women more, but on the other hand if he invited me in to watch a movie I wouldn't hate it so much . . . It's almost like he's cheating on me. A terrible feeling" (Member, Expecting mother's chat group) (Bridges, Bergner, Hesson-McInnis, 2003, p. 1).*

Educational efforts aimed at reducing the harmful effects of pornography need to be developed and evaluated. Special populations such as judges, police officers, doctors, and lawyers, on the one hand, and men who rape and assault women, on the other hand, may require specific research attention and intervention efforts. Teenagers are another important understudied group. But it is clear that psychologists can add much to the debate in our society about the effects of pornography.

OTHER FORMS OF GENDERED VIOLENCE AND EXPLOITATION

In many other arenas, unequal power relations between the sexes or among groups defined by their sexuality have harmful consequences for less powerful groups. In this section, we will briefly consider some of these: prostitution, anti-gay violence, female infanticide, female genital mutilation, and elder abuse. For the most part, psychology has only begun to contribute to an understanding of the causes and effects of these cases of gendered violence or exploitation.

Prostitution

Prostitution, or the exchange of sex for money, gifts, and favors, was first brought into the public discourse in the United States and Europe in the eighteenth and nineteenth centuries. At that time, it became subject to control and regulation by the medical and legal professions. Prostitutes were widely condemned as sources of physical and moral disease and subjected

to vice campaigns in which they were treated and examined for diseases and imprisoned as lawbreakers (Lorber, 1994). To this day, prostitution remains a socially stigmatized activity and a sign of debased moral identity virtually everywhere. Although it is legal in some countries (e.g., the Netherlands), it is usually an illegal way of making money.

Most prostitutes are girls and women, but boys and young men also offer sex for money. Prostitution is a gendered problem because, overwhelmingly, the people who buy sex are men, and it is men who control the trade wherever it is practiced. That is, men working as pimps and traffickers often set the conditions of employment or inservitude, reap the profits, and maintain tight control over the lives of prostitutes.

Some feminists argue that the very word *prostitute* is problematic because of its moralistic and stigmatized qualities, and advocate the substitution of the term *sex worker.* Margo St. James, for example, has campaigned to treat prostitution as freely chosen work (Lorber, 1994). Others suggest that prostitutes are not exploited by men, but rather exploit men's sexual interest in women. More commonly, however, the position is taken that prostitution is intrinsically sexually exploitive because it exists in societies in which women have less power and fewer resources, opportunities, and employment options than men.

Research strongly suggests that prostitution is not a freely chosen activity for the girls, boys, women, and men who engage in it. Studies show that prostitutes in the United States and Canada often begin their careers as adolescents, before meaningful choice is possible, and they are almost always manipulated if not coerced into this lifestyle by adults, often drug dealers, gangs, and pimps, on whom they are dependent. Child prostitution is on the rise, especially in the Third World and eastern Europe, where poverty, chaos, and porous borders have turned prostitution into a global growth industry. Disproportionately, prostitutes are found to come from the ranks of sexually abused children, runaway and homeless children, and drug addicts (Graham & Wish, 1994; Yates, MacKenzie, Pennbridge, & Swofford, 1991). It is associated with multiple drug abuse, depression, suicide attempts, and dissociative disorders, including multiple personality (Ross, Anderson, Herber, & Norton, 1990; Yates et al., 1991).

As Overall concludes, it may make sense to defend prostitutes' entitlement to do their work and thereby earn more money than they would otherwise, but it makes less sense to defend prostitution as a practice in societies characterized by widespread gender inequality (Overall, 1992).

Anti-Gay Violence

Recent surveys suggest that roughly two-thirds of people in the United States condemn same-sex sexual behavior as morally wrong or sinful. Many heterosexuals in the United States also reject gay people at the personal level, with only 45 percent stating that they "wouldn't mind" working around gay people (Herek, 1995). At the same time that there is widespread condemnation and avoidance of gay men and lesbians, people in the United States are increasingly reluctant to condone discrimination on the basis of sexual orientation and increasingly believe that gay men and women should have equal rights in terms of job opportunities (Colasanto, 1989). The brutal murder of a young gay man, Matthew Shepard, in Wyoming in 1998 brought the problem of *homophobia*—the intense and illogical fear of lesbians and gay men, along with negative and hostile reactions to gay people—into sharp relief. There were countless vigils for Matthew Shepard throughout the United States, bringing people of all ages, political parties, sexual orientations, and religious affiliations together in genuine grief and anger. A year later, Private First Class Barry Winchell was bludgeoned to death with a baseball bat while serving on a military base in Kentucky, an incident that brought homophobia and heterosexism in the military to the fore.

Despite survey evidence suggesting that women and men have become more tolerant about homosexuality over time, gay people still suffer discrimination, social ostracism, and physical violence because they are gay. One survey of 125 gay and lesbian college students indicated that 26 percent had been verbally insulted once and 50 percent twice or more, 26 percent had been threatened with physical violence, 17 percent had suffered property damage, and six respondents had experienced extreme violence. Most respondents reported that they expected harassment in the future and were driven to conceal their sexual orientation. Nearly half reported making specific life changes intended to decrease discrimination, harassment, and violence (D'Augelli, 1989).

Herek has offered a comprehensive model for understanding the causes of anti-gay violence and harassment based on a form of bias called *heterosexism* (Herek, 1995). **Heterosexism** is an ideological system that denies, denigrates, and stigmatizes any non-heterosexual form of behavior, identity, relationship, or community. It has two variations: cultural and psychological. *Cultural* or *institutional heterosexism* is pervasive in U.S. society and is seen in societal customs and institutions that render homosexuality invisible and, when it becomes visible, reprehensible. *Psychological heterosexism* is evident in individuals' attitudes and actions. Because of the interplay of cultural and psychological heterosexism, gay men and lesbians are frequently the targets of violence and exploitation. According to Herek, some people hold anti-gay attitudes and engage in anti-gay actions because they are functional; that is, they serve a purpose in people's lives. For instance, some anti-gay crimes serve an experimental function by enabling the attacker to make sense of negative past experiences with gay people. Others serve an expressive function by enabling attackers to feel better about their own groups and maintain status and affiliation with their peers. Anti-gay assaults are a means for some young men to affirm their heterosexuality or masculinity by attacking someone who represents an unacceptable aspect of their own personalities (e.g., homoerotic feelings or effeminate tendencies).

Herek believes that anti-gay attitudes and actions will diminish when they become dysfunctional, that is, when they no longer serve a purpose in people's lives, such as ego defense. This involves determining what psychological functions are served by a person's feelings or behavior and then intervening by helping individuals meet their needs in other, less destructive ways. Individual anti-gay attitudes and behaviors will become dysfunctional when they are no longer supported by religious and political institutions, and when they are not integral to society's images of sexuality and gender.

Recently, some investigators have argued that homophobia and heterosexism affect heterosexuals as well as lesbians and gay men, because they enforce traditional, rigid gender roles that limit the range of acceptable behaviors for all people (Garnets, 2004; Hyde & Jaffe, 2000). As Garnets suggests, a heterosexual woman may shun the label feminist or avoid mentioning that she is a member of a certain organization because she is afraid that she will be labeled a lesbian. Fear of being labeled gay can keep people from forming friendships or displaying affection for their friends, high prices to pay indeed.

Female Infanticide

Perhaps nowhere is the tragedy of gender inequality more evident than in the widespread practice of female infanticide: the killing of baby girls because they are girls. Throughout history, cultural, religious, social, and economic forces have served to devalue the lives of females. In almost all societies, this devaluation has lead to the widespread preference for male children. In some societies, the devaluation of females has led to more dire consequences for females: selective abortion of female fetuses, severe neglect of female babies relative to males, and murder of female babies.

Societies in which female infanticide is practiced vary in their characteristics but appear to have some features in common. In an exploratory study of female infanticide among the Kallar of Tamil Nadu, India, researchers identified the following reasons for the continuance of this practice: relatively low value placed on human life, perceived need for military strength against competing villages, marriage patterns that place heavy financial burdens on the bride's family, and a religious emphasis on the importance of sons (Krishnaswamky, 1984). Among the Canadian and North Alaskan Inuit (Eskimo) culture, it has been estimated that at various times between 15 and 50 percent of female babies are murdered (Schrire & Steiger, 1974). Female infanticide among Eskimos is commonly seen as economically based, with female children viewed as unproductive consumers who do not hunt and leave home to marry as soon as they reach an age at which they might be productive.

The sex ratios of men to women are deeply skewed in favor of men in today's China and parts of India. In China, economic practices and inheritance laws that strongly favor males and a traditional preference for sons, combined with China's restrictive one-child policy, have had devastating consequences for females. National surveys conducted in China indicate that 111 males are born for every 100 females, compared to a normal level of 106 males per 100 females (Hull, 1990). This means that more than 500,000 female babies are unaccounted for in China every year. There are probably several reasons for this reported sex imbalance, including selective abortions of females fetuses and the underreporting of females who were safely born and are still alive but are concealed from health care and school systems by parents who want sons. But a major factor in the missing females is infanticide (Herbert, 1997; Hull, 1990).

In northern India, the long-standing sex ratio imbalance in favor of males has reached a level that is becoming a major societal concern. After 20 years of taking "advantage of a mixture of technology and tradition to bear the child of their choice," some regions in India now have sex ratios of children as extreme as 750 girls to 1,000 boys (Rhode, 2003, p. 3). In India, there are sex imbalances favoring males among older people as well, with contributing factors being maternal mortality, suttee—the cultural practice of a wife immolating herself on her deceased husband's funeral pyre—murder, dowry murder, and forced suicide (Freed & Freed, 1989). There is obviously great potential for social upheaval and tragedy in imbalances this great. For example, it is not clear how societies that value marriage and family as much as China and India do will cope with the problem that will arise when boys of today reach marriageable age and cannot find mates. All the explanations for the sex ratio imbalances in favor of males throughout the world pose major challenges to the life, health, safety, and welfare of girls and women.

The Case of Female Genital Mutilation

An estimated 85 million to 114 million girls and women throughout the world are genitally mutilated; that is, they have undergone a procedure in which their clitorises are removed (clitoridectomy) or, more radically, the clitoris and surrounding tissues of the labia minora and the inner layers of the labia majora are excised, and the labia majora, the outer lips of the vagina, are stitched together to cover the urethral and vaginal openings (infibulation), with a small aperture to permit the flow of urine and menstrual blood and to allow intercourse. Before or during delivery of a child, an infibulated woman is "opened" to allow the passage of the baby.

Most of these girls and women live in Africa, where female genital mutilation (FGM) is found in at least 28 different countries (Abusharaf, 1998). Some live in the Middle East and parts of Asia. Increasingly, African immigrants migrate to the United States, Canada, and Europe, where they sometimes seek the procedure for themselves or their daughters (Toubia, 1993).

In the eyes of many scholars and activists around the globe, FGM is an extreme and outrageous example of efforts common in some societies to "suppress women's sexuality, ensure their subjugation and control their reproductive functions" (Toubia, 1993, p. 5). After decades of commentary and debate about this practice, a consensus has been reached among scholars, medical practitioners, policy makers, and women's health advocates throughout the world about the need to eliminate this practice. We treat this issue in Chapter 3, which explores cultural aspects of FGM, and Chapter 14, which discusses the historical use of clitoridectomy in England and the United States to control sexual impulses and other presumed mental disorders in women. We address it here because FGM is an important form of violence against women. Indeed, as an institutionalized form of violence against women that is tolerated by governments, encouraged if not enforced by culture, and represented—falsely—as sanctioned by religion, it is particularly problematic. As a practice, it is often brutal, conducted without anesthesia, in unsanitary conditions, using surgical implements such as knives, razor blades, or broken bottles wielded by people with no medical training. It leaves survivors vulnerable to numerous medical complications that can plague them throughout their lives, from recurrent infections to painful intercourse, infertility, and obstructed labor that can cause babies to be born dead or brain damaged (Abusharaf, 1998). As Pulitzer Prize–winning African American novelist

Alice Walker, who decried the practice in her best-selling novel, *Possessing the Secret of Joy,* has noted, "torture is not culture" (Nevid et al., 1995).

Genital cutting is entrenched in local customs and belief systems and is considered essential to women's identity—a primary signifier of chastity, cleanliness, fertility, beauty, and marriagiability. It cannot be meaningfully discussed without understanding indigenous cultures and showing sensitivity to its profound cultural, social, and psychological implications (Abusharaf, 1998). If the practice is to be eradicated, it will have to be done with the cooperation of African, Middle Eastern, and Asian communities, and without the sensationalism, condescension, and other signs of cultural insensitivity sometimes exhibited by Western writers and advocates. Indeed, changes in the acceptability of this practice are already under way in Uganda, among other African countries (Abusharaf, 1998).

Elder Abuse

It is increasingly recognized that in old age both men and women suffer from neglect and maltreatment from their caregivers. The most vulnerable group of elders is people over age 80, the most rapidly expanding age group in the United States. Because 70 to 80 percent of abused and neglected elders are women, maltreatment in old age is largely a female issue (Nadien, 1996).

Nadien (1996) has identified three types of abuse and neglect that dependent elders may suffer. The most commonly reported of these is physical maltreatment, including abusive acts, such as assaulting, shoving, and grabbing, and neglectful acts, such as depriving elders of the food or medicine that they need. Psychological maltreatment is believed to be the most common form of elder abuse, although it often goes unreported (Block & Sinnot, 1979). It includes abusive acts such as verbal aggression, threats, coercion, and ridicule, whereas psychological neglect includes deprivation of needed social acceptance and stimulation. Finally, maltreatment can be material, financial, or legal. Abuses in these areas occur when caregivers misappropriate elders' property or money, and neglect occurs when the elderly are deprived of needed information, legal advice, representation, or social support. Recent research suggests that elderly people who are abused, neglected, or exploited die sooner than same-age peers who are not mistreated, even when other relevant variables are controlled (Lacks et al., 1998).

Maltreatment of elders may be at the hands of adult children and grandchildren, spouses, more distant relatives, or paid home-care workers. In the case of institutionalized elders, there is potential for maltreatment by members of the staff, usually nurses and aides, but sometimes doctors as well. Because of severe stigmatization surrounding this problem, and fear of retaliation and institutionalization, a conspiracy of silence is maintained by victims as well as perpetrators of maltreatment. For these reasons, the

extent of elder abuse is not known (Kosberg, 1988). But if current demographic trends continue, an increasing proportion of Americans will be elderly, with growth most rapid among the "oldest old"—those over 80. With these trends comes an increase in the number of elderly, particularly elderly women, requiring caregiving and vulnerable to maltreatment. As Nadien (1996) suggests, we need to sensitize people to the nature and effects of elder abuse, combat negative stereotypes about the elderly and other effects of ageism, and eliminate the conditions that foster elder maltreatment, including reducing some of the unavoidable sources of stress that accompany elder care.

SUMMARY

In this chapter, we have seen how sexual harassment, rape, partner abuse, child sexual abuse, pornography, prostitution, anti-gay violence, female infanticide, female genital mutilation, and elder abuse can be usefully viewed as gendered forms of violence or exploitation. Although there are many potential causes of each of these problems, we locate the root cause of the oppression of girls and women in their relative lack of power, status, and resources in most societies. This chapter addressed central questions of how gender inequality creates personal and social contexts conducive to exploitation of, and violence against, women and girls. As we argued, the threat, fear, and reality of violence and exploitation change girls' and women's lives in countless ways, limiting their choices, opportunities, and possibilities.

Over the past 30 years, women throughout the world have joined in collective action against violence and exploitation. These actions range widely

from the formation of consciousness-raising groups about domestic violence to public speak-outs against forms of oppression. Women have established educational programs for thousands of law enforcement and health professionals. There are now thousands of organizations providing services around the country to women who have been raped or beaten by their partners. Neighborhood groups have formed networks of refuges, called safe houses or greenlight programs, wherein women attacked in the streets can find safety. Women have worked for legal reforms on many fronts, including changes in rape laws that make it easier for women to report crimes and obtain convictions. These efforts have been extraordinarily successful. But our analysis suggests that deeper societal changes are needed. As long as females are devalued in society relative to men, they will be victims of violence and exploitation by men.

KEY TERMS

Battered women (p. 392)
Date rape (p. 382)
Gender harassment (p. 370)
Heterosexism (p. 406)
Incest (p. 399)
Marital rape (p. 383)
Nonnormative rape (p. 379)

Normative rape (p. 379)
Pornography (p. 402)
Prostitution (p. 405)
Quid pro quo harassment (p. 370)
Rape (p. 379)
Rape myths (p. 387)
Rape trauma syndrome (p. 389)

Seduction theory (p. 399)
Seductive behavior (p. 370)
Sex-role spillover (p. 374)
Sexual abuse of children (p. 398)
Sexual harassment (p. 368)

DISCUSSION QUESTIONS

1. Why is sexual harassment often so difficult to identify in specific situations? Do you think that the context of unequal power relationships in which sexual harassment occurs is critical in defining harassment? Why or why not?

2. Do you think that there can be truly consensual sexual relationships between employers and employees, professors and students?

3. Men are generally far less likely to perceive a behavior as harassing than women are. Why do you think this is so?

4. Relatively few women who are harassed file formal complaints against their harassers. Why is this so?

5. Many women who are raped do not regard themselves as rape victims. Why? Why is it important to know that?

6. What are rape myths? Generate five or six rape myths, and explain how such myths support and maintain rape in a culture.

7. How does the existence of rape influence your thoughts, feelings, and behaviors? How do you think it affects people of the other sex?

8. Do you consider date rape as less serious or severe than other forms of rape? Why or why not?

9. Do you feel that there are circumstances in which a woman "deserves" to be raped, or in which rape is not that serious? If you do, what are those?

10. What images come to your mind when you hear the term *battered woman*? Do you find that you devalue women who have experienced abuse from their partners?

11. Why do you think that people are preoccupied with asking why abused women so often stay in their relationships?

12. Do you think it is possible for a person under the age of 18 to give meaningful consent to an adult at least six years older?

13. Why do you think so little pornography is targeted at and marketed to women?

14. Do you consider pornography a form of sex discrimination? Why or why not?

FURTHER READINGS

American Psychological Association Presidential Task Force. (1996). *Violence and the family: Report of the APA Presidential Task Force on Violence and the Family.* Washington, DC: American Psychological Association.

Donnerstein, E., & Malamuth, N. (1997). Pornography: Its consequences on the observer. In L. B. Schlesinger & E. Revitch (Eds.), *Sexual dynamics of antisocial behavior* (2nd ed., pp. 30–49). Springfield, IL: Thomas.

Dziech, B., & Hawkins, M. (1998). *Sexual harassment in higher education.* New York: Garland.

Funk, R. E. (1993). *Stopping rape: A challenge for men.* Philadelphia: New Society Publishers.

Herek, G. H. (1995). Psychological heterosexism and anti-gay violence: The social psychology of bigotry and bashing. In M. S. Kimmel & M. A. Messner (Eds.), *Men's lives* (3rd ed., pp. 341–353). Boston: Allyn and Bacon.

Maltz, W. (2001). *The sexual healing journey: A guide for survivors of sexual abuse.* New York: Harper Perennial.

Sipe, A. W. R. (1995). *Sex, priests, and power. Anatomy of a crisis.* New York: Brunner/Mazel.

CHAPTER 13

ISSUES IN MENTAL HEALTH

WITH SIGNIFICANT RESEARCH AND
WRITING CONTRIBUTIONS BY RACHEL GORMAN

The bulimia started the week after we got engaged. He (Charles) put his hand on my waistline and said: Oh, a little bit chubby here, aren't we? That triggered off something in me. And the Camilla thing—I was desperate, desperate.
—From *Diana: Her True Story* by Andrew Morton

Live as domestic a life as possible. Have your child with you all the time. Lie down an hour after each meal. Have but two hours intellectual life a day. And never touch pen, brush or pencil as long as you live.
—S. Weir Mitchell to Charlotte Perkins Gilman on treatment for her depression

But I'm not beautiful like you, I'm beautiful like me.
—Shirley Manson

It is not true that life is one damn thing after another . . . it's the same damn things over and over again.
—Edna St. Vincent Millay

Unfortunately, sometimes people don't hear you until you scream.
—Stefanie Powers

In 1892, only a little more than a century ago, Charlotte Perkins Gilman wrote a fictionalized account of her own treatment for depression in a novel entitled *The Yellow Wallpaper.* Both the illness and the prescribed treatment are understood by the physician—in this case the woman's husband—from a heavily androcentric perspective. The patient is confined to a bedroom with a vertiginous yellow wallpaper, which has all the earmarks of a cell. There is a heavy, immovable bedstead, barred windows, rings on the wall, and a gate at the head of the stairs. Her therapy is the "rest cure," which consists of fresh air, rest, and, to build up her strength, cod liver oil, lots of tonics, ale, wine, and rare meat. But perhaps its most important aspect is the protagonist's incarceration and immobilization. All activity, including even reading, writing, and conversation, is severely curtailed. It is not surprising, then, that instead of achieving the intended remission of symptoms, the "cure" produces the opposite result: The patient experiences a slow descent into "madness" as healthy forms of self-expression are taken from her (Gilman, 1975; Sechzer, Pfafflin, Denmark, Griffin, & Blumenthal, 1996).

The relationship between femininity and "insanity" has a long history that extends today. For over a century, feminists have disapproved of the mental health establishment and its treatment of women (Marecek & Hare-Mustin, 1991). Equating feminity and insanity were not always the conclusions of medical and scientific knowledge but rather "part of a cultural framework in which ideas about femininity and insanity were constructed" (Showalter, 1985). Of great importance to early mental health practitioners was the presumed different causes of madness in females and males. Even though both women and men presented similar symptomatology, the male malady was associated with the economic and intellectual pressures on highly civilized men, whereas the female malady was associated with sexuality and the essential nature of women. Women were considered to be more vulnerable than men and expressed insanity in particularly feminine ways (Showalter, 1985).

The rest cure prescribed for Gilman was one doctor's form of "paternalistic behavioral modification" in which the reality of being mentally ill was made to look so bad that women would be happy to return to their roles as wives and mothers. Women who were insane and who were not middle or upper class had "work therapy," which consisted of work as unpaid servants. However, in general, the medical profession maintained that it was affluent women who were the most vulnerable and susceptible to "madness." Working women and Black women were considered to be robust, in good health, and less susceptible to the same mental health disorders as women in the upper classes.

Another frequently used treatment during this era was based on the idea that insane women had something wrong with their reproductive organs. This resulted in treatments such as electrical stimulation of the uterus, clitoral cauterization, and prescribed weight gain to prevent the ovaries from slipping out of place. Clitoridectomy was used as a cure for masturbation, which was regarded as a disease. (Although illegal in the United States, clitoridectomy is still practiced in some parts of the world. The practice can be found in the United States due to immigration. Clitoridectomy is discussed further in Chapters 3, 12, and 14.) Accounts suggest that women who were institutionalized were forced into social conformity, because their insanity was deemed to result from their disagreeing with their families or husbands. For example, one doctor performed surgical operations on women whose "symptom" was the desire for divorce (Marecek & Hare-Mustin, 1991).

With the rise of neurology in the late nineteenth and early twentieth centuries, women came to be seen by the medical establishment as especially prone to nervous disorders. At this time women were thought to be especially vulnerable to becoming mentally ill because they did not have the mental capacity of men. This risk grew greatly if a woman attempted to better herself through education or too many activities (Ussher, 1992).

As described in Chapter 14, all mature women were considered vulnerable to hysteria, which was believed to originate in the uterus. For instance, the theory of the "wandering womb" developed during this time. This theory postulated that the womb itself wandered through a woman's body, acting as an enormous sponge that sucked energy and intelligence from defenseless women. Insanity became associated with menstruation, pregnancy, and menopause

(Ussher, 1992). Meanwhile, women continued to be seen as responsible for the emotional and moral sustenance of their husband and children. Religious authorities upheld this view by portraying traditional family structure as biblically and biologically ordained. And physicians followed these specified gender roles, especially in assigning different causes for mental disorders to women and men. For example, "uncontrolled passion" as a cause of insanity had a supposedly higher incidence in women. Thus, "woman" became synonymous with "madness."

The middle decades of the twentieth century were dominated by psychoanalysis and its deeply sexist view of women. Psychoanalysis focused on penis envy and the castration complex as central events in female development. Mothers were often blamed for the difficulties and disorders of childhood and adult life. Heterosexuality, marriage, and motherhood were equated with psychological maturity (Marecek & Hare-Mustin, 1991). One of Freud's most famous cases involved his analysis of Dora, a young woman who was brought in for treatment by her father. Dora told Freud about an experience in which a male friend of the family had made sexual advances toward her. When she accused the family friend, both the friend and her father asserted that Dora had imagined the sexual advances. Dora also confided to Freud that she suspected that her father was cheating on his wife with the wife of the family friend, and that this was a motivating factor in her father's willingness to take the friend's side. Freud famously stated that Dora both enjoyed and solicited the attention from the family friend and that Dora was jealous of her father's affair because she was in love with him. This case is one of great contention for feminists, who feel that psychoanalysis is yet another strategy for male control over the female, one that proclaims that the duty of the woman is to embrace sexual submission.

As the twentieth century progressed, new diagnostic techniques were developed, and science made important strides in elucidating the causes and treatment of mental disorders. As urbanization and industrialization spread, the position of women changed, especially after they won the right to vote. Representations of women in medicine, psychiatry, and psychology have similarly changed in ways that are more progressive and less sexist. But although women have made tremendous strides in diverse arenas, gender biases in psychiatry and clinical psychology still persist to this day, and many of the themes discussed earlier remain surprisingly relevant areas of inquiry. As we shall see, construal of symptoms, diagnosis, and reporting are not free from sexism even today.

ISSUES IN DIAGNOSIS

The *Diagnostic and Statistical Manual of Mental Disorders*

The *Diagnostic and Statistical Manual of Mental Disorders (DSM),* published by the American Psychiatric Association, is used by mental health professionals in psychology as well as in psychiatry to categorize symptoms of mental disorder. The most current edition (published in 2000) of the *DSM* is the *DSM-IV-TR.* This stands for the *DSM* (4th edition) *Text Revision.* It is called a text revision because it contains updated information from the DSM-IV, which was published in 1994. The goal of the *DSM* is to define mental disorders in an objective manner so as to remove as much guesswork as possible from diagnosis and to increase reliability. It provides a list and description of mental disorders, each with specific diagnostic code numbers. As such, it is a reference book of mental disorders.

The *DSM-IV-TR* is critical to mental health professionals because it standardizes diagnoses across clinicians and other diagnosticians. Diagnostic categories in medicine and psychology have traditionally provided the language and framework for therapists' judgments and actions. Criteria are supposed to be as objective as possible and based on overt, observable characteristics or self-reports from the person being diagnosed. The DSM is not concerned with causes of disorders or subjective interpretations of disorders. This ensures that agreement in diagnosis is consistent. However, when the criteria from the diagnostic categories outlined in the *DSM* are used, women are much more frequently diagnosed with mental disorders than are men. In particular, women are more likely than men to be diagnosed with anxiety and mood disorders, such as depression, as well as cer-

tain personality disorders (Klonoff, Landrine, & Campbell, 2000). On the other hand, men are more likely to be diagnosed with alcohol and other drug use disorders, and other personality disorders. Why is this?

The Double Standard of Labeling and Diagnosis

Although the DSM is useful for organizational purposes, applying a label to a diagnosis can be inherently problematic. Labels have the effect of putting the spotlight on the individual with the condition rather than on the social context that may have given rise to the disorder. Labeling also groups individuals into broad categories, which tends to magnify their similarities and obscure the unique aspects of their personalities. Because women are more frequently diagnosed with mental disorders than men, they also face a greater likelihood of stigmatization. Many labels carry a stigma, and people who have been labeled with diagnoses of mental disorders may also be the targets of discrimination. A label implying a mental disorder can prevent clinicians from seeing the qualities of a person that are not captured by the label.

Labels can also reduce the respect given to the person by others and the person's own self-esteem. In one experiment, psychotherapists watched a videotape of a man talking about his personal problems. They rated the man's level of adjustment as much less favorable when they were led to believe he was a mental patient than when they believed that he was not (Langer & Abelson, 1974). In another experiment, former mental patients performed more poorly in a social interaction when they believed that the person with whom they were interacting knew that they were once mental patients than when they believed that the person did not know anything about their past (Farina & Felner, 1973).

Additional problems with our current method of labeling lie in the fact that there are significant sex differences in the diagnosis of certain mental disorders. Gender stereotypes shape what is considered normal behavior for women and men. Personality traits equated with mental health are characteristics usually used to describe men, such as being rational, independent, and possessing leadership qualities.

Characteristics that are more common in women, such as being submissive, emotional, and conforming, are considered pathological. This can lead therapists either to trivialize women's problems, as when anxiety and depression are treated dismissively, or to exaggerate them, as when medications such as antidepressants are overprescribed for women (Simoni-Wastila, 1998). There is also concern that different diagnoses will cause a therapist to see clients in a different light. For example, a woman who has suffered sexual abuse, always seeks to be the center of attention, and shows inconsistency in her personal relationships could be diagnosed with histrionic personality disorder, which implies that something is inherently wrong with her. On the other hand, she could be diagnosed with posttraumatic stress disorder, which would imply that something external occurred which led to certain behaviors.

Reporting Bias

Another possibility for the sex differences present in the diagnosis of mental disorders is *reporting bias.* The diagnosis of anxiety and mood disorders depends to an extent on self-report measures. Men's social role dictates that they are supposed to be the "stronger" sex, which may cause them to be less likely to admit distress in an interview or questionnaire. They are also less likely to seek out treatment for mental health problems, leading women to have higher numbers of diagnoses. One line of research that supports this theory uses a scenario in which men and women were both subjected to a stressful situation: an exam at school. Both the men and women exhibited the same physiological levels of stress, but the women reported higher levels of anxiety (Polefrone & Manuck, 1987). Men may also deal with their anxious feelings by suppressing them with drugs or alcohol, whereas women are more likely to express them directly.

MAJOR DIAGNOSTIC CATEGORIES APPLIED TO WOMEN

As we have seen throughout this text, differences between females and males are often most usefully seen as a consequence of biological endowment and psy-

chological and social influences from the time of birth. When examining contributing factors to virtually all psychological disorders, many contemporary investigators advocate the use of the **biopsychosocial model,** which takes into account biological, psychological, and social factors. For those who espouse this model, biological variables, such as genes or hormones, are often considered *susceptibility factors* that place a group, for example, women, at greater risk for a given disorder. In this model, social and other environmental factors are *precipitating factors* that can trigger the disorder in people who are susceptible (Radloff & Rae, 1979). The fact is that in many instances biological, psychological, and social factors are not separable from each other. No one factor is necessarily more basic or more important than another. Rather, biological, psychological and social factors act together, or co-act, to influence the onset and course of a disorder.

One orientation toward women's mental health that has gained force in recent years is an outgrowth of social role theory that posits that women's social position, exposure to poverty and violence, and double duty in workplace and home contribute greatly to their higher levels of mental distress. The very things that lend women's lives such texture and richness— their jobs, families, and other caring relationships— are often significant sources of stress and conflict. Beyond this, women's overall lower social and economic status and other barriers to women's achievement, including various forms of physical and emotional abuse, are enormous sources of strain for many women. For ethnic minority and lesbian women, there are added stresses resulting from bias and discrimination.

Diagnostic categories, however biased they can be in insulating individuals from the social–cultural context and in seemingly "blaming the victim," have also been useful in organizing material on mental disorders. With these caveats in mind, we present some of the major disorders that are diagnosed in women. We will additionally examine disorders that affect women and girls in a perceptibly different way than men and boys. Biases in treatment and diversity issues are also considered. Disorders discussed are depression, eating disorders such as anorexia and bulimia, and anxiety disorders including agoraphobia and post-traumatic stress disorder (PTSD), which are diagnosed much more highly in women. Other disorders that affect women in different ways than men are discussed, such as suicide, parasuicide, personality disorders, and substance abuse.

DEPRESSION

Major **depression** is perhaps the most clinically important mental disorder. It affects about 16 percent of people in the United States over the course of their lifetime. This amounts to about 34 million adults (Bremner et al., 2003). Gender differences in incidence of depression exceed those in any other mental disorder. Typical estimates show that the prevalence of major depression among women is usually between one and one-half to three times that of men (Kessler, 2003; Nolen-Hoeksema & Keita, 2003). It has been estimated that the lifetime prevalence rate for major depressive disorder for women in the United States is 21.3 percent compared to 12.7 percent for men (Kessler, McGonagle, Swartz, Blazer, & Nelson, 1993). This finding is one of the most robust to emerge in well-designed epidemiological studies in the United States (Kessler et al., 1994; Robins & Regier, 1990). Depression has been called the leading cause of disability among women in the world today (Murray & Lopez, 1996).

Sex differences in the incidence of depression emerge in adolescence and continue through adulthood. They also cut across racial and ethnic backgrounds and economic status. The same ratio has been reported in other countries around the world and has been found using a variety of measures of depression. Further, data have shown that in the past few decades, the number of people with depression has increased drastically (Cross-National Collaborative Group, 1992).

A number of factors contribute to depression in both sexes. Men and women obviously differ in both sociocultural and biological factors (Kessler, 2003). But it is more likely that the increased rate of depression in women is due to sociocultural factors than biological factors. For instance, environmental and other stressors such as childhood adversity, social isolation,

and exposure to stressful life experiences may account for the increase. Psychological factors, such as cognitive styles, can also serve to make someone vulnerable to depression (Mazure, Keita, & Blehar, 2002). Before discussing theories of the causes of depression and the factors that contribute to the sex differences in this disorder, let us review the symptoms of depression.

Symptoms

According to the DSM-IV-TR, a major depressive episode consists of a period of at least two weeks during which there is either a depressed mood or the loss of interest or pleasure in nearly all activities (known as anhedonia). A depressed mood is characterized by a variety of symptoms that affect the whole individual; an episode of depression often includes emotional, behavioral, cognitive, and physical components.

Emotional symptoms are experienced as sad or gloomy feelings; feeling tearful, guilty, apathetic, irritable; and anhedonia (inability to experience pleasure). Cognitive symptoms include thoughts of inadequacy, worthlessness, self-blame, and pessimism. These depressed thoughts interfere with normal functioning, so that the individual has trouble concentrating and making decisions. Behavioral symptoms include decreased ability to do ordinary work, neglected personal appearance, decreased social contacts, and sleep disturbance. Many depressed people contemplate suicide (to be discussed later). Physical symptoms include difficulty with digestion, headaches, dizzy spells, fatigue, and pain. Weight gain or loss is also common (*DSM-IV-TR*). One woman describes her depression in stark terms in Box 13.1. See Table 13.1 for symptoms.

Reasons Why More Women Are Diagnosed with Depression

All the reasons that were offered earlier in the chapter for why it is difficult to evaluate the causes of sex differences in mental disorders apply to the case of depression. Men do not seek help as often as women, so they are diagnosed less frequently. *Clinician bias* may be one factor that contributes to the higher diag-

Box 13.1

Depression: I Am Not My Disease

You may not know it to look at me but I suffer from a disease called major depression. I have lived with this disease for most of my life; it defines the way I think about the world and maybe even the way the world looks at me. My disease is treated with medications but they do not make the symptoms go away, they just mask them. The medications distract me from suicidal ideation and thoughts of self-injury enough to get through each day most of the time. If you have ever felt depressed, you may think you can understand the intense feelings of clinical depression and to some extent you just might be able to. But just try to imagine these feelings hanging around all day, every day. Sometimes stronger, sometimes to a lesser extent, but they are always there. Always feeling depressed but unable to define any external reason is frustrating and lends itself to thoughts of suicide. It would be great to just find that

reason; then I might be able to problem-solve it away. I have tried to commit suicide a number of times and have spent considerable time and energy coming up with a plan. I still struggle with thoughts of suicide, but the thoughts cannot kill me. I work very hard to overcome these thoughts every day. Some days are easier than others. I have come to accept on some level that these thoughts and urges will probably never go away. Now I am learning how to redirect the energy spent on planning my death to something more healthful. It's not an easy task, trying to change a mind-set that has been with me for more than 30 years. The thought that I might be able to get through just one day without thinking of suicide is something I strive toward but I also fear. The fear of the unknown, of what will replace the thoughts of suicide. (Personal communication)

TABLE 13.1   Criteria for Depression

TYPE	SYMPTOMS
Mood Components	Loss of interest in activities and people An emotional emptiness or feeling of flatness A lack of responsiveness to the environment
Cognitive Components	Self-blame and reproach Guilt and self-deprecation Hopelessness and helplessness
Other Signs	Psychomotor retardation/agitation Loss of libido Sleep and appetite disturbances

Source: From "Depression in the Young," by D. Moreau, 1996, in *Women and Mental Health. Annals of the Academy of Sciences* (pp. 181–190), edited by J. A. Sechzer, S. M. Pfafflin, F. L. Denmark, A. Griffin, & S. Blumenthal. New York: The New York Academy of Sciences.

nosis of depression in women. Because men are considered to be the stronger sex, clinicians may be less likely to diagnose them with depression. Additionally, symptoms of depression differ in women and men. Women tend to report more emotional symptoms, such as crying and feelings of worthlessness, whereas men report more physical symptoms, such as sleep disorders and loss of sex drive (Oliver & Toner, 1990). Substance abuse and aggressive behavior may mask depression in men (Fausto-Sterling, 1992b). Partially because of this, men are diagnosed much more frequently as having substance abuse problems or antisocial personality disorder, whereas women are diagnosed with depression. As we have argued, all people are prone to gender schemas, women and men, professional and laypeople alike. Therapists have schemas for men that include men being autonomous, assertive, active, and striving, and so are hesitant to diagnose men with depression.

Reporting bias (females' and males' willingness to report depression) poses the question of whether the sex difference in depression is due to differential willingness to self-identify as depressed and seek help for the disorder. This apparently has been discounted as an explanation for the higher incidences of depression among women (Kendler et al., 1997). Kessler (2000b) tested for the number of depressed people in the general population, rather than in a clinical population, and still found that the 2 to 1 female-to-male ratio holds true.

Another line of research that is the subject of great contention is the idea that biological factors are at the heart of sex differences in depression. Because the large discrepancy in instances of depression begins to occur in adolescence, this has led some to raise questions about the role of sex hormones (Kessler, 2003). Additionally, women report mood changes surrounding other life events that include hormone fluctuations such as menstruation and the postpartum period. (Depression occurring postpartum, discussed in Chapter 10, is more widely accepted.) Although some researchers continue to find that biological theories of sex differences are in general persuasive, others view them as irrelevant in contributing to gender differences in instances of depression. Many reviewers state that systematic reviews of the literature show that biology alone cannot explain the great incidence of depression in women (Fivush & Buckner, 2000; Kessler, 2003; Worrell & Remer, 2003). Biological factors certainly contribute to depression in both women and men, but it remains unclear as to whether they affect them differently.

Major Theories and Factors Contributing to Depression

Role Theory. Social factors seem to be particularly salient contributing factors to depression. The *sex-role theory of depression* is that women are not necessarily

more predisposed to depression than men, but that they encounter more stressors in their daily lives that can promote depression (Barnett, Biener, & Baruch, 1987). The main thrust of this theory is that females are more depressed than males due to the higher levels of stress and lower levels of fulfillment they experience in female, as opposed to male, gender roles.

Until adolescence (age 11), the incidence of depression for females and males is about equal. It appears, however, that females have a more difficult time than males during early adolescence, and between the ages of 11 and 13, there is a steep increase in the number of girls with depression. By the age of 15, females are twice as likely to have experienced depression as males (Cyranowski, Frank, Young, & Shear, 2000). While this could be attributed solely to hormonal changes, adolescence is a time when roles and expectations for females and males change drastically, a phenomenon known as **gender intensification** (Hill & Lynch, 1983). Gender intensification refers to the fact that both females and males are increasingly concerned with adhering to female and male gender roles at this age.

The stressors that females encounter during adolescence can foster depression in someone who is biologically susceptible to the disorder. Young girls might face a decrease in their opportunities and choices, whether real or perceived. According to adolescents' own reports, parents restrict girls' more than boys' behaviors and have lower expectations for girls. Girls also feel that if they pursue male-stereotyped activities, such as math or competitive sports, they will be rejected by their peers. Adolescence is also the time when a female's appearance becomes very important and bodily changes accelerate (Nolen-Hoeksema, 2001). For young girls whose appearance deviates significantly from the ideal, adolescence is a particularly tough time, and eating disorders typically begin during this period.

Gender intensification occurs again for young adults who are married. This can be explained by the fact that when a woman is married, especially once she has children, there exists an even greater pressure to fulfill the roles slated for the female gender. Some of the duties involved in the female role include dual responsibilities at home and at work, potential single parenthood, and acting as the primary caregiver for children and aging parents. As we have stated, even in the most egalitarian households, the brunt of housework still falls on the women's shoulders. Housework confers little social power and respect and is boring and monotonous. Even in the workplace, when women have jobs comparable to men, their work is often undervalued. In their relationships, women often have unequal decision-making power. The social pressure on women to be physically attractive and to conform to unrealistic ideals of female beauty is a lifelong burden for many. Taken together, these stresses can be overwhelming and lead to burnout, which in turn leads to depression.

Cognitive Styles

Learned Helplessness. Eminent psychologist Martin Seligman coined the term *learned helplessness* to describe the sense of powerlessness that organisms come to experience when they learn that there is nothing they can do to improve a situation (Seligman & Maier, 1967). In these situations, people and animals often give up trying. Beyond that, they frequently generalize this response to other situations and literally learn to be helpless. One way of looking at the female gender role, with its low status and power, is as training for a sense of helplessness. Many women (and some powerless men) develop a generalized expectation that they cannot control events, that they should not even bother to try, and this situation can lead to the symptoms of depression—lowered motivation, passivity, self-esteem loss, and the inability to see opportunities to control the environment (Nolen-Hoeksema & Jackson, 2001). Over the past 20 years, a great deal of research has linked learned helplessness to the female gender role. For example, one study found that women who had low scores on masculinity ratings were least likely to try to control their environment after participating in a task over which they had little control, fostering learned helplessness (Baucom, 1983).

One particularly pernicious effect of gender roles is that there is a silencing of voice and suppression of anger that are fostered in women. This has been documented as having a negative effect on the emotional development of women (Crawford, Kippax, Onyx, Gault, & Benton, 1992). Women place interpersonal relationships at a higher priority than men do and often at a higher priority than their own happiness.

Expressing anger could potentially disrupt their relationships. Anger is then internalized, and this internalization is correlated with depression (Cox, Stabb, & Hulgus, 2000).

Rumination. There also exists some evidence that the way that females are reared fosters excessive worrying, or *rumination*. Susan Nolen-Hoeksema and her colleagues have proposed that when women are depressed, they are more likely than men to passively focus on the possible causes and consequences of their symptoms of anxiety or disappointment (Nolen-Hoeksema & Jackson, 2001). These ruminations prolong and deepen a negative mood, creating a negative bias that fosters predominately pessimistic ideas and eliminates positive ones. Ruminators are more likely to blame themselves and feel helpless, thus often making their problems more salient and even worse. Women are much more likely than men to use rumination as a coping strategy—to obsess about a negative event over and over again—whereas men are more likely to engage in escapist and avoidant behaviors, distract themselves, or find a solution to the problem than women are (Kohlmann, Weidner, Dotzauer, & Burns, 1997; Lazarus & Folkman, 1984).

Attributional Styles. Another cognitive factor that can increase vulnerability to depression is a *negative attributional* or *explanatory style*. People who have this style of understanding things that happen in their lives focus on interpretations of events and outcomes that represent problems, failures, and shortcomings. They see these problems as more internally caused, uncontrollable, and stable than they really are. Recall that we noted in Chapter 6 that women and men make different attributions for success and failure. Women are more likely to attribute their successes to luck, chance, or effort and their failures to their inabilities than men are, and men are more likely to attribute successes to their abilities, and failures to luck, chance, and lack of effort. Thus, women have a more negative attributional style than men do. Research shows that a negative attributional or explanatory style can interact with stressors to contribute to the development of depression. These cognitive models have received support from experimental studies of adults as well as children (Broderick & Korteland, 2002). These results support the importance of underlying cognitive or motivational states to the development of depressive disorders. In general, girls report experiencing more negative cognitive styles than boys, and more stressors than boys, from early adolescence onward. Thus, the presence of specific, gender-related preexisting cognitive styles in girls can make them more susceptible to depression when they confront the stresses of adolescence (Broderick & Korteland, 2002).

Interpersonal Styles. Some researchers point to sex differences in interpersonal styles as contributing to higher incidences of depression in women. One aspect of interpersonal style that has received a great deal of research attention is the concept of *unmitigated communion.* Unmitigated communion refers to a focus on other people so much that one loses one's sense of self (Helgeson, 1994; Helegeson & Fritz, 1998). According to Helgeson, many women become overly involved in the problems of their friends, partners, and family members, and take on these people's problems as their own. From childhood onward, it appears that there are differences in the importance that females and males place on interpersonal relationships. Whereas some theorists have emphasized that these intimate friendships are a source of empowerment and strength for women, others point to the negative effects of this approach. Some researchers have argued that women may become so involved with others' problems that they actually neglect their own needs and become dependent on others. One study showed that females who scored highly on measures of high interpersonal orientation, which is highly correlated with unmitigated communion, were more vulnerable to depression. Respondents high in interpersonal orientation were more likely than others to endorse such items as "I worry a lot about the people that are close to me" and "It hurts me a lot when people I love are unhappy" (Gore, Aseltine, & Colten, 1993). Because of this, women may also be at higher risk for depression than men when they are involved in problematic relationships or when their relationships end.

Unmitigated communion also can result in troubles in one's marital relationships. Because relationships are thought to be more central to a woman's self-concept than to a man's, women typically feel more responsible than men for making sure that a relationship goes well. This illustrates how women typically give more social support than they receive in a marriage. They may believe that they ought to behave unselfishly in a relationship rather than expressing their own personal preferences. However, marriage can also be a contributing factor to depression in women because women and men tend to have different notions of intimacy. The amount of disclosure and the quality of the relationship may be more central factors to women's self-esteem than to men's. Women tend to define intimacy through the amount of self-disclosure, whereas men might define it through shared activities. Additionally, men may not even view intimacy as a factor of paramount importance (Culp & Beach, 1998).

Sexual and Physical Assault. As we suggested in Chapter 12, due in part to women's lesser power in our society, they are more frequently the victims of traumas, including rape, battery, and sexual harassment. Violence against women has consistently been linked to higher rates of depression in women. Approximately 85 percent of the victims of nonfatal intimate assault are women (Greenfield, Rand, & Craven, 1998). The rate of women experiencing sexual assault is at least twice that of men (Nolen-Hoeksema, 2001). Women who experience other commonly occurring forms of abuse, such as physical abuse and sexual harassment, may experience higher rates of depression as well (Koss, Figueredo, and Prince, 2001).

Many theories connect sexual victimization with depression by looking at the cognitive impact of victimization, which may lead to depression by fostering feelings of helplessness, low self-esteem, self-blame, and feelings of isolation. Such thought processes promote maladaptive change in the central beliefs that give meaning to daily experience (Barker-Collo, Melnyk, & McDonald-Miszczak, 2000).

Male partner abuse is a cause of depression as well. It is the primary cause of injury to women requiring emergency medical treatment. Tragically, it is often repetitive—nearly 1 in 5 abused women has presented for medical treatment of trauma more than 11 times (Stark et al., 1981). Features of the abuse that may exacerbate the traumatic impact of the event include the duration of exposure to abuse, the extent of physical force and physical damage, and the nature or closeness of the relationship to the perpetrator. The psychological impact of rape is also quite severe and is affected by the degree of physical force employed, the use of weapons, and the perceived fear of death or injury (Koss, Koss, & Woodruff, 1991).

Studies show that women molested as children are more likely to have clinical depression at some time in their lives than women who were not molested (Silverman, Reinherz, & Giaconia, 1996). In addition, several studies document a higher incidence of depression among women who have been raped as adolescents or adults. Statistics show that it is more likely for sexual abuse to occur in females under the age of 18 (Tjaden & Thoennes, 1998). One study concluded that victims of childhood sexual abuse were more likely to meet criteria for major depressive disorder and PTSD at age 21, with 44 percent of abuse victims meeting criteria for two or more disorders (Silverman et al., 1996). Female children who experience sexual abuse are more likely to experience abuse again as adults. In fact, sexual assault during childhood has been more consistently linked with depression in adult women than sexual assault that first occurs during adulthood (Cutler & Nolen-Hocksema, 1991).

Rates of sexual assault are between 7 and 19 percent for females and between 3 and 7 percent for males (Cutler & Nolen-Hoeksema, 1991). It has been estimated that one consequence of this disparity is that as much as 35 percent of the sex difference in adult depression can be accounted for by the higher incidence of assault of girls relative to boys (Cutler & Nolen-Hoeksema, 1991). Children and adolescents who have experienced abuse, especially those who have endured repeated abuse over an extended period of time, tend to have inadequately regulated biological responses to stress. Children and adolescents who experience abuse also tend to have pessimistic perspectives on themselves and others, contributing to their vulnerability to depression (Zahn-Waxler, 2000). (See Chapter 14 for details about stress.)

Economic Inequality. The feminization of poverty has become associated with an increase in depression in women (Bogard, Trillo, Schwartz, & Gerstel,

2001). Even though women in the United States reside in one of the wealthiest nations in the world, the economic situations that many women face are becoming more and more problematic. Approximately one-fourth of African American and Latina women live in poverty (U.S. Census Bureau, 2001). Women's lower salaries and status on the job relative to men and the unequal division of household labor that keeps women working a double shift contribute to depression. In addition, the high proportion of single-parent households headed by women, the inadequacy or absence of child-support payments to divorced mothers, and the lack of good and affordable child care all contribute to the incidence of depression among women who are mothers. In fact, poverty is one of the single most consistent correlates of depression for both females and males (Belle & Doucet, 2003).

Women and children comprise nearly 75 percent of U.S. residents living in poverty (National Institute of Mental Health [NIMH], 2000). This low economic status lends itself to many stresses including isolation, uncertainty, and poor access to medical resources. Sadness and low morale are more common among persons with low incomes and those lacking social supports (NIMH, 2000). One study of current and recent welfare recipients found that over one-quarter of the mothers met diagnostic criteria for major depression. Rates of major depression in homeless and housed low-income mothers are about twice as high as in the general population of women (Siefert, Bowman, Heflin, Danziger, & Williams, 2000). Why is this? As has been discussed in Chapter 12, poor women exist in a more threatening and less predictable environment. Many have been physically or sexually abused. Depression has been linked to the experience of humiliating events, which are far more prevalent in the lives of poor women than middle-class women.

Biological Factors in Depression
Hormones.   Hormones fluctuate during the lives of women and men, but have mainly been studied as a cause of depression in women. Medical models maintain that women are particularly at risk for mental disorders, especially depression, during the times when they experience dramatic fluctuations in hormones:

menstruation, pregnancy, the postpregnancy or post-partum period, infertility, and menopause. Female hormones may play a role in some mood fluctuations. But comparative research suggests that they are not the only source of depression or of sex disparities in depression. For example, these hormonal fluctuations cannot account for the increased rates of depression over the past few decades. Additionally, sex differences in depression are not stable across all racial, ethnic, and cultural groups (Root, 1995). Sex differences are less consistent in developing countries than in highly developed countries, such as the United States (Whiffen, 2001).

Sex hormones as a cause of depression is an issue that is embroiled in much controversy. For many biologically oriented researchers, there is a clear link between hormonal fluctuations and female depression. They typically cite the increased rates of depression for women after puberty, as well as the link between mood and the menstrual cycle or reproduction, which seem to suggest a causal role for gonadal or sex hormones. Researchers with a more psychological or sociocultural orientation are quick to point out that it is unclear that depressions occurring during hormonal change are in fact due to the direct effects of hormonal changes on mood (Nolen-Hoeksema, 2001). They cite that these hormonal fluctuations are always accompanied by stressful life events that are the "true" causes of the increased depression. It is nonetheless the case that several forms of depression are labeled according to women's reproductive stages: premenstrual dysphoric disorder, postpartum depression, and menopausal syndrome.

Premenstrual Syndrome (PMS) and Premenstrual Dysphoric Disorder (PMDD).   Over the past two decades much attention has been given to **premenstrual syndrome (PMS)**, a poorly defined condition in which women become more emotionally erratic, irritable, and tired during the few days before menstruation. PMS has proved too vague a term to be of use to researchers. As Joan Chrisler (2000) states:

> *PMS is not a disease. There are no laboratory findings that can discriminate PMS sufferers from nonsufferers. The symptoms of PMS are not specific to it; some are common in men and in premenarcheal girls*

and postmenopausal women. The only clinical sign specific to PMS is that it is generally followed by menstruation. However, there are many menstruating women who don't experience PMS, and some women who don't menstruate complain of PMS. (p. 114)

A more severe form of PMS has captured the interest of researchers in depression and has been included in the research diagnostic criteria as **premenstrual dysphoric disorder (PMDD)** in the *DSM-IV* in 2000. This highlights the fact that some women have very distressing emotional symptoms before their menstrual period (Steiner, Dunn, & Born, 2003). As much as 75 percent of women report mild discomfort associated with the menstrual cycle, but only 3 to 8 percent of women are affected by PMDD (Angst, Sellaro, Merikangas, & Endicott, 2001). Women experiencing PMDD report that symptoms seriously interfere with their daily functioning and relationships. The etiology of PMDD is not known, but increasingly it is thought that normal cyclic ovarian function, rather than hormone imbalance per se, may trigger biochemical changes within the central nervous system that render women vulnerable to mood disorders (Rubinow, Schmidt and Roca, 1998).

Many feminists are concerned that the labeling of PMDD as a mental health problem diminishes all women and defines them as inferior because of their biology. The label suggests they are, at least for part of their cycle, less reliable and more emotional than men. One particular concern is that labels can impact how one perceives one's body. Recent research examined female college students who completed a "Menstrual Joy Questionnaire" or a "Menstrual Distress Questionnaire" prior to discussing menstrual attitudes. The women who had taken the "Menstrual Joy Questionnaire" reported more positive attitudes and stated that they had never before considered that menstruation could bring joy (Chrisler, Johnston, Champagne, & Preston, 1994). This highlights the possibility that discomfort and irritability surrounding menstruation may be related to our societal derogation and stigmatization of the event.

Postpartum Women and Depression.   Postpartum depression is the most common psychological complication of childbearing. Postpartum depression can range from transient "down" feelings to an episode of major depression to postpartum psychosis—a severe, incapacitating, psychotic depression. The "baby blues" occur in 26 to 85 percent of women, depending on the criteria used, and involve irritability and tearfulness that last up to two weeks postpartum (Steiner, Dunn, and Born, 2003). Postpartum depression occurs in 13 percent of women after delivery, which means that nearly a half million women experience this disorder every year (Pop, Essed, de Geus, van Son, & Komproe, 1993). Studies suggest that women who experience major depression after childbirth have often had prior depressive episodes.

Pregnancy and childbirth do have enormous combined psychological, physiological, and endocrine effects on a woman's body and mind. The rapid decline in the levels of reproductive hormones that occurs after delivery is believed to contribute to the development of depression in susceptible women. Because of the timing of postpartum depression, beginning in the first few weeks following delivery and resolving spontaneously within three to six months, there is good reason to think that hormones are implicated in this disorder (Steiner, 1998). Although there is not conclusive evidence for a direct causal relationship between hormones and postpartum moods, strategies for combining pharmacological and psychological treatment modalities are under development for postpartum depression (Miller, 2002).

Although it is tempting to attribute postpartum depression to hormonal decline, several other factors may predispose women to this condition. There may be some legitimacy in the medical model, but the problem with it is that it minimizes psychological, social, and cultural factors. Motherhood brings about profound changes in one's life. Many of the changes can be disruptive and difficult to adjust to, such as recovering from a painful delivery, sleep deprivation, adjusting to one's new role as a mother, and the demands of caring for a newborn (Johnston-Robledo, 2000). Additionally, stressful life events, past episodes of depression (not necessarily related to childbearing), and a family history of mood disorders, all recognized predictors of major depression in women, are also predictors of postpartum depression.

The likelihood of postpartum depression does not appear to be related to a woman's educational level, the sex of her infant, whether she breast-feeds, the mode of delivery, or whether the pregnancy was planned. Women are less likely to experience depression postpartum in cultures that recognize and support the efforts of new mothers (Zelkowitz, 1996). A dissatisfying marriage can also contribute to postpartum depression.

Menopause. It has long been believed that menopause causes depression, increased irritability, and nervousness (Avis, 2003). Women in the general population and clinicians believe that this is the case (Avis, 1996; Cowan, Warren, & Young, 1985), and, as we saw in Chapter 11, menopause in our society generally is considered to be a negative event. There are biomedical and sociological theories that attempt to explain the connection between menopause and changes in mood. Biomedical theories explain that depressed mood is caused by vasomotor symptoms and sleep disturbance associated with declining estrogen levels or that biochemical changes in the brain lead directly to depression (Schmidt & Rubinow, 1991; Stewart & Boydell, 1993). Other theories connect depression in menopause to the life events that coincide with menopause such as children leaving home, increased health problems, and illness and death of aging parents (Dennerstein, Dudley, & Burger, 1997).

Epidemiologic studies do not provide consistent evidence of an association between menopause and depression in the general population (Nicol-Smith, 1996; Pearce, Hawton, & Blake, 1995). Some theorists have found that depression may be related to discomfort resulting from symptoms associated with menopause such as hot flashes, night sweats, and menstrual problems. Studies have found that life stress and negative attitudes about menopause and aging may contribute to depressed feelings surrounding menopause (Nicol-Smith, 1996; Pearce, Hawton, & Blake, 1995). Previously, depression during menopause was considered a unique disorder, but research has shown that depression at menopause is no different than depression at other ages. The women most vulnerable to change-of-life depression are those with a history of past depressive episodes (NIMH, 2000).

Depression among Lesbian Women

Lesbian women are at higher risk for depression and depressive episodes than are straight women. A century of psychological research has assumed that lesbian women and gay men are at risk for "homosexual pathology," based on heterosexist and sexist assumptions about sexual orientation and mental health (Kitzinger, 1999). Increasingly, we recognize that it is homophobia and heterosexism that are problematic and not being gay. It is nonetheless the case that gay and heterosexual people inhabit different worlds and that the experiences of many gay people in our society are enough to cause profound distress in anyone. Possible explanations for higher rates of depression in gay people are the differences in life experiences between gay and heterosexual, or "straight," people, in particular, the harmful effects of heterosexism, homophobia, and anti-gay violence, which can lead to problems with self-image and self-esteem, and internalized homophobia (Cochran & Mays, 2000). Lesbians report a higher rate of substance abuse than is generally found for women (Sprock & Yoder, 1997). Cochran has noted that the mental health field has failed to appreciate lesbians' heightened risk for depression, and possible differences between lesbian and heterosexual women in presentation of symptoms and therapeutic issues (Cochran, 2001).

Aging Women and Depression

Several studies show that most older people feel more satisfied with their lives (Reynolds et al., 1999). Being older in and of itself is not a cause of depression. However, an estimated 10 to 20 percent of older women do experience clinically significant depressive symptoms (Blazer & Koenig, 1996). Rates are especially high for women dealing with the stress of caring for older relatives or family members with severe health problems as well as dementia. Elderly women are also experiencing a great deal of loss. Since women live longer than men and tend to marry men who are older than they are, they are more likely to be widowed. In addition, a number of physical and psychosocial changes

occur as people age, including the discomfort of menopause and the financial changes that occur as a result of retirement, which may negatively affect women. Here, too, mental health professionals have had difficulty recognizing depression because it may be difficult to determine which symptoms result from depression and which might result from health problems, cognitive decline, and dementia. Reciprocal relationships among those factors may also result in under-recognized and under-treated depression (Lebowitz et al., 1997). However, the most important risk factor for the onset and persistence of depression in older women appears to be health problems.

Ethnic Minority Women

Ethnic minority women experience comparable or higher rates of major depression compared with White women (Brown, Barrio, & Abe-Kim, 2003). The confounding of race and other demographic factors, particularly socioeconomic status, makes it difficult to assign a causal role to any one factor. However, it appears that several factors contribute to ethnic minority women's rates of depression. Members of racial minority groups have disproportionately high rates of poverty, which exposes them to chronic strains with fewer resources with which to resolve them (McLeod & Kessler, 1990). Minority women also have two sources of secondclass status in society with which to contend—being minority and being female. Perceived racial and ethnic discrimination has been found to be associated with depressive symptoms and poorer mental health in African American, Latina, Puerto Rican, and Asian American women (Klonoff, Landrine, & Ullman, 1999; Kuo, 1995; Rogler, Cortes, & Malgady, 1991). Additionally, ethnic minority women are diverse with respect to acculturation and immigration. Women who are raised in the United States have often been raised with the pull of culturally diverse social environments. Immigrants, on the other hand, have left the culture that provided a context for their behavior and self-schemas (Vega & Rumbaut, 1991).

A number of factors make it difficult to contrast rates of depression, including that cultural differences may obscure or exaggerate people's problems. Symptoms often present differently in people from different ethnic groups, and clinicians may be likely to underdiagnose depression in minority populations. For example, African American women with major depression reported greater impairment in physical functioning than have White women (Brown, Schulberg, & Madonia, 1996). A disorder found in Korean American women that corresponds closely with the diagnosis of major depressive disorder, called *hwa-byung,* includes symptoms such as constriction in the chest, heart palpitations, hot flashes, headache, dysphoria, anxiety, and irritability (Lin et al., 1992). These types of symptoms may make it more likely for sufferers to dismiss psychological factors as contributors to the problems and may make it less likely for them to seek psychological treatment.

Treatment for Depression

The most commonly used treatments for depression are psychotherapy, antidepressant medication, or a combination of the two. In general, more people are getting help for major depression than ever before, which might indicate that the stigmas associated with the disorder may be receding. However, while more people are getting help for depression, only a small percentage of those people are getting adequate help for their condition. Part of the problem is that antidepressant medications take several weeks to work, and that patients become frustrated with waiting for the medication to work or with the side effects, and decide to drop out of treatment (Windham, 2003).

Psychotherapy helps patients to gain insight into and resolve their problems through verbal interactions with their therapist. There are many different schools of thought concerning psychotherapy with depression, some of which can be difficult to test empirically. Controlled clinical trials have provided strong evidence for the efficacy of interpersonal and cognitive–behavioral interventions, as well as structured behavioral marital and family therapies (Hollon, Thase, & Markowitz, 2002). Interpersonal therapy attempts to change interpersonal relationships that may contribute to and worsen depression, and **cognitive–behavioral therapy** aims to help patients change negative styles of thinking and behaving that may contribute to depression.

There is little indication in the empirical literature to date that there are sex differences in responsiveness to type of psychotherapy (Hollon, in Summit, 2000); however, few studies have looked explicitly for sex differences in treatment for depression (Gorman & Rabinowitz, 2004). Regardless, psychotherapy is an effective way to treat women with depression (Hollon in Summit, 2000).

There have been many studies that validate the efficacy of antidepressant medication as a means for treating depression. Antidepressant medication does not cure depression, but it helps people to feel better by controlling certain symptoms. The most commonly used antidepressants are selective serotonin reuptake inhibiters (SSRIs). Their precursors, tricyclic antidepressants (TCAs) or monoamine oxidase inhibitors (MAOIs), are still used as a second-line choice. SSRIs increase the amount of the neurotransmitter serotonin in the brain, a chemical most scientists believe may affect depression and other mental conditions. Other neurotransmitters that are thought to play a role in depression are norepinephrine and dopamine.

New evidence is demonstrating that there are sex differences in the response to antidepressants (Yonkers, 2003). The differences may result from sex differences in endogenous central nervous system levels of serotonin (Nishizawa et al., 1997). Serotonin, which we have noted, is implicated as a cause of depression. This hypothesis is consistent with findings that women with chronic depression respond preferentially to SSRIs and men to tricyclics (Kornstein et al., 2001). Hormonal treatments are emerging as possible treatments for women experiencing perimenopausal and, as we have indicated, postpartum depression (Gregoire, Kumar, Everitt, Henderson, & Studd, 1996).

EATING DISORDERS

Weight, eating, and body image are issues of major concern for women in our society. Being thin is equated with attractiveness, and many women spend a great deal of time thinking about monitoring their food intake. Women who are overweight tend to be stigmatized in our society. Many women have body image problems and concern about eating, characterized by severe dieting and exercising. In some cases, this can lead to eating disorders such as anorexia and bulimia. So common is the concern about weight in this society, and so ubiquitous are diets and other weight loss schemas, that we find it useful to think of eating disorders not as discrete pathologies that are qualitatively different from normal behavior (Pike & Striegel-Moore, 1997). Rather, eating disorders exist on a continuum, with "normal" eating on one pole and disordered eating on the other. It is not clearly understood how and why a person loses control of her or his eating habits and comes to suffer from an eating disorder.

That said, eating disorders are real, treatable medical conditions in which certain maladaptive patterns of eating take on a life of their own. The main types of eating disorders are anorexia and bulimia. A third type, binge-eating disorder, has also been suggested (*DSM-IV-TR*). All of these disorders are much more frequently diagnosed in females than in males. Only an estimated 5 to 15 percent of people with anorexia or bulimia and an estimated 35 percent of those with binge-eating disorder are male (Andersen, 1995; Spitzer et al., 1992). These disorders typically develop during adolescence or early adulthood, though recent reports indicate that their onset is also occurring in childhood or later adulthood. See Box 13.2 for a personal communication regarding eating disorders.

Anorexia Nervosa

Anorexia nervosa is characterized by a refusal to maintain a minimally normal body weight. Often anorexia nervosa begins with the desire to be attractive and thin. Individuals will lose the desired amount of weight, but become involved in a destructive cycle in which they make their diets more and more restrictive. In industrialized societies, statistics show that one out of 100 young women suffers from anorexia. Over 90 percent of anorexics are females, and the usual age of onset is between 13 and 25 (Sokol & Gray, 1998).

Four basic criteria are associated with anorexia according to the *DSM-IV-TR*: (1) Individuals cannot maintain an appropriate minimum body weight for their height and age. Body weight less than 85 per-

---

BOX 13.2

Food Is The Enemy

Food is my enemy and I battle it every day. At the age of 16 I began my battle with food. It began with the typical teenage desire to lose weight; just a few pounds and everything will be OK. I started with restricting my intake of food; initially I did not eat for 3 weeks, just low calorie fluids and pickles were allowed. Then I allowed myself a whopping 500 calories a day, anything more resulting in purging (vomiting and laxatives) and increased exercise for a few days. I kept count of calories in a daily journal. In the journal I also kept tabs on the exercises I had done for the day and the amount of calories burned. In a matter of months I went from an initial weight of 125 lbs to my all time low of 85 lbs. I had 3 grand mal seizures due to my low body weight, lost my menstrual cycle, and was putting my life at risk. I was hospitalized for the seizures but never for my eating disorder. While an inpatient, a psychiatrist evaluated me but I knew how to play the game. I promised to follow up with counseling when discharged but never even made the initial appointment. By the third seizure the doctors were threatening me with intravenous feeding so I caved and began eating. This brought my weight back to an acceptable number but my battle had just begun. I despised the fact that everyone around me was monitoring my food intake. My eating disorder began to change; I began the ritual of eating and purging. I continued this for a number of years. My weight remained fairly stable and everyone began to leave me alone. As a result of my eating behaviors my metabolism is messed up. I can go for weeks without eating and not lose any weight—this is no exaggeration. Eating a "normal" amount of food causes me to gain weight. I have gained a lot of weight due to some of the medications that I have been on and now find myself overweight. This is truly a nightmare for me. I am having a hard time coping with the fact that I am overweight yet am still considered to have an eating disorder. When I hear someone say that they have an eating disorder, my initial reaction is to give her/him the "once over," and of course my first thought is that she/he is not that skinny. I don't think that others truly believe that I have an eating disorder because of my current weight. (Personal communication)

cent of expected weight is problematic. (2) Individuals have intense fear of becoming fat, even though they are already underweight. (3) Individuals think that they are fat (body distortion) and weight loss is not acknowledged. (4) Three consecutive periods are missed. See Table 13.2.

Anorexia nervosa is characterized by a pathological fear of obesity and intentional starvation. There is often a rapid weight loss of at least 25 percent of total body weight and 15 percent below the normal weight for one's age, height, and sex (American Psychiatric Association [APA], 1994). People diagnosed with anorexia see themselves as overweight even when they are dangerously thin. They may obsessively check their body weight and may use other means than food restriction to control their weight, such as obsessive exercise. Additionally, people who have anorexia often become very isolated and do not have many friends. They are preoccupied with hiding the behavior of watching their weight. One female describes her relationship with her anorexic suite mate at college, who, at 5 foot 2 inches, weighed 90 pounds.

> My friend would exercise three or four times a day, but would lie about it to her friends. She would get up before anyone else and go running, and then come back to the suite and pretend to be getting out of bed when everyone else was getting up. Then later on in the day she would announce that she needed to go for a run because she hadn't exercised in so long. She would always make up excuses to skip meals, and when she did eat, she was very concerned with the purity and clean-

TABLE 13.2 *DSM-IV-TR* Criteria for Anorexia Nervosa

1. Refusal to maintain body weight at or above a minimally normal weight for age and height.
2. Intense fear of gaining weight.
3. Disturbance in the way in which one's body weight and shape are experienced; undue influence of body weight on self-evaluation; or denial of the seriousness of current low body weight.
4. Amenorrhea (absence of menstrual cycle).

Source: Reprinted with permission from the *Diagnostic and Statistical Manual of Mental Disorders,* Text Revision, copyright 2000. American Psychiatric Association.

liness of her food. Often times if we were around campus late at night, we would see her running around the track in the dark. We gradually felt more distant and disconnected from her. (Personal communication)

People with anorexia also develop unusual relationships with food. They may avoid meals or spend excessive amounts of time choosing food and portioning out their meals. An anorexic person diets compulsively and may develop ritualistic behaviors surrounding eating and food. This compulsive diet is the result of a phobia of gaining any weight. The anorexic's body view is so severely distorted that she cannot tell that she is extremely thin and may describe herself as fat. In one study, females with anorexia were asked to draw their bodies, and all drew distorted versions of themselves in which they appeared much heavier than they actually were (Penner, Thompson, & Coovert, 1991).

The rapid and excessive loss of weight in anorexia can cause severe health complications. Starvation resulting from anorexia can result in heart disease, low blood pressure, kidney failure, or cardiac arrhythmias due to low body levels of electrolytes, which can result in death (Halmi, 1996; Penner et al., 1991). Anorexia is an extremely difficult disorder to treat because anorexics refuse to acknowledge that they have a problem. Some may recover after one episode, but for others, anorexia is a chronic condition. However, for those who do not recover, anorexia can be life threatening at its most severe state, and many anorexics may die later on in their lives because of complications resulting from their disease.

No other psychiatric disorder in women has a higher death rate than anorexia nervosa. The mortality rate among people with anorexia has been estimated at 0.56 percent per year, which is about 12 times higher than the annual death rate due to all causes of death among females ages 15 to 24 in the general population (NIMH, 2001).

Bulimia Nervosa

An estimated 1.1 to 4.2 percent of females have **bulimia nervosa** during their lives (APA Work Group on Eating Disorders, 2000). At least 90 percent of individuals with bulimia are female, and the disorder is

TABLE 13.3 *DSM-IV-TR* Criteria for Bulimia Nervosa

1. Recurrent episodes of binge eating with a sense of lack of control.
2. Recurrent use of inappropriate compensatory behavior to avoid weight gain (self-induced vomiting, laxative abuse, diuretic abuse).
3. A minimum average of two episodes of binge eating and two inappropriate compensatory behaviors a week for at least three months.
4. Self-evaluation is unduly influenced by body shape and weight.
5. The person does not meet the criteria for anorexia nervosa.

Source: Reprinted with permission from the *Diagnostic and Statistical Manual of Mental Disorders,* Text Revision, copyright 2000. American Psychiatric Association.

particularly prevalent on college campuses (Heffernan, 1998). Bulimia occurs at least five times more often than anorexia. Bulimia is also primarily found in women, though the age of onset of bulimia is slightly older than for anorexia (Pike & Striegel-Moore, 1997). See Table 13.3 for symptoms.

Bulimia is manifest by repeated episodes of binge eating, which is characterized by consumption of an excessive amount of food within a discrete period of time and by a sense of lack of control over eating during that episode. This is followed by inappropriate compensatory behaviors such as self-induced vomiting; misuse of laxatives, diuretics, or other medications; fasting; or excessive exercise. Those suffering from bulimia share the same dissatisfaction with their bodies as do those who are suffering from anorexia. They fear gaining weight and desire to be thinner. Often they are embarrassed by their behavior but feel a need to purge anyway. They purge in secret and feel very relieved afterward. See Box 13.3.

There are two subtypes of bulimics—those who binge and purge with recurrent self-induced vomiting, and those who binge but who do not purge regularly and instead diet and exercise vigorously (Pike & Striegel-Moore, 1997). The latter group seems to have less anxiety about eating and have less body image disturbance. The typical binger–purger will gorge on food, sometimes ingesting more than 4,000 calories at one time. Before the calories are absorbed into the

BOX 13.3

What Can We Do?

We don't know what to do. Do we say something, or not say something. She piles the pasta on her plate. We know what is going to happen. She doesn't try to hide it from us. We go shopping. The next morning all the food is gone, it's awful. We used to hear the wretching. Now we will smell something bad. We go in her room and find the bags of vomit in her drawers. It's awful. Sometimes it's crusted on the toilet seat or the vanity. I guess she plans to take the bags out and forgets. The phone doesn't ring much anymore. She doesn't seem to have as many friends as she did. (Personal communication)

body, vomiting is induced or laxatives are taken. These people continue to lose weight even though they spend hours gorging on food. However, someone who has been diagnosed with bulimia is often of average weight, which can be distinguished from an anorexic person, who is severely underweight (Siegel, Brisman, & Weinshel, 1997). Bulimia may cause numerous health problems affecting the gastrointestinal tract, heart, and liver and may also affect metabolism and cause erosion of dental enamel from the acids in vomit (Mitchell, 1995). It is usually not as life threatening as anorexia but can be equally as difficult to treat.

Binge-Eating Disorder

Binge-eating disorder is characterized by episodes of consuming an excessive amount of food within a discrete period of time and by a sense of lack of control over eating during that period. There are no attempts, as in bulimia, to get rid of the excess weight through purging (Marcus, 1995). The ratio for binge eating disorder is about 2.5:1 female to male, making the ratio still skewed in favor of women, but not nearly as much as the previous two disorders (Spitzer et al., 1992).

People with this disorder are often very isolated and are morbidly obese. Those with this disorder might feel very hurt or alone and abandoned. They want to relieve these feelings, so early in the day they might plan to binge that evening. On the way home from work they might stop at the store and buy donuts, cookies, ice cream, whatever it is that they like to eat. In the evening, by themselves, they often binge for several hours until they eventually feel numb and pass out. People with this disorder also eat faster than normal and eat alone because they do not feel good about the amount of food they have consumed. They feel disgusted, depressed, or guilty after overeating.

Binge-eating disorder is a relatively new concept. It was listed in the *DSM-IV-TR* as a category that needs further studying. There have been few studies on binge-eating disorder, but it appears that people with the disorder have higher rates of lifetime psychiatric disorders as do their families. The onset of binge-eating disorder is later in life than the onset for anorexia and bulimia. However, binge eaters tend to make a favorable recovery—much more so than those with anorexia or bulimia (Fairburn, Cooper, Doll, Normal, & O'Connor, 2000).

Demographics of Those with Eating Disorders

Age.   Anorexia and bulimia are seen now in younger and younger females. Girls as young as fifth grade are showing evidence of eating disorders and discussing with their peers the need to diet and be thinner. As children are growing up, they see their mothers' attempts to diet and exercise in order to remain thin with notes about "fat," "calories," and "carbs" attached to the refrigerator. Conversations about how not to gain

weight and what foods are the lowest in calories are all too frequent. Many children are brought up on diet foods (e.g., skim or 1 percent milk instead of whole milk, diet salad dressing, fat-free cookies and ice cream), further emphasizing the parents' preoccupation with weight. Such patterns serve as models for growing girls. Statistics show that two-thirds to three-fourths of high school girls in the United States are concerned with their weight and diet despite being of normal weight or underweight. Subgroups of women in which weight is particularly important, such as dancers, models, and professional athletes show higher rates of eating disorders than the average population (O'Mahoney and Hollwey, 1995). See Box 13.4.

Race and Class Issues.   Anorexia is a problem of industrialized nations, where obtaining food is not an issue. Previously, and to some extent still today, the typical anorexic woman was White and upper middle class. The desire for thinness was associated with higher income and higher social class. Recently, however, eating disorders have increased among women of color (Ofosu, Lafreniere, & Senn, 1998). For example, one study found that both European American and Asian American female college students reported that they were heavier than they actually were (Mintz & Kashubeck, 1999). Acculturation into the middle class seems to be a major contributor to disordered eating for ethnic minority women. One study that analyzed trends of Latina and Asian women who visited

---

BOX 13.4

"Flawless" Dancer in the Mirror

On payday, a group of ballerinas would go to their favorite pastry shop and gorge themselves on rich pastries and coffee. On returning to the ballet theater, they entered the bathroom and, in each cubicle, faced forward over the toilet and induced vomiting by pushing their fingers down into their throats. There was immediate relief that there would be no weight gain from their eating adventure.

This same pattern was repeated week after week without any apparent concern or recognition of the seriousness of this behavior.

The young woman who related this story to me said she was certain that many of these women did have guilt about their behavior but felt it was an easy way to maintain their weight as was required, even mandated, by the ballet master. She was so astounded at this recurring paradigm and became so frightened that she might be very vulnerable to this "seductive" method of weight control that she left the ballet and attended college. She is now an architect and interior designer. In working out her interest in ballet she frequently consults for ballet and opera companies on their scenic designs. (Personal communication)

health clinics found that those who had symptoms of anorexia, bulimia, or binge-eating disorder were more likely than their peers with other symptoms to speak English and to have mothers and fathers who were born in the United States (Cachelin, Veisel, Barzegarnazani, & Striegel-Moore, 2000). Other research also points to the social perspectives on women's weight from ones' country of origin. One study found that women who were from the Dominican Republic did not value thinness in the same way as a woman from an upper-class family in Argentina (Thompson, 1994). Hence, social class, country of origin, current residence, and level of acculturation all seem to contribute to how women perceive their bodies.

Studies show that Black women are less likely than White women to report dieting and vomiting, but equally or more likely to report binge eating. The lower reports of dieting and vomiting have been thought to reflect a lower risk for Black women of developing anorexia or bulimia (Striegel-Moore & Smolak, 1996). In general, Black women are more satisfied with their body image than are White women. Both Black females and males seem to prefer average-weight women over thin women. However, in recent years, the numbers of Black women with body image dissatisfaction and eating disorders seems to be on the upswing (Grant et al., 1999). Some studies seem to suggest that Black women are as preoccupied with their weight as White women, but that their preferred weight is simply higher than that of White women (Pomerleau, Zucker, & Stewart, 2001).

Gender.   We are now beginning to see eating disorders more frequently in men. Anorexia and bulimia are more common in male athletes such as wrestlers or jockeys, whose weight is important. Sexual orientation is also related to eating disorders in men; eating disorders are more common among gay men than straight men. Gay men also show higher body dissatisfaction than straight men. The same factors that are predictors of eating disorders in women, such as body dissatisfaction, are predictors for gay men (Andersen, 1995).

Risk Factors for Eating Disorders

There are many theories as to what factors cause eating disorders. Sexual abuse and trauma seem to be common in women suffering from eating disorders and can serve as triggers for women who are predisposed to the disorders. Other life stressors such as starting a new school or a new job, the breakup of a relationship, or even a critical comment from a friend can cause disordered eating. There is also some evidence to suggest that girls who mature early are at higher risks for developing eating disorders. Female development includes the development of breasts and hips, which may be perceived as being "fat" in comparison to their peers (Jacobi et al., 2004). There is often comorbidity between eating disorders and other psychiatric disorders, such as depression, substance abuse, and anxiety disorders.

The "Culture of Thinness."   The "culture of thinness" is a significant contributing factor to eating disorders. Culture of thinness refers to the extreme pressures on women to be thin. Societal pressures that lead women to diet increase their vulnerability to developing an eating disorder (Cooper, 1995). One recent study has found that 60 percent of high school aged females and over 80 percent of women in undergraduate universities are not satisfied with their bodies (Spitzer, 1999). Moreover, there is evidence that models and actresses are thinner now than ever before. For instance, although the average size of women has increased from the 1950s to the 1990s, the weight of *Playboy* centerfolds and Miss America contestants decreased during this time period. Strikingly, approximately a third of *Playboy* centerfolds meet the BMI (body mass index) criterion for anorexia (Spitzer, 1999).

The discrepancy between actual women and women in the media is getting larger. Every day, women encounter glamorous images of thin women. Thinness is equated with attractiveness, and the message is that if a woman is not thin, she should be. A recent study by Peggy Chin Evans (2003) found that women associate a thin female body type with success in life. This association seems to contribute to women's negative feelings about themselves after they compare themselves to "ideal" women. Results from her study suggest that women report more dissatisfaction about themselves and their futures after exposure to a "thin-ideal female."

It is often suggested that the mass media are the most pervasive distributors of sociocultural standards for thinness and beauty, many of which are impossible for average women to attain (Thompson & Heinberg, 1999). For example, 83 percent of teenage girls report spending 4.3 hours a week reading magazines, and most of these girls regard these magazines as important sources of beauty information. One study (Nichter & Vuckovic, 1994) asked teenage girls to describe their ideal female: She was 5 foot 7 inches, 100 pounds, and a size 5 with long blond hair and blue eyes. A woman of this size would be in the anorexic and amenorrheic range. Studies also have shown that girls who watched more than eight hours of television shows such as soap operas or music videos had higher rates of body dissatisfaction than other girls. Furthermore, when high school and college-aged women were exposed to photographs of models, they reported depression, stress, guilt, shame, insecurity, and body image dissatisfaction that was not evident for controls who were shown photos of average-sized women (Stice & Shaw, 1994). Another disorder which consists of a preoccupation with imagined or slight defects in one's appearance is called *body dysmorphic disorder* (BDD). In men, this often manifests itself as a disorder in which no matter how big and strong they are, they perceive themselves as small and weak.

Psychological and Sociological Factors.

One psychological theory of eating disorders is that they stem from feelings of a lack of autonomy, a lack of control, and a lack of sense of self, coupled with a desire for perfection and achievement (Rolls, Fedoroff, & Guthrie, 1991). Controlling weight loss and food intake is one way for sufferers to feel in control and to contribute to a sense of achievement. Eating disorders might emerge during adolescence because it is a tumultuous time characterized by feelings of loss of control, becoming very concerned with others' perceptions of them, and becoming aware of the limitations of the female gender role with respect to achievement. One way to deal with these stresses is to exert control over one's body and weight (Silverstein & Perlick, 1995).

Those who have eating disorders have been described as *perfectionistic*. They often set unrealistic standards for their appearance and try to meet the expectations that they or others have set for them (Smith, 1996). Obviously, not all perfectionists develop eating disorders. It is a vulnerability that, com-

bined with the proper stressor, leads to the development of an eating disorder. Perfectionists, though, see the world in black and white, so they see only two options for their bodies, thin or fat. Often, the cycle begins when a woman compares herself to others or sets impossibly high standards for her weight. She begins to feel badly about herself when she cannot meet her expectations. To escape from feeling badly and to feel that she can control the situation, she might begin to purge, exercise excessively, or heavily monitor her eating. These are very directed activities toward which perfectionistic people can focus all of their energy to make themselves feel better momentarily.

Eating disorders have also been linked with a high need for others' approval and a desire to please others. A psychoanalytic perspective describes that as girls grow up, they do not want to disappoint their families by no longer being the "little girl" in the family. Anorexia prevents young women from having to deal with puberty, "becoming a woman," and what this means in their family's and society's eyes. Eating disorders also are a means of expressing anger and frustration without explicitly verbalizing it. Disordered individuals instead internalize their negative feelings and take it out on themselves by controlling their eating or binging and purging.

Undoubtedly, biological factors play a role in the development of eating disorders. Eating disorders often run in families, which may signal a genetic link. Twin studies have shown higher rates of concordance among identical twins (56 percent) compared to fraternal twins (7 percent) (Fichter & Noegel, 1990). People with a mother or sister who has had anorexia nervosa are more likely than others with no history of that disorder to develop it themselves (Strober et al., 2000). When one identical twin has bulimia, the other twin is eight times more likely to develop bulimia than someone from the general population (Kendler et al., 1991). Those whose family members do not develop an eating disorder have a greater likelihood of developing other psychiatric problems (Nagel & Jones, 1992). Although these rates could result from genetic factors, they also may be a product of a shared environment. Families who are overly concerned about weight and appearance may contribute to their daughter's developing an eating disorder. Additionally, a mother's attitude about eating and about her own body can impact her daughter. Thus, a familial connection to eating disorders exists, either through genes, shared environment, or inherited personality traits. One therapist relates how this familial component affected her client:

> One adult bulimic describes how she grew up in a very wealthy and powerful family in a small town. Her mother always felt that the family was on display, and she was very concerned with her daughter's weight. Her older sister was sent to a "fat" camp even though she wasn't fat, and her mother was constantly monitoring her weight and offering her sugar free and fat free alternatives. Now as an adult, she vomits and uses laxatives to control her weight. (Personal communication)

Being surrounded by friends who are overly concerned about their weight, or having a girlfriend or boyfriend who is pressuring you to be thin, can also encourage eating disorders. It appears that bulimia in particular, is influenced by friendship networks and social norms (Pike, 1995). One study that examined eating behavior in a sorority showed that members' binging behaviors were correlated. As the school year went on, the girls became closer, and their behavior influenced each other more and more. The girls who binged the most were the most popular, and girls who originally did not binge as much increased their binging behavior so that it was more similar to that of the popular girls (Pike, 1995).

Treatment Patterns for Anorexia and Bulimia

Anorexia is one of the most difficult disorders to treat because people with anorexia usually see nothing wrong with their continued dieting or will not admit that they are ill. People with eating disorders may strongly resist getting and staying in treatment. Anorexics are particularly resolute, resisting changes in their behavior.

One example is a woman in her late forties who is 5 feet 5 inches and weighs 78 pounds. She is completely convinced that this is a healthy weight for her. Her bones stick out sharply, and she cannot even sit down on a hard surface because it hurts. When she eats she immediately gets cold because all of her blood is used for digestion, and so she has to stand under a heat

lamp. People stare at her wherever she goes. However, she responds negatively and with hostility to criticisms, appeals, and even warnings of the consequences of her behavior. This is often the case especially when criticisms come from anorexics' families. Unfortunately, such people frequently drop out of treatment (Szmuckler, Eislet, Russell, & Dare, 1985).

A multifaceted program for treatment of anorexia is necessary to achieve any success. Such a program includes medical treatment and behavioral, cognitive, and individual as well as family therapy (Halmi, 1994). Nutritional counseling and, when appropriate, psychopharmaceuticals may be helpful. However, there is an immediate need to treat the patient's emaciation and restore her nutritional state. Until some measure of normal nutrient status is achieved, psychotherapy, regardless of the approach, is extremely difficult due to the patient's psychological symptoms of **emaciation** (15 to 25 percent underweight): irritability, depression, continuing preoccupation with food, and sleep disturbances. Severely anorexic emaciated patients almost always require medical treatment and should be hospitalized (Halmi, 1994). Intravenous feeding may be necessary. The first phase must always include restoring the weight that was lost through the severe dieting. The second phase is treating the underlying psychological issues that contributed to the body image issues, such as low self-esteem or interpersonal conflicts.

Cognitive therapy for anorexia, first reported by Garner and Bemis (1982), is another approach to treatment. It involves assessing distorted cognition: the patient's feelings of low self-worth, poor body image, and the perception that the only way she can be effective is by dieting and losing weight. With behavior therapy, a critical concern is that behavioral treatment in a hospital setting may not carry over to the family situation (Garfinckel & Garner, 1982). Age is important in any treatment decision because patients under 18 fare best in family therapy, but patients older than 18 have not been found to benefit. Medication (antidepressants) may be needed as an adjunct to therapy (Russell, Szmuckler, & Dare, 1987).

Multifaceted treatment has also been carried out with bulimics, who can usually be treated as outpatients rather than being hospitalized, as is so frequently necessary with emaciated anorexics. A combination of cognitive–behavioral therapy and medication (e.g., antidepressants) seems to be the most effective, with the particular combination depending on the individual patient (Agras et al., 1992; McCann and Agras, 1990).

In both anorexia and bulimia there are frequent relapses. Weight gained in the hospital is difficult to maintain. Decreasing episodes of binging and especially purging requires constant self-monitoring, and this is very arduous for the recovering patient. Long-term remission and/or full recovery are possibilities, although positive outcomes are more likely with early diagnosis and treatment. Certain SSRIs have been shown to be beneficial for maintaining positive mood and weight maintenance.

ANXIETY DISORDERS

Anxiety disorders include phobias, panic disorder, generalized anxiety disorder, agoraphobia, and PTSD. A person with an anxiety disorder experiences persistent anxiety that causes intense suffering. The anxiety is irrational, uncontrollable, and disruptive. Anxiety disorders have both cognitive and physical components that are maladaptive, disrupting everyday activities, moods, and thought processes. Certain anxiety disorders such as specific phobias, panic disorder, and generalized anxiety disorder affect women more than men. They are discussed first because they are believed to have similar causes. Agoraphobia is discussed separately because it shows the largest sex gap of all anxiety disorders. Finally, posttraumatic stress disorder (PTSD) is discussed. Women do not necessarily experience PTSD more than men do, but the events that precipitate PTSD in women are particularly gendered (National Institutes of Health [NIH] Anxiety Disorders, 2002).

Specific Phobias and Panic Disorders

More than twice as many women as men suffer from specific phobias (Narrow, Rae, & Regier, 1988). A phobia is an intense, irrational fear triggered by a specific object or situation. When someone encounters the object or situation, a panic attack can ensue. **Panic attacks** are sudden episodes of extreme anxiety that escalate in intensity and are accompanied by severe physical symptoms such as pounding heart, rapid breathing, breathlessness, and a choking sensation. Additionally, the person may experience sweating, trembling, lightheadedness, chills, or hot flashes. People experiencing a panic attack sometimes feel as though they are losing their minds or on the verge of death (APA, 1994). Panic disorder affects about 2.4 million adult Americans and is twice as common in women as in men (Robins & Regier, 1991). People with panic disorder have feelings of terror that strike suddenly and repeatedly with no warning. They cannot predict when a panic attack will occur, and may develop intense anxiety between episodes, worrying when and where the next one will strike (NIH, 2002).

Generalized Anxiety Disorder

Generalized anxiety disorder (GAD) affects 4 million adult Americans and about twice as many women as men (Robins & Regier, 1991). It is characterized by a constant anticipation of disaster, worrying excessively about health, money, family, or work. The source of the anxiety can be hard to pinpoint. Sometimes just the thought of getting through the day provokes anxiety. People with GAD cannot seem to shake their concerns, even though they usually realize that their anxiety is more intense than the situation warrants. Their worries are accompanied by physical symptoms, especially fatigue, headaches, muscle tension, muscle aches, difficulty swallowing, trembling, twitching, irritability, sweating, and hot flashes (NIMH, 2002).

Possible Causes of Phobias and Generalized Anxiety Disorder. One potential explanation for the gender difference in anxiety disorders is that our society is less tolerant of fear in males than in females. Socialization for males promotes conquering fears, whereas women are socialized to avoid their fears (Gelfond, 1991). Women are also more likely to admit that they feel anxious or fearful. Some studies suggest that sex differences may exist because of this reporting bias (Richardson, 1991), but most researchers believe that sex differences in phobic avoidance are real (Schmidt & Koselka, 2000).

Other theories deal with the ways that males and females react to internal and external situational cues.

A possible explanation for the sex difference is that females may possess great reactivity, which could provide a greater opportunity for developing fear-of-arousal symptoms. Males more accurately perceive physiological changes than females and may be less likely to catastrophize about the meaning of these symptoms. Additionally, females may be more prone to focus on external cues in the context of fear, thereby creating increased estimations of panic likelihood across various situations (Schmidt & Koselka, 2000).

Agoraphobia

When panic results in phobic avoidance, the diagnosis becomes agoraphobia, which literally means "fear of the marketplace." Agoraphobia is a particularly debilitating phobia that occurs mainly in women. It often occurs concurrently with panic disorder, and women are diagnosed with this dual disorder three times as often as men (American Psychiatric Association, 1994). Crowds, standing in line, stores, or riding on a bus may trigger fears of agoraphobia. Because of this, those suffering from the disorder often become prisoners in their own homes. Agoraphobia can be triggered by a person having panic attacks; once the panic attacks start, those affected may fear that they will have one in a place where there is no means of escape (Arrindell et al., 2003). This concern leads to agoraphobia.

Agoraphobia receives the most attention of all the phobias from feminist researchers and clinicians, in part because it is so debilitating, but also because it seems to reflect a disadvantage in the female gender role (McHugh, 2000). Most theories positing the cause of agoraphobia focus on female role theory. Gender-role socialization often encourages girls from a young age to stay close to home and discourages venturing out in the world (Gelfond, 1991). Especially as young girls grow up, traditional societal mores promote dependency, shaping their behavior and aspirations by deemphasizing autonomy and mastery while fostering expectations of protection and guidance. Agoraphobics tend to display, sometimes in rather extreme ways, aspects of the feminine role: unassertiveness, compliant and dependent behavior, difficulty in expressing anger, and passive approaches to interpersonal problems. Boys, on the other hand, experience socialization that entails reinforcement for quite different behavior: Males are expected to be independent, confronting, and instrumental in their approach to the world (Fodor, 1974). This may be an important factor in understanding the different rates of agoraphobia.

A spin-off of role theory is that it is the lack of masculine traits in women rather than an intensification of feminine traits that results in high agoraphobic levels. Some societies offer both females and males greater opportunities for the fulfillment of multiple social roles. Arrindell et al. (2003) undertook a study that examined whether societies that provide females and males with equal opportunities for attaining mastery over their lives, as opposed to those that offer these possibilities to women at a lesser extent, would report lower levels of agoraphobic fears. It was found that countries where gender roles were very rigid and stereotyped, such as Japan, had higher rates of agoraphobic fear levels. Societies exemplified by Sweden, where it is acceptable for females to display characteristics of the masculine gender role and for men to display characteristics of the feminine gender role, showed the lowest rates of agoraphobia (Arindell et al., 2003).

Other theories focus on the relationship between agoraphobia and marital status. Some researchers state that marriage increases the instances of agoraphobia because it promotes the stereotypical women's role, including helplessness and dependency. A woman who is afraid to leave her own home also serves to allay her husband's anxieties about what she might be doing when she is out on her own. A related theory states that the conflict of dealing with the differences in role expectations for females in private versus public spaces may trigger agoraphobia (McHugh, 2000).

Gelfond (1991) states that the more we learn about the fears of women with agoraphobia, the more we can understand about the fears of women in our society in general. In fact, some researchers question whether there is really a qualitative difference between women with agoraphobia and those without the symptoms. They suggest that there is a continuum for these symptoms, and many of them occur among a wide range of women (Gelfond, 1991).

Posttraumatic Stress Disorder

Posttraumatic stress disorder (PTSD) is an anxiety disorder that results from an extreme physical or psychological trauma that produces intense feelings of helplessness. PTSD first became known as a disorder that affects war veterans, but recently, it is seen to result from many traumatic experiences. Women are more likely to develop PTSD than men (Davidson, 2000). Women who have been assaulted often show symptoms of PTSD. Symptoms include frequently recalling the event, avoiding stimuli or situations that tend to trigger memories of the experience, a general numbing of emotional responsiveness, and increased physical arousal associated with anxiety. PTSD can often cause depression, and comorbidity between substance abuse and PTSD is very common. This is extremely common among women who have been abused by their partners, women who have had childhood abuse, and refugee women. A random sample of women revealed that over 12 percent met the criteria for PTSD, a much higher percentage than previous estimates (Resnick, Kilpatrick, Walsh, & Veronen, 1993). For an example of how someone feels when experiencing PTSD, see Box 13.5.

A recent event that precipitated PTSD in many people was the September 11, 2001, terrorist attacks. Major studies which assessed the immediate mental health effects of the terrorist attacks found that posttraumatic stress disorder was one of the most pervasive public health problems resulting from the attacks (City Health Information, 2003; Schuster et al., 2002; Galea et al., 2003). However, it is interesting to note that stress reactions varied significantly according to sex, with more female respondents reporting stress reactions compared with males. Additionally, females were far more likely to seek out and receive postdisaster treatment than males (Boscarino et al., 2002). An additional study found that even female adolescents were more likely to report greater levels of distress following the attacks than were male adolescents (Foresto, in press).

SUICIDE

Almost 6,000 women ages 15 and older take their own lives annually in the United States, making sui-

---

BOX 13.5

The Stranger in Me

I was raped when I was 25 years old. For a long time, I spoke about the rape as though it was something that happened to someone else. I was aware that it had happened to me, but there was no feeling.

Then I started having flashbacks. They kind of came over me like a splash of water. I would be terrified. Suddenly I was reliving the rape. Every instant was startling. I wasn't aware of anything around me. I was in a bubble, just kind of floating. And it was scary. Having a flashback can wring you out.

The rape happened the week before Thanksgiving, and I can't believe the anxiety and fear I feel every year around the anniversary date. It's as though I've seen a werewolf. I can't relax, can't sleep, don't want to be with anyone. I wonder whether I'll ever be free of this terrible problem.

Source: National Institute of Mental Health, Anxiety Disorders 2002, p. 8.

---

cide the second leading cause of injurious death among women (*Mental Health Weekly Digest,* May 12, 2003). Major depression is implicated as the cause of at least half of all suicides. In addition to depression, suicide is linked to substance abuse. There is a positive correlation between difficult life events, such as ending a relationship or losing one's job, and suicide attempts. The divorce rate is also positively correlated with suicide, as is unemployment (Canetto & Lester, 1995). Suicide attempts and suicidal ideation are frequent for depressed girls and women; in fact, women attempt suicide twice as frequently as men, and the higher rate of attempted suicide is attributed to the elevated rate of mood disorders in women (Wannan & Fombonne, 1998; Hawton, 2000).

Suicide presents an interesting contradiction in that despite women's higher incidences of depression, men succeed in committing suicide at much higher rates. Men complete suicide at a rate four times that of women, yet women are twice as likely to experience major depression (Frierson et al., 2002). In the

United States in 1998, the suicide rate among women was 4.4 per 100,000, whereas for men it was 18.6 per 100,000. These rates hold fairly constant in most countries, with the notable exception of China, where the suicide rate is very high among females (Hawton, 2000). In 2000, suicide by firearms was the most common method for both women and men, accounting for 57 percent of all suicides. However, 80 percent of all firearm suicide deaths are White males (NIMH, 2003). This finding holds across most Western societies.

Why is there this discrepancy in attempted and successful suicides? Many of the theories addressing the discrepancy deal with male and female gender-role theory. One idea is that because it is difficult to classify suicides, some are listed as other causes of death, such as accidents, particularly for women because they use ambiguous and less successful methods. There is also the possibility men's suicide attempts are underreported.

Among men, committing suicide is considered to be a powerful response to some kind of failure; attempting but not completing suicide is often construed as weak behavior and thus is viewed negatively. Males are more likely than females to report being concerned with societal disapproval of suicide, which may explain why their attempts are successful (Canetto & Sakinofsky, 1998).

Women and men will tend to adopt the self-destructive behaviors that are congruent with the gender scripts of their culture (Canetto & Sakinofsky, 1998). The link between suicide and alcohol abuse is stronger in men, and the link between suicide and depression is stronger among women. Men are more likely to try to kill themselves in more violent ways, by using guns or jumping from high places, whereas women are more likely to take pills or try to slit their wrists (NIMH, 2003).

Another factor associated with suicide is a perceived lack of social support. Interpersonal relationships are central to women's self-concept, and those who feel unsatisfied in these relationships are more likely to attempt suicide. Women may also attempt suicide after experiencing abuse. The precipitating life events for women who attempt suicide tend to be interpersonal losses or crises in significant social or family relationships. It is interesting to note that, in the United States, women with professional careers have a higher incidence of suicide than women who are not professionals. For example, the suicide rate for female physicians is much higher than the rates of the general public. This is thought to result from high pressure, a strong sense of isolation, and a lack of support (Robinson, 2003).

Some evidence suggests that young women who commit suicide have an exaggerated need to depend on others. They need to develop a healthy sense of personal control. Female adolescents who try to kill themselves are very dissatisfied with their personal relationships. However, other theories suggest that women's lower numbers of completed suicide may have to do with their better social relationships and greater connectedness. They may have more of a network to help support them during difficult times in life, which may insulate them from suicide.

PARASUICIDE AND SELF-MUTILATION

Parasuicidal behavior is self-harmful or destructive behavior without the intent to kill oneself. Parasuicidal behavior is *not* a failed suicide attempt. One distinction is that a person who truly attempts suicide seeks to end all feelings, whereas a person who self-harms seeks to "feel better." Although some self-harmful behaviors are very invasive and result in permanent disfigurement, the more common type is superficial self-mutilation. The most common *self-injurious behavior* (SIB) is skin cutting, banging or hitting oneself, pulling out one's hair, and burning of skin (Hawton, Fagg, Simkin, Bole, & Bond, 1997). Parasuicidal behavior is becoming a significant health concern in the United States. Important risk factors include being of a young age, between 15 and 24, and being female. Parasuicidal behavior can be comorbid with many other psychiatric disorders. Additionally, approximately 4 percent of the nonclinical population has reported self-harm (Briere & Gil, 1998). Parasuicidal behavior is often comorbid with *borderline personality disorder,* which primarily affects women (Favazza & Rosenthal, 1993).

There are several reasons cited as to why someone might engage in SIB. A cutter may be experiencing extreme psychological pain that she cannot express verbally. Cutting allows her to focus the pain to one superficial area and to have the illusion that she is controlling the pain. It is seen as a means of releasing tension or expressing pain (Bowen & John, 2001). A psychodynamic perspective on SIB is that the sufferer is internalizing a person close to her, such as her mother. The mother may make her daughter very angry, but the daughter feels that she cannot verbally express her anger. By cutting herself, she is expressing anger and aggression to the internalized mother. One therapist describes a female patient who was a self-cutter. The patient's father was extremely rageful, and the mother was very passive. Whenever the mother tried to point out to the father that he was being aggressive, he would deny it. The patient never had any sort of model for regulating her emotions. When she became frustrated, angry, or upset, she would cut herself. It was the only way that she knew how to regulate her emotions. See Box 13.6 for a perspective on the feelings of release that a cutter might experience.

Once people begin to cut themselves, they also see the reaction that they are getting from others around them, that it makes other people anxious and it makes people pay attention to them. The understanding is that in instances in which SIB is used to elicit desirable behaviors from others in the environment, or used to communicate anger or distress, the reactions of others may also reinforce the behavior

---

Box 13.6

Beneath the Surface

I scratch. I do it when I'm alone, in the bathroom. I do it at dinner, under the table. Anytime. I do it till it bleeds. My ankles, inner thighs, legs, torso. The skin is scarred, and black and blue. Thickened in spots. It bleeds and scars. I know I am doing it. I can't control it. Sometimes I scratch into a frenzy. Actually it feels good. Doesn't hurt. After I feel relieved, relaxed, calm. My OBGyn was so upset, wanted to know what had happened to me down there. I know it's not normal, I just can't stop doing it. (Personal communication)

(Handerwek, Larzelere, Friman, & Mitchell, 1998). There has been considerable research highlighting the communicative quality of certain types of SIB. This is particularly relevant in younger female populations. Teenage incidences occurring within interpersonal contexts are often cited as examples of attempts to influence another person's affection (Collins, 1996).

PERSONALITY DISORDERS

Another dimension of diagnosis in the *DSM* is *personality disorders*. When a person behaves in an inflexible and maladaptive way, she or he may be diagnosed with a personality disorder. Personality disorders are associated with distress and impaired functioning. The *DSM-IV-TR* states that a personality disorder is an enduring pattern of inner experience and behavior that deviates markedly from the expectation of the individual's culture, is pervasive and inflexible, has an onset in adolescence or early adulthood, is stable over time, and leads to distress or impairment (American Psychiatric Association, 1994). Personality disorders are thought to originate during childhood and adolescence when people are taught maladaptive ways to deal with their environment. Three that are frequently diagnosed in women are borderline, dependent, and histrionic personality disorders (American Psychiatric Association, 1994).

Seventy-five percent of those diagnosed with **borderline personality disorder** (BPD) are women. The disorder is characterized by chronic instability in emotions, self-image, and relationships. Moods are uncontrollable, intense, and fluctuate quickly. One experiences pervasive feelings of emptiness and is desperately afraid of abandonment. There is a component of self-destructiveness that accompanies BPD, which is often manifested in parasuicidal behavior. See Box 13.7 for an example.

Dependent personality disorder is also diagnosed more frequently in females than males in clinical settings. Symptoms include great difficulty making everyday decisions. Those diagnosed tend to be passive and to allow other people to take the initiative and assume responsibility for most major areas of their lives. They have difficulty expressing disagreement with other people, especially with those

Box 13.7

The Fight Within

He gets so angry. Says such hurtful things. Awful things about me. It makes me feel so bad. It hurts so much. It's horrible the things he says to me. I feel I must be such an awful person. I had to hurt myself because I was so bad. I must deserve this. It just felt like the right thing to do, I deserved it. I did it. Just pushed the knife into my arm, watched it bleed. It was so weird. I just did it! (Personal communication)

---

on whom they are dependent. Individuals with this disorder are often preoccupied with fears of being left to care for themselves.

Histrionic personality disorder is characterized by pervasive and excessive emotionality and attention-seeking behavior. Those individuals with histrionic personality disorder are uncomfortable or feel unappreciated when they are not the center of attention. The appearance and behavior of individuals with this disorder are often inappropriately sexually provocative or seductive. People may appear overly flamboyant and attention seeking. This disorder is also diagnosed more frequently in females.

The diagnosis of personality disorders has been surrounded by a great deal of controversy. Part of the controversy stems from the fact that personality disorders are very difficult to test empirically. Another problem is that the personality disorders most frequently diagnosed in females are exaggerations of the female gender role, whereas those most frequently applied to males are exaggerations of the male gender role (Walker, 1994). One classic study examined clinicians who were presented with clinical vignettes of females and males with the same personality characteristics. Descriptions of women were found to receive more extreme ratings for histrionic personality disorder, even when the descriptions were identical (Hamilton et al., 1987). These disorders are very difficult to treat in psychotherapy because often the persons suffering from these disorders do not realize there is anything wrong with their behavior.

SUBSTANCE ABUSE

Substance abuse is often considered to be a "male disorder," and the statistics show that in general, it is. In all categories of substance abuse, men outnumber women (Opland, Winters, & Stinchfield, 1995). Because it is considered a male disorder, female abusers run the risk of being ignored or overlooked, or, alternatively, overly pathologized. However, females are unique users. The patterns and effects of substance abuse differ significantly for males and for females. Substance abuse can have significant health repercussions for females.

Substance abuse is characterized by the use of psychoactive substances, such as alcohol, amphetamines, marijuana, cocaine, hallucinogens, opiates, and others, leading to clinically significant impairment or distress manifested by one or more of the following during a 12-month period: (1) substance use resulting in failure to fulfill major role obligations, (2) substance use in situations in which it is physically hazardous, (3) substance-related legal problems, and (4) continued substance use despite having persistent or recurrent social or interpersonal problems caused by the effects of the substance. *Substance dependence* can also be diagnosed; it is less severe than abuse (*DSM-IV-TR*).

Substance abuse is of particular interest because many theorists consider substance abuse and depression to be manifestations of similar feelings. Men are said to be more likely to externalize their problems through delinquency and substance abuse, whereas women are more likely to internalize and manifest symptoms such as depression and low self-esteem. This is consistent with cultural gender-role norms (Huselid & Cooper, 1994).

Alcohol

Alcohol is the most frequently used and abused substance, and men drink more than women in all categories of drinking (USDHHS, 2000). Fourteen percent of men and 5 percent of women between the ages of 15 and 54 meet the criteria for an alcohol abuse disorder. Alcohol consumption is highly correlated with depressed mood. Why are there such significant differences in the use of alcohol between the sexes? For one, there is a double standard about the social acceptability of drinking (Warner, Weber, & Albanes, 1999). One study proposes three theories as to how this originated. The first theory discusses that women are often excluded from areas of public life, especially those related to leisure. The second theory states that women who drink pose a threat to traditional definitions of femininity. The third theory focuses on the linkages that many societies make between drinking and sexual disinhibition (Warner et al., 1999). Many studies show that the social environment is more accepting of male drinkers because drinking is considered a masculine activity. Drinking in females is not as socially acceptable, so women tend to find other outlets rather than substance abuse. Research conducted by Hope Landrine found that consuming alcohol and becoming intoxicated are considered aspects of the traditional male gender role (Landrine, Bardwell, & Dean, 1988). Another proposed theory is that women are more sensitive to the effects of alcohol, so they learn to use it more moderately than men do.

Tobacco

Another substance that is widely abused is tobacco. The number of female smokers is on the rise. In 2002, among youths aged 12 to 17, girls were slightly more likely than boys to smoke (National Survey on Drug Use and Health [NSDH], 2002). Females are also more likely than males to smoke in college. Females are vulnerable to start smoking because of several factors. Many women smoke because they feel that it helps them to maintain their weight. Because of this, restrained eaters are a particularly susceptible group. Unfortunately, tobacco usage can result in serious health problems. Tobacco usage contributes to osteoporosis, cervical cancer, and pregnancy complications. It is estimated that 20 percent of the cases of low birth weight, which is associated with numerous health problems in infancy, can be attributed to maternal cigarette smoking (Camp, Kleges, & Relyea, 1993). About 140,000 American women die each year from diseases related to smoking. It appears that smoking significantly increases the chance of lung cancer, heart disease, and strokes for women more than for men. This is discussed further in Chapter 14.

Other Substance Use

Illegal drug use is also higher among men than women, with men more likely than women to use and abuse drugs such as heroin, amphetamines, cocaine, and marijuana—a pattern that parallels their alcohol use (USDHHS, 2000). Women, however, are more likely than men to use prescription tranquilizers and sedatives. That is, women are more likely to describe symptoms to physicians, which leads to their diagnoses of having mental disorders treatable by drugs. The higher rate of prescription drug use by women and the greater use of illegal drugs by men result in similar rates but different patterns of substance use.

One interesting theory rooted in social role theory states that greater social conformity in women compared to men protects them from use of drugs (Kilbey & Burgermeister, 2001). One study of female marijuana users states that gender roles effectively restrict adolescent females in their access to and use of this particular drug. Sex differences exist because drugs are illegal, and therefore must be obtained through social networks linked to dealers. Women are virtually excluded from these dealing networks because males serve as both dealers and intermediaries. Women often get marijuana and smoke it with their boyfriends. When women do have access to drugs, they are much more likely to use them in a private setting, whereas men are more likely to use them in public (Warner et al., 1999).

Differences in Physiological Responses

Recent surveys indicate that 4.5 million women are alcoholics or abuse alcohol, 3.5 million misuse prescription drugs, and 3.1 million use illegal drugs (CASA, 1996). How do women's and men's physiological responses to drugs and alcohol differ? Women have different body compositions than men, with more body fat and less fluid, so their bodies react differently to different substances. Women and men have different physiological responses to substances, as women often become intoxicated after consuming smaller quantities of a substance than men do. Even if a woman consumes the same amount of alcohol as a male who weighs the same as she does, it will affect her differently (Frezza et al., 1990). Substance abuse can have different physiological side effects on women than they have on men. For example, menstrual disorders are associated with long-term heavy drinking or drug use. Long-term cocaine use disrupts normal menstrual cycles and may lead to amenorrhea (Yoffee, 2002). Additionally, substance abuse tends to impair judgment, leading to unprotected sex and STIs. Children born to alcoholic mothers are at risk for developing fetal alcohol syndrome. Alcoholism in women can increase sex hormones known to cause breast cancer.

Predictors of Substance Abuse

What are the predictors of drug and alcohol problems? Sexual and physical abuse are strong predictors for substance abuse. About 75 percent of female substance abusers have a history of sexual or physical assault (Kelley et al., 2001). One study examined female adult twins who had a history of three levels of childhood sexual abuse: nongenital, genital, and intercourse. Intercourse was associated with significantly increased odds ratios that reflected 2.5- to almost sixfold increases in major depressive disorder, GAD, panic disorder, bulimia nervosa, alcohol dependence, and drug dependence. The authors report that their data indicate that nongenital and genital childhood sexual abuse accounts for 6 percent of the variance and intercourse accounts for 12 percent of the variance in liability for the six psychiatric disorders measured (Kilbey & Burgermeister, 2001).

Women usually require a traumatic incident to sink into substance abuse such as divorce, desertion, infidelity, and so on. Women who are substance abusers are very likely to have partners who are substance abusers. Women experience much greater social disapproval for abusing substances than men do. Females are also diagnosed more often with comorbid psychiatric conditions than are men, but this could be related to the phenomenon discussed earlier in which men exhibiting signs of depression are diagnosed with substance abuse disorders whereas women with the same symptoms are diagnosed with depression. There is very high comorbidity between substance abuse and other mental disorders. Other contributing factors include genetic factors, history of childhood adversity—sexual or physical abuse—or

having a mood disorder. Depression often precedes alcohol use but may also be a consequence; someone with social anxiety may try to temper anxiety by drinking or have a husband or partner who is a drinker.

TREATMENT OF MENTAL DISORDERS

We have seen throughout this chapter how gender bias has played an important role in the diagnosis of mental disorders. Gender bias can also play a significant role in the treatment of mental disorders and in the therapist–patient relationship. Treatments for specific disorders have been discussed throughout the chapter. Here, we discuss treatment in a more general manner.

Most traditional types of psychotherapy involve a long-term relationship between patient and therapist in which the patient talks about his or her feelings, fears, attitudes, and behaviors. These problems are discussed and interpreted according to the theoretical orientation of the therapist and the type of therapy that she or he practices. Trust of the therapist is a major factor in the therapist–patient relationship. Often the therapist focuses on the early childhood of the patient as a determinant of the psychological problems presented. How adequately do these traditional therapies deal with the psychological problems of women, and how do the attitudes of therapists toward women and men influence the diagnosis and therapy their patients receive?

Over thirty years ago, Broverman and his associates addressed these questions in a classic study of the clinical judgments of 79 female and male psychologists, psychiatrists, and social workers. They found that these therapists made clear-cut distinctions between who were healthy females and males. Broverman, Broverman, Clarkeson, Rosenkrantz, and Vogel (1970) found no significant differences between standards for males and for all adults, but found significant differences between standards for females and all adults. Thus, the standards for mental health represent the male model, and females deviate from them. Broverman and his colleagues also found that more socially desirable personality attributes were assigned to men, with undesirable ones attributed to women. Of additional interest was the finding that there was no difference in the results whether the therapist was female or male, showing that women therapists may be just as biased as men (Broverman et al., 1970).

Traditional psychotherapy came under fire with the advent of the feminist movement in the 1960s. Feminist psychologists believed that psychotherapy, then usually performed by male therapists, worked to further the status quo. Regardless of the theoretical orientation used by the therapist, feminists noted that psychotherapy mischaracterized women as dependent and passive, judged social roles assigned to men as more desirable than those set aside for women, and ignored diversity among women (Rawlings & Carter, 1977). All of these worked to further the subjugation of women. Feminist psychologists objected to the idea that traditional therapy involves a hierarchical relationship that identifies the therapist as the expert.

Because psychotherapy involves discussing and interpreting the client's experiences according to the theoretical orientation of the therapist, the effect of the treatment is the interaction of both the orientation of the therapist and the therapist's personal beliefs. A therapist's own gender bias can inadvertently influence the way in which she or he practices. The most prevalent traditional psychotherapies are summarized next: psychodynamic, cognitive behavioral, and psychopharmacology.

Psychodynamic therapy originated from psychoanalysis, which is based on the tenets of Sigmund Freud. These have been discussed and reviewed in Chapters 4 and 5. Psychoanalysis is viewed as inherently sexist, and Freud himself acknowledged that his theories about women were the least developed part of his work (Slipp, 1993). Freud focused on the resolution of penis envy as a necessity for the healthy development of the adult female. He also proposed that women are *masochists,* people who derive pleasure from pain. However, some of the positive aspects of the psychodynamic orientation are examining how one's childhood and past relationships influence them currently. This is sometimes explored through interpretation of free association and dreams. Additionally, Freud was one of the first people to publicly acknowledge that women were sexual beings. While some feminists still dislike psychodynamic psycho-

therapy, its modern interpretations are considerably more gender neutral.

Concepts of *cognitive* and *behavioral therapy* are not inherently sexist. Nonetheless, in their focus on adaptiveness and appropriateness of behavior, some therapists may inadvertently reinforce gender-role stereotypes or introduce gender schema bias into treatment. Thus, an individual therapist may be sexist and introduce his or her bias into the therapy. For example, if a woman feels depressed because she does not feel socially competent, a therapist might give her a homework assignment to initiate several social interactions within the next week. However, the woman might feel better if she could come to understand that being social does not need to be central to her self-image for her to feel confident. The female gender role encourages interpersonal relationships to be held in high regard for women. Behavioral and cognitive therapists need to be aware of this so that any value judgments will be impartial for females and males.

Although this section is concerned with psychotherapies, it is necessary to include some mention of *psychopharmacology,* or drug therapy, which is becoming an increasingly important part of the treatment of mental disorders. We know that even when women and men present the same symptoms and receive the same psychiatric diagnosis, women are still more likely than men to have medications prescribed as part of their therapy. As critical as drug treatments appear to be in the management of psychiatric disorders, they have historically been viewed as paternalistic and dismissive responses to women's distress. We need to guard against this practice and assure that medications are prescribed appropriately for women with mental disorders.

Any type of therapy can be problematic depending on the therapist's attitudes toward women and femininity. If a therapist thinks that women should adhere to traditional gender roles, she or he can inadvertently foster and promote these sorts of roles. Of all traditional paradigms, only psychoanalysis takes gender seriously, and at least until recently, it has been profoundly sexist. These traditional paradigms do not address women's issues, issues of women of color, or issues of psychotherapy with lesbian and bisexual women. Since the advent of the women's movement, feminist therapy has emerged as an influential approach to psychotherapy.

In the 1960s, women began to organize consciousness-raising groups, which primarily served to identify sociocultural factors that influenced women and to promote solidarity. Violence against women was also a major organizing factor for consciousness-raising groups. Early examples of these consciousness-raising groups were rape crisis centers and battered woman shelters (Heise, 1996). There principles became integrated into an unstructured type of group psychotherapy with an emphasis on personal change and self-knowledge (Brown, 1994). Women gathered together to share personal experiences in the context of the larger social, political, economic, and legal contexts. This marked the beginning of feminist psychotherapy as a political entity, often summarized by the saying "the personal is political" (Worrell, 2000).

When these principles became incorporated more formally into psychotherapy, they first led to the proposal of gender-neutral or nonsexist therapy. The *non-sexist* approach contends that both women and men should be treated alike. Individual needs and abilities, rather than gender stereotypes, should guide a person's choices (Worrell & Remer, 1992). Nonsexist therapies are not inherently feminist, because feminist therapy is characterized by an ideological slant. As the women's movement has become less radical, feminist therapy has also become slightly less radical and more integrated into mainstream psychotherapy practices. Because of this, the idea of gender-neutral or nonsexist therapy has been rendered obsolete (Worrell & Johnson, 2001).

Feminist psychotherapy has emerged as a philosophy of therapy, not a set of specific techniques, nor a theoretical orientation (Wyche & Rice, 1997). Feminist psychotherapy can be performed with any traditional theoretical orientation. Nonetheless, there is some agreement as to basic tenets of feminist therapy. These are honoring the client's own perspective on her life; placing the person and her problems in a social context; attending to the power relationship in therapy; scrutinizing a client's situation for multiple sources of oppression in addition to gender; and fostering social change (Marecek, 2001). These tenets can be applied to any school of psychotherapy. Some

applications to traditional psychotherapy are self-disclosure on the side of the therapist, which is intended to disrupt any power imbalances inherent in traditional psychotherapy, as well as not using formal diagnostic labels from the *DSM*.

Several general schools of thought of feminist psychotherapy relate directly to varying causal factors for different mental disorders discussed earlier in the chapter. Some of the types of feminisms deal with the idea that oppression of women is caused by irrational prejudice, sex role socialization and male domination (Worrell, 2001). Other schools of thought deal with the idea that women and men have different experiences, with women's being more focused on interpersonal relationships and more welcoming of stereotypical women's qualities: gentleness and emotionality (Worrell, 2001). Those who use feminist therapy have used it to create interventions for disorders ranging from eating problems, sexual difficulties, and sexual abuse, to relationship violence. The main concepts of feminist therapy can be used with couples and families, and also can be extended for use with men (Marecek, 2001). One model of this type of therapy has been realized at the Stone Center at Wellesley College.

The Stone Center looks at dependency as a source of the empowerment of women. Instead of seeing dependency as a basis for their problems, members of the Stone Center reevaluated it and gave dependency a new interpretation as relationship skills: sensitivity, empathy, care of others. The group saw these skills as valuable not only to women's development but also to society as a whole. These skills develop during child rearing when girls are taught to emulate their mothers. They learn the capacity for care-taking and relationship development. Boys are taught to be the opposite of their mothers and are encouraged to be autonomous and discouraged from developing close relationships (Miller, 1976). The Stone Center group has demonstrated how empathy, mutual empowerment, and dependency can be valuable in treating several disorders. These include depression, anxiety, posttraumatic stress disorder, self-destructive behavior, and other problems that interfere with an individual's ability to function. Johnson and Ferguson, in their book *Trusting Ourselves: The Source-*

book on the *Psychology of Women* (1990), expressed the opinion that the Stone Center's work was a comprehensive pro-female psychological theory that could rival the pro-male perspective of Freud.

Multicultural feminist psychology actually developed in response to the women's movement (Comas-Diaz, 1991). Minority women criticized early feminists for their lack of perspective on situations involving women who were not White and middle class. Women of color are subject to oppression as women and as minorities. Additionally, women of color are faced with conflicting loyalties, in which solidarity with their racial or ethnic group often takes priority over gender. Being asked to view men as the source of women's oppression denies their sense of group bonding both with the boys and men that they love and with other men in their community and support networks (Comas-Diaz & Greene, 1994). These ideas provide part of the backbone of multicultural feminist therapy. A multicultural feminist therapist can help women of color to explore their experiences of racism and sexism from within and outside their communities. Additionally, they can examine their personal and cultural identities, internalization of their negative experiences with the dominant culture, and their need to distance or remain interconnected with their ethnoracial group (Worrell and Johnson, 2001, p. 322). Many of these women also deal with issues concerning an immigrant identity.

Does feminist therapy work? Feminist therapy has proliferated since the 1970s, but most of the work takes place in private practice and clinics. There has been little empirical research testing the efficacy of the theoretical positions described. If feminist therapy is to hold the weight of other major intervention approaches, it needs to establish its unique elements as well as empirical validity. Feminist psychotherapy has both its proponents and its opponents (Worrell and Johnson, 2001).

One question about feminist psychotherapy is whether it is significantly different from traditional therapy. Surveys conducted on feminist therapies have shown that feminist therapists do, in fact, focus more on a gender-role perspective, and that there are significant differences in empowerment and advocacy for women between feminist therapists and traditional therapists. One recent survey was conducted with over 200 clinicians, some of whom were women-centered and some of whom were not. Results showed that the therapists differed in five of the six measures: affirming the client, gender-role perspective, woman-centered activism, therapist self-disclosure, and egalitarian stance (Worrell and Johnson, 2001). Client studies have affirmed that these practitioners actually do employ these strategies in their practices. Clients who have received brief treatment have shown outcomes of increased empowerment and resilience.

There are several criticisms of feminist psychotherapy. Some feel that by helping women to function better in our society, they are sustaining and supporting the status quo rather than resisting and restructuring it. Others believe that the political nature of the feminist framework has no real place in psychotherapy. Others state that it can really be of help only to White middle-class women and is irrelevant to those less privileged. Other criticisms deal with feminist therapy's lack of defined theory driven procedures and its lack of established empirical validity (Worrell and Johnson, 2001).

Relational therapy has been criticized on several grounds. There are reservations about glorifying a woman's relational skills and creating a type of female chauvinism. Another criticism concerns placing such importance on women's nurturing and relational behaviors that it might reinforce the old concept of separate domains for men and women. There is also the question of whether relational therapy is useful for women of color or different ethnic groups. On the other hand, some proponents support this new model for women's psychology that challenges widespread and standardized models of psychological functioning in which male bias is evident. The Stone Center relational model assumes a distinct female psychology that has its own unique merits. The model asserts that female attributes have been undervalued and neglected although they are positive human traits that all people need to develop.

DIVERSITY ISSUES IN THERAPY

The United States is rapidly becoming one of the most ethnically and racially diverse countries in the world, and, in light of this, it is especially important to consider the needs of minority women in psychotherapy. It is important for therapists to recognize that ethnic minority women's understanding about mental health disorders is culturally informed, and this influences how they choose coping strategies. Minority women may be more inclined to use coping strategies such as prayer or seeking help from within a social network before attempting to find professional help (Brown et al., 2003). Common themes that emerge when examining the mental health of ethnic minority women are a social orientation, the importance of family and connection with the community, the centrality of spirituality as an aspect of psychological well-being and as a coping strategy, and the experience of ethnic and racial discrimination (Brown et al., 2003).

Studies have shown that Women of Color are less likely to seek out mental health services than are their European American counterparts for several reasons, including shame in talking about personal problems with strangers, suspicion about therapists, and economic barriers (Dinges & Cherry, 1995). Of minority women who do seek out psychotherapy, most will not be able to choose therapists from their own background. Unfortunately, at present, only about 5 percent of therapists belong to ethnic minority groups (Hall, 1997). As a result, most people of color must work with therapists whose life experiences have been very different from their own. Additionally, there is often the problem of language. For example, Asian clients may not be proficient enough in English to express their feelings and concerns; there are similar concerns for Latinas (Chisholm, 1996; Shum, 1996). It is documented that ethnic minority women may be more likely to present for treatment of mental disorders in primary care settings, which unfortunately may then run the risk of going unrecognized or being inadequately treated (Borowsky et al., 2000).

An additional consideration for training more therapists of color is to understand and help clients to cope with the stresses that are inevitable when people emigrate to another culture. Unless the new immigrant has relatives or friends in the United States, she will feel isolated, lonely, and often frightened, especially if she has difficulty with English. If she is a single mother and has children to support, the experience may well have profound psychological consequences. Even if the whole family immigrates, stresses are inevitable—new regulations to learn and fears about money and jobs, for example—all of which contribute to internal conflict. It is important that we encourage women of color to become psychotherapists. The need for these therapists will be even more evident as diversity in the United States continues to increase in the twenty-first century.

In addressing the needs of ethnic minority women, therapists must learn more about the cultures their clients come from and the degree to which their lifestyles are representative of the mores and philosophy of that culture. This can help the therapist to understand the cultural context of mental disorders, including the culturally accepted expressions of distress. The therapist has to be willing to discuss these issues with clients. The therapist must consider the extent of the identification of the women with their racial–ethnic groups, as well as how integrated they have become in U.S. society. Additionally, the practitioner should consider the role of multiple risk factors, such as life stress, health problems, interpersonal role strain, and other dimensions of social stress that result from having ethnic minority status. Migration status is an important consideration, because women may have experienced traumatic circumstances surrounding the transition, which could result in PTSD.

SUMMARY

We began this chapter by reviewing the historical and cultural perceptions and biases of mental illness that have existed over time, especially toward women. Although many changes have taken place and others have been initiated, we should ask what progress has actually been made in the treatment of mental disorders. However, the exploration of women's health and well being, as well as gender differences in mental disorders, has become far more of a focus in the United States over recent years.

Depression, considered the leading cause of disability among women today, is a significantly gendered disorder. Although gender has long been recognized as a critical variable in depression, it has not been rigorously studied. We have been involved in bringing the issue of sex and gender bias in depression to the forefront of research (Gorman and Rabinowitz, 2004; Sechzer et al., 1994). Other groups have also studied gender in various aspects of depression and have made important contributions to the progress in this area. Now that the National Institute of Health has mandated that both women and men be studied in disorders affecting both genders and data be compared and analyzed separately, we can look forward to more data about the earlier recognition and appropriate treatment, both medical and psychotherapeutic, of women and men with this disorder.

Previously considered upper middle class disorders, anorexia and bulimia are now affecting women at all socioeconomic levels and across race and ethnicity. Additionally, we are beginning to see men with eating disorders. The death rates from eating disorders, especially anorexia, have doubled in the last twenty years and are now one of the highest reported for any mental disorder. We have also made progress in evaluating many of the psychological and cultural factors that are highly associated with the onset of anorexia and bulimia.

The question of which therapies are appropriate for women, including women of different ethnic and racial groups, has also begun to be studied. More data is needed to evaluate the outcomes of these therapies, compare them to more "standard" therapies, and to consider the possible benefits of integrating facets of these therapies with traditional therapies.

Finally, psychology has begun to focus on diversity, poverty, and stresses of migration. Psychology has increasingly come to recognize the importance of knowledge by therapists about the different racial and ethnic cultures that compose an impressive proportion of the U.S. population.

KEY TERMS

Anorexia nervosa (p. 426)
Anxiety disorders (p. 433)
Behavior therapy (p. 437)
Biopsychosocial model (p. 415)
Binge eating disorder (p. 428)
Borderline personality disorder (p. 437)
Bulimia nervosa (p. 427)
Cognitive–behavioral therapy (p. 425)

Dependent personality disorder (p. 437)
Depression (p. 416)
Diagnostic and Statistical Manual of Mental Disorders (DSM) (p. 414)
Emaciation (p. 432)
Gender intensification (p. 418)
Histrionic personality disorder (p. 438)
Panic attacks (p. 433)

Parasuicidal behavior (p. 436)
Posttraumatic stress disorder (p. 435)
Premenstrual dysphoric disorder (PMDD) (p. 422)
Premenstrual syndrome (PMS) (p. 422)

DISCUSSION QUESTIONS

1. Do you know anyone who is or was anorexic or bulimic? Did you observe any of the behaviors described earlier in this chapter? What factors do you think were involved in their developing these eating disorders? What treatment was most effective for them?

2. Many people who are anorexic or bulimic do not understand the meaning of the behaviors they are practicing, whether they are restricting food, binging, or purging. How would you go about helping someone who you suspected was anorexic or bulimic to realize she or he had a serious disorder? What strategies would you use to help that person accept the problem and get help?

3. If you should need psychotherapy at some future date, have you thought about the kind of therapist you would prefer, given the criteria for selecting a therapist in this chapter? Would you see only a therapist of your own gender? What do you think are the advantages and disadvantages of seeing a therapist of your same gender?

4. Discuss the characteristics of depression. What factors do you think would be important in predicting whether a woman or man would become depressed? Are these factors different for men and women?

5. It has been suggested that male psychiatrists should not treat female patients because, for females, the psychotherapeutic relationship is just another power relationship in which the female must submit to the dominant male authority figure. Do you agree with this? If so, why? If not, why?

6. What kind of background and training do you feel a therapist will need to treat women of different race or ethnicity? Must the therapist be matched with a client who shares the same race or ethnicity?

FURTHER READINGS

Figert, A. E. (1996). *Women and the ownership of PMS: The structuring of a psychiatric disorder.* New York: Alvin de Gruyter.

Gaesser, G. A. (2002). *Big fat lies: The truth about your weight and your health.* Carlsbad, CA: Gurze.

Nathan, P. E., & Gorman, J. M. (Eds). (2002). *A guide to treatments that work* (2nd ed.). New York: Oxford University Press.

Simonds, S. L. (2001). *Depression in women: An integrative treatment approach.* New York: Springer.

CHAPTER 14

A GENDERED VIEW
OF PHYSICAL HEALTH

[W]omen's health care has always mirrored a male dominated world.
—Ann Douglas Wood

*As long as the course of scientific thought was judged to be exclusively
determined by its own logical and empirical necessities, there could be no
place for any signature, male or otherwise, in the system of knowledge.*
—Evelyn Fox Keller

*During the late eighteenth and nineteenth centuries the medical profession
became organized as a profession along traditional masculine lines. This
was particularly damaging to women healers and tended to undermine or
exclude traditional "female" characteristics from "official" medicine.*
—Ann Dally

*Medical textbooks have presented a view of women as neurotic
complainers, fostering the assumption in physicians that the symptoms
a woman describes may be "all in her head" and handled, not with
diagnostic testing, but with tranquilizers. This was to become deadly to
women in the AIDS epidemic.*
—Gena Corea

No matter what part of the media we turn to, we will surely find a headline or report on a new advance or finding in medicine which will affect women's health. But it was not always that way! In the 1980s and 1990s, most medical research studies that affect both women and men were carried out with male participants. For instance, reports on a study of more than 22,000 physicians showed a beneficial effect of an aspirin every other day on coronary heart disease (Steering Committee of the Physician's Health Study Research Group, 1989). That sounded terrific! However, on reading the details of the report it seems that no women were included in the study, even though cardiovascular disease is the leading cause of death for both women and men (Wenger, Speroff, & Packard, 1993). Two years after the Steering Committee report, Manson et al. (1991) suggested that aspirin *may* have a similar effect on women. Then, a more definitive study showed that aspirin does have a similar effect on women (Rich-Edwards, Manson, Hennekens, & Buring, 1995). Although women are the primary users of estrogen, another study investigated the role of estrogen in prevention of heart disease, but only in men (Healy, 1991; National Institutes of Health—Office of Research on Women's Health [NIH-ORWH], 1992). A review of women's health issues by Rodin and Ickovics (1990) provided still another example. These authors pointed out that, even when women are the primary users of a particular class of drugs, the majority of research studies either did not include women or included them in small numbers. When women were included, it was often in the late stages of the study, so long-term effects could not be determined (Abramson, 1990; Palca, 1990).

Even though the majority of research studies were conducted with male participants, the data were generalized, often with little justification, to females. One justification presented by scientists was that a woman's hormonal fluctuations resulted in different findings from men. Another was that it was more difficult to recruit women for studies. Still another concern was that women of reproductive age were not permitted to be tested in many studies, especially for drug studies (Food and Drug Administration [FDA], 1977). The reproductive test ban was abolished in 1993 (FDA Press Release April 5, 1993; Federal Register July 2, 1993). Generalization of data from male studies to females was the practice not only for studies with humans but also for studies carried out with male animals. Later on in this chapter we will return to this aspect of research.

Why were women ignored in research on diseases or disorders that affect both genders? Why has it been, and often still is, assumed that there are no differences in etiology, symptoms, or treatment responses between women and men? This is an extension of what we have already seen in other chapters in this book; women have generally been considered less normative than men and less important. In the case of health research, women have been understudied and sex and gender not considered important variables in the advancement of scientific and medical knowledge. Such gender stereotyping has permeated all phases of the life span of both females and males and, as we will see, has affected the physical health of both. As described earlier in this book, these stereotyped attitudes toward women and men, derived from mythological, religious, or sociocultural constructions of women and men in many societies, have also strongly influenced medical research and the medical community's treatment of women and men. Moreover, medical care and treatment of health problems, whether developing during infancy, adolescence, adulthood, or old age, show marked differences for females and males, not only in physical health but also in mental health, as shown in Chapter 13.

Why should psychologists be concerned about physical health? Is there really a mind–body relationship? Does the state of our health affect our mental processes and our behavior, and if so, how? Does the mind affect our health, and how? We will see that our state of physical health has psychological effects, many of which are related to issues of gender. We will also see that strategies for promoting health and well-being or for coping with physical problems involve behavioral changes in attitudes and practices.

In addressing these issues, we will define health and well-being and how gender stereotypes of women and men affect their health. We will explore the history of these stereotyped attitudes, adhered to by the medical profession, and how the care and treatment of women and men have been affected. A review of research studies concerning major disorders affecting both women and men will highlight the extent of gender bias in research and practice and the importance of taking a gendered perspective on health. We will describe attempts to change medical care for women in Western societies and how successful this has been.

THE POLITICS OF ILLNESS

Victorian Times

A Male-Dominated World. The neglect of women's health problems has a long history. In the last few decades, many reviews of the literature on medical care and the diseases of women have appeared. This has come from the efforts of feminist groups, increasing interest in women's studies, and the efforts of women and men in the U.S. Congress. According to Brieger, "women's health care has always mirrored a male-dominated world" (1984, p. 153). They perceived Victorian physicians "as maintaining a *status quo* by keeping women subordinate in domestic and maternal roles" (p. 153). Thus, two disorders diagnosed in the nineteenth century, *hysteria* and *neurasthenia,* have been considered the response to this male-dominated world.

Hysteria. From the late 1800s to the early 1900s, a new disease appeared in England and the United States and was subsequently labeled *hysteria.* Affected women would faint or throw their limbs about without control, their backs would arch, and their entire bodies would become rigid. In many cases, paralysis of a whole body part, such as one hand, arm, leg, or foot, was common. Such hysterical people lost their voice and appetite, screamed, and at times laughed uncontrollably (Dally, 1991; Ehrenreich & English, 1981).

Hysteria spread throughout Europe and was reported to affect women almost exclusively. In England, it was an ideal disease for the doctors, because it was never fatal and required endless amounts of medical attention. Physicians began to suspect that these symptoms of hysteria were only a clever charade, because there were few reports of these attacks when women were alone. Doctors did insist, however, that hysteria was a disease of the uterus (hysteria is derived from the Greek *hystera,* meaning womb or uterus). As the prevalence of the disease spread, doctors came to label every incident of a woman's nontraditional behavior as "hysterical" (Dally, 1991; Ehrenreich & English, 1981).

In the United States rich women routinely frequented health spas and saw prominent specialists for these problems. Women who were not as wealthy saw family physicians, took patent medicines such as Lydia Pinkham's tonic or Swamp Root, which were supposed to cure all manner of diseases (Fourcroy, 1994), and later resorted to popular advice books written by physicians on female health. Black women and poor women had little access to care. The belief that held from the midnineteenth century to the early twentieth century was that the normal state for women was to be sick. "Even though women were treated for diseases of the stomach, liver, heart, etc., these diseases will be found to be sympathetic reactions or symptoms of one disease, a disease of the womb" (Dirix, 1869, pp. 23–24).

Neurasthenia. While physicians struggled with attempts at understanding the symptoms of hysteria, another disorder, called *neurasthenia* (nerve weakness), appeared, with a vague syndrome of physical symptoms engulfing middle- and upper-class populations. Neurasthenia first appeared in the United

States, described in 1868 by George Beard, but soon spread throughout England and Europe. In general, this was not seen as a disease in the medical sense, but actually appeared to be a way of life. It was the way these women were expected to live their lives, a way that predisposed them to continue to live as society demanded them to. Neurasthenia encompassed a wide range of symptoms, some of which included blushing, vertigo, headaches and neuralgia, insomnia, anorexia, and depression (Showalter, 1985). The delicate but wealthy lady, dependent on her husband, set the "sexual romanticist ideal of femininity for women of all classes" (Ehrenreich & English, 1981, p. 330). Marriage for these women had become a "sexuo-economic relation in which women performed sexual and reproductive duties [in exchange] for financial support" (Ehrenreich & English, 1981, p. 331).

Physicians treating affected women considered female functions inherently pathological and concluded that menstruation was a serious hazard for women. Pregnant women were considered to be indisposed throughout their nine-month pregnancy. During pregnancy, a woman was cautioned to avoid sights that could shock her, any type of intellectual stimulation, anger, and lustful thoughts. She should not even smell alcohol or smoke on her husband's breath. These requirements were to be rigidly carried out to prevent the baby from developing a deformity or from becoming stunted during gestation. After childbirth and child rearing, all a woman could look forward to was her menopause, portrayed in the literature of the time as the "death of the woman in the woman" (Ehrenreich & English, 1981, p. 335). Physicians came to "establish" that women's sickness is innate and stems from the possession of a uterus and ovaries. Furthermore, a woman's personality and her behavior were seen as dominated by her ovaries, which could then be blamed for all possible female disorders.

Medical Treatments for Women

Ovariotomy.   In the latter part of the eighteenth century, medical treatment for these female disorders gave way to drastic surgery such as ovariotomy (surgical removal of the ovaries) and even clitoridectomy (removal of the clitoris), the female organ analogous to the male penis (Dally, 1991). Ovariotomy (now known as oophorectomy) was performed not only for gynecological symptoms but also for the purpose of controlling psychological disorders. In 1872, Robert Battey, an American surgeon, performed the first ovariotomy in the United States on a 23-year-old woman for relief of her nervous (psychological) symptoms, menstrual dysfunction, and convulsions. This procedure would in a short time become the "cure" for epilepsy, as well as all kinds of insanity. By 1906, it was estimated that 150,000 women had been subjected to this procedure to treat more than just ovarian disease. After 1906, the purpose of the procedure for psychological disorders was finally discredited (Dally, 1991).

Clitoridectomy.   Although clitoridectomy is an old cultural rite in many African and Middle Eastern cultures, it came to be a new fashion in England and later in the United States during the late nineteenth century and even into the twentieth century (see the Chapters 3 and 12 for a further discussion of clitoridectomy—female genital mutilation). In England the prevailing attitude toward women was that the clitoris was a source of psychological disturbance, and the obvious solution was to remove it, hence this procedure. Clitoridectomy removed a woman's sexual pleasure and restricted her sexuality to reproduction. The procedure was first performed in in England in the 1860s by Isaac Baker Brown, a prominent British surgeon. Clitoridectomy was to *cure* nymphomania, hysteria, epilepsy (then believed to be caused by masturbation), and insanity. The use of clitoridectomy increased for a time, but by 1867 Baker Brown was under attack. Although many physicians considered the surgery as "quackery," the main complaint was not the procedure or its rationale, but that Baker Brown performed it to excess and without suitable permission. It was then discredited in England, but Baker Brown came to the United States, where he found much support. Clitoridectomy to control sexuality became very popular in the United States until about 1925 (Dally, 1991). The last officially reported clitoridectomy procedure in the United States was carried out in 1948 on a 5-year-old girl in order to cure her masturbation (Ehrenreich &

English, 1981). Since 1996, this procedure is illegal in the United States but is still being performed under conditions of secrecy because many immigrants from other countries adhere to this practice (see Chapters 3 and 12).

Health Status of Women

Certainly, women of the nineteenth and early twentieth centuries were considerably sicker than women are today. They wore heavy, tight-laced corsets in the style of the day, so tight that in some cases the pelvic organs and liver were displaced and the ribs fractured. Another risk for women, particularly young women, was tuberculosis. The death rate was very high. The health of women who were needy or impoverished received little to no attention from the medical community despite high rates of childbearing diseases and tuberculosis.

But the medical profession in general maintained that it was affluent women who were the most delicate and in need of special medical care. Attitudes of society had made the middle- and upper-class women sickly; working women, on the other hand, were supposed to be robust, just as they were supposed to be coarse and immodest. Similarly, Black women who worked in middle- and upper-class homes were also considered to be in good health. Brieger (1984) makes an important point that men also complained of neglect during the nineteenth century. This attitude toward working-class and poor women, both White and Black, was apparently generalized to working-class and poor men, so these groups also received little medical care.

With all these treatments for hysteria and neurasthenia, their real cause continued to elude physicians. The conflict between hysterical and neurasthenic women and their physicians about the cause and treatment of these disorders and their symptoms remained unresolved. Meanwhile, Sigmund Freud in Vienna was developing a treatment that would eventually remove these diseases from the pelvis and reproductive system and from gynecologist's control, to "elevate them to mental disorders." Freud's insight into hysteria and neurasthenia and with it an understanding of women's resentment and rebelliousness

about their forced way of life helped psychologists and psychiatrists replace medical specialists as the dominant experts in women's lives. Still, for decades, physicians would continue to view menstruation, pregnancy, and menopause as physical diseases and intellectual liabilities (Dally, 1991).

Although women's intelligence and abilities would begin to be accepted, many of these prejudices about women and their health status, engendered by the medical society's stereotypes, would remain and be sustained to the present day. These prejudices then became part of the medical and scientific research enterprise, which began to expand after World War II when the National Institutes of Health and other federal agencies were established.

WOMEN, MEN, AND HEALTH

Physical Health and Well-Being

Health Defined. Health is a highly desired state. In 1973, Milton Rokeach began his classic studies of American values. Participants in the study were required to rank various states of being, such as wealth, power, and so on. Rokeach had originally planned to use health as one of these values. He found, however, that there was essentially no variance with regard to health because it was ranked first by almost everyone (Kaplan, Sallis, & Patterson, 1993). Even though health is such an important and cherished state, there have been many different approaches toward understanding precisely what health means. Many definitions arc negative, such as health is the "absence of disease" or "not being sick." Other definitions have included only the physical aspects (Kaplan et al., 1993). Are physical health and well-being just the absence of a disease, disorder, or injury, or are there other components? Soon after the World Health Organization (WHO) was established by the United Nations in 1948, it defined health as "a complete state of *physical, mental,* and *social well-being* and not merely the absence of disease or illness" (WHO, 1948). This definition implied that being healthy involves various dimensions other than the absence of disease or infirmity. Since that time, various definitions of health have been used, for example, a positive state of physical, mental, and social well-being. But as we have learned more about diseases and treatment, the emphasis has been on prevention and treatment strategies, the mind–body interaction, psychosocial intervention, and other approaches.

Gender-Role Stereotypes and the Consequences for Physical Health

There is an established relationship between gender and health. Stresses and pressures on a woman's and man's well-being are imposed by the general culture of which they are a product. Eighty years ago, Karen Horney wrote on the subject of a masculine civilization. Westkott (1998) has interpreted Horney's writing as referring to "the presumption within Western culture of male superiority and female inferiority" (p. 14) and the cultural assumptions and practices responsible for bringing these attitudes about. Even with the changes time has brought in 80 years, the same concept of male superiority and female inferiority has persisted. Psychologists and other social scientists have chronicled the ways in which these attitudes and practices have affected girls' and women's mental and physical health regardless of their cultural backgrounds or race or ethnicity (Helstrom & Blechman, 1998; Westkott, 1998).

More women than men suffer from physiological and psychological disorders, with gender differences reported in the incidence of many specific disorders (for psychological disorders, see Chapter 13). On the other hand, even though life expectancy for both females and males has increased over the course of the last century, life expectancy still favors women (see Chapter 11). In fact, since 1900 this difference in life expectancy between women and men has consistently widened (Brannon, 2002). How do we explain this?

Many of these differences have been associated with the perceived male gender role. The disparate lifestyles may be an important component of these differences in physical health between women and men. Whereas women seek help frequently, men tend to delay seeking medical help in an effort to avoid being a considered a "sissy" and to be stoic. Taking time off from work to recuperate or to see a physi-

cian may mean more financial loss for men than for women, because women's positions and salaries are generally inferior to those of men (Reddy, Fleming, & Adesso, 1992). In 1979, Scarf reported that about 60 percent of all medical appointments were made by women. This gender difference in medical visits does not appear in childhood, but increases in adolescence and then in adulthood. Even excluding physician visits for pregnancy and childbirth, according to Brannon (2002), women still have a higher incidence of physician visits. The reason for this difference is not clear. One explanation is that women may be more vulnerable and develop more diseases that require not only medical care but also longer medical care. Although men show a higher incidence of fatal chronic disease, women have higher rates of drug use and illness from acute disorders such as respiratory infections, infectious and parasitic diseases, and chronic conditions, such as arthritis, disorders of bone or cartilage, anemias, or varicosities.

There is a marked difference in diagnosis and treatment of the physical complaints of women and men. Physicians may show gender bias in their treatment of women and attribute a woman's physical complaints to psychogenic rather than organic causes. The reverse appears true for men (Brannon, 2002; Ratcliff, 2002). This may be one reason that mood-altering drugs are prescribed for women more than twice as often as for men. The fact that these drugs do not ameliorate women's physical symptoms may result in more frequent visits to their physicians for the same unrelieved symptomatology. Regardless of the frequency of physician's visits, women may live longer but they will not be as healthy as men (NIH-ORWH, 1992). We shall see this pattern continue in our discussion of bias in specific health problems for women.

Gender Comparisons in Morbidity and Mortality: A Crisis in Women's Health

As noted earlier in this chapter, the existing scientific paradigm that governs health research relevant to both women and men, including treatment, has been based on a male model. The failure to recognize sex and gender as important variables in health research reflects ongoing attitudes toward women by the medical and scientific communities. Implicit in this male model has been the assumption that with the obvious exception of disorders affecting only women, there are no differences in etiology, symptoms, or treatment responses between females and males in disorders affecting both sexes. Using this model, basic and clinical studies have usually been carried out with White males and results generalized to females as well as minority groups, often without any scientific rationale. The preference for male subjects in research was not limited to human participants; we see the same preference in animal studies, in which the predominant sex studied is also male. Data from male animal studies are also generalized to female animals of the same and different species and then to humans. Findings from basic animal research frequently form the basis for human clinical studies (Sechzer, Denmark, & Rabinowitz, 1993; Sechzer, Zmitrovich, & Denmark, 1985; Sechzer, Rabinowitz, Denmark, McGinn, Weeks, & Wilkens, 1994). Until the end of the 1980s, the importance of sex and gender as significant variables in research was totally neglected. Because of the dire consequences of such neglect, this issue attracted the concerted attention of the public, government agencies, and the medical and scientific communities (Sechzer, Griffin, & Pfafflin, 1994).

By the end of the 1980s, national statistics pointed to a crisis in women's health. It was generally known that heart disease, cancer, and stroke were the major causes of death for women and men, but the number of women who die each year from these diseases was startling. According to Wenger, Speroff, and Packard (1993), 500,000 women died annually of cardiovascular disease. By 1991, the number of deaths of women from cancer was more than 230,000 and still ranks first or second as the cause of death across all age groups. Four types of cancers accounted for about 70 percent of all cancers in women: breast, colon–rectal, lung, and uterine (gynecological cancers) (Anderson, 1998). Breast cancer alone accounted for 32 percent of cancers. Breast cancer was higher for White women than Black women, but survival was much lower for Black women. Since 1980 there has been a "2% increase in incidence" (Andersen, 1998, p. 570).

Treatment of these diseases was derived from studies of males and the research generalized to females (NIH-ORWH, 1992; Sechzer et al., 1992; Sechzer, Rabinowitz, Denmark, McGinn, Weeks, & Wilkens, 1994). Box 14.1 presents additional data on the report of the NIH—Office of Research on Women's Health. It summarizes the status of women's health as of 1992. The NIH also reviewed data on the health problems of ethnic and racially diverse women and their children. Box 14.2 describes the findings as of 1992. Later in this chapter we will report how the government and the scientific and medical communities responded to this crisis in medical care.

Box 14.1

Gender Comparisons for Women's Health

Although women will live longer than men, they will be sicker, isolated, and will suffer more from chronic diseases.

In their 1992 report, the National Institutes of Health—Office of Research on Women's Health (NIH-ORWH) studied data from a different perspective and asked whether there were differences in the health of men and women. This group found that health problems specific to women were worsening and that currently science and medicine do not have enough knowledge to reverse this trend. The NIH-ORWH reported the following: (1) Women will constitute the larger population and will be more susceptible to disease in the future; (2) overall, women have worse health than men; (3) certain health problems are more prevalent in women than in men; and (4) certain health problems are unique to women or affect women differently than they do men. Among these findings and those of others are data showing that, throughout their lives, the quality of life for women lags behind that for men. Women's activities are limited by health problems by approximately 25 percent more days each year than are men's activities. Women are bedridden 35 percent more days because of infectious and parasitic diseases, respiratory diseases, digestive conditions, injuries, and other acute conditions. These findings have been upheld even when reproductive problems are removed from the calculations.

Box 14.2

Ethnic and Racial Diversity in Women's Health

The NIH-ORWH 1992 report found that health status varies among the different subgroups of the U.S. population. Although data are lacking for many ethnic and racial subgroups for many health conditions, we know that many conditions and diseases occur with higher frequency in different groups of women.

Death from stroke occurs twice as often in Black women as in White women. The rate of death from coronary disease is higher for Black women than for White women, 172.9 versus 106.6 per 100,000 persons. The rate of death from complications of pregnancy and childbirth is 3.5 times greater for Black than for White women. Ectopic pregnancies are the main cause of pregnancy-related deaths among Black women.

Occurrence of adolescent pregnancies is highest among Blacks (23 percent) and lowest among Asian Americans (6 percent). Birth rate among Black girls under age 15 is seven times higher than for White girls. Systemic lupus erythematosus occurs three times more often in Black women than in White women.

The incidence of breast cancer is lower for Black women than for White women, but death rates from breast cancer are higher for Black women. Rates for lung cancer are higher for White women than for Black women. Black women have the highest incidence of gonorrhea and syphilis.

Although overall incidence of cancer is lower for Hispanic women, certain specific cancer rates are higher. The incidence of cervical cancer among Hispanic women is double that for non-Hispanic White women. Death due to stomach cancer is twice as high for Hispanics as for non-Hispanic Whites.

Among Hispanics, death rates from homicide, AIDS, and perinatal conditions are greater than for Whites. The incidence of tuberculosis for Blacks and Hispanics is four times that of non-Hispanic Whites.

The prevalence of noninsulin-dependent diabetes mellitus (NIDDM) is twice as high among Black women as White women. Hispanics have three times the risk of developing diabetes and greater metabolic severity than non-Hispanic Whites. Prevalence of noninsulin-dependent diabetes mellitus is two to five times higher among American Indians than among other U.S. populations; 68 percent of Pima Indian women 55 to 64 years of age have noninsulin-dependent diabetes mellitus.

Obesity is a major risk factor for cardiovascular disease, stroke, and other diseases; 44 percent of Black women, 42 percent of Mexican American women, 40 percent of Puerto Rican women, 31 percent of Cuban women, and 24 percent of White women are overweight.

STRESS

Stress and Stressors Defined

The ability to avoid, escape, or control stress is critical to the health and well-being of humans and animals. We have all been in situations in which we have experienced stress, whether preparing for a test, missing a train, or trying to handle job responsibilities and at the same time meeting the demands of one's children.

Stress has been defined as a negative emotional experience associated with physiological, psychological, environmental, and behavioral changes. How we respond to stress will indicate whether we adapt to some degree to the stressful event, alter it, or fail to adapt. Stress can also be defined as the effect produced by external (physical or environmen-

tal) or internal (physiological or psychological) *stressors* (National Research Council, 1992; Rice, 1987). Table 14.1 gives examples of potential stressors. Moreover, stress and an individual's response to it always involve the relationship between the individual and the environment. The individual then makes an assessment (sometimes unconsciously) as to whether she or he can meet the demands of the environmental stressor(s) and make a response. How an individual responds can vary according to age, sex, physiological and psychological state, past experience, and genetic profile (Rice, 1987; Taylor, 1995).

As we have noted throughout this book, women are generally subjected to and experience more stress than men. In addition to illness, conditions for women that are particularly stressful include hold-

TABLE 14.1 Examples of Potential Stressors

CAUSES OF PHYSIOLOGIC STRESS	CAUSES OF PSYCHOLOGIC STRESS	CAUSES OF ENVIRONMENTAL STRESS
Injury ⎫	Fear	Restraint
Surgery ⎬ Pain[a]	Anxiety	Noise
Disease ⎭	Boredom	Odors
Starvation	Loneliness	Habitat
Dehydration	Separation	Ecology
		People
		Other species
		Chemicals
		Pheromones

Source: Reprinted, with permission, from *Recognition and Alleviation of Pain and Distress in Laboratory Animals.* Copyright 1992 by the National Academy of Sciences. Courtesy of the National Academy Press, Washington, DC.

[a]Note that pain is shown as resulting from physiologic stressors. It could also result from environmental stressors (e.g., chemical) and be potentiated by psychologic stressors (e.g., fear).

ing low-status jobs; receiving unequal pay for equal and comparable work; juggling careers, family, and household activities; and being the targets of harassment and violence.

Early Contributions

Cannon and the Fight or Flight Response. Walter Cannon and Hans Selye are the two scientists usually associated with early research that helped to elucidate some of the mechanisms of stress. Cannon was the first to describe the **fight or flight response.** He proposed that when an organism perceives a threat (e.g., a woman facing an attacker), the body is rapidly aroused and changes in its internal environment take place. Heart rate increases; blood pressure, blood sugar, and respirations increase; blood circulating to the skin is decreased, while blood circulating to the muscles increases; and secretion of catecholamines (norepinephrine and dopamine) increases. This physiological response to a stressor mobilizes the organism to attack or to flee—the fight or flight response. Cannon concluded that the fight or flight response is an adaptive one because it enables the organism to respond quickly to the perceived threat. He also reasoned that stress can be harmful because it interferes with emotional and normal physiological functioning and could cause health

problems over time. Cannon also proposed that, when the organism is incapable of or prevented from making a fight or flight response and stress is prolonged, its state of physiological arousal is sustained and can form the basis for health problems (Cannon, 1929; DiMatteo & Martin, 2002; Rice, 1987; Taylor, 1995).

Selye and the General Adaptation Syndrome. Hans Selye also made major contributions to the field of stress with his concept of the **general adaptation syndrome.** He exposed rats to different and prolonged stressors, such as extreme cold and induced excessive fatigue. He measured their physiological responses to these stressors. All the stressors evoked the same pattern of response in the rats. They developed enlarged adrenal glands and increased amounts of corticosteroids from the adrenal glands. The thymus gland and lymph nodes appeared shrunken, and ulcers were produced in the stomach and small intestine. From these observations, Selye (1956) developed his theory of the general adaptation syndrome because the response to stress will be the same regardless of the situation or type of stressor as the individual's body prepares for some action (e.g., increased secretion of corticosteroids by the adrenal glands to activate the nervous system). Most important, under conditions of prolonged stress, the system can become exhausted and physiological resources depleted (Levine, 1985; Selye, 1956; Taylor, 1995) and problems become evident.

The importance and influence of both Cannon's and Selye's work are still evident today. They identified internal and external stressors and the mechanisms that established the foundation for a stress–disease relationship. Although they did not emphasize psychological factors, the involvement and importance of psychological responses became evident as research in this field continued. We have learned much about different kinds of stressors, the stress that can result, and the types of responses that they may elicit.

Distress Models and the Appearance of Maladaptive Behaviors. If stress is prolonged and the individual is unable to respond or adapt adequately to the stress caused by physiological, psychological, or environmental stressors, as displayed in Figure 14.1, she or he may become severely distressed and begin to show **maladaptive behaviors.** However, if the stressors involved are short term and the individual cannot make an appropriate response (to avoid, escape, or control) and displays maladaptive behaviors, these responses do not usually, but may, result in long-term harmful results.

There are two models of distress. In the first, *distress induced by pain* (Figure 14.1), the individual can only adapt to a certain extent as pain increases. When pain goes beyond the tolerance level and reaches the intolerance level, we could expect to see maladaptive behaviors.

The second model of distress is that of *distress not induced by pain* (Figure 14.2), but induced by stressors of various types (psychological, physiological, or environmental). This will bring about a state of stress. Again, as in the pain model, results depend

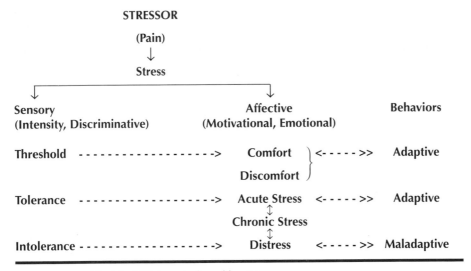

FIGURE 14.1 Model of Distress Induced by Pain

Note relationship between sensory discriminative component and affective emotional component. Sensory component of pain ranges from threshold to tolerance and then intolerance. In affective components, intensity of pain can proceed from a state of comfort to distress. Arrow paths indicate flow from sensation to affect to behaviors. This is the normal case, but under some conditions, behaviors can influence affect and thus modify the sensation. Double arrows emphasize that behavior is primarily influenced by affect. Direction of flow indicates schematized concept only, not neural pathways.

Source: Reprinted with permission from *Recognition and Alleviation of Pain and Distress in Laboratory Animals.* Copyright 1992 by the National Academy of Sciences. Courtesy of the National Academy Press, Washington, DC.

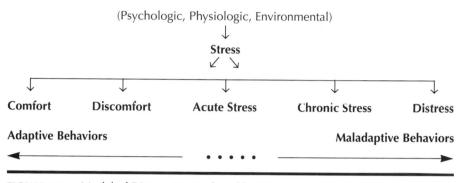

FIGURE 14.2   Model of Distress Not Induced by Pain

Stressors, leading to stress, can initiate various states in an individual ranging from comfort to distress. Adaptative stress will not interfere with an individual's state of comfort or well-being. When experiencing distress, maladaptive behaviors can result, varying in range and severity with increasing distress.

Source: Reprinted, with permission, from *Recognition and Alleviation of Pain and Distress in Laboratory Animals.* Copyright 1992 by the National Academy of Sciences. Courtesy of the National Academy Press, Washington, DC.

on the amount of stress that the individual can tolerate in an adaptive state with normal behavior. If the nature and duration of the stress increase and become chronic, the individual may be unable to adapt any longer and enter a state of distress. At this point, she or he will begin to show maladaptive behaviors.

Reinforcement of Maladaptive Behaviors and Consequences for Health.   If the maladaptive behaviors that appear as a response to stress partially or temporarily reduce stress, these maladaptive responses will be reinforced or conditioned and will reappear not only under the same conditions but also in similar conditions (drugs and alcohol). In this way, maladaptive behaviors can become a permanent part of an individual's repertoire. If these behaviors persist over a long-term period, they can seriously impair an individual's state of physical and mental health (DiMatteo & Martin, 2002; National Research Council, 1992; Weissberg, 1983). Women who are single mothers and work and care for their children or who are the victims of domestic violence over long periods may well begin to show maladaptive behaviors. These behaviors may include eating disorders; excessive anxiety or fear; and depression and inappropriate social behaviors such as aggression, passivity, or withdrawal, and, in some

cases, alcoholism or drug abuse. Men are more likely to become involved with drugs and alcohol and with aggressive behaviors than are women. These behaviors may also involve emotional, physical, or sexual child abuse; spouse abuse; father–daughter incest; and even suicide. Physical disorders in both women and men may appear and can include headaches, gastric and intestinal ulcers, immunosuppression (an important risk factor for cancer), or hypertension, which is a serious risk factor for cardiovascular disease (National Research Council, 1992).

Coping with Stress.   Coping with stress can result in altering or removing the problem or ameliorating the emotional aspects of the problem. "Coping is the process of changing thoughts and behaviors to manage situations that involve potential stressors" (Lazarus & Folkman, 1984, cited by Brannon, 2002, p. 373). Behavioral or cognitive therapeutic approaches, increasing social support, enhancing aspects of personal control, and exercise may reduce stress and the maladaptive responses to stress. Denial and disengagement from the problem as well as turning to religion may also serve as strategies. At some point medication may also be necessary. Benzodiazepines (i.e., tranquilizers such as Valium and Librium) reduce physiological arousal and reduce anxiety (Serafino, 1994). Because benzodiazepines can be addicting, they should be used only for short periods and under the strict supervision of a physician. Newer antianxiety drugs such as Ativan and Xanax may also be used but again are very addicting and must be taken under a physician's supervision. Relaxation techniques, biofeedback, and modeling have also been shown to be effective in reducing stress.

Women tend to seek social support as compared with men. However, both women and men who are employed may use problem-focused techniques as well as seeking social support. Although women may use more emotion-focused strategies, men use more instrumental type of focusing strategy. Financial situations may be an important factor in the type of coping resources selected. Women, especially single mothers, may not have the finances needed. Women and men who have lost jobs may also lack the finances to seek a particular strategy. Although there may be gender differences in the resources used by women and men, these differences may be due to the type of situations for each gender (Brannon, 2002). Thus, these differences appear to be small with considerable overlap.

Pain: A Major Stressor

Pain can be considered as an important source of stress. We should also consider pain as a state of stress itself. Every day, millions of people are disabled by pain that interferes with their productivity at work and at home and their overall quality of life. It is the most common reason for medical visits. It is also the major and most consistent reason for absence in the workplace.

Definition and Measurement of Pain.
Pain occurs in humans and other animals. **Pain** was defined very early by the International Association for the Study of Pain as an "unpleasant emotional experience associated with actual or potential tissue damage" (Mersky, 1976, p. 249). Before this, definitions of pain emphasized only the physiological aspect of the pain experience, but more recent ones, recognizing the psychological impact of pain, now include the word *emotional* in defining pain. Pain perception depends

on activation of a special set of nerve endings or receptors (nociceptors) by noxious or harmful stimuli (i.e., heat, mechanical, or chemical) and subsequent processing in the spinal cord and brain. The perception of pain and its intensity vary according to site, duration, frequency, and intensity and can be influenced by psychological states, previous experience, innate differences, or the state of physical health. The perceived intensity of pain based on the state of the individual certainly influences the ability to cope or adapt and, as discussed earlier, an inability to adapt and cope may well have dire consequences on the physical and mental health of the individual and may result in maladaptive behaviors.

The **pain threshold** is defined as the point at which pain is first perceived and represents minimal pain and is not usually associated with stress (Hardy, Wolff, & Goodell, 1952; Wolff, 1978). **Pain tolerance** is the upper limit or the highest intensity of pain that a human or animal will accept voluntarily (Wolff, 1978). Tolerance varies with different conditions (anxiety, fear, health status, motivation, previous experience with pain, etc.).

Types of Pain.
There are two major components of pain perception, the sensory (physiological) and the affective (emotional or psychological) (Gracely, McGrath, & Dubner, 1978; Kaplan, Sallis, & Patterson, 1993; Price & Dubner, 1977). There are also two types of pain: acute and chronic. *Acute pain* is typically associated with an active disease state or traumatic injury (Chapman & Bonica, 1985). When the damaged tissue heals, pain usually disappears. When healing takes place but pain still persists, this pain is referred to as *chronic pain*. Chapman and Bonica (1985) identified three types of chronic pain: (1) pain that lasts after normal healing of a disease or injury, (2) pain associated with a chronic medical condition, and (3) pain that develops and persists in the absence of any identifiable organic problem.

Sociocultural Differences in Perception of Pain.
Sociocultural studies have shown some evidence for cultural differences in behavioral responsiveness to pain. Several classic studies were conducted with different cultural groups in the 1960s and 1970s. Bloom

(1988) reviewed a number of these that clearly established the point that pain is a psychological as well as a physical process. Zola (1966) compared a group of Italian patients with Irish patients admitted to a medical clinic in Massachusetts. The Italian group complained of significantly more pain of a diffuse nature than did the Irish patients. Zola suggested that the ways of expressing illness and pain were a reflection of traditional customs of managing problems in their specific cultures. Sternback and Tursky (1965) and Tursky and Sternback (1967) contrasted four different groups of women—all housewives: Americans of British descent, native-born Italians, Jews, and Irish. Rather than studying people who were ill, they brought the groups into their laboratory and studied their responses to electric shock. The differences found between these groups seemed consistent with cultural norms in the various groups. The American women adapted more quickly to shock and appeared to have a "matter-of-fact orientation toward pain" (p. 239); Italian women had a lower threshold for pain and desired pain relief; and Irish women were more anxious, showed unwillingness to express their feelings, and tended to inhibit communicating their pain to others. Jewish women appeared highly concerned about the implications of their reactions and responses to pain. Similar to Zola, these investigators concluded that their findings were consistent with prevailing cultural norms. Obviously, such norms change over time and in different social contexts.

Zborowski (1969) studied a large group of men who were patients at a veterans' hospital in New York. The patients were representative of Italian, Irish, Jewish, and Anglo-Saxon Americans. Zborowski's findings were quite consistent with those of the studies just described. Italian and Jewish patients appeared more emotional than Anglo-Saxon and Irish patients and more diffuse in their complaints about pain. They also were more apprehensive about their physicians. When Zborowski selected the patients with regard to the seriousness of their pain, he found that the Italian and Jewish patients expressed their pain more than did the other groups. He concluded that, over a variety of illnesses, one's cultural background had an important, if not central, role in shaping responsiveness to pain and illness.

Later studies have focused on how societal factors appear to perpetuate pain, especially chronic pain. The long-term experience of pain involves processes that have important psychological components. Along with others, Steig and Williams (1983) have identified several societal factors that tend to increase the number of chronic pain patients seeking care. Some of these involve incentives provided by the medical and insurance professions, and such secondary gains from disability such as freedom from daily responsibilities and the elicitation of social support. In addition, job and economic stresses and changing family roles, including the division of household labor, all affect people's experience of pain (Bloom, 1988; Cohen, 1984; Steig & Williams, 1983).

A study of ethnic and racial differences in the characteristics and impact of chronic pain demonstrated marked differences between Caucasians (pain duration—9.9 years), African Americans (pain duration—7.6 years), and Hispanics (pain duration—6.5 years). African Americans missed more hours of work in a month than Caucasians or Hispanics. Hispanics reported less disturbed sleep or irritability, inability to participate in sports, and inability to do household chores than the other two groups. Yet, Hispanics were more likely than Caucasians and African Americans to feel that their pain had ruined their life, and that they felt like a burden or sometimes wished to die. Hispanics felt greater support from their families than did the other groups (Portnoy, 2003). Potential barriers to pain management were also suggested. One example was that language difficulties in describing pain affected proper treatment. Recognition of chronic pain in different racial and ethnic groups was necessary to understand the high prevalence and impact of their chronic pain. In reporting the results of this study, other authors were cited who found similar differences. Another study showed that African American patients with chronic pain do not receive proper care and suffer reduced function and quality of life. "African-Americans with chronic pain have more symptoms than Whites, more pain, more depression and greater impairment of their physical, emotional and social health" (Green, 2003, p. 1). Green and her colleagues believe that further research is needed to evaluate whether a pain care gap based on race exists with chronic pain.

Sex and Gender Differences in Pain Perception.

There are many sex differences in the perception of specific types of pain. Obviously, pain during labor and childbirth is unique to females. In diseases and disorders of both women and men, women experience a higher incidence of pain than men with arthritis, the neuralgias, migraine headaches, and cystitis. Men, on the other hand, show a higher proportion of pain with back problems, cardiac conditions, and cluster headaches (Bodner, 1998).

There is recent evidence showing sex differences in pain perception and analgesia. In females who have not reached menopause, pain mechanisms and pain perception appear to depend in part on estrogen receptors, and pain relief may operate through distinctly different pathways in females and males. Mogil, Sternberg, Kest, Marek, and Liebeskind (1993) found that a pathway involved in pain and pain relief relies on the presence of estrogen. In another study it was found that menstruating women and those taking hormone replacement therapy (HRT) had lower pain thresholds and tolerance than men and postmenopausal women not on HRT. Additional findings have also shown sex differences in response to different types of analgesic agents used to relieve pain in animals. In his review of this problem, Bodner believes it imperative that physicians understand these sex differences so that appropriate treatment will bring about the most effective pain relief (Bodner, 1998). This should include an understanding of pain mechanisms in pre- and postmenopausal women. This may mean that under certain conditions (e.g., age, reproductive status) drugs designed to relieve pain in men might not necessarily be effective in women.

Studies of sex differences in pain perception have found that differences appear primarily in situations with specific, experimentally manipulated pain stimuli (electrical or pressure stimulation). In these studies it was found that women generally have somewhat lower pain thresholds, lower pain tolerance, and are able to make finer discriminations between painful stimuli (Berkley, 1997). These differences, however, are small and are applicable to special situations. These differences may be hor-monal. Hormonal levels fluctuate in women while remaining relatively stable in men. In addition, the racial or ethnic group to which these patients belonged was not identified.

The Green (2003) study cited earlier was different in that it involved chronic pain, not experimentally induced pain. Green found that African American women with chronic pain experience more depressive symptoms and disability than Caucasian women. African American women were less likely than Caucasians to have a primary care physician and more likely to use the emergency room for pain than Caucasians. They also waited longer than Caucasians to see a physician for treatment of their pain.

Treatment of Pain and Coping Strategies.

Treatments for pain depend on the type of pain and the patient's responsiveness to pain. Drug treatment differs for acute and chronic pain, with concern for the patient becoming dependent or even addicted to the drug. Such drugs include peripherally and centrally acting analgesics, local anesthetics, and indirectly acting drugs that affect the emotional response to pain, which often contributes to the intensity of the pain, such as sedatives, tranquilizers, and antidepressants.

Surgery is the most radical treatment for controlling intractable chronic pain (e.g., tic doloreux). New, less risky techniques are in use for implanting fine tubes or pumps into special areas of the spinal cord that can deliver pain medication on a controlled basis to avoid overmedicating the patient. The pain controlled analgesia (PCA) method is a noninvasive technique in pain management. The patient has an intravenous system in place with a button that can be pressed whenever she or he has pain. A predetermined dose of pain medication will be delivered into the patient's vein. Drug dosage is calibrated to avoid any overdose of medication.

Behavioral and cognitive methods are being used to modify motivational and cognitive processes. These methods have been shown to help patients cope with their chronic pain. Other techniques involve relaxation, meditation, biofeedback, visual imagery, hypnosis, exercise, physical therapy, tai-chi, and qigong (Bloom, 1988; Rice, 1992). Because of the difficulty in following these patients after treatment is completed, results are difficult to evaluate precisely.

ISSUES OF BIAS IN WOMEN'S HEALTH RESEARCH

As we have stated earlier in this chapter, the prevailing paradigm of health and illness is premised on a male model. Such a model fails to recognize gender as salient in medical and scientific research. This neglect can be traced back to a historical exclusion of women from essentially all phases of the public domain. This practice extended into the sciences, where women not only were excluded from participation (in the behavioral as well as the biological and physical) but also were all but ignored as subjects of research. Thus, male scientists, selecting male subjects, constructed a male research model for science and medicine (Sechzer, Griffin, & Pfafflin, 1994). According to Keller (1982), "As long as the course of scientific thought was judged to be exclusively determined by its own logical and empirical necessities, there could be no place for any signature, male or otherwise, in that system of knowledge" (p. 312). Yet, according to many findings, scientific thought has not been exclusively determined by these criteria, and our system of knowledge does sustain a male signature. This male paradigm for disease is not only biological and behavioral; it is, as we have seen, also sociocultural (Sechzer, Griffin, & Pfafflin, 1994).

This section will review three major diseases that occur in both males and females, but for which sex and gender bias is evident and for which a gendered perspective may be useful. Because space constraints prevent us from providing an exhaustive discussion of all diseases and disorders in which sex or gender bias is evident, we have selected those that we feel to be of greatest concern for women: cardiovascular disease, lung cancer, and sexually transmitted infections.

Cardiovascular Disease

Cardiovascular disease (CVD) is the leading cause of death in the developing world for both men and women. Heart disease takes the lives of more women in the United States than stroke, breast cancer, ovarian or uterine cancer, and HIV combined. In 2002 more than 500,000 women died of cardiovascular disease in the United States. The American Heart Association (AHA) estimates that 1 in 9 women ages 45 to 64 have some sort of heart disease, but the ratio jumps to 1 in 3 for women over 65 (JAMA, 2002). Approximately 90 percent of all heart disease deaths among women occur after menopause. Although complete data are lacking for many ethnic and racial subgroups for many health conditions, it is known that many conditions and diseases occur with higher frequency in these diverse groups of women. African American women and Hispanic women are more likely to die from heart disease than are White women. And, women with diabetes are more likely to develop severe heart disease than are diabetic men.

In 2002, stroke was the third leading cause of death for women in the United States (cancer is the second leading cause). Stroke accounts for more deaths for White women than for White men, and deaths from stroke occur twice as often in African American women as in White women. The rates of death from coronary disease were higher for African American women than for White women. Deaths from CVD have decreased in the last 25 years, but death by stroke has decreased more rapidly.

These are startling statistics. Just what is cardiovascular disease and what are the conditions that contribute to its development in both women and men? Why do women with cardiovascular disease fare so poorly? Is it because they are misdiagnosed, diagnosed later, or not treated in the same way as men? And what research has been done in this area, and has it shown reasons for these striking differences?

CVD appears to be a disease of highly developed countries. One way to explain this is that people in more highly advanced countries live longer; that is, they live long enough to fall victim to CVD. The stresses and other risk factors for developing CVD, such as a high-fat diet and lack of exercise, seem to be much higher in modernized countries.

Kaplan et al. (1993) have provided a very clear description of cardiovascular disease. CVD is actually a group of diseases with many components in common.

1. Coronary artery disease occurs when the small arteries that supply blood to the heart muscle become blocked, usually with atherosclerotic plaques. Three types of coronary artery disease result from such blockage: (a) Primary cardiac arrest, in which blood cannot be pumped through the body, can result in sudden death before lifesaving techniques are begun; (b) myocardial infarction (MI), commonly called a *heart attack,* occurs when a blockage in a coronary artery cuts off the blood supply to a particular part of the heart, which then dies. How large a part of the heart is affected determines the patient's recovery or death. Myocardial infarction is usually accompanied by a great deal of pain in the chest; (c) angina pectoris is caused by restricted blood supply in the coronary arteries (not complete blockage) and manifests a type of pain similar to but not as severe as the pain experienced with MI.

2. Cerebrovascular disease is also known as *stroke* or a *cerebrovascular accident* (CVA). This disease occurs when blood flow to a part of the brain is altered because of either a blockage in an artery in the brain or a leak or breakage in a cerebral artery (an artery of the brain). When this occurs, that part of the brain dies. Consequences of stroke can vary widely, depending on the part of the brain affected. Disturbances may involve ability to speak, other language abilities, motor function, memory, sensation and perception, or paralysis. Due to the redundancy of the brain, patients can often recover some or a great deal of function over a period of time. However, this too depends on the seriousness of the CVA. Stroke is often fatal and is the third largest cause of death in the United States.

3. Peripheral artery disease (PAD), often accompanied by diabetes, is caused by diminished blood flow to the arms or legs. This results in pain and loss of function in the extremities. The reduced blood flow causes the affected tissue to die or in less severe cases to suffer a lack of oxygen. Function in the affected limb is severely curtailed and amputation may result.

Risk Factors. Risk factors for heart disease are the same in women and men. Genetic factors such as sex, age, anatomy of the heart and arteries, and inherited lipid and glucose metabolism all act to influence the risk of CVD. Lipid metabolism is the process by which fats and cholesterol are used and stored in the body. Glucose metabolism refers to how glucose is utilized in the body. People who have a genetic disposition to develop a disorder of glucose metabolism

may eventually present with diabetes mellitus. Diabetes is not only a serious disease in itself, but also increases the risk of CVD. Behavioral and environmental factors are also extremely important. Men are at greater risk for CVD than are women, at least until the time of menopause when it was thought that estrogen levels, which start to decline and cease altogether, are no longer preventing CVD in women. Women then catch up to men at an older age. High blood cholesterol, high blood pressure, and obesity are three well-documented physiological risk factors for development of CVD. Behavioral factors associated with CVD are cigarette smoking, poor diet, and a low level of physical activity. These factors are either direct risks or modify physiological processes. Stress is another important factor in CVD. Emotional components such as stress, anger, and hostility have also been implicated in the development of this disease. The type of occupation (e.g., working as an air traffic controller), environmental conditions, such as living in a crowded apartment or neighborhood, and low socioeconomic status have been shown to influence the development of CVD. Type A behavior (e.g., competitiveness, hostility, aggression, impatience, and a sense of time urgency) has also been implicated as a possible risk factor (Kaplan et al., 1993; Serafino, 1994).

Now that we know more about what CVD is and the associated risk factors involved, we can pursue the answers to the other questions that we asked by reviewing the research literature in this area and evaluating the results.

Bias Issues in Cardiovascular Research. As early as 1993, Wenger, Speroff, and Packard (1993) reported that 50 percent of all women with CVD died within a year, or 500,000 women. One-half of these deaths are due to *coronary heart disease.* Wenger et al. (1993) state that there is insufficient information about prevention, diagnostic tests, responses to treatment, or intervention in women. One reason for this is because there are few studies of sex differences in response to treatment, testing, or other therapies.

In 1994, the authors of this text began a comprehensive survey of the biomedical and behavioral research literature in several key areas including CVD, cancer, depression, and AIDS. The purpose of our study was to explore whether women were represented in research and testing in key areas of health. We analyzed patterns of subject use, representations of women and men, and the appropriateness of generalizing research findings to both females and males from either single-sex studies or from studies in which both sexes were included but not compared. We also evaluated whether patterns changed across an eight-year period from 1984 to 1992. Results of our survey of cardiovascular disease demonstrated exceptional gender bias across an eight-year period. We found that males were the predominant subjects in 1984 and 1992. Although women were included in most of the studies, they were included in small numbers. Data were not analyzed separately by sex, but combined, so evaluating responses to treatment by the women tested, as well as by men, was not possible. Moreover, in several studies, sex of the subjects was not even identified. These combined data were then generalized either implicitly or explicitly to both sexes. Little to no rationale for this practice was offered by authors of these studies. Unfortunately, there was little change across the eight-year period studied (Sechzer, Rabinowitz, Denmark, McGinn, Weeks, Wilkens, 1994).

Why Should Sex Differences Be Studied?   Johnson, Kayser, and Pedraza (1984) found that women and men with preoperative angina pain showed surprising differences after coronary bypass surgery was performed. Men experience better pain relief of their angina pain than do women. In a Canadian study, Hung et al. (1984) concluded that much of the available technology for assessing coronary artery disease in men may not be sensitive enough to diagnose the disease in women, because women present atypical symptoms (symptoms that differ from those commonly presented by males). By 1992, Hannan, Bernard, Kilburn, and O'Donnel reviewed sex differences in mortality for coronary artery bypass surgery, with more women dying than men. This study reviewed problems of smaller coronary arteries in women, making them more at risk for surgery. This is especially important, for it seems that heart disease in women has not been taken seriously, and as a result, by the time that women are diagnosed they may

be more seriously ill and thus at a greater risk than the average man of similar age.

Another follow-up study of men and women who had surgery (angioplasty or coronary bypass surgery) because of stenosis (blockage) in their coronary arteries was carried out by Faxon et al. (1992). This group of patients had re-stenosed. However, more women were treated medically to reduce stenosis than men, who, instead, had repeat surgery for a second or third stenosis. These types of studies exploring sex differences in diagnosis, treatment, and outcome for women and men have been too few in the research literature. Instead, as indicated earlier, data are combined so that we do not know the responses of men and of women to various treatments, including surgery and its outcome. Results are simply combined and generalized to males and females through a general statement in the conclusion of the study. Therefore, many of the generalizations made in these studies were rated as *questionable* or *inappropriate* (Sechzer, Rabinowitz, & Denmark et al., 1994).

However, things may be changing. More studies are being conducted to determine how women fare with intervention. These studies show that women with CVD enter the studies older, sicker, and with a higher incidence of other disorders than do men. This is probably due to later diagnosis and referral for treatment (Legato, 1994). Data, when analyzed separately, show that women have more complications of surgery than men, perhaps due to late intervention. Some progress is encouraging in the area of sex bias and CVD, although women still tend to be treated differently than men. Physicians refer men who report symptoms of CVD for further testing and treatment more often than they do women with similar symptoms. It should be noted that some of the differences in referrals for testing and treatment may involve an assessment of women's risks and poorer condition (Brannon, 2002). Yet women and the elderly are still underrepresented in clinical trials. This was despite government regulations in 1993, which mandated that in disorders affecting both sexes, women and men must be proportionally represented. More than one-third of myocardial infarction (MI) patients in the United States are older than 75 years and about 43 percent are women. These people have traditionally been left out of clinical trials that evaluate treatments for cardiovascular disease. Despite efforts by researchers to change this practice, women and the elderly are still underrepresented in heart studies. Peterson and colleagues evaluated 593 clinical trials of MI and angina carried out since 1966. Between 1966 and 1990, elderly patients comprised only 2 percent of participants in studies. From 1991 through 2000 the number of patients increased by only 9 percent—still well below the proportion of elderly MI patients in the United States. In this same time period, the number of women increased from 20 to 25 percent, also falling short of the proportion of female patients (Peterson et al., 2001). The researchers state that "Because safety and efficacy can vary as a function of sex and age, these enrollment biases undermine efforts to provide evidence-based care to all cardiac patients." The researchers also noted that cholesterol-lowering drugs have been widely prescribed to elderly patients without clinical trials to assess their effectiveness. Nevertheless, the greater attention being paid to gender bias in CVD and studies that not only evaluate CVD in women but also provide preventive instruction (e.g., the National Cholesterol Education program) indicate that progress is indeed being made. Such progress is important not only for the health of women but also for the health of men.

Attention is now being paid to hormone replacement therapy and the question of whether it prevents CVD. For some time now, scientists believed that a women's risk for heart disease increased after menopause as her estrogen levels declined and production ultimately ceased. Estrogen replacement therapy (ERT), which ameliorated the distressing symptoms of menopause, was also seen as the solution to replace estrogen and thus reduce the risk of CVD in women. And numerous studies over a period of years linked estrogen replacement with a reduced risk of heart disease. A large-scale, ongoing study at the NIH, the Women's Health Initiative, evaluated medical conditions in a large group of women. One group of participants was given estrogen pills (ERT, estrogen replacement therapy), while another group was given estrogen plus progestin pills (HRT, hormone replacement therapy). In 2001 this large-scale study found no link between estrogen and a reduced

risk of heart disease. In July 2002, the NIH stopped major clinical trials of risks and benefits of combined estrogen and progestin in menopausal women. This was because of increased risk of coronary heart disease, breast cancer, and pulmonary embolism in the HRT group as compared with the placebo group. On the positive side, there were fewer cases of hip fractures and fewer cases of colorectal cancer. Nevertheless, it was decided "that on balance, the harm was greater than the benefit" (Medication, Safety & Reliability, 2002; JAMA, 2002). Trials with estrogen alone are continuing (see Chapter 11 for additional information about HRT). In another study by Viscoli and colleagues, it was found that estradiol (another form of estrogen) does not reduce the risk of mortality or recurrence of stroke in postmenopausal women with cerebrovascular disease. The team also found that a higher risk for fatal stroke among women in the estradial group compared with the placebo group. Women who received estradiol and had a stroke showed more impaired neurological and functional deficits than women in the placebo group who experienced a stroke (Viscoli et al., 2001). So, even though progress is being made, there is still a long way to travel and many questions yet to be answered.

Treatment and Coping.   Dietary strategies are used for weight control for obese CVD patients and for patients with elevated cholesterol levels and blood pressures (hypertension). If adhered to, they can be highly effective. Drug therapy to reduce blood pressure and cholesterol levels is initiated when diet is not effective. Diet usually involves salt reduction for the elevated blood pressure and a low-fat diet to decrease cholesterol (the DASH diet). Exercise is important in control of weight and for reduction of hypertension. Relaxation therapy, biofeedback, meditation, yoga, and qi-gong are other strategies frequently used and can play an important role in reducing stress. Some programs address behavioral changes to improve the status of patients with CVD.

Over the past years, the Ornish program, under the direction of Dean Ornish, has received much attention. The program includes an extremely low-fat diet (10 percent of calories from fat) as well as caffeine-free beverages. It also emphasizes moderate exercise and helps smokers decrease and hopefully eliminate cigarettes from their lifestyle. The Ornish program includes relaxation and yoga exercise as a daily part of the program's routine. Results of this one-year program have been positive. Angina pain decreased and blockage in the coronary vessels decreased in the majority of patients. This is the first study to show that changing the behavioral lifestyle could lead to a reversal of blockage in coronary arteries that was due to atherosclerosis (Kaplan et al., 1993; Ornish et al., 1990). In 2003, studies of the Atkins diet were carried out at two university centers. This diet restricts carbohydrates and allows high fats and proteins and has demonstrated a significant weight loss in many groups. Data from these controlled studies showed not only a loss of weight but also a significant decrease in cholesterol and triglycerides. This diet is a new entry into the possible means of protection against cardiovascular disease (De Noon, 2003).

Individual or group therapy may also be necessary to help CVD patients cope with and reduce stress. Anger and hostility must be dealt with in therapy to understand the source of these emotions and deal with them in ways that will not further compromise health. Depending on the type of heart disease and the physical condition of the patient, different surgical procedures may be carried out; for example, coronary bypass surgery, implanting stents to prevent vessels in the heart from closing, implanting pacemakers, and so forth.

Lung Cancer

Cancer is the second leading cause of death in the United States, killing over 555,000 people each year. Lung cancer is the leading type of fatal cancer for both women and men. More men than women die of lung cancer. For women, there is an average of 191.1 deaths per 100,000 and for men an average of 219.5 per 100,000 in the United States (U.S. Census Bureau, 1999b), which includes individuals of all ages. More than 160,000 cases of lung cancer are diagnosed each year. The five-year survival rate is low, approximately 13 percent, but survival is three times as high if the disease is discovered while it is still localized. However, in lung cancer the malignant cells begin to

metastasize while still small and will usually have spread by the time the diagnosis is made. Although death rates for cancer in general have decreased, in lung cancer the death rate has not really changed.

Until recently, breast cancer was the leading cause of death from cancer for women. However, death from lung cancer has now surpassed that for breast cancer. Although lung cancer rates in men are still higher than those in women, they have begun to decline while the rate of lung cancer in women has continued to increase. The lung cancer rate for African American women and White women is approximately equal. Five-year survival rates for African American and White women are relatively low, but comparable, and higher than for males (NIH-ORWH, 1992). Although fewer people are smoking in industrialized countries, in less developed countries people are picking up the habit at very high levels. Smoking is highest among Asian men, especially in China and Vietnam. Global smoking deaths are now approaching 5 million people (Boyles, 2003).

What Is Lung Cancer and How Does It Develop? As in cardiovascular studies, some of the answers to these questions are to be found in the research literature. Cancer was certainly known at least as far back as the time of the ancient Greeks. The *Ebers Papyrus,* written around 1500 B.C.E., appears to be the first medical document to describe cancer, but it only characterized the swellings associated with some tumors. Hippocrates, in the third century B.C.E., gave the disease the name **cancer,** and several hundred years later in the second century C.E., the Roman physician Galen first used the word **tumor** (Brannon & Feist, 1992).

Cancer is a large group of diseases characterized by uncontrolled growth and spread of abnormal cells (American Cancer Society, 1991) that can affect any part of the body. Cancer cells may differ in different parts of the body, but they all have a common characteristic: the appearance of *neoplastic cells* (new and abnormal growth). In contrast to normal cells, neoplastic cells show new and unlimited growth and are able to multiply uncontrollably and invade and overwhelm normal tissue. In this way, cancer cells spread or metastasize to other sites in the body. Once cells become cancerous, their growth and site in the body are no longer controlled by the same processes that control normal cells. Neoplastic cells can be **malignant** (cells that can metastasize), or they can be **benign** (cells that grow but are limited to a single tumor) (Brannon & Feist, 1992).

Risk Factors. Lung cancer is almost entirely due to cigarette smoking (American Cancer Society, 1999); although other variables, such as genetic factors, environmental carcinogens (air pollution), or cancer-causing substances that women and men encounter in the workplace (such as asbestos and insecticides), may play a role in lung cancer (Taylor, 1995). Stress may also play a role in that it may decrease the functioning of the immune system, making the person more vulnerable to carcinogens.

Today, more young women become smokers than do young men. Recent evidence has also shown that smokers not only put themselves at risk but also put others at risk who are exposed to their *passive smoking* or secondhand smoke. Findings have suggested that women smokers are twice as likely as male smokers to develop lung cancer. This may be due in part to women's smaller lungs receiving a more concentrated dose of smoke with its carcinogens, which may make them more vulnerable (NIH-ORWH, 1992).

Bias Issues in Lung Cancer Research. In 1992, the Women's Health Initiative, under the aegis of the National Institutes of Health, was set in motion by Dr. Bernadine Healy, the then-director of the NIH. The Initiative is a 14-year study and includes some 150,000 women at 45 clinical centers across the country. The purpose of this expansive study is to decrease the prevalence of cancer, especially breast cancer, cardiovascular disease, and osteoporosis among women. Yet, despite the fact that lung cancer is more lethal for women than breast cancer, and the death rate may have already exceeded that for men, there is no comparable large-scale lung cancer study under way or even planned that is comparable to the Women's Health Initiative. Not only is the quantity of research in lung cancer generally insufficient, but in the research that was carried out, inadequate attention has

been paid to gender (Denmark, Sechzer, Rabinowitz et al., 1994). However, in 1995 a study at several medical centers began to investigate whether a CT scan of the lungs would show lung cancer earlier than an X-ray. Simultaneously an X-ray and a CT scan were taken of each participant (smokers, past smokers, and those who had never smoked). Dr. Henschke, head of the study at the Weill-Cornell Medical College, was able to demonstrate that CT scans were able to identify lung cancer before X-rays did. This study involved both women and men, but the sex comparison of the data, if analyzed, has not yet been made available (Henschke, 2003).

Well before the 1995 study began, Denmark, Sechzer, Rabinowitz, et al. (1994) continued to explore the question of sex and gender bias in science. Studies of lung cancer research published in 1984 and 1992 were reviewed and compared. Two leading cancer journals were examined, the *Journal of Clinical Oncology* and *Cancer.* For both years, although sample size was usually adequate, the sex of the subjects was frequently unspecified. Just as in the cardiovascular studies, when sex was identified, male subjects predominated both in 1984 and in 1992. Moreover, even when sex was specified, there was little or no description of treatment responses by sex. Similarly, there was little or no identification of toxic effects of drugs used on women or on men; nor was there any indication of how many women and how many men died after a specific period of survival. In statements about the number or percentage of patients that responded well to treatment and improved, again there was no indication of how many women and how many men responded positively. The typical study combined data for both females and males and then generalized the results, implicitly or explicitly, to both sexes. This was usually found at the end of the discussion or in the conclusions at the end of the report. Generalizations of data from such studies were rated as *questionable* or *inappropriate.* Lung cancer studies did show somewhat more progress toward gender-fair research than in cardiovascular studies. However, on reviewing animal studies cited as a basis for human research in some areas of lung cancer, we found that the animals used were either predominately male or were unidentified as to their sex (Denmark et al., 1994, 1995; Sechzer, 1993; Sechzer, Rabinowitz, Denmark, McGinn, Weeks, Wilkens et al., 1994).

Of particular interest is that females generally have better immune systems than males. With the recent focus on the relevance of the immune system in cancer, exploration of sex differences should have been made, because this may be an important factor in treatment response. In addition to sex differences in immunity, females and males may also have different thresholds for toxicity in the drugs used for treatment. Milano et al. (1992) studied sex and age differences in the drug fluorouracil (5FU), one of the oldest anticancer drugs. These investigators found that, whereas age and 5FU were not correlated, clearance of the drug is slower in women. This raises questions of dosage and toxicity. If it takes longer for women to clear 5FU from their bodies than for men, then repeated dosage would increase the concentration of the drug in their systems. This would place women at greater risk for developing toxicity to the drug and might affect their response and recovery. In some of the studies that involved 5FU treatment, toxicity was reported, but with no indication of the sex of the patients affected. An additional study by Waits et al. (1992) indicated sex differences in the drug etoposide, another drug used for lung cancer. In this study, women were found to be apparently more responsive to the drug than men. Sex differences might exist for other drugs, but would need to be tested for such differences to be evident.

Although some progress has been made in this area of cancer research, it is still obvious that researchers prefer male participants. Yet, as in cardiovascular studies, even when women were included, data were not analyzed separately for females and males and were generalized. We have seen in the cancer studies reviewed that there are differences between females and males in areas of drug toxicity and in the immune system that are based on biological differences. These findings underscore the need for sex comparative studies. Learning about which drugs women and men respond best to, and taking toxicity factors into account, should result in better treatment of the disease, with the patients suffering fewer side effects.

Treatment and Coping. Treatments for lung cancer include (1) surgery—lobe and lung removal; (2) radio-

therapy—when radiation is used; (3) chemotherapy—drug therapy; and (4) palliative care—symptom and pain management. There are negative side effects to most of these procedures. In addition to these four treatment choices, there are clinical trials available with access to cutting-edge treatments not yet approved for general use by the public. Taking part in a clinical trial exposes the patient to unavailable treatment options. Gene therapy is another option to improve the function of the immune system and correct genetic damage. Angiogenesis (the ability to grow blood vessels) and thalidomide (inhibits growth of blood vessels) are starting to be used.

The diagnosis of cancer always has a heightened psychological impact on the patient. When a person is told that she or he has cancer, it often seems like a death sentence, regardless of whether the patient knows a little or a great deal about the disease. Fear and anxiety usually accompany cancer at some stage of the patient's illness. Helping patients to cope with the disease and the potential side effects of treatment, which are usually highly stressful, is an important task for psychologists and health care providers. Many people with cancer become depressed, although levels of depression are varied. Sexual problems are not uncommon. Pain is also a frequent and severe problem for cancer patients, and proper pain management is crucial. In addition to analgesics (pain-relieving drugs), it is necessary to help patients acquire coping skills during the stressful effects of the disease. Some of these include individual or group therapy (which have been found to have positive effects on cancer patients and may improve survival) and relaxation training and meditation to reduce pain and to relieve some of the psychological effects of cancer. When patients are terminal, therapy and support are necessary to help the patients accept their forthcoming death (Kaplan et al., 1993; Serafino, 1994).

Prevention. Although it was previously believed that a diagnosis of lung cancer was a death sentence, we know that progress has been made in the survival rate of many cancers. Many cancers are thought to be avoidable through behavioral changes, most notably a cessation of smoking or a decision not to initiate smoking. Early and consistent screening now with CT scans, particularly in low-income and minority groups, is another crucial preventive strategy. With the ability to detect lung cancer earlier with a CT scan, survival rates should increase, and with very early treatment with new drugs continuing to be available, cure rates should increase as well.

Today's woman who smokes is at a greater risk of dying from a smoking-related disease than her counterpart in the 1960s, because it is highly likely that she began smoking at a younger age and therefore has more past years of smoking in her lifetime.

The most important issue in lung cancer is prevention. Tobacco smoke is generally recognized as the single most documented risk factor in lung cancer, but it is important for women and men to know that smoking is also a risk factor for cervical, bladder, and other cancers. To decrease smoking initiation and increase smoking cessation, research should focus on cigarette advertising, weight control without cigarette use, and social supports. Of special concern is advertising that specifically targets minority women such as African American and Hispanic women (NIH-ORWH, 1992). Developing and implementing innovative prevention and cessation programs will be an exceptional task. The continuing crackdown on tobacco companies has decreased cigarette sales in the United States but not overseas. The European Community will need to address these issues as its lung cancer rates and lung cancer deaths increase.

Sexually Transmitted Infections

Sexually transmitted infections (STIs) are defined as those diseases that are spread by sexual contact, vaginal or anal intercourse, or oral sex. Some STIs can also be transmitted through nonsexual means; for example, sharing contaminated needles can spread AIDS and viral hepatitis. According to Rathus et al. (2002), STIs are rampant. The World Health Organization has estimated that at least 333 million people worldwide are stricken with curable STIs each year (WHO, 1995, cited in Rathus et al., 2002). In the industrialized world, the United States seems to have the highest rate of STIs. Ten million to 12 million new cases of STIs are reported in this country each year, including 2.5 million adolescents. Approximately one in four Americans is likely to contract an STI at some point in her or his life (Rathus, Nevid, & Fichner-Rathus 2002). Some people have an STI but do not realize it because some infections do not produce evident symptoms. Yet if the infection is not diagnosed, it can be harmful or even fatal, as in the case of HIV/AIDS. The rapid increase in the incidence of STIs is due to the increased numbers of people who engage in intercourse and do not use condoms. Also, some infected people without symptoms unknowingly pass their STIs on to their partners. In addition, drug users are more likely to partake in risky sexual practices and either infect their partners or become infected by their partners. A 2001 study found that nearly 1 in 5 teenage girls has an undiagnosed STI (Wiesenfeld, 2001).

Today, the most alarming STI is HIV/AIDS. In addition to HIV/AIDS, the most common STIs in the United States are syphilis, gonorrhea, chlamydia, and HPV (human papilloma virus) (Rathus et al., 2002).

AIDS/HIV Infection. The prevalence of the **acquired immune deficiency syndrome (AIDS)** has now reached epidemic proportions, not only in the United States but also globally. AIDS is a fatal infection caused by the human immunodeficiency virus **(HIV).** It was first described in medical reports and journals in 1981 and has since spread rapidly around the world. As of the end of 2002, an estimated 42 million people worldwide—38.6 million adults and 3.2 million children younger than 15 years—were living with HIV/AIDS. About 70 percent of these people (29.4 million) live in sub-Saharan Africa; another 17 percent (7.2 million) live in Asia (National Institute of Arthritis and Infectious Diseases, 2002).

Worldwide. Approximately 50 percent of adults living with HIV/AIDS worldwide are women. An estimated 5 million new HIV infections occurred worldwide during 2002—or 14,000 infections each day. Over 95 percent of these new infections occurred in developing countries. In 2002 alone, HIV/AIDS-associated illnesses caused the deaths of approximately 3.1 million people worldwide, which included an estimated 610,000 children younger than 15 years (National Institute of Arthritis and Infectious Diseases, 2002).

United States. The Centers for Disease Control and Prevention (CDC) (2000a) estimate that 850,000 to 950,000 U.S. residents are living with HIV infection, and one-quarter of these people are unaware of their infection. Approximately 40,000 new HIV infections occur each year in the United States—70 percent among men and 30 percent among women. Sixty percent of men were infected through homosexual sex, 25 percent through injection drug use, and 15 percent through heterosexual sex. Of these new infections, about 50 percent are Black, 30 percent White, 20 percent Hispanic, and a small percent are members of other racial–ethnic groups.

From 1985 to 2001, the proportion of adult/adolescent AIDS cases reported in women increased from 7 to 25 percent. As of the end of 2001, 467,910 deaths among people with AIDS had been reported to the CDC. AIDS is now the fifth leading cause of death in the United States among people aged 25 to 44 and is the leading cause of death for Black men in this group. The estimated annual number of AIDS-related deaths in the United States fell approximately 70 percent from 1995 to 2001, from 51,670 deaths in 1995 to 15,603 deaths in 2001. Of these deaths, 52 percent were among Blacks, 29 percent among Whites, 18 percent among Hispanics, and less than 1 percent among Asian/Pacific Islanders and American Indians/Alaska Natives (National Institute of Arthritis and Infectious Diseases, 2002).

The data presented here give a clear explanation of the most recent information available regarding HIV/AIDS worldwide and in the United States. Women have become the fastest growing population with AIDS, with the primary modes of transmission being intravenous (IV) drug use and sexual contact (Rathus et al., 2002). People who have unprotected male–female sex comprise about 40 percent of cases in the United States (Rathus et al., 2002). The main route of transmission in Asia is heterosexual intercourse, and in countries such as Thailand and India, the commercial sex trade is the main mode of contact.

The global HIV/AIDS epidemic constitutes a global emergency and one of the most formidable challenges to human life and dignity. Its rapid growth has been accompanied by steady changes in its demographic distribution. In 1981, when we were just becoming acquainted with the terms *HIV* and *AIDS* and reports began to appear in the medical literature, fewer than 100 people had died. By 1993, the CDC estimated that there were more than 253,448 cases of AIDS in the United States (Cohen & Alfonso, 1994). By 1995, more than 74,000 new cases of AIDS were diagnosed in this country. And in 1996 alone, more than 548,000 Americans were diagnosed with AIDS and 338,000 died, and, as indicated, it became the leading killer of Americans age 25 to 44. In 1998 an estimated 1.5 million Americans or people living in the United States were infected with HIV (CDC, 1996; Rathus, Nevid, & Fichner-Rathus, 1997). The CDC (1998) also reported that between 1992 and 1997, the number of persons living with AIDS had increased. This was due to the expanded case definition of the disease and to the improved survival rates with new drug treatment. Of all the AIDS cases, the number of women infected increased from 13.8 percent in 1992 to 19.1 percent in 1997; the number of Black people living with AIDS increased from 32.7 percent to 39.2 percent during this period, which is almost identical to the number of White people living with AIDS (CDC, 1998). There was a dramatic *decrease* in pediatric AIDS in the United States, due in large part to the Public Health Service guidelines for treatment with the drug *zidovudine* during pregnancy, which has reduced the perinatal transmission of HIV. With the development of new drugs, anti-retroviral and others, those who can obtain these drugs may delay the development of full-blown AIDS and will undoubtedly live longer with an improved quality of life. Yet, many infected people will go on to develop AIDS and die.

In the beginning of the epidemic in the United States, it was believed that AIDS predominately affected men who have sex with men and were intravenous drug users. But now HIV/AIDS is not limited to discrete populations but also to subgroups of intravenous drug users and the incidence from male–female contact is increasing. African Americans and Hispanics are among the fastest-growing infected population in the United States. Among these, women have become an increasing group of HIV-infected people. Of the number of Americans who have developed AIDS, approximately 46 percent of men and 75 percent women are African Americans or Hispanic Americans (Rathus et al., 1997). Although HIV/AIDS infection was first observed in men, it is now the fastest-growing disease for women in this country and abroad, as noted earlier. In 1990, 25 percent of all seropositive adults worldwide were women, and in 1992, 40 percent of all seropositive adults were women. Now, at least half of infected people are women. In 1996, HIV/AIDS was the fourth leading cause of death among U.S. women aged 25 to 44 but the leading cause of death among African American women in the same age group. And, although AIDS-related deaths among women are decreasing as a result of advances in treatment, AIDS-related deaths among women are not declining as rapidly as AIDS-related deaths in men. Moreover, recent data for 25 states showed that a substantial number of women were newly diagnosed with HIV infection. There was a larger percentage of HIV cases diagnosed in Women of Color. African American and Hispanic women represent less than one-fourth of all women in the United States, yet they account for more than three-fourths of AIDS cases reported to date among U.S. women (CDC, 1998).

What is AIDS, and why do so many of the affected people die? Why is AIDS in women increasing? Why is the incidence higher in African Americans? Has the research being conducted found anything different in women as compared with men in the development of AIDS?

What Is AIDS, and How Do People Get It? The human immunodeficiency virus is spread through sexual contact, through exposure to HIV-contaminated blood and blood products, and from mother to child through prenatal contact. Kaplan et al. (1993) have provided a clear understanding of how AIDS develops. These authors inform us that it takes at least eight weeks for the **antibodies** to HIV to develop and to be identified on a blood test. However, on contact, HIV rapidly enters the body. It attaches and enters cells in the host's body, usually CD4 helper–inducer **T cell** lymphocytes. These CD4 T cells are an important component of the white blood cells, a part of the **immune system.** Under normal conditions, when a virus (e.g., a cold virus) enters the body, the CD4

cells alert the immune system to this invasion by a foreign body, the cold virus. The normal response of the CD4 cells is to multiply on contact with the cold virus. However, when the HIV has already entered the body and is attached to the CD4 cells, HIV will multiply when the CD4 cells multiply, which is the normal response of the immune system. Thus, the life cycle of HIV contains a set of steps in which it uses the host's own cells to multiply and produces a tremendous number of new HIV viruses. As more and more CD4 cells become infected, the immune system becomes unable to respond to infectious agents. Individuals then die of other infections that the immune system cannot fight off. HIV also infects a number of other cells in the immune system, as well as in the skin, lymph nodes, and brain. As the body weakens, its immune system is no longer able to fight, and opportunistic infections and tumors appear, which define full-blown AIDS. The final appearance of AIDS varies for different people.

Diagnosis in Women and Men. People with AIDS do not show any symptoms (are **asymptomatic**) until long after their initial infection with the HIV virus. Once infected, antibodies to the virus will be made but may not appear until at least eight weeks or longer after exposure. The appearance of symptoms differs widely with the individual. The appearance of symptoms characteristic of AIDS can take years. Major infections will begin to appear when the immune system is severely compromised and include Kaposi's sarcoma (cancer), *Pneumocystis carinii* pneumonia (a parasitic infection), tuberculosis (a bacterial infection), and *Cryptosporidium* (a parasitic infection), which deplete the body further. These symptoms when presented confirm the diagnosis of AIDS.

Transmission of the disease is of major importance to women, medically and psychologically. AIDS/HIV infection was first observed in men and the definition (known as the *case definition*) was developed around the symptoms presented by men. The significant gaps in the case definition of AIDS/HIV seriously compromised women. Until 1994, the case definition by the CDC did not include medical illnesses frequently presented by women in the early stages of the disease, especially recurrent pelvic inflammatory disease and other pelvic infections.

Therefore, by the time AIDS was diagnosed in women, they were more likely to be sicker than men, in whom the diagnosis is usually made much earlier. Thus, women diagnosed later than men died sooner than their male counterparts (Cohen & Alfonso, 1994). Whether this change has facilitated earlier diagnoses of AIDS in women remains to be determined. There are still many physicians, especially gynecologists, who treat patients for medical problems that include pelvic inflammatory disease, rather than consider and test for HIV infection.

High-Risk Behaviors and Prevention. As a means of protection against exposure to HIV infection, everyone should know the high-risk behaviors involved. **High-risk behaviors** include any unprotected sexual intercourse; vaginal, anal, and oral forms are all unsafe without *barrier protection*. The risk seems to be highest for the receptive partner of anal intercourse. Sharing needles with intravenous drug users can transmit the HIV virus. This dangerous behavior may also expose an IV drug user's partner to the HIV virus. Women partners who are HIV positive and become pregnant may transmit the virus to their unborn or newborn infant. Women who are sex workers and have been exposed to the HIV virus may then infect their male partners. Although abstinence is the safest way to avoid HIV exposure, this is not satisfactory or acceptable for many adolescents or adults. Use of condoms, especially those lubricated with the now available virucidal spermicide, can lower the risk. However, there is always the possibility of the condom leaking or breaking. Another means of protection is to have mutually monogamous relationships. General public awareness has not been adequate to change behavior to a safer lifestyle (Cohen & Alfonso, 1994; Grodsky, 1995). Chapter 8 provides a full discussion of a safer lifestyle.

Although now a negligible risk in developed countries, contaminated blood products during transfusions should still be regarded as a potential source of exposure. Efforts should be made to use gloves and other protective garments, especially where there is a cut in the skin. In undeveloped countries where screening of blood donors is not routinely carried out, there is a very high risk of contamination (Cohen & Alfonso, 1994; Kaplan et al., 1993).

Treatment: Medical and Psychological. At present, there is no medical cure for AIDS. The drug that has been continually in use is AZT (azidothymidine or zidovudine), which slows the progress of the HIV virus, but does not effect a cure. AZT does seem to prevent HIV infection of the brain (encephalopathy) and does lengthen survival considerably. Patients will still develop **opportunistic infections** associated with decreased immune function.

There are now many new approaches to treat HIV/AIDS that have come about with the development of *antiretroviral drugs*. These drugs, protein inhibitors, act against HIV, which is a *retrovirus*. They suppress the viral load and increase T/CD4 cell counts. One combination of drugs (indinavir, zidovudine, and lamivudine) given simultaneously (not sequentially) showed a marked antiretroviral response in 78 percent of patients tested (97 patients were enrolled in the study), markedly suppressing HIV replication for long periods of time, up to two years. However, the duration of HIV suppression varies among affected individuals (Gulik, Mellors, Havlir et al., 1998). In another study, antiretroviral treatment (ART) was given to HIV-infected drug users. Four sites were set up in different areas but all provided easy access. The results demonstrated that when sites for treatment were made accessible, ART compliance improved and the patients did not develop the AIDS complex (Rompalo, 2001). The results of the study cited, as well as results from other studies, showed qualitative and quantitative changes in the immune system that were associated with improvements in immune responses. Although patients receiving antiretroviral drugs are not cured of HIV, they appear to have a great deal of protection against most AIDS-related opportunistic infections (Powderly, Landay, & Lederman, 1998). However, only in industrialized or developed countries is health care funding adequate to treat the large number of people with AIDS (Cohen & Fauci, 1998).

Although antiretroviral therapy has significantly decreased the mortality rate for AIDS patients, the incidence of new HIV infections has not decreased as significantly in the United States. In 1997, almost 6 million people worldwide became HIV infected and, importantly, over 90 percent of these people lived in developing countries. In these countries, the amount of money spent on health care is extremely small, and access to antiretroviral therapy virtually nonexistent. These facts make the development of a vaccine a pressing need. Many vaccines are in development with some actually in clinical trials. But it will probably be years before an effective vaccine is developed given the many varieties of HIV subtypes (Cohen & Fauci, 1998).

Psychological interventions for AIDS patients have been developed. Cognitive–behavioral stress management with gay men after they were notified that they were **HIV positive** showed a decrease in depression and an increase in immune functioning (Antoni et al., 1991). Other encouraging programs include relaxation and stress management training, biofeedback, and visual imagery, some of which resulted in a decline of HIV-related symptoms (Taylor, 1995).

Psychological and Sociocultural Issues for Women with AIDS. There are important sociocultural and psychological issues concerning women with AIDS. A large study of male and female heterosexuals showed a surprisingly low proportion of condom use, particularly for women with high-risk behaviors (Catania et al., 1992). Catania et al. concluded that women either do not understand the risks of HIV transmission or are in denial of their personal risk. But this may also represent a lack of empowerment to enforce safe sex practices with their partner(s). Teenagers are also among populations at particular risk because they frequently succumb to peer pressure not only to have sexual intercourse but also to use drugs. Women in all these groups need to understand that they have the ability to choose a method of contraception. But attitudes and beliefs often lead high-risk women to willingly avoid using contraception. The fear of loss of love, companionship, home, and financial support may influence their decision. Violence or even death may occur if some women insist on using barrier protection. **HIV-seropositive** women should be aware that there is a chance that their baby will be born infected with HIV if they do not choose contraception. Obviously, sexual behavior is not cognitive activity and therefore does not lend itself easily to behavior change based on information alone. Efforts to educate and increase awareness about AIDS and its transmission have not been successful in altering behaviors (Cohen & Alfonso, 1994; Grodsky, 1995).

Compounding the devastating illness caused by AIDS, which results in profound emaciation, weakness, depression, pneumonia and other immune disorders, pain, disfigurement, and untimely death, there is the new form of discrimination called *AIDSism* (or AIDS-related stigma). This type of discrimination appears to be more devastating for HIV-infected women than for infected men. Discrimination against people with AIDS is well known; homophobia and fear of contagion are severe. Once the diagnosis has been made, infected people may become isolated, shunned, or homeless and may no longer be accepted at shelters. The stress and psychological effects on women are so great that they are at much higher risk for suicide. Sexual partners of injecting drug users are even at higher risk for suicide than are other infected people (Cohen & Alfonso, 1994; Kirschner, 1995).

Gender Issues in AIDS Research. In addition to the vulnerability of affected women and their being ignored in diagnosis and in medical treatment, women have also been underrepresented in clinical trials of AIDS drugs and treatment. When AIDS became highly manifest in the early and middle 1980s, biomedical, behavioral, and social research on AIDS/HIV infection in the United States and in other Western countries was concentrated overwhelmingly on gay and bisexual men as research participants. Although this focus was highly understandable, given the nature of the early stages of the epidemic, the trend has continued, even with the rapid rise in the number of AIDS-infected women.

Important differences in biological factors, transmission patterns, clinical manifestations, and survival times are evident between men and women infected with the HIV virus. Men and women also differ on many psychosocial variables that may affect their immune function and hasten the progress of the disease. Questions are now being raised about whether research findings obtained primarily in men can be reliably generalized to women with AIDS/HIV infection.

In a survey of AIDS/HIV research published in scientific journals in 1984 and in 1991, Rabinowitz (1993) and Rabinowitz, Sechzer, Denmark, and Weeks

(1994) found that males are still the predominant research subjects. In 1991, nearly four times as many males as females were studied, and in almost 25 percent of the studies the participants were not identified according to gender. Although 41 percent of the studies included both males and females, most of them featured inadequate representation of one gender, virtually always females. The authors also found that when women were included, data were not analyzed separately by gender but combined and generalized to both males and females without any justification or rationale (Rabinowitz et al., 1994). Thus, women, who comprise 52 percent of the adult population, are not only underinsured, underdiagnosed, and undertreated by the medical profession, but are also particularly underrepresented in clinical trials, many of which involve drug treatment for AIDS. To address these needs for women, it will be necessary to redefine AIDS in order to include diseases most frequently appearing in infected women. There is a crucial need to develop a comprehensive program of education and clinical care that will deal with the special needs of women and children. It is also critical to include more women of all ages in clinical research trials so that a gender-comparative analysis of results can determine when and what type of treatment are necessary for women.

A major issue concerning a woman's risk for developing AIDS addresses the time to begin treatment. Results of a 1998 study show that infected women may be at a more advanced stage of infection with HIV than men are, even though the results of their blood tests are identical and, according to federal guidelines, treatment is not yet indicated. This suggests that infected women are treated at a more advanced stage of infection than men and are at a greater risk for developing AIDS when compared to men (Grady 1998). Aspects of this critical finding are provided in Box 14.3.

Transmission of HIV between Women. Little attention has been given to the transmission of HIV between women because the main focus has been on the "standard" transmission behaviors, such as drug use and sharing of needles and sex among men. It has been assumed that the sexual transmission of HIV from woman to women is low. However, a recent report by

Kennedy et al. (1998) has raised questions about the prevalence of HIV transmission between women. A multisite study was conducted by these authors with 871 HIV-infected women, who were then followed for up to three and a half years. Details of this interesting and informative study are provided in Box 14.4.

Other Sexually Transmitted Infections. As early as 1994 Borgatta emphasized that many screening and treatment programs for sexually transmitted infections (STIs) other than HIV/AIDS were directed at women, and, because of this, there may be the inadvertent perception that these infections were wholly female problems. Except for the gay and lesbian population, screening and prevention programs for men were virtually nonexistent. Undoubtedly, many of the secondary and tertiary effects of STIs are unique to women: chronic pelvic inflammatory disease, tubal infertility, cervical cancer, preterm birth, and neonatal infection. In many other infections, the behavior that increases the risk of the infection is considered an undesirable one, and patients can be counseled for strategies to change and decrease risk-taking behavior. Unfortunately, there has been and still is little "unanimity on what constitutes appropriate sexual behavior" (Borgatta, 1994, p. 102), especially to reduce the incidence of STIs. Some of the choices might range from people keeping a monogamous relationship, delaying initial sexual activity, decreasing the lifetime number of sexual partners, using barrier or other protection against infection, to encouraging alternate sexual practices. This issue is problematic because it is adolescents who are at the highest risk for STIs and AIDS. Although some adolescents may have information about STIs and HIV, their behavior has not seemed to change and adolescents are still at very high risk for these diseases (Borgatta, 1994). The question of whether there should be different approaches for females and males has also been raised.

Other sexually transmitted infections have not had as much publicity and public concern as has HIV/AIDS but are still prevalent and of serious concern. Like HIV/AIDS, these other sexually transmitted infections (STIs) have become widespread and, in certain areas, uncontrollable. In 1995, the World Health Organization estimated that approximately 333

BOX 14.3

HIV-Infected Women at a Greater Risk for Developing AIDS Than Men

HIV-infected women may be at a greater risk for developing AIDS than men even though their blood tests are identical and, according to federal guidelines, they do not need to start treatment. A study carried out at Johns Hopkins School of Public Health measured the *virus load,* or level of virus present in the bloodstream of HIV-infected men and women. This test is important in deciding when to start treatment with antiviral drugs to prevent or delay the onset of AIDS. Guidelines issued by the U.S. Public Health Service recommend beginning treatment for both genders when the viral load rises to 10,000 copies of HIV per millimeter. This level of HIV infection is taken to indicate that the immune system is losing ground to the infection.

The results of the study showed that at a given stage of HIV infection a woman's viral load was lower than a man's even though the immune system of a woman showed as much damage as a man's. Thus, using the viral load as a marker for initiating treatment may very well delay treatment for women, with the result that when their virus load reaches the treatment point, they will be much sicker than men beginning treatment at the same virus level. Researchers who conducted the study recommended that official guidelines be changed to begin treatment earlier for women.

This finding in 650 men and women who are drug users adds fuel to the ongoing debate about just when to begin treatment. Some scientists or physicians feel that treatment with antiviral drugs should be started as soon as possible to prevent damage to the immune system; others, concerned about the side effects of antiviral drugs and drug resistance, feel that treatment should be postponed as long as possible. Still others say that, although the findings are important (and other groups have found similar differences between the sexes), it was premature to change treatment guidelines (Grady, 1998).

The results of this study may have parallels to a woman's risk for developing lung cancer described earlier in this chapter. Findings have suggested that women smokers are twice as likely to develop lung cancer. This may be due in part to women's smaller lungs receiving a more concentrated dose of smoke with its carcinogens, which may make them more vulnerable. Further studies with HIV-infected women will bring a greater understanding of this gender difference. In the meantime, establishing new procedures to detect the stage of HIV infection as an adjunct to measuring viral load may be a valuable guide in determining when to start treatment in women as well as in men.

---

million people worldwide are infected with STIs each year (WHO, 1995). In the United States alone it was been reported that at least 13 million people are affected including a large proportion of adolescents with chlamydia (Burstein, Gaydos et al., 1997). These other sexually transmitted infections that we will discuss include syphilis, gonorrhea, chlamydia, and the human papilloma virus. As indicated earlier, the estimated number of new cases of STIs per year in the United States, including HIV/AIDS, is now 15.3 million.

Syphilis. Syphilis is a bacterial infection. Syphilis and other STIs are frequently spread by drug users, prostitutes, and their sex partners by vaginal, oral, or anal activity or by contact with an infectious chancre. With the development of penicillin during World War II, the incidence of syphilis decreased. Despite this new drug, there was a resurgence during the

1980s, and by 1990 the rate of number of cases in the United States reached 50,000 a year. Again, in the 1990s, syphilis decreased to about 8,500 cases per year (Rathus et. al., 2002). The incidence of syphilis has since continued to rise. By 1993, there was a total of 35,000 cases, an increase of about 6 percent from the year before (USDHHS, 1994). By 2000, the estimated number of new cases per year was 70,000. The increase has paralleled the rise in cocaine use and HIV infection. Diagnosis, primarily by serologic (blood) tests, is highly reliable but may not give positive results during the early phase of the disease. Darkfield examinations (microscopic examination of the syphilitic lesions) are specific for syphilis and provide the earliest possible testing. Such examinations require expensive microscopic equipment and may not be available at many primary care facilities. If early diagnosis is made and treatment given, blood

Box 14.4

HIV Transmission between Women

The sexual behavior of women with the human immunodeficiency virus (HIV) has been largely ignored as a subject of investigation due to the belief that sexual contact between women is an unlikely transmission route for HIV. In the past, studies reported that the majority of women who became infected with HIV had engaged in high-risk behaviors, such as drug injection or sexual contact with men. However, current research indicates that female-to-female sex may be more prevalent than previously envisaged and therefore constitutes a larger risk factor for the spread of HIV than previously surmised.

Responding to this scarcity of information, the HIV Epidemiologic Research Study reported on the sexual behaviors of women infected with HIV. All 871 HIV-positive women who participated in the study met at least one of the following criteria: drug injection since 1985, sex with five or more partners in the last five years, sex with an at-risk male, or sex to obtain money or drugs. Of this group, 250 (29 percent) HIV-infected women reported having had sex with a woman, and 67 of these women engaged in sexual behavior with one steady female partner.

The study also investigated the prevention practices employed by women to protect their partners from vaginal secretions that could spread the HIV virus. Sex-toy use and receptive oral sex were examined. Thirty-four percent of women with a steady sex partner reported using sex toys and 80 percent reported receiving oral sex. Almost every participant engaged in the prevention measure of cleaning sex toys before using them again. However, using a barrier, such as a dental dam, during oral sex was not consistently practiced among these women. Thirty-one percent of this group reported using a barrier "sometimes" during oral sex, whereas 26 percent reported "always" using a barrier, and 43 percent "never" used a barrier. In contrast, the consistent use of a barrier as a prevention measure is much higher among women from a cohort group who have sex with men. Fifty-three percent of these women reported always using a condom during sexual contact with men. The authors of this study (Kennedy et al., 1998) caution readers about the generalizability of the data because of the small number of women studied. Nevertheless, the sexual behavior and prevention practices among women who have sex with other women is an area that merits significant concern in this era of the AIDS epidemic.

---

tests may return to negative. Serologic tests are almost always positive during the secondary stage of the disease but cannot distinguish between secondary and tertiary stages. This distinction is important because patients in the secondary stage will be cured with one or several injections of penicillin. Tertiary syphilis with organ infection will require more extensive treatment.

More research is still needed to develop improved diagnostic tests for early detection of syphilis and to distinguish between the different stages of the disease. Treatment is with penicillin or with doxycycline, tetracycline, or erythromycin for nonpregnant penicillin-allergic patients.

Gonorrhea.   Gonorrhea is also a bacterial infection. Known as "the clap" or "the drip," it was once very widespread. Although the incidence of gonorrhea declined by the mid-1990s in most portions of the population due to safer sex practice, the incidence increased again by the late 1990s. There has also been an increase in penicillin-resistant gonorrhea. Gonorrhea is transmitted by vaginal, oral, or anal sexual activity or to the newborn by the mother at the time of delivery. The diagnosis of gonorrhea is usually made early because about 50 percent of males and females with early infection *are* symptomatic. This facilitates early diagnosis and treatment. Treatments for gonorrhea have improved, with many effective agents such as antibiotics, ceftriaxone, ciprofloxacin, cefixime, and ofloxacin. In comparison with the other STI's, treatment options for this disease are effective (Borgalta 1994).

Chlamydia.   Chlamydia is another bacterial infection. The incidence of chlamydia is now much more frequent than syphilis or gonorrhea. Prevalence may be as high as 10 percent in some populations. The

CDC (1998) has estimated that there are nearly 4 million new infections a year in the United States. Chlamydia is present throughout all socioeconomic groups in the United States, in contrast to gonorrhea and syphilis, which have been associated with low socioeconomic groups. There is a high prevalence and incidence of chlamydia among adolescent females who are at the highest risk for infection (Burstein et al., 1998). Transmission is by vaginal, oral, or anal activity; from the mother to the newborn during delivery; or by touching the eye after touching infected genitals. Chlamydia is asymptomatic in women and frequently in men. Because of this, the organisms may reside in the subject for a prolonged period during which the disease may be transmitted. The causative organism of chlamydia lives in the cells and cannot be cultured by usual procedures. When symptomatic it tends to cause a low-grade illness, but the disease may progress. This may lead to urethral and epididymal scarring in men and in woman to painful urination, tubal damage, which may lead to infertility, ectopic pregnancy, or chronic pelvic infection.

Because of the asymptomatic nature of the disease and concern for progression, effective prevention and screening are essential. Current screening for the disease is expensive. The Abbott Testpack analyzes a cervical smear in women and an extract of fluid from the penis in men. There are several treatments available including antibiotics, azithromycin, doxycycline, ofloxacin, and amoxicillin (Rathus et al., 2002).

Human Papilloma Virus (HPV) or Genital Warts. It is estimated that the human papilloma virus (HPV) is present in 10 to 20 percent of women of reproductive age in the United States. Infection rates are greater than rates for all other STIs. In 2000, the CDC (2000a) estimated that 5.5 million people in the United States are infected each year and that approximately 20 million people are already infected. HPV is not a reportable disease and may be asymptomatic. Various subgroups of HPV are associated with warts of the genitalia of both men and women and with flat warts that are associated with changes in the vulva, vagina, cervix, penile skin, and with cancerous lesions in these sites. Transmission is by sexual contact

and with infected towels or clothing. Direct viral tests are difficult and very expensive, so diagnosis is based on clinical identification of the warts and an abnormal Pap smear. There is no specific test for HPV at the present time. Although there are several treatment options for HPV, none is completely effective and recurrences are not unusual. Treatment can include cryotherapy (freezing), podophyllin, trichloroacetic acid (TCA) or buchloroacetic acid (BCA), burning, and surgical removal (Rathus et al., 2002). At present there is no optimal treatment approach. Although there is much research in this area, many unanswered questions remain.

Prevention. In the area of primary prevention of STIs, there are a number of issues associated with condom use and spermicide effectiveness. Although condom use has increased and free condom distribution has even further increased their use (Cates, Stewart, & Russell, 1992), formal education apparently does not make a significant difference. In some studies, women at highest risk used condoms less frequently than women at lower risk. The new "female condom" may be a possibility for some women (Cates et al., 1992). More efficient spermicides are also needed for primary protection. Spermicides that are basically detergents act differently against the different STI organisms. The development of specific spermicides for each of the infections does not seem to be evident in the very near future.

Thus, primary prevention for all STI's is the same as just described, but for secondary prevention and control of the infection, the identification and treatment of different STIs are specific for each. Tertiary prevention from the development of sequelae such as infertility and tubal disease is crucial but, according to Borgatta (1994), programs planned to prevent or reduce tubal disease may be poorly funded and treatment for acute pelvic infection may be inadequate and lead to chronic disease. Newer antibiotics have been proposed to treat STIs and more effectively control sequelae.

Many issues need to be addressed, such as the impact of immediate diagnosis through tests conducted in a physician's office versus delay in diagnosis by use of an outside laboratory, the question of turnaround time for such diagnostic tests, and many questions regarding the treatment of those identified with STIs and their partners. In many settings the patient is given medication for her or his partner. Should this be done or should the partner be made to appear in person and be tested? The partner who has had no contact with the physician needs treatment. The partner may also have need to be educated about STIs and their prevention, although education alone, as noted above, does not seem to make a difference. Effective means of prevention are avoiding high risk behavior, practicing monogamy, having regular medical checkups, and seeking educational information for the latest strategies to prevent STIs including HIV/AIDS.

There is little information on STIs in homosexual women. Whether they can transmit vaginitis or chlamydia is unknown. It is assumed however that viral diseases like HPV, herpes, and HIV can be transmitted. Because lesbians, like heterosexual women, are not likely to maintain a monogamous relationship for their lifetime, the majority of lesbians have also had some heterosexual contact at some time during their life. Some lesbians have also had bisexual relationships. On the whole, the majority of women having sex with women will probably not seek treatment from the standard health care system, especially if they are not bisexual and not at risk for unintended pregnancy.

DISEASES PRIMARILY AFFECTING WOMEN

This section will describe two diseases that are unique to women: breast cancer and osteoporosis. Although men do develop these diseases they represent a very small proportion of the affected population. Both breast cancer and osteoporosis are considered to be primarily women's diseases.

Breast Cancer

Breast cancer is a high mortality illness and is a major health problem in the United States as well as in other parts of the world. For women in this country, breast cancer is the second leading cause of cancer deaths, after lung cancer. Breast cancer alone now accounts for almost 40 percent of cancer deaths in women with

one in nine women in the United States expected to develop the disease (CDC, 2002). In specific numbers, 211,300 American women are expected to be diagnosed with breast cancer in 2003, and 40,200 are expected to die (Stein, 2003). Although death rates from this cancer are continuing to fall, the number of new cases is growing (Warner, 2003). Obviously not all women with breast cancer will die of the disease. One explanation for the incidence of breast cancer continuing to increase is the advances in cancer screening techniques. Early diagnosis with these advanced techniques also contributes to the decline in death rates (Warner, 2003). The causative factors have not been precisely defined, so the prevention of breast cancer still remains difficult.

What Is Breast Cancer, and How Does It Develop?
Cancer begins when cells in a particular site become altered and are capable of uncontrolled growth. The type of cancer cell that becomes *neoplastic* depends on the site in which it develops.

Kemeny (1994) has provided an excellent review of breast cancer and its treatment. Breast cancer usually starts inside the ducts and then enlarges locally. When confined to the ducts, it is known as *in situ carcinoma.* Once the cancer penetrates the lining of the ducts or the basement membrane, it is then able to invade the tissue around it and becomes an *invasive cancer.* Invasive cancer then has the capacity to enter the lymphatic stream, seeding cancer cells into the lymph nodes, and then seeding them into the bloodstream, by which they travel to other parts of the body (metastasis). The most common sites for *metastasis* from breast cancer are the lungs, liver, and bones (especially the vertebrae) (Kemeny, 1994).

Risk Factors. The major **risk factors** for breast cancer do not appear to be related to lifestyle. Breast cancer rates increase with age from 14.2 per 100,000 women by age 35 to 44, to 204.9 per 100,000 women age 85 and over (Brannon, 2002). Women with a sister, mother, or daughter with breast cancer have an above average risk of developing the disease, but the risk is not as great as has been thought. In fact, most women with a family history will never get the disease (Beral, 2001). Most women with breast cancer do not have a family history. "For women with one close relative with breast cancer, the lifetime risk of the disease was 8.0%. The risk was 13.3% for women with 2 first degree relatives and 21.1% for those with three affected relatives" (Beral, 2001). Menstrual cycle factors, including early menarche and late menopause, increase the relative risk from 1.1 to 1.9. Age at first full-term pregnancy for women over 30 years of age also increases the risk to more than 2.0. Pregnancy factors and the menstrual cycle, especially early onset have been interpreted in terms of exposure to endogenous estrogen (Travis, 1988; McAnulty & Burnette, 2004), and estrogen replacement therapy has also been associated with some increased breast cancer risk. Alcohol consumption has been considered a risk factor. Although dietary fat has been assumed to be a risk factor, more recent studies do not support this association (Colditz, 1993). On the other hand, postmenopausal obesity does increase the relative risk of breast cancer. Other proposed risk factors, such as breast injury, sexual stimulation, or breast-feeding, which many women feel increases breast cancer risk, have not been supported with any empirical data (American Cancer Society, 1994).

Psychosocial aspects of breast cancer are beginning to be addressed, albeit with a small number of studies. These are described in Box 14.5.

Treatment.   Treatment for breast cancer is based on how far the cancer has spread or the stages of the disease. Kemeny (1994) has described four stages. Stage I is a small cancer confined to the breast; stage II is a larger breast cancer that may have already involved the axillary (under the arm) lymph nodes on the same side as the breast cancer; stage III is a much more advanced cancer that has spread into the skin and chest wall and may have more extensive lymph node involvement; stage IV is a breast cancer that has metastasized or spread into organs outside the breast such as the lungs, liver, or bones.

Stages I and II are considered curable with surgery. Not all of these cancers are 100 percent curable, but surgery should cure approximately 50 percent of these tumors with no further treatment. Stage III breast cancer is generally not considered curable by surgery alone, but must have additional treatment with chemotherapy or radiation therapy or both. With a stage IV cancer, surgery is not indicated because the

---

BOX 14.5

Psychosocial Aspects of Breast Cancer

Although written about and commented on in the popular press, it appears that the medical community has not generally studied the psychosocial and psychosexual aspects of breast cancer. From the few small studies available, women seem more comfortable with lumpectomy and tend to adjust better as far as their body image and feelings about their own sexuality are concerned than women who have had mastectomies.

In a California study of women who had undergone either lumpectomy or mastectomy, there were large differences in the sexual and body image states of the two groups. As would be expected, women with mastectomies felt much more negative about their nude appearance and more self-conscious in groups of women. These women also felt less sexually desirable and were more dissatisfied with their body image when compared with women having undergone lumpectomies. However,

there was no difference in concern about the recurrence of their cancer. Neither group showed evidence of undue depression, anxiety, or other psychological stresses.

Thus, the women with lumpectomies appeared better adjusted psychosexually and were not more concerned about recurrence of their cancer. Although other studies have reported similar results, there has as yet been no large nationwide study to examine these and other questions.

The psychosexual and psychological well-being of women with breast cancer is a critical concern. These aspects have often been overlooked in rehabilitating women with the disease or in the process of a woman making an informed choice between lumpectomy and mastectomy. These concerns must be considered before any treatment for breast cancer begins (Kemeny, Wellisch, & Schain, 1988).

cancer has already spread outside the breast (Kemeny, 1994).

Early in the the twentieth century, *radical mastectomy* (removal of the entire breast, chest muscle, and all the lymph nodes) was the considered cure for the disease, and this became the standard procedure for tumors that had not spread beyond the breast. In the 1960s total rather than radical mastectomy was tested; the major chest muscle was not removed. Results over 20 years showed no difference in survival rates. More recently, the *lumpectomy* procedure was developed and tested. The breast is not removed, but only the cancer with a rim of normal breast tissue around it. After studying results for more than 10 years with more than 2,000 women, there was no significant difference in disease-free survival between all these variations of treatment (Fisher, Redmond, & Poisson, 1989). Radiation treatment after any of these surgical procedures is often carried out to help prevent the cancer from recurring. Other treatments include antiestrogen medications such as tamoxifen. Evidence has shown that tamoxifen has decreased the incidence of a cancer recurring in the other breast. Raloxifene (Evista), a drug for osteoporosis, has also been shown to decrease the incidence of breast cancer. Two recent studies have shown a decreased risk for breast cancer. In the first study, the drug letrozole cut the relapse risk for postmenopausal women for more than five years. These women all had the standard treatment for early stage breast cancer (Stein, 2003). The second study showed that cholesterol-lowering drugs might reduce the risk of breast cancer as well as of heart disease (Rubin, 2003).

Other new medical approaches have included self-help groups that meet on a regular basis to exchange various forms of support, from information and tangible help to building self-esteem and addressing other psychological needs. One study found that survival increased for at least two years in these women compared with women who have not been involved with such support groups. In 2003, letrozole, a new drug, has been shown to reduce the risk or recurrence of breast cancer (Stein, 2003).

Prevention. At the present time there is no way to prevent breast cancer other than by trying to reduce risk factors. Unlike lung cancer, no carcinogenic agent has been identified with breast cancer. However, research with tamoxifen (an antiestrogen medication) has yielded surprising results. The new drug letrozole may also yield positive results. Although there are contradicting reports on its efficacy in preventing cancer recurrence, all studies have shown a decrease in the incidence of a second breast cancer in the other breast. Recent research with tamoxifen is investigating whether it might prevent breast cancer for women who are at high risk. This series of investigations is known as the Breast Chemoprevention Trial, the first chemoprevention trial in the United States. In late 1998, tamoxifen was approved by the FDA for women at high risk for breast cancer and for women who have had breast cancer. It may signal a new trend toward preventative medicine in the United States, which is long overdue for women. Another drug, raloxifene (Evista), was approved in the United States for the prevention of osteoporosis. Results of clinical trials demonstrated not only an increase in bone density in women with osteoporosis, but also a decrease in breast cancer (Smith, 2003).

Osteoporosis

Osteoporosis is a global health problem and is estimated to affect over 200 million people worldwide. This disease affects more than 25 million Americans, 80 percent of whom are women. Osteoporosis accounts for approximately 1.5 million new fractures each year. One-third to one-half of all postmenopausal women have some degree of osteoporosis, and the rates for this disease increase dramatically with age at an estimated cost of $10 billion for rehabilitation and extended treatment.

What Is Osteoporosis? **Osteoporosis** is characterized by decreased skeletal mass and poor bone quality, which leads to increased fractures, typically of the hip, spine, and wrist (Barefield, 1996; Galsworthy, 1994; NIH-ORWH, 1992). Each year 1.5 million fractures are attributed to osteoporosis, including 250,000 to 300,000 hip fractures. Hip fractures are the most serious consequence of osteoporosis. The incidence of fractures in African American and Hispanic women is one-half that of Caucasian and Asian women, but their risk is still serious. A study carried out in the state of Washington found that over 5 percent of all hospitalizations for injuries of patients who were 65 years or older were the results of falls. More women were injured than men. One of the results of such injuries was that approximately one-half of patients with injuries due to falls were placed in nursing facilities (Kaplan et al., 1993; Riggs & Melton, 1992).

Osteoporosis is one of the few medical conditions not described by Hippocrates. This is probably because very few women and men lived long enough—past menopause—to develop the disease. Even in the late 1800s, women's fragile skeletons were considered a normal part of the aging process, along with changes in posture showing a dowager's hump. These changes were common in elderly Caucasian women. In the 1920s, reports and discussions about weakened bones started to appear in the German literature. The incidence of wrist fractures in women was attributed to the hazards of the long skirts worn by women during this time. Astley Cooper, a British surgeon, also noted fragility of bones in aged cadavers. However, in 1941, Fuller Albright concluded that "osteoporosis resulted from inadequate formation and/or excessive breakdown of bone" (Galsworthy, 1994, p. 159). Although his hypothesis was published in the *American Journal of Medicine,* little attention was given during the early 1900s to the problem of this chronic illness primarily in women (Galsworthy, 1994).

In the 1960s, medicine began to focus not only on women but also on elderly women and men. Although women who presented problems of osteoporosis were helped with pain relief and rehabilitation, physicians did not have sophisticated tools with which to make a diagnosis. When the technology for bone scanning was developed in the 1970s, it was possible to identify patients with osteoporosis, and the disease became well known across the country and abroad.

Risk Factors.   Osteoporosis is often thought of as a silent disorder because symptoms first occur in advanced stages of the disease: wrist fractures, painful and deforming vertebral fractures, and the pain and

morbidity of hip fractures. Therefore, physicians will evaluate patients on a profile of risk factors that might predict the future development of the disease. This profile is not as accurate a predictor of fracture risks as are bone density evaluations. However, some of the risk factors commonly used include female, Caucasian, Asian, Northern European, light hair and complexion, diet limited in calcium, sedentary lifestyle, postmenopausal, fracture history of spine, wrist, and hip, and family history of osteoporosis. To this list may be added the past and current medications and especially the use of steroidal and other drugs that cause bone resorption such as cortisone and cortisone-like drugs. Some chemotherapeutic drugs may also reduce bone density.

Diagnosis.   Diagnosis of osteoporosis is confirmed primarily by bone density measurements. This procedure has been shown to be a more accurate predictor of fracture risk than any other assessments. There are a variety of bone density techniques. These measurements confirm the presence of osteoporosis and determine the type of intervention that is necessary (e.g., diet, drugs, exercise, etc.).

Because bone is a living tissue, it remodels continually during one's lifespan. Remodeling is characterized by rapid resorption (when bone tissue is removed from specific areas in the body) and then a slower phase when bone tissue is reformed at these sites. In older people, reformation may be deficient, and more and more bone tissue is lost primarily from sites in the wrist, spine, and hip in proportion to bone reformation (National Osteoporosis Foundation, 1991).

Prevention and Treatment.   For women (and men) with osteoporosis or who are at risk for developing osteoporosis, there are many treatment options. Dietary supplementation of calcium, vitamin D, and calcium-rich foods are used. Drugs are now available that protect the bones by either preventing resorptive mechanisms or building bone mass. In this way, bone loss is inhibited and the skeleton can rebuild, albeit slowly. There are many new drugs developed to prevent bone loss and to help reform bone tissue, all of which will help prevent fractures. Estrogen replacement therapy for postmenopausal women has shown protection from bone loss, but does not build bone. It is one of the few positive effects of this hormone. There are other drugs waiting FDA clearance that should be available within the next few years. Exercise is also very important, especially weight-bearing exercise. Of these, walking is considered very effective, as is a treadmill or a stair climber, which have been shown not only to prevent bone loss but also to increase bone density in the spine and hips, depending on the frequency and intensity of use.

Prevention for younger people consists of building up their bone density levels before menopause to prevent bone loss. This includes adequate calcium and vitamin D intake and aerobic and weight-bearing exercise on a regular basis. These strategies should become part of one's lifestyle. The National Institutes of Health has made specific recommendations for calcium intake. Of special interest here are those recommendations for women 25 to 50 years of age (1,000 mg/day) and for postmenopausal women (1,000 to 1,500 mg/day).

Men must also be included in treatment for and prevention of bone loss to help prevent hip and other fractures. According to a recent report, men are seldom treated for osteoporosis following a hip fracture (Kiebzak et al., 2002). The study showed that men typically experienced a hip fracture about a year younger than women, but only 4.5 percent of men received osteoporosis treatment after discharge from the hospital. Five years later, only 11 percent of men received a bone mineral density test and 27 percent were taking osteoporosis medication. The basic treatment was calcium and vitamin D. Moreover, men had nearly double the one-year mortality rate of women following a hip fracture.

Although osteoporosis as a health problem has reached virtually epidemic proportions, there is sufficient knowledge to undertake effective therapeutic action immediately. For young women (and men), strategies to prevent bone loss should be pursued throughout their lifespan.

A CHANGING VIEW OF WOMEN'S HEALTH

During the 1980s concern about women's health had gathered enough momentum and began to effect changes in medical care and research. These changes came about as a result of responses and concerns about women's health by women in positions of authority and by pressure from scientists, both men and women, special-interest groups, the media, and the general public (LaRosa, 1994; Sechzer, Griffin, & Pfafflin, 1994). The increase in the number of women physicians has also been significant. In most medical schools, almost 40 percent or more of the students are women preparing for all specialties, including nontraditional disciplines such as surgery and urology.

Changes in Government Regulations

One of the first changes came about in 1990 with the creation of the Office of Research on Women's Health (ORWH) at the National Institutes of Health (NIH). The ORWH directs programs and initiatives concerned with a research agenda on women's health across all the institutes that comprise the NIH and encourages clinical research trials to include adequate numbers of women when the disease or disorder studied is applicable to both sexes. The ORWH also focuses on the recruitment and advancement of women in biomedical centers. With these three goals, the ORWH stimulates more research on women's health issues to prevent disease and improve the quality of life for women and promotes the identification and treatment of disease with the most advanced gender-sensitive information available (LaRosa, 1994).

A second change in 1991 was the new policy of the NIH and the Alcohol, Drug, and Mental Health Administration (ADAMHA) stating that clinical research studies must include both sexes so that results are applicable to the general population (NIH, 1991). The exceptions are those diseases or conditions that affect only one sex. Thus, we have a mandate to include adequate numbers of women (as well as men) in clinical research studies of conditions or disorders that affect both females and males. Adequate justification must be given if the researchers feel that only one sex can be used.

The Food and Drug Administration (FDA) also made changes in its policies regarding the approval of drugs for use in the general population. As of 1993, all drug testing must "include women in reasonable numbers in studies and provide the FDA with information about any significant differences found between women and men in their responses to drugs" (Fourcroy, 1994, p. 186). This mandate no longer excludes women of childbearing age from participation in early phases of clinical trials. The research results must also include an analysis of gender-specific differences (Fourcroy, 1994). This action by the FDA essentially reversed a policy that had been in effect since 1977. These changes were made to have an impact on research with human participants in order to assure that sex and gender differences found in studies will be made available to physicians for improved care and treatment of women. These changes should also be valuable for men's health. In the section on bias in health research, we showed that data for both women and men (when women were included) were combined and generalized to both sexes. Those studies did not identify results by sex, so any adverse effects for either women or men were not evident. Subsequent treatment by health care providers has relevance for potential harm in their treatment of patients, whether female or male. It will be important to determine the outcome of research with these regulations in force.

Progress has definitely been made. But "more also needs to be done to study differences *between* the sexes" (Pardue, 2001, p. 6). Pardue believes that the research community has paid little attention to the fact that a female or male is much more than having different hormonal and reproductive systems. This is in total agreement with the position that we three have been espousing since 1994 and demonstrating with results of our research on sex and gender bias reviewed in this chapter (Sechzer, Rabinowitz, et al., 1994). As a variable, sex and gender have been understudied and undervalued, which has been detrimental to the validity of research findings. Thus, studying differences *between* females and males may result in crucial improvements in the progress of science in the practice of science by the research community.

SUMMARY

This chapter reviewed several different aspects of physical health ranging from the nineteenth through the twenty-first century. Early treatment of the physical health problems of women certainly affected their psychological state. As we continued to move forward in time, we saw that physical health cannot be considered apart from psychological health. This is particularly true for women who have found so many impediments to appropriate health care. We have examined the social construction of illness, beginning with Victorian times in the nineteenth century, and described how particular attitudes toward women and the practices borne of this and earlier eras have continued into the present and have affected women's physical and mental health, their medical care, and the research on the diseases and disorders that they develop.

We recounted how the attitudes of male society in general and of physicians in particular dominated the life of women during Victorian times. We showed how women accepted their roles and inferior status, thus helping society fix and maintain these views into present times. To our twenty-first-century readers, it may be hard to understand how these women accepted their socially constrained roles and how a sexuoeconomic relationship with men developed.

Building on these historical associations, we described health problems of women and how they compare with those of men. We attempted to explain why women are sicker than men with the same health problems. The problem of stress and pain was reviewed, as well as the maladaptive behaviors that can develop in response to long-term stressful situations.

The next section of this chapter reviewed issues of gender bias in women's health from a variety of approaches. We described major illnesses that affect both women and men, cardiovascular disease, lung cancer, HIV/AIDS infection, and the gender differences in these illnesses. We also described research on these diseases to determine whether the treatment of data for women and men was biased and whether this pattern changed across an eight-year period. We discussed the inherent gender bias we found not only in subject selection for the studies but also in evaluating and generalizing results of such studies to women and men without any justification. In doing so, we also evaluated the consequences of gender bias on the health of women. Breast cancer and osteoporosis, diseases primarily affecting women, were also reviewed.

In the last section of this chapter, we explored some important changes in the way women's health was viewed and speculated about the apparent attention these changes are bringing to gender differences in health research and in diagnosis and treatment.

We stated that progress had definitely been made but added that more needs to be done to study the differences between the sexes. We believe that our research studies on sex and gender bias, conducted in 1994, heightened the importance of studying and testing the difference between the sexes in behavioral and biomedical research. The changes in viewing women's health that have started should lead to important findings for the health of men as well as for women.

KEY TERMS

Acquired immunodeficiency syndrome (AIDS) (p. 468)
Antibody (p. 470)
Asymptomatic (p. 470)
Benign (p. 466)
Cancer (p. 465)
Cerebrovascular disease (p. 462)
Coronary artery disease (p. 461)
Fight or flight response (p. 455)
General adaptation syndrome (p. 455)

High-risk or unsafe behavior (p. 471)
HIV (p. 468)
HIV positive (HIV+) (p. 472)
HIV-seropositive (p. 472)
Immune system (p. 470)
Maladaptive behaviors (p. 456)
Malignant (p. 466)
Opportunistic infections (p. 471)
Osteoporosis (p. 479)
Pain (p. 458)

Pain threshold (p. 458)
Pain tolerance (p. 458)
Peripheral artery disease (p. 462)
Risk factor (p. 477)
Sexually transmitted infections (STIs) (p. 468)
Stress (p. 454)
T cell (p. 470)
Tumor (p. 465)

DISCUSSION QUESTIONS

1. As a women, if you were faced with the diagnosis of breast cancer, what would be your choice of treatment? How would you make this decision? With whom would you consult? Would you consider having a second opinion? A third? What would you want from your spouse or significant other? Would you tell your friends?

2. As a man, how do you think you would react if your spouse, significant other, or current girlfriend informed you that she has been diagnosed with breast cancer?

3. Do you currently see a male physician for either gynecological care and/or medical care? Have you experienced any bias or overt sexism in his treatment and attitude toward you? What do you consider the most important issues of bias and prejudice that one should look for when being treated by a male physician? If you had your choice, would you prefer to be treated by a women physician if she were on the same level of expertise as the male physician?

4. Do you think that over the next ten years female physicians will outnumber male physicians. Why? And will they be better physicians? If yes, why?

5. Recent statistics have shown that, while smoking among males has decreased along with a decrease in lung cancer, smoking by women has increased with a concomitant increase in lung cancer. In fact, lung cancer now kills more women than breast cancer. What social and psychological factors do you think have contributed to this turn for the worse for women?

6. In many states, all newborn babies are tested anonymously for HIV infection to estimate the dimensions of the epidemic. When an infant tests positively for HIV, it is a valid indication that the mother is also infected, even though most states do not inform the mother because of individual privacy rights. Do you agree with this provision, or do you feel that the mother should be notified of her HIV status? Is it possible to notify the mother without violating her privacy rights? What are the benefits of informing the mother as well as the drawbacks?

7. If you were a therapist and learned that your patient was infected with HIV but refused to inform his or her partner even though they were having sex together, how would you handle this situation?

8. Heart disease is now the number-one killer of both men and women, but it seems not only that men are treated differently from women but also that many tests or treatments are not very effective for women. Although some progress is being made to be more gender fair in treatment, what would you do if you were diagnosed with a heart condition and worried that the treatment you were receiving was gender biased or that it would not be effective for you as a women?

FURTHER READINGS

Cadden, J. (1993). *The meaning of sex differences in the middle Ages.* Cambridge, UK: Cambridge University Press.

Corea, G. (1992). *The invisible epidemic: The story of women and AIDS.* New York: HarperCollins.

Love, S. M. (1990). *Dr. Susan Love's breast book.* Reading, MA: Addison-Wesley.

Shilts, R. (1987). *And the band played on.* New York: Penguin.

Steele, G. D., Winchester, D. P., Menck, H. R., & Murphy, G. P. (1993). *National Cancer Data Base—Annual review of patient care.* American Cancer Society, American College of Surgeons Commission on Cancer.

A REFLECTION ON THE FUTURE

The times are changing. Change may be occurring too quickly for some, but change is not occurring fast enough for many boys and girls limited by their gender roles to less than full lives.
—Carol Nagy Jacklin

And how do you look backward. By looking forward. And what do they see. As they look forward. They see what they had to do before they could look backward. And there we have it all.
—Gertrude Stein

Living each day as a preparation for the next is an exciting way to live. Looking forward to something is much more fun than looking back at something—much more constructive. If we prepare ourselves so that we never have to think, "Oh, if I had only known, if I had only been ready," our lives can really be the great adventure that we so passionately want them to be.
—Hortense Odlum

The future depends entirely on what each of us does each day . . . a movement is only people moving.
—Gloria Steinem

On what basis could we form a coalition is still an open question. The idea of basing it on sexual preferences strikes me as somewhat dubious, strikes me as being less than a firm foundation. It seems to me that a coalition has to be based on the grounds of human dignity. . . . There's nothing in me that is not in everybody else, and nothing in everybody else that is not in me. . . . I'm saying I have nothing to prove. The world also belongs to me. . . . If you don't live the only life you have, you won't live some other life; you won't live any life at all.
—James Baldwin

Where, after all, do universal human rights begin? . . . In small places, close to home. . . . Such are the places where every man, woman, and child seeks equal justice, equal opportunity, equal dignity.
—Eleanor Roosevelt

Everyone has inside . . . a piece of good news. The good news is that you don't know how great you can be! How much you can love! What you can accomplish! And what your potential is!
—Anne Frank

CRITICAL ISSUES FOR THE FUTURE
  Images of Women
  Occupational Barriers
  Housework: The Revolution Left Undone

Redefining Masculinity
CHANGES IN THE FIELD OF PSYCHOLOGY
SMALL WORLD: INTERNATIONAL REALM
OF WOMEN'S ACTIVITIES

Psychology is evolving to become a discipline that reflects and encompasses the behavior of *all* people in a social context, not just men, as it has in the past. In the not too distant past, the psychology of women and the psychology of gender were marginalized areas within psychology, but now research findings in these fields are being incorporated into the general domain of psychology. Indeed, these findings have altered, if not revolutionized, theory and method in psychology and other behavioral and social sciences. Topics such as rape, parenting, and the division of household labor, once deemed "women's issues," are now seen as part of the human montage.

The dawn of the twenty-first century is a time of rapid social change throughout the world, with profound implications for changing gender roles. As we have discussed throughout this book, this is evident in many areas of life, including education, home, family, the workplace, science, mental and physical health, and global issues affecting women. The conditions and concerns of women in other cultures are more visible to all of us than ever before. Gendered perspectives on all issues are increasingly valued by scientists and laypeople, although, as we have suggested, many women in the United States and other countries do not consider gender the most central source of oppression in their lives. And, as we see with cases such as mothers of young children working outside the home, there is no uniform women's perspective, because gender interacts with culture to produce different viewpoints and practices. But the inequalities and inequities that women have endured and the equalities and equities that they pursue command the attention of more and more psychologists and other social scientists today.

If the future looks progressively better for both girls and women, it is a future filled with challenges and dangers. The preceding chapters identified problems that need to be addressed and resolved at the individual, social, and societal levels. The issues within these chapters indicate areas of needed reenergizing, rethinking, and reform. Regardless of whether one locates the causes of women's oppression in political, economic, sociological, or psychological factors, we must join forces to fight what some have called a backlash against feminism and feminists. Bearing this in mind, let us turn to certain issues that merit special attention in a future psychology of women and gender.

CRITICAL ISSUES FOR THE FUTURE

Images of Women

Sexism is on the defensive, but it is still openly permissible in contexts in which racism or ethnocentrism would not be tolerated. Women are subjected to representations in religion, education, science, and the media that are inaccurate and often demeaning. As we have seen vividly in Chapter 2, most religions relegate women to a secondary role in the official activities of the congregation and perpetuate women's devalued status. As we saw in Chapter 6, educators still treat children on the basis of presumed innate sex differences, rather than on the basis of individual differences. Gender-based expectations that teachers have of students may foster gender-differentiated skills and self-perceptions that limit them later on. Throughout this book, we have pointed out that although some biological differences between women and men may have important implications for some behaviors, there are in fact very few of these instances, and the effects of historical, cultural, and social contexts are too often ignored, minimized, or deemed trivial.

Perhaps nowhere are stereotyped images of women more ubiquitous—and damaging—than in the popular media, in which women are still too often valued and defined by their physical attractiveness, and in which older women, women with disabilities, and others who do not conform to rigidly defined standards of appropriate female appearances and behavior are invisible. Psychology can do its part to change negative, inaccurate, and harmful images of women with a gendered analysis of such issues, based on solid empirical research, that educates people about the effects of gender schemas on all aspects of life, particularly the impact of media sexism on body image and self-esteem, negative portrayals of older women the effects of the social importance of looks coupled with impossible standards of appearance, and the harmful effects on women and men of the objectification, subordination, and sexualization of women.

Occupational Barriers

Women today do obtain positions in occupations that are traditionally dominated by men. There is, however, a cost for many women entering fields that have been unoccupied by women or occupied by only a few women. As we have discussed in Chapters 7 and 12, sexual harassment, lack of advancement, and a hostile atmosphere may greet the most competent and ambitious women. The expectation among contemporary young women is that barriers have been removed; the reality is quite different.

In 1980, women earned approximately 60 percent of men's wages. By 2003, this had increased to 76 percent of men's wages. Despite these gains, pay equity remains a critical goal for women in all occupations. Recent research indicates that women increasingly start out equal to men in many professions, but sex disparities in salary and status emerge early in career paths and grow over time. To increase gender diversity in the workplace, we need to continue to support affirmative action programs and policies that break the glass ceiling and bring women into leadership roles within organizations. Psychologists can help us to achieve a better understanding of how such policies can be successfully justified and implemented.

There is increasing recognition of the need for family-oriented policies for men and women in the workplace by both the government and private industries. In 1993, President Clinton proposed and Congress passed the Family Leave Act, which allows 12 weeks of unpaid leave for reasons related to care of a family member in all companies of over 50 employees. Unfortunately, family-supported policies are still more the exception than the rule in U.S. businesses and organizations. And even where such policies exist, they are often not used by workers. The reasons for this are many and complex, but certainly include that the leave is inadequate for many people's needs and may stigmatize or marginalize workers who choose to take it. It appears that policies and laws do not always achieve their purposes in contemporary society.

Moreover, in the United States, where high-quality day care is scarce, many women feel that they cannot pursue high-powered careers once they start their families, and this leads them to forego high-powered careers—or child rearing. Recent research suggests that many women—around 40 percent of all the women in academia, for example—forego having children altogether, a much higher percentage than is found among women generally and of men in academia. This glaring sex disparity reflects some of the difficulties that women perceive about combining work and family.

Housework: The Revolution Left Undone

Perhaps nothing better represents the power inequity between women and men than the traditional division of household labor by sex. It is doubtful that gender roles outside the home can change very much if they do not change within the home. Some recent studies show that men have reported an increase in their chores at home to the point of near parity with women. Other studies, however, which rely on couples, with women and men separately writing down what they actually do each day, show little change in men's participation in family chores. As we have stated, the higher a couple's income and education are, the more equal the household responsibilities are, in part because of the greater likelihood of affording outside help. But it is still the case that women do more than men around the house, even when they make more money than their male partners. Young women need to understand that if past trends persist and their household budgets are limited, they may be working two shifts, one at work and one at home. Will that satisfy them? Are these the lives we envision for our daughters? What can be done to make the division of household labor more gender fair?

Redefining Masculinity

It has been a theme of this book that there continue to be significant limitations placed on the female gender role, including low pay, status, and power in the home, workplace, and larger world. There are significant problems men face with the male gender role as well. To name a few: limited personal and social relationships and physical health problems stemming from overwork and unhealthy lifestyle choices. The culture of masculinity and its negative impact on

men, women, and children require careful and sustained study, and need to be brought into national discourse.

CHANGES IN THE FIELD OF PSYCHOLOGY

A number of trends in psychology merit attention. One significant trend concerns psychology as both a discipline that studies women and a discipline that attracts female students. An increasing number of psychologists are women. A number of implications flow from this, some of them troubling, but more of them positive. Some psychologists are concerned that as a profession becomes more "feminized"— that is, when the proportion of women increases beyond 70 percent—the status and pay of the profession decline. However, as we have seen, the perspectives and experiences of women are appropriately changing what psychologists study and how it is studied. Clearly, many benefits to psychology come from the influx of feminist women. Such women will be able not only to impart survival strategies to women through mentoring and networking, but also to nurture feminist psychologists who challenge the status quo (Denmark, 1992).

Another particularly noteworthy trend in psychology generally is the increased focus on the biological bases of behaviors, including social and interpersonal behavior. On the positive side, we have learned a great deal in recent years about how hormones influence the behavior of both women and men. The value of some prescription drugs in helping people think, feel, and behave in ways that are more beneficial to them has led many clinical psychologists to advocate for obtaining prescription privileges. In recent years, psychologists have seemingly "rediscovered" emotions and now regularly study emotions, motivation, and mood in connection with cognition and behavior, often using sophisticated technological and physiological measures. On the negative side, the new emphasis on finding biological substrates of behavior has led some to argue that the complex sex differences in social behavior are mainly due to inborn biological mechanisms, presumably shaped through evolutionary processes. As we have argued, evidence for evolutionary psychology explanations of sex differences falls considerably short of its promise. There are inherent dangers in an approach that looks at differences in the present and works backward to determine the possible causes in the distant past. To date, many psychologists who study women and gender do not find these evolutionary psychology explanations of sex differences persuasive.

Finally, the practices of science itself, particularly research methods, have been subjected to increasing scrutiny and critique by feminist psychologists. The experimental method, for example, was once thought to characterize the only approach for a scientific psychology. Although this method is appropriate for many basic research questions, it is limited in the study of major status characteristics such as gender, race, ethnicity, and class to which people cannot be randomly assigned. Furthermore, the experimental method presents its own problems and difficulties, which were previously buried in the mythology that all science was "objective" and "value-free." Indeed, feminist reviews of research methods demonstrate the fallibility of such thinking (Rabinowitz & Sechzer, 1993; Rabinowitz & Martin, 2001; Rabinowitz & Weseen, 2001). While some psychologists may mourn any erosion of the authority of the experimental method, other psychologists have developed scientific skepticism about the overreliance on classical methods. The result is a willingness to consider what was once heretical: qualitative research methods. The use of such qualitative research methods as ethnography, discourse analysis, and clinical interviews is increasing and enriching the field. Some psychologists consider the integration of quantitative and qualitative methods as representing the best approach to many research questions.

SMALL WORLD: INTERNATIONAL REALM OF WOMEN'S ACTIVITIES

As we highlighted in Chapter 3 and mainstreamed throughout this book, gender interacts with culture, race, ethnicity, and class, and to consider it apart from these rich variables is to miss its essence. There is no "ideal" or prototypical woman or man. Women and men from around the world come in different ethnicities, cultural backgrounds, social classes, and so on. It is only at the intersections of these variables that we get a glimpse of the variations and possibilities that exist within gender categories. The psychology of the future needs to find more and better ways to conceptualize and study gender at the intersections. Indeed, the journey to gender equality may be quite different in different societies and cultures. As Burn (1996) notes, "Countries that are openly stratified and accepting of class differences may foster a greater acceptance of inequality. Women's movements in these countries may have to rely on a different rationale than those in Western counties in order to garner support" (p. 151).

As we contemplate women's issues across cultures, we need to consider that Western-style feminist values may conflict with the values of cherishing cultural diversity. But just as we must not impose Western values on others, we must also continue to champion universal values such as the equality of all people and challenge cultural practices that are sexist, racist, heterosexist, or discriminatory in other ways. Promoting equality and well-being among all people in a multicultural world is a central challenge for psychology, particularly for feminist psychology, in the twenty-first century.

GLOSSARY

Ablatio penis   Accidental destruction of the penis.

Acculturation   The adoption by an individual or a group of the culture patterns of another group; a process of social change caused by the interaction of significantly diverse cultures.

Achievement motivation   The desire to accomplish something of importance due to one's own efforts, the desire to excel at what one does.

Acquired immune deficiency syndrome (AIDS)   A progressive deterioration of the immune system by the HIV (human immunodeficiency virus), which suppresses the immune system's ability to fight various infections and malignancies. A diagnosis of HIV/AIDS is made on the basis of a blood test.

Adolescence   Refers to social and psychological events and is defined by society as the period between childhood and maturity.

African American   Descendants of Africans who were brought to the United States as slaves.

Ageism   Discrimination on the basis of age.

American Indian   Overinclusive term referring to anyone whose ancestors are from one of the 587 American Indian tribes.

Androcentric bias   The discipline of psychology is largely focused on men and describes men as superior and women as inferior.

Androgens   Hormones such as testosterone that develop and sustain secondary sex characteristics in males. Androgens are considered the male hormones.

Anorexia nervosa   A serious eating disorder characterized by an intense fear of obesity, intentional starvation, and a distorted body image.

Antibody   A special protein created by the body's immune system that fights specific agents causing infections in the body. With HIV infections, the infecting virus cannot be destroyed by antibodies.

Anxiety disorders   Characterized by persistent anxiety that causes intense suffering.

Apostle   Any of the 12 disciples sent out by Christ to teach the gospel (the Christian doctrine of the redemption of man through Jesus as Christ).

Asian American   Overinclusive term referring to people whose ancestors are from China, Japan, Korea, India, Southeast Asia, and South Asia.

Assimilation   The process by which immigrants or other newcomers become accepted by the people of the culture to which they have adapted.

Asymptomatic   Without obvious symptoms. In a case of HIV, it means that a person can be infected with the virus but have no signs or symptoms. However, even though asymptomatic, an infected individual can still infect others.

Attributions   Social psychologists have determined that people make judgments about the likely causes of their successes and failures. Attributions differ along the dimensions of internality, stability, and controllability. In achievement situations, they are generally made to ability, effort, luck, or task-difficulty.

Aversive racism   A phenomenon whereby covert forms of discrimination prevail even among those who loudly proclaim their egalitarianism.

B.C.E.   Before the common era, or was referred to as B.C. (Before Christ).

Battered women   Women subjected to physical and emotional abuse. A somewhat problematic term because it puts the focus on the victims and their stigmatized identities rather than on the perpetrators and may keep victims silent and ashamed.

Behavior setting   A basic environmental unit that entails the naturally occurring spatial and temporal features that surround behavior and the appropriate behavioral match.

Behavior therapy   A system of therapies based on principles of learning theory.

Benevolent sexism   Is a subjectively favorable, chivalrous ideology that offers protection and affection to women who embrace conventional roles, roles that perpetuate their inequality in a patriarchal society.

Benign tumors   Cells that are encapsulated and do not spread. They can be removed completely.

Bias in research methods   Bias occurs in every part of the research process—from question formulation and research design to data analysis and interpretation.

Binge eating disorder   Characterized by episodes of consuming an excessive amount of food within a discrete period of time and by a sense of lack of control over eating during that period.

Biopsychosocial model   A model for examining the etiology of mental disorders which takes into account biological, psychological, and social factors.

Bisexuality   Sexual activity with and/or desire for people of both sexes.

Black   Term used for African Americans, people from the Caribbean (e.g., West Indians), Black Hispanics, and recent immigrants from Africa

Blatant sexism   Occurs when women are treated in a transparently harmful and unequal way.

Borderline personality disorder   Characterized by chronic instability in emotions, self image, and relationships.

Brahma   The supreme and eternal essence or spirit of the universe.

Brass ceiling   Women's exclusion from combat, which precludes their advancement in the military.

Bronze Age   The Bronze Age came between the Stone Age and the Iron Age. During this period bronze tools and weapons were developed.

Bulimia nervosa   A serious eating disorder characterized by cycles of binging and purging, episodes of self-induced vomiting, and the habitual use of laxatives.

Burqa   A full body and head covering worn by Afghani women under the Taliban regime. The face area has a veiled inset permitting the women to see out.

C.E.   The Common Era, or was referred to as A.D. (*anno domini,* in the year of the Lord).

Cesarean section   A surgical method in which delivery occurs through an incision in the abdominal wall and uterus.

Cancer   A large group of diseases characterized by uncontrolled growth and spread of abnormal cells independent of the rest of the body that metastasize to other parts of the body (see also *tumor*).

Capacitation   The process that makes the sperm capable of penetrating the ovum.

Cerebrovascular accident (CVA)   Cerebrovascular accident occurs when blood flow to a part of the brain is altered because of either a blockage in an artery or a leak or break in an artery of the brain.

Chicanos and Chicanas   Men and women of Mexican origin.

Chromosomes   The genetic material in the nucleus of every cell of the body. The sperm and ova each have 23 cells; all the other cells of the body have 46.

Class   The socioeconomic status of an individual or group.

Classism   A society that stigmatizes poor people, working-class people, and their cultures while valuing the affluent and their culture solely because of their relative wealth.

Climacteric   The aging process between 45 and 65 years of age.

Cognitive therapy   A type of psychotherapy that attempts to identify and restructure dysfunctional thoughts.

Cohabitation   Unmarried couples living together.

Cohort   A group of people born within the same year or years.

Conception   The union of a sperm cell and a viable ovum; the onset of pregnancy, marked by implantation of the blastocyst (zygote) in the endometrium of the uterus.

Contextualistic behaviorism   A perspective that emphasizes that "behaviors" have no a priori categorical meanings but must be understood and defined through a careful analysis of the context in which the behavior occurs.

Contingent worker   An individual who is working part time as a temporary employee or on a per diem basis.

Contraceptives   Methods of birth control. These vary in their levels of effectiveness, cost and ease of use, sharing of responsibility between males and females, and protection from sexually transmitted infections (STIs).

Conventional reasoning   The second level of moral development in Kohlberg's theory. At this level, individuals abide by internal moral standards that are based entirely on those of parents and/or society.

Coronary artery disease   Illnesses caused by atherosclerosis, a narrowing of the coronary arteries supplying blood to the heart. Atherosclerotic plaques deposited in the vessels of the heart narrow the vessels until little or no blood can pass through.

Covert sexism   A form of sexism that is intentional, hidden, and often hostile.

Cultural approach   Explains the origin of gender stereotypes from a sociocultural perspective in which children are socialized to act in accordance with their cultural dictates.

Cultural deprivation model   Explains the condition of African Americans within the context of racism, prejudice, and discrimination by arguing that problems of ethnic identity, self-esteem, school failure, chronic unemployment, family disturbances, and higher rates of more serious psychiatric disorders are caused by oppressive environmental circumstances.

Cultural feminism   Emphasizes characteristics and qualities of women, that have been devalued and ignored in our society.

Culture A group's program for survival in and adaptation to its environment; the cultural program consists of knowledge, concepts, and values shared by group members through systems of communication.

Cunnilingus Oral–genital sexual activity performed on women.

Date rape Rape in the context of a dating or romantic relationship.

Dependent personality disorder Characterized by passivity and allowing other people to take the initiative and assume responsibility for most major areas of one's life.

Depression An affective disorder characterized by sadness, loss of interest in situations usually pleasant, a negative view of self, feelings of hopelessness, helplessness, passivity, loss of weight and appetite, and sleep disturbances.

Diagnostic and Statistical Manual of Mental Disorders (DSM) A reference book of mental disorders used by mental health professionals, which standardizes diagnoses across clinicians and diagnosticians.

Division 35 The American Psychological Association's Division of the Psychology of Women, which was established in 1973.

Dominant culture Owns and controls the means of production and commerce; has the power to grant and take away livelihoods; owns and controls the channels of communication in the society; decides what, how, and who gets addressed in the media; promotes those aspects of culture in the media that are considered valuable; denigrates, or makes invisible those aspects of culture that it considers inferior or of lesser value.

Dominant generation Comprised of individuals in their middle years who are responsible for the caretaking of both the young and the old.

Double standard of aging The differential standards applied to aging men and women. Typically, aging women are devalued for their reduced physical attractiveness, while aging men remain highly valued for their continued competence and autonomy.

Ecological model Theoretical perspective in psychology in which human behavior is understood in terms of the interaction between the person and the environment.

Effect size A statistic that tells us how large the effect of a variable is or how large a difference between two groups is. The most commonly used measure of effect size is Cohen's *d*. Effect sizes below 0.3 are considered small, between 0.3 and 0.7 moderate, and above 0.7 large.

Egalitarian marriages Relatively uncommon marriages in which the husbands and wives are partners in the truest sense of the term. Neither spouse is dominant or submissive, roles are flexible, and responsibilities are shared.

Emaciation A state of weight loss of at least 25 percent of total body weight and 15 percent below the normal weight for one's age, height, and gender.

Embryo The fertilized ovum that will eventually become the offspring. It is called an embryo from the second week after fertilization until the end of the eighth week of pregnancy.

Emic Attributes and traits that are culturally specific.

Empty nest syndrome When children leave the home and parents are left to cope with their absence.

Endogamy The custom of marrying only within one's tribe or clan.

Engendering psychology Cultivating a psychology in which gender considerations are mainstreamed throughout the discipline.

Epistle Any of the letters in the New Testament written by an Apostle; a selection from the Epistles reads as part of the Mass or communion in church.

Estrogen A hormone present in both females and males, but with its highest concentration in females. It is considered the female hormone. It is produced by the ovaries and adrenal glands in the female and by the testes and the adrenals in the male; in the female it stimulates breast growth at puberty, maintains the lining of the uterus, and controls the menstrual cycle.

Ethnicity Describes a sense of commonality transmitted over generations by the family and reinforced by the surrounding community based on perceived similarity by virtue of their common ancestry.

Ethnocultural group A population of people that is largely self-perpetuating, shares fundamental cultural values, makes up a field of communication and interaction, and has a membership that identifies itself, and is identified by others, as constituting a category distinguishable from other categories of the same order.

Etic Attributes and traits that are universal.

Evolutionary psychology Theory developed by Wilson that holds that psychological traits are selected through an evolutionary process. Adaptive traits are selected because they serve to perpetuate the species.

Exchange theory A theory of interpersonal attraction that holds that people pursue relationships in which the value of the resources that they will obtain from their partner is greatest relative to the value of the resources that they can offer in return.

Exogamy The custom of marrying only outside of one's tribe or clan, i.e., outbreeding.

Fear of success   A construct named by Matina Horner to explain why women do not achieve as well as men. According to Horner, women feel that success involves loss of femininity and social rejection. Research has not generally supported the idea that women fear success more than men do.

Fellatio   Oral–genital sexual activity performed on men.

Feminism   The belief that women and men are equal and should be equally valued and have equal rights.

Feminization of poverty   An increasing trend over time for women to be overrepresented among the poor in the United States.

Fetal alcohol syndrome   Symptoms presented by an infant exposed to heavy amounts of alcohol during gestation, which include growth deficiencies and nervous system alterations.

Fetus   The unborn offspring in the postembryonic period from the ninth week after fertilization until birth.

Fight or flight response   A response by which the body is swiftly aroused, usually in response to an external threatening stimulus. The response is initiated through the sympathetic nervous and endocrine systems resulting in the individual either fighting or fleeing the object of the threat.

First wave of feminism   Feminism began in 1903 with the founding of the Women's Social and Political Union.

Follicular phase   The first phase begins when ovarian follicles begin to mature.

Foreplay   The general name given for a variety of acts that are intended to be sexually arousing and a prelude for later intercourse.

Frequency distribution   An array, often graphically depicted, of the range of possible scores or values and number of times that score or value was achieved.

Gender   A concept that refers to how differences between boys and girls and men and women are arranged in the social context of society. Psychological features and social categories created by human cultures to describe the traits and behaviors that are regarded by the culture as appropriate to women and men.

Gendered division of labor   A phenomenon in which the division of occupations into two genders is grounded in stereotypes of innate sex differences in traits and abilities.

Gender harassment   Generalized sexist remarks and behavior that convey insulting, degrading, or prejudiced attitudes toward women.

Gender identity   The process, occurring in early childhood, of coming to identify oneself as female or male.

Gender identity disorder   A disorder in which the individual displays an array of marked cross-gender role behaviors and often expresses the wish to belong to the other sex.

Gender intensification   A time period when both females and males are increasingly concerned with adhering to female and male gender roles.

Gender schemas   Structures that allow a person to organize information related to gender by linking gender labels to objects, traits, and behaviors.

Gender schema theory   A theory proposed by Bem suggesting that children create knowledge structures that organize gender-related information in memory and are used to evaluate new information according to gender.

Gender stereotype   Cognitive representation of males and females; an organized set of beliefs about the psychological traits and characteristics as well as the activities appropriate to men or women.

General adaptation syndrome   Hans Selye first described this syndrome as a means by which an individual responds to stress. The syndrome is characterized by (1) a nonspecific mobilization stage that initiates sympathetic nervous system activity; (2) a resistance stage, by which the individual attempts to cope with the threat; (3) a stage of exhaustion, which takes place if the individual cannot overcome the threat and thus its physiological responses are depleted.

Genital mutilation   A practice occurring in many parts of Africa and the Middle East in which girls and young women have the foreskin of the clitoris removed and/or the clitoris and labia removed; the two sides of the vulva are sewn together with unsterilized equipment and without anesthesia as part of a rite of passage.

Glass ceiling   Refers to the phenomenon in the workplace whereby women are unable to attain the highest level in the corporate ladder hierarchy.

Globalization   To extend to other or all parts of the globe; make worldwide.

Grafenberg or G-spot   A hypothesized place in the vagina that when stimulated, presumably produces a distinct and powerful orgasm in women. Evidence for the existence of a G-spot is not conclusive.

Graying of America   The phenomenon in the United States whereby increased medical awareness and technology cause increased longevity for individuals.

Hegemony   The political domination and power, especially the leadership or domination of one state over others in a group or groups.

Heilman's lack of fit model The idea that gender biases stem largely from an incongruity between an applicant's perceived attributes and the requirements of the position.

Heterosexism An ideological system that denies, denigrates, and stigmatizes any nonheterosexual form of behavior, identity, relationship, or community.

High-risk or unsafe behavior In the case of HIV/AIDS and other sexually transmitted diseases, specific sexual or drug-related activities that increase the chances of contracting or transmitting HIV or other viruses. High-risk behaviors are those that allow blood, semen, or vaginal fluid of one person to contact the blood or mucous membranes (in the eyes, mouth, rectum, vagina) of another person. HIV can also be transmitted through breast milk. Two of the highest-risk behaviors are having intercourse without using a condom (barrier protection) and sharing intravenous (IV) needles in drug use. Unprotected anal intercourse is a particularly high-risk behavior.

Hispanic Refers to all people of Spanish origin and includes a variety of nationalities, ethnicities, and races.

Histrionic personality disorder Characterized by pervasive and excessive emotionality and attention seeking behavior.

HIV The abbreviation for human immunodeficiency virus. HIV is a slow-acting virus that is believed to be the cause of AIDS.

HIV positive (HIV+), HIV seropositive Terms used to describe a person infected with HIV.

Homogamy The notion that people tend to marry others highly similar to themselves on demographic, physical, and psychological characteristics.

Horizontal hostility Members of a subordinate group expressing self-hatred and hostility in a horizontal direction toward one's own kind (e.g., infighting among members of a subordinate group, violence and crime directed toward members of their group).

Hormone A chemical substance secreted by the endocrine system of females and males and carried directly to the organ or tissue on which it acts.

Hostile sexism Resembles other forms of prejudice typically directed toward groups who are seen as threats to the in-group's status and power and involves a pejorative devaluation of women, and women's work, which creates a diminished quality of life for them, or in extreme cases, threatens their very lives.

Immune system The system that protects the body from infection. Specialized cells in the immune system and proteins in the blood and in other bodily fluids work together to eliminate disease-causing agents or other toxic foreign substances from the body.

Incest Sexual relations between people of any age who are so closely related that such relations are prohibited and punishable by law.

Inferiority model Comprises a vast array of theories that explicitly or implicitly link African Americans' status in society to inherent genetic defects.

Infertility If successful pregnancy has not occurred after a period of one year or more of sexual intercourse without contraceptives, there may be an infertility problem.

Insider's perspective A research perspective based on the ideas, hypotheses of an "insider" social scientist who is from the culture or group being researched.

Involuntary minority Are people and their descendants who were originally forced against their will by Euro-Americans through slavery, conquest, and colonization to marginally participate in American society; they tend to define themselves and their cultures in opposition to the cultural values of the majority.

Iron Age The period after the Bronze Age during which iron tools and weapons were developed.

Issei First-generation Japanese Americans born and raised in Japan.

Karma That a person's actions in any one of his or her states of existence will determine his or her fate and status in the next life. Karma is also considered one's destiny.

Late midlife astonishment Occurs when a woman in her fifties realizes the onset and stigma of aging.

Lateralization The extent to which one hemisphere of the brain organizes particular abilities or functions.

Latinos and Latinas Men and women from Latin America; some politically conscious men and women prefer the term *Latino/Latina* to Hispanic.

Liberal feminism Focuses on equality of women and men.

Linguistic sexism The perpetuation and reinforcement of sexist ideology through the content of a language.

Luteal phase The third phase of the menstrual cycle, which begins after ovulation. The corpus luteum produces large amounts of progesterone and estrogen to prepare the uterus for the implantation of the fertilized egg.

Maladaptive behaviors Behaviors inappropriate to the typical behavior of the individual. This can occur as a response to stress or stressors when the individual is unable to adapt or cope with these.

Malignant tumors   Cells that grow diffusely through normal tissue and are difficult to remove and continue to spread (*metastasize*) to other parts of the body.

Marianismo   A concept that considers women morally and spiritually superior to men and, therefore, capable of enduring male-inflicted suffering.

Marital rape   Very severe kinds of rape; marital rape occurs when a husband has sexual relations with his wife against her will. Marital rape is not recognized as rape in many countries and is often not taken seriously in our own society.

Marriage gradient   The tendency for men to *marry down* in age and social and economic class, whereas women tend to *marry up* on these dimensions.

Masturbation   Solitary sexual activity practiced by means of manual stimulation of the genitals, with or without the aid of artificial stimulation.

Matching hypothesis   The idea that people tend to develop romantic relationships with those who are similar to them, especially in physical attractiveness.

Men's movement   Includes military, political, religious, and economic events that have benefited men.

Menarche   The onset of the menstrual period.

Menopause   The time when a woman's menstrual cycle slows down and finally stops. This usually occurs sometime between a woman's late forties and early fifties.

Menstrual cycle   This cycle occurs approximately every month and continues until about the late forties or early fifties. The menstrual cycle has four phases.

Menstrual phase   The fourth phase of the menstrual cycle. A flow of blood begins from the lining of the uterus in females after they have reached puberty.

Mesolithic Age   *Meso* means mid or middle. The Mesolithic Age refers to the period between the Paleolithic and Neolithic ages during which certain animals and plants were domesticated. The Mesolithic Age ranged from 10,000 B.C.E. until approximately 7000 B.C.E.

Meta-analysis   A statistical technique that combines the data from different studies that test the same hypothesis in order to determine whether there was an overall effect of a variable.

Midwifery   A health profession in which individuals, both women and men, are trained to assist in the birthing process.

Model minority   Stereotypic belief that Asian Americans have overcome discrimination and are a successful model minority.

Modern marriage   Senior partner–junior partner relationships that capture the notion that husbands and wives are almost equals in most respects, but in important matters, the husband's will predominates.

Monotheism   The doctrine or belief that there is only one God.

Morality of constraint   The first stage in Piaget's theory. This stage characterizes children's moral judgments until they are approximately 9 or 10 years of age. In this stage, children base their moral judgments on what is deemed appropriate by the adults surrounding them.

Morality of cooperation   The second stage in Piaget's theory. Children in this stage base their moral judgments on intentions rather than consequences, moving from an objective to a subjective orientation.

Mosque   A Moslem (Muslim) temple or place of worship.

Motherhood mandate   The enormous social pressure that girls and women experience to have children; the belief that females must have children in order to be real and complete women.

Motherhood mystique   Idealized images and stereotypes that surround the notion of motherhood; for instance, the notions that only women are loving and nurturing enough to raise children, that mothering means subordinating personal goals to the children's and family's needs, and that motherhood is uniquely joyous and fulfilling for women.

Multicultural perspective   Incorporates knowledge about group differences with respect to culture, ethnicity, and race into constructs of major basic and applied theoretical models of psychology and psychological research.

Myotonia   The contraction of muscles that occurs during sexual arousal.

Neolithic Age   *Neo* means new, recent, latest. The Neolithic Age refers to the latest period of the Stone Age, from approximately 7000 B.C.E. to about 3500 B.C.E. These people created metal tools, pottery, weaving, and rearing of stock and development of agriculture.

Nirvana   The state of perfect blessedness achieved by the extinction of all desires and pleasures culminating in the ultimate absorption of the soul after death into the supreme spirit (Brahma).

Nisei   Second-generation Japanese Americans who were born in the United States and experienced American backlash during World War II resulting in the internment of many Japanese Americans.

Nonnormative rape   Rape that is not supported or tolerated by society; this conforms to the stereotypical notion of rape: the "surprise attack on a virtuous woman."

Nonoverlapping distributions Frequency distributions in which virtually all members of one group score higher or lower than the other group.

Normal distribution A frequency distribution with a bell-like shape, with most scores clustered around the middle or mean, and progressively fewer scores at either extreme. Many psychological traits, including IQ, are normally distributed in the population.

Normative rape Rape that is supported or at least tolerated by society; it includes rape by intimates, such as husbands, as well as punitive rape and rape during wartime.

Occupational segregation A phenomenon in which specific occupations are characterized as either female or male.

Opportunistic infections Infections that develop in people whose immune systems are weakened, as in AIDS. Some of the more common opportunistic infections identified with AIDS in both men and women are *Pneumocystis carinii* pneumonia (PCP), *Mycobacterium intracellulare* (MAI), toxoplasmosis, and Kaposi's sarcoma (usually a rare form of cancer). Women presenting with gynecological problems that have been associated with HIV/AIDS are pelvic inflammatory disease (PID), human papilloma virus (HPV), cervical cancer, candida infections of the vagina and cervix, genital herpes.

Osteoporosis (1) A disorder primarily seen in postmenopausal women. It is characterized by decreased bone mass and increased incidence of spinal and hip fracture. The loss of estrogen after menopause is associated with this problem. (2) The process of bone demineralization and thinning of the bones that results in a high risk of vertebral and/or hip fracture. It is especially seen in older women and those who have been on medications such as cortisone, which depletes calcium from the bones.

Ostrich effect A phenomenon in which women believe that sex bias operates in society, but deny having personally experienced its disadvantages.

Outsider's perspective A research perspective based on the ideas, hypotheses, of an "outsider" social scientist who is not from the culture or group he or she researches.

Ovaries Paired reproductive glands in the female located on each side of the uterus that contain and release eggs or ova and secrete hormones such as estrogen and progesterone. These are the female gonads.

Ovulation phase The second phase of the menstrual cycle when the egg or ovum is released from the ovary.

Ovum The female egg.

Pain An unpleasant emotional response associated with actual or potential tissue damage.

Pain threshold The point at which pain is first perceived.

Pain tolerance The upper limit or the highest intensity of pain that a human or animal will accept.

Paleolithic Age *Paleo* means ancient or "old world." The Paleolithic Age represents an old-world cultural period—the earliest part of the Stone Age—going back at least as far as 25,000 B.C.E. During this period man developed flint, stone, and bone tools and lived by hunting, fishing, and gathering plant foods. This period lasted until approximately 10,000 B.C.E., when the Mesolithic Age began.

Panethnicity Refers to the development of coalitions among ethic–racial subgroups.

Panic attacks Sudden episodes of extreme anxiety that escalate in intensity and are accompanied by severe physical symptoms.

Pantheism The doctrine that God is not a personality but that all the laws, forces, and manifestations of the universe are God.

Parasuicide Self-harmful or destructive behavior without the intent to kill oneself.

Parental imperative Parental roles force female and male adults into positions consistent with their respective gender roles.

Parthenogenesis The belief that reproduction took place by the development of an unfertilized ovum, seed, or spore.

Paul A Jew of Tarsus (a city of southern Turkey near the Mediterranean Sea) who became the apostle of Christianity to the Gentiles. Paul wrote several Epistles in the New Testament. He lived sometime in the 60s C.E.

Pauline Characteristic of the Apostle Paul; his writings or doctrines.

Peripheral artery disease (PAD) Peripheral artery disease is diminished blood flow to the arms or legs resulting in pain and or loss of function in the extremities.

Polyandry The practice of having two or more husbands at the same time.

Polygamy The practice of having two or more wives at the same time.

Polytheism The belief in and worship of many gods and goddesses.

Pornography   Sexually explicit material whose primary purpose is to produce sexual arousal for commercial purposes; it objectifies people by reducing them to their body parts.

Postconventional reasoning   The highest level of moral development in Kohlberg's theory. At this level, morality is completely internalized and based on abstract principles and values.

Postpartum experience   Literally *after birth*, this denotes a period of time ranging from the first days to the first year following delivery when women are adjusting to what it means to be a mother.

Posttraumatic stress disorder   An anxiety disorder that results from an extreme physical or psychological trauma that produces intense feelings of helplessness.

Preconventional reasoning   The first level of moral development in Kohlberg's theory, in which children base moral decisions on the consequences of their actions.

Premenstrual dysphoric disorder (PMDD)   A disorder in which some women have very distressing emotional symptoms before their menstrual period that seriously interfere with their daily functioning and relationships.

Premenstrual syndrome (PMS)   A syndrome of psychological and physical symptoms including anxiety, depression, hyperirritability, retention of fluid, weight gain, and discomfort that some women experience a few days before menstruation.

Progesterone   A hormone produced in both sexes, but it is primarily known as a female hormone and during pregnancy is present in a high concentration.

Prostitution   The exchange of sex for money, gifts, and favors; prostitution is characterized by widespread gender inequality.

Pseudohermaphrodite   A person who is born with ambiguous genitalia, the gonads of one sex and the genitals of the other sex.

Puberty   The period of most rapid physical growth that humans experience, excluding prenatal and early postnatal life.

Puritan   A member of a Protestant group in England and the American colonies who, in the sixteenth and seventeenth centuries, wanted a greater reformation of the church in order to purify it of elaborate ceremonies and forms.

Quaker   A popular name for a member of the Society of Friends. It is a Christian religion founded by George Fox. The Friends have no formal creed, rites, liturgy, or priesthood and reject violence in all relationships, including war. The word *Quaker* is said to originate from George Fox's admonition to "quake" at the word of the Lord.

Quid pro quo harassment   Sexual bribery or sexual coercion, referring to sexual harassment that has rewards or punishments attached to it.

Racism   The subordination of certain groups of people based on their origins and physical characteristics.

Radical feminism   Focuses on the control of women by men. Radical feminism is based on the belief that men's oppression of women is primary and serves as a model for all other oppression.

Rape   Vaginal, oral, or anal penetration by an object or body part, against consent and through force or threat of bodily harm or when the individual is unable to give consent.

Rape myths   Attitudes and beliefs that are generally false but are widely and persistently held and serve to deny and justify male sexual aggression against females.

Rape trauma syndrome   A particular form of posttraumatic stress disorder characterized by two phases: an acute phase, usually lasting for several weeks, in which rape survivors exhibit severe disorganization; and a second, long-term reorganization, which may take several years, characterized by fears of recurrence, frightening dreams, and mistrust in personal relationships.

Reentry women   Middle-aged women who return to school or work once their children have left the home.

Refractory period   The time following orgasm during which an individual is unable to experience orgasm again.

Reincarnation   The belief that after death, the soul will undergo a rebirth in another body.

Risk factor   Condition or factor that will increase the likelihood of developing a disease or disorder.

Role overload   An index of internal stress or negative emotional affect that is felt in response to multiple work and family demands.

Romantic love   A powerful notion in Western culture, this kind of love is marked by strong physiological or sexual arousal paired with an idealized image of the beloved.

Safe(r) sex   Sexual practices that eliminate or substantially reduce the chances that HIV or other STIs will be transmitted from an infected to an uninfected person

Sandwich generation   The same as the dominant generation; that is, middle-aged individuals caring for both their parents and their children.

Sansei   Third-generation Japanese Americans.

Scarcity hypothesis   Human beings have a set amount of time and energy.

Science   A knowledge-based activity that depends on facts accumulated through systematic and objective questioning, hypothesis testing, methodological study, analysis, and presentation.

Seduction theory   An early notion of Freud's; this theory proposed that women's neuroses were caused by actual childhood sexual abuse, rather than by distorted wishes or desires.

Seductive behavior   Unwanted sexual advances for which there is no penalty attached to a women's non-compliance.

Semenarche   A boy's first ejaculation.

Sex   Refers to the biological differences in the genetic composition and reproductive structures and functions of men and women.

Sex discrimination   The harmful and unequal treatment of individuals due to their sex.

Sexism   (1) Differential treatment of individuals based on their sex. (2) The subordination of women and the assumption of the superiority of men solely on the basis of sex or gender.

Sex-role spillover   A carryover into the workplace (or academy) of gender-based expectations for behavior; for example, the expectation that women will be nurturant, compliant, or sexy.

Sexual abuse of children   Any form of sexual contact that occurs before age 18, with a relative, a person at least five years older than the child, or someone who forces himself or herself on the child, regardless of the age difference.

Sexual dimorphism   Physical and behavioral characteristics that differ in females and males.

Sexual dysfunction   In women it is often defined as inability to experience orgasms under any circumstances, including high levels of stimulation (primary dysfunction) or vaginal intercourse (secondary dysfunction); inhibited sexual desire, or a general lack of interest in sex.

Sexual fantasy   Any mental imagery that people find sexually arousing.

Sexual harassment   Unwelcome sexual advances, requests for sexual favors, or other verbal or physical contact of a sexual nature when (1) such behavior is made a term of employment, (2) submission to such terms is used as the basis for employment conditions, or (3) the verbal or physical conduct creates a hostile environment.

Sexual orientation   The focus of one's sexual and romantic desires and behaviors toward the other sex, one's own sex, or both.

Sexually transmitted infections (STIs)   Infectious diseases spread through sexual contact such as HIV/AIDS, other viral infections, bacterial infections, fungal and parasitic diseases. Sharing contaminated needles can also spread AIDS and viral hepatitis.

Shakti   After the Indian goddess Shakti. To have shakti means to have the energy of creation and destruction.

Social constructionism   This view, largely credited to Foucault, holds that human behavior is determined by historical, cultural, and social conditions.

Socialist feminism   Focuses on social relations and how social institutions preserve and promote male dominance.

Sociobiology   See Evolutionary psychology.

Sperm   The male germ cell as compared with the female ovum. Sperm are produced by the testes.

Statistically significant differences   Differences between or among groups that are reliable or reproducible; that is, that are unlikely to be due to chance alone.

Stereotypes   Generalized and oversimplified beliefs about groups of people.

Stereotype threat   The apprehension experienced by minority group members that their behavior might confirm a cultural stereotype.

Stereotyping   Cognitive perspective used to describe gender differences. People learn to streamline information processing by grouping people into categories based on some similarity among members.

Stone Age   The period of human culture during which stone implements were developed and used. The Stone Age is usually divided into the *Paleolithic, Mesolithic,* and *Neolithic* periods. *Litho* means stone or rock; *lithic* refers to a particular period or stage in the use of stone.

Stress   Stress is the effect produced by external (i.e., physical or environmental) events or by internal (i.e., physiological or psychological) factors referred to as *stressors,* which alter an organism's biological equilibrium.

Structural approach   Emphasizes the common positions that certain groups occupy within the social structure. Focus is on structural constraints that channel our experience, from the family to the societal level.

Subtle sexism   Harmful and unequal treatment of women that is less apparent and less visible to others and ourselves.

Suttee   A now outlawed Hindu custom of self-immolation whereby the widow threw herself while still alive onto the funeral pyre of her husband's body and was cremated with him.

Symbolic ethnicity   Suggests that ethnicity has shifted from the center of identity to the periphery, and involves more visible aspects of ethnic heritage (e.g., acknowledging ceremonial holidays, eating ethnic food, wearing ethnic clothing on ceremonial occasions) without binding the individual to adhere to the shared customs, and traditions of the past.

Symbolic racism   Refers to subtler forms of prejudice in which race is not directly expressed but nonetheless is the subtext for opposition to policy changes/issues related to race relations.

T cell   (Also called CD4 cell). A type of lymphocyte (white blood cell) that is crucial for normal functioning of the person's immune system. T cells, or CD4 cells, are the primary target of HIV. The nature of this virus is such that it is able to encode itself into the genetic material of the T cell/CD4 cell and later can use the machinery of the cell to replicate new virus particles. The body's immune system becomes weakened and eventually destroyed CD4/T cells are the main control mechanisms of the immune system. Because HIV can reduce the number of T/CD4 cells, a test to determine the number of T/CD4 cells is used as a marker of the severity of HIV and the condition of the immune system.

Talmud   Means "learning." The Talmud refers to the collection of Hebrew or Jewish writings that constitute the Jewish civil and religious law.

Testes   The pair of male reproductive glands contained in the scrotum, called the male gonads.

Testosterone   In sexual function, this hormone is considered the most important. It is present in both females and males, but has its highest concentration in males. It is referred to as the male hormone and is secreted by the testes and adrenal glands in the male and by the ovaries and adrenals in the female.

Tokenism   The hiring of women as "tokens" in the workplace to satisfy antidiscrimination laws.

Torah   The complete body of Jewish religious literature.

Traditional marriage   Increasingly uncommon, this is a marriage in which the husband is the dominant partner and the wife submissive; the husband basically supports the family economically, and marital roles are relatively rigid.

Trimester   The three-month period used to describe the progression of a pregnancy in three periods.

Trophy wives   Young, highly attractive women whom men stereotypically marry during the midlife crisis period.

Tumor   A neoplasm or new growth. A mass of cells that grows independently of the rest of the body.

Uterus   The hollow muscular organ in the female in which menstruation occurs, as well as implantation of the fertilized ovum, nourishment and growth of the fetus, and finally the last stage of pregnancy, labor, through which the infant is delivered.

Vagina   The tubular organ in the female composed of muscle located between the urinary bladder and the rectum. It is the vestibule for sexual intercourse and serves as a vehicle for sperm to reach the ova in the fallopian tubes. It also serves as the passage for the infant from the uterus to the outside world during labor.

Vasocongestion   Increased blood supply to the genitals that causes the penis, vaginal lips, and clitoris to swell.

Vedic   An old Indian language and precursor of Sanskrit. The early sacred literature was written in Vedic. Before the development of Hinduism, the people of this time were called Vedic.

Viagra   A drug introduced by the Pfizer pharmaceutical company as a solution to male impotency.

Visual–spatial ability   An umbrella category for three classes of abilities: spatial visualization, which requires finding a figure embedded in a complex background; spatial perception, which requires locating a true vertical or horizontal line in the midst of distracting information; and mental rotation, which requires correctly identifying a figure that has been rotated so that it is presented at a different angle.

Voluntary minority   Are people, and their descendants, who have voluntarily come to the United States because they believe that the move will ultimately lead to more economic opportunities and greater political freedom; they apparently do not interpret their presence and/or reception in the United States in terms of having been forced on them by Euro-Americans.

White   Subsumes many ethnocultural groups (e.g., Anglo Americans, Irish Americans, Polish Americans).

White privilege   Unearned advantages/privileges and conferred dominance for White people based on their fair skin color, which operate basically outside their awareness but nevertheless perpetuate oppressive conditions for people of color.

Zona pellucida   A jellylike substance surrounding the mature ovum.

Zygote   The single cell produced by the penetration of the ovum by the sperm; the union of the two gametes.

REFERENCES

AARP (2001). Census 2000 data about Grandparent Headed Households. Retrieved March 12, 2004, from www. aarp.org/Articles/a2004-01-16-census2000data.html.

Abbey, A. (1982). Sex differences in attributions for friendly behavior. Do males misperceive females' friendliness? *Journal of Personality and Social Personality, 42,* 830–838.

Abbey, A., & Melby, C. (1986). The effect of nonverbal cues on gender differences in perceptions of sexual intent. *Sex Roles, 15,* 283–298.

Abbey, A., Andrews, F., & Halman, L. J. (1991). Gender's role in responses to infertility. *Psychology of Women Quarterly, 15,* 295–316.

Abe-Kim, J., Okazaki, S., & Goto, S. G. (2001). Unidimensional versus multidimensional approaches to the assessment of acculturation for Asian American populations. *Cultural Diversity and Ethnic Minority Psychology, 7*(3), 203–206.

Abel, G., Gore, D., Holland, C., Camp, N., Becker, J., & Rathner, J. (1989). The measurement of the cognitive distortion of child molesters. *Annals of Sex Research, 2,* 135–152.

Abramson, L. (1990, May 4). Uncaring women's health care. *New York Times.*

Abreu, J. M. (2001). Theory and research on stereotypes and perceptual bias: A resource guide for multicultural counseling trainers. *Counseling Psychologist, 29,* 487–512.

Abusharaf, R. (1998, March/April). Unmasking tradition. *The Sciences,* 22–27.

Acker, J. (1990). Hierarchies, jobs, bodies: A theory of gendered organizations. *Gender & Society, 4,* 139–158.

Adami, H. O. (1992). Long-term consequences of estrogen and estrogen-progestin replacement. *Cancer Causes and Control, 3,* 83–90.

Adams, C. J. (Ed.) (1965). *A reader's guide to the great religions.* New York: Free Press, p. 287f. Cited by Noss & Noss, 1984, p. 496.

Adams, J. W., Kottke, J. L., & Padgitt, J. S. (1983). Sexual harassment of university students. *Journal of College Student Personnel, 24,* 484–490.

Adelmann, P. (1993). Psychological well-being and homemaker vs. retiree identity among older women. *Sex Roles, 29*(3/4), 195–212.

Adelmann, P. K., Antonucci, T. C., Crohan, S. E., & Coleman, L. M. (1989). Empty nest, cohort, and employment in the well-being of midlife women. *Sex Roles, 20,* 173–189.

Adkins-Regan, E. (1988). Sex hormones and sexual orientation in animals. *Psychobiology, 16,* 335–347.

Adler, L. L. (1999). Autonomy in a cross-cultural perspective. In M. B. Nadien & F. L. Denmark (Eds.), *Females and autonomy: A Life-span perspective* (p. 14). Boston: Allyn and Bacon.

Adler, N., David, H. P., Major, B. N., Rot, S. H., Russo, N. F., & Wyatt, G. E. (1990, April 6). Psychological responses after abortion. *Science, 248,* 41–44.

Adler, P. A., Kless, S. J., & Adler, P. (1992). Socialization to gender roles: Popularity among elementary school boys and girls. *Sociology of Education, 65,* 169–187.

Agras, W. S., Rossiter, E. M., Arnow, B., Schneider, J. A., Telch, C. F., Raeburn, S. D., Bruce, B., Perl, M., & Koran, L. M. (1992). Pharmacologic and cognitive-behavioral treatment for bulimia nervosa: A controlled comparison. *American Journal of Psychiatry, 149,* 82–87.

Agrawal, R., & Kumar, A. (1992). Everyday memory in adulthood. *Psychological Studies, 37*(2/3), 161–172.

Ahlstrom, S. E. (1972). *A religious history of the American people.* New Haven, CT: Yale University Press.

AIDS surveillance update. (1994, October). New York City Department of Health.

Aitken, L. S., Fenaughty, A. M., West, S. G., Johnson, J. J., & Luckett, T. L. (1995). Perceived determinants of risk for breast cancer and the relations among objective risk, perceived risk, and screening behavior over time. *Women's Health: Research on Gender, Behavior, and Policy, 1*(1), 27–50.

Akman, D. E., Toner, B. B., Stuckless, N., Ali, A., Emmott, S. D., & Downie, F. P. (2001). Feminist issues in research methodology: The development of a cognitive scale. *Feminism & Psychology, 11*(2), 209–227.

Alan Guttmacher Institute. (1991). *Facts in brief.* New York: Author.

Alan Guttmacher Institute. (2002). *Facts in brief: Induced abortion.* New York: Author.

Albert, S. M., Glied, S., & Andrews, H. (2001). Primary care expenditures before the onset of Alzheimer's Disease. *Neurology, 59*(4), 573–578.

Alington, D. E., & Troll, L. E. (1984). Social change and equality: The roles of women and economics. In G. Baruch & J. Brooks-Gunn (Eds.), *Women in midlife* (pp. 181–202). New York: Plenum Press.

Allen, E. (1988). West Indians. In L. Comas-Diaz & E. Griffith (Eds.), *Clinical guidelines in cross-cultural mental health* (pp. 305–333). New York: Wiley.

Allen, L. S., Hines, M., Shryne, J. E., & Gorski, R. A. (1989). Two sexually dimorphic cell groups in the human brain. *Journal of Neuroscience, 9,* 497–506.

Allgeier, E. R., & McCormick, N. B. (1983). *Changing boundaries: Gender roles and sexual behavior.* Palo Alto, CA: Mayfield.

Allison, J. A., & Wrightsman, L. S. (1993). *Rape: The misunderstood crime.* Newbury Park, CA: Sage.

Almquist, E. M. (1989). The experiences of minority women in the United States: Intersections of race, gender and class. In J. Freeman (Ed.), *Women: A feminist perspective* (4th ed., pp. 414–445). Mountain View, CA: Mayfield.

Alterman, E. (1997, November). Sex in the 90's. *Elle,* pp. 128–134.

Alton-Lee, A., Nuthall, G., & Patrick, J. (1993). Reframing classroom research: A lesson from the private world of children. *Harvard Educational Review, 63*(1), 50–84.

Alvarez, L. (2003, October 21). Norway leads industrial nations back to breast-feeding. *New York Times.*

Alvidrez, J., & Weinstein, R. S. (1993, March). Early teacher expectations and later academic achievement. Paper presented at the biennial meeting of the Society for Research in Child Development, New Orleans.

Amaro, H. (1988). Considerations for prevention of HIV infection among Hispanic women. *Psychology of Women Quarterly, 12,* 429–443.

Amaro, H. (1995). Love, sex, and power: Considering women's realities in HIV prevention. *American Psychologist, 50,* 437–447.

Amaro, H., & Russo, N. F. (1987). Hispanic women and mental health: An overview of contemporary issues in research and practice. *Psychology of Women Quarterly, 11,* 393–407.

Amatea, E. S., & Fong-Beyette, M. L. (1987). Through a different lens: Examining professional women's interrole coping by focus and mode. *Sex Roles, 17*(5/6), 237–252.

Amato, P. R., Johnson, D. R., Booth, A., & Rogers, S. J. (2003). Continuity and change in marital quality between 1980 and 2000. *Journal of Marriage and the Family, 65*(1), 1–22.

American Association of University Women. (AAUW). (1992). *The AAUW report: How schools shortchange girls.* Washington, DC: AAUW.

American Association of University Women. (AAUW). (1993). *Hostile hallways: The AAUW survey on sexual harassment in America's schools.* Washington, DC: American Association of University Women Educational Foundation.

American Association of University Women. (AAUW). (1998). The AAUW report: Separated by sex: A critical look at single-sex education for girls. Washington, DC: AAUW Educational Foundation.

American Cancer Society. (1991). *Cancer facts and figures.* Atlanta, GA: American Cancer Society.

American Cancer Society. (1994a). Breast cancer: Cause and prevention. *American Cancer Society Cancer Response System.* #407068.

American Cancer Society. (1994b). Breast cancer: Methods of detection. *American Cancer Society Cancer Response System.* #407013.

American Cancer Society. (1999). *Lung cancer disease entirely due to smoking.* Atlanta, GA: American Cancer Society.

American Catholic. (2003, September 27). The Catholic Church and sexual abuse by priests. Retrieved December 4, 2003, from www.americancatholic.org/News/Clergy/Sex_abuse.

American Heritage Dictionary of the English Language (4th ed.). (2000). Boston: Houghton Mifflin.

American Psychiatric Association. (1994). *Diagnostic and statistical manual of mental disorders* (4th ed.). Washington, DC: Author.

American Psychiatric Association Task Force on DSM-IV. (2000). *Diagnostic and statistical manual of mental disorders* (revised 4th ed.). Washington, DC: American Psychiatric Association Task Force on DSM-IV.

American Psychiatric Association Work Group on Eating Disorders. (2000). Practice guideline for the treatment of patients with eating disorders (revision). *American Journal of Psychiatry, 157* (1 Suppl.), 1–39.

American Psychological Association. (April 2002). *Summit on women and depression: Proceedings and recommendations.* American Psychological Association.

American Psychological Association. (2003). Guidelines on multicultural education, training, research, practice, and organizational change for psychologists. *American Psychologist, 58,* 377–402.

American Psychological Association Committee on Lesbian and Gay Concerns. (1986). Cited by B. Greene, 1994b.

Anas, E., Anderson, R., Hsiang-Ching, K., Murphy, S. L., & Kochanek, K. D. (2003). National vital statistics reports. *Centers for Disease Control, 52*(3), 1–116.

Anatomy *is* destiny. (1997, March 17). *New York Post,* p. 17.

Anatomy of a cover-up. (2003, May 26). *Daily News,* p. 3.

Andersen, A. E. (1995). Eating disorders in males. In K. D. Brownell & C. G. Fairburn (Eds.), *Eating disorders and obesity* (pp. 177–187). New York: Guilford Press.

Anderson, B. L. (1998). Breast cancer: Biobehavioral aspects. In A. E. Blechman & K. D. Brownell (Eds.), *Behavioral Medicine and Women: A comprehensive handbook* (pp. 570–576). New York: Guilford Press.

Anderson, B. S., & Zinsser, J. P. (1988). *A history of their own: Women in Europe from prehistory to the present* (Vol. 1, pp. 53–54). New York: Harper & Row.

Andrews, L. B. (1984). *New conceptions.* New York: St. Martin's.

Aneshensel, C. S., Frerichs, R. R., & Clark, V. A. (1981). Family roles and sex differences in depression. *Journal of Health and Social Behavior, 22,* 379–393.

Angier, N. (1991, August 30). Zone of brain linked to men's sexual orientation. *New York Times,* pp. A1, D18. Cited by Rathus, Nevid, & Fichner-Rathus, 1998, p. 189.

Angier, N. (1999). *Woman: An intimate geography.* Boston: Houghton Mifflin.

Angst, J., Scllaro, R., Merikangas, K. R., & Endicott, J. (2001). The epidemiology of perimenstural psychological symptoms. *Acta Psychiatrica Scandinavica, 104,* 110–116.

An-Naim, A. (2002). The Islamic counter reformation. *New Perspectives Quarterly, 19*(1), p. 1–6.

Antill, J. K. (1983). Sex role complementarity versus similarity in married couples. *Journal of Personality and Social Psychology, 45,* 145–155.

Antoni, M. H., Schneiderman, N., Klimas, N., La Perriere, A., Ironson, G., & Fletcher, M. (1991). Disparities in psychological, neuroendocrine, and immunologic patterns in asymptomatic HIV-1 seropositive and seronegative gay men. *Biological Psychiatry, 29,* 1023–1041. Cited by Taylor, 1995.

Anzaldúa, G. (Ed.). (1990). *Making face, making soul—Haciendo caras: Creative and critical perspectives by feminists of color.* San Francisco: Aunt Lute Foundation.

Apfelbaum, E. (1979). Relations of domination and movements for liberation: An analysis of power between groups. In W. G. Austin & S. Worchel (Eds.), *The social psychology of intergroup relations* (pp. 188–204). Monterey, CA: Brooks/Cole.

Arber, S., & Ginn, J. (1994). Women and aging. *Reviews in Clinical Gerontology, 4*(4), 349–358.

Arditti, J. A. (1995). No regrets: Custodial mother's accounts of the difficulties and benefits of divorce. *Contemporary Family Therapy: An International Journal, 17*(2), 229–248.

Arias, I., & Pape, K. T. (1994). Physical abuse. In L. L'Abate (Ed.), *Handbook of developmental family psychology and psychopathology* (pp. 284–308). New York: Wiley.

Aries, F. (1962). *Centuries of childhood.* New York: Knopf.

Arling, G. (1976a). The elderly widow and her family, neighbors, and friends. *Journal of Marriage and Family, 38,* 757–769.

Arling, G. (1976b). Resistance to isolation among elderly widows. *International Journal of Aging and Human Development, 7,* 67–76.

Arrighi, B. A. and Maume, D. J. Jr. (2000). Workplace subordination and men's avoidance of housework. *Journal of Family Issues, 21*(4), 464–487.

Arrindell, W. A., Eisemann, M., Richter, J., Oei, T. P. S., Caballo, V. E., van der Ende, J., Sanavio, E., Bages, N., Feldman, L., Torres, B., Sica, C., Iwawaki, S., & Hatzichristou, C. (2003). Cultural Clinical Psychology Study Group. Masculinity–femininity as a national characteristic and its relationship with national agoraphobic fear levels: Fodor's sex role hypothesis revitalized. *Behavior Research and Therapy, 41,* 795–807.

Asch, S. E. (1951). Effects of group pressure upon the modification and distortion of judgments. In H. Guetzkow (Ed.), *Groups, leadership and men* (pp. 177–190). Pittsburgh, PA: Carnegie Press.

Associated Press. (2000, August 29). After years of decline, Caesareans are on the rise again. *The Associated Press online.*

Associated Press. (2003, June 25). U.S. birthrate falls to a record low. *Milwaukee Journal Sentinal.* Retrieved November 1, 2003, from www.jsonline.com/lifestyle/parenting/jun03/150733.asp.

Atkinson, D. R., & Hackett, G. (1998). *Counseling Diverse Populations.* Boston: McGraw-Hill.

Atkinson, D. R., Morton, G., & Sue, D. W. (1998). *Counseling American minorities.* Boston: McGraw Hill.

Attie, I., & Brooks-Gunn, J. (1989). The development of eating problems in adolescent girls: A longitudinal study. *Developmental Psychology, 25,* 70–79.

Avis, N. E. (1996). Women's perceptions of the menopause. *European Menopause Journal, 3,* 80–84.

Avis, N. E. (1999). Women's health at midlife. In S. L. Willis & J. D. Reid (Eds.), *Life in the middle: Psychological and social development in middle age* (pp. 105–146). San Diego: Academic Press.

Avis, N. E. (2003). Depression during the menopausal transition. *Psychology of Women Quarterly, 27,* 91–100.

Azibo, D. A. (1988). Understanding the proper and improper usage of the comparative research framework. *Journal of Black Psychology, 15,* 81–91.

Babchuk, N., & Anderson, T. (1989). Older widows and married women: Their intimates and confidantes. *International Journal of Aging and Human Development, 28*(1), 21–33.

Baber, K. M., & Allen, K. R. (1992). *Women and families: Feminist reconstructions.* New York: Guilford.

Bachman, R., & Saltzman, L. E. (1996). *Violence against women: Estimates form the redesigned survey.* [Bureau of Justice Statistics special report]. Rockville, MD: U.S. Department of Justice.

Bacquet, C. R., Horm, J. W., Gibbs, T., & Greenwald, P. (1991). Socioeconomic factors and cancer incidence among blacks and whites. *Journal of the National Cancer Institute, 83,* 551–557.

Bader, M. (2002). Priests, sexual abuse and illusions of innocence. *Alternet.org.,* March 13, 2002. Available: www.alternet.org/story.html? StoryID=12625

Bailey, J. M., et al. (1999). A family history study of male sexual orientation using three independent samples. *Behavior Genetics, 29*(2), 79–86.

Bailey, J. M., & Pillard, R. C. (1991). A genetic study of male sexual orientation. *Archives of General Psychiatry, 48,* 1083–1096.

Bailey, J. M., Pillard, R. C., Neale, M. C., & Agyei, Y. (1993). Heritable factors influence sexual orientation in women. *Archives of General Psychiatry, 50,* 217–223.

Baltes, P. B., Smith, J., & Staudinger, U. M. (1992). Wisdom and successful aging. In T. B. Sonderegger (Ed.), *Nebraska Symposium on Motivation 1991: Psychology and aging, 39,* 123–167. Lincoln, NE: University of Nebraska Press.

Bambara, T. C. (Ed.). (1970). *The Black woman: An anthology.* New York: Signet.

Banerjee, R. (2000). Boys will be boys: The effect of social evaluation concerns on gender-typing. *Social Development, 9*(3), 397–408.

Barbanel, L. (1990). Women therapists at midlife. *Psychotherapy in Private Practice, 8*(2), 79–85.

Barbee, A. P., Cunningham, M. R., Winstead, B. A., Derlega, V. J., Gulley, M. R., Yankeelov, P. A., & Druen, P. B. (1993). Effects of gender role expectations on the social support process. *Journal of Social Issues, 49,* 175–190.

Barber, J. S., & Axinn, W. G. (1998). Gender role attitudes and marriage among young women. *The Sociological Quarterly, 39,* 11–31.

Barba, R., & Cardinale, L. (1991). Are females invisible students: An investigation of teacher-student questioning interactions. *School Science and Mathematics, 91,* 306–310.

Bardwell, J. R., Cochran, S. W., & Walker, S. (1986). Relationship of parental education, race, and gender to sex-role stereotyping in five-year-old kindergartners. *Sex Roles, 15,* 275–281.

Barer, B. M. (1994). Men and women aging differently. *International Journal of Aging and Human Development, 38*(1), 29–40.

Bargh, J. A., Raymond, P., Pryor, J. B., & Strack, F. (1995). Attractiveness of the underling: An automatic power–sex association and its consequences for sexual harassment and aggression. *Journal of Personality and Social Psychology, 68,* 768–781.

Barile, C. A. (2001). The never-married, Caucasian, American women in mid-life as a departure from the stereotypes of the old maid spinster. *Dissertation Abstracts International, 61*(9B), 4969.

Barker, K. (1993). Changing assumptions and contingent solutions: The costs and benefits of women working full- and part-time. *Sex Roles, 1/2,* 47–71.

Barker, K. (1998). Toiling for piece-rates and accumulating deficits: Contingent work in higher education. In K. Barker & K. Christensen (Eds.), *Contingent work: American employment relations in transition* (p. xx). Ithaca, NY: ILR/Cornell University Press

Barker, K., & Christensen, K. (1998). Introduction. In K. Barker & K. Christensen (Eds.), *Contingent work: American employment relations in transition* (p. xx). Ithaca, NY: ILR/Cornell University Press.

Barker, R. (1968). *Ecological psychology.* Stanford, CA: Stanford University Press.

Barker-Benfield, G. J. (1976). The horrors of half-known life: Male attitudes toward women and sexuality in nineteenth-century America. New York: Harper and Row. Cited by Brieger, (1984). History of medicine. In *A guide to the culture of science, technology, and medicine* (pp. 121–194). New York: Free Press.

Barker-Collo, S., Melnyk, W., & McDonald-Miszczak, L. (2000). A cognitive-behavioral model of posttraumatic stress for sexually abused females. *Journal of Interpersonal Violence, 15*(4), 375 392.

Barnes, N. S. (1987). Buddhism. In A. Sharma (Ed.), *Women in World Religions* (pp. 105–133). Albany: State University of New York Press.

Barnett, O. W., & La Violette, A. D. (1993). *It could happen to anyone: Why battered women stay.* Newbury Park, CA: Sage.

Barnett, R. C., & Baruch, G. K. (1987). Mothers' participation in childcare: Patterns and consequences. In F. J. Crosby (Ed.), *Spouse, parent and worker* (pp. 91–108). New Haven, CT: Yale University Press.

Barnett, R. C., Biener, G. K., & Baruch, G. K. (1987). *Gender and stress.* New York: Free Press.

Barnett, R. C., Marshall, N. L., Raudenbush, S. W., & Brennan, R. T. (1983). Gender and the relationship between job experience and psychological distress: A study of dual-earner couples. *Journal of Personality and Social Psychology, 64,* 794–806.

Barnett, R. C., & Rivers, C. (1996). *She works/He works: How two-income families are happier, healthier, and better off.* San Francisco: HarperSanFrancisco.

Baron, L., & Straus, M. A. (1989). *Four theories of marital rape in American society: A state-level analysis.* New Haven, CT: Yale University Press.

Barringer, F. (1992, October 7). Family-leave debate: A profound ambivalence. *New York Times,* pp. A1, A22L.

Barringer, F. (1993, April 15). Sex survey of American males finds 1 percent are gay. *New York Times,* pp. A1, A9.

Bart, P. B. (1971). Depression in middle-aged women. In V. G. Gornick & B. K. Moran (Eds.), *Women in sexist society.* New York: Basic Books.

Bart, P. B., & Grossman, M. (1978). Menopause. In M. T. Notman & C. C. Nadelson (Eds.), *The woman patient: Medical and psychological interfaces* (pp. 337–354). New York: Plenum Press.

Bar-Tal, D., & Saxe, L. (1976). Perceptions of similarly and dissimilarly attractive couples and individuals. *Journal of Personality and Social Psychology, 33,* 772–781.

Barth, F. (1969). *Ethnic groups and boundaries.* Boston: Little, Brown.

Bartsch, R. A. (2000). Gender representation in television commercials: Updating an update. *Sex Roles, 43*(9–10), 735–743.

Baruch, G. K., Beiner, L., & Barnett, R. C. (1987). Women and gender in research on work and family stress. *American Psychologist, 42,* 130–136.

Baskin, J. (1985). The separation of Jewish women in rabbinic Judaism. In Y. Y. Haddad & E. B. Findley (Eds.), *Women, religion and social change* (pp. 4–5). Albany: State University of New York Press.

Basow, S. A. (1986). *Gender stereotypes: Traditions and alternatives.* Monterey, CA: Brooks/Cole.

Basow, S. A. (1992). *Gender: Stereotypes and roles* (3rd ed.). Pacific Grove, CA: Brooks/Cole.

Basow, S. A. (2004). Gender dynamics in the classroom. In J. C. Chrisler, C. Golden, & P. D. Rozee (Eds.), *Lectures on the psychology of women* (3rd ed.). New York: McGraw-Hill.

Bates, G. (1981). On the nature of the hot flash. *Clinical Obstetrics and Gynecology, 24*(1), 231–241.

Baucom, D. H. (1983). Personality process and individual differences: Sex role identity and the decision to regain control among women: A learned helplessness investigation. *Journal of Personality and Social Psychology, 44,* 334–343.

Baum, M. J., Erskine, M. S., Kornberg, E., & Weaver, C. E. (1990). Prenatal and neonatal testosterone exposure interact to affect differentiation of sexual behavior and partner preference in female ferrets. *Behavioral Neuroscience, 104,* 185–198.

Baxter, J. (1992). Power attitudes and time: The domestic division of labour. *Journal of Comparative Family Studies, 23,* 165–182.

Bazzini, D. G., McIntosh, W., Smith, S., Cook, S., & Harris, C. (1997). The aging woman in popular film: Underrepresented, unattractive, unfriendly, and unintelligent. *Sex Roles, 36,* 531–543.

Beal, C. (1994). *Boys and girls: The development of gender roles.* New York: McGraw-Hill.

Beckman, L. J., & Houser, B. B. (1982). The consequences of childlessness on the social-psychological well-being of older women. *Journal of Gerontology, 37*(2), 243–250.

Begley, S. (February 13, 1995). Three is not enough. *Newsweek,* pp. 67–69.

Beitzig, L. (1989). Causes of conjugal dissolution: A cross-cultural study. *Current Anthropology, 30,* 654–676.

Belcastro, P. A. (1985). Sexual behavior differences between black and white adolescents. *Journal of Sex Research, 21,* 56–67.

Belenky, M. F., Clinchy, B. M., Goldberg, N. R., & Tarole, J. M. (1986). *Women's ways of knowing: The development of self, voice, and mind.* New York: Basic Books.

Belgrave, F. Z., van Oss Marian, B., & Chambers, D. B. (2000). Cultural, contextual, and intrapersonal predictors of risky sexual attitudes among urban African American girls in early adolescence. *Cultural Diversity and Ethnic Minority Psychology, 6*(3), 309–322.

Belkin, L. (2003, October 26). The opt-out revolution. *New York Times Magazine,* pp. 42ff.

Bell, A. P., & Weinberg, M. S. (1978). *Homosexualities: A study of diversity among men and women.* New York: Simon & Schuster.

Bell, A. P., Weinberg, M. S., & Hammersmith, S. K. (1901). *Sexual preference.* Bloomington, IN: Indiana University Press.

Bell, I. P. (1989). The double standard: Age. In J. Freeman (Ed.), *Women: A feminist perspective* (4th ed., pp. 236–244). Mountain View, CA: Mayfield.

Bell, J. (Ed.). (1995). *Famous Black quotations.* New York: Warner Books.

Belle, D., & Doucet, J. (2003). Poverty, inequality, and discrimination as sources of depression among U.S. women. *Psychology of Women Quarterly, 27,* 101–113.

Beller, M., & Gafni, N. (1996). The 1991 international assessment of educational progress in mathematics and sciences: The gender differences perspective. *Journal of Educational Psychology, 88,* 365–377.

Belsky, J. (1979). Mother–father–infant interaction: A naturalistic observation study. *Developmental Psychology, 15,* 601–607.

Belsky, J. (1992). The research findings on gender issues in aging men and women. In B. R. Wainrib (Ed.), *Gender issues across the life cycle.* New York: Springer.

Belsky, J., & Rovine, M. (1990). Patterns of marital change across the transition to parenthood. *Journal of Marriage and the Family, 52*(1), 5–19.

Bem, D. J. (1996). Exotic becomes erotic: A developmental theory of sexual orientation. *Psychological Review, 103,* 320–335.

Bem, S. L. (1974). The measurement of psychological androgyny. *Journal of Consulting and Clinical Psychology, 42*(2), 155–162.

Bem, S. L. (1981). Gender schema theory: A cognitive account of sex typing. *Psychological Review, 88,* 354–364.

Bem, S. L. (1994, August 17). In a male-centered world, female differences are transformed into female disadvantages. *Chronicle of Higher Education,* pp. B1–B3.

Benbow, C. P., & Stanley, J. C. (1980). Sex differences in mathematical ability: Fact or artifact? *Science, 210,* 1262–1264.

Beneke, T. (1993). Men on rape. In A. Minas (Ed.), *Gender basics: Feminist perspectives on women and men* (pp. 352–357). Belmont, CA: Wadsworth.

Benin, M., & Agostinelli, J. (1988). Husbands' and wives' satisfaction with the division of labor. *Journal of Marriage and the Family, 50,* 349–361.

Benjamin, J. (1988). *The bonds of love: Psychoanalysis, feminism, and the problem of domination.* New York: Pantheon Books.

Bennett, A. (1989). *Death of the organization.* New York: William Morrow.

Bennett, N. G., Blanc, A. K., & Bloom, D. E. (1988). Commitment and the modern union: Assessing the link between premarital cohabitation and subsequent marital stability. *American Sociological Review, 53,* 127–138.

Benokraitis, N. V., & Feagin, J. R. (1995). *Modern sexism: Blatant, subtle, and covert discrimination* (2nd ed.). Englewood Cliffs, NJ: Prentice Hall.

Benson, R. C. (1983). *Handbook of obstetrics and gynecology.* Los Altos, CA: Lange Medical.

Benward, J., & Densen-Gerber, J. (1975). Incest as a causative factor in antisocial behavior: An exploratory study. *Contemporary Drug Problems, 4,* 323–340.

Beral. (2001). Most women with family history of breast cancer do not get cancer. *Lancet,* 358:1389–1399.

Berardo, D. H., Shehan, C. L., & Leslie, G. R. (1987). A residue of transition: Jobs, careers, and spouse's time in housework. *Journal of Marriage and the Family, 49,* 381–390.

Berger, C. R. (1988). Uncertainty and information exchange in developing relationships. In S. Duck & D. F. Hay (Eds.), *Handbook of personal relationships: Theory, research, and interventions* (pp. 239–255). Chichester, UK: John Wiley & Sons.

Bergmann, T. J., Grahn, J. L., & Wyatt, G. (1986, Summer). Relationship of employment status to employee job satisfaction. *Akron Business Review,* pp. 45–50.

Berk, R., & Berk, S. (1979). *Labor and leisure at home: Content and organization of the household day.* Beverly Hills, CA: Sage.

Bernard, J. (1972). *The future of marriage.* New York: World.

Berndt, T. J. (1992). Friendships and friends' influence in adolescence. *Current Directions in Psychological Science, 1,* 156–159.

Bernstein, A. (2003). *Health snapshot: More diabetes, longer life.* Hyattsville, MD: National Center for Health Statistics.

Bernstein, D. (1993). The female superego: A different perspective. In N. Freedman & B. Distler (Eds.), *Female identity conflict in clinical practice* (pp. 69–100). Northvale, NJ: Jason Aronson.

Bernstein, N. (March 7, 2004). Behind fall in pregnancy, a new teenage culture of restraint. *The New York Times,* pp. A1, 36, 37.

Berscheid, E. (1988). Some comments on love's autonomy—Or whatever happened to old-fashioned lust? In R. J. Sternberg & M. L. Barnes (Eds.), *The psychology of love* (pp. 359–374). New Haven, CT: Yale University Press.

Bertilson, H., Springer, K., & Fierke, K. (1982). Underrepresentation of female referents as pronouns: Examples and pictures in introductory college textbooks. *Psychological Reports, 51,* 923–931.

Betancourt, H., & Lopez, S. R. (1993). The study of culture, ethnicity, and race in American psychology. *American Psychologist, 48,* 629–637.

Beyer, S. (1990). Gender differences in the accuracy of self-evaluations of performance. *Journal of Personality and Social Psychology, 59,* 960–970.

Bhatia, M. S., Dhar, N. K., Singhal, P. K., Nigam, V. R., et al. (1990). Temper tantrums: Prevalence and etiology in a non-referral outpatient setting. *Clinical Pediatrics, 29*(6), 311–315.

Bhattacharjee, N. (1999). Through the looking glass: Gender socialization in a primary school. In T. S. Saraswathi (Ed.), *Culture, socialization and human development: Theory, research and applications in India* (pp. 336–355). Thousand Oaks, CA: Sage Publications.

Biaggio, M. K. (1999) Personal communication.

Bianchi, S. (1995). The changing demographic and socioeconomic characteristics of single-parent families. In S. Hanson et al. (Eds.), *Single-parent families: Diversities, myths and realities* (pp. 71–97). New York: Hayworth Press.

Bianchi, S. M., Milkie, M. A., Sayer, L. C., & Robinson, J. P. (2000). Is anyone doing the housework? Trends in the gender division of household labor. *Social Forces, 79,* 191–228.

Bieber, I., Dair, H. J., Dince, P. R., Drellich, M. G., Grand, H. G., Grundlach, R. H., Kremer, M. W., Rifkin, A. H., Wilbur, C. B., & Bieber, T. B. (1962). *Homosexuality: A psychoanalytic study of male homosexuals.* New York: Basic Books.

Biernat, M. (1991). Gender stereotypes and the relationship between masculinity and femininity: A developmental analysis. *Journal of Personality and Social Psychology, 61*(3), 351–365.

Biernat, M., & Wortman, C. B. (1991). Sharing of home responsibilities between professionally employed women and their husbands. *Journal of Personality and Social Psychology, 60*(6), 844–860.

Bigler, R. S., & Liben, L. S. (1992). Cognitive mechanisms in children's gender stereotyping: Theoretical and educational implications of a cognitive-based intervention. *Child Development, 63,* 1351–1363.

Biladeau, M. A. (2003, March). A phenomenological study of men at later midlife. *Dissertation Abstracts International, 63*(8B), 3955.

Biller, H. B. (1981). Father absence, divorce, and personality development. In M. E. Lamb (Ed.), *The role of the father in child development* (2nd ed., pp. 489–552). New York: Wiley.

Billy, J. O. G., Tanfer, K., Grady, W. R., & Keplinger, D. H. (1993). The sexual behavior of men in the United States. *Family Planning Perspectives, 25*(2), 52–60.

Bingham S. G., & Scherer, L. L. (1993). Factors associated with responses to sexual harassment and satisfaction with outcome. *Sex Roles, 29,* 239–269.

Binion, V. J. (1990). Psychological androgyny: A black female perspective. *Sex Roles, 22*(7/8), 487–507.

Biological Imperatives (1973, January 8.) *Time,* pp. 34–35.

Birchler, G. R., Fals-Stewart, W., & Hersen, M. (1996). Marital discord. In V. B. Van Hasselt et al. (Ed.), *Psychological treatment of older adults: An introductory text* (pp. 315–333). New York: Plenum Press.

Birenbaum, M., Kelly, A. E., & Levi-Keren, M. (1994). Stimulus features and sex differences in mental rotation test performance. *Intelligence, 19,* 51–64.

Bisagno, V., Bowman, R. E., & Luine, V. N. (2003). Functional aspects of estrogen neuroprotection. *Endocrine, 21,* 33–41.

Bishop, K., & Wahlsten, D. (1997). Sex differences in the human corpus callosum: Myth and reality. *Neuroscience and Biobehavioral Review, 21,* 581–601.

Black, S. M., & Hill, C. E. (1984). The psychological well-being of women in their middle years. *Psychology of Women Quarterly, 8,* 282–292.

Blackwell, A., Kwoh, S., & Pastor, M. (2002). *Searching for the uncommon common ground: New dimensions on race in America.* New York: W. W. Norton.

Blader, J. C., & Marshall, W. L. (1989). Is assessment of sexual arousal in rapists worthwhile? A critique of current methods and the development of a response compatibility approach. *Clinical Psychology Review, 9,* 569–587.

Blau, F. D., & Ferber, M. A. (1987). Occupations and earnings of women workers. In S. Koziara, M. Moskow, & L. D. Tanner (Eds.), *Working women: Past, present, future* (pp. 37–68). Washington, DC: Bureau of National Affairs.

Blazer, D. G., & Koenig, H. G. (1996). Mood disorders. In E. W. Busse & D. G. Blazer (Eds.), *Textbook of geriatric psychiatry* (pp. 235–263). Washington, DC: American Psychiatric Press.

Blier, R. (1984). *Science and gender: A critique of biology and its theories on women.* New York: Pergamon Press.

Block, M. R., & Sinnot, J. D. (Eds.). (1979). *The battered elder syndrome.* College Park, MD: University of Maryland Press.

Bloom, B. L. (1988). *Health psychology: a psychosocial perspective.* Englewood Cliffs, NJ: Prentice Hall.

Blosser, F. (2000, June 1). Working women face high risks from work stress, musculoskeletal injuries, other disorders, NIOSH finds. *National Institute for Occupational Safety and Health Report.*

Blumstein, P., & Schwartz, P. (1983). *American couples: Money, work, and sex.* New York: William Morrow.

Blumstein, P., & Schwartz, P. (1990). Intimate relationships and the creation of sexuality. In D. P. McWhirter, S. A. Sanders, & J. M. Reinish (Eds.), *Homosexuality/heterosexuality: Concepts of sexual orientation* (pp. 307–320). New York: Oxford University Press.

Blumstein, P. W., & Schwartz, P. (1976). Bisexuality in women. *Archives of Sexual Behavior, 5,* 171–181.

Blyth, D. A., & Foster-Clark, F. S. (1987). Gender differences in perceived intimacy with different members of adolescents' social networks. *Sex Roles, 17,* 595–605.

Bodner, R. J. (1998). Pain. In E. A. Blechman & K. D. Brownell (Eds.), *Behavioral medicine and women* (pp. 695–699). New York: Guilford Press.

Bogard, C. J., Trillo, A., Schwartz, M., & Gerstel, N. (2001). Future employment among homeless single mothers: The effects of full-time work experience and depressive symptomatology. *Women and Health, 32* (1/2), 137–157.

Bohan, J. (1996). *Psychology and sexual orientation.* New York: Routledge.

Bohan, J. S. (1992). *Seldom seen, rarely heard: Women's place in psychology.* Boulder, CO: Westview Press.

Bohannan, P. (Ed.). (1970). *Divorce and after.* Garden City, NY: Doubleday.

Bolumar, F. (1996). Smoking reduces fecundity: A European multicenter study on infertility and subfecundity. *American Journal of Epidemiology, 143,* 578–587.

Bonnadonna, G., Valagussa, P., & Rossi, A. (1985). Ten-year experience with CMF-based adjuvant chemotherapy in resectable breast cancer. *Breast Cancer Research and Treatment, 2,* 95–115.

Bono, A., (2004). John Jay study reveals extent of abuse problem: Four percent of priests serving over last 50 years accused of abuse. *Catholic News Service.* Retrieved April 3, 2004, from www.americancatholic.org/news/clergysexabuse/johnjaycns.asp

Booth-Butterfield, M. (1986). Stifle or stimulate? The effects of communication task structure on apprehension in non-apprehensive students. *Communication Education, 35*(4), 337–348.

Borgatta, L. (1994). Sexually transmitted diseases. In J. A. Sechzer, A. Griffin, & S. M. Pfafflin (Eds.), *Forging a women's health research agenda: Policy issues for the 1990's: Annals of the New York Academy of Sciences, 736,* 102–113. New York: The New York Academy of Sciences.

Born, M. P., Bleichrodt, N., & van der Fleir, H. (1987). Cross-cultural comparison of sex-related differences on intelligence tests. *Journal of Cross-Cultural Psychology, 18,* 283–314.

Borowsky, S. J., Rubenstein, L. V., Meredith, L. S., Camp, P., Jackson-Triche, M., & Wells, K. B. (2000). Who is at risk of nondetection of mental health problems in primary care? *Journal of General Internal Medicine, 15,* 381–388.

Boscarino, J. A., Galea, S., Ahern, J. (2002). Utilization of mental health services following the September 11th terrorist attacks in Manhattan, New York City. *International Journal of Emergency Mental Health, 4*(3), 143–156.

Bose, U. (1985). Child-rearing attitudes of working and non-working mothers. *Psychological Research Journal, 9*(2), 54–61.

Boston Women's Health Book Collective. (1984). *The new our bodies, ourselves.* New York: Simon & Schuster.

Boston Women's Health Book Collective. (1992). *The new our bodies, ourselves.* New York: Simon & Schuster.

Boston Women's Health Book Collective. (1998). *Our bodies, ourselves for the new century: A book by and for women.* New York: Touchstone.

Boswell, J. (1988). *The kindness of strangers: The abandonment of children in Western Europe from late antiquity to the Renaissance.* New York: Pantheon.

Bowd, A. D. (2003). Stereotypes of elderly persons in narrative jokes. *Research on Aging, 25*(1), 22–35.

Bowen, A. C. L., & John, A. M. H. (2001). Gender differences in presentation and conceptualization of adolescent self-injurious behavior: Implications for therapeutic practice. *Counseling Psychology Quarterly, 4,* 357–379.

Boyles, S. (2003, September 11). Global smoking deaths approach 5 million. *WebMd Medical News,* Retrieved April 4, 2004 from http://aolsvc.health.webmd.aol.com/content/article/73/88935.htm?cobrand=aol

Bradshaw, C. (1994). Asian and Asian American women: Historical and political considerations in psychotherapy. In L. Comas-Diaz & B. Greene (Eds.), *Women of color: Integrating ethnic and gender identities in psychotherapy* (pp. 72–113.) New York: Guilford Press.

Brannon, L. (1996). *Gender: Psychological perspectives.* Boston: Allyn and Bacon.

Brannon, L. (1999). *Gender: Psychological perspectives.* Boston: Allyn and Bacon.

Brannon, L. (2002). *Gender: Psychological perspectives.* Boston, Allyn and Bacon.

Brannon, L., & Feist, J. (1992). *Health psychology: An introduction to behavior and health.* Belmont, CA: Wadsworth.

Brannon, R. C. (1976). No "sissy stuff": The stigma of anything vaguely feminine. In D. David & R. Brannon (Eds.), *The forty-nine percent majority* (pp. 235–249). Reading, MA: Addison-Wesley. Cited by Harrison, Chen, & Ficarrotto, 1995.

Breckenridge, J. N., Gallagher, D., Thompson, L. W., & Peterson, J. (1986). Characteristic depressive symptoms of bereaved elders. *Journal of Gerontology, 41,* 163–168.

Brehm, S., Miller, R. S., Perlman, D., & Campbell, S. M. (2002). *Intimate relationships.* Boston: McGraw-Hill.

Bremner, J. D., Vythilingam, M., Ng, C. K., Vermetten, E., Nazeer, A., Oren, D. A., et al. (2003). Regional brain metabolic correlates of methylparatyrosine-induced depressive symptoms. *Journal of the American Medical Association, 289*(23), 3125–3134.

Brewer, M. B., Dull, V., & Lui, L. (1981). Perceptions of the elderly: Stereotypes as prototypes. *Journal of Personality and Social Psychology, 41,* 656–670.

Brice, J. (1982). West Indians. In M. McGoldrick., J. K. Pearce, & J. Giordano (Eds.), *Ethnicity and family therapy* (pp. 123–133). New York: Guilford Press.

Brickman, P., Janoff-Bulman, R., & Rabinowitz, V. C. (1987). Meaning and value. In P. Brickman (Ed.), *Commitment, conflict, and caring* (pp. 59–105). Englewood Cliffs, NJ: Prentice Hall.

Bridgeman, B., & Moran, R. (1996). Success in college for students with discrepancies between performance on multiple choice and essay tests. *Journal of Educational Psychology, 88,* 333–340.

Bridges, A. J., Bergner, R. M., & Hesson-McInnis, M. (2003). Romantic partners' use of pornography. *Journal of Sex and Marital Therapy, 29,* 1–14.

Bridges, J. S. (1993). Pink or blue: Gender-stereotypic perception of infants as conveyed by birth congratulations cards. *Psychology of Women Quarterly, 17*(2), 193–205.

Bridges, J. S., & McGrail, C. A. (1989). Attributions of responsibility for date and stranger rape. *Sex Roles, 21,* 273–286.

Brieger, G. H. (1984). History of Medicine. In P. T. Durbin (Ed.), *A Guide to the Culture of Science, Technology and Medicine.* New York: Free Press, pp. 121–194.

Briere J., & Gil, E. (1998). Self-mutilation in clinical and general population samples: Prevalence, correlates, and functions. *American Journal of Orthopsychiatry, 68,* 609–620.

Briere, J., & Runtz, M. (1989). University males' sexual interest in children: Predicting potential incidences of "pedophilia" in a nonforensic sample. *Child Abuse and Neglect, 13,* 65–75.

Brittanica Book of the Year. (1987). Chicago: Encyclopedia Brittanica, p. 338. Cited by Carmody, 1989, p. 134.

Brod, H. (1995). Pornography and the alienation of male sexuality. In M. Kimmel & M. Messner (Eds.), *Men's lives* (3rd ed.). Boston: Allyn and Bacon.

Broderick, P. C., & Korteland, C. (2002). Coping style and depression in early adolescence: Relationships to gender, gender role, and implicit beliefs. *Sex Roles, 46,* 201–213.

Brody, J. (1994, March 21). Notions of beauty transcend culture. *New York Times,* p. A14.

Brody, J. E. (1998, September 15). Teen-agers and sex: Younger and more at risk. *The New York Times online.*

Brooks-Gunn, J. (1987). The impact of puberty and sexual activity upon the health and education of adolescent girls and boys. *Peabody Journal of Education, 64,* 88–112.

Brooks-Gunn, J. (1988). Antecedents and consequences of variations in girls' maturational timing. *Journal of Adolescent Health Care, 9,* 365–373.

Brooks-Gunn, J., & Furstenberg, F. F. (1989). Adolescent sexual behavior. *American Psychologist, 44,* 249–257.

Brooks-Gunn, J., & Matthews, W. S. (1979). *He and she: How children develop their sex role identity.* Englewood Cliffs, NJ: Prentice Hall.

Brooks-Gunn, J., & Ruble, D. N. (1983). Dysmenorrhea in adolescence. In S. Golub (Ed.), *Menarche: The transition from girl to woman* (pp. 251–261). Lexington, MA: Lexington Books.

Brooks-Gunn, J., Samelson, M., Warren, M. P., & Fox, R. (1986). Physical similarity of and disclosure of menarcheal status to friends: Effects of age and pubertal status. *Journal of Early Adolescence, 6,* 3–14.

Brooks-Gunn, J., & Warren, M. P. (1988). The psychological significance of secondary sexual characteristics in nine- to eleven-year-old girls. *Child Development, 59,* 1061–1069.

Brooks-Gunn, J., & Zahaykevich, M. (1989). Parent–daughter relationships in early adolescence: A developmental perspective. In K. Kreppner & R. Lerner (Eds.), *Family systems and life-span development* (pp. 223–246). Hillsdale, NJ: Erlbaum.

Brophy, J. (1985). Interactions of male and female teachers. In L. C. Wilinson & C. B. Marrett (Eds.), *Gender influences in classroom interactions* (pp. 115–142). Orlando, FL: Academic Press.

Broverman, I., Broverman, D. M., Clarkson, F. E., Rosenkrantz, P. S., & Vogel, S. R. (1970). Sex-role stereotypes and clinical judgments of mental health. *Journal of Consulting and Clinical Psychology, 34,* 1–7.

Broverman, I. K., Vogel, S. R., Broverman, D. M., Clarkson, F. E., & Rosenkrantz, P. S. (1972). Sex-role stereotypes: A current appraisal. *Journal of Social Issues, 28,* 59–78.

Brown, C., Abe-Kim, J. S., & Barrio, C. (2003). Depression in ethnically diverse women: Implications for treatment in primary care settings. *Professional Psychology: Research and Practice, 34*(1), 10–19.

Brown, C., Schulberg, H. C., & Madonia, M. J. (1996). Clinical presentations of major depression by African Americans and Whites in primary medical care practice. *Journal of Affective Disorders, 41*(3), 181–191.

Brown, D. R., & Gary, L. E. (1985). Social support network differentials among married and nonmarried black families. *Psychology of Women Quarterly, 9,* 229–241.

Brown, J. (2000, March 31). A crack appears in the Navy's ceiling. *The Christian Science Monitor.*

Brown, J. K. (1982). A cross-cultural exploration of the end of the childbearing years. In A. M. Voda, M. Dinnerstein, & S. R. O'Donnell (Eds.), *Changing perspectives on menopause* (pp. 51–59). Austin, TX: University of Texas Press.

Brown, L. S. (1994). *Subversive dialogues: Theory in feminist therapy.* New York: Basic Books.

Brown, M. S. (1981). Culture and childrearing. In A. N. Clark (Ed.), *Culture and childrearing* (pp. 3–35). Philadelphia: F. A. Davis.

Brown, N. M., & Amatea, E. S. (2000). *Love and intimate relationships: Journeys of the heart.* Philadelphia, PA: Brunner/Mazel.

Browne, A. (1987). *When battered women kill.* New York: Macmillan/Free Press.

Browne, A. (1993). Violence against women by male partners: Prevalence, outcomes, and policy implications. *American Psychologist, 48,* 1077–1087.

Browne, A., & Finkelhor, D. (1986). Impact of child sexual abuse: A review of the research. *Psychological Bulletin, 99,* 66–77.

Browning, C., Reynolds, A. L., & Dworkin, S. H. (1991). Affirmative psychotherapy for lesbian women. *Counseling Psychology, 19,* 177–196.

Browning, J. R., Hatfield, E., Kessler, D., & Levine, T. (2000). Sexual motives, gender, and sexual behavior. *Archives of Sexual Behavior, 29*(2), 135–153.

Brownmiller, S. (1975). *Against our will: Men, women, and rape,* New York: Simon & Schuster.

Bryant, J., & Brown, D. (1989). Uses of pornography. In D. Zillman & J. Bryant (Eds.), *Pornography: Research advances and policy considerations* (pp. 25–55). Hillsdale, NJ: Erlbuam.

Buhrmester, D., & Furman, W. (1987). The development of companionship and intimacy. *Child Development, 58,* 1101–1113.

Bullivant, M. (1984). *Cultural maintenance and evolution.* Clevedon, UK: Multilingual Matters.

Bullough, V. L. (1974). *The subordinate sex.* Baltimore: Books on Demand. Cited by Swidler, 1976, p. 7.

Bumpass, L. (1995, July 6). Cited in Steinhauer, J. No marriage, no apologies. *New York Times,* pp. C1, C7.

Bumpass, L. L., Sweet, J. A., & Cherlin, A. (1991). The role of cohabitation in declining rates of marriage. *Journal of Marriage and the Family, 53,* 913–927.

Burack, R. C., & Liang, J. (1987). The early detection of cancer in the primary care setting: actors associated with the acceptance and completion of recommended procedures. *Preventive Medicine, 16,* 739–751.

Bureau of Labor Statistics. (2001). *Current population survey data for 2000 by detailed occupation and sex.* Retrieved February 2002 from ftp://ftp.bls.gov/pub/special.requests/1f.aat11.txt.

Burgess, A. W., & Holmstrom, L. L. (1974). Rape trauma syndrome. *American Journal of Psychiatry, 131,* 981–986.

Burn, S. M. (1996). *The social psychology of gender.* New York: McGraw-Hill.

Burns, L. H. (1999). Sexual counseling and infertility. In L. H. Burns & S. N. Covington (Eds.), *Infertility counseling: A comprehensive handbook for clinicians* (p. 630). New York: Parthenon.

Burt, M. R. (1980). Cultural myths and supports for rape. *Journal of Personality and Social Psychology, 38,* 217–230.

Busch, C. M., Zonderman, A. B., & Costa, P. T. (1994). Menopausal transition and psychological distress in a nationally representative sample: Is menopause associated with psychological distress? *Journal of Aging and Health, 6,* 209–228.

Bush, T. L. (1990). The epidemiology of cardiovascular disease in postmenopausal women. In M. Flint, F. Kronenberg, & W. Utian (Eds.), *Multidisciplinary perspectives on menopause. Annals of the New York Academy of Sciences, 592,* 263–271.

Buss, D. M. (1988). The evolution of human intrasexual competition: Tactics of mate attraction. *Journal of Personality & Social Psychology, 54*(4), 618–628.

Buss, D. M. (1989). Sex differences in human mate preferences: Evolutionary hypotheses tested in 37 cultures. *Behavioral and Brain Sciences, 12,* 1–49.

Buss, D. M. (1994). What do people desire in a mate? The evolution of human sexual strategies. *Journal of NIH Research, 6,* 37–40.

Buss, D. M., & Kendrick, D. T. (1998). Evolutionary social psychology. In D. T. Gilbert, S. T. Fiske, & G. Lindzey (Eds.), *The handbook of social psychology* (4th ed., Vol. 2, pp. 982–1026). New York: McGraw-Hill.

Bussey, K., & Bandura, A. (1984). Influence of gender constancy and social power on sex-linked modeling. *Journal of Personality and Social Psychology, 47,* 1292–1302.

Bussey, K., & Bandura, A. (1992). Self-regulatory mechanisms governing gender development. *Child Development, 63,* 1236–1250.

Buunk, B. P. (2002). Age and gender differences in mate selection criteria for various involvement levels. *Personal Relationships, 9*(3), 271–278.

Cachelin, F. M., Veisel, C., Barzegarnazani, E., & Striegel-Moore, R. H. (2000). Disordered eating, acculturation, and treatment-seeking in a community sample of Hispanic, Asian, Black, and White women. *Psychology of Women Quarterly, 24,* 244–253.

Cadden, J. (1993). *Meanings of sex difference in the Middle Ages: Medicine, science and culture.* Cambridge, UK: Cambridge University Press. Cambridge & London.

Cahill, T. (1998). *The gifts of the Jews.* New York: Bantam Doubleday Dell.

Cameron, P., & Biber, H., (1973). Sexual thought throughout the life span. *Gerontologist, 13,* 144–147.

Camp, D. E., Klesges, R. C., & Relyea, G. (1993). The relationship between body weight concerns and adolescent smoking. *Health Psychology, 12,* 24–32.

Campbell, A. (1993). *Men, women, and aggression.* New York: Basic Books.

Campbell, B. (1993). To be black, gifted, and alone. In V. Cyrus (Ed.), *Experiencing race, class, and gender in the United States.* Mountain View, CA: Mayfield.

Campbell, D. T. (1967). Stereotypes and the perception of group differences. *American Psychologist, 22,* 817–829.

Campbell, E. K., & Campbell, P. G. (1997). Family size and sex preferences and eventual fertility in Botswana. *Journal of Biosocial Science, 29,* 191–204.

Campbell, G., Jr. (1996). Bridging the ethnic and gender gaps in engineering. *NACME Research Letter, 6*(1), 1.

Campbell, J. (1962). *The masks of God: Oriental mythology.* New York: Viking.

Campbell, J. (1964). *The masks of God: Occidental mythology.* New York: Viking.

Campbell, S. M., Peplau, L., & De Bro, S. C. (1992). Women, men, and condoms: Attitudes and experiences of college students. *Psychology of Women Quarterly, 16,* 273–288.

Canetto, S. S., & Lester, D. (1995, Spring). Gender and the primary prevention of suicide mortality. *Suicide & Life-Threatening Behavior, 25*(1), 58–69.

Canetto, S. S., Kaminski, P. L., & Felicio, D. M. (1995). Typical and optimal aging in women and men: Is there a double standard? *International Journal of Aging and Human Development, 40*(3), 187–207.

Canetto, S. S., & Sakinofsky, I. (1998). The gender paradox in suicide. *American Association of Suicidology, 28*(1), 58–69.

Cannon, W. (1929). *Bodily changes in pain, hunger, fear and rage: An account of recent researches into the function of emotional excitement.* New York: Appelton Press.

Caplan, P. J., & Hall-McCorquodale, I. (1985). The scapegoating of mothers: A call for change. *American Journal of Orthopsychiatry, 55,* 610–613.

Cappella, J. N., & Palmer, M. T. (1990). Attitude similarity, relational history, and attraction: The mediating effects of kinesic and vocal behaviors. *Communication Monographs, 5,* 161–183.

Carlson, N. R. (2002). *Foundations of physiological psychlogy.* Boston: Allyn and Bacon.

Carmody, D. L. (1989). *Women and world religions* (2nd ed.). Englewood Cliffs, NJ: Prentice Hall.

Carrere, S., Buehlman, K. T., Gottman, J. M., Coan, J. A., & Ruckstuhl, L. (2000). Predicting marital stability and divorce in newlywed couples. *Journal of Family Psychology, 14*(1), 42–58.

Carroll, J. L., Volk, K. D., & Hyde, J. S. (1985). Differences between males and females in motives for engaging in sexual intercourse. *Archives of Sexual Behavior, 14,* 131–139.

Carroll, J. L., & Wolpe, P. R. (1996). *Sexuality and gender in society.* New York: HarperCollins.

Carroll, T. F. (1983). *Women, religion, and development in the Third World.* New York: Praeger.

Carson, R. (1969). *Interaction concepts of personality.* Chicago: Aldine.

Carter, B. (1992). Stonewalling feminism. *Family Therapy Networker, 16,* 64–69.

CASA Report. (1996). National Center on Addiction and Substance Abuse at Columbia University, New York.

Cascardi, M., Langhinrichsen, J., & Vivian, D. (1992). Marital aggression: Impact, injury, and health correlates for husbands and wives. *Archives of Internal Medicine, 152,* 357–363.

Cash, T. F., Gillen, B., & Burns, D. S. (1977). Sexism and "beautyism" in personnel consultant decision making. *Journal of Applied Psychology, 62,* 301–310.

Castles, S., & Miller, M. J. (1998). *The age of migration: International population movements in the modern world.* New York: The Guilford Press.

Catania, J. A., Coates, T., Stall, R., Bye, L., Kegeles, S., Capell, F., Henne, J., McKusick, L., Morin, S., Turner, H., & Pollack, L. (1991). Changes in condom use among homosexual men in San Francisco. *Health Psychology, 10,* 190–199.

Catania, J. A., Coates, T. J., Stall, R., Turner, H., Peterson, J., Hearst, N., Dolcini, M. M., Hudes, E., Gagnon, J., Wiley, J., & Groves, R. (1992). Prevalence of AIDS-related risk factors and condom use in the United States. *Science, 258,* 1101–1106.

Catell, J. M. (1903). Cited in A. Fausto-Sterling, 1992b.

Cates, W., Stewart, F. H., & Russell, J. (1992). Commentary: The quest for women's prophylactic methods—Hope vs. science. *American Journal of Public Health, 82*(11), 1479–1482.

Catsambis, S. (1999). The path to math: Gender and racial–ethnic differences in mathematics participation from middle school to high school. In L. A. Peplau, S. C. DeBro, R. C. Veniegas, & P. L. Taylor (Eds.), *Gender, culture, and ethnicity: Current research about women and men* (pp. 102–120). Mountain View, CA: Mayfield.

Cauchon, D. (1991, April 4). Women will break through glass ceiling. *USA Today,* p. 9A.

Cauchon, D. (2004, March 10). Civil unions gain support, poll says. *USA Today.* Retrieved March 14, 2004 from www.keepmedia.com.

Cazenave, N. A., & Zahn, M. A. (1992). Women, murder, and male domination: Police reports of domestic violence in Chicago and Philadelphia. In E. C. Viano (Ed.), *Intimate violence: Interdisciplinary perspectives* (pp. 83–97). Washington, DC: Hemisphere Publication Corporation.

Centers for Disease Control and Prevention. (1989). Trends in lung cancer incidence—United States, 1973–1986. *Morbidity and Mortality Weekly Report 38,* 505–513.

Centers for Disease Control and Prevention. (1990). Heterosexual behaviors and factors that influence condom use among patients attending a sexually transmitted disease clinic—San Francisco. *Morbidity and Mortality Weekly Report, 39,* 685–689.

Centers for Disease Control and Prevention. (1993). HIV/AIDS surveillance—fourth quarter edition—U.S. AIDS cases reported through December 1992. Washington, DC: U.S. Department of Health and Human Services.

Centers for Disease Control and Prevention. (1996, September 1). Aids Hotline.

Centers for Disease Control and Prevention. (1998). *HIV/AIDS Surveillance Report.* Atlanta, GA: Centers for Disease Control and Prevention.

Centers for Disease Control and Prevention. (2000a). HIV/AIDS surveillance report: U.S. HIV and AIDS cases reported through December 1999 *11*(2).

Centers for Disease Control and Prevention. (2000b, June 9). Youth risk behavior surveillance— United States, 1999. *Morbidity and Mortality Weekly Report, 49*(SS05) 1–96.

Centers for Disease Control and Prevention. (2001). *HIV/AIDS Surveillance Report, 13* (No. 1). Atlanta, GA: Centers for Disease Control and Prevention.

Centers for Disease Control and Prevention. (2002). *Fact Sheet: Youth Risk Behavior Trends.* Atlanta: Centers for Disease Control and Prevention.

Centers for Disease Control and Prevention. (2003, October 10). Cancer death rates falling, but slowly. Atlanta: Centers for Disease Control and Prevention.

Centers for Disease Control and Prevention, National Center for HIV, STD and TB Prevention. (2004). HIV/AIDS Surveillance Report, 13, 2, p. 1–2, Retrieved February 29, 2004 from www.cdc.gov/hiv/stats/hasr1302/table7.htm.

Centers for Disease Control and Prevention, the Alan Guttmacher Institute. Child Trends Databank. Cited in Bernstein, N., Behind fall in pregnancy, a new teenage culture of restraint. *The New York Times,* March 7, 2004, pp. A1, 36, 37.

Chambers, D. L. (1989). Accommodation and satisfaction: Women and men lawyers and the balance of work and family. *Law and Social Inquiry, 14,* 251–287.

Chan, C. S. (1987). Asian American women: Psychological responses to sexual exploitation and cultural stereotypes. *Women & Therapy, 6,* 33–38.

Chan, C. S. (1991). *Asian Americans: An interpretive history.* Boston: Twayne.

Chan, D. W. (1990). Sex knowledge, attitudes, and experiences of Chinese medical students in Hong Kong. *Archives of Sexual Behavior, 19,* 73–93.

Cherlin, A., & Furstenberg, F. F. (1985). Styles and strategies of grandparenting. In V. L. Bengston & J. F. Robertson (Eds.), *Grandparenthood* (pp. 97–116). Beverly Hills, CA: Sage.

Cherry, F., & Deaux, K. (1978). Fear of success versus fear of gender-inappropriate behavior. *Sex Roles, 4,* 97–101.

Chideya, F. (1995). *Don't believe the hype.* New York: Penguin Books.

Chin, J. L., & Russo, N. F. (1997). Feminist curriculum development: Principles and resources. In J. Worell & N. G. Johnson (Eds.), *Shaping the future of feminist psychology* (pp. 93–201). Washington, DC: American Psychological Association.

Chisholm, J. F. (1996). Mental health issues in African-American women. In J. A. Sechzer, S. M. Pfafflin, F. L. Denmark, A. Griffin, & S. J. Blumenthal (Eds.), *Women and mental health. Annals of the New York Academy of Sciences, 789,* 167–168.

Chodorow, N. (1978). *The reproduction of motherhood: Psychoanalysis and the sociology of gender.* Berkeley, CA: University of California Press.

Chodorow, N. (1979). Feminism and difference: Gender, relation and difference in psychoanalytic perspective. *Socialist Review, 9*(4), 51–70.

Chodorow, N. (1989). *Feminism and psychoanalytic theory.* New Haven: Yale University Press.

Chow, E. N. L. (1985). The acculturation experience of Asian American women. In A. Sargeant (Ed.), *Beyond sex roles* (2nd ed., pp. 238–261). St. Paul, MN: West.

Chrisler, J. C. (2000/2004). PMS as a culture bound syndrome. In J. C. Chrisler, C. Golder, & P. D. Rozee (Eds.), *Lectures on the psychology of women.* New York: McGraw-Hill.

Chrisler, J. C., Golden, C., & Rozee, P. D. (Eds). (2004). *Lectures on the Psychology of Women* (3rd ed.). New York: McGraw Hill.

Chrisler, J. C., Johnston, I. K., Champagne, N. M., & Preston, K. E. (1994). Menstrual joy: The construct and its consequences. *Psychology of Women Quarterly, 18,* 375–387.

Christensen, K., & Murphree, M. (1988). Introduction to conference proceedings. In K. Christensen & M. Murphree (Eds.), *Flexible workstyles: A look at contingent labor. Conference Summary* (pp. 1–4). Washington, DC: U.S. Department of Labor, Women's Bureau.

Chu, J. (1988). Social and economic profile of Asian Pacific American women: Los Angeles County. In G. Y. Okihito, S. Hume, A. A. Hansen, & J. M. Liu (Eds.), *Reflections on shattered windows: Promises and prospects for Asian American studies* (pp. 193–205). Pullman, WA: Washington State University Press.

Chuang, Y. C. (2002). Sex differences in mate selection preference and sexual strategy: Tests for evolutionary hypotheses. *Chinese Journal of Psychology, 44*(1), 75–93.

City Health Information. (2003). The New York City Department of Health and Mental Hygiene 22(1).

Clarke-Stewart, K. A. (1978). And Daddy makes three: The father's impact on mother and young child. *Child Development, 49,* 466–478.

Cloud, J. (2003, October, 27). Inside the New SAT. *Time,* pp. 48–53.

Coates, S. W. (1995). Gender identity disorder in boys: The interface of constitution and early experience. *Psychoanalytic Inquiry, 15*(1), 6–38.

Cobbs, P. (1972). Ethnotherapy in groups. In L. Soloman & B. Berson (Eds.), *New perspectives on encounter groups* (pp. 383–403). San Francisco: Jossey-Bass.

Cochran, S. C. (2001). Emerging issues in research on lesbians' and gay men's mental health: Does sexual orientation really matter? *American Psychologist, 56*(11), 931–947.

Cochran, S. C., & Mays, V. M. (2000). Prevalence of psychiatric disorders and treatment utilization among lesbian, gay, and bisexual individuals in the National Survey of Midlife Development in the United States. Manuscript submitted for publication.

Cohen, J. (1969). *Statistical power analysis for the behavioral sciences.* New York: Academic Press.

Cohen, M. A. A., & Alfonso, C. A. (1994). Dissemination of HIV: How serious is it for women, medically and psychologically? In J. A. Sechzer, A. Griffin, & S. M. Pfafflin (Eds.), *Forging a women's health research agenda: Policy issues for the 1990's. Annals of the New York Academy of Sciences, 736,* 114–121.

Cohen, O. J., & Fauci, A. S. (1998). HIV/AIDS in 1998—Gaining the upper hand? *Journal of the American Medical Association. 280*(1) 87–88.

Cohen, P. (1998, July 11). Daddy dearest: Do you really matter? *New York Times,* pp. B7, B9.

Cohen, S. (1984). The chronic intractable benign pain syndrome. *Drug abuse and alcoholism newsletter, 13*(4), 240.

Colasanto, D. (1989, October 25). Gay rights support has grown since 1982, Gallup poll finds. *San Francisco Chronicle,* p. A21.

Colditz, G. A. (1993). Epidemiology of breast cancer: Findings from the Nurses' Health Study. *Cancer, 7* (Suppl.), 1480–1489.

Cole, C., Hill, F., & Dayley, L. (1983). Do masculine pronouns used generically lead to thoughts of men? *Sex Roles, 9,* 737–750.

Cole, J. (Ed.). (1986). *All American women: Lives that divide, ties that bind.* New York: Macmillan.

Cole, M., Gay, J., Glick, J. A., & Sharp, D. (1971). *The cultural context of learning and thinking: An exploration in experimental anthropology.* New York: Basic Books.

Cole, S. S., & Cole, T. M. (1993). Sexuality, disability, and reproductive issues through the lifespan. *Sexuality and Disability, 11*(3), 189–205.

Coles, R., & Stokes, G. (1985). *Sex and the American teenager.* New York: Harper & Row.

Collaer, M. L., & Hines, M. (1995). Human behavioral sex differences: A role for gonadal hormones during early development? *Psychological Bulletin, 118,* 55–107.

Collins, D. (1996). Attacks on the body: How can we understand self-harm? *Psychodynamic Counseling, 2*(4), 463–475.

Collins, P. H. (1990). *Black feminist thought.* Boston: Unwin Hyman.

Coltraine, S. (2000). The perpetuation of subtle prejudice: Race and gender imagery in 1990s television advertising. *Sex Roles, 42*(5/6), 363–389.

Coltrane, S. (1997). Families and gender equity. *National Forum, 77,* 31–34.

Columbia Encyclopedia (5th ed.). (1993). *Mary, mother of Jesus.* New York: Columbia University Press.

Comas-Diaz, L. (1991). Feminism and diversity in psychology: The case of women of color. *Psychology of Women Quarterly, 15,* 597–610.

Comas-Diaz, L. (1992, Spring). The future of psychotherapy with ethnic minorities. *Psychotherapy, 29*(1), 88–94.

Comas-Diaz, L. (2001). Hispanics, Latinos, or Americanos: The evolution of identity. *Cultural Diversity and Ethnic Minority Psychology, 7*(2), 115–120.

Comas-Diaz, L., & Greene, B. (Eds.) (1994). *Women of color: Integrating ethnic and gender identities in psychotherapy.* New York: Guilford Press.

Comas-Diaz, L., & Jacobsen, F. (1991). Ethnocultural transference and countertransference in the therapeutic dyad. *American Journal of Orthopsychiatry, 61*(3), 392–402.

Combahee River Collective. (1979). A Black feminist statement. In Z. Eisenstein (Ed.), *Capitalist patriarchy and the case for socialist feminism* (pp. 135–139). New York: Monthly Review Press.

Comfort, A. (1974). *More joy of sex.* New York: Simon & Schuster.

Constantinople, A. (1979). Sex-role acquisition: In search of the elephant. *Sex Roles, 5,* 121–133.

Cook, E. (1990). Gender and psychological distress. *Journal of Counseling and Development, 2,* 371–375.

Coombs, R. H., & Kenkel, W. F., (1996). Sex differences in dating aspirations and satisfaction with computer-selected partners. *Journal of Marriage and the Family, 28,* 62–66.

Cooper, A., Scherer, C. R., Boies, S. C., & Gordon, B. L. (1999). Sexuality on the Internet: From sexual exploration to pathological expression. *Professional Psychology: Research and Practice, 30,* 154–164.

Cooper, Z. (1995). The development and maintenance of eating disorders. In K. D. Brownell & C. G. Fairburn (Eds.), *Eating disorders and obesity.* New York: Guilford Press.

Cordua, G. D., McGraw, K. O., & Drabman, R. S. (1979). Doctor or nurse: Children's perceptions of sex-typed occupations. *Child Development, 50,* 590–593.

Corea, G. (1992). *The invisible epidemic: The story of women and AIDS.* New York: HarperCollins.

Cosentino, C. E., & Collins, M. (1996). Sexual abuse of children: Prevalence, effects, and treatment. In J. A. Sechzer, S. M. Pfafflin, F. L. Denmark, A. Griffin, & S. J. Blumenthal (Eds.), *Women and mental health. Annals of the New York Academy of Sciences, 789,* 45–65.

Cosse, W. J. (1992). Who's who and what's what? The effects of gender on development in adolescence. In B. R. Wainrib (Ed.), *Gender issues across the life cycle.* New York: Springer.

Costello, C. B., & Stone, A. J. (2001). *The American woman 2001–2002: Getting to the top.* New York: W. W. Norton.

Courtney, A. E., & Whipple, T. W. (1985). Female role portrayals in advertising and communication effectiveness: A review. *Journal of Advertising, 14*(3), 4–8, 17.

Cowan, C. P., & Cowan, P. A. (1992). *When partners become parents: The big life change for couples.* New York: Basic Books.

Cowan, G., Warren, L. G., & Young, J. L. (1985). Medical perceptions of menopausal symptoms. *Psychology of Women Quarterly, 9,* 3–14.

Cowell, P. E., Allen, L. S., Zalatimo, N. S., & Denenberg, V. H. (1992). A developmental study of sex and age interactions in the human corpus callosum. *Developmental Brain Research, 66,* 187–192.

Cox, D. L., Stabb, S. D., & Hulgus, J. F. (2000). Anger and depression in girls and boys. *Psychology of Women Quarterly, 24,* 110–112.

Cozby, P. C. (1973). Self-disclosure: A literature review. *Psychological Bulletin, 79,* 73–91.

Craik, F. I. M. (1977). Age differences in human memory. In J. E. Birren & K. W. Schaie (Eds.), *Handbook of the psychology of aging.* New York: Van Nostrand Reinhold.

Crandall, V. C. (1969). Sex differences in expectancy of intellectual and academic reinforcement. In C. P. Smith (Ed.), *Achievement-related motives in children* (pp. 11–45). New York: Russell Sage Foundation.

Crandall, V. C. (1978, August). Expecting sex differences and sex differences in expectancies: A developmental analysis. Paper presented at the meeting of the American Psychological Association, Toronto, Canada.

Crawford, J., Kippax, S., Onyx, J., Gault, U., & Benton, P. (1992). *Emotion and gender.* London: Sage.

Crawford, M., & Chaffin, R. (1997). The meanings of difference: Cognition in social and cultural context. In P. J. Caplan, M. Crawford, J. S. Hyde, & J. T. E. Richardson (Eds.), *Gender differences in human cognition* (pp. 81–130). New York: Oxford University Press.

Crawford, M., & Kimmel, E. (1999). Promoting methodological diversity in feminist research (pp. 1–6). In M. Crawford & E. Kimmel (Eds.), *Innovations in feminist research* (Special Issue). *Psychology of Women Quarterly, 23,* 1.

Crawford, M., & Marecek, J. (1989). Psychology reconstructs the female: 1968–1988. *Psychology of Women Quarterly, 13,* 147–165.

Crawford, M., & McLeod, M. (1990). Gender in the college classroom: An assessment of the chilly climate for women. *Sex Roles, 23,* 101–122.

Crawford, N. (2003). Understanding children's atypical gender behavior. *American Psychological Association Monitor on Psychology, 34*(8), 40–42.

Crockett, L. J., & Petersen, A. C. (1987). Pubertal status and psychosocial development: Findings from the early adolescent study. In R. M. Lerner & T. T. Foch (Eds.), *Biological–psychosocial interactions in early adolescence* (pp. 173–188). Hillsdale, NJ: Erlbaum.

Crosby, F. (1982). *Relative deprivation and working women.* New York: Oxford University Press.

Crosby, F. (1984). Relative deprivation in organizational settings. In B. Staw & L. L. Cummings (Eds.), *Research in organizational behavior* (Vol. 6, pp. 51–93). Greenwich, CT: JAI Press.

Crosby, F. (1991). *Juggling: The unexpected advantages of balancing career and home for women and their families.* New York: Free Press.

Crosby, F., Clayton, S., Alkinis, O., & Hemker, K. (1986). Cognitive biasis in the perception of discrimination: The importance of format. *Sex Roles, 14,* 637–646.

Crosby, F. J., Pufall, A., Snyder, R. C., O'Connell, M., & Whalen, P. (1989). The denial of personal disadvantage among you, me and all the other ostriches. In M. Crawford & M. Gentry (Eds.), *Gender and thought: Psychological perspectives* (pp. 79–99). New York: Springer-Verlag.

Cross-National Collaborative Group. (1992). The changing rate of major depression: Cross-national comparisons. *Journal American Medical Association, 268,* 3098–3105.

Crouter, A. C., McHale, S. M., & Bartko, W. T. (1993). Gender as an organizing feature in parent–child relationships. *Journal of Social Issues, 49,* 161–174.

Culp L. N., & Beach, S. R. H. (1998). Marriage and depressive symptoms. *Psychology of Women Quarterly, 22,* 647–663.

Cunningham, M. (2001). Parental influence on the gendered division of housework. *American Sociological Review, 66*(2), 184–203.

Curran, B. A. (1986). American lawyers in the 1980: A profession in transition. *Law and Society Review, 20,* 19–52.

Cutler, S., & Nolen-Hoeksema, S. (1991). Accounting for sex differences in depression through female victimization: Childhood sexual abuse. *Sex Roles, 24,* 425–438.

Cyranowski, J. M., Frank, E., Young, E., & Shear, M. K. (2000). Adolescent onset of the gender difference in lifetime rates of major depression. *Archives of General Psychiatry, 57,* 21–27.

Cyrus, V. (Ed.). (1993). *Experiencing race, class, and gender in the United States.* Mountain View, CA: Mayfield.

Dally, A. (1991) *Women under the knife.* London: Hutchinson Radius.

Dan, A. J., & Bernhard, L. A. (1989). Menopause and other health issues for midlife women. In S. Hunter & M. Sundel (Eds.), *Midlife myths: Issues, findings, and practice implications.* Newbury Park, CA: Sage.

Dansky, B. S., & Kilpatrick, D. G. (1997). Effects of sexual harassment. In W. O'Donahue (Ed.), *Sexual harassment: Theory, research, and treatment* (pp. 152–174). Boston: Allyn and Bacon.

Danza, R. (1983). Menarche: Its effects on mother–daughter and father–daughter interactions. In S. Golub (Ed.), *Menarche* (pp. 99–105). Lexington, MA: Lexington Books.

D'Augelli, A. R. (1989). Homophobia in a university community: Views of prospective resident assistants. *Journal of College Student Development, 30,* 546–552.

D'Augelli, A. R. (1994). Lesbian and gay male development: Steps toward an analysis of lesbians' and gay men's lives. In B. Greene & G. M. Herek (Eds.), *Lesbian and gay psychology: Theory, research, and clinical applications* (pp. 118–132). Psychological Perspectives on Lesbian and Gay Issues, Vol. 1. Thousand Oaks, CA: Sage.

D'Augelli, A. R., & Garnets, L. (1995). Lesbian, gay, and bisexual communities. In A. R. D'Augelli & C. J. Patterson (Eds.), *Lesbian, gay and bisexual identities across the lifespan.* New York: Oxford University Press.

Davenport, D. S., & Yurich, J. (1991). Multicultural gender issues. *Journal of Counseling and Development, 70,* 64–71.

Davidson, J. M. (1989). Sexual emotions, hormones, and behavior. *Advances, 6*(2), 56–58.

Davidson, J. R. (2000). Trauma: The impact of post-traumatic stress disorder. *Journal of Psychopharmacology, 14*(2 Suppl. 1), S5–S12.

Davies, M., & McCartney, S. (2003). Effects of gender and sexuality on judgements of victim blame and rape myth acceptance in a depicted male rape. *Journal of Community & Applied Social Psychology,13*(5), 391–398.

Davis, A. Y. (1981). *Women, race & class.* New York: Random House.

Davis, S. (1990). Men as success objects and women as sex objects: A study of personal advertisements. *Sex Roles, 23,* 43–50.

Dawood, K., Pillard, R., Horvath, C., Revelle, W., & Bailey, J. M. (2000). Familial aspects of male homosexuality. *Archives of Sexual Behavior, 29*(2), 155–163.

Day, K. (1999). Strangers in the night: Women's fear of sexual assault on urban college campuses. *Journal of Architecture and Planning Research, 16,* 289–312.

De Angelis, B. (1997). *The real rules: How to find the right man for the real you.* New York: Bantam Doubleday Dell.

Dearwater, R. R., Coben, J. H., Campbell, J. C., Nah, G., Glass, N., McLoughlin, E., & Bekemeier, B. (1998). Prevalence of intimate partner abuse in women treated at community hospital emergency departments. *Journal of the American Medical Association, 280,* 433–438.

Deaux, K. (1995). How basic can you be? The evolution of research on gender stereotypes. *Journal of Social Issues, 51,* 11–20.

Deaux, K., & Emswiller, T. (1974). Explanations of successful performance in sex-linked tasks: What is skill for the male is luck for the female. *Journal of Personality and Social Psychology, 29,* 80–85.

Deaux, K., & Hanna, R. (1984). Courtship in the personal column: The influence of gender and sexual orientation. *Sex Roles, 1,* 363–375.

Deaux, K., & Kite, M. (1993). Gender stereotypes. In F. L. Denmark & M. A. Paludi (Eds.), *Psychology of women: A handbook of issues and theories* (pp. 107–139). Westport, CT: Greenwood Press.

Deaux, K., White, L., & Farris, E. (1975). Skill vs. luck: Field and lab studies of male and female preferences. *Journal of Personality and Social Psychology, 32,* 629–636.

Debold, E., Wilson, M., & Malave, I. (1993). *Mother–daughter revolution: From betrayal to power.* Reading, MA: Addison-Wesley.

DeFour, D. C. (1996). The interface of racism and sexism on college campuses. In M. A. Paludi et al. (Eds.), *Sexual harassment on college campuses: Abusing the ivory tower.* Albany: State University of New York Press.

Dege, K., & Gretzinger, J. (1982). Attitudes of families toward menopause. In A. M. Voda, M. Dinnerstein, & S. R. O'Donnell (Eds.), *Changing perspectives on menopause* (pp. 60–69). Austin, TX: University of Texas Press.

De Groot, S. C. (1980). Female and male returnees: Glimpses of two distinct populations. *Psychology of Women Quarterly, 5,* 358–361.

DeKeseredy, W. S., & Kelly, K. (1995). Sexual abuse in Canadian university and college dating relationships: The contribution of male peer support. *Journal of Family Violence. 10*(1), 41–53.

DeKeseredy, W., & Kelly, K. (1993). The incidence and prevalence of woman abuse in Canadian university and college dating relationships. *Canadian Journal of Sociology, 18,* 137–159.

Delamont, S. (1990). *Sex roles and the school* (2nd ed.). London: Routledge.

Delaney, J., Lupton, M. J., & Toth, E. (1988). *The curse: A cultural history of menstruation* (rev. ed.). Urbana, IL: University of Illinois.

Delgado, J. L., & Trevino, F. (1985). The state of Hispanic health in the United States. In *The state of Hispanic America,* Vol. II. Oakland, CA: National Hispanic Center for Advanced Studies and Policy Analysis.

DeLorey, C. (1984). Health care and midlife women. In G. Baruch & J. Brooks-Gunn (Eds.), *Women in midlife* (pp. 277–301). New York: Plenum Press.

Denmark, F. L. (1980). From rocking the cradle to rocking the boat. *American Psychologist, 35*(12), 1057–1065.

Denmark, F. L. (1975). Growing up male. In E. Zuckerman (Ed.), *Women and men: Roles, attitudes, and power relationships.* New York: Radcliffe Club.

Denmark, F. L. (1976). The psychology of women: Its definition and the development of the field. Invited address presented at the Eastern Psychological Association, New York.

Denmark, F. L. (1992, August). *Changing sex roles psychology: For better or for worse?* Paper presented at the meeting of the American Psychological Association, Washington DC.

Denmark, F. L. (1994). Engendering psychology. *American Psychologist, 49*(4), 329–334.

Denmark, F. L. (1999). From enhancing the development of adolescent girls. In N. G. Johnson, M. C. Roberts, & J. Worell (Eds.), *Beyond appearance: A new look at adolescent girls* (pp. 377–404). Washington, DC: APA.

Denmark, F. L. (2002). Myths of aging. *Eye on Psi Chi, 7*(1), 14–21.

Denmark, F. L. (2003). The older woman: Myths and realities about ageing and death. In R. Roth, L. Lowenstein, & D. Trent (Eds.), Catching the future: Women and men in global psychology. Lengerich: Pabst Science Publishers.

Denmark, F. L., & Fernandez, L. C. (1993). Historical development of the psychology of women. In F. L. Denmark & M. A. Paludi (Eds.), *Psychology of women: A handbook of issues and theories* (pp. 3–22). Westport, CT: Greenwood Press.

Denmark, F. L., & Francois, F. (1987). Research context of studies for sex differences in mathematics performance. In J. A. Sechzer & S. M. Pfafflin (Eds.), *Psychology and educational policy. Annals of the New York Academy of Sciences, 517,* 61–68.

Denmark, F. L., Nielson, K. A., & Scholl, K. (1993). Life in the United States of America. In L. L. Adler (Ed.), *International handbook of gender roles* (pp. 452–467). Westport, CT: Greenwood Press.

Denmark, F. L., Novick, K., & Pinto, A. (1996). *Women, work, and family: Mental health issues. Annals of the New York Academy of Sciences, 789,* 101–117.

Denmark, F. L., & Paludi, M. A. (1993). *The psychology of women: A handbook of issues and theories.* CT: Greenwood Press.

Denmark, F. L., Rabinowitz, V., & Sechzer, J. (Eds.). (2000). *Engendering psychology.* New York: Allyn & Bacon.

Denmark, F. L., Russo, N. F., Frieze, I. H., & Sechzer, J. A. (1988). Guidelines for avoiding sexism in psychological research: A report of the Ad Hoc Committee on Nonsexist Research. *American Psychologist, 43,* 582–585.

Denmark, F. L., Sechzer, J. A., & Rabinowitz, V. C. (1994). *Studies of sex and gender in lung cancer research.* American Psychological Association Conference on Psychosocial and Behavioral Factors in Women's Health. Washington, DC.

Denmark, F. L., Sechzer, J. A., & Rabinowitz, V. C. (1995). Studies of sex and gender in lung cancer research II. *Annual Convention of the American Psychological Society.* New York: Appelton Press.

Denmark, F. L., Shaw, J. S., & Ciali, S. D. (1985). The relationship among sex roles, living arrangements, and the division of household responsibilities. *Sex Roles, 12* (5/6), 617–625.

Denmark, F. L., & Waters, J. A. (1977). Male and female in children's readers: A cross-cultural analysis. In Y. H. Poortinga (Ed.), *Basic problems in cross-cultural psychology.* Amsterdam: Swets and Zeitlinger B. V.

Dennerstein, L., Dudley, E., & Burger, H. (1997). Well-being and the menopausal transition. *Journal of Psychosomatic Obstetrics and Gynaecology, 18,* 95–101.

Denney, N., Field, J., & Quadagno, D. (1984). Sex differences in sexual needs and desires. *Archives of Sexual Behavior, 13,* 233–245.

DeNoon, D. (2003, May 21). Atkins diet lesson: Watch those carbs. *WebMd Medical News.* Retrieved April 6, 2004 from http://my.webmd.com/content/article/65/72694. htm?lastseletedguid=(5FE84E90-BC77-40 . . .)

Derlega, V. J., Winstead, B. A., Wong, P. T. P., & Hunter, S. (1985). Gender effects in an initial encounter: A case where men exceed women in disclosure. *Journal of Personal and Social Relations, 2,* 25–44.

DeVellis, B. M., Wallston, B. S., & Acker, I. (1984). Childfree by choice: Attitudes and adjustment of sterilized women. *Population and Environment: Behavioral and Social Issues, 1,* 152–162.

DeVoe, E. R. & Borges, G. (2004). Domestic violence and Jewish women. Available: www.columbia.edu/cu/csswp/research/descriptions/DeVoe.htm

De Young, M. (1982). *The sexual victimization of children.* Jefferson, NC: McFarland.

Diamond, M. (1982). Sexual identity, monozygotic twins reared in discordant sex roles and a BBC follow-up. *Archives of Sexual Behavior, 11,* 181–186.

Diamond, M. (1993). Homosexuality and bisexuality in different populations. *Archives of Sexual Behavior 22,* 291–310.

Diamond, M., & Sigmundson, K. (1997). Sex reassignment at birth. *Archives of Pediatric and Adolescent Medicine, 151,* 298–304.

Diamond, N. (1973). The status of women in Taiwan: One step forward, two steps back. In M. B. Young (Ed.), *Women in China.* Ann Arbor, MI: Center for Chinese Studies, University of Michigan.

Diehl, L. A. (1988). The paradox of G. Stanley Hall: Foe of coeducation and educator of women. In L. T. Benjamin (Ed.), *A history of psychology: Original sources and contemporary research* (pp. 295–310). New York: McGraw-Hill.

Dietz, T. L. (1998). An examination of violence and gender role portrayals in video games: Implications for gender socialization and aggressive behavior. *Sex Roles, 38*(5/6), 425–442.

Digest of educational statistics. (1976). Washington, DC: U.S. Department of Health, Education, and Welfare, Education Division, National Center for Educational Statistics.

Digest of educational statistics. (1992). Washington, DC: U.S. Department of Health, Education, and Welfare, Educational Division, National Center for Educational Statistics.

DiMaggio, P., & Mohr, J. (1985). Cultural capital, educational attainment, and marital selection. *American Journal of Sociology, 90,* 1231–1261.

DiMatteo, M. R., & Martin, L. R. (2002). *Health psychology.* Boston: Allyn and Bacon.

Dinges, N. G., & Cherry, D. (1995). Symptom expression and the use of mental health services among American ethnic minorities. In J. F. Aponte, R. Y. Rivers, & J. Wohl (Eds.), *Psychological interventions and cultural diversity* (pp. 40–56). Boston: Allyn and Bacon.

Dinnerstein, D. (1976). *The mermaid and the minotaur.* New York: Harper and Row.

Dion, K. K., & Dion, K. L. (2001). Gender and relationships. In R. Unger (Ed.), *Handbook on the psychology of woman and gender* (pp. 256–271). New York: Wiley.

Dirix, M. E. (1869). *Woman's complete guide to health.* New York: W. A. Townsend and Adams, pp. 23–24. Cited by Ehrenreich and English, 1981, p. 340.

Dix, T. (1993). Attributing dispositions to children: An interactional analysis of attribution in socialization. *Personality and Social Psychology Bulletin, 19*(5), 633–643.

Dodson, B. (1987). *Sex for one: The joy of selfloving.* New York: Crown.

Done, R. S. (2000). Self-control and deviant behavior in organizations: The case of sexually harassing behavior. Unpublished doctoral dissertation, University of Arizona, Tuscon.

Donnerstein, E. (1983). Erotica and human aggression. In R. Green & E. Donnerstein (Eds.), *Aggression: Theoretical and empirical reviews.* New York: Academic Press.

Donnerstein, E., & Berkowitz, L. (1982). Victim reactions in aggressive–erotic films as a factor in violence against women. *Journal of Personality and Social Psychology, 41,* 710–724.

Donnerstein, E., & Linz, D. (1993). Sexual violence in the mass media. In M. Costanzo & S. Oskamp (Eds.), *Violence and the law* (pp. 9–36). Thousand Oaks, CA: Sage.

Donnerstein, E., & Linz, D. (1995). Mass media sexual violence and male viewers: Current theory and research. In M. S. Kimmel & M. A. Messner (Eds.), *Men's lives* (3rd ed., pp. 381–392). Boston: Allyn and Bacon.

Doress, P. B., Siegal, D. L., & the Midlife and Old Women Book Project. (1987). *Ourselves, growing older.* New York: Simon & Schuster.

Dornbusch, S. M., Gross, R. T., Duncan, P. D., & Ritter, P. L. (1987). Stanford studies of adolescence using the national health examination survey. In R. M. Lerner & T. T. Foch (Eds.), *Biological–psychosocial interactions in early adolescence* (pp. 189–205). Hillsdale, NJ: Erlbaum.

Douglas, M. (1969). *Purity and danger: An analysis of the concept of pollution and taboo.* London: Ark Publications.

Dovidio, J. F., & Gaertner, S. L. (1986). *Prejudice, discrimination, and racism.* New York: Academic Press.

Downing, N. E., & Roush, K. L. (1985). From passive acceptance to active commitment: A model of feminist identity for women. The Counseling Psychologist, 13, 695–709.

Downs, W. R. (1993). Developmental considerations for the effects of childhood sexual abuse. *Journal of Interpersonal Violence, 8,* 331–345.

Downs, W. R., Miller, B. A., Testa, M., & Panek, D. (1992). Long-term effects of parent-to-child violence for women. *Journal of Interpersonal Violence, 7,* 365–382.

Doyle, J. A. (1989). *The male experience* (2nd ed.). Dubuque, IA: William C. Brown.

Dresden, M. J. (1961). Mythology of ancient Iran. In S. N. Kramer (Ed.), *Mythology of the ancient world* (pp. 342–344). New York: Doubleday.

DuBois, C. L. Z., Knapp, D. E., Faley, R. H., & Kustis, G. A. (1998). An empirical examination of same—and other—gender sexual harassment in the workplace. *Sex Roles, 39,* 731–749.

Dubow, E. F., Huesmann, L. R., & Eron, L. D. (1987). Childhood correlates of adult ego development. *Child Development, 58,* 859–869.

Dubowitz, H. (2001). Father involvement and children's functioning at age 6 years: A multisite study. *Child Maltreatment, 6*(4), 300–309.

Dunn, M. E., & Trost, J. E. (1989). Male multiple orgasms: A descriptive study. *Archives of Sexual Behavior, 18,* 377–387.

Dunn, W. (1992). *The Baby Bust: A Generation Comes of Age.* Primedia Business Magazines & Media.

Durex. (2001). *Global survey, 2001.* London: Durex Co.

DuRivage, V. L. (1992). New policies for the part-time and contingent workforce. In V. L. duRivage (Ed.), *New policies for the part-time and contingent workforce* (pp. 89–122). Armonk, NY: M. E. Sharpe.

Durkin, K. F. (1997). Misuse of the Internet by pedophiles: Implications for law enforcement and probation practice. *Federal Probation, 61,* 14–18.

Durret, M. E., O'Bryant, S., & Pennebaker, J. W. (1975). Child-rearing report of white, black, and Mexican American families. *Developmental Psychology, 2,* 871.

Dutton, D. G., & Painter, S. (1981). Traumatic bonding: The development of emotional attachments in battered women and other relationships of intermittent abuse. *Victimology: An International Journal, 1,* 139–155.

Dyson, A. H. (1994). The Ninjas, the X-men, and the ladies: Playing with power and identity in an urban primary school. *Teachers College Record, 96*(2), 219–239.

Dziech, B. W., & Weiner, L. L. (1984). *The lecherous professor: Sexual harassment on campus.* Boston: Beacon Press.

Dziech, B. W., & Weiner, L. (1990). *The lecherous professor: Sexual harassment on campus* (2nd ed.). Urbana: University of Illinois Press.

Eagly, A. (1987). *Sex differences in social behavior: A social-role interpretation.* Hillsdale, NJ: Erlbaum.

Eagly, A., & Mladinic, A. (1998). Are people prejudiced against women? Some answers from research on attitudes, gender stereotypes, and judgments of competence. In W. Stroebe and M. Hewstone (Eds.), *European review of social psychology* (pp. 1–63). New York: Wiley.

Eagly, A. H. (1995a). Reflections on the commenters' views. *American Psychologist, 50,* 169–171.

Eagly, A. H. (1995b). The science and politics of comparing women and men. *American Psychologist, 50,* 145–158.

Eals, M., & Silverman, I. (1994). The hunter-gatherer theory of spatial sex differences: Proximate factors mediating the female advantage in recall of object arrays. *Ethology and Sociobiology, 15*(2), 95–105.

Eccles, J. S. (1987). Gender roles and women's achievement-related decisions. *Psychology of Women Quarterly, 11,* 135–172.

Eckholm, E. (1992, October 6). What happens to infants when their mothers go to work. *New York Times,* pp. A1, A21.

Eckholm, E. (2002, June 21). Desire for sons drives use of prenatal scans in China. *New York Times,* p. A3.

Edwards, T. M. (2000, August 28). Single by choice. *Time Magazine online, 156*(9).

Ehrenreich, B., & English, D. (1979). *For her own good: 150 years of the experts' advice to women.* London: Pluto Press.

Ehrenreich, B., & English, D. (1981). The sexual politics of illness. In P. Conrad & R. Kern (Eds.), *The sociology of health and illness: Critical perspectives* (pp. 327–350). New York: St. Martin's Press.

Ehrenreich, B., & Hochschild, A. R. (2002). *Global women: Nannies, maids and sex workers in the new economy.* London: Granta Books.

Ehrhardt, A. A., Grisanti, G. C., & Meyer-Bahlburg, H. F. (1977). Prenatal exposure to medroxyprogesterone acetate (MPA) in girls. *Psychoneuroendocrinology, 2,* 391–398.

Ehrhardt, A. A., Meyer-Balburg, H. F. L., Rosen, L. R., Feldman, J. F., Veridiano, N. P., Zimmerman, I., & McEwen, B. S. (1985). Sexual orientation after prenatal exposure to exogenous estrogen. *Archives of Sexual Behavior, 14,* 57–77.

Eisenberg, N., Martin, C. L., & Fables, R. A. (1996). Gender development and gender effects. In D.C. Berliner & R. C.

Calfee (Eds.), *The handbook of educational psychology* (pp. 358–396). New York: Simon & Schuster.

Elder, G. H., Caspi, A., & Downey, G. (1986). Problem behavior and family relationships: A multigenerational analysis. In A. Sorensen, F. Weinert, & L. Sherrod (Eds.), *Human development and the life course.* Hillside, NJ: Erlbaum.

Elias, M. (1984, February 7). Women pay for working hard. *USA Today.*

Elias, M. (1997, April 4). Day care not harmful to growth or bonding. *USA Today,* p. 01.A.

Ellis, L., & Ames, M. A. (1987). Neurohormonal functioning and sexual orientation: A theory of homosexuality–heterosexuality. *Psychological Bulletin, 101,* 233–258.

Ember, C. R., & Ember, M. (1990). *Anthropology* (6th ed.; Instructor's ed.). Englewood Cliffs, NJ: Prentice-Hall.

Enarson, E. P. (1984). *Woods-working women: Sexual integration in the U.S. forest service.* Birmingham: University of Alabama Press.

Encyclopedia Britannica. (1999, July 12). *Hebrew.* Retrieved July 14, 1999 from http://search.eb.com/bol/topic?thes_id=182911.

Encyclopedia Britannica. (1999, July 12). *Christianity.* Retrieved July 24, 1999 from http://search.eb.com/bol/topic?map_id=41297000&tmap_typ=ai.

Epstein, C. F. (1986). Family and career: Why women can "have it all." In C. Tavris (Ed.), *Everywoman's emotional well-being: Heart and mind, body and soul.* Englewood Cliffs, NJ: Prentice Hall.

Equal Employment Opportunity Commission. (2003). Sexual Harassment Changes EEOC and FEPA Combined FY 1992-FY003. Retrieved March 8, 2004 from www.eeoc.gov/stats/harass.html

Equal Opportunity Employment Commission. (1999, January 14). *Report on sexual harassment.* Retrieved from www.eeoc.gov/stats/harass.html

Erikson, E. (1950). *Childhood and society.* New York: W. W. Norton.

Escobar, J. I. (1993). Psychiatric epidemiology. In A. C. Gaw (Ed.), *Culture, ethnicity and mental illness* (pp. 43–73). Washington, DC: American Psychiatric Press.

Espin, O. M. (1994). Feminist approaches. In L. Comas-Diaz & B. Greene (Eds.), *Women of color: Integrating ethnic and gender identities in psychotherapy* (pp. 265–286). New York: Guilford Press.

Espiritu, Y. L. (1992). *Asian American panethnicity: Bridging institutions and identities.* Philadelphia: Temple University Press.

Estrich, S. (1987). *Real rape.* Cambridge, MA: Harvard University Press.

Etaugh, C. (1993). Women in the middle and later years. In F. L. Denmark & M. A. Paludi (Eds.), *Psychology of women: A handbook of issues and theories* (pp. 213–246). Westport, CT: Greenwood Press.

Etaugh, C., Levine, D., & Mennella, A. (1984). Development of sex biases in children: 40 years later. *Sex Roles, 10,* 911–922.

Etaugh, C., & Liss, M. B. (1992). Home, school, and playroom: Training grounds for adult gender roles. *Sex Roles, 26,* 129–146.

Etienne, M., & Leacock, E. (1980). *Women and colonization: Anthropological perspectives.* New York: Praeger.

Ettinger, B. (1993). Use of low-dosage 17 beta-estradiol for the prevention of osteoporosis. *Clinical Therapy, 15,* 950–962.

Evans, L. (2000). No sissy boys here: A context analysis of the representation of masculinity in elementary school reading textbooks. *Sex Roles, 42*(3/4), 255–270.

Evans, P. C. (2003). "If only I were thin like her, maybe I could be happy like her": The self-implications of associating a thin female ideal with life success. *Psychology of Women Quarterly, 27,* 209–214.

Evans, R. J. (1976). *The feminist movement in Germany.* London: Sage.

Evans-Pritchard, E. E. (1937). *Witchcraft, oracles, and magic among the Azande.* Oxford, UK: Oxford University Press.

Ewing, W. (1993). The civic advocacy of violence. In A. Minas (Ed.), *Gender basics: Feminist perspectives on women and men* (pp. 200–205). Belmont, CA: Wadsworth.

Eyer, D. (1994). Mother–infant bonding: A scientific fiction. *Human Nature, 5*(1), 69–94.

Fabe, M., & Wikler, N. (1978). *Up against the clock.* New York: Random House.

Fagot, B., Hagan, R., Leinbach, M., & Kronsberg, S. (1985). Differential reactions to assertive and communicative acts of toddler boys and girls. *Child Development, 56,* 1499–1505.

Fagot, B. I. (1985). Changes in thinking about early sex-role development. *Developmental Review, 5,* 83–98.

Fagot, B. I. (1991, April). *Peer relations in boys and girls from two to seven.* Paper presented at the biennial meeting of the Society for Research in Child Development, Seattle, WA.

Fagot, B. I., Leinbach, M. D., & O'Boyle, C. (1992). Gender labeling, gender stereotyping, and parenting behaviors. *Developmental Psychology, 28*(2), 225–230.

Fahrenkamp, E. J. (2001). Age, gender, and perceived social support of married and never-married persons as predictors of self-esteem. *Dissertation Abstracts International, 62*(2B), 1130.

Fain, T. C., & Anderton, D. L. (1987). Sexual harassment: Organizational context and diffuse status. *Sex Roles, 5/6,* 291–311.

Fairburn, C. G., Cooper, Z., Doll, H. A., Normal, P., & O'Connor, M. (2000). The natural course of bulimia nervosa and binge eating disorder in young women. *Archives of General Psychiatry, 57,* 659–665.

Faludi, S. (1991). *Backlash: The undeclared war against American women.* New York: Crown.

Fantini, M., & Cardenas, R. (1980). *Parenting in a multicultural society.* New York: Longman.

Farina A., & Felner, R. D. (1973). Employment interviewer reactions to former mental patients. *Journal of Abnormal Psychology, 82,* 268–272.

Fausto-Sterling, A. (1992a). Hormones and aggression. In A. Fausto-Sterling (Ed.), *Myths of gender: Biological theories about women and men* (2nd ed.) (pp. 123–154). New York: Basic Books.

Fausto-Sterling, A. (1992b). *Myths of gender: Biological theories about women and men* (2nd ed.). New York: Basic Books.

Fausto-Sterling, A. (1993, March/April). The five sexes: Why male and female are not enough. *The Sciences,* pp. 20–25.

Favazza, A. R., & Rosenthal, R. J. (1993). Diagnostic issues in self-mutilation. *Hospital Community Psychiatry, 44,* 134–140.

Faxon, D. P., Ghalilli, K., Jacobs, A. K., Ruocco, N. A., Christellis, E. M., Kellett, M. A. , Jr., Varrichione, T. R., & Ryan, T. J. (1992). The degree of vascularization and outcome after multivessel coronary angioplasty. *American Heart Journal, 123* (4, Pt. 1), 854–859.

Feather, N. T., & Simon, J. G. (1975). Reactions to male and female success and failure in sex-linked occupations: Impressions of personality, causal attributions, and perceived likelihood of different consequences. *Journal of Personality and Social Psychology, 31,* 20–31.

Featherston, E. (Ed.). (1994). *Skin deep: Women writing on color, culture and identity.* Freedom, CA: Crossing Press.

Federal Register. (2003, July 2). Guideline for the study and evaluation of gender differences in the clinical evaluation of drugs. 58(139), 39406–39416.

Federbush, M. (1974). The sex problems of school math books. In J. Stacey, S. Beraud, & J. Daniels (Eds.), *And Jill came tumbling after: Sexism in American education.* New York: Dell.

Fein, E., & Schneider, S. (1995). *The rules: Time-tested secrets for capturing the heart of Mr. Right.* New York: Warner Books.

Fein, E., & Schneider, S. (1997). *The rules II: More rules to live and love by.* New York: Warner Books.

Feingold, A. (1988). Cognitive gender differences are disappearing. *American Psychologist, 43,* 95–103.

Feingold, A. (1991). Sex differences in the effect of similarity and physical attractiveness on opposite-sex attraction. *Basic and Applied Social Psychology, 12,* 357–367.

Feingold, A. (1993). Cognitive gender differences: A developmental perspective. *Sex Roles, 29,* 91–112.

Feldman-Summers, S., & Kiesler, S. B. (1974). Those who are number two try harder: The effects of sex on attributions of causality. *Journal of Personality and Social Psychology, 30,* 846–855.

Fennema, E., & Sherman, J. (1977). Sex-related differences in mathematics, achievement, spatial visualization, and affective factors. *American Vocational Research Journal, 14,* 51–71.

Ferre, M. M., & Hall, E. J. (1990). Visual imagery of American society: Gender and race in introductory sociology textbooks. *Gender & Society, 4,* 500–533.

Festinger, L. (1957). *A theory of cognitive dissonance.* Palo Alto, CA: Stanford University Press.

Fichter, M. M., & Noegel, R. (1990). Concordance for bulimia nervosa in twins. *International Journal of Eating Disorders, 9,* 255–263.

Fidell, L. S. (1980). Sex role stereotypes and the American physician. *Psychology of Women Quarterly, 4,* 313–330.

Fidell, L. S. (1984). Sex roles in medicine. In C. Widom (Ed.), *Sex roles and psychopathology* (pp. 375–389). New York: Plenum Press.

Field, D. (1999). Continuity and change in friendships in advanced age: Findings from the Berkeley Older Generation Study. *International Journal of Aging and Human Development, 48,* 325–346.

Field, T. (1978). Interaction behaviors of primary versus secondary caretaker fathers. *Developmental Psychology, 14,* 183–184.

Fields, J., & Casper, L. (2001). *America's families and living arrangements.* Washington DC: U.S. Census Bureau.

Fine, M. (1988). Sexuality, schooling, and adolescent females: The missing discourse of desire. *Harvard Educational Review, 58,* 29–53.

Fine, M., & Asch, A. (1981). Disabled women: Sexism without the pedestal. *Journal of Sociology and Social Welfare, 8,* 233–248.

Fine, M., & Asch, A. (1988). *Women with disabilities: Essays in psychology, culture, and politics.* Philadelphia: Temple University Press.

Fine, M., Weis, L., Powell, C., & Wong, L. M. (1997). *Off white: Readings on race, power, and society.* New York: Routledge.

Finkel, S. K. & Olswang, S. G. (1996). Childrearing as a career impediment to women assistant professors. *Review of Higher Education, 19*(2), 123–141.

Finkelhor, D. (1979). *Sexually victimized children.* New York: Free Press.

Finkelhor, D. (Ed.). (1984). *Child sexual abuse: Theory and research.* New York: Free Press.

Finkelhor, D. (1986). Sexual abuse: Beyond the family systems approach. *Journal of Psychotherapy and the Family, 2,* 53–65.

Finkelhor, D. (1990). Early and long term effects of child sexual abuse: An update. *Professional Psychology: Research and Practice, 21,* 325–330.

Finkelhor, D., & Hotaling, G. T. (1984). Sexual abuse in the national incidence study of child abuse and neglect: An appraisal. *Child Abuse and Neglect, 8,* 23–32.

Finkelhor, D., & Russell, D. (1984). Women as perpetrators: Review of the evidence. In D. Finkelhor (Ed.), *Child sexual abuse: Theory and research.* New York: Free Press.

Finkelhor, D., & Yllo, K. (1982). Forced sex in marriage: A preliminary research report. *Crime and Delinquency, 28,* 459–478.

Fischer, J. L., & Narus, L. R. (1981). Sex-role development in late adolescence and adulthood. *Sex Roles, 7,* 97–106.

Fischer, T. D. (1987). Family communication and the sexual behavior and attitudes of college students. *Journal of Youth and Adolescence, 16,* 481–495.

Fishbein, H. D., & Imai, S. (1993). Preschoolers select playmates on the basis of gender and race. *Journal of Applied Developmental Psychology, 14*(3), 303–316.

Fisher, B., Redmond, C., & Poisson, R. (1989). Eight-year results of a randomized clinical trial comparing total mastectomy and lumpectomy with or without irradiation in the treatment of breast cancer. *New England Journal of Medicine, 320,* 822–828.

Fisher, B., Redmond, C., & Risher, E. R. (1985). Ten-year results of a randomized clinical trial comparing radical mastectomy and total mastectomy with or without radiation. *New England Journal of Medicine, 312,* 674–681.

Fisher, S. W. (2000). The stay-at-home dad. *Christianity Today International/Marriage Partnership, 17*(3), 24.

Fiske, S. T., Bersoff, D. N., Borgida, E., Deaux, K., & Heilman, M. E. (1991). Social science research on trial: Use of sex stereotyping research in *Price Waterhouse v. Hopkins. American Psychologist, 46,* 1049–1060.

Fiske, S. T., & Glick, P. (1995). Ambivalence and stereotypes cause sexual harassment: A theory with implications for organizational change. *Journal of Social Issues, 51*(1), 97–115.

Fiske, S. T., & Taylor, S. E. (1991). *Social cognition* (2nd ed.). New York: McGraw-Hill.

Fitting, M. D., Salisbury, S., Davies, N., & Mayelin, D. K. (1978). Self-concept and sexuality of spinal cord injured women. *Archives of Sexual Behavior, 7,* 143–156.

Fitzgerald, L. F. (1993). Sexual harassment: Violence against women in the workplace. *American Psychologist, 48,* 1070–1076.

Fitzgerald, L. F. (1996). Sexual harassment: The definition and measurement of a construct. In M. A. Paludi (Ed.), *Sexual harassment on college campuses: Abusing the ivory power* (pp. 25–47). Albany: State University of New York Press.

Fitzgerald, L. F., Dragow, F., Hulin, C. F., Gelfand, M. J., & Magley, V. J. (1997). Antecedents and consequences of sexual harassment in organizations: A test of an integrated model. *Journal of Applied Psychology, 82*(4), 578–589.

Fitzgerald, L. F., Magley, V. J., Drasgow, F., & Waldo, C. R. (1999). Measuring sexual harassment in the military: The Sexual Experiences Questionnaire (SEQ-DOD). *Military Psychology, 11,* 243–264.

Fitzgerald, L. F., & Ormerod, A. J. (1991). Perceptions of sexual harassment: The influence of gender and context. *Psychology of Women Quarterly, 15,* 281–294.

Fitzgerald, L. F., & Ormerod, A. J. (1993). Breaking silence: The sexual harassment of women in academia and the workplace. In F. L. Denmark & M. A. Paludi (Eds.), *Psychology of women: A handbook of issues and theories* (pp. 553–581). Westport, CT: Greenwood Press.

Fitzgerald, L. F., & Shullman, S. L. (1993). Sexual harassment: A research analysis and agenda for the 1990's. *Journal of Vocational Behavior, 42,* 5–27.

Fitzgerald, L. F., Shullman, S. L., Bailey, N., Richards, M., Swecker, J., Gold, A., Ormerod, A. J., & Weitzman, L. (1988). The incidence and dimensions of sexual harassment in academia and the workplace. *Journal of Vocational Behavior, 32,* 152–175.

Fitzgerald, L. F., & Weitzman, L. M. (1990). Men who harass: Speculation and data. In M. A. Paludi, et al. (Ed.), *Ivory power: Sexual harassment on campus* (pp. 125–140). Albany: State University of New York Press.

Fitzgerald, L. F., Weitzman, L. M., Gold, Y., & Ormerod, M. (1988). Academic harassment: Sex and denial in scholarly garb. *Psychology of Women Quarterly, 12,* 329–340.

Fivush, R., & Buckner, J. P. (2000). Gender, sadness, and depression: Developmental and sociocultural perspectives. In A. Fischer (Ed.), *Emotion and gender.* New York: Cambridge University Press.

Flaks, D. K., Ficher, I., Masterpasqua, F., & Joseph, G. (1995). Lesbians choosing motherhood: A comparative study of lesbian and heterosexual parents and their children. *Developmental Psychology, 31,* 105–114.

Flower, L. (1997). *The elements of world religions.* New York: Element Books.

Fodor, I. G. (1974). The phobic syndrome in women: Implications for treatment. In V. Franks & V. Burtle (Eds.), *Women in therapy: New psychotherapies for a changing society.* New York: Brunner/Mazel.

Follingstad, D. R., Brennan, A. F., Hause, E. S., Polek, D. S., & Rutledge, L. L. (1991). Factors moderating physical and psychological symptoms of battered women. *Journal of Family Violence, 6,* 81–95.

Foos, P. W., & Clark, M. C. (2000). Old age, inhibition, and the part-set cuing effect. *Educational Gerontology, 26*(2), 155–160.

Forcey, L. R. (1987). *Mothers of sons: Towards an understanding of responsibility.* New York: Praeger.

Foresto, L. A. (in press). Adolescent responses to the 9/11/01 terrorist attacks. *New York State Psychologist, 16*(3), 38–41.

Forman, F., & Maier, C. (1997). Jewish women's voices: Past and present: A bibliography. Available: www.utoronto.ca/wjudaism/journal/vollnlform.htm

Forster, N. (2001). A case study of women's academic views on equal opportunity career prospects and work family-conflicts in a UK university. *Career Development International, 6*(1), 28–38.

Fortes, M. (1962). *The web of kinship among the Tallensi.* London: Oxford University Press.

Foster, C., Squyres, S., & Jacobs, N. (Eds.). (1996). Women's changing role. *The information series on current topics.* New York: Wylie—Information Plus.

Foster, V., Kimmel, M., & Skelton, C. (2001). "What about the boys?" An overview of the debates. In W. Martino & B. Meyenn (Eds), *What about the boys? Issues of masculinity in schools* (pp. 1–23). Buckingham, UK: Open University Press.

Foucault, M. (1978). *The history of sexuality,* Vol. 1 (Robert Hurley, trans.). New York: Pantheon.

Fourcroy, J. L. (1994). Women and the development of drugs: Why can't a woman be more like a man? In J. A. Sechzer, A. Griffin, & S. M. Pfafflin (Eds.), *Forging a women's health research agenda: Policy issues for the 1990's. Annals of the New York Academy of Sciences, 736,* 174–195.

Fowers, B. J. (1991). His and her marriages: A multivariate study of gender and marital satisfaction. *Sex Roles, 24,* 209–221.

Fowlkes, M. R. (1987). The myth of merit and male professional careers: The roles of wives. In N. Gerstel & H. E. Ross (Eds.), *Work and families* (pp. 347–360). Philadelphia: Temple University Press.

Fox, L. H. (1987). Sex differences among the mathematically gifted. In J. A. Sechzer & S. M. Pfafflin (Eds.) *Psychology and educational policy. Annals of the New York Academy of Sciences, 517,* 99–112.

Fox, M., Gibbs, M., & Auerbach, D. (1985). Age and gender dimensions of friendship. *Psychology of Women Quarterly, 9,* 489–502.

Fox, R. (1996). Bisexuality in perspective: A review of theory and research. In B. A. Firestein (Ed.), *Bisexuality: The psychology and politics of an invisible minority.* Thousand Oaks, CA: Sage.

Franz, C. E., & Stewart, A. J. (1994). *Women creating lives: Identities, resilience, and resistance.* Boulder, CO: Westview Press.

Frayser, S. (1985). *Varieties of sexual experience: An anthropological perspective on human sexuality.* New Haven, CT: Human Relations Area Files Press.

Freed, R. S., & Freed, S. A. (1989). Beliefs and practices resulting in female deaths and fewer females than males in India. *Population and Environment, 10,* 144–161.

Freedman, R. (1986). *Beauty bond.* Lexington, MA: Health.

Freeman, W. E., Boxer, A. S., Rickels, K., Tureck, R., & Mastroianni, L., Jr. (1985). Psychological evaluation and support in a program of in vitro fertilization and embryo transfer. *Fertility and Sterility, 43,* 48–53.

Freiberg, P. (1991). Self-esteem gender gap widens in adolescence. *APA Monitor, 22*(4), 29.

Frenkel, K. A. (1990, April). Women and computing. *Computer Select.*

Freud, S. (1912). The psychology of love. In J. Strachey (Ed.), *The standard edition of the complete psychological works of Sigmund Freud,* Vol. 11, p. 189. Ernest Jones (Ed.), London: Hogarth Ltd., p. 189.

Freud, S. (1924/1961). The dissolution of the Oedipus complex. In Ernest Jones (Ed.), *The standard edition of the complete psychological works of Sigmund Freud* (Vol. 19, pp. 172–179). London: Hogarth Ltd.

Freud, S. (1925/1961). Some psychical consequences of the anatomical distinction between the sexes. In J. Strachey (Ed.), *The standard edition of the complete psychological works of Sigmund Freud* (Vol. 19, pp. 243–258). London: Hogarth Press and the Institute of Psychoanalysis.

Freud, S. (1931). Female sexuality. In J. Strachey (Ed.), *Sigmund Freud, collected papers* (Vol. 5, pp. 252–272). London: Hogarth Press and the Institute of Psychoanalysis.

Freud, S. (1959). Some psychological consequences of the anatomical distinction between the sexes. In J. Strachey (Ed.) *The Collected Papers* (Vol. 5, p. 186). London: Hogarth Press and the Institute of Psycho-Analysis.

Frey, K. S., & Ruble, D. N. (1992). Gender constancy and the "cost" of sex-typed behavior: A test of the conflict hypothesis. *Developmental Psychology, 28*(4), 714–721.

Frezza, M., di Padova, C., Pozzato, G., Terpin, M., Baraona, E., & Lieber, C. S. (1990). High blood alcohol levels in women: The role of decreased gastric alcohol dehydrogenase activity and first-pass metabolism. *New England Journal of Medicine, 322,* 95–99.

Friedan, B. (1993). *The fountain of age.* New York: Simon & Schuster.

Friedman, A., Tzukerman, Y., Wienberg, H., & Todd, J. The shift in power with age: Changes in perception of the power of women and men over the life cycle. *Psychology of Women Quarterly, 16*(4), 513–525.

Friend, R., Rafferty, Y., & Bramel, D. (1990). A puzzling interpretation of the Asch "conformity" study. *European Journal of Social Psychology, 20,* 29–44.

Frierson, R. L., Melikian, M., & Wadman, P. C. (2002). Principles of suicide risk management. *Postgraduate medicine, 112*(3), 65–71.

Frieze, I. H. (1983). Investigating the causes and consequences of marital rape. *Signs, 8,* 532–552.

Frieze, I. H., Whitley, B. E., Jr., Hanusa, B. H., & McHugh, M. C. (1982). Assessing the theoretical models for sex differences in causal attributions for success and failure. *Sex Roles, 8,* 333–343.

Fritner, M. P., & Rubinson, L. (1993). Acquaintance rape: The influence of alcohol, fraternity membership, and sports team membership. *Journal of Sex Education and Therapy, 19,* 272–284.

Frost-Knappman, E. (1994). *The ABC-CLIO companion to women's progress in America.* Santa Barbara, CA: ABC-CLIO.

Fuhrer, R., Antonucci, T. C., & Dartigues, J. F. (1992). The co-occurrence of depressive symptoms and cognitive impairment in a French community: Are there gender differences? *European Archives of Psychiatry and Clinical Neuroscience, 242*(2/3), 161–171.

Fujitomi, S., & Wong, D. (1976). The new Asian American woman. In S. Cox (Ed.), *Female psychology: The emerging self* (pp. 236–248). Chicago: Science Research Associates.

Fuller, A. H. (1961). *Buraji: Portrait of a Lebanese Moslem village.* Cambridge, MA: Harvard University Press.

Funk, R. E. (1993). *Stopping rape: A challenge for men.* Philadelphia: New Society Publishers.

Gaddis, A., & Brooks-Gunn, J. (1985). The male experience of pubertal change. *Journal of Youth and Adolescence, 14,* 61–69.

Gagnon, J. H. (1977). *Human sexualities.* Glenview, IL: Scott, Foresman.

Gagnon, J. H., & Simon, W. (1973). *Sexual conduct: The social origins of human sexuality.* Chicago: Aldine.

Galea, S., Vlahov, D., Resnick, H., Ahern, J., Susser, E., Gold, J., Bucuvalas, M., Kilpatrick, D. (2003). Trends of probable post-traumatic stress disorder in New York City after the

September 11 terrorist attacks. *American Journal of Epidemiology, 158,* 514–524.

Gallo, L. C., Troxel, W. M., Mathews, K. A., & Kuller, L. H. (2003). Marital status and quality in middle-aged women: Associations with levels and trajectories of cardiovascular risk factors. *Health Psychology, 22*(5), 453–463.

Galsworthy, T. D. (1994). Osteoporosis: Statistics, intervention and prevention. In J. A. Sechzer, A. Griffin, & S. M. Pfafflin (Eds.), Forging a woman's health research agenda: Policy issues for the 1990's. *Annals of the New York Academy of Sciences, 736,* 158–164.

Gans, H. J. (1979, January). Symbolic ethnicity: The future of ethnic groups and cultures in America. *Ethnic and Racial Studies 2,* 1–20.

Garb, H. (1997). Race bias, social class bias, and gender bias in clinical judgment. *Clinical Psychology: Science and Practice, 4*(2), 99–120.

Garber, M. (1995). *Vice versa: Bisexuality and the eroticism of everyday life.* New York: Simon and Schuster.

Garcia, L. T. (1986). Exposure to pornography and attitudes about women and rape: A correlational study. *Journal of Sex Research, 22,* 378–385.

Garfinkel, P. E., & Garner, D. M. (1982). *Anorexia nervosa: A multidimensional perspective.* New York: Bruner/Mazel.

Garland, A. W. (1988). *Women activists: Challenging the abuse of power.* New York: Feminist Press.

Garner, D. M., & Bemis, K. M. (1982). A cognitive-behavioral approach to anorexia nervosa. *Cognitive Therapy Research, 6,* 1223–1250.

Garnets, L. D. (2004). Life as a lesbian. In J. D. Chrisler, C. Golden, & P. D. Rozee (Eds.), *Lectures on the psychology of women* (3rd ed.). New York: McGraw-Hill.

Gary, L. E. (1987). Attitudes of Black adults toward community mental health centers. *Hospital and Community Psychiatry, 38,* 1100–1105.

Gates, G. J., & Sonenstein, F. L. (2000). Heterosexual genital sexual activity among adolescent males. *Family Planning Perspectives, 32*(6), 295–297, 304.

Gazetas, P., Estabrook, A., O'Neil, J., & Sciacca, R. (1994). Importance of adequate staging and of hormone receptors in women over age 70 with breast cancer. *Columbia University Medical Center,* New York.

Gelfond, M. (1991). Reconceptualizing agoraphobia: A case study of epistemological bias in clinical research. *Feminism & Psychology, 1,* 247–262.

Gelles, R. J., & Straus, M. A. (1988). *Intimate violence.* New York: Simon & Schuster.

Gendercide. (2002). *Female Infanticide.* Retrieved from http://gendercide.org/case_infanticide.html.

Genesis Rabbah, 18, 2. Cited by Swidler, 1976, p. 72.

Gerdes, E. P. (1995). Women preparing for traditionally male professions: Physical and psychological symptoms associated with work and home stress. *Sex Roles, 32*(11/12), 787–814.

Geringer, W. M., et al. (1993). Knowledge, attitudes and behavior related to condom use and STDs in a high risk population. *Journal of Sex Research, 30,* 75–83.

Gerrard, M. (1987). Sex, sex guilt, and contraceptive use revisited: The 1980s. *Journal of Personality and Social Psychology, 52,* 975–980.

Gibbons, J. L., Lynn, M., Stiles, D. A., de Berducido, E. J., Richter, R., Walker, K., & Wiley, D. (1993). Guatemalan, Filipino, and U.S. adolescents' images of women as office workers and homemakers. *Psychology of Women Quarterly, 17*(4), 373–388.

Gidycz, C. A., & Koss, M. P. (1990). A comparison of group and individual sexual assault victims. *Psychology of Women Quarterly, 14,* 325–342.

Gilbert, L. A. (1993). Women at midlife: Current theoretical perspectives and research. *Women and Therapy, 14*(1/2), 105–115.

Gillen, K., & Muncer, S. J. (1995). Sex differences in the perceived causal structure of date rape: A preliminary report. *Aggressive Behavior, 21,* 101–112.

Gilligan, C. (1982). *In a different voice: Psychological theory and women's development.* Cambridge, MA: Harvard University Press.

Gilligan, C. (2002). *The Birth of Pleasure* (1st Ed.). New York: Knopf.

Gilligan, C., & Attanucci, J. (1988). Two moral orientations: Gender differences and similarities. *Merrill–Palmer Quarterly, 34,* 223–237.

Gilman, A. G., Rall, T. W., Nies, A. S., & Taylor, P. (Eds.). (1990). *Goodman and Gilman's pharmological basis of therapeutics* (8th ed.). New York: Pergamon Press.

Gilman, C. P. (1975). *The living of Charlotte Perkins Gilman: An autobiography.* New York: Harper Books.

Gimbutas, M. (1982). Prehistoric religions: Old Europe. In *The Encyclopedia of Religion* (Vol. II, pp. 506–515); *The goddesses and gods of Old Europe.* Berkeley: University of California Press. Cited by Carmody, 1989, pp. 14–21.

Ginorio, A. B., Gutierrez, L., Cauce, A. M., & Acosta, M. (1995). Psychological issues for Latinas. In H. Landrine (Ed.), *Bringing cultural diversity to feminist psychology: Theory, research, and practice* (pp. 241–264). Washington, DC: American Psychological Association.

Gitlin, M. J., & Pasnau, R. O. (1989). Psychiatric syndromes linked to reproductive function in women: A review of current knowledge. *American Journal of Psychiatry, 146,* 1413–1422.

Gittings, J. (2002) Growing sex imbalance shocks China. *The Guardian,* May 13, 2002.

Giuliano, T. A., Popp, K. E., & Knight, J. L. (2000). Footballs versus Barbies: Childhood play activities as predictors of sports participation by women. *Sex Roles, 42,* 159–182.

Glascock, J. (2001). Gender roles on prime-time network television: Demographics and behaviors. *Journal of Broadcasting and Electric Media, 45*(4), 656–669.

Glasman, L. (2002). Mother "there for" me: Female-identity development in the context of the mother–daughter relationship. A qualitative study. *Dissertation Abstracts International, 62*(7B), 3377.

Glass, S. P., & Wright, T. L. (1992). Justifications of extramarital relationships: The associations between attitudes, behaviors, and gender. *Journal of Sex Research, 29,* 361–387.

Glazer, N., & Moynihan, D. P. (1970). *Beyond the melting pot* (2nd ed.). Cambridge, MA: MIT Press.

Glenn, E. N. (1986). *Issei, nisei, war bride: Three generations of Japanese American women in domestic service.* Philadelphia: Temple University Press.

Glick, P. (1991). Trait-based and sex-based discrimination in occupational prestige, occupational salary, and hiring. *Sex Roles, 25*(5/6), 351–378.

Glick, P. C., & Lin, S. L. (1986). Recent changes in divorce and remarriage. *Journal of Marriage and Family, 48*(4), 737–747.

Glick, P., & Fiske, S. (2001). An ambivalent alliance: Hostile and benevolent sexism as complementary justifications for gender inequality. *American Psychologist, 56,* 109–118.

Glick, P., & Fiske, S. T. (1996). The ambivalent sexism inventory: Differentiating hostile and benevolent sexism. *Journal of Personality & Social Psychology, 70*(3), 491–512.

Goffman, E. (1959). *The presentation of self in everyday life.* Oxford, England: Doubleday.

Goffman, E. (1979). *Gender advertisements.* Cambridge, MA: Harvard University Press.

Golan, N. (1986). *The perilous bridge.* New York: Free Press.

Gold, D., & Andres, D. (1978). Developmental comparisons between ten-year-old children with employed and non-employed mothers. *Child Development, 49,* 75–84.

Goldberg, H. (1980). *The new male: From self-destruction to self-care.* New York: Signet.

Goldenberg, N. R. (1985). *Changing of the gods: Feminism and the end of traditional religions.* Boston: Beacon Press.

Goldman, B. D. (1978). Developmental influences of hormones on neuroendocrine mechanisms of sexual behavior: Comparisons with other sexually dimorphic behaviors. In J. B. Hutchinson (Ed.), *Biological determinants of sexual behavior* (pp. 127–152). New York: HarperCollins. Cited by Masters, Johnson, & Kolodny, 1995, p. 203.

Gondolf, E. W., & Hanneken, J. (1987). The gender warriors: Reformed batterers on abuse, treatment, and change. *Journal of Family Violence, 2,* 177–191.

Goodchilds, J. D., Zellman, G. L., Johnson, P. B., & Giarusso, R. (1988). Adolescents and their perception of sexual interactions. In A. W. Burgess (Ed.), *Rape and sexual assault* (Vol. 2, pp. 245–270). New York: Garland.

Goode, E. (1996). Gender and courtship entitlement: Responses to personal ads. *Sex Roles, 34*(3/4), 141–169.

Goode, W. J. (1974). A theory of strain. *American Sociological Review, 25,* 483–496.

Gooden, A. M. (2001). Gender representation in notable children's picture books: 1995–1999. *Sex Roles, 45*(1/2), 89–101.

Goodman, J., & Croyle, R. T. (1989). Social framework testimony in employment discrimination cases. *Behavioral Science and the Law, 7,* 227–241.

Goodman, L. A., Koss, M. P., Fitzgerald, L. F., Russo, N. F., & Keita, G. P. (1993). Male violence against women: Current research and future directions. *American Psychologist, 48,* 1054–1058.

Goodson, P., McCormick, D., & Evans, A. (2001). Searching for sexually explicit materials on the Internet: An exploratory study of college students' behavior and attitudes. *Archives of Sexual Behavior, 30,* 101–118.

Gordon, M. (1978). *Human nature, class, and ethnicity.* New York: Oxford University Press.

Gordon, M. J., & Riger, S. (1989). *The female fear.* New York: Free Press.

Gordon, R. R., & Gordon, K. K. (1967). Factors in postpartum emotional adjustment. *American Journal of Orthopsychiatry, 37,* 359–360.

Gore, S., Aseltine, R. H., Jr., & Colten, M. E. (1993). Gender, social–relational involvement, and depression. *Journal of Research on Adolescence, 3,* 101–125.

Gore, S., & Mangione, T. W. (1983). Social roles, sex roles, and psychological distress: Additive and interactive models of sex differences. *Journal of Health and Social Behavior, 24,* 300–312.

Gormly, A. V., Gormly, J. B., & Weiss, H. (1987). Motivations for parenthood among young adult college students. *Sex Roles, 16,* 31–39.

Gorski, R. A., Gordon, J. H., Shryne, J. E., & Southam, M. A. (1978). Evidence for a morphological sex difference within the medial preoptic area of the rat brain. *Brain Research, 148,* 333–346.

Gottfredson, L. S. (1981). Circumscription and compromise: A developmental theory of occupational aspirations. *Journal of Counseling Psychology Monograph, 28,* 545–579.

Gottman, J., Coan, J., Carrere, S., & Swanson, C. (1998). Predicting marital happiness and stability from newlywed interaction. *Journal of Marriage and the Family, 60,* 5–23.

Gouchie, C., & Kimura, D. (1991). The relationship between testosterone levels and cognitive ability patterns. *Psychoneuroendocrinology, 16,* 323–334.

Government of South Africa. Girls Education Movement. Available: http://gem.giv.za.

Gracely, R. H., McGrath, P., & Dubner, R. (1978). Ratio scales of sensory and affective verbal pain descriptors. *Pain, 5,* 5–18.

Grady, D. (1998, November 6). Study says HIV tests underestimate women's risk. *New York Times* p. A18.

Graham, N., & Wish, E. D. (1994). Drug use among female arrestees: Onset, pattern, and relationship to prostitution. *Journal of Drug Issues, 24,* 315–329.

Graham, S. (1992). Most of the subjects were White and middle class. *American Psychologist, 47*(5), 629–639.

Grambs, J. D. (1989). *Women over forty: Visions and realities.* New York: Springer.

Grant, K., Lyons, A., Landis, D., Cho, M. H., Scudiero, M., Reynolds, L., Murphy, J., & Bryant, H. (1999). Gender, body image, and depressive symptoms among low-income African American adolescents. *Journal of Social Issues, 55*(2), 299–316.

Graves, J. L., Jr. (2001). *The emperor's new clothes: Biological theories of race at the millennium.* New Brunswick, NJ: Princeton University Press.

Gray, P. (1993, February 15). What is love? *Time,* pp. 47–49.

Green, B. L., & Russo, N. F. (1993). Work and family roles: Selected issues. In F. L. Denmark & M. A. Paludi (Eds.), *Psychology of Women: A handbook of issues and theories.* Westport, CT: Greenwood.

Green, P. (2003). Compared to white patients with chronic pain African-Americans have more symptoms, greater impairment. *Anesthesiology News, 29*(7), 1.

Green, R. (1980). Native American women. *Signs: Journal of Women in Culture and Society, 6,* 248–267.

Greenberg, J., & Mitchell, S. (1983). *Object relations in psychoanalytic theory.* Cambridge, MA: Harvard University Press.

Greenblatt, R. (1979). Update on the male and female climacteric. *American Geriatrics Society, 27*(11), 481–490. Cited by Masters, Johnson, & Kolodny, 1995, p. 268.

Greene, B. (1992). Black feminist psychotherapy. In E. Wright (Ed.), *Feminism and psychoanalysis.* Oxford, UK: Blackwell.

Greene, B. (1994a). African American women. In L. Comas-Diaz & B. Greene (Eds.), *Women of color: Integrating ethnic and gender identities in psychotherapy.* New York: Guilford Press, pp. 10–29.

Greene, B. (1994b). Lesbian and gay sexual orientations: Implications for clinical training, practice, and research. In B. Greene & G. M. Herek's (Eds.), *Lesbian and gay psychology: Theory, research, and clinical applications.* Psychological perspectives on lesbian and gay issues, Vol. 1. (pp. 1–24). Sage: Thousand Oaks, CA: Sage.

Greene, J. G., & Cooke, D. J. (1980). Life stress and symptoms at the climacterium. *British Journal of Psychiatry, 136,* 486–491.

Greenfield, L. A., Rand, M. R., & Craven, D. (1998). Violence by intimates: Analysis of data on crimes by current or self-reported major depression. *Psychiatric Services, 50*(2), 257–259.

Greenfield, P. (1994). Independence and interdependence as developmental scripts: Implications for theory, research and practice. In P. Greenfield & R. Cocking (Eds.), *Cross-cultural roots of minority child development* (pp. 1–37). Hillsdale, NJ: Erlbaum.

Greenhaus, J. H., & Parasuraman, S. (1993). Job performance attributions and career advancement prospects. An examination of race and gender effects. *Organizational Behavior and Human Decision Processes, 55,* 273–297.

Gregoire, A. J., Kumar, R., Everitt, B., Henderson, A. F., & Studd, J. W. (1996). Transdermal estrogen for treatment of severe postnatal depression. *Lancet, 347,* 930–933.

Grief, J. B. (1979). Fathers, children, and joint custody. *American Journal of Orthopsychiatry, 49,* 311–319.

Griffen, J. (1979). A cross-cultural investigation of behavioral changes at menopause. In J. Williams (Ed.), *Psychology of women.* New York: W. W. Norton.

Griffin, S. (1979). *Rape: The power of consciousness.* San Francisco: Harper & Row.

Griffith, E., & Baker, F. (1993). Psychiatric care of African Americans. In A. Gaw (Ed.), *Culture, ethnicity, and mental illness.* Washington, DC: American Psychiatric Press.

Grodsky, P. B. (1995). Personal communication.

Gross, A., Smith, R., & Wallston, B. (1983). The men's movement: Personal vs. political. In J. Freeman (Ed.), *Social movements of the sixties and seventies.* New York: Longman.

Groth, A. N., & Birnbaum, H. J. (1979). *Men who rape: The psychology of the offender.* New York: Plenum Press.

Groth, A. N., & Burgess, A. W. (1980). Male rape: Offenders and victims. *American Journal of Psychiatry, 137,* 806–810.

Gruber, J. E. (1990). Methodological problems and policy implications in sexual harassment research. *Population Research Political Review, 9,* 235–254.

Gruber, J. S., & Bjorn, L. (1982). Blue-collar blues: The sexual harassment of women auto workers. *Work and Occupations, 9,* 271–298.

Guinier, L., Fine, M., Balin, J., Bartow, A., & Stachel, D. L. (1994). Becoming gentlemen: Women's experiences at one Ivy League law school. *University of Pennsylvania Law Review, 143* (1), 1–110.

Gulik, R. M., Mellors, J. W., Havlir, D., Enron, J. J., Gonzalez, C., McMahon, D., Jonas, L., Meibohm, A., Holder, D., Schleif, W. A., Condra, J. H., Emini, E., Isaacs, R., Chodakowitz, J. A., & Richman, D. D. (1998). Simultaneous *vs* sequential initiation of therapy with indivir, zidovudine and lamivudine for HIV-I infection: 100 week follow-up. *Journal of the American Medical Association, 280*(1), 35–41.

Gump, L. S. (2000). Cultural and gender differences in moral judgment: A study of Mexican Americans and Anglo-Americans. *Hispanic Journal of Behavioral Sciences, 22*(1), 78–93.

Gutek, B. A. (1985). *Sex in the workplace.* San Francisco: Jossey-Bass.

Gutek, B. A. (1993). Responses to sexual harassment. In S. Oskamp & M. Costanzo (Eds.), *Gender issues in contemporary society* (pp. 197–216). Newbury Park, CA: Sage.

Gutek, B. A. (1996). Sexual harassment at work: When an organization fails to respond. In M. S. Stockdale (Ed.), *Sexual harassment in the workplace: Perspectives, frontiers, and response strategies* (pp. 272–290). Thousand Oaks, CA: Sage.

Gutek, B. A., & Done, R. S. (2001). Sexual harassment. In R. K. Unger (Ed.), *Handbook of the psychology of women and gender* (pp. 367–387). New York: Wiley.

Gutek, B. A., & Koss, M. (1993). Changed women and changed organizations: Consequences of and coping with sexual harassment. *Journal of Vocational Behavior, 42,* 28–48.

Gutek, B. A., & Morasch, B. (1982). Sex ratios, sex-role spillover, and sexual harassment of women at work. *Journal of Social Issues, 38,* 55–74.

Gutmann, D. (1987). *Reclaimed powers: Towards a psychology of later life.* New York: Basic Books.

Habila, H. (2003, October 4). Justice, Nigeria's Way. *The New York Times,* p. A13.

Hackel, L., & Ruble, D. N. (1992). Change in the marital relationship after first baby: Predicting the impact of expectancy disconfirmation. *Journal of Personality and Social Psychology, 62,* 944–957.

Hacker, A. (2003, June 20). How the B.A. gap widens the chasm between men and women. *The Chronicle of Higher Education,* pp. B10–B11.

Haddad, Y. Y. (1985). Islam, women, and revolution in twentieth-century Arab thought. In *Women, religion and social change* (pp. 275–306). Y. Y. Haddad & E. B. Findley (Eds.), Albany: State University of New York Press.

Hagan, J., Zatz, M., Arnold, B., & Kay, F. (1991). Cultural, capital, gender, and structural transformation of legal practice. *Law and Society Review, 25,* 239–262.

Hagen, R. I., & Kahn, A. (1975). Discrimination against competent women. *Journal of Applied Social Psychology, 5,* 362–367.

Halkitis, P. N., Parsons, J. T., & Wilton, L. (2003). Barebacking among gay and bisexual men in New York City: Explanations for the emergence of intentional unsafe behavior. *Archives of Sexual Behavior, 32*(4), 351–357.

Hall, C. C. I. (1997). Cultural malpractice: The growing obsolescence of psychology with the changing U.S. population. *American Psychologist, 52,* 642–651.

Hall, D. T., & Gordon, F. E. (1973). Effects of career choices on married women. *Journal of Applied Psychology, 58,* 42–48.

Hall, G. C. N., & Hirschman, R. (1991). Toward a theory of sexual aggression: A quadripartite model. *Journal of Consulting and Clinical Psychology, 59,* 662–669.

Hall, G. C. N., Shondrick, D. D., & Hirschman, R. (1993). The role of sexual arousal in sexually aggressive behavior: A meta-analysis. *Journal of Consulting and Clinical Psychology, 61,* 1091–1095.

Hall, G. S. (1904). Adolescence: Its psychology and its relations to physiology, anthropology, sociology, sex, crime, religion, and education (Vols. 1 and 2). New York: Appleton.

Hall, G. S. (1906, June 4). Coeducation. *American Academy of Medicine,* 1–4.

Hall, G. S. (1908). Feminization in school and home. *World's Work, 16,* 10237–10244.

Hall, J. A. (1984). *Nonverbal sex differences.* Baltimore: Johns Hopkins University Press.

Hall, J. A. (1985). *Nonverbal sex differences: Communication accuracy and expressive style.* Baltimore: Johns Hopkins University Press.

Hall, J. A. Y., & Kimura, D. (1995). Sexual orientation and performance on sexually dimorphic motor tasks. *Archives of Sexual Behavior, 24,* 395–407.

Hall, R. M., & Sandler, B. R. (1982, July 7). *The classroom climate: A chilly one for women?* Washington, DC: Project on the Status and Education of Women, Association of American Colleges.

Hallak, M. Personal communications, July 16, 2003.

Haller, J. S., & Haller, R. M. (1974). *The physician and sexuality in Victorian America.* Urbana, IL: University of Illinois Press.

Halmi, K. A. (1994). A multimodal model for understanding and treating eating disorders. *Journal of Women's Health, 3*(6), 487–493.

Halmi, K. A. (1996). Eating disorder research in the past decade. In J. A. Sechzer, S. M. Plafflin, F. L. Denmark, A. Griffin, & S. J. Blumenthal (Eds.), *Women and mental health. Annals of the New York Academy of Sciences, 575,* xi.

Halpern, D. F. (1986). *Sex differences in cognitive abilities.* Hillsdale, NJ: Erlbaum.

Halpern, D. F. (1997). Sex differences in intelligence: Implications for education. *American Psychologist, 52* (10) 1091–1102.

Halpern, D. F. (2000). *Sex differences in cognitive abilities* (3rd ed.). Mahwah, NJ: Erlbaum.

Halpern, D. F., & Wright, T. (1996). A process-oriented model of cognitive sex differences [Special issue]. *Learning and Individual Differences, 8,* 3–24.

Halvorsen, R. (1998). The ambiguity of lesbian and gay marriages: Change and continuity in the symbolic order. *Journal of Homosexuality, 35*(3–4), 207–231.

Hamberger, L. K. (1997). Female offenders in domestic violence: A look at actions in their context. In R. Geffner, S. B. Sorenson, & P. K. Lundberg-Love (Eds.), *Violence and sexual abuse at home: Current issues in spousal battering and child maltreatment* (pp. 117–130). New York: Haworth Press.

Hamilton, L. H., Brooks-Gunn, J., Warren, M. P., & Hamilton, W. G. (1987, December). The impact of thinness and dieting on the professional ballet dancer. *Journal of Medical Problems of Performing Artists,* 117–122.

Hamilton, M. C. & Mayfield, B. (1999, March). *Son daughter preferences of primiparous married couples, non pregnant married couples, and college students.* Paper presented at the meeting of the Association for Women in Psychology, Providence, RI.

Hamilton, S., Rothbart, M., & Dawes, R. M. (1986). Sex bias, diagnosis, and DSM-III. *Sex Roles, 15*(5–6), 269–274.

Hampson, E. (1990). Estrogen-related variations in human spatial and articulatory-motor skills. *Psychoneuroendocrinology, 15,* 97–111.

Handerwerk, M. L., Larzelere, R. E., Friman, P. C., & Mitchell, A. M. (1998). The relationship between lethality of attempted suicide and prior communications in a sample of residential youth. *Journal of Adolescence, 21,* 407–414.

Hannan, E. L., Bernard, H. R., Kilburn, H. C., & O'Donnel, J. F. (1992). Gender differences in mortality rates for coronary bypass surgery. *American Heart Journal, 123*(4, pt. 1), 855–872.

Hanson, R. K. (1990). The psychological impact of sexual assault on women and children: A review. *Annals of Sex Research, 3,* 187–232.

Hanson, S. (1986). Chapter 10: Father–child relationships: Beyond *Kramer vs. Kramer.* In R. A. Lewis & M. D. Sussman (Eds.), *Men's changing roles in the family* (pp. 135–150). New York: Haworth Press.

Harding, M. E. (1971). *Women's mysteries: Ancient and modern.* New York: Putnam.

Harding, S. (1986). *The science question in feminism.* Ithaca, NY: Cornell University Press.

Hardy, J. D., Wolff, H. G., & Goodell, H. (1952). *Pain sensation and reactions.* Baltimore: Williams & Wilkins.

Hardy, R., & Kuh, D. (2002). Change in psychological and vasomotor symptom reporting during menopause. *Social Science and Medicine, 55*(11), 1975–1988.

Hare-Mustin, R., & Marecek, J. (1988). The meaning of difference: Gender theory, postmodernism, and psychology. *American Psychologist, 43*(6), 455–464.

Hariton, E. B., & Singer, J. L., (1974). Women's fantasies during sexual intercourse: Normative and theoretical implications. *Journal of Consulting and Clinical Psychology, 42,* 313–322.

Harmon, A. (1999, March 22). With the best of intentions, a game maker fails. *New York Times Business Day.*

Harney, P. A., & Muelenhard, C. L. (1991). Rape. In E. Grauerholtz & M. A. Koralewski (Eds.), *Sexual coercion: A sourcebook on its nature, causes, and prevention* (pp. 3–16). Lexington, MA: Lexington Books.

Harold, S. (1992). Education in later life: The case of older women. *Educational Gerontology, 18*(5), 511–527.

Harper, E. B. (1969). Fear and status of the woman. *Southwestern Journal of Anthropology, 25,* 81–95.

Harré, R., & Lamb, R. (1986). *The dictionary of personality and social psychology.* Cambridge, MA: MIT Press.

Harrington, N. T., & Leitenberg, H. (1994). Relationship between alcohol consumption and victim behaviors immediately preceding sexual aggression by an acquaintance. *Violence and Victims, 9,* 315–324.

Harris, L. (1997). *The Metropolitan Life survey of the American teacher 1997: Examining gender issues in public schools.* New York: Louis Harris and Associates.

Harris, M. B., Begay, C., & Page, P. (1989). Activities, family relationships, and feelings about aging in a multicultural elderly sample. *International Journal of Aging and Human Development, 29*(2), 103–117.

Harrison, A. A., & Saeed, L. (1977). Let's make a deal: An analysis of revelations and stipulations in lonely hearts advertisements. *Journal of Personality and Social Psychology, 35,* 257–264.

Harrison, J., Chin, J., & Ficarrotto, T. (1995). Warning: Masculinity may be dangerous to your health. In M. S. Kimmel & Michael A. Messner (Eds.), *Mens lives* (pp. 237–249). Boston: Allyn and Bacon.

Hatcher, R. A., et al. (1994). *Contraceptive technology 1992–1994* (16th rev. ed.). New York: Irvington Publishers.

Hatcher, R. A., et al. (1998). *Contraceptive technology* (17th rev. ed.). New York: Ardent Media.

Hatfield, E., & Rapson, R. (1996). *Love and sex: Cross-cultural perspectives.* Boston: Allyn and Bacon.

Hatfield, E., & Sprecher, S. (1986). Measuring passionate love in intimate relationships. *Journal of Adolescence, 9,* 383–410.

Hawton, K. (2000). Sex and suicide. *British Journal of Psychiatry, 177,* 484–485.

Hawton, K., Fagg, J., Simkin, S., Bale, E., & Bond, A. (1997). Trends in deliberate self-harm in Oxford, 1985–1995: Implications for clinical services and the prevention of suicide. *British Journal of Psychiatry, 171,* 556–560.

Hayden-Thompson, L., Rubin, K. H., & Hymel, S. (1987). Sex preferences in sociometric choices. *Developmental Psychology, 23,* 558–562.

Haynes, S. G., Harvey, C., Montes, H., Nickens, H., & Cohen, B. (1990). Patterns of cigarette smoking among Hispanics in the United States: Results from the NHANES, 1982–1984. *American Journal of Public Health, 80,* 47–53.

Hays, H. R. (1964). *The dangerous sex: The myth of feminine evil.* New York: Putnam.

Healy, B. (1991). The Yentyl syndrome. *New England Journal of Medicine, 325,* 274–276.

Healy, M., & staff and wire reports. (2002, August 1). Grandparents carry big child-care load, *USA Today,* section 7D.

Heaton, T. B. (2002). Factors contributing to increasing marital stability in the U.S. *Journal of Family Issues, 23*(3), 392–409.

Hedges, L. V., & Nowell, A. (1995). Sex differences in mental test scores, variability, and number of high-scoring individuals. *Science, 269,* 41–45.

Heffernan, K. (1998). Bulimia nervosa. In E. A. Blechman & K. D. Brownell (Eds.), *Behavioral medicine and women: A comprehensive handbook* (pp. 358–363). New York: Guilford Press.

Hegeler, S., & Mortesen, M. (1977). Sexual behavior in elderly Danish males. In R. Gemme & C. Wheeler (Eds.), *Progress in sexology* (pp. 285–292). New York: Plenum Press.

Heider, F. (1958). *The psychology of interpersonal relations.* New York: Wiley.

Heilman, M. (1983). Sex bias in work settings: The lack of fit model. *Research and Organizational Behavior, 5,* 269–298.

Heilman, M. E. (1994). Affirmative action: Some unintended consequences for working women. *Research in Organizational Behavior, 16,* 125–169.

Heinz, J. P., & Laumann, E. O. (1982). *Chicago lawyers: The social structure of the bar.* New York: Russell Sage.

Heise, L. (1994). *Violence against women: The hidden health burden.* Washington, DC: WorldBank Discussion Papers. From Landes, Foster, & Cessna, 1995.

Heise, L. L. (1996). Violence against women: Global organizing for change. In J. L. Edleson & Z. C. Eisikovits (Eds.), *Future interventions with battered women and their families* (pp. 7–33). Thousand Oaks, CA: Sage.

Helgeson, V. S. (1994). Relation of agency and communion to well-being: Evidence and potential explanations. *Psychological Bulletin, 116,* 412–428.

Helgeson, V. S., & Fritz, H. L. (1998). A theory of unmitigated communion. *Personality and Social Psychology Review, 2,* 173–183.

Helms, J. E. (1984). Toward a theoretical explanation of the effects of race on counseling. A Black and White model. *The Counseling Psychologist, 13,* 695–710.

Helms, J. E. (1990). *Black and White racial identity: Theory, research, and practice.* Westport, CT: Greenwood Press.

Helms, J. E. (1995). An update of Helms's White and people of color racial identity models. In J. G. Ponterotto, J. M. Casas, L. A. Suzuki, & C. M. Alexander (Eds.), *Handbook of multicultural counseling* (pp. 181–198). Thousand Oaks, CA: Sage.

Helms, J. E., & Talleyrand, R. M. (1997). Race is not ethnicity. *American Psychologist, 52,* 1246–1247.

Helson, R., Mitchell, V., & Moane, G. (1984). Personality and patterns of adherence and nonadherence to the social clock. *Journal of Personality and Social Psychology, 46,* 1079–1096.

Helstrom, A. W., & Blechman, A. E. (1998). Section editor's overview. In A. E. Blechman & K. D. Brownell (Eds.), *Behavioral medicine and women: A comprehensive handbook* (pp. 813–815). New York: Guilford Press.

Hemming, H. (1985). Women in a man's world: Sexual harassment. *Human Behavior, 38,* 67–79.

Hendrick, C., & Hendrick, S. (1986). A theory and method of love. *Journal of Personality and Social Psychology, 50,* 392–402.

Henry, T. (1998, October 14). Girls lagging as gender gap widens in tech education. *USA Today,* p. 4D.

Henschke, C. (2003, March 21). Role of CT screening for lung cancer, Part 1, pros and cons persist. *Medscape Radiology,* pp. 1–6. Retrieved April 7, 2004 from www.medscape.com/viewarticle/450877?src=search.

Henshaw, S. K., & Silverman, J. (1988). The characteristics and prior contraceptive use of U.S. abortion patients. *Family Planning Perspectives, 20,* 158–168.

Herbert, B. (1997, October 30). China's missing girls. *New York Times,* p. A31.

Herek, G. H. (1995). Psychological heterosexism and anti-gay violence: The social psychology of bigotry and bashing. In M. S. Kimmel & M. A. Messner (Eds.), *Men's lives* (3rd ed., pp. 341–353). Boston: Allyn and Bacon.

Herrnstein, R. J., & Murray, C. (1994). *The bell curve: Intelligence and class structure in American life.* New York: Free Press.

Hersch, P. (1991, January/February). Secret lives: Lesbian and gay teens in fear of discovery. *The Family Therapy Networker,* pp. 36–39, 41–43.

Hess, B. B., Markson, E. W., & Stein, P. J. (1993). *Sociology,* 4th edition. New York: MacMillan.

Hetherington, E. M. (1967). The effects of familial variables on sex-typing, on parent–child similarity, and on imitation in children. In J. P. Hill (Ed.), *Minnesota symposia on child psychology* (Vol. 1). Minneapolis: University of Minnesota Press.

Hetherington, E. M. (1989). Coping with family transitions: Winners, losers, and survivors. *Child Development, 60,* 1–14.

Hetherington, E. M., Cox, M., & Cox, R. (1982). Effects of divorce on parents and children. In M. Lamb (Ed.), *Nontraditional families* (pp. 233–288). Hillsdale, NJ: Erlbaum.

Hewlett, S. A., (2002). *Creating a life: Professional women and the quest for children.* New York: Talk Miramax.

Higginbotham, E. (1997). Introduction. In A. Stromberg, B. A. Gutek, & L. Larwood (Eds.), *Women and work: Exploring race, ethnicity and class* (Vol. 6, pp. xv–xxxii). Beverly Hills, CA: Sage.

Hill, C. T., Peplau, L. A., & Rubin, Z. (1981). Differing perceptions in dating couples: Sex roles vs. alternative explanations. *Psychology of Women Quarterly, 5,* 418–434.

Hill, I. (1989). *The bisexual spouse.* New York: Harper & Row.

Hill, J. P. (1988). Adapting to menarche: Familial control and conflict. In M. R. Gunnar & W. A. Collins (Eds.). *Development during the transition to adolescence. Minnesota symposia on child development* Vol. 21, (pp. 207–223). Hillsdale, NJ: Erlbaum.

Hill, J. P., & Holmbeck, G. N. (1987). Familial adaptation to biological change during adolescence. In R. M. Lerner & T. T. Foch (Eds.), *Biological–psychosocial interactions in early adolescence* (pp. 207–223). Hillsdale, NJ: Erlbaum.

Hill, J. P., & Lynch, M. E. (1983). The intensification of gender-related role expectations during early adolescence. In J. Brooks-Gunn & A. C. Petersen (Eds.), *Girls at puberty* (pp. 201–228). New York: Plenum Press.

Hill, M. E., & Augoustinos, M. (1997). Re examining gender bias in achievement attributions. *Australian Journal of Psychology, 49,* 85–90.

Hilton, T. L. (1987). Demography, demagoguery, and test performance. In J. A. Sechzer & S. M. Pfafflin (Eds.), *Psychology and educational policy. Annals of the New York Academy of Sciences, 517,* 29–38.

Hines, M. (1990). Gonadal hormones and human cognitive development. In J. Balthazart (Ed.), *Brain and behavior in vertebrates 1: Sexual differentiation, neuroanatomical aspects, neurotransmitters and neuropeptides* (pp. 51–63). Basel, Switzerland: Karger.

Hines, P., & Boyd-Franklin, N. (1982). Black families. In M. McGoldrick, J. K. Pearce, & J. Giordano (Eds.), *Ethnicity and family therapy* (pp. 84–107). New York: Guilford Press.

Hite, S. (1981). *The Hite report on male sexuality.* New York: Knopf.

Hitt, J. (1998, January). Who will do abortions here? *New York Times Magazine,* pp. 20ff.

Hochschild, A. (1989). *The second shift.* New York: Viking.

Hochschild, A. (1997). *The time bind: When work becomes home and home becomes work.* New York: Metropolitan Books.

Hochschild, A. R. (1978). *The unexpected community: Portrait of an old-age subculture.* Berkeley: University of California Press.

Hodson, S., & Pryor, B. (1984). Sex discrimination in the courtroom: Attorney's gender and credibility. *Psychological Reports, 55,* 483–486.

Hoeffer, B. (1981). Children's acquisition of sex-role behavior in lesbian-mother families. *American Journal of Orthopsychiatry, 51,* 536–544.

Hoffman, C. & Hurst, N. (1990). Gender stereotypes. *Journal of Personality and Social Psychology, 58,* 197–208.

Hoffman, L. (1972). Early childhood experiences and women's achievement motives. *Journal of Social Issues, 28,* 129–155.

Hoffman, L. W. (1989). Effects of maternal employment in the two-person family. *American Psychologist, 44,* 283–292.

Hoffman, L., Clinebell, S., & Kilpatrick, J. (1997). Office romances: The new battleground over employees' rights to privacy and the employer's right to intervene. *Employee Responsibilities and Rights Journal, 10,* 263–275.

Hofman, M. A., & Swaab, D. F. (1989). The sexually dimorphic nucleus in the preoptic area in the human brain: a comparative morphometric study. *Journal of Anatomy, 164,* 55–72.

Hogg, J., & Frank, M. (1992). Toward an interpersonal model of codependence and contradependence. *Journal of Counseling and Development, 70,* 371–375.

Holcomb, D. R., Holcomb, L. C., Sondag, K., & Williams, N. (1991). Attitudes about date rape: Gender differences among college students. *College Student Journal, 25,* 434–439.

Holden, C. (1997). Changing sex is hard to do. *Science, 275,* 1745.

Holden, C. (1997, April 25). Early puberty getting more common. *Science, 276,* 537.

Hollingworth, L. S. (1914). Functional periodicity: An experimental study of the mental and motor abilities of women during menstruation. *Teachers College Contributions to Education, 69.*

Hollingworth, L. S. (1916). Social devices for impelling women to bear and rear children. *American Journal of Sociology, 22,* 19–29.

Hollis, L. A. (1994). Women's issues in later adulthood: Psychosocial adjustment, satisfaction, and health. Poster paper presented at the American Psychological Association Women's Health Conference, Washington, DC.

Hollon, S. D., Thase, M. E., Markowitz, J. C. (2002, November). Treatment and prevention of depression. *Psychological Science, 3*(2), 39–77.

Holloway, M. H. (1994, August). Trends in women's health: A global view. *Scientific American,* pp. 76–83.

Hong, L. K., & Duff, R. W. (1994). Widows in retirement communities: The social context of subjective well-being. *The Gerontologist, 34,* 347–352.

hooks, b. (1981). *Ain't I a woman?* Boston: South End Press.

hooks, b. (1984). *Feminist theory: From margin to center.* Boston: South End Press.

hooks, b. (1992). Eating the other. In b. hooks, *Black looks: Race and representation* (pp. 21–39). Boston: Gloria Watkins/South End Press.

hooks, b. (1993a). *Sisters of the yam.* Boston: South End Press.

hooks, b. (1993b). Violence in intimate relationships: A feminist perspective. In A. Minas (Ed.), *Gender basics: A feminist perspective on women and men* (pp. 205–209). Belmont, CA: Wadsworth.

Hopkins v. Price Waterhouse, 618 F. Supp. 1109 (D.D.C. 1985).

Hopkins, J., Campbell, B., & Marcus, M. (1987). Role of infant related stressors in post-partum depression. *Journal of Abnormal Psychology, 96,* 237–241.

Hopps, J. (1982). Oppression based on color. *Social Work, 27,* 1, 3–5.

Horn, J. L., & Donaldson, G. (1980). Cognitive development II: Adulthood development of human abilities. In O. G. Brim & J. Kagan (Eds.), *Constancy and change in human development.* Cambridge, MA: Harvard University Press.

Horner, M. (1969, June). Fail bright women. *Psychology Today,* p. 36.

Hornsey, M., & Hogg, M. (2000). Assimilation and diversity: An integrative model of subgroup relations. *Personality and Social Psychology Review, 4,* 143–156.

Hossain, Z., & Roopnarine, J. L. (1993). Division of household labor and child care in dual-earner African-American families with infants. *Sex Roles, 29,* 571–583.

Hotaling, C. T., & Sugarman, D. B. (1986). An analysis of risk markers in husband and wife violence: The current state of knowledge. *Violence and Victims, 1,* 101–124.

House, W. C. (1974). Actual and perceived differences in male and female expectancies and minimal goal levels as a function of competition. *Journal of Personality, 42,* 493–509.

Houseknecht, S. K. (1979). Timing of the decision to remain voluntarily childless: Evidence for continuous socialization. *Psychology of Women Quarterly, 4,* 81–96.

Howard, J. A., Blumstein, P., & Schwartz, P. (1987). Social or evolutionary theories: Some observations on preferences in human mate selection. *Journal of Personality and Social Psychology, 53,* 194–200.

Hoyenga, K. B., & Hoyenga, K. T. (1993). *Gender related differences: Origins and outcome.* Boston: Allyn and Bacon.

Hrdy, S. B. (1997). Raising Darwin's Consciousness: Female sexuality and the prehominid origins of patriarchy. *Human Nature, 8*(1) 1–49.

Huang, K., & Uba, L. (1992). Premarital sexual behavior among Chinese college students in the United States. *Archives of Sexual Behavior, 21,* 227–240.

Huff, C. W., & Cooper, J. (1987, June). Sex bias in educational software: The effects of designers' stereotypes on the software they design. *Journal of Applied Social Psychology, 17,* 519–532.

Hughes, J. O., & Sandler, B. R. (1988). Peer harassment: Hassles for women on campus. *Project on the status and education of women.* Washington, DC: Association of American Colleges.

Hull, L. W. H. (1959). *History and philosophy of science* (pp. 1–33). London: William Cloves and Sons, Ltd.

Hull, T. H. (1990). Recent trends in sex ratios at birth in China. *Population and Development Review, 16,* 63–83.

Hultin, M. (2003). Some take the glass escalator, some hit the glass ceiling? Career consequences of occupational sex segregation. *Work and Occupations, 30*(1), 30–61.

Human Rights Watch News. (2000). *Taking cover: Women in post-Taliban Afghanistan.* Retrieved www.hrw.org/backgrounder/wrd/afghan-women-2k2.htm.

Humm, M. (1992). First wave feminism. In M. Humm (Ed.), *Modern feminisms: Political, literary, cultural.* New York: Columbia University Press.

Hung, J., Chaitman, B. R., Lam, J., Lesperance, J., Dupras, G., Fines, P., & Bourassa, M. G. (1984). Noninvasive diagnostic test choices for the evaluation of coronary artery disease in women: A multivariate comparison of cardiac fluoroscopy, exercise electrocardiography and exercise thallium myocardial perfusion scintigraphy. *Journal of the American College of Cardiology, 4*(1), 8–22.

Hunt, M. (1974). *Sexual behavior in the 1970's.* New York: Dell Books.

Hunter College Women's Studies Collective. (in press). *Women's realities, women's choices* (3rd ed.). New York: Oxford University Press.

Hunter College Women's Studies Collective. (1995). *Women's realities; Women's choices* (2nd ed.). New York: Oxford.

Hunter, M. S., & Liao, K. L. M. (1994). Intentions to use hormone replacement therapy in a community sample of 45-year-old women. *Maturitas, 20*(1), 13–23.

Hunter, R. H. F. (1995). *Sex determination, differentiation and intersexuality in placental mammals.* Cambridge, UK: Cambridge University Press.

Hurtado, A., Hayes-Bastista, D. E., Burciaga, D. Valdez, R., & Hernandez, A. (1992). *Redefining California: Latino social engagement in a multicultural society.* Los Angeles, CA: UCLA Chicano Studies Research Center.

Huselid, R. F., & Cooper, M. L. (1994). Gender roles as mediators of sex differences in expressions of pathology. *Journal of Abnormal Psychology, 103,* 595–603.

Huston, A. C., & Alvarez, M. (1990). The socialization context of gender role development in early development. In R. Montemayer, G. R. Adams, & T. P. Gullota (Eds.), *From childhood to adolescence: A transitional period?* (pp. 156–179). Newbury Park, CA: Sage.

Hyde, J. (1984). How large are gender differences in aggression? A developmental meta-analysis. *Developmental Psychology, 20,* 722–736.

Hyde, J., & Jaffe, S. (2000). Becoming a heterosexual adult: The experiences of young women. *Journal of Social Issues, 56*(2), 283–296.

Hyde, J. S. (1981). How large are cognitive gender differences? A meta-analysis using w2 and d. *American Psychologist, 36,* 892–901.

Hyde, J. S. (1984). Children's understanding of sexist language. *Developmental Psychology, 20*(4), 697–706.

Hyde, J. S. (1985). *Half the human experience.* Lexington, MA., D. C. Heath.

Hyde, J. S. (1996). *Understanding human sexuality.* New York: McGraw-Hill.

Hyde, J. S., & DeLamater, J. (1999). *Understanding human sexuality.* New York: McGraw-Hill.

Hyde, J. S., & Essex, M. J. (Eds.). (1991). *Parental leave and childcare: Setting a research and policy agenda.* Philadelphia: Temple University Press.

Hyde, J. S., Essex, M. J., & Horton, F. (1993). Fathers' parental leave: Attitudes and experiences. *Journal of Family Issues, 14,* 616–638.

Hyde, J. S., Fennema, E., & Lamon, S. J. (1990). Gender differences in mathematics performance: A meta-analysis. *Psychological Bulletin, 107,* 139–155.

Hyde, J. S., Fennema, E., Ryan, M., Frost, L., & Hopp, C. (1990). Gender comparisons of mathematics attitudes and affects: A meta-analysis. *Psychology of Women Quarterly, 14,* 299–324.

Hyde, J. S., Klein, M. H., Essex, M. J., & Clark, R. (1995). Maternity leave and women's mental health. *Psychology of Women Quarterly, 19,* 257–285.

Hyde, J. S., Krajnik, M., & Skuldt-Niederberger, K. (1991). Androgyny across the life span: A replication and longitudinal follow-up. *Developmental Psychology, 27,* 516–519.

Hyde, J. S., & Linn, M. C. (Eds.). (1986). *The psychology of gender: Advances through meta-analysis.* Baltimore: Johns Hopkins University Press.

Hyde, J. S., & Plant, E. A. (1995). Magnitude of psychological gender differences. *American Psychologist, 50,* 159–161.

Ickovics, J. R., & Rodin, J. (1992). Women and AIDS in the United States: Epidemiology, natural history, and mediating mechanisms. *Health Psychology, 11,* 1–16.

Iglitzen, L. B., & Ross, R. (Eds.). (1986). *Women in the world 1975–1985: The women's decade.* Santa Barbara, CA: ABC/Clio.

Iijima Hall, C. (1997). Cultural malpractice: The growing obsolescence of psychology with the changing U.S. population. *American Psychologist, 52*(6), 642–651.

Imamoglu, E. O., Kuller, R., Imamoglu, V., & Kuller, M. (1993). The social psychological worlds of Swedes and Turks in and around retirement. *Journal of Cross-Cultural Psychology, 24*(1), 26–41.

Imperato-McGinley, J., & Peterson, R. (1976). Male pseudohermaphroditism: The complexities of male phenotypic development. *American Journal of Medicine, 61,* 251–272.

Imperato-McGinley, J., Peterson, R. E., Gaultieret, T., & Sturla, E. (1979). Androgens and the evolution of male gender identity among male pseudohermaphrodites with 5α-reductase deficiency. *New England Journal of Medicine, 300*(22), 1233–1237.

Indian Health Service. (1989). *Indian health service: Trends in Indian health.* Washington, DC: U.S. Department of Health and Human Services.

Ingrassia, M. (1995, April 24). The body of the beholder. *Newsweek,* pp. 66–67.

Ingrassia, M., & Beck, M. (1994, July 4). Patterns of abuse. *Newsweek,* pp. 26–33.

Ippolitov, F. W. (1973). Interanalyser differences in sensitivity–strength parameter for vision, hearing, and cutaneous modalities. In V. D. Nebylitsyn & J. A. Gray (Eds.), *Biological bases of individual behaviour* (pp. 43–61). New York: Academic Press.

Ireland, M. S. (1993). *Reconceiving women: Separating motherhood from female identity.* New York: Guilford.

Irvine, J. J. (1986). Teacher–student interactions: Effects of student race, sex, and grade level. *Journal of Educational Psychology, 78*(1), 14–21.

Irwin, J. L. (1979). *Womanhood in radical Protestantism 1525–1675.* Toronto, Canada: Edwin Mellon Press.

Isay, R. A. (1990). Psychoanalytic theory and the therapy of gay men. In D. P. McWhirter, S. A. Sanders, & J. A. M. Reinisch (Eds.), *Homosexuality/heterosexuality: Concepts of sexual orientation* (pp. 283–303). New York: Oxford University Press.

Ishii-Kuntz, M., & Coltrane, S. (1992). Predicting the sharing of household labor: Are parenting and housework distinct? *Sociological Perspectives, 35,* 629–647.

Israel, J., Poland, N., Reame, N., & Warner, D. (1980). *Surviving the change: A practical guide to menopause.* Detroit: Cinnabar.

Iwao, S. (1993). *The Japanese woman: Traditional image and changing reality.* New York: Free Press.

Jaccoma, G., & Denmark, F. L. (1974). Boys or girls: The hows and whys. Unpublished master's thesis, Hunter College, New York, NY.

Jacklin, C. N. (1981). Methodological issues in the study of sex-related differences. *Developmental Review, 1,* 266–273.

Jackson, A. (1990, Fall). Evolution of ethnocultural psychotherapy. *Psychotherapy, 27*(3), 428–435.

Jackson, A. P. (1993). Black, single, working mothers in poverty: Preferences for employment, well-being, and perceptions of preschool-age children. *Social Work, 38*(1), 26–34.

Jackson, L. A., & Ervin, K. S. (1992). Height stereotypes of women and men: The liabilities of shortness for both sexes. *Journal of Social Psychology, 132,* 433–445.

Jackson, L. C., & Greene, B. (2000). *Psychotherapy with African American women: Innovations in psychodynamic perspectives and practice.* New York: The Guilford Press.

Jackson, M. (1987). "Facts of life" or the eroticization of women's oppression? Sexology and the social construction of homosexuality. In P. Caplan (Ed.), *The cultural construction of sexuality* (pp. 52–61). London: Tavistock.

Jackson, P. R. (1988). Personal networks, support mobilization and unemployment. *Psychological Medicine, 18*(2), 397–404.

Jacob, I. (2002). *My sisters' voices: Teenage girls of color speak out.* New York: Holt.

Jacobi, C., Hayward, C., & de Zwaan, M. (2004). Coming to terms with risk factors for eating disorders: Application of risk terminology and suggestions for a general taxonomy. *Psychological Bulletin, 130*(1), 19–65.

Jacobs, G., Dauphinais, P., Gross, S., & Guzman, L. (1991). *American Psychological Association site visitation report.* Washington, DC: American Psychological Association.

Jacobs, J. A., & Gerson, K. (2001). Overworked individuals or overworked families? Explaining trends in work, leisure, and family time. *Work & Occupations, 28*(1), 40–63.

Jacobs, J. A.; & Labov, T. (2002). Gender differentials in intermarriage among sixteen race and ethnic groups. *Sociological Forum, 17*(4), 621–646.

Jacobs, P. A. (1969). The chromosome basis of some types of intersexuality in man. *Journal of Reproduction and Fertility* (Suppl. 7), 73–78. Cited by Hunter, 1995, p. 214.

Jacobs, R. H. (1994). His and her aging: Differences, difficulties, dilemmas, delights. *Journal of Geriatric Psychiatry, 27*(1), 113–128.

Jacobson, M. F. (1998). *Whiteness of a different color: European immigrants and the alchemy of race.* Cambridge, MA: Harvard University Press.

Jaffee, S., & Hyde, J. S. (2000). Gender differences in moral orientation: A meta-analysis. *Psychological Bulletin, 126*(5), 703–726.

Jaimes, M. A. (1982). Towards a new image of American Indian women. *Journal of American Indian Education, 22*(1), 18–32.

Jalilvand, M. (2000). Married women, work, and values. *Monthly Labor Review, 123*(8), 26–31.

James, A. N. (2001). Educating boys: A comparison of educational attitudes of male graduates of single-sex and coed schools. *Dissertation Abstracts International, 62*(1A), 77.

Janelli, L. M. (1993). Are there body image differences between older men and women? *Western Journal of Nursing Research, 15*(3), 327–339.

Janowsky, J. S., Oviatt, S. K., & Orwoll, E. S. (1994). Testosterone influences in spatial cognition in older men. *Behavioral Neuroscience, 108,* 325–332.

Janus, S. S., & Janus, C. L. (1993). *The Janus report on sexual behavior.* New York: Wiley.

Jaques, E. (1965). Death and the mid-life crisis. *The International Journal of Psycho-Analysis and the Bulletin of the International Psycho-Analytic Association, 46*(4), 502–512.

Jeffe, S. B. (1995, April 20). Equity the key for women. *USA Today,* p. 13A.

Jensen, A. R. (1985). The nature of the black–white difference on various psychometric tests: Spearman's hypothesis. *Behavioral and Brain Sciences, 8,* 193–263.

Jewish population of the world. *Jewish Virtual Library of the American-Israeli Cooperative Enterprise.* (2004).

Jeynes, W. H. (2001). The effects of recent parental divorce on their children's consumption of alcohol. *Journal of Youth and Adolescence, 30*(3), 305–319.

Johansson, S., & Nygren, O. (1991) The missing girls of China: A new demographic account. *Population and Development Review, 17*(1) 40–41.

Johnson, C. L. (1994). Differential expectations and realities: Race, socioeconomic status, and health of the oldest old. *International Journal of Ageing and Human Development, 38,* 13–27.

Johnson, K., and Ferguson, T. (1990). *Trusting Ourselves: The Sourcebook on the Psychology of Women.* Atlantic Monthly Press.

Johnson, M. Personal communications, May 15, 1998.

Johnson, M. M. (1963). Sex role learning in the nuclear family. *Child Development, 34,* 319–333.

Johnson, M. M. (1977). Fathers, mothers, and sex typing. In E. M. Hetherington & R. D. Parke (Eds.), *Contemporary readings in child psychology.* New York: McGraw-Hill.

Johnson, P. (1976). Women and power: Toward a theory of effectiveness. *Journal of Social Issues, 32,* 99–110.

Johnson, W. D., Kayser, K. L., & Pedraza, P. M. (1984). Angina pectoris and coronary bypass surgery: Patterns of prevalence and recurrence in 3,105 consecutive patients followed up to 11 years. *American Heart Journal 108*(4), 1190–1197.

Johnston-Robledo, I. (2000). From postpartum depression to the empty nest syndrome. In J. C. Chrisler, C. Golden, & P. D. Rozee (Eds.), *Lectures on the psychology of women.* New York: McGraw-Hill.

Jones, E. F., et al. (1985). Teenage pregnancy in developed countries: Determinants and policy implications. *Family Planning Perspectives, 17,* 53–62.

Jones, J. (1985). *Labor of love, labor of sorrow: Black women, work, and family from slavery to the present.* New York: Basic Books.

Jones, J. M. (1991). Psychological models of race: What have they been and what should they be? In J. Goodchilds (Ed.), *Psychological perspectives on human diversity in America* (pp. 3–46). Washington, DC: American Psychological Association.

Journal of the American Medical Association. (2002). Women and heart disease, vol. 288, 3230.

Jue, D., Meador, K. J., Zamrini, E. Y., Allen, M. E., et al. (1992). Differential effects of aging on directional and absolute errors in visuospatial memory. *Neuropsychology, 6*(4), 331–339.

Just for Catholics. (2003, September 27). *Priests and sexual abuse.* Retrieved January 7, 2004, from www.justforcatholics.org/a104.htm.

Kahn, A. S., & Yoder, J. D. (1989). The psychology of women and conservatism: Rediscovering social change. *Psychology of Women Quarterly, 13,* 417–432.

Kaiser, K. (1990). Cross-cultural perspectives on menopause. In M. Flint, F. Kronenberg, & W. Utian (Eds.), *Multidiscipli-nary perspectives on menopause. Annals of the New York Academy of Sciences, 592,* 430–432.

Kalb, M. (2002). Does sex matter? The confluence of gender and transference in analytic space. *Psychoanalytic Psychology, 19*(1), 118–143.

Kalick, S. M., & Hamilton, T. E. (1986). The matching hypothesis reexamined. *Journal of Personality and Social Psychology, 51,* 673–682.

Kalleburg, A. L., & VanBuren, M. E. (1996). Is bigger better? Explaining the relationship between organization size and job rewards. *American Sociological Review,* 47–66.

Kallman, F. J. (1952). Comparative twin study on the genetic aspects of male homosexuality. *Journal of Nervous and Mental Disease, 115,* 283–298.

Kammeyer, K. C. W. (1990). *Marriage and family: A foundation for personal decisions* (2nd ed.). Boston: Allyn & Bacon.

Kanamine, L. (1997, March 11). Citadel punishes 10 for harassment. *USA Today,* p. 1A.

Kanter, R. M. (1977a). *Men and women of the corporation.* New York: Basic Books.

Kanter, R. M. (1977b). Some effects of proportions on group life: Skewed sex ratios and responses to token women. *American Journal of Sociology, 82,* 965–990.

Kantrowitz, B. (March 1, 2004). The new face of marriage. *Newsweek.* Retrieved March 14, 2004 from www.keepmedia.com.

Kantrowitz, B., & Kalb, B. (1988, May 11). Boys will be boys. *Newsweek,* pp. 54–60.

Kantrowitz, B., & Springen, K. (2003, October 13). Free at last! *Newsweek,* pp. 62–64.

Kaplan, D. L., & Keys, C. B. (1997). Sex and relationship variables as predictors of sexual attraction in cross-sex platonic friendships between young heterosexual adults. *Journal of Social and Personal Relationships, 14,* 191–206.

Kaplan, H. S. (1979). *Disorders of sexual desire.* New York: Simon & Schuster.

Kaplan, H. S. (1987). *Sexual aversion, sexual phobias, and panic disorder.* New York: Brunner/Mazel.

Kaplan, R. M., Sallis J. F., Jr., & Patterson, T. L. (1993). *Health and human behavior* (pp. 162–164). New York, New York: McGraw-Hill.

Karkau, K. (1973). *Sexism in the fourth grade.* Pittsburgh, PA: Know, Inc.

Kaslow, F. W., Hansson, K., & Lunblad, A. M. (1994). Long term marriages in Sweden: And some comparisons with similar couples in the United States. *Contemporary Family Therapy: An International Journal, 16,* 521–537.

Kassing, L. R., & Prieto, L. R. (2003). The rape myth and blame-based beliefs of counselors-in-training toward male victims of rape. *Journal of Counseling and Development, 81*(4), 455–461.

Katz, D. M. (1997). Too young to date? In A. M. Meehan & E. Astor-Stetson (Eds.), *Adolescent psychology* (pp. 162–163). Guilford, CT: Dushkin Publishing Group/Brown & Benchmark Publishers.

Katz, P. A. (1979). The development of female identity. In C. B. Kopp & M. Kirpatrick (Eds.), *Becoming female: Perspectives on development* (pp. 3–28). New York: Plenum Press.

Katz, P. A., & Ksansnak, K. R. (1994). Developmental aspects of gender role flexibility and traditionality in middle childhood and adolescence. *Developmental Psychology, 30*(2), 272–282.

Kaufert, P. (1982). Myth and the menopause. *Sociology of Health and Illness, 4,* 141–166.

Kaufman, J. (1998). Adolescent females' perception of autonomy and control. In M. B. Nadien & F. L. Denmark (Eds.), *Females and autonomy: A life-span perspective* (pp. 43–72). Boston: Allyn and Bacon.

Kaw, E. (1993). Medicalization of racial features: Asian American women and cosmetic surgery. *Medical Anthropology Quarterly, 7,* 74–89.

Keith, J. B., et al. (1991). Sexual activity and contraceptive use among low-income urban Black adolescent females. *Adolescence, 26,* 269–785.

Keller, E. F. (1982). Feminism and science. In N. O. Koehane et al. (Eds.), *Feminist theory: A critique of ideology.* Brighton: Harvester.

Keller, E. F. (1992). Feminism and science. In M. Humm (Ed.), *Modern feminisms: Political, literary, cultural.* (pp. 312–317). New York: Columbia University Press.

Kelley, K., & Streeter, D. (1992). The roles of gender in organizations. In K. Kelley (Ed.), *Issues, theory, and research in industrial/organizational psychology.* Amsterdam: Elsevier Science Publishers.

Kelly, G. F. (2004). *Sexuality today: The human perspective* (7th ed.). New York: McGraw-Hill.

Kelly, M. P., Strassberg, D. S., & Kircher, J. R. (1990). Attitudinal and experiential correlates of anorgasmia. *Archives of Sexual Behavior, 19,* 165–177.

Kelly, P. J., Blacksin, B., & Mason, E. (2001). Factors affecting substance abuse treatment completion for women. *Issues in Mental Health Nursing, 22,* 287–304.

Kemeny, M. M. (1994). Breast cancer in the United States. In J. A. Sechzer, A. Griffin, & S. M. Pfafflin (Eds.), *Forging a women's health research agenda: Policy issues for the 1990's. Annals of the New York Academy of Sciences, 736,* pp. 122–130.

Kemeny, M. M., Wellisch, D. K., & Schain, W. S. (1988) Psychosocial outcome in a randomized surgical trial for treatment of primary breast cancer. *Cancer, 62,* 1231–1237.

Kendall, D. (1997). *Race, class, and gender in a diverse society.* Boston: Allyn and Bacon.

Kendler, K. S., et al. (2000). Child sexual abuse and adult psychiatric and substance abuse disorders in women: An epidemiological and co-twin control analysis. *Archives of General Psychiatry, 57*(10), 953–959.

Kendler, K. S., Davis, C. G., & Kessler, R. C. (1997). The familial aggregation of common psychiatric and substance abuse disorders in the National Comorbidity Survey: A family history study. *British Journal of Psychiatry, 170,* 541–548.

Kendler, K. S., MacLean, C., Neale, M., Kessler, R., Heath, A., & Eaves, L. (1991). The genetic epidemiology of bulimia nervosa. *American Journal of Psychiatry, 148,* 1627–1637.

Kennedy, M., Moore, J., Schuman, P., Schoenbaum, E., Zierler, S., Rompalo, A., & Chu, S. Y. (1998). Sexual behavior of HIV-infected women reporting recent sexual contact with women. *Journal of the American Medical Association, 280*(1), 29–30.

Kerig, P. K., Cowan, P. A., & Cowan, C. P. (1993). Marital quality and gender differences in parent–child interaction. *Developmental Psychology, 29*(6), 931–939.

Kerwin, C., & Ponterotto, J. G. (1995). Biracial identity development: theory and research. In J. G. Ponterotto, J. M. Casas, L. A. Suzuki, & C. M. Alexander (Eds.), *Handbook of multicultural counseling* (pp. 199–217). Thousand Oaks, CA: Sage.

Kessler, R. C. (2000a). Gender differences in major depression: Epidemiological findings. In E. Frank (Ed.), *Gender and its effects on psychopathology* (pp. 61–84). Washington, DC: American Psychiatric Press.

Kessler, R. C. (2000b). Gender differences in the prevalence and correlates of mood disorders in the general population. In M. Steiner, K. A. Yonkers, & E. Eriksson (Eds.), *Mood disorders in women* (pp. 15–33). London: Martin Dunitz.

Kessler, R. C. (2003). Epidemiology of women and depression. *Journal of Affective Disorders, 74,* 5–13.

Kessler, R. C., McGonagle, K. A., Swartz, M., Blazer, D. G., & Nelson, C. B. (1993). Sex and depression in the National Comorbidity Survey I: Lifetime prevalence, chronicity, and recurrence. *Journal of Affective Disorders, 29,* 85–96.

Kessler, R. C., McGonagle, K. A., Zhao, S., Nelson, C. B., et al. (1994). Lifetime and 12-month prevalence of DSM-III-R psychiatric disorders in the United States: Results from the National Comorbidity Study. *Archives of General Psychiatry, 51*(1), 8–19.

Keye, W. R. (1999). Medical aspects on infertility for the counselor. In L. H. Burns & S. N. Covington (Eds.), *Infertility counseling: A comprehensive handbook for clinicians* (pp. 27–46). New York: Parthenon.

Khan, D., & Mohajer, S. (2003, October 13). Never had a chance. *Newsday,* p. A3.

Kibria, N., Barnett, R. C., Baruch, G. K., Marshall, N. L., & Pleck, J. H. (1990). Homemaking-role quality and the psychological well-being and distress of employed women. *Sex Roles, 22*(5/6), 327–347.

Kidder, L. H., Lafleur, R. A., & Wells, C. V. (1995). Recalling harassment, reconstructing experience. *Journal of Social Issues, 51,* 117–138.

Kiebzak, G. M., et al. (2002). Undertreatment of osteoporosis in men with hip fracture. *Archives of Internal Medicine, 12,* 2217–2222.

Kilbey, M. M., & Burgermeister, D. (2001). Substance abuse. In *Encyclopedia of women and gender* (Vol. 2). New York: Academic Press.

Kilbourne, J. (1987). *Killing us softly: Advertising images of women.* Film available from Jean Kilbourne, P. O. Box 385, Cambridge, MA: Cambridge Documentary Films.

Kilmartin, C. T. (1994). *The masculine self.* New York: Macmillan.

Kim, E. H., & Otani, J. (1983). Asian women in America. In E. H. Kim (Ed.), *With silk wings: Asian American women at work.* Oakland, CA: Asian Women United of California.

Kim, T. L. (1993). Life in Korea. In L. L. Adler (Ed.), *International handbook on gender roles* (pp. 187–198). Westport, CT: Greenwood Press.

Kimball, M. M. (1995). *Feminist visions of gender similarities and differences.* Binghamton, NY: Haworth Press.

Kimmel, D.C. (1988). Ageism, psychology, and public policy. *American Psychologist, 43,* 175–178.

Kimura, D. (1987). Are men's and women's brains really different? *Canadian Journal of Psychology, 28,* 133–147.

Kimura, D. (1996). Sex, sexual orientation, and sex hormones influence human cognitive function. *Current Opinion in Neurobiology, 6,* 259–263.

Kimura, D., & Hampson, E. (1994). Cognitive patterns in men and women is influenced by fluctuations in sex hormones. *Psychological Science, 3,* 57–61.

Kincaid-Elders, E. (1982). Bad maps for an unknown region: Menopause from a literary perspective. In A. M. Voda, M. Dinnerstein, & S. R. O'Donnell (Eds.), *Changing perspectives on menopause* (pp. 24–38). Austin, TX: University of Texas Press.

King, M. C. (1992). Occupational segregation by race and sex, 1940–1988. *Monthly Labor Review, 115*(4), 30–37.

Kinsey, A. C., Pomeroy, W. B., & Martin, C. E. (1948). *Sexual behavior in the human male.* Philadelphia: Saunders.

Kinsey, A. C., Pomeroy, W. B., Martin, C. E., & Gebhard, P. H. (1953). *Sexual behavior in the human female.* Philadelphia: Saunders.

Kirschner, J. T. (1995). AIDS and suicide. *Journal of Family Practice, 41*(5), 493–496.

Kistner, J., Metzler, A., Gatlin, D., & Risi, S. (1993). Classroom racial proportions and children's peer relations: Race and gender effects. *Journal of Educational Psychology, 85*(3), 446–452.

Kitson, G. C., & Sussman, M. B. (1982). Marital complaints, demographic characteristics and symptoms of mental distress in divorce. *Journal of Marriage and the Family, 44*(1), 87–101.

Kitzinger, C. (1999). Lesbian and gay psychology: Is it critical? *Annual Review of Critical Psychology, 1,* 50–66.

Kitzinger, S. (1978). *Women as mothers: How they see themselves in different cultures.* New York: Random House.

Kitzinger, S. (1983). *Women's experience of sex.* London: Dorling Kindersley.

Klein, J. (1980). *Jewish identity and self esteem: Healing wounds through ethnotherapy.* New York: Institute on Pluralism and Group Identity.

Klein, L. (1990). Women and computing. *Communications of the Association for Computing Machinery, 33,* 34–36.

Klein, V. (1950). The stereotype of femininity. *Journal of Social Issues, 6,* 3–12.

Kleinfield, J. S. (1998, May). *The myth that schools shortchange girls: Social science in the service of deception.* Prepared for the Women's Freedom Network. Available from the author, College of Liberal Arts, University of Alaska–Fairbanks, Fairbanks, AK 99775.

Kleinke, C. L., & Meyer, C. (1990). Evaluation of rape victims by men and women with high and low beliefs in a just world. *Psychology of Women Quarterly, 14,* 343–353.

Klesse, C. (2003). Bisexuality in the United States. *Sexualities, 6*(2), 268–270.

Klinger, L. J. (2001). Children's perceptions of aggressive and gender-specific content in toy commercials. *Social Behavior and Personality, 29*(1), 11–20.

Klonoff, E. A., & Landrine, H. (1995). The schedule of sexist events: A measure of lifetime and recent sexist discrimination in women's lives. *Psychology of Women Quarterly, 19,* 439–472.

Klonoff, E. A., Landrine H., & Campbell, R. (2000). Sexist discrimination may account for well-known gender differences in psychiatric symptoms. *Psychology of Women Quarterly, 24,* 93–99.

Klonoff, E. A., Landrine, H., & Ullman, J. B. (1999). Racial discrimination and psychiatric symptoms among blacks. *Cultural Diversity and Ethnic Minority Psychology, 5*(4), 329–339.

Knafo, D., & Jaffe, Y. (1984). Sexual fantasizing in males and females. *Journal of Research in Personality, 18,* 451–467.

Knox, D., Zusman, M. E., & Nieves, W. (1997). College students' monogamous preferences for a date and mate. *College Student Journal, 31*(4), 445–448.

Knudsen, D. D. (1991). Child sexual coercion. In E. Grauerholz & M. A. Koralewski (Eds.), *Sexual coercion: A sourcebook on its nature, causes, and prevention* (pp. 17–28). Lexington, MA: Lexington Books.

Koelega, H. S., & Koster, E. P. (1974). Some experiments on sex differences in odor perception. *Annals of the New York Academy of Sciences, 237,* 234–246.

Koestner, R., & Wheeler, L. (1988). Self-presentation in personal advertisements: The influence of implicit notions of attraction and role expectations. *Journal of Personal Relationships, 5,* 149–160.

Koff, E., Rierdan, J., & Silverstone, E. (1978). Changes in representation of body image as a function of menarcheal status. *Developmental Psychology, 14,* 635–642.

Kohlberg, L. (1966). A cognitive-developmental analysis of children's sex-role concepts and attitudes. In E. Maccoby (Ed.), *The development of sex differences* (pp. 82–173). Stanford, CA: Stanford University Press.

Kohlberg, L. (1976). Moral stages and moralization: The cognitive-developmental approach. In T. Lickona (Ed.),

Moral development and behavior (pp. 31–53). New York: Holt, Rinehart & Winston.

Kohlberg, L. (1981). *The philosophy of moral development.* San Francisco: Harper & Row.

Kohlmann, C. W., Weidner, G., Dotzauer, E., & Burns, L. R. (1997). Gender differences in health behaviors: The role of avoidant coping. *European Review of Applied Psychology, 47,* 115–120.

Kohn, A. (1987). Shattered innocence. *Psychology Today. 21*(2), 54–58.

Kolata, G. (1998, September 9). Researchers report success in method to pick baby's sex. *New York Times,* p. A1.

Konrad, A. M., & Gutek, B. (1986). Impact of work experiences on attitudes towards sexual harassment. *Administration Science Quarterly, 3*(3), 422–438.

Koran 81.i–14 (cp. Rev. 6.12–14); Pelican trs., p. 17, II.3–11. Cited by Ringgren & Strom, 1967, p. 181.

Kornstein, S. G., Schatzberg, A. F., Thase, M. E., Yonkers, K. A., McCullough, J. P., Keitner, G. I., Gelenberg, A. J., Davis, S. M., & Keller, M. B. (2001). Gender differences in treatment response to sertaline versus imipramine in chronic depression: Reply. *American Journal of Psychiatry, 158*(9), 1532–1533.

Kortenhaus, C. M., & Demarest, J. (1993). Gender role stereotyping in children's literature: An update. *Sex Roles, 28,* 219–232.

Kosberg, J. I. (1988). Preventing elder abuse: Identification of high risk factors prior to placement decisions. *Gerontologist, 28,* 43–50.

Koss, M. P. (1990). Changed lives: The psychological impact of sexual harassment. In M. Paludi (Ed.), *Ivory power: Sex and gender harassment in the academy* (pp. 73–92). Albany, NY: State University of New York Press.

Koss, M. P. (1993a). Changed lives: The psychological impact of sexual harassment. In M. Paludi (Ed.), *Ivory power: Sex and gender harassment in the academy* (pp. 73–92). Albany: State University of New York Press.

Koss, M. P. (1993b). Rape: Scope, impact, intervention, and public policy responses. *American Psychologist, 48,* 1062–1069.

Koss, M. P., & Dinero, T. E. (1989). Discriminant analysis of risk factors for sexual victimization among a national sample of college women. *Journal of Consulting and Clinical Psychology, 57,* 242–250.

Koss, M. P., Dinero, T. E., Seibel, C., & Cox, S. (1988). Stranger and acquaintance rape: Are there differences in the victim's experience? *Psychology of Women Quarterly, 12,* 1–24.

Koss, M. P., Figueredo, A. J., & Prince, R. J. (2001). *A cognitive mediational model of rape's mental, physical, and social health impact: Preliminary specification and evaluation in cross-sectional data.* Manuscript submitted for publication.

Koss, M. P., Gidycz, C. A., & Wisniewski, N. (1987). The scope of rape: Incidence and prevalence of sexual aggression and victimization in a national sample of higher education stu-

dents. *Journal of Consulting and Clinical Psychology, 55,* 162–170.

Koss, M. P., Heise, L., & Russo, N. F. (1994). The global health burden of rape. *Psychology of Women Quarterly, 18,* 509–537.

Koss, M. P., & Heslet, L. (1992). Somatic consequences of violence against women. *Archives of Family Medicine, 1,* 53–59.

Koss, M. P., Koss, P. G., & Woodruff, W. J. (1991). Relation of criminal victimization to health perceptions among women medical patients. *Journal of Consulting and Clinical Psychology, 58,* 158–162.

Krause, N., & Markides, K. S. (1985). Employment and psychological well-being in Mexican-American women. *Journal of Health and Social Behavior, 26,* 15–26.

Kravitz, J. (1975). The relationship of attitudes to discretionary physician and dentist use by race and income. In R. Anderson, J. Kravitz, & O. W. Anderson (Eds.), *Equity in health services: empirical analyses in social policy* (pp. 73–93). Cambridge, MA: Ballinger.

Krefting, L. A., Berger, P. K., & Wallace, M. J., Jr. (1978). The contribution of sex distribution, job content, and occupational classification to job sextyping: Two studies. *Journal of Vocational Behavior, 13,* 181–191.

Krishnaswamky, S. (1984). A note on female infanticide: An anthropological inquiry. *Indian Journal of Social Work, 45,* 297–302.

Kritchevsky, D. (1990). Nutrition and breast cancer. *Cancer, 66,* 1321–1325.

Kronenberg, F. (1990). Hot flashes: epidemiology and physiology. In M. Flint, F. Kronenberg, & W. Utian (Eds.), *Multidisciplinary perspectives on menopause. Annals of the New York Academy of Sciences, 592,* pp. 52–87.

Kruger, A. (1994). The midlife transition: Crisis or chimera? *Psychological Reports, 75,* 1299–1305.

Kuhn, T. (1970). *The structure of scientific revolutions.* Chicago: University of Chicago Press.

Kulik, L. B. (1998). Effect of gender and social environment of gender role perceptions and identity: Comparative study of kibbutz and urban adolescents in Israel. *Journal of Community Psychology, 26*(6), 533–548.

Kumekawa, E. (1993). Sansei ethnic identity and the consequences of perceived unshared suffering for third generation Japanese Americans. In Y. Song & E. Kim (Eds.), *American mosaic: Selected readings on America's multicultural heritage* (pp. 204–214). Upper Saddle River, NJ: Prentice Hall.

Kuo, W. H. (1984). Prevalence of depression among Asian-Americans. *The Journal of Nervous and Mental Disease, 172,* 449–457.

Kuo, W. H. (1995). Coping with racial discrimination: The case of Asian Americans. *Ethnic and Racial Studies, 18*(1), 109–127.

Kurdek, L. A. (1993). The allocation of household labor in gay, lesbian, and heterosexual married couples. *Journal of Social Issues, 49,* 127–139.

Kurdek, L. A. (1994). The nature and correlates of relationship quality in gay, lesbian, and heterosexual cohabiting couples: A test of the individual difference, interdependence, and discrepancy models. In B. Greene & G. M. Herek (Eds.), *Lesbian and gay psychology: Theory, research, and clinical applications* (pp. 133–155). Psychological Perspectives on Lesbian and Gay Issues, Vol. 1. Thousand Oaks, CA: Sage.

Kutner, N. G. (1984). Women with disabling health conditions: The significance of employment. *Women and Health, 9*(4), 21–31.

Lackey, P. N. (1989). Adults' attitudes about assignments of household chores to male and female children. *Sex Roles, 20*(5/6), 271–280.

Lacks, M. S., Williams, C. S., O'Brien, S., Pillemer, K. A., & Charlson, M. E. (1998). The mortality of elder mistreatment. *Journal of the American Medical Association, 280,* 428–432.

Lafontaine, E., & Tredeau, L. (1986). The frequency, sources, and correlates of sexual harassment among women in traditional male occupations. *Sex Roles, 15.*

LaFromboise, T., Bennett, C., James, A., & Running Wolf, P. (1995). American Indian women and psychology. In H. Landrine (Ed.), *Bringing cultural diversity to feminist psychology: Theory, research, and practice* (pp. 197–239). Washington, DC: American Psychological Association.

LaFromboise, T., Berman, J., & Sohi, B. (1994). American Indian women. In L. Comas-Diaz & B. Greene (Eds.), *Women of Color: Integrating ethnic and gender identities in psychotherapy* (pp. 30–71). New York: Guilford Press.

LaFromboise, T. D., Heyle, A. M., & Ozer, E. J. (1990). Changing and diverse roles of women in American Indian cultures. *Sex Roles, 22,* 455–476.

Lamanna, M. A., & Reidmann, A. (1997). *Marriage and families* (6th ed.). Belmont, CA: Wadsworth.

Lamb, M. (Ed.). (1987). *The father's role: Cross-cultural perspectives.* Hillsdale, NJ: Erlbaum.

Lamb, M. E. (1979). Paternal influences and the father's role. *American Psychologist, 34,* 938–943.

Lamm, B. (1977). Men's movement hype. In J. Snodgrass (Ed.), *For men against sexism.* Albion, CA: Times Change Press.

Landes, A., Foster, C., & Cessna, C. (Eds.). (1994). Women's changing role. *The information series on current topics.* New York: Wylie—Information Plus.

Landes, A., Foster, C., & Cessna, C. (Eds.). (1995). Violent relationships: Battering and abuse among adults. *The information series on current topics.* New York: Wylie—Information Plus.

Landrine, H. (1985). Race × class stereotypes of women. *Sex Roles, 13,* 65–75.

Landrine, H. (Ed.). (1995). *Bringing cultural diversity to feminist psychology: Theory, research, and practice.* Washington, DC: American Psychological Association.

Landrine, H., Bardwell, S., & Dean, T. (1988). Gender expectations for alcohol use: A study of the significance of the masculine role. *Sex Roles, 19,* 703–712.

Laner, M. R. (2000). Dating scripts revisited. *Journal of Family Issues, 21*(4), 488–500.

Langer, E. J., & Abelson, R. P. (1974). A patient by any other name . . . : Clinician group differences in labeling bias. *Journal of Consulting and Clinical Psychology, 42,* 4–9.

Langer, W. L. (Ed.). (1948). *An encyclopedia of world history.* Boston: Houghton Mifflin.

Lanzito, C., (2002, July/August). Embracing the future. *AARP Exclusive,* p. 76.

LaRosa, J. H. (1994). Office of Research on Women's Health: National Institutes of Health and the women's health agenda. In J. A. Sechzer, A. Griffin, & S. M. Pfafflin (eds.). Forging a Women's Health Research Agenda: Policy Issues for the 1990's. *Annals of the New York Academy of Sciences, 736,* 196–204.

LaRossa, R., & LaRossa, M. M. (1981). *How infants change families.* Beverly Hills, CA: Sage.

Larrabee, G. J., & Crook, T. H. (1993). Do men show more rapid age-associated decline in simulated everyday verbal memory than do women? *Psychology and Aging, 8*(1), 68–71.

Larson, R. J., Csikszentmihalyi, N., & Graef, R. (1982). Time alone in daily experience: Loneliness or renewal? In L. A. Peplau & D. Perlman (Eds.), *Loneliness: A sourcebook of current theory, research and therapy.* New York: Wiley.

Lauer, K. O. (1985). His husband, her wife: The dynamics of the pride system in marriage. *Journal of Evolutionary Psychology, 6,* 329–340.

Laumann, E. O., Gagnon, J. H., Michael, R. T., & Michaels, S. (1994). *The social organization of sexuality: Sexual practices in the United States.* Chicago: University of Chicago Press.

Lauritsen, J. L., & Swicegood, C. G. (1997). The consistency of self-reported initiation of sexual activity. *Family Planning Perspectives, 29*(5), 215–221.

Law, D., Pellegrino. J. W., & Hunt, E. B. (1993). Comparing the tortoise and the hare: Gender differences and experience in dynamic spatial reasoning tasks. *Psychological Science, 4,* 35–41.

Laws, J. L., & Schwartz, P. (1977). *Sexual scripts.* Hinsdale, IL: Dryden.

Lawson, C. (1992, August 6). Violence at home: "They don't want anyone to know." *New York Times,* pp. C1–C7.

Lazarus, A. A. (2000). Working effectively and efficiently with couples. *Family Journal—Counseling and Therapy for Couples and Families, 8*(3), 222–228.

Lazarus, R. S., & Folkman, S. (1984). Stress, appraisal and coping. *Journal of Adolescence, 14,* 119–133.

Leaper, C. (1999). Communication patterns of African American girls and boys from low-income, urban backgrounds. *Child Development, 70*(6), 1489–1503.

Leaper, C., Hauser, S. T., Kremen, A., Powers, S., Jacobson, A. M., Noam, G. G., Weiss-Perry, B., & Follansbee, D.

(1989). Adolescent–parent interactions in relation to adolescents' gender and ego developmental pathway: A longitudinal study. *Journal of Early Adolescence, 9,* 335–361.

Leaper, C., Smith, L., Sprague, R., & Schwartz, R. (1991). *Single-parent mothers, married mothers, married fathers, and the socialization of gender in preschool children.* Paper presented at the biennial meeting of the Society for Research in Child Development, Seattle, WA.

Lebowitz, B. C., Pearson, J. L., Schneider, L. S., Reynolds, C. F., Alexopoulos, G. S., Bruce, M. L., Conwell, Y. L., Katz, I. R., Meyers, B. S., Morrison, M. F., Mossey, J., Niederehe, G., & Parmelee, P. (1997). Diagnosis and treatment of depression in later life: Consensus statement update. *Journal of the American Medical Association, 278,* 1186–1190.

Lederer, W. (1968). *The fear of women.* New York: Grune and Stratton.

Lee, C., & Owens, R. G. (2002). Men, work, and gender. *Australian Psychologist, 37*(1), 13–19.

Lee, P. Y., Alexander, K. P., Hammill, B. G., Pasquali, S. K., & Peterson, E. D. (2001). Representation of elderly persons and women in published randomized trials of acute coronary syndromes, *Journal of the American Medical Association, 286,* 708–713.

Lee, V. E., & Marks, H. M. (1990). Sustained effects of the single-sex secondary school experience on attitudes, behaviors, and values in college. *Journal of Educational Psychology, 82,* 578–592.

Lee, V. E., Marks, H. M., & Byrd, T. (1994). Sexism in single-sex and coeducational independent secondary school classrooms. *Sociology of Education, 67,* 92–120.

Legato, M. A. (1994). Cardiovascular disease in women: What's different? What's new? What's unresolved? In J. A. Sechzer, A. Griffin, & S. M. Pfafflin (Eds.), *Forging a women's health research agenda: Policy issues for the 1990's. Annals of the New York Academy of Sciences,* Vol. 736, pp. 147–157.

Lego, S. (1992). Masochism: Implications for psychiatric nursing. *Archives of Psychiatric Nursing, 6,* 224–229.

Lehrner, J. P. (1993). Gender differences in long-term odor recognition memory: Verbal versus sensory influences and the consistency of label use. *Chemical Sciences, 18,* 17–26.

Leidner, R. (1991). Selling hamburgers and selling insurance: Gender, work, and identity in interactive service jobs. *Gender & Society, 5*(2), 154–177.

Leigh, W. (1994). The health status of women of color. In C. Costello & A. Stone (Eds.), *The American woman: 1994–95 where we stand—Women and health* (pp. 154–196). New York: W. W. Norton.

Leitenberg, H., & Henning, K. (1995). Sexual fantasy. *Psychological Bulletin, 117,* 469–496.

Lempers, J. D., Clark-Lempers, D., & Simons, R. L. (1989). Economic hardship, parenting, and distress in adolescence. *Child Development, 60,* 25–39.

LePage-Lees, P. (1997). Struggling with a nontraditional past: Academically successful women from disadvantaged backgrounds discuss their relationship with "disadvantage." *Psychology of Women Quarterly, 21,* 365–385.

Lerner, M. J. (1980). *The belief in a just world: A fundamental delusion.* New York: Plenum Press.

Lerner, R. M., & Olson, C. K. (1997). "My body is so ugly!" In A. M. Meehan & E. Astor-Stetson (Eds.), *Adolescent psychology* (pp. 20–22). Guilford, CT: Dushkin Publishing Group/Brown & Benchmark Publishers.

Lester, B. M., Latasse, L. E., & Seifer, R. (1998). Cocaine exposure and children: The meaning of subtle effects. *Science, 282,* 633–634.

LeVay, S. (1991). A difference in hypothalamic structure between heterosexual and homosexual men. *Science, 253,* 1034–1037.

LeVay, S. (1996). *Queer science: The use and abuse of research into homosexuality.* Cambridge, MA: MIT Press.

Levenson, R. W., Carstensen, L. L., & Gottman, J. M. (1993). Long-term marriage: Age, gender, and satisfaction. *Psychology and Aging, 8*(2), 301–313.

Levenson, R. W., & Gottman, J. (1985). Physiological and affective predictors of change in relationship satisfaction. *Journal of Personality & Social Psychology, 49,* 85–94.

Levine, S. A. (1985). A definition of stress. In G. Moberg (Ed.), *Animal stress.* Bethesda, MD: American Physiological Society.

Levinson, D. J., Darrow, C. N., Klein, E. B., Levinson, M. H., & McKee, B. (1978). *The seasons of a man's life.* New York: Knopf.

Levi-Strauss, C. (1969). *The elementary structures of kinship.* London: Eyre & Spotiswoode.

Levy, J. (1969). Possible basis for the evolution of lateral specialization of the human brain. *Nature, 224,* 614–618.

Levy, J. (1990). Regulation and generation of perception in the asymmetric brain. In C. B. Trevarthen (Ed.), *Brain circuits and functions of the mind.* (pp. 231–248). Cambridge, UK: Cambridge University Press.

Lewin, K. (1935). *A dynamic theory of personality.* New York: McGraw-Hill.

Lewin, M., & Tragos, L. M. (1987). Has the feminist movement influenced adolescent sex role attitudes? A reassessment after a quarter century. *Sex Roles, 16*(34), 125–135.

Lewin, T. (1991, February 8). Studies on teen-age sex cloud condom debate. *New York Times,* p. A14.

Lewin, T. (1998, March 12). All-girl schools questioned as a way to attain equity. *New York Times.* p. A12.

Lewis, M. (1972). Parents and children: Sex-role development. *School Review, 80,* 229–240.

Lewis, P. H. (1995, July 3). Critics troubled by computer study on pornography. *New York Times,* pp. 37, 40.

Lewittes, H. J. (1988). Just being friendly means a lot: Women, friendship, and aging. *Women & Health, 14,* 139–159.

Lexis Nexis Academic. (2003, May 12). Mental Health Weekly Digest via NewsRx.com and newsRx.net.

Liang, J. (1982). Sex differences in life satisfaction among the elderly. *Journal of Gerontology, 37,* 100–108.

Libby, M. N., & Aries, E. (1989). Gender differences in preschool children's narrative fantasy. *Psychology of Women Quarterly, 13*, 293–306.

Liben, L. S., & Signorella, M. L. (1993). Gender-schematic processing in children: The role of initial interpretations of stimuli. *Developmental Psychology, 29*(1), 141–149.

Liebler, C. A. (2002). Gender differences in the exchange of social support with friends, neighbors, and co-workers at midlife. *Social Sciences Research, 31*(3), 364–391.

Liefer, M. (1977). Psychological changes accompanying pregnancy and motherhood. *Genetic Psychology Monographs, 95*, 55–96.

Liefer, M. (1980). *Psychological effects of motherhood: A study of first pregnancy.* New York: Praeger.

Life magazine home page. The mystery of Mary. July 9, 1999. Available: www.pathfinder.com@fil7w/gcA86aAOQaQLife/essay/Mary/01.html

Lim, T. K. (1994). Gender-related differences in intelligence: Application of confirmatory factor analysis. *Intelligence, 19*, 179–192.

Lin, K. M., Lau, J. K., Yamamoto, J., Zheng, Y. P., Kim, H. S., Cho, K. H., & Nakasaki, G. (1992). *Hwa-byung.* A community study of Korean Americans. *Journal of Nervous and Mental Disease, 180*(6), 386–391.

Lindgren, J. R., & Taub, N. (1993). *The law of sex discrimination.* Minneapolis, MN: West.

Lindsay, R. (1993). Hormone replacement therapy for prevention and treatment of osteoporosis. *American Journal of Medicine, 95*, 37S-39S.

Lindsey, B. (Ed.). (1980). *Comparative perspectives of Third World women: The impact of race, sex, and class.* New York: Praeger.

Linn, M. C., & Petersen, A. C. (1985). Emergence and characterization of sex differences in spatial ability: A meta-analysis. *Child Development, 56*, 1479–1498.

Linz, C. (1992). Setting the stage: Facts and figures. In J. A., Krentz, (Ed.), *Dangerous men and adventurous women: Romance writers on the appeal of romance.* Philadelphia: University of Pennsylvania.

Linz, D. G., Donnerstein, E., & Penrod, J. (1984). The effects of multiple exposures to filmed violence against women. *Journal of Communication, 34*, 130–147.

Lips, H. (Ed.). (1993). *Sex and gender: An introduction* (2nd ed.). Mountain View, CA: Mayfield.

Lobel, T. E., Agami-Rozenblatt, O., & Bempechat, J. (1993). Personality correlates of career choice in the kibbutz: A comparison of career and non-career women. *Sex Roles, 29*(5/6), 359–370.

Lobel, T. E., & Menashri, J. (1993). Relations of conceptions of gender-role transgressions and gender constancy to gender-typed toy preferences. *Developmental Psychology, 29*(1), 150–155.

Lock, J., & Steiner, H. (1999). Gay, lesbian, and bisexual youth risks for emotional, physical, and social problems: Results from a community-based survey. *Journal of the American Academy of Child and Adolescent Psychiatry, 38*, 297–304.

Loftus, E. F. (1991). Resolving legal questions with psychological data. *American Psychologist, 46*, 1046–1048.

Loftus, E. F. (1993). The reality of repressed memories. *American Psychologist, 48*, 518–537.

Lollis, C. M., Johnson, E. H., Antoni, M. H., & Hinkle, Y. (1996). Characteristics of African Americans with multiple risk factors associated with HIV/AIDS. *Journal of Behavioral Medicine, 19*, 55–71.

Long, E. C. J., & Andrews, D. W. (1990). Perspective taking as a predictor of marital adjustment. *Journal of Personality & Social Psychology, 59*, 126–131.

Long, J., & Porter, K. L. (1984). Multiple roles of midlife women. In G. Baruch & J. Brooks-Gunn (Eds.), *Women in midlife* (pp. 109–159). New York: Plenum Press.

Lonsway, K. A. (1996). Preventing acquaintance rape through education: What do we know? *Psychology of Women Quarterly, 20*, 229–265.

Lonsway, K. A., & Fitzgerald, L. F. (1994). Rape myths: In review. *Psychology of Women Quarterly, 18*, 133–164.

Lopata, H. (1971). *Occupation housewife.* New York: Oxford University Press.

Lopata, H. Z. (1973). *Widowhood in an American city.* Cambridge, MA: Schenckman.

LoPiccolo, J., & Stock, W. E. (1986). Treatment of sexual dysfunction. *Journal of Consulting & Clinical Psychology, 54*, 158–167.

Lorber, J. (1994). *Paradoxes of gender.* New Haven, CT: Yale University Press.

Lord, C., Ross, L., & Lepper, M. (1979). Biased assimilation and attitude polarization: The effects of prior theories on subsequently considered evidence. *Journal of Personality and Social Psychology, 37*, 2098–2109.

Lorde, A. (1984). *Sister outsider.* Freedom, CA: Frossing Press.

Los Cocco, K. A., & Spitze, G. (1990). Working conditions, social support, and the well-being of female and male factory workers. *Journal of Health & Social Behavior, 31*, 313–327.

Lott, B. L. (1991). *Women's lives: Themes and variations in gender learning* (2nd ed.). Monterey, CA: Brooks/Cole.

Lott, B. (1994). *Women's lives: Themes and variations in gender learning* (3rd ed.). Pacific Grove, CA: Brooks/Cole.

Lott, B. (1995). Distancing from women: Interpersonal sexist discrimination. In B. Lott & D. Maluso (Eds.), *The social psychology of interpersonal discrimination* (pp. 12–49). New York: Guilford Press.

Lottes, I. L., & Kuriloff, P. J. (1994). Sexual socialization differences by gender, Greek membership, ethnicity and religious background. *Psychology of Women Quarterly, 18*, 203–219.

Low, B. S. (1989). Cross-cultural patterns in the training of children: An evolutionary perspective. *Journal of Comparative Psychology, 103*, 311–319.

Lowie, R., & Hollingworth, L. S. (1916). Science and feminism. *Scientific Monthly, 3*, 277–284.

Lown, J., & Dolan, E. (1988). Financial challenges in remarriage. *Lifestyles: Family & Economic Issues, 9,* 73–88.

Luine, V., & Rodriguez, M. (1994). Effects of estradiol in radial arm maze performance of young and aged rats. *Behavioral and Neural Biology, 62,* 230–236.

Luine, V., Rentas, L., Sterback, L., & Beck, K. (1996). Estradiol effects of rat spatial memory. *Society of Neuroscience Abstracts, 22,* 1387.

Lummis, M., & Stevenson, H. W. (1990). Gender differences in beliefs and achievement: A cross-cultural study. *Developmental Psychology, 26,* 254–263.

Maccoby, E., & Jacklin, C. (1974). *The psychology of sex differences.* Stanford, CA.: Stanford University Press.

MacDonald, B., & Rich, C. (1983). *Look me in the eye: Old women, aging, and ageism.* San Francisco: Spinsters Ink.

MacKinnon, C. A. (1979). *Sexual harassment of working women.* New Haven, CT: Yale University Press.

Magnusson, D., Strattin, H., & Allen, V. L. (1985). Biological maturation and social development: A longitudinal study of some adjustment processes from mid-adolescence to adulthood. *Journal of Youth & Adolescence, 14,* 267–283.

Malamuth, N. M. (1981). Rape fantasies as a function of exposure to violent–sexual stimuli. *Archives of Sexual Behavior, 10,* 33–47.

Malamuth, N. M., & Check, J. V. P. (1983). Sexual arousal to rape depictions: Individual differences. *Journal of Abnormal Psychology, 92,* 55–67.

Malamuth, N. M., & Donnerstein, E. (1982). The effects of aggressive pornographic mass media stimuli. In L. Berkowitz (Ed.), *Advances in experimental social psychology* (Vol. 15). New York: Academic Press.

Malamuth, N. M., Haber, S., & Feshback, S. (1980). Testing hypotheses regarding rape: Exposure to sexual violence, sex differences and the "normality" of rapists. *Journal of Research in Personality, 14,* 121–137.

Malamuth, N. M., Sockloskie, R. J., Koss, M. P., & Tanaka, J. S. (1991). Characteristics of aggressors against women: Testing a model using a national sample of college women. *Journal of Consulting & Clinical Psychology, 59,* 670–681.

Malgady, R., Rogler, L., & Constantino, G. (1987). Ethnocultural and linguistic bias in mental health evaluation of Hispanics. *American Psychologist, 42,* 228–234.

Maltz, W., & Holman, B. (1987). *Incest and sexuality: A guide to understanding and healing.* Lexington, MA: Lexington Books/D. C. Heath.

Mandler, G. (1980). Recognizing the judgment of previous occurrence. *Psychology Review, 87,* 252–271.

Mann, J. (1997, April 11). Falling short of equality. *Washington Post,* p. E3.

Manning, J. T. (1998). Age difference between husbands and wives as a predictor of rank, sex of first child, and asymmetry of daughters. *Evolution of Human Behavior, 19*(2), 99–110.

Mansfield, P. K., & Voda, A. M. (1993). From Edith Bunker to the 6:00 News: How and what midlife women learn about menopause. *Women & Therapy, 14*(1/2), 89–104.

Manson, J. E., Stampfer, M. J., Colditz, G. A., Willett, W. C., Rosner, B., Speizer, F. E., & Hennekens, C. H. (1991). A prospective study of aspirin use and primary prevention of cardiovascular disease in women. *Journal of the American Medical Association, 266,* 521–527.

Mantecon, V. H. (1993). Where are the archetypes? Searching for symbols of women's midlife passage. *Women & Therapy, 14*(1/2), 77–88.

Marano, H. E. (1993, November/December). Inside the heart of marital violence. *Psychology Today,* 48–91.

Marano, H. E. (1997, July 1). Puberty may start at 6 as hormones surge. *New York Times,* p. C1.

Marantz, S. A., & Mansfield, A. F. (1977). Maternal employment and the development of sex-role stereotyping in five-to-eleven-year-old girls. *Child Development, 48,* 668–673.

Marcus, M. D. (1995). Binge eating and obesity. In K. D. Brownell, & C. G. Fairburn (Eds.), *Eating disorders and obesity: A comprehensive handbook* (pp. 441–449). New York: Guilford Press.

Marecek, J. (2001). Disorderly constructs: Feminist frameworks for clinical psychology. In R. Unger (Ed.), *Handbook of the psychology of women and gender.* (pp. 303–316). New York: Wiley.

Marecek, J., & Hare-Mustin, R. T. (1991). A short history of the future: Feminism and clinical psychology. *Psychology of Women Quarterly, 15,* 521–536.

Marecek, J., Kimmel, E. B., Crawford, M., & Hare-Mustin, R. T. (2003). Psychology of women and gender. In D. K. Freedheim (Ed.), *Handbook of psychology. History of psychology* (pp. 249–268). New York: Wiley.

Margolin, L. (1989). Gender and the prerogatives of dating and marriage: An experimental assessment of a sample of college students. *Sex Roles, 20,* 91–102.

Markson, E. W., & Gognalons-Nicolet, M. (1990). Midlife: Crisis or nodal point? Some cross-cultural views. In B. B. Hess, & E. W. Markson (Eds.), *Growing old in America* (4th ed.). New Brunswick, NJ: Transaction.

Markson, E. W., & Taylor, C. A. (1993). Real versus reel world: Older women and the Academy awards. *Women & Therapy, 14*(1/2), 77–88.

Marshall, E. (1993). Search for a killer: Focus shifts from fat to hormones. *Science, 259,* 618–621.

Marshall, M. P. (2000). Peer influence on adolescent alcohol use: The moderation role of parental support and discipline. *Applied Developmental Science 4*(2), 80–88.

Marshall, W. A., & Tanner, J. M. (1969). Variation in the pattern of pubertal changes in girls. *Archives of Disease in Childhood, 44,* 291–303.

Martin, C. L., & Little, J. K. (1990). The relation of gender understanding to children's sex-typed preferences and gender stereotypes. *Child Development, 61,* 1427–1439.

Martin, E. (1991). The egg and the sperm: How science has constructed a romance based on stereotypical male–female roles. *Signs, 16,* 485–501.

Marx, D. M., & Roman, J. S. (2002). Female role models: Protecting women's math test performance. *Personality and Social Psychology Bulletin, 28,* 1183–1193.

Maspero, G. (1914). Chansons populaires. In G. Maspero, *Chansons populaires recueillies dans la Haute-Egypte: De 1900 à 1914.* Cairo. Imprimerie de l'Institute Francais d'Archeologie Orientale.

Masson, J. M. (1984, February). Freud and the seduction theory. *The Atlantic,* 12.

Masters, W. H., & Johnson, V. E. (1966). *Human sexual response.* Boston: Little, Brown.

Masters, W. H., & Johnson, V. E. (1979). *Homosexuality in perspective.* Boston: Little, Brown.

Masters, W. H., & Johnson, V. E., & Kolodny, R. C. (1994). *Heterosexuality.* New York: Harper Collins.

Masters, W. H., & Johnson, V. E., & Kolodny, R. C., (1995). *Human sexuality* (5th ed.) New York: Harper Collins.

Mathews, A. W., and Hensley, S. (October 8, 2003). Hormone-therapy debate grows. *The Wall Street Journal,* Health and Family, Section D7.

Matthews, V. H. & Benjamin, D. (1995). *Social world of ancient Israel:1250–587* BCE. Peabody, MA: Hendrickson Publications.

Maybach, K. L., & Gold, S. R. (1994). Hyperfemininity and attraction to macho and non-macho men. *Journal of Sex Research, 31*(2), 91–98.

Mayekiso, T., & Bhana, K. (1997). Sexual harassment: Perceptions of students at the University of Transkei. *South African Journal of Psychology, 27,* 230–235.

Mazure, C. M., Keita, G. P., & Blehar, M. C. (2002). *Summit on women and depression: Proceedings and recommendations.* Washington, DC: American Psychological Association.

Mbawa, K. (1992). Botswana children's career aspirations and views of sex roles. *Journal of Social Psychology, 133*(4), 587–588.

McAdoo, J. L. (1986). Chapter 9: A Black perspective on the father's role in child development. In R. A. Lewis & M. D. Sussman (Eds.), *Men's changing roles in the family* (pp. 117–134). New York: Haworth Press.

McAnulty, R. D., & Burnette, M. M. (2004). *Exploring human sexuality: Making healthy decisions* (2nd ed.). Pearson Education.

McCann, U. D., & Agras, W. S. (1990). Successful treatment of nonpurging bulimia nervosa with desipramine: A double-blind, placebo controlled study. *American Journal of Psychiatry, 147,* 1509–1513.

McCarthy, B. (2003). Marital sex as it ought to be. *Journal of Family Psychotherapy, 14*(2), 1–12.

McClelland, D. C., Atkinson, J. W., Clark, R. A., & Lowell, F. L. (1953). *The achievement motive.* New York: Appleton Century-Croft.

McConatha, J. T. (1999). Description of older adults as depicted in magazine advertisements. *Psychological Reports, 85*(3, pt. 1), 1051–1056.

McCormick, N. B., (1987). Sexual scripts: Social and therapeutic implications. *Sexual and Marital Therapy, 2,* 3–27.

McCusker, J., & Morrow, G. R. (1980). Factors relevant to the use of cancer early detection techniques. *Preventive Medicine, 9,* 388–397.

McDonald, K., & Parke, R. D. (1986). Parent–child physical play: The effects of sex and age on children and parents. *Sex Roles, 15,* 367–378.

McDonald, S. M. (1989). Sex bias in the representation of male and female characters in children's picture books. *Journal of Genetic Psychology, 150,* 389–401.

McDougall, J. (1999). Parental preference for sex of children in Canada. *Sex Roles, 41*(7/8), 615–626.

McElmurry, B. J., & Huddleston, D. (1987). *The perimenopausal woman: Perceived threats to sexuality and self-care responses.* Paper presented at the Seventh Conference of the Society for Menstrual Cycle Research, Ann Arbor, MI.

McEwan, B. (1981). Neuronal gonadal steroid actions. *Science, 211*(4488), 1303–1311.

McGoldrick, M., Pearce, J. K., & Giordano, J. (Eds.). (1982). *Ethnicity and family therapy.* New York: Guilford Press.

McHale, S. M. and Crouter, A. C. (1992, August). You can't always get what you want: Incongruence between sex-role attitudes and family work roles and its implications for marriage. *Journal of Marriage and the Family, 54*(3), 537–547.

McHale, S., & Huston, T. (1985). A longitudinal study of the transition to parenthood and its effects on the marriage relationship. *Journal of Family Issues, 6,* 409–433.

McHugh, M. C. (2000). A feminist approach to agoraphobia: Challenging traditional views of women at home. In J. C. Chrisler, C. Golden, & P. D. Rozee (Eds.), *Lectures on the psychology of women* (pp. 341–359). New York: McGraw-Hill.

McHugh, M. C., & Bartoszek, T. A. R. (2000). Intimate violence. In M. K. Biaggio & M. Hersen (Eds.), *Issues in the psychology of women* (pp. 115–142) New York: Kluwer Academic/Plenum Publishers.

McIntosh, P. (1988). White privilege: Unpacking the invisible knapsack. Reprinted in P. Rothenberg (Ed.), *White privilege: Essential readings on the other side of racism* (pp. 97–101).

McKee, L. (1982). Fathers' participation in infant care, a critique. In L. McKee & M. O'Brien (Eds.), *The father figure* (pp. 120–138). London: Tavistock.

McKinley, J. C. (2003, September 25). Gay marriages are still far from approval by Albany. *New York Times,* p. B5.

McKinnon, J. (April, 2003). The Black Population in the United States: March 2002. Current Population Reports. U.S. Census Bureau, 1–8.

McLaren, A. (1984). *Reproductive rituals: The perception of fertility in England from the sixteenth century to the nineteenth century.* London and New York: Methuen.

McLaughlin, D. K., & Lichter, D. (1997). Poverty and the marital behavior of young women. *Journal of Marriage and the Family, 59,* 582–594.

McLaughlin, M., Cormier, L. S., & Cormier, W. H. (1988). Relation between coping strategies and distress, stress, and marital adjustment of multiple role women. *Journal of Counseling Psychology, 35*(2), 187–193.

McLean, V. (2002). Stress, depression and role conflict in working mothers. *South African Psychiatry Review, 5*(2), 13–16.

McLemore, S. D. (1991). *Racial and ethnic relations in America.* Boston: Allyn and Bacon.

McLeod, J. D., & Kessler, R. C. (1990). Socioeconomic status differences in vulnerability to undesirable life events. *Journal of Health and Social Behavior, 31*(2), 162–172.

McMahon, M. (1995). *Engendering motherhood: Identity and self-transformation in women's lives.* New York: Guilford Press.

McMellon, C. A., & Schiffman, L. G. (2002). Cybersenior empowerment: How some older individuals are taking control of their lives. *Journal of Applied Gerontology, 21*(2), 157–175.

Medication Safety and Reliability. (2002, August). Women's health initiative and HERS II studies find risks of long-term HRT outweigh benefits. *Formulary, 37,* 381.

Mednick, M. T., & Thomas, V. G. (1993). Women and the psychology of achievement: a view from the eighties. In F. L. Denmark & M. A. Paludi (Eds.), *Psychology of women: A handbook of issues and theories.* Westport, CT: Greenwood Press.

Meehan, A. M. (1984). A meta-analysis of sex differences in formal operational thought. *Child Development, 55,* 1110–1124.

Menning, B. E. (1977). *Infertility: A guide for the childless couple.* Englewood Cliffs, NJ: Prentice Hall.

Mensch, B. S. (2003). Gender-role attitudes among Egyptian adolescents. *Studies in Family Planning, 34*(1), pp. 8–18.

Mersky, H. (1976). Pain terms: A list with definitions and notes on usage. *Pain, 6,* 249–250.

Meyer, B. (1980). The development of girls' sex-role attitudes. *Child Development, 51,* 508–514.

Meyer, V. F. (1991). A critique of adolescent pregnancy prevention research: The invincible white male. *Adolescence, 26,* 217–222.

Michael, R. T., Gagnon, J. H., Laumann, E. O., & Kolata, G. (1994). *Sex in America: A definitive survey.* Boston: Little, Brown.

Milano, G., Etienne, M. C., Cassuto-Viguier, E., Thyss, A., Santini, J., Frenay, M., Renee, N., Schneider, M. & Demard, F. (1992). Influence of sex and age on fluorouracil clearance. *Journal of Clinical Oncology, 10*(7), 1171–1175.

Miller, J. (1976). *Toward a new psychology of women.* Boston: Beacon Press.

Miller, K. E. (1993, March). Same-sex and opposite-sex friendship quality and perceived social competence: Developmental overlap. Paper presented at the biennial meeting of the Society for Research in Child Development, New Orleans.

Miller, L. J. (2002). Postpartum depression. *Journal of the American Medical Association, 287,* 762–765.

Miller, P. N., Darryl, W., & McKibbin, E. M. (1999). Stereotypes of the elderly in magazine advertisements 1956–1996. *International Journal of Aging and Human Development, 49*(4), 319–337.

Millner, D. (1997). *The sistahs' rules: Secrets for meeting, getting, and keeping a good black man.* New York: Quill/William Morrow.

Mintz, L. B., & Kashubeck, S. (1999). Body image and disordered eating among Asian American and Caucasian college students. *Psychology of Women Quarterly, 23,* 782–796.

Mirowsky, J., & Ross, C. E. (1980). Minority status, ethnic culture and distress: A comparison of Blacks, Whites, Mexicans and Mexican Americans. *American Journal of Sociology, 86,* 479–495.

Mitchell, J. E. (1995). Medical complications of bulimia nervosa. In K. D. Brownell & C. G. Fairburn (Eds.), *Eating disorders and obesity: A comprehensive handbook* (pp. 271–275). New York: Guilford Press.

Mitchell, V., & Helson, R. (1990). Women's prime of life: Is it the 50s? *Psychology of Women Quarterly, 14,* 451–470.

Mittwoch, U. (1977). To be right is to be born male. *New Scientist, 73,* 74–76.

Moen, P. (1992). *Women's two roles: A contemporary dilemma.* New York: Auburn House.

Mogil, J. S., Sternberg, W. F., Kest, B., Marek, P., & Liebeskind, J. C. (1993). Sex differences in the antagonism of swim stress-induced analgesia: Effects of gonadectomy and estrogen replacement. *Pain, 53,* 17–25.

Mohn, J. K., Tingle, L. R., & Finger, R. (2002). An analysis of the causes of the decline in non-marital birth and pregnancy rates for teens from 1991 to 1995. *Adolescent and Family Health, 3*(1), 39–47.

Momsen, J. H. (1999). *Gender. migration and domestic service.* London: Routledge.

Mona, L. R., Gardos, M. A., & Brown, R. C. (1994). Sexual self-views of women with disabilities: The relationship among age-of-onset, nature of disability, and sexual self-esteem. *Sexuality and Disability, 12,* 261–275.

Money, J. (1975). Ablatio penis: Normal male infant sex-reassigned as a girl. *Archives of Sexual Behavior, 4,* 65–72.

Money, J. (1987). Propaedeutics of diecious G-1/R: Theoretical foundations for understanding dimorphic gender-identity/role. In J. M. Reinisch, L. A. Rosenblum, & S. A. Sanders (Eds.), *Masculinity/femininity: Basic perspectives* (pp. 13–28). New York: Oxford University Press.

Money, J. (1988). *Gay, straight and in-between.* New York: Oxford University Press.

Money, J. (1990). Agenda and credenda of the Kinsey Scale. In D. P. McWirter et al. (Eds.), *Homosexuality/heterosexuality:*

Concepts of sexual orientation (pp. 41–60). New York: Oxford University Press.

Money, J., & Ehrhardt, A. E. (1972). *Man & woman, boy & girl.* Baltimore: Johns Hopkins University Press.

Money, J., & Tucker, P. (1975). *Sexual signatures: On being a man or woman* (pp. 95–98). Boston: Little, Brown. Cited by Diamond & Sigmundson, 1997, pp. 298–304.

Montague, H., & Hollingworth, L. S. (1914). The comparative variability of the sexes at birth. *American Journal of Sociology, 20,* 335–370.

Moore, M. (2000, October 29). The problems of Turkey rest on women's heads. *Washington Post Foreign Service,* p. A32.

Morahan-Martin, J. (1991). Consider the children: Is parenthood being devalued? *The Psychological Record, 41,* 303–314.

Moran, M. (2001, August 7). Clinical trials: unequal representation. *WebMD, Medical News Archives,* 1–3.

Morford, M. P. O., & Lenardon, R. J. (1995). *Classical mythology.* (5th ed.). White Plains, NY: Longman.

Morgan, K. S., & Brown, L. S. (1993). Lesbian career development, work behavior, and vocational counseling. In L. D. Garrets & D. C. Kimmel (Eds.), *Psychological perspectives on lesbian and gay male experiences* (pp. 267–286). New York: Columbia University Press.

Morin, R. (2002, June 9). The baby boy payoff. *Washington Post,* p. B05.

Morris, L. B. (2000, June 25). For the partum blues, a question of whether to medicate. *New York Times online.*

Morrison, M. F. (2000). Effects of estrogen on mood and cognition in aging women. *Psychiatric Annals, 30*(2), 113–119.

Morse, D. (1969). *The peripheral worker.* New York: Columbia University Press.

Morton, T. U. (1978). Intimacy and reciprocity of exchange: A comparison of spouses and strangers. *Journal of Personality and Social Psychology, 36,* 72–81.

Mowder, B. (2003, July 30). Personal communication.

Moynihan, D. P. (1965). *The Negro family: The case for national action.* Washington, DC: U.S. Department of Labor.

Mueller, K. A., & Yoder, J. D. (1997). Gendered norms for family size, employment, and occupation: Are there personal costs for violating them? *Sex Roles, 36,* 901–919.

Mullins, L. C., & Mushel, M. (1992). The existence and emotional closeness of relationships with children, friends, and spouses: The effect of loneliness among older persons. *Research on Aging, 14*(4), 448–470.

Mullis, I. V. S., & Others (1993). *NAEP 1992—Reading report card for the nation and the states: Data from the national and trial state assessments.* Princeton, NJ: National Assessment of Educational Progress.

Mundy, L. (2000, July 16). Sex and sensibility. *Washington Post online.*

Murell, A. J. (1996). Sexual harassment and women of color: Issues, challenges, and future directions. In M. S. Stockdale (Ed.), *Sexual harassment in the workplace: Perspectives,* *frontiers, and response strategies* (pp. 51–66). Thousand Oaks, CA: Sage.

Murguia, A., Zea, M., Reisen, C., & Peterson, R. (2000). The development of the cultural health attributions questionnaire (CHAQ). *Cultural Diversity and Ethnic Minority Psychology, 6,* (3), 268–283.

Murray, B. (1998, October). Survey reveals concerns of today's girls. *APA Monitor, 29,* 12.

Murray, C. J., & Lopez, A. D. (1996). Alternative visions of the future: Projecting mortality and disability, 1990–2020. In C. J. Murray & A. D. Lopez (Eds.), *The global burden of disease: A comprehensive assessment of mortality and disability from diseases, injuries, and risk factors in 1990 and projected to 2020* (pp. 325–395). Boston: Harvard University Press.

Mussen, P. H., & Rutherford, E. (1963). Parent–child relations and parental personality in relation to young children's sex-role preferences. *Child Development, 34,* 489–507.

Muster, N. J. (1992). Treating the adolescent victim-turned-offender. *Adolescence, 27,* 441–450.

Myer, M. H. (1985). A new look at mothers of incest victims. *Journal of Social Work and Human Sexuality, 3,* 47–58.

Myers, H., Lesser, I., Rodriguez, N., Mira, C. B., Hwang, W., Camp, C., Anderson, D., Erickson, L., & Wohl, M. (2002). Ethnic differences in clinical presentation of depression in adult women. *Cultural Diversity and Ethnic Minority Psychology, 8*(2), 138–156.

Nadien, M. (1996). Aging women: Issues of mental health and maltreatment. In J. A. Sechzer & S. M. Pfaffin (Eds.), *Women and Mental Health.* New York, NY: New York Academy of Sciences.

Nadien, M. B., & Denmark, F. L. (1999). Aging women: Stability or change in perceptions of personal control. In M. B. Nadien & F. L. Denmark, *Females and autonomy: A life-span perspective* (pp. 130–154). Boston: Allyn and Bacon.

Nagel, K. L., & Jones, K. H. (1992). Predisposition factors in anorexia nervosa. *Adolescence, 27,* 381–386.

Narroll, R. (1964). Ethnic unit classification. *Current Anthropology, 5*(4), 283–312.

Narrow, W. E., Rae, D. S., & Regier, D. A. (1998) NIMH epidemiology note: Prevalence of anxiety disorders. One-year prevalence best estimates calculated from ECA and NCS data. Population estimates based on U.S. Census estimated residential population age 18 to 54 on July 1, 1998. Unpublished.

National Center for Health Statistics. (1991). *Health, United States, 1990.* Hyattsville, MD: Public Health Service.

National Center for Health Statistics. (1997). Vital statistics in the United States. Retrieved March 12, 2004, from www.census.gov/prod/3/97pubs/97statab/vitstat.pdf

National Center for Health Statistics. (2003). *Health, United States, 2003.* Hyattsville, MD: Public Health Service.

National Crime Victimization Survey. (1995). *U.S. Bureau of Justice Statistics.* Washington, DC: U.S. Department of Justice.

National Institute for Occupational Safety and Health (NIOSH). (1999). *Stress . . . at Work* (Publication No. 99–101). Washington, DC: U.S. Department of Health and Human Services.

National Institute of Allergy and Infectious Diseases, National Institutes of Health. (2002). *Fact sheet: Treatment of HIV infection.* Retrieved December 10, 2002 from www.niaid.nih.gov/factsheets/treat-hiv.htm

National Institute of Mental Health. (2000). *Depression: What every woman should know.* Bethesda, MD: Author.

National Institute of Mental Health (2001). *Eating disorders: Facts about eating disorders and the search for solutions.*

National Institute of Mental Health. (2002). *Anxiety Disorders* (Rev. Ed.)[Brochure]. Hendrix, M. L.: Author.

National Institute of Mental Health. (2003). *Suicide facts.* Retrieved September 26, 2003, from www.nimh.nih.gov/research/suifact.htm.

National Institutes of Health, National Institute on Aging. (1993, May). *In search of the secrets of aging* (NIH Publication No. 93–2756). Washington, DC.

National Institutes of Health. (1991, February 3). *Guide for grants and contracts.* NIH/ADAMHA policy concerning inclusion of women in study populations.

National Institutes of Health—National Institute on Aging. (1993, May). *In search of the secrets of aging* (NIH Publicaton No. 93-2756). Washington, DC: Author.

National Institutes of Health—Office of Research on Women's Health. (NIH Publication No. 92-3457A). (1992, September). *Opportunities for research on women's health.* U.S. Department of Health & Human Services, Public Health Service, National Institutes of Health.

National Osteoporosis Foundation. (1991). *Boning up on osteoporosis: A guide to prevention and treatment.* Washington, DC: National Osteoporosis Foundation.

National Research Council. (1992). *Recognition and alleviation of pain and distress in laboratory animals.* Washington, DC: National Academy Press.

National Research Council. (1993). *Losing generations: Adolescents in high-risk settings.* Washington, DC: National Academy Press.

National Survey on Drug Use and Health. (2002). U.S. Department of Health and Human Services. Retrieved on April 9, 2004 from www.samhsa.gov/ORS/nhsda/2k2nsdvh/Results/2k2Results.htm#toc.

Naveh-Benjamin, M. (2002). Age-related differences in cued recall: Effects of support at encoding and retrieval. *Aging, Neuropsychology and Cognition, 9*(4), 276–287.

Neft, N., & Levine, A. (1997). *Where women stand: An international report on the status of women in 140 countries, 1997–1998.* New York: Random House.

Nelson, A. (2000). The pink dragon is female: Halloween costumes and gender markers. *Psychology of Women Quarterly, 24*(2), pp. 137–144.

Nelson, C., & Tienda, M. (1985). The structuring of Hispanic ethnicity: Historical and contemporary perspectives. *Ethnic and Racial Studies, 8,* 49–73.

Nelson, D. L., & Burke, R. J. (2002). Gender, Work Stress, and Health. Washington DC: American Psychological Association.

Neto, F., Williams, J. E., & Widner, S. C. (1991). Portugese children's knowledge of sex stereotypes. Effects of age, gender, and socioeconomic status. *Journal of Cross-Cultural Psychology, 22*(3), 376–388.

Neugarten, B. L. (Ed.). 1967. *Middle age and aging: A reader in social psychology.* Chicago: University of Chicago Press.

Neugarten, B. L., & Kraines, R. J. (1965). "Menopausal symptoms" in women of various ages. *Psychosomatic Medicine, 27,* 266.

Neugarten, B. L., Havighurst, R. J., & Tobin, S. S. (1968). Personality and patterns of aging. In B. L. Neugarten (Ed.), *Middle age and aging* (pp. 173–180). Chicago: University of Chicago Press.

Nevid, J. S. (1984). Sex differences in factors of romantic attraction. *Sex Roles, 11,* 401–411.

Nevid, J. S., Fichner-Rathus, L., & Rathus, S. (1995). *Human sexuality in a world of diversity* (2nd ed.). Boston: Allyn and Bacon.

Newcombe, N., Mathason, L., & Terlecki, M. (2002). Maximization of spatial competence: More important than finding the cause of sex differences. In A. McGillicuddy-De Lisi & R. De Lisi (Eds.), *Biology, society, and behavior: The development of sex differences in cognition* (pp. 183–206). Westport, CT: Ablex.

Newmann, J. P. (1986). Gender, life-strains, and depression. *Journal of Health and Social Behavior, 27,* 161–178.

Nichter, M., & Vuckovic, N. (1994). Fat talk: Body image among adolescent girls. In N. Sault (Ed.), *Many mirrors: Body image and social relations* (pp. 109–131). New Brunswick, NJ: Rutgers University Press.

Nicol-Smith, L. (1996). Causality, menopause, and depression: A critical review of the literature. *British Medical Journal, 313,* 1229–1232.

Niditch, S. (1991). Portrayal of women in the Hebrew Bible. In J. Baskin (Ed.), *Jewish women in historical perspective.* (pp. 25–42). Detroit, MI: Wayne State University Press.

Nielson, M. E. (2000). Psychology of Religion in the USA. (http://www.psywww.com/psyrelig/USA.html.)

Niemela, P., & Lento, R. (1993). The significance of the 50th birthday for women's individuation. *Women and Therapy, 14*(1/2), 117–127.

Nieto-Gomez, A. (1976). A heritage of LaHembra. In S. Cox (Ed.), *Female psychology: The emerging self* (pp. 226–235). Chicago: Science Research Associates.

Nilsen, A., et al. (1977). *Sexism and language.* Urbana, IL: National Council of Teachers of English.

Nilson, L. (1978). The social standing of a housewife. *Journal of Marriage and the Family, 40,* 541–548.

Nisbett, R. E., & Gurwitz, S. B. (1970). Weight, sex and the eating behavior of human newborns. *Journal of Comparative and Physiological Psychology, 73,* 245–253.

Nishizawa, S., Benkelfat, C., Young, S., Leyton, M., Mzengeza, S., Montigny, C. D., Blier, P., & Diksic, M. (1997). Differences between males and females in rates of serotonin synthesis in the human brain. *Proceedings of the National Academy of Sciences, 94,* 5308–5313.

Nock, S. L. (1995). A comparison of marriages and cohabiting relationships. *Journal of Family Issues, 16*(1), 53–76.

Nolen-Hoeksema, S. (2001). Gender differences in depression. *Psychological Science, 10,* 173–176.

Nolen-Hoeksema, S., & Jackson, B. (2001). Mediators of the gender difference in rumination. *Psychology of Women Quarterly, 25,* 37–47.

Nolen-Hoeksema, S., & Keita, G. (2003). Women and depression: Introduction. *Psychology of Women Quarterly, 27,* 89–90.

Nosaka, A. (2000). Effects of child gender preference on contraceptive use in rural Bangladesh. *Journal of Comparative Family Studies, 31*(4), 485–501.

Nosek, M. A., Howland, C. A., Young, M. E., Georgiou, D., Rintala, D. H., Foley, C. C., Bennett, L. L., & Smith, Q. (1994). Wellness models and sexuality among women with disabilities. *Journal of Applied Rehabilitation Counseling, 25*(1), 50–58.

Noss, J. B. (1949). Early Hinduism. In J. B. Noss & D. S. Noss (Eds.), *Man's religions.* New York: Macmillan.

Noss, J. B. (1974). *Man's religions* (5th ed.). New York: Macmillan.

Noss, J. B., & Noss, D. S. (1984). *Man's religions,* (7th ed.). New York: Macmillan.

Nyberg, K. L., & Alston, J. P. (1976–1977). Analysis of public attitudes toward homosexual behavior. *Journal of Homosexuality, 2,* 99–107.

Oakley, A. (1980). *Women confined.* New York: Schocken.

Obermeyer, C. M. (1996). Fertility norms and son preference in Morocco and Tunisia: Does women's status matter? *Journal of Biosocial Science, 28*(1), 57–72.

O'Boyle, M. W., & Hoff, E. J. (1987). Gender and handedness differences in mirror-tracing random forms. *Neuropsychologia, 25,* 977–982.

O'Connor, P. (1992). *Friendships between women.* New York: Guilford Press.

Offen, K. (1988). Defining feminism: A comparative historical approach. *Signs, 14,* 119–157.

Offer, D., Ostrov, E., Howard, K. I., & Atkinson, R. (1988). *The teenage world. Adolescents' self-image in ten countries.* New York: Plenum Press.

Ofosu, H. B., Lafreniere, K. D., & Senn, C. Y. (1998). Body image perception among women of African descent: A normative context? *Feminism & Psychology, 8,* 303–323.

Ogbu, J. (1994). From cultural differences to differences in cultural frame of reference. In P. Greenfield & R. Cocking (Eds.), *Cross-cultural roots of minority child development* (pp. 365–391). Hillsdale, NJ: Erlbaum.

Ogbu, J. U. (1982). Black education: A cultural–ecological perspective. In H. McAdoo (Ed.), *Black families* (pp. 139–154). Beverly Hills, CA: Sage.

Ogozalek, V. Z. (1991). The social impacts of computing: Computer technology and the graying of America. *Social Science Computer Review, 9*(4), 655–666.

O'Hare, W. P. (1992). America's minorities—The demographics of diversity. *Population Bulletin, 47,* 4, 1–47.

O'Hare, W. P., & Felt, J. C. (1991). *Asian Americans: America's fastest growing minority group.* Washington, DC: Population Reference Bureau.

Ohno, S. (1979). *Major sex-determining genes.* Berlin: Springer-Verlag.

Okazawa-Rey, M., Robinson, T., & Ward, J. (1987). Black women and the politics of skin color and hair. *Women & Therapy, 6,* pp. 89–102.

O'Leary, K. D., & Cascardi, M. (1998). Physical aggression in marriage: A developmental analysis. In T. N. Bradbury (Ed.), *The developmental course of marital dysfunction* (pp. 343–374). New York: Cambridge University Press.

O'Leary, K. D., Barling, J., Arias, I., Rosenbaum, A., Malone, J., & Tyree, A. (1989). Prevalence and stability of physical aggression between spouses: A longitudinal analysis. *Journal of Consulting and Clinical Psychology, 57,* 263–268.

Oliver, M. B., & Hyde, J. S. (1993). Gender differences in sexuality: A meta-analysis. *Psychological Bulletin, 114,* 29–51.

Oliver, S. J., & Toner, B. B. (1990). The influence of gender role typing in the expression of depressive symptoms. *Sex Roles, 22,* 775–790.

O'Mahony, J. F. & Hollwey, S. (1995). Eating problems and interpersonal functioning among several groups of women. *Journal of Clinical Psychology, 51*(3), 345–351.

Opland, E. A., Winters, K. C., & Stinchfield, R. D. (1995). Examining gender differences in drug-abusing adolescents. *Psychology of Addictive Behaviors, 9,* 167–175.

Oquendo, M., Horwath, E., & Martinez, A. (1992). *Ataques de nervios:* Proposed diagnostic criteria for a culture-specific syndrome. *Culture, Medicine, and Psychiatry, 16,* 367–376.

Orenstein, P. (1994). *Schoolgirls: Young women, self-esteem, and the confidence gap.* New York: Doubleday.

Orenstein, P. (1995, April 27). Show girls equity at work: Shattering the glass ceiling needed in the classroom as well as in the boardroom. *USA Today,* p. 13A.

Orlofsky, J. L. (1982). Psychological androgyny, sex-typing, and sex-role ideology as predictors of male–female interpersonal attraction. *Sex Roles, 8,* 1057–1073.

Ornish, D., Brown, S. E., Sherwitz, L. W., Billings, J. H., Armstrong, W. T., Ports, T. A., McLanahan, S. M., Kirkeeide, R. L., Brand, R. J., & Gould, K. L. (1990). Can lifestyle changes reverse coronary heart disease? *Lancet, 336,* 129–133.

Orr, E., & Ben-Eliahu, E. (1993). Gender differences in idiosyncratic sex-typed self-images and self-esteem. *Sex Roles, 29*(3/4), 271–296.

O'Sullivan, C. (1995). Fraternities and the rape culture. In M. S. Kimmel & M. A. Messner (Eds.), *Men's lives* (3rd ed., pp. 354–357). Boston: Allyn and Bacon.

Ortiz, V. (1994). Women of color: A demographic overview. In M. Zinn & G. Dill (Eds.), *Women of color in U.S. society* (pp. 13–40). Philadelphia: Temple University Press.

Overall, C. (1992). What's wrong with prostitution? Evaluating sex work. *Signs, 17,* 705–724.

Ozawa, M. N. and Yoon, H. (2002). The economic benefit of remarriage: Gender and income class. *Journal of Divorce & Remarriage, 36*(3–4), 21–39.

Packer, J. (1986). *Sex differences in the perception of street harassment. The dynamics of feminist therapy* (pp. 331–338). New York: Haworth.

Padilla, A. M., Salgado de Snyder, N. V., Cervantes, R. C., & Baezconde-Garbanati, L. (1987, Summer). Self regulation and risk-taking behavior: A Hispanic perspective. In *Research Bulletin* (pp. 1–5). Los Angeles: Spanish Speaking Mental Health Research Center.

Padilla, E. R., & O'Grady, K. E. (1987). Sexuality among Mexican-Americans: A case of sexual stereotyping. *Journal of Personality and Social Psychology, 52,* 5–10.

Pagelow, M. D. (1992). Adult victims of domestic violence: Battered women. *Journal of Interpersonal Violence, 7*(1), 87–120.

Pal, R. M. (2000). Women's movement in Islamic countries. *PUCL Bulletin,* December 2000.

Palca, J. (1990). Women left out at NIH. *Science, 248,* 1601–1602.

Palmore, E. (1971). Attitudes toward aging as shown by humor. *Gerontologist, 11,* 181–186.

Palmore, E. B., Burchett, B., Fillenbaum, G. G., George, L., & Wallman, L. M. (1985). *Retirement: Causes and consequences.* New York: Springer.

Paludi, M. (1992). *The psychology of women.* New York: Brown & Benchmark.

Paludi, M. A. (1984). Psychometric properties and underlying assumptions of four objective measures of fear of success. *Sex Roles, 10,* 765–781.

Paludi, M. A. (2004). Sexual harassment of college students: Cultural Similarities and differences. In J. C. Chrisler, C. Golden, & P. D. Rozee (Eds.), *Lectures on the psychology of women* (pp. 332–355). New York: McGraw Hill.

Pandey, G. (2003). Domestic abuse hits India's elite. *BBC News World Edition.* Available: www.news.bbc.co.uk/2/hi/south_asia/2946760.stm

Paradise, L. V., & Wall, S. M. (1986). Children's perceptions of male and female principals and teachers. *Sex Roles, 14,* 1–7.

Pardue, M. L. (2001, July 9). Studying the differences between the sexes may spur improvements in medicine. *The Scientist, 15*(14).

Parke, R. D. (1978). Perspectives on father–infant interaction. In J. D. Osofsky (Ed.), *Handbook of infancy* (pp. 549–590). New York: Wiley.

Parks, M. R., Stan, C. M., & Eggert, L. L. (1983). Romantic involvement and social network involvement, *Social Psychology Quarterly, 46*(2), 116–131.

Parrinder, G. (1983). *World religions: From ancient history to the present.* New York: Facts on File.

Patlak, M. (1997). The long and short of it. New medications for growth disorders. In A. M. Meehan & E. Astor-Stetson (Eds.), *Adolescent psychology* (pp. 37–39). Guilford, CT: Dushkin Publishing Group/Brown & Benchmark Publishers.

Patterson, C. (1992). Children of lesbian and gay parents. *Child Development, 63,* 1025–1042.

Patterson, C. (1994). Children of the lesbian baby-boom: Behavioral adjustment, self-concepts, and sex-role identity. In B. Greene & G. M. Herek (Eds.), *Lesbian and gay psychology: Theory, research, and clinical applications.* (pp. 156–175). Psychological Perspectives on Lesbian and Gay Issues, Vol. 1. Thousand Oaks, CA: Sage.

Patterson, C. J. (2000). Family relationships of lesbians and gay men. *Journal of Marriage & the Family, 62*(4), 1052–1069.

Patterson, C. J., & Redding, R. E. (1996). Lesbian and gay families with children: Implications of social science research for policy. *Journal of Social Issues, 52*(3), 29–50.

Patterson, C. J., & Schwartz, P. (1994). The social construction of conflict in intimate same-sex couples. In D. D. Cahn (Ed.), *Conflict in personal relationships* (pp. 3–26). Hillsdale, NJ: Erlbaum.

Payne, D. E., & Mussen, P. H. (1956). Parent–child relations and father identification among adolescent boys. *Journal of Abnormal and Social Psychology, 52,* 358–362.

Pearce, J., Hawton, K., & Blake, F. (1995). Psychological and sexual symptoms associated with menopause and the effects of hormone replacement therapy. *British Journal of Psychiatry, 167,* 163–173.

Pearlman, S. F. (1992). Heterosexual mothers/lesbian daughters: Parallels and similarities. *Journal of Feminist Family Therapy, 4*(2), 1–25.

Pearlman, S. F. (1993). Late mid-life astonishment: Disruptions to identity and self-esteem. *Women & Therapy, 14*(1/2), 1–12.

Pease, J. (1993). Professor Mom: Woman's work in a man's world. *Sociological Forum, 8*(1), 133–139.

Peirce, K. (1999). Aunt Jemima isn't keeping up with the Energizer bunny: Stereotyping of animated spokes-characters in advertising. *Sex Roles, 40*(11/12), 959–968.

Penner, L. A., Thompon, J. K., & Coovert, D. L. (1991). Size overestimation among anorexics: Much ado about very little? *Journal of Abnormal Psychology, 100,* 90–93.

Penning, M. J., & Strain, L. A. (1994). Gender differences in disability, assistance, and subjective well-being in later life. *Journal of Gerontology, 49*(4), 202–208.

Peplau, L. A. (1991). Lesbian and gay relationships. In J. Gonsiorek & J. Weinrich (Eds.), *Homosexuality: Research implications for public policy* (pp. 177–196). Newbury Park, CA: Sage.

Peplau, L. A., & Cochran, S. D. (1990). A relational perspective on homosexuality. In D. P. McWhirter, S. A. Sanders, & J. M. Reinisch (Eds.), *Homosexuality/heterosexuality: Con-*

cepts of sexual orientation (pp. 321–349). New York: Oxford University Press.

Peplau, L. A., & Gordon, S. L. (1985). Women and men in love: Gender differences in close heterosexual relationships. In V. E. O'Leary, R. K. Unger, & B. S. Wallston (Eds.), *Women, gender, and social psychology* (pp. 257–291). Hillsdale, NJ: Erlbaum.

Peplau, L. A., Garnets, L. D., Spalding, L. H., Conley, T. D., & Vienegas, R. C. (1998). Critique of Bem's "Exotic becomes Erotic" theory of sexual orientation. *Psychological Review, 105,* 387–394.

Peplau, L. A., Padesky, C. & Hamilton, M. (1982). Satisfaction in lesbian relationships. *Journal of Homosexuality, 8,* 23–35.

Peplau, L. A., Rubin, Z., & Hill, C. T. (1977). Sexual intimacy in dating relationships. *Journal of Social Issues, 33,* 86–109.

Perkins, W. (1596). *A discourse on the damned art of witchcraft.* London: n.p. Cited by Reuther, R. R. (1983). Women and religion in America Vol. 2, The colonial and revolutionary period. (pp. 222–224) New York: Harper Collins.

Perlini, A. H. (2001). The effects of male age and physical appearance on evaluations of attractiveness, social desirability and resourcefulness. *Social Behavior and Personality, 29*(3), 277–287.

Perrett, D. I. (1994). Nature. Cited by Brody, J. E. (1994, March 21). Notions of beauty transcend culture, new study suggests. *New York Times,* p. A14.

Perry, J. D., & Whipple, B. (1981). Pelvic muscle strength of female ejaculation: Evidence in support of a new theory of orgasm. *Journal of Sex Research, 17,* 22–39.

Persson, I., Adami, H. O., Bergkvist, L., Lindgren, A., Petterson, B., Hoover, R., & Schairer, C. (1989). Risk of endometrial cancer after treatment with estrogens alone or in conjunction with progestins: Results of a prospective study. *British Medical Journal, 298,* 147–151.

Petersen, A. C. (1983). Menarche: Meaning of measures and measuring meaning. In S. Golub (Ed.), *Menarche: The transition from girl to woman* (pp. 63–76). Lexington, MA: Lexington Books.

Peterson, A. C., & Crockett, L. J. (1987). Biological correlates of spatial ability and mathematical performance. In J. A. Sechzer & S. M. Pfafflin (Eds.), *Psychology and Educational Policy. Annals of the New York Academy of Sciences, 517,* 69–86.

Petersen, K. (2002, May, 23), When Grandpa and Grandma divorce the grandkids can be hurt, too. *USA Today,* section 11D.

Petrakis, N. (1988). Chinese and breast cancer. In *Summary of Breaking the Barriers Conference by Asian American Health Forum, Inc.* San Francisco: AAHF.

Pharr, S. (1988). *Homophobia: A weapon of sexism.* Inverness, CA: Chardon Press.

Philliber, W., & Hiller, D. (1983). Relative occupational attainment of spouses and later changes in marriage and wife's work experience. *Journal of Marriage and the Family, 45,* 161–170.

Phinney, J. S. (1996). When we talk about American ethnic groups, what do we mean? *American Psychologist, 51,* 918–927.

Piaget, J. (1932). *The moral judgment of the child.* London: Kegan, Paul, Trench, & Trubner.

Piedmont, R. L. (1995). Another look at fear of success, fear of failure, and test anxiety: A motivational analysis using the five-factor model. *Sex Roles, 32,* 139–158.

Pike, K. (1995). Bulimic symptomatology in high school girls: Toward a model of cumulative risk. *Psychology of Women Quarterly, 19,* 373–396.

Pike, K. M., & Striegel-Moore, R. H. (1997). Disordered eating and eating disorders. In S. J. Gallant, G. P. Keita, & R. Royak-Schaler (Eds.), *Health care for women: Psychological, social, and behavioral influences* (pp. 97–114). Washington, DC: American Psychological Association.

Pillard, R. C., & Weinrich, J. D. (1986). Evidence of a familial nature of male homosexuality. *Archives of Sexual Behavior, 43,* 808–812.

Pimental, E. E. (2000). Just how much do I love thee? Marital relations in urban China. *Journal of Marriage and the Family, 62,* 32–48.

Pinderhughes, E. (1989). *Understanding race, ethnicity, and power: The key to efficacy in clinical practice.* New York: Free Press.

Pine, F. (1990). *Drive, ego, object, self.* New York: Basic Books.

Pinel, J. P. J. (1993). *Biopsychology* (2nd ed.). Boston: Allyn and Bacon.

Pinel, J. P. J. (2003) *Biopsychology* (5th ed.). Boston: Allyn and Bacon.

Pinquart, M. (2003). Loneliness in married, widowed, divorced, and never-married older adults. *Journal of Social and Personal Relationships, 20*(1), 31–53.

Pipher, M. (1994). *Reviving Ophelia: Saving the selves of adolescent girls.* New York: Grosset/Putnam.

Pleck, J. H., Sonenstein, F. L., & Ku, L. (1993). Masculinity ideology: Its impact on adolescent males' heterosexual relationships. *Journal of Social Issues, 49,* 11–19.

Polatnick, M. R. (1993). Why men don't rear children. In A. Minas (Ed.), *Gender basics: Feminist perspectives on women and men* (pp. 500–508). Belmont, CA: Wadsworth.

Polefrone, J. M., & Manuck, S. B. (1987). Gender differences in cardiovascular and neuroendocrine response to stressors. In R. C. Barnett, L. Biener, & G. K. Baruch (Eds.), *Gender and stress* (pp. 13–38). New York: Free Press.

Pomerleau, C. S., Zucker, A. N., & Stewart, A. J. (2001). Characterizing concerns about post-cessation weight gain: Results from a national survey of women smokers. *Nicotine and Tobacco Research, 3,* 51–60.

Pool, R. (1993). Evidence for homosexuality gene. *Science, 261,* 291–292.

Pop, V. J. M., Essed, G. G., de Geus, C. A., vanSon, M. M., & Komproe, I. H. (1993). Prevalence of post-partum depression—or is it post-puerperium depression? *Acta Obstet. Gynecol. Scand, 72,* 354–358.

Portes, A., & Truelove, C. (1987). Making sense of diversity: Recent research on Hispanic minorities in the United States. *Annual Review of Sociology, 13,* 359–385.

Portnoy, R. (2003, July 29). *Anesthesiology News,* p. 4.

Poulin-Dubois, D., Serbin, L. A., Kenyon, B., & Derbyshire, A. (1994). Infants' intermodal knowledge about gender. *Developmental Psychology, 30*(3), 436–442.

Powderly, W. G., Landay, A., & Lederman, M. M. (1998). Recovery of the immune system with antiviral therapy: The end of opportunism? *Journal of the American Medical Association, 280*(1), 72–77.

Powell, E. (1991). *Talking back to sexual pressure.* Minneapolis, MN: Compcare Publishers.

Powell, G. N. (1986). Effects of sex role identity and sex on definitions of sexual harassment. *Sex Roles, 14,* 9–19.

Power, T. G., McGrath, M. P., Hughes, S. O., & Manire, S. H. (1994). Compliance and self-assertion: Young children's responses to mothers versus fathers. *Developmental Psychology, 30*(6), 980–989.

Powlishta, K. K., Serbin, L. A., Doyle, A. B., & White, D. R. (1994). Gender, ethnic, and body type biases: The generality of prejudice in childhood. *Developmental Psychology, 30*(4), 526–536.

Press, J. E., & Townsley, E. (1998). Wives' and husbands' housework reporting: Gender, class and social desirability. *Gender and Society, 12*(2), 188–218.

Preston, K., & Stanley, K. (1987). "What's the worst thing . . . ?": Gender-directed insults. *Sex Roles, 17,* 209–219.

Price, D. D., & Dubner, R. (1977). Neurons that subserve the sensory-discriminative aspects of pain. *Pain, 3,* 307–338.

Price, J. H., & Miller, P. A., (1984). Sexual fantasies of Black and White college students. *Psychological Reports, 54,* 1007–1014.

Price, S. J., & McKenry, P. C. (1988). *Divorce.* Newbury Park, CA: Sage.

Prilleltensky, I. (1989). Psychology and the status quo. *American Psychologist, 44,* 795–802.

Pryor, J. B. (1987). Sexual harassment proclivities in men. *Sex Roles, 17,* 269–290.

Purcell, P., & Stewart, L. (1990). Dick and Jane in 1989. *Sex Roles, 22,* 177–185.

Pyant, C. T., & Yanico, B. J. (1991). Relationship of racial identity and gender role attitudes to black women's psychological well-being. *Journal of Counseling Psychology, 38,* 315–322.

Quina, K. (1996). Sexual harassment and rape: A continuum of exploitation. In M. A. Paludi (Ed.), *Sexual harassment on college campuses: Abusing the ivory power.* Albany: State University of New York Press.

Rabin, R. (2004, March 3). NIH halts study of estrogen therapy. *Newsday.*

Rabinowitz, V. C. (1993). *Sex bias in human research: More questions about generalization.* Symposium on "Sex Bias in Research: Are Males and Females the Same?" Annual Meeting of the American Association for the Advancement of Science. Boston, MA.

Rabinowitz, V. C. (1996). Coping with sexual harassment. In M. A. Paludi (Ed.), *Sexual harassment on college campuses: Abusing the ivory power* (pp. 199–213). New York: State University of New York Press.

Rabinowitz, V. C. (2003, August 26). *Sex disparities in academia: Advice for department chairs.* Part of a symposium on family-friendly policies in academia at the annual meeting of the American Political Science Association. Philadelphia, PA.

Rabinowitz, V. C., & Gorman, R. (2004). *By numbers and narratives: Representations of women in depression research.* Manuscript in preparation.

Rabinowitz, V. C., & Martin, D. (2001). Choices and consequences: Methodological issues in the study of gender. In R. K. Unger (Ed.), *The handbook of the psychology of women and gender* (pp. 29–52). New York: Wiley.

Rabinowitz, V. C., & Sechzer, J. A. (1993). Feminist perspectives on research methods. In F. L. Denmark & M. A. Paludi (Eds.), *The psychology of women: A handbook of issues and theories* (pp. 23–66). Westport, CT: Greenwood Press.

Rabinowitz, V. C., Sechzer, J. A., Denmark, F. L., & Weeks, B. M. (1994). *Sex and gender bias in AIDS research: A content analysis.* American Psychological Association Conference on Psychosocial and Behavioral Factors in Women's Health. Washington, DC.

Rabinowitz, V. C., & Weseen, S. (1997). Elu(ci)d(at)ing Epistemological Impasses: Re-viewing the qualitative/quantitative debates in psychology. *Journal of Social Issues, 53*(4), 605–630.

Rabinowitz, V. C., & Weseen, S. (2001). Power, politics, and the qualitative/quantitative debates in psychology. In M. Brydon-Miller and D. L. Tolman (Eds.), *From subjects to subjectivities: A handbook of interpretive and participatory methods* (pp. 12–28). New York: NYU Press.

Radloff, L. S., & Rae, D. S. (1979). Susceptibility and precipitating factors in depression: Sex differences and similarities. *Journal of Abnormal Psychology, 88,* 174–181.

Raisman, G., & Field, P. M. (1971). Sexual dimorphism in the preoptic areas of the rat. *Science, 173,* 20–22.

Ramirez, R. R. and de la Cruz, G. P. (June, 2003). The Hispanic population in the United States: March 2002. Current population reports. US Census Bureau.

Ramsey, P. G. (1991). Young children's awareness and understanding of social class differences. *Journal of Genetic Psychology, 152*(1), 71–82.

Rape, Abuse, and Incest National Network. (2003). *Rape and sexual assault charts and data sets.* Retrieved April 3, 2004, from www.rainn.org/2003facts.pdf

Ratcliff, K. S. (2002). Women and health: Power, technology, inequality, and conflict in a gendered world. Boston: Allyn & Bacon.

Rathus, S. A. (1988). *Human sexuality.* New York: Holt, Rinehart and Winston.

Rathus, S. A., Nevid, J. S., & Fichner-Rathus, L., (1997). *Human sexuality in a world of diversity* (3rd ed.). Boston: Allyn and Bacon.

Rathus, S..A., Nevid, J. S. & Fichner-Rathus, L. (1998). *Essentials of human sexuality.* Boston: Allyn and Bacon.

Rathus, S. A., Nevid, J. S., & Fichner-Rathus, L.(2002). Human sexuality in a world of diversity, (5th ed.). Boston: Allyn and Bacon.

Ratner, R. (2000). *Bearing life: Women's writings on childlessness.* New York: Feminist Press.

Rawlings, E. I., & Carter, D. (1977). *Psychotherapy for women: Treatment toward equality.* Springfield, IL: Thomas.

Rawlings, S., & Saluter, A. (1995). Household and family characteristics. Washington, DC: U.S. Bureau of the Census.

Reddy, D. M., Fleming, R., & Adesso, V. J. (1992). Gender and health. In S. Maes, H. Leventhal, & M. Johnston (Eds.), *International review of health psychology* (Vol. 2, pp. 3–32). West Sussex, England: Wiley.

Reed, R. (1988). Education and achievement of young black males. In J. T. Gibbs (Ed.), *Young, black, and male in America* (pp. 37–96). Dover, MA: Auburn.

Reedy, M. N., Birren, J. E., & Schaie, K. W. (1981). Age and sex differences in satisfying relationships across the life span. *Human Development, 24,* 52–66.

Reeves, T. and Bennett, C. (May, 2002). The Asian and Pacific Islander population in the United States: March 2002. Current Population Reports. US Census Bureau, pp. 1–8.

Regier, D. A., Narrow, W. E., Rae, D. S., Manderscheid, R. W., Locke, B. Z., & Goodwin, F. K. (1993). The de facto U.S. mental and addictive disorders service system. *Archives of General Psychiatry, 50,* 85–94.

Reid, J. D. (1995). Development in later life: Older lesbians and gay lives. In A. R. D'Augelli & C. J. Patterson (Eds.), *Lesbian, gays, and bisexual identities over the life span: Psychological perspectives* (pp. 215–242). New York: Oxford University Press.

Reid, P. T. (1993). Poor women in psychological research: Shut up and shut out. *Psychology of Women Quarterly, 17,* 133–150.

Reid, P. T. (2002). Multicultural psychology: Bringing together gender and ethnicity. *Cultural Diversity and Ethnic Minority Psychology, 8*(2), 103–114.

Reid, P. T., & Paludi, M. A. (1993). Developmental psychology of women: Conception to adolescence. In F. L. Denmark & M. A. Paludi (Eds.), *Psychology of women: A handbook of issues and theories* (pp. 191–212). Westport, CT: Greenwood Press.

Reilly, M. E., Lott, B., & Gallogly, S. M. (1986). Sexual harassment of university students. *Sex Roles, 15,* 333–358.

Rein, M. (2001). *Minorities: A changing role in American society.* Farmington Hills, MI: Gale Group.

Reiner, W. (1997). To be male or female—That is the question. *Archives of Pediatric & Adolescent Medicine, 151,* 224–225.

Reinisch, J. M. (1990). *The Kinsey Institute new report on sex: What you must know to be sexually literate.* New York: St. Martin's Press.

Reis, H. T., Senchak, M., & Solomon, B. (1985). Sex differences in the intimacy of social interaction: Further examination of potential explanations. *Journal of Personality and Social Psychology, 48,* 1204–1217.

Reis, P., & Stone, A. J. (Eds.). (1992). *American women 1992–93: A status report.* New York: W. W. Norton.

Reiss, I. L. (1986). *Journey into sexuality: An exploratory voyage.* Englewood Cliffs, NJ: Prentice Hall.

Reitz, R. (1981). *Menopause: A positive approach.* London: Unwin.

Ren, P. (2004). Beyond orgasm: Dare to be honest about the sex you really want. *Archives of Sexual Behavior, 33*(1), 75–76.

Reskin, B. F. (1993). Sex segregation in the workplace. In J. Blake & J. Hagen (Eds.), *American sociological review* (Vol. 19, pp. 241–270). Palo Alto, CA: Annual Reviews.

Reskin, B. F., & Hartmann, H. I. (1986). *Women's work, men's work: Sex segregation on the job.* Washington, DC: National Academy Press.

Reskin, B. F., & Padavic, I. (1994). *Women and men at work.* Thousand Oaks, CA: Pine Forge Press.

Reskin, B. F., & Roos, P. A. (1987). Sex segregation and status hierarchies. In C. Bose & G. Spitze (Eds.), *Ingredients for women's employment policy* (pp. 3–21). Albany: State University of New York Press.

Resnick, H. S., Kilpatrick, D. G., Dansky, B. S., Saunders, B. E., & Best, C. L. (1993). Prevalence of victim trauma and post-traumatic stress disorder in a representative national sample of women. *Journal of Consulting and Clinical Psychology, 61,* 984–991.

Resnick, H. S., Kilpatrick, D. G., Walsh, C., & Veronen, L. J. (1991). Marital rape. In R. T. Ammerman & M. Hersen (Eds.), *Case studies in family violence* (pp. 329–355). New York: Plenum Press.

Reuther, R. R. (1983). Women and religion. Vol. 2. The colonial and revolutionary period. New York: HarperCollins.

Reynolds, C. F., Miller, M. D., Pasternak, R. E., Frank, E., Perel, J. M., Cornes, C., Houck, P. R., Mazumdar, S., Dew, M. A., & Kupfer, D. J. (1999). Treatment of bereavement-related major depressive episodes in later life: A controlled study of acute and continuation treatment with nortiptyline and interpersonal psychotherapy. *American Journal of Psychiatry, 156,* 202–208.

Reynolds, A. L., & Pope, R. L. (1991). The complexities of diversity: Exploring multiple oppressions. *Journal of Counseling and Development, 70,* 174–180.

Rhode, D. (2003, October 26). India steps up effort to halt abortions of female fetuses. *New York Times,* p. A3.

Rhodes, A. L. (1983). Effects of religious denominations on sex differences in occupational expectations. *Sex Roles, 9,* 93–108.

Rice, J. K., & Hemmings, A. (1988, Spring). Women's colleges and women achievers: An update. *Signs: Journal of Women in Cultures, 13,* 3.

Rice, P. L. (1987). *Stress and health.* Pacific Grove, CA: Brooks/Cole.

Rice, P. L. (1992). *Stress and health* (2nd ed.). Pacific Grove, CA: Brooks Cole.

Rich, A. (1977). *Of women born.* New York: Bantam.

Rich, A. (1980). Compulsory sexuality and lesbian existence. *Signs: Journal of Women in Culture, 5,* 647–650.

Richardson, J. T. E. (1991). Gender differences in imagery, cognition, and memory. In R. H. Logie & M. Denis (Eds.), *Mental images in human cognition* (pp. 107–121). San Diego: Academic Press.

Richardson, L., & Taylor, V. (Eds.). (1993). *Feminist frontiers III.* New York: McGraw-Hill.

Rich-Edwards, J. W., Manson, J. E., Hennekins, C. H., & Buring, J. E. (1995). The primary protection of coronary heart disease in women. *New England Journal of Medicine, 332*(26), 1758–1766.

Richmond-Abbott, M. (1992). *Masculine and feminine: Gender roles across the life cycle* (2nd ed.). New York: McGraw-Hill.

Riege, W. H., & Inman, V. (1981). Age differences in nonverbal memory tasks. *Journal of Gerontology, 36,* 51–58.

Riger, S. (1992). Epistemological debates, feminist voices: Science, social values, and the study of women. *American Psychologist, 47,* 730–740.

Riggs, B. L., & Melton, J. III. (1992). The prevention and treatment of osteoporosis. *The New England Journal of Medicine, 327,* 620–627.

Ringgren, H., & Strom, A. V. (1967). *Religions of mankind,* (pp. 44–50). Philadelphia: Fortress Press.

Risman, B. J. (1987). Intimate relationships from a microcultural perspective: Men who mother. *Gender & Society, 1,* 6–32.

Rivers, R. (1995). Clinical issues and interventions with ethnic minority women. In J. Aponte, R. Rivers, & J. Wohl (Eds.), *Psychological interventions and cultural diversity* (pp. 181–198). Boston: Allyn and Bacon.

Robert, M., & Ohlmann, T. (1994). Water-level representation by men and women as a function of rod-and-frame test proficiency and visual and postural information. *Perception, 23,* 1321–1333.

Roberts, T. (1991). Gender and the influence of evaluations on self-assessments in achievement settings. *Psychological Bulletin, 19,* 297–308.

Robins, L. N., & Regier, D. A. (Eds.). (1990). *Psychiatric disorders in America.* Ontario: Collier MacMillan Canada.

Robins L. N., & Regier, D. A. (Eds.). (1991). *Psychiatric disorders in America: The Epidemiologic Catchment Area Study.* New York: Free Press.

Robinson, G. E. (2003). Stresses on women physicians: Consequences and coping techniques. *Depression & Anxiety, 17*(3), 180–189.

Robinson, J. G., & McIlwee, J. S. (1989). Women in engineering: A promise unfulfilled? *Social Problems, 36,* 455–472.

Robinson, S. P. (1985). Hindu paradigms of women: Images and values. In Y. Y. Haddad & E. B. Findley (Eds.), *Women, religion and social change* (pp. 190–194). Albany: State University of New York Press.

Rodgers, C. S., Fagot, B. I., & Winebarger, A. (1998). Gender-typed toy play in dizygotic twin pairs: A test of hormone transfer theory. *Sex Roles, 39,* 173–184.

Rodin, J., & Ickovics, J. R. (1990). Women's health: Review and research agenda as we approach the 21st century. *American Psychologist, 45,* 1018–1034.

Rogers, K. (1966). *The troublesome helpmate: A history of misogyny in literature.* Seattle: University of Washington Press. Cited by Williams, J., 1987.

Rogers, R. W. (1908). *The religion of Babylonia and Assyria.* New York: Eaton & Mains. Cited by Noss, J. B., 1985, pp. 140–143.

Rogler, L. H., Cortes, D. C., & Malgady, R. G. (1991). Acculturation and mental health status among Hispanics: Convergence and new directions for research. *American Psychologist, 46,* 585–597.

Rohrbaugh, J. B. (1979).*Women: Psychology's puzzle.* New York: Basic Books.

Roizblatt, A. (1999). Long lasting marriages in Chile. *Contemporary Family Therapy: An International Journal, 21*(1), 113–129.

Rollins, B. C. (1989). Marital quality at midlife. In S. Hunter & M. Sundel (Eds.), *Midlife myths: Issues, findings, and practice implications.* Newbury Park, CA: Sage.

Rollins, J. H. (1996). *Women's minds, women's bodies. The psychology of women in a biosocial context.* Upper Saddle River, NJ: Prentice Hall.

Rolls, B. J., Fedoroff, I. C., & Guthrie, J. F. (1991). Gender differences in eating behavior and body weight regulation. *Health Psychology, 10,* 133–142.

Root, M. (1992). Reconstructing the impact of trauma on personality. In L. S. Brown & M. Ballou (Eds.)., *Personality and psychopathology: Feminist reappraisals* (pp. 229–266). New York: Guilford Press.

Root, M. (1995). The psychology of Asian American women. In H. Landrine (Ed.), *Bringing cultural diversity to feminist psychology: Theory, research, and practice* (pp. 265–301). Washington, DC: American Psychological Association.

Rosaldo, M. Z., & Lamphere, L. (1974). *Woman, culture and society.* Stanford, CA: Stanford University Press.

Roscoe, B., Diana, M. S., & Brooks, R. H. (1987). Early, middle, and late adolescents' views on dating and factors influencing partner selection. *Adolescence, 22,* 59–68.

Rosen, B. N., & Peterson, L. (1990). Gender differences in children's outdoor play injuries: A review and an integration. *Clinical Psychology Review, 10,* 187–205.

Rosenberg, J., Perlstadt, H., & Phillips, W. R. F. (1993). Now that we are here: Discrimination, disparagement, and harassment at work and the experience of women lawyers. *Gender & Society, 7*(3), 415–433.

Rosenberg, R. (1982). *Beyond separate spheres: Intellectual roots of modern feminism.* New Haven, CT: Yale University Press.

Rosenthal, E. (2000). China's widely flouted one-child policy undercuts its census. *The New York Times,* April 14, 2002.

Rosenthal, E. (2002, April 14) China's widely flouted one-child policy undercuts its census. *The New York Times.*

Rosenthal, R., & Jacobson, L. (1968). *Pygmalion in the classroom: Teacher expectations and pupils' intellectual development.* New York: Holt, Rinehart & Winston.

Ross, C. A., Anderson, G., Heber, S., & Norton, G. R. (1990). Dissociation and abuse among multiple personality patients, prostitutes, and exotic dancers. *Hospital and Community Psychiatry, 41,* 328–330.

Ross, C. E., & Mirowsky, J. (1988). Child care and emotional adjustment to wives' employment. *Journal of Health and Social Behavior, 29,* 127–138.

Ross, H., & Taylor, H. (1989). Do boys prefer Daddy or his physical style of play? *Sex Roles, 20,* 23–31.

Ross, S. I., & Jackson, J. M. (1991). Teachers' expectations for Black males' and Black females' academic achievement. *Personality and Social Psychology Bulletin, 17,* 78–82.

Rosser, S. V. (1992). *Biology and feminism: A dynamic interaction.* New York: Twayne.

Rossi, A. (1979). Transition to parenthood. In P. Rose (Ed.), *Socialization and the life cycle* (pp. 132–145). New York: St. Martin's Press.

Rossi, A. S. (1980). Life-span theories and women's lives. *Signs, 6,* 4–32.

Rostovsky, S. S., & Travis, C. B. (1996). Menopause research and the dominance of the biomedical model 1984–1994. *Psychology of Women Quarterly, 20,* 285–312.

Rothbaum, B. O., Foa, E. B., Riggs, D. S., Murdock, T., & Walsh, W. (1992). A prospective examination of post-traumatic stress disorder in rape victims. *Journal of Traumatic Stress, 5,* 455–475.

Rothblum, E. D. (1988). Introduction: Lesbianism as a model of a positive lifestyle for women. *Women & Therapy, 8,* 1–12.

Rothblum, E. D. (1994). Lesbians and physical appearance: Which model applies? In B. Greene & G. M. Herek (Eds.), *Lesbian and gay psychology: Theory, research, and clinical applications.* Psychological Perspectives on Lesbian and Gay Issues. Thousand Oaks, CA: Sage.

Rothenberg, P. (Ed.). (2001). *Race, class and gender in the United States.* New York: Worth.

Rothstein, E. (1997, February 17). Software for girls: Glaring gender differences. *New York Times CyberTimes.* Retrieved September 18, 1999 from http://search.nytimes.com/search/daily.

Rowe, M. P. (1996). Dealing with harassment: A systems approach. In M. S. Stockdale (Ed.), *Sexual harassment in the workplace: Perspectives, frontiers, and response strategies* (pp. 241–271). Thousand Oaks, CA: Sage.

Rowe, W., Behrens, J., & Leach, M. (1995). Racial/ethnic identity and racial consciousness: Looking back and looking forward. In J. G. Ponterotto and J. M. Casas (Eds.). *Handbook of multicultural counseling.* (pp. 218–235). Thousand Oaks, CA; Sage.

Rozee, P. D. (1993). Forbidden or forgiven? Rape in cross-cultural perspective. *Psychology of Women Quarterly, 17,* 499–514.

Rozee, P. D. (2000). Sexual victimization: Harassment and rape. In M. K. Biaggio & M. Herson (Eds.) *Issues in the psychology of women.* (pp. 93–113). New York: Kluwer Academic/Plenum Publishers.

Rozee, P. D. (2004). Women's fear of rape: Causes, consequences, and coping. In J. C. Chrisler, C. Golden, & P. D. Rozee (Eds.), *Lectures on the psychology of women* (pp. 276–291). New York: McGraw Hill.

Rozee, P. D., & Koss, M. P. (2001). Rape: A century of resistance. *Psychology of Women Quarterly. 25*(4), 295–311.

Rozin, P., & Fallon, A. (1988). Body image, attitudes to weight, and misperceptions of figure preferences of the opposite sex: A comparison of men and women in two generations. *Journal of Abnormal Psychology, 97,* 342–345.

Rubin, J., Provenzano, F., & Luria, Z. (1974). The eye of the beholder: Parents' views on sex of newborns. *American Journal of Orthopsychiatry, 44,* 512–519.

Rubin, L. (1980). Blue-collar marriage and the sexual revolution. In A. Skolnik & J. Skolnik (Eds.), *The family in transition* (3rd ed., p. 160). Boston: Little, Brown.

Rubin, R. (2003, October). Cholesterol drugs may cut breast cancer risk. *USA Today,* p. 6D.

Rubin, R., Reinisch, J., and Haskett, R. (1981). Postnatal gonadal steroid effects on human behavior. *Science, 211*(4488), 1318–1324.

Rubin, Z., Peplau, L. A., & Hill, C. T. (1981). Loving and leaving: Sex differences in romantic attachments. *Sex Roles, 7,* 821–835.

Rubinow, D. R., Schmidt, P. J., & Roca, C. A. (1998, November). Estrogen-serotonin interactions: Implications for effective regulation. *Biological Psychiatry, 44*(9), 839–850.

Rudman, L. A., & Borgida, E. (1995). The afterglow of construct accessibility: The behavioral consequences of priming men to view women as sexual objects. *Journal of Experimental Social Psychology, 31,* 493–517.

Ruiz, A. S. (1990). Ethnic identity: Crisis and resolution. *Journal of Multicultural Counseling and Development, 18,* 29–40.

Rusbult, C. E., & Martz, J. M. (1995). Remaining in an abusive relationship: An investment model analysis of nonvoluntary dependence. *Personality and Social Psychology Bulletin, 21,* 558–571.

Russell, D. (1986). *The secret trauma: Incest in the lives of girls and women.* New York: Basic Books.

Russell, D. (1993). *Against pornography.* Berkeley, CA: Russell Publications.

Russell, G. F. M., Szmuckler, G. I., & Dare, C. (1987). An evaluation of family therapy and anorexia nervosa and bulimia nervosa. *Archives of General Psychiatry, 44,* 1047–1056.

Russo, N., & Denmark, F. (1984). Women, psychology, and public policy. *American Psychologist, 39*(10), 161–165.

Russo, N., & Green, B. (1993). Women and mental health. In F. Denmark & M. Paludi (Eds.), *Psychology of women: A handbook of issues and theories* (pp. 379–436). Westport, CT: Greenwood Press.

Russo, N. F. (1976). The motherhood mandate. *Journal of Social Issues, 32,* 143–153.

Russo, N. F. (2004). Understanding emotional responses after abortion. In J. C. Chrisler, C. G. Golden, & P. D. Rozee (Eds.), *Lectures on the psychology of women* (pp. 129–143). New York: McGraw-Hill.

Russo, N. F., & Denmark, F. L. (1987). Contributions of women to psychology. *Annual Review of Psychology, 38,* 279–298.

Ryan, E. B., & Carranza, M. A. (1975). Valuative reactions of adolescents toward speakers of standard English and Mexican-American accented English. *Journal of Personality and Social Psychology, 31,* 855–863.

Ryan, E. B., Carranza, M. A., & Moffie, R. W. (1977). Reactions towards varying degrees of accentedness in the speech of Spanish-English bilinguals. *Language and Speech, 20,* 24–26.

Ryan, W. (1971). *Blaming the victim.* New York: Random House.

Rybarczyk, B. (1994). Diversity among American men: The impact of aging, ethnicity, and race. In C. T. Kilmartin (Ed.), *The masculine self* (pp. 113–131). New York: Macmillan.

Saal, F. E., Johnson, C. B., & Weber, N. (1989). Friendly or sexy? It may depend on whom you ask. *Psychology of Women Quarterly, 13,* 263–276.

Sadker, M., & Sadker, D. (1994). *Failing at fairness: How America's schools cheat girls.* New York: Scribner's Sons.

Sadker, M., Sadker, D., & Klein, S. (1991). The issue of gender in elementary and secondary education. In G. Grant (Ed.), *Review of research in education* (Vol. 17, pp. 269–334). Washington, DC: American Educational Research Association.

Safilios-Rothschild, C. (1979). *Sex-role socialization and discrimination: A synthesis and critique of the literature.* Washington, DC: National Institute of Education.

Sagan, E. (1988). *Freud, women, and morality.* New York: Basic Books.

Salant, K. (2003, October 11). Home-improvement projects let elderly parents stay close, but not too close. *Washington Post,* section F3.

Salgado de Snyder, V. N., Cervantes, R. C. & Padilla, A. M. (1990). Gender and ethnic differences in psychosocial stress and generalized distress among Hispanics. *Sex Roles, 22,* 441–453.

Sanday, P. R. (1981). The socio-cultural context of rape: A cross-cultural study. *Journal of Social Issues, 37,* 5–27.

Sanders, S. A., & Reinisch, J. M. (1999). Would you say you "had sex" if . . . ? *Journal of the American Medical Association, 28*(3), 275–277.

Sanderson, S. L. (2000). Factors influencing paternal involvement in child rearing. *Dissertation Abstracts International, 60*(11B), 57–90.

Santelli, J. S., Lindberg, L. D., Abma, J., McNeely, J. S., & Resnick, M. (2000, July/August). Adolescent sexual behavior: Estimates and trends from four nationally representative surveys. *Family Planning Perspectives, 32*(4), 156–194.

Sarafino, E. R. (1994). *Health psychology: Biopsychosocial interactions.* New York: Wiley.

Saravate, S. (2000, June 16). Dowries the root cause of abuse of women in India. *Pacific News Service,* pp. 1–3.

Sargent, C., & Harris, M. (1992). Gender ideology, childrearing, and child health in Jamaica. *American Ethnologist, 19*(3), 523–537.

Satterfield, A. T., & Muehlenhard, C. L. (1997). The effects of an authority figure's flirtatiousness on women's and men's self-rated creativity. *Psychology of Women Quarterly, 21,* 395–416.

Satyaswaroop, P. G., Zaino, R. J., & Mortel, R. (1983). Human endometrial adenocarcinoma transplanted into nude mice: Growth regulation by estradiol. *Science, 219,* 58–60.

Savin-Williams, R. C. (1979). Dominance hierarchies in groups of early adolescents. *Child Development, 50,* 923–935.

Scanzoni, L., & Scanzoni, J. J. (1976). *Men, women, and change: A sociology of marriage and the family.* New York: McGraw-Hill.

Scarf, M. (1979). The more sorrowful sex. *Psychology Today, 12*(11), 44–52, 89.

Scarr, S. (1988). Race and gender as psychological variables. *American Psychologist, 43,* 56–59.

Schaefer, R. T. (2001). *Race and ethnicity in the United States.* Upper Saddle River, NJ: Prentice Hall.

Schaie, K. W. (1987). Aging and human performance. In M. W. Riley, J. D. Matarazzo, & A. Baum (Eds.), *Perspectives and behavioral medicine: The aging dimension* (pp. 29–37). Hillsdale, NJ: Erlbaum.

Schaie, K. W. (1994). *The course of adult intellectual development.* Unpublished manuscript, Pennsylvania State University, University Park, PA.

Schatten, G., & Schatten, H. (1983). The energetic egg. *The Sciences, 23*(5), 28–34.

Schatz, M. S., & Bane, W. (1991). Empowering the parents of children in substitute care: A training model. *Child Welfare, 70,* 665–678.

Schlegal, A. (1973). The adolescent socialization of the Hopi girl. *Ethnology, 12,* 449–462.

Schlegal, A., & Barry, H., III. (1991). *Adolescence: An anthropological inquiry.* New York: Plenum Press.

Schlesinger, B. (1982). Lasting marriages in the 1980s. *Conciliation Courts Review, 20,* 43–49.

Schlossberg, N. K. (1984). The midlife woman as student. In G. Baruch & J. Brooks-Gunn (Eds.), *Women in midlife* (pp. 315–339). New York: Plenum Press.

Schmidt, N. B., & Koselka, M. (2000). Gender differences in patients with panic disorder: Evaluating cognitive mediation of phobic avoidance. *Cognitive Therapy and Research, 24,* 533 550.

Schmidt, P. J., & Rubinow, D. R. (1991). Menopause-related affective disorders: A justification for further study. *American Journal of Psychiatry, 148,* 844–852.

Schneider, B. F. (1987). Graduate women, sexual harassment, and university policy. *General Hospital Psychiatry, 58,* 46–65.

Schneir, M. (Ed.). (1972). *Feminism: The essential historial writings.* New York: Vintage.

Schoen, R., Astone, N., & Rothert, K. (2002). Women's employment, marital happiness, and divorce. *Social Forces, 81*(2), 643–662.

Schrire, C., & Steiger, W. L. (1974). A matter of life and death: An investigation into the practice of female infanticide in the Arctic. *Man, 9,* 161–184.

Schuette, C. T. (2000). Children's evaluations of gender roles in a home context. *Dissertation Abstracts International, 61*(1B), 556.

Schur, E. M. (1984). *Labeling women deviant: Gender, stigma and control.* Philadelphia: Temple University Press.

Schuster, M. A., Stein, B. D., Jaycox, L. H., Collins, R. L., Marshall, G. N., Elliott, M. N., Zhou, A. J., Kanouse, D. E., Morrison, J. L., & Berry, S. II. (2001). A National Survey of Stress Reactions after the September 11, 2001, Terrorist Attacks. *New England Journal of Medicine, 345,* 1507–1512.

Schwartz, R. A. (1986). Abortion on request: The psychiatric implications. In J. D. Butler & D. F. Walbert (Eds.), *Abortion and the law* (3rd ed., pp. 323–337). Dublin, Ireland: Round Hall Sweet & Maxwell.

Scrimshaw, S. (1984). Infanticide in human populations: Social and individual concerns. In G. Haustater & S. Hrdy (Eds.), *Infanticide: Comparative and evolutionary perspectives* (pp. 463–486). New York: Aldine.

Searles, P., & Berger, R. J. (1987). The current status of rape reform legislation: An examination of state statutes. *Women's Rights Law Reporter, 10,* 25–43.

Seavey, C. A., Katz, P. A., & Zalk, S. R. (1975). Baby X: The effects of gender labels on adult responses to infants. *Sex Roles, 1,* 103–109.

Sechzer, J. (2000). Gender and physical health: Issues across the lifespan. In C. Sedikides, & M. Brewer, (Eds.), *Individual self, relational self, collective self.* Philadelphia: Brunner-Routledge.

Sechzer, J. A., with the National Research Council Committee on Pain and Distress in Laboratory Animals, Institute of Laboratory Animal Resources. (1992). *Recognition and allevia-*

tion of pain and distress in laboratory animals. Washington, DC: National Academy Press.

Sechzer, J. A. (1993). *Sex bias in animal research: A question of generalization.* Symposium on "Sex Bias in Research: Are Males and Females the Same?" Annual Meeting of the American Association for the Advancement of Science. Boston, MA.

Sechzer, J. A. (2004). History and interpretations of Islamic women's status. *Sex Roles.* Special edition on "Islam and Women: Where Tradition Meets Modernity" (In Press).

Sechzer, J. A. Griffin, A., & Pflafflin, S. M. (1994). Women's health and paradigm change. In J. A. Sechzer, A. Griffin, & S. M. Pflafflin (Eds.), *Forging a women's health research agenda: Policy issues for the 1990's. Annals of the New York Academy of Sciences, 736,* 2–20.

Sechzer, J. A., Denmark, F. L., & Rabinowitz, V. C. (1993). Gender bias in women's health research. Proceedings of the NIH—Office of Research on Women's Health. *Recruitment and retention of women in clinical trials.* Huntsville, MD.

Sechzer, J. A., Pfafflin, S. M., Denmark, F. L., Griffin, A., & Blumenthal, S. J. (1996). Women and mental health: An introduction. In J. A. Sechzer, S. M. Pfafflin, F. L. Denmark, A. Griffin, & S. J. Blumenthal (Eds.), *Women and mental health. Annals of the New York Academy of Sciences, 789,* vii–x.

Sechzer, J. A., Rabinowitz, V. C., Denmark, F. L., McGinn, M. F., Weeks, B. M., & Wilkens, C. L. (1994). Sex and gender bias in animal research and in clinical studies of cancer, cardiovascular disease, and depression. In J. A. Sechzer, A. Griffin, & S. M. Pfafflin (Eds.), *Forging a women's health research agenda: Policy issues for the 1990's. Annals of the New York Academy of Sciences, 736,* 21–48.

Sechzer, J. A., Zmitrovich, A., & Denmark, F. L. (1985, October). Sex bias in research. Symposium on "Sex and Gender Bias in Psychological Research." *Program of the Section of Psychology of the New York Academy of Sciences.* New York, NY.

Sechzer, J., Pfafflin, S., & Denmark, F. L. (1996). *Women and Mental Health.* New York: New York Academy of Science.

Sedikides, C., & Brewer, M. (2001). *Individual self, relational self, collective self.* Philadelphia: Brunner-Routledge.

Seed, M. (1994). Postmenopausal hormone replacement therapy, coronary heart disease and plasma lipoproteins. *Drugs, 47*(Suppl. 2), 25–34.

Seegmiller, B. (1993). Pregnancy. In F. Denmark & M. Paludi (Eds.), *Psychology of women: A handbook of issues and theories* (pp. 437–474). Westport, CT: Greenwood Press.

Seligman, M. E. (1992). *Helplessness: On depression, development, and death.* New York: Freeman.

Seligman, M. E., & Maier, S. F. (1967). Failure to escape traumatic shock. *Journal of Experimental Psychology 74*(1), 1–9.

Seller, M. (1981). G. Stanley Hall & Edward Thorndike on the education of women: Theory and policy in the progressive era. *Educational Studies, 11,* 365–374.

Selye, H. (1956). *The stress of life.* New York: McGraw-Hill.

Serafino, E. P. (1994). *Health psychology: Biopsychosocial interactions.* New York: Wiley.

Serbin, L. A. (2001). Gender stereotyping in infancy: Visual preferences for and knowledge of gender-stereotyped toys in the second year. *International Journal of Behavioral Development, 25*(1), 7–15.

Serbin, L. A., Connor, J. M., Buchardt, C. J., & Citron, C. C. (1979). Effects of peer presence on sex-typing of children's play behavior. *Journal of Experimental Child Psychology, 27,* 303–309.

Serbin, L. A., Moller, L., Powlishta, K., & Gulko, J. (1991, April). *The emergence of gender segregation and behavioral compatibility in toddlers' peer preferences.* Paper presented at the biennial meeting of the Society for Research in Child Development, Seattle, WA.

Serbin, L. A., O'Leary, K. D., Kent, R., & Tonick, I. (1973). A comparison of teacher response to preacademic and problem behavior of boys and girls. *Child Development, 44,* 796–804.

Serril, M. S. (1993, June 21). Defiling the children. *Newsweek,* pp. 52–55.

Severne, L. (1982). Psychosocial aspects of menopause. In A. M. Voda, M. Dinnerstein, & S. R. O'Donnell (Eds.), *Changing perspectives on menopause* (pp. 239–247). Austin, TX: University of Texas Press.

Shaffer, D. R., & Wegley, C. (1974). Success orientation and sex role congruence as determinants of the attractiveness of competent women. *Journal of Personality, 42,* 586–600.

Shafter, R. (1992). Women and masochism: An introduction to trends in psychoanalytic thinking. *Issues in Ego Psychology, 15,* 56–62.

Shapiro, H. I. (1988). *The new birth-control book: A complete guide for women and men.* Englewood Cliffs, NJ: Prentice Hall.

Shaywitz, B. A., Shaywitz, S. E., Pugh, K. R., Constable, R. T., Skudlarski, P., Fulbright, R. K., Bronen, R. A., Fletcher, J. M., Shankweller, D. P., Katz, L., & Gore, G. C. (1995). Sex differences in the functional organization of the brain for language. *Nature, 373,* 607–609.

Shellenbarger, S. (1997, April 16). For many, work seems like a retreat compared with home. *Wall Street Journal,* p. B1.

Shenk, D., & Fullmer, E. (1996). Significant relationships among older women: Cultural and personal constructions of lesbianism. In K. A. Roberto (Ed.), *Relationships between women in later life* (pp. 75–89). New York: Harrington Park Press/Haworth Press.

Shepard, G. B. (1991). A glimpse of kindergarten—Chinese style. *Young Children, 47,* 11–15.

Sherwin, B. B. (1998). Estrogen and cognitive functioning in women. *Estrogen and Cognition, 217,* 17–22.

Sherwin, L. N. (1987). *Psychosocial dimensions of the pregnant family.* New York: Springer.

Shields, S. (1975). Functionalism, Darwinism, and the psychology of women. *American Psychologist, 30,* 739–754.

Shlapentokh, V. (1984, February 4). In Soviet Union, women emerge superior. *New York Times,* p. 23.

Shockley, W. (1971). Negro I.Q. deficit: Failure of a malicious coincidence model warrants new research proposals. *Review of Educational Research, 41,* 227–248.

Short, R. V. (1982). Sex determination and differentiation. In C. R. Austin & R. V. Short (Eds.), *Reproduction in mammals* (2nd ed., Vol. 2, pp. 70–113). London: Cambridge University Press.

Shorter, E. (1975). *The making of the modern family.* New York: Basic Books.

Showalter, E. (1985). *The female malady: Women, madness, and culture, 1830–1980.* New York: Penguin Books.

Shum, L. M. (1996). Asian-American women: Cultural and mental health issues. In J. A. Sechzer & S. M. Pfafflin (Eds.), *Women and mental health* (pp. 181–190). New York, NY: New York Academy of Sciences.

Sidanius, J., Bobo, L., & Pratto, F. (1996). Racism, conservatism, affirmative action, and intellectual sophistication: A matter of principled conservatism or group dominance? *Journal of Personality and Social Psychology. 70*(3), 476–490.

Sidel, R. (1993). Who are the poor? In V. Cyrus (Ed.), *Experiencing race, class, and gender in the United States* (pp. 123–128). Mountain View, CA: Mayfield.

Sidorowicz, L. S., & Lunney, G. S. (1980). Baby X revisited. *Sex Roles, 6,* 67–73.

Siefert, K., Bowman, P. J., Heflin, C. M., Danziger, S., & Willimas, D. R. (2000). Social and environmental predictors of maternal depression in current and recent welfare recipients. *American Journal of Orthopsychiatry, 70*(4), 510–522.

Siegel, M., Brisman, J., & Weinshel, M. (1997). *Surviving an eating disorder: Strategies for family and friends* (rev. ed.). New York: HarperCollins.

Signorelli, N. (1989). Television and conceptions about sex roles: Maintaining conventionality and the status quo. *Sex Roles, 21*(5/6), 341–352.

Silver, J. (1998). Taking domestic violence to task. Available: www.ou.org/publications/ja/5758/spring98/silver1.htm

Silverman, A. B., Reinherz, H. Z., & Giaconia, R. M. (1996). The long-term sequelae of child and adolescent abuse: A longitudinal community study. *Child Abuse and Neglect, 20,* 709–723.

Silverman, I., & Eals, M. (1992). Sex differences in spatial abilities: Evolutionary theory and data. In J. Barkow, L. Cosmides, & J. Tooby (Eds.), *The adapted mind: Evolutionary psychology and the generation of culture* (pp. 533–549). New York: Oxford University Press.

Silverstein, B., & Perlick, D. (1995). *The cost of competence: Why inequality causes depression, eating disorders, and illness in women.* New York: Oxford University Press.

Silverstein, L. B. (1996). Fathering is a feminist issue. *Psychology of Women Quarterly, 20,* 3–37.

Silverstein, L. B., & Auerbach, C. F. (2002). The myth of the "normal family." *Annual Editions: The Family 02/03* (pp. 13–15). Dubuque, IA: McGraw-Hill/Dushkin.

Simmons, R. G., & Blyth, D. A. (1987). *Moving into adolescence: The impact of pubertal change and school context.* New York: Aldine De Gruyter.

Simmons, R. G., Blyth, D. A., Van Cleave, E. F., & Bush, D. M. (1979). Entry into early adolescence: The impact of school structure, puberty, and early dating on self-esteem. *American Sociological Review, 44,* 948–967.

Simoni-Wastila, L. (1998). Gender and psychotropic drug use. *Medical Care, 36*(1), 88–94.

Singer, J., & Singer, I. (1972). Types of female orgasm. *Journal of Sex Research, 8,* 255–267.

Singh, D. (1993). Adaptive significance of waist-to-hip ratio and female physical attractiveness. *Journal of Personality and Social Psychology, 65,* 293–307.

Singh, S. (1994). Gender differences in work values and personality characteristics among Indian executives. *Journal of Social Psychology, 134*(5), 699–700.

Singh, S., & Darroch, J. E. (1999). Trends in sexual activity among adolescent American women: 1982–1995. *Family Planning Perspectives, 31*(5), 212–219.

Slipp, S. (1993). *The Freudian mystique: Freud, women, and feminism.* New York, NY: University Press.

Slochower, J. (1996). *Holding and psychoanalysis: A relational perspective.* Hillsdale, NJ: Analytic Press.

Slonim-Nevo, V. (1992). First premarital intercourse among Mexican-American and Anglo-American adolescent women: Interpreting ethnic differences. *Journal of Adolescent Research, 7,* 332–351.

Small, M. F. (1999). A woman's curse. *The Sciences, 39*(1), 24–29.

Smart, J. F., & Smart, D. W. (1995). Acculturative stress: The experience of the Hispanic immigrant. *The Counseling Psychologist, 23,* 25–42.

Smetana, J. G. (1988). Concepts of self and social convention: Adolescents' and parents' reasoning about hypothetical and actual family conflicts. In M. Gunnar & W. A. Collins (Eds.), *Development during the transition to adolescence: Minnesota symposia on child psychology* (Vol. 21, pp. 79–119). Hillsdale, NJ: Erlbaum.

Smith, A. D. (1977). Adult age differences in cued recall. *Developmental Psychology, 13,* 326–331.

Smith, C. A. (1996). Women, weight, and body image. In J. C. Chrisler, C. Golden, & P. D. Rozee (Eds.), *Lectures on the psychology of women* (pp. 91–104). New York: McGraw-Hill.

Smith, G. J. (1985). Facial and full-length ratings of attractiveness related to the social interactions of young children. *Sex Roles, 12,* 287–293.

Smith, H. (1994). *World's religions: A guide to our wisdom traditions.* New York: HarperCollins.

Smith, H. S., Handy, R. T., & Loetscher, L. A. (1960). *American Christianity, Volume I. 1607–1620.* New York: Charles Scribner.

Smith, J. I. (1985). Women, religion and social change in early Islam. In Y. Y. Haddad & E. B. Findly (Eds.), *Women, religion and social change* (pp. 19–36). Albany: State University of New York Press.

Smith, M. (2002). Atkins diet heart-healthy after all? *WebMD Medical News Archive.* Retrieved April 7, 2004 from http://my.webmd.com/content/article/53/61344.html?

Smith, W. D., Burlew, A. K., Mosley, M. H., & Whitney, W. M. (1978). *Minority issues in mental health.* Reading, MA: Addison-Wesley.

Smock, P. J. (2000). Annual review of sociology. Cited in Nagourney, E. (2000, February 15). Study finds families bypassing marriage. *New York Times,* p. F8.

Smuts, B. (1995). The evolutionary origins of patriarchy. *Human Nature, 6,* 1–32.

Snipp, C. M., & Aytac, I. A. (1990). The labor force participation of American Indian women. *Research in Human Capital and Development, 6,* 189–211.

Sochting, I., Fairbrother, N., & Koch, W. J. (2004). Sexual assault of women: Prevention efforts and risk factors. *Violence Against Women, 10*(1), 73–93.

Sohoni, N. K. (1994). Where are all the girls? *MS, 5*(96).

Sokol, M. S., & Gray, N. S. (1998). Anorexia nervosa. In E. A. Blechman & K. D. Brownell (Eds.), *Behavioral medicine and women: A comprehensive handbook* (pp. 350–357). New York: Guilford Press.

Sommers, C. H. (1994). *Who stole feminism? How women have betrayed women.* New York: Simon & Schuster.

Sommers, C. H. (2000). *The war against boys: How misguided feminism is harming our young men.* New York: Simon & Schuster.

Song, Y. (1993). Asian American women's experience in the crossfire of cultural conflict. In Y. Song & E. Kim (Eds.), *American mosaic: Selected readings on America's multicultural heritage* (pp. 186–203). Upper Saddle River, NJ: Prentice Hall.

Sonnert, G., & Holton, G. (1996). Career patterns of women and men in the sciences. *American Scientist, 84,* 63–71.

Spalter-Roth, R., Kalleberg, A. L., Rasell, E., Cassirer, N., Reskin, B. F., Hudson, K., Applebaum, E., & Dooley, B. L. (1997). *Managing work and family: Nonstandard work arrangements among managers and professionals.* Washington, DC: Economic Policy Institute.

Specter, M. (1998, July 10). The baby bust: A special report: Population implosion worries a graying Europe. *The New York Times,* pp. A1, A6.

Spelman, E. V. (1988). *The inessential woman: Problems of exclusion in feminist thought.* Boston: Beacon Press.

Spence, J. T., Helmreich, R. L., & Stapp, J. (1974). The personal attributes questionnaire: A measure of sex-role stereotypes and masculinity/femininity. *JSAS Catalog of Selected Documents in Psychology, 4,* 43.

Spencer, P. (2003, November). Changing lanes. *Woman's Day.*

Spickard, P. R. (1992). The illogic of American racial categories. In M. P. P. Root (Ed.), *Racially mixed people in America* (pp. 12–23). Newbury Park, CA: Sage.

Spitzer, B. L. (1999). Gender differences in population versus media body sizes: A comparison over four decades. *Sex Roles, 40,* 545–565.

Spitzer, R. L., Devlin, M., Walsh, B. T., Hasin, D., Wing, R., Marcus, M., et al. (1992). Binge-eating disorder: A multisite field trial of the diagnostic criteria. *International Journal of Eating Disorders, 11,* 191–203.

Spitzer, R. L., Yanovski, S., Wadden, T., Wing, R., Marcus, M. D., Stunkard, A., Devlin, M., Mitchell, J., Hasin, D., & Horne, R. L. (1993). Binge eating disorder: Its further validation in a multisite study. *International Journal of Eating Disorders, 13*(2), 137–153.

Spraggins, R. (2003, March). Women and men in the United States: March 2002, Population Characteristics. US Census Bureau, pp. 1–5.

Sprecher, S., Regan, P. C., & McKinney, K. (1998). Beliefs about the outcomes of extramarital sexual relationships as a function of the gender of the "cheating spouse." *Sex Roles, 38,* 301–311.

Sprock, J., & Yoder, C. Y. (1997). Women and depression: An update on the report of the APA task force. *Sex Roles, 36,* 269–303.

Spurlock, J. (1984). Black women in the middle years. In G. Baruch & J. Brooks-Gunn (Eds.), *Women in midlife* (pp. 245–260). New York: Plenum Press.

Squyres, S., Jacobs, N., & Quiram, J. (Eds.). (1996). Minorities: A changing role in American society. *The information series on current topics.* New York: Wylie—Information Plus.

Stacey, R. D., Prisbell, M., & Tollefsrud, K. (1992). A comparison of attitudes among college students toward sexual violence committed by strangers and by acquaintances: A research report. *Journal of Sex Education and Therapy, 18,* 257–263.

Stack, C. (1974). *All our kin.* New York: Harper & Row.

Stack, S., & Eshleman, J. R. (1998). Marital status and happiness: A 17-nation study. *Journal of Marriage and the Family, 60,* 527–537.

Stahly, G. B. (1996). Battered women: Why don't they just leave? In J. C. Chrisler, C. Golden, & P. D. Rozee (Eds.), *Lectures on the psychology of women.* New York: McGraw-Hill.

Stahly, G. B. (2004). Battered women: Why don't they just leave? In J. D. Chrisler, C. Golden, & P. D. Rozee (Eds.), *Lectures on the psychology of women* (3rd ed.). New York: McGraw-Hill.

Stanley, J. (1977). Paradigmatic woman: The prostitute. In D. Shores (Ed.), *Papers in language variation.* Birmingham: University of Alabama Press.

Stanley, J. C. (1993). Boys and girls who reason well mathematically. In G. R. Bock & K. Ackrill (Eds.), *The Origin and development of high ability* (pp. 119–138). New York: Wiley.

Stanley, J. C., Benbow, C. P., Brody, L. E., Dauber, S., & Lupkowski, A. (1992). Gender differences on eighty-six nationally standardized aptitude and achievement tests. In N. Colangelo, S. G. Assouline, & D. L. Ambroson (Eds.), *Talent development, Vol. 1: Proceedings from the 1991 Henry B. and Jocelyn Wallace National Research Symposium on Talent Development* (pp. 42–65). Unionville, NY: Trillium Press.

Stark, E., & Flitcraft, A. (1988). Violence among intimates: An epidemiological review. In V. B. Van Hasselt & R. L. Morrison (Eds.), *Handbook of family violence* (pp. 293–317). New York: Plenum Press.

Stark, E., Flitcraft, A., Zuckerman, D., Grey, A., Robison, J., & Frazier, W. (1981). *Wife abuse in the medical setting: An introduction for health personnel* (Monograph 7). Rockville, MD: National Clearinghouse on Domestic Violence.

Statistics Canada. (2000). *Women in Canada 2000: A gender-based statistical report.* Canada: Author.

Stattin, H., & Klackenberg-Larsson, I. (1991). The short and long term implications for parent–child relations of parents' prenatal preferences for their child's gender. *Developmental Psychology, 27,* 141–147.

Stay-at-home dads—A growing trend. (1998, April 15). *U.S. News and World Report.*

Stead, D. (1996, January 7). Breaking the glass ceiling with the power of words. *New York Times,* p. 6F.

Steckel, A. (1987). Psychosocial development of children of lesbian mothers. In F. N. Bozett (Ed.), *Gay and lesbian parents* (pp. 75–85). New York: Praeger.

Steele, C. M. (1997). A threat in the air: How stereotypes shape intellectual identity and performance. *American Psychologist, 52,* 613–629.

Steele, C. M., & Aronson, J. (1995). Stereotype threat and the intellectual test performance of African Americans. *Journal of Personality and Social Psychology, 69,* 797–811.

Steering Committee of the Physician's Health Study Research Group. (1989). Final report from the aspirin component of the ongoing physician's health study. *New England Journal of Medicine, 321,* 129–135.

Steig, R. L., & Williams, R. C. (1983). Chronic pain as a biosocial cultural phenomenon: Implications for treatment. *Seminars in Neurology, 3,* 370–376.

Steil, J. M. (1997). *Marital equality: Its relationship to the well-being of husbands and wives.* Thousand Oaks, CA: Sage.

Steil, J. M., & Turetsky, B. (1987). Marital influence levels and symptomatology among wives. In F. Crosby (Ed.), *Relative deprivation and working women* (pp. 74–90). New York: Oxford University Press.

Stein, J. H., & Reiser, L. W. (1994). A study of white middle-class adolescent boys' responses to "semenarche" (the first ejaculation). *Journal of Youth and Adolescence, 23,* 373–384.

Stein, R. (2003, October 10). Breast cancer drug reduces relapse risk. *Washington Post*, p. A1.

Steinbacher, R., & Gilroy, F. D. (1996). Technology for sex selection: Current status and utilization. *Psychological Reports, 79*, 728–730.

Steinberg, L. (1981). Transformations in family relations at puberty. *Developmental Psychology, 17*, 833–840.

Steinberg, L. (1993). *Adolescence* (3rd ed.). New York: McGraw-Hill.

Steiner, M. (1998). Perinatal mood disorders: Position paper. *Psychopharmacological Bulletin, 34*, 301–306.

Steiner, M., Dunn, E., & Born, L. (2003). Hormones and mood: From menarche to menopause and beyond. *Journal of Affective Disorders, 74*(1), 67–83.

Steinhart, E. (1992). The effects of perceived status and degree of accentedness on listeners' social judgments. Unpublished doctoral project, Pace University, New York.

Steinhauer, J. (1995, July 6). No marriage, no apologies. *New York Times*, pp. C1, C7.

Steinmetz, S. K., & Lucca, J. S. (1988). Husband battering. In V. B. Van Hasselt, R. L. Morrisson, A. S. Bellack, & M. Hersen (Eds.), *Handbook of family violence* (pp. 233–246). New York: Plenum Press.

Sternback, R. A., & Tursky, B. (1965). Ethnic differences among housewives in psychological and skin potential responses to electric stimuli. *Psychophysiology 1*, 241–246.

Sternberg, R. (1988). Triangulating love. In R. J. Sternberg & M. L. Barnes (Eds.), *The psychology of love* (pp. 119–138). New Haven, CT.: Yale University Press.

Sternberg, R. J., & McGrane, P. A. (1993). *Intellectual development across the life span*. Unpublished manuscript, Yale University, New Haven, CT.

Stevens, E. (1973). Machismo and marianismo. *Transaction Society, 10*(6), 57–63.

Stevens, E. (1993). Marianismo: The other face of machismo in Latin America. In A. Minas (Ed.), *Gender basics: Feminist perspectives on women and men*. Belmont, CA: Wadsworth.

Stevenson, M. R., & Black, K. N. (1988). Paternal absence and sex-role development: A meta-analysis. *Child Development, 59*(3), 793–814.

Stewart, A. J. (1998). Doing personality research: How can feminist theories help? In B. M. Clinchy & J. K. Norem (Eds.), *The gender and psychology reader* (pp. 54–68). New York: New York University Press.

Stewart, D. C., & Boydell, K. M. (1993). Psychologic distress during menopause: Associations across the reproductive life cycle. *International Journal of Psychiatry in Medicine, 23*, 157–162.

Stice, E., & Shaw, H. (1994). Adverse effects of media portrayed thin-ideal on women and linkages to bulimic symptomatology. *Journal of Social and Clinical Psychology, 13*, 288–308.

Stieg, R. L., & Williams, R. C. (1983). Chronic pain as a biosociocultural phenomenon: Implications for treatment. *Seminars in Neurology, 3*, 370–376. Cited by Bloom, 1988.

Stockard, J., & Johnson, M. M. (1992). *Sex and gender in society*. Englewood Cliffs, NJ: Prentice Hall.

Stockdale, M. S., Visio, M., & Batra, L. (1999). The sexual harassment of men: Evidence for a broader theory of sexual harassment and sex discrimination. *Psychology, Public Policy & Law, 5*(3), 630–664.

Stolberg, S. (1998, April 3). Rise in smoking by young blacks erodes a success story. *New York Times*, p. A24.

Stoller, E. P., & Cutler, S. J. (1992). The impact of gender on configurations of care among married elderly couples. *Research on Aging, 14*(3), 313–330.

Stoltzman, S. M. (1986). Menstrual attitudes, beliefs, and symptom experiences of adolescent females, their peers, and their mothers. *Health Care for Women International, 7*, 97–114.

Stone, G. C. (1979). Health and the health system: A historical overview and conceptual framework. In G. C. Stone, F. Cohen, & N. E. Adler (Eds.), *Health psychology: A handbook* (pp. 1–17). San Francisco: Jossey-Bass.

Storer, J. H. (1992). Gender and kin role transposition as an accommodation to father-daughter incest. In T. L. Whitehead & B. V. Reid (Eds.), *Gender constructs and social issues* (pp. 70–102). Urbana, IL: University of Illinois Press.

Storms, M. D. (1981). A theory of erotic orientation development. *Psychological Review, 88*, 340–353.

Straus, M., Gelles, R., & Steinmetz, S. (1980). *Behind closed doors: Violence in America*. Garden City, NY: Doubleday.

Strawbridge, W. J., Kaplan, G. A., Camacho, T., & Cohen, R. D. (1992). The dynamics of disability and functional change in an elderly cohort: Results from the Alameda County Study. *Journal of the American Geriatrics Society, 40*(8), 799–806.

Stricken, L. J., Rock, D. A., & Burton, N. W. (1993). Sex differences in predictions of college grades from scholastic aptitude scores. *Journal of Educational Psychology, 85*, 710–718.

Striegel-Moore, R. H., & Smolak, L. (1996). The role of race in the development of eating disorders. In L. Smolak, M. Levine, & R. H. Striegel-Moore (Eds.), *The developmental psychopathology of eating disorders: Implications for research, treatment, and prevention* (pp. 259–284). Hillsdale, NJ: Erlbaum.

Strober, M., Freeman, R., & Lampert, C. (2000). Controlled family study of anorexia nervosa and bulimia nervosa: Evidence of shared liability and transmission of partial syndromes. *American Journal of Psychiatry, 157*(3), 393–401.

Stroebe, M. S. (1998). New directions in bereavement research: Exploration of gender differences. *Palliative Medicine, 12*, 5–12.

Struckman-Johnson, C. (1991). Male victims of acquaintance rape. In A. Parrot & L. Bechofer (Eds.), *Acquaintance rape: The hidden crime* (pp. 192–213). New York: Wiley.

Stuenkel, C. A. (1989). Menopause and estrogen replacement therapy. *Psychiatric Clinics of North America, 12*(1), 133–152.

Stueve, A., & O'Donnell, L. (1984). The daughter of aging parents. In G. Baruch & J. Brooks-Gunn (Eds.), *Women in midlife* (pp. 203–225). New York: Plenum Press.

Stumpf, H., & Jackson D. N. (1994). Gender-related differences in cognitive abilities: Evidence from a medical school admission testing program. *Personality and Individual Differences, 17,* 335–344.

Sudarkasa, N. (1988). Interpreting the African heritage in Afro-American family organization. In H. P. McAdoo (Ed.), *Black families* (2nd ed., pp. 27–43). Newbury Park, CA: Sage.

Sue, S. (1988). Psychotherapeutic services for ethnic minorities. *American Psychologist, 43,* 301–308.

Sukemune, S., Shiraishi, T., Shirakawa, Y., & Matsumi, J. T. (1993). Life in Japan. In L. L. Adler (Ed.), *International handbook of gender roles* (pp. 174–186). Westport, CT: Greenwood Press.

Sullivan, J. P., & Mosher, D. L. (1990). Acceptance of guided imagery of marital rape as a function of macho personality. *Violence and Victims, 5,* 275–286.

Swaab, D. F., & Fliers, E. (1985). A sexually dimorphic nucleus in the human brain. *Science, 188,* 1112–1115.

Swain, C. M. (2002). *The new white nationalism in America: Its challenge to integration.* Cambridge, UK: Cambridge University Press.

Swartzman, L. C., Edelberg, R., & Kemmann, E. (1990). The menopausal hot flash: Symptom reports and concomitant physiological changes. *Journal of Behavioral Medicine, 13*(1), 15–30.

Swerdlow, M., (1989). Men's accommodations to women entering a nontraditional occupation: A case of rapid transit operatives. *Gender & Society, 3,* 373–387.

Swidler, L. (1976). *Women in Judaism: The status of women in formative Judaism.* Metuchen, NJ: Scarecrow Press.

Swim, J. K., & Sanna, L. J. (1996). He's skilled; she's lucky: A meta-analysis of observers' attributions for women's and men's successes and failures. *Personality and Social Psychology Bulletin, 22,* 507–519.

Symons, D. (1979). *The evolution of human sexuality.* New York: Anchor Press/Doubleday.

Szmuckler, G. I., Eislet, I., Russell, G. F. M., & Dare, C. (1985). Anorexia nervosa, "parental expressed emotion" and dropping out of treatment. *British Journal of Psychiatry, 147,* 265–271.

Taeuber, C. (Ed.). (1991). *Statistical handbook on women in America.* Phoenix, AZ: Oryx Press.

Tafoya, T. (1989). Circles and cedar: Native Americans and family therapy. In G. W. Saba, B. M. Karrer, & K. V. Hardy (Eds.), *Minorities and family therapy* (pp. 71–96). Binghamton, NY: Haworth House.

Talbani, A. (2000). Adolescent females between tradition and modernity: Gender role socialization in south Asian immigrant culture. *Journal of Adolescence, 23*(5), 615–627.

Tallichet, S. E. (1995). Gendered relations in the mines and the division of labor underground. *Gender & Society, 9*(6), 697–711.

Tamir, L. M. (1982). *Men in their forties: The transition to middle age.* New York: Springer.

Tang, C. S., Critelli, J. W., & Porter, J. E. (1995). Sexual aggression and victimization in dating relationships among Chinese college students. *Archives of Sexual Behavior, 24,* 47–53.

Tangri, S., & Hayes, S. M. (1997). Theories of sexual harassment. In W. O'Donohue (Ed.), *Sexual harassment: Theory, research, and treatment* (pp. 112–128). Boston: Allyn and Bacon.

Tangri, S., Burt, M. R., & Johnson, L. B. (1982). Sexual harassment at work: Three explanatory models. *Journal of Social Issues, 38,* 33–54.

Tannahill, R. (1982). *Sex in history.* Briarcliff Manor, NY: Stein & Day.

Tannen, D. (1990). *You just don't understand: Men and women in conversation.* New York: William Morrow.

Task Force on DSM-IV. (2000). *Diagnostic and statistical manual of mental disorders DSM-IV-TR.* Washington, DC: American Psychiatric Association.

Tavard, G. (1973). *Woman in Christian tradition.* Notre Dame, IN: Notre Dame Press. Cited by Swidler, 1976, pp. 27–28.

Tavris, C. (1992). *The mismeasure of women: Why women are not the better sex, the inferior sex, or the opposite sex.* New York: Touchstone/Simon & Schuster.

Tavris, C., & Sadd, S. (1977). *The Redbook report on female sexuality.* New York: Delacorte.

Taylor, S. E. (1995). *Health psychology* (3rd ed.). New York: McGraw-Hill.

Te Velde, E. R., & van Leusden, H. A. I. M. (1994). Hormonal treatment for the climacteric: Alleviation of symptoms and prevention of postmenopausal disease. *The Lancet, 343,* 654–656.

Templeton, L. (1999). Gender schemas and children's interpretations of ambiguous situations (stereotyping). *Dissertation Abstracts International, 59*(11B), 6096.

Terpstra, D. E. (1986). Organizational costs of sexual harassment. *Journal of Employment Counseling, 23,* 112–119.

Terpstra, D. E., & Baker, D. D. (1986). A framework for the study of sexual harassment. *Basic and Applied Social Psychology, 7,* 17–34.

The catholic church and the scandal of sex abuse by priests. *AmericanCatholic.org.,* (2003). Available: www.americancatholic.org/News/ClergySexAbuse

The eHarlequin.com Story. Retrieved February 27, 2004 from www.eHarlequin.com/Article.jhtm

Thoits, P. A. (1987a). Gender and marital status differences in control and distress: Common stress versus unique stress explanations. *Journal of Health and Social Behavior, 28,* 7–22.

Thoits, P. A. (1987b). Position paper. In A. Eichler & D. L. Parron (Eds.), *Women's mental health: Research agenda for the future* (DHHS publication number ADM 87–1542). Washington, DC: U.S. Government Printing Office.

Thomas, A., & Sillen, S. (1979). *Racism and psychiatry*. Secaucus, NJ: Citadel Press.

Thompson, B. (1994). Food, bodies, and growing up female: Childhood lessons about culture, race, and class. In P. Fallon, M. A. Katzman, & S. C. Wooley (Eds.), *Feminist perspectives on eating disorders* (pp. 355–378). New York: Guilford Press.

Thompson, B. (1994). Childhood lessons: Culture, race, class, and sexuality. In B. W. Thompson (Ed.), *A hunger so wide and so deep: American women speak out on eating problems* (pp. 27–45). Minneapolis: University of Minnesota Press.

Thompson, J. K., & Heinberg, L. J. (1999). The media's influence on body image disturbance and eating disorders: We reviled them, now can we rehabilitate them? *Journal of Social Issues, 55*(2), 339–353.

Thompson, L. (1991). Family work: Women's sense of fairness. *Journal of Family Issues, 12,* 181–196.

Thornhill, N. W., & Thornhill, R. (1991). Coercive sexuality of men: Is there psychological adaptation to rape? In E. Grauerhoz & M. A. Koralewski (Eds.), *Sexual coercion: A sourcebook in its nature, causes, and prevention* (pp. 91–107). Lexington, MA: Lexington Books/D. C. Heath.

Thornhill, R., & Palmer, C. T. (2000). *A natural history of rape: Biological bases of sexual coercion*. Cambridge, MA: MIT Press.

Thorpe, T. C. (1989). Caregiving: What do midlife lesbians view as important? *Journal of Gay and Lesbian Psychotherapy, 1*(1), 87–103.

Thurston, B. (1998). *Women in the New Testament: Questions and commentary*. New York: Crossroad-Herder.

Tidball, M. E. (1973). Perspective on academic women and affirmative action. *Educational Record, 54,* 130–135.

Till, F. J. (1980). *Sexual harassment: A report on the sexual harassment of students*. Report of the National Advisory Council on Women's Educational Programs. U.S. Department of Education.

Time. (1973, January 8). Cited by Diamond & Sigmundson, 1997, Sex reassignment at birth. p. 299.

Tivis, L. J. (2001). Estrogen replacement therapy: A perspective on cognitive impact. *Assessment, 8*(4), 403–416.

Tjaden, P., & Thoennes, N. (1998). *Prevalence, incidence, and consequences of violence against women: Findings from the National Violence Against Women Survey. Research in Brief*. Washington, DC: National Institute of Justice, U.S. Department of Justice.

Tobin-Richards, M. H., Boxer, A. M., & Petersen, A. C. (1983). The psychological significance of pubertal change: Sex differences in perceptions of self during early adolescence. In J. Brooks-Gunn & A. C. Petersen (Eds.), *Girls at puberty* (pp. 127–154). New York: Plenum Press.

Todd, J., Friedman, A., & Kariuki P. W. (1990). Women growing stronger with age: The effect of status in the United States and Kenya. *Psychology of Women Quarterly, 14,* 567–577.

Tolman, D. L. (1992). Voicing the body: A psychological study of adolescent girls' sexual desire. Unpublished dissertation, Harvard University.

Tolman, D. L. (2002). *Dilemmas of desire*. Cambridge, MA: Harvard University Press.

Tolman, D. L., & Diamond, L. M. (2002). Desegregating sexuality research: Cultural and biological perspectives on gender and desire. *Annual Review of Sex Research, 12,* 33–74.

Tomkiewicz, J., & Hughes, R. E. (1993). Women who choose business administration versus women who choose administrative services: How they differ. *Journal of Applied Social Psychology, 23*(11), 867–874.

Tong, R. (1982). Feminism, pornography, and censorship. *Social Theory and Practice, 8,* 1–17.

Tong, R. (1989). *Feminist thought: A comprehensive introduction*. Boulder, CO: Westview Press.

Torack, R. M. (1982). Historical aspects of normal and abnormal brain fluids. *Archives of Neurology, 39,* 197–201.

Toubia, N. (1993). *Female genital mutilation: Call for global action*. New York: Women, Inc.

Touchette, N. (1993). Estrogen signals a novel route to pain relief. *Journal of NIH Research, 5,* 53–58.

Townsend, J. M. (1995). Sex without emotional involvement: An evolutionary interpretation of sex differences. *Archives of Sexual Behavior, 24,* 173–206.

Travis, C. B. (1988). *Women and health psychology: Biomedical issues*. Hillsdale, NJ: Erlbaum.

Triandis, H. (1994). *Culture and social behavior*. New York: McGraw-Hill.

Troll, L. E. (1989). Myths of midlife intergenerational relationships. In S. Hunter & M. Sundel (Eds.), *Midlife myths* (pp. 210–231). Newbury Park, CA: Sage.

Turkel, A. R. (2002). From victim to heroine: Children's stories revisited. *Journal of the American Academy of Psychoanalysis, 30*(1), 71–81.

Turner, B., & Turner, C. (1992, April). Who treats minorities? Paper presented at the meeting of the Eastern American Psychological Association. Boston, MA.

Tursky, B., & Sternback, R. A. (1967). Further physiological correlates of ethnic differences in responses to shock. *Psychophysiology 4,* 67–74.

Uchitelle, L. (1996, August 23). Despite drop, rate of layoff remains high. *New York Times*, p. A1.

Udall, L. (1977). *Me and mine: The life story of Helen Sekequaptewa*. Tucson: University of Arizona Press.

Udry, J. R., & Billy, J. O. G. (1987). Initiation of coitus in early adolescence. *American Sociological Review, 52,* 841–855.

Udry, J. R., & Talbert, L. M. (1988). Sex hormone effects on personality at puberty. *Journal of Personality and Social Psychology, 54,* 291–295.

Udry, J. R., Billy, J. O. G., Morris, N. M., Groff, T. R., Raj, M. H. (1985). Serum androgenic hormones motivate sexual behavior in adolescent boys. *Fertility and Sexuality, 43,* 90–94.

Udvardy, M. (1992). The fertility of the post-fertile: Concepts of gender, aging, and reproductive health among the Giriama of Kenya. *Journal of Cross-Cultural Gerontology, 7*(4), 289–306.

Unger, R., & Crawford, M. (1996). *Women and gender: A feminist psychology* (2nd ed.). New York: McGraw-Hill.

Unger, R. K. (1979). *Female and male psychological perspectives.* New York: Harper & Row.

Unger, R. K. (1981). Sex as a social reality: Field and laboratory research. *Psychology of Women Quarterly, 5,* 645–653.

Unger, R. K. (1995). Conclusion: Cultural diversity and the future of feminist psychology. In H. Landrine (Ed.), *Bringing cultural diversity to feminist psychology: Theory, research, and practice* (pp. 413–431). Washington, DC: American Psychological Association.

United Nations Children's Fund (UNICEF) (2003). Girls' Education, Making Investments Count. New York: The United Nations Children's Fund (UNICEF).

United Nations. (1991). *The world's women 1970–1990: Trends and statistics.* New York.

United Nations. (2001). *The World Population Prospects.*

U.S. Census Bureau. (1988). *Current population reports: Population profile of the United States, 1987* (Special Studies, Series P-23, No. 150). Washington, DC: U.S. Government Printing Office.

U.S. Census Bureau. (1990). *Statistical abstract of the United States,* Washington, DC: U.S. Government Printing Office.

U.S. Census Bureau. (1992). Current population reports, series P-20, No. 459. *The Asian and Pacific Islander population in the United States: March 1991 and 1990.* Washington, DC: U.S. Government Printing Office.

U.S. Census Bureau. (1998a, February 18). Press-Release ch. 98–126.

U.S. Census Bureau. (1998b, July 27). Current population survey.

U.S. Census Bureau. (1998). *Statistical abstract of the United States, 118th edition.* Washington, DC: U.S. Government Printing Office.

U.S. Census Bureau. (1999a). Marital status and living arrangements: March 1998 (Update). Population Division, Fertility and Family Statistics Branch: Washington, DC.

U.S. Census Bureau. (1999b). *Statistical abstract of the United States, 119th edition.* Washington, DC: U.S. Government Printing Office.

U.S. Census Bureau. (2000, March). *America's families and living arrangements* (Report P20–537, Table A1). Retrieved May 12, 2001, from www.census.gov/population www.socdemo/race.html

U.S. Census Bureau. (2001). *Statistical abstract of the United States.* Washington, DC: U.S. Government Printing Office.

U.S. Census Bureau. (2001a). *Poverty in the United States: 2000. Current population reports* (Series P60–214). Washington, DC: U.S. Government Printing Office.

U.S. Census Bureau. (2001b, June 29). U.S. adults postponing marriage. Census Bureau Reports, United States Department of Commerce News, Jason Fields, Public Information Office.

U.S. Census Bureau. (2002). *Statistical abstract of the United States, 122nd edition.* Washington, DC: U.S. Government Printing Office.

U.S. Census Bureau. (2003, May 20). About one-half of older married couples have incomes of $35,000 or more. Census Bureau Reports, United States Department of Commerce News, Robert Bernstein, Public Information Office.

U.S. Department of Commerce (1990). Section 4. Education. Available: www.census.gov/prod/2002pubs/01statab/educ.pdf

U.S. Department of Commerce. (1998). *U.S. Census Bureau: The official statistics.* Washington, DC: U.S. Government Printing Office.

U.S. Department of Education (1996). The third international mathematics and science study. Washington, DC. Available at www.ed.gov/nces

U.S. Department of Education (1997). *National assessment of educational progress* (Indicator 32: Writing Proficiency; prepared by the Educational Testing Service). Washington, DC. Available at www.ed.gov/nces

U.S. Department of Health and Human Services (USDHHS). (2000). *Health, United States, 2000.* Washington, DC: U.S. Government Printing Office.

U.S. Department of Health and Human Services, Centers for Disease Control, Operational Research Section, Behavioral and Prevention Research Branch, Division of STD/HIV Prevention, Center for Prevention Services. (1992). *What we have learned from the AIDS Community Demonstration Projects.* Atlanta, GA: Centers for Disease Control.

U.S. Department of Health and Human Services. (1996). Vol. 46, No. 11.

U.S. Department of Justice, Federal Bureau of Investigation. (1996). *Crimes in the United States: Uniform Crime Report.* Washington, DC: U.S. Government Printing Office.

U.S. Department of Labor. (1993). *20 facts on women workers.* Washington, DC: U.S. Government Printing Office.

U.S. Department of Labor, Bureau of Labor Statistics. *Highlights of Women's Earnings in 2002.* Report 972. September, 2003, pp. 1–37.

U.S. Department of Labor, Bureau of Labor Statistics. (2002, May). *Highlights of women's earnings in 2001,* Report 960.

U.S. Department of Labor, Employment Standards and Administration Wage and Hour Division. (2003, October 30). Report.

U.S. Food and Drug Administration. (1977). General considerations for the clinical evaluation of drugs. (Publication No. HEW) FDA 77–3040. Washington, DC: U.S. Government Printing Office.

U.S. Merit Systems Protection Board. (1981). *Sexual harassment in the federal workplace: Is it a problem?* Washington, DC: U.S. Government Printing Office.

U.S. Merit Systems Protection Board. (1988). *Sexual harassment in the federal workplace: An update.* Washington, DC: U.S. Government Printing Office.

U.S. Merit Systems Protection Board. (1995). *Sexual harassment in the federal workplace: Trends, progress, continuing challenges.* Washington, DC: U.S. Government Printing Office.

United States v. Wong Kim Ark, 169 U.S. 649 (1898).

Urbancic, J. C. (1987). Incest trauma. *Journal of Psychosocial Nursing, 25,* 33–35.

Ussher, J. (1989). *The psychology of the female body.* London: Routledge.

Ussher, J. M. (1992). *Women's madness: Misogyny or mental illness?* Amherst, MA: University of Massachusetts Press.

Utsey, S. O., Chae, M., Brown, C., & Kelly, D. (2002). Effect of ethnic group membership on ethnic identity, race-related stress, and quality of life. *Cultural Diversity and Ethnic Minority Psychology, 8*(4), 366–377.

Utsey, S. O., & Payne, Y. A. (2000). Differential psychological and emotional impacts of race-related stress. *Journal of African American Men, 5,* 56–72.

Utsey, S. O., Ponterotto, J. G., Reynolds, A. L., & Cancelli, A. A. (2000). Racial discrimination, coping, life satisfaction, and self-esteem among African Americans. *Journal of Counseling and Development, 78,* 72–80.

Utz, R. L., Carr, D., & Nesse, R. (2002). The effect of widowhood on older adults' social participation: An evaluation of activity, disengagement, and continuity theories. *Gerontologist, 42*(4), 522–533.

Valian, V. (1998). *Why so slow? The advancement of women.* Cambridge, MA: MIT Press.

Van Goozen, S. H. M., Cohen-Kettenis, P. T., Gooren, L. J. G., Frijda, N. H., & Van de Poll, N. E. (1995). Gender differences in behavior: Activating effects of cross-sex hormones. *Psychoneuroendocrinology, 20,* 343–363.

Van Keep, P. A. (1976). Psychosocial aspects of the climacteric. In P. A. Van Keep, R. B. Greenblatt, & M. Albeaux-Fernet (Eds.), *Consensus on menopause research.* Baltimore: University Park Press.

Vannoy, D. (1991). Social differentiation, contemporary marriage, and human development. *Journal of Family Issues, 12*(3), 251–267.

Vascioli, C. M., et al. (2001). HRT not helpful for secondary prevention of cerebrovascular disease. *New England Journal of Medicine, 345,* 1243–1249.

Vasquez, M. (1994). Latinas. In L. Comas-Diaz & B. Greene (Eds.), *Women of color: Integrating ethnic and gender identities in psychotherapy* (pp. 114–138). New York: Guilford Press.

Vasta, R., Knott, J. A., & Gaze, C. E. (1996). Can spatial training erase the gender differences on the water-level task? *Psychology of Women Quarterly, 20,* 549–568.

Vaughn, B. E., Block, J. H., & Block, J. (1988). Parental agreement on child rearing during early childhood and the psychological characteristics of adolescents. *Child Development, 59,* 1020–1033.

Vazquez-Nuttall, E., Romero-Garcia, I., & DeLeon, B. (1987). Sex roles and perceptions of feminity and masculinity of Hispanic women: A review of the literature. *Psychology of Women Quarterly, 11,* 409–426.

Vega, W. A., & Rumbaut, R. G. (1991). Ethnic minorities and mental health. *Annual Review of Sociology, 17,* 351–383.

Vega, W. A., Warheit, G. J., & Meinhardt, K. (1984). Marital disruption and the prevalence of depressive symptomatology among Anglos and Mexican Americans. *Journal of Marriage and Family, 46,* 817–824.

Veniegas, R. C., & Peplau, L. A. (1997). Power and the quality of same-sex friendships. *Psychology of Women Quarterly, 21,* 279–297.

Verbrugge, L. M. (1979). Female illness rates and illness behavior. *Women and Health, 4*(1), 61–75.

Verbrugge, L. M. (1980). Sex differences in complaints and diagnoses. *Journal of Behavioral Medicine, 3*(4), 327–355.

Vierck, C. J., Jr. (1976). Extrapolations from the pain research literature to problems of adequate veterinary care. *Journal of the American Veterinary Association, 168*(6), 510–513.

Villalon, D. (2002, October 6). *Rape drug detectors: California UWCA branch distributes devices to spot date-rape drugs.* Retrieved October 20, 2002, from http://abcnews .go.com/sections/scitech/DailyNews/daterape_ detection121006.html

Villarosa, L. (Ed.). (1994). *Body & soul: The Black women's guide to physical health and emotional well-being.* New York: HarperPerennial.

Viscoli, C. M., Brass, L. M., Kernan, W. N., Sarrel, P. M., Suissa, S., & Horwitz, R. I. (2001, October 25). A clinical trial of estrogen replacement therapy after ischemic stroke. *New England Journal of Medicine, 345*(17), 1243–1249.

Voda, A. M., & Eliasson, M. (1983). Menopause: The closure of menstrual life. *Women & Health, 8*(2/3), 137–156.

Voyer, D. (1996). On the magnitude of laterality and sex differences in functional literalities. *Laterality, 1,* 51–83.

Voyer, D., Voyer, S., & Bryden, M. P. (1995). Magnitude of sex differences in spatial abilities: A meta-analysis and consideration of critical variables. *Psychological Bulletin, 117,* 250–270.

Wade, C., & Tavris, C. (1994). The longest war: Gender and culture. In W. J. Lonner & R. S. Malpass (Eds.), *Psychology and culture* (pp. 121–126). Boston: Allyn & Bacon.

Wade, N. (July 15, 2003). Why we die: Why we live: A new theory on aging. *The New York Times,* Section F, P. 3.

Waits, T. M., Johnson, D. H., Hainsworth, J. D., Hande, K. R., Thomasa, M., & Grieco, E. A. (1992). Prolonged administration of oral etoposide in non-small cell lung cancer: A phase II trial. *Journal of Clinical Oncology, 10*(2), 292–296.

Wakefield, H., & Underwager, R. (1991). Female child sexual abusers: A critical review of the literature. *American Journal of Forensic Psychology, 9,* 43–69.

Waldron, I. (1976). Why do women live longer than men? *Social Science and Medicine, 10,* 349–362.

Walker, A. J., Pratt, C. C., & Wood, B. (1993). Perceived frequency of role conflict and relationship quality for caregiving daughters. *Psychology of Women Quarterly, 17,* 207–221.

Walker, L. E. (1994). Are personality disorders gender biased? In S. A. Kirk & S. D. Einbinder (Eds.), *Controversial issues in mental health* (pp. 75–96). Washington, DC: American Psychological Association.

Walker, L. E. A. (1979). *The battered woman.* New York: Harper & Row.

Wallerstein, J. S. (1997, June 27). *New York Times.*

Wallerstein, J., & Lewis, J. (1998, July). The long-term impact of divorce on children: A first report from a 25-year study. *Family & Conciliation Courts Review, 36*(3), 368–383.

Wallerstein, J. S., & Blakeslee, S. (1989). *Second chances: Men, women and children a decade after divorce.* New York: Ticknor and Fields.

Wallerstein, J. S., & Kelly, J. B. (1980). *Surviving the breakup: How children and parents cope with divorce.* New York: Basic Books.

Wallston, B. S., DeVellis, B. M., & Wallston, K. (1983). Licensed practical nurses' sex role stereotypes. *Psychology of Women Quarterly, 7,* 199–208.

Walsh, P., & Connor, C. L. (1979). Old men and young women: How objectively are their skills assessed? *Journal of Gerontology, 34,* 561–568.

Wang, H. (2000). Predictors of divorce adjustment: Stressors, resources, and definitions. *Journal of Marriage and the Family, 62*(3), 655–668.

Wannan, G., & Fombonne, E. (1998). Gender differences in rates and correlates of suicidal behavior amongst child psychiatric outpatients. *Journal of Adolescence, 21,* 371–381.

Ward, M. C. (1999). *A world full of women* (2nd ed.). Boston: Allyn and Bacon.

Warner, J. (2003, September 2). Cancer death rates falling but slowly. *WebMD, Medical News,* p. 1.

Warner, J., Weber, T. R., & Albanes, R. (1999). "Girls are retarded when they're stoned." Marijuana and the construction of gender roles among adolescent females. *Sex Roles, 40,* 25–43.

Warner, R. L., & Steel, B. S. (1999). Child-rearing as a mechanism for social change: The relationship of child gender to parent's commitment to gender equity. *Gender & Society, 13,* 503–517.

Warren, C. W., et al. (1990). Assessing the reproductive behavior of on- and off-reservation American Indian females: Characteristics of two groups in Montana. *Social Biology, 37,* 69–83.

Waterman, J. (1986). Family dynamics of incest with young children. In K. MacFarlane & J. Waterman (Eds.), *Sexual abuse of children: Evaluation and treatment* (pp. 197–203). New York: Guilford Press.

Waterman, J., & Lusk, R. (1986). Scope of the problem. In K. MacFarlane & J. Waterman (Eds.), *Sexual abuse of children: Evaluation and treatment* (pp. 3–14). New York: Guilford Press.

Watson, C. M. (2002). Career aspirations of adolescent girls: Effects of achievement level, grade, and single-sex school environment. *Sex Roles, 46*(9/10), 323–335.

Webb, G. (2001). Sex and the Internet. Yahoo! *Internet Life, 7*(5), 88–98.

Wechsler, D. (1972). "Hold" and "don't hold" test. In S. M. Chown (Ed.), *Human aging* (pp. 25–34). New York: Penguin.

Wechsler, D. (1991). *Wechsler Intelligence Scale for Children (3rd ed.),* San Antonio, TX: Psychological Corporation.

Weidiger, P. (1975). *Menstruation and menopause.* New York: Knopf.

Weinber, D. H. (2003, September 26). Income and Poverty 2002 Press Briefing. U.S. Census Bureau.

Weinberg, M. S., Williams, C. J., & Pryor, D. W. (1994). *Dual attraction: Understanding bisexuality.* New York: Oxford University Press.

Weiner, B. (1974). *Achievement motivation and attribution theory.* Morristown, NJ: General Learning Press.

Weiner, B. (1986). *An attributional theory of motivation and emotion.* New York: Springer-Verlag.

Weinraub, M., & Frankel, J. (1977). Sex differences in parent–infant interaction during free play, departure, and separation. *Child Development, 48,* 1240–1249.

Weissberg, M. P. (1983). *Dangerous secrets: Maladaptive responses to stress.* New York: W. W. Norton.

Weisz, A. N. (2003). Gender and moral reasoning: African American youths respond to dating dilemmas. *Journal of Human Behavior in the Social Environment, 6*(3), 17–34.

Welch, D. (1987). American Indian women: Reaching beyond the myth. In C. Calloway (Ed.), *New directions in American Indian history* (pp. 31–48). Norman, OK: University of Oklahoma Press.

Welsh, D. P., & Powers, S. I. (1991). Gender differences in family interaction. In R. M. Lerner, A. C. Petersen, & J. Brooks-Gunn (Eds.) *Encyclopedia of adolescence* (pp. 334–339). New York: Garland Press.

Wendell, S. (1993). Toward a feminist theory of disability. In A. Minas (Ed.), *Gender basics: Feminist perspectives on women and men* (pp. 50–58). Belmont, CA: Wadsworth.

Wenger, N. K., Speroff, L., & Packard, B. P. (1993). Cardiovascular health and disease in women. *New England Journal of Medicine, 329*(4), 247–256.

Weseen, S. (2000). Secrets mothers keep. In L. Weis & M. Fine (Eds.), *Speed bumps: A student-friendly guide to qualitative research.* New York: Teachers College Press.

Weskott, M. (1998). Culture and women's health. In A. E. Blechman & K. D. Brownell (Eds.), *Behavioral medicine and women: A comprehensive handbook* (pp. 816–820). New York: Guilford Press.

Wesner, M. (2001). Aging advantages at using spatial cues in contrast discrimination search tasks. *Proceedings of the Third International Conference on Cognitive Science* (pp. 302–306). Beijing, China: Press of USTC.

West, C. (1994). *Race matters.* New York: Random House.

West, C., & Zimmerman, D. H. (1987). Going gender. *Gender and Society, 1,* 125–151.

Wheeler, L., Reis, H. T., & Bond, M. H. (1989). Collectivism–individualism in everyday social life: The middle kingdom and the melting pot. *Journal of Personality and Social Psychology, 45,* 945–953.

Wheeler, M. (1974). *No-fault divorce.* Boston: Beacon Press.

Whelan, T. A., & Lally, C. M. E. (2002). Paternal commitment and father's quality of life. *Journal of Family Studies, 8*(2), 181–196.

Whiffen, V. E. (2001). Depression. In J. Worell (Ed.), *Encyclopedia of Sex and Gender* (pp. 303–314). New York: Academic Press.

White, E. (Ed.). (1994). *The Black women's health book: Speaking for ourselves* (2nd ed.). Seattle, WA: Seal Press.

White, J. W., Donat, P. L. N., & Bondurant, B. (2001). A developmental examination of violence against girls and women. In R. Unger (Ed.), *Handbook of the psychology of women and gender* (pp. 343–357). New York: McGraw-Hill.

White, K. M., Speisman, J. C., Jackson, D., Bartis, S., & Costos, D. (1986). Intimacy maturity and its correlates in young married couples. *Journal of Personality and Social Psychology, 50,* 152–162.

White, M. (1998). "The pink's run out!" The place of artmaking in young children's construction of the gendered self. In Y. Nicola (Ed.), *Gender in Early Childhood, 223–248.* Florena, KY: Taylor & Francis/Routledge.

White, S. W., & Kowalski, R. M. (1994). Deconstructing the myth of the nonaggressive woman: A feminist analysis. *Psychology of Women Quarterly, 18*(4), 487–508.

Wickelgren, I. (1997). Estrogen stakes claim to cognition. *Science, 276,* 675–678.

Wiergacz, K. J., & Lucas, J. L. (2003). Wonder women: The portrayal of women in television soap operas. *Psi Chi Journal of Undergraduate Research, 8*(2), 70–74.

Wiesenfeld, H. (2001). Study found nearly 1 in 5 teenage girls have an undiagnosed STD. *Sexually Transmitted Disease 28*(6): 321–325.

Wilbur, J., Dan, A., Hedricks, C., & Holm, K. (1990). The relationship among menopausal status, menopausal symptoms, and physical activity in midlife women. *Family and Community Health, 13*(3), 67–78.

Will, J., Self, P., & Datan, N. (1976). Maternal behavior and perceived sex of infant. *American Journal of Orthopsychiatry, 46,* 135–139.

Willett, W. C., Hunter, D. J., Stampfer, M. J., Colditz, G., Manson, J. E., Speigelman, D., Rosner, B. M., Hennekens, C. H., & Speiser, F. E. (1992). Dietary fat and fiber in relation to risk of breast cancer. *Journal of the American Medical Association, 268,* 2037–2044.

Williams, A. (1998). Communication of ageism. In M. L. Hecht (Ed.), *Communicating prejudice* (pp. 136–160). Thousand Oaks, CA: Sage.

Williams, C. L. (1989). *Gender differences at work: Women and men in nontraditional occupations.* Berkeley: University of California Press.

Williams, E., Radin, N., & Allegro, T. (1992). Sex role attitudes of adolescents raised primarily by their fathers: An 11-year follow-up. *Merrill–Palmer Quarterly, 38*(4), 457–476.

Williams, G. H. (Ed.). (1962). *The radical reformation.* Philadelphia: Westminster Press.

Williams, J. E. (1990). *Sex and psyche: Gender and self viewed cross-culturally.* Newbury Park, CA: Sage.

Williams, J. E., & Best, D. L. (1982). *Measuring sex stereotypes: A thirty nation study.* Beverly Hills, CA: Sage.

Williams, J. E., & Best, D. L. (1990). *Measuring sex stereotypes: A multination study* (rev. ed.). Newbury Park, CA: Sage.

Williams, J. H. (1987). *Psychology of women.* New York: W. W. Norton.

Williams, P. (1997, December 29). Of race and risk. *The Nation.*

Willingham, W. W., & Cole, N. S. (1997). *Gender and fair assessment.* Hillsdale, NJ: Erlbaum.

Wilmoth, G., & Adelstein, D. (1988). Psychological sequelae of abortion and public policy. Paper presented at the 96th American Psychological Association Convention, Atlanta, GA.

Wilson, E. O. (1975). *Sociobiology: The new synthesis.* Cambridge, MA: Harvard University Press.

Wilson, E. O. (1978). *On human nature.* Cambridge, MA: Harvard University Press.

Wilson, J. (1978). *Religion in American society.* Englewood Cliffs, NJ: Prentice Hall.

Wilson, J. D. (1990). Androgens. In A. G. Gilman, T. W. Rall, A. S. Nies, & P. Taylor (Eds.), *Goodman and Gilman's pharmacological basis of therapeutics* (8th Ed., pp. 1414–1418). New York: Pergamon Press.

Wincze, J. P., Hoon, E. F., & Hoon, P. W. (1976). Physiological responsivity of normal and sexually dysfunctional women during erotic stimulus exposure. *Journal of Psychosomatic Research, 20,* 445–451.

Windham, C. (2003). More people treated for depression. *Wall Street Journal,* Wednesday, June 18, 2003, p. D3.

Wines, M. (1992, May 21). Views on single motherhood are multiple at White House. *New York Times,* pp. 1, B16.

Winkler, A. E. (1998). Earnings of husbands and wives in dual-earner families. *Monthly Labor Review, 121*(4).

Winkler, K. J. (1990, October 10). Evidence of "cultural vitality." *Chronicle of Higher Education,* pp. A5, A8.

Wise, L. L., Steel, L., & MacDonald, C. (1979). *Origins and career consequences of sex differences in high school mathematics achievement.* Palo Alto, CA: American Institutes for Research.

Wise, P. M., et al. (2001). Estradiol is a protective factor in the adult and aging brain. *Brain Research Review, 37,* 313–319.

Wise, T. (2002). Membership has its privileges: Thoughts on acknowledging and challenging whiteness. In P. Rothenberg (Ed.), *White privilege: Essential readings on the other side of racism* (pp. 107–111). London, UK: Worth Publishing.

Witherington, B., III. (1984). *Women in the ministry of Jesus.* Cambridge, MA: Cambridge University Press. Cited by Carmody, 1989.

Witt, S. D. (2000). The influence of peers on children's socialization to gender roles. *Early Child Development and Care, 162,* 1–7.

Witt, S. H. (1976). Native women today: Sexism and the Indian woman. In S. Cox (Ed.), *Female psychology: The emerging self* (pp. 249–259). Chicago: Science Research Associates.

Wolf, N. (1991). *The beauty myth: How images of beauty are used against women.* New York: William Morrow.

Wolff, B. B. (1978). Behavioral measurement of human pain. In R. A. Sternbach (Ed.), *The psychology of pain* (pp. 129–168). New York: Raven Press.

Wolff, C. (1971). *Love between women.* New York: Harper & Row.

Wolff, P. H. (1969). The natural history of crying and other vocalizations in early infancy. In B. M. Foss (Ed.), *Determinants of infant behaviour* (Vol. 3, pp. 113–138). London: Methuen.

Women's Health Initiative. (2002). Risks and benefits of estrogen plus progestin in healthy postmenopausal women. *Journal of the American Medical Association, 288*(3), 321–333.

Wong, D. Y. (1983). Asian/Pacific American women: Legal issues. In *Civil rights issues of Asian and Pacific Americans: Myths and realities* (pp. 153–164). Washington, DC: U.S. Government Printing Office.

Wong, D. Y., & Hayashi, D. (1989). Behind unmarked doors: Developments in the garment industry. In Asian American Women United of California (Ed.), *Making waves: An anthology of writings by and about Asian American women* (pp. 159–171). Boston: Beacon Press.

Wood, A. D. (1973, Summer). The fashionable diseases: Woman's complaints and their treatment in nineteenth century America. *Journal of Interdisciplinary History, 4,* 25–42.

Wood, E. (2002). The impact of parenting experience on gender stereotyped toy play of children. *Sex Roles, 47*(1/2), 39–49.

Wood, J. T. (2001). *Gendered lives: Communication, gender, and culture* (4th ed.). Belmont, CA: Wadsworth.

Woodhouse, A. (1982). Sexuality, femininity, and fertility control. *Women's Studies International Forum, 5,* 1–15.

World Bank. (1993). *World development report 1993: Investing in health.* New York: Oxford University Press.

World Health Organization. (1948). *Constitution of the World Health Organization.* Geneva, Switzerland: WHO Basic Documents.

World Jewish population: Year 2002. *JewishPeople.net.,* (2002). Available: www.jewishpeople.net/jewpopofworl.html

Worobey, J. L., & Angel, R. J. (1990). Functional capacity and living arrangements of unmarried elderly persons. *Journal of Gerontology, 45*(3), 95–101.

Worrell, J. (2000). Feminist interventions: Life beyond symptoms reduction. *Psychology of Women Quarterly, 24.*

Worrell, J. (2001). Feminist interventions: Accountability beyond symptom reduction. *Psychology of Women Quarterly, 25*(4). Special Issue: Women's lives, feminist research, and the decade of behavior, pp. 335–343.

Worrell, J., & Johnson, D. (2001). Therapy with women: Feminist frameworks. In R. Unger (Ed.), *Handbook of the psychology of women and gender* (pp. 317–329). New York: Academic Press.

Worrell, J., & Remer, P. (1992). *Feminist perspectives in therapy: An empowerment model for women.* New York: Wiley.

Worrell, J., & Remer, P. (2003). *Feminist perspectives in therapy: Empowering diverse women* (2nd ed.). New York: John Wiley & Sons.

Wu, X., & DeMaris, A. (1996). Gender and marital status differences in depression: The effects of chronic strains. *Sex Roles, 34*(5/6), 299–319.

Wyatt, G. E. (1989). Reexamining factors predicting Afro-American and white American women's age at first coitus. *Archives of Sexual Behavior, 18,* 271–298.

Wyatt, G. E. (1992). The sociocultural context of African American and White American women's rape. *Journal of Social Issues, 48,* 77–91.

Wyatt, G. E. (1994). The sociocultural relevance of sex research: Challenges for the 1990s and beyond. *American Psychologist, 49,* 748–754.

Wyche, K. F., & Rice, J. K. (1997). Feminist therapy: From dialogue to tenets. In J. Worell & N. G. Johnson (Eds.), *Shaping the future of feminist psychology: Education, research, and practice* (pp. 57–71). Washington, DC: American Psychological Association.

Yalom, I. D. (1980). *Existential psychotherapy.* New York: Basic Books.

Yamada, M. (1983). Asian Pacific American women and feminism. In C. Moraga & G. Anzaldira (Eds.), *This bridge called my back: Writings by radical women of color.* New York: Kitchen Table—Women of Color Press.

Yankelovich, D. (1981). *New rules.* New York: Random House.

Yarkin, K. L., Town, J. P., & Wallston, B. S. (1982). Blacks and women must try harder: Stimulus persons' race and sex and attributions of causality. *Personality and Social Psychology Bulletin, 8,* 21–24.

Yates, G. L., MacKenzie, R. G., Pennbridge, J., & Swofford, A. (1991). A risk profile comparison of homeless youth involved in prostitution and homeless youth not involved (Special Issue: Homeless Youth). *Journal of Adolescent Health, 12,* 545–548.

Yee, B. W. (1990). Gender and family issues in minority groups. *Generations, 14*(3), 39–42.

Yoder, J. D. (1999). *Women and gender: Transforming psychology.* Upper Saddle River, NJ: Prentice Hall.

Yoder, J. D., & Schleicher, T. L. (1996). Undergraduates regard deviation from occupational gender stereotypes as costly for women. *Sex Roles, 34,* 171–188.

Yoffee, L. (2002, November 7). Addiction medicine: Important to recognize that addiction, abuse in females is different. *Women's Health Weekly* via NewsRx.com and NewsRX.net (Expanded Reporting p. 8). Retrieved August 8, 2003 from http://web.lexis-nexis.com/universe/document?_m= 2dda1af615ef723ce0c5db7d9b768b5c&_docnum= 1&wchp=dGLbVzb-zSkVb&_md5= e4c61307e654b376601be94b85fd9329

Yonkers, K. A. (2003). Special issues related to the treatment of depression in women. *Journal of Clinical Psychiatry, 64*(18), 8–13.

Young, C. (1989). Psychodynamics of coping and survival of the African American female in a changing world. *Journal of Black Studies, 20,* 208–223.

Young, K. K. (1987). Introduction to women in world religions. In A. Sharma (Ed.), *Women in World Religions* (pp. 1–36). Albany: State University of New York Press.

Younger, B. L. (2002). A study of women and the relationships among self-esteem, androgyny, and transformational leadership behavior. *Dissertation Abstracts International, 63*(5B), 2628.

Yu, A. Y. (1993). Life in Hong Kong. In L. L. Adler (Ed.), *International handbook on gender roles* (pp. 108–121). Westport, CT: Greenwood Press.

Yu, L. C., & Carpenter, L. (1991). Women in China. In L. L. Adler (Ed.), *Women in cross-cultural perspective* (pp. 189–203). Westport, CT: Praeger.

Zaehner, R. C. (1958). *The comparison of religions.* Boston: Beacon Press.

Zahaykevich, M., Sirey, A. R., & Brooks-Gunn, J. (2000). Unpublished manuscript.

Zahn-Waxler, C. (2000). The development of empathy, guilt, and internalization of distress: Implications for gender differences in internalizing and externalizing problems. In R. Davidson (Ed.), *Wisconsin Symposium on Emotion: Vol. 1. Anxiety, depression, and emotion* (pp. 222–265). Oxford, UK: Oxford University Press.

Zalk, S. R. (1996). Men in the academy: A psychological profile of harassers. In M. A. Paludi (Ed.), *Sexual harassment on college campuses: Abusing the ivory power* (pp. 81–113). Albany: State University of New York Press.

Zborowski, M. (1969). *People in Pain.* San Francisco, CA: Jossey-Bass Press.

Zelinski, E. M., Gilewski, M. J., & Schaie, K. W. (1993). Individual differences in cross-sectional and 3-year longitudinal memory performance across the adult life span. *Psychology and Aging, 8*(2), 176–186.

Zelkowitz, P. (1996). Childbearing and women's mental health. Transcultural Psychiatric Research Review. 33.(4), 391–412.

Zeman, N. (1990, Summer/Fall). The new rules of courtship (Special Edition). *Newsweek,* pp. 24–27.

Zillman, D., & Bryant, J. (1982). Pornography, sexual callousness, and the trivialization of rape. *Journal of Communication, 32,* 10–21.

Zillman, D., & Bryant, J. (1984). Effects of massive exposure to pornography. In N. H. Malamuth & E. Donnerstein (Eds.), *Pornography and sexual aggression* (pp. 115–138). New York: Academic Press.

Zimiles, H., & Lee, V. E. (1991). Adolescent family structure and educational progress. *Developmental Psychology, 27,* 314–320.

Zola, I. K. (1966). Culture and symptoms: An analysis of patients presenting complaints. *American Sociological Review, 31,* 615–630.

Zucker, K. J., Bradley, S. J., Lowry Sullivan, C. B., Kuksis, M., Birkenfeld-Adams, A., & Mitchell, J. N. (1993). A gender identity interview for children. *Journal of Personality Assessment, 61*(3), 443–456.

Zunzunegui, M., Alvarado, B. E., & Del Ser, T. (2003). Social networks, social integration, and social engagement determine cognitive decline in community-dwelling Spanish older adults. *Journals of Gerontology, 58B*(2), S93–S100.

Author Index

SUBJECT INDEX